The Individual Investor's Guide to

Low-Load

Mutual
Funds

The American Association
of Individual Investors

16th
Edition
1997

The American Association of Individual Investors is an independent, not-for-profit corporation formed in 1978 for the purpose of assisting individuals in becoming effective managers of their own assets through programs of education, information, and research.

American Association of Individual Investors
625 North Michigan Avenue
Chicago, Illinois 60611
(312) 280-0170
www.aaii.org

ISBN 1-883328-00-4
Library of Congress Catalog Number: 95-75595

Data in this guide was provided by Micropal and directly from the funds. While the material in this *Guide* cannot be guaranteed to be error free, it has been obtained from sources believed to be reliable.

Preface

Inside the *Guide* are the information and performance statistics you will need to make well-informed decisions on your mutual fund investments. Our goal is to provide pertinent information, organized to minimize your time spent collecting and comparing information on the increasingly large universe of mutual funds.

Information for this *Guide* was gathered in part from each fund's prospectus and annual report, and from direct contact with funds. Micropal Inc. supplied performance and share statistics. As always, our objective is full, accurate, and timely disclosure of investment information. The 1997 edition of the *Low-Load Mutual Fund Guide* covers 866 mutual funds.

John Bajkowski oversaw the development of the fund analysis format. Marie Swick supervised the data collection and verification. Jean Henrich and Anna M. Chan provided copy editing and Kurt A. Zauke designed the cover. Carol A. Monk served as project editor for the *Guide*.

Chicago
March 1997

John Markese, Ph.D.
President

Table of Contents

How to Use This Guide   1

Selecting a mutual fund, while less time-consuming than investing in individual securities, does require some homework. No one should put money into an investment that is not understood. This does not require a detailed investigation of the fund's investments, but it does require an understanding of the investment objectives and strategies and the possible risks and returns.

This *Guide* is designed to provide you with that understanding. We have kept the chapters brief and to the point, so that individuals new to mutual fund investing will not be overwhelmed with unnecessary details.

Chapters 2 through 5 deal with the basics of investing in mutual funds—diversification; loads; various categories of mutual funds and what they mean; how to read a mutual fund's prospectus and annual report, as well as any other material they send you; and how to evaluate the risk of a mutual fund.

Those who are familiar with mutual funds may want to skip directly to Chapter 6, which describes how the mutual funds were chosen for inclusion in the *Guide*. Chapter 7 is a key to the terms used in the performance tables and the mutual fund data pages, and includes an explanation of how the returns were calculated and what the different risk measures mean.

Chapter 8 presents the performance tables, which include the historical performance of different categories of mutual funds and their corresponding benchmarks. While past performance is no indication of future performance, it may indicate the quality and consistency of fund management. From this section, you should pick out several mutual funds that meet your investment objectives and risk tolerance. These funds can then be examined more closely in the mutual fund data pages.

Chapter 9 contains the individual fund listings. The funds are listed alphabetically; their ticker symbol and investment category are indicated at the top of the page after the fund's name. These pages provide 10 years of per share data, performance statistics along with risk measures, portfolio information, and shareholder services provided by the fund. Use the address, telephone numbers, and e-mail addresses provided to call or write the funds to request a copy of the prospectus and annual report. Make sure you read the prospectus carefully before investing in any mutual fund.

At the back of the *Guide* is a list of special category funds that includes asset allocation, funds investing in other mutual funds, global, index, sector, small capitalization stocks, socially conscious, and state specific tax-exempt bond funds. And finally, there is a list of fund changes, including fund name changes, investment category changes, and funds that were dropped from the *Guide*.

Investing in Mutual Funds 2

A mutual fund is an investment company that pools investors' money to invest in securities. An open-end mutual fund continuously issues new shares when investors want to invest in the fund, and it redeems shares when investors want to sell. A mutual fund trades directly with its shareholders, and the share price of the fund represents the market value of the securities that the fund holds.

There are several advantages that mutual funds offer individual investors. They provide:

- Professional investment management at a low cost, even for small accounts;
- A diversified group of securities that only a large portfolio can provide;
- Information through prospectuses and annual reports that facilitates comparisons among funds;
- Special services such as check writing, dividend reinvestment plans, telephone switching, and periodic withdrawal and investment plans;
- Account statements that make it easy to track the value of your investment and that ease the paperwork at tax time.

Successful investing takes time and effort, and it requires special knowledge and relevant, up-to-date information. Investors must spend a considerable amount of energy searching for opportunities and monitoring each investment. Professional investment management is relatively cheap with mutual funds. The typical adviser charges about 0.5% annually for managing a fund's assets. For an individual making a $10,000 investment, that comes to only $50 a year.

Of course, mutual fund investing does not preclude investing in securities on your own. One useful strategy would be to invest in mutual funds and individual securities. The mutual funds would ensure your participation in overall market moves and lend diversification to your portfolio, while the individual securities would provide you with the opportunity to apply your specific investment analysis skills.

DIVERSIFICATION

If there is one ingredient to successful investing that is universally agreed upon, it is the benefit of diversification. This is a concept that is backed by a great deal of research, market experience, and common sense. Diversification reduces risk. Risk to investors is frequently defined as volatility of return—in other words, how much an investment's return might vary over a year. Investors prefer returns that are relatively predictable, and thus less volatile. On the other hand, they want returns that are high, but higher returns are accompanied by higher risks. Diversification eliminates some of the risk without reducing potential returns.

Mutual funds, because of their size and the laws governing their operation, provide investors with diversification that might be difficult for an individual to duplicate. This is true not only for common stock funds, but also for bond funds, municipal bond funds, gold funds, international bond and stock funds—in fact, for almost all mutual funds. Even the sector funds that invest only within one industry offer diversification within that industry. The degree of diversification will vary among funds, but most will provide investors with some amount of diversification.

AVOIDING EXCESSIVE CHARGES

This book is dedicated to no-load and low-load mutual funds. Investors should realize that:

- A load is a sales commission that goes to the seller of the fund shares;
- A load does not go to anyone responsible for managing the fund's assets and does not serve as an incentive for the fund manager to perform better;
- Funds with loads, on average, consistently underperform no-load funds when the load is taken into consideration in performance calculations;
- For every high-performing load fund, there exists a similar no-load or low-load fund that can be purchased more cheaply;
- Loads understate the real commission charged because they reduce the total amount being invested: $10,000 invested in a 6% front-end load fund results in a $600 sales charge and only a $9,400 investment in the fund;
- If a load fund is held over a long time period, the effect of the load, if paid up front, is not diminished as quickly as many people believe; if the money paid for the load had been working for you, as in a no-load fund, it would have been compounding over the whole time period.

The bottom line in any investment is how it performs for you, the investor, and that performance includes consideration of all loads, fees, and expenses. There may be some load funds that will do even better factoring in the load, but you have no way of finding that fund in advance. The only guide you have is historical performance, which is not necessarily an indication of future performance. With a heavily loaded fund, you are starting your investment with a significant loss—the load. Avoid unnecessary charges whenever possible.

SORTING OUT CHARGES

It is best to stick with no-load or low-load funds, but they are becoming more difficult to distinguish from heavily loaded funds. The use of high front-end loads has declined, and funds are now turning to other kinds of charges. Some mutual funds sold by brokerage firms, for example, have lowered their front-end loads to 5%, and others have introduced back-end loads (deferred sales charges), which are sales commissions paid when exiting the fund. In both instances, the load is often accompanied by annual charges.

On the other hand, some no-load funds have found that to compete, they must market themselves much more aggressively. To do so, they have introduced charges of their own.

The result has been the introduction of low loads, redemption fees, and annual charges. Low loads—up to 3%—are sometimes added instead of the annual charges. In addition, some funds have instituted a charge for investing or withdrawing money.

Redemption fees work like back-end loads: You pay a percentage of the value of your fund when you get out. Loads are on the amount you have invested, while redemption fees are calculated against the value of your fund assets. Some funds have sliding scale redemption fees, so that the longer you remain invested, the lower the charge when you leave. Some funds use redemption fees to discourage short-term trading, a policy that is designed to protect longer-term investors. These funds usually have redemption fees that disappear after six months.

Probably the most confusing charge is the annual charge, the 12b-1 plan. The adoption of a 12b-1 plan by a fund permits the adviser to use fund assets to pay for distribution costs, including advertising, distribution of fund literature such as prospectuses and annual reports, and sales commissions paid to brokers. Some funds use 12b-1 plans as masked load charges: They levy very high rates on the fund and use the money to pay brokers to sell the fund. Since the charge is annual and based on the value of the investment, this can result in a total cost to a long-term investor that exceeds a high up-front sales load. A fee table is required in all prospectuses to clarify the impact of a 12b-1 plan and other charges.

The fee table makes the comparison of total expenses among funds easier. Selecting a fund based solely on expenses, including loads and charges, will not give you optimal results, but avoiding funds with high expenses and unnecessary charges is important for long-term performance.

Mutual Fund Categories 3

Mutual funds come in all shapes and sizes; there are over 850 funds covered in this book alone, each with its own characteristics. Many mutual funds, however, have shared investment objectives that generally lead to other characteristics that are similar.

These shared characteristics allow us to divide mutual funds into several broad categories. This chapter defines the mutual fund categories we used for this book. In this guide, the individual fund data pages appear alphabetically; the fund's category is indicated beneath the fund's name.

The following table summarizes some important characteristics of funds by category. Averages for expense ratio, income to assets ratio, portfolio turnover, returns and risk (see Chapter 5: "Understanding Risk" on page 19) illustrate some of the differences in the categories.

Investment Category	Expense Ratio (%)	Yield (%)	Portfolio Turnover (%)	Beta (%)	Maturity (yrs)	Standard Deviation (%)
Aggressive Growth	1.37	0.21	123	0.94	na	14.3
Growth	1.13	0.71	86	0.87	na	10.4
Growth & Income	0.91	2.00	59	0.85	na	9.3
Balanced	0.93	3.31	94	0.63	na	6.8
Corporate Bond	0.73	6.41	160	na	7.7	4.6
Corp. High-Yield Bond	0.94	8.63	120	na	7.1	4.6
Government Bond	0.63	5.18	146	na	8.1	4.1
Mortgage-Backed Bond	0.73	6.34	145	na	12.1	3.8
General Bond	0.78	6.07	168	na	6.7	3.8
Tax-Exempt Bond	0.61	4.90	53	na	12.6	5.6
International Stock	1.46	0.91	76	0.69	na	10.3
International Bond	1.17	6.52	269	na	8.4	7.0
Gold	1.58	1.50	48	0.61	na	25.0
Domestic Equity Fund	1.16	0.88	91	0.89	na	10.5
Small-Cap Stock	1.28	0.33	76	0.78	na	11.3
Domestic Taxable Bond	0.74	6.12	155	na	8.1	3.9

AGGRESSIVE GROWTH FUNDS

The investment objective of aggressive growth funds is maximum capital gains. They invest aggressively in common stocks and tend to stay fully invested over the market cycle. Sometimes, these funds will borrow money to purchase securities, and some may engage in trading stock options or take positions in stock index futures.

Aggressive growth funds typically provide low income distributions. This is because they tend to be fully invested in common stocks and do not earn a significant amount of interest income. In addition, the common stocks they invest in are generally growth-oriented stocks that pay little or no cash dividends.

Many aggressive growth funds concentrate their assets in particular industries or segments of the market, and their degree of diversification may not be as great as other types of funds. These investment strategies result in increased risk. Thus, they tend to perform better than the overall market during bull markets but fare worse during bear markets.

In general, long-term investors who need not be concerned with monthly or yearly variation in investment return will find investment in this class of funds rewarding. Because of the extreme volatility of return, however, risk-averse investors with a short-term investment horizon may find that these mutual funds lie well outside their comfort zones. During prolonged market declines, aggressive growth funds can sustain severe declines in net asset value.

Market timing is not a strategy we recommend, particularly over the short term. Although the transaction costs of switching in and out of no-load mutual funds are near zero, it can create significant tax liabilities. In addition, the ability to consistently time the market correctly in the short term, after adjusting for risk, costs, and taxes, has not been demonstrated. However, aggressive growth funds, with their high volatility and fully invested position, do make ideal vehicles for those who believe they know the next market move.

GROWTH FUNDS

The investment objective of growth funds is to obtain long-term growth of invested capital. They generally do not engage in speculative tactics such as using financial leverage. On occasion, these funds will use stock or index options or futures to reduce risk by hedging their portfolio positions.

Growth funds typically are more stable than aggressive growth funds. Generally, they invest in growth-oriented firms that are more mature and that pay cash dividends.

The degree of concentration of assets is not as severe as with aggressive growth funds. Additionally, these funds may move from effectively fully invested to larger cash positions during uncertain market environments.

In general, growth fund performance tends to mirror the market during bull and bear markets. Some growth funds have been able to perform relatively well during recent bear markets because their managers were able to change portfolio composition by a much greater degree or to maintain much higher cash positions than aggressive growth fund managers. However, higher cash positions can also cause the funds to underperform aggressive growth funds during bull markets.

Aggressive investors should consider holding both growth fund shares and aggressive growth fund shares in their overall portfolios. This is an especially appealing strategy for investors who hold aggressive growth mutual funds that invest in small stock growth firms. The portfolios of these funds complement the portfolios of growth funds, leading to greater overall diversification. The combination produces overall returns that will tend to be less volatile than an investment in only aggressive growth funds.

As with aggressive growth funds, these funds can sustain severe declines during prolonged bear markets. Since some portfolio managers of growth funds attempt to time the market over the longer market cycle, using these funds to move in and out of the market for timing purposes may be counterproductive.

GROWTH AND INCOME FUNDS

Growth and income funds generally invest in the common stocks and convertible securities of seasoned, well-established, cash-dividend-paying companies. The funds attempt to provide shareholders with significant income along with long-term growth. They generally attempt to avoid excessive fluctuations in return. One tends to find a high concentration of public utility common stocks and sometimes convertible securities in the portfolios of growth and income funds. The funds also provide higher income distributions, less variability in return, and greater diversification than growth and aggressive growth funds. Names such as equity-income, income, and total return have been attached to funds that have characteristics of growth and income funds. Because of the high current income offered by these kinds of funds, potential investors should keep the tax consequences in mind.

BALANCED FUNDS

The balanced fund category has become less distinct in recent years, and a significant overlap in fund objectives exists between growth and income funds and balanced funds. In general, the portfolios of balanced funds consist of investments in common stocks and substantial investments in bonds and convertible securities. The proportion of stocks and bonds that will be held is usually stated in the investment objective, but usually the portfolio manager has the option of allocating the proportions between some stated range. Some asset allocation funds—funds that have a wide latitude of portfolio composition change—can also be found in the balanced category. Balanced funds are generally less volatile than aggressive growth, growth, and growth and income funds. As with growth and income funds, balanced funds provide a high dividend yield.

BOND FUNDS

Bond mutual funds are attractive to investors because they provide diversification and liquidity, which may not be as readily attainable in direct bond investments.

Bond funds have portfolios with a wide range of average maturities. Many funds use their names to characterize their maturity structure. Generally, short term means that the portfolio has a weighted average maturity of less than three years. Intermediate implies an average maturity of three to 10 years, and long term is over 10 years. The longer the maturity, the greater the change in fund value when interest rates change. Longer-term bond funds are riskier than shorter-term funds, and they tend to offer higher yields.

Bond funds are principally categorized by the types of bonds they hold. Corporate bond funds invest primarily in investment grade corporate bonds of various maturities; however, corporate high-yield bond funds provide high income and invest generally in corporate bonds rated below investment grade.

Government bond funds invest in the bonds of the U.S. government and its agencies, while mortgage-backed bond funds invest primarily in mortgage-backed securities. General bond funds invest in a mix of government and agency bonds, corporate bonds, and mortgage-backed securities. Tax-exempt bond funds invest in bonds whose income is exempt from federal income tax. Some tax-exempt funds may invest in bonds whose income is also exempt from the income tax of a specific state.

INTERNATIONAL BOND AND STOCK FUNDS

International funds invest in bonds and stocks of foreign firms and governments. Some funds specialize in regions, such as the Pacific or Europe, and others invest in multiple foreign regions. In addition, some funds—usually termed "global funds"—invest in both foreign and U.S. securities. We have two classifications of international funds—international stock funds and international bond funds.

International funds provide investors with added diversification. The most important factor when diversifying a portfolio is selecting assets that do not behave similarly to each other under similar economic scenarios. Within the U.S., investors can diversify by selecting securities of firms in different industries. In the international realm, investors take the diversification process one step further by holding securities of firms in different countries. The more independently these foreign markets move in relation to the U.S. stock market, the greater will be the diversification benefit, and the lower the risk.

In addition, international funds overcome some of the difficulties investors face in making foreign investments directly. For instance, individuals have to thoroughly understand the foreign brokerage process, be familiar with the various foreign marketplaces and their economies, be aware of currency fluctuation trends, and have access to reliable financial information. This can be a monumental task for the individual investor.

There are some risks unique to investing internationally. In addition to the risk inherent in investing in any security, there is an additional exchange rate risk. The return to a U.S. investor from a foreign security depends on both the security's return in its own currency and the rate at which that currency can be exchanged for U.S. dollars. Another uncertainty is political risk, which includes government restriction, taxation, or even total prohibition of the exchange of one currency into another. Of course, the more the mutual fund is diversified among various countries, the less the risk involved.

GOLD FUNDS

Gold mutual funds specialize in investments in both foreign and domestic companies that mine gold and other precious metals. Some funds also hold gold directly through investments in gold coins or bullion. Gold options are another method used to invest in the industry. Mutual fund investments in precious metals range from the conservative to the highly speculative.

Gold and other precious metals mutual funds allow investors interested in this area to invest in a more liquid and diversified vehicle than would be available through a direct purchase.

The appeal of gold and precious metals is that they have performed well during extreme inflationary periods. Over the short term, the price of gold moves in response to a variety of political, economic, and psychological forces. As world tension and anxiety rise, so may the price of gold. In periods of peace and stability, the price of gold may decline. Silver and platinum react in a similar fashion to gold. Precious metals funds, like the metals themselves, are very volatile, often shooting from the bottom to the top and back to the bottom in fund rankings over the years. Investors should understand, however, that because most gold funds invest in the stock of gold mining companies, they are still subject to some stock market risk.

OTHER TYPES OF FUNDS

There are many specialized mutual funds that do not have their own categories. Instead, they will be found in one of the various categories mentioned above. These funds are classified by their investment objectives rather than by their investment strategies. For instance, several funds specialize in specific sectors or industries, but one industry-specific fund does not necessarily appear in the same category as another industry-specific sector fund. For example, a technology sector fund would likely appear in the aggressive growth category while a utility sector fund would be found in the growth and income category. Specialized funds include small company funds, "socially conscious" funds, index funds, funds investing in funds, and asset allocation funds.

Asset allocation funds, for example, are usually one of two types. Some allocation funds are designed to provide diversification among the various categories of investments and within each investment category. For example, an asset allocation fund may hold minimum percentages in stocks, bonds, cash, and international investments. The second asset allocation strategy used by some funds is to move money around according to what the fund managers believe to be optimal proportions given their expectations for the economy, interest rates, and other market factors. These latter asset allocation funds are market timing funds, distinctly different and with greater risk than the asset allocation funds striving solely for diversification. These market-timing asset allocation funds are noted in the book.

One other fund type deserves a special mention—the index fund. An example of an index fund is Vanguard's Index Trust—500, categorized as a growth and income fund. This fund is designed to match the Standard & Poor's 500 stock index and does so by investing in all 500 stocks in the S&P 500; the amounts invested in each stock are proportional to the firm's market value representation in the S&P 500. Statistics on index funds are quite useful for comparison with other funds, since indexes represent a widely followed segment of the market. Index funds are available covering most major segments of the bond and stock markets, domestic and international. Because they are unmanaged, they make no research efforts to select particular stocks or bonds, nor do they make timing decisions. This passive management approach makes the cost of managing an index fund relatively low. A list of specialized funds appear in Appendix A: "Special Types of Funds" on page 924 at the back of this *Guide*.

Understanding Mutual Fund Statements

4

One of the advantages of mutual fund investing is the wealth of information that mutual funds provide to fund investors and prospective investors. Taken together, the various reports provide investors with vital information concerning financial matters and how the fund is managed, both key elements in the selection process. In fact, mutual fund prospectuses, annual reports, and performance statistics are key sources of information most investors will need in the selection and monitoring process.

To new mutual fund investors, the information may seem overwhelming. However, regulations governing the industry have standardized the reports: Once you know where to look for information, the location will hold true for almost all funds.

There are basically five types of statements produced by the mutual fund: the prospectus; the statement of additional information; annual, semiannual, and quarterly reports; marketing brochures; and account statements. Actually, the second report—the statement of additional information—is part of the prospectus. However, the Securities and Exchange Commission allows mutual funds to simplify and streamline the prospectus, if they choose, by dividing it into two parts: Part A, which all prospective investors must receive if requested, and Part B—the statement of additional information—which the fund must send investors if they specifically request it. Some fund families also currently offer an abbreviated profile prospectus. In practice, when reference is made to the prospectus, it is to Part A. For simplicity, that is what we will do here as well.

THE PROSPECTUS

The prospectus is the single most important document produced by the mutual fund, and it is must-reading for investors before investing. Current shareholders must be sent new prospectuses when they are updated, at least once every 14 months.

The prospectus is generally organized into sections, and although it must cover specific topics, the overall structure may differ somewhat among funds. The cover usually gives a quick synopsis of the fund: investment category, sales or redemption charges, minimum investment, retirement plans available, address and telephone number. More detailed descriptions are in the body of the prospectus.

Fee Table: All mutual fund prospectuses must include a table near the front that delineates all fees and charges to the investor. The table contains three sections: The first section lists all transaction charges to the investor, including all front-end and back-end loads and redemption fees; the second section lists all annual fund operating expenses, including management fees and any 12b-1 charges, as a percentage of net assets; and the third section is an illustration of the total cost of these fees and charges to an investor over time. The illustration assumes an initial investment of $1,000 and a 5% growth rate for the fund, and states the total dollar cost to an investor if he were to redeem his shares at the end of one year, three years, five years, and 10 years.

Selected Per Share Data and Ratios: One of the most important sections of the prospectus contains the selected per share data and ratios, which provides statistics on income and capital changes per share of the fund. The per share figures are given for the life of the fund or 10 years, whichever is less. Also included are important statistical summaries of investment activities throughout each period. Occasionally these financial statements are only

The Prospectus Fee Table: An Example

CONSOLIDATED DISCLOSURE OF FUND FEES AND EXPENSES

Shareholder Transaction Expenses

Maximum Sales Load Imposed on Purchases (as a percentage of offering price)	None
Maximum Sales Load Imposed on Reinvested Dividends (as a percentage of offering price)	None
Deferred Sales Load (as a percentage of original purchase price or redemption proceeds, if applicable) ..	None
Redemption Fees (as a percent of redemption proceeds, if applicable)	None
Exchange Fee [1]	None

Annual Fund Operating Expenses[2] *(as a percentage of average net assets)*

Management Fees	0.65%
12b-1 Fees	None
Other Expenses	0.09%
Total Fund Operating Expenses	0.74%

[1] There is a $5 fee for telephone exchanges only.

[2] Annual Fund Operating Expenses are based on expenses incurred for the year ended March 31, 1996.

EXAMPLE

	One Year	Three Years	Five Years	Ten Years
A shareholder would pay the following expenses on a $1,000 investment, assuming: (1) 5% annual return and (2) redemption at the end of each period.	$8	$24	$41	$92

This Example should not be considered a representation of past or future expenses. Actual expenses may be greater or lesser than those shown.

The purpose of the table is to assist the prospective investor in understanding the various costs and expenses that an investor in the Fund will bear directly and indirectly. For a description of "Management Fees" and "Other Expenses," see "Investment Adviser."

Source: Nicholas Fund prospectus, July 31, 1996.

Selected Per Share Data and Ratios: An Example

	500 PORTFOLIO									
	Year Ended December 31,									
	1995	1994	1993	1992	1991	1990	1989	1988	1987	1986
Net Asset Value, Beginning of Year..	$42.97	$43.83	$40.97	$39.32	$31.24	$33.64	$27.18	$24.65	$24.27	$22.99
Investment Operations										
Net Investment Income	1.22	1.18	1.13	1.12	1.15	1.17	1.20	1.08	.88	.89
Net Realized and Unrealized Gain (Loss) on Investments	14.76	(.67)	2.89	1.75	8.20	(2.30)	7.21	2.87	.36	3.30
Total from Investment Operations	15.98	.51	4.02	2.87	9.35	(1.13)	8.41	3.95	1.24	4.19
Distributions										
Dividends from Net Investment Income	(1.22)	(1.17)	(1.13)	(1.12)	(1.15)	(1.17)	(1.20)	(1.10)	(.69)	(.89)
Distributions from Realized Capital Gains	(.13)	(.20)	(.03)	(.10)	(.12)	(.10)	(.75)	(.32)	(.17)	(2.02)
Total Distributions	(1.35)	(1.37)	(1.16)	(1.22)	(1.27)	(1.27)	(1.95)	(1.42)	(.86)	(2.91)
Net Asset Value, End of Year	$57.60	$42.97	$43.83	$40.97	$39.32	$31.24	$33.64	$27.18	$24.65	$24.27
Total Return*	37.45%	1.18%	9.89%	7.42%	30.22%	(3.32)%	31.36%	16.22%	4.71%	18.06%
Ratios/Supplemental Data										
Net Assets, End of Year (Millions) . .	$17,372	$9,356	$8,273	$6,547	$4,345	$2,173	$1,804	$1,055	$826	$485
Ratio of Expenses to Average Net Assets	.20%	.19%	.19%	.19%	.20%	.22%	.21%	.22%	.26%	.28%
Ratio of Net Investment Income to Average Net Assets	2.38%	2.72%	2.65%	2.81%	3.07%	3.60%	3.62%	4.08%	3.15%	3.40%
Portfolio Turnover Rate	4%†	6%†	6%†	4%†	5%†	23%†	8%	10%	15%	29%

* Total return figures do not reflect the annual account maintenance fee of $10.
† Portfolio turnover rates excluding in-kind redemptions were 2%, 4%, 2%, 1%, 1% and 6%, respectively.

Source: Vanguard Index Trust—500 prospectus, April 30, 1996.

referred to in the prospectus and are actually contained in the annual report, which in this instance would accompany the prospectus.

The per share section summarizes the financial activity over the fund's fiscal year, which may or may not correspond to the calendar year, to arrive at the end-of-year net asset value for the fund. The financial activity summarized includes increases in net asset value due to dividend and interest payments received and capital gains from investment activity. Decreases in net asset value are due to capital losses from investment activity, investment expenses, and payouts to fund shareholders in the form of distributions.

Potential investors may want to note the line items in this section. *Investment income* represents the dividends and interest earned by the fund during its fiscal year. *Expenses* reflect such fund costs as the management fee, legal fees, and transfer agent fees. These expenses are given in detail in the statement of operations section of the annual report.

Net investment income is investment income less expenses. This line is important for investors to note because it reflects the level and stability of net income over the time period. A high net investment income would most likely be found in funds that have income rather than growth as their investment category. Since net investment income must be distributed to shareholders to avoid direct taxation of the fund, a high net investment income has the potential of translating into a high tax liability for the investor.

Net realized and unrealized gain (loss) on investments is the change in the value of investments that have been sold (realized) during the year or that continue to be held (unrealized) by the fund.

Distributions to fund shareholders are also detailed. These distributions will include dividends from net investment income for the current fiscal period. Tax law requires that income earned must be distributed in the calendar year earned. Also included in distributions will be any realized net capital gains.

The last line in the per share section will be the *net asset value* at the end of the year, which reflects the value of one share of the fund. It is calculated by determining the total assets of the fund and dividing by the number of mutual fund shares outstanding. The figure will change for a variety of reasons, including changes in investment income, expenses, gains, losses, and distributions. Depending upon the source of change, a decline in net asset value may or may not be due to poor performance. For instance, a decline in net asset value may be due to a distribution of net realized gains on securities.

The financial ratios at the bottom of the per share financial data are important indicators of fund performance and strategy. The *expense ratio* relates expenses incurred by the fund to average net assets. These expenses include the investment advisory fee, legal and accounting fees, and 12b-1 charges to the fund; they do not include fund brokerage costs, loads, or redemption fees. A high expense ratio detracts from your investment return. In general, common stock funds have higher expense ratios than bond funds, and smaller funds have higher expense ratios than larger funds. International funds also tend to have higher expense ratios than domestic funds. Index funds usually have the lowest expense ratios. The average expense ratio for common stock funds is 1.15%, and for bond funds (taxable and non-taxable) about 0.67%.

The *ratio of net investment income to average net assets* is very similar to a dividend yield. This, too, should reflect the investment category of the fund. Common stock funds with income as a significant part of their investment objective would be expected to have a ratio in the 2% to 4% range under current market conditions, and aggressive growth funds would have a ratio closer to 0%. Bond funds would normally have ratios more than twice those of common stock funds.

The *portfolio turnover rate* is the lower of purchases or sales divided by average net assets. It reflects how frequently securities are bought and sold by the fund. For purposes of determining the turnover rate for common stock funds, fixed-income securities with a maturity of less than a year are excluded, as are all government securities, short- and long-term. For bond funds, however, long-term U.S. government bonds are included.

Investors should take note of the portfolio turnover rate, because the higher the turnover, the greater the brokerage costs incurred by the fund. Brokerage costs are not reflected in the expense ratio but instead are directly reflected as a decrease in net asset value. In addition, mutual funds with high turnover rates generally have higher capital gains distributions—a potential tax liability. Aggressive growth mutual funds are most likely to have high turnover rates. Some bond funds also have very high portfolio turnover rates. A 100% portfolio turnover rate indicates that the value of the portfolio was completely turned over in a year; a 200% portfolio turnover indicates that the value of the portfolio was completely turned over twice in a year. The portfolio turnover rate for the average mutual fund is around 100% but varies with market conditions and investment category.

Investment Objective/Policy: The investment objective section of the prospectus elaborates on the brief sentence or two from the prospectus cover. In this section, the fund describes the types of investments it will make—whether it is bonds, stocks, convertible securities, options, etc.—along with some general guidelines as to the proportions these securities will represent in the fund's portfolio. The investment objective statement usually indicates whether it will be oriented toward capital gains or income. In this section, the management will also briefly discuss its approach to market timing, risk assumption, and the anticipated level of portfolio turnover. Some prospectuses may indicate any investment restrictions they have placed on the fund, such as purchasing securities on margin, selling short, concentrating in firms or industries, trading foreign securities, and lending securities; this section may also state the allowable proportions in certain investment categories. The restrictions section is usually given in more detail in the statement of additional information.

Fund Management: The fund management section names the investment adviser and gives the advisory fee schedule. Most advisers charge a management fee on a sliding scale that decreases as assets under management increase. Occasionally, some portion of the fund adviser's fees are subject to the fund's performance relative to the market.

Some prospectuses will describe the fund's officers and directors with a short biography of affiliations and relevant experience. For most funds, however, this information is provided in more detail in the statement of additional information. The board of directors is elected by fund shareholders; the fund adviser is selected by the board of directors. The adviser is usually a firm operated by or affiliated with officers of the fund. Information on fund officers and directors is not critical to fund selection. In the prospectus the portfolio manager for the fund is named. The portfolio manager is responsible for the day-to-day investment decisions of the fund and is employed by the fund adviser. Who the portfolio manager is and how long the manager has been in the position can be useful in judging historical performance.

Other Important Sections: There are several other sections in a mutual fund prospectus of which investors should be aware. They will appear under various headings, depending upon the prospectus, but they are not difficult to find.

Mutual funds that have 12b-1 plans must describe them in the prospectus. Under SEC rules, a description of these plans must be prominently and clearly placed in the prospectus, usually in a section titled "Distribution Plan." The distribution plan details the marketing aspects of the fund and how it relates to fund expenses. For instance, advertising, distribution of fund literature, and any arrangements with brokers would be included in the marketing plan; the 12b-1 plan pays for these distribution expenses. The distribution plan section specifies the maximum annual 12b-1 charge that can be made. Funds often charge less than the maximum. The actual charge to the fund of a 12b-1 plan is listed at the front of the prospectus in the fee table.

The *capital stock* section, or *fund share characteristics* section, provides shareholders with a summary of their voting rights, participation in dividends and distributions, and the number of authorized and issued shares of the fund. Often, a separate section will discuss the tax treatment that will apply to fund distributions, which may include dividends, interest, and capital gains.

The *how-to-buy-shares* section gives the minimum initial investment and any subsequent minimums; it will also list load charges or fees. In addition, information on mail, wire, and telephone purchases is provided, along with distribution reinvestment options, automatic exchange, investment and withdrawal plans, and retirement options.

The *how-to-redeem-shares* section discusses telephone, written, and wire redemption options, including automatic withdrawal plans, with a special section on signature guarantees and other documents that may be needed. Also detailed are any fees for reinvestment or redemption. Shareholder services are usually outlined here, with emphasis on exchanges among funds in a family of funds. This will include any fees for exchanging, any limits on the number of exchanges allowed, and any other exchange restrictions.

STATEMENT OF ADDITIONAL INFORMATION

This document elaborates on the prospectus. The investment objectives section is more in-depth, with a list and description of investment restrictions. The management section gives brief biographies of directors and officers, and provides the number of fund shares owned beneficially by the officers and directors named. The investment adviser section, while reiterating the major points made in the prospectus, gives all the expense items and contract provisions of the agreement between the adviser and the fund. If the fund has a 12b-1 plan, further details will likely be in the statement of additional information.

Many times, the statement of additional information will include much more information on the tax consequences of mutual fund distributions and investment. Conditions under which withholding for federal income tax will take place are also provided. The fund's financial statements are incorporated by reference to the annual report to shareholders and generally do not appear in the statement of additional information. Finally, the independent auditors give their opinion on the accuracy of the fund's financial statements.

ANNUAL, SEMIANNUAL, AND QUARTERLY REPORTS

All funds must send their shareholders audited annual and semiannual reports. Mutual funds are allowed to combine their prospectus and annual report; some do this, but many do not.

The annual report describes the fund activities over the past year and provides a listing of all investments of the fund at market value as of the end of the fiscal year. Sometimes the cost basis of each investment is also given. Looking in-depth at the individual securities held by the fund is probably a waste of time. However, it is helpful to be aware of the overall investment categories. For instance, investors should look at the percentage invested in common stocks, bonds, convertible bonds, and any other holdings. In addition, a look at the types of common stocks held and the percentage of fund assets by industry classification gives the investor some indication of how the portfolio will fare in various market environments.

The annual report will also have a balance sheet, listing all assets and liabilities of the fund by general category. This holds little interest for investors.

The statement of operations, similar to an income statement, is of interest only in that the fund expenses are broken down. For most funds, the management fee is by far the largest expense; the expense ratio in the prospectus conveys much more useful information. The statement of changes in net assets is very close to the financial information provided in the prospectus, but the information is not on a per share basis. Per share information will, however, frequently be detailed in the annual report in a separate section. Footnotes to the financial statements elaborate on the entries, but other than any pending litigation against the fund, they are most often routine.

The quarterly or semiannual reports are current accounts of the investment portfolio and provide more timely views of the fund's investments than does the annual report.

MARKETING BROCHURES AND ADVERTISEMENTS

These will generally provide a brief description of the fund. However, the most important bit of information is the telephone number to call and request the fund prospectus and annual report, if you have not received them already.

The SEC has tightened and standardized the rules regarding mutual fund advertising. All mutual funds that use performance figures in their ads must now include one-, three-, five-, and 10-year total return figures. Bond funds that quote yields must use a standardized method for computing yield, and they must include total return figures as well. Finally, any applicable sales commissions must be mentioned in the advertisement.

ACCOUNT STATEMENTS

Mutual funds send out periodic account statements detailing reinvestment of dividend and capital gains distributions, new purchases or redemptions, and any other account activity such as service fees. This statement provides a running account balance by date with share accumulations, an account value to date, and a total of distributions made to date. *These statements are invaluable for tax purposes and should be saved.* The fund will also send out, in January, a Form 1099-DIV for any distributions made in the previous year and a Form 1099-B if any mutual fund shares were sold.

Understanding Risk 5

Risk tolerance refers to the level of volatility of an investment that an investor finds acceptable. The anticipated holding period of an investment is important because it should affect the investor's risk tolerance. Time is a form of diversification; longer holding periods provide greater diversification across different market environments. Investors who anticipate longer holding periods can take on more risk.

The liquidity needs of an investor similarly help define the types of funds that the investor should consider. Liquidity implies preservation of capital, and if liquidity is important, then mutual funds with smaller variations in value should be considered. A liquid mutual fund is one in which withdrawals from the fund can be made at any time with a reasonable certainty that the per share value will not have dropped sharply. Highly volatile aggressive growth funds are the least liquid, and short-term fixed-income funds are the most liquid.

A LOOK AT RISK

Risk is the most difficult concept for many investors to grasp, and yet much of the mutual fund investment decision depends on an understanding of risk. There are many different ways to categorize investment risk and numerous approaches to the measurement of risk. If we can assume that the volatility of the return on your mutual fund investment is the concern you grapple with when you think of risk, the task of making decisions about risk becomes easier.

Questions about how much value a mutual fund is likely to lose in a down market or how certain it is that a fund will be worth a given amount at the end of the year are the same concerns as volatility of return. Changes in the domestic and international economies, interest rates, exchange rates, corporate profits, consumer confidence, and general expectations all combine to move markets up and down, creating volatility, or risk.

Total risk for a mutual fund measures variation in return from all sources. As an example, variation in return for common stocks is caused by factors unique to the firm, industry variables, and conditions affecting all stocks. Market risk refers to the variables such as interest rates, inflation, and the business cycle that affect all stocks to some degree. In well-diversified portfolios of common stock, the firm and industry risk of the various stocks in the portfolio offset each other; thus, these portfolios tend to have lower total risk, and this total risk is usually composed almost entirely of market risk. For less diversified portfolios, funds that hold very few stocks, or sector funds that concentrate investment in one industry, total risk is usually higher and is composed of firm and industry risk in addition to market risk.

Risk levels based upon total risk are given for all funds with 36 months of performance data. The five categories (high, above average, average, below average, and low) serve as a way to compare the risk inherent in common stock funds, international funds, sector funds, bond funds, or any type of mutual fund. Shorter-term bond funds would be expected to have relatively low total risk while some of the concentrated, less-diversified, aggressive common stock funds would likely be ranked in the high total risk category.

The total risk measure will enable you to construct a portfolio of funds that reflects your risk tolerance and the holding period you anticipate for your portfolio. Portfolios for individuals with low risk tolerance and short holding periods should be composed predominantly of funds that are less volatile, with lower total risk. Individuals with high risk tolerances and longer holding periods can form appropriate portfolios by combining mutual funds with higher total risk.

STANDARD DEVIATION

Total risk is measured by the standard deviation statistic, a numerical measure of how much the return on a mutual fund has varied, no matter what the cause, from the historical average return of the fund. Higher standard deviations indicate higher total risk. The category risk rank measures the total risk of a fund to the average total risk for all funds in the same investment category. The rankings for category risk are high, above average, average, below average, and low. Funds ranked above average and high for category risk should produce returns above the average for the investment category.

The risk index indicates the magnitude of the standard deviation for a fund relative to the average standard deviation for funds in the category. A risk index of 1.2, for example, means that the standard deviation for a fund is 20% higher than the average standard deviation for the category.

MARKET RISK

Market risk is a part of total risk but measures only the sensitivity of the fund to movements in the general market. This is valuable information to the individual investor, particularly when combined with use of the total risk and category risk rank measures, to judge how a mutual fund will perform in different market situations. The market risk measure used for common stock funds is beta; for bond funds, average maturity is used.

BETA

Beta is a measure of the relative volatility inherent in a mutual fund investment. This volatility is compared to some measure of the market such as Standard & Poor's index of 500 common stocks. The market's beta is always 1.0 by definition, and a money market fund's beta is always 0. If you hold a mutual fund with a beta of 1.0, it will move, on average, in tandem with the market. If the market is up 10%, the fund will be up, on average, 10%, and if the market drops 10%, the fund will drop, on average, 10%. A mutual fund with a beta of 1.5 is 50% more volatile than the market: If the market is up 10%, the fund will be up, on average, 50% more, or 15%; conversely, if the market is down 10%, the fund, on average, will be down 15%. A negative beta, a rare occurrence, implies that the mutual fund moves in the opposite direction of the market's movement.

The higher the fund's beta, the greater the volatility of the investment in the fund and the less appropriate the fund would be for shorter holding periods or to meet liquidity needs. Remember that beta is a relative measure: A low beta only implies that the fund's movement is not volatile relative to the market. Its return, however, may be quite variable, resulting in high total risk. For instance, industry-specific sector fund moves may not be related to market volatility, but changes in the industry may cause these funds' returns to fluctuate widely. For a well-diversified stock fund, beta is a very useful measure of risk, but for concentrated funds, beta only captures a portion of the variability that the fund may experience. Betas for gold funds, for example, can be very misleading. Gold funds often have relatively low betas, but these funds are extremely volatile. Their volatility stems from factors that do not affect the common stock market as much. In addition, the betas of gold funds sometimes change significantly from year to year.

AVERAGE MATURITY

For all bond funds, the average maturity of the bonds in the portfolio is reported as a market risk measure, rather than beta. The volatility of a bond fund is determined by how the fund reacts primarily to changes in interest rates, although high-yield (junk) bond funds and international bond funds can be affected significantly by factors other than interest rates. When interest rates rise, bond funds fall in value, and conversely, when interest rates fall, bond mutual funds rise in value. The longer the average maturity of the bond fund, the greater will be the variation in the return on the bond fund when interest rates change. Bond mutual fund investors with less risk tolerance and shorter holding periods should seek shorter maturity funds, and longer-term bond fund investors who are more risk tolerant will find funds with longer maturities a better match.

In the case where a bond fund holds mortgage-backed securities, average maturity may not capture the potential for decline in effective maturity when interest rates fall and mortgages are refinanced. Some mortgage funds also use derivatives, highly leveraged financial instruments that derive their value from movements in specific interest rates or indexes, which further complicate an analysis of their risk. Bond funds that hold corporate bonds and municipal bonds also face changing effective maturities when interest rates decline and bond issuers call bonds before maturity.

Which Funds Were Included

The funds that appear in *The Individual Investor's Guide to Low-Load Mutual Funds* were selected from a large universe of funds. Following are the various screens we used to arrive at the final selection.

SIZE

Funds must appear on the National Association of Securities Dealers mutual fund list found in most major newspapers. New funds are required to have an initial minimum of $50 million in assets to qualify for inclusion in the *Guide*. Funds with total assets that fall below $25 million for two consecutive years are dropped from the *Guide*.

LOADS

The decision as to what constitutes a significant load is difficult, but we took this approach in the *Guide*:

- All funds with front-end loads, back-end loads, or redemption fees of 3% or less were included if the fund did not also have a 12b-1 charge. Funds with redemption fees that disappear after six months that also have 12b-1 charges appear in this *Guide*.
- Funds with 12b-1 plans and no front- or back-end loads were included in the *Guide*; we note, however, if the fund has a 12b-1 plan and what the maximum annual charge is. Investors should carefully assess these plans individually.
- Funds that impose a load that exceeds 3% or increase an existing load above 3% are dropped from the *Guide*.

A Key to Terms and Statistics

Most of the information used in the mutual fund data pages and performance tables is provided by Micropal, but some may come from mutual fund reports (the prospectus and annual and quarterly reports) and solicitation of information directly from the fund. Any data source has the potential for error, however, and before investing in any mutual fund, the prospectus for the fund should be read and the annual report examined.

When *na* appears in the performance tables or on the mutual fund page, it indicates that the number was not available or does not apply in that particular instance. For example, the 10-year annual return figure would not be available for funds that have been operating less than 10 years. For three-year annual return, category risk, standard deviation, total risk, and beta, funds operating less than three years would not have the number available. We do not compile the bull and bear ratings for funds not operating during the entire bull or bear market period. Dashes (—) are used generally during years when the fund was not in operation or did not have a complete calendar year of operations. All numbers are truncated rather than rounded when necessary, unless noted otherwise in the following descriptions.

The following provides an explanation of the terms we have used in the performance tables and mutual fund data pages. The explanations are listed in the order in which the data and information appear on the mutual fund pages.

Fund Name: The funds are presented alphabetically by fund name.

Ticker: The ticker symbol for each fund is given in parentheses for those investors who may want to access on-line data with their computer or touch-tone phone. The ticker is four letters and is usually followed by an "X," indicating that this is a mutual fund. For example, the Acorn fund ticker symbol is ACRNX.

Investment Category: The fund's investment category is indicated at the top of the page next to the fund's ticker symbol. After evaluating the information and statistics, we placed all mutual funds in exclusive categories by investment category and type of investment. For more complete definitions of the mutual fund investment categories used in the *Guide*, see Chapter 3: "Mutual Fund Categories" on page 5.

Fund Address, Telephone Number(s), and Internet and Web Address: The management company address, telephone number, and Internet and Web address (if applicable) where investors can write or call to have specific questions answered or to obtain a copy of the prospectus.

Fund Inception Date: The day the fund was made available to the public for purchase.

Performance

Return (%): Return percentages for the periods below.

3yr Annual: Assuming an investment on January 1, 1994, the annual total return if held through December 31, 1996.

5yr Annual: Assuming an investment on January 1, 1992, the annual total return if held through December 31, 1996.

10yr Annual: Assuming an investment on January 1, 1987, the annual total return if held through December 31, 1996.

Bull: This return reflects the fund's performance in the most recent bull market, starting July 1, 1994, and continuing through December 31, 1996.

Bear: This return reflects the fund's performance in the most recent bear market, from February 1, 1994, through June 30, 1994.

Differ from category (+/–): The difference between the return for the fund and average return for all funds in the same investment category for the *3yr Annual, 5yr Annual, 10yr Annual, Bull,* and *Bear* periods. When the difference from category is negative, the fund underperformed the average fund in its investment category for the period by the percent indicated. The rankings, with possibilities of high, above average, average, below average, and low, are relative to all other funds within the same investment category. A rank of high, for example, would indicate that the return is in the highest 20% for that time period of all funds in the investment category.

Total Risk: The total risk of a fund relative to the total risk of all funds in the *Guide,* measured over the last three years. A high total risk indicates that the fund was in the group that had the greatest volatility of return for all funds, and a low total risk puts it into the group with the lowest volatility of return. Possibilities are high, above average, average, below average, and low.

Standard Deviation: A measure of total risk, expressed as an annual return, that indicates the degree of variation in return experienced relative to the average return for a fund as measured over the last three years. The higher the standard deviation, the greater the total risk of the fund. Standard deviation of any fund can be compared to any other fund.

Category Risk: The total risk of the fund relative to the average total risk for funds within the same investment category as measured over the last three years. High category risk would, for example, indicate one of the highest total risks in the investment category. The possibilities are high, above average, average, below average, and low.

Risk Index: A numerical measure of relative category risk, the risk index is a ratio of the total risk of the fund to the average total risk of funds in the category as measured over the last three years. Ratios above 1.0 indicate higher than average risk and ratios below 1.0 indicate lower than average risk for the category. Numbers are rounded rather than truncated.

Beta: A risk measure that relates the fund's volatility of returns to the market. The higher the beta of a fund, the higher the market risk of the fund. The figure is based on monthly returns for 36 months. A beta of 1.0 indicates that the fund's returns will on average be as volatile as the market and move in the same direction; a beta higher than 1.0 indicates that if the market rises or falls, the fund will rise or fall respectively but to a greater degree; a beta of less than 1.0 indicates that if the market rises or falls, the fund will rise or fall to a lesser degree. The S&P 500 index always has a beta of 1.0 because it is the measure we selected to represent the overall stock market. Beta is a meaningful figure of risk only for well-diversified common stock portfolios. For sector funds and other concentrated portfolios, beta is less useful than total risk as a measure of risk. Beta was not calculated for bond funds since they do not react in the same way to the factors that affect the stock market. For bond funds, the average maturity of the bond portfolio is more indicative of market risk, so it is used in place of beta.

Avg Mat: For bond funds, average maturity in years is an indication of market risk. When interest rates rise, bond prices fall and when interest rates fall, bond prices rise. The longer the average maturity of the bonds held in the portfolio, the greater will be the sensitivity of the fund to interest rate changes and thus the greater the risk. The refinancing of mortgages and the calling of outstanding bonds can affect average maturity when interest rates decline. An *na* indicates that the mutual fund did not provide an average maturity figure.

Return (%): This is a total return figure, expressed as a percentage. All distributions were assumed to have been reinvested. Rate of return is calculated on the basis of the calendar year. Return figures do not take into account front-end and back-end loads, redemption fees, or one-time or annual account charges, if any. The 12b-1 charge, as part of the expense ratio, is reflected in the return figure.

Differ from Category (+/–): The difference between the return for the fund and average return for all funds in the same investment category for the time period.

Return, Tax-Adjusted (%): Annual return after adjusting for the maximum federal income tax (39.6%) on income and short-term capital gains distributions and the federal income tax distributions (28%) on long-term capital gains.

Per Share Data

Dividends, Net Income ($): Per share income distributions for the calendar year.

Distrib'ns, Cap Gains ($): Per share distributions for the calendar year from realized capital gains after netting out realized losses. These distributions vary each year with both the investment success of the fund and the amount of securities sold.

Net Asset Value ($): Calendar year-end net asset value is the sum of all securities held, based on their market value, divided by the number of mutual fund shares outstanding.

Expense Ratio (%): The sum of administrative fees plus adviser management fees and 12b-1 fees divided by the average net asset value of the fund, stated as a percentage. Brokerage costs incurred by the fund are not included in the expense ratio but are instead reflected directly in net asset value. Front-end loads, back-end loads, redemption fees, and account activity charges are not included in this ratio.

Annual Yield (%): The per share annual income distribution made by the fund divided by the sum of the year-ending net asset value plus any capital gains distributions made during the year. This ratio is similar to a dividend yield and would be higher for income-oriented funds and lower for growth-oriented funds. The figure only reflects income; it is not total return. For some funds the yield may be distorted if the fund reports short-term capital gains as income.

Portfolio Turnover (%): A measure of the trading activity of the fund, which is computed by dividing the lesser of purchases or sales for the year by the monthly average value of the securities owned by the fund during the year. Securities with maturities of less than one year are excluded from the calculation. The result is expressed as a percentage, with 100% implying a complete portfolio turnover within one year.

Total Assets (Millions $): Aggregate fund value in millions of dollars at the end of the calendar year.

Portfolio

Portfolio Manager: The name of the portfolio manager(s) and the year when the senior manager(s) began managing the fund are noted, providing additional information useful in evaluating past performance. (Senior managers are listed first.) Funds managed by a committee are so noted. For some funds, a recent change in the portfolio manager(s) may indicate that the long-term annual performance figures and other performance classifications are less meaningful.

Investm't Category: Notes the investment category of the fund. Following this is the geographical distribution, and any special emphasis of the fund. The possible choices in the section include:

Geographical Distribution: Domestic, Foreign

Special Emphasis: Asset Allocation, Index, Sector, and State Specific

Investment Style: Investment style can be categorized by the size of firms the fund invests in and the investment approach employed by the fund, either growth or value. The investment style attributed to the fund indicates that the historical performance of the fund most closely follows the style checked (listed below). More than one style may be checked, indicating a blend of size and/or approach of the fund's investments. Style is *only* calculated for equity funds with three or more years of performance data, otherwise this section appears in gray.

Style Categories: Large-Cap Growth, Large-Cap Value, Mid-Cap Growth, Mid-Cap Value, Small-Cap Growth, Small-Cap Value ('Cap' denotes capitalization.)

Portfolio: The portfolio composition classifies investments by type and gives the percentage of the total portfolio invested in each. Due to rounding of the percentages and the practice of leverage (borrowing) to buy securities, the portfolio total percentage may not equal 100.0%.

Shareholder Information

Minimum Investment and Minimum IRA Investment: The minimum initial and subsequent investments, by mail, in the fund are detailed. Minimum investment by telephone or by wire may be different. Often, funds will have a lower minimum IRA investment; this is also indicated.

Maximum Fees:

Load: The maximum load is given, if any, and whether the load is front-end or back-end is indicated.

12b-1: If a fund has a 12b-1 plan, the maximum percentage that can be charged is given; service charges, if any, are included in the 12b-1 charge figure.

Other: Redemption fees are given along with the time period, if appropriate. The symbol *f* denotes dollar charges, such as an annual account fee, an account start-up fee, an account close-out fee, or a below minimum balance fee. The symbol *ff* is used to note the $7.50 redemption fee charged by the Fidelity Select Funds for the redemption of shares held for 30 days or more.

Distributions: The months in which income and capital gains distributions are made are indicated, when available.

Exchange Options:

Number Per Year: Indicates the maximum number of exchanges allowed.

Fee: Indicates any fees charged for exchanges.

Telephone: Indicates whether telephone exchanges with other funds in the family are permitted. If exchange privileges are allowed, we have indicated whether exchanges are available with a money market fund (money market fund available).

Services: Investor services provided by the fund are detailed. These include the availability for IRA (IRA) and other pension plans (pension); whether the fund allows for an automatic exchange between funds in the family (auto exchange); whether the fund allows for automatic investments through an investor's checking account (auto invest); and whether the fund allows the automatic and systematic withdrawal of money from the fund (auto withdraw). Since all funds have automatic reinvestment of distributions options, this service was not specifically noted.

Fund Performance Rankings

When choosing among mutual funds, most investors start with performance statistics: How well have the various mutual funds performed in the past? If past performance alone could perfectly predict future performance, selection would be easy.

What past performance can tell you is how well the fund's management has handled different market environments, how consistent the fund has been, and how well the fund has done relative to its risk level, relative to other similar funds, and relative to the market.

We present performance statistics in several different forms. First, we provide an overall picture, with the average performance of each mutual fund category for the last five years, along with benchmarks for large and small company domestic stocks, international stocks, bonds, and Treasury bills. The top 20 and bottom 20 mutual fund performers for 1996 are given as a recent reference of performance. The list changes each year and reflects the cyclical nature of financial markets and the changing success of individual mutual fund managers. Lists of the top 50 mutual funds ranked by annual return over the last 10 years, five years, and three years are given for a long-term perspective on investment performance.

Since the performance of a fund must be judged relative to similar funds, we have also grouped the funds by investment category and ranked them according to their total return performance for 1996. To make the comparison easier, we have also provided other data. The fund's annual returns for the last three years, five years, and 10 years give a longer-term perspective on the performance of the fund; category and total risk ranks are also given to judge performance. (To maintain ranking accuracy, funds are sorted by more precise numbers than those published in the *Guide*.)

Key to Fund Categories used in Performance Tables

AG-Aggressive Growth	**B-CHY-**Corp. High-Yield Bond	**IntlS-**International Stock
Grth-Growth	**B-Gov-**Government Bond	**IntlB-**International Bond
GI-Growth & Income	**B-MB-**Mortgage-Backed Bond	**Gld-**Gold
Bal-Balanced	**B-Gen-**General Bond	
B-Cor-Corporate Bond	**B-TE-**Tax-Exempt Bond	

Total Risk and Return Performance
for Different Mutual Fund Categories

Fund Investment Category	Annual Return (%) 1996	1995	1994	1993	1992	5yr	Total Return (%) Bull	Bear	Std Dev (%)	Total Risk
Aggressive Growth	19.1	34.3	0.0	19.3	11.7	15.3	71.1	-10.6	14.3	high
Growth	20.1	30.3	-0.3	14.0	11.8	14.3	62.4	-6.7	10.4	abv av
Growth & Income	19.7	30.1	-1.3	13.8	10.7	13.9	59.8	-6.4	9.3	av
Balanced	14.2	24.6	-1.6	14.4	8.9	11.4	45.1	-5.7	6.8	blw av
Corporate Bond	5.2	18.0	-3.1	11.8	8.9	8.3	24.8	-5.1	4.6	low
Corporate High-Yield Bond	15.3	17.5	-2.9	18.9	16.1	12.1	33.1	-5.4	4.6	low
Government Bond	1.5	19.6	-4.4	11.6	6.7	6.6	22.0	-6.4	4.1	low
Mortgage-Backed Bond	4.4	14.7	-1.7	6.9	6.2	6.0	21.1	-3.6	3.8	low
General Bond	3.9	14.9	-2.3	9.1	6.5	6.1	20.3	-4.2	3.8	low
Tax-Exempt Bond	3.7	15.2	-5.3	11.8	8.3	6.4	18.4	-5.4	5.6	blw av
International Stock	14.8	9.1	-3.1	39.6	-3.8	10.0	24.3	-7.2	10.3	abv av
International Bond	11.3	16.0	-7.6	15.3	5.2	6.6	31.2	-9.5	7.0	av
Gold	11.2	5.0	-12.1	87.8	-15.3	9.6	14.9	-10.2	25.0	high
Domestic Equity	19.6	31.5	-0.5	15.6	11.5	14.5	64.4	-7.8	10.5	abv av
Small Capitalization Stock	19.9	31.4	0.2	17.4	14.9	15.2	68.3	-9.5	11.3	abv av
Domestic Taxable Bond	4.4	16.6	-2.9	10.4	7.5	6.9	22.2	-4.8	3.9	low
Average For All Funds	**13.1**	**22.3**	**-2.5**	**17.3**	**8.2**	**11.0**	**41.5**	**-6.7**	**8.7**	**av**
Index Comparisons										
S&P 500	22.9	37.5	1.3	10.0	7.6	15.1	77.3	-6.6	9.7	abv av
Russell 2000*	16.4	28.4	-1.9	18.9	18.4	15.6	57.0	-9.3	12.1	high
MS EAFE**	6.3	11.5	8.0	32.9	-11.9	8.4	17.7	0.4	11.0	abv av
Lehman Brothers bond indexes										
Corporate	3.2	22.2	-4.0	12.1	8.6	8.1	27.7	-6.9	5.8	blw av
Corporate High Yield	11.3	19.1	-1.1	17.1	15.7	12.2	34.3	-4.4	4.4	low
Government	2.7	18.3	-3.4	10.6	7.2	6.8	22.5	-5.5	4.7	blw av
Mortgage Backed	5.3	16.8	-1.7	6.8	6.9	6.7	24.7	-4.0	4.0	low
Municipal	4.4	17.4	-5.2	12.2	8.8	6.4	17.1	-5.6	5.3	blw av
Treasury Bills	5.2	5.6	3.9	2.9	3.3	4.2	13.6	1.4	0.3	low

*Index of small company stocks
**Europe, Australia, Far East Index

Total Risk & Return for Domestic Taxable Bond Mutual Funds by Maturity

Maturity Category	Annual Return (%) 1996	1995	1994	1993	1992	5yr	Total Return (%) Bull	Bear	Std Dev (%)	Total Risk
Short-Term Bond Funds	4.8	10.2	0.0	6.0	5.5	5.1	16.5	-1.5	1.9	low
Intermediate-Term Bond Funds	5.3	17.0	-3.2	11.0	8.2	7.2	23.2	-5.1	4.4	low
Long-Term Bond Funds	2.2	22.3	-4.8	13.2	7.6	7.7	26.1	-7.2	6.2	blw av

The Top 20 Performers: 1996

Type	Fund Name	Annual Return (%)				Category Risk	Total Risk
		1996	3yr	5yr	10yr		
AG	Warburg Pincus Small Co Value	56.1	na	na	na	na	na
AG	PBHG Technology & Communications	54.4	na	na	na	na	na
AG	Fidelity Sel Energy Service	49.0	28.2	21.4	11.1	abv av	high
AG	Fremont US Micro Cap	48.7	na	na	na	na	na
GI	CGM Realty	44.0	na	na	na	na	na
AG	Fidelity Sel Electronics	41.7	41.0	36.4	20.0	high	high
IntlB	Fidelity New Markets Income	41.3	8.4	na	na	high	high
IntlS	Robertson Stephens Glbl Natrl Res	41.2	na	na	na	na	na
IntlS	Fidelity Hong Kong & China	40.9	na	na	na	na	na
Gld	INVESCO Strat Port—Gold	40.6	4.5	12.6	3.8	high	high
AG	Oakmark Small Cap	39.7	na	na	na	na	na
AG	Fidelity Sel Brokerage & Investment	39.6	12.6	17.5	11.3	abv av	high
AG	INVESCO Strat Port—Energy	38.8	15.5	9.3	8.1	av	high
Grth	Fidelity Export	38.6	na	na	na	na	na
GI	Cohen & Steers Realty Shares	38.4	18.5	18.8	na	high	high
Grth	Legg Mason Value Trust/Prim	38.4	25.4	19.6	14.3	high	high
AG	Dreyfus Grth & Value: Emerging Ldrs	37.4	na	na	na	na	na
AG	Montgomery Small Cap Opportunities	37.2	na	na	na	na	na
AG	Fidelity Sel Home Finance	36.8	29.1	34.0	21.8	blw av	high
GI	Fidelity Real Estate Investment Port	36.2	15.5	15.6	11.8	high	abv av

The Bottom 20 Performers: 1996

Type	Fund Name	Annual Return (%)				Category Risk	Total Risk
		1996	3yr	5yr	10yr		
Gld	United Service Gold Shares	-25.5	-19.1	-10.2	-7.7	high	high
IntlS	Fidelity Japan Small Companies	-24.6	na	na	na	na	na
IntlS	Warburg Pincus Japan OTC—Common	-13.1	na	na	na	na	na
IntlS	Fidelity Japan	-11.2	0.4	na	na	high	high
IntlS	T. Rowe Price Int'l: Japan	-11.0	-0.3	0.7	na	high	high
IntlS	Japan Fund	-11.0	-3.8	-1.8	3.4	high	high
B-Gov	Benham Target Maturities Trust: 2020	-8.5	6.7	12.3	na	high	high
IntlS	Vanguard Int'l Equity Index: Pacific	-7.9	2.3	3.4	na	high	high
B-TE	Fundamental New York Muni	-7.8	-5.3	1.3	3.2	high	av
B-Gov	Benham Target Maturities Trust: 2015	-6.1	7.2	11.6	9.2	high	high
B-Gov	Benham Target Maturities Trust: 2010	-3.6	6.6	10.9	9.8	high	high
IntlS	Fidelity Pacific Basin	-2.8	-4.0	6.0	5.4	abv av	high
Gld	American Century Global Gold	-2.8	-4.1	7.9	na	abv av	high
AG	Dreyfus Special Growth—Investor	-2.6	1.3	9.5	10.3	abv av	high
B-Gov	T. Rowe Price US Treasury Long-Term	-2.4	5.7	7.1	na	high	av
B-Gov	Benham Long-Term Treasury	-1.4	4.9	na	na	high	av
B-Gov	Vanguard Long-Term US Treas	-1.3	5.9	8.3	8.7	high	av
B-Gov	Benham Target Maturities Trust: 2005	-1.3	6.0	9.7	9.7	high	abv av
GI	Warburg Pincus Grth & Inc—Common	-1.2	8.5	13.5	na	high	high
IntlS	INVESCO Int'l Fds: Pacific Basin	-1.2	2.4	5.8	6.3	abv av	high

The Top 50 Performers: 10 Years, 1987-1996

Type	Fund Name	Annual Return (%)				Category Risk	Total Risk
		10yr	5yr	3yr	1996		
AG	Fidelity Sel Home Finance	21.8	34.0	29.1	36.8	blw av	high
AG	Twentieth Century Giftrust	21.7	20.8	18.4	5.7	high	high
AG	PBHG Growth	21.2	26.6	20.0	9.8	high	high
AG	INVESCO Strat Port—Health Science	21.0	7.1	21.3	11.4	av	high
Grth	Fidelity Sel Regional Banks	20.9	26.9	25.9	35.8	high	high
AG	INVESCO Strat Port—Technology	20.4	20.6	23.1	21.7	av	high
Grth	Fidelity Contrafund	20.2	18.2	18.0	21.9	av	abv av
AG	Fidelity Sel Software & Computer	20.2	26.2	21.3	21.7	high	high
AG	Twentieth Century Ultra	20.1	13.2	14.7	13.8	abv av	high
AG	Fidelity Sel Electronics	20.0	36.4	41.0	41.7	high	high
Grth	VanguardSpecPort: Health Care	19.9	16.2	24.5	21.3	av	abv av
AG	Fidelity Sel Health Care	19.7	11.5	26.9	15.4	blw av	high
Grth	INVESCO Strat Port—Financial Svcs	19.4	20.8	19.6	30.2	abv av	abv av
AG	Kaufmann	19.3	18.8	21.7	20.9	av	high
AG	CGM Capital Development	19.2	16.0	11.6	28.1	abv av	high
Grth	Brandywine	19.2	19.1	19.2	24.9	high	high
AG	Fidelity Sel Computers	18.7	30.4	33.9	31.6	high	high
AG	Fidelity Sel Medical Delivery	18.2	10.0	20.7	11.0	abv av	high
AG	Columbia Special	18.1	15.6	14.3	13.0	av	high
AG	Berger One Hundred	18.0	11.1	8.8	13.7	blw av	abv av
AG	Fidelity Sel Food & Agriculture	18.0	13.6	17.9	13.3	low	av
Grth	Fidelity Sel Telecommunications	17.8	16.3	12.5	5.3	av	abv av
AG	Fidelity Growth Co	17.3	14.8	16.8	16.8	blw av	abv av
GI	Fidelity Growth & Income Port	17.3	17.2	18.4	20.0	blw av	av
Grth	Mairs & Power Growth	17.2	19.3	25.8	26.4	abv av	abv av
AG	INVESCO Strat Port—Leisure	17.2	14.9	6.2	9.0	low	abv av
AG	Fidelity Sel Biotechnology	17.0	3.0	8.8	5.5	abv av	high
AG	Fidelity Sel Multimedia	17.0	18.6	12.0	1.0	blw av	high
AG	Fidelity OTC Port	16.9	15.6	18.5	23.7	blw av	high
AG	Fidelity Sel Retailing	16.7	12.1	8.7	20.8	abv av	high
GI	SAFECO Equity	16.6	19.7	19.8	25.0	av	av
Grth	Founders Growth	16.5	16.5	17.9	16.5	high	high
AG	Janus Twenty	16.5	11.3	17.5	27.8	blw av	high
Grth	Janus Fund	16.4	12.6	15.2	19.6	low	av
AG	INVESCO Dynamics	16.4	16.0	15.9	15.6	blw av	abv av
AG	Fidelity Sel Technology	16.3	20.9	22.7	15.8	high	high
AG	T. Rowe Price New Horizons	16.2	19.7	22.1	17.0	av	high
Grth	Strong Schafer Value	16.2	18.4	16.5	23.2	av	abv av
Grth	Fidelity Magellan	16.2	14.8	14.4	11.6	abv av	abv av
Grth	Fidelity Sel Chemicals	16.2	15.7	19.2	21.5	abv av	abv av
Grth	Acorn Invest Trust: Acorn	16.1	17.6	11.0	22.5	av	abv av
GI	Sequoia	16.0	16.5	21.1	21.7	high	abv av
AG	Sit Mid Cap Growth	15.8	11.4	17.4	21.8	abv av	high
Grth	T. Rowe Price New America Growth	15.8	15.6	17.0	20.0	high	high
AG	Janus Venture	15.8	11.0	12.9	8.0	av	high
Grth	William Blair Mutual Fds: Growth	15.7	15.0	17.4	17.9	abv av	abv av
Grth	Columbia Growth	15.7	15.0	16.8	20.8	abv av	abv av
Grth	Fidelity Sel Financial Services	15.6	25.7	23.3	32.1	high	high
Grth	Gabelli Asset	15.6	14.6	12.2	13.3	low	av
AG	Founders Special	15.4	11.6	11.2	15.3	av	high

The Top 50 Performers: 5 Years, 1992-1996

Type	Fund Name	5yr	10yr	3yr	1996	Category Risk	Total Risk
AG	Fidelity Sel Electronics	36.4	20.0	41.0	41.7	high	high
AG	Fidelity Sel Home Finance	34.0	21.8	29.1	36.8	blw av	high
AG	Fidelity Sel Computers	30.4	18.7	33.9	31.6	high	high
Grth	Fidelity Sel Regional Banks	26.9	20.9	25.9	35.8	high	high
AG	PBHG Growth	26.6	21.2	20.0	9.8	high	high
AG	Fidelity Sel Software & Computer	26.2	20.2	21.3	21.7	high	high
Grth	Fidelity Sel Financial Services	25.7	15.6	23.3	32.1	high	high
Grth	Oakmark	25.6	na	17.2	16.2	blw av	av
AG	T. Rowe Price Science & Technology	24.8	na	27.1	14.2	abv av	high
AG	Heartland Value	22.0	15.2	16.8	20.9	low	abv av
AG	Fidelity Sel Industrial Equipment	21.7	12.3	18.6	26.7	av	high
Grth	First Eagle Fund of America	21.4	na	19.7	29.3	abv av	abv av
AG	Fidelity Sel Energy Service	21.4	11.1	28.2	49.0	abv av	high
AG	Fidelity Sel Technology	20.9	16.3	22.7	15.8	high	high
Grth	INVESCO Strat Port—Financial Svcs	20.8	19.4	19.6	30.2	abv av	abv av
AG	Twentieth Century Giftrust	20.8	21.7	18.4	5.7	high	high
Grth	Fidelity Low Priced Stock	20.8	na	18.4	26.8	low	av
AG	Skyline: Special Equities Port	20.7	na	13.6	30.3	low	abv av
AG	INVESCO Strat Port—Technology	20.6	20.4	23.1	21.7	av	high
Gld	Midas	20.4	10.8	11.1	21.2	high	high
AG	Baron Asset	20.0	na	21.0	21.9	blw av	high
Grth	Longleaf Partners	19.8	na	18.9	21.0	low	av
GI	SAFECO Equity	19.7	16.6	19.8	25.0	av	av
AG	T. Rowe Price New Horizons	19.7	16.2	22.1	17.0	av	high
Grth	Legg Mason Value Trust/Prim	19.6	14.3	25.4	38.4	high	high
Grth	Mairs & Power Growth	19.3	17.2	25.8	26.4	abv av	abv av
AG	Fidelity Sel Defense & Aerospace	19.2	9.8	23.3	25.0	blw av	high
Grth	Brandywine	19.1	19.2	19.2	24.9	high	high
Grth	Brandywine Blue	19.1	na	18.6	23.2	high	high
AG	Strong Common Stock	19.1	na	16.6	20.4	low	abv av
AG	Fidelity Sel Developing Communications	19.0	na	15.6	14.5	high	high
Grth	Fidelity Value	18.9	14.2	16.9	16.8	low	av
GI	Cohen & Steers Realty Shares	18.8	na	18.5	38.4	high	high
Bal	Third Avenue Value	18.8	na	16.5	21.9	high	av
AG	Kaufmann	18.8	19.3	21.7	20.9	av	high
AG	SteinRoe Capital Opportunities	18.8	14.6	21.9	20.3	abv av	high
Grth	T. Rowe Price Small Cap Value	18.8	na	16.6	24.6	low	av
AG	Fidelity Sel Multimedia	18.6	17.0	12.0	1.0	blw av	high
Grth	Sound Shore	18.6	14.7	20.1	33.2	blw av	av
AG	Crabbe Huson Special	18.6	na	9.4	5.9	low	abv av
GI	Babson Value	18.6	14.5	18.3	22.7	blw av	av
Grth	Strong Schafer Value	18.4	16.2	16.5	23.2	av	abv av
Grth	Fidelity Contrafund	18.2	20.2	18.0	21.9	av	abv av
Grth	Vanguard PRIMECAP	18.0	15.0	21.3	18.3	high	high
Grth	Neuberger & Berman Partners	18.0	14.7	18.8	26.4	abv av	abv av
GI	Vanguard Windsor	17.9	14.0	17.9	26.3	high	abv av
AG	Royce: Micro-Cap	17.9	na	12.5	15.5	low	av
Grth	Acorn Invest Trust: Acorn	17.6	16.1	11.0	22.5	av	abv av
AG	IAI Emerging Growth	17.6	na	17.0	6.9	high	high
Grth	Neuberger & Berman Focus	17.5	14.9	16.8	16.2	high	high

The Top 50 Performers: Three Years, 1994-1996

Type	Fund Name	Annual Return (%)				Category Risk	Total Risk
		3yr	5yr	10yr	1996		
AG	Fidelity Sel Electronics	41.0	36.4	20.0	41.7	high	high
AG	Fidelity Sel Computers	33.9	30.4	18.7	31.6	high	high
AG	Fidelity Sel Home Finance	29.1	34.0	21.8	36.8	blw av	high
AG	PBHG Emerging Growth	29.0	na	na	17.0	high	high
AG	Fidelity Sel Energy Service	28.2	21.4	11.1	49.0	abv av	high
AG	T. Rowe Price Science & Technology	27.1	24.8	na	14.2	abv av	high
AG	Fidelity Sel Health Care	26.9	11.5	19.7	15.4	blw av	high
AG	Robertson Stephens Value + Growth	26.0	na	na	14.0	high	high
Grth	Fidelity Sel Regional Banks	25.9	26.9	20.9	35.8	high	high
Grth	Mairs & Power Growth	25.8	19.3	17.2	26.4	abv av	abv av
Grth	Strong Growth	25.4	na	na	19.5	high	high
Grth	Legg Mason Value Trust/Prim	25.4	19.6	14.3	38.4	high	high
Grth	VanguardSpecPort: Health Care	24.5	16.2	19.9	21.3	av	abv av
AG	Fidelity New Millennium	23.6	na	na	23.1	av	high
Grth	Fidelity Sel Financial Services	23.3	25.7	15.6	32.1	high	high
AG	Fidelity Sel Defense & Aerospace	23.3	19.2	9.8	25.0	blw av	high
AG	INVESCO Strat Port—Technology	23.1	20.6	20.4	21.7	av	high
Grth	Fidelity Dividend Growth	23.1	na	na	30.1	abv av	abv av
AG	Fidelity Sel Technology	22.7	20.9	16.3	15.8	high	high
AG	T. Rowe Price New Horizons	22.1	19.7	16.2	17.0	av	high
AG	SteinRoe Capital Opportunities	21.9	18.8	14.6	20.3	abv av	high
Grth	Janus Mercury	21.9	na	na	17.6	high	high
Grth	Vanguard US Growth Port	21.9	12.9	14.7	26.0	blw av	abv av
AG	SSgA: Small Cap	21.8	na	na	28.7	low	abv av
AG	Kaufmann	21.7	18.8	19.3	20.9	av	high
Grth	Montgomery Growth—R	21.5	na	na	20.2	blw av	av
Grth	Dreyfus Appreciation	21.5	13.6	14.8	25.6	blw av	abv av
Grth	Yacktman	21.3	na	na	26.0	low	av
AG	INVESCO Strat Port—Health Science	21.3	7.1	21.0	11.4	av	high
Grth	Vanguard PRIMECAP	21.3	18.0	15.0	18.3	high	high
AG	Fidelity Sel Software & Computer	21.3	26.2	20.2	21.7	high	high
Bal	Value Line Asset Allocation	21.2	na	na	26.6	high	av
GI	Sequoia	21.1	16.5	16.0	21.7	high	abv av
AG	Wasatch Mid-Cap	21.1	na	na	3.5	high	high
AG	Berger Small Co Growth	21.1	na	na	16.7	abv av	high
GI	T. Rowe Price Blue Chip Growth	21.0	na	na	27.7	av	av
AG	Baron Asset	21.0	20.0	na	21.9	blw av	high
Grth	T. Rowe Price Mid-Cap Growth	20.8	na	na	24.8	abv av	abv av
Grth	Vanguard Index Trust: Growth Port	20.7	na	na	23.8	av	abv av
AG	Fidelity Sel Medical Delivery	20.7	10.0	18.2	11.0	abv av	high
GI	Selected American Shares	20.4	14.2	14.9	30.7	high	abv av
AG	USAA Aggressive Growth	20.2	11.4	13.1	16.4	high	high
Grth	Sound Shore	20.1	18.6	14.7	33.2	blw av	av
GI	Preferred Value	20.1	na	na	25.2	av	av
Grth	Clover Capital Equity Value	20.0	15.8	na	22.8	low	av
AG	PBHG Growth	20.0	26.6	21.2	9.8	high	high
GI	SAFECO Equity	19.8	19.7	16.6	25.0	av	av
Grth	First Eagle Fund of America	19.7	21.4	na	29.3	abv av	abv av
GI	American Century Value	19.7	na	na	24.2	blw av	av
GI	Dodge & Cox Stock	19.6	17.5	15.3	22.2	abv av	abv av

Aggressive Growth Funds
Ranked by 1996 Total Returns

Fund Name	Annual Return (%)				Category Risk	Total Risk
	1996	3yr	5yr	10yr		
Warburg Pincus Small Co Value	56.1	na	na	na	na	na
PBHG Technology & Communications	54.4	na	na	na	na	na
Fidelity Sel Energy Service	49.0	28.2	21.4	11.1	abv av	high
Fremont US Micro Cap	48.7	na	na	na	na	na
Fidelity Sel Electronics	41.7	41.0	36.4	20.0	high	high
Oakmark Small Cap	39.7	na	na	na	na	na
Fidelity Sel Brokerage & Investment	39.6	12.6	17.5	11.3	abv av	high
INVESCO Strat Port—Energy	38.8	15.5	9.3	8.1	av	high
Dreyfus Grth & Value: Emerging Ldrs	37.4	na	na	na	na	na
Montgomery Small Cap Opportunities	37.2	na	na	na	na	na
Fidelity Sel Home Finance	36.8	29.1	34.0	21.8	blw av	high
PBHG Core Growth	32.8	na	na	na	na	na
Fidelity Sel Computers	31.6	33.9	30.4	18.7	high	high
Loomis Sayles Small Cap	30.3	16.4	17.3	na	blw av	abv av
Skyline: Special Equities Port	30.3	13.6	20.7	na	low	abv av
Turner Small Cap	28.8	na	na	na	na	na
SSgA: Small Cap	28.7	21.8	na	na	low	abv av
Lindner Bulwark	28.7	na	na	na	na	na
Legg Mason Special Investment Trust/Prim	28.6	11.0	14.4	14.5	av	high
SteinRoe Special Venture	28.6	na	na	na	na	na
CGM Capital Development	28.1	11.6	16.0	19.2	abv av	high
PBHG Select Equity	27.9	na	na	na	na	na
Bonnel Growth	27.9	na	na	na	na	na
Janus Twenty	27.8	17.5	11.3	16.5	blw av	high
Caldwell & Orkin Market Opportunity	27.2	13.6	14.2	na	low	av
Van Wagoner Emerging Growth	26.8	na	na	na	na	na
T. Rowe Price Health Sciences	26.7	na	na	na	na	na
Robertson Stephens Information Age	26.7	na	na	na	na	na
Fidelity Sel Industrial Equipment	26.7	18.6	21.7	12.3	av	high
Vanguard Horizon Fd: Aggressive Growth	25.1	na	na	na	na	na
Fidelity Sel Defense & Aerospace	25.0	23.3	19.2	9.8	blw av	high
Scudder Small Co Value	23.8	na	na	na	na	na
Fidelity OTC Port	23.7	18.5	15.6	16.9	blw av	high
Ariel Growth	23.5	11.9	11.2	13.9	low	av
Oberweis Emerging Growth Port	23.1	19.2	16.1	na	high	high
Fidelity New Millennium	23.1	23.6	na	na	av	high
SAFECO Growth	22.8	15.0	12.5	14.5	av	high
Strong Small Cap	22.6	na	na	na	na	na
Rainier Investment: Small/Mid Cap Equity	22.5	na	na	na	na	na
Value Line Leveraged Growth Investors	22.3	17.3	12.8	14.3	blw av	high
Baron Asset	21.9	21.0	20.0	na	blw av	high
Sit Mid Cap Growth	21.8	17.4	11.4	15.8	abv av	high
Fidelity Sel Software & Computer	21.7	21.3	26.2	20.2	high	high
INVESCO Strat Port—Technology	21.7	23.1	20.6	20.4	av	high
Janus Olympus	21.7	na	na	na	na	na
Robertson Stephens Emerging Growth	21.5	16.4	10.5	na	high	high
Northern Select Equity	21.5	na	na	na	na	na
Founders Discovery	21.2	13.6	13.3	na	high	high
T. Rowe Price OTC	21.0	17.4	16.9	12.3	low	abv av
Heartland Value	20.9	16.8	22.0	15.2	low	abv av
Kaufmann	20.9	21.7	18.8	19.3	av	high

Aggressive Growth Funds
Ranked by 1996 Total Returns

Fund Name	Annual Return (%)				Category Risk	Total Risk
	1996	3yr	5yr	10yr		
Fidelity Sel Retailing	20.8	8.7	12.1	16.7	abv av	high
Dreyfus Grth & Value: Aggressive Grth	20.6	na	na	na	na	na
Marshall Mid Cap Stock	20.6	15.0	na	na	av	high
Strong Common Stock	20.4	16.6	19.1	na	low	abv av
Preferred Small Cap	20.4	na	na	na	na	na
SteinRoe Capital Opportunities	20.3	21.9	18.8	14.6	abv av	high
Galaxy II: Small Co Index	19.6	15.3	13.9	na	low	abv av
Montgomery Micro Cap	19.1	na	na	na	na	na
Northern Small Cap	18.9	na	na	na	na	na
Heartland Small Cap Contrarian	18.8	na	na	na	na	na
WPG Tudor	18.8	14.8	12.5	13.7	abv av	high
SteinRoe Special	18.8	10.8	13.3	15.1	low	av
INVESCO Strat Port—Environmental	18.7	14.0	2.8	na	av	high
Montgomery Small Cap	18.6	13.0	14.4	na	av	high
Vanguard Index Trust: Small Cap Stock	18.1	14.7	16.2	12.4	blw av	abv av
Dreyfus New Leaders	17.3	14.9	14.2	14.3	low	abv av
Warburg Pincus Post-Vent Cap—Common	17.2	na	na	na	na	na
PBHG Emerging Growth	17.0	29.0	na	na	high	high
T. Rowe Price New Horizons	17.0	22.1	19.7	16.2	av	high
Fidelity Growth Co	16.8	16.8	14.8	17.3	blw av	abv av
Berger Small Co Growth	16.7	21.1	na	na	abv av	high
T. Rowe Price Capital Opportunity	16.7	na	na	na	na	na
USAA Aggressive Growth	16.4	20.2	11.4	13.1	high	high
Fidelity Sel Automotive	16.0	4.7	17.0	14.1	blw av	high
Fidelity Fifty	15.9	16.7	na	na	low	abv av
Fidelity Sel Technology	15.8	22.7	20.9	16.3	high	high
Fidelity Emerging Growth	15.7	16.2	15.3	na	abv av	high
INVESCO Dynamics	15.6	15.9	16.0	16.4	blw av	abv av
Fidelity Sel Environmental Services	15.6	9.6	5.2	na	abv av	high
Royce: Micro-Cap	15.5	12.5	17.9	na	low	av
Schwab Capital Trust: Small Cap Index	15.4	12.6	na	na	blw av	high
Fidelity Sel Health Care	15.4	26.9	11.5	19.7	blw av	high
Founders Special	15.3	11.2	11.6	15.4	av	high
Twentieth Century Growth	15.0	10.8	6.2	13.8	blw av	high
Sit Small Cap Growth	14.9	na	na	na	na	na
Fidelity Sel Developing Communications	14.5	15.6	19.0	na	high	high
Founders Frontier	14.3	15.0	14.0	na	av	high
T. Rowe Price Science & Technology	14.2	27.1	24.8	na	abv av	high
Robertson Stephens Value + Growth	14.0	26.0	na	na	high	high
Vanguard Explorer	14.0	13.2	13.6	12.9	blw av	abv av
Fidelity Sel Industrial Materials	14.0	12.4	14.1	11.3	av	high
Twentieth Century Ultra	13.8	14.7	13.2	20.1	abv av	high
Berger One Hundred	13.7	8.8	11.1	18.0	blw av	abv av
Wasatch Micro-Cap	13.6	na	na	na	na	na
Fidelity Small Cap Stock	13.6	11.6	na	na	abv av	high
Vanguard Horizon Fd: Capital Opportunity	13.4	na	na	na	na	na
Fidelity Sel Leisure	13.4	10.3	16.8	14.6	low	abv av
Fidelity Sel Food & Agriculture	13.3	17.9	13.6	18.0	low	av
Fidelity Sel Construction & Housing	13.2	7.0	14.2	12.5	blw av	abv av
Fidelity Sel Consumer Industries	13.1	10.4	12.7	na	blw av	high
Columbia Special	13.0	14.3	15.6	18.1	av	high

Aggressive Growth Funds
Ranked by 1996 Total Returns

Fund Name	Annual Return (%)				Category Risk	Total Risk
	1996	3yr	5yr	10yr		
INVESCO Diversified Fds: Small Co	12.4	11.9	na	na	low	abv av
Janus Enterprise	11.6	15.6	na	na	av	high
INVESCO Emerging Growth	11.6	11.7	16.7	na	abv av	high
INVESCO Strat Port—Health Science	11.4	21.3	7.1	21.0	av	high
Fidelity Sel Medical Delivery	11.0	20.7	10.0	18.2	abv av	high
Chesapeake Growth	10.8	15.5	na	na	high	high
Scudder Development	10.0	16.2	10.8	14.7	high	high
Merger	9.9	10.3	10.7	7.1	low	low
Warburg Pincus Emerging Grth—Common	9.8	16.5	15.9	na	av	high
PBHG Growth	9.8	20.0	26.6	21.2	high	high
Fairmont	9.5	14.5	14.6	8.2	abv av	high
Fidelity Sel Transportation	9.5	9.4	15.9	14.0	low	abv av
INVESCO Strat Port—Leisure	9.0	6.2	14.9	17.2	low	abv av
Janus Venture	8.0	12.9	11.0	15.8	av	high
Twentieth Century Vista	7.5	18.0	11.1	15.1	high	high
Value Line Special Situations	7.2	11.7	8.7	8.5	av	high
Fidelity Sel Paper & Forest Products	7.0	14.2	14.6	10.0	abv av	high
IAI Emerging Growth	6.9	17.0	17.6	na	high	high
GIT Equity Trust: Special Growth	6.9	7.8	8.9	9.8	low	abv av
Crabbe Huson Special	5.9	9.4	18.6	na	low	abv av
Twentieth Century Giftrust	5.7	18.4	20.8	21.7	high	high
Fidelity Sel Biotechnology	5.5	8.8	3.0	17.0	abv av	high
Wasatch Aggressive Equity	5.1	12.4	12.7	13.8	blw av	high
Wasatch Mid-Cap	3.5	21.1	na	na	high	high
KEY Capital Growth	3.5	9.7	na	na	abv av	high
Cappiello-Rushmore Emerging Growth	1.9	8.8	na	na	high	high
Fidelity Sel Air Transportation	1.2	8.1	12.0	9.9	high	high
Fidelity Sel Multimedia	1.0	12.0	18.6	17.0	blw av	high
Bull & Bear Special Equities	1.0	5.8	12.0	9.9	high	high
Dreyfus Special Growth—Investor	-2.6	1.3	9.5	10.3	abv av	high
Aggressive Growth Fund Average	**19.1**	**15.8**	**15.3**	**15.0**	**av**	**high**

Growth Funds
Ranked by 1996 Total Returns

Fund Name	Annual Return (%)				Category Risk	Total Risk
	1996	3yr	5yr	10yr		
Fidelity Export	38.6	na	na	na	na	na
Legg Mason Value Trust/Prim	38.4	25.4	19.6	14.3	high	high
Fidelity Sel Regional Banks	35.8	25.9	26.9	20.9	high	high
SteinRoe Young Investor	35.0	na	na	na	na	na
Fidelity Sel Natural Gas	34.3	17.7	na	na	high	high
Vanguard Spec Port: Energy	33.9	18.2	17.2	15.0	high	high
Sound Shore	33.2	20.1	18.6	14.7	blw av	av
Fidelity Sel Energy	32.4	17.3	13.4	11.3	high	high
Fidelity Sel Financial Services	32.1	23.3	25.7	15.6	high	high
Gintel	31.0	12.7	12.7	10.4	high	high
Longleaf Partners Small Cap	30.6	17.1	15.5	na	low	av

Growth Funds
Ranked by 1996 Total Returns

Fund Name	Annual Return (%)				Category Risk	Total Risk
	1996	3yr	5yr	10yr		
INVESCO Strat Port—Financial Svcs	30.2	19.6	20.8	19.4	abv av	abv av
Fidelity Dividend Growth	30.1	23.1	na	na	abv av	abv av
Eclipse Financial Asset Tr: Equity	29.8	13.9	15.6	na	av	abv av
Neuberger & Berman Genesis	29.8	17.5	16.4	na	blw av	abv av
First Eagle Fund of America	29.3	19.7	21.4	na	abv av	abv av
T. Rowe Price Value	28.5	na	na	na	na	na
Babson Enterprise II	27.6	12.3	14.7	na	abv av	abv av
American Century Equity Growth	27.3	19.5	14.6	na	blw av	av
Fidelity Low Priced Stock	26.8	18.4	20.8	na	low	av
Skyline: Special Equities II	26.5	14.6	na	na	abv av	abv av
Neuberger & Berman Partners	26.4	18.8	18.0	14.7	abv av	abv av
Mairs & Power Growth	26.4	25.8	19.3	17.2	abv av	abv av
Vanguard US Growth Port	26.0	21.9	12.9	14.7	blw av	abv av
Yacktman	26.0	21.3	na	na	low	av
Dreyfus Appreciation	25.6	21.5	13.6	14.8	blw av	abv av
Fremont Growth	25.0	18.8	na	na	av	abv av
Brandywine	24.9	19.2	19.1	19.2	high	high
T. Rowe Price Mid-Cap Growth	24.8	20.8	na	na	abv av	abv av
T. Rowe Price Small Cap Value	24.6	16.6	18.8	na	low	av
Northeast Investors Growth	24.6	19.3	11.5	13.2	av	abv av
T. Rowe Price New Era	24.2	16.4	13.1	12.1	blw av	av
Vanguard Index Trust: Growth Port	23.8	20.7	na	na	av	abv av
Ariel Appreciation	23.7	12.0	11.4	na	av	abv av
Fidelity Sel Insurance	23.7	18.4	17.1	14.4	av	abv av
PBHG Large Cap Growth	23.3	na	na	na	na	na
Vanguard/Morgan Growth	23.3	18.1	14.1	14.5	abv av	abv av
Warburg Pincus Cap Apprec—Common	23.2	18.2	15.5	na	av	abv av
Brandywine Blue	23.2	18.6	19.1	na	high	high
Strong Schafer Value	23.2	16.5	18.4	16.2	av	abv av
Scudder Equity Trust: Value	22.9	17.6	na	na	blw av	av
Clover Capital Equity Value	22.8	20.0	15.8	na	low	av
Sentry	22.8	15.7	12.0	12.6	low	av
Acorn Invest Trust: Acorn	22.5	11.0	17.6	16.1	av	abv av
Value Line	22.5	15.6	11.5	14.5	abv av	abv av
Dreyfus Growth Opportunity	22.2	13.6	7.4	11.3	av	abv av
Tweedy Browne American Value	22.1	18.2	na	na	low	av
Fidelity Contrafund	21.9	18.0	18.2	20.2	av	abv av
IAI Value	21.8	11.2	13.4	13.2	blw av	abv av
L. Roy Papp Stock	21.8	16.8	12.9	na	av	abv av
Nicholas Ltd Edition	21.8	15.4	14.3	na	abv av	abv av
Babson Growth	21.8	16.7	13.8	12.3	low	av
T. Rowe Price Growth Stock	21.7	17.1	14.5	13.2	blw av	av
Fidelity Large Cap Stock	21.5	na	na	na	na	na
Fidelity Sel Chemicals	21.5	19.2	15.7	16.2	abv av	abv av
Dreyfus Core Value/Investor	21.4	18.2	14.8	12.2	blw av	abv av
Babson Shadow Stock	21.3	12.8	14.2	na	low	av
VanguardSpecPort: Health Care	21.3	24.5	16.2	19.9	av	abv av
Babson Enterprise	21.2	13.0	15.9	14.0	low	av
World Fds: Vontobel US Value	21.2	19.4	15.9	na	blw av	av
MSB	21.1	14.1	14.7	12.2	blw av	av
Longleaf Partners	21.0	18.9	19.8	na	low	av

Growth Funds
Ranked by 1996 Total Returns

Fund Name	1996	3yr	5yr	10yr	Category Risk	Total Risk
INVESCO Growth	20.9	12.6	11.6	12.9	av	abv av
SteinRoe Growth Stock	20.9	16.4	11.9	14.0	av	abv av
Vanguard Tax Managed Capital Apprec Port	20.9	na	na	na	na	na
Columbia Growth	20.8	16.8	15.0	15.7	abv av	abv av
AARP Capital Growth	20.6	12.3	11.4	13.2	abv av	abv av
KEY Fund	20.4	14.6	14.1	13.0	low	av
Montgomery Growth—R	20.2	21.5	na	na	blw av	av
T. Rowe Price New America Growth	20.0	17.0	15.6	15.8	high	high
Loomis Sayles Growth	19.8	14.7	11.3	na	high	high
Harbor Capital Appreciation	19.8	19.5	16.0	na	high	high
Nicholas	19.7	16.3	13.4	13.9	blw av	av
Janus Fund	19.6	15.2	12.6	16.4	low	av
Scudder Equity Trust: Capital Growth	19.5	12.3	12.7	14.0	av	abv av
Strong Growth	19.5	25.4	na	na	high	high
Gradison-McDonald Opportunity Value	19.4	13.9	13.4	12.3	blw av	abv av
Clipper	19.4	19.1	16.8	14.9	abv av	abv av
Gabelli Growth	19.4	15.2	12.2	na	av	abv av
Nicholas II	19.3	15.7	12.5	13.3	av	abv av
Gradison-McDonald Established Value	19.3	14.8	15.0	13.0	low	av
Brundage Story & Rose Equity	19.2	14.7	11.2	na	av	abv av
Turner Growth Equity	19.2	13.1	na	na	high	high
Twentieth Century Select	19.2	10.3	8.0	11.6	abv av	abv av
Preferred Growth	18.7	14.6	na	na	high	high
Weitz Series Value Port	18.7	13.9	15.0	13.1	av	abv av
Stonebridge Growth	18.4	12.7	7.6	10.9	low	av
Dreyfus Midcap Index	18.4	14.0	13.5	na	abv av	abv av
Vanguard PRIMECAP	18.3	21.3	18.0	15.0	high	high
Schwartz Value	18.2	8.8	13.7	12.2	low	av
Scudder Quality Growth	18.2	15.6	10.5	na	abv av	abv av
Strong Opportunity	18.1	15.7	17.1	14.8	blw av	abv av
Royce: Premier	18.1	12.8	14.6	na	low	blw av
Fidelity Mid Cap Stock	18.1	na	na	na	na	na
William Blair Mutual Fds: Growth	17.9	17.4	15.0	15.7	abv av	abv av
Northern Growth Equity	17.8	na	na	na	na	na
USAA Growth	17.8	17.1	13.7	13.2	high	high
Janus Mercury	17.6	21.9	na	na	high	high
Vanguard Index Trust: Extended Market	17.6	15.6	14.7	na	abv av	abv av
Capstone Growth	17.2	11.7	8.3	11.9	blw av	av
Fidelity Stock Selector	17.1	17.2	16.2	na	abv av	high
Fiduciary Capital Growth	17.1	14.1	14.3	11.6	blw av	av
Fidelity Trend	16.9	10.0	13.1	13.2	abv av	abv av
Reich & Tang Equity	16.8	15.0	15.0	13.5	blw av	av
Fidelity Value	16.8	16.9	18.9	14.2	low	av
Strong Value	16.8	na	na	na	na	na
T. Rowe Price Capital Appreciation	16.8	14.1	13.4	13.3	low	blw av
IAI Midcap Growth	16.5	15.8	na	na	abv av	abv av
Founders Growth	16.5	17.9	16.5	16.5	high	high
Wasatch Growth	16.5	18.8	14.3	14.1	abv av	abv av
Neuberger & Berman Focus	16.2	16.8	17.5	14.9	high	high
Oakmark	16.2	17.2	25.6	na	blw av	av
IAI Regional	15.7	15.6	11.7	14.4	av	abv av

Guide to Low-Load Mutual Funds

Growth Funds
Ranked by 1996 Total Returns

Fund Name	Annual Return (%)				Category Risk	Total Risk
	1996	3yr	5yr	10yr		
Fidelity Blue Chip Growth	15.3	17.6	16.5	na	abv av	abv av
Twentieth Century Heritage	15.3	11.0	12.6	na	high	high
Fidelity Capital Appreciation	15.1	11.9	16.8	15.4	blw av	abv av
Fidelity Disciplined Equity	15.1	15.2	14.5	na	av	abv av
SAFECO Northwest	15.0	10.8	9.4	na	blw av	av
Weston Century Capital Port	14.5	13.6	10.9	na	av	abv av
Berwyn	14.2	12.2	15.9	12.8	abv av	abv av
Marshall Value Equity	13.9	13.3	na	na	blw av	av
Gabelli Asset	13.3	12.2	14.6	15.6	low	av
Royce: Penn Mutual	12.8	9.9	11.4	11.4	low	av
Scout Regional	12.5	10.7	9.8	6.2	low	av
Wayne Hummer Growth	11.8	11.4	9.6	11.9	blw av	av
Selected Special Shares	11.8	13.5	11.9	12.2	high	high
Crabbe Huson Equity—Prim	11.7	12.0	15.5	na	av	abv av
Marshall Stock	11.7	11.9	na	na	blw av	abv av
Fidelity Magellan	11.6	14.4	14.8	16.2	abv av	abv av
API Trust: Growth	11.3	9.7	9.7	10.5	av	abv av
FAM Value	11.2	12.4	12.2	12.8	low	av
Meridian	11.1	11.0	12.3	14.3	blw av	abv av
Harbor Growth	11.0	10.7	8.5	11.8	high	high
Neuberger & Berman Manhattan	9.8	11.5	12.4	12.7	high	high
Rightime Fund	8.5	11.5	9.2	10.4	low	blw av
Fidelity Retirement Growth	8.3	10.4	12.7	14.6	blw av	av
Cappiello-Rushmore Growth	7.2	15.3	na	na	high	high
Flex Muirfield Fd	5.7	10.9	9.5	na	low	av
Fidelity Sel Telecommunications	5.3	12.5	16.3	17.8	av	abv av
Monetta	1.6	6.8	5.2	12.4	high	high
Strong Discovery	1.4	8.8	9.9	na	high	high
Mathers	-0.1	0.2	1.1	7.4	low	blw av
Growth Fund Average	**20.1**	**15.7**	**14.3**	**13.9**	av	abv av

Growth and Income Funds
Ranked by 1996 Total Returns

Fund Name	Annual Return (%)				Category Risk	Total Risk
	1996	3yr	5yr	10yr		
CGM Realty	44.0	na	na	na	na	na
Cohen & Steers Realty Shares	38.4	18.5	18.8	na	high	high
Fidelity Real Estate Investment Port	36.2	15.5	15.6	11.8	high	abv av
Legg Mason Total Return Trust/Prim	31.1	16.6	15.6	12.1	high	abv av
Selected American Shares	30.7	20.4	14.2	14.9	high	abv av
Legg Mason American Leading Cos	28.3	14.7	na	na	av	abv av
Reynolds Blue Chip Growth	28.2	19.2	9.9	na	high	high
T. Rowe Price Blue Chip Growth	27.7	21.0	na	na	av	av
Lexington Growth & Income	26.4	14.5	13.8	11.5	abv av	abv av
Vanguard Windsor	26.3	17.9	17.9	14.0	high	abv av
Janus Growth & Income	26.0	17.7	12.9	na	high	abv av
T. Rowe Price Growth & Income	25.6	17.9	16.4	13.5	low	av

Growth and Income Funds
Ranked by 1996 Total Returns

Fund Name	1996	3yr	5yr	10yr	Category Risk	Total Risk
T. Rowe Price Dividend Growth	25.3	19.0	na	na	low	av
Preferred Value	25.2	20.1	na	na	av	av
SAFECO Equity	25.0	19.8	19.7	16.6	av	av
WPG Growth & Income	24.4	16.0	14.2	13.8	abv av	abv av
Founders Blue Chip	24.3	17.2	13.0	13.7	av	av
Dreyfus Third Century	24.3	16.0	10.8	13.5	high	abv av
1784 Growth & Income	24.2	17.2	na	na	high	abv av
American Century Value	24.2	19.7	na	na	blw av	av
Vanguard Windsor II	24.1	19.4	16.7	14.6	abv av	abv av
American Century Income & Growth	23.9	19.0	15.1	na	av	av
SSgA: Matrix Equity	23.6	16.4	na	na	av	av
American Century Equity Income	23.3	na	na	na	na	na
Lindner Utility	23.1	14.7	na	na	high	high
Vanguard Quantitative Port	23.0	18.4	15.1	15.2	abv av	abv av
Sit Large Cap Growth	23.0	18.5	12.5	13.0	high	abv av
USAA Growth & Income	23.0	17.9	na	na	av	av
Vanguard Tax Managed Grth & Inc Port	23.0	na	na	na	na	na
Vanguard Index Trust: 500 Port	22.8	19.5	15.0	15.0	abv av	abv av
Babson Value	22.7	18.3	18.6	14.5	blw av	av
T. Rowe Price Equity Index	22.6	19.3	14.7	na	abv av	abv av
SSgA: S&P 500 Index	22.6	19.4	na	na	abv av	abv av
Fidelity Market Index	22.5	19.2	14.8	na	abv av	abv av
Galaxy II: Large Co Index	22.5	19.2	14.7	na	abv av	abv av
Dreyfus S&P 500 Index	22.3	18.9	14.7	na	abv av	abv av
Dodge & Cox Stock	22.2	19.6	17.5	15.3	abv av	abv av
Scudder Growth & Income	22.1	18.0	15.8	14.3	blw av	av
Domini Social Equity	21.8	17.9	14.4	na	av	av
SteinRoe Growth & Income	21.8	16.5	14.4	na	low	av
Vanguard Index Trust: Value Port	21.7	18.3	na	na	abv av	abv av
Sequoia	21.7	21.1	16.5	16.0	high	abv av
AARP Growth & Income	21.6	18.2	15.8	13.8	blw av	av
Schwab 1000	21.5	18.3	14.5	na	av	abv av
SSgA: Growth & Income	21.4	15.9	na	na	abv av	abv av
Vanguard/Trustees' Equity—US Port	21.2	15.7	14.1	12.8	high	abv av
Marshall Equity Income	21.1	16.9	na	na	low	av
Loomis Sayles Growth & Income	21.1	17.5	15.6	na	abv av	abv av
Fidelity Equity Income	21.0	16.9	17.3	13.4	blw av	av
Lindner Growth	21.0	12.9	14.2	12.9	abv av	abv av
Vanguard Index Trust: Total Stock Market	20.9	17.9	na	na	abv av	abv av
Columbia Common Stock	20.8	17.2	15.6	na	blw av	av
American Gas Index	20.7	12.4	13.0	na	abv av	abv av
T. Rowe Price Spectrum: Growth	20.5	16.6	15.5	na	blw av	av
Aquinas Equity Income	20.4	na	na	na	na	na
T. Rowe Price Equity Income	20.3	18.8	17.0	14.4	low	av
IAI Growth & Income	20.2	13.3	10.7	12.3	av	av
Value Line Convertible	20.2	11.8	12.8	10.5	low	blw av
Fidelity Growth & Income Port	20.0	18.4	17.2	17.3	blw av	av
Harbor Value	20.0	17.8	13.7	na	blw av	av
Northern Income Equity	19.9	na	na	na	na	na
Fidelity Fund	19.8	17.7	15.9	14.4	av	av
Maxus Equity	19.2	13.6	15.7	na	low	av

Growth and Income Funds
Ranked by 1996 Total Returns

Fund Name	Annual Return (%)				Category Risk	Total Risk
	1996	3yr	5yr	10yr		
KEY Convertible Securities	19.1	11.4	13.1	na	low	blw av
Fidelity Equity Income II	18.7	15.6	16.9	na	blw av	av
WPG Quantitative Equity	18.5	16.6	na	na	av	av
INVESCO Value: Value Equity	18.4	17.2	13.2	13.5	blw av	av
Bartlett Capital Trust: Basic Value	18.4	16.0	13.9	11.5	blw av	av
Homestead Value	17.9	17.3	16.5	na	av	av
Neuberger & Berman Guardian	17.8	16.1	16.3	15.4	high	abv av
USAA Income Stock	17.8	14.6	12.6	na	low	av
Vanguard Equity Income	17.3	16.6	14.7	na	blw av	av
Hotchkis & Wiley Equity Income	17.3	15.0	14.9	na	high	abv av
Century Shares Trust	17.1	15.0	14.0	13.4	high	abv av
Royce: Equity Income	16.4	9.4	12.1	na	low	blw av
Dreyfus	15.8	11.1	9.0	10.7	high	abv av
Analytic Optioned Equity	15.6	12.9	10.3	10.2	low	blw av
Berger Growth & Income	15.6	9.2	11.0	11.8	av	av
Vanguard Convertible Securites	15.4	8.3	11.4	9.7	blw av	av
Dreyfus LifeTime Port: Grth & Inc—Retail	15.2	na	na	na	na	na
Fidelity Convertible Securities	15.0	10.5	14.1	na	low	av
Dreyfus Growth & Income	14.4	10.6	14.0	na	blw av	av
Stratton Growth	14.1	18.9	13.8	12.2	blw av	av
Strong Total Return	14.0	12.6	11.9	10.6	high	abv av
INVESCO Strat Port—Utilities	12.7	8.3	11.2	10.8	low	av
Philadelphia	12.7	9.5	13.1	10.6	low	av
Scout Stock	12.2	11.3	10.3	11.0	low	av
Fidelity Utilities Income	11.4	11.2	12.0	na	blw av	av
Fidelity Sel Utilities Growth	11.4	11.4	11.5	11.9	blw av	av
Markman Moderate Growth	11.1	na	na	na	na	na
Gateway Index Plus	10.5	9.0	7.9	9.8	low	low
Stratton Monthly Dividend Shares	8.5	5.6	6.7	7.6	av	av
Vanguard Preferred Stock	8.4	7.9	9.0	8.9	low	blw av
Strong American Utilities	8.3	13.0	na	na	av	av
Americas Utility	5.4	6.6	na	na	abv av	abv av
Vanguard Spec Port: Utilities Income	5.2	8.8	na	na	blw av	av
Copley	4.8	6.8	9.6	8.9	low	av
American Century Utilities	4.5	8.3	na	na	av	abv av
Galaxy II: Utility Index	3.4	9.0	na	na	abv av	abv av
Warburg Pincus Grth & Inc—Common	-1.2	8.5	13.5	na	high	high
Growth & Income Fund Average	**19.7**	**15.3**	**13.9**	**12.7**	**av**	**av**

Balanced Funds
Ranked by 1996 Total Returns

Fund Name	Annual Return (%)				Category Risk	Total Risk
	1996	3yr	5yr	10yr		
Baron Growth & Income	27.7	na	na	na	na	na
Value Line Asset Allocation	26.6	21.2	na	na	high	av
SAFECO Income	23.9	16.9	14.9	11.3	high	av
CGM Mutual	23.6	11.5	12.3	13.8	high	abv av
Greenspring	22.6	14.4	14.8	12.0	low	blw av
USAA Invest Trust: Growth Strategy	22.1	na	na	na	na	na
Third Avenue Value	21.9	16.5	18.8	na	high	av
Northeast Investors Trust	20.1	12.9	15.8	10.6	low	blw av
Buffalo Balanced	19.3	na	na	na	na	na
Founders Balanced	18.7	14.6	14.2	12.4	abv av	av
USAA Invest Trust: Cornerstone Strategy	17.8	11.3	12.6	10.6	abv av	av
Fidelity Asset Manager: Growth	17.5	9.3	14.4	na	high	av
Value Line Income	17.3	12.3	9.3	10.6	abv av	av
SteinRoe Balanced	17.0	11.2	10.7	10.7	av	blw av
INVESCO Industrial Income	16.7	12.6	10.9	14.7	abv av	av
Vanguard Wellington	16.1	15.4	13.4	12.5	high	av
Vanguard STAR	16.1	14.2	12.8	12.1	av	blw av
Vanguard Asset Allocation	15.7	15.2	13.3	na	high	av
Jurika & Voyles Balanced /J	15.4	12.3	na	na	high	av
Vanguard LifeStrategy: Growth Port	15.4	na	na	na	na	na
Megatrend	15.3	11.5	8.7	na	abv av	av
Janus Balanced	15.3	13.6	na	na	low	blw av
Aquinas Balanced	15.2	na	na	na	na	na
Fidelity Puritan	15.1	12.4	14.8	12.5	abv av	av
Preferred Asset Allocation	15.0	14.1	na	na	high	av
Dreyfus Asset Allocation Total Return	14.9	13.0	na	na	abv av	av
IAI Balanced	14.7	10.2	na	na	abv av	av
INVESCO Multiple Asset: Balanced	14.6	19.0	na	na	av	blw av
T. Rowe Price Balanced	14.5	11.9	11.4	11.0	blw av	blw av
Schwab Asset Director: High Growth	14.4	na	na	na	na	na
T. Rowe Price Personal Strat Fds: Bal	14.2	na	na	na	na	na
AARP Balanced Stock & Bond	14.1	na	na	na	na	na
Dodge & Cox Balanced	14.0	14.1	13.7	13.0	abv av	av
Berwyn Income	13.9	10.9	14.2	na	low	blw av
Vanguard Balanced Index	13.9	13.0	na	na	av	blw av
American Century Capital Manager	13.0	na	na	na	na	na
Eclipse Financial Asset Tr: Balanced	12.9	11.5	12.7	na	blw av	blw av
Warburg Pincus Balanced—Common	12.8	14.5	12.3	na	high	av
Montgomery Asset Allocation—R	12.8	na	na	na	na	na
Fidelity Asset Manager	12.7	7.5	11.5	na	av	av
Vanguard LifeStrategy: Moderate Grth	12.7	na	na	na	na	na
American Century Balanced Investors	12.6	10.9	6.5	na	abv av	av
INVESCO Value Trust: Total Return	12.3	13.9	12.8	na	av	blw av
Vanguard Tax Managed Balanced Port	12.2	na	na	na	na	na
Weston Century I Port	12.0	10.3	9.7	na	blw av	blw av
Columbia Balanced	11.8	11.8	11.6	na	blw av	blw av
T. Rowe Price Personal Strat Fds: Inc	11.7	na	na	na	na	na
Hotchkis & Wiley Balanced Income	11.7	12.0	11.5	11.2	blw av	blw av
Dreyfus Balanced	11.6	13.2	na	na	blw av	blw av
Scudder Portfolio Trust: Balanced	11.5	11.2	na	na	high	av
Lindner Dividend	11.5	9.4	12.7	11.2	blw av	blw av

Balanced Funds
Ranked by 1996 Total Returns

Fund Name	1996	3yr	5yr	10yr	Category Risk	Total Risk
		Annual Return (%)				
Schwab Asset Director: Balanced Growth	11.1	na	na	na	na	na
USAA Invest Trust: Growth & Tax Strategy	11.1	9.9	9.6	na	low	blw av
BB&K Diversa	10.6	6.5	8.9	7.7	av	blw av
Strong Asset Allocation	10.4	9.8	9.4	8.8	blw av	blw av
Pax World	10.3	13.5	7.8	10.7	av	blw av
Vanguard LifeStrategy: Conservative Grth	10.3	na	na	na	na	na
Vanguard Wellesley Income	9.4	10.4	10.9	11.0	av	av
Fidelity Balanced	9.3	5.9	8.8	10.5	blw av	blw av
Maxus Income	9.2	6.6	7.2	7.9	low	low
Fidelity Asset Manager: Income	7.8	7.4	na	na	low	low
Vanguard LifeStrategy: Income Port	7.6	na	na	na	na	na
T. Rowe Price Spectrum: Income	7.6	8.0	8.8	na	low	low
Crabbe Huson Asset Allocation—Prim	6.8	8.3	11.0	na	av	blw av
Permanent Portfolio	1.6	4.4	6.1	5.5	low	blw av
USAA Income	1.3	6.1	7.3	9.2	blw av	blw av
Balanced Fund Average	**14.2**	**11.7**	**11.4**	**10.8**	**av**	**blw av**

Corporate Bond Funds
Ranked by 1996 Total Returns

Fund Name	1996	3yr	5yr	10yr	Category Risk	Total Risk
		Annual Return (%)				
CGM Fixed Income	15.3	10.5	na	na	high	av
Loomis Sayles Bond	10.2	11.7	14.2	na	high	av
Janus Flexible Income	6.8	7.9	10.2	na	abv av	blw av
Janus Short-Term Bond	6.1	4.7	na	na	low	low
Dreyfus Short-Term Income	6.1	5.7	na	na	low	low
Strong Corporate Bond	5.5	9.3	10.7	7.7	high	blw av
Homestead Short-Term Bond	5.1	5.2	na	na	low	low
Fidelity Spartan Short-Term Bond	5.0	3.2	na	na	blw av	low
SteinRoe Income	4.8	6.4	8.3	8.9	av	low
Vanguard Short-Term Corporate	4.7	5.6	6.2	7.6	blw av	low
Fidelity Short-Term Bond	4.7	3.3	5.2	6.5	blw av	low
INVESCO Income—Select Income	4.7	7.6	8.9	8.4	av	low
AmSouth Mutual Fds: Ltd Maturity	3.6	4.7	5.4	na	blw av	low
Wayne Hummer Income	3.5	5.2	na	na	av	low
Vanguard Interm-Term Corporate Bond	2.7	6.1	na	na	abv av	blw av
Dreyfus A Bonds Plus	2.6	5.0	7.5	8.3	abv av	blw av
Benham Bond	2.4	5.5	6.4	na	abv av	blw av
Vanguard Long-Term Corporate	1.1	6.6	8.7	9.4	high	av
Corporate Bond Fund Average	**5.2**	**6.3**	**8.3**	**8.1**	**av**	**low**

Corporate High-Yield Funds
Ranked by 1996 Total Returns

Fund Name	Annual Return (%)				Category Risk	Total Risk
	1996	3yr	5yr	10yr		
Strong High Yield Bond	26.8	na	na	na	na	na
Janus High Yield	24.0	na	na	na	na	na
Value Line Aggressive Income Trust	19.7	11.2	12.9	9.1	av	low
Legg Mason High Yield	14.9	na	na	na	na	na
Fidelity Spartan High Income	14.1	11.7	15.6	na	blw av	low
INVESCO Income—High Yield Port	13.9	8.4	11.1	9.3	high	blw av
Nicholas Income	12.3	9.2	10.1	8.9	low	low
T. Rowe Price High Yield	11.5	5.9	10.6	8.7	high	blw av
Fidelity Capital & Income	11.4	7.4	14.6	10.5	abv av	blw av
SAFECO High Yield Bond	10.3	7.6	10.6	na	blw av	low
Vanguard High Yield Corporate	9.5	8.6	11.6	9.5	abv av	low
Corporate High-Yield Fund Average	**15.3**	**8.7**	**12.1**	**9.3**	**av**	**low**

Government Bond Funds
Ranked by 1996 Total Returns

Fund Name	Annual Return (%)				Category Risk	Total Risk
	1996	3yr	5yr	10yr		
Analytic Short-Term Gov't	5.3	5.2	na	na	low	low
Vanguard Admiral Short-Term US Treas	4.4	5.2	na	na	low	low
Vanguard Short-Term US Treas	4.3	5.2	5.7	na	blw av	low
Permanent Treasury Bill Portfolio	4.2	4.1	3.5	na	low	low
Fidelity Spartan Short Interm Gov't	4.2	5.2	na	na	blw av	low
Benham Short-Term Gov't	4.1	4.6	4.4	6.0	low	low
Fidelity Spartan Ltd Maturity Gov't	4.1	5.5	5.7	na	blw av	low
Benham Interm-Term Treasury	4.0	4.9	5.8	6.7	blw av	low
Dreyfus 100% US Treasury Short-Term	4.0	4.9	5.7	na	low	low
Fidelity Short—Interm Gov't	4.0	4.7	4.8	na	blw av	low
Schwab Short/Interm Gov't Bond	4.0	3.8	5.0	na	blw av	low
Dreyfus Short—Interm Gov't	3.9	5.1	5.9	na	blw av	low
Columbia US Gov't Securities	3.8	4.5	5.0	6.6	low	low
Benham Short-Term Treasury	3.5	4.4	na	na	low	low
Dreyfus 100% US Treasury Interm-Term	3.0	4.6	6.4	na	av	low
Northern US Gov't	3.0	na	na	na	na	na
Fidelity Spartan Gov't Income	2.6	5.3	6.0	na	av	blw av
T. Rowe Price US Treasury Interm	2.3	5.0	5.8	na	av	low
Founders Gov't Securities	2.3	1.7	3.9	na	av	low
Warburg Pincus Interm Maturity Gov't	2.2	5.3	5.9	na	av	low
Galaxy II: US Treasury Index—Retail	2.2	5.1	6.4	na	av	low
Fidelity Gov't Securities	2.0	4.5	6.7	7.8	abv av	blw av
Vanguard Admiral Interm US Treas	2.0	5.6	na	na	abv av	blw av
Benham Target Maturities Trust: 2000	1.9	4.6	7.5	8.7	abv av	blw av
Vanguard Interm-Term US Treas	1.9	5.5	7.1	na	abv av	blw av
INVESCO Value: Interm Gov't Bond	1.3	5.1	6.0	7.0	av	low
Dreyfus 100% US Treasury Long-Term	0.8	4.5	7.4	na	abv av	av
Scudder Zero Coupon 2000	0.6	3.3	6.7	7.9	abv av	blw av
Janus Interm Gov't Sec	0.5	3.5	3.5	na	av	low
US Gov't Securities	-0.5	4.5	7.4	8.4	abv av	av

Government Bond Funds
Ranked by 1996 Total Returns

	Annual Return (%)				Category	Total
Fund Name	1996	3yr	5yr	10yr	Risk	Risk
Vanguard Admiral Long-Term US Treas	-1.1	6.2	na	na	high	av
Benham Target Maturities Trust: 2005	-1.3	6.0	9.7	9.7	high	abv av
Vanguard Long-Term US Treas	-1.3	5.9	8.3	8.7	high	av
Benham Long-Term Treasury	-1.4	4.9	na	na	high	av
T. Rowe Price US Treasury Long-Term	-2.4	5.7	7.1	na	high	av
Benham Target Maturities Trust: 2010	-3.6	6.6	10.9	9.8	high	high
Benham Target Maturities Trust: 2015	-6.1	7.2	11.6	9.2	high	high
Benham Target Maturities Trust: 2020	-8.5	6.7	12.3	na	high	high
Government Bond Fund Average	**1.5**	**4.9**	**6.6**	**8.0**	**av**	**low**

Mortgage-Backed Funds
Ranked by 1996 Total Returns

	Annual Return (%)				Category	Total
Fund Name	1996	3yr	5yr	10yr	Risk	Risk
Smith Breeden Short Duration US Gov't Series	6.2	5.5	na	na	low	low
Benham Adjustable Rate Gov't Sec	5.8	4.4	4.4	na	low	low
Lexington GNMA Income	5.6	6.2	6.3	8.0	av	low
Fidelity Mortgage Securities	5.4	7.9	7.2	8.2	blw av	low
Vanguard GNMA	5.2	6.8	6.6	8.5	abv av	low
Benham GNMA	5.2	6.2	6.5	8.3	av	low
Montgomery Short Gov't Bond	5.1	5.8	na	na	low	low
Smith Breeden Interm Duration US Gov't	5.0	6.3	na	na	abv av	low
Sit US Gov't Securities	4.9	6.0	6.1	na	low	low
Fidelity Spartan Ginnie Mae	4.9	6.4	6.4	na	abv av	low
Fidelity Ginnie Mae	4.8	6.2	6.2	7.7	abv av	low
Dreyfus Basic GNMA	4.8	6.5	7.0	na	av	low
Vanguard Short-Term Federal	4.7	5.2	5.7	na	blw av	low
AARP GNMA & US Treasury	4.4	5.0	5.5	7.2	blw av	low
Dreyfus GNMA	4.4	5.3	5.8	7.3	blw av	low
Scudder GNMA	4.2	5.5	5.9	7.6	high	low
Brundage Story & Rose Sh Interm Fxd Inc	4.0	5.5	6.2	na	blw av	low
SAFECO GNMA	3.9	4.7	5.6	7.2	high	low
Value Line US Gov't Securities	3.9	2.0	4.4	7.1	high	blw av
T. Rowe Price GNMA	3.1	6.1	6.1	7.6	high	low
Marshall Gov't Income	3.0	5.4	na	na	high	low
USAA Invest Trust: GNMA	2.9	6.3	6.4	na	av	low
1784 US Gov't Medium-Term Income	2.0	4.4	na	na	abv av	low
Mortgage-Backed Bond Fund Average	**4.4**	**5.6**	**6.0**	**7.7**	**av**	**low**

General Bond Funds
Ranked by 1996 Total Returns

Fund Name	1996	3yr	5yr	10yr	Category Risk	Total Risk
	Annual Return (%)				**Category**	**Total**
Fund Name	**1996**	**3yr**	**5yr**	**10yr**	**Risk**	**Risk**
Strong Short-Term Bond	6.7	5.5	6.5	na	blw av	low
Blanchard Short-Term Flexible Income	6.6	5.5	na	na	low	low
Strong Advantage	6.6	5.8	6.7	na	low	low
Dreyfus Strategic Income	6.6	6.4	8.6	9.7	high	blw av
USAA Short-Term Bond	6.3	5.7	na	na	blw av	low
Harbor Short Duration	6.3	5.4	na	na	low	low
Hotchkis & Wiley Low Duration	6.2	8.0	na	na	low	low
Blanchard Flexible Income	5.8	4.8	na	na	av	low
Analytic Master Fixed Income	5.6	6.7	na	na	av	low
Warburg Pincus Fixed Income—Common	5.5	6.4	7.4	na	av	low
SSgA: Yield Plus	5.4	5.3	na	na	low	low
Fremont Bond	5.2	6.9	na	na	high	blw av
Marshall Short-Term Income	4.9	5.2	na	na	low	low
Harbor Bond	4.9	6.3	8.0	na	abv av	low
Neuberger & Berman Ultra Short Bond	4.8	4.6	4.1	5.8	low	low
Preferred Short-Term Gov't Securities	4.7	4.2	na	na	blw av	low
SteinRoe Interm Bond	4.5	5.9	6.9	7.8	av	low
Vanguard Bond Index Short-Term Bond	4.5	na	na	na	na	na
Neuberger & Berman Ltd Maturity Bond	4.5	4.8	5.2	6.8	blw av	low
Legg Mason US Gov't Interm/Prim	4.4	5.2	5.7	na	blw av	low
Babson Bond Trust: Port S	4.4	5.1	6.1	na	av	low
IAI Reserve	4.4	4.6	4.1	5.8	low	low
Hotchkis & Wiley Total Return	4.3	na	na	na	na	na
1784 Short-Term Income	4.3	na	na	na	na	na
Legg Mason Invest Grade/Prim	4.3	6.0	7.2	na	high	blw av
T. Rowe Price Short-Term US Gov't	4.2	4.8	4.2	na	blw av	low
IAI Bond	4.1	4.7	6.6	8.1	high	blw av
Capstone Gov't Income	3.9	3.5	3.4	4.5	low	low
T. Rowe Price Short-Term Bond	3.9	3.4	4.3	6.2	blw av	low
T. Rowe Price Summit Fds: Ltd Term Bond	3.9	3.4	na	na	blw av	low
Scudder Short-Term Bond	3.8	3.7	4.9	6.9	blw av	low
WPG Gov't Securities	3.8	2.3	4.2	6.7	abv av	low
SSgA: Interm	3.6	4.9	na	na	av	low
Fidelity Interm Bond	3.6	4.6	6.3	7.4	av	low
Dodge & Cox Income	3.6	6.5	7.7	na	high	blw av
Vanguard Bond Index Total Bond Mkt	3.5	6.0	6.9	8.0	abv av	low
Scout Bond	3.5	4.5	5.7	6.9	av	low
Scudder Portfolio Trust: Income	3.4	5.3	7.0	8.2	high	blw av
Columbia Fixed Income Securities	3.3	5.9	7.2	8.3	abv av	low
Babson Bond Trust: Port L	3.1	4.9	6.7	7.8	abv av	low
Fidelity Spartan Investment Grade Bond	3.1	5.0	na	na	high	blw av
William Blair Mutual Fds: Income	3.0	5.3	6.2	na	blw av	low
Fidelity Investment Grade Bond	3.0	4.0	7.2	8.1	abv av	low
Preferred Fixed Income	2.9	5.7	na	na	abv av	low
IAI Gov't	2.9	3.9	5.1	na	av	low
Aquinas Fixed Income	2.8	na	na	na	na	na
Strong Gov't Securities	2.8	5.9	7.9	8.8	high	blw av
AARP High Quality Bond	2.7	4.7	6.2	7.6	abv av	low
1784 Income	2.6	na	na	na	na	na
SteinRoe Gov't Income	2.6	5.1	5.7	7.3	abv av	low
Northern Fixed Income	2.5	na	na	na	na	na

Guide to Low-Load Mutual Funds

General Bond Funds
Ranked by 1996 Total Returns

Fund Name	Annual Return (%)				Category Risk	Total Risk
	1996	3yr	5yr	10yr		
Vanguard Bond Index Interm-Term Bond	2.5	na	na	na	na	na
AmSouth Mutual Fds: Bond	2.5	5.5	6.7	na	high	blw av
Marshall Interm Bond	2.4	4.6	na	na	av	low
T. Rowe Price New Income	2.3	5.8	6.3	7.7	abv av	low
Heartland US Gov't Securities	2.0	3.1	7.2	na	high	blw av
INVESCO Income—US Gov't Securities	0.4	4.4	5.8	6.4	high	blw av
Vanguard Bond Index Long-Term Bond	-0.3	na	na	na	na	na
General Bond Fund Average	**3.9**	**5.1**	**6.1**	**7.3**	**av**	**low**

Tax-Exempt Bond Funds
Ranked by 1996 Total Returns

Fund Name	Annual Return (%)				Category Risk	Total Risk
	1996	3yr	5yr	10yr		
Benham CA High Yield Muni	5.8	5.8	7.9	6.5	av	blw av
Sit Minnesota Tax-Free Income	5.8	6.0	na	na	low	low
Sit Tax-Free Income	5.6	5.8	7.1	na	low	low
Vanguard CA Tax-Free Ins Interm Term	5.4	na	na	na	na	na
USAA Tax-Exempt CA Bond	5.3	5.2	7.2	na	high	blw av
Strong High Yield Muni Bond	5.1	6.0	na	na	blw av	low
USAA Tax-Exempt Virginia Bond	5.0	4.8	7.0	na	av	blw av
T. Rowe Price Tax-Free High Yield	4.9	5.3	7.6	7.8	blw av	low
Vanguard CA Tax-Free Ins Long-Term	4.9	5.4	7.6	7.4	high	blw av
Fidelity Muni Income	4.9	4.1	6.7	7.2	abv av	blw av
Strong Short-Term Muni Bond	4.8	2.8	4.4	na	low	low
Dreyfus Basic Interm Muni Bond	4.8	na	na	na	na	na
Strong Muni Advantage	4.8	na	na	na	na	na
Fidelity Spartan CA Muni Income	4.7	4.2	7.0	na	high	blw av
Fidelity CA Muni Income	4.7	4.3	7.0	6.9	high	blw av
Janus Federal Tax-Exempt	4.7	3.8	na	na	abv av	blw av
1784 Rhode Island Tax-Exempt Income	4.7	na	na	na	na	na
T. Rowe Price Summit Fds: Muni Interm	4.6	5.3	na	na	low	low
Fidelity Spartan CA Interm Muni Income	4.6	4.7	na	na	blw av	blw av
Dreyfus Basic Muni Bond	4.5	na	na	na	na	na
Fidelity Spartan Interm Muni Income	4.5	4.3	na	na	blw av	low
Fidelity Spartan Muni Income	4.5	4.4	7.1	na	high	blw av
T. Rowe Price CA Tax-Free Bond	4.5	4.9	7.2	6.4	av	blw av
SteinRoe Muni Trust: High Yield Muni	4.5	5.6	6.5	7.6	blw av	blw av
USAA Tax-Exempt Interm-Term	4.4	4.8	6.8	7.0	blw av	low
USAA Tax-Exempt Long-Term	4.4	4.4	6.8	7.3	abv av	blw av
Vanguard Muni Bond Fd: High Yield	4.4	5.4	7.7	8.1	abv av	blw av
USAA Tax-Exempt Short-Term	4.4	4.4	4.9	5.4	low	low
Scudder Muni Tr: High Yield Tax-Free	4.4	4.5	7.5	na	high	blw av
Vanguard Muni Bond Fd: Long-Term	4.4	5.3	7.6	8.0	abv av	blw av
USAA Florida Tax Free Income	4.3	3.7	na	na	high	av
Vanguard Penn Tax-Free Ins Long-Term	4.3	5.0	7.5	7.8	av	blw av
Schwab CA Long-Term Tx Fr Bond	4.3	4.4	na	na	high	blw av
Fidelity Spartan NY Muni Income	4.3	4.4	7.1	na	high	blw av

Tax-Exempt Bond Funds
Ranked by 1996 Total Returns

Fund Name	Annual Return (%)				Category Risk	Total Risk
	1996	3yr	5yr	10yr		
Fidelity Ltd Term Muni Income	4.3	4.4	6.7	6.8	blw av	blw av
Warburg Pincus NY Interm Muni	4.3	4.3	6.0	na	low	low
Dreyfus General CA Muni Bond	4.2	4.5	7.1	na	high	blw av
1784 Tax-Exempt Medium-Term Income	4.2	4.9	na	na	blw av	low
Benham CA Interm-Term Tax-Free	4.2	4.4	6.1	6.2	blw av	low
Fidelity Spartan Conn Muni Income	4.2	4.3	6.7	na	abv av	blw av
Fidelity Ohio Muni Income	4.2	4.6	6.9	7.3	av	blw av
Vanguard Ohio Tax-Free Ins Long-Term	4.2	4.9	7.3	na	abv av	blw av
Dreyfus Short—Interm Muni Bond	4.2	3.6	4.8	na	low	low
Vanguard Muni Bond Fd: Interm-Term	4.1	5.0	7.0	7.6	low	low
Fidelity Spartan Aggressive Muni	4.1	4.8	na	na	av	blw av
SteinRoe Muni Trust: Interm Muni	4.1	4.3	6.3	6.7	blw av	low
Dreyfus Penn Interm Muni Bond	4.1	5.7	na	na	blw av	low
Schwab Long-Term Tax-Free Bond	4.1	4.5	na	na	abv av	blw av
First Hawaii Muni Bond	4.1	4.2	6.4	na	blw av	low
Vanguard Florida Insured Tax-Free	4.1	5.3	na	na	high	blw av
Dreyfus NY Interm Tax-Exempt	4.1	4.0	6.5	na	blw av	low
Scudder Ohio Tax-Free	4.1	4.8	7.1	na	av	blw av
T. Rowe Price Tax-Free Ins Interm Bond	4.1	4.6	na	na	low	low
Scudder Muni Trust: Managed Muni Bond	4.1	4.6	7.1	7.8	abv av	blw av
T. Rowe Price VA Tax-Free Bond	4.1	4.9	7.2	na	av	blw av
Vanguard NY Insured Tax-Free Fd	4.0	4.9	7.4	7.4	abv av	blw av
Vanguard Muni Bond Fd: Ltd Term	4.0	4.1	5.0	na	low	low
Scudder MA Tax-Free	4.0	4.8	7.8	na	abv av	blw av
Fidelity Spartan NJ Muni Income	4.0	4.2	6.8	na	av	blw av
Vanguard Muni Bond Fd: Ins Long-Term	4.0	5.2	7.5	8.0	high	blw av
Scudder Muni Trust: Med-Term Tax-Free	4.0	4.6	6.7	6.6	blw av	low
Fidelity Spartan Penn Muni Income	4.0	5.0	7.4	7.4	av	blw av
Dreyfus MA Tax-Exempt Bond	4.0	4.1	6.4	6.4	av	blw av
T. Rowe Price Tax-Free Short Interm	4.0	4.1	4.9	5.2	low	low
Scudder Ltd Term Tax-Free	3.9	na	na	na	na	na
Benham Interm-Term Tax-Exempt	3.9	4.4	5.8	na	low	low
Fidelity Spartan Florida Muni Income	3.9	4.7	na	na	high	blw av
Dupree KY Tx Fr Short-To-Medium	3.9	3.7	4.7	na	low	low
Calvert Tax-Free Reserves Ltd Term Port/A	3.9	3.9	4.1	5.1	low	low
Benham CA Ltd-Term Tax-Free	3.9	3.8	na	na	low	low
T. Rowe Price GA Tax-Free Bond	3.9	4.8	na	na	abv av	blw av
Schwab CA Short Interm Tx Fr Bond	3.9	3.9	na	na	low	low
Fidelity Spartan NY Interm Muni Income	3.8	4.4	na	na	blw av	low
Fidelity Spartan Short Interm Muni Inc	3.8	4.0	5.0	5.1	low	low
Fidelity Spartan MD Muni Income	3.8	4.2	na	na	abv av	blw av
Fidelity CA Insured Muni Income	3.8	3.6	6.7	6.6	high	av
Dreyfus Muni Bond	3.8	3.7	6.4	6.9	av	blw av
Dreyfus Interm Muni Bond	3.8	4.2	6.5	6.8	blw av	low
Benham Interm-Term Tax-Free	3.8	4.1	5.9	6.5	low	low
Heartland Wisconsin Tax-Free	3.8	4.5	na	na	abv av	blw av
Fidelity NY Muni Income	3.7	4.5	7.0	7.1	high	blw av
SteinRoe Muni Trust: Managed Muni	3.7	4.6	6.6	7.4	av	blw av
T. Rowe Price MD Tax-Free Bond	3.7	4.7	7.0	na	av	blw av
Fidelity Minnesota Muni Income	3.7	4.2	6.4	6.5	av	blw av
Columbia Muni Bond	3.7	4.1	5.8	6.8	blw av	low

Tax-Exempt Bond Funds
Ranked by 1996 Total Returns

Fund Name	Annual Return (%)				Category Risk	Total Risk
	1996	3yr	5yr	10yr		
Fidelity NY Insured Muni Income	3.7	4.2	6.7	6.8	high	blw av
T. Rowe Price NY Tax-Free Bond	3.7	4.6	7.4	7.0	av	blw av
Benham Arizona Interm-Term Muni	3.7	na	na	na	na	na
Dreyfus Conn Interm Muni Bond	3.7	4.1	na	na	blw av	low
USAA Tax-Exempt NY Bond	3.7	3.6	6.6	na	high	blw av
Benham Ltd-Term Tax-Exempt	3.7	4.2	na	na	low	low
1784 Conn Tax-Exempt Income	3.7	na	na	na	na	na
Benham CA Insured Tax-Free	3.7	4.8	7.3	6.8	high	blw av
AARP Insured Tax-Free General Bond	3.6	4.1	6.6	7.2	abv av	blw av
Vanguard Muni Bond Fd: Short-Term	3.6	3.7	3.9	5.0	low	low
Fidelity Insured Muni Income	3.6	4.3	6.8	7.0	high	blw av
Dupree KY Tax-Free Income	3.6	4.7	7.1	7.3	blw av	low
Fremont CA Interm Tax-Free	3.6	4.2	5.9	na	blw av	low
T. Rowe Price FL Ins Interm Tax-Free	3.6	4.5	na	na	low	low
Dreyfus CA Interm Muni Bond	3.6	3.5	na	na	blw av	low
Fidelity MA Muni Income	3.5	4.6	7.2	7.2	abv av	blw av
Benham CA Long-Term Tax-Free	3.5	5.0	7.3	7.0	abv av	blw av
Neuberger & Berman Muni Securities Trust	3.5	3.8	5.5	na	low	low
Scudder CA Tax-Free	3.5	4.5	7.2	7.6	high	blw av
Fidelity Aggressive Muni	3.5	3.8	6.8	7.7	av	blw av
Value Line Tax-Exempt High Yield Port	3.5	3.9	6.2	6.9	abv av	blw av
Schwab Short/Interm Tax-Free Bond	3.5	3.8	na	na	low	low
Scudder Penn Tax-Free	3.5	4.5	7.1	na	av	blw av
Dreyfus MA Interm Muni Bond	3.4	3.5	na	na	blw av	blw av
Babson Tax-Free Income: Port S	3.4	3.5	4.7	5.6	low	low
Dreyfus CA Tax-Exempt Bond	3.4	3.1	5.5	6.0	av	blw av
T. Rowe Price MD Sh Term Tax Free	3.4	3.8	na	na	low	low
Dreyfus NJ Muni Bond	3.4	3.8	6.6	na	av	blw av
1784 MA Tax-Exempt Income	3.3	3.5	na	na	blw av	blw av
Northern Interm Tax-Exempt	3.3	na	na	na	na	na
Fidelity Michigan Muni Income	3.3	3.3	6.5	6.9	abv av	blw av
Scudder MA Ltd TF	3.3	na	na	na	na	na
Dreyfus Florida Interm Muni Bond	3.3	3.8	na	na	blw av	blw av
Dreyfus NJ Interm Muni Bond	3.3	3.7	na	na	blw av	blw av
Scudder NY Tax-Free	3.2	4.1	7.0	7.4	high	blw av
Babson Tax-Free Income: Port L	3.2	3.6	6.2	6.8	av	blw av
T. Rowe Price Tax-Free Income	3.2	4.7	7.2	6.6	av	blw av
T. Rowe Price NJ Tax-Free Bond	3.2	4.2	7.2	na	av	blw av
SAFECO Muni Bond	3.1	4.6	7.0	7.8	high	av
Vanguard NJ Tax Free Insured Long	3.1	4.6	7.3	na	abv av	blw av
GIT Tax-Free Trust: Virginia Port	3.1	3.1	5.8	na	abv av	blw av
Dreyfus General Muni Bond	3.1	3.8	6.8	7.4	abv av	blw av
Benham Long-Term Tax-Exempt	3.1	4.8	6.8	na	av	blw av
California Tax-Free Income	3.1	4.3	7.2	7.4	high	blw av
Dreyfus General NY Muni Bond	3.0	3.6	6.9	6.9	abv av	blw av
Crabbe Huson Oregon Tax-Free—Prim	2.9	3.9	5.6	5.9	low	low
GIT Tax-Free Trust: National Port	2.9	2.6	5.5	5.9	abv av	blw av
Rushmore Fund for Tax-Free Invest: VA	2.9	3.9	6.2	6.0	blw av	blw av
Northern Tax-Exempt	2.8	na	na	na	na	na
Rushmore Fund for Tax-Free Invest: MD	2.8	3.6	6.1	6.0	blw av	blw av
SAFECO CA Tax-Free Income	2.5	5.5	7.5	7.6	high	av

Tax-Exempt Bond Funds
Ranked by 1996 Total Returns

Fund Name	Annual Return (%)				Category Risk	Total Risk
	1996	3yr	5yr	10yr		
Dreyfus NY Tax-Exempt Bond	2.4	3.4	6.3	6.5	abv av	blw av
Strong Muni Bond	2.4	2.8	6.4	6.2	av	blw av
INVESCO Tax-Free Long Term Bond	2.3	3.7	6.4	7.3	av	blw av
Value Line NY Tax-Exempt Trust	2.3	3.4	6.6	na	high	blw av
Dreyfus Insured Muni Bond	2.2	2.6	5.5	6.2	high	blw av
Benham Long-Term Tax-Free	2.2	4.1	7.1	6.7	abv av	blw av
Dreyfus NY Insured Tax-Exempt	2.1	3.2	5.8	na	abv av	blw av
Fundamental New York Muni	-7.8	-5.3	1.3	3.2	high	av
Tax-Exempt Bond Fund Average	**3.7**	**4.2**	**6.4**	**6.7**	**av**	**blw av**

International Stock Funds
Ranked by 1996 Total Returns

Fund Name	Annual Return (%)				Category Risk	Total Risk
	1996	3yr	5yr	10yr		
Robertson Stephens Glbl Natrl Res	41.2	na	na	na	na	na
Fidelity Hong Kong & China	40.9	na	na	na	na	na
Artisan Int'l	34.3	na	na	na	na	na
Harbor Int'l Growth	32.0	14.8	na	na	high	high
Twentieth Century Int'l Discovery	31.1	na	na	na	na	na
INVESCO European Small Co	31.0	na	na	na	na	na
Scudder Greater Europe Growth	30.8	na	na	na	na	na
Fidelity Latin America	30.7	-5.7	na	na	high	high
INVESCO Int'l Fds: European	29.6	14.4	11.5	9.4	abv av	abv av
Robertson Stephens Glbl Low Priced Stk	29.3	na	na	na	na	na
Janus Overseas	28.8	na	na	na	na	na
Scudder Int'l: Latin America	28.3	1.5	na	na	high	high
Oakmark Int'l	28.0	8.0	na	na	abv av	high
Janus Worldwide	26.4	16.8	17.4	na	blw av	abv av
Fidelity Europe Capital Appreciation	25.8	15.5	na	na	abv av	high
T. Rowe Price Int'l: European Stock	25.8	16.8	13.9	na	blw av	av
INVESCO Latin American Growth	25.8	na	na	na	na	na
Fidelity Europe	25.6	16.6	14.4	12.1	low	av
Neuberger & Berman Int'l	23.6	na	na	na	na	na
T. Rowe Price Int'l: Latin America	23.3	-5.6	na	na	high	high
Robertson Stephens Contrarian	21.6	14.5	na	na	high	high
Scudder Global Discovery	21.4	9.7	12.7	na	av	abv av
Vanguard Int'l Equity Index: European	21.2	14.7	13.5	na	blw av	abv av
Robertson Stephens Developing Century	21.0	na	na	na	na	na
Acorn Invest Trust: Int'l	20.6	8.1	na	na	low	av
Montgomery Select 50—R	20.4	na	na	na	na	na
Tweedy Browne Global Value	20.2	11.5	na	na	low	av
Montgomery Global Opportunities	20.1	8.8	na	na	abv av	high
Harbor Int'l	20.1	13.6	16.3	na	av	abv av
Founders Passport	20.0	10.2	na	na	av	abv av
Fidelity Diversified Int'l	20.0	12.6	11.0	na	av	abv av
USAA Invest Trust: Int'l	19.1	9.8	13.0	na	av	abv av
USAA Invest Trust: World Growth	19.0	10.5	na	na	av	abv av

International Stock Funds
Ranked by 1996 Total Returns

Fund Name	Annual Return (%)				Category Risk	Total Risk
	1996	3yr	5yr	10yr		
Fidelity Worldwide	18.7	9.4	13.6	na	low	av
Scout Worldwide	18.3	12.1	na	na	low	av
Loomis Sayles Int'l Equity	18.3	8.1	10.6	na	low	av
Hotchkis & Wiley Int'l	18.2	11.2	14.3	na	low	av
Preferred Int'l	17.2	9.0	na	na	abv av	abv av
World Fds: Vontobel Europacific	16.9	7.0	11.0	na	abv av	abv av
INVESCO Worldwide Communications	16.8	na	na	na	na	na
Columbia Int'l Stock	16.6	6.1	na	na	av	abv av
USAA Invest Trust: Emerging Markets	16.5	na	na	na	na	na
Legg Mason Int'l Equity Trust/Prim	16.5	na	na	na	na	na
Lexington Global	16.4	9.4	10.7	na	blw av	av
Bartlett Capital Trust: Value Int'l	16.0	8.0	10.1	na	blw av	abv av
T. Rowe Price Int'l: Stock	15.9	8.6	11.6	11.1	av	abv av
Fidelity Canada	15.9	6.8	8.2	na	abv av	high
Vanguard Int'l Equity Index: Emerging Mkts	15.9	na	na	na	na	na
First Eagle Int'l	15.9	na	na	na	na	na
Vanguard Horizon Fd: Global Equity	15.5	na	na	na	na	na
American Century Glbl Natural Resources	15.4	na	na	na	na	na
Montgomery Int'l Small Cap	14.9	3.6	na	na	abv av	high
SSgA: Emerging Markets	14.8	na	na	na	na	na
Vanguard World: Int'l Growth Port	14.6	9.8	12.5	10.0	av	abv av
Scudder Int'l	14.5	7.6	10.6	9.8	blw av	abv av
Twentieth Century Int'l Growth	14.4	6.8	12.7	na	av	abv av
Fremont Global	13.9	9.2	10.3	na	low	blw av
Founders Worldwide Growth	13.9	10.3	12.1	na	av	abv av
T. Rowe Price Int'l: Discovery	13.8	0.2	6.5	na	av	abv av
1784 Int'l Equity	13.6	na	na	na	na	na
Scudder Global	13.6	9.4	12.4	12.7	low	av
T. Rowe Price Int'l: New Asia	13.5	-1.7	13.6	na	high	high
Babson-Stewart Ivory Int'l	13.4	8.9	11.1	na	blw av	av
Blanchard Global Growth	13.3	5.7	8.1	8.3	low	av
Fidelity Overseas	13.0	7.6	9.1	8.9	low	av
Fremont Int'l Growth	13.0	na	na	na	na	na
Fidelity Int'l Growth & Income	12.6	7.0	9.9	9.2	low	av
Montgomery Emerging Markets—R	12.3	-1.9	na	na	high	high
INVESCO Int'l Fds: Int'l Growth	11.9	6.8	6.4	na	blw av	abv av
Dreyfus Global Growth	11.9	5.0	6.6	na	blw av	av
T. Rowe Price Int'l: Emerging Mkts Stock	11.8	na	na	na	na	na
Warburg Pincus Int'l Equity—Common	10.5	6.9	12.0	na	abv av	high
Sit Int'l Growth	10.3	5.3	12.2	na	av	abv av
Vanguard/Trustees' Equity—Intl Port	10.2	8.3	8.6	10.4	blw av	av
William Blair Mutual Fds: Intl Growth	10.2	5.7	na	na	low	av
Fidelity Southeast Asia	10.1	-1.2	na	na	high	high
Fidelity Emerging Markets	9.9	-4.4	10.9	na	high	high
Vanguard Horizon Fd: Global Asset Alloc	9.9	na	na	na	na	na
Warburg Pincus Emerging Mkts—Common	9.9	na	na	na	na	na
Schroder Capital Int'l—Inv	9.9	6.9	11.3	9.1	blw av	abv av
BB&K Int'l Equity	9.5	2.5	5.6	3.5	blw av	av
Fidelity Int'l Value	9.5	na	na	na	na	na
Schwab Capital Trust: Int'l Index	9.1	8.9	na	na	blw av	abv av
Gabelli Global Telecommunications	8.9	6.8	na	na	blw av	abv av

International Stock Funds
Ranked by 1996 Total Returns

Fund Name	Annual Return (%)				Category Risk	Total Risk
	1996	3yr	5yr	10yr		
Dreyfus Int'l Growth	8.4	1.0	na	na	av	abv av
IAI Int'l	8.4	5.9	9.2	na	blw av	abv av
SteinRoe Int'l	8.3	na	na	na	na	na
Strong Int'l Stock	8.1	4.7	na	na	abv av	abv av
Montgomery Global Communications	8.0	3.0	na	na	abv av	high
Fidelity Global Balanced	7.7	2.0	na	na	low	av
Lexington Worldwide Emerging Mkts	7.3	-4.6	8.0	8.3	high	high
Scudder Int'l: Pacific Opport Fd	6.4	-3.7	na	na	high	high
Northern Int'l Growth Equity	5.0	na	na	na	na	na
Nomura Pacific Basin	3.0	3.6	6.4	9.4	abv av	high
Northern Int'l Select Equity	2.8	na	na	na	na	na
Strong Asia Pacific	2.1	0.8	na	na	abv av	high
INVESCO Int'l Fds: Pacific Basin	-1.2	2.4	5.8	6.3	abv av	high
Fidelity Pacific Basin	-2.8	-4.0	6.0	5.4	abv av	high
Vanguard Int'l Equity Index: Pacific	-7.9	2.3	3.4	na	high	high
Japan Fund	-11.0	-3.8	-1.8	3.4	high	high
T. Rowe Price Int'l: Japan	-11.0	-0.3	0.7	na	high	high
Fidelity Japan	-11.2	0.4	na	na	high	high
Warburg Pincus Japan OTC—Common	-13.1	na	na	na	na	na
Fidelity Japan Small Companies	-24.6	na	na	na	na	na
International Stock Fund Average	**14.8**	**6.3**	**10.0**	**8.6**	**av**	**abv av**

International Bond Funds
Ranked by 1996 Total Returns

Fund Name	Annual Return (%)				Category Risk	Total Risk
	1996	3yr	5yr	10yr		
Fidelity New Markets Income	41.3	8.4	na	na	high	high
Scudder Emerging Markets Income	34.5	13.9	na	na	high	high
Loomis Sayles Global Bond	15.0	9.1	8.4	na	high	av
Lexington Ramirez Global Income	13.3	8.3	8.4	7.6	av	blw av
Strong Short-Term Global Bond	10.0	na	na	na	na	na
Warburg Pincus Global Fixed Income	9.9	6.4	8.0	na	blw av	low
Bull & Bear Global Income	8.7	1.4	8.0	4.8	abv av	av
BB&K Int'l Bond Fd	8.4	1.8	5.3	na	high	av
Legg Mason Global Gov't Trust/Prim	8.2	8.8	na	na	av	blw av
Strong Int'l Bond	7.9	na	na	na	na	na
T. Rowe Price Int'l: Bond	7.1	8.1	9.2	10.0	av	blw av
T. Rowe Price Int'l: Global Gov't Bd	6.5	6.8	6.9	na	blw av	blw av
Benham European Gov't Bond	6.3	10.3	na	na	abv av	av
Payden & Rygel Global Fixed Income—A	5.7	6.5	na	na	low	low
Scudder Int'l Bond	3.5	0.8	5.0	na	blw av	blw av
Fidelity Global Bond	3.4	-2.7	3.2	7.0	abv av	av
Scudder Global Bond	3.1	3.1	4.3	na	low	low
International Bond Fund Average	**11.3**	**6.0**	**6.6**	**7.3**	**av**	**av**

Gold Funds
Ranked by 1996 Total Returns

Fund Name	Annual Return (%)				Category	Total
	1996	3yr	5yr	10yr	Risk	Risk
INVESCO Strat Port—Gold	40.6	4.5	12.6	3.8	high	high
Scudder Gold	32.1	11.4	14.9	na	blw av	high
Blanchard Precious Metals	24.3	3.3	12.5	na	abv av	high
Midas	21.2	11.1	20.4	10.8	high	high
Fidelity Sel American Gold	19.9	4.0	14.3	8.5	av	high
United Service World Gold	19.5	4.7	15.7	6.0	blw av	high
Lexington Goldfund	7.8	-0.7	7.8	5.2	low	high
Fidelity Sel Precious Metals & Minerals	5.4	0.2	10.7	6.3	blw av	high
Bull & Bear Gold Investors Ltd	4.2	-5.3	5.7	3.1	abv av	high
USAA Invest Trust: Gold	0.0	-2.0	6.5	0.9	av	high
Vanguard Spec Port: Gold & Prec Metals	-0.8	-3.6	6.9	6.1	low	high
American Century Global Gold	-2.8	-4.1	7.9	na	abv av	high
United Service Gold Shares	-25.5	-19.1	-10.2	-7.7	high	high
Gold Fund Average	**11.2**	**0.3**	**9.6**	**4.3**	**av**	**high**

Small Stock Funds
Ranked by 1996 Total Returns

Fund Name	Annual Return (%)				Category	Category	Total
	1996	3yr	5yr	10yr	Category	Risk	Risk
Warburg Pincus Small Co Value	56.1	na	na	na	AG	na	na
Fremont US Micro Cap	48.7	na	na	na	AG	na	na
Oakmark Small Cap	39.7	na	na	na	AG	na	na
Dreyfus Grth & Value: Emerging Ldrs	37.4	na	na	na	AG	na	na
Montgomery Small Cap Opportunities	37.2	na	na	na	AG	na	na
Longleaf Partners Small Cap	30.6	17.1	15.5	na	Grth	low	av
Loomis Sayles Small Cap	30.3	16.4	17.3	na	AG	blw av	abv av
Skyline: Special Equities Port	30.3	13.6	20.7	na	AG	low	abv av
Eclipse Financial Asset Tr: Equity	29.8	13.9	15.6	na	Grth	av	abv av
Neuberger & Berman Genesis	29.8	17.5	16.4	na	Grth	blw av	abv av
Turner Small Cap	28.8	na	na	na	AG	na	na
SSgA: Small Cap	28.7	21.8	na	na	AG	low	abv av
Legg Mason Special Invest Trust/Prim	28.6	11.0	14.4	14.5	AG	av	high
SteinRoe Special Venture	28.6	na	na	na	AG	na	na
Babson Enterprise II	27.6	12.3	14.7	na	Grth	abv av	abv av
Caldwell & Orkin Market Opportunity	27.2	13.6	14.2	na	AG	low	av
Fidelity Low Priced Stock	26.8	18.4	20.8	na	Grth	low	av
Skyline: Special Equities II	26.5	14.6	na	na	Grth	abv av	abv av
T. Rowe Price Small Cap Value	24.6	16.6	18.8	na	Grth	low	av
Scudder Small Company Value	23.8	na	na	na	AG	na	na
Ariel Growth	23.5	11.9	11.2	13.9	AG	low	av
Oberweis Emerging Growth Port	23.1	19.2	16.1	na	AG	high	high
SAFECO Growth	22.8	15.0	12.5	14.5	AG	av	high
Strong Small Cap	22.6	na	na	na	AG	na	na
Rainier Investment: Small/Mid Cap	22.5	na	na	na	AG	na	na
Acorn Invest Trust: Acorn	22.5	11.0	17.6	16.1	Grth	av	abv av
Baron Asset	21.9	21.0	20.0	na	AG	blw av	high
Nicholas Ltd Edition	21.8	15.4	14.3	na	Grth	abv av	abv av
Robertson Stephens Emerging Growth	21.5	16.4	10.5	na	AG	high	high

Small Stock Funds
Ranked by 1996 Total Returns

Fund Name	1996	3yr	5yr	10yr	Category	Category Risk	Total Risk
Babson Shadow Stock	21.3	12.8	14.2	na	Grth	low	av
Babson Enterprise	21.2	13.0	15.9	14.0	Grth	low	av
Founders Discovery	21.2	13.6	13.3	na	AG	high	high
T. Rowe Price OTC	21.0	17.4	16.9	12.3	AG	low	abv av
Heartland Value	20.9	16.8	22.0	15.2	AG	low	abv av
Kaufmann	20.9	21.7	18.8	19.3	AG	av	high
Preferred Small Cap	20.4	na	na	na	AG	na	na
SteinRoe Capital Opportunities	20.3	21.9	18.8	14.6	AG	abv av	high
Galaxy II: Small Co Index	19.6	15.3	13.9	na	AG	low	abv av
Gradison-McDonald Opport Value	19.4	13.9	13.4	12.3	Grth	blw av	abv av
Montgomery Micro Cap	19.1	na	na	na	AG	na	na
Northern Small Cap	18.9	na	na	na	AG	na	na
Heartland Small Cap Contrarian	18.8	na	na	na	AG	na	na
Montgomery Small Cap	18.6	13.0	14.4	na	AG	av	high
Schwartz Value	18.2	8.8	13.7	12.2	Grth	low	av
Royce: Premier	18.1	12.8	14.6	na	Grth	low	blw av
Vanguard Index Trust: Small Cap Stock	18.1	14.7	16.2	12.4	AG	blw av	abv av
Vanguard Index Trust: Ext Market	17.6	15.6	14.7	na	Grth	abv av	abv av
Dreyfus New Leaders	17.3	14.9	14.2	14.3	AG	low	abv av
PBHG Emerging Growth	17.0	29.0	na	na	AG	high	high
T. Rowe Price New Horizons	17.0	22.1	19.7	16.2	AG	av	high
Berger Small Co Growth	16.7	21.1	na	na	AG	abv av	high
USAA Aggressive Growth	16.4	20.2	11.4	13.1	AG	high	high
Fidelity Emerging Growth	15.7	16.2	15.3	na	AG	abv av	high
Royce: Micro-Cap	15.5	12.5	17.9	na	AG	low	av
Schwab Capital Trust: Small Cap Index	15.4	12.6	na	na	AG	blw av	high
Sit Small Cap Growth	14.9	na	na	na	AG	na	na
Founders Frontier	14.3	15.0	14.0	na	AG	av	high
Robertson Stephens Value + Growth	14.0	26.0	na	na	AG	high	high
Vanguard Explorer	14.0	13.2	13.6	12.9	AG	blw av	abv av
Wasatch Micro-Cap	13.6	na	na	na	AG	na	na
Fidelity Small Cap Stock	13.6	11.6	na	na	AG	abv av	high
Columbia Special	13.0	14.3	15.6	18.1	AG	av	high
Royce: Penn Mutual	12.8	9.9	11.4	11.4	Grth	low	av
Scout Regional	12.5	10.7	9.8	6.2	Grth	low	av
INVESCO Diversified Fds: Small Co	12.4	11.9	na	na	AG	low	abv av
INVESCO Emerging Growth	11.6	11.7	16.7	na	AG	abv av	high
FAM Value	11.2	12.4	12.2	12.8	Grth	low	av
Meridian	11.1	11.0	12.3	14.3	Grth	blw av	abv av
Scudder Development	10.0	16.2	10.8	14.7	AG	high	high
Warburg Pincus Emrg Grth—Common	9.8	16.5	15.9	na	AG	av	high
PBHG Growth	9.8	20.0	26.6	21.2	AG	high	high
Janus Venture	8.0	12.9	11.0	15.8	AG	av	high
Twentieth Century Vista	7.5	18.0	11.1	15.1	AG	high	high
IAI Emerging Growth	6.9	17.0	17.6	na	AG	high	high
GIT Equity Trust: Special Growth	6.9	7.8	8.9	9.8	AG	low	abv av
Crabbe Huson Special	5.9	9.4	18.6	na	AG	low	abv av
Twentieth Century Giftrust	5.7	18.4	20.8	21.7	AG	high	high
Cappiello-Rushmore Emrg Growth	1.9	8.8	na	na	AG	high	high
Monetta	1.6	6.8	5.2	12.4	Grth	high	high
Small Stock Fund Average	**19.9**	**15.1**	**15.2**	**14.3**	—	—	**abv av**

Individual Fund Listings 9

1784 Conn Tax-Exempt Income (SCTEX)

Tax-Exempt Bond

680 E. Swedesford Road
Wayne, PA 19087
800-252-1784, 610-254-1000
www.1784funds.com

PERFORMANCE

fund inception date: 8/1/94

	3yr Annual	5yr Annual	10yr Annual	Bull	Bear
Return (%)	na	na	na	na	na
Differ from Category (+/-)	na	na	na	na	na

Total Risk	Standard Deviation	Category Risk	Risk Index	Avg Mat
na	na	na	na	6.7 yrs

	1996	1995	1994	1993	1992	1991	1990	1989	1988	1987
Return (%)	3.7	14.6	—	—	—	—	—	—	—	—
Differ from Category (+/-)	0.0	-0.6	—	—	—	—	—	—	—	—
Return, Tax-Adjusted (%)	3.7	14.6	—	—	—	—	—	—	—	—

PER SHARE DATA

	1996	1995	1994	1993	1992	1991	1990	1989	1988	1987
Dividends, Net Income ($)	0.51	0.51	—	—	—	—	—	—	—	—
Distrib'ns, Cap Gain ($)	0.00	0.00	—	—	—	—	—	—	—	—
Net Asset Value ($)	10.39	10.54	—	—	—	—	—	—	—	—
Expense Ratio (%)	0.75	0.52	—	—	—	—	—	—	—	—
Yield (%)	4.90	4.83	—	—	—	—	—	—	—	—
Portfolio Turnover (%)	20	36	—	—	—	—	—	—	—	—
Total Assets (Millions $)	92	72	—	—	—	—	—	—	—	—

PORTFOLIO (as of 9/30/96)

Portfolio Manager: David H. Thompson - 1994

Investm't Category: Tax-Exempt Bond

✔ Domestic	Index
Foreign	Sector
Asset Allocation	✔ State Specific

Investment Style

Large-Cap Growth	Large-Cap Value
Mid-Cap Growth	Mid-Cap Value
Small-Cap Growth	Small-Cap Value

Portfolio

5.5% cash	0.0% corp bonds
0.0% stocks	0.0% gov't bonds
0.0% preferred	94.5% muni bonds
0.0% conv't/warrants	0.0% other

SHAREHOLDER INFORMATION

Minimum Investment
Initial: $1,000   Subsequent: $250

Minimum IRA Investment
Initial: na   Subsequent: na

Maximum Fees
Load: none   12b-1: 0.25%
Other: none

Distributions
Income: monthly   Capital Gains: Dec

Exchange Options
Number Per Year: no limit   Fee: none
Telephone: yes (money market fund available)

Services
auto invest, auto withdraw

1784 Growth & Income

(SEGWX)

Growth & Income

680 E. Swedesford Road
Wayne, PA 19087
800-252-1784, 610-254-1000
www.1784funds.com

	3yr Annual	5yr Annual	10yr Annual	Bull	Bear
Return (%)	17.2	na	na	68.5	-8.3
Differ from Category (+/-)	1.9 av	na	na	8.7 abv av	-1.9 blw av

Total Risk	Standard Deviation		Category Risk	Risk Index		Beta
abv av	11.0%		high	1.2		1.00

	1996	1995	1994	1993	1992	1991	1990	1989	1988	1987
Return (%)	24.2	29.8	-0.2	—	—	—	—	—	—	—
Differ from Category (+/-)	4.5	-0.3	1.1	—	—	—	—	—	—	—
Return, Tax-Adjusted (%)	23.2	29.3	-0.9	—	—	—	—	—	—	—

PER SHARE DATA

	1996	1995	1994	1993	1992	1991	1990	1989	1988	1987
Dividends, Net Income ($)	0.09	0.11	0.11	—	—	—	—	—	—	—
Distrib'ns, Cap Gain ($)	0.33	0.00	0.08	—	—	—	—	—	—	—
Net Asset Value ($)	16.30	13.47	10.47	—	—	—	—	—	—	—
Expense Ratio (%)	0.94	0.94	0.35	—	—	—	—	—	—	—
Yield (%)	0.54	0.81	1.04	—	—	—	—	—	—	—
Portfolio Turnover (%)	39	38	31	—	—	—	—	—	—	—
Total Assets (Millions $)	381	271	193	—	—	—	—	—	—	—

PORTFOLIO (as of 9/30/96)

Portfolio Manager: Ted Ober, Eugene Takach - 1993

Investm't Category: Growth & Income

✔ Domestic	Index
Foreign	Sector
Asset Allocation	State Specific

Investment Style

✔ Large-Cap Growth	Large-Cap Value
✔ Mid-Cap Growth	Mid-Cap Value
Small-Cap Growth	Small-Cap Value

Portfolio

4.0% cash	0.0% corp bonds
96.0% stocks	0.0% gov't bonds
0.0% preferred	0.0% muni bonds
0.0% conv't/warrants	0.0% other

SHAREHOLDER INFORMATION

Minimum Investment
Initial: $1,000   Subsequent: $250

Minimum IRA Investment
Initial: $250   Subsequent: $1

Maximum Fees
Load: none   12b-1: 0.25%
Other: none

Distributions
Income: quarterly   Capital Gains: Dec

Exchange Options
Number Per Year: no limit   Fee: none
Telephone: yes (money market fund available)

Services
IRA, pension, auto invest, auto withdraw

1784 Income (SEINX)

General Bond

680 E. Swedesford Road
Wayne, PA 19087
800-252-1784, 610-254-1000
www.1784funds.com

PERFORMANCE

fund inception date: 7/1/94

	3yr Annual	5yr Annual	10yr Annual	Bull	Bear
Return (%)	na	na	na	na	na
Differ from Category (+/-)	na	na	na	na	na

Total Risk	Standard Deviation	Category Risk	Risk Index	Avg Mat
na	na	na	na	12.9 yrs

	1996	1995	1994	1993	1992	1991	1990	1989	1988	1987
Return (%)	2.6	17.9	—	—	—	—	—	—	—	—
Differ from Category (+/-)	-1.3	3.0	—	—	—	—	—	—	—	—
Return, Tax-Adjusted (%)	0.0	14.8	—	—	—	—	—	—	—	—

PER SHARE DATA

	1996	1995	1994	1993	1992	1991	1990	1989	1988	1987
Dividends, Net Income ($)	0.63	0.65	—	—	—	—	—	—	—	—
Distrib'ns, Cap Gain ($)	0.08	0.12	—	—	—	—	—	—	—	—
Net Asset Value ($)	10.11	10.57	—	—	—	—	—	—	—	—
Expense Ratio (%)	0.80	0.55	—	—	—	—	—	—	—	—
Yield (%)	6.18	6.08	—	—	—	—	—	—	—	—
Portfolio Turnover (%)	100	80	—	—	—	—	—	—	—	—
Total Assets (Millions $)	331	211	—	—	—	—	—	—	—	—

PORTFOLIO (as of 9/30/96)

Portfolio Manager: Jack A. Ablin - 1994

Investm't Category: General Bond

✔ Domestic	Index
✔ Foreign	Sector
Asset Allocation	State Specific

Investment Style

Large-Cap Growth	Large-Cap Value
Mid-Cap Growth	Mid-Cap Value
Small-Cap Growth	Small-Cap Value

Portfolio

64.5% cash	2.0% corp bonds
0.0% stocks	21.6% gov't bonds
10.0% preferred	1.9% muni bonds
0.0% conv't/warrants	0.0% other

SHAREHOLDER INFORMATION

Minimum Investment
Initial: $1,000   Subsequent: $250

Minimum IRA Investment
Initial: $250   Subsequent: $1

Maximum Fees
Load: none   12b-1: 0.25%
Other: none

Distributions
Income: monthly   Capital Gains: Dec

Exchange Options
Number Per Year: no limit   Fee: none
Telephone: yes (money market fund available)

Services
IRA, pension, auto invest, auto withdraw

1784 Int'l Equity (SEEQX)

International Stock

680 E. Swedesford Road
Wayne, PA 19087
800-252-1784, 610-254-1000
www.1784funds.com

PERFORMANCE

fund inception date: 1/3/95

	3yr Annual	5yr Annual	10yr Annual	Bull	Bear
Return (%)	na	na	na	na	na
Differ from Category (+/-)	na	na	na	na	na

Total Risk	Standard Deviation	Category Risk	Risk Index	Beta
na	na	na	na	na

	1996	1995	1994	1993	1992	1991	1990	1989	1988	1987
Return (%)	13.6	—	—	—	—	—	—	—	—	—
Differ from Category (+/-)	-1.2	—	—	—	—	—	—	—	—	—
Return, Tax-Adjusted (%)	13.1	—	—	—	—	—	—	—	—	—

PER SHARE DATA

	1996	1995	1994	1993	1992	1991	1990	1989	1988	1987
Dividends, Net Income ($)	0.09	—	—	—	—	—	—	—	—	—
Distrib'ns, Cap Gain ($)	0.06	—	—	—	—	—	—	—	—	—
Net Asset Value ($)	12.36	—	—	—	—	—	—	—	—	—
Expense Ratio (%)	1.13	—	—	—	—	—	—	—	—	—
Yield (%)	0.72	—	—	—	—	—	—	—	—	—
Portfolio Turnover (%)	15	—	—	—	—	—	—	—	—	—
Total Assets (Millions $)	431	—	—	—	—	—	—	—	—	—

PORTFOLIO (as of 9/30/96)

Portfolio Manager: Kenton Ide - 1995

Investm't Category: International Stock
Domestic	Index
✔ Foreign	Sector
Asset Allocation	State Specific

Investment Style
Large-Cap Growth	Large-Cap Value
Mid-Cap Growth	Mid-Cap Value
Small-Cap Growth	Small-Cap Value

Portfolio
5.2% cash	0.0% corp bonds
94.8% stocks	0.0% gov't bonds
0.0% preferred	0.0% muni bonds
0.0% conv't/warrants	0.0% other

SHAREHOLDER INFORMATION

Minimum Investment
Initial: $1,000   Subsequent: $250

Minimum IRA Investment
Initial: $250   Subsequent: $1

Maximum Fees
Load: none   12b-1: 0.25%
Other: none

Distributions
Income: annual   Capital Gains: Dec

Exchange Options
Number Per Year: no limit   Fee: none
Telephone: yes (money market fund available)

Services
IRA, pension, auto invest, auto withdraw

1784 MA Tax-Exempt Income (SEMAX)

680 E. Swedesford Road
Wayne, PA 19087
800-252-1784, 610-254-1000
www.1784funds.com

Tax-Exempt Bond

PERFORMANCE

fund inception date: 6/14/93

	3yr Annual	5yr Annual	10yr Annual	Bull	Bear
Return (%)	3.5	na	na	16.2	-5.4
Differ from Category (+/-)	-0.7 low	na	na	-2.2 blw av	0.0 av

Total Risk	Standard Deviation	Category Risk	Risk Index	Avg Mat
blw av	4.8%	blw av	0.9	8.2 yrs

	1996	1995	1994	1993	1992	1991	1990	1989	1988	1987
Return (%)	3.3	13.7	-5.5	—	—	—	—	—	—	—
Differ from Category (+/-)	-0.4	-1.5	-0.2	—	—	—	—	—	—	—
Return, Tax-Adjusted (%)	3.3	13.7	-5.5	—	—	—	—	—	—	—

PER SHARE DATA

	1996	1995	1994	1993	1992	1991	1990	1989	1988	1987
Dividends, Net Income ($)	0.47	0.46	0.47	—	—	—	—	—	—	—
Distrib'ns, Cap Gain ($)	0.00	0.00	0.00	—	—	—	—	—	—	—
Net Asset Value ($)	9.99	10.14	9.35	—	—	—	—	—	—	—
Expense Ratio (%)	0.80	0.80	0.33	—	—	—	—	—	—	—
Yield (%)	4.70	4.53	5.02	—	—	—	—	—	—	—
Portfolio Turnover (%)	47	34	13	—	—	—	—	—	—	—
Total Assets (Millions $)	126	95	55	—	—	—	—	—	—	—

PORTFOLIO (as of 9/30/96)

Portfolio Manager: Susan Sanderson - 1993

Investm't Category: Tax-Exempt Bond
- ✔ Domestic
- Foreign
- Asset Allocation
- Index
- Sector
- ✔ State Specific

Investment Style
- Large-Cap Growth
- Mid-Cap Growth
- Small-Cap Growth
- Large-Cap Value
- Mid-Cap Value
- Small-Cap Value

Portfolio
3.8% cash	0.0% corp bonds
0.0% stocks	0.0% gov't bonds
0.0% preferred	96.2% muni bonds
0.0% conv't/warrants	0.0% other

SHAREHOLDER INFORMATION

Minimum Investment
Initial: $1,000   Subsequent: $250

Minimum IRA Investment
Initial: na   Subsequent: na

Maximum Fees
Load: none   12b-1: 0.25%
Other: none

Distributions
Income: monthly   Capital Gains: Dec

Exchange Options
Number Per Year: no limit   Fee: none
Telephone: yes (money market fund available)

Services
auto invest, auto withdraw

1784 Rhode Island Tax-Exempt Income

680 E. Swedesford Road
Wayne, PA 19087
800-252-1784, 610-254-1000
www.1784funds.com

(SERIX) *Tax-Exempt Bond*

PERFORMANCE

fund inception date: 8/1/94

	3yr Annual	5yr Annual	10yr Annual	Bull	Bear
Return (%)	na	na	na	na	na
Differ from Category (+/-)	na	na	na	na	na

Total Risk	Standard Deviation	Category Risk	Risk Index	Avg Mat
na	na	na	na	6.7 yrs

	1996	1995	1994	1993	1992	1991	1990	1989	1988	1987
Return (%)	4.7	14.1	—	—	—	—	—	—	—	—
Differ from Category (+/-)	1.0	-1.1	—	—	—	—	—	—	—	—
Return, Tax-Adjusted (%)	4.7	14.1	—	—	—	—	—	—	—	—

PER SHARE DATA

	1996	1995	1994	1993	1992	1991	1990	1989	1988	1987
Dividends, Net Income ($)	0.52	0.52	—	—	—	—	—	—	—	—
Distrib'ns, Cap Gain ($)	0.00	0.00	—	—	—	—	—	—	—	—
Net Asset Value ($)	10.31	10.36	—	—	—	—	—	—	—	—
Expense Ratio (%)	0.77	0.54	—	—	—	—	—	—	—	—
Yield (%)	5.04	5.01	—	—	—	—	—	—	—	—
Portfolio Turnover (%)	19	58	—	—	—	—	—	—	—	—
Total Assets (Millions $)	46	34	—	—	—	—	—	—	—	—

PORTFOLIO (as of 9/30/96)

Portfolio Manager: David H. Thompson - 1995

Investm't Category: Tax-Exempt Bond
✔ Domestic   Index
Foreign   Sector
Asset Allocation   ✔ State Specific

Investment Style
Large-Cap Growth   Large-Cap Value
Mid-Cap Growth   Mid-Cap Value
Small-Cap Growth   Small-Cap Value

Portfolio
5.5% cash   0.0% corp bonds
0.0% stocks   0.0% gov't bonds
0.0% preferred   94.5% muni bonds
0.0% conv't/warrants 0.0% other

SHAREHOLDER INFORMATION

Minimum Investment
Initial: $1,000   Subsequent: $250

Minimum IRA Investment
Initial: na   Subsequent: na

Maximum Fees
Load: none   12b-1: 0.25%
Other: none

Distributions
Income: monthly   Capital Gains: Dec

Exchange Options
Number Per Year: no limit   Fee: none
Telephone: yes (money market fund available)

Services
auto invest, auto withdraw

1784 Short-Term Income
(SESTX)
General Bond

680 E. Swedesford Road
Wayne, PA 19087
800-252-1784, 610-254-1000
www.1784funds.com

PERFORMANCE

fund inception date: 7/1/94

	3yr Annual	5yr Annual	10yr Annual	Bull	Bear
Return (%)	na	na	na	na	na
Differ from Category (+/-)	na	na	na	na	na

Total Risk	Standard Deviation	Category Risk	Risk Index	Avg Mat
na	na	na	na	2.5 yrs

	1996	1995	1994	1993	1992	1991	1990	1989	1988	1987
Return (%)	4.3	11.3	—	—	—	—	—	—	—	—
Differ from Category (+/-)	0.4	-3.6	—	—	—	—	—	—	—	—
Return, Tax-Adjusted (%)	2.0	8.7	—	—	—	—	—	—	—	—

PER SHARE DATA

	1996	1995	1994	1993	1992	1991	1990	1989	1988	1987
Dividends, Net Income ($)	0.58	0.61	—	—	—	—	—	—	—	—
Distrib'ns, Cap Gain ($)	0.00	0.03	—	—	—	—	—	—	—	—
Net Asset Value ($)	10.04	10.20	—	—	—	—	—	—	—	—
Expense Ratio (%)	0.63	0.48	—	—	—	—	—	—	—	—
Yield (%)	5.77	5.96	—	—	—	—	—	—	—	—
Portfolio Turnover (%)	95	84	—	—	—	—	—	—	—	—
Total Assets (Millions $)	142	75	—	—	—	—	—	—	—	—

PORTFOLIO (as of 9/30/96)

Portfolio Manager: Mary K. Werler - 1994

Investm't Category: General Bond
- ✔ Domestic
- ✔ Foreign
- Asset Allocation
- Index
- Sector
- State Specific

Investment Style
- Large-Cap Growth
- Mid-Cap Growth
- Small-Cap Growth
- Large-Cap Value
- Mid-Cap Value
- Small-Cap Value

Portfolio
79.6% cash	0.0% corp bonds
0.0% stocks	4.1% gov't bonds
0.0% preferred	15.7% muni bonds
0.0% conv't/warrants	0.6% other

SHAREHOLDER INFORMATION

Minimum Investment
Initial: $1,000   Subsequent: $250

Minimum IRA Investment
Initial: $250   Subsequent: $1

Maximum Fees
Load: none   12b-1: 0.25%
Other: none

Distributions
Income: monthly   Capital Gains: Dec

Exchange Options
Number Per Year: no limit   Fee: none
Telephone: yes (money market fund available)

Services
IRA, pension, auto invest, auto withdraw

1784 Tax-Exempt Medium-Term Income

(SETMX) *Tax-Exempt Bond*

680 E. Swedesford Road
Wayne, PA 19087
800-252-1784, 610-254-1000
www.1784funds.com

PERFORMANCE

fund inception date: 6/14/93

	3yr Annual	5yr Annual	10yr Annual	Bull	Bear
Return (%)	4.9	na	na	18.9	-3.9
Differ from Category (+/-)	0.7 high	na	na	0.5 av	1.5 high

Total Risk	Standard Deviation	Category Risk	Risk Index	Avg Mat
low	4.3%	blw av	0.8	5.9 yrs

	1996	1995	1994	1993	1992	1991	1990	1989	1988	1987
Return (%).	4.2	14.3	-3.1	—	—	—	—	—	—	—
Differ from Category (+/-) . .	0.5	-0.9	2.2	—	—	—	—	—	—	—
Return, Tax-Adjusted (%). . .	4.0	14.1	-3.1	—	—	—	—	—	—	—

PER SHARE DATA

	1996	1995	1994	1993	1992	1991	1990	1989	1988	1987
Dividends, Net Income ($).	0.50	0.49	0.47	—	—	—	—	—	—	—
Distrib'ns, Cap Gain ($) . . .	0.07	0.06	0.00	—	—	—	—	—	—	—
Net Asset Value ($)	10.18	10.34	9.56	—	—	—	—	—	—	—
Expense Ratio (%).	0.79	0.80	0.32	—	—	—	—	—	—	—
Yield (%)	4.87	4.71	4.91	—	—	—	—	—	—	—
Portfolio Turnover (%). . . .	37	74	98	—	—	—	—	—	—	—
Total Assets (Millions $). . .	228	192	90	—	—	—	—	—	—	—

PORTFOLIO (as of 9/30/96)

Portfolio Manager: David H. Thompson - 1993

Investm't Category: Tax-Exempt Bond
- ✔ Domestic
- Foreign
- Asset Allocation
- Index
- Sector
- State Specific

Investment Style
- Large-Cap Growth
- Mid-Cap Growth
- Small-Cap Growth
- Large-Cap Value
- Mid-Cap Value
- Small-Cap Value

Portfolio
5.5% cash	0.0% corp bonds
0.0% stocks	0.0% gov't bonds
0.0% preferred	94.5% muni bonds
0.0% conv't/warrants	0.0% other

SHAREHOLDER INFORMATION

Minimum Investment
Initial: $1,000   Subsequent: $250

Minimum IRA Investment
Initial: na   Subsequent: na

Maximum Fees
Load: none   12b-1: 0.25%
Other: none

Distributions
Income: monthly   Capital Gains: Dec

Exchange Options
Number Per Year: no limit   Fee: none
Telephone: yes (money market fund available)

Services
auto invest, auto withdraw

1784 US Gov't Medium-Term Income (SEGTX)

Mortgage-Backed Bond

680 E. Swedesford Road
Wayne, PA 19087
800-252-1784, 610-254-1000
www.1784funds.com

PERFORMANCE

fund inception date: 6/7/93

	3yr Annual	5yr Annual	10yr Annual	Bull	Bear
Return (%)	4.4	na	na	18.6	-5.2
Differ from Category (+/-)	-1.2 low	na	na	-2.5 blw av	-1.6 low

Total Risk	Standard Deviation	Category Risk	Risk Index	Avg Mat
low	4.1%	abv av	1.1	4.6 yrs

	1996	1995	1994	1993	1992	1991	1990	1989	1988	1987
Return (%).	2.0	15.8	-3.8	—	—	—	—	—	—	—
Differ from Category (+/-) .	-2.4	1.1	-2.1	—	—	—	—	—	—	—
Return, Tax-Adjusted (%). .	-0.4	13.2	-6.1	—	—	—	—	—	—	—

PER SHARE DATA

	1996	1995	1994	1993	1992	1991	1990	1989	1988	1987
Dividends, Net Income ($) .	0.59	0.59	0.56	—	—	—	—	—	—	—
Distrib'ns, Cap Gain ($) . . .	0.00	0.00	0.00	—	—	—	—	—	—	—
Net Asset Value ($)	9.45	9.86	9.06	—	—	—	—	—	—	—
Expense Ratio (%).	0.80	0.80	0.31	—	—	—	—	—	—	—
Yield (%)	6.24	5.98	6.18	—	—	—	—	—	—	—
Portfolio Turnover (%). . . .	158	142	144	—	—	—	—	—	—	—
Total Assets (Millions $). . .	197	157	109	—	—	—	—	—	—	—

PORTFOLIO (as of 9/30/96)

Portfolio Manager: Jack A. Ablin - 1993

Investm't Category: Mortgage-Backed Bond
- ✔ Domestic
- Foreign
- Asset Allocation
- Index
- Sector
- State Specific

Investment Style
- Large-Cap Growth
- Mid-Cap Growth
- Small-Cap Growth
- Large-Cap Value
- Mid-Cap Value
- Small-Cap Value

Portfolio
19.3% cash	0.0% corp bonds
0.0% stocks	80.7% gov't bonds
0.0% preferred	0.0% muni bonds
0.0% conv't/warrants	0.0% other

SHAREHOLDER INFORMATION

Minimum Investment
Initial: $1,000   Subsequent: $250

Minimum IRA Investment
Initial: $250   Subsequent: $1

Maximum Fees
Load: none   12b-1: 0.25%
Other: none

Distributions
Income: monthly   Capital Gains: Dec

Exchange Options
Number Per Year: no limit   Fee: none
Telephone: yes (money market fund available)

Services
IRA, pension, auto invest, auto withdraw

AARP Balanced Stock & Bond (ABSBX)

Two International Place
Boston, MA 02110
800-322-2282, 617-295-1000

Balanced

PERFORMANCE

fund inception date: 2/1/94

	3yr Annual	5yr Annual	10yr Annual	Bull	Bear
Return (%)	na	na	na	44.5	na
Differ from Category (+/-)	na	na	na	-0.6 av	na

Total Risk	Standard Deviation	Category Risk	Risk Index	Beta
na	na	na	na	na

	1996	1995	1994	1993	1992	1991	1990	1989	1988	1987
Return (%)	14.1	23.8	—	—	—	—	—	—	—	—
Differ from Category (+/-)	-0.1	-0.8	—	—	—	—	—	—	—	—
Return, Tax-Adjusted (%)	12.1	21.7	—	—	—	—	—	—	—	—

PER SHARE DATA

	1996	1995	1994	1993	1992	1991	1990	1989	1988	1987
Dividends, Net Income ($)	0.68	0.61	—	—	—	—	—	—	—	—
Distrib'ns, Cap Gain ($)	0.21	0.21	—	—	—	—	—	—	—	—
Net Asset Value ($)	18.32	16.86	—	—	—	—	—	—	—	—
Expense Ratio (%)	na	1.01	—	—	—	—	—	—	—	—
Yield (%)	3.66	3.57	—	—	—	—	—	—	—	—
Portfolio Turnover (%)	na	63	—	—	—	—	—	—	—	—
Total Assets (Millions $)	443	277	—	—	—	—	—	—	—	—

PORTFOLIO (as of 9/30/96)

Portfolio Manager: Hoffman, Hutchinson, Thorndike - 1994

Investm't Category: Balanced
- ✔ Domestic
- ✔ Foreign
-   Asset Allocation

  Index
  Sector
  State Specific

Investment Style

Large-Cap Growth	Large-Cap Value
Mid-Cap Growth	Mid-Cap Value
Small-Cap Growth	Small-Cap Value

Portfolio

3.0% cash	12.0% corp bonds
55.0% stocks	27.0% gov't bonds
2.0% preferred	0.0% muni bonds
0.0% conv't/warrants	1.0% other

SHAREHOLDER INFORMATION

Minimum Investment
Initial: $500   Subsequent: $1

Minimum IRA Investment
Initial: $250   Subsequent: $1

Maximum Fees
Load: none   12b-1: none
Other: none

Distributions
Income: quarterly   Capital Gains: annual

Exchange Options
Number Per Year: no limit   Fee: none
Telephone: yes (money market fund available)

Services
IRA, pension, auto invest, auto withdraw

AARP Capital Growth
(ACGFX)
Growth

Two International Place
Boston, MA 02110
800-322-2282, 617-295-1000

PERFORMANCE

fund inception date: 11/30/84

	3yr Annual	5yr Annual	10yr Annual	Bull	Bear
Return (%)	12.3	11.4	13.2	60.3	-11.5
Differ from Category (+/-)	-3.4 blw av	-2.9 low	-0.7 av	-2.1 av	-4.8 low

Total Risk	Standard Deviation	Category Risk	Risk Index	Beta
abv av	11.3%	abv av	1.1	1.07

	1996	1995	1994	1993	1992	1991	1990	1989	1988	1987
Return (%)	20.6	30.5	-10.1	15.9	4.7	40.5	-15.8	33.4	27.3	0.2
Differ from Category (+/-)	0.5	0.2	-9.8	1.9	-7.1	4.5	-9.7	7.3	9.2	-1.8
Return, Tax-Adjusted (%)	17.2	29.5	-10.7	13.3	3.4	38.9	-18.2	30.9	26.5	-1.8

PER SHARE DATA

	1996	1995	1994	1993	1992	1991	1990	1989	1988	1987
Dividends, Net Income ($)	0.41	0.39	0.01	0.05	0.14	0.23	0.59	0.19	0.09	0.15
Distrib'ns, Cap Gain ($)	3.99	0.51	0.64	2.90	1.21	0.94	1.79	1.93	0.42	1.23
Net Asset Value ($)	42.07	38.46	30.15	34.24	32.09	31.94	23.57	30.83	24.72	19.84
Expense Ratio (%)	na	0.95	0.97	1.05	1.13	1.17	1.11	1.16	1.23	1.24
Yield (%)	0.89	1.00	0.03	0.13	0.42	0.69	2.32	0.57	0.35	0.71
Portfolio Turnover (%)	na	98	79	100	89	100	83	64	45	54
Total Assets (Millions $)	902	709	631	682	491	284	173	187	89	80

PORTFOLIO (as of 9/30/96)

Portfolio Manager: William Gadsden, Bruce Beaty - 1989

Investm't Category: Growth
- ✔ Domestic
- ✔ Foreign
- Asset Allocation
- Index
- Sector
- State Specific

Investment Style
- ✔ Large-Cap Growth
- Mid-Cap Growth
- Small-Cap Growth
- Large-Cap Value
- Mid-Cap Value
- Small-Cap Value

Portfolio
2.0% cash	0.0% corp bonds
98.0% stocks	0.0% gov't bonds
0.0% preferred	0.0% muni bonds
0.0% conv't/warrants	0.0% other

SHAREHOLDER INFORMATION

Minimum Investment
Initial: $500   Subsequent: $1

Minimum IRA Investment
Initial: $250   Subsequent: $1

Maximum Fees
Load: none   12b-1: none
Other: none

Distributions
Income: Dec   Capital Gains: annual

Exchange Options
Number Per Year: no limit   Fee: none
Telephone: yes (money market fund available)

Services
IRA, pension, auto invest, auto withdraw

AARP GNMA & US Treasury (AGNMX)

Two International Place
Boston, MA 02110
800-322-2282, 617-295-1000

Mortgage-Backed Bond

PERFORMANCE

fund inception date: 1/31/85

	3yr Annual	5yr Annual	10yr Annual	Bull	Bear
Return (%)	5.0	5.5	7.2	19.4	-4.1
Differ from Category (+/-)	-0.6 blw av	-0.5 low	-0.5 blw av	-1.7 blw av	-0.5 av

Total Risk	Standard Deviation	Category Risk	Risk Index	Avg Mat
low	3.2%	blw av	0.8	6.1 yrs

	1996	1995	1994	1993	1992	1991	1990	1989	1988	1987
Return (%).	4.4	12.8	-1.7	5.9	6.5	14.3	9.7	11.6	7.0	2.7
Differ from Category (+/-) . .	0.0	-1.9	0.0	-1.0	0.3	-0.1	-0.1	-1.0	-0.4	0.7
Return, Tax-Adjusted (%). . .	1.8	10.0	-4.1	3.1	3.5	11.0	6.3	8.1	3.4	-0.9

PER SHARE DATA

	1996	1995	1994	1993	1992	1991	1990	1989	1988	1987
Dividends, Net Income ($).	0.97	1.01	0.94	1.09	1.21	1.25	1.29	1.30	1.36	1.46
Distrib'ns, Cap Gain ($) . . .	0.00	0.00	0.00	0.00	0.00	0.00	0.00	0.00	0.00	0.00
Net Asset Value ($)	15.04	15.36	14.56	15.77	15.93	16.13	15.28	15.18	14.82	15.14
Expense Ratio (%).	na	0.67	0.66	0.70	0.72	0.74	0.79	0.79	0.81	0.88
Yield (%)	6.44	6.57	6.45	6.91	7.59	7.74	8.44	8.56	9.17	9.64
Portfolio Turnover (%). . . .	na	70	114	105	74	87	61	48	85	51
Total Assets (Millions $). .	4,910	5,257	5,248	6,629	5,546	3,735	2,662	2,526	2,745	2,718

PORTFOLIO (as of 9/30/96)

Portfolio Manager: David H. Glen, Mark Boyadjian - 1984

Investm't Category: Mortgage-Backed Bond
- ✔ Domestic
- Foreign
- Asset Allocation
- Index
- Sector
- State Specific

Investment Style
- Large-Cap Growth
- Mid-Cap Growth
- Small-Cap Growth
- Large-Cap Value
- Mid-Cap Value
- Small-Cap Value

Portfolio
1.0% cash	0.0% corp bonds
0.0% stocks	99.0% gov't bonds
0.0% preferred	0.0% muni bonds
0.0% conv't/warrants	0.0% other

SHAREHOLDER INFORMATION

Minimum Investment
Initial: $500   Subsequent: $1

Minimum IRA Investment
Initial: $250   Subsequent: $1

Maximum Fees
Load: none   12b-1: none
Other: none

Distributions
Income: monthly   Capital Gains: annual

Exchange Options
Number Per Year: no limit   Fee: none
Telephone: yes (money market fund available)

Services
IRA, pension, auto invest, auto withdraw

AARP Growth & Income
(AGIFX)
Growth & Income

Two International Place
Boston, MA 02110
800-322-2282, 617-295-1000

PERFORMANCE
fund inception date: 1/2/85

	3yr Annual	5yr Annual	10yr Annual	Bull	Bear
Return (%)	18.2	15.8	13.8	65.1	-3.9
Differ from Category (+/-)	2.9 abv av	1.9 abv av	1.1 abv av	5.3 av	2.5 high

Total Risk	Standard Deviation	Category Risk	Risk Index	Beta
av	9.0%	blw av	1.0	0.87

	1996	1995	1994	1993	1992	1991	1990	1989	1988	1987
Return (%)	21.6	31.8	3.0	15.6	9.2	26.4	-2.1	26.6	10.9	0.8
Differ from Category (+/-)	1.9	1.7	4.3	1.8	-1.5	-2.7	3.8	3.1	-5.9	0.6
Return, Tax-Adjusted (%)	19.2	29.6	0.7	14.2	7.6	24.1	-4.2	24.5	8.8	-2.0

PER SHARE DATA

	1996	1995	1994	1993	1992	1991	1990	1989	1988	1987
Dividends, Net Income ($)	1.18	1.10	0.97	0.83	0.92	1.01	1.22	1.06	1.03	0.94
Distrib'ns, Cap Gain ($)	1.72	0.84	1.22	0.21	0.30	0.47	0.13	0.00	0.00	0.77
Net Asset Value ($)	45.38	39.77	31.74	32.94	29.41	28.08	23.45	25.36	20.90	19.79
Expense Ratio (%)	na	0.72	0.76	0.84	0.91	0.96	1.03	1.04	1.06	1.08
Yield (%)	2.50	2.70	2.94	2.50	3.09	3.53	5.17	4.17	4.92	4.57
Portfolio Turnover (%)	na	31	31	17	36	54	58	55	61	43
Total Assets (Millions $)	4,622	3,259	2,298	1,752	881	458	265	239	209	252

PORTFOLIO (as of 9/30/96)

Portfolio Manager: Robert T. Hoffman - 1991

Investm't Category: Growth & Income
- ✔ Domestic
- ✔ Foreign
-   Asset Allocation
-   Index
-   Sector
-   State Specific

Investment Style

Large-Cap Growth	✔ Large-Cap Value
Mid-Cap Growth	✔ Mid-Cap Value
Small-Cap Growth	Small-Cap Value

Portfolio

2.1% cash	0.1% corp bonds
91.7% stocks	0.0% gov't bonds
2.8% preferred	0.0% muni bonds
3.3% conv't/warrants	0.0% other

SHAREHOLDER INFORMATION

Minimum Investment
Initial: $500   Subsequent: $1

Minimum IRA Investment
Initial: $250   Subsequent: $1

Maximum Fees
Load: none   12b-1: none
Other: none

Distributions
Income: quarterly   Capital Gains: annual

Exchange Options
Number Per Year: no limit   Fee: none
Telephone: yes (money market fund available)

Services
IRA, pension, auto invest, auto withdraw

AARP High Quality Bond
(AGBFX)
General Bond

Two International Place
Boston, MA 02110
800-322-2282, 617-295-1000

PERFORMANCE

fund inception date: 1/31/85

	3yr Annual	5yr Annual	10yr Annual	Bull	Bear
Return (%)	4.7	6.2	7.6	21.1	-6.7
Differ from Category (+/-)	-0.4 blw av	0.1 av	0.3 av	0.8 av	-2.5 low

Total Risk	Standard Deviation	Category Risk	Risk Index	Avg Mat
low	4.7%	abv av	1.2	7.8 yrs

	1996	1995	1994	1993	1992	1991	1990	1989	1988	1987
Return (%)	2.7	17.2	-4.5	10.9	6.2	15.4	7.5	12.3	8.0	1.8
Differ from Category (+/-)	-1.2	2.3	-2.2	1.8	-0.3	0.7	0.2	0.6	0.4	-0.5
Return, Tax-Adjusted (%)	0.5	14.7	-6.6	8.0	3.4	12.6	4.5	9.0	4.6	-1.8

PER SHARE DATA

	1996	1995	1994	1993	1992	1991	1990	1989	1988	1987
Dividends, Net Income ($)	0.91	0.94	0.85	0.91	1.00	1.06	1.15	1.22	1.24	1.45
Distrib'ns, Cap Gain ($)	0.00	0.00	0.00	0.37	0.18	0.00	0.00	0.00	0.00	0.00
Net Asset Value ($)	15.99	16.48	14.92	16.51	16.07	16.29	15.12	15.20	14.68	14.77
Expense Ratio (%)	na	0.95	0.95	1.01	1.13	1.17	1.14	1.16	1.17	1.18
Yield (%)	5.69	5.70	5.69	5.39	6.15	6.50	7.60	8.02	8.44	9.81
Portfolio Turnover (%)	na	201	63	100	63	90	47	58	24	193
Total Assets (Millions $)	513	544	529	622	413	234	159	134	122	114

PORTFOLIO (as of 9/30/96)

Portfolio Manager: Glen, Hutchinson, Wohler - 1984

Investm't Category: General Bond
- ✔ Domestic
- Foreign
- Asset Allocation
- Index
- Sector
- State Specific

Investment Style
- Large-Cap Growth
- Mid-Cap Growth
- Small-Cap Growth
- Large-Cap Value
- Mid-Cap Value
- Small-Cap Value

Portfolio
11.0%	cash	24.0%	corp bonds
0.0%	stocks	59.0%	gov't bonds
0.0%	preferred	0.0%	muni bonds
0.0%	conv't/warrants	6.0%	other

SHAREHOLDER INFORMATION

Minimum Investment
Initial: $500   Subsequent: $1

Minimum IRA Investment
Initial: $250   Subsequent: $1

Maximum Fees
Load: none   12b-1: none
Other: none

Distributions
Income: monthly   Capital Gains: annual

Exchange Options
Number Per Year: no limit   Fee: none
Telephone: yes (money market fund available)

Services
IRA, pension, auto invest, auto withdraw

AARP Insured Tax-Free General Bond (AITGX)

Tax-Exempt Bond

Two International Place
Boston, MA 02110
800-322-2282, 617-295-1000

PERFORMANCE

fund inception date: 1/31/85

	3yr Annual	5yr Annual	10yr Annual	Bull	Bear
Return (%)	4.1	6.6	7.2	19.1	-6.4
Differ from Category (+/-)	-0.1 blw av	-0.2 blw av	0.5 abv av	0.7 av	-1.0 blw av

Total Risk	Standard Deviation	Category Risk	Risk Index	Avg Mat
blw av	5.8%	abv av	1.0	11.0 yrs

	1996	1995	1994	1993	1992	1991	1990	1989	1988	1987
Return (%)	3.6	16.1	-6.3	12.6	8.5	12.2	6.3	10.7	12.2	-1.0
Differ from Category (+/-)	-0.1	0.9	-1.0	0.8	0.2	0.8	-0.1	1.7	2.2	0.4
Return, Tax-Adjusted (%)	3.4	16.1	-6.3	11.9	7.8	11.9	6.3	10.2	12.2	-1.0

PER SHARE DATA

	1996	1995	1994	1993	1992	1991	1990	1989	1988	1987
Dividends, Net Income ($)	0.87	0.86	0.86	0.87	0.93	0.98	1.03	1.07	1.07	1.17
Distrib'ns, Cap Gain ($)	0.09	0.00	0.00	0.40	0.42	0.16	0.00	0.25	0.00	0.00
Net Asset Value ($)	17.98	18.29	16.54	18.54	17.62	17.52	16.68	16.70	16.31	15.55
Expense Ratio (%)	na	0.69	0.68	0.72	0.74	0.77	0.80	0.84	0.92	1.00
Yield (%)	4.81	4.70	5.19	4.59	5.15	5.54	6.17	6.31	6.56	7.52
Portfolio Turnover (%)	na	17	38	47	62	32	48	149	164	135
Total Assets (Millions $)	1,766	1,839	1,748	2,128	1,570	1,160	827	564	352	250

PORTFOLIO (as of 9/30/96)

Portfolio Manager: Donald Carleton, Philip Condon - 1986

Investm't Category: Tax-Exempt Bond
- ✔ Domestic
- Foreign
- Asset Allocation
- Index
- Sector
- State Specific

Investment Style
- Large-Cap Growth
- Mid-Cap Growth
- Small-Cap Growth
- Large-Cap Value
- Mid-Cap Value
- Small-Cap Value

Portfolio
5.7% cash	0.0% corp bonds	
0.0% stocks	0.0% gov't bonds	
0.0% preferred	94.3% muni bonds	
0.0% conv't/warrants	0.0% other	

SHAREHOLDER INFORMATION

Minimum Investment
Initial: $500   Subsequent: $1

Minimum IRA Investment
Initial: na   Subsequent: na

Maximum Fees
Load: none   12b-1: none
Other: none

Distributions
Income: monthly   Capital Gains: annual

Exchange Options
Number Per Year: no limit   Fee: none
Telephone: yes (money market fund available)

Services
auto invest, auto withdraw

API Trust: Growth
(APITX)
Growth

P.O. Box 2529
2303 Yorktown Ave.
Lynchburg, VA 24501
800-544-6060, 804-846-1361

PERFORMANCE   fund inception date: 6/14/85

	3yr Annual	5yr Annual	10yr Annual	Bull	Bear
Return (%)	9.7	9.7	10.5	43.4	-11.0
Differ from Category (+/-)	-6.0 low	-4.6 low	-3.4 low	-19.0 low	-4.3 low

Total Risk	Standard Deviation	Category Risk	Risk Index	Beta
abv av	10.2%	av	1.0	0.88

	1996	1995	1994	1993	1992	1991	1990	1989	1988	1987
Return (%)	11.3	22.9	-3.5	18.2	1.9	45.9	-12.7	15.6	25.9	-7.7
Differ from Category (+/-)	-8.8	-7.4	-3.2	4.2	-9.9	9.9	-6.6	-10.5	7.8	-9.7
Return, Tax-Adjusted (%)	7.6	20.3	-6.0	16.7	0.9	42.7	-12.7	9.6	25.1	-12.4

PER SHARE DATA

	1996	1995	1994	1993	1992	1991	1990	1989	1988	1987
Dividends, Net Income ($)	0.00	0.00	0.00	0.00	0.00	0.00	0.00	0.08	0.15	0.05
Distrib'ns, Cap Gain ($)	1.66	1.01	1.11	0.57	0.37	0.95	0.00	2.05	0.00	1.87
Net Asset Value ($)	12.66	12.85	11.28	12.83	11.34	11.49	8.53	9.76	10.25	8.26
Expense Ratio (%)	2.24	2.06	2.24	2.05	1.97	2.38	2.60	2.66	2.74	2.41
Yield (%)	0.00	0.00	0.00	0.00	0.00	0.00	0.00	0.67	1.46	0.49
Portfolio Turnover (%)	63	91	90	157	99	206	118	163	165	190
Total Assets (Millions $)	69	65	50	49	44	35	24	34	28	23

PORTFOLIO (as of 9/30/96)

Portfolio Manager: David D. Basten - 1985

Investm't Category: Growth
✔ Domestic   Index
✔ Foreign   Sector
  Asset Allocation State Specific

Investment Style
  Large-Cap Growth   Large-Cap Value
✔ Mid-Cap Growth   Mid-Cap Value
✔ Small-Cap Growth   Small-Cap Value

Portfolio
  0.3% cash   0.0% corp bonds
  0.0% stocks   0.0% gov't bonds
  0.0% preferred   0.0% muni bonds
  0.0% conv't/warrants 99.7% other

SHAREHOLDER INFORMATION

Minimum Investment
Initial: $500   Subsequent: $100

Minimum IRA Investment
Initial: $500   Subsequent: $100

Maximum Fees
Load: none   12b-1: 1.00%
Other: none

Distributions
Income: annual   Capital Gains: annual

Exchange Options
Number Per Year: no limit   Fee: none
Telephone: none

Services
IRA, pension, auto invest, auto withdraw

Acorn Invest Trust: Acorn
(ACRNX)
Growth

227 W. Monroe
Suite 300
Chicago, IL 60606
800-922-6769, 312-634-9200

PERFORMANCE
fund inception date: 6/10/70

	3yr Annual	5yr Annual	10yr Annual	Bull	Bear
Return (%)	11.0	17.6	16.1	50.6	-9.5
Differ from Category (+/-)	-4.7 low	3.3 high	2.2 high	-11.8 blw av	-2.8 blw av

Total Risk	Standard Deviation	Category Risk	Risk Index	Beta
abv av	9.9%	av	1.0	0.73

	1996	1995	1994	1993	1992	1991	1990	1989	1988	1987
Return (%)	22.5	20.8	-7.5	32.3	24.2	47.3	-17.6	24.9	24.6	4.4
Differ from Category (+/-)	2.4	-9.5	-7.2	18.3	12.4	11.3	-11.5	-1.2	6.5	2.4
Return, Tax-Adjusted (%)	19.1	18.0	-9.0	30.5	22.6	46.0	-19.7	22.9	20.9	3.4

PER SHARE DATA

	1996	1995	1994	1993	1992	1991	1990	1989	1988	1987
Dividends, Net Income ($)	0.11	0.09	0.11	0.06	0.13	0.10	0.13	0.11	0.16	0.15
Distrib'ns, Cap Gain ($)	1.47	1.08	0.56	0.59	0.34	0.15	0.44	0.36	0.63	1.08
Net Asset Value ($)	15.04	13.60	12.24	13.95	11.06	9.32	6.51	8.58	7.27	6.48
Expense Ratio (%)	na	0.57	0.62	0.65	0.67	0.72	0.82	0.73	0.80	0.82
Yield (%)	0.66	0.61	0.85	0.41	1.14	1.05	1.86	1.22	2.02	1.98
Portfolio Turnover (%)	na	29	18	20	25	25	36	26	36	52
Total Assets (Millions $)	2,863	2,399	1,982	2,034	1,449	1,150	769	854	562	418

PORTFOLIO (as of 9/30/96)

Portfolio Manager: R. Wange, C. McQuaid, T. Hogan - 1970

Investm't Category: Growth
✔ Domestic	Index
✔ Foreign	Sector
Asset Allocation	State Specific

Investment Style
Large-Cap Growth	Large-Cap Value
Mid-Cap Growth	Mid-Cap Value
✔ Small-Cap Growth	✔ Small-Cap Value

Portfolio
6.6% cash	0.0% corp bonds
91.9% stocks	0.0% gov't bonds
1.1% preferred	0.0% muni bonds
0.4% conv't/warrants	0.0% other

SHAREHOLDER INFORMATION

Minimum Investment
Initial: $1,000   Subsequent: $100

Minimum IRA Investment
Initial: $200   Subsequent: $100

Maximum Fees
Load: none   12b-1: none
Other: none

Distributions
Income: Jul, Dec   Capital Gains: Dec

Exchange Options
Number Per Year: 4   Fee: none
Telephone: yes (money market fund available)

Services
IRA, pension, auto exchange, auto invest, auto withdraw

Acorn Invest Trust: Int'l
(ACINX)
International Stock

227 W. Monroe
Suite 300
Chicago, IL 60606
800-922-6769, 312-634-9200

PERFORMANCE

fund inception date: 9/23/92

	3yr Annual	5yr Annual	10yr Annual	Bull	Bear
Return (%)	8.1	na	na	29.6	-6.5
Differ from Category (+/-)	1.8 abv av	na	na	5.3 abv av	0.7 av

Total Risk	Standard Deviation	Category Risk	Risk Index	Beta
av	9.2%	low	0.9	0.56

	1996	1995	1994	1993	1992	1991	1990	1989	1988	1987
Return (%)	20.6	8.9	-3.8	49.1	—	—	—	—	—	—
Differ from Category (+/-)	5.8	-0.2	-0.7	9.5	—	—	—	—	—	—
Return, Tax-Adjusted (%)	19.8	8.8	-4.0	49.1	—	—	—	—	—	—

PER SHARE DATA

	1996	1995	1994	1993	1992	1991	1990	1989	1988	1987
Dividends, Net Income ($)	0.12	0.00	0.01	0.00	—	—	—	—	—	—
Distrib'ns, Cap Gain ($)	0.28	0.01	0.09	0.00	—	—	—	—	—	—
Net Asset Value ($)	19.61	16.59	15.24	15.94	—	—	—	—	—	—
Expense Ratio (%)	na	1.20	1.20	1.20	—	—	—	—	—	—
Yield (%)	0.60	0.00	0.06	0.00	—	—	—	—	—	—
Portfolio Turnover (%)	na	26	20	19	—	—	—	—	—	—
Total Assets (Millions $)	1,751	1,276	1,364	906	—	—	—	—	—	—

PORTFOLIO (as of 9/30/96)

Portfolio Manager: Ralph Wanger, Leah J. Zell - 1992

Investm't Category: International Stock
- Domestic
- ✔ Foreign
- Asset Allocation
- Index
- Sector
- State Specific

Investment Style
- Large-Cap Growth
- Mid-Cap Growth
- Small-Cap Growth
- Large-Cap Value
- Mid-Cap Value
- Small-Cap Value

Portfolio
6.7% cash	0.0% corp bonds	
89.9% stocks	0.0% gov't bonds	
3.3% preferred	0.0% muni bonds	
0.1% conv't/warrants	0.0% other	

SHAREHOLDER INFORMATION

Minimum Investment
Initial: $1,000   Subsequent: $100

Minimum IRA Investment
Initial: $200   Subsequent: $100

Maximum Fees
Load: none   12b-1: none
Other: none

Distributions
Income: Jul, Dec   Capital Gains: Dec

Exchange Options
Number Per Year: 4   Fee: none
Telephone: yes (money market fund available)

Services
IRA, pension, auto exchange, auto invest, auto withdraw

American Century Balanced Investors (TWBIX)

Balanced

4500 Main St., 14th Floor
P.O. Box 418210
Kansas City, MO 64141
800-345-2021, 816-531-5575
www.americancentury.com

PERFORMANCE

fund inception date: 10/20/88

	3yr Annual	5yr Annual	10yr Annual	Bull	Bear
Return (%)	10.9	6.5	na	41.0	-6.6
Differ from Category (+/-)	-0.8 blw av	-4.9 low	na	-4.1 blw av	-0.9 blw av

Total Risk	Standard Deviation	Category Risk	Risk Index	Beta
av	7.4%	abv av	1.1	0.68

	1996	1995	1994	1993	1992	1991	1990	1989	1988	1987
Return (%)	12.6	21.3	-0.1	7.2	-6.1	46.8	1.8	25.6	—	—
Differ from Category (+/-)	-1.6	-3.3	1.5	-7.2	-15.0	22.7	2.7	7.5	—	—
Return, Tax-Adjusted (%)	9.2	18.2	-1.7	6.2	-7.0	45.6	0.4	23.0	—	—

PER SHARE DATA

	1996	1995	1994	1993	1992	1991	1990	1989	1988	1987
Dividends, Net Income ($)	0.48	0.48	0.43	0.37	0.34	0.35	0.41	0.42	—	—
Distrib'ns, Cap Gain ($)	1.38	1.00	0.27	0.00	0.00	0.00	0.00	0.32	—	—
Net Asset Value ($)	17.26	16.99	15.27	16.00	15.28	16.64	11.62	11.83	—	—
Expense Ratio (%)	na	0.98	1.00	1.00	1.00	1.00	1.00	1.00	—	—
Yield (%)	2.57	2.66	2.76	2.31	2.22	2.10	3.52	3.45	—	—
Portfolio Turnover (%)	na	85	94	95	100	116	104	171	—	—
Total Assets (Millions $)	904	839	689	683	700	351	74	35	—	—

PORTFOLIO (as of 6/30/96)

Portfolio Manager: committee - 1988

Investm't Category: Balanced
✔ Domestic   Index
✔ Foreign   Sector
  Asset Allocation State Specific

Investment Style
Large-Cap Growth   Large-Cap Value
Mid-Cap Growth   Mid-Cap Value
Small-Cap Growth   Small-Cap Value

Portfolio
3.2% cash	0.0% corp bonds
58.0% stocks	0.0% gov't bonds
0.0% preferred	0.0% muni bonds
0.0% conv't/warrants	38.8% other

SHAREHOLDER INFORMATION

Minimum Investment
Initial: $2,500   Subsequent: $100

Minimum IRA Investment
Initial: $1,000   Subsequent: $100

Maximum Fees
Load: none   12b-1: none
Other: none

Distributions
Income: quarterly   Capital Gains: Dec

Exchange Options
Number Per Year: 6   Fee: none
Telephone: yes (money market fund available)

Services
IRA, pension, auto exchange, auto invest, auto withdraw

American Century Capital Manager (BCMFX)

Balanced

4500 Main St., 14th Floor
P.O. Box 418210
Kansas City, MO 64141
800-345-2021, 415-965-4222
www.americancentury.com

PERFORMANCE

fund inception date: 12/1/94

	3yr Annual	5yr Annual	10yr Annual	Bull	Bear
Return (%)	na	na	na	na	na
Differ from Category (+/-)	na	na	na	na	na

Total Risk	Standard Deviation	Category Risk	Risk Index	Beta
na	na	na	na	na

	1996	1995	1994	1993	1992	1991	1990	1989	1988	1987
Return (%)	13.0	19.8	—	—	—	—	—	—	—	—
Differ from Category (+/-)	-1.2	-4.8	—	—	—	—	—	—	—	—
Return, Tax-Adjusted (%)	10.1	17.8	—	—	—	—	—	—	—	—

PER SHARE DATA

	1996	1995	1994	1993	1992	1991	1990	1989	1988	1987
Dividends, Net Income ($)	0.39	0.37	—	—	—	—	—	—	—	—
Distrib'ns, Cap Gain ($)	0.64	0.18	—	—	—	—	—	—	—	—
Net Asset Value ($)	12.00	11.56	—	—	—	—	—	—	—	—
Expense Ratio (%)	na	1.01	—	—	—	—	—	—	—	—
Yield (%)	3.08	3.15	—	—	—	—	—	—	—	—
Portfolio Turnover (%)	na	100	—	—	—	—	—	—	—	—
Total Assets (Millions $)	82	53	—	—	—	—	—	—	—	—

PORTFOLIO (as of 6/30/96)

Portfolio Manager: Jeffrey Tyler - 1994

Investm't Category: Balanced

✔ Domestic	Index
✔ Foreign	Sector
Asset Allocation	State Specific

Investment Style

Large-Cap Growth	Large-Cap Value
Mid-Cap Growth	Mid-Cap Value
Small-Cap Growth	Small-Cap Value

Portfolio

15.3% cash	3.4% corp bonds
43.9% stocks	31.4% gov't bonds
0.0% preferred	0.0% muni bonds
0.0% conv't/warrants	6.1% other

SHAREHOLDER INFORMATION

Minimum Investment
Initial: $2,500   Subsequent: $100

Minimum IRA Investment
Initial: $1,000   Subsequent: $100

Maximum Fees
Load: none   12b-1: none
Other: none

Distributions
Income: quarterly   Capital Gains: Dec

Exchange Options
Number Per Year: 6   Fee: none
Telephone: yes (money market fund available)

Services
IRA, pension, auto exchange, auto invest, auto withdraw

American Century Equity Growth (BEQGX)

Growth

4500 Main St., 14th Floor
P.O. Box 418210
Kansas City, MO 64141
800-345-2021, 415-965-4222
www.americancentury.com

PERFORMANCE

fund inception date: 5/9/91

	3yr Annual	5yr Annual	10yr Annual	Bull	Bear
Return (%)	19.5	14.6	na	76.8	-5.6
Differ from Category (+/-)	3.8 high	0.3 av	na	14.4 abv av	1.1 abv av

Total Risk	Standard Deviation	Category Risk	Risk Index	Beta
av	9.2%	blw av	0.9	0.91

	1996	1995	1994	1993	1992	1991	1990	1989	1988	1987
Return (%).	27.3	34.5	-0.3	11.4	4.1	—	—	—	—	—
Differ from Category (+/-) . .	7.2	4.2	0.0	-2.6	-7.7	—	—	—	—	—
Return, Tax-Adjusted (%). .	22.9	31.2	-1.9	9.0	2.9	—	—	—	—	—

PER SHARE DATA

	1996	1995	1994	1993	1992	1991	1990	1989	1988	1987
Dividends, Net Income ($).	0.26	0.22	0.29	0.23	0.32	—	—	—	—	—
Distrib'ns, Cap Gain ($) . . .	1.85	1.01	0.25	0.65	0.02	—	—	—	—	—
Net Asset Value ($)	15.96	14.24	11.53	12.12	11.68	—	—	—	—	—
Expense Ratio (%).	na	0.71	0.75	0.75	0.75	—	—	—	—	—
Yield (%)	1.45	1.44	2.46	1.80	2.73	—	—	—	—	—
Portfolio Turnover (%).	na	125	94	96	114	—	—	—	—	—
Total Assets (Millions $). . .	261	159	97	96	73	—	—	—	—	—

PORTFOLIO (as of 6/30/96)

Portfolio Manager: Steven Colton - 1991

Investm't Category: Growth
- ✔ Domestic
- Foreign
- Asset Allocation
- Index
- Sector
- State Specific

Investment Style
- Large-Cap Growth
- Mid-Cap Growth
- Small-Cap Growth
- ✔ Large-Cap Value
- Mid-Cap Value
- Small-Cap Value

Portfolio
- 1.1% cash
- 98.9% stocks
- 0.0% preferred
- 0.0% conv't/warrants
- 0.0% corp bonds
- 0.0% gov't bonds
- 0.0% muni bonds
- 0.0% other

SHAREHOLDER INFORMATION

Minimum Investment
Initial: $2,500   Subsequent: $100

Minimum IRA Investment
Initial: $1,000   Subsequent: $100

Maximum Fees
Load: none   12b-1: none
Other: none

Distributions
Income: quarterly   Capital Gains: Dec

Exchange Options
Number Per Year: 6   Fee: none
Telephone: yes (money market fund available)

Services
IRA, pension, auto exchange, auto invest, auto withdraw

American Century Equity Income (TWEIX)

Growth & Income

4500 Main St., 14th Floor
P.O. Box 418210
Kansas City, MO 64141
800-345-2021, 816-531-5575
www.americancentury.com

PERFORMANCE

fund inception date: 8/1/94

	3yr Annual	5yr Annual	10yr Annual	Bull	Bear
Return (%)	na	na	na	na	na
Differ from Category (+/-)	na	na	na	na	na

Total Risk	Standard Deviation	Category Risk	Risk Index	Beta
na	na	na	na	na

	1996	1995	1994	1993	1992	1991	1990	1989	1988	1987
Return (%)	23.3	29.6	—	—	—	—	—	—	—	—
Differ from Category (+/-)	3.6	-0.5	—	—	—	—	—	—	—	—
Return, Tax-Adjusted (%)	19.4	25.5	—	—	—	—	—	—	—	—

PER SHARE DATA

	1996	1995	1994	1993	1992	1991	1990	1989	1988	1987
Dividends, Net Income ($)	0.18	0.19	—	—	—	—	—	—	—	—
Distrib'ns, Cap Gain ($)	0.54	0.45	—	—	—	—	—	—	—	—
Net Asset Value ($)	6.34	5.76	—	—	—	—	—	—	—	—
Expense Ratio (%)	0.98	na	—	—	—	—	—	—	—	—
Yield (%)	2.61	3.05	—	—	—	—	—	—	—	—
Portfolio Turnover (%)	170	na	—	—	—	—	—	—	—	—
Total Assets (Millions $)	179	96	—	—	—	—	—	—	—	—

PORTFOLIO (as of 6/30/96)

Portfolio Manager: Zuger, Davidson - 1994

Investm't Category: Growth & Income
✔ Domestic   Index
✔ Foreign   Sector
  Asset Allocation State Specific

Investment Style

Large-Cap Growth   Large-Cap Value
Mid-Cap Growth   Mid-Cap Value
Small-Cap Growth   Small-Cap Value

Portfolio

0.0% cash	0.0% corp bonds
80.3% stocks	0.0% gov't bonds
4.4% preferred	0.0% muni bonds
0.0% conv't/warrants	15.3% other

SHAREHOLDER INFORMATION

Minimum Investment
Initial: $2,500   Subsequent: $50

Minimum IRA Investment
Initial: $1,000   Subsequent: $50

Maximum Fees
Load: none   12b-1: none
Other: none

Distributions
Income: quarterly   Capital Gains: Dec

Exchange Options
Number Per Year: 6   Fee: none
Telephone: yes (money market fund available)

Services
IRA, pension, auto exchange, auto invest, auto withdraw

American Century Global Gold (BGEIX)

Gold

4500 Main St., 14th Floor
P.O. Box 418210
Kansas City, MO 64141
800-345-2021, 415-965-4222
www.americancentury.com

PERFORMANCE

fund inception date: 8/17/88

	3yr Annual	5yr Annual	10yr Annual	Bull	Bear
Return (%)	-4.1	7.9	na	2.7	-14.1
Differ from Category (+/-)	-4.4 blw av	-1.7 av	na	-12.2 blw av	-3.9 blw av

Total Risk	Standard Deviation	Category Risk	Risk Index	Beta
high	26.6%	abv av	1.1	0.68

	1996	1995	1994	1993	1992	1991	1990	1989	1988	1987
Return (%)	-2.8	9.2	-16.8	81.2	-8.7	-11.3	-19.5	29.9	—	—
Differ from Category (+/-)	-14.0	4.2	-4.7	-6.6	6.6	-6.7	2.8	5.5	—	—
Return, Tax-Adjusted (%)	-4.4	9.2	-16.9	81.1	-8.8	-11.4	-19.8	29.7	—	—

PER SHARE DATA

	1996	1995	1994	1993	1992	1991	1990	1989	1988	1987
Dividends, Net Income ($)	0.05	0.00	0.02	0.01	0.01	0.01	0.05	0.04	—	—
Distrib'ns, Cap Gain ($)	0.63	0.00	0.02	0.00	0.00	0.00	0.02	0.00	—	—
Net Asset Value ($)	11.33	12.37	11.33	13.67	7.55	8.28	9.35	11.71	—	—
Expense Ratio (%)	na	0.61	0.61	0.72	0.75	0.75	0.96	1.00	—	—
Yield (%)	0.41	0.00	0.17	0.07	0.13	0.12	0.53	0.34	—	—
Portfolio Turnover (%)	na	28	41	28	53	56	21	34	—	—
Total Assets (Millions $)	455	540	570	618	161	124	104	61	—	—

PORTFOLIO (as of 6/30/96)

Portfolio Manager: William Martin - 1992

Investm't Category: Gold

✔ Domestic
✔ Foreign
  Asset Allocation

  Index
✔ Sector
  State Specific

Investment Style

Large-Cap Growth	Large-Cap Value
Mid-Cap Growth	Mid-Cap Value
Small-Cap Growth	Small-Cap Value

Portfolio

1.1% cash	0.0% corp bonds
98.9% stocks	0.0% gov't bonds
0.0% preferred	0.0% muni bonds
0.0% conv't/warrants	0.0% other

SHAREHOLDER INFORMATION

Minimum Investment
Initial: $2,500   Subsequent: $100

Minimum IRA Investment
Initial: $1,000   Subsequent: $100

Maximum Fees
Load: none   12b-1: none
Other: none

Distributions
Income: Jun, Dec   Capital Gains: Dec

Exchange Options
Number Per Year: 6   Fee: none
Telephone: yes (money market fund available)

Services
IRA, pension, auto exchange, auto invest, auto withdraw

American Century Glbl Natural Resources (BGRIX)

International Stock

4500 Main St., 14th Floor
P.O. Box 418210
Kansas City, MO 64141
800-345-2021, 415-965-4222
www.americancentury.com

PERFORMANCE

fund inception date: 9/15/94

	3yr Annual	5yr Annual	10yr Annual	Bull	Bear
Return (%)	na	na	na	na	na
Differ from Category (+/-)	na	na	na	na	na

Total Risk	Standard Deviation	Category Risk	Risk Index	Beta
na	na	na	na	na

	1996	1995	1994	1993	1992	1991	1990	1989	1988	1987
Return (%)	15.4	14.4	—	—	—	—	—	—	—	—
Differ from Category (+/-)	0.6	5.3	—	—	—	—	—	—	—	—
Return, Tax-Adjusted (%)	14.2	13.3	—	—	—	—	—	—	—	—

PER SHARE DATA

	1996	1995	1994	1993	1992	1991	1990	1989	1988	1987
Dividends, Net Income ($)	0.16	0.15	—	—	—	—	—	—	—	—
Distrib'ns, Cap Gain ($)	0.21	0.16	—	—	—	—	—	—	—	—
Net Asset Value ($)	11.91	10.66	—	—	—	—	—	—	—	—
Expense Ratio (%)	na	0.76	—	—	—	—	—	—	—	—
Yield (%)	1.32	1.38	—	—	—	—	—	—	—	—
Portfolio Turnover (%)	na	39	—	—	—	—	—	—	—	—
Total Assets (Millions $)	50	30	—	—	—	—	—	—	—	—

PORTFOLIO (as of 12/31/96)

Portfolio Manager: William Martin - 1994

Investm't Category: International Stock
- ✔ Domestic
- ✔ Foreign
- Asset Allocation
- Index
- Sector
- State Specific

Investment Style
- Large-Cap Growth
- Mid-Cap Growth
- Small-Cap Growth
- Large-Cap Value
- Mid-Cap Value
- Small-Cap Value

Portfolio
2.0% cash	0.0% corp bonds
98.0% stocks	0.0% gov't bonds
0.0% preferred	0.0% muni bonds
0.0% conv't/warrants	0.0% other

SHAREHOLDER INFORMATION

Minimum Investment
Initial: $2,500   Subsequent: $100

Minimum IRA Investment
Initial: $1,000   Subsequent: $100

Maximum Fees
Load: none   12b-1: none
Other: none

Distributions
Income: Jun, Dec   Capital Gains: Dec

Exchange Options
Number Per Year: 6   Fee: none
Telephone: yes (money market fund available)

Services
IRA, pension, auto exchange, auto invest, auto withdraw

American Century Income & Growth

(BIGRX) *Growth & Income*

4500 Main St., 14th Floor
P.O. Box 418210
Kansas City, MO 64141
800-345-2021, 415-965-4222
www.americancentury.com

PERFORMANCE

fund inception date: 12/17/90

	3yr Annual	5yr Annual	10yr Annual	Bull	Bear
Return (%)	19.0	15.1	na	75.7	-6.5
Differ from Category (+/-)	3.7 high	1.2 abv av	na	15.9 high	-0.1 av

Total Risk	Standard Deviation	Category Risk	Risk Index	Beta
av	9.1%	av	1.0	0.92

	1996	1995	1994	1993	1992	1991	1990	1989	1988	1987
Return (%)	23.9	36.8	-0.6	11.3	7.8	39.0	—	—	—	—
Differ from Category (+/-)	4.2	6.7	0.7	-2.5	-2.9	9.9	—	—	—	—
Return, Tax-Adjusted (%)	20.7	34.0	-2.9	9.7	6.5	37.1	—	—	—	—

PER SHARE DATA

	1996	1995	1994	1993	1992	1991	1990	1989	1988	1987
Dividends, Net Income ($)	0.40	0.42	0.43	0.42	0.41	0.48	—	—	—	—
Distrib'ns, Cap Gain ($)	1.43	0.75	0.63	0.18	0.03	0.00	—	—	—	—
Net Asset Value ($)	20.16	17.81	13.92	15.08	14.11	13.53	—	—	—	—
Expense Ratio (%)	na	0.67	0.73	0.75	0.75	0.50	—	—	—	—
Yield (%)	1.85	2.26	2.95	2.75	2.89	3.54	—	—	—	—
Portfolio Turnover (%)	na	69	67	31	63	140	—	—	—	—
Total Assets (Millions $)	716	372	224	229	140	58	—	—	—	—

PORTFOLIO (as of 6/30/96)

Portfolio Manager: Steven Colton - 1990

Investm't Category: Growth & Income
- ✔ Domestic
- Foreign
- Asset Allocation
- Index
- Sector
- State Specific

Investment Style
- Large-Cap Growth
- Mid-Cap Growth
- Small-Cap Growth
- ✔ Large-Cap Value
- Mid-Cap Value
- Small-Cap Value

Portfolio
1.6% cash	0.0% corp bonds
98.4% stocks	0.0% gov't bonds
0.0% preferred	0.0% muni bonds
0.0% conv't/warrants	0.0% other

SHAREHOLDER INFORMATION

Minimum Investment
Initial: $2,500   Subsequent: $100

Minimum IRA Investment
Initial: $1,000   Subsequent: $100

Maximum Fees
Load: none   12b-1: none
Other: none

Distributions
Income: monthly   Capital Gains: Dec

Exchange Options
Number Per Year: 6   Fee: none
Telephone: yes (money market fund available)

Services
IRA, pension, auto exchange, auto invest, auto withdraw

Guide to Low-Load Mutual Funds

American Century Utilities (BULIX)

Growth & Income

4500 Main St., 14th Floor
P.O. Box 418210
Kansas City, MO 64141
800-345-2021, 415-965-4222
www.americancentury.com

PERFORMANCE

fund inception date: 3/1/93

	3yr Annual	5yr Annual	10yr Annual	Bull	Bear
Return (%)	8.3	na	na	40.6	-10.0
Differ from Category (+/-)	-7.0 low	na	na	-19.2 low	-3.6 low

Total Risk	Standard Deviation	Category Risk	Risk Index	Beta
abv av	9.5%	av	1.0	0.64

	1996	1995	1994	1993	1992	1991	1990	1989	1988	1987
Return (%)	4.5	35.2	-10.1	—	—	—	—	—	—	—
Differ from Category (+/-)	-15.2	5.1	-8.8	—	—	—	—	—	—	—
Return, Tax-Adjusted (%)	3.0	33.4	-11.8	—	—	—	—	—	—	—

PER SHARE DATA

	1996	1995	1994	1993	1992	1991	1990	1989	1988	1987
Dividends, Net Income ($)	0.42	0.38	0.43	—	—	—	—	—	—	—
Distrib'ns, Cap Gain ($)	0.00	0.00	0.00	—	—	—	—	—	—	—
Net Asset Value ($)	11.51	11.44	8.79	—	—	—	—	—	—	—
Expense Ratio (%)	na	0.75	0.75	—	—	—	—	—	—	—
Yield (%)	3.64	3.32	4.89	—	—	—	—	—	—	—
Portfolio Turnover (%)	na	68	61	—	—	—	—	—	—	—
Total Assets (Millions $)	148	217	152	—	—	—	—	—	—	—

PORTFOLIO (as of 6/30/96)

Portfolio Manager: Steven Colton - 1993

Investm't Category: Growth & Income
✔ Domestic   Index
  Foreign   Sector
  Asset Allocation   State Specific

Investment Style
  Large-Cap Growth   ✔ Large-Cap Value
  Mid-Cap Growth   Mid-Cap Value
  Small-Cap Growth   Small-Cap Value

Portfolio
  1.6% cash   0.0% corp bonds
  97.2% stocks   0.0% gov't bonds
  0.0% preferred   0.0% muni bonds
  0.0% conv't/warrants   1.2% other

SHAREHOLDER INFORMATION

Minimum Investment
Initial: $2,500   Subsequent: $100

Minimum IRA Investment
Initial: $1,000   Subsequent: $100

Maximum Fees
Load: none   12b-1: none
Other: none

Distributions
Income: monthly   Capital Gains: Dec

Exchange Options
Number Per Year: 6   Fee: none
Telephone: yes (money market fund available)

Services
IRA, pension, auto exchange, auto invest, auto
withdraw

American Century Value

(TWVLX)

Growth & Income

4500 Main St., 14th Floor
P.O. Box 418210
Kansas City, MO 64141
800-345-2021, 816-531-5575
www.americancentury.com

PERFORMANCE

fund inception date: 9/1/93

	3yr Annual	5yr Annual	10yr Annual	Bull	Bear
Return (%)	19.7	na	na	72.1	-3.6
Differ from Category (+/-)	4.4 high	na	na	12.3 high	2.8 high

Total Risk	Standard Deviation	Category Risk	Risk Index	Beta
av	8.7%	blw av	0.9	0.79

	1996	1995	1994	1993	1992	1991	1990	1989	1988	1987
Return (%)	24.2	32.7	3.9	—	—	—	—	—	—	—
Differ from Category (+/-)	4.5	2.6	5.2	—	—	—	—	—	—	—
Return, Tax-Adjusted (%)	20.6	28.9	1.4	—	—	—	—	—	—	—

PER SHARE DATA

	1996	1995	1994	1993	1992	1991	1990	1989	1988	1987
Dividends, Net Income ($)	0.11	0.13	0.12	—	—	—	—	—	—	—
Distrib'ns, Cap Gain ($)	0.60	0.47	0.27	—	—	—	—	—	—	—
Net Asset Value ($)	6.59	5.90	4.92	—	—	—	—	—	—	—
Expense Ratio (%)	0.97	1.00	1.00	—	—	—	—	—	—	—
Yield (%)	1.52	2.04	2.31	—	—	—	—	—	—	—
Portfolio Turnover (%)	145	94	79	—	—	—	—	—	—	—
Total Assets (Millions $)	1,476	652	153	—	—	—	—	—	—	—

PORTFOLIO (as of 6/30/96)

Portfolio Manager: Peter Zuger, Phil Davidson - 1993

Investm't Category: Growth & Income
✔ Domestic   Index
✔ Foreign   Sector
  Asset Allocation State Specific

Investment Style
  Large-Cap Growth   ✔ Large-Cap Value
  Mid-Cap Growth   ✔ Mid-Cap Value
  Small-Cap Growth   Small-Cap Value

Portfolio
0.2% cash   0.0% corp bonds
97.6% stocks   0.0% gov't bonds
0.0% preferred   0.0% muni bonds
0.0% conv't/warrants   2.2% other

SHAREHOLDER INFORMATION

Minimum Investment
Initial: $2,500   Subsequent: $50

Minimum IRA Investment
Initial: $1,000   Subsequent: $50

Maximum Fees
Load: none   12b-1: none
Other: none

Distributions
Income: quarterly   Capital Gains: Dec

Exchange Options
Number Per Year: 6   Fee: none
Telephone: yes (money market fund available)

Services
IRA, pension, auto exchange, auto invest, auto withdraw

American Gas Index
(GASFX)

Growth & Income

4922 Fairmont Ave.
Bethesda, MD 20814
800-621-7874, 301-657-1500

PERFORMANCE

fund inception date: 5/10/89

	3yr Annual	5yr Annual	10yr Annual	Bull	Bear
Return (%)	12.4	13.0	na	54.6	-10.1
Differ from Category (+/-)	-2.9 blw av	-0.9 blw av	na	-5.2 blw av	-3.7 low

Total Risk	Standard Deviation	Category Risk	Risk Index	Beta
abv av	10.1%	abv av	1.1	0.81

	1996	1995	1994	1993	1992	1991	1990	1989	1988	1987
Return (%)	20.7	30.5	-9.8	16.5	11.4	3.2	-10.5	—	—	—
Differ from Category (+/-)	1.0	0.4	-8.5	2.7	0.7	-25.9	-4.6	—	—	—
Return, Tax-Adjusted (%)	19.3	28.7	-11.3	14.8	9.4	1.4	-12.5	—	—	—

PER SHARE DATA

	1996	1995	1994	1993	1992	1991	1990	1989	1988	1987
Dividends, Net Income ($)	0.44	0.46	0.44	0.39	0.41	0.46	0.54	—	—	—
Distrib'ns, Cap Gain ($)	0.00	0.00	0.00	0.06	0.13	0.00	0.10	—	—	—
Net Asset Value ($)	15.22	13.01	10.36	11.96	10.65	10.09	10.24	—	—	—
Expense Ratio (%)	0.85	0.85	0.84	0.85	0.85	0.79	0.75	—	—	—
Yield (%)	2.89	3.53	4.24	3.24	3.80	4.55	5.22	—	—	—
Portfolio Turnover (%)	10	8	11	21	30	30	25	—	—	—
Total Assets (Millions $)	232	212	176	230	162	145	115	—	—	—

PORTFOLIO (as of 9/30/96)

Portfolio Manager: committee - 1989

Investm't Category: Growth & Income
- ✔ Domestic
- ✔ Index
- Foreign
- ✔ Sector
- Asset Allocation
- State Specific

Investment Style
- Large-Cap Growth
- ✔ Large-Cap Value
- Mid-Cap Growth
- ✔ Mid-Cap Value
- Small-Cap Growth
- Small-Cap Value

Portfolio
- 2.0% cash
- 0.0% corp bonds
- 98.0% stocks
- 0.0% gov't bonds
- 0.0% preferred
- 0.0% muni bonds
- 0.0% conv't/warrants
- 0.0% other

SHAREHOLDER INFORMATION

Minimum Investment
Initial: $2,500   Subsequent: $1

Minimum IRA Investment
Initial: $500   Subsequent: $1

Maximum Fees
Load: none   12b-1: none
Other: none

Distributions
Income: quarterly   Capital Gains: annual

Exchange Options
Number Per Year: no limit   Fee: none
Telephone: yes (money market fund available)

Services
IRA, pension, auto exchange, auto invest, auto withdraw

America's Utility (AMUTX)
Growth & Income

901 E. Byrd St.
P.O. Box 26501
Richmond, VA 23261
800-487-3863, 804-649-1315

PERFORMANCE

fund inception date: 5/5/92

	3yr Annual	5yr Annual	10yr Annual	Bull	Bear
Return (%)	6.6	na	na	43.2	-13.3
Differ from Category (+/-)	-8.7 low	na	na	-16.6 low	-6.9 low

Total Risk	Standard Deviation	Category Risk	Risk Index	Beta
abv av	10.0%	abv av	1.1	0.62

	1996	1995	1994	1993	1992	1991	1990	1989	1988	1987
Return (%)	5.4	32.2	-13.1	13.3	—	—	—	—	—	—
Differ from Category (+/-)	-14.3	2.1	-11.8	-0.5	—	—	—	—	—	—
Return, Tax-Adjusted (%)	3.8	30.2	-14.8	11.1	—	—	—	—	—	—

PER SHARE DATA

	1996	1995	1994	1993	1992	1991	1990	1989	1988	1987
Dividends, Net Income ($)	0.96	0.96	0.96	0.92	—	—	—	—	—	—
Distrib'ns, Cap Gain ($)	0.00	0.00	0.00	0.40	—	—	—	—	—	—
Net Asset Value ($)	25.07	24.72	19.50	23.54	—	—	—	—	—	—
Expense Ratio (%)	na	1.21	1.21	1.21	—	—	—	—	—	—
Yield (%)	3.82	3.88	4.92	3.84	—	—	—	—	—	—
Portfolio Turnover (%)	na	27	28	21	—	—	—	—	—	—
Total Assets (Millions $)	144	161	123	133	—	—	—	—	—	—

PORTFOLIO (as of 9/30/96)

Portfolio Manager: John Davenport - 1995

Investm't Category: Growth & Income
- ✔ Domestic
- Foreign
- Asset Allocation
- Index
- ✔ Sector
- State Specific

Investment Style
- Large-Cap Growth
- Mid-Cap Growth
- Small-Cap Growth
- ✔ Large-Cap Value
- ✔ Mid-Cap Value
- Small-Cap Value

Portfolio
5.0% cash	9.5% corp bonds
85.5% stocks	0.0% gov't bonds
0.0% preferred	0.0% muni bonds
0.0% conv't/warrants	0.0% other

SHAREHOLDER INFORMATION

Minimum Investment
Initial: $1,000   Subsequent: $100

Minimum IRA Investment
Initial: $1,000   Subsequent: $100

Maximum Fees
Load: none   12b-1: none
Other: none

Distributions
Income: quarterly   Capital Gains: annual

Exchange Options
Number Per Year: none   Fee: na
Telephone: na

Services
IRA, pension

AmSouth Mutual Fds: Bond (AOBDX)

3435 Stelzer Road
Columbus, OH 43219
800-451-8382, 614-470-8000

General Bond

PERFORMANCE

fund inception date: 12/1/88

	3yr Annual	5yr Annual	10yr Annual	Bull	Bear
Return (%)	5.5	6.7	na	21.7	-4.7
Differ from Category (+/-)	0.4 abv av	0.6 abv av	na	1.4 abv av	-0.5 av

Total Risk	Standard Deviation	Category Risk	Risk Index	Avg Mat
blw av	4.8%	high	1.3	9.3 yrs

	1996	1995	1994	1993	1992	1991	1990	1989	1988	1987
Return (%)	2.5	18.4	-3.3	9.8	7.2	15.3	6.9	12.3	—	—
Differ from Category (+/-)	-1.4	3.5	-1.0	0.7	0.7	0.6	-0.4	0.6	—	—
Return, Tax-Adjusted (%)	0.2	15.4	-5.9	7.2	3.8	12.4	3.9	9.5	—	—

PER SHARE DATA

	1996	1995	1994	1993	1992	1991	1990	1989	1988	1987
Dividends, Net Income ($)	0.64	0.68	0.69	0.69	0.72	0.73	0.78	0.69	—	—
Distrib'ns, Cap Gain ($)	0.00	0.10	0.03	0.03	0.32	0.04	0.01	0.02	—	—
Net Asset Value ($)	10.71	11.09	10.08	11.17	10.84	11.11	10.37	10.48	—	—
Expense Ratio (%)	0.75	0.75	0.78	0.78	0.82	0.93	0.84	1.10	—	—
Yield (%)	5.97	6.07	6.82	6.16	6.45	6.54	7.51	6.57	—	—
Portfolio Turnover (%)	9	17	30	14	240	181	53	0	—	—
Total Assets (Millions $)	138	102	90	67	61	25	20	11	—	—

PORTFOLIO (as of 9/30/96)

Portfolio Manager: committee - 1988

Investm't Category: General Bond
- ✔ Domestic
- ✔ Foreign
- Asset Allocation
- Index
- Sector
- State Specific

Investment Style
- Large-Cap Growth
- Mid-Cap Growth
- Small-Cap Growth
- Large-Cap Value
- Mid-Cap Value
- Small-Cap Value

Portfolio

0.8% cash	0.0% corp bonds
0.0% stocks	99.2% gov't bonds
0.0% preferred	0.0% muni bonds
0.0% conv't/warrants	0.0% other

SHAREHOLDER INFORMATION

Minimum Investment
Initial: $1,000   Subsequent: $1

Minimum IRA Investment
Initial: $250   Subsequent: $25

Maximum Fees
Load: 3.00% front   12b-1: none
Other: none

Distributions
Income: monthly   Capital Gains: annual

Exchange Options
Number Per Year: 4   Fee: none
Telephone: yes (money market fund available)

Services
IRA, pension, auto invest

AmSouth Mutual Fds: Ltd Maturity (AOLMX)

3435 Stelzer Road
Columbus, OH 43219
800-451-8382, 614-470-8000

Corporate Bond

PERFORMANCE

fund inception date: 2/1/89

	3yr Annual	5yr Annual	10yr Annual	Bull	Bear
Return (%)	4.7	5.4	na	17.3	-3.2
Differ from Category (+/-)	-1.6 low	-2.9 low	na	-7.5 blw av	1.9 abv av

Total Risk	Standard Deviation	Category Risk	Risk Index	Avg Mat
low	2.7%	blw av	0.6	2.0 yrs

	1996	1995	1994	1993	1992	1991	1990	1989	1988	1987
Return (%)	3.6	12.7	-1.9	7.1	6.0	11.9	8.5	—	—	—
Differ from Category (+/-)	-1.6	-5.3	1.2	-4.7	-2.9	-5.3	4.5	—	—	—
Return, Tax-Adjusted (%)	1.4	10.3	-4.0	4.7	3.3	8.9	5.5	—	—	—

PER SHARE DATA

	1996	1995	1994	1993	1992	1991	1990	1989	1988	1987
Dividends, Net Income ($)	0.58	0.58	0.55	0.55	0.66	0.72	0.76	—	—	—
Distrib'ns, Cap Gain ($)	0.00	0.00	0.00	0.12	0.08	0.08	0.00	—	—	—
Net Asset Value ($)	10.33	10.54	9.89	10.63	10.57	10.69	10.31	—	—	—
Expense Ratio (%)	0.76	0.80	0.79	0.69	0.68	0.85	1.02	—	—	—
Yield (%)	5.61	5.50	5.56	5.11	6.19	6.68	7.37	—	—	—
Portfolio Turnover (%)	29	38	48	141	35	85	119	—	—	—
Total Assets (Millions $)	44	63	47	48	41	13	7	—	—	—

PORTFOLIO (as of 9/30/96)

Portfolio Manager: committee - 1989

Investm't Category: Corporate Bond
✔ Domestic   Index
✔ Foreign   Sector
  Asset Allocation State Specific

Investment Style
Large-Cap Growth   Large-Cap Value
Mid-Cap Growth   Mid-Cap Value
Small-Cap Growth   Small-Cap Value

Portfolio
1.5% cash   79.4% corp bonds
0.0% stocks   19.1% gov't bonds
0.0% preferred   0.0% muni bonds
0.0% conv't/warrants 0.0% other

SHAREHOLDER INFORMATION

Minimum Investment
Initial: $1,000   Subsequent: $1

Minimum IRA Investment
Initial: $250   Subsequent: $25

Maximum Fees
Load: 3.00% front   12b-1: none
Other: none

Distributions
Income: monthly   Capital Gains: annual

Exchange Options
Number Per Year: 4   Fee: none
Telephone: yes (money market fund available)

Services
IRA, pension, auto invest

Analytic Master Fixed Income (ANMFX)
General Bond

700 S. Flower St.
Suite 2400
Los Angeles, CA 90017
800-374-2633, 213-688-3015

PERFORMANCE

fund inception date: 7/1/93

	3yr Annual	5yr Annual	10yr Annual	Bull	Bear
Return (%)	6.7	na	na	25.4	-3.9
Differ from Category (+/-)	1.6 high	na	na	5.1 high	0.3 av

Total Risk	Standard Deviation	Category Risk	Risk Index	Avg Mat
low	3.8%	av	1.0	6.6 yrs

	1996	1995	1994	1993	1992	1991	1990	1989	1988	1987
Return (%).	5.6	16.4	-1.1	—	—	—	—	—	—	—
Differ from Category (+/-). .	1.7	1.5	1.2	—	—	—	—	—	—	—
Return, Tax-Adjusted (%). . .	3.0	13.8	-3.6	—	—	—	—	—	—	—

PER SHARE DATA

	1996	1995	1994	1993	1992	1991	1990	1989	1988	1987
Dividends, Net Income ($).	0.58	0.61	0.64	—	—	—	—	—	—	—
Distrib'ns, Cap Gain ($) . . .	0.12	0.00	0.00	—	—	—	—	—	—	—
Net Asset Value ($)	10.27	10.41	9.50	—	—	—	—	—	—	—
Expense Ratio (%).	na	0.69	0.60	—	—	—	—	—	—	—
Yield (%)	5.58	5.85	6.73	—	—	—	—	—	—	—
Portfolio Turnover (%).	na	31	44	—	—	—	—	—	—	—
Total Assets (Millions $). . . .	28	24	6	—	—	—	—	—	—	—

PORTFOLIO (as of 9/30/96)

Portfolio Manager: John A. Flom CFA - 1993

Investm't Category: General Bond
✔ Domestic	Index
✔ Foreign	Sector
Asset Allocation	State Specific

Investment Style
Large-Cap Growth	Large-Cap Value
Mid-Cap Growth	Mid-Cap Value
Small-Cap Growth	Small-Cap Value

Portfolio
5.0% cash	8.0% corp bonds
22.0% stocks	42.0% gov't bonds
0.0% preferred	0.0% muni bonds
4.0% conv't/warrants	19.0% other

SHAREHOLDER INFORMATION

Minimum Investment
Initial: $5,000   Subsequent: $1

Minimum IRA Investment
Initial: $1   Subsequent: $1

Maximum Fees
Load: none   12b-1: none
Other: none

Distributions
Income: monthly   Capital Gains: annual

Exchange Options
Number Per Year: no limit   Fee: none
Telephone: yes (money market fund available)

Services
IRA, pension, auto withdraw

Analytic Optioned Equity

(ANALX)

Growth & Income

700 S. Flower St.
Suite 2400
Los Angeles, CA 90017
800-374-2633, 213-688-3015

PERFORMANCE

fund inception date: 7/3/78

	3yr Annual	5yr Annual	10yr Annual	Bull	Bear
Return (%)	12.9	10.3	10.2	45.0	-3.5
Differ from Category (+/-)	-2.4 blw av	-3.6 low	-2.5 low	-14.8 blw av	2.9 high

Total Risk	Standard Deviation	Category Risk	Risk Index	Beta
blw av	5.8%	low	0.6	0.58

	1996	1995	1994	1993	1992	1991	1990	1989	1988	1987
Return (%)	15.6	21.5	2.5	6.7	6.1	13.3	1.5	17.7	15.5	4.2
Differ from Category (+/-)	-4.1	-8.6	3.8	-7.1	-4.6	-15.8	7.4	-5.8	-1.3	4.0
Return, Tax-Adjusted (%)	13.4	20.6	-0.5	4.1	3.4	10.1	-1.7	14.5	12.4	-3.1

PER SHARE DATA

	1996	1995	1994	1993	1992	1991	1990	1989	1988	1987
Dividends, Net Income ($)	0.20	0.23	0.31	0.71	0.28	0.39	0.48	0.51	0.41	1.48
Distrib'ns, Cap Gain ($)	0.74	0.00	0.82	0.10	0.78	0.80	0.78	0.65	0.65	1.45
Net Asset Value ($)	14.38	13.26	11.12	11.96	11.97	12.29	11.92	13.00	12.06	11.38
Expense Ratio (%)	na	1.38	1.10	1.07	1.02	1.10	1.11	1.09	1.13	1.17
Yield (%)	1.32	1.73	2.59	5.88	2.19	2.97	3.77	3.73	3.22	11.53
Portfolio Turnover (%)	na	32	48	36	82	76	72	61	66	84
Total Assets (Millions $)	54	42	48	77	92	102	107	106	103	74

PORTFOLIO (as of 9/30/96)

Portfolio Manager: Charles L. Dobson - 1978

Investm't Category: Growth & Income
- ✔ Domestic
- Foreign
- Asset Allocation
- Index
- Sector
- State Specific

Investment Style
- Large-Cap Growth
- Mid-Cap Growth
- Small-Cap Growth
- ✔ Large-Cap Value
- Mid-Cap Value
- Small-Cap Value

Portfolio
- 7.6% cash
- 92.4% stocks
- 0.0% preferred
- 0.0% conv't/warrants
- 0.0% corp bonds
- 0.0% gov't bonds
- 0.0% muni bonds
- 0.0% other

SHAREHOLDER INFORMATION

Minimum Investment
Initial: $5,000   Subsequent: $1

Minimum IRA Investment
Initial: $1   Subsequent: $1

Maximum Fees
Load: none   12b-1: none
Other: none

Distributions
Income: quarterly   Capital Gains: annual

Exchange Options
Number Per Year: no limit   Fee: none
Telephone: yes (money market fund not available)

Services
IRA, pension, auto withdraw

Analytic Short-Term Gov't (ANSGX)

Government Bond

700 S. Flower St.
Suite 2400
Los Angeles, CA 90017
800-374-2633, 213-688-3015

PERFORMANCE

fund inception date: 7/1/93

	3yr Annual	5yr Annual	10yr Annual	Bull	Bear
Return (%)	5.2	na	na	17.7	-1.8
Differ from Category (+/-)	0.3 abv av	na	na	-4.3 blw av	4.6 high

Total Risk	Standard Deviation	Category Risk	Risk Index	Avg Mat
low	1.9%	low	0.5	1.8 yrs

	1996	1995	1994	1993	1992	1991	1990	1989	1988	1987
Return (%)	5.3	10.5	0.0	—	—	—	—	—	—	—
Differ from Category (+/-)	3.8	-9.1	4.4	—	—	—	—	—	—	—
Return, Tax-Adjusted (%)	2.7	8.1	-1.9	—	—	—	—	—	—	—

PER SHARE DATA

	1996	1995	1994	1993	1992	1991	1990	1989	1988	1987
Dividends, Net Income ($)	0.65	0.56	0.47	—	—	—	—	—	—	—
Distrib'ns, Cap Gain ($)	0.00	0.00	0.00	—	—	—	—	—	—	—
Net Asset Value ($)	9.83	9.97	9.55	—	—	—	—	—	—	—
Expense Ratio (%)	na	0.50	0.45	—	—	—	—	—	—	—
Yield (%)	6.61	5.61	4.92	—	—	—	—	—	—	—
Portfolio Turnover (%)	na	10	3	—	—	—	—	—	—	—
Total Assets (Millions $)	24	27	24	—	—	—	—	—	—	—

PORTFOLIO (as of 9/30/96)

Portfolio Manager: John A. Flom CFA - 1993

Investm't Category: Government Bond
- ✔ Domestic
- ✔ Foreign
- Asset Allocation
- Index
- Sector
- State Specific

Investment Style
- Large-Cap Growth
- Mid-Cap Growth
- Small-Cap Growth
- Large-Cap Value
- Mid-Cap Value
- Small-Cap Value

Portfolio
2.0% cash	8.0% corp bonds
0.0% stocks	90.0% gov't bonds
0.0% preferred	0.0% muni bonds
0.0% conv't/warrants	0.0% other

SHAREHOLDER INFORMATION

Minimum Investment
Initial: $5,000   Subsequent: $1

Minimum IRA Investment
Initial: $1   Subsequent: $1

Maximum Fees
Load: none   12b-1: none
Other: none

Distributions
Income: monthly   Capital Gains: annual

Exchange Options
Number Per Year: no limit   Fee: none
Telephone: yes (money market fund available)

Services
IRA, pension, auto withdraw

Aquinas Balanced

(AQBLX)

Balanced

5310 Harvest Hill Road
Suite 248
Dallas, TX 75230
800-423-6369, 214-233-6655

PERFORMANCE

fund inception date: 1/3/94

	3yr Annual	5yr Annual	10yr Annual	Bull	Bear
Return (%)	na	na	na	45.3	-7.6
Differ from Category (+/-)	na	na	na	0.2 av	-1.9 blw av

Total Risk	Standard Deviation	Category Risk	Risk Index	Beta
na	na	na	na	na

	1996	1995	1994	1993	1992	1991	1990	1989	1988	1987
Return (%)	15.2	23.1	—	—	—	—	—	—	—	—
Differ from Category (+/-)	1.0	-1.5	—	—	—	—	—	—	—	—
Return, Tax-Adjusted (%)	11.9	21.0	—	—	—	—	—	—	—	—

PER SHARE DATA

	1996	1995	1994	1993	1992	1991	1990	1989	1988	1987
Dividends, Net Income ($)	0.26	0.32	—	—	—	—	—	—	—	—
Distrib'ns, Cap Gain ($)	0.91	0.23	—	—	—	—	—	—	—	—
Net Asset Value ($)	11.53	11.03	—	—	—	—	—	—	—	—
Expense Ratio (%)	na	1.46	—	—	—	—	—	—	—	—
Yield (%)	2.09	2.84	—	—	—	—	—	—	—	—
Portfolio Turnover (%)	na	118	—	—	—	—	—	—	—	—
Total Assets (Millions $)	30	26	—	—	—	—	—	—	—	—

PORTFOLIO (as of 9/30/96)

Portfolio Manager: committee - 1994

Investm't Category: Balanced

✔ Domestic   Index
   Foreign   Sector
   Asset Allocation   State Specific

Investment Style

Large-Cap Growth   Large-Cap Value
Mid-Cap Growth   Mid-Cap Value
Small-Cap Growth   Small-Cap Value

Portfolio

2.8%	cash	17.0%	corp bonds
59.7%	stocks	17.1%	gov't bonds
0.0%	preferred	0.0%	muni bonds
0.0%	conv't/warrants	3.4%	other

SHAREHOLDER INFORMATION

Minimum Investment
Initial: $1,000   Subsequent: $250

Minimum IRA Investment
Initial: $500   Subsequent: $50

Maximum Fees
Load: none   12b-1: none
Other: none

Distributions
Income: quarterly   Capital Gains: Dec

Exchange Options
Number Per Year: 4   Fee: none
Telephone: yes (money market fund not available)

Services
IRA, pension, auto invest, auto withdraw

Aquinas Equity Income

(AQEIX)

Growth & Income

5310 Harvest Hill Road
Suite 248
Dallas, TX 75230
800-423-6369, 214-233-6655

PERFORMANCE

fund inception date: 1/3/94

	3yr Annual	5yr Annual	10yr Annual	Bull	Bear
Return (%)	na	na	na	65.4	-5.2
Differ from Category (+/-)	na	na	na	5.6 av	1.2 abv av

Total Risk	Standard Deviation	Category Risk	Risk Index	Beta
na	na	na	na	na

	1996	1995	1994	1993	1992	1991	1990	1989	1988	1987
Return (%)	20.4	35.6	—	—	—	—	—	—	—	—
Differ from Category (+/-)	0.7	5.5	—	—	—	—	—	—	—	—
Return, Tax-Adjusted (%)	17.9	32.6	—	—	—	—	—	—	—	—

PER SHARE DATA

	1996	1995	1994	1993	1992	1991	1990	1989	1988	1987
Dividends, Net Income ($)	0.22	0.28	—	—	—	—	—	—	—	—
Distrib'ns, Cap Gain ($)	0.74	0.59	—	—	—	—	—	—	—	—
Net Asset Value ($)	13.26	11.83	—	—	—	—	—	—	—	—
Expense Ratio (%)	na	1.37	—	—	—	—	—	—	—	—
Yield (%)	1.57	2.25	—	—	—	—	—	—	—	—
Portfolio Turnover (%)	na	40	—	—	—	—	—	—	—	—
Total Assets (Millions $)	54	42	—	—	—	—	—	—	—	—

PORTFOLIO (as of 9/30/96)

Portfolio Manager: committee - 1994

Investm't Category: Growth & Income

✔ Domestic   Index
    Foreign   Sector
    Asset Allocation   State Specific

Investment Style

Large-Cap Growth	Large-Cap Value
Mid-Cap Growth	Mid-Cap Value
Small-Cap Growth	Small-Cap Value

Portfolio

4.3% cash	0.0% corp bonds
96.1% stocks	0.0% gov't bonds
0.0% preferred	0.0% muni bonds
0.0% conv't/warrants	0.0% other

SHAREHOLDER INFORMATION

Minimum Investment
Initial: $1,000   Subsequent: $250

Minimum IRA Investment
Initial: $500   Subsequent: $50

Maximum Fees
Load: none   12b-1: none
Other: none

Distributions
Income: quarterly   Capital Gains: Dec

Exchange Options
Number Per Year: 4   Fee: none
Telephone: yes (money market fund not available)

Services
IRA, pension, auto invest, auto withdraw

Aquinas Fixed Income
(AQFIX)
General Bond

5310 Harvest Hill Road
Suite 248
Dallas, TX 75230
800-423-6369, 214-233-6655

PERFORMANCE

fund inception date: 1/3/94

	3yr Annual	5yr Annual	10yr Annual	Bull	Bear
Return (%)	na	na	na	19.9	-5.5
Differ from Category (+/-)	na	na	na	-0.4 av	-1.3 blw av

Total Risk	Standard Deviation	Category Risk	Risk Index	Avg Mat
na	na	na	na	12.6 yrs

	1996	1995	1994	1993	1992	1991	1990	1989	1988	1987
Return (%)	2.8	16.2	—	—	—	—	—	—	—	—
Differ from Category (+/-)	-1.1	1.3	—	—	—	—	—	—	—	—
Return, Tax-Adjusted (%)	0.6	13.9	—	—	—	—	—	—	—	—

PER SHARE DATA

	1996	1995	1994	1993	1992	1991	1990	1989	1988	1987
Dividends, Net Income ($)	0.54	0.53	—	—	—	—	—	—	—	—
Distrib'ns, Cap Gain ($)	0.00	0.00	—	—	—	—	—	—	—	—
Net Asset Value ($)	9.90	10.17	—	—	—	—	—	—	—	—
Expense Ratio (%)	na	0.98	—	—	—	—	—	—	—	—
Yield (%)	5.45	5.21	—	—	—	—	—	—	—	—
Portfolio Turnover (%)	na	126	—	—	—	—	—	—	—	—
Total Assets (Millions $)	36	35	—	—	—	—	—	—	—	—

PORTFOLIO (as of 9/30/96)

Portfolio Manager: committee - 1994

Investm't Category: General Bond
- ✔ Domestic
- ✔ Foreign
- Asset Allocation
- Index
- Sector
- State Specific

Investment Style
- Large-Cap Growth
- Mid-Cap Growth
- Small-Cap Growth
- Large-Cap Value
- Mid-Cap Value
- Small-Cap Value

Portfolio

3.6% cash	41.9% corp bonds
0.0% stocks	45.5% gov't bonds
0.0% preferred	0.0% muni bonds
0.0% conv't/warrants	9.0% other

SHAREHOLDER INFORMATION

Minimum Investment
Initial: $1,000   Subsequent: $250

Minimum IRA Investment
Initial: $500   Subsequent: $50

Maximum Fees
Load: none   12b-1: none
Other: none

Distributions
Income: monthly   Capital Gains: Dec

Exchange Options
Number Per Year: 4   Fee: none
Telephone: yes (money market fund not available)

Services
IRA, pension, auto invest, auto withdraw

Ariel Appreciation

(CAAPX)

Growth

307 N. Michigan Ave.
Suite 500
Chicago, IL 60601
800-292-7435, 312-726-0140

	3yr Annual	5yr Annual	10yr Annual	Bull	Bear
Return (%)	12.0	11.4	na	48.4	-5.5
Differ from Category (+/-)	-3.7 low	-2.9 low	na	-14.0 low	1.2 abv av

Total Risk	Standard Deviation	Category Risk	Risk Index	Beta
abv av	9.7%	av	0.9	0.71

	1996	1995	1994	1993	1992	1991	1990	1989	1988	1987
Return (%)	23.7	24.1	-8.4	7.9	13.2	33.1	—	—	—	—
Differ from Category (+/-)	3.6	-6.2	-8.1	-6.1	1.4	-2.9	—	—	—	—
Return, Tax-Adjusted (%)	21.8	21.1	-10.3	7.3	13.0	32.6	—	—	—	—

PER SHARE DATA

	1996	1995	1994	1993	1992	1991	1990	1989	1988	1987
Dividends, Net Income ($)	0.07	0.19	0.06	0.05	0.08	0.16	—	—	—	—
Distrib'ns, Cap Gain ($)	1.36	1.76	1.39	0.34	0.00	0.02	—	—	—	—
Net Asset Value ($)	26.07	22.24	19.51	22.89	21.60	19.15	—	—	—	—
Expense Ratio (%)	1.36	1.36	1.35	1.37	1.44	1.50	—	—	—	—
Yield (%)	0.25	0.79	0.28	0.21	0.37	0.83	—	—	—	—
Portfolio Turnover (%)	26	18	12	56	2	20	—	—	—	—
Total Assets (Millions $)	142	139	128	219	179	90	—	—	—	—

PORTFOLIO (as of 9/30/96)

Portfolio Manager: Eric McKissack - 1990

Investm't Category: Growth
- ✔ Domestic
- Foreign
- Asset Allocation
- Index
- Sector
- State Specific

Investment Style
- Large-Cap Growth
- ✔ Mid-Cap Growth
- ✔ Small-Cap Growth
- Large-Cap Value
- ✔ Mid-Cap Value
- ✔ Small-Cap Value

Portfolio
0.6% cash	0.0% corp bonds
99.4% stocks	0.0% gov't bonds
0.0% preferred	0.0% muni bonds
0.0% conv't/warrants	0.0% other

SHAREHOLDER INFORMATION

Minimum Investment
Initial: $1,000   Subsequent: $50

Minimum IRA Investment
Initial: $250   Subsequent: $50

Maximum Fees
Load: none   12b-1: 0.25%
Other: none

Distributions
Income: annual   Capital Gains: annual

Exchange Options
Number Per Year: 5   Fee: none
Telephone: yes (money market fund available)

Services
IRA, pension, auto invest, auto withdraw

Ariel Growth (ARGFX)

Aggressive Growth

307 N. Michigan Ave.
Suite 500
Chicago, IL 60601
800-292-7435, 312-726-0140

PERFORMANCE

fund inception date: 9/29/86

	3yr Annual	5yr Annual	10yr Annual	Bull	Bear
Return (%)	11.9	11.2	13.9	48.9	-6.8
Differ from Category (+/-)	-3.9 blw av	-4.1 low	-1.1 blw av	-22.2 blw av	3.8 abv av

Total Risk	Standard Deviation	Category Risk	Risk Index	Beta
av	9.3%	low	0.7	0.65

	1996	1995	1994	1993	1992	1991	1990	1989	1988	1987
Return (%)	23.5	18.5	-4.3	8.7	11.7	32.7	-16.1	25.0	39.9	11.4
Differ from Category (+/-)	4.4	-15.8	-4.3	-10.6	0.0	-19.4	-10.7	-3.4	23.5	13.8
Return, Tax-Adjusted (%)	21.6	13.5	-6.2	6.6	8.8	30.9	-16.6	24.1	38.8	9.9

PER SHARE DATA

	1996	1995	1994	1993	1992	1991	1990	1989	1988	1987
Dividends, Net Income ($)	0.00	0.43	0.23	0.29	0.74	0.47	0.28	0.38	0.15	0.05
Distrib'ns, Cap Gain ($)	1.78	4.18	1.70	1.73	1.92	0.79	0.00	0.12	0.38	0.74
Net Asset Value ($)	31.96	27.32	26.98	30.19	29.74	29.10	22.94	27.68	22.55	16.50
Expense Ratio (%)	1.31	1.37	1.25	1.16	1.23	1.25	1.31	1.41	1.56	1.20
Yield (%)	0.00	1.36	0.80	0.90	2.33	1.57	1.22	1.36	0.65	0.29
Portfolio Turnover (%)	17	16	9	13	19	39	20	14	22	60
Total Assets (Millions $)	121	120	130	225	254	262	207	180	36	6

PORTFOLIO (as of 9/30/96)

Portfolio Manager: John W. Rogers Jr. - 1986

Investm't Category: Aggressive Growth

✔ Domestic	Index
Foreign	Sector
Asset Allocation	State Specific

Investment Style

Large-Cap Growth	Large-Cap Value
Mid-Cap Growth	Mid-Cap Value
✔ Small-Cap Growth	✔ Small-Cap Value

Portfolio

0.8% cash	0.0% corp bonds
98.9% stocks	0.0% gov't bonds
0.0% preferred	0.0% muni bonds
0.0% conv't/warrants	0.2% other

SHAREHOLDER INFORMATION

Minimum Investment
Initial: $1,000   Subsequent: $50

Minimum IRA Investment
Initial: $250   Subsequent: $50

Maximum Fees
Load: none   12b-1: 0.25%
Other: none

Distributions
Income: annual   Capital Gains: annual

Exchange Options
Number Per Year: no limit   Fee: none
Telephone: yes (money market fund available)

Services
IRA, pension, auto invest, auto withdraw

Artisan Int'l (ARTIX)
International Stock

1000 N. Water St.
Suite 1770
Milwaukee, WI 53202
800-344-1770, 414-390-6100

PERFORMANCE

fund inception date: 12/28/95

	3yr Annual	5yr Annual	10yr Annual	Bull	Bear
Return (%)	na	na	na	na	na
Differ from Category (+/-)	na	na	na	na	na

Total Risk	Standard Deviation	Category Risk	Risk Index	Beta
na	na	na	na	na

	1996	1995	1994	1993	1992	1991	1990	1989	1988	1987
Return (%).............	34.3	—	—	—	—	—	—	—	—	—
Differ from Category (+/-).	19.5	—	—	—	—	—	—	—	—	—
Return, Tax-Adjusted (%)...	33.9	—	—	—	—	—	—	—	—	—

PER SHARE DATA

	1996	1995	1994	1993	1992	1991	1990	1989	1988	1987
Dividends, Net Income ($).	0.00	—	—	—	—	—	—	—	—	—
Distrib'ns, Cap Gain ($) ...	0.11	—	—	—	—	—	—	—	—	—
Net Asset Value ($)	13.32	—	—	—	—	—	—	—	—	—
Expense Ratio (%).........	na	—	—	—	—	—	—	—	—	—
Yield (%)	0.00	—	—	—	—	—	—	—	—	—
Portfolio Turnover (%).....	na	—	—	—	—	—	—	—	—	—
Total Assets (Millions $)...	170	—	—	—	—	—	—	—	—	—

PORTFOLIO (as of 9/30/96)

Portfolio Manager: Mark L. Yockey - 1995

Investm't Category: International Stock

Domestic	Index
✔ Foreign	Sector
Asset Allocation	State Specific

Investment Style

Large-Cap Growth	Large-Cap Value
Mid-Cap Growth	Mid-Cap Value
Small-Cap Growth	Small-Cap Value

Portfolio

1.9% cash	0.0% corp bonds
98.1% stocks	0.0% gov't bonds
0.0% preferred	0.0% muni bonds
0.0% conv't/warrants	0.0% other

SHAREHOLDER INFORMATION

Minimum Investment
Initial: $1,000   Subsequent: $50

Minimum IRA Investment
Initial: $1,000   Subsequent: $50

Maximum Fees
Load: none   12b-1: none
Other: none

Distributions
Income: annual   Capital Gains: annual

Exchange Options
Number Per Year: no limit   Fee: none
Telephone: yes (money market fund available)

Services
IRA, pension, auto invest, auto withdraw

BB&K Diversa (DVERX)

Balanced

2755 Campus Drive
San Mateo, CA 94403
800-882-8383, 415-571-5800

PERFORMANCE

fund inception date: 12/18/86

	3yr Annual	5yr Annual	10yr Annual	Bull	Bear
Return (%)	6.5	8.9	7.7	31.5	-9.8
Differ from Category (+/-)	-5.2 low	-2.5 blw av	-3.1 low	-13.6 low	-4.1 low

Total Risk	Standard Deviation	Category Risk	Risk Index	Beta
blw av	6.8%	av	1.0	0.65

	1996	1995	1994	1993	1992	1991	1990	1989	1988	1987
Return (%).	10.6	20.5	-9.4	21.5	4.4	15.9	-9.6	12.7	6.6	8.5
Differ from Category (+/-).	-3.6	-4.1	-7.8	7.1	-4.5	-8.2	-8.7	-5.4	-5.6	5.8
Return, Tax-Adjusted (%). .	6.2	17.4	-10.4	20.4	3.3	14.0	-10.7	10.9	4.8	6.1

PER SHARE DATA

	1996	1995	1994	1993	1992	1991	1990	1989	1988	1987
Dividends, Net Income ($).	0.43	0.35	0.31	0.30	0.30	0.46	0.30	0.45	0.45	0.51
Distrib'ns, Cap Gain ($) . . .	1.38	0.76	0.00	0.00	0.00	0.00	0.00	0.00	0.00	0.13
Net Asset Value ($)	12.43	12.89	11.64	13.18	11.11	10.94	9.85	11.20	10.35	10.14
Expense Ratio (%).	na	1.85	1.82	1.70	1.90	1.46	1.46	1.34	1.26	1.02
Yield (%)	3.11	2.56	2.66	2.27	2.70	4.20	3.04	4.01	4.34	4.96
Portfolio Turnover (%).	na	166	137	96	94	254	235	100	89	66
Total Assets (Millions $). . . .	37	41	41	50	49	56	71	105	103	86

PORTFOLIO (as of 9/30/96)

Portfolio Manager: committee - 1991

Investm't Category: Balanced
- ✔ Domestic   Index
- ✔ Foreign   Sector
- ✔ Asset Allocation   State Specific

Investment Style

Large-Cap Growth	Large-Cap Value
Mid-Cap Growth	Mid-Cap Value
Small-Cap Growth	Small-Cap Value

Portfolio

2.0% cash	0.0% corp bonds
55.5% stocks	32.9% gov't bonds
0.0% preferred	0.0% muni bonds
0.0% conv't/warrants	9.6% other

SHAREHOLDER INFORMATION

Minimum Investment
Initial: $5,000   Subsequent: $100

Minimum IRA Investment
Initial: $5,000   Subsequent: $100

Maximum Fees
Load: none   12b-1: none
Other: none

Distributions
Income: quarterly   Capital Gains: Dec

Exchange Options
Number Per Year: no limit   Fee: none
Telephone: yes (money market fund not available)

Services
IRA, pension, auto withdraw

BB&K Int'l Bond Fd
(BBIFX)

International Bond

2755 Campus Drive
San Mateo, CA 94403
800-882-8383, 415-571-5800

PERFORMANCE

fund inception date: 10/4/90

	3yr Annual	5yr Annual	10yr Annual	Bull	Bear
Return (%)	1.8	5.3	na	29.7	-18.9
Differ from Category (+/-)	-4.2 blw av	-1.3 av	na	-1.5 av	-9.4 low

Total Risk	Standard Deviation	Category Risk	Risk Index	Avg Mat
av	7.6%	high	1.1	5.6 yrs

	1996	1995	1994	1993	1992	1991	1990	1989	1988	1987
Return (%)	8.4	20.6	-19.3	14.7	6.9	13.9	—	—	—	—
Differ from Category (+/-)	-2.9	4.6	-11.7	-0.6	1.7	-1.1	—	—	—	—
Return, Tax-Adjusted (%)	5.0	14.4	-21.8	10.3	2.7	9.8	—	—	—	—

PER SHARE DATA

	1996	1995	1994	1993	1992	1991	1990	1989	1988	1987
Dividends, Net Income ($)	0.70	1.21	0.65	1.11	1.10	1.03	—	—	—	—
Distrib'ns, Cap Gain ($)	0.00	0.00	0.00	0.00	0.00	0.00	—	—	—	—
Net Asset Value ($)	8.15	8.18	7.81	10.45	10.10	10.47	—	—	—	—
Expense Ratio (%)	na	1.16	1.12	0.42	0.64	0.53	—	—	—	—
Yield (%)	8.58	14.79	8.32	10.62	10.89	9.83	—	—	—	—
Portfolio Turnover (%)	na	179	319	157	140	89	—	—	—	—
Total Assets (Millions $)	51	62	104	172	110	81	—	—	—	—

PORTFOLIO (as of 9/30/96)

Portfolio Manager: Arthur Micheletti - 1992

Investm't Category: International Bond

Domestic	Index
✔ Foreign	Sector
Asset Allocation	State Specific

Investment Style

Large-Cap Growth	Large-Cap Value
Mid-Cap Growth	Mid-Cap Value
Small-Cap Growth	Small-Cap Value

Portfolio

5.5% cash	0.0% corp bonds
0.0% stocks	0.0% gov't bonds
0.0% preferred	0.0% muni bonds
0.0% conv't/warrants	94.5% other

SHAREHOLDER INFORMATION

Minimum Investment
Initial: $5,000   Subsequent: $100

Minimum IRA Investment
Initial: $5,000   Subsequent: $100

Maximum Fees
Load: none   12b-1: none
Other: none

Distributions
Income: quarterly   Capital Gains: Dec

Exchange Options
Number Per Year: no limit   Fee: none
Telephone: yes (money market fund not available)

Services
IRA, pension, auto withdraw

BB&K Int'l Equity (BBIEX)
International Stock

2755 Campus Drive
San Mateo, CA 94403
800-882-8383, 415-571-5800

PERFORMANCE   fund inception date: 9/4/79

	3yr Annual	5yr Annual	10yr Annual	Bull	Bear
Return (%)	2.5	5.6	3.5	17.4	-9.7
Differ from Category (+/-)	-3.8 blw av	-4.4 low	-5.1 low	-6.9 blw av	-2.5 blw av

Total Risk	Standard Deviation	Category Risk	Risk Index	Beta
av	9.3%	blw av	0.9	0.70

	1996	1995	1994	1993	1992	1991	1990	1989	1988	1987
Return (%)	9.5	12.4	-12.6	37.8	-11.5	1.8	-19.2	14.0	11.7	2.6
Differ from Category (+/-)	-5.3	3.3	-9.5	-1.8	-7.7	-11.4	-9.1	-8.6	-3.2	-9.6
Return, Tax-Adjusted (%)	7.4	9.3	-12.6	37.8	-12.1	1.2	-20.2	14.0	11.7	-19.8

PER SHARE DATA

	1996	1995	1994	1993	1992	1991	1990	1989	1988	1987
Dividends, Net Income ($)	0.05	0.06	0.00	0.00	0.08	0.00	0.17	0.00	0.00	3.07
Distrib'ns, Cap Gain ($)	0.36	0.53	0.00	0.00	0.00	0.10	0.00	0.00	0.00	12.63
Net Asset Value ($)	5.94	5.80	5.70	6.52	4.73	5.43	5.43	6.92	6.07	5.43
Expense Ratio (%)	na	1.53	1.39	0.68	1.05	1.22	1.30	1.22	1.24	0.88
Yield (%)	0.79	0.94	0.00	0.00	1.69	0.00	3.13	0.00	0.00	na
Portfolio Turnover (%)	na	174	176	131	77	81	134	86	96	121
Total Assets (Millions $)	120	108	148	219	94	148	72	na	na	na

PORTFOLIO (as of 9/30/96)

Portfolio Manager: Rosemary Macedo - 1995

Investm't Category: International Stock
Domestic	Index
✔ Foreign	Sector
Asset Allocation	State Specific

Investment Style
Large-Cap Growth	Large-Cap Value
Mid-Cap Growth	Mid-Cap Value
Small-Cap Growth	Small-Cap Value

Portfolio
3.3% cash	0.0% corp bonds
96.7% stocks	0.0% gov't bonds
0.0% preferred	0.0% muni bonds
0.0% conv't/warrants	0.0% other

SHAREHOLDER INFORMATION

Minimum Investment
Initial: $5,000   Subsequent: $100

Minimum IRA Investment
Initial: $5,000   Subsequent: $100

Maximum Fees
Load: none   12b-1: none
Other: none

Distributions
Income: Dec   Capital Gains: Dec

Exchange Options
Number Per Year: no limit   Fee: none
Telephone: yes (money market fund not available)

Services
IRA, pension, auto withdraw

Babson Bond Trust: Port L

(BABIX)

General Bond

3 Crown Center
2440 Pershing Road
Kansas City, MO 64108
800-422-2766, 816-471-5200

PERFORMANCE
fund inception date: 8/2/45

	3yr Annual	5yr Annual	10yr Annual	Bull	Bear
Return (%)	4.9	6.7	7.8	20.6	-5.3
Differ from Category (+/-)	-0.2 av	0.6 abv av	0.5 abv av	0.3 av	-1.1 blw av

Total Risk	Standard Deviation	Category Risk	Risk Index	Avg Mat
low	4.4%	abv av	1.2	13.0 yrs

	1996	1995	1994	1993	1992	1991	1990	1989	1988	1987
Return (%)	3.1	15.9	-3.3	11.1	7.9	14.9	7.7	13.1	7.1	1.9
Differ from Category (+/-)	-0.8	1.0	-1.0	2.0	1.4	0.2	0.4	1.4	-0.5	-0.4
Return, Tax-Adjusted (%)	0.6	13.2	-5.8	7.5	4.8	11.5	4.4	9.4	3.2	-1.9

PER SHARE DATA

	1996	1995	1994	1993	1992	1991	1990	1989	1988	1987
Dividends, Net Income ($)	0.10	0.10	0.10	0.11	0.12	0.13	0.13	0.14	0.15	0.16
Distrib'ns, Cap Gain ($)	0.00	0.00	0.00	0.05	0.01	0.00	0.00	0.00	0.00	0.00
Net Asset Value ($)	1.53	1.59	1.47	1.63	1.62	1.63	1.54	1.56	1.51	1.56
Expense Ratio (%)	na	0.97	0.97	0.98	0.99	0.98	0.97	0.97	0.97	0.97
Yield (%)	6.53	6.28	6.80	6.54	7.36	7.97	8.44	8.97	9.93	10.25
Portfolio Turnover (%)	na	50	40	80	54	75	51	51	42	54
Total Assets (Millions $)	141	161	139	160	144	114	91	77	66	64

PORTFOLIO (as of 9/30/96)

Portfolio Manager: Edward L. Martin - 1984

Investm't Category: General Bond
- ✔ Domestic
- Foreign
- Asset Allocation
- Index
- Sector
- State Specific

Investment Style
- Large-Cap Growth
- Mid-Cap Growth
- Small-Cap Growth
- Large-Cap Value
- Mid-Cap Value
- Small-Cap Value

Portfolio
1.0% cash	61.0% corp bonds
0.0% stocks	38.0% gov't bonds
0.0% preferred	0.0% muni bonds
0.0% conv't/warrants	0.0% other

SHAREHOLDER INFORMATION

Minimum Investment
Initial: $500   Subsequent: $50

Minimum IRA Investment
Initial: $250   Subsequent: $50

Maximum Fees
Load: none   12b-1: none
Other: none

Distributions
Income: monthly   Capital Gains: Dec

Exchange Options
Number Per Year: no limit   Fee: none
Telephone: yes (money market fund available)

Services
IRA, pension, auto exchange, auto invest, auto withdraw

Babson Bond Trust:
Port S (BBDSX)

General Bond

3 Crown Center
2440 Pershing Road
Kansas City, MO 64108
800-422-2766, 816-471-5200

PERFORMANCE   fund inception date: 3/31/88

	3yr Annual	5yr Annual	10yr Annual	Bull	Bear
Return (%)	5.1	6.1	na	19.3	-3.8
Differ from Category (+/-)	0.0 av	0.0 av	na	-1.0 blw av	0.4 abv av

Total Risk	Standard Deviation	Category Risk	Risk Index	Avg Mat
low	3.1%	av	0.8	10.2 yrs

	1996	1995	1994	1993	1992	1991	1990	1989	1988	1987
Return (%)...............	4.4	13.6	-2.1	8.4	6.9	14.5	8.0	10.8	—	—
Differ from Category (+/-)..	0.5	-1.3	0.2	-0.7	0.4	-0.2	0.7	-0.9	—	—
Return, Tax-Adjusted (%)...	1.6	10.5	-4.8	5.2	3.9	11.2	4.6	7.5	—	—

PER SHARE DATA

	1996	1995	1994	1993	1992	1991	1990	1989	1988	1987
Dividends, Net Income ($).	0.68	0.72	0.69	0.71	0.75	0.80	0.84	0.81	—	—
Distrib'ns, Cap Gain ($) ...	0.00	0.00	0.00	0.15	0.05	0.02	0.00	0.00	—	—
Net Asset Value ($)	9.67	9.94	9.42	10.33	10.34	10.45	9.90	9.98	—	—
Expense Ratio (%).........	na	0.67	0.67	0.68	0.65	0.66	0.78	0.91	—	—
Yield (%)	7.03	7.24	7.32	6.77	7.21	7.64	8.48	8.11	—	—
Portfolio Turnover (%).....	na	57	42	147	47	60	35	27	—	—
Total Assets (Millions $)....	34	33	29	37	28	15	7	5	—	—

PORTFOLIO (as of 9/30/96)

Portfolio Manager: Edward L. Martin - 1988

Investm't Category: General Bond
- ✔ Domestic
-   Foreign
-   Asset Allocation
-   Index
-   Sector
-   State Specific

Investment Style
Large-Cap Growth	Large-Cap Value
Mid-Cap Growth	Mid-Cap Value
Small-Cap Growth	Small-Cap Value

Portfolio
4.0% cash	56.0% corp bonds
0.0% stocks	40.0% gov't bonds
0.0% preferred	0.0% muni bonds
0.0% conv't/warrants	0.0% other

SHAREHOLDER INFORMATION

Minimum Investment
Initial: $500   Subsequent: $50

Minimum IRA Investment
Initial: $250   Subsequent: $50

Maximum Fees
Load: none   12b-1: none
Other: none

Distributions
Income: monthly   Capital Gains: Dec

Exchange Options
Number Per Year: no limit   Fee: none
Telephone: yes (money market fund available)

Services
IRA, pension, auto exchange, auto invest, auto withdraw

Babson Enterprise

(BABEX)

Growth

3 Crown Center
2440 Pershing Road
Kansas City, MO 64108
800-422-2766, 816-471-5200

this fund is closed to new investors

PERFORMANCE

fund inception date: 12/2/83

	3yr Annual	5yr Annual	10yr Annual	Bull	Bear
Return (%)	13.0	15.9	14.0	48.9	-4.4
Differ from Category (+/-)	-2.7 blw av	1.6 abv av	0.1 av	-13.5 low	2.3 abv av

Total Risk	Standard Deviation	Category Risk	Risk Index	Beta
av	8.7%	low	0.8	0.53

	1996	1995	1994	1993	1992	1991	1990	1989	1988	1987
Return (%)	21.2	16.4	2.4	16.2	24.5	43.0	-15.9	22.4	32.4	-9.2
Differ from Category (+/-)	1.1	-13.9	2.7	2.2	12.7	7.0	-9.8	-3.7	14.3	-11.2
Return, Tax-Adjusted (%)	16.4	12.7	-0.6	14.0	19.6	40.7	-17.0	20.0	29.9	-13.4

PER SHARE DATA

	1996	1995	1994	1993	1992	1991	1990	1989	1988	1987
Dividends, Net Income ($)	0.00	0.11	0.03	0.05	0.08	0.07	0.12	0.19	0.05	0.08
Distrib'ns, Cap Gain ($)	2.66	1.84	1.69	1.10	2.33	0.76	0.30	0.69	0.75	1.68
Net Asset Value ($)	16.31	15.66	15.15	16.51	15.22	14.19	10.55	13.06	11.39	9.22
Expense Ratio (%)	na	1.09	1.08	1.09	1.11	1.17	1.22	1.24	1.37	1.35
Yield (%)	0.00	0.62	0.17	0.28	0.45	0.46	1.10	1.38	0.41	0.73
Portfolio Turnover (%)	na	13	15	17	28	15	10	15	41	24
Total Assets (Millions $)	201	201	190	220	184	133	79	86	53	35

PORTFOLIO (as of 9/30/96)

Portfolio Manager: Peter Schliemann, Lance James - 1985

Investm't Category: Growth

✔ Domestic	Index
Foreign	Sector
Asset Allocation	State Specific

Investment Style

Large-Cap Growth	Large-Cap Value
Mid-Cap Growth	Mid-Cap Value
✔ Small-Cap Growth	✔ Small-Cap Value

Portfolio

3.0% cash	0.0% corp bonds
97.0% stocks	0.0% gov't bonds
0.0% preferred	0.0% muni bonds
0.0% conv't/warrants	0.0% other

SHAREHOLDER INFORMATION

Minimum Investment
Initial: $1,000   Subsequent: $100

Minimum IRA Investment
Initial: $250   Subsequent: $50

Maximum Fees
Load: none   12b-1: none
Other: none

Distributions
Income: Dec   Capital Gains: Dec

Exchange Options
Number Per Year: no limit   Fee: none
Telephone: yes (money market fund available)

Services
IRA, pension, auto exchange, auto invest, auto withdraw

Babson Enterprise II

(BAETX)

Growth

3 Crown Center
2440 Pershing Road
Kansas City, MO 64108
800-422-2766, 816-471-5200

PERFORMANCE

fund inception date: 8/5/91

	3yr Annual	5yr Annual	10yr Annual	Bull	Bear
Return (%)	12.3	14.7	na	50.5	-7.9
Differ from Category (+/-)	-3.4 blw av	0.4 av	na	-11.9 blw av	-1.2 blw av

Total Risk	Standard Deviation	Category Risk	Risk Index	Beta
abv av	11.0%	abv av	1.1	0.73

	1996	1995	1994	1993	1992	1991	1990	1989	1988	1987
Return (%)	27.6	19.8	-7.4	19.7	17.2	—	—	—	—	—
Differ from Category (+/-)	7.5	-10.5	-7.1	5.7	5.4	—	—	—	—	—
Return, Tax-Adjusted (%)	22.8	18.0	-7.6	19.1	17.1	—	—	—	—	—

PER SHARE DATA

	1996	1995	1994	1993	1992	1991	1990	1989	1988	1987
Dividends, Net Income ($)	0.11	0.05	0.02	0.00	0.00	—	—	—	—	—
Distrib'ns, Cap Gain ($)	2.98	0.94	0.08	0.32	0.03	—	—	—	—	—
Net Asset Value ($)	20.37	18.40	16.19	17.60	14.97	—	—	—	—	—
Expense Ratio (%)	na	1.45	1.50	1.60	1.83	—	—	—	—	—
Yield (%)	0.47	0.25	0.12	0.00	0.00	—	—	—	—	—
Portfolio Turnover (%)	na	15	9	18	14	—	—	—	—	—
Total Assets (Millions $)	45	40	36	30	12	—	—	—	—	—

PORTFOLIO (as of 9/30/96)

Portfolio Manager: Peter Schliemann, Lance James - 1991

Investm't Category: Growth

✔ Domestic	Index
Foreign	Sector
Asset Allocation	State Specific

Investment Style

Large-Cap Growth	Large-Cap Value
✔ Mid-Cap Growth	✔ Mid-Cap Value
✔ Small-Cap Growth	✔ Small-Cap Value

Portfolio

2.0%	cash	0.0% corp bonds
98.0%	stocks	0.0% gov't bonds
0.0%	preferred	0.0% muni bonds
0.0%	conv't/warrants	0.0% other

SHAREHOLDER INFORMATION

Minimum Investment
Initial: $1,000   Subsequent: $100

Minimum IRA Investment
Initial: $250   Subsequent: $50

Maximum Fees
Load: none   12b-1: none
Other: none

Distributions
Income: Dec   Capital Gains: Dec

Exchange Options
Number Per Year: no limit   Fee: none
Telephone: yes (money market fund available)

Services
IRA, pension, auto exchange, auto invest, auto withdraw

Babson Growth (BABSX)

Growth

3 Crown Center
2440 Pershing Road
Kansas City, MO 64108
800-422-2766, 816-471-5200

PERFORMANCE

fund inception date: 3/9/60

	3yr Annual	5yr Annual	10yr Annual	Bull	Bear
Return (%)	16.7	13.8	12.3	64.4	-5.9
Differ from Category (+/-)	1.0 av	-0.5 av	-1.6 blw av	2.0 abv av	0.8 av

Total Risk	Standard Deviation	Category Risk	Risk Index	Beta
av	8.9%	low	0.9	0.90

	1996	1995	1994	1993	1992	1991	1990	1989	1988	1987
Return (%).............	21.8	31.4	-0.6	10.2	9.1	26.0	-9.5	22.1	15.9	3.4
Differ from Category (+/-)..	1.7	1.1	-0.3	-3.8	-2.7	-10.0	-3.4	-4.0	-2.2	1.4
Return, Tax-Adjusted (%)..	17.4	28.9	-3.0	8.3	7.6	25.0	-11.7	17.3	9.7	-1.3

PER SHARE DATA

	1996	1995	1994	1993	1992	1991	1990	1989	1988	1987
Dividends, Net Income ($).	0.11	0.15	0.20	0.19	0.20	0.21	0.26	0.28	0.30	0.45
Distrib'ns, Cap Gain ($) ...	2.13	0.85	0.81	0.55	0.32	0.03	0.54	1.45	2.14	1.50
Net Asset Value ($)	15.43	14.66	11.97	13.08	12.58	12.02	9.75	11.61	10.97	11.59
Expense Ratio (%)........	0.85	0.85	0.86	0.86	0.86	0.86	0.86	0.86	0.81	0.74
Yield (%)	0.62	0.96	1.56	1.39	1.55	1.74	2.52	2.14	2.28	3.43
Portfolio Turnover (%).....	33	17	10	13	12	22	23	33	26	14
Total Assets (Millions $)...	313	271	226	245	244	256	221	273	240	219

PORTFOLIO (as of 9/30/96)

Portfolio Manager: David G. Kirk, James B. Gribbell - 1995

Investm't Category: Growth

✔ Domestic	Index
Foreign	Sector
Asset Allocation	State Specific

Investment Style

✔ Large-Cap Growth	✔ Large-Cap Value
Mid-Cap Growth	Mid-Cap Value
Small-Cap Growth	Small-Cap Value

Portfolio

1.0% cash	0.0% corp bonds
99.0% stocks	0.0% gov't bonds
0.0% preferred	0.0% muni bonds
0.0% conv't/warrants	0.0% other

SHAREHOLDER INFORMATION

Minimum Investment
Initial: $500   Subsequent: $50

Minimum IRA Investment
Initial: $250   Subsequent: $50

Maximum Fees
Load: none   12b-1: none
Other: none

Distributions
Income: Jun, Dec   Capital Gains: Jun, Dec

Exchange Options
Number Per Year: no limit   Fee: none
Telephone: yes (money market fund available)

Services
IRA, pension, auto exchange, auto invest, auto withdraw

Babson Shadow Stock

(SHSTX)

Growth

3 Crown Center
2440 Pershing Road
Kansas City, MO 64108
800-422-2766, 816-471-5200

PERFORMANCE

fund inception date: 9/10/87

	3yr Annual	5yr Annual	10yr Annual	Bull	Bear
Return (%)	12.8	14.2	na	52.2	-8.3
Differ from Category (+/-)	-2.9 blw av	-0.1 av	na	-10.2 blw av	-1.6 blw av

Total Risk	Standard Deviation	Category Risk	Risk Index	Beta
av	8.1%	low	0.8	0.52

	1996	1995	1994	1993	1992	1991	1990	1989	1988	1987
Return (%)	21.3	23.6	-4.3	15.2	17.4	39.9	-19.4	11.2	22.4	—
Differ from Category (+/-)	1.2	-6.7	-4.0	1.2	5.6	3.9	-13.3	-14.9	4.3	—
Return, Tax-Adjusted (%)	17.5	20.9	-9.5	12.4	16.9	39.4	-19.8	9.6	21.3	—

PER SHARE DATA

	1996	1995	1994	1993	1992	1991	1990	1989	1988	1987
Dividends, Net Income ($)	0.08	0.10	0.11	0.09	0.08	0.08	0.09	0.16	0.12	—
Distrib'ns, Cap Gain ($)	1.35	0.75	2.12	1.02	0.05	0.00	0.00	0.26	0.09	—
Net Asset Value ($)	11.70	10.89	9.52	12.32	11.72	10.11	7.29	9.14	8.60	—
Expense Ratio (%)	1.14	1.13	1.28	1.25	1.26	1.31	1.29	1.33	1.51	—
Yield (%)	0.61	0.85	0.94	0.67	0.67	0.79	1.23	1.70	1.38	—
Portfolio Turnover (%)	25	19	43	15	23	0	16	15	7	—
Total Assets (Millions $)	38	38	33	37	31	24	18	27	17	—

PORTFOLIO (as of 9/30/96)

Portfolio Manager: P.C. Schliemann, R.W. Whitridge - 1987

Investm't Category: Growth
- ✔ Domestic
- Foreign
- Asset Allocation
- Index
- Sector
- State Specific

Investment Style
- Large-Cap Growth
- Mid-Cap Growth
- Small-Cap Growth
- Large-Cap Value
- Mid-Cap Value
- ✔ Small-Cap Value

Portfolio
1.0% cash	0.0% corp bonds
99.0% stocks	0.0% gov't bonds
0.0% preferred	0.0% muni bonds
0.0% conv't/warrants	0.0% other

SHAREHOLDER INFORMATION

Minimum Investment
Initial: $2,500   Subsequent: $100

Minimum IRA Investment
Initial: $250   Subsequent: $50

Maximum Fees
Load: none   12b-1: none
Other: none

Distributions
Income: Jun   Capital Gains: Jun

Exchange Options
Number Per Year: no limit   Fee: none
Telephone: yes (money market fund available)

Services
IRA, pension, auto exchange, auto invest, auto withdraw

Babson Tax-Free Income: Port L (BALTX)

Tax-Exempt Bond

3 Crown Center
2440 Pershing Road
Kansas City, MO 64108
800-422-2766, 816-471-5200

PERFORMANCE

fund inception date: 2/22/80

	3yr Annual	5yr Annual	10yr Annual	Bull	Bear
Return (%)	3.6	6.2	6.8	18.4	-7.0
Differ from Category (+/-)	-0.6 low	-0.2 blw av	0.1 av	0.0 av	-1.6 low

Total Risk	Standard Deviation	Category Risk	Risk Index	Avg Mat
blw av	5.6%	av	1.0	13.5 yrs

	1996	1995	1994	1993	1992	1991	1990	1989	1988	1987
Return (%)	3.2	16.4	-7.5	12.2	8.4	12.2	6.2	8.7	11.6	-1.4
Differ from Category (+/-)	-0.5	1.2	-2.2	0.4	0.1	0.8	-0.2	-0.3	1.6	0.0
Return, Tax-Adjusted (%)	3.1	16.4	-7.6	10.9	7.3	12.1	6.2	8.7	11.6	-2.0

PER SHARE DATA

	1996	1995	1994	1993	1992	1991	1990	1989	1988	1987
Dividends, Net Income ($)	0.41	0.41	0.42	0.44	0.49	0.52	0.55	0.60	0.64	0.66
Distrib'ns, Cap Gain ($)	0.02	0.00	0.02	0.40	0.36	0.03	0.00	0.00	0.00	0.19
Net Asset Value ($)	8.91	9.06	8.16	9.28	9.05	9.17	8.70	8.73	8.60	8.31
Expense Ratio (%)	1.01	1.02	1.02	1.00	0.99	0.98	1.00	0.99	1.00	0.99
Yield (%)	4.59	4.52	5.13	4.54	5.20	5.65	6.32	6.87	7.44	7.76
Portfolio Turnover (%)	39	34	53	126	128	116	121	172	168	123
Total Assets (Millions $)	27	29	26	33	31	29	28	27	22	20

PORTFOLIO (as of 9/30/96)

Portfolio Manager: Joel M. Vernick - 1986

Investm't Category: Tax-Exempt Bond
✔ Domestic   Index
  Foreign   Sector
  Asset Allocation State Specific

Investment Style
  Large-Cap Growth   Large-Cap Value
  Mid-Cap Growth   Mid-Cap Value
  Small-Cap Growth   Small-Cap Value

Portfolio
  0.0% cash   0.0% corp bonds
  0.0% stocks   0.0% gov't bonds
  0.0% preferred   100.0% muni bonds
  0.0% conv't/warrants 0.0% other

SHAREHOLDER INFORMATION

Minimum Investment
Initial: $1,000   Subsequent: $100

Minimum IRA Investment
Initial: na   Subsequent: na

Maximum Fees
Load: none   12b-1: none
Other: none

Distributions
Income: monthly   Capital Gains: Jun, Dec

Exchange Options
Number Per Year: no limit   Fee: none
Telephone: yes (money market fund available)

Services
auto exchange, auto invest, auto withdraw

Babson Tax-Free Income: Port S (BASTX)

Tax-Exempt Bond

3 Crown Center
2440 Pershing Road
Kansas City, MO 64108
800-422-2766, 816-471-5200

PERFORMANCE

fund inception date: 2/22/80

	3yr Annual	5yr Annual	10yr Annual	Bull	Bear
Return (%)	3.5	4.7	5.6	13.2	-2.7
Differ from Category (+/-)	-0.7 low	-1.7 low	-1.1 low	-5.2 low	2.7 high

Total Risk	Standard Deviation	Category Risk	Risk Index	Avg Mat
low	2.7%	low	0.5	5.0 yrs

	1996	1995	1994	1993	1992	1991	1990	1989	1988	1987
Return (%)	3.4	9.3	-1.8	6.6	6.3	9.4	6.6	6.9	5.3	4.0
Differ from Category (+/-)	-0.3	-5.9	3.5	-5.2	-2.0	-2.0	0.2	-2.1	-4.7	5.4
Return, Tax-Adjusted (%)	3.2	9.2	-1.8	6.4	6.0	9.0	6.6	6.9	5.2	3.7

PER SHARE DATA

	1996	1995	1994	1993	1992	1991	1990	1989	1988	1987
Dividends, Net Income ($)	0.44	0.44	0.45	0.47	0.51	0.57	0.60	0.64	0.66	0.67
Distrib'ns, Cap Gain ($)	0.05	0.02	0.00	0.05	0.11	0.13	0.00	0.00	0.02	0.09
Net Asset Value ($)	10.75	10.88	10.40	11.05	10.87	10.84	10.58	10.51	10.45	10.59
Expense Ratio (%)	1.01	1.01	1.02	1.00	1.00	0.99	0.99	0.99	1.00	0.99
Yield (%)	4.07	4.03	4.32	4.23	4.64	5.19	5.67	6.08	6.30	6.27
Portfolio Turnover (%)	41	34	21	47	81	98	74	115	131	66
Total Assets (Millions $)	24	27	28	31	25	19	17	17	17	16

PORTFOLIO (as of 9/30/96)

Portfolio Manager: Joel M. Vernick - 1986

Investm't Category: Tax-Exempt Bond

✔ Domestic	Index
Foreign	Sector
Asset Allocation	State Specific

Investment Style

Large-Cap Growth	Large-Cap Value
Mid-Cap Growth	Mid-Cap Value
Small-Cap Growth	Small-Cap Value

Portfolio

2.0% cash	0.0% corp bonds
0.0% stocks	0.0% gov't bonds
0.0% preferred	98.0% muni bonds
0.0% conv't/warrants	0.0% other

SHAREHOLDER INFORMATION

Minimum Investment
Initial: $1,000   Subsequent: $100

Minimum IRA Investment
Initial: na   Subsequent: na

Maximum Fees
Load: none   12b-1: none
Other: none

Distributions
Income: monthly   Capital Gains: Jun, Dec

Exchange Options
Number Per Year: no limit   Fee: none
Telephone: yes (money market fund available)

Services
auto exchange, auto invest, auto withdraw

Babson Value (BVALX)

Growth & Income

3 Crown Center
2440 Pershing Road
Kansas City, MO 64108
800-422-2766, 816-471-5200

PERFORMANCE

fund inception date: 12/21/84

	3yr Annual	5yr Annual	10yr Annual	Bull	Bear
Return (%)	18.3	18.6	14.5	64.3	-3.7
Differ from Category (+/-)	3.0 abv av	4.7 high	1.8 high	4.5 av	2.7 high

Total Risk	Standard Deviation	Category Risk	Risk Index	Beta
av	8.9%	blw av	1.0	0.84

	1996	1995	1994	1993	1992	1991	1990	1989	1988	1987
Return (%)	22.7	31.7	2.5	22.8	15.3	28.9	-11.4	18.2	18.9	3.1
Differ from Category (+/-)	3.0	1.6	3.8	9.0	4.6	-0.2	-5.5	-5.3	2.1	2.9
Return, Tax-Adjusted (%)	21.5	30.4	1.0	20.6	13.5	27.1	-13.0	16.9	16.6	1.2

PER SHARE DATA

	1996	1995	1994	1993	1992	1991	1990	1989	1988	1987
Dividends, Net Income ($)	0.49	0.56	0.47	0.53	0.62	0.71	0.71	0.50	0.76	0.66
Distrib'ns, Cap Gain ($)	0.60	0.34	0.60	0.91	0.32	0.00	0.00	0.03	0.08	0.04
Net Asset Value ($)	37.74	31.68	24.78	25.22	21.75	19.67	15.85	18.68	16.27	14.38
Expense Ratio (%)	na	0.98	0.99	1.00	1.01	1.01	1.04	1.06	1.11	1.08
Yield (%)	1.27	1.74	1.85	2.02	2.80	3.60	4.47	2.67	4.64	4.57
Portfolio Turnover (%)	na	6	14	26	17	31	6	17	24	52
Total Assets (Millions $)	763	308	121	45	35	27	22	21	10	12

PORTFOLIO (as of 9/30/96)

Portfolio Manager: Roland W. Whitridge - 1984

Investm't Category: Growth & Income
- ✔ Domestic
- Foreign
- Asset Allocation
- Index
- Sector
- State Specific

Investment Style
- Large-Cap Growth
- Mid-Cap Growth
- Small-Cap Growth
- ✔ Large-Cap Value
- Mid-Cap Value
- Small-Cap Value

Portfolio
- 6.0% cash
- 94.0% stocks
- 0.0% preferred
- 0.0% conv't/warrants
- 0.0% corp bonds
- 0.0% gov't bonds
- 0.0% muni bonds
- 0.0% other

SHAREHOLDER INFORMATION

Minimum Investment
Initial: $1,000   Subsequent: $100

Minimum IRA Investment
Initial: $250   Subsequent: $50

Maximum Fees
Load: none   12b-1: none
Other: none

Distributions
Income: quarterly   Capital Gains: Dec

Exchange Options
Number Per Year: no limit   Fee: none
Telephone: yes (money market fund available)

Services
IRA, pension, auto exchange, auto invest, auto withdraw

Babson-Stewart Ivory Int'l

(BAINX)

International Stock

3 Crown Center
2440 Pershing Road
Kansas City, MO 64108
800-422-2766, 816-471-5200

PERFORMANCE

fund inception date: 12/14/87

	3yr Annual	5yr Annual	10yr Annual	Bull	Bear
Return (%)	8.9	11.1	na	25.6	-2.7
Differ from Category (+/-)	2.6 abv av	1.1 av	na	1.3 av	4.5 high

Total Risk	Standard Deviation	Category Risk	Risk Index	Beta
av	9.5%	blw av	0.9	0.57

	1996	1995	1994	1993	1992	1991	1990	1989	1988	1987
Return (%).............	13.4	12.5	1.3	33.4	-1.8	15.0	-9.4	26.9	3.4	—
Differ from Category (+/-).	-1.4	3.4	4.4	-6.2	2.0	1.8	0.7	4.3	-11.5	—
Return, Tax-Adjusted (%)..	12.2	11.4	-0.4	32.5	-2.3	14.6	-9.9	25.9	3.1	—

PER SHARE DATA

	1996	1995	1994	1993	1992	1991	1990	1989	1988	1987
Dividends, Net Income ($).	0.07	0.17	0.04	0.05	0.14	0.11	0.06	0.06	0.00	—
Distrib'ns, Cap Gain ($) ...	0.61	0.36	0.92	0.32	0.02	0.00	0.14	0.28	0.08	—
Net Asset Value ($)	18.41	16.85	15.45	16.20	12.43	12.81	11.24	12.63	10.26	—
Expense Ratio (%)........	1.26	1.30	1.32	1.57	1.58	1.75	1.75	2.68	4.77	—
Yield (%)	0.36	0.98	0.24	0.30	1.12	0.85	0.52	0.46	0.00	—
Portfolio Turnover (%).....	33	37	60	49	44	52	42	40	18	—
Total Assets (Millions $)....	89	71	55	43	20	13	10	7	3	—

PORTFOLIO (as of 9/30/96)

Portfolio Manager: John Wright - 1988

Investm't Category: International Stock
Domestic	Index
✔ Foreign	Sector
Asset Allocation	State Specific

Investment Style
Large-Cap Growth	Large-Cap Value
Mid-Cap Growth	Mid-Cap Value
Small-Cap Growth	Small-Cap Value

Portfolio
6.0% cash	0.0% corp bonds
94.0% stocks	0.0% gov't bonds
0.0% preferred	0.0% muni bonds
0.0% conv't/warrants	0.0% other

SHAREHOLDER INFORMATION

Minimum Investment
Initial: $2,500   Subsequent: $100

Minimum IRA Investment
Initial: $250   Subsequent: $50

Maximum Fees
Load: none   12b-1: none
Other: none

Distributions
Income: Jun   Capital Gains: Jun

Exchange Options
Number Per Year: no limit   Fee: none
Telephone: yes (money market fund available)

Services
IRA, pension, auto exchange, auto invest, auto withdraw

Baron Asset (BARAX)

Aggressive Growth

767 Fifth Ave.
24th Floor
New York, NY 10153
800-992-2766, 212-759-7700

PERFORMANCE

fund inception date: 6/12/87

	3yr Annual	5yr Annual	10yr Annual	Bull	Bear
Return (%)	21.0	20.0	na	83.3	-5.4
Differ from Category (+/-)	5.2 high	4.7 high	na	12.2 abv av	5.2 high

Total Risk	Standard Deviation	Category Risk	Risk Index	Beta
high	12.9%	blw av	0.9	0.81

	1996	1995	1994	1993	1992	1991	1990	1989	1988	1987
Return (%).............	21.9	35.2	7.4	23.4	13.9	34.0	-18.5	24.9	34.4	—
Differ from Category (+/-)..	2.8	0.9	7.4	4.1	2.2	-18.1	-13.1	-3.5	18.0	—
Return, Tax-Adjusted (%)..	21.8	35.1	6.5	21.9	13.6	33.8	-19.1	21.7	32.4	—

PER SHARE DATA

	1996	1995	1994	1993	1992	1991	1990	1989	1988	1987
Dividends, Net Income ($).	0.00	0.00	0.00	0.31	0.00	0.03	0.19	0.15	0.04	—
Distrib'ns, Cap Gain ($) ...	0.03	0.03	0.65	0.45	0.16	0.00	0.00	1.25	0.65	—
Net Asset Value ($)	36.23	29.74	22.01	21.11	17.73	15.71	11.75	14.66	12.87	—
Expense Ratio (%)........	1.40	1.40	1.60	1.80	1.70	1.70	1.80	2.10	2.50	—
Yield (%)	0.00	0.00	0.00	1.43	0.00	0.19	1.61	0.94	0.29	—
Portfolio Turnover (%).....	19	35	55	108	96	143	98	149	242	—
Total Assets (Millions $).	1,276	353	87	64	47	46	42	49	15	—

PORTFOLIO (as of 9/30/96)

Portfolio Manager: Ronald S. Baron - 1987

Investm't Category: Aggressive Growth

✔ Domestic	Index
Foreign	Sector
Asset Allocation	State Specific

Investment Style

Large-Cap Growth	Large-Cap Value
✔ Mid-Cap Growth	Mid-Cap Value
✔ Small-Cap Growth	Small-Cap Value

Portfolio

2.6% cash	0.0% corp bonds
92.0% stocks	0.0% gov't bonds
0.9% preferred	0.0% muni bonds
4.5% conv't/warrants	0.0% other

SHAREHOLDER INFORMATION

Minimum Investment
Initial: $2,000   Subsequent: $1

Minimum IRA Investment
Initial: $2,000   Subsequent: $1

Maximum Fees
Load: none   12b-1: 0.25%
Other: none

Distributions
Income: Dec   Capital Gains: Dec

Exchange Options
Number Per Year: no limit   Fee: none
Telephone: yes

Services
IRA, auto invest

Baron Growth & Income

(BGINX)

Balanced

767 Fifth Ave.
24th Floor
New York, NY 10153
800-992-2766, 212-759-7700

PERFORMANCE   fund inception date: 1/3/95

	3yr Annual	5yr Annual	10yr Annual	Bull	Bear
Return (%)	na	na	na	na	na
Differ from Category (+/-)	na	na	na	na	na

Total Risk	Standard Deviation	Category Risk	Risk Index	Beta
na	na	na	na	na

	1996	1995	1994	1993	1992	1991	1990	1989	1988	1987
Return (%)	27.7	—	—	—	—	—	—	—	—	—
Differ from Category (+/-)	13.5	—	—	—	—	—	—	—	—	—
Return, Tax-Adjusted (%)	27.1	—	—	—	—	—	—	—	—	—

PER SHARE DATA

	1996	1995	1994	1993	1992	1991	1990	1989	1988	1987
Dividends, Net Income ($)	0.09	—	—	—	—	—	—	—	—	—
Distrib'ns, Cap Gain ($)	0.16	—	—	—	—	—	—	—	—	—
Net Asset Value ($)	19.04	—	—	—	—	—	—	—	—	—
Expense Ratio (%)	1.50	—	—	—	—	—	—	—	—	—
Yield (%)	0.46	—	—	—	—	—	—	—	—	—
Portfolio Turnover (%)	40	—	—	—	—	—	—	—	—	—
Total Assets (Millions $)	235	—	—	—	—	—	—	—	—	—

PORTFOLIO (as of 9/30/96)

Portfolio Manager: Ronald S. Baron - 1995

Investm't Category: Balanced

✔ Domestic	Index
✔ Foreign	Sector
Asset Allocation	State Specific

Investment Style

Large-Cap Growth	Large-Cap Value
Mid-Cap Growth	Mid-Cap Value
Small-Cap Growth	Small-Cap Value

Portfolio

2.0% cash	0.6% corp bonds
91.6% stocks	0.0% gov't bonds
1.3% preferred	0.0% muni bonds
0.0% conv't/warrants	0.0% other

SHAREHOLDER INFORMATION

Minimum Investment
Initial: $2,000   Subsequent: $1

Minimum IRA Investment
Initial: $2,000   Subsequent: $1

Maximum Fees
Load: none   12b-1: 0.25%
Other: none

Distributions
Income: Dec   Capital Gains: Dec

Exchange Options
Number Per Year: no limit   Fee: none
Telephone: yes

Services
IRA, auto invest

Bartlett Capital Trust: Basic Value (MBBVX)

Growth & Income

7 E. Redwood
10th Floor
Baltimore, MD 21202
800-800-3609, 410-539-3400

PERFORMANCE

fund inception date: 5/5/83

	3yr Annual	5yr Annual	10yr Annual	Bull	Bear
Return (%)	16.0	13.9	11.5	58.3	-4.9
Differ from Category (+/-)	0.7 av	0.0 av	-1.2 blw av	-1.5 blw av	1.5 abv av

Total Risk	Standard Deviation	Category Risk	Risk Index	Beta
av	8.3%	blw av	0.9	0.72

	1996	1995	1994	1993	1992	1991	1990	1989	1988	1987
Return (%)	18.4	31.5	0.4	11.6	10.2	25.9	-9.7	11.6	26.2	-3.8
Differ from Category (+/-)	-1.3	1.4	1.7	-2.2	-0.5	-3.2	-3.8	-11.9	9.4	-4.0
Return, Tax-Adjusted (%)	15.5	28.9	-2.2	10.6	8.6	24.4	-11.4	8.4	21.4	-6.2

PER SHARE DATA

	1996	1995	1994	1993	1992	1991	1990	1989	1988	1987
Dividends, Net Income ($)	0.26	0.31	0.24	0.22	0.32	0.39	0.52	0.84	0.52	0.45
Distrib'ns, Cap Gain ($)	1.39	0.83	1.03	0.14	0.28	0.00	0.00	0.18	1.14	0.39
Net Asset Value ($)	18.84	17.34	14.10	15.28	14.02	13.28	10.87	12.58	12.18	11.01
Expense Ratio (%)	1.17	1.20	1.20	1.21	1.22	1.21	1.19	1.23	1.57	1.28
Yield (%)	1.28	1.70	1.58	1.42	2.23	2.93	4.78	6.58	3.90	3.94
Portfolio Turnover (%)	25	26	33	43	49	92	77	99	97	58
Total Assets (Millions $)	131	122	93	100	96	90	84	109	95	73

PORTFOLIO (as of 9/30/96)

Portfolio Manager: James A. Miller, Woodrow Uible - 1983

Investm't Category: Growth & Income
- ✔ Domestic
- ✔ Foreign
- Asset Allocation
- Index
- Sector
- State Specific

Investment Style
Large-Cap Growth	✔ Large-Cap Value
Mid-Cap Growth	✔ Mid-Cap Value
Small-Cap Growth	Small-Cap Value

Portfolio
7.3% cash	0.0% corp bonds
92.0% stocks	0.0% gov't bonds
0.7% preferred	0.0% muni bonds
0.0% conv't/warrants	0.0% other

SHAREHOLDER INFORMATION

Minimum Investment
Initial: $5,000   Subsequent: $100

Minimum IRA Investment
Initial: $250   Subsequent: $100

Maximum Fees
Load: none   12b-1: none
Other: none

Distributions
Income: quarterly   Capital Gains: annual

Exchange Options
Number Per Year: 6   Fee: none
Telephone: yes (money market fund available)

Services
IRA, pension, auto exchange, auto invest, auto withdraw

Bartlett Capital Trust: Value Int'l (BVLIX)

International Stock

7 E. Redwood
10th Floor
Baltimore, MD 21202
800-800-3609, 410-539-3400

PERFORMANCE

fund inception date: 10/6/89

	3yr Annual	5yr Annual	10yr Annual	Bull	Bear
Return (%)	8.0	10.1	na	27.0	-7.3
Differ from Category (+/-)	1.7 av	0.1 av	na	2.7 av	-0.1 av

Total Risk	Standard Deviation	Category Risk	Risk Index	Beta
abv av	9.9%	blw av	1.0	0.67

	1996	1995	1994	1993	1992	1991	1990	1989	1988	1987
Return (%).............	16.0	9.1	-0.6	31.3	-1.9	21.4	-14.6	—	—	—
Differ from Category (+/-)..	1.2	0.0	2.5	-8.3	1.9	8.2	-4.5	—	—	—
Return, Tax-Adjusted (%)..	13.9	7.6	-2.3	31.0	-2.4	20.2	-16.4	—	—	—

PER SHARE DATA

	1996	1995	1994	1993	1992	1991	1990	1989	1988	1987
Dividends, Net Income ($).	0.09	0.15	0.08	0.07	0.11	0.22	0.45	—	—	—
Distrib'ns, Cap Gain ($) ...	0.75	0.37	0.61	0.00	0.00	0.02	0.00	—	—	—
Net Asset Value ($)	13.21	12.13	11.60	12.33	9.45	9.73	8.22	—	—	—
Expense Ratio (%)........	1.83	1.83	1.88	2.00	2.00	1.99	1.41	—	—	—
Yield (%)	0.64	1.20	0.65	0.56	1.16	2.25	5.47	—	—	—
Portfolio Turnover (%).....	38	24	19	19	27	39	155	—	—	—
Total Assets (Millions $)....	79	67	56	45	26	18	21	—	—	—

PORTFOLIO (as of 9/30/96)

Portfolio Manager: Madelyn Matlock - 1989

Investm't Category: International Stock

Domestic	Index
✔ Foreign	Sector
Asset Allocation	State Specific

Investment Style

Large-Cap Growth	Large-Cap Value
Mid-Cap Growth	Mid-Cap Value
Small-Cap Growth	Small-Cap Value

Portfolio

6.8% cash	0.0% corp bonds
93.2% stocks	0.0% gov't bonds
0.0% preferred	0.0% muni bonds
0.0% conv't/warrants	0.0% other

SHAREHOLDER INFORMATION

Minimum Investment
Initial: $5,000   Subsequent: $100

Minimum IRA Investment
Initial: $250   Subsequent: $100

Maximum Fees
Load: none   12b-1: none
Other: none

Distributions
Income: quarterly   Capital Gains: annual

Exchange Options
Number Per Year: 6   Fee: none
Telephone: yes (money market fund available)

Services
IRA, pension, auto exchange, auto invest, auto withdraw

Benham Adjustable Rate Gov't Sec (BARGX)

Mortgage-Backed Bond

4500 Main St., 14th Floor
P.O. Box 418210
Kansas City, MO 64141
800-345-2021, 415-965-4222
www.americancentury.com

PERFORMANCE

fund inception date: 9/3/91

	3yr Annual	5yr Annual	10yr Annual	Bull	Bear
Return (%)	4.4	4.4	na	14.5	-1.2
Differ from Category (+/-)	-1.2 low	-1.6 low	na	-6.6 low	2.4 high

Total Risk	Standard Deviation	Category Risk	Risk Index	Avg Mat
low	1.7%	low	0.5	21.5 yrs

	1996	1995	1994	1993	1992	1991	1990	1989	1988	1987
Return (%)	5.8	8.8	-1.2	3.5	5.2	—	—	—	—	—
Differ from Category (+/-)	1.4	-5.9	0.5	-3.4	-1.0	—	—	—	—	—
Return, Tax-Adjusted (%)	3.6	6.4	-3.1	1.2	2.8	—	—	—	—	—

PER SHARE DATA

	1996	1995	1994	1993	1992	1991	1990	1989	1988	1987
Dividends, Net Income ($)	0.52	0.54	0.46	0.56	0.60	—	—	—	—	—
Distrib'ns, Cap Gain ($)	0.00	0.00	0.00	0.00	0.00	—	—	—	—	—
Net Asset Value ($)	9.52	9.51	9.26	9.84	10.05	—	—	—	—	—
Expense Ratio (%)	0.60	0.57	0.51	0.45	0.00	—	—	—	—	—
Yield (%)	5.46	5.67	4.96	5.69	5.97	—	—	—	—	—
Portfolio Turnover (%)	221	60	91	82	82	—	—	—	—	—
Total Assets (Millions $)	254	313	446	1,080	1,520	—	—	—	—	—

PORTFOLIO (as of 6/30/96)

Portfolio Manager: Newlin Rankin - 1995

Investm't Category: Mortgage-Backed Bond

✔ Domestic
Foreign
Asset Allocation

Index
Sector
State Specific

Investment Style

Large-Cap Growth
Mid-Cap Growth
Small-Cap Growth

Large-Cap Value
Mid-Cap Value
Small-Cap Value

Portfolio

3.0% cash	0.0% corp bonds
0.0% stocks	97.0% gov't bonds
0.0% preferred	0.0% muni bonds
0.0% conv't/warrants	0.0% other

SHAREHOLDER INFORMATION

Minimum Investment
Initial: $2,500   Subsequent: $50

Minimum IRA Investment
Initial: $1,000   Subsequent: $50

Maximum Fees
Load: none   12b-1: none
Other: none

Distributions
Income: monthly   Capital Gains: Dec

Exchange Options
Number Per Year: 6   Fee: none
Telephone: yes (money market fund available)

Services
IRA, pension, auto exchange, auto invest, auto withdraw

Benham Arizona Interm-Term Muni

(BEAMX) *Tax-Exempt Bond*

4500 Main St., 14th Floor
P.O. Box 418210
Kansas City, MO 64141
800-345-2021, 415-965-4222
www.americancentury.com

PERFORMANCE

fund inception date: 4/11/94

	3yr Annual	5yr Annual	10yr Annual	Bull	Bear
Return (%)	na	na	na	17.7	na
Differ from Category (+/-)	na	na	na	-0.7 blw av	na

Total Risk	Standard Deviation	Category Risk	Risk Index	Avg Mat
na	na	na	na	6.8 yrs

	1996	1995	1994	1993	1992	1991	1990	1989	1988	1987
Return (%)	3.7	13.1	—	—	—	—	—	—	—	—
Differ from Category (+/-)	0.0	-2.1	—	—	—	—	—	—	—	—
Return, Tax-Adjusted (%)	3.7	13.1	—	—	—	—	—	—	—	—

PER SHARE DATA

	1996	1995	1994	1993	1992	1991	1990	1989	1988	1987
Dividends, Net Income ($)	0.47	0.52	—	—	—	—	—	—	—	—
Distrib'ns, Cap Gain ($)	0.00	0.00	—	—	—	—	—	—	—	—
Net Asset Value ($)	10.49	10.58	—	—	—	—	—	—	—	—
Expense Ratio (%)	0.14	0.00	—	—	—	—	—	—	—	—
Yield (%)	4.48	4.91	—	—	—	—	—	—	—	—
Portfolio Turnover (%)	35	33	—	—	—	—	—	—	—	—
Total Assets (Millions $)	27	23	—	—	—	—	—	—	—	—

PORTFOLIO (as of 9/30/96)

Portfolio Manager: David MacEwen - 1994

Investm't Category: Tax-Exempt Bond
✔ Domestic   Index
   Foreign   Sector
   Asset Allocation   ✔ State Specific

Investment Style
Large-Cap Growth   Large-Cap Value
Mid-Cap Growth   Mid-Cap Value
Small-Cap Growth   Small-Cap Value

Portfolio
3.3% cash   0.0% corp bonds
0.0% stocks   0.0% gov't bonds
0.0% preferred   96.7% muni bonds
0.0% conv't/warrants   0.0% other

SHAREHOLDER INFORMATION

Minimum Investment
Initial: $5,000   Subsequent: $50

Minimum IRA Investment
Initial: na   Subsequent: na

Maximum Fees
Load: none   12b-1: none
Other: none

Distributions
Income: monthly   Capital Gains: Dec

Exchange Options
Number Per Year: 6   Fee: none
Telephone: yes (money market fund available)

Services
auto exchange, auto invest, auto withdraw

Benham Bond (TWLBX)

Corporate Bond

4500 Main St., 14th Floor
P.O. Box 418210
Kansas City, MO 64141
800-345-2021, 816-531-5575
www.americancentury.com

PERFORMANCE

fund inception date: 3/2/87

	3yr Annual	5yr Annual	10yr Annual	Bull	Bear
Return (%)	5.5	6.4	na	23.7	-6.5
Differ from Category (+/-)	-0.8 av	-1.9 blw av	na	-1.1 av	-1.4 blw av

Total Risk	Standard Deviation	Category Risk	Risk Index	Avg Mat
blw av	5.2%	abv av	1.2	11.0 yrs

	1996	1995	1994	1993	1992	1991	1990	1989	1988	1987
Return (%)...............	2.4	20.2	-4.6	10.1	5.5	17.4	6.0	13.9	8.3	—
Differ from Category (+/-).	-2.8	2.2	-1.5	-1.7	-3.4	0.2	2.0	4.5	-1.0	—
Return, Tax-Adjusted (%)..	-0.2	17.4	-7.0	7.0	2.5	14.2	2.6	10.3	4.7	—

PER SHARE DATA

	1996	1995	1994	1993	1992	1991	1990	1989	1988	1987
Dividends, Net Income ($).	0.59	0.60	0.58	0.62	0.63	0.72	0.79	0.81	0.83	—
Distrib'ns, Cap Gain ($) ...	0.09	0.01	0.00	0.18	0.15	0.00	0.00	0.00	0.00	—
Net Asset Value ($)	9.51	9.97	8.85	9.88	9.73	9.98	9.18	9.46	9.07	—
Expense Ratio (%).........	na	0.78	0.88	1.00	0.98	0.96	1.00	1.00	1.00	—
Yield (%)	6.14	6.01	6.55	6.16	6.37	7.21	8.60	8.56	9.15	—
Portfolio Turnover (%).....	na	105	78	113	186	219	98	216	280	—
Total Assets (Millions $)...	142	153	118	158	142	121	85	67	27	—

PORTFOLIO (as of 9/30/96)

Portfolio Manager: committee - 1987

Investm't Category: Corporate Bond

✔ Domestic   Index
✔ Foreign   Sector
  Asset Allocation   State Specific

Investment Style

Large-Cap Growth   Large-Cap Value
Mid-Cap Growth   Mid-Cap Value
Small-Cap Growth   Small-Cap Value

Portfolio

13.2% cash	57.5% corp bonds
0.0% stocks	29.3% gov't bonds
0.0% preferred	0.0% muni bonds
0.0% conv't/warrants	0.0% other

SHAREHOLDER INFORMATION

Minimum Investment
Initial: $2,500   Subsequent: $50

Minimum IRA Investment
Initial: $1,000   Subsequent: $50

Maximum Fees
Load: none   12b-1: none
Other: none

Distributions
Income: monthly   Capital Gains: Dec

Exchange Options
Number Per Year: 6   Fee: none
Telephone: yes (money market fund available)

Services
IRA, pension, auto exchange, auto invest, auto withdraw

Benham CA High Yield Muni (BCHYX)

Tax-Exempt Bond

4500 Main St., 14th Floor
P.O. Box 418210
Kansas City, MO 64141
800-345-2021, 415-965-4222
www.americancentury.com

PERFORMANCE
fund inception date: 12/30/86

	3yr Annual	5yr Annual	10yr Annual	Bull	Bear
Return (%)	5.8	7.9	6.5	23.2	-5.1
Differ from Category (+/-)	1.6 high	1.5 high	-0.2 blw av	4.8 high	0.3 abv av

Total Risk	Standard Deviation	Category Risk	Risk Index	Avg Mat
blw av	5.4%	av	1.0	20.5 yrs

	1996	1995	1994	1993	1992	1991	1990	1989	1988	1987
Return (%)	5.8	18.2	-5.4	13.1	9.1	10.9	5.6	9.6	12.4	-11.1
Differ from Category (+/-)	2.1	3.0	-0.1	1.3	0.8	-0.5	-0.8	0.6	2.4	-9.7
Return, Tax-Adjusted (%)	5.8	18.2	-5.4	12.7	9.1	10.9	5.6	9.6	12.4	-11.1

PER SHARE DATA

	1996	1995	1994	1993	1992	1991	1990	1989	1988	1987
Dividends, Net Income ($)	0.55	0.56	0.55	0.57	0.57	0.59	0.61	0.65	0.65	0.68
Distrib'ns, Cap Gain ($)	0.00	0.00	0.00	0.12	0.00	0.00	0.00	0.00	0.00	0.00
Net Asset Value ($)	9.48	9.50	8.54	9.60	9.12	8.90	8.58	8.72	8.57	8.23
Expense Ratio (%)	na	0.51	0.51	0.55	0.56	0.50	0.24	0.00	0.00	0.00
Yield (%)	5.80	5.89	6.44	5.86	6.25	6.62	7.10	7.45	7.58	8.26
Portfolio Turnover (%)	na	40	42	27	33	47	104	50	143	57
Total Assets (Millions $)	158	130	96	116	89	68	46	38	17	8

PORTFOLIO (as of 9/30/96)

Portfolio Manager: Steve Permut - 1987

Investm't Category: Tax-Exempt Bond
✔ Domestic	Index
Foreign	Sector
Asset Allocation	✔ State Specific

Investment Style
Large-Cap Growth	Large-Cap Value
Mid-Cap Growth	Mid-Cap Value
Small-Cap Growth	Small-Cap Value

Portfolio
2.7% cash	0.0% corp bonds
0.0% stocks	0.0% gov't bonds
0.0% preferred	97.3% muni bonds
0.0% conv't/warrants	0.0% other

SHAREHOLDER INFORMATION

Minimum Investment
Initial: $5,000   Subsequent: $50

Minimum IRA Investment
Initial: na   Subsequent: na

Maximum Fees
Load: none   12b-1: none
Other: none

Distributions
Income: monthly   Capital Gains: Dec

Exchange Options
Number Per Year: 6   Fee: none
Telephone: yes (money market fund available)

Services
auto exchange, auto invest, auto withdraw

Benham CA Insured Tax-Free (BCINX)

Tax-Exempt Bond

4500 Main St., 14th Floor
P.O. Box 418210
Kansas City, MO 64141
800-345-2021, 415-965-4222
www.americancentury.com

PERFORMANCE

fund inception date: 12/30/86

	3yr Annual	5yr Annual	10yr Annual	Bull	Bear
Return (%)	4.8	7.3	6.8	22.6	-7.2
Differ from Category (+/-)	0.6 high	0.9 high	0.1 av	4.2 high	-1.8 low

Total Risk	Standard Deviation	Category Risk	Risk Index	Avg Mat
blw av	6.4%	high	1.1	17.4 yrs

	1996	1995	1994	1993	1992	1991	1990	1989	1988	1987
Return (%)	3.7	19.0	-6.6	13.4	9.1	11.2	6.7	10.3	10.1	-6.1
Differ from Category (+/-)	0.0	3.8	-1.3	1.6	0.8	-0.2	0.3	1.3	0.1	-4.7
Return, Tax-Adjusted (%)	3.7	19.0	-6.6	12.6	9.1	11.2	6.7	10.3	10.1	-6.1

PER SHARE DATA

	1996	1995	1994	1993	1992	1991	1990	1989	1988	1987
Dividends, Net Income ($)	0.53	0.53	0.52	0.54	0.66	0.57	0.58	0.59	0.63	0.64
Distrib'ns, Cap Gain ($)	0.00	0.00	0.00	0.27	0.00	0.00	0.00	0.00	0.00	0.00
Net Asset Value ($)	10.24	10.41	9.23	10.43	9.94	9.74	9.30	9.29	8.98	8.75
Expense Ratio (%)	na	0.50	0.49	0.52	0.55	0.59	0.61	0.66	0.00	0.00
Yield (%)	5.17	5.09	5.63	5.04	6.63	5.85	6.23	6.35	7.01	7.31
Portfolio Turnover (%)	na	40	47	60	54	38	117	74	145	21
Total Assets (Millions $)	195	190	161	222	154	114	66	47	32	15

PORTFOLIO (as of 9/30/96)

Portfolio Manager: David MacEwen - 1991

Investm't Category: Tax-Exempt Bond
- ✔ Domestic
- Foreign
- Asset Allocation
- Index
- Sector
- ✔ State Specific

Investment Style

Large-Cap Growth	Large-Cap Value
Mid-Cap Growth	Mid-Cap Value
Small-Cap Growth	Small-Cap Value

Portfolio

8.8% cash	0.0% corp bonds
0.0% stocks	0.0% gov't bonds
0.0% preferred	91.2% muni bonds
0.0% conv't/warrants	0.0% other

SHAREHOLDER INFORMATION

Minimum Investment
Initial: $5,000   Subsequent: $50

Minimum IRA Investment
Initial: na   Subsequent: na

Maximum Fees
Load: none   12b-1: none
Other: none

Distributions
Income: monthly   Capital Gains: Dec

Exchange Options
Number Per Year: 6   Fee: none
Telephone: yes (money market fund available)

Services
auto exchange, auto invest, auto withdraw

Benham CA Interm-Term Tax-Free (BCITX)

Tax-Exempt Bond

4500 Main St., 14th Floor
P.O. Box 418210
Kansas City, MO 64141
800-345-2021, 415-965-4222
www.americancentury.com

PERFORMANCE

fund inception date: 11/9/83

	3yr Annual	5yr Annual	10yr Annual	Bull	Bear
Return (%)	4.4	6.1	6.2	17.7	-4.3
Differ from Category (+/-)	0.2 av	-0.3 blw av	-0.5 blw av	-0.7 blw av	1.1 abv av

Total Risk	Standard Deviation	Category Risk	Risk Index	Avg Mat
low	4.0%	blw av	0.7	7.6 yrs

	1996	1995	1994	1993	1992	1991	1990	1989	1988	1987
Return (%).	4.2	13.5	-3.8	10.6	7.0	10.3	6.9	7.9	5.9	0.7
Differ from Category (+/-). .	0.5	-1.7	1.5	-1.2	-1.3	-1.1	0.5	-1.1	-4.1	2.1
Return, Tax-Adjusted (%). . .	4.1	13.5	-3.8	10.3	6.9	10.3	6.9	7.9	5.9	0.7

PER SHARE DATA

	1996	1995	1994	1993	1992	1991	1990	1989	1988	1987
Dividends, Net Income ($)	0.54	0.54	0.53	0.55	0.57	0.59	0.62	0.62	0.62	0.62
Distrib'ns, Cap Gain ($) . . .	0.03	0.00	0.00	0.08	0.01	0.00	0.00	0.00	0.00	0.00
Net Asset Value ($)	11.16	11.27	10.43	11.38	10.88	10.74	10.30	10.23	10.08	10.12
Expense Ratio (%).	na	0.48	0.48	0.50	0.52	0.55	0.58	0.60	0.64	0.67
Yield (%)	4.82	4.79	5.08	4.79	5.23	5.49	6.01	6.06	6.15	6.12
Portfolio Turnover (%).	na	25	43	26	49	29	20	40	47	52
Total Assets (Millions $). . .	443	426	393	468	329	260	203	181	163	140

PORTFOLIO (as of 9/30/96)

Portfolio Manager: David MacEwen - 1991

Investm't Category: Tax-Exempt Bond
- ✔ Domestic
- Foreign
- Asset Allocation
- Index
- Sector
- ✔ State Specific

Investment Style
- Large-Cap Growth
- Mid-Cap Growth
- Small-Cap Growth
- Large-Cap Value
- Mid-Cap Value
- Small-Cap Value

Portfolio
2.9% cash	0.0% corp bonds
0.0% stocks	0.0% gov't bonds
0.0% preferred	97.1% muni bonds
0.0% conv't/warrants	0.0% other

SHAREHOLDER INFORMATION

Minimum Investment
Initial: $5,000   Subsequent: $50

Minimum IRA Investment
Initial: na   Subsequent: na

Maximum Fees
Load: none   12b-1: none
Other: none

Distributions
Income: monthly   Capital Gains: Dec

Exchange Options
Number Per Year: 6   Fee: none
Telephone: yes (money market fund available)

Services
auto exchange, auto invest, auto withdraw

Benham CA Long-Term Tax-Free (BCLTX)

Tax-Exempt Bond

4500 Main St., 14th Floor
P.O. Box 418210
Kansas City, MO 64141
800-345-2021, 415-965-4222
www.americancentury.com

PERFORMANCE

fund inception date: 11/9/83

	3yr Annual	5yr Annual	10yr Annual	Bull	Bear
Return (%)	5.0	7.3	7.0	22.2	-6.5
Differ from Category (+/-)	0.8 high	0.9 high	0.3 av	3.8 high	-1.1 blw av

Total Risk	Standard Deviation	Category Risk	Risk Index	Avg Mat
blw av	6.2%	abv av	1.1	18.9 yrs

	1996	1995	1994	1993	1992	1991	1990	1989	1988	1987
Return (%)	3.5	19.7	-6.6	13.7	8.1	11.7	6.7	9.7	10.4	-4.6
Differ from Category (+/-)	-0.2	4.5	-1.3	1.9	-0.2	0.3	0.3	0.7	0.4	-3.2
Return, Tax-Adjusted (%)	3.4	19.7	-6.8	12.6	7.4	11.7	6.7	9.7	10.4	-4.6

PER SHARE DATA

	1996	1995	1994	1993	1992	1991	1990	1989	1988	1987
Dividends, Net Income ($)	0.61	0.61	0.61	0.65	0.68	0.69	0.71	0.72	0.73	0.75
Distrib'ns, Cap Gain ($)	0.01	0.00	0.05	0.43	0.27	0.00	0.00	0.00	0.00	0.00
Net Asset Value ($)	11.32	11.56	10.21	11.63	11.21	11.28	10.75	10.78	10.51	10.21
Expense Ratio (%)	na	0.49	0.48	0.49	0.52	0.55	0.57	0.58	0.63	0.65
Yield (%)	5.38	5.27	5.94	5.38	5.92	6.11	6.60	6.67	6.94	7.34
Portfolio Turnover (%)	na	59	61	55	72	38	74	78	35	82
Total Assets (Millions $)	302	295	249	323	291	260	227	201	160	157

PORTFOLIO (as of 9/30/96)

Portfolio Manager: David MacEwen - 1991

Investm't Category: Tax-Exempt Bond
- ✔ Domestic
- Foreign
- Asset Allocation
- Index
- Sector
- ✔ State Specific

Investment Style
- Large-Cap Growth
- Mid-Cap Growth
- Small-Cap Growth
- Large-Cap Value
- Mid-Cap Value
- Small-Cap Value

Portfolio
- 6.4% cash
- 0.0% stocks
- 0.0% preferred
- 0.0% conv't/warrants
- 0.0% corp bonds
- 0.0% gov't bonds
- 93.6% muni bonds
- 0.0% other

SHAREHOLDER INFORMATION

Minimum Investment
Initial: $5,000   Subsequent: $50

Minimum IRA Investment
Initial: na   Subsequent: na

Maximum Fees
Load: none   12b-1: none
Other: none

Distributions
Income: monthly   Capital Gains: Dec

Exchange Options
Number Per Year: 6   Fee: none
Telephone: yes (money market fund available)

Services
auto exchange, auto invest, auto withdraw

Benham CA Ltd-Term Tax-Free (BCSTX)

Tax-Exempt Bond

4500 Main St., 14th Floor
P.O. Box 418210
Kansas City, MO 64141
800-345-2021, 415-965-4222
www.americancentury.com

PERFORMANCE

fund inception date: 6/1/92

	3yr Annual	5yr Annual	10yr Annual	Bull	Bear
Return (%)	3.8	na	na	12.7	-1.4
Differ from Category (+/-)	-0.4 blw av	na	na	-5.7 low	4.0 high

Total Risk	Standard Deviation	Category Risk	Risk Index	Avg Mat
low	1.8%	low	0.3	2.9 yrs

	1996	1995	1994	1993	1992	1991	1990	1989	1988	1987
Return (%)	3.9	8.3	-0.7	5.9	—	—	—	—	—	—
Differ from Category (+/-)	0.2	-6.9	4.6	-5.9	—	—	—	—	—	—
Return, Tax-Adjusted (%)	3.9	8.3	-0.7	5.8	—	—	—	—	—	—

PER SHARE DATA

	1996	1995	1994	1993	1992	1991	1990	1989	1988	1987
Dividends, Net Income ($)	0.43	0.42	0.38	0.37	—	—	—	—	—	—
Distrib'ns, Cap Gain ($)	0.00	0.00	0.00	0.03	—	—	—	—	—	—
Net Asset Value ($)	10.25	10.29	9.90	10.35	—	—	—	—	—	—
Expense Ratio (%)	na	0.51	0.51	0.36	—	—	—	—	—	—
Yield (%)	4.19	4.08	3.83	3.56	—	—	—	—	—	—
Portfolio Turnover (%)	na	49	65	54	—	—	—	—	—	—
Total Assets (Millions $)	108	100	106	125	—	—	—	—	—	—

PORTFOLIO (as of 9/30/96)

Portfolio Manager: David MacEwen - 1992

Investm't Category: Tax-Exempt Bond

✔ Domestic	Index
Foreign	Sector
Asset Allocation	✔ State Specific

Investment Style

Large-Cap Growth	Large-Cap Value
Mid-Cap Growth	Mid-Cap Value
Small-Cap Growth	Small-Cap Value

Portfolio

23.3% cash	0.0% corp bonds
0.0% stocks	0.0% gov't bonds
0.0% preferred	76.7% muni bonds
0.0% conv't/warrants	0.0% other

SHAREHOLDER INFORMATION

Minimum Investment
Initial: $5,000   Subsequent: $50

Minimum IRA Investment
Initial: na   Subsequent: na

Maximum Fees
Load: none   12b-1: none
Other: none

Distributions
Income: monthly   Capital Gains: Dec

Exchange Options
Number Per Year: 6   Fee: none
Telephone: yes (money market fund available)

Services
auto exchange, auto invest, auto withdraw

Benham European Gov't Bond (BEGBX)

International Bond

4500 Main St., 14th Floor
P.O. Box 418210
Kansas City, MO 64141
800-345-2021, 415-965-4222
www.americancentury.com

PERFORMANCE

fund inception date: 1/7/92

	3yr Annual	5yr Annual	10yr Annual	Bull	Bear
Return (%)	10.3	na	na	34.3	-1.1
Differ from Category (+/-)	4.3 high	na	na	3.1 abv av	8.4 high

Total Risk	Standard Deviation	Category Risk	Risk Index	Avg Mat
av	7.0%	abv av	1.0	5.5 yrs

	1996	1995	1994	1993	1992	1991	1990	1989	1988	1987
Return (%)	6.3	24.4	1.5	11.7	—	—	—	—	—	—
Differ from Category (+/-)	-5.0	8.4	9.1	-3.6	—	—	—	—	—	—
Return, Tax-Adjusted (%)	3.5	20.9	-0.8	10.5	—	—	—	—	—	—

PER SHARE DATA

	1996	1995	1994	1993	1992	1991	1990	1989	1988	1987
Dividends, Net Income ($)	0.72	0.90	0.60	0.11	—	—	—	—	—	—
Distrib'ns, Cap Gain ($)	0.15	0.00	0.01	0.26	—	—	—	—	—	—
Net Asset Value ($)	11.79	11.95	10.36	10.82	—	—	—	—	—	—
Expense Ratio (%)	na	0.82	0.86	0.85	—	—	—	—	—	—
Yield (%)	6.03	7.53	5.78	0.99	—	—	—	—	—	—
Portfolio Turnover (%)	na	167	166	310	—	—	—	—	—	—
Total Assets (Millions $)	253	252	193	356	—	—	—	—	—	—

PORTFOLIO (as of 6/30/96)

Portfolio Manager: Robert Brown - 1994

Investm't Category: International Bond
Domestic	Index
✔ Foreign	Sector
Asset Allocation	State Specific

Investment Style
Large-Cap Growth	Large-Cap Value
Mid-Cap Growth	Mid-Cap Value
Small-Cap Growth	Small-Cap Value

Portfolio
12.4% cash	0.0% corp bonds
0.0% stocks	0.0% gov't bonds
0.0% preferred	0.0% muni bonds
0.0% conv't/warrants	87.6% other

SHAREHOLDER INFORMATION

Minimum Investment
Initial: $2,500   Subsequent: $100

Minimum IRA Investment
Initial: $1,000   Subsequent: $100

Maximum Fees
Load: none   12b-1: none
Other: none

Distributions
Income: quarterly   Capital Gains: Dec

Exchange Options
Number Per Year: 6   Fee: none
Telephone: yes (money market fund available)

Services
IRA, pension, auto exchange, auto invest, auto withdraw

Benham GNMA (BGNMX)

Mortgage-Backed Bond

4500 Main St., 14th Floor
P.O. Box 418210
Kansas City, MO 64141
800-345-2021, 415-965-4222
www.americancentury.com

PERFORMANCE

fund inception date: 9/23/85

	3yr Annual	5yr Annual	10yr Annual	Bull	Bear
Return (%)	6.2	6.5	8.3	23.3	-3.6
Differ from Category (+/-)	0.6 abv av	0.5 high	0.6 high	2.2 abv av	0.0 av

Total Risk	Standard Deviation	Category Risk	Risk Index	Avg Mat
low	3.8%	av	1.0	na

	1996	1995	1994	1993	1992	1991	1990	1989	1988	1987
Return (%).	5.2	15.8	-1.7	6.5	7.6	15.5	10.1	13.8	8.5	2.7
Differ from Category (+/-). .	0.8	1.1	0.0	-0.4	1.4	1.1	0.3	1.2	1.1	0.7
Return, Tax-Adjusted (%). . .	2.5	12.8	-4.2	3.9	4.6	12.1	6.6	10.1	4.9	-0.8

PER SHARE DATA

	1996	1995	1994	1993	1992	1991	1990	1989	1988	1987
Dividends, Net Income ($).	0.71	0.74	0.67	0.70	0.81	0.86	0.89	0.90	0.88	0.87
Distrib'ns, Cap Gain ($) . .	0.00	0.00	0.00	0.01	0.00	0.00	0.00	0.00	0.00	0.06
Net Asset Value ($)	10.49	10.68	9.90	10.76	10.78	10.80	10.15	10.08	9.69	9.76
Expense Ratio (%).	0.58	0.58	0.54	0.56	0.62	0.72	0.75	0.75	0.73	0.74
Yield (%)	6.76	6.92	6.76	6.49	7.51	7.96	8.76	8.92	9.08	8.85
Portfolio Turnover (%). . . .	63	119	48	70	97	207	433	497	497	566
Total Assets (Millions $).	1,142	1,111	952	1,260	997	702	353	281	257	245

PORTFOLIO (as of 6/30/96)

Portfolio Manager: Casey Colton, Jeffrey R. Tyler - 1994

Investm't Category: Mortgage-Backed Bond
- ✔ Domestic
- Foreign
- Asset Allocation
- Index
- Sector
- State Specific

Investment Style
- Large-Cap Growth
- Mid-Cap Growth
- Small-Cap Growth
- Large-Cap Value
- Mid-Cap Value
- Small-Cap Value

Portfolio
5.2% cash	0.0% corp bonds
0.0% stocks	94.8% gov't bonds
0.0% preferred	0.0% muni bonds
0.0% conv't/warrants	0.0% other

SHAREHOLDER INFORMATION

Minimum Investment
Initial: $2,500   Subsequent: $50

Minimum IRA Investment
Initial: $1,000   Subsequent: $50

Maximum Fees
Load: none   12b-1: none
Other: none

Distributions
Income: monthly   Capital Gains: Dec

Exchange Options
Number Per Year: 6   Fee: none
Telephone: yes (money market fund available)

Services
IRA, pension, auto exchange, auto invest, auto withdraw

Benham Interm-Term Tax-Exempt (TWTIX)

Tax-Exempt Bond

4500 Main St., 14th Floor
P.O. Box 418210
Kansas City, MO 64141
800-345-2021, 816-531-5575
www.americancentury.com

PERFORMANCE

fund inception date: 3/2/87

	3yr Annual	5yr Annual	10yr Annual	Bull	Bear
Return (%)	4.4	5.8	na	16.8	-3.5
Differ from Category (+/-)	0.2 av	-0.6 low	na	-1.6 blw av	1.9 high

Total Risk	Standard Deviation	Category Risk	Risk Index	Avg Mat
low	3.6%	low	0.6	7.3 yrs

	1996	1995	1994	1993	1992	1991	1990	1989	1988	1987
Return (%)	3.9	11.9	-2.1	9.0	7.1	10.0	6.2	6.6	6.0	—
Differ from Category (+/-)	0.2	-3.3	3.2	-2.8	-1.2	-1.4	-0.2	-2.4	-4.0	—
Return, Tax-Adjusted (%)	3.8	11.7	-2.4	8.6	6.9	10.0	6.2	6.6	6.0	—

PER SHARE DATA

	1996	1995	1994	1993	1992	1991	1990	1989	1988	1987
Dividends, Net Income ($)	0.48	0.48	0.47	0.47	0.47	0.52	0.56	0.56	0.54	—
Distrib'ns, Cap Gain ($)	0.02	0.07	0.08	0.13	0.07	0.00	0.00	0.00	0.00	—
Net Asset Value ($)	10.37	10.48	9.88	10.66	10.35	10.19	9.76	9.73	9.67	—
Expense Ratio (%)	na	0.60	0.60	0.72	0.98	0.96	1.00	1.00	1.00	—
Yield (%)	4.61	4.54	4.71	4.35	4.50	5.10	5.73	5.75	5.58	—
Portfolio Turnover (%)	na	32	74	38	36	62	102	74	86	—
Total Assets (Millions $)	80	81	76	97	78	50	26	21	15	—

PORTFOLIO (as of 9/30/96)

Portfolio Manager: committee - 1995

Investm't Category: Tax-Exempt Bond
✔ Domestic   Index
  Foreign   Sector
  Asset Allocation State Specific

Investment Style
  Large-Cap Growth   Large-Cap Value
  Mid-Cap Growth   Mid-Cap Value
  Small-Cap Growth   Small-Cap Value

Portfolio
  4.3% cash   0.0% corp bonds
  0.0% stocks   0.0% gov't bonds
  0.0% preferred   95.7% muni bonds
  0.0% conv't/warrants 0.0% other

SHAREHOLDER INFORMATION

Minimum Investment
Initial: $5,000   Subsequent: $50

Minimum IRA Investment
Initial: na   Subsequent: na

Maximum Fees
Load: none   12b-1: none
Other: none

Distributions
Income: monthly   Capital Gains: Dec

Exchange Options
Number Per Year: 6   Fee: none
Telephone: yes (money market fund available)

Services
auto exchange, auto invest, auto withdraw

Benham Interm-Term Tax-Free (BNTIX)

Tax-Exempt Bond

4500 Main St., 14th Floor
P.O. Box 418210
Kansas City, MO 64141
800-345-2021, 415-965-4222
www.americancentury.com

PERFORMANCE

fund inception date: 7/31/84

	3yr Annual	5yr Annual	10yr Annual	Bull	Bear
Return (%)	4.1	5.9	6.5	16.4	-4.2
Differ from Category (+/-)	-0.1 blw av	-0.5 blw av	-0.2 blw av	-2.0 blw av	1.2 abv av

Total Risk	Standard Deviation	Category Risk	Risk Index	Avg Mat
low	3.8%	low	0.7	7.1 yrs

	1996	1995	1994	1993	1992	1991	1990	1989	1988	1987
Return (%).	3.8	12.7	-3.5	10.1	7.1	11.6	6.8	8.2	6.6	2.2
Differ from Category (+/-). .	0.1	-2.5	1.8	-1.7	-1.2	0.2	0.4	-0.8	-3.4	3.6
Return, Tax-Adjusted (%). . .	3.8	12.7	-3.6	9.8	6.8	11.2	6.8	8.2	6.6	2.2

PER SHARE DATA

	1996	1995	1994	1993	1992	1991	1990	1989	1988	1987
Dividends, Net Income ($).	0.52	0.51	0.49	0.51	0.53	0.58	0.61	0.61	0.63	0.63
Distrib'ns, Cap Gain ($) . . .	0.00	0.00	0.03	0.11	0.10	0.11	0.00	0.00	0.00	0.00
Net Asset Value ($)	10.83	10.95	10.19	11.11	10.67	10.58	10.14	10.10	9.92	9.91
Expense Ratio (%).	0.70	0.66	0.67	0.72	0.65	0.50	0.50	0.50	0.50	0.50
Yield (%)	4.80	4.65	4.79	4.54	4.92	5.42	6.01	6.03	6.35	6.35
Portfolio Turnover (%).	45	47	46	36	85	55	142	49	54	26
Total Assets (Millions $). . . .	64	64	62	78	55	42	28	23	21	22

PORTFOLIO (as of 9/30/96)

Portfolio Manager: David MacEwen - 1991

Investm't Category: Tax-Exempt Bond
- ✔ Domestic
- Foreign
- Asset Allocation
- Index
- Sector
- State Specific

Investment Style
- Large-Cap Growth
- Mid-Cap Growth
- Small-Cap Growth
- Large-Cap Value
- Mid-Cap Value
- Small-Cap Value

Portfolio
- 0.8% cash
- 0.0% stocks
- 0.0% preferred
- 0.0% conv't/warrants
- 0.0% corp bonds
- 0.0% gov't bonds
- 99.2% muni bonds
- 0.0% other

SHAREHOLDER INFORMATION

Minimum Investment
Initial: $5,000   Subsequent: $50

Minimum IRA Investment
Initial: na   Subsequent: na

Maximum Fees
Load: none   12b-1: none
Other: none

Distributions
Income: monthly   Capital Gains: Dec

Exchange Options
Number Per Year: 6   Fee: none
Telephone: yes (money market fund available)

Services
auto exchange, auto invest, auto withdraw

Benham Interm-Term Treasury (CPTNX)

Government Bond

4500 Main St., 14th Floor
P.O. Box 418210
Kansas City, MO 64141
800-345-2021, 415-965-4222
www.americancentury.com

PERFORMANCE

fund inception date: 5/16/80

	3yr Annual	5yr Annual	10yr Annual	Bull	Bear
Return (%)	4.9	5.8	6.7	18.8	-3.8
Differ from Category (+/-)	0.0 av	-0.8 blw av	-1.3 blw av	-3.2 av	2.6 av

Total Risk	Standard Deviation	Category Risk	Risk Index	Avg Mat
low	3.5%	blw av	0.9	5.4 yrs

	1996	1995	1994	1993	1992	1991	1990	1989	1988	1987
Return (%)	4.0	13.7	-2.4	7.9	6.5	13.7	9.2	11.9	5.2	-1.1
Differ from Category (+/-)	2.5	-5.9	2.0	-3.7	-0.2	-2.0	2.9	-3.4	-3.1	3.3
Return, Tax-Adjusted (%)	1.8	11.3	-4.3	5.3	3.1	10.9	6.2	8.7	2.2	-4.2

PER SHARE DATA

	1996	1995	1994	1993	1992	1991	1990	1989	1988	1987
Dividends, Net Income ($)	0.57	0.58	0.50	0.49	0.59	0.71	0.75	0.77	0.74	0.72
Distrib'ns, Cap Gain ($)	0.00	0.00	0.00	0.27	0.47	0.00	0.00	0.00	0.00	0.18
Net Asset Value ($)	10.31	10.48	9.76	10.51	10.46	10.85	10.22	10.09	9.74	9.97
Expense Ratio (%)	0.53	0.53	0.51	0.53	0.59	0.73	0.75	0.75	0.75	0.93
Yield (%)	5.52	5.53	5.12	4.54	5.39	6.54	7.33	7.63	7.59	7.09
Portfolio Turnover (%)	167	92	212	299	149	70	217	386	465	396
Total Assets (Millions $)	341	307	296	388	360	300	129	95	66	42

PORTFOLIO (as of 9/30/96)

Portfolio Manager: Schroeder, Colton, Rankin - 1992

Investm't Category: Government Bond
- ✔ Domestic
- Foreign
- Asset Allocation
- Index
- Sector
- State Specific

Investment Style
- Large-Cap Growth
- Mid-Cap Growth
- Small-Cap Growth
- Large-Cap Value
- Mid-Cap Value
- Small-Cap Value

Portfolio
- 1.1% cash
- 0.0% stocks
- 0.0% preferred
- 0.0% conv't/warrants
- 0.0% corp bonds
- 98.9% gov't bonds
- 0.0% muni bonds
- 0.0% other

SHAREHOLDER INFORMATION

Minimum Investment
Initial: $2,500   Subsequent: $50

Minimum IRA Investment
Initial: $1,000   Subsequent: $50

Maximum Fees
Load: none   12b-1: none
Other: none

Distributions
Income: monthly   Capital Gains: Dec

Exchange Options
Number Per Year: 6   Fee: none
Telephone: yes (money market fund available)

Services
IRA, pension, auto exchange, auto invest, auto withdraw

Benham Long-Term Tax-Exempt (TWTLX)

Tax-Exempt Bond

4500 Main St., 14th Floor
P.O. Box 418210
Kansas City, MO 64141
800-345-2021, 816-531-5575
www.americancentury.com

PERFORMANCE

fund inception date: 3/2/87

	3yr Annual	5yr Annual	10yr Annual	Bull	Bear
Return (%)	4.8	6.8	na	21.2	-5.9
Differ from Category (+/-)	0.6 abv av	0.4 av	na	2.8 high	-0.5 av

Total Risk	Standard Deviation	Category Risk	Risk Index	Avg Mat
blw av	5.6%	av	1.0	16.9 yrs

	1996	1995	1994	1993	1992	1991	1990	1989	1988	1987
Return (%)	3.1	18.4	-5.6	12.1	7.6	11.1	6.1	9.5	10.3	—
Differ from Category (+/-)	-0.6	3.2	-0.3	0.3	-0.7	-0.3	-0.3	0.5	0.3	—
Return, Tax-Adjusted (%)	3.1	18.4	-5.8	11.1	7.1	11.1	6.1	9.2	10.3	—

PER SHARE DATA

	1996	1995	1994	1993	1992	1991	1990	1989	1988	1987
Dividends, Net Income ($)	0.53	0.53	0.51	0.52	0.52	0.56	0.60	0.62	0.60	—
Distrib'ns, Cap Gain ($)	0.00	0.00	0.04	0.34	0.16	0.00	0.00	0.09	0.00	—
Net Asset Value ($)	10.63	10.85	9.64	10.80	10.43	10.35	9.86	9.88	9.70	—
Expense Ratio (%)	na	0.59	0.60	0.73	0.98	0.96	1.00	1.00	1.00	—
Yield (%)	4.98	4.88	5.26	4.66	4.90	5.40	6.08	6.21	6.18	—
Portfolio Turnover (%)	na	61	66	81	88	110	144	120	215	—
Total Assets (Millions $)	61	59	49	68	62	41	29	21	13	—

PORTFOLIO (as of 9/30/96)

Portfolio Manager: committee - 1995

Investm't Category: Tax-Exempt Bond

✔ Domestic	Index
Foreign	Sector
Asset Allocation	State Specific

Investment Style

Large-Cap Growth	Large-Cap Value
Mid-Cap Growth	Mid-Cap Value
Small-Cap Growth	Small-Cap Value

Portfolio

3.4% cash	0.0% corp bonds
0.0% stocks	0.0% gov't bonds
0.0% preferred	96.6% muni bonds
0.0% conv't/warrants	0.0% other

SHAREHOLDER INFORMATION

Minimum Investment
Initial: $5,000   Subsequent: $50

Minimum IRA Investment
Initial: na   Subsequent: na

Maximum Fees
Load: none   12b-1: none
Other: none

Distributions
Income: monthly   Capital Gains: Dec

Exchange Options
Number Per Year: 6   Fee: none
Telephone: yes (money market fund available)

Services
auto exchange, auto invest, auto withdraw

Benham Long-Term Tax-Free (BTFLX)

Tax-Exempt Bond

4500 Main St., 14th Floor
P.O. Box 418210
Kansas City, MO 64141
800-345-2021, 415-965-4222
www.americancentury.com

PERFORMANCE

fund inception date: 7/31/84

	3yr Annual	5yr Annual	10yr Annual	Bull	Bear
Return (%)	4.1	7.1	6.7	19.5	-6.6
Differ from Category (+/-)	-0.1 blw av	0.7 abv av	0.0 blw av	1.1 av	-1.2 blw av

Total Risk	Standard Deviation	Category Risk	Risk Index	Avg Mat
blw av	5.8%	abv av	1.0	17.2 yrs

	1996	1995	1994	1993	1992	1991	1990	1989	1988	1987
Return (%)	2.2	17.7	-6.2	14.2	9.2	12.8	6.6	9.6	11.1	-6.8
Differ from Category (+/-)	-1.5	2.5	-0.9	2.4	0.9	1.4	0.2	0.6	1.1	-5.4
Return, Tax-Adjusted (%)	2.2	17.7	-6.4	13.6	8.4	12.2	6.3	9.4	11.1	-6.8

PER SHARE DATA

	1996	1995	1994	1993	1992	1991	1990	1989	1988	1987
Dividends, Net Income ($)	0.60	0.61	0.60	0.62	0.64	0.68	0.72	0.73	0.76	0.79
Distrib'ns, Cap Gain ($)	0.00	0.00	0.05	0.24	0.29	0.23	0.09	0.04	0.00	0.00
Net Asset Value ($)	11.58	11.93	10.70	12.10	11.38	11.31	10.88	11.00	10.78	10.41
Expense Ratio (%)	0.70	0.66	0.67	0.72	0.65	0.50	0.50	0.50	0.50	0.50
Yield (%)	5.18	5.11	5.58	5.02	5.48	5.89	6.56	6.61	7.05	7.58
Portfolio Turnover (%)	49	34	39	105	148	150	215	69	76	102
Total Assets (Millions $)	56	56	45	66	46	42	32	37	29	25

PORTFOLIO (as of 9/30/96)

Portfolio Manager: David MacEwen - 1991

Investm't Category: Tax-Exempt Bond
- ✔ Domestic
- Foreign
- Asset Allocation
- Index
- Sector
- State Specific

Investment Style
- Large-Cap Growth
- Mid-Cap Growth
- Small-Cap Growth
- Large-Cap Value
- Mid-Cap Value
- Small-Cap Value

Portfolio
- 3.3% cash
- 0.0% stocks
- 0.0% preferred
- 0.0% conv't/warrants
- 0.0% corp bonds
- 0.0% gov't bonds
- 96.7% muni bonds
- 0.0% other

SHAREHOLDER INFORMATION

Minimum Investment
Initial: $5,000   Subsequent: $50

Minimum IRA Investment
Initial: na   Subsequent: na

Maximum Fees
Load: none   12b-1: none
Other: none

Distributions
Income: monthly   Capital Gains: Dec

Exchange Options
Number Per Year: 6   Fee: none
Telephone: yes (money market fund available)

Services
auto exchange, auto invest, auto withdraw

Benham Long-Term Treasury (BLAGX)

Government Bond

4500 Main St., 14th Floor
P.O. Box 418210
Kansas City, MO 64141
800-345-2021, 415-965-4222
www.americancentury.com

PERFORMANCE

fund inception date: 9/8/92

	3yr Annual	5yr Annual	10yr Annual	Bull	Bear
Return (%)	4.9	na	na	28.6	-12.3
Differ from Category (+/-)	0.0 av	na	na	6.6 high	-5.9 low

Total Risk	Standard Deviation	Category Risk	Risk Index	Avg Mat
av	9.2%	high	2.3	21.3 yrs

	1996	1995	1994	1993	1992	1991	1990	1989	1988	1987
Return (%).	-1.4	29.2	-9.3	17.6	—	—	—	—	—	—
Differ from Category (+/-) .	-2.9	9.6	-4.9	6.0	—	—	—	—	—	—
Return, Tax-Adjusted (%). .	-3.7	26.4	-11.6	13.2	—	—	—	—	—	—

PER SHARE DATA

	1996	1995	1994	1993	1992	1991	1990	1989	1988	1987
Dividends, Net Income ($).	0.60	0.60	0.59	0.65	—	—	—	—	—	—
Distrib'ns, Cap Gain ($) . .	0.00	0.00	0.00	0.59	—	—	—	—	—	—
Net Asset Value ($)	9.78	10.55	8.69	10.22	—	—	—	—	—	—
Expense Ratio (%).	0.67	0.67	0.57	0.00	—	—	—	—	—	—
Yield (%)	6.13	5.68	6.78	6.01	—	—	—	—	—	—
Portfolio Turnover (%). . . .	112	146	200	56	—	—	—	—	—	—
Total Assets (Millions $). . .	127	104	28	23	—	—	—	—	—	—

PORTFOLIO (as of 9/30/96)

Portfolio Manager: Schroeder, Colton, Rankin - 1992

Investm't Category: Government Bond
- ✔ Domestic
- Foreign
- Asset Allocation
- Index
- Sector
- State Specific

Investment Style
- Large-Cap Growth
- Mid-Cap Growth
- Small-Cap Growth
- Large-Cap Value
- Mid-Cap Value
- Small-Cap Value

Portfolio
1.2% cash	0.0% corp bonds
0.0% stocks	98.8% gov't bonds
0.0% preferred	0.0% muni bonds
0.0% conv't/warrants	0.0% other

SHAREHOLDER INFORMATION

Minimum Investment
Initial: $2,500   Subsequent: $50

Minimum IRA Investment
Initial: $1,000   Subsequent: $50

Maximum Fees
Load: none   12b-1: none
Other: none

Distributions
Income: monthly   Capital Gains: Dec

Exchange Options
Number Per Year: 6   Fee: none
Telephone: yes (money market fund available)

Services
IRA, pension, auto exchange, auto invest, auto withdraw

Benham Ltd-Term Tax-Exempt (TWTSX)

Tax-Exempt Bond

4500 Main St., 14th Floor
P.O. Box 418210
Kansas City, MO 64141
800-345-2021, 816-531-5575
www.americancentury.com

PERFORMANCE

fund inception date: 3/1/93

	3yr Annual	5yr Annual	10yr Annual	Bull	Bear
Return (%)	4.2	na	na	12.5	0.2
Differ from Category (+/-)	0.0 av	na	na	-5.9 low	5.6 high

Total Risk	Standard Deviation	Category Risk	Risk Index	Avg Mat
low	1.0%	low	0.2	2.3 yrs

	1996	1995	1994	1993	1992	1991	1990	1989	1988	1987
Return (%)	3.7	6.7	2.4	—	—	—	—	—	—	—
Differ from Category (+/-)	0.0	-8.5	7.7	—	—	—	—	—	—	—
Return, Tax-Adjusted (%)	3.7	6.7	2.4	—	—	—	—	—	—	—

PER SHARE DATA

	1996	1995	1994	1993	1992	1991	1990	1989	1988	1987
Dividends, Net Income ($)	0.42	0.44	0.37	—	—	—	—	—	—	—
Distrib'ns, Cap Gain ($)	0.00	0.00	0.00	—	—	—	—	—	—	—
Net Asset Value ($)	10.08	10.14	9.93	—	—	—	—	—	—	—
Expense Ratio (%)	na	0.60	0.00	—	—	—	—	—	—	—
Yield (%)	4.16	4.33	3.72	—	—	—	—	—	—	—
Portfolio Turnover (%)	na	78	42	—	—	—	—	—	—	—
Total Assets (Millions $)	50	58	61	—	—	—	—	—	—	—

PORTFOLIO (as of 9/30/96)

Portfolio Manager: committee - 1995

Investm't Category: Tax-Exempt Bond

✔ Domestic   Index
  Foreign   Sector
  Asset Allocation   State Specific

Investment Style
  Large-Cap Growth   Large-Cap Value
  Mid-Cap Growth   Mid-Cap Value
  Small-Cap Growth   Small-Cap Value

Portfolio

23.0%	cash	0.0%	corp bonds
0.0%	stocks	0.0%	gov't bonds
0.0%	preferred	77.1%	muni bonds
0.0%	conv't/warrants	0.0%	other

SHAREHOLDER INFORMATION

Minimum Investment
Initial: $5,000   Subsequent: $50

Minimum IRA Investment
Initial: na   Subsequent: na

Maximum Fees
Load: none   12b-1: none
Other: none

Distributions
Income: monthly   Capital Gains: Dec

Exchange Options
Number Per Year: 6   Fee: none
Telephone: yes (money market fund available)

Services
auto exchange, auto invest, auto withdraw

Benham Short-Term Gov't (TWUSX)

Government Bond

4500 Main St., 14th Floor
P.O. Box 418210
Kansas City, MO 64141
800-345-2021, 816-531-5575
www.americancentury.com

PERFORMANCE

fund inception date: 12/15/82

	3yr Annual	5yr Annual	10yr Annual	Bull	Bear
Return (%)	4.6	4.4	6.0	16.1	-2.1
Differ from Category (+/-)	-0.3 blw av	-2.2 low	-2.0 low	-5.9 low	4.3 abv av

Total Risk	Standard Deviation	Category Risk	Risk Index	Avg Mat
low	2.0%	low	0.5	2.0 yrs

	1996	1995	1994	1993	1992	1991	1990	1989	1988	1987
Return (%)	4.1	10.4	-0.5	4.1	4.3	11.6	7.5	9.9	5.6	3.8
Differ from Category (+/-)	2.6	-9.2	3.9	-7.5	-2.4	-4.1	1.2	-5.4	-2.7	8.2
Return, Tax-Adjusted (%)	1.9	8.1	-2.4	2.7	2.5	9.0	4.1	6.3	2.1	3.4

PER SHARE DATA

	1996	1995	1994	1993	1992	1991	1990	1989	1988	1987
Dividends, Net Income ($)	0.51	0.51	0.44	0.33	0.42	0.59	0.78	0.82	0.82	0.79
Distrib'ns, Cap Gain ($)	0.00	0.00	0.00	0.00	0.00	0.00	0.00	0.00	0.00	0.12
Net Asset Value ($)	9.45	9.58	9.16	9.65	9.59	9.60	9.17	9.29	9.24	9.53
Expense Ratio (%)	na	0.70	0.81	1.00	0.99	0.99	1.00	1.00	1.00	1.00
Yield (%)	5.39	5.32	4.80	3.41	4.37	6.14	8.50	8.82	8.87	8.18
Portfolio Turnover (%)	na	128	470	413	391	779	620	567	578	468
Total Assets (Millions $)	347	390	382	493	538	557	472	447	424	355

PORTFOLIO (as of 9/30/96)

Portfolio Manager: Bud Hoops, Robert Gahagan - 1989

Investm't Category: Government Bond

✔ Domestic   Index
  Foreign   Sector
  Asset Allocation State Specific

Investment Style

Large-Cap Growth   Large-Cap Value
Mid-Cap Growth   Mid-Cap Value
Small-Cap Growth   Small-Cap Value

Portfolio

17.5% cash	0.0% corp bonds
0.0% stocks	82.5% gov't bonds
0.0% preferred	0.0% muni bonds
0.0% conv't/warrants	0.0% other

SHAREHOLDER INFORMATION

Minimum Investment
Initial: $2,500   Subsequent: $50

Minimum IRA Investment
Initial: $1,000   Subsequent: $50

Maximum Fees
Load: none   12b-1: none
Other: none

Distributions
Income: monthly   Capital Gains: Dec

Exchange Options
Number Per Year: 6   Fee: none
Telephone: yes (money market fund available)

Services
IRA, pension, auto exchange, auto invest, auto withdraw

Benham Short-Term Treasury (BSTAX)

Government Bond

4500 Main St., 14th Floor
P.O. Box 418210
Kansas City, MO 64141
800-345-2021, 415-965-4222
www.americancentury.com

PERFORMANCE

fund inception date: 9/8/92

	3yr Annual	5yr Annual	10yr Annual	Bull	Bear
Return (%)	4.4	na	na	14.6	-1.2
Differ from Category (+/-)	-0.5 low	na	na	-7.4 low	5.2 high

Total Risk	Standard Deviation	Category Risk	Risk Index	Avg Mat
low	1.9%	low	0.5	1.9 yrs

	1996	1995	1994	1993	1992	1991	1990	1989	1988	1987
Return (%)	3.5	9.9	0.1	5.3	—	—	—	—	—	—
Differ from Category (+/-)	2.0	-9.7	4.5	-6.3	—	—	—	—	—	—
Return, Tax-Adjusted (%)	1.3	7.6	-1.7	3.6	—	—	—	—	—	—

PER SHARE DATA

	1996	1995	1994	1993	1992	1991	1990	1989	1988	1987
Dividends, Net Income ($)	0.51	0.54	0.44	0.38	—	—	—	—	—	—
Distrib'ns, Cap Gain ($)	0.03	0.00	0.00	0.03	—	—	—	—	—	—
Net Asset Value ($)	9.75	9.95	9.57	10.00	—	—	—	—	—	—
Expense Ratio (%)	0.67	0.67	0.58	0.00	—	—	—	—	—	—
Yield (%)	5.21	5.42	4.59	3.78	—	—	—	—	—	—
Portfolio Turnover (%)	224	140	261	157	—	—	—	—	—	—
Total Assets (Millions $)	35	37	30	23	—	—	—	—	—	—

PORTFOLIO (as of 9/30/96)

Portfolio Manager: Robert V. Gahagan - 1996

Investm't Category: Government Bond
- ✔ Domestic
-   Index
-   Foreign
-   Sector
-   Asset Allocation
-   State Specific

Investment Style
- Large-Cap Growth
- Large-Cap Value
- Mid-Cap Growth
- Mid-Cap Value
- Small-Cap Growth
- Small-Cap Value

Portfolio

21.3% cash	0.0% corp bonds
0.0% stocks	78.7% gov't bonds
0.0% preferred	0.0% muni bonds
0.0% conv't/warrants	0.0% other

SHAREHOLDER INFORMATION

Minimum Investment
Initial: $2,500   Subsequent: $50

Minimum IRA Investment
Initial: $1,000   Subsequent: $50

Maximum Fees
Load: none   12b-1: none
Other: none

Distributions
Income: monthly   Capital Gains: Dec

Exchange Options
Number Per Year: 6   Fee: none
Telephone: yes (money market fund available)

Services
IRA, pension, auto exchange, auto invest, auto withdraw

Benham Target Maturities Trust: 2000 (BTMTX)

Government Bond

4500 Main St., 14th Floor
P.O. Box 418210
Kansas City, MO 64141
800-345-2021, 415-965-4222
www.americancentury.com

PERFORMANCE

fund inception date: 3/25/85

	3yr Annual	5yr Annual	10yr Annual	Bull	Bear
Return (%)	4.6	7.5	8.7	22.8	-8.5
Differ from Category (+/-)	-0.3 blw av	0.9 high	0.7 abv av	0.8 abv av	-2.1 blw av

Total Risk	Standard Deviation	Category Risk	Risk Index	Avg Mat
blw av	6.0%	abv av	1.5	4.1 yrs

	1996	1995	1994	1993	1992	1991	1990	1989	1988	1987
Return (%)	1.9	20.7	-6.9	15.4	8.4	20.6	6.3	19.8	11.4	-6.0
Differ from Category (+/-)	0.4	1.1	-2.5	3.8	1.7	4.9	0.0	4.5	3.1	-1.6
Return, Tax-Adjusted (%)	-0.6	18.3	-8.7	11.4	5.8	18.6	4.4	17.2	11.4	-8.4

PER SHARE DATA

	1996	1995	1994	1993	1992	1991	1990	1989	1988	1987
Dividends, Net Income ($)	0.00	0.00	0.00	0.00	0.00	0.00	0.00	0.00	0.00	0.00
Distrib'ns, Cap Gain ($)	0.00	0.00	0.00	0.00	0.00	0.00	0.00	0.00	0.00	0.00
Net Asset Value ($)	82.01	80.41	66.60	71.53	61.95	57.11	47.33	44.52	37.16	33.33
Expense Ratio (%)	0.53	0.63	0.59	0.60	0.66	0.66	0.70	0.70	0.70	0.70
Yield (%)	0.00	0.00	0.00	0.00	0.00	0.00	0.00	0.00	0.00	0.00
Portfolio Turnover (%)	29	52	89	76	93	67	79	49	163	73
Total Assets (Millions $)	272	299	255	286	186	95	70	48	14	6

PORTFOLIO (as of 9/30/96)

Portfolio Manager: David W. Schroeder - 1990

Investm't Category: Government Bond
- ✔ Domestic
- Foreign
- Asset Allocation
- Index
- Sector
- State Specific

Investment Style
- Large-Cap Growth
- Mid-Cap Growth
- Small-Cap Growth
- Large-Cap Value
- Mid-Cap Value
- Small-Cap Value

Portfolio
5.3% cash	0.0% corp bonds
0.0% stocks	94.7% gov't bonds
0.0% preferred	0.0% muni bonds
0.0% conv't/warrants	0.0% other

SHAREHOLDER INFORMATION

Minimum Investment
Initial: $2,500   Subsequent: $50

Minimum IRA Investment
Initial: $1,000   Subsequent: $50

Maximum Fees
Load: none   12b-1: none
Other: none

Distributions
Income: Dec   Capital Gains: Dec

Exchange Options
Number Per Year: 6   Fee: none
Telephone: yes (money market fund available)

Services
IRA, pension, auto exchange, auto invest, auto withdraw

Benham Target Maturities Trust: 2005 (BTFIX)

Government Bond

4500 Main St., 14th Floor
P.O. Box 418210
Kansas City, MO 64141
800-345-2021, 415-965-4222
www.americancentury.com

PERFORMANCE

fund inception date: 3/25/85

	3yr Annual	5yr Annual	10yr Annual	Bull	Bear
Return (%)	6.0	9.7	9.7	32.0	-12.7
Differ from Category (+/-)	1.1 high	3.1 high	1.7 high	10.0 high	-6.3 low

Total Risk	Standard Deviation	Category Risk	Risk Index	Avg Mat
abv av	10.0%	high	2.5	9.1 yrs

	1996	1995	1994	1993	1992	1991	1990	1989	1988	1987
Return (%)..............	-1.3	32.6	-9.0	21.5	9.5	21.4	3.5	23.8	14.4	-10.4
Differ from Category (+/-).	-2.8	13.0	-4.6	9.9	2.8	5.7	-2.8	8.5	6.1	-6.0
Return, Tax-Adjusted (%)..	-3.8	30.3	-11.2	13.2	6.1	18.8	2.3	21.1	14.4	-12.9

PER SHARE DATA

	1996	1995	1994	1993	1992	1991	1990	1989	1988	1987
Dividends, Net Income ($).	0.00	0.00	0.00	0.00	0.00	0.00	0.00	0.00	0.00	0.00
Distrib'ns, Cap Gain ($) ...	0.00	0.00	0.00	0.00	0.00	0.00	0.00	0.00	0.00	0.00
Net Asset Value ($)	60.35	61.11	46.07	50.57	41.60	37.97	31.26	30.18	24.36	21.28
Expense Ratio (%)........	0.58	0.71	0.64	0.62	0.63	0.70	0.70	0.70	0.70	0.70
Yield (%)	0.00	0.00	0.00	0.00	0.00	0.00	0.00	0.00	0.00	0.00
Portfolio Turnover (%).....	31	34	68	49	64	85	186	72	27	68
Total Assets (Millions $)...	252	228	101	128	167	190	75	30	8	3

PORTFOLIO (as of 9/30/96)

Portfolio Manager: David W. Schroeder - 1990

Investm't Category: Government Bond
✔ Domestic   Index
  Foreign   Sector
  Asset Allocation State Specific

Investment Style
  Large-Cap Growth   Large-Cap Value
  Mid-Cap Growth   Mid-Cap Value
  Small-Cap Growth   Small-Cap Value

Portfolio
5.3% cash   0.0% corp bonds
0.0% stocks   94.7% gov't bonds
0.0% preferred   0.0% muni bonds
0.0% conv't/warrants 0.0% other

SHAREHOLDER INFORMATION

Minimum Investment
Initial: $2,500   Subsequent: $50

Minimum IRA Investment
Initial: $1,000   Subsequent: $50

Maximum Fees
Load: none   12b-1: none
Other: none

Distributions
Income: Dec   Capital Gains: Dec

Exchange Options
Number Per Year: 6   Fee: none
Telephone: yes (money market fund available)

Services
IRA, pension, auto exchange, auto invest, auto withdraw

Benham Target Maturities Trust: 2010 (BTTNX)

Government Bond

4500 Main St., 14th Floor
P.O. Box 418210
Kansas City, MO 64141
800-345-2021, 415-965-4222
www.americancentury.com

PERFORMANCE

fund inception date: 3/25/85

	3yr Annual	5yr Annual	10yr Annual	Bull	Bear
Return (%)	6.6	10.9	9.8	40.1	-17.0
Differ from Category (+/-)	1.7 high	4.3 high	1.8 high	18.1 high	-10.6 low

Total Risk	Standard Deviation	Category Risk	Risk Index	Avg Mat
high	13.4%	high	3.3	13.9 yrs

	1996	1995	1994	1993	1992	1991	1990	1989	1988	1987
Return (%).	-3.6	42.0	-11.6	26.2	9.7	21.0	0.2	28.0	15.7	-15.3
Differ from Category (+/-). .	-5.1	22.4	-7.2	14.6	3.0	5.3	-6.1	12.7	7.4	-10.9
Return, Tax-Adjusted (%). .	-6.6	40.1	-13.5	20.1	6.1	18.9	-1.6	24.4	15.7	-16.2

PER SHARE DATA

	1996	1995	1994	1993	1992	1991	1990	1989	1988	1987
Dividends, Net Income ($)	0.00	0.00	0.00	0.00	0.00	0.00	0.00	0.00	0.00	0.00
Distrib'ns, Cap Gain ($) . .	0.00	0.00	0.00	0.00	0.00	0.00	0.00	0.00	0.00	0.00
Net Asset Value ($)	45.20	46.86	32.98	37.29	29.53	26.90	22.22	22.16	17.31	14.96
Expense Ratio (%).	0.67	0.71	0.68	0.66	0.70	0.70	0.70	0.70	0.70	0.70
Yield (%)	0.00	0.00	0.00	0.00	0.00	0.00	0.00	0.00	0.00	0.00
Portfolio Turnover (%). . . .	24	26	35	131	95	131	191	88	259	84
Total Assets (Millions $). . .	117	120	55	60	54	52	47	65	9	9

PORTFOLIO (as of 9/30/96)

Portfolio Manager: David W. Schroeder - 1990

Investm't Category: Government Bond
- ✔ Domestic
- Foreign
- Asset Allocation
- Index
- Sector
- State Specific

Investment Style
- Large-Cap Growth
- Mid-Cap Growth
- Small-Cap Growth
- Large-Cap Value
- Mid-Cap Value
- Small-Cap Value

Portfolio
- 5.3% cash
- 0.0% stocks
- 0.0% preferred
- 0.0% conv't/warrants
- 0.0% corp bonds
- 94.7% gov't bonds
- 0.0% muni bonds
- 0.0% other

SHAREHOLDER INFORMATION

Minimum Investment
Initial: $2,500   Subsequent: $50

Minimum IRA Investment
Initial: $1,000   Subsequent: $50

Maximum Fees
Load: none   12b-1: none
Other: none

Distributions
Income: Dec   Capital Gains: Dec

Exchange Options
Number Per Year: 6   Fee: none
Telephone: yes (money market fund available)

Services
IRA, pension, auto exchange, auto invest, auto withdraw

Benham Target Maturities Trust: 2015 (BTFTX)

Government Bond

4500 Main St., 14th Floor
P.O. Box 418210
Kansas City, MO 64141
800-345-2021, 415-965-4222
www.americancentury.com

PERFORMANCE

fund inception date: 9/1/86

	3yr Annual	5yr Annual	10yr Annual	Bull	Bear
Return (%)	7.2	11.6	9.2	47.3	-19.6
Differ from Category (+/-)	2.3 high	5.0 high	1.2 high	25.3 high	-13.2 low

Total Risk	Standard Deviation	Category Risk	Risk Index	Avg Mat
high	16.8%	high	4.1	19.1 yrs

	1996	1995	1994	1993	1992	1991	1990	1989	1988	1987
Return (%).............	-6.1	52.7	-14.1	30.5	7.7	22.4	-3.4	33.4	11.0	-20.2
Differ from Category (+/-).	-7.6	33.1	-9.7	18.9	1.0	6.7	-9.7	18.1	2.7	-15.8
Return, Tax-Adjusted (%)..	-8.5	48.7	-15.3	18.6	4.3	19.4	-5.6	31.8	11.0	-21.7

PER SHARE DATA

	1996	1995	1994	1993	1992	1991	1990	1989	1988	1987
Dividends, Net Income ($).	0.00	0.00	0.00	0.00	0.00	0.00	0.00	0.00	0.00	0.00
Distrib'ns, Cap Gain ($)...	0.00	0.00	0.00	0.00	0.00	0.00	0.00	0.00	0.00	0.00
Net Asset Value ($).....	34.60	36.82	24.11	28.06	21.50	19.95	16.29	16.86	12.63	11.37
Expense Ratio (%)........	0.65	0.71	0.68	0.63	0.62	0.61	0.70	0.70	0.70	0.70
Yield (%)	0.00	0.00	0.00	0.00	0.00	0.00	0.00	0.00	0.00	0.00
Portfolio Turnover (%).....	17	69	64	138	103	40	81	48	188	509
Total Assets (Millions $)...	125	140	123	74	118	212	322	318	11	2

PORTFOLIO (as of 9/30/96)

Portfolio Manager: David W. Schroeder - 1990

Investm't Category: Government Bond

✔ Domestic	Index
Foreign	Sector
Asset Allocation	State Specific

Investment Style

Large-Cap Growth	Large-Cap Value
Mid-Cap Growth	Mid-Cap Value
Small-Cap Growth	Small-Cap Value

Portfolio

5.3% cash	0.0% corp bonds
0.0% stocks	94.7% gov't bonds
0.0% preferred	0.0% muni bonds
0.0% conv't/warrants	0.0% other

SHAREHOLDER INFORMATION

Minimum Investment
Initial: $2,500   Subsequent: $50

Minimum IRA Investment
Initial: $1,000   Subsequent: $50

Maximum Fees
Load: none   12b-1: none
Other: none

Distributions
Income: Dec   Capital Gains: Dec

Exchange Options
Number Per Year: 6   Fee: none
Telephone: yes (money market fund available)

Services
IRA, pension, auto exchange, auto invest, auto withdraw

Benham Target Maturities Trust: 2020 (BTTTX)

Government Bond

4500 Main St., 14th Floor
P.O. Box 418210
Kansas City, MO 64141
800-345-2021, 415-965-4222
www.americancentury.com

PERFORMANCE

fund inception date: 12/29/89

	3yr Annual	5yr Annual	10yr Annual	Bull	Bear
Return (%)	6.7	12.3	na	49.7	-21.8
Differ from Category (+/-)	1.8 high	5.7 high	na	27.7 high	-15.4 low

Total Risk	Standard Deviation	Category Risk	Risk Index	Avg Mat
high	19.7%	high	4.8	24.0 yrs

	1996	1995	1994	1993	1992	1991	1990	1989	1988	1987
Return (%)..............	-8.5	61.3	-17.7	35.6	8.3	17.3	-4.5	—	—	—
Differ from Category (+/-)	-10.0	41.7	-13.3	24.0	1.6	1.6	-10.8	—	—	—
Return, Tax-Adjusted (%).	-10.6	60.0	-18.1	30.0	5.2	14.9	-5.1	—	—	—

PER SHARE DATA

	1996	1995	1994	1993	1992	1991	1990	1989	1988	1987
Dividends, Net Income ($).	0.00	0.00	0.00	0.00	0.00	0.00	0.00	—	—	—
Distrib'ns, Cap Gain ($) ...	0.00	0.00	0.00	0.00	0.00	0.00	0.00	—	—	—
Net Asset Value ($)	24.04	26.25	16.27	19.76	14.57	13.45	11.46	—	—	—
Expense Ratio (%)........	0.61	0.72	0.70	0.70	0.66	0.67	0.70	—	—	—
Yield (%)	0.00	0.00	0.00	0.00	0.00	0.00	0.00	—	—	—
Portfolio Turnover (%).....	47	78	116	178	144	151	189	—	—	—
Total Assets (Millions $)...	985	726	125	48	38	77	77	—	—	—

PORTFOLIO (as of 9/30/96)

Portfolio Manager: David W. Schroeder - 1990

Investm't Category: Government Bond

✔ Domestic
  Foreign
  Asset Allocation

  Index
  Sector
  State Specific

Investment Style

Large-Cap Growth
Mid-Cap Growth
Small-Cap Growth

Large-Cap Value
Mid-Cap Value
Small-Cap Value

Portfolio

5.3% cash	0.0% corp bonds
0.0% stocks	94.7% gov't bonds
0.0% preferred	0.0% muni bonds
0.0% conv't/warrants	0.0% other

SHAREHOLDER INFORMATION

Minimum Investment
Initial: $2,500   Subsequent: $50

Minimum IRA Investment
Initial: $1,000   Subsequent: $50

Maximum Fees
Load: none   12b-1: none
Other: none

Distributions
Income: Dec   Capital Gains: Dec

Exchange Options
Number Per Year: 6   Fee: none
Telephone: yes (money market fund available)

Services
IRA, pension, auto exchange, auto invest, auto withdraw

Berger Growth & Income
(BEOOX)
Growth & Income

210 University Blvd.
Suite #900
Denver, CO 80206
800-333-1001, 303-329-0200

PERFORMANCE

fund inception date: 12/12/66

	3yr Annual	5yr Annual	10yr Annual	Bull	Bear
Return (%)	9.2	11.0	11.8	43.3	-11.0
Differ from Category (+/-)	-6.1 low	-2.9 low	-0.9 blw av	-16.5 low	-4.6 low

Total Risk	Standard Deviation	Category Risk	Risk Index	Beta
av	9.3%	av	1.0	0.81

	1996	1995	1994	1993	1992	1991	1990	1989	1988	1987
Return (%).............	15.6	23.9	-9.1	23.5	4.8	60.9	-8.0	20.3	5.3	-2.9
Differ from Category (+/-) .	-4.1	-6.2	-7.8	9.7	-5.9	31.8	-2.1	-3.2	-11.5	-3.1
Return, Tax-Adjusted (%)..	11.5	23.2	-9.6	23.1	4.6	56.2	-8.7	18.7	3.3	-5.3

PER SHARE DATA

	1996	1995	1994	1993	1992	1991	1990	1989	1988	1987
Dividends, Net Income ($).	0.18	0.18	0.13	0.08	0.04	0.23	0.12	0.24	0.18	0.41
Distrib'ns, Cap Gain ($) ...	1.63	0.00	0.00	0.00	0.00	0.74	0.00	0.00	0.17	0.68
Net Asset Value ($)	13.30	13.08	10.71	11.92	9.72	9.32	6.47	7.16	6.17	6.19
Expense Ratio (%)........	1.56	1.63	1.81	2.10	2.56	2.66	2.48	2.00	2.00	1.79
Yield (%)	1.20	1.37	1.21	0.67	0.41	2.28	1.85	3.35	2.84	5.96
Portfolio Turnover (%)....	112	85	23	62	42	143	139	132	159	241
Total Assets (Millions $)...	323	349	368	189	43	7	5	1	1	2

PORTFOLIO (as of 9/30/96)

Portfolio Manager: Rod Linafelter - 1990

Investm't Category: Growth & Income
- ✔ Domestic
- ✔ Foreign
- Asset Allocation
- Index
- Sector
- State Specific

Investment Style
- ✔ Large-Cap Growth
- ✔ Mid-Cap Growth
- Small-Cap Growth
- ✔ Large-Cap Value
- ✔ Mid-Cap Value
- Small-Cap Value

Portfolio
9.0% cash	0.0% corp bonds
77.0% stocks	0.0% gov't bonds
0.0% preferred	0.0% muni bonds
10.0% conv't/warrants	4.0% other

SHAREHOLDER INFORMATION

Minimum Investment
Initial: $500   Subsequent: $50

Minimum IRA Investment
Initial: $500   Subsequent: $50

Maximum Fees
Load: none   12b-1: 0.25%
Other: none

Distributions
Income: quarterly   Capital Gains: Dec

Exchange Options
Number Per Year: 4   Fee: none
Telephone: yes (money market fund available)

Services
IRA, pension, auto exchange, auto invest, auto withdraw

Berger One Hundred

(BEONX)

Aggressive Growth

210 University Blvd.
Suite #900
Denver, CO 80206
800-333-1001, 303-329-0200

PERFORMANCE

fund inception date: 11/10/66

	3yr Annual	5yr Annual	10yr Annual	Bull	Bear
Return (%)	8.8	11.1	18.0	51.0	-16.3
Differ from Category (+/-)	-7.0 low	-4.2 low	3.0 abv av	-20.1 blw av	-5.7 low

Total Risk	Standard Deviation	Category Risk	Risk Index	Beta
abv av	11.9%	blw av	0.8	0.92

	1996	1995	1994	1993	1992	1991	1990	1989	1988	1987
Return (%).	13.7	21.3	-6.7	21.1	8.5	88.8	-5.6	48.2	1.6	15.6
Differ from Category (+/-).	-5.4	-13.0	-6.7	1.8	-3.2	36.7	-0.2	19.8	-14.8	18.0
Return, Tax-Adjusted (%). .	9.4	19.6	-6.7	21.1	8.5	88.1	-7.7	43.9	1.2	13.3

PER SHARE DATA

	1996	1995	1994	1993	1992	1991	1990	1989	1988	1987
Dividends, Net Income ($)	0.00	0.00	0.00	0.00	0.00	0.00	0.00	0.01	0.00	0.00
Distrib'ns, Cap Gain ($) . . .	2.77	0.92	0.00	0.00	0.00	0.17	0.58	0.89	0.07	1.58
Net Asset Value ($)	17.83	18.10	15.69	16.81	13.87	12.78	6.87	7.98	5.99	5.97
Expense Ratio (%).	1.42	1.48	1.70	1.69	1.89	2.24	2.13	1.62	1.72	1.61
Yield (%)	0.00	0.00	0.00	0.00	0.00	0.00	0.00	0.11	0.00	0.00
Portfolio Turnover (%). . . .	122	114	64	74	51	78	145	83	166	106
Total Assets (Millions $). .	2,068	2,152	2,112	1,648	760	192	15	14	10	10

PORTFOLIO (as of 9/30/96)

Portfolio Manager: Rod Linafelter - 1990

Investm't Category: Aggressive Growth
- ✔ Domestic
- ✔ Foreign
-   Asset Allocation
-   Index
-   Sector
-   State Specific

Investment Style
-   Large-Cap Growth
- ✔ Mid-Cap Growth
- ✔ Small-Cap Growth
-   Large-Cap Value
-   Mid-Cap Value
-   Small-Cap Value

Portfolio
6.0% cash	0.0% corp bonds
94.0% stocks	0.0% gov't bonds
0.0% preferred	0.0% muni bonds
0.0% conv't/warrants	0.0% other

SHAREHOLDER INFORMATION

Minimum Investment
Initial: $500   Subsequent: $50

Minimum IRA Investment
Initial: $500   Subsequent: $50

Maximum Fees
Load: none   12b-1: 0.25%
Other: none

Distributions
Income: Dec   Capital Gains: Dec

Exchange Options
Number Per Year: 4   Fee: none
Telephone: yes (money market fund available)

Services
IRA, pension, auto exchange, auto invest, auto withdraw

Berger Small Co Growth
(BESCX)
Aggressive Growth

210 University Blvd.
Suite #900
Denver, CO 80206
800-333-1001, 303-329-0200

PERFORMANCE

fund inception date: 12/30/93

	3yr Annual	5yr Annual	10yr Annual	Bull	Bear
Return (%)	21.1	na	na	88.2	-8.9
Differ from Category (+/-)	5.3 high	na	na	17.1 abv av	1.7 abv av

Total Risk	Standard Deviation	Category Risk	Risk Index	Beta
high	17.1%	abv av	1.2	0.78

	1996	1995	1994	1993	1992	1991	1990	1989	1988	1987
Return (%)	16.7	33.8	13.7	—	—	—	—	—	—	—
Differ from Category (+/-)	-2.4	-0.5	13.7	—	—	—	—	—	—	—
Return, Tax-Adjusted (%)	15.3	33.8	13.7	—	—	—	—	—	—	—

PER SHARE DATA

	1996	1995	1994	1993	1992	1991	1990	1989	1988	1987
Dividends, Net Income ($)	0.00	0.00	0.00	—	—	—	—	—	—	—
Distrib'ns, Cap Gain ($)	0.19	0.00	0.00	—	—	—	—	—	—	—
Net Asset Value ($)	4.24	3.80	2.84	—	—	—	—	—	—	—
Expense Ratio (%)	1.68	1.89	2.05	—	—	—	—	—	—	—
Yield (%)	0.00	0.00	0.00	—	—	—	—	—	—	—
Portfolio Turnover (%)	91	109	na	—	—	—	—	—	—	—
Total Assets (Millions $)	808	570	291	—	—	—	—	—	—	—

PORTFOLIO (as of 9/30/96)

Portfolio Manager: William Keithler - 1994

Investm't Category: Aggressive Growth
- ✔ Domestic
- ✔ Foreign
- Asset Allocation
- Index
- Sector
- State Specific

Investment Style
- Large-Cap Growth
- ✔ Mid-Cap Growth
- ✔ Small-Cap Growth
- Large-Cap Value
- Mid-Cap Value
- Small-Cap Value

Portfolio
10.0% cash	0.0% corp bonds
90.0% stocks	0.0% gov't bonds
0.0% preferred	0.0% muni bonds
0.0% conv't/warrants	0.0% other

SHAREHOLDER INFORMATION

Minimum Investment
Initial: $500   Subsequent: $50

Minimum IRA Investment
Initial: $500   Subsequent: $50

Maximum Fees
Load: none   12b-1: 0.25%
Other: none

Distributions
Income: Dec   Capital Gains: Dec

Exchange Options
Number Per Year: 4   Fee: none
Telephone: yes (money market fund available)

Services
IRA, pension, auto exchange, auto invest, auto withdraw

Berwyn (BERWX)

Growth

1189 Lancaster Ave.
Berwyn, PA 19312
800-824-2249, 610-296-7222

PERFORMANCE

fund inception date: 5/4/84

	3yr Annual	5yr Annual	10yr Annual	Bull	Bear
Return (%)	12.2	15.9	12.8	44.6	-8.1
Differ from Category (+/-)	-3.5 blw av	1.6 abv av	-1.1 blw av	-17.8 low	-1.4 blw av

Total Risk	Standard Deviation	Category Risk	Risk Index	Beta
abv av	11.0%	abv av	1.1	0.74

	1996	1995	1994	1993	1992	1991	1990	1989	1988	1987
Return (%)	14.2	19.2	3.8	22.9	20.6	43.5	-23.9	16.5	21.5	2.7
Differ from Category (+/-)	-5.9	-11.1	4.1	8.9	8.8	7.5	-17.8	-9.6	3.4	0.7
Return, Tax-Adjusted (%)	10.5	16.8	2.5	21.8	17.7	42.3	-25.8	14.4	20.0	-2.0

PER SHARE DATA

	1996	1995	1994	1993	1992	1991	1990	1989	1988	1987
Dividends, Net Income ($)	0.00	0.01	0.00	0.00	0.04	0.10	0.13	0.09	0.07	0.16
Distrib'ns, Cap Gain ($)	2.50	1.44	0.77	0.58	1.30	0.27	0.71	0.79	0.47	1.85
Net Asset Value ($)	19.69	19.44	17.55	17.67	14.85	13.46	9.66	13.82	12.62	10.84
Expense Ratio (%)	na	1.23	1.33	1.37	1.38	1.38	1.46	1.42	1.45	1.52
Yield (%)	0.00	0.04	0.00	0.00	0.24	0.72	1.25	0.61	0.53	1.26
Portfolio Turnover (%)	na	32	24	24	45	33	24	25	20	43
Total Assets (Millions $)	95	97	63	47	31	18	11	14	11	8

PORTFOLIO (as of 9/30/96)

Portfolio Manager: Robert Killen - 1984

Investm't Category: Growth
- ✔ Domestic | Index
- ✔ Foreign | Sector
-   Asset Allocation | State Specific

Investment Style

Large-Cap Growth	Large-Cap Value
Mid-Cap Growth	Mid-Cap Value
Small-Cap Growth	✔ Small-Cap Value

Portfolio

1.3% cash	0.0% corp bonds
97.2% stocks	0.0% gov't bonds
0.8% preferred	0.0% muni bonds
0.6% conv't/warrants	0.0% other

SHAREHOLDER INFORMATION

Minimum Investment
Initial: $10,000   Subsequent: $250

Minimum IRA Investment
Initial: $1,000   Subsequent: $250

Maximum Fees
Load: 1.00% redemption   12b-1: none
Other: redemption fee applies for 1 year

Distributions
Income: annual   Capital Gains: annual

Exchange Options
Number Per Year: 4   Fee: none
Telephone: yes (money market fund available)

Services
IRA, pension, auto invest, auto withdraw

Berwyn Income (BERIX)

Balanced

1189 Lancaster Ave.
Berwyn, PA 19312
800-824-2249, 610-296-7222

this fund is closed to new investors

PERFORMANCE

fund inception date: 9/3/87

	3yr Annual	5yr Annual	10yr Annual	Bull	Bear
Return (%)	10.9	14.2	na	39.2	-5.4
Differ from Category (+/-)	-0.8 blw av	2.8 high	na	-5.9 blw av	0.3 av

Total Risk	Standard Deviation	Category Risk	Risk Index	Beta
blw av	5.2%	low	0.8	0.39

	1996	1995	1994	1993	1992	1991	1990	1989	1988	1987
Return (%)	13.9	21.0	-1.1	16.9	21.7	22.9	-0.2	11.8	11.3	—
Differ from Category (+/-)	-0.3	-3.6	0.5	2.5	12.8	-1.2	0.7	-6.3	-0.9	—
Return, Tax-Adjusted (%)	10.1	17.6	-3.7	12.8	17.4	18.7	-3.6	8.4	7.9	—

PER SHARE DATA

	1996	1995	1994	1993	1992	1991	1990	1989	1988	1987
Dividends, Net Income ($)	0.80	0.70	0.72	0.65	0.70	0.93	0.82	0.79	0.76	—
Distrib'ns, Cap Gain ($)	0.47	0.31	0.03	0.68	0.55	0.05	0.04	0.05	0.05	—
Net Asset Value ($)	12.31	11.95	10.74	11.63	11.12	10.20	9.14	10.03	9.75	—
Expense Ratio (%)	na	0.73	0.93	1.07	1.34	1.34	1.46	1.50	1.75	—
Yield (%)	6.25	5.70	6.68	5.28	5.99	9.07	8.93	7.83	7.75	—
Portfolio Turnover (%)	na	39	30	83	46	14	14	3	17	—
Total Assets (Millions $)	138	119	55	30	12	5	3	3	2	—

PORTFOLIO (as of 9/30/96)

Portfolio Manager: Ed Killen - 1994

Investm't Category: Balanced
- ✔ Domestic
- ✔ Foreign
- ✔ Asset Allocation
- Index
- Sector
- State Specific

Investment Style
- Large-Cap Growth
- Mid-Cap Growth
- Small-Cap Growth
- Large-Cap Value
- Mid-Cap Value
- Small-Cap Value

Portfolio
5.7% cash	27.9% corp bonds
19.3% stocks	0.0% gov't bonds
15.1% preferred	0.0% muni bonds
32.0% conv't/warrants	0.0% other

SHAREHOLDER INFORMATION

Minimum Investment
Initial: $10,000   Subsequent: $250

Minimum IRA Investment
Initial: $1,000   Subsequent: $250

Maximum Fees
Load: none   12b-1: none
Other: none

Distributions
Income: quarterly   Capital Gains: annual

Exchange Options
Number Per Year: 4   Fee: none
Telephone: yes (money market fund available)

Services
IRA, pension, auto invest, auto withdraw

Blanchard Flexible Income

(BLFIX)

General Bond

Federated Investors Tower
1001 Liberty Ave.
Pittsburgh, PA 15222
800-245-0242, 412-288-1900

PERFORMANCE

fund inception date: 11/2/92

	3yr Annual	5yr Annual	10yr Annual	Bull	Bear
Return (%)	4.8	na	na	21.0	-5.7
Differ from Category (+/-)	-0.3 av	na	na	0.7 av	-1.5 blw av

Total Risk	Standard Deviation	Category Risk	Risk Index	Avg Mat
low	3.8%	av	1.0	6.6 yrs

	1996	1995	1994	1993	1992	1991	1990	1989	1988	1987
Return (%)	5.8	15.4	-5.6	13.8	—	—	—	—	—	—
Differ from Category (+/-)	1.9	0.5	-3.3	4.7	—	—	—	—	—	—
Return, Tax-Adjusted (%)	3.3	12.7	-8.0	10.0	—	—	—	—	—	—

PER SHARE DATA

	1996	1995	1994	1993	1992	1991	1990	1989	1988	1987
Dividends, Net Income ($)	0.30	0.30	0.31	0.42	—	—	—	—	—	—
Distrib'ns, Cap Gain ($)	0.00	0.00	0.00	0.07	—	—	—	—	—	—
Net Asset Value ($)	4.90	4.93	4.55	5.15	—	—	—	—	—	—
Expense Ratio (%)	1.56	1.58	1.30	0.20	—	—	—	—	—	—
Yield (%)	6.12	6.08	6.81	8.04	—	—	—	—	—	—
Portfolio Turnover (%)	431	455	346	129	—	—	—	—	—	—
Total Assets (Millions $)	184	229	272	690	—	—	—	—	—	—

PORTFOLIO (as of 9/30/96)

Portfolio Manager: Jack D. Burks - 1992

Investm't Category: General Bond

✔ Domestic	Index
✔ Foreign	Sector
Asset Allocation	State Specific

Investment Style

Large-Cap Growth	Large-Cap Value
Mid-Cap Growth	Mid-Cap Value
Small-Cap Growth	Small-Cap Value

Portfolio

2.5% cash	35.4% corp bonds
0.0% stocks	53.8% gov't bonds
0.0% preferred	0.0% muni bonds
0.0% conv't/warrants	8.3% other

SHAREHOLDER INFORMATION

Minimum Investment
Initial: $3,000   Subsequent: $200

Minimum IRA Investment
Initial: $2,000   Subsequent: $200

Maximum Fees
Load: none   12b-1: 0.25%
Other: none

Distributions
Income: monthly   Capital Gains: annual

Exchange Options
Number Per Year: no limit   Fee: none
Telephone: yes (money market fund available)

Services
IRA, pension, auto invest, auto withdraw

Blanchard Global Growth
(BGGFX)
International Stock

Federated Investors Tower
1001 Liberty Ave.
Pittsburgh, PA 15222
800-245-0242, 412-288-1900

PERFORMANCE   fund inception date: 5/30/86

	3yr Annual	5yr Annual	10yr Annual	Bull	Bear
Return (%)	5.7	8.1	8.3	26.1	-9.0
Differ from Category (+/-)	-0.6 blw av	-1.9 blw av	-0.3 blw av	1.8 av	-1.8 blw av

Total Risk	Standard Deviation	Category Risk	Risk Index	Beta
av	8.0%	low	0.8	0.66

	1996	1995	1994	1993	1992	1991	1990	1989	1988	1987
Return (%)	13.3	12.7	-7.6	24.4	0.7	10.7	-6.4	15.6	7.3	16.3
Differ from Category (+/-)	-1.5	3.6	-4.5	-15.2	4.5	-2.5	3.7	-7.0	-7.6	4.1
Return, Tax-Adjusted (%)	6.5	12.3	-8.4	20.6	-1.1	9.3	-7.8	12.6	6.3	13.6

PER SHARE DATA

	1996	1995	1994	1993	1992	1991	1990	1989	1988	1987
Dividends, Net Income ($)	0.21	0.08	0.19	0.00	0.30	0.31	0.20	0.37	0.10	0.11
Distrib'ns, Cap Gain ($)	2.26	0.00	0.03	1.28	0.19	0.00	0.20	0.50	0.18	0.65
Net Asset Value ($)	9.52	10.59	9.47	10.48	9.47	9.89	9.22	10.28	9.69	9.29
Expense Ratio (%)	2.54	2.51	2.61	2.40	2.31	2.36	2.28	2.29	2.28	3.10
Yield (%)	1.78	0.75	2.00	0.00	3.10	3.13	2.12	3.43	1.01	1.10
Portfolio Turnover (%)	91	221	166	138	109	78	88	85	119	69
Total Assets (Millions $)	69	73	93	95	98	149	206	253	246	217

PORTFOLIO (as of 9/30/96)

Portfolio Manager: Charles J. Jacklin - 1996

Investm't Category: International Stock
- ✔ Domestic   Index
- ✔ Foreign   Sector
- ✔ Asset Allocation State Specific

Investment Style

Large-Cap Growth	Large-Cap Value
Mid-Cap Growth	Mid-Cap Value
Small-Cap Growth	Small-Cap Value

Portfolio

11.0% cash	30.6% corp bonds
33.6% stocks	14.3% gov't bonds
0.8% preferred	0.0% muni bonds
0.3% conv't/warrants	9.4% other

SHAREHOLDER INFORMATION

Minimum Investment
Initial: $3,000   Subsequent: $200

Minimum IRA Investment
Initial: $2,000   Subsequent: $200

Maximum Fees
Load: none   12b-1: 0.75%
Other: none

Distributions
Income: annual   Capital Gains: annual

Exchange Options
Number Per Year: no limit   Fee: none
Telephone: yes (money market fund available)

Services
IRA, pension, auto invest, auto withdraw

Blanchard Precious Metals

(BLPMX)

Gold

Federated Investors Tower
1001 Liberty Ave.
Pittsburgh, PA 15222
800-245-0242, 412-288-1900

PERFORMANCE

fund inception date: 6/22/88

	3yr Annual	5yr Annual	10yr Annual	Bull	Bear
Return (%)	3.3	12.5	na	21.1	-7.7
Differ from Category (+/-)	3.0 abv av	2.9 abv av	na	6.2 abv av	2.5 abv av

Total Risk	Standard Deviation	Category Risk	Risk Index	Beta
high	26.4%	abv av	1.1	0.61

	1996	1995	1994	1993	1992	1991	1990	1989	1988	1987
Return (%)	24.3	4.4	-15.0	100.4	-18.5	-2.4	-22.9	8.0	—	—
Differ from Category (+/-)	13.1	-0.6	-2.9	12.6	-3.2	2.2	-0.6	-16.4	—	—
Return, Tax-Adjusted (%)	14.0	4.4	-18.5	100.4	-18.5	-2.4	-22.9	7.4	—	—

PER SHARE DATA

	1996	1995	1994	1993	1992	1991	1990	1989	1988	1987
Dividends, Net Income ($)	0.30	0.00	0.00	0.00	0.00	0.00	0.00	0.03	—	—
Distrib'ns, Cap Gain ($)	2.25	0.00	1.18	0.00	0.00	0.00	0.00	0.10	—	—
Net Asset Value ($)	6.46	7.30	6.99	9.64	4.81	5.90	6.04	7.83	—	—
Expense Ratio (%)	2.36	2.49	2.46	3.24	3.09	3.05	2.95	3.99	—	—
Yield (%)	3.44	0.00	0.00	0.00	0.00	0.00	0.00	0.37	—	—
Portfolio Turnover (%)	176	116	174	66	62	57	56	20	—	—
Total Assets (Millions $)	82	70	77	72	20	25	30	34	—	—

PORTFOLIO (as of 9/30/96)

Portfolio Manager: Kevin McLean - 1988

Investm't Category: Gold

✔ Domestic   Index
✔ Foreign   ✔ Sector
  Asset Allocation   State Specific

Investment Style

Large-Cap Growth   Large-Cap Value
Mid-Cap Growth   Mid-Cap Value
Small-Cap Growth   Small-Cap Value

Portfolio

2.7% cash	0.0% corp bonds
82.6% stocks	14.7% gov't bonds
0.0% preferred	0.0% muni bonds
0.0% conv't/warrants	0.0% other

SHAREHOLDER INFORMATION

Minimum Investment
Initial: $3,000   Subsequent: $200

Minimum IRA Investment
Initial: $2,000   Subsequent: $200

Maximum Fees
Load: none   12b-1: 0.75%
Other: none

Distributions
Income: annual   Capital Gains: annual

Exchange Options
Number Per Year: no limit   Fee: none
Telephone: yes (money market fund available)

Services
IRA, pension, auto invest, auto withdraw

Blanchard Short-Term Flexible Income (BSTBX)

General Bond

Federated Investors Tower
1001 Liberty Ave.
Pittsburgh, PA 15222
800-245-0242, 412-288-1900

PERFORMANCE

fund inception date: 4/16/93

	3yr Annual	5yr Annual	10yr Annual	Bull	Bear
Return (%)	5.5	na	na	17.5	-0.9
Differ from Category (+/-)	0.4 abv av	na	na	-2.8 blw av	3.3 high

Total Risk	Standard Deviation	Category Risk	Risk Index	Avg Mat
low	1.6%	low	0.4	2.4 yrs

	1996	1995	1994	1993	1992	1991	1990	1989	1988	1987
Return (%)	6.6	9.1	1.0	—	—	—	—	—	—	—
Differ from Category (+/-)	2.7	-5.8	3.3	—	—	—	—	—	—	—
Return, Tax-Adjusted (%)	4.4	7.0	-0.9	—	—	—	—	—	—	—

PER SHARE DATA

	1996	1995	1994	1993	1992	1991	1990	1989	1988	1987
Dividends, Net Income ($)	0.16	0.15	0.14	—	—	—	—	—	—	—
Distrib'ns, Cap Gain ($)	0.00	0.00	0.00	—	—	—	—	—	—	—
Net Asset Value ($)	3.01	2.98	2.88	—	—	—	—	—	—	—
Expense Ratio (%)	1.44	1.38	0.63	—	—	—	—	—	—	—
Yield (%)	5.31	5.03	4.86	—	—	—	—	—	—	—
Portfolio Turnover (%)	291	84	212	—	—	—	—	—	—	—
Total Assets (Millions $)	154	19	24	—	—	—	—	—	—	—

PORTFOLIO (as of 9/30/96)

Portfolio Manager: Jack D. Burks - 1993

Investm't Category: General Bond
- ✔ Domestic   Index
- ✔ Foreign   Sector
-   Asset Allocation   State Specific

Investment Style
Large-Cap Growth   Large-Cap Value
Mid-Cap Growth   Mid-Cap Value
Small-Cap Growth   Small-Cap Value

Portfolio
7.9% cash	23.0% corp bonds
0.0% stocks	60.3% gov't bonds
0.0% preferred	0.0% muni bonds
0.0% conv't/warrants	8.8% other

SHAREHOLDER INFORMATION

Minimum Investment
Initial: $3,000   Subsequent: $200

Minimum IRA Investment
Initial: $2,000   Subsequent: $200

Maximum Fees
Load: none   12b-1: 0.25%
Other: none

Distributions
Income: monthly   Capital Gains: annual

Exchange Options
Number Per Year: no limit   Fee: none
Telephone: yes (money market fund available)

Services
IRA, pension, auto invest, auto withdraw

Bonnel Growth (ACBGX)

Aggressive Growth

P.O. Box 29467
7900 Callaghan Road
San Antonio, TX 78229
800-426-6635, 210-308-1234
www.usfunds.com

PERFORMANCE

fund inception date: 10/17/94

	3yr Annual	5yr Annual	10yr Annual	Bull	Bear
Return (%)	na	na	na	na	na
Differ from Category (+/-)	na	na	na	na	na

Total Risk	Standard Deviation	Category Risk	Risk Index	Beta
na	na	na	na	na

	1996	1995	1994	1993	1992	1991	1990	1989	1988	1987
Return (%)	27.9	45.2	—	—	—	—	—	—	—	—
Differ from Category (+/-)	8.8	10.9	—	—	—	—	—	—	—	—
Return, Tax-Adjusted (%)	27.5	43.3	—	—	—	—	—	—	—	—

PER SHARE DATA

	1996	1995	1994	1993	1992	1991	1990	1989	1988	1987
Dividends, Net Income ($)	0.06	0.00	—	—	—	—	—	—	—	—
Distrib'ns, Cap Gain ($)	0.10	0.65	—	—	—	—	—	—	—	—
Net Asset Value ($)	17.68	13.95	—	—	—	—	—	—	—	—
Expense Ratio (%)	na	2.48	—	—	—	—	—	—	—	—
Yield (%)	0.33	0.00	—	—	—	—	—	—	—	—
Portfolio Turnover (%)	na	145	—	—	—	—	—	—	—	—
Total Assets (Millions $)	96	36	—	—	—	—	—	—	—	—

PORTFOLIO (as of 9/30/96)

Portfolio Manager: Arthur Bonnel - 1994

Investm't Category: Aggressive Growth

✔ Domestic	Index
✔ Foreign	Sector
Asset Allocation	State Specific

Investment Style

Large-Cap Growth	Large-Cap Value
Mid-Cap Growth	Mid-Cap Value
Small-Cap Growth	Small-Cap Value

Portfolio

0.5% cash	0.0% corp bonds
99.6% stocks	0.0% gov't bonds
0.0% preferred	0.0% muni bonds
0.0% conv't/warrants	0.0% other

SHAREHOLDER INFORMATION

Minimum Investment
Initial: $5,000   Subsequent: $50

Minimum IRA Investment
Initial: $1   Subsequent: $1

Maximum Fees
Load: none   12b-1: 0.25%
Other: none

Distributions
Income: semiannual   Capital Gains: annual

Exchange Options
Number Per Year: no limit   Fee: $5
Telephone: yes (money market fund available)

Services
IRA, pension, auto invest

Guide to Low-Load Mutual Funds

Brandywine (BRWIX)

Growth

3908 Kennett Pike
Greenville, DE 19807
800-656-3017, 302-656-6200

PERFORMANCE

fund inception date: 12/30/85

	3yr Annual	5yr Annual	10yr Annual	Bull	Bear
Return (%)	19.2	19.1	19.2	80.6	-10.4
Differ from Category (+/-)	3.5 high	4.8 high	5.3 high	18.2 high	-3.7 low

Total Risk	Standard Deviation	Category Risk	Risk Index	Beta
high	14.8%	high	1.4	1.06

	1996	1995	1994	1993	1992	1991	1990	1989	1988	1987
Return (%)	24.9	35.7	0.0	22.5	15.6	49.1	0.5	32.9	17.6	2.6
Differ from Category (+/-)	4.8	5.4	0.3	8.5	3.8	13.1	6.6	6.8	-0.5	0.6
Return, Tax-Adjusted (%)	23.5	31.1	-1.7	18.9	14.8	44.8	-1.9	31.3	17.4	0.4

PER SHARE DATA

	1996	1995	1994	1993	1992	1991	1990	1989	1988	1987
Dividends, Net Income ($)	0.00	0.00	0.00	0.00	0.01	0.12	0.28	0.03	0.03	0.00
Distrib'ns, Cap Gain ($)	1.34	3.84	1.45	2.87	0.54	2.11	0.99	0.68	0.00	0.88
Net Asset Value ($)	33.69	28.08	23.50	24.97	22.74	20.17	15.17	16.41	12.87	10.97
Expense Ratio (%)	1.06	1.07	1.10	1.10	1.10	1.09	1.12	1.13	1.20	1.20
Yield (%)	0.00	0.00	0.00	0.00	0.04	0.53	1.73	0.17	0.23	0.00
Portfolio Turnover (%)	202	193	190	150	189	188	158	91	107	147
Total Assets (Millions $)	6,628	4,210	2,299	1,527	839	623	312	165	124	91

PORTFOLIO (as of 9/30/96)

Portfolio Manager: Foster Friess - 1985

Investm't Category: Growth

✔ Domestic	Index
✔ Foreign	Sector
Asset Allocation	State Specific

Investment Style

Large-Cap Growth	Large-Cap Value
✔ Mid-Cap Growth	Mid-Cap Value
✔ Small-Cap Growth	Small-Cap Value

Portfolio

0.8% cash	0.0% corp bonds
99.2% stocks	0.0% gov't bonds
0.0% preferred	0.0% muni bonds
0.0% conv't/warrants	0.0% other

SHAREHOLDER INFORMATION

Minimum Investment
Initial: $25,000   Subsequent: $1,000

Minimum IRA Investment
Initial: $0   Subsequent: $0

Maximum Fees
Load: none   12b-1: none
Other: none

Distributions
Income: Oct, Dec   Capital Gains: Oct, Dec

Exchange Options
Number Per Year: no limit   Fee: none
Telephone: none

Services
IRA, auto withdraw

Brandywine Blue (BLUEX)

Growth

3908 Kennett Pike
Greenville, DE 19807
800-656-3017, 302-656-6200

PERFORMANCE

fund inception date: 1/10/91

	3yr Annual	5yr Annual	10yr Annual	Bull	Bear
Return (%)	18.6	19.1	na	75.5	-8.4
Differ from Category (+/-)	2.9 abv av	4.8 high	na	13.1 abv av	-1.7 blw av

Total Risk	Standard Deviation	Category Risk	Risk Index	Beta
high	14.1%	high	1.4	1.00

	1996	1995	1994	1993	1992	1991	1990	1989	1988	1987
Return (%).............	23.2	32.3	2.3	27.2	13.1	—	—	—	—	—
Differ from Category (+/-)..	3.1	2.0	2.6	13.2	1.3	—	—	—	—	—
Return, Tax-Adjusted (%)..	23.2	30.4	2.1	22.8	13.1	—	—	—	—	—

PER SHARE DATA

	1996	1995	1994	1993	1992	1991	1990	1989	1988	1987
Dividends, Net Income ($).	0.00	0.00	0.00	0.00	0.00	—	—	—	—	—
Distrib'ns, Cap Gain ($) ...	0.00	1.10	0.10	2.33	0.00	—	—	—	—	—
Net Asset Value ($)	26.47	21.48	17.05	16.77	15.08	—	—	—	—	—
Expense Ratio (%)........	1.13	1.31	1.80	2.00	2.00	—	—	—	—	—
Yield (%)	0.00	0.00	0.00	0.00	0.00	—	—	—	—	—
Portfolio Turnover (%)....	196	174	220	144	191	—	—	—	—	—
Total Assets (Millions $)...	385	190	32	8	4	—	—	—	—	—

PORTFOLIO (as of 9/30/96)

Portfolio Manager: Foster Friess - 1991

Investm't Category: Growth
✔ Domestic	Index
Foreign	Sector
Asset Allocation	State Specific

Investment Style
Large-Cap Growth	Large-Cap Value
✔ Mid-Cap Growth	Mid-Cap Value
Small-Cap Growth	Small-Cap Value

Portfolio
1.0% cash	0.0% corp bonds
99.0% stocks	0.0% gov't bonds
0.0% preferred	0.0% muni bonds
0.0% conv't/warrants	0.0% other

SHAREHOLDER INFORMATION

Minimum Investment
Initial: $100,000   Subsequent: $1,000

Minimum IRA Investment
Initial: $0   Subsequent: $0

Maximum Fees
Load: none   12b-1: none
Other: none

Distributions
Income: Oct, Dec   Capital Gains: Oct, Dec

Exchange Options
Number Per Year: no limit   Fee: none
Telephone: none

Services
IRA, auto withdraw

Brundage Story & Rose Equity (BREQX)

Growth

312 Walnut St.
21st Floor
Cincinnati, OH 45202
800-545-0103, 513-629-2070

PERFORMANCE

fund inception date: 1/2/91

	3yr Annual	5yr Annual	10yr Annual	Bull	Bear
Return (%)	14.7	11.2	na	59.1	-8.0
Differ from Category (+/-)	-1.0 av	-3.1 low	na	-3.3 av	-1.3 blw av

Total Risk	Standard Deviation	Category Risk	Risk Index	Beta
abv av	10.0%	av	1.0	0.95

	1996	1995	1994	1993	1992	1991	1990	1989	1988	1987
Return (%)	19.2	27.2	-0.6	10.2	2.4	—	—	—	—	—
Differ from Category (+/-)	-0.9	-3.1	-0.3	-3.8	-9.4	—	—	—	—	—
Return, Tax-Adjusted (%)	16.2	25.4	-2.1	9.0	1.3	—	—	—	—	—

PER SHARE DATA

	1996	1995	1994	1993	1992	1991	1990	1989	1988	1987
Dividends, Net Income ($)	0.06	0.05	0.06	0.09	0.11	—	—	—	—	—
Distrib'ns, Cap Gain ($)	1.42	0.68	0.55	0.37	0.31	—	—	—	—	—
Net Asset Value ($)	15.67	14.44	11.94	12.63	11.89	—	—	—	—	—
Expense Ratio (%)	na	1.45	0.50	0.50	0.50	—	—	—	—	—
Yield (%)	0.35	0.33	0.48	0.69	0.90	—	—	—	—	—
Portfolio Turnover (%)	na	42	57	29	24	—	—	—	—	—
Total Assets (Millions $)	27	24	18	19	16	—	—	—	—	—

PORTFOLIO (as of 9/30/96)

Portfolio Manager: Greg Ratte - 1994

Investm't Category: Growth
- ✔ Domestic
- ✔ Foreign
- Asset Allocation
- Index
- Sector
- State Specific

Investment Style
- ✔ Large-Cap Growth
- ✔ Mid-Cap Growth
- Small-Cap Growth
- ✔ Large-Cap Value
- ✔ Mid-Cap Value
- Small-Cap Value

Portfolio
0.7% cash	0.0% corp bonds
99.3% stocks	0.0% gov't bonds
0.0% preferred	0.0% muni bonds
0.0% conv't/warrants	0.0% other

SHAREHOLDER INFORMATION

Minimum Investment
Initial: $1,000   Subsequent: $1

Minimum IRA Investment
Initial: $250   Subsequent: $1

Maximum Fees
Load: none   12b-1: 0.25%
Other: none

Distributions
Income: quarterly   Capital Gains: annual

Exchange Options
Number Per Year: no limit   Fee: none
Telephone: yes (money market fund available)

Services
IRA, pension, auto invest, auto withdraw

Brundage Story & Rose Sh Interm Fxd Inc (BRSFX)

Mortgage-Backed Bond

312 Walnut St.
21st Floor
Cincinnati, OH 45202
800-545-0103, 513-629-2070

PERFORMANCE

fund inception date: 1/2/91

	3yr Annual	5yr Annual	10yr Annual	Bull	Bear
Return (%)	5.5	6.2	na	20.3	-3.4
Differ from Category (+/-)	-0.1 blw av	0.2 av	na	-0.8 av	0.2 abv av

Total Risk	Standard Deviation	Category Risk	Risk Index	Avg Mat
low	3.3%	blw av	0.9	4.2 yrs

	1996	1995	1994	1993	1992	1991	1990	1989	1988	1987
Return (%).............	4.0	15.5	-2.3	8.3	6.4	—	—	—	—	—
Differ from Category (+/-) .	-0.4	0.8	-0.6	1.4	0.2	—	—	—	—	—
Return, Tax-Adjusted (%)...	1.7	12.9	-4.5	5.8	3.8	—	—	—	—	—

PER SHARE DATA

	1996	1995	1994	1993	1992	1991	1990	1989	1988	1987
Dividends, Net Income ($).	0.61	0.64	0.59	0.63	0.68	—	—	—	—	—
Distrib'ns, Cap Gain ($) ...	0.00	0.00	0.00	0.03	0.00	—	—	—	—	—
Net Asset Value ($)	10.58	10.78	9.92	10.76	10.56	—	—	—	—	—
Expense Ratio (%).........	na	0.60	0.50	0.50	0.50	—	—	—	—	—
Yield (%)	5.76	5.93	5.94	5.83	6.43	—	—	—	—	—
Portfolio Turnover (%).....	na	39	57	29	24	—	—	—	—	—
Total Assets (Millions $)....	33	35	33	43	29	—	—	—	—	—

PORTFOLIO (as of 9/30/96)

Portfolio Manager: H. Dean Benner - 1991

Investm't Category: Mortgage-Backed Bond
- ✔ Domestic
- Foreign
- Asset Allocation
- Index
- Sector
- State Specific

Investment Style
- Large-Cap Growth
- Mid-Cap Growth
- Small-Cap Growth
- Large-Cap Value
- Mid-Cap Value
- Small-Cap Value

Portfolio
3.3% cash	18.5% corp bonds
0.0% stocks	78.2% gov't bonds
0.0% preferred	0.0% muni bonds
0.0% conv't/warrants	0.0% other

SHAREHOLDER INFORMATION

Minimum Investment
Initial: $1,000   Subsequent: $1

Minimum IRA Investment
Initial: $250   Subsequent: $1

Maximum Fees
Load: none   12b-1: 0.25%
Other: none

Distributions
Income: monthly   Capital Gains: annual

Exchange Options
Number Per Year: no limit   Fee: none
Telephone: yes (money market fund available)

Services
IRA, pension, auto invest, auto withdraw

Buffalo Balanced (BUFBX)

Balanced

3 Crown Center
2440 Pershing Road
Kansas City, MO 64108
800-492-8332, 816-471-5200

PERFORMANCE

fund inception date: 8/12/94

	3yr Annual	5yr Annual	10yr Annual	Bull	Bear
Return (%)	na	na	na	na	na
Differ from Category (+/-)	na	na	na	na	na

Total Risk	Standard Deviation	Category Risk	Risk Index	Beta
na	na	na	na	na

	1996	1995	1994	1993	1992	1991	1990	1989	1988	1987
Return (%)	19.3	20.3	—	—	—	—	—	—	—	—
Differ from Category (+/-)	5.1	-4.3	—	—	—	—	—	—	—	—
Return, Tax-Adjusted (%)	14.3	16.4	—	—	—	—	—	—	—	—

PER SHARE DATA

	1996	1995	1994	1993	1992	1991	1990	1989	1988	1987
Dividends, Net Income ($)	0.73	0.64	—	—	—	—	—	—	—	—
Distrib'ns, Cap Gain ($)	0.83	0.40	—	—	—	—	—	—	—	—
Net Asset Value ($)	10.86	10.46	—	—	—	—	—	—	—	—
Expense Ratio (%)	1.11	1.06	—	—	—	—	—	—	—	—
Yield (%)	6.24	5.89	—	—	—	—	—	—	—	—
Portfolio Turnover (%)	61	33	—	—	—	—	—	—	—	—
Total Assets (Millions $)	41	45	—	—	—	—	—	—	—	—

PORTFOLIO (as of 9/30/96)

Portfolio Manager: na

Investm't Category: Balanced

✔ Domestic	Index
Foreign	Sector
Asset Allocation	State Specific

Investment Style

Large-Cap Growth	Large-Cap Value
Mid-Cap Growth	Mid-Cap Value
Small-Cap Growth	Small-Cap Value

Portfolio

5.0% cash	35.0% corp bonds
30.0% stocks	0.0% gov't bonds
0.0% preferred	0.0% muni bonds
0.0% conv't/warrants	0.0% other

SHAREHOLDER INFORMATION

Minimum Investment

Initial: $2,500   Subsequent: $100

Minimum IRA Investment

Initial: $250   Subsequent: $100

Maximum Fees

Load: none   12b-1: none
Other: none

Distributions

Income: quarterly   Capital Gains: annual

Exchange Options

Number Per Year: no limit   Fee: none
Telephone: yes (money market fund available)

Services

IRA, pension, auto exchange, auto invest, auto withdraw

Bull & Bear Global Income

(BBGLX)

International Bond

11 Hanover Square
10th Floor
New York, NY 10005
800-847-4200, 212-363-1100

fund inception date: 9/1/83

	3yr Annual	5yr Annual	10yr Annual	Bull	Bear
Return (%)	1.4	8.0	4.8	20.7	-15.0
Differ from Category (+/-)	-4.6 blw av	1.4 abv av	-2.5 blw av	-10.5 blw av	-5.5 blw av

Total Risk	Standard Deviation	Category Risk	Risk Index	Avg Mat
av	7.5%	abv av	1.1	7.4 yrs

	1996	1995	1994	1993	1992	1991	1990	1989	1988	1987
Return (%)	8.7	10.8	-13.5	24.9	13.1	17.9	-3.1	-3.1	4.9	-6.5
Differ from Category (+/-)	-2.6	-5.2	-5.9	9.6	7.9	2.9	-13.6	-6.3	0.6	-16.7
Return, Tax-Adjusted (%)	6.0	7.8	-16.2	21.5	9.5	14.0	-7.4	-7.7	0.3	-11.2

PER SHARE DATA

	1996	1995	1994	1993	1992	1991	1990	1989	1988	1987
Dividends, Net Income ($)	0.54	0.60	0.66	0.72	0.75	0.74	0.96	1.20	1.29	1.61
Distrib'ns, Cap Gain ($)	0.00	0.00	0.00	0.00	0.00	0.00	0.00	0.00	0.00	0.00
Net Asset Value ($)	8.33	8.19	7.97	9.94	8.59	8.29	7.71	8.93	10.43	11.19
Expense Ratio (%)	2.18	2.21	1.98	1.95	1.93	1.95	1.72	1.68	1.71	1.50
Yield (%)	6.48	7.32	8.28	7.24	8.73	8.92	12.45	13.43	12.36	14.38
Portfolio Turnover (%)	585	385	223	172	206	555	134	122	124	85
Total Assets (Millions $)	31	36	41	57	41	44	42	61	110	132

PORTFOLIO (as of 9/30/96)

Portfolio Manager: Steven A. Landis - 1995

Investm't Category: International Bond
- ✔ Domestic
- ✔ Foreign
- Asset Allocation
- Index
- Sector
- State Specific

Investment Style

Large-Cap Growth	Large-Cap Value
Mid-Cap Growth	Mid-Cap Value
Small-Cap Growth	Small-Cap Value

Portfolio

0.0% cash	63.4% corp bonds
0.0% stocks	0.0% gov't bonds
5.7% preferred	0.0% muni bonds
31.8% conv't/warrants	0.0% other

SHAREHOLDER INFORMATION

Minimum Investment
Initial: $1,000   Subsequent: $100

Minimum IRA Investment
Initial: $500   Subsequent: $100

Maximum Fees
Load: 1.00% redemption   12b-1: 0.50%
Other: redemption fee applies for 1 month

Distributions
Income: monthly   Capital Gains: Dec

Exchange Options
Number Per Year: no limit   Fee: none
Telephone: yes (money market fund available)

Services
IRA, pension, auto invest, auto withdraw

Bull & Bear Gold Investors Ltd (BBGIX)

Gold

11 Hanover Square
10th Floor
New York, NY 10005
800-847-4200, 212-363-1100

PERFORMANCE

fund inception date: 9/10/58

	3yr Annual	5yr Annual	10yr Annual	Bull	Bear
Return (%)	-5.3	5.7	3.1	0.1	-13.4
Differ from Category (+/-)	-5.6 low	-3.9 low	-1.2 blw av	-14.8 blw av	-3.2 blw av

Total Risk	Standard Deviation	Category Risk	Risk Index	Beta
high	26.7%	abv av	1.1	0.60

	1996	1995	1994	1993	1992	1991	1990	1989	1988	1987
Return (%)	4.2	-5.5	-13.9	87.6	-17.2	-1.2	-22.2	19.3	-13.6	30.4
Differ from Category (+/-)	-7.0	-10.5	-1.8	-0.2	-1.9	3.4	0.1	-5.1	5.5	-1.8
Return, Tax-Adjusted (%)	-1.1	-8.7	-16.1	87.2	-17.2	-1.4	-22.3	18.9	-13.7	27.3

PER SHARE DATA

	1996	1995	1994	1993	1992	1991	1990	1989	1988	1987
Dividends, Net Income ($)	0.00	0.00	0.00	0.00	0.00	0.05	0.03	0.13	0.03	0.00
Distrib'ns, Cap Gain ($)	2.27	1.61	1.45	0.11	0.00	0.00	0.00	0.00	0.00	1.39
Net Asset Value ($)	10.33	12.10	14.50	18.52	9.93	11.99	12.18	15.69	13.26	15.37
Expense Ratio (%)	2.93	2.93	2.57	3.01	2.96	2.59	2.62	2.46	2.33	2.46
Yield (%)	0.00	0.00	0.00	0.00	0.00	0.41	0.24	0.82	0.22	0.00
Portfolio Turnover (%)	61	158	129	156	97	95	65	60	52	66
Total Assets (Millions $)	24	26	38	56	21	28	34	46	42	54

PORTFOLIO (as of 9/30/96)

Portfolio Manager: Kjeld R. Thygesen - 1995

Investm't Category: Gold
- ✔ Domestic
- ✔ Foreign
- Asset Allocation

- Index
- ✔ Sector
- State Specific

Investment Style

Large-Cap Growth	Large-Cap Value
Mid-Cap Growth	Mid-Cap Value
Small-Cap Growth	Small-Cap Value

Portfolio

0.0% cash	0.0% corp bonds
101.2% stocks	0.0% gov't bonds
0.0% preferred	0.0% muni bonds
0.0% conv't/warrants	1.5% other

SHAREHOLDER INFORMATION

Minimum Investment
Initial: $1,000   Subsequent: $100

Minimum IRA Investment
Initial: $500   Subsequent: $100

Maximum Fees
Load: 1.00% redemption   12b-1: 10.00%
Other: redemption fee applies for 1 month

Distributions
Income: Dec   Capital Gains: Dec

Exchange Options
Number Per Year: no limit   Fee: none
Telephone: yes (money market fund available)

Services
IRA, pension, auto invest, auto withdraw

Bull & Bear Special Equities (BBSEX)

Aggressive Growth

11 Hanover Square
10th Floor
New York, NY 10005
800-847-4200, 212-363-1100

PERFORMANCE

fund inception date: 3/20/86

	3yr Annual	5yr Annual	10yr Annual	Bull	Bear
Return (%)	5.8	12.0	9.9	53.1	-22.8
Differ from Category (+/-)	-10.0 low	-3.3 blw av	-5.1 low	-18.0 blw av	-12.2 low

Total Risk	Standard Deviation	Category Risk	Risk Index	Beta
high	19.5%	high	1.4	1.24

	1996	1995	1994	1993	1992	1991	1990	1989	1988	1987
Return (%)	1.0	40.4	-16.6	16.3	28.3	40.5	-36.4	42.2	22.7	-6.5
Differ from Category (+/-)	-18.1	6.1	-16.6	-3.0	16.6	-11.6	-31.0	13.8	6.3	-4.1
Return, Tax-Adjusted (%)	-2.0	38.3	-16.9	9.9	28.3	40.5	-36.4	35.9	20.6	-6.5

PER SHARE DATA

	1996	1995	1994	1993	1992	1991	1990	1989	1988	1987
Dividends, Net Income ($)	0.00	0.00	0.00	0.00	0.00	0.00	0.00	0.00	0.00	0.00
Distrib'ns, Cap Gain ($)	2.71	1.39	0.19	5.64	0.00	0.00	0.00	4.05	1.14	0.00
Net Asset Value ($)	22.96	25.42	19.11	23.13	24.88	19.38	13.79	21.68	18.17	15.75
Expense Ratio (%)	na	2.88	2.92	2.74	3.07	2.83	3.10	3.50	2.94	3.01
Yield (%)	0.00	0.00	0.00	0.00	0.00	0.00	0.00	0.00	0.00	0.00
Portfolio Turnover (%)	na	319	309	256	261	384	475	433	514	751
Total Assets (Millions $)	52	56	46	73	69	16	8	6	2	2

PORTFOLIO (as of 9/30/96)

Portfolio Manager: Brett B. Sneed - 1988

Investm't Category: Aggressive Growth
- ✔ Domestic   Index
- ✔ Foreign   Sector
-    Asset Allocation   State Specific

Investment Style
-    Large-Cap Growth   Large-Cap Value
-    Mid-Cap Growth   Mid-Cap Value
- ✔ Small-Cap Growth   ✔ Small-Cap Value

Portfolio
0.0% cash	0.0% corp bonds
107.8% stocks	0.0% gov't bonds
0.0% preferred	0.0% muni bonds
0.7% conv't/warrants	0.0% other

SHAREHOLDER INFORMATION

Minimum Investment
Initial: $1,000   Subsequent: $100

Minimum IRA Investment
Initial: $500   Subsequent: $100

Maximum Fees
Load: 1.00% redemption   12b-1: 1.00%
Other: redemption fee applies for 1 month

Distributions
Income: Dec   Capital Gains: Dec

Exchange Options
Number Per Year: no limit   Fee: none
Telephone: yes (money market fund available)

Services
IRA, pension, auto invest, auto withdraw

CGM Capital Development (LOMCX)

Aggressive Growth

222 Berkeley St.
Suite 1013
Boston, MA 02116
800-345-4048, 617-859-7714
cgmfunds.com

this fund is closed to new investors

PERFORMANCE

fund inception date: 6/22/61

	3yr Annual	5yr Annual	10yr Annual	Bull	Bear
Return (%)	11.6	16.0	19.2	64.1	-22.0
Differ from Category (+/-)	-4.2 blw av	0.7 abv av	4.2 high	-7.0 av	-11.4 low

Total Risk	Standard Deviation	Category Risk	Risk Index	Beta
high	18.0%	abv av	1.3	1.34

	1996	1995	1994	1993	1992	1991	1990	1989	1988	1987
Return (%)	28.1	41.0	-23.0	28.6	17.4	99.2	1.3	17.8	-0.3	15.8
Differ from Category (+/-)	9.0	6.7	-23.0	9.3	5.7	47.1	6.7	-10.6	-16.7	18.2
Return, Tax-Adjusted (%)	21.9	38.6	-23.9	20.8	14.1	82.3	1.1	16.9	-1.8	3.3

PER SHARE DATA

	1996	1995	1994	1993	1992	1991	1990	1989	1988	1987
Dividends, Net Income ($)	0.07	0.01	0.06	0.06	0.20	0.06	0.09	0.34	0.62	0.14
Distrib'ns, Cap Gain ($)	5.86	1.68	0.71	7.51	2.67	11.07	0.00	0.00	0.01	10.09
Net Asset Value ($)	29.08	27.33	20.58	27.71	27.43	25.80	18.53	18.37	15.87	16.56
Expense Ratio (%)	na	0.85	0.84	0.85	0.86	0.88	0.94	0.92	0.92	0.82
Yield (%)	0.20	0.03	0.28	0.17	0.66	0.16	0.48	1.85	3.90	0.52
Portfolio Turnover (%)	na	271	146	143	163	272	226	254	301	187
Total Assets (Millions $)	648	521	401	523	394	325	175	189	194	231

PORTFOLIO (as of 9/30/96)

Portfolio Manager: G. Kenneth Heebner - 1976

Investm't Category: Aggressive Growth
✔ Domestic   Index
  Foreign   Sector
  Asset Allocation State Specific

Investment Style
  Large-Cap Growth   Large-Cap Value
✔ Mid-Cap Growth   ✔ Mid-Cap Value
  Small-Cap Growth   Small-Cap Value

Portfolio
  2.6% cash   0.0% corp bonds
  97.4% stocks   0.0% gov't bonds
  0.0% preferred   0.0% muni bonds
  0.0% conv't/warrants 0.0% other

SHAREHOLDER INFORMATION

Minimum Investment
Initial: $2,500   Subsequent: $50

Minimum IRA Investment
Initial: $1,000   Subsequent: $50

Maximum Fees
Load: none   12b-1: none
Other: none

Distributions
Income: Dec   Capital Gains: Dec

Exchange Options
Number Per Year: 4   Fee: none
Telephone: yes (money market fund available)

Services
IRA, pension, auto exchange, auto invest, auto withdraw

CGM Fixed Income (CFXIX)

Corporate Bond

222 Berkeley St.
Suite 1013
Boston, MA 02116
800-345-4048, 617-859-7714
cgmfunds.com

PERFORMANCE

fund inception date: 3/17/92

	3yr Annual	5yr Annual	10yr Annual	Bull	Bear
Return (%)	10.5	na	na	42.7	-9.0
Differ from Category (+/-)	4.2 high	na	na	17.9 high	-3.9 low

Total Risk	Standard Deviation	Category Risk	Risk Index	Avg Mat
av	7.8%	high	1.7	8.1 yrs

	1996	1995	1994	1993	1992	1991	1990	1989	1988	1987
Return (%)	15.3	27.2	-8.1	18.3	—	—	—	—	—	—
Differ from Category (+/-)	10.1	9.2	-5.0	6.5	—	—	—	—	—	—
Return, Tax-Adjusted (%)	10.8	24.3	-10.7	15.0	—	—	—	—	—	—

PER SHARE DATA

	1996	1995	1994	1993	1992	1991	1990	1989	1988	1987
Dividends, Net Income ($)	0.76	0.69	0.73	0.61	—	—	—	—	—	—
Distrib'ns, Cap Gain ($)	0.75	0.00	0.00	0.32	—	—	—	—	—	—
Net Asset Value ($)	11.60	11.41	9.57	11.17	—	—	—	—	—	—
Expense Ratio (%)	na	0.85	0.85	0.85	—	—	—	—	—	—
Yield (%)	6.15	6.04	7.62	5.30	—	—	—	—	—	—
Portfolio Turnover (%)	na	148	129	149	—	—	—	—	—	—
Total Assets (Millions $)	40	31	28	32	—	—	—	—	—	—

PORTFOLIO (as of 9/30/96)

Portfolio Manager: G. Kenneth Heebner, Janice Saul - 1992

Investm't Category: Corporate Bond
- ✔ Domestic
- ✔ Foreign
-   Asset Allocation
-   Index
-   Sector
-   State Specific

Investment Style
Large-Cap Growth	Large-Cap Value
Mid-Cap Growth	Mid-Cap Value
Small-Cap Growth	Small-Cap Value

Portfolio
2.3% cash	45.7% corp bonds
0.0% stocks	18.7% gov't bonds
22.4% preferred	0.0% muni bonds
10.9% conv't/warrants	0.0% other

SHAREHOLDER INFORMATION

Minimum Investment
Initial: $2,500   Subsequent: $50

Minimum IRA Investment
Initial: $1,000   Subsequent: $50

Maximum Fees
Load: none   12b-1: none
Other: none

Distributions
Income: monthly   Capital Gains: Dec

Exchange Options
Number Per Year: 4   Fee: none
Telephone: yes (money market fund available)

Services
IRA, pension, auto exchange, auto invest, auto withdraw

CGM Mutual (LOMMX)

Balanced

222 Berkeley St.
Suite 1013
Boston, MA 02116
800-345-4048, 617-859-7714
cgmfunds.com

PERFORMANCE

fund inception date: 11/5/29

	3yr Annual	5yr Annual	10yr Annual	Bull	Bear
Return (%)	11.5	12.3	13.8	49.5	-9.9
Differ from Category (+/-)	-0.2 av	0.9 av	3.0 high	4.4 abv av	-4.2 low

Total Risk	Standard Deviation	Category Risk	Risk Index	Beta
abv av	10.1%	high	1.5	0.82

	1996	1995	1994	1993	1992	1991	1990	1989	1988	1987
Return (%).............	23.6	24.3	-9.8	21.8	6.0	40.8	1.1	21.6	3.1	13.6
Differ from Category (+/-)	.9.4	-0.3	-8.2	7.4	-2.9	16.7	2.0	3.5	-9.1	10.9
Return, Tax-Adjusted (%).	.18.6	22.0	-11.3	18.4	3.1	35.6	-0.6	18.4	0.9	6.2

PER SHARE DATA

	1996	1995	1994	1993	1992	1991	1990	1989	1988	1987
Dividends, Net Income ($).	0.74	0.77	1.04	0.85	0.93	0.97	0.93	0.93	1.10	1.06
Distrib'ns, Cap Gain ($) ...	4.15	0.89	0.00	1.93	1.42	2.64	0.00	0.95	0.00	4.51
Net Asset Value ($)	31.42	29.43	25.05	28.88	26.02	26.80	21.64	22.34	19.94	20.40
Expense Ratio (%)........	na	0.91	0.92	0.93	0.93	0.93	0.97	0.97	1.01	0.94
Yield (%)	2.08	2.53	4.15	2.75	3.38	3.29	4.29	3.99	5.51	4.25
Portfolio Turnover (%).....	na	291	173	97	121	201	159	218	218	197
Total Assets (Millions $)..	1,243	1,154	1,063	947	548	401	295	312	292	303

PORTFOLIO (as of 9/30/96)

Portfolio Manager: G. Kenneth Heebner - 1989

Investm't Category: Balanced
✔ Domestic   Index
  Foreign   Sector
✔ Asset Allocation State Specific

Investment Style
  Large-Cap Growth   Large-Cap Value
  Mid-Cap Growth   Mid-Cap Value
  Small-Cap Growth   Small-Cap Value

Portfolio
  0.0% cash   4.4% corp bonds
  74.4% stocks   21.5% gov't bonds
  0.0% preferred   0.0% muni bonds
  0.0% conv't/warrants 0.0% other

SHAREHOLDER INFORMATION

Minimum Investment
Initial: $2,500   Subsequent: $50

Minimum IRA Investment
Initial: $1,000   Subsequent: $50

Maximum Fees
Load: none   12b-1: none
Other: none

Distributions
Income: quarterly   Capital Gains: Dec

Exchange Options
Number Per Year: 4   Fee: none
Telephone: yes (money market fund available)

Services
IRA, pension, auto exchange, auto invest, auto withdraw

CGM Realty (CGMRX)

Growth & Income

222 Berkeley St.
Suite 1013
Boston, MA 02116
800-345-4048, 617-859-7714
cgmfunds.com

PERFORMANCE

fund inception date: 5/13/94

	3yr Annual	5yr Annual	10yr Annual	Bull	Bear
Return (%)	na	na	na	73.1	na
Differ from Category (+/-)	na	na	na	13.3 high	na

Total Risk	Standard Deviation	Category Risk	Risk Index	Beta
na	na	na	na	na

	1996	1995	1994	1993	1992	1991	1990	1989	1988	1987
Return (%)	44.0	19.7	—	—	—	—	—	—	—	—
Differ from Category (+/-)	24.3	-10.4	—	—	—	—	—	—	—	—
Return, Tax-Adjusted (%)	40.5	16.9	—	—	—	—	—	—	—	—

PER SHARE DATA

	1996	1995	1994	1993	1992	1991	1990	1989	1988	1987
Dividends, Net Income ($)	0.67	0.68	—	—	—	—	—	—	—	—
Distrib'ns, Cap Gain ($)	0.38	0.00	—	—	—	—	—	—	—	—
Net Asset Value ($)	14.50	10.89	—	—	—	—	—	—	—	—
Expense Ratio (%)	na	1.00	—	—	—	—	—	—	—	—
Yield (%)	4.50	6.24	—	—	—	—	—	—	—	—
Portfolio Turnover (%)	na	85	—	—	—	—	—	—	—	—
Total Assets (Millions $)	129	47	—	—	—	—	—	—	—	—

PORTFOLIO (as of 9/30/96)

Portfolio Manager: G. Kenneth Heebner - 1994

Investm't Category: Growth & Income
✔ Domestic   Index
  Foreign   ✔ Sector
  Asset Allocation   State Specific

Investment Style
Large-Cap Growth   Large-Cap Value
Mid-Cap Growth   Mid-Cap Value
Small-Cap Growth   Small-Cap Value

Portfolio
0.5% cash   0.0% corp bonds
99.5% stocks   0.0% gov't bonds
0.0% preferred   0.0% muni bonds
0.0% conv't/warrants 0.0% other

SHAREHOLDER INFORMATION

Minimum Investment
Initial: $2,500   Subsequent: $50

Minimum IRA Investment
Initial: $1,000   Subsequent: $50

Maximum Fees
Load: none   12b-1: none
Other: none

Distributions
Income: quarterly   Capital Gains: Dec

Exchange Options
Number Per Year: 4   Fee: none
Telephone: yes (money market fund available)

Services
IRA, pension, auto invest, auto withdraw

Caldwell & Orkin Market Opportunity

(COAGX) *Aggressive Growth*

2050 Tower Place
3340 Peachtree Road
Atlanta, GA 30326
800-237-7073, 404-239-0707

PERFORMANCE

fund inception date: 3/11/91

	3yr Annual	5yr Annual	10yr Annual	Bull	Bear
Return (%)	13.6	14.2	na	47.3	-2.2
Differ from Category (+/-)	-2.2 blw av	-1.1 av	na	-23.8 low	8.4 high

Total Risk	Standard Deviation	Category Risk	Risk Index	Beta
av	7.6%	low	0.5	0.16

	1996	1995	1994	1993	1992	1991	1990	1989	1988	1987
Return (%)	27.2	16.5	-1.0	14.9	15.2	—	—	—	—	—
Differ from Category (+/-)	8.1	-17.8	-1.0	-4.4	3.5	—	—	—	—	—
Return, Tax-Adjusted (%)	22.2	15.3	-2.4	9.0	13.9	—	—	—	—	—

PER SHARE DATA

	1996	1995	1994	1993	1992	1991	1990	1989	1988	1987
Dividends, Net Income ($)	0.50	0.34	0.26	0.04	0.00	—	—	—	—	—
Distrib'ns, Cap Gain ($)	1.65	0.00	0.22	2.69	0.51	—	—	—	—	—
Net Asset Value ($)	14.65	13.27	11.71	12.31	13.17	—	—	—	—	—
Expense Ratio (%)	1.56	1.18	1.21	1.30	1.64	—	—	—	—	—
Yield (%)	na	2.56	2.17	0.26	0.00	—	—	—	—	—
Portfolio Turnover (%)	222	331	292	223	50	—	—	—	—	—
Total Assets (Millions $)	43	33	35	18	15	—	—	—	—	—

PORTFOLIO (as of 9/30/96)

Portfolio Manager: Michael B. Orkin - 1992

Investm't Category: Aggressive Growth
- ✔ Domestic
- Foreign
- Asset Allocation
- Index
- Sector
- State Specific

Investment Style
- Large-Cap Growth
- Mid-Cap Growth
- ✔ Small-Cap Growth
- Large-Cap Value
- Mid-Cap Value
- ✔ Small-Cap Value

Portfolio
- 51.0% cash
- 49.0% stocks
- 0.0% preferred
- 0.0% conv't/warrants
- 0.0% corp bonds
- 0.0% gov't bonds
- 0.0% muni bonds
- 0.0% other

SHAREHOLDER INFORMATION

Minimum Investment
Initial: $10,000   Subsequent: $1,000

Minimum IRA Investment
Initial: $2,000   Subsequent: $1,000

Maximum Fees
Load: none   12b-1: none
Other: none

Distributions
Income: annual   Capital Gains: annual

Exchange Options
Number Per Year: no limit   Fee: none
Telephone: none

Services
IRA, pension

California Tax-Free Income (CFNTX)

Tax-Exempt Bond

44 Montgomery St.
Suite 2100
San Francisco, CA 94104
800-225-8778, 415-398-2727
www.caltrust.com

PERFORMANCE

fund inception date: 12/4/85

	3yr Annual	5yr Annual	10yr Annual	Bull	Bear
Return (%)	4.3	7.2	7.4	22.2	-8.2
Differ from Category (+/-)	0.1 av	0.8 high	0.7 high	3.8 high	-2.8 low

Total Risk	Standard Deviation	Category Risk	Risk Index	Avg Mat
blw av	6.9%	high	1.2	15.2 yrs

	1996	1995	1994	1993	1992	1991	1990	1989	1988	1987
Return (%)	3.1	20.6	-8.7	14.7	8.8	12.1	6.7	9.9	11.3	-1.3
Differ from Category (+/-)	-0.6	5.4	-3.4	2.9	0.5	0.7	0.3	0.9	1.3	0.1
Return, Tax-Adjusted (%)	3.1	20.6	-9.2	14.0	8.6	12.1	6.7	9.9	11.3	-1.3

PER SHARE DATA

	1996	1995	1994	1993	1992	1991	1990	1989	1988	1987
Dividends, Net Income ($)	0.61	0.61	0.62	0.67	0.71	0.73	0.76	0.79	0.80	0.89
Distrib'ns, Cap Gain ($)	0.00	0.00	0.19	0.28	0.08	0.00	0.00	0.00	0.00	0.00
Net Asset Value ($)	12.64	12.88	11.23	13.18	12.36	12.13	11.52	11.54	11.25	10.86
Expense Ratio (%)	na	0.62	0.60	0.60	0.60	0.60	0.59	0.60	0.61	0.39
Yield (%)	4.82	4.73	5.42	4.97	5.70	6.01	6.59	6.84	7.11	8.19
Portfolio Turnover (%)	na	32	31	25	45	44	42	48	102	87
Total Assets (Millions $)	213	207	185	281	226	167	92	76	47	27

PORTFOLIO (as of 9/30/96)

Portfolio Manager: Phillip McClanahan - 1985

Investm't Category: Tax-Exempt Bond
- ✔ Domestic
- Foreign
- Asset Allocation
- Index
- Sector
- ✔ State Specific

Investment Style
- Large-Cap Growth
- Mid-Cap Growth
- Small-Cap Growth
- Large-Cap Value
- Mid-Cap Value
- Small-Cap Value

Portfolio
8.2% cash	0.0% corp bonds	
0.0% stocks	0.0% gov't bonds	
0.0% preferred	91.8% muni bonds	
0.0% conv't/warrants	0.0% other	

SHAREHOLDER INFORMATION

Minimum Investment
Initial: $10,000   Subsequent: $250

Minimum IRA Investment
Initial: na   Subsequent: na

Maximum Fees
Load: none   12b-1: none
Other: none

Distributions
Income: monthly   Capital Gains: Oct

Exchange Options
Number Per Year: no limit   Fee: none
Telephone: yes (money market fund available)

Services
auto invest, auto withdraw

Calvert Tax-Free Reserves Ltd Term Port/A

4550 Montgomery Ave.
Suite 1000 N.
Bethesda, MD 20814
800-368-2745, 301-951-4800
www.calvertgroup.com/cal-
vert.htm

(CTFLX) *Tax-Exempt Bond*

PERFORMANCE

fund inception date: 3/31/81

	3yr Annual	5yr Annual	10yr Annual	Bull	Bear
Return (%)	3.9	4.1	5.1	11.1	0.7
Differ from Category (+/-)	-0.3 blw av	-2.3 low	-1.6 low	-7.3 low	6.1 high

Total Risk	Standard Deviation	Category Risk	Risk Index	Avg Mat
low	0.5%	low	0.1	1.0 yrs

	1996	1995	1994	1993	1992	1991	1990	1989	1988	1987
Return (%)	3.9	5.5	2.4	4.0	4.9	6.4	6.5	7.1	6.8	3.5
Differ from Category (+/-)	0.2	-9.7	7.7	-7.8	-3.4	-5.0	0.1	-1.9	-3.2	4.9
Return, Tax-Adjusted (%)	3.9	5.5	2.4	4.0	4.9	6.4	6.5	7.1	6.8	3.5

PER SHARE DATA

	1996	1995	1994	1993	1992	1991	1990	1989	1988	1987
Dividends, Net Income ($)	0.44	0.44	0.38	0.38	0.49	0.62	0.66	0.67	0.59	0.58
Distrib'ns, Cap Gain ($)	0.00	0.00	0.00	0.00	0.00	0.00	0.00	0.00	0.00	0.00
Net Asset Value ($)	10.69	10.72	10.59	10.72	10.68	10.65	10.61	10.61	10.55	10.45
Expense Ratio (%)	na	0.70	0.66	0.67	0.71	0.73	0.77	0.78	0.81	0.76
Yield (%)	4.11	4.10	3.58	3.54	4.58	5.82	6.22	6.31	5.59	5.55
Portfolio Turnover (%)	na	33	27	14	5	1	12	21	68	52
Total Assets (Millions $)	565	457	547	653	567	291	151	132	145	147

PORTFOLIO (as of 6/30/96)

Portfolio Manager: Reno Martini, David
Rochat - 1991

Investm't Category: Tax-Exempt Bond
✔ Domestic   Index
  Foreign   Sector
  Asset Allocation   State Specific

Investment Style
  Large-Cap Growth   Large-Cap Value
  Mid-Cap Growth   Mid-Cap Value
  Small-Cap Growth   Small-Cap Value

Portfolio
32.0% cash   0.0% corp bonds
 0.0% stocks   0.0% gov't bonds
 0.0% preferred   68.0% muni bonds
 0.0% conv't/warrants 0.0% other

SHAREHOLDER INFORMATION

Minimum Investment
Initial: $2,000   Subsequent: $250

Minimum IRA Investment
Initial: na   Subsequent: na

Maximum Fees
Load: 2.00% front   12b-1: none
Other: none

Distributions
Income: monthly   Capital Gains: annual

Exchange Options
Number Per Year: 8   Fee: none
Telephone: yes (money market fund available)

Services
auto exchange, auto invest, auto withdraw

Cappiello-Rushmore Emerging Growth (CREGX)

4922 Fairmont Ave.
Bethesda, MD 20814
800-621-7874, 301-657-1517

Aggressive Growth

PERFORMANCE

fund inception date: 10/6/92

	3yr Annual	5yr Annual	10yr Annual	Bull	Bear
Return (%)	8.8	na	na	55.5	-22.1
Differ from Category (+/-)	-7.0 low	na	na	-15.6 blw av	-11.5 low

Total Risk	Standard Deviation	Category Risk	Risk Index	Beta
high	19.9%	high	1.4	1.14

	1996	1995	1994	1993	1992	1991	1990	1989	1988	1987
Return (%)	1.9	35.9	-7.0	22.5	—	—	—	—	—	—
Differ from Category (+/-)	-17.2	1.6	-7.0	3.2	—	—	—	—	—	—
Return, Tax-Adjusted (%)	-2.9	35.6	-7.0	22.1	—	—	—	—	—	—

PER SHARE DATA

	1996	1995	1994	1993	1992	1991	1990	1989	1988	1987
Dividends, Net Income ($)	0.00	0.00	0.00	0.00	—	—	—	—	—	—
Distrib'ns, Cap Gain ($)	2.65	0.10	0.00	0.13	—	—	—	—	—	—
Net Asset Value ($)	13.36	15.73	11.65	12.52	—	—	—	—	—	—
Expense Ratio (%)	1.50	1.50	1.50	1.50	—	—	—	—	—	—
Yield (%)	0.00	0.00	0.00	0.00	—	—	—	—	—	—
Portfolio Turnover (%)	121	96	128	67	—	—	—	—	—	—
Total Assets (Millions $)	33	48	19	12	—	—	—	—	—	—

PORTFOLIO (as of 9/30/96)

Portfolio Manager: Frank Cappiello - 1992

Investm't Category: Aggressive Growth

✔ Domestic	Index
Foreign	Sector
Asset Allocation	State Specific

Investment Style

Large-Cap Growth	Large-Cap Value
✔ Mid-Cap Growth	Mid-Cap Value
✔ Small-Cap Growth	Small-Cap Value

Portfolio

3.9% cash	0.0% corp bonds
96.1% stocks	0.0% gov't bonds
0.0% preferred	0.0% muni bonds
0.0% conv't/warrants	0.0% other

SHAREHOLDER INFORMATION

Minimum Investment
Initial: $2,500   Subsequent: $1

Minimum IRA Investment
Initial: $500   Subsequent: $1

Maximum Fees
Load: none   12b-1: none
Other: *f*

Distributions
Income: Dec   Capital Gains: Dec

Exchange Options
Number Per Year: no limit   Fee: none
Telephone: yes (money market fund available)

Services
IRA, pension, auto invest

Cappiello-Rushmore Growth (CRGRX)

Growth

4922 Fairmont Ave.
Bethesda, MD 20814
800-621-7874, 301-657-1517

PERFORMANCE

fund inception date: 10/6/92

	3yr Annual	5yr Annual	10yr Annual	Bull	Bear
Return (%)	15.3	na	na	59.7	-9.7
Differ from Category (+/-)	-0.4 av	na	na	-2.7 av	-3.0 blw av

Total Risk	Standard Deviation	Category Risk	Risk Index	Beta
high	14.1%	high	1.4	0.98

	1996	1995	1994	1993	1992	1991	1990	1989	1988	1987
Return (%)	7.2	37.0	4.5	14.3	—	—	—	—	—	—
Differ from Category (+/-)	-12.9	6.7	4.8	0.3	—	—	—	—	—	—
Return, Tax-Adjusted (%)	6.2	37.0	4.4	14.3	—	—	—	—	—	—

PER SHARE DATA

	1996	1995	1994	1993	1992	1991	1990	1989	1988	1987
Dividends, Net Income ($)	0.00	0.00	0.01	0.00	—	—	—	—	—	—
Distrib'ns, Cap Gain ($)	0.58	0.00	0.00	0.00	—	—	—	—	—	—
Net Asset Value ($)	17.05	16.45	12.00	11.49	—	—	—	—	—	—
Expense Ratio (%)	1.50	1.50	1.50	1.05	—	—	—	—	—	—
Yield (%)	0.00	0.00	0.08	0.00	—	—	—	—	—	—
Portfolio Turnover (%)	74	70	119	na	—	—	—	—	—	—
Total Assets (Millions $)	28	26	15	4	—	—	—	—	—	—

PORTFOLIO (as of 9/30/96)

Portfolio Manager: Frank Cappiello - 1992

Investm't Category: Growth
- ✔ Domestic
- Foreign
- Asset Allocation
- Index
- Sector
- State Specific

Investment Style
- Large-Cap Growth
- ✔ Mid-Cap Growth
- ✔ Small-Cap Growth
- Large-Cap Value
- Mid-Cap Value
- Small-Cap Value

Portfolio
10.0% cash	0.0% corp bonds
84.5% stocks	0.0% gov't bonds
0.0% preferred	0.0% muni bonds
5.5% conv't/warrants	0.0% other

SHAREHOLDER INFORMATION

Minimum Investment
Initial: $2,500   Subsequent: $1

Minimum IRA Investment
Initial: $500   Subsequent: $1

Maximum Fees
Load: none   12b-1: none
Other: f

Distributions
Income: Dec   Capital Gains: Dec

Exchange Options
Number Per Year: no limit   Fee: none
Telephone: yes (money market fund available)

Services
IRA, pension, auto invest

Capstone Gov't Income

(CGVIX)

General Bond

5847 San Felipe
Suite 4100
Houston, TX 77057
800-262-6631, 713-260-9000
www.capstonefinancial.com

PERFORMANCE

fund inception date: 6/7/68

	3yr Annual	5yr Annual	10yr Annual	Bull	Bear
Return (%)	3.5	3.4	4.5	10.9	-0.5
Differ from Category (+/-)	-1.6 low	-2.7 low	-2.8 low	-9.4 low	3.7 high

Total Risk	Standard Deviation	Category Risk	Risk Index	Avg Mat
low	0.8%	low	0.2	0.4 yrs

	1996	1995	1994	1993	1992	1991	1990	1989	1988	1987
Return (%)	3.9	5.5	1.1	3.3	3.5	6.5	-1.2	7.2	11.7	3.7
Differ from Category (+/-)	0.0	-9.4	3.4	-5.8	-3.0	-8.2	-8.5	-4.5	4.1	1.4
Return, Tax-Adjusted (%)	3.0	3.1	0.1	2.5	2.7	5.0	-4.7	3.5	8.3	-0.2

PER SHARE DATA

	1996	1995	1994	1993	1992	1991	1990	1989	1988	1987
Dividends, Net Income ($)	0.10	0.28	0.12	0.09	0.09	0.17	0.44	0.48	0.43	0.52
Distrib'ns, Cap Gain ($)	0.00	0.00	0.00	0.00	0.00	0.00	0.00	0.00	0.00	0.00
Net Asset Value ($)	4.79	4.71	4.73	4.80	4.74	4.67	4.55	5.05	5.17	5.03
Expense Ratio (%)	na	0.77	0.87	0.93	0.96	1.67	1.40	1.24	1.29	1.29
Yield (%)	2.08	5.94	2.53	1.87	1.89	3.64	9.67	9.50	8.31	10.33
Portfolio Turnover (%)	na	309	285	596	633	754	82	70	100	102
Total Assets (Millions $)	79	25	8	88	29	30	16	20	23	21

PORTFOLIO (as of 9/30/96)

Portfolio Manager: Howard S. Potter - 1991

Investm't Category: General Bond
- ✔ Domestic
- Foreign
- Asset Allocation
- Index
- Sector
- State Specific

Investment Style
- Large-Cap Growth
- Mid-Cap Growth
- Small-Cap Growth
- Large-Cap Value
- Mid-Cap Value
- Small-Cap Value

Portfolio
32.9% cash	0.0% corp bonds
0.0% stocks	67.1% gov't bonds
0.0% preferred	0.0% muni bonds
0.0% conv't/warrants	0.0% other

SHAREHOLDER INFORMATION

Minimum Investment
Initial: $200   Subsequent: $1

Minimum IRA Investment
Initial: $200   Subsequent: $1

Maximum Fees
Load: none   12b-1: 0.20%
Other: none

Distributions
Income: Dec   Capital Gains: Dec

Exchange Options
Number Per Year: 12   Fee: none
Telephone: yes

Services
IRA, pension, auto invest, auto withdraw

Capstone Growth (TRDFX)

Growth

5847 San Felipe
Suite 4100
Houston, TX 77057
800-262-6631, 713-260-9000
www.capstonefinancial.com

PERFORMANCE

fund inception date: 1/14/52

	3yr Annual	5yr Annual	10yr Annual	Bull	Bear
Return (%)	11.7	8.3	11.9	54.2	-10.8
Differ from Category (+/-)	-4.0 low	-6.0 low	-2.0 low	-8.2 blw av	-4.1 low

Total Risk	Standard Deviation	Category Risk	Risk Index	Beta
av	9.5%	blw av	0.9	0.95

	1996	1995	1994	1993	1992	1991	1990	1989	1988	1987
Return (%)	17.2	29.1	-7.8	6.1	0.7	34.8	-3.3	30.7	12.4	7.7
Differ from Category (+/-)	-2.9	-1.2	-7.5	-7.9	-11.1	-1.2	2.8	4.6	-5.7	5.7
Return, Tax-Adjusted (%)	11.9	24.2	-8.5	3.7	-0.5	31.0	-5.7	26.0	10.5	5.8

PER SHARE DATA

	1996	1995	1994	1993	1992	1991	1990	1989	1988	1987
Dividends, Net Income ($)	0.22	0.17	0.10	0.18	0.20	0.31	0.38	0.40	0.30	0.31
Distrib'ns, Cap Gain ($)	2.28	1.91	0.16	0.94	0.32	1.17	0.57	1.37	0.28	0.28
Net Asset Value ($)	13.74	13.81	12.46	13.81	14.14	14.56	12.02	13.48	11.71	10.95
Expense Ratio (%)	na	1.31	1.28	1.24	1.10	0.97	0.94	0.95	1.01	0.94
Yield (%)	1.37	1.08	0.79	1.22	1.38	1.97	3.01	2.69	2.50	2.76
Portfolio Turnover (%)	na	119	12	45	22	38	48	50	62	56
Total Assets (Millions $)	62	88	75	102	101	103	82	87	87	90

PORTFOLIO (as of 9/30/96)

Portfolio Manager: Albert Santa Luca, Dan Watson - 1994

Investm't Category: Growth

✔ Domestic	Index
✔ Foreign	Sector
Asset Allocation	State Specific

Investment Style

✔ Large-Cap Growth	✔ Large-Cap Value
Mid-Cap Growth	Mid-Cap Value
Small-Cap Growth	Small-Cap Value

Portfolio

21.4% cash	0.0% corp bonds
78.5% stocks	0.0% gov't bonds
0.0% preferred	0.0% muni bonds
0.2% conv't/warrants	0.0% other

SHAREHOLDER INFORMATION

Minimum Investment
Initial: $200   Subsequent: $1

Minimum IRA Investment
Initial: $200   Subsequent: $1

Maximum Fees
Load: none   12b-1: 0.25%
Other: none

Distributions
Income: Nov   Capital Gains: Nov

Exchange Options
Number Per Year: 12   Fee: none
Telephone: yes

Services
IRA, pension, auto withdraw

Century Shares Trust
(CENSX)

One Liberty Square
Boston, MA 02109
800-321-1928, 617-482-3060

Growth & Income

PERFORMANCE

fund inception date: 3/1/28

	3yr Annual	5yr Annual	10yr Annual	Bull	Bear
Return (%)	15.0	14.0	13.4	60.7	-7.6
Differ from Category (+/-)	-0.3 blw av	0.1 av	0.7 av	0.9 av	-1.2 blw av

Total Risk	Standard Deviation	Category Risk	Risk Index	Beta
abv av	11.2%	high	1.2	0.91

	1996	1995	1994	1993	1992	1991	1990	1989	1988	1987
Return (%)	17.1	35.2	-4.0	-0.4	26.9	31.5	-7.9	41.6	15.6	-8.1
Differ from Category (+/-)	-2.6	5.1	-2.7	-14.2	16.2	2.4	-2.0	18.1	-1.2	-8.3
Return, Tax-Adjusted (%)	15.3	33.2	-5.8	-2.3	25.3	29.4	-9.8	38.8	10.5	-11.7

PER SHARE DATA

	1996	1995	1994	1993	1992	1991	1990	1989	1988	1987
Dividends, Net Income ($)	0.46	0.41	0.45	0.45	0.42	0.47	0.51	0.50	0.54	0.50
Distrib'ns, Cap Gain ($)	1.11	0.92	0.88	1.10	0.56	0.56	0.57	0.71	1.90	1.61
Net Asset Value ($)	31.30	28.07	21.77	24.04	25.68	21.03	16.82	19.42	14.62	14.76
Expense Ratio (%)	na	0.94	1.01	0.82	0.84	0.95	1.03	0.94	0.87	0.81
Yield (%)	1.41	1.41	1.98	1.78	1.60	2.17	2.93	2.48	3.26	3.05
Portfolio Turnover (%)	na	5	2	19	5	0	3	3	3	2
Total Assets (Millions $)	278	267	206	233	259	157	130	150	110	109

PORTFOLIO (as of 9/30/96)

Portfolio Manager: Allan Fulkerson, William Dyer - 1976

Investm't Category: Growth & Income
- ✔ Domestic
- Foreign
- Asset Allocation
- Index
- ✔ Sector
- State Specific

Investment Style
- Large-Cap Growth
- Mid-Cap Growth
- Small-Cap Growth
- ✔ Large-Cap Value
- ✔ Mid-Cap Value
- Small-Cap Value

Portfolio
- 1.4% cash
- 98.2% stocks
- 0.0% preferred
- 0.0% conv't/warrants
- 0.0% corp bonds
- 0.4% gov't bonds
- 0.0% muni bonds
- 0.0% other

SHAREHOLDER INFORMATION

Minimum Investment
Initial: $500   Subsequent: $25

Minimum IRA Investment
Initial: $500   Subsequent: $25

Maximum Fees
Load: none   12b-1: none
Other: none

Distributions
Income: Jun, Dec   Capital Gains: Dec

Exchange Options
Number Per Year: none   Fee: na
Telephone: na

Services
IRA, pension, auto invest, auto withdraw

Chesapeake Growth

(CPGRX)

Aggressive Growth

105 N. Washington St.
P.O. Drawer 69
Rocky Mount, NC 27802
800-525-3863, 919-972-9922

this fund is closed to new investors

PERFORMANCE

fund inception date: 1/11/93

	3yr Annual	5yr Annual	10yr Annual	Bull	Bear
Return (%)	15.5	na	na	65.8	-13.7
Differ from Category (+/-)	-0.3 av	na	na	-5.3 av	-3.1 blw av

Total Risk	Standard Deviation	Category Risk	Risk Index	Beta
high	20.1%	high	1.4	1.14

	1996	1995	1994	1993	1992	1991	1990	1989	1988	1987
Return (%)	10.8	30.2	7.0	—	—	—	—	—	—	—
Differ from Category (+/-)	-8.3	-4.1	7.0	—	—	—	—	—	—	—
Return, Tax-Adjusted (%)	9.0	27.5	7.0	—	—	—	—	—	—	—

PER SHARE DATA

	1996	1995	1994	1993	1992	1991	1990	1989	1988	1987
Dividends, Net Income ($)	0.00	0.00	0.00	—	—	—	—	—	—	—
Distrib'ns, Cap Gain ($)	1.06	1.31	0.00	—	—	—	—	—	—	—
Net Asset Value ($)	17.84	17.09	14.03	—	—	—	—	—	—	—
Expense Ratio (%)	na	1.43	1.49	—	—	—	—	—	—	—
Yield (%)	0.00	0.00	0.00	—	—	—	—	—	—	—
Portfolio Turnover (%)	na	75	66	—	—	—	—	—	—	—
Total Assets (Millions $)	510	425	235	—	—	—	—	—	—	—

PORTFOLIO (as of 9/30/96)

Portfolio Manager: Gardner, Lewis - 1993

Investm't Category: Aggressive Growth
- ✔ Domestic
- ✔ Foreign
-   Asset Allocation
-   Index
-   Sector
-   State Specific

Investment Style
-   Large-Cap Growth
- ✔ Mid-Cap Growth
- ✔ Small-Cap Growth
-   Large-Cap Value
-   Mid-Cap Value
-   Small-Cap Value

Portfolio
1.5% cash	0.0% corp bonds
98.5% stocks	0.0% gov't bonds
0.0% preferred	0.0% muni bonds
0.0% conv't/warrants	0.0% other

SHAREHOLDER INFORMATION

Minimum Investment
Initial: $25,000   Subsequent: $500

Minimum IRA Investment
Initial: $25,000   Subsequent: $500

Maximum Fees
Load: 3.00% front   12b-1: none
Other: none

Distributions
Income: quarterly   Capital Gains: annual

Exchange Options
Number Per Year: no limit   Fee: none
Telephone: none

Services
IRA, auto invest, auto withdraw

Clipper (CFIMX)

Growth

9601 Wilshire Blvd.
Suite 800
Beverly Hills, CA 90210
800-420-7556, 310-247-3940

PERFORMANCE

fund inception date: 2/29/84

	3yr Annual	5yr Annual	10yr Annual	Bull	Bear
Return (%)	19.1	16.8	14.9	77.2	-8.2
Differ from Category (+/-)	3.4 high	2.5 high	1.0 abv av	14.8 high	-1.5 blw av

Total Risk	Standard Deviation	Category Risk	Risk Index	Beta
abv av	10.9%	abv av	1.1	1.03

	1996	1995	1994	1993	1992	1991	1990	1989	1988	1987
Return (%)	19.4	45.2	-2.5	11.1	15.9	32.5	-7.6	22.1	19.6	2.8
Differ from Category (+/-)	-0.7	14.9	-2.2	-2.9	4.1	-3.5	-1.5	-4.0	1.5	0.8
Return, Tax-Adjusted (%)	16.8	41.2	-4.2	6.8	13.3	29.8	-8.8	19.9	17.0	-4.4

PER SHARE DATA

	1996	1995	1994	1993	1992	1991	1990	1989	1988	1987
Dividends, Net Income ($)	0.83	0.75	0.70	0.75	0.95	1.24	1.14	1.00	0.95	3.41
Distrib'ns, Cap Gain ($)	4.26	5.42	2.00	6.72	3.01	1.91	0.21	1.54	1.68	5.75
Net Asset Value ($)	67.57	60.74	46.09	50.02	51.74	48.10	38.80	43.45	37.74	33.76
Expense Ratio (%)	na	1.11	1.11	1.11	1.12	1.15	1.15	1.17	1.24	1.25
Yield (%)	1.15	1.13	1.45	1.32	1.73	2.47	2.92	2.22	2.40	8.63
Portfolio Turnover (%)	na	31	45	64	46	42	23	26	33	140
Total Assets (Millions $)	558	403	247	271	209	161	125	128	85	75

PORTFOLIO (as of 9/30/96)

Portfolio Manager: J. Gipson, M. Sandler, B. Veaco - 1984

Investm't Category: Growth
- ✔ Domestic
- ✔ Foreign
- Asset Allocation
- Index
- Sector
- State Specific

Investment Style
- ✔ Large-Cap Growth
- Mid-Cap Growth
- Small-Cap Growth
- ✔ Large-Cap Value
- Mid-Cap Value
- Small-Cap Value

Portfolio
25.0%	cash	0.0%	corp bonds
75.0%	stocks	0.0%	gov't bonds
0.0%	preferred	0.0%	muni bonds
0.0%	conv't/warrants	0.0%	other

SHAREHOLDER INFORMATION

Minimum Investment
Initial: $5,000   Subsequent: $1,000

Minimum IRA Investment
Initial: $2,000   Subsequent: $200

Maximum Fees
Load: none   12b-1: none
Other: none

Distributions
Income: annual   Capital Gains: annual

Exchange Options
Number Per Year: none   Fee: na
Telephone: na

Services
IRA, pension, auto invest, auto withdraw

Clover Capital Equity Value (CCEVX)

Growth

680 E. Swedesford Road
Wayne, PA 19087
800-932-7781, 610-254-1000

PERFORMANCE

fund inception date: 12/6/91

	3yr Annual	5yr Annual	10yr Annual	Bull	Bear
Return (%)	20.0	15.8	na	67.7	-1.6
Differ from Category (+/-)	4.3 high	1.5 abv av	na	5.3 abv av	5.1 high

Total Risk	Standard Deviation	Category Risk	Risk Index	Beta
av	8.4%	low	0.8	0.56

	1996	1995	1994	1993	1992	1991	1990	1989	1988	1987
Return (%)	22.8	21.3	16.0	12.5	7.3	—	—	—	—	—
Differ from Category (+/-)	2.7	-9.0	16.3	-1.5	-4.5	—	—	—	—	—
Return, Tax-Adjusted (%)	20.8	18.0	13.5	11.7	6.7	—	—	—	—	—

PER SHARE DATA

	1996	1995	1994	1993	1992	1991	1990	1989	1988	1987
Dividends, Net Income ($)	0.20	0.23	0.11	0.08	0.12	—	—	—	—	—
Distrib'ns, Cap Gain ($)	0.74	1.21	0.92	0.20	0.04	—	—	—	—	—
Net Asset Value ($)	16.88	14.55	13.19	12.30	11.20	—	—	—	—	—
Expense Ratio (%)	1.10	1.10	1.14	1.18	1.20	—	—	—	—	—
Yield (%)	1.13	1.45	0.77	0.64	1.06	—	—	—	—	—
Portfolio Turnover (%)	51	84	58	83	na	—	—	—	—	—
Total Assets (Millions $)	90	54	27	16	10	—	—	—	—	—

PORTFOLIO (as of 9/30/96)

Portfolio Manager: Paul W. Spindler, Michael Jones - 1991

Investm't Category: Growth
✔ Domestic
  Foreign
  Asset Allocation
  Index
  Sector
  State Specific

Investment Style
  Large-Cap Growth
✔ Mid-Cap Growth
✔ Small-Cap Growth
  Large-Cap Value
  Mid-Cap Value
  Small-Cap Value

Portfolio
17.0% cash
80.8% stocks
1.4% preferred
0.8% conv't/warrants
0.0% corp bonds
0.0% gov't bonds
0.0% muni bonds
0.0% other

SHAREHOLDER INFORMATION

Minimum Investment
Initial: $2,000   Subsequent: $100

Minimum IRA Investment
Initial: $500   Subsequent: $100

Maximum Fees
Load: none   12b-1: none
Other: none

Distributions
Income: quarterly   Capital Gains: annual

Exchange Options
Number Per Year: no limit   Fee: none
Telephone: yes (money market fund not available)

Services
IRA, auto invest, auto withdraw

Individual Fund Listings   171

Cohen & Steers Realty Shares (CSRSX)

757 Third Ave.
New York, NY 10017
800-437-9912, 212-832-3232

Growth & Income

PERFORMANCE

fund inception date: 7/1/91

	3yr Annual	5yr Annual	10yr Annual	Bull	Bear
Return (%)	18.5	18.8	na	55.3	5.6
Differ from Category (+/-)	3.2 abv av	4.9 high	na	-4.5 blw av	12.0 high

Total Risk	Standard Deviation	Category Risk	Risk Index	Beta
high	12.3%	high	1.3	0.08

	1996	1995	1994	1993	1992	1991	1990	1989	1988	1987
Return (%)	38.4	11.1	8.3	18.6	20.0	—	—	—	—	—
Differ from Category (+/-)	18.7	-19.0	9.6	4.8	9.3	—	—	—	—	—
Return, Tax-Adjusted (%)	35.8	8.8	6.2	14.9	17.0	—	—	—	—	—

PER SHARE DATA

	1996	1995	1994	1993	1992	1991	1990	1989	1988	1987
Dividends, Net Income ($)	1.88	1.83	1.66	1.51	1.80	—	—	—	—	—
Distrib'ns, Cap Gain ($)	0.55	0.00	0.00	1.68	0.23	—	—	—	—	—
Net Asset Value ($)	45.09	34.62	32.90	31.92	29.58	—	—	—	—	—
Expense Ratio (%)	na	1.12	1.14	1.18	1.25	—	—	—	—	—
Yield (%)	4.11	5.28	5.04	4.49	6.03	—	—	—	—	—
Portfolio Turnover (%)	na	22	39	65	15	—	—	—	—	—
Total Assets (Millions $)	1,636	793	458	155	49	—	—	—	—	—

PORTFOLIO (as of 9/30/96)

Portfolio Manager: Martin Cohen, Bob Steers - 1991

Investm't Category: Growth & Income
- ✔ Domestic
- ✔ Foreign
-   Asset Allocation
-   Index
- ✔ Sector
-   State Specific

Investment Style
- Large-Cap Growth
- Mid-Cap Growth
- Small-Cap Growth
- Large-Cap Value
- Mid-Cap Value
- ✔ Small-Cap Value

Portfolio
7.5% cash	0.0% corp bonds
92.5% stocks	0.0% gov't bonds
0.0% preferred	0.0% muni bonds
0.0% conv't/warrants	0.0% other

SHAREHOLDER INFORMATION

Minimum Investment
Initial: $10,000   Subsequent: $500

Minimum IRA Investment
Initial: na   Subsequent: na

Maximum Fees
Load: none   12b-1: none
Other: none

Distributions
Income: quarterly   Capital Gains: annual

Exchange Options
Number Per Year: none   Fee: na
Telephone: na

Services

Columbia Balanced
(CBALX)
Balanced

1301 S.W. 5th Ave.
P.O. Box 1350
Portland, OR 97207
800-547-1707, 503-222-3606

PERFORMANCE
fund inception date: 9/12/91

	3yr Annual	5yr Annual	10yr Annual	Bull	Bear
Return (%)	11.8	11.6	na	44.1	-5.1
Differ from Category (+/-)	0.1 av	0.2 av	na	-1.0 av	0.6 av

Total Risk	Standard Deviation	Category Risk	Risk Index	Beta
blw av	6.0%	blw av	0.9	0.58

	1996	1995	1994	1993	1992	1991	1990	1989	1988	1987
Return (%)	11.8	25.0	0.0	13.6	8.8	—	—	—	—	—
Differ from Category (+/-)	-2.4	0.4	1.6	-0.8	-0.1	—	—	—	—	—
Return, Tax-Adjusted (%)	8.4	22.1	-1.5	11.2	7.2	—	—	—	—	—

PER SHARE DATA

	1996	1995	1994	1993	1992	1991	1990	1989	1988	1987
Dividends, Net Income ($)	0.76	0.73	0.64	0.56	0.56	—	—	—	—	—
Distrib'ns, Cap Gain ($)	1.34	0.74	0.00	0.59	0.08	—	—	—	—	—
Net Asset Value ($)	20.32	20.08	17.28	17.91	16.80	—	—	—	—	—
Expense Ratio (%)	na	0.69	0.72	0.73	0.81	—	—	—	—	—
Yield (%)	3.50	3.50	3.70	3.02	3.31	—	—	—	—	—
Portfolio Turnover (%)	na	108	98	107	138	—	—	—	—	—
Total Assets (Millions $)	679	486	249	186	90	—	—	—	—	—

PORTFOLIO (as of 9/30/96)

Portfolio Manager: Michael W. Powers - 1991

Investm't Category: Balanced
✔ Domestic
✔ Foreign
✔ Asset Allocation
Index
Sector
State Specific

Investment Style
Large-Cap Growth
Mid-Cap Growth
Small-Cap Growth
Large-Cap Value
Mid-Cap Value
Small-Cap Value

Portfolio
3.0% cash
50.9% stocks
0.0% preferred
0.0% conv't/warrants
0.0% corp bonds
27.6% gov't bonds
0.0% muni bonds
18.5% other

SHAREHOLDER INFORMATION

Minimum Investment
Initial: $1,000
Subsequent: $100

Minimum IRA Investment
Initial: $1,000
Subsequent: $100

Maximum Fees
Load: none
Other: none
12b-1: none

Distributions
Income: quarterly
Capital Gains: Dec

Exchange Options
Number Per Year: 4
Fee: none
Telephone: yes (money market fund available)

Services
IRA, pension, auto exchange, auto invest, auto withdraw

Columbia Common Stock

(CMSTX)

Growth & Income

1301 S.W. 5th Ave.
P.O. Box 1350
Portland, OR 97207
800-547-1707, 503-222-3606

PERFORMANCE

fund inception date: 9/12/91

	3yr Annual	5yr Annual	10yr Annual	Bull	Bear
Return (%)	17.2	15.6	na	65.6	-5.6
Differ from Category (+/-)	1.9 av	1.7 abv av	na	5.8 av	0.8 abv av

Total Risk	Standard Deviation	Category Risk	Risk Index	Beta
av	8.9%	blw av	1.0	0.85

	1996	1995	1994	1993	1992	1991	1990	1989	1988	1987
Return (%)	20.8	30.8	2.0	16.4	9.9	—	—	—	—	—
Differ from Category (+/-)	1.1	0.7	3.3	2.6	-0.8	—	—	—	—	—
Return, Tax-Adjusted (%)	15.8	28.3	1.0	14.1	8.8	—	—	—	—	—

PER SHARE DATA

	1996	1995	1994	1993	1992	1991	1990	1989	1988	1987
Dividends, Net Income ($)	0.23	0.26	0.25	0.21	0.24	—	—	—	—	—
Distrib'ns, Cap Gain ($)	2.96	0.95	0.19	0.84	0.17	—	—	—	—	—
Net Asset Value ($)	19.26	18.59	15.16	15.29	14.04	—	—	—	—	—
Expense Ratio (%)	na	0.80	0.84	0.84	0.86	—	—	—	—	—
Yield (%)	1.03	1.33	1.62	1.30	1.68	—	—	—	—	—
Portfolio Turnover (%)	na	75	64	90	68	—	—	—	—	—
Total Assets (Millions $)	532	358	124	100	51	—	—	—	—	—

PORTFOLIO (as of 9/30/96)

Portfolio Manager: Alan Folkman - 1996

Investm't Category: Growth & Income
✔ Domestic   Index
✔ Foreign   Sector
   Asset Allocation   State Specific

Investment Style
Large-Cap Growth   ✔ Large-Cap Value
Mid-Cap Growth   ✔ Mid-Cap Value
Small-Cap Growth   Small-Cap Value

Portfolio
5.9% cash	0.0% corp bonds
94.1% stocks	0.0% gov't bonds
0.0% preferred	0.0% muni bonds
0.0% conv't/warrants	0.0% other

SHAREHOLDER INFORMATION

Minimum Investment
Initial: $1,000   Subsequent: $100

Minimum IRA Investment
Initial: $1,000   Subsequent: $100

Maximum Fees
Load: none   12b-1: none
Other: none

Distributions
Income: quarterly   Capital Gains: Dec

Exchange Options
Number Per Year: 4   Fee: none
Telephone: yes (money market fund available)

Services
IRA, pension, auto exchange, auto invest, auto withdraw

Columbia Fixed Income Securities (CFISX)

General Bond

1301 S.W. 5th Ave.
P.O. Box 1350
Portland, OR 97207
800-547-1707, 503-222-3606

PERFORMANCE

fund inception date: 1/6/83

	3yr Annual	5yr Annual	10yr Annual	Bull	Bear
Return (%)	5.9	7.2	8.3	23.8	-5.4
Differ from Category (+/-)	0.8 abv av	1.1 high	1.0 high	3.5 abv av	-1.2 blw av

Total Risk	Standard Deviation	Category Risk	Risk Index	Avg Mat
low	4.7%	abv av	1.2	5.9 yrs

	1996	1995	1994	1993	1992	1991	1990	1989	1988	1987
Return (%).	3.3	18.9	-3.4	10.4	7.9	16.8	8.2	14.3	7.7	1.3
Differ from Category (+/-) .	-0.6	4.0	-1.1	1.3	1.4	2.1	0.9	2.6	0.1	-1.0
Return, Tax-Adjusted (%). . .	0.8	16.0	-5.9	7.1	4.3	13.3	5.0	10.9	4.3	-2.4

PER SHARE DATA

	1996	1995	1994	1993	1992	1991	1990	1989	1988	1987
Dividends, Net Income ($).	0.85	0.88	0.83	0.84	0.95	0.99	1.02	1.03	1.03	1.03
Distrib'ns, Cap Gain ($) . . .	0.00	0.00	0.00	0.36	0.40	0.18	0.00	0.00	0.00	0.27
Net Asset Value ($)	13.08	13.51	12.16	13.44	13.28	13.59	12.72	12.75	12.11	12.23
Expense Ratio (%).	na	0.65	0.66	0.66	0.66	0.69	0.73	0.74	0.77	0.82
Yield (%)	6.49	6.51	6.82	6.08	6.94	7.18	8.01	8.07	8.50	8.24
Portfolio Turnover (%).	na	137	139	118	196	159	132	114	133	114
Total Assets (Millions $). . .	360	315	252	300	262	207	133	110	102	100

PORTFOLIO (as of 9/30/96)

Portfolio Manager: Thomas L. Thomsen - 1983

Investm't Category: General Bond

✔ Domestic
  Foreign
  Asset Allocation
  Index
  Sector
  State Specific

Investment Style

Large-Cap Growth
Mid-Cap Growth
Small-Cap Growth
Large-Cap Value
Mid-Cap Value
Small-Cap Value

Portfolio

4.8%	cash	22.7%	corp bonds
0.0%	stocks	70.1%	gov't bonds
0.0%	preferred	0.0%	muni bonds
0.0%	conv't/warrants	2.4%	other

SHAREHOLDER INFORMATION

Minimum Investment
Initial: $1,000   Subsequent: $100

Minimum IRA Investment
Initial: $1,000   Subsequent: $100

Maximum Fees
Load: none   12b-1: none
Other: none

Distributions
Income: monthly   Capital Gains: Dec

Exchange Options
Number Per Year: 4   Fee: none
Telephone: yes (money market fund available)

Services
IRA, pension, auto exchange, auto invest, auto withdraw

Columbia Growth (CLMBX)

Growth

1301 S.W. 5th Ave.
P.O. Box 1350
Portland, OR 97207
800-547-1707, 503-222-3606

PERFORMANCE

fund inception date: 6/16/67

	3yr Annual	5yr Annual	10yr Annual	Bull	Bear
Return (%)	16.8	15.0	15.7	69.5	-8.8
Differ from Category (+/-)	1.1 abv av	0.7 abv av	1.8 high	7.1 abv av	-2.1 blw av

Total Risk	Standard Deviation	Category Risk	Risk Index	Beta
abv av	11.1%	abv av	1.1	1.01

	1996	1995	1994	1993	1992	1991	1990	1989	1988	1987
Return (%).............	20.8	32.9	-0.7	13.0	11.8	34.2	-3.4	29.0	10.8	14.7
Differ from Category (+/-) . .	0.7	2.6	-0.4	-1.0	0.0	-1.8	2.7	2.9	-7.3	12.7
Return, Tax-Adjusted (%). .	15.7	29.2	-2.3	9.4	8.3	30.3	-4.8	23.5	8.8	7.1

PER SHARE DATA

	1996	1995	1994	1993	1992	1991	1990	1989	1988	1987
Dividends, Net Income ($).	0.17	0.28	0.26	0.18	0.20	0.39	0.48	0.54	0.52	0.60
Distrib'ns, Cap Gain ($) . . .	5.16	2.88	1.11	3.02	2.98	2.44	0.46	3.40	0.64	5.33
Net Asset Value ($)	30.74	29.84	24.84	26.38	26.18	26.26	21.68	23.40	21.21	20.19
Expense Ratio (%).	na	0.75	0.81	0.82	0.86	0.90	0.96	0.96	1.04	1.04
Yield (%)	0.47	0.85	1.00	0.61	0.68	1.35	2.16	2.01	2.37	2.35
Portfolio Turnover (%).	na	94	79	105	116	164	172	166	179	197
Total Assets (Millions $). .	1,101	848	591	605	518	431	270	266	204	193

PORTFOLIO (as of 9/30/96)

Portfolio Manager: Alexander S. Macmillan - 1992

Investm't Category: Growth

✔ Domestic	Index
Foreign	Sector
Asset Allocation	State Specific

Investment Style

Large-Cap Growth	Large-Cap Value
✔ Mid-Cap Growth	✔ Mid-Cap Value
Small-Cap Growth	Small-Cap Value

Portfolio

6.3% cash	0.0% corp bonds
93.4% stocks	0.0% gov't bonds
0.0% preferred	0.0% muni bonds
0.3% conv't/warrants	0.0% other

SHAREHOLDER INFORMATION

Minimum Investment
Initial: $1,000   Subsequent: $100

Minimum IRA Investment
Initial: $1,000   Subsequent: $100

Maximum Fees
Load: none   12b-1: none
Other: none

Distributions
Income: Dec   Capital Gains: Dec

Exchange Options
Number Per Year: 4   Fee: none
Telephone: yes (money market fund available)

Services
IRA, pension, auto exchange, auto invest, auto withdraw

Columbia Int'l Stock
(CMISX)
International Stock

1301 S.W. 5th Ave.
P.O. Box 1350
Portland, OR 97207
800-547-1707, 503-222-3606

PERFORMANCE

fund inception date: 9/10/92

	3yr Annual	5yr Annual	10yr Annual	Bull	Bear
Return (%)	6.1	na	na	17.5	-3.3
Differ from Category (+/-)	-0.2 av	na	na	-6.8 blw av	3.9 high

Total Risk	Standard Deviation	Category Risk	Risk Index	Beta
abv av	10.7%	av	1.0	0.61

	1996	1995	1994	1993	1992	1991	1990	1989	1988	1987
Return (%)	16.6	5.1	-2.5	33.3	—	—	—	—	—	—
Differ from Category (+/-)	1.8	-4.0	0.6	-6.3	—	—	—	—	—	—
Return, Tax-Adjusted (%)	13.4	5.1	-3.0	32.4	—	—	—	—	—	—

PER SHARE DATA

	1996	1995	1994	1993	1992	1991	1990	1989	1988	1987
Dividends, Net Income ($)	0.23	0.00	0.00	0.00	—	—	—	—	—	—
Distrib'ns, Cap Gain ($)	1.13	0.00	0.21	0.31	—	—	—	—	—	—
Net Asset Value ($)	13.86	13.07	12.43	12.96	—	—	—	—	—	—
Expense Ratio (%)	na	1.54	1.52	1.71	—	—	—	—	—	—
Yield (%)	1.53	0.00	0.00	0.00	—	—	—	—	—	—
Portfolio Turnover (%)	na	156	138	144	—	—	—	—	—	—
Total Assets (Millions $)	124	100	118	73	—	—	—	—	—	—

PORTFOLIO (as of 9/30/96)

Portfolio Manager: James M. McAlear - 1992

Investm't Category: International Stock
- ✔ Domestic
- ✔ Foreign
- Asset Allocation
- Index
- Sector
- State Specific

Investment Style
Large-Cap Growth	Large-Cap Value
Mid-Cap Growth	Mid-Cap Value
Small-Cap Growth	Small-Cap Value

Portfolio
4.9% cash	0.0% corp bonds
88.4% stocks	0.0% gov't bonds
3.3% preferred	0.0% muni bonds
3.4% conv't/warrants	0.0% other

SHAREHOLDER INFORMATION

Minimum Investment
Initial: $1,000   Subsequent: $100

Minimum IRA Investment
Initial: $1,000   Subsequent: $100

Maximum Fees
Load: none   12b-1: none
Other: none

Distributions
Income: Dec   Capital Gains: Dec

Exchange Options
Number Per Year: 4   Fee: none
Telephone: yes (money market fund available)

Services
IRA, pension, auto exchange, auto invest, auto withdraw

Columbia Muni Bond
(CMBFX)
Tax-Exempt Bond

1301 S.W. 5th Ave.
P.O. Box 1350
Portland, OR 97207
800-547-1707, 503-222-3606

PERFORMANCE
fund inception date: 5/23/84

	3yr Annual	5yr Annual	10yr Annual	Bull	Bear
Return (%)	4.1	5.8	6.8	17.9	-5.2
Differ from Category (+/-)	-0.1 blw av	-0.6 low	0.1 blw av	-0.5 blw av	0.2 abv av

Total Risk	Standard Deviation	Category Risk	Risk Index	Avg Mat
low	4.5%	blw av	0.8	12.1 yrs

	1996	1995	1994	1993	1992	1991	1990	1989	1988	1987
Return (%)	3.7	14.1	-4.7	10.7	6.4	11.7	6.8	8.9	10.1	1.2
Differ from Category (+/-)	0.0	-1.1	0.6	-1.1	-1.9	0.3	0.4	-0.1	0.1	2.6
Return, Tax-Adjusted (%)	3.5	13.9	-4.7	10.5	6.1	11.6	6.7	8.8	10.0	1.2

PER SHARE DATA

	1996	1995	1994	1993	1992	1991	1990	1989	1988	1987
Dividends, Net Income ($)	0.60	0.63	0.64	0.66	0.69	0.72	0.74	0.76	0.76	0.76
Distrib'ns, Cap Gain ($)	0.06	0.07	0.00	0.08	0.12	0.03	0.01	0.01	0.03	0.00
Net Asset Value ($)	12.15	12.37	11.48	12.71	12.17	12.22	11.65	11.64	11.42	11.11
Expense Ratio (%)	na	0.57	0.57	0.58	0.59	0.59	0.60	0.61	0.63	0.66
Yield (%)	4.91	5.06	5.57	5.16	5.61	5.87	6.34	6.52	6.63	6.84
Portfolio Turnover (%)	na	21	19	9	18	15	7	11	10	21
Total Assets (Millions $)	381	383	339	430	341	285	207	166	140	118

PORTFOLIO (as of 9/30/96)

Portfolio Manager: Thomas L. Thomsen - 1984

Investm't Category: Tax-Exempt Bond

✔ Domestic	Index
Foreign	Sector
Asset Allocation	State Specific

Investment Style

Large-Cap Growth	Large-Cap Value
Mid-Cap Growth	Mid-Cap Value
Small-Cap Growth	Small-Cap Value

Portfolio

2.5% cash	0.0% corp bonds
0.0% stocks	0.0% gov't bonds
0.0% preferred	97.5% muni bonds
0.0% conv't/warrants	0.0% other

SHAREHOLDER INFORMATION

Minimum Investment
Initial: $1,000   Subsequent: $100

Minimum IRA Investment
Initial: na   Subsequent: na

Maximum Fees
Load: none   12b-1: none
Other: none

Distributions
Income: monthly   Capital Gains: Dec

Exchange Options
Number Per Year: 4   Fee: none
Telephone: yes (money market fund available)

Services
auto exchange, auto invest, auto withdraw

Columbia Special (CLSPX)

Aggressive Growth

1301 S.W. 5th Ave.
P.O. Box 1350
Portland, OR 97207
800-547-1707, 503-222-3606

PERFORMANCE

fund inception date: 8/13/85

	3yr Annual	5yr Annual	10yr Annual	Bull	Bear
Return (%)	14.3	15.6	18.1	54.9	-7.3
Differ from Category (+/-)	-1.5 av	0.3 av	3.1 abv av	-16.2 blw av	3.3 abv av

Total Risk	Standard Deviation	Category Risk	Risk Index	Beta
high	13.7%	av	1.0	0.92

	1996	1995	1994	1993	1992	1991	1990	1989	1988	1987
Return (%)	13.0	29.3	2.2	21.6	13.6	50.4	-12.4	31.9	42.5	3.0
Differ from Category (+/-)	-6.1	-5.0	2.2	2.3	1.9	-1.7	-7.0	3.5	26.1	5.4
Return, Tax-Adjusted (%)	7.2	25.1	0.3	16.6	11.9	48.6	-12.5	29.2	36.8	3.0

PER SHARE DATA

	1996	1995	1994	1993	1992	1991	1990	1989	1988	1987
Dividends, Net Income ($)	0.00	0.02	0.07	0.01	0.00	0.00	0.01	0.01	0.00	0.00
Distrib'ns, Cap Gain ($)	4.38	2.71	1.19	3.32	1.04	0.77	0.00	1.05	1.86	0.00
Net Asset Value ($)	19.85	21.44	18.69	19.51	18.79	17.45	12.12	13.85	11.32	9.26
Expense Ratio (%)	na	0.98	1.05	1.12	1.19	1.22	1.32	1.35	1.38	1.44
Yield (%)	0.00	0.08	0.35	0.04	0.00	0.00	0.08	0.06	0.00	0.00
Portfolio Turnover (%)	na	182	178	154	117	115	147	124	244	333
Total Assets (Millions $)	1,638	1,384	889	772	470	264	121	95	30	20

PORTFOLIO (as of 9/30/96)

Portfolio Manager: Chad Fleischman - 1995

Investm't Category: Aggressive Growth

✔ Domestic	Index
✔ Foreign	Sector
Asset Allocation	State Specific

Investment Style

Large-Cap Growth	Large-Cap Value
✔ Mid-Cap Growth	Mid-Cap Value
✔ Small-Cap Growth	Small-Cap Value

Portfolio

11.9% cash	0.0% corp bonds
88.1% stocks	0.0% gov't bonds
0.0% preferred	0.0% muni bonds
0.0% conv't/warrants	0.0% other

SHAREHOLDER INFORMATION

Minimum Investment

Initial: $2,000   Subsequent: $100

Minimum IRA Investment

Initial: $2,000   Subsequent: $100

Maximum Fees

Load: none   12b-1: none
Other: none

Distributions

Income: Dec   Capital Gains: Dec

Exchange Options

Number Per Year: 4   Fee: none
Telephone: yes (money market fund available)

Services

IRA, pension, auto exchange, auto invest, auto withdraw

Columbia US Gov't Securities (CUGGX)

Government Bond

1301 S.W. 5th Ave.
P.O. Box 1350
Portland, OR 97207
800-547-1707, 503-222-3606

PERFORMANCE   fund inception date: 10/14/86

	3yr Annual	5yr Annual	10yr Annual	Bull	Bear
Return (%)	4.5	5.0	6.6	15.2	-1.3
Differ from Category (+/-)	-0.4 blw av	-1.6 blw av	-1.4 low	-6.8 low	5.1 high

Total Risk	Standard Deviation	Category Risk	Risk Index	Avg Mat
low	2.0%	low	0.5	2.5 yrs

	1996	1995	1994	1993	1992	1991	1990	1989	1988	1987
Return (%).	3.8	10.2	-0.1	5.9	5.8	12.7	9.2	9.6	5.3	4.1
Differ from Category (+/-) . .	2.3	-9.4	4.3	-5.7	-0.9	-3.0	2.9	-5.7	-3.0	8.5
Return, Tax-Adjusted (%). . .	1.8	8.0	-1.9	3.8	3.3	8.6	6.3	6.5	2.6	1.7

PER SHARE DATA

	1996	1995	1994	1993	1992	1991	1990	1989	1988	1987
Dividends, Net Income ($).	0.41	0.44	0.36	0.31	0.38	0.53	0.60	0.63	0.56	0.51
Distrib'ns, Cap Gain ($) . . .	0.00	0.00	0.00	0.16	0.21	0.46	0.00	0.00	0.00	0.00
Net Asset Value ($)	8.24	8.34	7.99	8.36	8.35	8.47	8.43	8.30	8.17	8.30
Expense Ratio (%).	na	0.79	0.81	0.75	0.76	0.76	0.85	0.85	0.85	0.85
Yield (%)	4.97	5.27	4.50	3.63	4.43	5.93	7.11	7.59	6.85	6.14
Portfolio Turnover (%).	na	253	253	254	289	309	222	159	394	147
Total Assets (Millions $). . . .	41	41	33	35	35	34	22	13	9	7

PORTFOLIO (as of 9/30/96)

Portfolio Manager: Thomas L. Thomsen - 1986

Investm't Category: Government Bond
✔ Domestic   Index
  Foreign   Sector
  Asset Allocation State Specific

Investment Style
  Large-Cap Growth   Large-Cap Value
  Mid-Cap Growth   Mid-Cap Value
  Small-Cap Growth   Small-Cap Value

Portfolio
  2.7% cash   0.0% corp bonds
  0.0% stocks   97.3% gov't bonds
  0.0% preferred   0.0% muni bonds
  0.0% conv't/warrants 0.0% other

SHAREHOLDER INFORMATION

Minimum Investment
Initial: $1,000   Subsequent: $100

Minimum IRA Investment
Initial: $1,000   Subsequent: $100

Maximum Fees
Load: none   12b-1: none
Other: none

Distributions
Income: monthly   Capital Gains: Dec

Exchange Options
Number Per Year: 4   Fee: none
Telephone: yes (money market fund available)

Services
IRA, pension, auto exchange, auto invest, auto withdraw

Copley (COPLX)
Growth & Income

P.O. Box 3287
315 Pleasant St., 5th Floor
Fall River, MA 02724
508-674-8459

PERFORMANCE

fund inception date: 1/31/80

	3yr Annual	5yr Annual	10yr Annual	Bull	Bear
Return (%)	6.8	9.6	8.9	35.8	-8.8
Differ from Category (+/-)	-8.5 low	-4.3 low	-3.8 low	-24.0 low	-2.4 low

Total Risk	Standard Deviation	Category Risk	Risk Index	Beta
av	8.1%	low	0.9	0.45

	1996	1995	1994	1993	1992	1991	1990	1989	1988	1987
Return (%)	4.8	26.0	-7.7	10.1	17.6	17.1	-1.6	17.8	19.8	-8.3
Differ from Category (+/-)	-14.9	-4.1	-6.4	-3.7	6.9	-12.0	4.3	-5.7	3.0	-8.5
Return, Tax-Adjusted (%)	4.8	26.0	-7.7	10.1	17.6	17.1	-1.6	17.8	19.8	-8.3

PER SHARE DATA

	1996	1995	1994	1993	1992	1991	1990	1989	1988	1987
Dividends, Net Income ($)	0.00	0.00	0.00	0.00	0.00	0.00	0.00	0.00	0.00	0.00
Distrib'ns, Cap Gain ($)	0.00	0.00	0.00	0.00	0.00	0.00	0.00	0.00	0.00	0.00
Net Asset Value ($)	26.05	24.85	19.71	21.35	19.38	16.47	14.06	14.28	12.12	10.11
Expense Ratio (%)	1.03	1.09	1.51	1.14	1.38	1.50	1.86	1.38	1.72	1.43
Yield (%)	0.00	0.00	0.00	0.00	0.00	0.00	0.00	0.00	0.00	0.00
Portfolio Turnover (%)	4	31	10	5	7	16	3	24	10	16
Total Assets (Millions $)	75	79	73	80	36	33	27	28	23	25

PORTFOLIO (as of 9/30/96)

Portfolio Manager: Irving Levine - 1978

Investm't Category: Growth & Income
- ✔ Domestic
- Foreign
- Asset Allocation
- Index
- Sector
- State Specific

Investment Style
- Large-Cap Growth
- Mid-Cap Growth
- Small-Cap Growth
- ✔ Large-Cap Value
- ✔ Mid-Cap Value
- Small-Cap Value

Portfolio
11.0% cash	0.0% corp bonds
87.0% stocks	0.0% gov't bonds
2.0% preferred	0.0% muni bonds
0.0% conv't/warrants	0.0% other

SHAREHOLDER INFORMATION

Minimum Investment
Initial: $1,000   Subsequent: $100

Minimum IRA Investment
Initial: $1,000   Subsequent: $100

Maximum Fees
Load: none   12b-1: none
Other: none

Distributions
Income: none   Capital Gains: none

Exchange Options
Number Per Year: none   Fee: na
Telephone: na

Services
IRA, pension, auto withdraw

Crabbe Huson Asset Allocation—Prim (CHAAX)

Balanced

One Financial Center
121 S.W. Morrison, Ste. 1415
Portland, OR 97204
800-541-9732, 503-295-0919
www.contrarian.com

PERFORMANCE

fund inception date: 1/31/89

	3yr Annual	5yr Annual	10yr Annual	Bull	Bear
Return (%)	8.3	11.0	na	31.7	-5.8
Differ from Category (+/-)	-3.4 low	-0.4 av	na	-13.4 low	-0.1 av

Total Risk	Standard Deviation	Category Risk	Risk Index	Beta
blw av	6.9%	av	1.0	0.61

	1996	1995	1994	1993	1992	1991	1990	1989	1988	1987
Return (%)	6.8	20.2	-0.9	18.2	12.1	21.2	-0.8	—	—	—
Differ from Category (+/-)	-7.4	-4.4	0.7	3.8	3.2	-2.9	0.1	—	—	—
Return, Tax-Adjusted (%)	4.4	16.5	-2.9	15.8	10.2	18.8	-2.6	—	—	—

PER SHARE DATA

	1996	1995	1994	1993	1992	1991	1990	1989	1988	1987
Dividends, Net Income ($)	0.28	0.32	0.31	0.21	0.32	0.46	0.45	—	—	—
Distrib'ns, Cap Gain ($)	0.73	1.12	0.46	0.71	0.30	0.18	0.00	—	—	—
Net Asset Value ($)	13.01	13.15	12.17	13.07	11.87	11.15	9.78	—	—	—
Expense Ratio (%)	na	1.48	1.44	1.46	1.52	1.76	1.90	—	—	—
Yield (%)	2.03	2.24	2.45	1.52	2.62	4.06	4.60	—	—	—
Portfolio Turnover (%)	na	225	149	116	155	158	162	—	—	—
Total Assets (Millions $)	125	142	107	91	55	26	13	—	—	—

PORTFOLIO (as of 9/30/96)

Portfolio Manager: committee - 1989

Investm't Category: Balanced
- ✔ Domestic
- ✔ Foreign
- ✔ Asset Allocation
- Index
- Sector
- State Specific

Investment Style
- Large-Cap Growth
- Mid-Cap Growth
- Small-Cap Growth
- Large-Cap Value
- Mid-Cap Value
- Small-Cap Value

Portfolio
8.8% cash	11.7% corp bonds
56.1% stocks	23.4% gov't bonds
0.0% preferred	0.0% muni bonds
0.0% conv't/warrants	0.0% other

SHAREHOLDER INFORMATION

Minimum Investment
Initial: $2,000   Subsequent: $500

Minimum IRA Investment
Initial: $2,000   Subsequent: $500

Maximum Fees
Load: none   12b-1: 0.25%
Other: none

Distributions
Income: quarterly   Capital Gains: Dec

Exchange Options
Number Per Year: 10   Fee: none
Telephone: yes (money market fund available)

Services
IRA, pension, auto invest, auto withdraw

Crabbe Huson Equity— Prim (CHEYX)

Growth

One Financial Center
121 S.W. Morrison, Ste. 1415
Portland, OR 97204
800-541-9732, 503-295-0919
www.contrarian.com

PERFORMANCE

fund inception date: 1/31/89

	3yr Annual	5yr Annual	10yr Annual	Bull	Bear
Return (%)	12.0	15.5	na	42.8	-4.8
Differ from Category (+/-)	-3.7 low	1.2 abv av	na	-19.6 low	1.9 abv av

Total Risk	Standard Deviation	Category Risk	Risk Index	Beta
abv av	9.9%	av	1.0	0.79

	1996	1995	1994	1993	1992	1991	1990	1989	1988	1987
Return (%)	11.7	23.8	1.5	25.9	16.4	35.0	-1.6	—	—	—
Differ from Category (+/-)	-8.4	-6.5	1.8	11.9	4.6	-1.0	4.5	—	—	—
Return, Tax-Adjusted (%)	9.2	21.7	0.7	24.0	14.6	32.0	-3.0	—	—	—

PER SHARE DATA

	1996	1995	1994	1993	1992	1991	1990	1989	1988	1987
Dividends, Net Income ($)	0.06	0.16	0.14	0.07	0.15	0.13	0.34	—	—	—
Distrib'ns, Cap Gain ($)	1.53	0.94	0.24	0.78	0.54	0.82	0.00	—	—	—
Net Asset Value ($)	18.85	18.32	15.69	15.84	13.27	12.00	9.64	—	—	—
Expense Ratio (%)	na	1.40	1.45	1.49	1.55	1.84	1.93	—	—	—
Yield (%)	0.29	0.83	0.87	0.42	1.08	1.01	3.52	—	—	—
Portfolio Turnover (%)	na	92	106	114	180	171	265	—	—	—
Total Assets (Millions $)	447	429	155	41	15	7	3	—	—	—

PORTFOLIO (as of 9/30/96)

Portfolio Manager: committee - 1989

Investm't Category: Growth
- ✔ Domestic
- ✔ Foreign
- Asset Allocation
- Index
- Sector
- State Specific

Investment Style
- Large-Cap Growth
- ✔ Mid-Cap Growth
- ✔ Small-Cap Growth
- Large-Cap Value
- ✔ Mid-Cap Value
- ✔ Small-Cap Value

Portfolio
8.2% cash	0.0% corp bonds
91.8% stocks	0.0% gov't bonds
0.0% preferred	0.0% muni bonds
0.0% conv't/warrants	0.0% other

SHAREHOLDER INFORMATION

Minimum Investment
Initial: $2,000   Subsequent: $500

Minimum IRA Investment
Initial: $2,000   Subsequent: $500

Maximum Fees
Load: none   12b-1: 0.25%
Other: none

Distributions
Income: Dec   Capital Gains: Dec

Exchange Options
Number Per Year: 10   Fee: none
Telephone: yes (money market fund available)

Services
IRA, pension, auto invest, auto withdraw

Crabbe Huson Oregon Tax-Free—Prim (ORBFX)

Tax-Exempt Bond

One Financial Center
121 S.W. Morrison, Ste. 1415
Portland, OR 97204
800-541-9732, 503-295-0919
www.contrarian.com

PERFORMANCE

fund inception date: 10/3/84

	3yr Annual	5yr Annual	10yr Annual	Bull	Bear
Return (%)	3.9	5.6	5.9	15.6	-4.0
Differ from Category (+/-)	-0.3 blw av	-0.8 low	-0.8 low	-2.8 low	1.4 abv av

Total Risk	Standard Deviation	Category Risk	Risk Index	Avg Mat
low	3.8%	low	0.7	9.5 yrs

	1996	1995	1994	1993	1992	1991	1990	1989	1988	1987
Return (%)	2.9	12.1	-2.7	8.9	7.3	9.8	6.3	7.5	7.6	0.7
Differ from Category (+/-)	-0.8	-3.1	2.6	-2.9	-1.0	-1.6	-0.1	-1.5	-2.4	2.1
Return, Tax-Adjusted (%)	2.9	12.1	-2.9	8.9	7.0	9.5	6.1	7.4	7.3	0.6

PER SHARE DATA

	1996	1995	1994	1993	1992	1991	1990	1989	1988	1987
Dividends, Net Income ($)	0.54	0.54	0.53	0.56	0.61	0.64	0.64	0.67	0.65	0.68
Distrib'ns, Cap Gain ($)	0.00	0.00	0.06	0.00	0.10	0.09	0.06	0.02	0.09	0.01
Net Asset Value ($)	12.56	12.74	11.87	12.82	12.31	12.16	11.77	11.75	11.60	11.48
Expense Ratio (%)	na	0.98	0.98	1.05	1.11	1.21	1.38	1.04	1.21	1.31
Yield (%)	4.29	4.23	4.44	4.36	4.91	5.22	5.40	5.69	5.56	5.91
Portfolio Turnover (%)	na	22	20	11	25	53	58	45	31	18
Total Assets (Millions $)	26	28	26	30	20	19	18	18	20	14

PORTFOLIO (as of 9/30/96)

Portfolio Manager: Richard S. Huson, Garth Nisbet - 1995

Investm't Category: Tax-Exempt Bond
- ✔ Domestic
- Foreign
- Asset Allocation
- Index
- Sector
- ✔ State Specific

Investment Style
- Large-Cap Growth
- Mid-Cap Growth
- Small-Cap Growth
- Large-Cap Value
- Mid-Cap Value
- Small-Cap Value

Portfolio
1.4% cash	0.0% corp bonds
0.0% stocks	0.0% gov't bonds
0.0% preferred	98.6% muni bonds
0.0% conv't/warrants	0.0% other

SHAREHOLDER INFORMATION

Minimum Investment
Initial: $2,000   Subsequent: $500

Minimum IRA Investment
Initial: na   Subsequent: na

Maximum Fees
Load: none   12b-1: 0.25%
Other: none

Distributions
Income: monthly   Capital Gains: Dec

Exchange Options
Number Per Year: 10   Fee: none
Telephone: yes (money market fund available)

Services
auto invest, auto withdraw

Crabbe Huson Special
(CHSPX)
Aggressive Growth

One Financial Center
121 S.W. Morrison, Ste. 1415
Portland, OR 97204
800-541-9732, 503-295-0919
www.contrarian.com

PERFORMANCE

fund inception date: 4/9/87

	3yr Annual	5yr Annual	10yr Annual	Bull	Bear
Return (%)	9.4	18.6	na	28.2	-5.0
Differ from Category (+/-)	-6.4 low	3.3 abv av	na	-42.9 low	5.6 high

Total Risk	Standard Deviation	Category Risk	Risk Index	Beta
abv av	10.9%	low	0.8	0.54

	1996	1995	1994	1993	1992	1991	1990	1989	1988	1987
Return (%).	5.9	10.7	11.7	34.5	33.3	17.0	3.8	17.0	19.8	—
Differ from Category (+/-)	-13.2	-23.6	11.7	15.2	21.6	-35.1	9.2	-11.4	3.4	—
Return, Tax-Adjusted (%). . .	4.8	8.8	10.5	33.5	33.3	5.7	1.2	12.0	19.8	—

PER SHARE DATA

	1996	1995	1994	1993	1992	1991	1990	1989	1988	1987
Dividends, Net Income ($)	0.14	0.21	0.04	0.00	0.00	0.04	0.15	0.25	0.00	—
Distrib'ns, Cap Gain ($) . . .	0.32	0.57	0.45	0.32	0.00	3.74	0.68	1.41	0.00	—
Net Asset Value ($)	14.33	13.98	13.34	12.40	9.47	7.10	9.45	9.92	9.90	—
Expense Ratio (%).	na	1.40	1.44	1.57	1.74	1.92	2.00	2.00	3.94	—
Yield (%)	0.95	1.44	0.29	0.00	0.00	0.36	1.48	2.20	0.00	—
Portfolio Turnover (%).	na	122	146	73	102	256	314	275	155	—
Total Assets (Millions $). . .	450	919	377	29	7	3	3	3	4	—

PORTFOLIO (as of 9/30/96)

Portfolio Manager: James E. Crabbe, John Johnson - 1990

Investm't Category: Aggressive Growth
- ✔ Domestic
- ✔ Foreign
- Asset Allocation
- Index
- Sector
- State Specific

Investment Style
Large-Cap Growth	Large-Cap Value
Mid-Cap Growth	Mid-Cap Value
Small-Cap Growth	✔ Small-Cap Value

Portfolio
0.0% cash	0.0% corp bonds
71.6% stocks	0.0% gov't bonds
0.0% preferred	0.0% muni bonds
0.0% conv't/warrants	28.4% other

SHAREHOLDER INFORMATION

Minimum Investment
Initial: $2,000   Subsequent: $500

Minimum IRA Investment
Initial: $2,000   Subsequent: $500

Maximum Fees
Load: none   12b-1: 0.25%
Other: none

Distributions
Income: Dec   Capital Gains: Dec

Exchange Options
Number Per Year: 10   Fee: none
Telephone: yes (money market fund available)

Services
IRA, pension, auto invest, auto withdraw

Dodge & Cox Balanced

(DODBX)

Balanced

One Sansome St.
35th Floor
San Francisco, CA 94104
800-621-3979, 415-981-1710

PERFORMANCE

fund inception date: 1/1/31

	3yr Annual	5yr Annual	10yr Annual	Bull	Bear
Return (%)	14.1	13.7	13.0	50.9	-5.2
Differ from Category (+/-)	2.4 abv av	2.3 abv av	2.2 high	5.8 abv av	0.5 av

Total Risk	Standard Deviation	Category Risk	Risk Index	Beta
av	7.6%	abv av	1.1	0.73

	1996	1995	1994	1993	1992	1991	1990	1989	1988	1987
Return (%).	14.0	28.0	1.9	15.9	10.5	20.7	0.9	23.0	11.5	7.1
Differ from Category (+/-).	-0.2	3.4	3.5	1.5	1.6	-3.4	1.8	4.9	-0.7	4.4
Return, Tax-Adjusted (%). .	12.3	25.5	0.1	13.6	8.7	18.4	-1.3	20.2	8.9	2.7

PER SHARE DATA

	1996	1995	1994	1993	1992	1991	1990	1989	1988	1987
Dividends, Net Income ($).	2.04	2.18	1.79	1.67	1.73	1.76	1.81	1.76	1.68	1.70
Distrib'ns, Cap Gain ($) . . .	0.24	0.91	0.33	1.06	0.07	0.28	0.33	0.71	0.46	2.67
Net Asset Value ($)	59.82	54.60	45.21	46.40	42.44	40.09	35.03	36.85	32.09	30.72
Expense Ratio (%).	na	0.57	0.58	0.60	0.63	0.65	0.70	0.72	0.77	0.72
Yield (%)	3.39	3.92	3.93	3.51	4.06	4.35	5.11	4.68	5.16	5.09
Portfolio Turnover (%).	na	20	20	15	6	10	10	12	9	15
Total Assets (Millions $). .	3,349	1,800	725	486	268	179	82	50	39	34

PORTFOLIO (as of 9/30/96)

Portfolio Manager: na

Investm't Category: Balanced

✔ Domestic	Index
Foreign	Sector
Asset Allocation	State Specific

Investment Style

Large-Cap Growth	Large-Cap Value
Mid-Cap Growth	Mid-Cap Value
Small-Cap Growth	Small-Cap Value

Portfolio

3.7% cash	13.0% corp bonds
57.4% stocks	25.7% gov't bonds
0.2% preferred	0.0% muni bonds
0.0% conv't/warrants	0.0% other

SHAREHOLDER INFORMATION

Minimum Investment
Initial: $2,500   Subsequent: $100

Minimum IRA Investment
Initial: $1,000   Subsequent: $100

Maximum Fees
Load: none   12b-1: none
Other: none

Distributions
Income: quarterly   Capital Gains: Mar, Dec

Exchange Options
Number Per Year: no limit   Fee: none
Telephone: yes

Services
IRA, auto invest, auto withdraw

Dodge & Cox Income

(DODIX)

General Bond

One Sansome St.
35th Floor
San Francisco, CA 94104
800-621-3979, 415-981-1710

PERFORMANCE

fund inception date: 1/2/89

	3yr Annual	5yr Annual	10yr Annual	Bull	Bear
Return (%)	6.5	7.7	na	25.8	-5.4
Differ from Category (+/-)	1.4 high	1.6 high	na	5.5 high	-1.2 blw av

Total Risk	Standard Deviation	Category Risk	Risk Index	Avg Mat
blw av	5.1%	high	1.4	11.1 yrs

	1996	1995	1994	1993	1992	1991	1990	1989	1988	1987
Return (%)	3.6	20.2	-2.9	11.3	7.7	17.9	7.4	—	—	—
Differ from Category (+/-)	-0.3	5.3	-0.6	2.2	1.2	3.2	0.1	—	—	—
Return, Tax-Adjusted (%)	1.1	17.1	-5.6	8.2	4.6	14.7	4.3	—	—	—

PER SHARE DATA

	1996	1995	1994	1993	1992	1991	1990	1989	1988	1987
Dividends, Net Income ($)	0.74	0.81	0.76	0.78	0.82	0.82	0.81	—	—	—
Distrib'ns, Cap Gain ($)	0.00	0.03	0.05	0.17	0.09	0.03	0.01	—	—	—
Net Asset Value ($)	11.68	12.02	10.74	11.89	11.55	11.59	10.61	—	—	—
Expense Ratio (%)	na	0.54	0.54	0.60	0.62	0.64	0.69	—	—	—
Yield (%)	6.33	6.72	7.04	6.46	7.04	7.05	7.62	—	—	—
Portfolio Turnover (%)	na	53	55	26	12	15	13	—	—	—
Total Assets (Millions $)	494	303	195	180	136	96	52	—	—	—

PORTFOLIO (as of 9/30/96)

Portfolio Manager: committee - 1989

Investm't Category: General Bond
- ✔ Domestic
- Foreign
- Asset Allocation
- Index
- Sector
- State Specific

Investment Style
- Large-Cap Growth
- Mid-Cap Growth
- Small-Cap Growth
- Large-Cap Value
- Mid-Cap Value
- Small-Cap Value

Portfolio

3.3% cash	32.7% corp bonds
0.0% stocks	64.0% gov't bonds
0.0% preferred	0.0% muni bonds
0.0% conv't/warrants	0.0% other

SHAREHOLDER INFORMATION

Minimum Investment
Initial: $2,500   Subsequent: $100

Minimum IRA Investment
Initial: $1,000   Subsequent: $100

Maximum Fees
Load: none   12b-1: none
Other: none

Distributions
Income: quarterly   Capital Gains: Mar, Dec

Exchange Options
Number Per Year: no limit   Fee: none
Telephone: yes

Services
IRA, auto invest, auto withdraw

Dodge & Cox Stock
(DODGX)
Growth & Income

One Sansome St.
35th Floor
San Francisco, CA 94104
800-621-3979, 415-981-1710

PERFORMANCE
fund inception date: 12/31/64

	3yr Annual	5yr Annual	10yr Annual	Bull	Bear
Return (%)	19.6	17.5	15.3	71.4	-5.4
Differ from Category (+/-)	4.3 high	3.6 high	2.6 high	11.6 abv av	1.0 abv av

Total Risk	Standard Deviation	Category Risk	Risk Index	Beta
abv av	10.3%	abv av	1.1	0.98

	1996	1995	1994	1993	1992	1991	1990	1989	1988	1987
Return (%)	22.2	33.3	5.1	18.3	10.8	21.4	-5.1	26.8	13.7	11.9
Differ from Category (+/-)	2.5	3.2	6.4	4.5	0.1	-7.7	0.8	3.3	-3.1	11.7
Return, Tax-Adjusted (%)	20.7	30.9	3.7	15.8	9.7	19.5	-6.6	24.7	11.4	9.2

PER SHARE DATA

	1996	1995	1994	1993	1992	1991	1990	1989	1988	1987
Dividends, Net Income ($)	1.29	1.46	1.14	1.04	1.11	1.24	1.35	1.23	1.07	1.04
Distrib'ns, Cap Gain ($)	1.68	2.46	0.89	2.84	0.16	0.87	0.28	0.82	1.11	1.57
Net Asset Value ($)	79.81	67.83	53.94	53.23	48.37	44.85	38.79	42.57	35.26	32.94
Expense Ratio (%)	na	0.60	0.61	0.62	0.64	0.64	0.65	0.65	0.69	0.65
Yield (%)	1.58	2.07	2.07	1.85	2.28	2.71	3.45	2.83	2.94	3.01
Portfolio Turnover (%)	na	13	7	15	7	5	7	4	10	12
Total Assets (Millions $)	2,227	1,227	543	435	335	281	172	125	81	67

PORTFOLIO (as of 9/30/96)

Portfolio Manager: committee - 1965

Investm't Category: Growth & Income
- ✔ Domestic
- Foreign
- Asset Allocation
- Index
- Sector
- State Specific

Investment Style
- Large-Cap Growth
- Mid-Cap Growth
- Small-Cap Growth
- ✔ Large-Cap Value
- Mid-Cap Value
- Small-Cap Value

Portfolio
7.3% cash	0.0% corp bonds
92.7% stocks	0.0% gov't bonds
0.0% preferred	0.0% muni bonds
0.0% conv't/warrants	0.0% other

SHAREHOLDER INFORMATION

Minimum Investment
Initial: $2,500   Subsequent: $100

Minimum IRA Investment
Initial: $1,000   Subsequent: $100

Maximum Fees
Load: none   12b-1: none
Other: none

Distributions
Income: quarterly   Capital Gains: Mar, Dec

Exchange Options
Number Per Year: no limit   Fee: none
Telephone: yes

Services
IRA, auto invest, auto withdraw

Domini Social Equity

(DSEFX)

Growth & Income

6 St. James Ave.
Boston, MA 02116
800-762-6814,

PERFORMANCE

fund inception date: 6/3/91

	3yr Annual	5yr Annual	10yr Annual	Bull	Bear
Return (%)	17.9	14.4	na	71.3	-6.7
Differ from Category (+/-)	2.6 abv av	0.5 av	na	11.5 abv av	-0.3 av

Total Risk	Standard Deviation	Category Risk	Risk Index	Beta
av	9.3%	av	1.0	0.94

	1996	1995	1994	1993	1992	1991	1990	1989	1988	1987
Return (%).	21.8	35.1	-0.4	6.5	12.0	—	—	—	—	—
Differ from Category (+/-) . .	2.1	5.0	0.9	-7.3	1.3	—	—	—	—	—
Return, Tax-Adjusted (%). .	21.2	34.4	-1.3	5.8	11.5	—	—	—	—	—

PER SHARE DATA

	1996	1995	1994	1993	1992	1991	1990	1989	1988	1987
Dividends, Net Income ($).	0.15	0.15	0.20	0.14	0.12	—	—	—	—	—
Distrib'ns, Cap Gain ($) . . .	0.11	0.08	0.08	0.07	0.01	—	—	—	—	—
Net Asset Value ($)	19.35	16.11	12.10	12.43	11.87	—	—	—	—	—
Expense Ratio (%).	0.98	0.90	0.75	0.75	0.75	—	—	—	—	—
Yield (%)	0.77	0.92	1.64	1.12	1.01	—	—	—	—	—
Portfolio Turnover (%).	5	6	8	4	3	—	—	—	—	—
Total Assets (Millions $). . .	111	69	33	26	10	—	—	—	—	—

PORTFOLIO (as of 6/30/96)

Portfolio Manager: na

Investm't Category: Growth & Income
- ✔ Domestic
- Foreign
- Asset Allocation
- Index
- Sector
- State Specific

Investment Style
- ✔ Large-Cap Growth
- Mid-Cap Growth
- Small-Cap Growth
- Large-Cap Value
- Mid-Cap Value
- Small-Cap Value

Portfolio

0.0% cash	0.0% corp bonds
100.0% stocks	0.0% gov't bonds
0.0% preferred	0.0% muni bonds
0.0% conv't/warrants	0.0% other

SHAREHOLDER INFORMATION

Minimum Investment
Initial: $1,000   Subsequent: $1

Minimum IRA Investment
Initial: $250   Subsequent: $1

Maximum Fees
Load: none   12b-1: 0.25%
Other: none

Distributions
Income: Jun, Dec   Capital Gains: Dec

Exchange Options
Number Per Year: none   Fee: na
Telephone: na

Services
IRA, pension, auto invest, auto withdraw

Dreyfus (DREVX)
Growth & Income

The Pan Am Building
200 Park Ave., 7th Floor
New York, NY 10166
800-782-6620, 516-794-5451
www.dreyfus.com/funds

PERFORMANCE

fund inception date: 5/24/51

	3yr Annual	5yr Annual	10yr Annual	Bull	Bear
Return (%)	11.1	9.0	10.7	44.6	-8.5
Differ from Category (+/-)	-4.2 low	-4.9 low	-2.0 blw av	-15.2 low	-2.1 blw av

Total Risk	Standard Deviation	Category Risk	Risk Index	Beta
abv av	10.4%	high	1.1	0.94

	1996	1995	1994	1993	1992	1991	1990	1989	1988	1987
Return (%)	15.8	23.7	-4.3	6.3	5.5	28.0	-3.4	23.6	8.7	8.6
Differ from Category (+/-)	-3.9	-6.4	-3.0	-7.5	-5.2	-1.1	2.5	0.1	-8.1	8.4
Return, Tax-Adjusted (%)	12.4	13.4	-5.8	3.9	4.0	26.0	-6.0	20.4	6.5	0.4

PER SHARE DATA

	1996	1995	1994	1993	1992	1991	1990	1989	1988	1987
Dividends, Net Income ($)	0.08	0.22	0.21	0.32	0.24	0.34	0.51	0.58	0.45	0.77
Distrib'ns, Cap Gain ($)	1.15	4.07	0.39	0.66	0.34	0.28	0.36	0.35	0.16	2.56
Net Asset Value ($)	10.82	10.42	11.93	13.10	13.27	13.14	10.80	12.07	10.55	10.28
Expense Ratio (%)	na	0.74	0.74	0.74	0.74	0.78	0.77	0.75	0.77	0.71
Yield (%)	0.66	1.51	1.70	2.32	1.76	2.53	4.56	4.66	4.20	5.99
Portfolio Turnover (%)	na	269	27	39	55	80	99	104	179	110
Total Assets (Millions $)	2,837	2,654	2,447	2,850	3,174	2,996	2,525	2,723	2,258	2,364

PORTFOLIO (as of 9/30/96)

Portfolio Manager: Ernest G. Wiggins Jr. - 1995

Investm't Category: Growth & Income
- ✔ Domestic
- ✔ Foreign
-   Asset Allocation
-   Index
-   Sector
-   State Specific

Investment Style
-   Large-Cap Growth
-   Mid-Cap Growth
-   Small-Cap Growth
- ✔ Large-Cap Value
- ✔ Mid-Cap Value
-   Small-Cap Value

Portfolio
0.9% cash	0.0% corp bonds
99.2% stocks	0.0% gov't bonds
0.0% preferred	0.0% muni bonds
0.0% conv't/warrants	0.0% other

SHAREHOLDER INFORMATION

Minimum Investment
Initial: $2,500   Subsequent: $100

Minimum IRA Investment
Initial: $750   Subsequent: $1

Maximum Fees
Load: none   12b-1: none
Other: none

Distributions
Income: quarterly   Capital Gains: annual

Exchange Options
Number Per Year: no limit   Fee: none
Telephone: yes (money market fund available)

Services
IRA, pension, auto exchange, auto invest, auto withdraw

Dreyfus 100% US Treasury Interm-Term (DRGIX)

Government Bond

The Pan Am Building
200 Park Ave., 7th Floor
New York, NY 10166
800-782-6620, 516-794-5451
www.dreyfus.com/funds

PERFORMANCE

fund inception date: 3/27/87

	3yr Annual	5yr Annual	10yr Annual	Bull	Bear
Return (%)	4.6	6.4	na	18.7	-4.6
Differ from Category (+/-)	-0.3 blw av	-0.2 av	na	-3.3 av	1.8 av

Total Risk	Standard Deviation	Category Risk	Risk Index	Avg Mat
low	4.1%	av	1.0	9.4 yrs

	1996	1995	1994	1993	1992	1991	1990	1989	1988	1987
Return (%)	3.0	15.7	-4.0	11.0	7.1	15.2	8.5	12.8	5.7	—
Differ from Category (+/-)	1.5	-3.9	0.4	-0.6	0.4	-0.5	2.2	-2.5	-2.6	—
Return, Tax-Adjusted (%)	0.5	12.8	-6.7	8.1	4.1	11.8	4.9	9.1	2.1	—

PER SHARE DATA

	1996	1995	1994	1993	1992	1991	1990	1989	1988	1987
Dividends, Net Income ($)	0.82	0.89	0.91	0.94	1.00	1.06	1.12	1.13	1.15	—
Distrib'ns, Cap Gain ($)	0.00	0.00	0.00	0.00	0.00	0.00	0.00	0.00	0.00	—
Net Asset Value ($)	12.69	13.13	12.16	13.60	13.12	13.22	12.48	12.59	12.22	—
Expense Ratio (%)	na	0.84	0.89	0.73	0.52	0.62	0.80	0.80	0.47	—
Yield (%)	6.46	6.77	7.48	6.91	7.62	8.01	8.97	8.97	9.41	—
Portfolio Turnover (%)	na	492	696	333	116	22	4	6	21	—
Total Assets (Millions $)	197	196	184	254	229	183	71	60	62	—

PORTFOLIO (as of 9/30/96)

Portfolio Manager: Gerald E. Thunelius - 1994

Investm't Category: Government Bond
- ✔ Domestic
- Foreign
- Asset Allocation
- Index
- Sector
- State Specific

Investment Style
- Large-Cap Growth
- Mid-Cap Growth
- Small-Cap Growth
- Large-Cap Value
- Mid-Cap Value
- Small-Cap Value

Portfolio
36.0% cash	0.0% corp bonds
0.0% stocks	64.0% gov't bonds
0.0% preferred	0.0% muni bonds
0.0% conv't/warrants	0.0% other

SHAREHOLDER INFORMATION

Minimum Investment
Initial: $2,500   Subsequent: $100

Minimum IRA Investment
Initial: $750   Subsequent: $1

Maximum Fees
Load: none   12b-1: 0.25%
Other: none

Distributions
Income: monthly   Capital Gains: annual

Exchange Options
Number Per Year: no limit   Fee: none
Telephone: yes (money market fund available)

Services
IRA, pension, auto exchange, auto invest, auto withdraw

Dreyfus 100% US Treasury Long-Term (DRGBX)

Government Bond

The Pan Am Building
200 Park Ave., 7th Floor
New York, NY 10166
800-782-6620, 516-794-5451
www.dreyfus.com/funds

PERFORMANCE

fund inception date: 3/27/87

	3yr Annual	5yr Annual	10yr Annual	Bull	Bear
Return (%)	4.5	7.4	na	23.1	-8.8
Differ from Category (+/-)	-0.4 blw av	0.8 high	na	1.1 abv av	-2.4 blw av

Total Risk	Standard Deviation	Category Risk	Risk Index	Avg Mat
av	7.4%	abv av	1.8	16.4 yrs

	1996	1995	1994	1993	1992	1991	1990	1989	1988	1987
Return (%)	0.8	24.9	-9.2	16.5	7.5	18.2	7.0	16.2	8.1	—
Differ from Category (+/-)	-0.7	5.3	-4.8	4.9	0.8	2.5	0.7	0.9	-0.2	—
Return, Tax-Adjusted (%)	-1.8	22.0	-11.8	13.6	4.5	14.8	3.6	12.5	4.5	—

PER SHARE DATA

	1996	1995	1994	1993	1992	1991	1990	1989	1988	1987
Dividends, Net Income ($)	0.98	0.96	1.00	1.02	1.07	1.13	1.16	1.16	1.16	—
Distrib'ns, Cap Gain ($)	0.00	0.00	0.00	0.00	0.00	0.00	0.00	0.00	0.00	—
Net Asset Value ($)	14.61	15.50	13.26	15.68	14.37	14.42	13.26	13.56	12.74	—
Expense Ratio (%)	na	0.87	0.98	0.78	0.56	0.25	0.00	0.00	0.00	—
Yield (%)	6.70	6.19	7.54	6.50	7.44	7.83	8.74	8.55	9.10	—
Portfolio Turnover (%)	na	634	1,213	420	97	21	31	40	19	—
Total Assets (Millions $)	138	145	124	215	239	217	42	24	9	—

PORTFOLIO (as of 9/30/96)

Portfolio Manager: Gerald E. Thunelius - 1994

Investm't Category: Government Bond
- ✔ Domestic
- Foreign
- Asset Allocation
- Index
- Sector
- State Specific

Investment Style
- Large-Cap Growth
- Mid-Cap Growth
- Small-Cap Growth
- Large-Cap Value
- Mid-Cap Value
- Small-Cap Value

Portfolio
11.2% cash	0.0% corp bonds
0.0% stocks	88.8% gov't bonds
0.0% preferred	0.0% muni bonds
0.0% conv't/warrants	0.0% other

SHAREHOLDER INFORMATION

Minimum Investment
Initial: $2,500   Subsequent: $100

Minimum IRA Investment
Initial: $750   Subsequent: $1

Maximum Fees
Load: none   12b-1: 0.25%
Other: none

Distributions
Income: monthly   Capital Gains: annual

Exchange Options
Number Per Year: no limit   Fee: none
Telephone: yes (money market fund available)

Services
IRA, pension, auto exchange, auto invest, auto withdraw

Dreyfus 100% US Treasury Short-Term (DRTSX)

Government Bond

The Pan Am Building
200 Park Ave., 7th Floor
New York, NY 10166
800-782-6620, 516-794-5451
www.dreyfus.com/funds

PERFORMANCE

fund inception date: 9/10/87

	3yr Annual	5yr Annual	10yr Annual	Bull	Bear
Return (%)	4.9	5.7	na	16.2	-1.3
Differ from Category (+/-)	0.0 av	-0.9 blw av	na	-5.8 blw av	5.1 high

Total Risk	Standard Deviation	Category Risk	Risk Index	Avg Mat
low	2.1%	low	0.5	2.3 yrs

	1996	1995	1994	1993	1992	1991	1990	1989	1988	1987
Return (%)...............	4.0	11.3	-0.4	7.0	7.0	12.9	6.2	12.7	7.8	—
Differ from Category (+/-)..	2.5	-8.3	4.0	-4.6	0.3	-2.8	-0.1	-2.6	-0.5	—
Return, Tax-Adjusted (%)...	1.6	8.5	-3.3	3.8	3.6	10.0	3.3	9.5	4.6	—

PER SHARE DATA

	1996	1995	1994	1993	1992	1991	1990	1989	1988	1987
Dividends, Net Income ($).	0.90	1.02	1.14	1.25	1.35	1.12	1.13	1.18	1.18	—
Distrib'ns, Cap Gain ($) ...	0.00	0.00	0.00	0.00	0.00	0.00	0.00	0.00	0.00	—
Net Asset Value ($)	14.82	15.13	14.55	15.75	15.91	16.18	15.40	15.62	14.96	—
Expense Ratio (%)........	na	0.65	0.35	0.11	0.03	0.00	0.00	0.00	0.00	—
Yield (%)	6.07	6.74	7.83	7.93	8.48	6.92	7.33	7.55	7.88	—
Portfolio Turnover (%).....	na	480	499	322	138	60	na	na	na	—
Total Assets (Millions $)...	191	187	172	188	142	29	0	0	0	—

PORTFOLIO (as of 9/30/96)

Portfolio Manager: Gerald E. Thunelius - 1994

Investm't Category: Government Bond

✔ Domestic	Index
Foreign	Sector
Asset Allocation	State Specific

Investment Style

Large-Cap Growth	Large-Cap Value
Mid-Cap Growth	Mid-Cap Value
Small-Cap Growth	Small-Cap Value

Portfolio

23.3% cash	0.0% corp bonds
0.0% stocks	76.7% gov't bonds
0.0% preferred	0.0% muni bonds
0.0% conv't/warrants	0.0% other

SHAREHOLDER INFORMATION

Minimum Investment
Initial: $2,500   Subsequent: $100

Minimum IRA Investment
Initial: $750   Subsequent: $1

Maximum Fees
Load: none   12b-1: 0.25%
Other: none

Distributions
Income: monthly   Capital Gains: annual

Exchange Options
Number Per Year: no limit   Fee: none
Telephone: yes (money market fund available)

Services
IRA, pension, auto exchange, auto invest, auto withdraw

Dreyfus A Bonds Plus

(DRBDX)

Corporate Bond

The Pan Am Building
200 Park Ave., 7th Floor
New York, NY 10166
800-782-6620, 516-794-5451
www.dreyfus.com/funds

PERFORMANCE

fund inception date: 6/25/76

	3yr Annual	5yr Annual	10yr Annual	Bull	Bear
Return (%)	5.0	7.5	8.3	23.8	-8.1
Differ from Category (+/-)	-1.3 blw av	-0.8 av	0.2 av	-1.0 av	-3.0 low

Total Risk	Standard Deviation	Category Risk	Risk Index	Avg Mat
blw av	5.6%	abv av	1.2	7.8 yrs

	1996	1995	1994	1993	1992	1991	1990	1989	1988	1987
Return (%)..............	2.6	20.3	-6.2	14.9	8.2	18.7	4.7	14.2	9.0	-0.4
Differ from Category (+/-).	-2.6	2.3	-3.1	3.1	-0.7	1.5	0.7	4.8	-0.3	-2.8
Return, Tax-Adjusted (%)...	0.2	17.5	-8.8	11.0	4.9	15.4	1.4	10.6	5.4	-4.4

PER SHARE DATA

	1996	1995	1994	1993	1992	1991	1990	1989	1988	1987
Dividends, Net Income ($).	0.87	0.93	0.94	1.00	1.07	1.10	1.15	1.18	1.19	1.34
Distrib'ns, Cap Gain ($) ...	0.00	0.00	0.07	0.58	0.20	0.00	0.00	0.00	0.00	0.21
Net Asset Value ($)	14.41	14.92	13.24	15.18	14.62	14.74	13.44	13.98	13.34	13.36
Expense Ratio (%)........	0.93	0.99	0.90	0.93	0.88	0.85	0.86	0.94	0.88	0.84
Yield (%)	6.03	6.23	7.06	6.34	7.21	7.46	8.55	8.44	8.92	9.87
Portfolio Turnover (%)....	165	172	93	81	67	26	40	66	49	79
Total Assets (Millions $)...	617	610	485	631	522	466	336	304	263	239

PORTFOLIO (as of 9/30/96)

Portfolio Manager: Garitt Kono - 1994

Investm't Category: Corporate Bond
✔ Domestic   Index
✔ Foreign   Sector
  Asset Allocation   State Specific

Investment Style
  Large-Cap Growth   Large-Cap Value
  Mid-Cap Growth   Mid-Cap Value
  Small-Cap Growth   Small-Cap Value

Portfolio
  8.1% cash   48.5% corp bonds
  0.0% stocks   32.5% gov't bonds
  0.0% preferred   0.0% muni bonds
  0.0% conv't/warrants 10.9% other

SHAREHOLDER INFORMATION

Minimum Investment
Initial: $2,500   Subsequent: $100

Minimum IRA Investment
Initial: $750   Subsequent: $1

Maximum Fees
Load: none   12b-1: 0.25%
Other: none

Distributions
Income: monthly   Capital Gains: annual

Exchange Options
Number Per Year: no limit   Fee: none
Telephone: yes (money market fund available)

Services
IRA, pension, auto exchange, auto invest, auto withdraw

Dreyfus Appreciation
(DGAGX)
Growth

The Pan Am Building
200 Park Ave., 7th Floor
New York, NY 10166
800-782-6620, 516-794-5452
www.dreyfus.com/funds

PERFORMANCE   fund inception date: 1/18/84

	3yr Annual	5yr Annual	10yr Annual	Bull	Bear
Return (%)	21.5	13.6	14.8	88.5	-7.4
Differ from Category (+/-)	5.8 high	-0.7 av	0.9 abv av	26.1 high	-0.7 av

Total Risk	Standard Deviation	Category Risk	Risk Index	Beta
abv av	9.6%	blw av	0.9	0.95

	1996	1995	1994	1993	1992	1991	1990	1989	1988	1987
Return (%).	25.6	37.8	3.6	0.7	4.6	38.4	-1.9	27.2	16.6	4.5
Differ from Category (+/-) . .	5.5	7.5	3.9	-13.3	-7.2	2.4	4.2	1.1	-1.5	2.5
Return, Tax-Adjusted (%). .	25.1	36.9	2.8	-0.1	4.1	37.0	-4.5	24.7	15.6	2.8

PER SHARE DATA

	1996	1995	1994	1993	1992	1991	1990	1989	1988	1987
Dividends, Net Income ($).	0.25	0.33	0.27	0.26	0.12	0.20	0.23	0.16	0.16	0.14
Distrib'ns, Cap Gain ($) . .	0.00	0.02	0.00	0.06	0.07	0.24	0.78	0.69	0.08	0.95
Net Asset Value ($)	25.58	20.55	15.17	14.92	15.15	14.67	10.95	12.20	10.28	9.03
Expense Ratio (%).	na	0.92	0.96	1.07	1.14	1.30	1.24	1.18	1.74	1.63
Yield (%)	0.97	1.60	1.77	1.73	0.78	1.34	1.96	1.24	1.54	1.40
Portfolio Turnover (%).	na	4	6	9	3	13	179	130	137	179
Total Assets (Millions $). . .	893	460	233	237	208	80	40	44	40	39

PORTFOLIO (as of 9/30/96)

Portfolio Manager: Fayez Sarofim - 1990

Investm't Category: Growth
- ✔ Domestic
- ✔ Foreign
-   Asset Allocation
-   Index
-   Sector
-   State Specific

Investment Style
- ✔ Large-Cap Growth
-   Mid-Cap Growth
-   Small-Cap Growth
-   Large-Cap Value
-   Mid-Cap Value
-   Small-Cap Value

Portfolio
4.2% cash	0.0% corp bonds
95.3% stocks	0.0% gov't bonds
0.6% preferred	0.0% muni bonds
0.0% conv't/warrants	0.0% other

SHAREHOLDER INFORMATION

Minimum Investment
Initial: $2,500   Subsequent: $100

Minimum IRA Investment
Initial: $750   Subsequent: $1

Maximum Fees
Load: none   12b-1: 0.20%
Other: none

Distributions
Income: annual   Capital Gains: annual

Exchange Options
Number Per Year: no limit   Fee: none
Telephone: yes (money market fund available)

Services
IRA, pension, auto exchange, auto invest, auto withdraw

Dreyfus Asset Allocation Total Return (DRAAX)

Balanced

The Pan Am Building
200 Park Ave., 7th Floor
New York, NY 10166
800-782-6620, 516-794-5451
www.dreyfus.com/funds

PERFORMANCE

fund inception date: 7/1/93

	3yr Annual	5yr Annual	10yr Annual	Bull	Bear
Return (%)	13.0	na	na	47.1	-4.4
Differ from Category (+/-)	1.3 abv av	na	na	2.0 abv av	1.3 abv av

Total Risk	Standard Deviation	Category Risk	Risk Index	Beta
av	7.6%	abv av	1.1	0.69

	1996	1995	1994	1993	1992	1991	1990	1989	1988	1987
Return (%)	14.9	23.5	1.6	—	—	—	—	—	—	—
Differ from Category (+/-)	0.7	-1.1	3.2	—	—	—	—	—	—	—
Return, Tax-Adjusted (%)	12.5	17.9	0.3	—	—	—	—	—	—	—

PER SHARE DATA

	1996	1995	1994	1993	1992	1991	1990	1989	1988	1987
Dividends, Net Income ($)	0.34	0.38	0.36	—	—	—	—	—	—	—
Distrib'ns, Cap Gain ($)	0.63	1.95	0.05	—	—	—	—	—	—	—
Net Asset Value ($)	13.98	13.02	12.48	—	—	—	—	—	—	—
Expense Ratio (%)	1.25	0.67	na	—	—	—	—	—	—	—
Yield (%)	2.32	2.53	2.87	—	—	—	—	—	—	—
Portfolio Turnover (%)	370	160	na	—	—	—	—	—	—	—
Total Assets (Millions $)	60	63	50	—	—	—	—	—	—	—

PORTFOLIO (as of 9/30/96)

Portfolio Manager: Timothy M. Ghriskey - 1996

Investm't Category: Balanced
- ✔ Domestic
- Foreign
- ✔ Asset Allocation
- Index
- Sector
- State Specific

Investment Style
- Large-Cap Growth
- Mid-Cap Growth
- Small-Cap Growth
- Large-Cap Value
- Mid-Cap Value
- Small-Cap Value

Portfolio
6.8%	cash	5.4% corp bonds
60.1%	stocks	27.8% gov't bonds
0.0%	preferred	0.0% muni bonds
0.0%	conv't/warrants	0.0% other

SHAREHOLDER INFORMATION

Minimum Investment
Initial: $2,500   Subsequent: $100

Minimum IRA Investment
Initial: $750   Subsequent: $1

Maximum Fees
Load: none   12b-1: 0.25%
Other: none

Distributions
Income: annual   Capital Gains: annual

Exchange Options
Number Per Year: no limit   Fee: none
Telephone: yes (money market fund available)

Services
IRA, pension, auto exchange, auto invest, auto withdraw

Dreyfus Basic GNMA

(DIGFX)

Mortgage-Backed Bond

The Pan Am Building
200 Park Ave., 7th Floor
New York, NY 10166
800-782-6620, 516-794-5451
www.dreyfus.com/funds

PERFORMANCE

fund inception date: 8/5/87

	3yr Annual	5yr Annual	10yr Annual	Bull	Bear
Return (%)	6.5	7.0	na	23.3	-2.9
Differ from Category (+/-)	0.9 high	1.0 high	na	2.2 abv av	0.7 abv av

Total Risk	Standard Deviation	Category Risk	Risk Index	Avg Mat
low	3.7%	av	1.0	21.1 yrs

	1996	1995	1994	1993	1992	1991	1990	1989	1988	1987
Return (%)	4.8	16.6	-1.0	8.7	7.0	13.2	8.5	8.4	10.5	—
Differ from Category (+/-)	0.4	1.9	0.7	1.8	0.8	-1.2	-1.3	-4.2	3.1	—
Return, Tax-Adjusted (%)	2.2	13.7	-3.8	5.8	4.0	10.3	5.2	5.0	6.8	—

PER SHARE DATA

	1996	1995	1994	1993	1992	1991	1990	1989	1988	1987
Dividends, Net Income ($)	0.98	1.02	1.07	1.11	1.16	1.05	1.20	1.22	1.34	—
Distrib'ns, Cap Gain ($)	0.00	0.00	0.00	0.00	0.00	0.00	0.00	0.00	0.00	—
Net Asset Value ($)	15.14	15.42	14.16	15.39	15.20	15.34	14.55	14.55	14.59	—
Expense Ratio (%)	na	0.50	0.06	0.00	0.00	0.00	0.00	0.00	0.00	—
Yield (%)	6.47	6.61	7.55	7.21	7.63	6.84	8.24	8.38	9.18	—
Portfolio Turnover (%)	na	254	290	34	31	40	na	288	1,026	—
Total Assets (Millions $)	58	55	44	54	45	25	0	0	2	—

PORTFOLIO (as of 9/30/96)

Portfolio Manager: Garitt Kono - 1992

Investm't Category: Mortgage-Backed Bond

✔ Domestic	Index
Foreign	Sector
Asset Allocation	State Specific

Investment Style

Large-Cap Growth	Large-Cap Value
Mid-Cap Growth	Mid-Cap Value
Small-Cap Growth	Small-Cap Value

Portfolio

3.2% cash	0.0% corp bonds
0.0% stocks	96.8% gov't bonds
0.0% preferred	0.0% muni bonds
0.0% conv't/warrants	0.0% other

SHAREHOLDER INFORMATION

Minimum Investment

Initial: $10,000   Subsequent: $1,000

Minimum IRA Investment

Initial: $5,000   Subsequent: $1,000

Maximum Fees

Load: none   12b-1: 0.25%
Other: none

Distributions

Income: monthly   Capital Gains: annual

Exchange Options

Number Per Year: 4   Fee: $5.00
Telephone: yes (money market fund available)

Services

IRA, pension, auto exchange, auto invest, auto withdraw

Dreyfus Basic Interm Muni Bond (DBIMX)

Tax-Exempt Bond

The Pan Am Building
200 Park Ave., 7th Floor
New York, NY 10166
800-782-6620, 516-794-5451
www.dreyfus.com/funds

PERFORMANCE

fund inception date: 5/4/94

	3yr Annual	5yr Annual	10yr Annual	Bull	Bear
Return (%)	na	na	na	19.5	na
Differ from Category (+/-)	na	na	na	1.1 av	na

Total Risk	Standard Deviation	Category Risk	Risk Index	Avg Mat
na	na	na	na	8.4 yrs

	1996	1995	1994	1993	1992	1991	1990	1989	1988	1987
Return (%)	4.8	13.8	—	—	—	—	—	—	—	—
Differ from Category (+/-)	1.1	-1.4	—	—	—	—	—	—	—	—
Return, Tax-Adjusted (%)	4.7	13.8	—	—	—	—	—	—	—	—

PER SHARE DATA

	1996	1995	1994	1993	1992	1991	1990	1989	1988	1987
Dividends, Net Income ($)	0.66	0.67	—	—	—	—	—	—	—	—
Distrib'ns, Cap Gain ($)	0.02	0.00	—	—	—	—	—	—	—	—
Net Asset Value ($)	13.05	13.13	—	—	—	—	—	—	—	—
Expense Ratio (%)	0.39	0.11	—	—	—	—	—	—	—	—
Yield (%)	5.04	5.10	—	—	—	—	—	—	—	—
Portfolio Turnover (%)	54	34	—	—	—	—	—	—	—	—
Total Assets (Millions $)	52	45	—	—	—	—	—	—	—	—

PORTFOLIO (as of 9/30/96)

Portfolio Manager: Doug J. Gaylor - 1996

Investm't Category: Tax-Exempt Bond
- ✔ Domestic
- Foreign
- Asset Allocation
- Index
- Sector
- State Specific

Investment Style
- Large-Cap Growth
- Mid-Cap Growth
- Small-Cap Growth
- Large-Cap Value
- Mid-Cap Value
- Small-Cap Value

Portfolio
0.0% cash	0.0% corp bonds
0.0% stocks	0.0% gov't bonds
0.0% preferred	88.1% muni bonds
0.0% conv't/warrants	11.9% other

SHAREHOLDER INFORMATION

Minimum Investment
Initial: $10,000   Subsequent: $1,000

Minimum IRA Investment
Initial: na   Subsequent: na

Maximum Fees
Load: none   12b-1: 0.25%
Other: none

Distributions
Income: monthly   Capital Gains: annual

Exchange Options
Number Per Year: 4   Fee: $5.00
Telephone: yes (money market fund available)

Services
auto exchange, auto invest, auto withdraw

Guide to Low-Load Mutual Funds

Dreyfus Basic Muni Bond

(DRMBX)

Tax-Exempt Bond

The Pan Am Building
200 Park Ave., 7th Floor
New York, NY 10166
800-782-6620, 516-794-5451
www.dreyfus.com/funds

PERFORMANCE

fund inception date: 5/6/94

	3yr Annual	5yr Annual	10yr Annual	Bull	Bear
Return (%)	na	na	na	22.9	na
Differ from Category (+/-)	na	na	na	4.5 high	na

Total Risk	Standard Deviation	Category Risk	Risk Index	Avg Mat
na	na	na	na	21.1 yrs

	1996	1995	1994	1993	1992	1991	1990	1989	1988	1987
Return (%)	4.5	19.2	—	—	—	—	—	—	—	—
Differ from Category (+/-)	0.8	4.0	—	—	—	—	—	—	—	—
Return, Tax-Adjusted (%)	4.3	19.1	—	—	—	—	—	—	—	—

PER SHARE DATA

	1996	1995	1994	1993	1992	1991	1990	1989	1988	1987
Dividends, Net Income ($)	0.73	0.74	—	—	—	—	—	—	—	—
Distrib'ns, Cap Gain ($)	0.09	0.04	—	—	—	—	—	—	—	—
Net Asset Value ($)	13.28	13.52	—	—	—	—	—	—	—	—
Expense Ratio (%)	0.39	0.20	—	—	—	—	—	—	—	—
Yield (%)	5.45	5.45	—	—	—	—	—	—	—	—
Portfolio Turnover (%)	59	58	—	—	—	—	—	—	—	—
Total Assets (Millions $)	69	49	—	—	—	—	—	—	—	—

PORTFOLIO (as of 9/30/96)

Portfolio Manager: Doug J. Gaylor - 1996

Investm't Category: Tax-Exempt Bond
- ✔ Domestic
- Foreign
- Asset Allocation
- Index
- Sector
- State Specific

Investment Style
- Large-Cap Growth
- Mid-Cap Growth
- Small-Cap Growth
- Large-Cap Value
- Mid-Cap Value
- Small-Cap Value

Portfolio

0.0% cash	0.0% corp bonds
0.0% stocks	0.0% gov't bonds
0.0% preferred	93.7% muni bonds
0.0% conv't/warrants	6.3% other

SHAREHOLDER INFORMATION

Minimum Investment
Initial: $10,000   Subsequent: $1,000

Minimum IRA Investment
Initial: na   Subsequent: na

Maximum Fees
Load: none   12b-1: 0.25%
Other: none

Distributions
Income: monthly   Capital Gains: annual

Exchange Options
Number Per Year: 4   Fee: $5.00
Telephone: yes (money market fund available)

Services
auto exchange, auto invest, auto withdraw

Dreyfus Balanced (DRBAX)

Balanced

The Pan Am Building
200 Park Ave., 7th Floor
New York, NY 10166
800-782-6620, 516-794-5451
www.dreyfus.com/funds

PERFORMANCE   fund inception date: 9/30/92

	3yr Annual	5yr Annual	10yr Annual	Bull	Bear
Return (%)	13.2	na	na	46.7	-2.9
Differ from Category (+/-)	1.5 abv av	na	na	1.6 abv av	2.8 high

Total Risk	Standard Deviation	Category Risk	Risk Index	Beta
blw av	6.0%	blw av	0.9	0.54

	1996	1995	1994	1993	1992	1991	1990	1989	1988	1987
Return (%)	11.6	25.0	3.9	10.8	—	—	—	—	—	—
Differ from Category (+/-)	-2.6	0.4	5.5	-3.6	—	—	—	—	—	—
Return, Tax-Adjusted (%)	9.3	21.7	2.2	9.2	—	—	—	—	—	—

PER SHARE DATA

	1996	1995	1994	1993	1992	1991	1990	1989	1988	1987
Dividends, Net Income ($)	0.43	0.57	0.46	0.40	—	—	—	—	—	—
Distrib'ns, Cap Gain ($)	0.63	0.75	0.12	0.13	—	—	—	—	—	—
Net Asset Value ($)	16.04	15.37	13.39	13.46	—	—	—	—	—	—
Expense Ratio (%)	na	1.04	0.69	na	—	—	—	—	—	—
Yield (%)	2.57	3.53	3.40	2.94	—	—	—	—	—	—
Portfolio Turnover (%)	na	72	58	na	—	—	—	—	—	—
Total Assets (Millions $)	289	196	92	59	—	—	—	—	—	—

PORTFOLIO (as of 9/30/96)

Portfolio Manager: Ernest Wiggins - 1995

Investm't Category: Balanced

✔ Domestic	Index
Foreign	Sector
Asset Allocation	State Specific

Investment Style

Large-Cap Growth	Large-Cap Value
Mid-Cap Growth	Mid-Cap Value
Small-Cap Growth	Small-Cap Value

Portfolio

0.1% cash	18.8% corp bonds
56.8% stocks	24.4% gov't bonds
0.0% preferred	0.0% muni bonds
0.0% conv't/warrants	0.0% other

SHAREHOLDER INFORMATION

Minimum Investment
Initial: $2,500   Subsequent: $100

Minimum IRA Investment
Initial: $750   Subsequent: $1

Maximum Fees
Load: none   12b-1: none
Other: none

Distributions
Income: quarterly   Capital Gains: annual

Exchange Options
Number Per Year: no limit   Fee: none
Telephone: yes (money market fund available)

Services
IRA, pension, auto exchange, auto invest, auto withdraw

Dreyfus CA Interm Muni Bond (DCIMX)

Tax-Exempt Bond

The Pan Am Building
200 Park Ave., 7th Floor
New York, NY 10166
800-782-6620, 516-794-5451
www.dreyfus.com/funds

PERFORMANCE

fund inception date: 4/20/92

	3yr Annual	5yr Annual	10yr Annual	Bull	Bear
Return (%)	3.5	na	na	16.0	-5.5
Differ from Category (+/-)	-0.7 low	na	na	-2.4 low	-0.1 av

Total Risk	Standard Deviation	Category Risk	Risk Index	Avg Mat
low	4.6%	blw av	0.8	8.5 yrs

	1996	1995	1994	1993	1992	1991	1990	1989	1988	1987
Return (%)	3.6	13.4	-5.6	14.4	—	—	—	—	—	—
Differ from Category (+/-)	-0.1	-1.8	-0.3	2.6	—	—	—	—	—	—
Return, Tax-Adjusted (%)	3.6	13.4	-5.6	14.4	—	—	—	—	—	—

PER SHARE DATA

	1996	1995	1994	1993	1992	1991	1990	1989	1988	1987
Dividends, Net Income ($)	0.60	0.63	0.67	0.73	—	—	—	—	—	—
Distrib'ns, Cap Gain ($)	0.00	0.00	0.00	0.00	—	—	—	—	—	—
Net Asset Value ($)	13.44	13.56	12.54	13.97	—	—	—	—	—	—
Expense Ratio (%)	0.65	0.32	0.04	0.00	—	—	—	—	—	—
Yield (%)	4.46	4.64	5.34	5.22	—	—	—	—	—	—
Portfolio Turnover (%)	41	17	6	6	—	—	—	—	—	—
Total Assets (Millions $)	222	235	238	306	—	—	—	—	—	—

PORTFOLIO (as of 9/30/96)

Portfolio Manager: Lawrence Troutman - 1992

Investm't Category: Tax-Exempt Bond
✔ Domestic   Index
  Foreign   Sector
  Asset Allocation ✔ State Specific

Investment Style
  Large-Cap Growth   Large-Cap Value
  Mid-Cap Growth   Mid-Cap Value
  Small-Cap Growth   Small-Cap Value

Portfolio
  0.0% cash   0.0% corp bonds
  0.0% stocks   0.0% gov't bonds
  0.0% preferred   77.7% muni bonds
  0.0% conv't/warrants 22.3% other

SHAREHOLDER INFORMATION

Minimum Investment
Initial: $2,500   Subsequent: $100

Minimum IRA Investment
Initial: na   Subsequent: na

Maximum Fees
Load: none   12b-1: 0.25%
Other: none

Distributions
Income: monthly   Capital Gains: annual

Exchange Options
Number Per Year: no limit   Fee: none
Telephone: yes (money market fund available)

Services
auto exchange, auto invest, auto withdraw

Dreyfus CA Tax-Exempt Bond (DRCAX)

Tax-Exempt Bond

The Pan Am Building
200 Park Ave., 7th Floor
New York, NY 10166
800-782-6620, 516-794-5451
www.dreyfus.com/funds

PERFORMANCE

fund inception date: 7/26/83

	3yr Annual	5yr Annual	10yr Annual	Bull	Bear
Return (%)	3.1	5.5	6.0	15.0	-6.0
Differ from Category (+/-)	-1.1 low	-0.9 low	-0.7 low	-3.4 low	-0.6 av

Total Risk	Standard Deviation	Category Risk	Risk Index	Avg Mat
blw av	5.5%	av	1.0	19.4 yrs

	1996	1995	1994	1993	1992	1991	1990	1989	1988	1987
Return (%)	3.4	14.0	-7.2	11.8	6.6	10.3	6.7	8.5	9.6	-1.7
Differ from Category (+/-)	-0.3	-1.2	-1.9	0.0	-1.7	-1.1	0.3	-0.5	-0.4	-0.3
Return, Tax-Adjusted (%)	3.4	14.0	-7.3	11.4	6.3	10.2	6.7	8.5	9.6	-1.7

PER SHARE DATA

	1996	1995	1994	1993	1992	1991	1990	1989	1988	1987
Dividends, Net Income ($)	0.73	0.79	0.82	0.86	0.90	0.95	1.01	1.03	1.05	1.06
Distrib'ns, Cap Gain ($)	0.00	0.00	0.04	0.16	0.15	0.03	0.00	0.00	0.00	0.00
Net Asset Value ($)	14.43	14.69	13.61	15.56	14.86	14.96	14.50	14.58	14.42	14.15
Expense Ratio (%)	0.69	0.71	0.70	0.69	0.68	0.69	0.69	0.70	0.71	0.70
Yield (%)	5.05	5.37	6.00	5.47	5.99	6.33	6.96	7.06	7.28	7.49
Portfolio Turnover (%)	56	39	28	41	46	56	35	40	60	32
Total Assets (Millions $)	1,425	1,521	1,431	1,846	1,781	1,729	1,547	1,463	1,281	1,127

PORTFOLIO (as of 9/30/96)

Portfolio Manager: Joseph P. Darcy - 1995

Investm't Category: Tax-Exempt Bond

✔ Domestic	Index
Foreign	Sector
Asset Allocation	✔ State Specific

Investment Style

Large-Cap Growth	Large-Cap Value
Mid-Cap Growth	Mid-Cap Value
Small-Cap Growth	Small-Cap Value

Portfolio

0.0% cash	0.0% corp bonds
0.0% stocks	0.0% gov't bonds
0.0% preferred	100.0% muni bonds
0.0% conv't/warrants	0.0% other

SHAREHOLDER INFORMATION

Minimum Investment
Initial: $2,500   Subsequent: $100

Minimum IRA Investment
Initial: na   Subsequent: na

Maximum Fees
Load: none   12b-1: 0.25%
Other: none

Distributions
Income: monthly   Capital Gains: annual

Exchange Options
Number Per Year: no limit   Fee: none
Telephone: yes (money market fund available)

Services
auto exchange, auto invest, auto withdraw

Dreyfus Conn Interm Muni Bond (DCTIX)

Tax-Exempt Bond

The Pan Am Building
200 Park Ave., 7th Floor
New York, NY 10166
800-782-6620, 516-794-5451
www.dreyfus.com/funds

PERFORMANCE

fund inception date: 6/26/92

	3yr Annual	5yr Annual	10yr Annual	Bull	Bear
Return (%)	4.1	na	na	17.4	-4.9
Differ from Category (+/-)	-0.1 blw av	na	na	-1.0 blw av	0.5 abv av

Total Risk	Standard Deviation	Category Risk	Risk Index	Avg Mat
low	4.7%	blw av	0.8	8.8 yrs

	1996	1995	1994	1993	1992	1991	1990	1989	1988	1987
Return (%)	3.7	14.2	-4.7	12.7	—	—	—	—	—	—
Differ from Category (+/-)	0.0	-1.0	0.6	0.9	—	—	—	—	—	—
Return, Tax-Adjusted (%)	3.7	14.2	-4.7	12.7	—	—	—	—	—	—

PER SHARE DATA

	1996	1995	1994	1993	1992	1991	1990	1989	1988	1987
Dividends, Net Income ($)	0.59	0.60	0.66	0.68	—	—	—	—	—	—
Distrib'ns, Cap Gain ($)	0.00	0.00	0.00	0.00	—	—	—	—	—	—
Net Asset Value ($)	13.51	13.61	12.47	13.77	—	—	—	—	—	—
Expense Ratio (%)	0.72	0.34	0.01	0.00	—	—	—	—	—	—
Yield (%)	4.36	4.40	5.29	4.93	—	—	—	—	—	—
Portfolio Turnover (%)	19	31	11	37	—	—	—	—	—	—
Total Assets (Millions $)	131	134	124	139	—	—	—	—	—	—

PORTFOLIO (as of 9/30/96)

Portfolio Manager: Stephen Kris - 1992

Investm't Category: Tax-Exempt Bond
- ✔ Domestic
- Foreign
- Asset Allocation
- Index
- Sector
- ✔ State Specific

Investment Style

Large-Cap Growth	Large-Cap Value
Mid-Cap Growth	Mid-Cap Value
Small-Cap Growth	Small-Cap Value

Portfolio

0.0% cash	0.0% corp bonds
0.0% stocks	0.0% gov't bonds
0.0% preferred	94.7% muni bonds
0.0% conv't/warrants	5.3% other

SHAREHOLDER INFORMATION

Minimum Investment
Initial: $2,500   Subsequent: $100

Minimum IRA Investment
Initial: na   Subsequent: na

Maximum Fees
Load: none   12b-1: 0.25%
Other: none

Distributions
Income: monthly   Capital Gains: annual

Exchange Options
Number Per Year: no limit   Fee: none
Telephone: yes (money market fund available)

Services
auto exchange, auto invest, auto withdraw

Dreyfus Core Value/ Investor (DCVIX)

Growth

The Pan Am Building
200 Park Ave., 7th Floor
New York, NY 10166
800-782-6620, 516-794-5451

PERFORMANCE

fund inception date: 2/6/47

	3yr Annual	5yr Annual	10yr Annual	Bull	Bear
Return (%)	18.2	14.8	12.2	66.7	-5.6
Differ from Category (+/-)	2.5 abv av	0.5 av	-1.7 blw av	4.3 abv av	1.1 abv av

Total Risk	Standard Deviation	Category Risk	Risk Index	Beta
abv av	9.7%	blw av	0.9	0.94

	1996	1995	1994	1993	1992	1991	1990	1989	1988	1987
Return (%).	21.4	35.5	0.3	16.5	4.0	22.8	-13.5	24.9	19.5	0.2
Differ from Category (+/-). .	1.3	5.2	0.6	2.5	-7.8	-13.2	-7.4	-1.2	1.4	-1.8
Return, Tax-Adjusted (%). .	15.6	31.7	-3.4	14.3	0.8	21.2	-14.4	16.7	16.5	-6.1

PER SHARE DATA

	1996	1995	1994	1993	1992	1991	1990	1989	1988	1987
Dividends, Net Income ($).	0.30	0.45	0.66	0.29	0.35	0.49	0.54	0.55	0.59	1.32
Distrib'ns, Cap Gain ($) . . .	5.76	2.62	2.70	1.53	2.63	0.56	0.06	7.60	1.87	5.36
Net Asset Value ($)	30.40	30.13	24.55	27.80	25.46	27.40	23.20	27.49	28.65	26.07
Expense Ratio (%).	na	1.13	1.11	1.15	1.22	1.20	1.26	1.23	1.31	0.95
Yield (%)	0.82	1.37	2.42	0.98	1.24	1.75	2.32	1.56	1.93	4.19
Portfolio Turnover (%). . . .	na	54	73	75	66	157	180	111	24	46
Total Assets (Millions $). . .	494	402	318	349	431	508	472	648	520	432

PORTFOLIO (as of 9/30/96)

Portfolio Manager: Guy R. Scott - 1991

Investm't Category: Growth

✔ Domestic   Index
✔ Foreign   Sector
  Asset Allocation State Specific

Investment Style

Large-Cap Growth	✔ Large-Cap Value
Mid-Cap Growth	✔ Mid-Cap Value
Small-Cap Growth	Small-Cap Value

Portfolio

2.0% cash	0.0% corp bonds
97.8% stocks	0.0% gov't bonds
0.2% preferred	0.0% muni bonds
0.0% conv't/warrants	0.0% other

SHAREHOLDER INFORMATION

Minimum Investment
Initial: $2,500   Subsequent: $100

Minimum IRA Investment
Initial: $750   Subsequent: $1

Maximum Fees
Load: none   12b-1: 0.25%
Other: none

Distributions
Income: quarterly   Capital Gains: annual

Exchange Options
Number Per Year: no limit   Fee: none
Telephone: yes (money market fund available)

Services
IRA, pension, auto exchange, auto invest, auto withdraw

Dreyfus Florida Interm Muni Bond (DFLIX)

Tax-Exempt Bond

The Pan Am Building
200 Park Ave., 7th Floor
New York, NY 10166
800-782-6620, 516-794-5451
www.dreyfus.com/funds

PERFORMANCE

fund inception date: 1/21/92

	3yr Annual	5yr Annual	10yr Annual	Bull	Bear
Return (%)	3.8	na	na	16.4	-5.0
Differ from Category (+/-)	-0.4 blw av	na	na	-2.0 blw av	0.4 abv av

Total Risk	Standard Deviation	Category Risk	Risk Index	Avg Mat
blw av	4.8%	blw av	0.9	8.1 yrs

	1996	1995	1994	1993	1992	1991	1990	1989	1988	1987
Return (%)	3.3	13.9	-5.0	12.8	—	—	—	—	—	—
Differ from Category (+/-)	-0.4	-1.3	0.3	1.0	—	—	—	—	—	—
Return, Tax-Adjusted (%)	3.3	13.9	-5.0	12.7	—	—	—	—	—	—

PER SHARE DATA

	1996	1995	1994	1993	1992	1991	1990	1989	1988	1987
Dividends, Net Income ($)	0.61	0.62	0.65	0.70	—	—	—	—	—	—
Distrib'ns, Cap Gain ($)	0.00	0.00	0.00	0.01	—	—	—	—	—	—
Net Asset Value ($)	13.45	13.62	12.52	13.85	—	—	—	—	—	—
Expense Ratio (%)	na	0.69	0.48	0.20	—	—	—	—	—	—
Yield (%)	4.53	4.55	5.19	5.05	—	—	—	—	—	—
Portfolio Turnover (%)	na	25	18	13	—	—	—	—	—	—
Total Assets (Millions $)	380	425	408	538	—	—	—	—	—	—

PORTFOLIO (as of 9/30/96)

Portfolio Manager: Stephen Kris - 1992

Investm't Category: Tax-Exempt Bond
- ✔ Domestic
- Foreign
- Asset Allocation
- Index
- Sector
- ✔ State Specific

Investment Style
- Large-Cap Growth
- Mid-Cap Growth
- Small-Cap Growth
- Large-Cap Value
- Mid-Cap Value
- Small-Cap Value

Portfolio
- 0.0% cash
- 0.0% stocks
- 0.0% preferred
- 0.0% conv't/warrants
- 0.0% corp bonds
- 0.0% gov't bonds
- 90.0% muni bonds
- 10.0% other

SHAREHOLDER INFORMATION

Minimum Investment
Initial: $2,500   Subsequent: $100

Minimum IRA Investment
Initial: na   Subsequent: na

Maximum Fees
Load: none   12b-1: 0.25%
Other: none

Distributions
Income: monthly   Capital Gains: annual

Exchange Options
Number Per Year: no limit   Fee: none
Telephone: yes (money market fund available)

Services
auto exchange, auto invest, auto withdraw

Dreyfus GNMA (DRGMX)

Mortgage-Backed Bond

The Pan Am Building
200 Park Ave., 7th Floor
New York, NY 10166
800-782-6620, 516-794-5451
www.dreyfus.com/funds

PERFORMANCE

fund inception date: 5/29/85

	3yr Annual	5yr Annual	10yr Annual	Bull	Bear
Return (%)	5.3	5.8	7.3	20.3	-3.8
Differ from Category (+/-)	-0.3 blw av	-0.2 blw av	-0.4 blw av	-0.8 blw av	-0.2 av

Total Risk	Standard Deviation	Category Risk	Risk Index	Avg Mat
low	3.6%	blw av	1.0	22.5 yrs

	1996	1995	1994	1993	1992	1991	1990	1989	1988	1987
Return (%)	4.4	15.1	-2.8	7.1	6.3	14.4	9.7	11.5	6.3	2.5
Differ from Category (+/-)	0.0	0.4	-1.1	0.2	0.1	0.0	-0.1	-1.1	-1.1	0.5
Return, Tax-Adjusted (%)	1.9	12.3	-5.3	4.4	3.4	11.0	6.2	7.9	2.7	-1.2

PER SHARE DATA

	1996	1995	1994	1993	1992	1991	1990	1989	1988	1987
Dividends, Net Income ($)	0.93	0.97	0.94	1.03	1.12	1.23	1.28	1.29	1.29	1.45
Distrib'ns, Cap Gain ($)	0.00	0.00	0.00	0.00	0.00	0.00	0.00	0.00	0.00	0.02
Net Asset Value ($)	14.53	14.84	13.79	15.15	15.12	15.32	14.54	14.49	14.21	14.59
Expense Ratio (%)	0.96	0.97	0.95	0.94	0.95	0.97	0.97	0.99	1.01	1.01
Yield (%)	6.40	6.53	6.81	6.79	7.40	8.02	8.80	8.90	9.07	9.92
Portfolio Turnover (%)	144	362	211	155	61	26	272	473	288	257
Total Assets (Millions $)	1,340	1,445	1,427	1,792	1,828	1,823	1,545	1,557	1,762	1,977

PORTFOLIO (as of 9/30/96)

Portfolio Manager: Garitt Kono - 1992

Investm't Category: Mortgage-Backed Bond
✔ Domestic	Index
Foreign	Sector
Asset Allocation	State Specific

Investment Style
Large-Cap Growth	Large-Cap Value
Mid-Cap Growth	Mid-Cap Value
Small-Cap Growth	Small-Cap Value

Portfolio
1.2% cash	0.0% corp bonds
0.0% stocks	98.8% gov't bonds
0.0% preferred	0.0% muni bonds
0.0% conv't/warrants	0.0% other

SHAREHOLDER INFORMATION

Minimum Investment
Initial: $2,500   Subsequent: $100

Minimum IRA Investment
Initial: $750   Subsequent: $1

Maximum Fees
Load: none   12b-1: 0.20%
Other: none

Distributions
Income: monthly   Capital Gains: annual

Exchange Options
Number Per Year: no limit   Fee: none
Telephone: yes (money market fund available)

Services
IRA, pension, auto exchange, auto invest, auto withdraw

Dreyfus General CA Muni Bond (GCABX)

Tax-Exempt Bond

The Pan Am Building
200 Park Ave., 7th Floor
New York, NY 10166
800-782-6620, 516-794-5452
www.dreyfus.com/funds

PERFORMANCE

fund inception date: 10/11/89

	3yr Annual	5yr Annual	10yr Annual	Bull	Bear
Return (%)	4.5	7.1	na	20.9	-6.8
Differ from Category (+/-)	0.3 abv av	0.7 abv av	na	2.5 abv av	-1.4 blw av

Total Risk	Standard Deviation	Category Risk	Risk Index	Avg Mat
blw av	6.2%	high	1.1	20.5 yrs

	1996	1995	1994	1993	1992	1991	1990	1989	1988	1987
Return (%)	4.2	18.0	-7.1	13.6	8.6	10.9	7.7	—	—	—
Differ from Category (+/-)	0.5	2.8	-1.8	1.8	0.3	-0.5	1.3	—	—	—
Return, Tax-Adjusted (%)	3.7	17.6	-7.3	13.4	8.4	10.9	7.7	—	—	—

PER SHARE DATA

	1996	1995	1994	1993	1992	1991	1990	1989	1988	1987
Dividends, Net Income ($)	0.68	0.71	0.76	0.80	0.84	0.88	0.92	—	—	—
Distrib'ns, Cap Gain ($)	0.24	0.15	0.08	0.06	0.08	0.00	0.00	—	—	—
Net Asset Value ($)	13.29	13.66	12.36	14.19	13.28	13.11	12.66	—	—	—
Expense Ratio (%)	na	0.76	0.76	0.64	0.37	0.21	0.00	—	—	—
Yield (%)	5.02	5.14	6.10	5.61	6.28	6.71	7.26	—	—	—
Portfolio Turnover (%)	na	83	29	30	24	3	10	—	—	—
Total Assets (Millions $)	303	333	296	433	388	299	131	—	—	—

PORTFOLIO (as of 9/30/96)

Portfolio Manager: Paul Disdier - 1989

Investm't Category: Tax-Exempt Bond
- ✔ Domestic
- Foreign
- Asset Allocation
- Index
- Sector
- ✔ State Specific

Investment Style
- Large-Cap Growth
- Mid-Cap Growth
- Small-Cap Growth
- Large-Cap Value
- Mid-Cap Value
- Small-Cap Value

Portfolio
0.0% cash	0.0% corp bonds
0.0% stocks	0.0% gov't bonds
0.0% preferred	82.1% muni bonds
0.0% conv't/warrants	17.9% other

SHAREHOLDER INFORMATION

Minimum Investment
Initial: $2,500   Subsequent: $100

Minimum IRA Investment
Initial: na   Subsequent: na

Maximum Fees
Load: none   12b-1: 0.25%
Other: none

Distributions
Income: monthly   Capital Gains: annual

Exchange Options
Number Per Year: no limit   Fee: none
Telephone: yes (money market fund available)

Services
auto exchange, auto invest, auto withdraw

Individual Fund Listings   **207**

Dreyfus General Muni Bond (GMBDX)

Tax-Exempt Bond

The Pan Am Building
200 Park Ave., 7th Floor
New York, NY 10166
800-782-6620, 516-794-5452
www.dreyfus.com/funds

PERFORMANCE

fund inception date: 3/21/84

	3yr Annual	5yr Annual	10yr Annual	Bull	Bear
Return (%)	3.8	6.8	7.4	19.1	-6.9
Differ from Category (+/-)	-0.4 blw av	0.4 av	0.7 abv av	0.7 av	-1.5 blw av

Total Risk	Standard Deviation	Category Risk	Risk Index	Avg Mat
blw av	5.9%	abv av	1.1	21.4 yrs

	1996	1995	1994	1993	1992	1991	1990	1989	1988	1987
Return (%)	3.1	17.2	-7.4	13.3	9.8	14.6	7.6	11.4	12.5	-5.6
Differ from Category (+/-)	-0.6	2.0	-2.1	1.5	1.5	3.2	1.2	2.4	2.5	-4.2
Return, Tax-Adjusted (%)	2.6	17.1	-7.7	12.8	9.5	14.5	7.6	11.4	12.5	-6.1

PER SHARE DATA

	1996	1995	1994	1993	1992	1991	1990	1989	1988	1987
Dividends, Net Income ($)	0.79	0.81	0.86	0.91	0.99	1.06	1.09	1.01	0.96	0.98
Distrib'ns, Cap Gain ($)	0.25	0.02	0.12	0.22	0.14	0.04	0.00	0.00	0.00	0.24
Net Asset Value ($)	14.59	15.20	13.72	15.84	15.02	14.76	13.90	13.97	13.48	12.87
Expense Ratio (%)	0.88	0.87	0.82	0.41	0.01	0.00	0.28	0.80	0.80	0.77
Yield (%)	5.32	5.32	6.21	5.66	6.53	7.16	7.84	7.22	7.12	7.47
Portfolio Turnover (%)	114	67	59	64	38	50	110	218	67	105
Total Assets (Millions $)	835	966	829	1,260	1,072	683	270	77	34	33

PORTFOLIO (as of 9/30/96)

Portfolio Manager: Paul Disdier - 1988

Investm't Category: Tax-Exempt Bond

✔ Domestic   Index
  Foreign   Sector
  Asset Allocation State Specific

Investment Style

Large-Cap Growth   Large-Cap Value
Mid-Cap Growth   Mid-Cap Value
Small-Cap Growth   Small-Cap Value

Portfolio

0.0% cash   0.0% corp bonds
0.0% stocks   0.0% gov't bonds
0.0% preferred   99.0% muni bonds
0.0% conv't/warrants 1.0% other

SHAREHOLDER INFORMATION

Minimum Investment
Initial: $2,500   Subsequent: $100

Minimum IRA Investment
Initial: na   Subsequent: na

Maximum Fees
Load: none   12b-1: 0.20%
Other: none

Distributions
Income: monthly   Capital Gains: annual

Exchange Options
Number Per Year: no limit   Fee: none
Telephone: yes (money market fund available)

Services
auto exchange, auto invest, auto withdraw

Dreyfus General NY Muni Bond (GNYMX)

Tax-Exempt Bond

The Pan Am Building
200 Park Ave., 7th Floor
New York, NY 10166
800-782-6620, 516-794-5452
www.dreyfus.com/funds

PERFORMANCE

fund inception date: 11/19/84

	3yr Annual	5yr Annual	10yr Annual	Bull	Bear
Return (%)	3.6	6.9	6.9	17.3	-6.1
Differ from Category (+/-)	-0.6 low	0.5 av	0.2 av	-1.1 blw av	-0.7 av

Total Risk	Standard Deviation	Category Risk	Risk Index	Avg Mat
blw av	6.1%	abv av	1.1	20.1 yrs

	1996	1995	1994	1993	1992	1991	1990	1989	1988	1987
Return (%)	3.0	16.5	-7.2	14.1	10.0	14.0	6.6	6.5	5.9	1.3
Differ from Category (+/-)	-0.7	1.3	-1.9	2.3	1.7	2.6	0.2	-2.5	-4.1	2.7
Return, Tax-Adjusted (%)	2.8	16.3	-7.4	13.6	9.6	14.0	6.6	6.5	5.9	1.3

PER SHARE DATA

	1996	1995	1994	1993	1992	1991	1990	1989	1988	1987
Dividends, Net Income ($)	1.00	1.04	1.12	1.16	1.21	1.29	1.35	1.05	1.00	1.04
Distrib'ns, Cap Gain ($)	0.12	0.13	0.11	0.29	0.26	0.00	0.00	0.00	0.00	0.00
Net Asset Value ($)	19.66	20.20	18.40	21.14	19.85	19.44	18.25	18.43	18.31	18.25
Expense Ratio (%)	na	0.86	0.76	0.69	0.62	0.36	0.07	1.32	1.10	0.89
Yield (%)	5.05	5.11	6.05	5.41	6.01	6.63	7.39	5.69	5.46	5.69
Portfolio Turnover (%)	na	65	24	23	43	19	60	27	32	67
Total Assets (Millions $)	309	335	293	401	323	226	114	36	44	52

PORTFOLIO (as of 9/30/96)

Portfolio Manager: Monica Wieboldt - 1988

Investm't Category: Tax-Exempt Bond
- ✔ Domestic
- Foreign
- Asset Allocation
- Index
- Sector
- ✔ State Specific

Investment Style
- Large-Cap Growth
- Mid-Cap Growth
- Small-Cap Growth
- Large-Cap Value
- Mid-Cap Value
- Small-Cap Value

Portfolio
- 0.0% cash
- 0.0% stocks
- 0.0% preferred
- 0.0% conv't/warrants
- 0.0% corp bonds
- 0.0% gov't bonds
- 90.3% muni bonds
- 9.7% other

SHAREHOLDER INFORMATION

Minimum Investment
Initial: $2,500   Subsequent: $100

Minimum IRA Investment
Initial: na   Subsequent: na

Maximum Fees
Load: none   12b-1: 0.20%
Other: none

Distributions
Income: monthly   Capital Gains: annual

Exchange Options
Number Per Year: no limit   Fee: none
Telephone: yes (money market fund available)

Services
auto exchange, auto invest, auto withdraw

Dreyfus Global Growth
(DSWIX)
International Stock

The Pan Am Building
200 Park Ave., 7th Floor
New York, NY 10166
800-782-6620, 516-794-5451
www.dreyfus.com/funds

PERFORMANCE

fund inception date: 4/10/87

	3yr Annual	5yr Annual	10yr Annual	Bull	Bear
Return (%)	5.0	6.6	na	23.1	-9.5
Differ from Category (+/-)	-1.3 blw av	-3.4 blw av	na	-1.2 av	-2.3 blw av

Total Risk	Standard Deviation	Category Risk	Risk Index	Beta
av	9.4%	blw av	0.9	0.81

	1996	1995	1994	1993	1992	1991	1990	1989	1988	1987
Return (%).............	11.9	12.0	-7.5	21.9	-2.8	17.5	5.7	21.0	15.4	—
Differ from Category (+/-) .	-2.9	2.9	-4.4	-17.7	1.0	4.3	15.8	-1.6	0.5	—
Return, Tax-Adjusted (%)...	6.7	12.0	-7.5	21.9	-2.8	17.5	5.7	21.0	15.4	—

PER SHARE DATA

	1996	1995	1994	1993	1992	1991	1990	1989	1988	1987
Dividends, Net Income ($)	0.24	0.00	0.00	0.00	0.00	0.00	0.00	0.00	0.00	—
Distrib'ns, Cap Gain ($) ...	6.49	0.00	0.00	0.00	0.00	0.00	0.00	0.00	0.00	—
Net Asset Value ($)	34.62	36.97	32.99	35.66	29.24	30.06	25.58	24.18	19.98	—
Expense Ratio (%).........	na	1.46	1.40	1.50	1.61	1.62	1.50	1.50	1.50	—
Yield (%)	0.58	0.00	0.00	0.00	0.00	0.00	0.00	0.00	0.00	—
Portfolio Turnover (%).....	na	225	147	187	439	420	566	452	452	—
Total Assets (Millions $)...	101	104	134	159	111	54	25	17	18	—

PORTFOLIO (as of 9/30/96)

Portfolio Manager: Ronald Chapman - 1995

Investm't Category: International Stock
- ✔ Domestic
- ✔ Foreign
- Asset Allocation
- Index
- Sector
- State Specific

Investment Style
- Large-Cap Growth
- Mid-Cap Growth
- Small-Cap Growth
- Large-Cap Value
- Mid-Cap Value
- Small-Cap Value

Portfolio
2.8% cash	0.0% corp bonds
96.6% stocks	0.0% gov't bonds
0.6% preferred	0.0% muni bonds
0.0% conv't/warrants	0.0% other

SHAREHOLDER INFORMATION

Minimum Investment
Initial: $2,500   Subsequent: $100

Minimum IRA Investment
Initial: $750   Subsequent: $1

Maximum Fees
Load: none   12b-1: 0.25%
Other: none

Distributions
Income: annual   Capital Gains: annual

Exchange Options
Number Per Year: no limit   Fee: none
Telephone: yes (money market fund available)

Services
IRA, pension, auto exchange, auto invest, auto withdraw

Dreyfus Growth & Income

(DGRIX)

Growth & Income

The Pan Am Building
200 Park Ave., 7th Floor
New York, NY 10166
800-782-6620, 516-794-5451
www.dreyfus.com/funds

PERFORMANCE

fund inception date: 12/31/91

	3yr Annual	5yr Annual	10yr Annual	Bull	Bear
Return (%)	10.6	14.0	na	44.2	-9.2
Differ from Category (+/-)	-4.7 low	0.1 av	na	-15.6 low	-2.8 low

Total Risk	Standard Deviation	Category Risk	Risk Index	Beta
av	8.8%	blw av	1.0	0.78

	1996	1995	1994	1993	1992	1991	1990	1989	1988	1987
Return (%).	14.4	25.0	-5.2	18.5	20.1	—	—	—	—	—
Differ from Category (+/-) .	-5.3	-5.1	-3.9	4.7	9.4	—	—	—	—	—
Return, Tax-Adjusted (%). . .	9.6	22.9	-6.3	17.4	19.2	—	—	—	—	—

PER SHARE DATA

	1996	1995	1994	1993	1992	1991	1990	1989	1988	1987
Dividends, Net Income ($).	0.34	0.44	0.36	0.35	0.27	—	—	—	—	—
Distrib'ns, Cap Gain ($) . . .	2.65	0.50	0.16	0.04	0.00	—	—	—	—	—
Net Asset Value ($)	18.16	18.55	15.63	17.04	14.73	—	—	—	—	—
Expense Ratio (%).	na	1.05	1.14	1.24	1.02	—	—	—	—	—
Yield (%)	1.63	2.30	2.27	2.04	1.83	—	—	—	—	—
Portfolio Turnover (%).	na	132	97	85	127	—	—	—	—	—
Total Assets (Millions $). .	2,088	1,860	1,621	1,277	134	—	—	—	—	—

PORTFOLIO (as of 9/30/96)

Portfolio Manager: Richard Hoey - 1991

Investm't Category: Growth & Income
- ✔ Domestic
- ✔ Foreign
- Asset Allocation
- Index
- Sector
- State Specific

Investment Style
- Large-Cap Growth
- ✔ Mid-Cap Growth
- Small-Cap Growth
- Large-Cap Value
- ✔ Mid-Cap Value
- Small-Cap Value

Portfolio
7.9% cash	0.0% corp bonds
66.5% stocks	0.0% gov't bonds
9.0% preferred	0.0% muni bonds
16.6% conv't/warrants	0.0% other

SHAREHOLDER INFORMATION

Minimum Investment
Initial: $2,500   Subsequent: $100

Minimum IRA Investment
Initial: $750   Subsequent: $1

Maximum Fees
Load: none   12b-1: 0.25%
Other: none

Distributions
Income: quarterly   Capital Gains: annual

Exchange Options
Number Per Year: no limit   Fee: none
Telephone: yes (money market fund available)

Services
IRA, pension, auto exchange, auto invest, auto withdraw

Dreyfus Grth & Value: Aggressive Grth (DGVAX)

Aggressive Growth

The Pan Am Building
200 Park Ave., 7th Floor
New York, NY 10166
800-782-6620, 516-794-5451
www.dreyfus.com/funds

PERFORMANCE

fund inception date: 9/29/95

	3yr Annual	5yr Annual	10yr Annual	Bull	Bear
Return (%)	na	na	na	na	na
Differ from Category (+/-)	na	na	na	na	na

Total Risk	Standard Deviation	Category Risk	Risk Index	Beta
na	na	na	na	na

	1996	1995	1994	1993	1992	1991	1990	1989	1988	1987
Return (%).	20.6	—	—	—	—	—	—	—	—	—
Differ from Category (+/-) . .	1.5	—	—	—	—	—	—	—	—	—
Return, Tax-Adjusted (%). .	20.6	—	—	—	—	—	—	—	—	—

PER SHARE DATA

	1996	1995	1994	1993	1992	1991	1990	1989	1988	1987
Dividends, Net Income ($).	0.00	—	—	—	—	—	—	—	—	—
Distrib'ns, Cap Gain ($) . . .	0.00	—	—	—	—	—	—	—	—	—
Net Asset Value ($)	19.70	—	—	—	—	—	—	—	—	—
Expense Ratio (%).	1.16	—	—	—	—	—	—	—	—	—
Yield (%)	0.00	—	—	—	—	—	—	—	—	—
Portfolio Turnover (%). . . .	125	—	—	—	—	—	—	—	—	—
Total Assets (Millions $). . . .	91	—	—	—	—	—	—	—	—	—

PORTFOLIO (as of 9/30/96)

Portfolio Manager: Michael L. Schonberg - 1995

Investm't Category: Aggressive Growth
- ✔ Domestic
- ✔ Foreign
- Asset Allocation
- Index
- Sector
- State Specific

Investment Style
- Large-Cap Growth
- Mid-Cap Growth
- Small-Cap Growth
- Large-Cap Value
- Mid-Cap Value
- Small-Cap Value

Portfolio
0.0% cash	0.0% corp bonds
117.3% stocks	0.0% gov't bonds
0.0% preferred	0.0% muni bonds
0.0% conv't/warrants	0.0% other

SHAREHOLDER INFORMATION

Minimum Investment
Initial: $2,500   Subsequent: $100

Minimum IRA Investment
Initial: $750   Subsequent: $1

Maximum Fees
Load: none   12b-1: 0.25%
Other: none

Distributions
Income: annual   Capital Gains: annual

Exchange Options
Number Per Year: no limit   Fee: none
Telephone: yes (money market fund available)

Services
IRA, pension, auto exchange, auto invest, auto withdraw

Dreyfus Grth & Value: Emerging Ldrs (DRELX)

Aggressive Growth

The Pan Am Building
200 Park Ave., 7th Floor
New York, NY 10166
800-782-6620, 516-794-5451
www.dreyfus.com/funds

PERFORMANCE

fund inception date: 9/28/95

	3yr Annual	5yr Annual	10yr Annual	Bull	Bear
Return (%)	na	na	na	na	na
Differ from Category (+/-)	na	na	na	na	na

Total Risk	Standard Deviation	Category Risk	Risk Index	Beta
na	na	na	na	na

	1996	1995	1994	1993	1992	1991	1990	1989	1988	1987
Return (%)	37.4	—	—	—	—	—	—	—	—	—
Differ from Category (+/-)	18.3	—	—	—	—	—	—	—	—	—
Return, Tax-Adjusted (%)	34.9	—	—	—	—	—	—	—	—	—

PER SHARE DATA

	1996	1995	1994	1993	1992	1991	1990	1989	1988	1987
Dividends, Net Income ($)	0.00	—	—	—	—	—	—	—	—	—
Distrib'ns, Cap Gain ($)	1.40	—	—	—	—	—	—	—	—	—
Net Asset Value ($)	20.39	—	—	—	—	—	—	—	—	—
Expense Ratio (%)	1.16	—	—	—	—	—	—	—	—	—
Yield (%)	0.00	—	—	—	—	—	—	—	—	—
Portfolio Turnover (%)	203	—	—	—	—	—	—	—	—	—
Total Assets (Millions $)	53	—	—	—	—	—	—	—	—	—

PORTFOLIO (as of 9/30/96)

Portfolio Manager: Thomas A. Frank - 1995

Investm't Category: Aggressive Growth

✔ Domestic	Index
✔ Foreign	Sector
Asset Allocation	State Specific

Investment Style

Large-Cap Growth	Large-Cap Value
Mid-Cap Growth	Mid-Cap Value
Small-Cap Growth	Small-Cap Value

Portfolio

7.6% cash	0.0% corp bonds
92.4% stocks	0.0% gov't bonds
0.0% preferred	0.0% muni bonds
0.0% conv't/warrants	0.0% other

SHAREHOLDER INFORMATION

Minimum Investment
Initial: $2,500   Subsequent: $100

Minimum IRA Investment
Initial: $750   Subsequent: $1

Maximum Fees
Load: none   12b-1: 0.25%
Other: none

Distributions
Income: annual   Capital Gains: annual

Exchange Options
Number Per Year: no limit   Fee: none
Telephone: yes (money market fund available)

Services
IRA, pension, auto exchange, auto invest, auto withdraw

Dreyfus Growth Opportunity (DREQX)

Growth

The Pan Am Building
200 Park Ave., 7th Floor
New York, NY 10166
800-782-6620, 516-794-5451
www.dreyfus.com/funds

PERFORMANCE

fund inception date: 2/4/72

	3yr Annual	5yr Annual	10yr Annual	Bull	Bear
Return (%)	13.6	7.4	11.3	57.3	-9.0
Differ from Category (+/-)	-2.1 blw av	-6.9 low	-2.6 low	-5.1 av	-2.3 blw av

Total Risk	Standard Deviation	Category Risk	Risk Index	Beta
abv av	10.6%	av	1.0	0.96

	1996	1995	1994	1993	1992	1991	1990	1989	1988	1987
Return (%).	22.2	28.3	-6.4	1.7	-4.2	51.4	-6.6	14.7	17.8	6.7
Differ from Category (+/-). .	2.1	-2.0	-6.1	-12.3	-16.0	15.4	-0.5	-11.4	-0.3	4.7
Return, Tax-Adjusted (%). .	17.9	23.3	-11.5	-3.9	-4.3	50.8	-7.7	10.6	15.8	-0.4

PER SHARE DATA

	1996	1995	1994	1993	1992	1991	1990	1989	1988	1987
Dividends, Net Income ($).	0.08	0.12	0.08	0.00	0.02	0.13	0.27	0.46	0.41	0.42
Distrib'ns, Cap Gain ($) . . .	1.28	1.27	1.84	2.60	0.00	0.00	0.01	0.80	0.03	2.06
Net Asset Value ($)	9.71	9.09	8.18	10.74	13.14	13.73	9.16	10.12	9.94	8.81
Expense Ratio (%).	1.04	1.10	1.09	1.00	0.95	0.98	1.00	1.04	0.91	0.95
Yield (%)	0.72	1.15	0.79	0.00	0.15	0.94	2.94	4.21	4.11	3.86
Portfolio Turnover (%). . . .	268	242	194	90	57	147	126	83	129	73
Total Assets (Millions $). . .	463	408	365	485	635	704	428	581	566	431

PORTFOLIO (as of 9/30/96)

Portfolio Manager: Timothy M. Ghriskey - 1996

Investm't Category: Growth
- ✔ Domestic
- ✔ Foreign
- Asset Allocation
- Index
- Sector
- State Specific

Investment Style
- Large-Cap Growth
- Mid-Cap Growth
- Small-Cap Growth
- ✔ Large-Cap Value
- ✔ Mid-Cap Value
- Small-Cap Value

Portfolio
4.1%	cash	0.0%	corp bonds
95.9%	stocks	0.0%	gov't bonds
0.0%	preferred	0.0%	muni bonds
0.0%	conv't/warrants	0.0%	other

SHAREHOLDER INFORMATION

Minimum Investment
Initial: $2,500   Subsequent: $100

Minimum IRA Investment
Initial: $750   Subsequent: $1

Maximum Fees
Load: none   12b-1: 0.25%
Other: none

Distributions
Income: annual   Capital Gains: annual

Exchange Options
Number Per Year: no limit   Fee: none
Telephone: yes (money market fund available)

Services
IRA, pension, auto exchange, auto invest, auto withdraw

Dreyfus Insured Muni Bond (DTBDX)

Tax-Exempt Bond

The Pan Am Building
200 Park Ave., 7th Floor
New York, NY 10166
800-782-6620, 516-794-5451
www.dreyfus.com/funds

PERFORMANCE

fund inception date: 6/25/85

	3yr Annual	5yr Annual	10yr Annual	Bull	Bear
Return (%)	2.6	5.5	6.2	15.7	-8.0
Differ from Category (+/-)	-1.6 low	-0.9 low	-0.5 blw av	-2.7 low	-2.6 low

Total Risk	Standard Deviation	Category Risk	Risk Index	Avg Mat
blw av	6.6%	high	1.2	23.3 yrs

	1996	1995	1994	1993	1992	1991	1990	1989	1988	1987
Return (%)...............	2.2	15.5	-8.7	12.5	7.7	11.3	7.0	8.7	10.1	-2.0
Differ from Category (+/-) .	-1.5	0.3	-3.4	0.7	-0.6	-0.1	0.6	-0.3	0.1	-0.6
Return, Tax-Adjusted (%)...	2.2	15.5	-8.7	11.4	7.3	11.3	7.0	8.7	10.1	-2.0

PER SHARE DATA

	1996	1995	1994	1993	1992	1991	1990	1989	1988	1987
Dividends, Net Income ($).	0.87	0.91	0.95	1.02	1.08	1.10	1.15	1.16	1.19	1.21
Distrib'ns, Cap Gain ($) ...	0.00	0.00	0.00	0.70	0.21	0.00	0.00	0.00	0.00	0.00
Net Asset Value ($)	17.62	18.11	16.51	19.08	18.54	18.46	17.63	17.60	17.30	16.83
Expense Ratio (%)........	0.85	0.94	0.93	0.94	0.96	0.96	0.99	1.00	0.90	0.84
Yield (%)	4.93	5.02	5.75	5.15	5.76	5.95	6.52	6.59	6.87	7.18
Portfolio Turnover (%).....	82	41	34	80	51	62	67	68	96	75
Total Assets (Millions $)...	212	241	215	288	263	244	204	191	182	175

PORTFOLIO (as of 9/30/96)

Portfolio Manager: Lawrence Troutman - 1985

Investm't Category: Tax-Exempt Bond
✔ Domestic   Index
  Foreign   Sector
  Asset Allocation   State Specific

Investment Style
  Large-Cap Growth   Large-Cap Value
  Mid-Cap Growth   Mid-Cap Value
  Small-Cap Growth   Small-Cap Value

Portfolio
  0.0% cash   0.0% corp bonds
  0.0% stocks   0.0% gov't bonds
  0.0% preferred   91.9% muni bonds
  0.0% conv't/warrants   8.1% other

SHAREHOLDER INFORMATION

Minimum Investment
Initial: $2,500   Subsequent: $100

Minimum IRA Investment
Initial: na   Subsequent: na

Maximum Fees
Load: none   12b-1: 0.20%
Other: none

Distributions
Income: monthly   Capital Gains: annual

Exchange Options
Number Per Year: no limit   Fee: none
Telephone: yes (money market fund available)

Services
auto exchange, auto invest, auto withdraw

Dreyfus Interm Muni Bond

(DITEX) *Tax-Exempt Bond*

The Pan Am Building
200 Park Ave., 7th Floor
New York, NY 10166
800-782-6620, 516-794-5451
www.dreyfus.com/funds

PERFORMANCE   fund inception date: 8/11/83

	3yr Annual	5yr Annual	10yr Annual	Bull	Bear
Return (%)	4.2	6.5	6.8	17.1	-4.6
Differ from Category (+/-)	0.0 av	0.1 blw av	0.1 av	-1.3 blw av	0.8 abv av

Total Risk	Standard Deviation	Category Risk	Risk Index	Avg Mat
low	4.5%	blw av	0.8	9.6 yrs

	1996	1995	1994	1993	1992	1991	1990	1989	1988	1987
Return (%).	3.8	14.2	-4.6	11.5	8.7	11.1	6.7	8.7	8.0	1.1
Differ from Category (+/-) . .	0.1	-1.0	0.7	-0.3	0.4	-0.3	0.3	-0.3	-2.0	2.5
Return, Tax-Adjusted (%). . .	3.5	14.1	-4.8	11.1	8.0	10.9	6.7	8.7	8.0	1.1

PER SHARE DATA

	1996	1995	1994	1993	1992	1991	1990	1989	1988	1987
Dividends, Net Income ($)	0.72	0.72	0.75	0.77	0.84	0.90	0.93	0.95	0.96	0.97
Distrib'ns, Cap Gain ($) . . .	0.11	0.02	0.06	0.16	0.30	0.07	0.00	0.00	0.00	0.00
Net Asset Value ($)	13.91	14.22	13.14	14.61	13.97	13.95	13.48	13.54	13.37	13.30
Expense Ratio (%).	0.71	0.73	0.70	0.71	0.70	0.69	0.71	0.71	0.73	0.71
Yield (%)	5.13	5.05	5.68	5.21	5.88	6.41	6.89	7.01	7.18	7.29
Portfolio Turnover (%).	48	42	36	60	48	31	40	34	49	50
Total Assets (Millions $). .	1,454	1,550	1,447	1,832	1,558	1,379	1,143	1,105	1,048	983

PORTFOLIO (as of 9/30/96)

Portfolio Manager: Monica Wieboldt - 1985

Investm't Category: Tax-Exempt Bond
✔ Domestic   Index
  Foreign   Sector
  Asset Allocation   State Specific

Investment Style
  Large-Cap Growth   Large-Cap Value
  Mid-Cap Growth   Mid-Cap Value
  Small-Cap Growth   Small-Cap Value

Portfolio
  0.0% cash   0.0% corp bonds
  0.0% stocks   0.0% gov't bonds
  0.0% preferred   88.8% muni bonds
  0.0% conv't/warrants 11.2% other

SHAREHOLDER INFORMATION

Minimum Investment
Initial: $2,500   Subsequent: $100

Minimum IRA Investment
Initial: na   Subsequent: na

Maximum Fees
Load: none   12b-1: 0.25%
Other: none

Distributions
Income: monthly   Capital Gains: annual

Exchange Options
Number Per Year: no limit   Fee: none
Telephone: yes (money market fund available)

Services
auto exchange, auto invest, auto withdraw

Dreyfus Int'l Growth
(DITFX)
International Stock

The Pan Am Building
200 Park Ave., 7th Floor
New York, NY 10166
800-782-6620, 516-794-5451
www.dreyfus.com/funds

PERFORMANCE

fund inception date: 6/29/93

	3yr Annual	5yr Annual	10yr Annual	Bull	Bear
Return (%)	1.0	na	na	6.6	-7.6
Differ from Category (+/-)	-5.3 blw av	na	na	-17.7 low	-0.4 av

Total Risk	Standard Deviation	Category Risk	Risk Index	Beta
abv av	10.1%	av	1.0	0.66

	1996	1995	1994	1993	1992	1991	1990	1989	1988	1987
Return (%).............	8.4	0.7	-5.5	—	—	—	—	—	—	—
Differ from Category (+/-).	-6.4	-8.4	-2.4	—	—	—	—	—	—	—
Return, Tax-Adjusted (%)...	6.8	0.7	-6.1	—	—	—	—	—	—	—

PER SHARE DATA

	1996	1995	1994	1993	1992	1991	1990	1989	1988	1987
Dividends, Net Income ($).	0.11	0.00	0.03	—	—	—	—	—	—	—
Distrib'ns, Cap Gain ($)...	0.62	0.00	0.25	—	—	—	—	—	—	—
Net Asset Value ($).....	14.85	14.38	14.28	—	—	—	—	—	—	—
Expense Ratio (%)........	2.04	1.92	na	—	—	—	—	—	—	—
Yield (%)	0.71	0.00	0.20	—	—	—	—	—	—	—
Portfolio Turnover (%).....	96	40	na	—	—	—	—	—	—	—
Total Assets (Millions $)....	93	107	160	—	—	—	—	—	—	—

PORTFOLIO (as of 9/30/96)

Portfolio Manager: John Christopher Whitaker - 1995

Investm't Category: International Stock
- Domestic
- ✔ Foreign
- Asset Allocation
- Index
- Sector
- State Specific

Investment Style
- Large-Cap Growth
- Mid-Cap Growth
- Small-Cap Growth
- Large-Cap Value
- Mid-Cap Value
- Small-Cap Value

Portfolio
0.0% cash	0.0% corp bonds
98.7% stocks	0.0% gov't bonds
1.8% preferred	0.0% muni bonds
0.0% conv't/warrants	0.0% other

SHAREHOLDER INFORMATION

Minimum Investment
Initial: $2,500   Subsequent: $100

Minimum IRA Investment
Initial: $750   Subsequent: $1

Maximum Fees
Load: none   12b-1: 0.75%
Other: none

Distributions
Income: annual   Capital Gains: annual

Exchange Options
Number Per Year: no limit   Fee: none
Telephone: yes (money market fund available)

Services
IRA, pension, auto exchange, auto invest, auto withdraw

Dreyfus LifeTime Port: Grth & Inc—Retail (DGIRX)

Growth & Income

The Pan Am Building
200 Park Ave., 7th Floor
New York, NY 10166
800-782-6620, 516-794-5451

PERFORMANCE

fund inception date: 3/31/95

	3yr Annual	5yr Annual	10yr Annual	Bull	Bear
Return (%)	na	na	na	na	na
Differ from Category (+/-)	na	na	na	na	na

Total Risk	Standard Deviation	Category Risk	Risk Index	Beta
na	na	na	na	na

	1996	1995	1994	1993	1992	1991	1990	1989	1988	1987
Return (%)	15.2	—	—	—	—	—	—	—	—	—
Differ from Category (+/-)	-4.5	—	—	—	—	—	—	—	—	—
Return, Tax-Adjusted (%)	13.6	—	—	—	—	—	—	—	—	—

PER SHARE DATA

	1996	1995	1994	1993	1992	1991	1990	1989	1988	1987
Dividends, Net Income ($)	0.34	—	—	—	—	—	—	—	—	—
Distrib'ns, Cap Gain ($)	0.30	—	—	—	—	—	—	—	—	—
Net Asset Value ($)	15.51	—	—	—	—	—	—	—	—	—
Expense Ratio (%)	na	—	—	—	—	—	—	—	—	—
Yield (%)	2.15	—	—	—	—	—	—	—	—	—
Portfolio Turnover (%)	na	—	—	—	—	—	—	—	—	—
Total Assets (Millions $)	135	—	—	—	—	—	—	—	—	—

PORTFOLIO (as of 9/30/96)

Portfolio Manager: na

Investm't Category: Growth & Income
- ✔ Domestic
- ✔ Foreign
- Asset Allocation

- Index
- Sector
- State Specific

Investment Style

Large-Cap Growth	Large-Cap Value
Mid-Cap Growth	Mid-Cap Value
Small-Cap Growth	Small-Cap Value

Portfolio

0.0% cash	0.0% corp bonds
68.8% stocks	37.2% gov't bonds
0.0% preferred	0.0% muni bonds
11.8% conv't/warrants	0.0% other

SHAREHOLDER INFORMATION

Minimum Investment
Initial: $2,500   Subsequent: $100

Minimum IRA Investment
Initial: $750   Subsequent: $1

Maximum Fees
Load: none   12b-1: 0.25%
Other: none

Distributions
Income: annual   Capital Gains: annual

Exchange Options
Number Per Year: no limit   Fee: none
Telephone: yes (money market fund available)

Services
IRA, pension, auto exchange, auto invest, auto withdraw

Dreyfus MA Interm Muni Bond (DMAIX)

Tax-Exempt Bond

The Pan Am Building
200 Park Ave., 7th Floor
New York, NY 10166
800-782-6620, 516-794-5451
www.dreyfus.com/funds

PERFORMANCE

fund inception date: 6/26/92

	3yr Annual	5yr Annual	10yr Annual	Bull	Bear
Return (%)	3.5	na	na	15.8	-5.4
Differ from Category (+/-)	-0.7 low	na	na	-2.6 low	0.0 av

Total Risk	Standard Deviation	Category Risk	Risk Index	Avg Mat
blw av	4.9%	blw av	0.9	8.4 yrs

	1996	1995	1994	1993	1992	1991	1990	1989	1988	1987
Return (%)	3.4	14.6	-6.5	12.5	—	—	—	—	—	—
Differ from Category (+/-)	-0.3	-0.6	-1.2	0.7	—	—	—	—	—	—
Return, Tax-Adjusted (%)	3.4	14.6	-6.6	12.5	—	—	—	—	—	—

PER SHARE DATA

	1996	1995	1994	1993	1992	1991	1990	1989	1988	1987
Dividends, Net Income ($)	0.58	0.58	0.62	0.67	—	—	—	—	—	—
Distrib'ns, Cap Gain ($)	0.00	0.00	0.01	0.00	—	—	—	—	—	—
Net Asset Value ($)	13.26	13.39	12.22	13.72	—	—	—	—	—	—
Expense Ratio (%)	0.75	0.49	0.06	0.00	—	—	—	—	—	—
Yield (%)	4.37	4.33	5.06	4.88	—	—	—	—	—	—
Portfolio Turnover (%)	31	9	4	9	—	—	—	—	—	—
Total Assets (Millions $)	64	70	66	91	—	—	—	—	—	—

PORTFOLIO (as of 9/30/96)

Portfolio Manager: Lawrence Troutman - 1992

Investm't Category: Tax-Exempt Bond
- ✔ Domestic
- Foreign
- Asset Allocation
- Index
- Sector
- ✔ State Specific

Investment Style
- Large-Cap Growth
- Mid-Cap Growth
- Small-Cap Growth
- Large-Cap Value
- Mid-Cap Value
- Small-Cap Value

Portfolio
- 0.0% cash
- 0.0% stocks
- 0.0% preferred
- 0.0% conv't/warrants
- 0.0% corp bonds
- 0.0% gov't bonds
- 96.2% muni bonds
- 3.8% other

SHAREHOLDER INFORMATION

Minimum Investment
Initial: $2,500   Subsequent: $100

Minimum IRA Investment
Initial: na   Subsequent: na

Maximum Fees
Load: none   12b-1: 0.25%
Other: none

Distributions
Income: monthly   Capital Gains: annual

Exchange Options
Number Per Year: no limit   Fee: none
Telephone: yes (money market fund available)

Services
auto exchange, auto invest, auto withdraw

Dreyfus MA Tax-Exempt Bond (DMEBX)

Tax-Exempt Bond

The Pan Am Building
200 Park Ave., 7th Floor
New York, NY 10166
800-782-6620, 516-794-5451
www.dreyfus.com/funds

fund inception date: 6/11/85

	3yr Annual	5yr Annual	10yr Annual	Bull	Bear
Return (%)	4.1	6.4	6.4	18.8	-6.3
Differ from Category (+/-)	-0.1 blw av	0.0 blw av	-0.3 blw av	0.4 av	-0.9 blw av

Total Risk	Standard Deviation	Category Risk	Risk Index	Avg Mat
blw av	5.6%	av	1.0	23.7 yrs

	1996	1995	1994	1993	1992	1991	1990	1989	1988	1987
Return (%)	4.0	15.5	-6.1	12.4	7.4	12.6	6.0	7.6	10.5	-3.5
Differ from Category (+/-)	0.3	0.3	-0.8	0.6	-0.9	1.2	-0.4	-1.4	0.5	-2.1
Return, Tax-Adjusted (%)	4.0	15.5	-6.1	11.6	7.4	12.6	6.0	7.6	10.5	-3.5

PER SHARE DATA

	1996	1995	1994	1993	1992	1991	1990	1989	1988	1987
Dividends, Net Income ($)	0.86	0.89	0.90	0.93	0.97	1.03	1.08	1.07	1.08	1.09
Distrib'ns, Cap Gain ($)	0.00	0.00	0.00	0.44	0.00	0.00	0.00	0.00	0.00	0.00
Net Asset Value ($)	16.39	16.62	15.21	17.13	16.51	16.30	15.44	15.62	15.54	15.09
Expense Ratio (%)	0.79	0.80	0.80	0.81	0.84	0.81	0.83	0.83	0.79	0.64
Yield (%)	5.24	5.35	5.91	5.29	5.87	6.31	6.99	6.85	6.94	7.22
Portfolio Turnover (%)	60	38	29	85	68	50	55	18	71	39
Total Assets (Millions $)	157	158	146	192	171	149	111	103	92	77

PORTFOLIO (as of 9/30/96)

Portfolio Manager: Joseph P. Darcy - 1996

Investm't Category: Tax-Exempt Bond
- ✔ Domestic
- Foreign
- Asset Allocation
- Index
- Sector
- ✔ State Specific

Investment Style
- Large-Cap Growth
- Mid-Cap Growth
- Small-Cap Growth
- Large-Cap Value
- Mid-Cap Value
- Small-Cap Value

Portfolio
0.0% cash	0.0% corp bonds
0.0% stocks	0.0% gov't bonds
0.0% preferred	97.1% muni bonds
0.0% conv't/warrants	2.9% other

SHAREHOLDER INFORMATION

Minimum Investment
Initial: $2,500   Subsequent: $100

Minimum IRA Investment
Initial: na   Subsequent: na

Maximum Fees
Load: none   12b-1: 0.25%
Other: none

Distributions
Income: monthly   Capital Gains: annual

Exchange Options
Number Per Year: no limit   Fee: none
Telephone: yes (money market fund available)

Services
auto exchange, auto invest, auto withdraw

Dreyfus Midcap Index
(PESPX)
Growth

The Pan Am Building
200 Park Ave., 7th Floor
New York, NY 10166
800-782-6620, 516-794-5451
www.dreyfus.com/funds

PERFORMANCE

fund inception date: 6/19/91

	3yr Annual	5yr Annual	10yr Annual	Bull	Bear
Return (%)	14.0	13.5	na	60.3	-9.7
Differ from Category (+/-)	-1.7 blw av	-0.8 av	na	-2.1 av	-3.0 blw av

Total Risk	Standard Deviation	Category Risk	Risk Index	Beta
abv av	10.7%	abv av	1.0	0.94

	1996	1995	1994	1993	1992	1991	1990	1989	1988	1987
Return (%)	18.4	30.3	-4.0	13.5	11.9	—	—	—	—	—
Differ from Category (+/-)	-1.7	0.0	-3.7	-0.5	0.1	—	—	—	—	—
Return, Tax-Adjusted (%)	16.3	27.9	-5.9	11.8	10.7	—	—	—	—	—

PER SHARE DATA

	1996	1995	1994	1993	1992	1991	1990	1989	1988	1987
Dividends, Net Income ($)	0.27	0.30	0.28	0.27	0.26	—	—	—	—	—
Distrib'ns, Cap Gain ($)	0.99	0.87	0.75	0.55	0.25	—	—	—	—	—
Net Asset Value ($)	21.23	19.00	15.48	17.19	15.87	—	—	—	—	—
Expense Ratio (%)	na	0.50	0.40	0.09	0.00	—	—	—	—	—
Yield (%)	1.21	1.50	1.72	1.52	1.61	—	—	—	—	—
Portfolio Turnover (%)	na	20	19	16	16	—	—	—	—	—
Total Assets (Millions $)	182	128	74	74	48	—	—	—	—	—

PORTFOLIO (as of 9/30/96)

Portfolio Manager: Steven A. Falci - 1996

Investm't Category: Growth
- ✔ Domestic
- ✔ Index
- Foreign
- Sector
- Asset Allocation
- State Specific

Investment Style
- Large-Cap Growth
- Large-Cap Value
- ✔ Mid-Cap Growth
- ✔ Mid-Cap Value
- Small-Cap Growth
- Small-Cap Value

Portfolio
3.8% cash	0.0% corp bonds
96.2% stocks	0.0% gov't bonds
0.0% preferred	0.0% muni bonds
0.0% conv't/warrants	0.0% other

SHAREHOLDER INFORMATION

Minimum Investment
Initial: $2,500   Subsequent: $100

Minimum IRA Investment
Initial: $750   Subsequent: $1

Maximum Fees
Load: 1.00% redemption   12b-1: 0.25%
Other: redemption fee applies for 6 months

Distributions
Income: annual   Capital Gains: annual

Exchange Options
Number Per Year: no limit   Fee: none
Telephone: none

Services
IRA, pension, auto invest

Dreyfus Muni Bond

(DRTAX)

Tax-Exempt Bond

The Pan Am Building
200 Park Ave., 7th Floor
New York, NY 10166
800-782-6620, 516-794-5451
www.dreyfus.com/funds

PERFORMANCE

fund inception date: 10/4/76

	3yr Annual	5yr Annual	10yr Annual	Bull	Bear
Return (%)	3.7	6.4	6.9	18.2	-6.7
Differ from Category (+/-)	-0.5 low	0.0 blw av	0.2 av	-0.2 av	-1.3 blw av

Total Risk	Standard Deviation	Category Risk	Risk Index	Avg Mat
blw av	5.6%	av	1.0	20.7 yrs

	1996	1995	1994	1993	1992	1991	1990	1989	1988	1987
Return (%)	3.8	15.6	-7.0	12.7	8.4	11.9	6.4	9.3	11.4	-1.8
Differ from Category (+/-)	0.1	0.4	-1.7	0.9	0.1	0.5	0.0	0.3	1.4	-0.4
Return, Tax-Adjusted (%)	3.8	15.6	-7.2	11.9	7.8	11.9	6.4	9.3	11.4	-1.8

PER SHARE DATA

	1996	1995	1994	1993	1992	1991	1990	1989	1988	1987
Dividends, Net Income ($)	0.68	0.70	0.73	0.77	0.82	0.85	0.89	0.90	0.91	0.92
Distrib'ns, Cap Gain ($)	0.00	0.00	0.07	0.33	0.27	0.00	0.00	0.00	0.00	0.00
Net Asset Value ($)	12.48	12.71	11.63	13.36	12.87	12.92	12.35	12.48	12.27	11.86
Expense Ratio (%)	0.71	0.70	0.68	0.69	0.68	0.67	0.67	0.68	0.71	0.68
Yield (%)	5.44	5.50	6.23	5.62	6.24	6.57	7.20	7.21	7.41	7.75
Portfolio Turnover (%)	64	51	36	45	68	36	28	36	51	67
Total Assets (Millions $)	3,777	3,938	3,625	4,571	4,283	4,117	3,684	3,580	3,346	3,107

PORTFOLIO (as of 9/30/96)

Portfolio Manager: Richard Moynihan - 1976

Investm't Category: Tax-Exempt Bond

✔ Domestic   Index
   Foreign   Sector
   Asset Allocation   State Specific

Investment Style

Large-Cap Growth   Large-Cap Value
Mid-Cap Growth   Mid-Cap Value
Small-Cap Growth   Small-Cap Value

Portfolio

0.0% cash	0.0% corp bonds
0.0% stocks	0.0% gov't bonds
0.0% preferred	94.1% muni bonds
0.0% conv't/warrants	5.9% other

SHAREHOLDER INFORMATION

Minimum Investment
Initial: $2,500   Subsequent: $100

Minimum IRA Investment
Initial: na   Subsequent: na

Maximum Fees
Load: none   12b-1: 0.25%
Other: none

Distributions
Income: monthly   Capital Gains: annual

Exchange Options
Number Per Year: no limit   Fee: none
Telephone: yes (money market fund available)

Services
auto exchange, auto invest, auto withdraw

Dreyfus NJ Interm Muni Bond (DNJIX)

Tax-Exempt Bond

The Pan Am Building
200 Park Ave., 7th Floor
New York, NY 10166
800-782-6620, 516-794-5451
www.dreyfus.com/funds

PERFORMANCE

fund inception date: 6/26/92

	3yr Annual	5yr Annual	10yr Annual	Bull	Bear
Return (%)	3.7	na	na	16.4	-5.4
Differ from Category (+/-)	-0.5 blw av	na	na	-2.0 blw av	0.0 abv av

Total Risk	Standard Deviation	Category Risk	Risk Index	Avg Mat
blw av	4.7%	blw av	0.9	7.7 yrs

	1996	1995	1994	1993	1992	1991	1990	1989	1988	1987
Return (%)	3.3	14.1	-5.3	12.4	—	—	—	—	—	—
Differ from Category (+/-)	-0.4	-1.1	0.0	0.6	—	—	—	—	—	—
Return, Tax-Adjusted (%)	3.3	14.1	-5.3	12.4	—	—	—	—	—	—

PER SHARE DATA

	1996	1995	1994	1993	1992	1991	1990	1989	1988	1987
Dividends, Net Income ($)	0.59	0.61	0.65	0.68	—	—	—	—	—	—
Distrib'ns, Cap Gain ($)	0.00	0.00	0.00	0.00	—	—	—	—	—	—
Net Asset Value ($)	13.53	13.69	12.56	13.93	—	—	—	—	—	—
Expense Ratio (%)	0.72	0.45	0.06	0.00	—	—	—	—	—	—
Yield (%)	4.36	4.45	5.17	4.88	—	—	—	—	—	—
Portfolio Turnover (%)	13	35	5	na	—	—	—	—	—	—
Total Assets (Millions $)	226	230	212	242	—	—	—	—	—	—

PORTFOLIO (as of 9/30/96)

Portfolio Manager: Stephen Kris - 1992

Investm't Category: Tax-Exempt Bond

✔ Domestic	Index
Foreign	Sector
Asset Allocation	✔ State Specific

Investment Style

Large-Cap Growth	Large-Cap Value
Mid-Cap Growth	Mid-Cap Value
Small-Cap Growth	Small-Cap Value

Portfolio

0.0% cash	0.0% corp bonds
0.0% stocks	0.0% gov't bonds
0.0% preferred	93.3% muni bonds
0.0% conv't/warrants	6.7% other

SHAREHOLDER INFORMATION

Minimum Investment
Initial: $2,500   Subsequent: $100

Minimum IRA Investment
Initial: na   Subsequent: na

Maximum Fees
Load: none   12b-1: 0.25%
Other: none

Distributions
Income: monthly   Capital Gains: annual

Exchange Options
Number Per Year: no limit   Fee: none
Telephone: yes (money market fund available)

Services
auto exchange, auto invest, auto withdraw

Dreyfus NJ Muni Bond

(DRNJX)

Tax-Exempt Bond

The Pan Am Building
200 Park Ave., 7th Floor
New York, NY 10166
800-782-6620, 516-794-5451
www.dreyfus.com/funds

PERFORMANCE   fund inception date: 11/6/87

	3yr Annual	5yr Annual	10yr Annual	Bull	Bear
Return (%)	3.8	6.6	na	17.6	-5.9
Differ from Category (+/-)	-0.4 blw av	0.2 av	na	-0.8 blw av	-0.5 av

Total Risk	Standard Deviation	Category Risk	Risk Index	Avg Mat
blw av	5.2%	av	0.9	19.1 yrs

	1996	1995	1994	1993	1992	1991	1990	1989	1988	1987
Return (%)...............	3.4	15.2	-6.1	12.9	8.7	11.9	7.9	9.1	12.5	—
Differ from Category (+/-).	-0.3	0.0	-0.8	1.1	0.4	0.5	1.5	0.1	2.5	—
Return, Tax-Adjusted (%)...	2.9	15.2	-6.2	12.8	8.2	11.8	7.9	9.0	12.5	—

PER SHARE DATA

	1996	1995	1994	1993	1992	1991	1990	1989	1988	1987
Dividends, Net Income ($).	0.71	0.74	0.77	0.78	0.79	0.80	0.83	0.83	0.87	—
Distrib'ns, Cap Gain ($) ...	0.22	0.00	0.01	0.02	0.20	0.04	0.00	0.04	0.00	—
Net Asset Value ($)	13.01	13.52	12.41	14.03	13.17	13.06	12.47	12.36	12.16	—
Expense Ratio (%).........	na	0.80	0.77	0.72	0.73	0.75	0.77	0.82	0.39	—
Yield (%)	5.36	5.47	6.19	5.55	5.90	6.10	6.65	6.69	7.15	—
Portfolio Turnover (%).....	na	24	10	6	34	23	25	35	61	—
Total Assets (Millions $)...	601	651	576	725	613	515	350	256	174	—

PORTFOLIO (as of 9/30/96)

Portfolio Manager: Samuel Weinstock - 1987

Investm't Category: Tax-Exempt Bond

✔ Domestic	Index
Foreign	Sector
Asset Allocation	✔ State Specific

Investment Style

Large-Cap Growth	Large-Cap Value
Mid-Cap Growth	Mid-Cap Value
Small-Cap Growth	Small-Cap Value

Portfolio

0.0% cash	0.0% corp bonds
0.0% stocks	0.0% gov't bonds
0.0% preferred	97.0% muni bonds
0.0% conv't/warrants	3.0% other

SHAREHOLDER INFORMATION

Minimum Investment

Initial: $2,500   Subsequent: $100

Minimum IRA Investment

Initial: na   Subsequent: na

Maximum Fees

Load: none   12b-1: 0.25%

Other: none

Distributions

Income: monthly   Capital Gains: annual

Exchange Options

Number Per Year: no limit   Fee: none

Telephone: yes (money market fund available)

Services

auto exchange, auto invest, auto withdraw

224   *Guide to Low-Load Mutual Funds*

Dreyfus NY Insured Tax-Exempt (DNYBX)

Tax-Exempt Bond

The Pan Am Building
200 Park Ave., 7th Floor
New York, NY 10166
800-782-6620, 516-794-5451
www.dreyfus.com/funds

PERFORMANCE

fund inception date: 2/18/87

	3yr Annual	5yr Annual	10yr Annual	Bull	Bear
Return (%)	3.2	5.8	na	16.3	-6.6
Differ from Category (+/-)	-1.0 low	-0.6 low	na	-2.1 blw av	-1.2 blw av

Total Risk	Standard Deviation	Category Risk	Risk Index	Avg Mat
blw av	6.0%	abv av	1.1	23.6 yrs

	1996	1995	1994	1993	1992	1991	1990	1989	1988	1987
Return (%)	2.1	15.3	-6.7	11.0	8.5	13.0	5.9	8.7	11.3	—
Differ from Category (+/-)	-1.6	0.1	-1.4	-0.8	0.2	1.6	-0.5	-0.3	1.3	—
Return, Tax-Adjusted (%)	1.6	15.3	-6.7	10.4	8.4	13.0	5.9	8.7	11.3	—

PER SHARE DATA

	1996	1995	1994	1993	1992	1991	1990	1989	1988	1987
Dividends, Net Income ($)	0.54	0.58	0.59	0.60	0.62	0.65	0.71	0.70	0.72	—
Distrib'ns, Cap Gain ($)	0.17	0.00	0.00	0.21	0.04	0.00	0.00	0.00	0.00	—
Net Asset Value ($)	11.19	11.68	10.66	12.04	11.60	11.33	10.64	10.75	10.56	—
Expense Ratio (%)	na	0.99	0.98	0.96	0.90	0.88	0.50	0.50	0.23	—
Yield (%)	4.75	4.96	5.53	4.89	5.32	5.73	6.67	6.51	6.81	—
Portfolio Turnover (%)	na	31	12	19	16	16	63	54	32	—
Total Assets (Millions $)	145	157	151	198	179	147	92	66	44	—

PORTFOLIO (as of 9/30/96)

Portfolio Manager: Lawrence Troutman - 1987

Investm't Category: Tax-Exempt Bond

✔ Domestic
  Foreign
  Asset Allocation

  Index
  Sector
✔ State Specific

Investment Style

Large-Cap Growth
Mid-Cap Growth
Small-Cap Growth

Large-Cap Value
Mid-Cap Value
Small-Cap Value

Portfolio

0.0% cash	0.0% corp bonds
0.0% stocks	0.0% gov't bonds
0.0% preferred	96.1% muni bonds
0.0% conv't/warrants	3.9% other

SHAREHOLDER INFORMATION

Minimum Investment
Initial: $2,500   Subsequent: $100

Minimum IRA Investment
Initial: na   Subsequent: na

Maximum Fees
Load: none   12b-1: 0.25%
Other: none

Distributions
Income: monthly   Capital Gains: annual

Exchange Options
Number Per Year: no limit   Fee: none
Telephone: yes (money market fund available)

Services
auto exchange, auto invest, auto withdraw

Dreyfus NY Interm Tax-Exempt (DRNIX)

Tax-Exempt Bond

The Pan Am Building
200 Park Ave., 7th Floor
New York, NY 10166
800-782-6620, 516-794-5451
www.dreyfus.com/funds

	3yr Annual	5yr Annual	10yr Annual	Bull	Bear
Return (%)	4.0	6.5	na	16.6	-4.5
Differ from Category (+/-)	-0.2 blw av	0.1 blw av	na	-1.8 blw av	0.9 abv av

Total Risk	Standard Deviation	Category Risk	Risk Index	Avg Mat
low	4.6%	blw av	0.8	9.0 yrs

	1996	1995	1994	1993	1992	1991	1990	1989	1988	1987
Return (%)	4.1	14.0	-5.2	11.5	9.3	11.1	6.0	9.3	9.5	—
Differ from Category (+/-)	0.4	-1.2	0.1	-0.3	1.0	-0.3	-0.4	0.3	-0.5	—
Return, Tax-Adjusted (%)	3.8	14.0	-5.2	11.4	9.1	10.9	5.9	9.3	9.5	—

PER SHARE DATA

	1996	1995	1994	1993	1992	1991	1990	1989	1988	1987
Dividends, Net Income ($)	0.84	0.84	0.85	0.89	0.97	1.02	1.11	1.10	1.08	—
Distrib'ns, Cap Gain ($)	0.17	0.00	0.00	0.03	0.10	0.08	0.05	0.00	0.00	—
Net Asset Value ($)	18.08	18.37	16.89	18.69	17.63	17.15	16.48	16.68	16.32	—
Expense Ratio (%)	0.84	0.96	0.89	0.85	0.85	0.60	0.30	0.24	0.00	—
Yield (%)	4.60	4.57	5.03	4.75	5.47	5.91	6.71	6.59	6.61	—
Portfolio Turnover (%)	47	29	20	17	29	56	38	7	1	—
Total Assets (Millions $)	366	371	337	421	232	147	105	82	48	—

PORTFOLIO (as of 9/30/96)

Portfolio Manager: Monica Wieboldt - 1987

Investm't Category: Tax-Exempt Bond
- ✔ Domestic
- Foreign
- Asset Allocation
- Index
- Sector
- ✔ State Specific

Investment Style
- Large-Cap Growth
- Mid-Cap Growth
- Small-Cap Growth
- Large-Cap Value
- Mid-Cap Value
- Small-Cap Value

Portfolio
- 0.0% cash
- 0.0% stocks
- 0.0% preferred
- 0.0% conv't/warrants
- 0.0% corp bonds
- 0.0% gov't bonds
- 84.9% muni bonds
- 15.1% other

SHAREHOLDER INFORMATION

Minimum Investment
Initial: $2,500   Subsequent: $100

Minimum IRA Investment
Initial: na   Subsequent: na

Maximum Fees
Load: none   12b-1: 0.25%
Other: none

Distributions
Income: monthly   Capital Gains: annual

Exchange Options
Number Per Year: no limit   Fee: none
Telephone: yes (money market fund available)

Services
auto exchange, auto invest, auto withdraw

Dreyfus NY Tax-Exempt Bond (DRNYX)

Tax-Exempt Bond

The Pan Am Building
200 Park Ave., 7th Floor
New York, NY 10166
800-782-6620, 516-794-5451
www.dreyfus.com/funds

PERFORMANCE

fund inception date: 7/26/83

	3yr Annual	5yr Annual	10yr Annual	Bull	Bear
Return (%)	3.4	6.3	6.5	16.8	-6.2
Differ from Category (+/-)	-0.8 low	-0.1 blw av	-0.2 blw av	-1.6 blw av	-0.8 blw av

Total Risk	Standard Deviation	Category Risk	Risk Index	Avg Mat
blw av	5.9%	abv av	1.1	17.9 yrs

	1996	1995	1994	1993	1992	1991	1990	1989	1988	1987
Return (%)	2.4	16.2	-7.0	12.6	8.8	12.4	5.5	8.9	10.1	-2.7
Differ from Category (+/-)	-1.3	1.0	-1.7	0.8	0.5	1.0	-0.9	-0.1	0.1	-1.3
Return, Tax-Adjusted (%)	2.2	16.1	-7.2	11.9	8.4	12.4	5.5	8.9	10.1	-2.7

PER SHARE DATA

	1996	1995	1994	1993	1992	1991	1990	1989	1988	1987
Dividends, Net Income ($)	0.77	0.80	0.85	0.90	0.98	1.02	1.05	1.06	1.07	1.08
Distrib'ns, Cap Gain ($)	0.07	0.04	0.10	0.37	0.22	0.00	0.00	0.00	0.00	0.00
Net Asset Value ($)	14.99	15.48	14.09	16.15	15.51	15.40	14.67	14.94	14.73	14.39
Expense Ratio (%)	0.71	0.72	0.71	0.70	0.69	0.70	0.70	0.69	0.72	0.71
Yield (%)	5.11	5.15	5.99	5.44	6.23	6.62	7.15	7.09	7.26	7.50
Portfolio Turnover (%)	81	49	35	51	40	26	31	38	57	38
Total Assets (Millions $)	1,784	1,879	1,699	2,134	1,992	1,881	1,657	1,679	1,559	1,417

PORTFOLIO (as of 9/30/96)

Portfolio Manager: Monica Wieboldt - 1985

Investm't Category: Tax-Exempt Bond
- ✔ Domestic
- Foreign
- Asset Allocation
- Index
- Sector
- ✔ State Specific

Investment Style
- Large-Cap Growth
- Mid-Cap Growth
- Small-Cap Growth
- Large-Cap Value
- Mid-Cap Value
- Small-Cap Value

Portfolio
- 0.0% cash
- 0.0% stocks
- 0.0% preferred
- 0.0% conv't/warrants
- 0.0% corp bonds
- 0.0% gov't bonds
- 100.0% muni bonds
- 0.0% other

SHAREHOLDER INFORMATION

Minimum Investment
Initial: $2,500   Subsequent: $100

Minimum IRA Investment
Initial: na   Subsequent: na

Maximum Fees
Load: none   12b-1: 0.25%
Other: none

Distributions
Income: monthly   Capital Gains: annual

Exchange Options
Number Per Year: no limit   Fee: none
Telephone: yes (money market fund available)

Services
auto exchange, auto invest, auto withdraw

Dreyfus New Leaders

(DNLDX)

Aggressive Growth

The Pan Am Building
200 Park Ave., 7th Floor
New York, NY 10166
800-782-6620, 516-794-5451
www.dreyfus.com/funds

PERFORMANCE

fund inception date: 1/29/85

	3yr Annual	5yr Annual	10yr Annual	Bull	Bear
Return (%)	14.9	14.2	14.3	57.4	-5.6
Differ from Category (+/-)	-0.9 av	-1.1 av	-0.7 av	-13.7 av	5.0 high

Total Risk	Standard Deviation	Category Risk	Risk Index	Beta
abv av	10.5%	low	0.7	0.74

	1996	1995	1994	1993	1992	1991	1990	1989	1988	1987
Return (%)	17.3	29.7	-0.2	17.0	9.4	45.3	-11.9	31.2	23.3	-5.2
Differ from Category (+/-)	-1.8	-4.6	-0.2	-2.3	-2.3	-6.8	-6.5	2.8	6.9	-2.8
Return, Tax-Adjusted (%)	15.0	26.8	-2.5	14.0	6.6	41.7	-13.6	29.2	22.8	-5.6

PER SHARE DATA

	1996	1995	1994	1993	1992	1991	1990	1989	1988	1987
Dividends, Net Income ($)	0.00	0.07	0.07	0.07	0.14	0.22	0.47	0.38	0.22	0.17
Distrib'ns, Cap Gain ($)	3.07	3.10	2.60	3.34	2.93	2.74	1.07	1.08	0.00	0.00
Net Asset Value ($)	40.74	37.39	31.33	34.13	32.17	32.29	24.25	29.27	23.41	19.16
Expense Ratio (%)	na	1.19	1.16	1.22	1.21	1.29	1.42	1.37	1.50	1.41
Yield (%)	0.00	0.17	0.20	0.18	0.39	0.62	1.85	1.25	0.93	0.88
Portfolio Turnover (%)	na	108	94	127	119	108	129	114	120	177
Total Assets (Millions $)	784	608	392	338	232	194	102	184	112	79

PORTFOLIO (as of 9/30/96)

Portfolio Manager: Thomas A. Frank - 1985

Investm't Category: Aggressive Growth
- ✔ Domestic   Index
- ✔ Foreign   Sector
-   Asset Allocation State Specific

Investment Style
Large-Cap Growth	Large-Cap Value
Mid-Cap Growth	Mid-Cap Value
✔ Small-Cap Growth	✔ Small-Cap Value

Portfolio
6.2% cash	0.0% corp bonds
93.6% stocks	0.0% gov't bonds
0.2% preferred	0.0% muni bonds
0.0% conv't/warrants	0.0% other

SHAREHOLDER INFORMATION

Minimum Investment
Initial: $2,500   Subsequent: $100

Minimum IRA Investment
Initial: $750   Subsequent: $1

Maximum Fees
Load: 1.00% redemption   12b-1: 0.25%
Other: redemption fee applies for 6 months

Distributions
Income: annual   Capital Gains: annual

Exchange Options
Number Per Year: no limit   Fee: none
Telephone: yes (money market fund available)

Services
IRA, pension, auto exchange, auto invest, auto withdraw

Dreyfus Penn Interm Muni Bond (DPABX)

Tax-Exempt Bond

The Pan Am Building
200 Park Ave., 7th Floor
New York, NY 10166
800-782-6620, 516-794-5451
www.dreyfus.com/funds

PERFORMANCE

fund inception date: 12/16/93

	3yr Annual	5yr Annual	10yr Annual	Bull	Bear
Return (%)	5.7	na	na	18.9	-3.4
Differ from Category (+/-)	1.5 high	na	na	0.5 av	2.0 high

Total Risk	Standard Deviation	Category Risk	Risk Index	Avg Mat
low	4.5%	blw av	0.8	8.3 yrs

	1996	1995	1994	1993	1992	1991	1990	1989	1988	1987
Return (%)	4.1	15.2	-1.6	—	—	—	—	—	—	—
Differ from Category (+/-)	0.4	0.0	3.7	—	—	—	—	—	—	—
Return, Tax-Adjusted (%)	4.1	15.2	-1.6	—	—	—	—	—	—	—

PER SHARE DATA

	1996	1995	1994	1993	1992	1991	1990	1989	1988	1987
Dividends, Net Income ($)	0.59	0.62	0.63	—	—	—	—	—	—	—
Distrib'ns, Cap Gain ($)	0.00	0.00	0.00	—	—	—	—	—	—	—
Net Asset Value ($)	13.11	13.17	12.00	—	—	—	—	—	—	—
Expense Ratio (%)	na	0.48	na	—	—	—	—	—	—	—
Yield (%)	4.50	4.70	5.25	—	—	—	—	—	—	—
Portfolio Turnover (%)	na	5	20	—	—	—	—	—	—	—
Total Assets (Millions $)	50	41	23	—	—	—	—	—	—	—

PORTFOLIO (as of 9/30/96)

Portfolio Manager: Doug J. Gaylor - 1995

Investm't Category: Tax-Exempt Bond

✔ Domestic   Index
   Foreign   Sector
   Asset Allocation   ✔ State Specific

Investment Style

Large-Cap Growth   Large-Cap Value
Mid-Cap Growth   Mid-Cap Value
Small-Cap Growth   Small-Cap Value

Portfolio

0.0% cash	0.0% corp bonds
0.0% stocks	0.0% gov't bonds
0.0% preferred	97.7% muni bonds
0.0% conv't/warrants	2.3% other

SHAREHOLDER INFORMATION

Minimum Investment
Initial: $2,500   Subsequent: $100

Minimum IRA Investment
Initial: na   Subsequent: na

Maximum Fees
Load: none   12b-1: 0.25%
Other: none

Distributions
Income: monthly   Capital Gains: annual

Exchange Options
Number Per Year: no limit   Fee: none
Telephone: yes (money market fund available)

Services
auto exchange, auto invest, auto withdraw

Dreyfus S&P 500 Index
(PEOPX)
Growth & Income

The Pan Am Building
200 Park Ave., 7th Floor
New York, NY 10166
800-782-6620, 516-794-5451
www.dreyfus.com/funds

PERFORMANCE   fund inception date: 1/2/90

	3yr Annual	5yr Annual	10yr Annual	Bull	Bear
Return (%)	18.9	14.7	na	74.6	-6.9
Differ from Category (+/-)	3.6 high	0.8 av	na	14.8 high	-0.5 av

Total Risk	Standard Deviation	Category Risk	Risk Index	Beta
abv av	9.7%	abv av	1.0	0.99

	1996	1995	1994	1993	1992	1991	1990	1989	1988	1987
Return (%)	22.3	36.7	0.6	9.5	7.7	29.8	—	—	—	—
Differ from Category (+/-)	2.6	6.6	1.9	-4.3	-3.0	0.7	—	—	—	—
Return, Tax-Adjusted (%)	20.5	35.4	-2.8	7.5	6.5	28.5	—	—	—	—

PER SHARE DATA

	1996	1995	1994	1993	1992	1991	1990	1989	1988	1987
Dividends, Net Income ($)	0.37	0.32	0.41	0.31	0.40	0.38	—	—	—	—
Distrib'ns, Cap Gain ($)	0.66	0.21	1.33	0.66	0.03	0.00	—	—	—	—
Net Asset Value ($)	22.22	19.00	14.29	15.93	15.43	14.73	—	—	—	—
Expense Ratio (%)	na	0.55	0.61	0.39	0.00	0.00	—	—	—	—
Yield (%)	1.61	1.66	2.62	1.86	2.58	2.57	—	—	—	—
Portfolio Turnover (%)	na	3	18	3	3	1	—	—	—	—
Total Assets (Millions $)	662	378	209	276	97	76	—	—	—	—

PORTFOLIO (as of 9/30/96)

Portfolio Manager: Steven A. Falci - 1996

Investm't Category: Growth & Income
- ✔ Domestic
- ✔ Index
- Foreign
- Sector
- Asset Allocation
- State Specific

Investment Style
- ✔ Large-Cap Growth
- ✔ Large-Cap Value
- Mid-Cap Growth
- Mid-Cap Value
- Small-Cap Growth
- Small-Cap Value

Portfolio
11.7% cash	0.0% corp bonds
88.3% stocks	0.0% gov't bonds
0.0% preferred	0.0% muni bonds
0.0% conv't/warrants	0.0% other

SHAREHOLDER INFORMATION

Minimum Investment
Initial: $2,500   Subsequent: $100

Minimum IRA Investment
Initial: $750   Subsequent: $1

Maximum Fees
Load: 1.00% redemption   12b-1: 0.25%
Other: redemption fee applies for 6 months

Distributions
Income: annual   Capital Gains: annual

Exchange Options
Number Per Year: no limit   Fee: none
Telephone: none

Services
IRA, pension, auto invest

Dreyfus Short—Interm Gov't (DSIGX)

Government Bond

The Pan Am Building
200 Park Ave., 7th Floor
New York, NY 10166
800-782-6620, 516-794-5451
www.dreyfus.com/funds

PERFORMANCE

fund inception date: 4/6/87

	3yr Annual	5yr Annual	10yr Annual	Bull	Bear
Return (%)	5.1	5.9	na	17.4	-1.7
Differ from Category (+/-)	0.2 av	-0.7 av	na	-4.6 blw av	4.7 high

Total Risk	Standard Deviation	Category Risk	Risk Index	Avg Mat
low	2.4%	blw av	0.6	2.3 yrs

	1996	1995	1994	1993	1992	1991	1990	1989	1988	1987
Return (%)...............	3.9	12.6	-0.8	7.3	7.0	13.4	10.0	11.2	5.5	—
Differ from Category (+/-)..	2.4	-7.0	3.6	-4.3	0.3	-2.3	3.7	-4.1	-2.8	—
Return, Tax-Adjusted (%)...	1.5	9.8	-3.5	4.5	3.6	9.9	6.5	7.5	2.2	—

PER SHARE DATA

	1996	1995	1994	1993	1992	1991	1990	1989	1988	1987
Dividends, Net Income ($).	0.65	0.72	0.75	0.77	0.81	0.83	0.98	1.02	0.94	—
Distrib'ns, Cap Gain ($) ...	0.00	0.00	0.00	0.05	0.27	0.20	0.00	0.00	0.00	—
Net Asset Value ($)	10.87	11.10	10.53	11.37	11.39	11.69	11.28	11.20	11.03	—
Expense Ratio (%).........	na	0.66	0.47	0.40	0.35	0.49	0.00	0.00	0.00	—
Yield (%)	5.97	6.48	7.12	6.74	6.94	6.98	8.68	9.10	8.52	—
Portfolio Turnover (%).....	na	387	695	317	226	132	25	17	89	—
Total Assets (Millions $)...	579	574	472	541	340	137	74	33	19	—

PORTFOLIO (as of 9/30/96)

Portfolio Manager: Gerald E. Thunelius - 1994

Investm't Category: Government Bond
✔ Domestic   Index
  Foreign   Sector
  Asset Allocation State Specific

Investment Style
  Large-Cap Growth   Large-Cap Value
  Mid-Cap Growth   Mid-Cap Value
  Small-Cap Growth   Small-Cap Value

Portfolio
16.9% cash   0.0% corp bonds
0.0% stocks   83.1% gov't bonds
0.0% preferred   0.0% muni bonds
0.0% conv't/warrants 0.0% other

SHAREHOLDER INFORMATION

Minimum Investment
Initial: $2,500   Subsequent: $100

Minimum IRA Investment
Initial: $750   Subsequent: $1

Maximum Fees
Load: none   12b-1: 0.25%
Other: none

Distributions
Income: monthly   Capital Gains: annual

Exchange Options
Number Per Year: no limit   Fee: none
Telephone: yes (money market fund available)

Services
IRA, pension, auto exchange, auto invest, auto withdraw

Dreyfus Short—Interm Muni Bond (DSIBX)

Tax-Exempt Bond

The Pan Am Building
200 Park Ave., 7th Floor
New York, NY 10166
800-782-6620, 516-794-5451
www.dreyfus.com/funds

PERFORMANCE

fund inception date: 4/30/87

	3yr Annual	5yr Annual	10yr Annual	Bull	Bear
Return (%)	3.6	4.8	na	11.7	-1.1
Differ from Category (+/-)	-0.6 low	-1.6 low	na	-6.7 low	4.3 high

Total Risk	Standard Deviation	Category Risk	Risk Index	Avg Mat
low	1.4%	low	0.3	2.1 yrs

	1996	1995	1994	1993	1992	1991	1990	1989	1988	1987
Return (%)...............	4.2	7.1	-0.4	6.6	6.7	8.2	6.6	6.5	5.7	—
Differ from Category (+/-)..	0.5	-8.1	4.9	-5.2	-1.6	-3.2	0.2	-2.5	-4.3	—
Return, Tax-Adjusted (%)...	4.2	7.1	-0.4	6.5	6.6	8.2	6.6	6.5	5.7	—

PER SHARE DATA

	1996	1995	1994	1993	1992	1991	1990	1989	1988	1987
Dividends, Net Income ($).	0.57	0.57	0.56	0.58	0.65	0.71	0.78	0.78	0.74	—
Distrib'ns, Cap Gain ($) ...	0.00	0.00	0.00	0.01	0.01	0.00	0.00	0.00	0.00	—
Net Asset Value ($)	12.97	13.01	12.70	13.31	13.05	12.88	12.58	12.55	12.54	—
Expense Ratio (%)........	0.68	0.70	0.74	0.75	0.72	0.59	0.50	0.43	0.00	—
Yield (%)	4.39	4.38	4.40	4.35	4.97	5.51	6.20	6.21	5.90	—
Portfolio Turnover (%).....	44	37	34	31	64	67	100	126	63	—
Total Assets (Millions $)...	335	336	426	575	339	157	77	61	61	—

PORTFOLIO (as of 9/30/96)

Portfolio Manager: Samuel Weinstock - 1987

Investm't Category: Tax-Exempt Bond

✔ Domestic
   Foreign
   Asset Allocation

   Index
   Sector
   State Specific

Investment Style

Large-Cap Growth
Mid-Cap Growth
Small-Cap Growth

Large-Cap Value
Mid-Cap Value
Small-Cap Value

Portfolio

0.0% cash
0.0% stocks
0.0% preferred
0.0% conv't/warrants

0.0% corp bonds
0.0% gov't bonds
96.3% muni bonds
3.7% other

SHAREHOLDER INFORMATION

Minimum Investment
Initial: $2,500   Subsequent: $100

Minimum IRA Investment
Initial: na   Subsequent: na

Maximum Fees
Load: none   12b-1: 0.10%
Other: none

Distributions
Income: monthly   Capital Gains: annual

Exchange Options
Number Per Year: no limit   Fee: none
Telephone: yes (money market fund available)

Services
auto exchange, auto invest, auto withdraw

Dreyfus Short-Term Income (DSTIX)

Corporate Bond

The Pan Am Building
200 Park Ave., 7th Floor
New York, NY 10166
800-782-6620, 516-794-5451
www.dreyfus.com/funds

PERFORMANCE

fund inception date: 8/18/92

	3yr Annual	5yr Annual	10yr Annual	Bull	Bear
Return (%)	5.7	na	na	19.2	-2.0
Differ from Category (+/-)	-0.6 av	na	na	-5.6 blw av	3.1 high

Total Risk	Standard Deviation	Category Risk	Risk Index	Avg Mat
low	2.2%	low	0.5	3.1 yrs

	1996	1995	1994	1993	1992	1991	1990	1989	1988	1987
Return (%)	6.1	11.1	0.1	9.1	—	—	—	—	—	—
Differ from Category (+/-)	0.9	-6.9	3.2	-2.7	—	—	—	—	—	—
Return, Tax-Adjusted (%)	3.4	8.4	-2.6	6.1	—	—	—	—	—	—

PER SHARE DATA

	1996	1995	1994	1993	1992	1991	1990	1989	1988	1987
Dividends, Net Income ($)	0.82	0.79	0.83	0.91	—	—	—	—	—	—
Distrib'ns, Cap Gain ($)	0.00	0.00	0.00	0.00	—	—	—	—	—	—
Net Asset Value ($)	11.95	12.06	11.60	12.42	—	—	—	—	—	—
Expense Ratio (%)	0.80	0.61	0.24	1.12	—	—	—	—	—	—
Yield (%)	6.86	6.55	7.15	7.32	—	—	—	—	—	—
Portfolio Turnover (%)	291	511	74	na	—	—	—	—	—	—
Total Assets (Millions $)	213	199	222	321	—	—	—	—	—	—

PORTFOLIO (as of 9/30/96)

Portfolio Manager: Kevin M. McClintock - 1996

Investm't Category: Corporate Bond
- ✔ Domestic
- ✔ Foreign
-   Asset Allocation

- Index
- Sector
- State Specific

Investment Style

Large-Cap Growth	Large-Cap Value
Mid-Cap Growth	Mid-Cap Value
Small-Cap Growth	Small-Cap Value

Portfolio

13.5% cash	65.2% corp bonds
0.0% stocks	10.3% gov't bonds
0.0% preferred	0.0% muni bonds
0.0% conv't/warrants	11.0% other

SHAREHOLDER INFORMATION

Minimum Investment
Initial: $2,500   Subsequent: $100

Minimum IRA Investment
Initial: $750   Subsequent: $1

Maximum Fees
Load: none   12b-1: 0.20%
Other: none

Distributions
Income: monthly   Capital Gains: annual

Exchange Options
Number Per Year: no limit   Fee: none
Telephone: yes (money market fund available)

Services
IRA, pension, auto exchange, auto invest, auto withdraw

Dreyfus Special Growth— Investor (DSGRX)

Aggressive Growth

The Pan Am Building
200 Park Ave., 7th Floor
New York, NY 10166
800-782-6620, 516-794-5451

PERFORMANCE

fund inception date: 5/3/82

	3yr Annual	5yr Annual	10yr Annual	Bull	Bear
Return (%)	1.3	9.5	10.3	17.5	-11.8
Differ from Category (+/-)	-14.5 low	-5.8 low	-4.7 low	-53.6 low	-1.2 av

Total Risk	Standard Deviation	Category Risk	Risk Index	Beta
high	15.7%	abv av	1.1	0.89

	1996	1995	1994	1993	1992	1991	1990	1989	1988	1987
Return (%)	-2.6	30.4	-18.3	20.0	26.1	29.2	-4.9	18.8	21.4	-3.9
Differ from Category (+/-)	-21.7	-3.9	-18.3	0.7	14.4	-22.9	0.5	-9.6	5.0	-1.5
Return, Tax-Adjusted (%)	-5.7	30.4	-18.4	16.9	22.5	23.3	-5.0	13.5	20.3	-12.5

PER SHARE DATA

	1996	1995	1994	1993	1992	1991	1990	1989	1988	1987
Dividends, Net Income ($)	0.00	0.00	0.00	0.00	0.18	0.00	0.02	0.24	0.33	0.81
Distrib'ns, Cap Gain ($)	2.08	0.00	0.04	1.78	1.61	2.82	0.00	2.36	0.00	4.09
Net Asset Value ($)	16.51	19.11	14.65	17.97	16.45	14.59	13.56	14.28	14.27	12.02
Expense Ratio (%)	na	1.40	1.42	1.73	1.57	1.70	1.62	1.72	1.58	1.49
Yield (%)	0.00	0.00	0.00	0.00	0.99	0.00	0.14	1.44	2.31	5.02
Portfolio Turnover (%)	na	68	133	94	112	141	222	184	183	322
Total Assets (Millions $)	51	66	64	83	64	41	43	40	34	29

PORTFOLIO (as of 9/30/96)

Portfolio Manager: Michael L. Schonberg - 1995

Investm't Category: Aggressive Growth
- ✔ Domestic
- ✔ Foreign
-   Asset Allocation
-   Index
-   Sector
-   State Specific

Investment Style
Large-Cap Growth	Large-Cap Value
Mid-Cap Growth	Mid-Cap Value
✔ Small-Cap Growth	✔ Small-Cap Value

Portfolio
0.6% cash	0.0% corp bonds
99.4% stocks	0.0% gov't bonds
0.0% preferred	0.0% muni bonds
0.0% conv't/warrants	0.0% other

SHAREHOLDER INFORMATION

Minimum Investment
Initial: $2,500   Subsequent: $100

Minimum IRA Investment
Initial: $750   Subsequent: $1

Maximum Fees
Load: none   12b-1: 0.25%
Other: none

Distributions
Income: annual   Capital Gains: annual

Exchange Options
Number Per Year: 6   Fee: none
Telephone: yes (money market fund available)

Services
IRA, pension, auto exchange, auto invest, auto withdraw

Dreyfus Strategic Income

(DSINX)

General Bond

The Pan Am Building
200 Park Ave., 7th Floor
New York, NY 10166
800-782-6620, 516-794-5451
www.dreyfus.com/funds

PERFORMANCE

fund inception date: 10/3/86

	3yr Annual	5yr Annual	10yr Annual	Bull	Bear
Return (%)	6.4	8.6	9.7	29.6	-8.7
Differ from Category (+/-)	1.3 high	2.5 high	2.4 high	9.3 high	-4.5 low

Total Risk	Standard Deviation	Category Risk	Risk Index	Avg Mat
blw av	5.3%	high	1.4	8.3 yrs

	1996	1995	1994	1993	1992	1991	1990	1989	1988	1987
Return (%)	6.6	20.8	-6.4	15.0	8.9	19.0	5.5	13.8	11.0	5.5
Differ from Category (+/-)	2.7	5.9	-4.1	5.9	2.4	4.3	-1.8	2.1	3.4	3.2
Return, Tax-Adjusted (%)	3.8	17.9	-9.0	11.4	5.7	15.4	2.0	10.0	7.1	0.9

PER SHARE DATA

	1996	1995	1994	1993	1992	1991	1990	1989	1988	1987
Dividends, Net Income ($)	1.00	0.92	0.94	1.00	1.05	1.15	1.17	1.20	1.24	1.32
Distrib'ns, Cap Gain ($)	0.00	0.00	0.00	0.36	0.07	0.00	0.00	0.00	0.00	0.37
Net Asset Value ($)	14.42	14.51	12.84	14.70	14.00	13.92	12.75	13.26	12.77	12.66
Expense Ratio (%)	na	1.04	0.94	0.84	0.85	0.87	0.50	0.50	0.49	0.26
Yield (%)	6.93	6.34	7.32	6.64	7.46	8.26	9.17	9.04	9.71	10.13
Portfolio Turnover (%)	na	176	161	118	73	16	16	93	155	76
Total Assets (Millions $)	295	321	309	385	164	64	43	42	39	32

PORTFOLIO (as of 9/30/96)

Portfolio Manager: Garitt Kono - 1994

Investm't Category: General Bond
- ✔ Domestic
- ✔ Foreign
-   Asset Allocation

-   Index
-   Sector
-   State Specific

Investment Style
- Large-Cap Growth
- Mid-Cap Growth
- Small-Cap Growth

- Large-Cap Value
- Mid-Cap Value
- Small-Cap Value

Portfolio
0.0% cash	21.9% corp bonds
0.0% stocks	55.5% gov't bonds
1.7% preferred	0.0% muni bonds
6.2% conv't/warrants	14.7% other

SHAREHOLDER INFORMATION

Minimum Investment
Initial: $2,500   Subsequent: $100

Minimum IRA Investment
Initial: $750   Subsequent: $1

Maximum Fees
Load: none   12b-1: 0.25%
Other: none

Distributions
Income: monthly   Capital Gains: annual

Exchange Options
Number Per Year: no limit   Fee: none
Telephone: yes (money market fund available)

Services
IRA, pension, auto exchange, auto invest, auto withdraw

Dreyfus Third Century

(DRTHX)

Growth & Income

The Pan Am Building
200 Park Ave., 7th Floor
New York, NY 10166
800-782-6620, 516-794-5451
www.dreyfus.com/funds

PERFORMANCE

fund inception date: 3/29/72

	3yr Annual	5yr Annual	10yr Annual	Bull	Bear
Return (%)	16.0	10.8	13.5	70.2	-10.6
Differ from Category (+/-)	0.7 av	-3.1 low	0.8 av	10.4 abv av	-4.2 low

Total Risk	Standard Deviation	Category Risk	Risk Index	Beta
abv av	11.0%	high	1.2	1.03

	1996	1995	1994	1993	1992	1991	1990	1989	1988	1987
Return (%)	24.3	35.8	-7.5	5.2	1.9	38.0	3.4	17.3	23.2	2.6
Differ from Category (+/-)	4.6	5.7	-6.2	-8.6	-8.8	8.9	9.3	-6.2	6.4	2.4
Return, Tax-Adjusted (%)	19.4	33.1	-11.2	2.9	1.5	36.5	1.7	15.1	19.5	-5.0

PER SHARE DATA

	1996	1995	1994	1993	1992	1991	1990	1989	1988	1987
Dividends, Net Income ($)	0.02	0.04	0.06	0.04	0.04	0.08	0.12	0.18	0.30	0.35
Distrib'ns, Cap Gain ($)	1.39	0.57	1.00	0.61	0.05	0.22	0.22	0.19	0.26	1.27
Net Asset Value ($)	8.82	8.24	6.53	8.26	8.48	8.42	6.33	6.45	5.82	5.18
Expense Ratio (%)	1.11	1.12	1.17	1.11	1.08	1.04	1.05	1.04	1.02	0.99
Yield (%)	0.19	0.45	0.79	0.45	0.46	0.92	1.83	2.71	4.93	5.42
Portfolio Turnover (%)	92	133	71	67	48	73	163	53	37	33
Total Assets (Millions $)	587	419	348	463	529	360	199	181	164	137

PORTFOLIO (as of 9/30/96)

Portfolio Manager: na

Investm't Category: Growth & Income
- ✔ Domestic
- Foreign
- Asset Allocation
- Index
- Sector
- State Specific

Investment Style
- ✔ Large-Cap Growth
- ✔ Mid-Cap Growth
- Small-Cap Growth
- Large-Cap Value
- Mid-Cap Value
- Small-Cap Value

Portfolio
- 10.6% cash
- 89.4% stocks
- 0.0% preferred
- 0.0% conv't/warrants
- 0.0% corp bonds
- 0.0% gov't bonds
- 0.0% muni bonds
- 0.0% other

SHAREHOLDER INFORMATION

Minimum Investment
Initial: $2,500   Subsequent: $100

Minimum IRA Investment
Initial: $750   Subsequent: $1

Maximum Fees
Load: none   12b-1: 0.25%
Other: none

Distributions
Income: annual   Capital Gains: annual

Exchange Options
Number Per Year: no limit   Fee: none
Telephone: yes (money market fund available)

Services
IRA, pension, auto exchange, auto invest, auto withdraw

Dupree KY Tax-Free Income (KYTFX)

Tax-Exempt Bond

125 S. Mill St.
Suite 100
Lexington, KY 40507
800-866-0614, 606-254-7741
www.dupree-funds.com

PERFORMANCE

fund inception date: 7/2/79

	3yr Annual	5yr Annual	10yr Annual	Bull	Bear
Return (%)	4.7	7.1	7.3	19.6	-5.1
Differ from Category (+/-)	0.5 abv av	0.7 abv av	0.6 abv av	1.2 blw av	0.3 abv av

Total Risk	Standard Deviation	Category Risk	Risk Index	Avg Mat
low	4.3%	blw av	0.8	17.1 yrs

	1996	1995	1994	1993	1992	1991	1990	1989	1988	1987
Return (%)	3.6	14.2	-3.0	12.6	9.0	10.6	7.4	10.7	10.3	-1.0
Differ from Category (+/-)	-0.1	-1.0	2.3	0.8	0.7	-0.8	1.0	1.7	0.3	0.4
Return, Tax-Adjusted (%)	3.6	14.0	-3.0	12.4	9.0	10.6	7.4	10.7	10.3	-1.0

PER SHARE DATA

	1996	1995	1994	1993	1992	1991	1990	1989	1988	1987
Dividends, Net Income ($)	0.39	0.40	0.40	0.41	0.43	0.44	0.45	0.46	0.47	0.48
Distrib'ns, Cap Gain ($)	0.00	0.04	0.00	0.04	0.00	0.00	0.00	0.00	0.00	0.00
Net Asset Value ($)	7.49	7.62	7.09	7.72	7.28	7.09	6.83	6.80	6.58	6.41
Expense Ratio (%)	0.62	0.63	0.69	0.67	0.71	0.75	0.76	0.78	0.81	0.79
Yield (%)	5.20	5.25	5.64	5.28	5.90	6.20	6.58	6.76	7.14	7.48
Portfolio Turnover (%)	4	18	30	31	12	18	36	44	87	54
Total Assets (Millions $)	315	293	246	271	194	142	98	77	64	54

PORTFOLIO (as of 9/30/96)

Portfolio Manager: William Griggs - 1989

Investm't Category: Tax-Exempt Bond

✔ Domestic
  Index
  Foreign
  Sector
  Asset Allocation
✔ State Specific

Investment Style

Large-Cap Growth   Large-Cap Value
Mid-Cap Growth   Mid-Cap Value
Small-Cap Growth   Small-Cap Value

Portfolio

0.0% cash	0.0% corp bonds
0.0% stocks	0.0% gov't bonds
0.0% preferred	100.0% muni bonds
0.0% conv't/warrants	0.0% other

SHAREHOLDER INFORMATION

Minimum Investment
Initial: $100   Subsequent: $100

Minimum IRA Investment
Initial: na   Subsequent: na

Maximum Fees
Load: none   12b-1: none
Other: none

Distributions
Income: quarterly   Capital Gains: Dec

Exchange Options
Number Per Year: no limit   Fee: none
Telephone: yes

Services
auto exchange, auto invest, auto withdraw

Dupree KY Tx Fr Short-To-Medium (KYSMX)

Tax-Exempt Bond

125 S. Mill St.
Suite 100
Lexington, KY 40507
800-866-0614, 606-254-7741
www.dupree-funds.com

PERFORMANCE

fund inception date: 9/15/87

	3yr Annual	5yr Annual	10yr Annual	Bull	Bear
Return (%)	3.7	4.7	na	12.1	-1.5
Differ from Category (+/-)	-0.5 low	-1.7 low	na	-6.3 low	3.9 high

Total Risk	Standard Deviation	Category Risk	Risk Index	Avg Mat
low	1.8%	low	0.3	6.1 yrs

	1996	1995	1994	1993	1992	1991	1990	1989	1988	1987
Return (%).	3.9	6.2	1.0	5.6	6.8	7.2	6.8	7.3	5.1	—
Differ from Category (+/-) . .	0.2	-9.0	6.3	-6.2	-1.5	-4.2	0.4	-1.7	-4.9	—
Return, Tax-Adjusted (%). . .	3.9	6.2	1.0	5.6	6.8	7.2	6.8	7.3	5.1	—

PER SHARE DATA

	1996	1995	1994	1993	1992	1991	1990	1989	1988	1987
Dividends, Net Income ($).	0.21	0.20	0.20	0.21	0.24	0.26	0.29	0.29	0.28	—
Distrib'ns, Cap Gain ($) . . .	0.00	0.00	0.00	0.00	0.00	0.00	0.00	0.00	0.00	—
Net Asset Value ($)	5.24	5.25	5.15	5.30	5.23	5.13	5.04	5.00	4.94	—
Expense Ratio (%).	0.75	0.72	0.72	0.76	0.76	0.76	0.76	0.75	0.75	—
Yield (%)	4.00	3.80	3.88	3.96	4.58	5.06	5.75	5.80	5.66	—
Portfolio Turnover (%).	57	4	17	22	29	26	58	41	103	—
Total Assets (Millions $). . . .	59	55	61	70	42	22	8	6	5	—

PORTFOLIO (as of 9/30/96)

Portfolio Manager: William Griggs - 1989

Investm't Category: Tax-Exempt Bond
✔ Domestic   Index
  Foreign   Sector
  Asset Allocation ✔ State Specific

Investment Style
  Large-Cap Growth   Large-Cap Value
  Mid-Cap Growth   Mid-Cap Value
  Small-Cap Growth   Small-Cap Value

Portfolio
  1.2% cash   0.0% corp bonds
  0.0% stocks   0.0% gov't bonds
  0.0% preferred   98.8% muni bonds
  0.0% conv't/warrants 0.0% other

SHAREHOLDER INFORMATION

Minimum Investment
Initial: $100   Subsequent: $100

Minimum IRA Investment
Initial: na   Subsequent: na

Maximum Fees
Load: none   12b-1: none
Other: none

Distributions
Income: monthly   Capital Gains: Dec

Exchange Options
Number Per Year: no limit   Fee: none
Telephone: yes

Services
auto exchange, auto invest, auto withdraw

Eclipse Financial Asset Tr: Balanced (EBALX)

Balanced

144 E. 30th St.
New York, NY 10016
800-872-2710, 212-696-4130
www.eclipsefund.com

PERFORMANCE

fund inception date: 5/1/89

	3yr Annual	5yr Annual	10yr Annual	Bull	Bear
Return (%)	11.5	12.7	na	43.1	-5.0
Differ from Category (+/-)	-0.2 av	1.3 abv av	na	-2.0 av	0.7 abv av

Total Risk	Standard Deviation	Category Risk	Risk Index	Beta
blw av	6.2%	blw av	0.9	0.58

	1996	1995	1994	1993	1992	1991	1990	1989	1988	1987
Return (%).............	12.9	23.0	-0.1	17.0	12.0	20.9	1.4	—	—	—
Differ from Category (+/-).	-1.3	-1.6	1.5	2.6	3.1	-3.2	2.3	—	—	—
Return, Tax-Adjusted (%)...	9.4	20.6	-1.8	13.8	8.7	18.9	-0.6	—	—	—

PER SHARE DATA

	1996	1995	1994	1993	1992	1991	1990	1989	1988	1987
Dividends, Net Income ($).	0.77	0.64	0.55	0.63	0.73	0.71	0.76	—	—	—
Distrib'ns, Cap Gain ($) ...	1.43	0.56	0.31	1.04	0.93	0.00	0.00	—	—	—
Net Asset Value ($)	21.00	20.59	17.75	18.63	17.37	17.02	14.69	—	—	—
Expense Ratio (%)........	na	0.81	0.80	0.69	0.52	0.66	1.00	—	—	—
Yield (%)	3.43	3.02	3.04	3.20	3.98	4.17	5.17	—	—	—
Portfolio Turnover (%).....	na	74	94	65	95	101	120	—	—	—
Total Assets (Millions $). ...	83	85	27	21	14	10	4	—	—	—

PORTFOLIO (as of 9/30/96)

Portfolio Manager: Wesley G. McCain - 1989

Investm't Category: Balanced
- ✔ Domestic
- ✔ Foreign
- Asset Allocation
- Index
- Sector
- State Specific

Investment Style
Large-Cap Growth   Large-Cap Value
Mid-Cap Growth   Mid-Cap Value
Small-Cap Growth   Small-Cap Value

Portfolio
2.2% cash	38.3% corp bonds
59.6% stocks	0.0% gov't bonds
0.0% preferred	0.0% muni bonds
0.0% conv't/warrants	0.0% other

SHAREHOLDER INFORMATION

Minimum Investment
Initial: $1,000   Subsequent: $1

Minimum IRA Investment
Initial: $1,000   Subsequent: $1

Maximum Fees
Load: none   12b-1: none
Other: none

Distributions
Income: quarterly   Capital Gains: annual

Exchange Options
Number Per Year: no limit   Fee: none
Telephone: yes (money market fund available)

Services
IRA, pension, auto invest, auto withdraw

Eclipse Financial Asset Tr: Equity (EEQFX)

Growth

144 E. 30th St.
New York, NY 10016
800-872-2710, 212-696-4130
www.eclipsefund.com

PERFORMANCE

fund inception date: 1/12/87

	3yr Annual	5yr Annual	10yr Annual	Bull	Bear
Return (%)	13.9	15.6	na	60.1	-10.5
Differ from Category (+/-)	-1.8 blw av	1.3 abv av	na	-2.3 av	-3.8 low

Total Risk	Standard Deviation	Category Risk	Risk Index	Beta
abv av	10.4%	av	1.0	0.73

	1996	1995	1994	1993	1992	1991	1990	1989	1988	1987
Return (%)	29.8	19.5	-4.7	17.0	19.3	31.1	-13.7	16.4	12.7	—
Differ from Category (+/-)	9.7	-10.8	-4.4	3.0	7.5	-4.9	-7.6	-9.7	-5.4	—
Return, Tax-Adjusted (%)	21.2	18.0	-6.6	12.5	17.2	30.4	-14.9	13.6	10.9	—

PER SHARE DATA

	1996	1995	1994	1993	1992	1991	1990	1989	1988	1987
Dividends, Net Income ($)	0.13	0.06	0.02	0.07	0.15	0.16	0.32	0.27	0.41	—
Distrib'ns, Cap Gain ($)	3.98	0.51	0.86	2.02	0.65	0.00	0.00	0.63	0.00	—
Net Asset Value ($)	13.47	13.56	11.83	13.35	13.20	11.73	9.07	10.86	10.12	—
Expense Ratio (%)	na	1.14	1.12	1.12	1.15	1.18	1.18	1.09	1.12	—
Yield (%)	0.74	0.42	0.15	0.45	1.08	1.36	3.52	2.34	4.05	—
Portfolio Turnover (%)	na	74	92	101	111	119	154	46	31	—
Total Assets (Millions $)	168	174	195	197	163	148	108	184	161	—

PORTFOLIO (as of 9/30/96)

Portfolio Manager: Wesley G. McCain - 1987

Investm't Category: Growth
✔ Domestic   Index
✔ Foreign   Sector
  Asset Allocation State Specific

Investment Style
  Large-Cap Growth   Large-Cap Value
  Mid-Cap Growth   Mid-Cap Value
✔ Small-Cap Growth   Small-Cap Value

Portfolio
  1.5% cash   0.0% corp bonds
  98.5% stocks   0.0% gov't bonds
  0.0% preferred   0.0% muni bonds
  0.0% conv't/warrants 0.0% other

SHAREHOLDER INFORMATION

Minimum Investment
Initial: $1,000   Subsequent: $1

Minimum IRA Investment
Initial: $1,000   Subsequent: $1

Maximum Fees
Load: none   12b-1: none
Other: none

Distributions
Income: annual   Capital Gains: annual

Exchange Options
Number Per Year: no limit   Fee: none
Telephone: yes (money market fund available)

Services
IRA, pension, auto invest, auto withdraw

FAM Value (FAMVX)

Growth

111 N. Grand St.
Cobleskill, NY 12043
800-453-4392, 518-234-7400

PERFORMANCE

fund inception date: 10/31/86

	3yr Annual	5yr Annual	10yr Annual	Bull	Bear
Return (%)	12.4	12.2	12.8	46.2	-3.8
Differ from Category (+/-)	-3.3 blw av	-2.1 blw av	-1.1 blw av	-16.2 low	2.9 abv av

Total Risk	Standard Deviation	Category Risk	Risk Index	Beta
av	8.4%	low	0.8	0.51

	1996	1995	1994	1993	1992	1991	1990	1989	1988	1987
Return (%)	11.2	19.7	6.8	0.2	25.0	47.6	-5.4	20.3	35.5	-17.2
Differ from Category (+/-)	-8.9	-10.6	7.1	-13.8	13.2	11.6	0.7	-5.8	17.4	-19.2
Return, Tax-Adjusted (%)	10.2	18.8	5.7	-0.1	23.9	45.4	-5.7	19.9	34.2	-17.7

PER SHARE DATA

	1996	1995	1994	1993	1992	1991	1990	1989	1988	1987
Dividends, Net Income ($)	0.17	0.20	0.12	0.09	0.10	0.08	0.07	0.05	0.25	0.10
Distrib'ns, Cap Gain ($)	0.62	0.39	0.62	0.04	0.48	0.81	0.01	0.06	0.00	0.02
Net Asset Value ($)	26.53	24.58	21.04	20.40	20.50	16.87	12.06	12.85	10.78	8.14
Expense Ratio (%)	na	1.25	1.39	1.39	1.50	1.49	1.53	1.51	1.48	1.54
Yield (%)	0.62	0.80	0.55	0.44	0.47	0.45	0.57	0.38	2.31	1.22
Portfolio Turnover (%)	na	9	2	5	10	14	9	15	12	16
Total Assets (Millions $)	251	266	210	220	44	13	6	4	2	1

PORTFOLIO (as of 9/30/96)

Portfolio Manager: na

Investm't Category: Growth
- ✔ Domestic
- Foreign
- Asset Allocation
- Index
- Sector
- State Specific

Investment Style
- Large-Cap Growth
- Mid-Cap Growth
- ✔ Small-Cap Growth
- Large-Cap Value
- Mid-Cap Value
- ✔ Small-Cap Value

Portfolio
4.5% cash	0.0% corp bonds
95.5% stocks	0.0% gov't bonds
0.0% preferred	0.0% muni bonds
0.0% conv't/warrants	0.0% other

SHAREHOLDER INFORMATION

Minimum Investment
Initial: $2,000   Subsequent: $50

Minimum IRA Investment
Initial: $100   Subsequent: $50

Maximum Fees
Load: none   12b-1: none
Other: none

Distributions
Income: annual   Capital Gains: annual

Exchange Options
Number Per Year: none   Fee: na
Telephone: na

Services
IRA, pension, auto invest

Fairmont (FAIMX)
Aggressive Growth

1346 S. Third St.
Louisville, KY 40208
800-262-9936, 502-636-5633

PERFORMANCE

fund inception date: 9/2/81

	3yr Annual	5yr Annual	10yr Annual	Bull	Bear
Return (%)	14.5	14.6	8.2	40.2	-1.8
Differ from Category (+/-)	-1.3 av	-0.7 av	-6.8 low	-30.9 low	8.8 high

Total Risk	Standard Deviation	Category Risk	Risk Index	Beta
high	16.4%	abv av	1.1	1.01

	1996	1995	1994	1993	1992	1991	1990	1989	1988	1987
Return (%)	9.5	27.9	7.2	15.5	14.0	40.5	-22.2	6.8	3.1	-7.8
Differ from Category (+/-)	-9.6	-6.4	7.2	-3.8	2.3	-11.6	-16.8	-21.6	-13.3	-5.4
Return, Tax-Adjusted (%)	6.2	23.5	7.2	15.5	14.0	40.2	-23.0	6.2	2.4	-8.0

PER SHARE DATA

	1996	1995	1994	1993	1992	1991	1990	1989	1988	1987
Dividends, Net Income ($)	0.00	0.00	0.00	0.00	0.00	0.08	0.30	0.20	0.23	0.17
Distrib'ns, Cap Gain ($)	3.14	3.76	0.00	0.00	0.00	0.00	0.00	0.00	0.00	0.08
Net Asset Value ($)	26.45	27.02	24.06	22.43	19.41	17.02	12.17	16.02	15.19	14.96
Expense Ratio (%)	na	1.70	1.74	1.78	1.79	1.79	1.68	1.37	1.25	1.18
Yield (%)	0.00	0.00	0.00	0.00	0.00	0.47	2.46	1.24	1.51	1.13
Portfolio Turnover (%)	na	2	275	155	132	115	128	90	158	145
Total Assets (Millions $)	30	28	22	18	16	17	15	42	64	79

PORTFOLIO (as of 9/30/96)

Portfolio Manager: Morton H. Sachs - 1981

Investm't Category: Aggressive Growth
- ✔ Domestic
- Foreign
- Asset Allocation
- Index
- Sector
- State Specific

Investment Style
- Large-Cap Growth
- Mid-Cap Growth
- ✔ Small-Cap Growth
- Large-Cap Value
- Mid-Cap Value
- ✔ Small-Cap Value

Portfolio
- 7.6% cash
- 92.4% stocks
- 0.0% preferred
- 0.0% conv't/warrants
- 0.0% corp bonds
- 0.0% gov't bonds
- 0.0% muni bonds
- 0.0% other

SHAREHOLDER INFORMATION

Minimum Investment
Initial: $1,000   Subsequent: $1

Minimum IRA Investment
Initial: $1,000   Subsequent: $1

Maximum Fees
Load: none   12b-1: none
Other: none

Distributions
Income: annual   Capital Gains: annual

Exchange Options
Number Per Year: no limit   Fee: none
Telephone: none

Services
IRA, pension

Fidelity Aggressive Muni

(FATFX)

Tax-Exempt Bond

82 Devonshire St.
Mail Zone F9A
Boston, MA 02109
800-544-6666, 801-534-1910
www.fidelity.com

PERFORMANCE   fund inception date: 9/13/85

	3yr Annual	5yr Annual	10yr Annual	Bull	Bear
Return (%)	3.8	6.8	7.7	17.4	-5.7
Differ from Category (+/-)	-0.4 blw av	0.4 av	1.0 high	-1.0 blw av	-0.3 av

Total Risk	Standard Deviation	Category Risk	Risk Index	Avg Mat
blw av	5.3%	av	1.0	17.3 yrs

	1996	1995	1994	1993	1992	1991	1990	1989	1988	1987
Return (%).	3.5	14.8	-5.9	13.7	9.1	11.7	7.4	9.5	13.4	1.4
Differ from Category (+/-) .	-0.2	-0.4	-0.6	1.9	0.8	0.3	1.0	0.5	3.4	2.8
Return, Tax-Adjusted (%). . .	3.5	14.8	-6.1	12.8	8.7	11.5	7.4	9.5	13.4	1.4

PER SHARE DATA

	1996	1995	1994	1993	1992	1991	1990	1989	1988	1987
Dividends, Net Income ($).	0.69	0.70	0.76	0.78	0.83	0.86	0.88	0.88	0.89	0.90
Distrib'ns, Cap Gain ($) . . .	0.00	0.00	0.05	0.34	0.13	0.06	0.00	0.00	0.00	0.00
Net Asset Value ($)	11.36	11.67	10.81	12.34	11.88	11.80	11.43	11.49	11.33	10.82
Expense Ratio (%).	na	0.64	0.63	0.64	0.64	0.69	0.66	0.69	0.73	0.74
Yield (%)	6.07	5.99	6.99	6.15	6.91	7.25	7.69	7.65	7.85	8.31
Portfolio Turnover (%).	na	39	40	54	43	30	46	46	46	68
Total Assets (Millions $). . .	866	907	793	948	759	650	548	543	452	352

PORTFOLIO (as of 9/30/96)

Portfolio Manager: Tanya M. Roy - 1995

Investm't Category: Tax-Exempt Bond
✔ Domestic
   Foreign
   Asset Allocation
   Index
   Sector
   State Specific

Investment Style
Large-Cap Growth   Large-Cap Value
Mid-Cap Growth   Mid-Cap Value
Small-Cap Growth   Small-Cap Value

Portfolio
1.0% cash   0.0% corp bonds
0.0% stocks   0.0% gov't bonds
0.0% preferred   99.0% muni bonds
0.0% conv't/warrants   0.0% other

SHAREHOLDER INFORMATION

Minimum Investment
Initial: $2,500   Subsequent: $250

Minimum IRA Investment
Initial: na   Subsequent: na

Maximum Fees
Load: 1.00% redemption   12b-1: none
Other: redemption fee applies for 6 months; *f*

Distributions
Income: monthly   Capital Gains: Feb, Dec

Exchange Options
Number Per Year: 4   Fee: none
Telephone: yes (money market fund available)

Services
auto exchange, auto invest, auto withdraw

Fidelity Asset Manager

(FASMX)

Balanced

82 Devonshire St.
Mail Zone F9A
Boston, MA 02109
800-544-6666, 801-534-1910
www.fidelity.com

PERFORMANCE
fund inception date: 12/28/88

	3yr Annual	5yr Annual	10yr Annual	Bull	Bear
Return (%)	7.5	11.5	na	32.6	-9.2
Differ from Category (+/-)	-4.2 low	0.1 av	na	-12.5 low	-3.5 low

Total Risk	Standard Deviation	Category Risk	Risk Index	Beta
av	7.0%	av	1.0	0.64

	1996	1995	1994	1993	1992	1991	1990	1989	1988	1987
Return (%)	12.7	18.1	-6.7	23.2	12.7	23.6	5.3	15.6	—	—
Differ from Category (+/-)	-1.5	-6.5	-5.1	8.8	3.8	-0.5	6.2	-2.5	—	—
Return, Tax-Adjusted (%)	9.8	16.7	-8.1	20.5	10.7	20.6	2.9	13.4	—	—

PER SHARE DATA

	1996	1995	1994	1993	1992	1991	1990	1989	1988	1987
Dividends, Net Income ($)	0.62	0.46	0.40	0.59	0.48	0.45	0.65	0.38	—	—
Distrib'ns, Cap Gain ($)	0.75	0.00	0.17	0.43	0.19	0.50	0.00	0.24	—	—
Net Asset Value ($)	16.47	15.85	13.83	15.40	13.37	12.46	10.87	10.94	—	—
Expense Ratio (%)	0.93	0.97	1.04	1.09	1.17	1.17	1.17	1.58	—	—
Yield (%)	3.60	2.90	2.85	3.72	3.53	3.47	5.97	3.39	—	—
Portfolio Turnover (%)	131	137	109	98	134	134	105	167	—	—
Total Assets (Millions $)	11,237	11,165	11,075	9,094	3,407	1,016	372	299	—	—

PORTFOLIO (as of 9/30/96)

Portfolio Manager: Habermann, Vander-heiden, Gray - 1996

Investm't Category: Balanced
- ✔ Domestic
- ✔ Foreign
- ✔ Asset Allocation
- Index
- Sector
- State Specific

Investment Style

Large-Cap Growth	Large-Cap Value
Mid-Cap Growth	Mid-Cap Value
Small-Cap Growth	Small-Cap Value

Portfolio

16.6% cash	37.6% corp bonds
45.8% stocks	0.0% gov't bonds
0.0% preferred	0.0% muni bonds
0.0% conv't/warrants	0.0% other

SHAREHOLDER INFORMATION

Minimum Investment
Initial: $2,500   Subsequent: $250

Minimum IRA Investment
Initial: $500   Subsequent: $250

Maximum Fees
Load: none   12b-1: none
Other: *f*

Distributions
Income: quarterly   Capital Gains: Dec

Exchange Options
Number Per Year: 4   Fee: none
Telephone: yes (money market fund available)

Services
IRA, pension, auto exchange, auto invest, auto withdraw

Fidelity Asset Manager: Growth (FASGX)

Balanced

82 Devonshire St.
Mail Zone F9A
Boston, MA 02109
800-544-6666, 801-534-1910
www.fidelity.com

PERFORMANCE

fund inception date: 12/30/91

	3yr Annual	5yr Annual	10yr Annual	Bull	Bear
Return (%)	9.3	14.4	na	39.8	-10.1
Differ from Category (+/-)	-2.4 blw av	3.0 high	na	-5.3 blw av	-4.4 low

Total Risk	Standard Deviation	Category Risk	Risk Index	Beta
av	8.9%	high	1.3	0.80

	1996	1995	1994	1993	1992	1991	1990	1989	1988	1987
Return (%).	17.5	19.9	-7.4	26.3	19.0	—	—	—	—	—
Differ from Category (+/-) . .	3.3	-4.7	-5.8	11.9	10.1	—	—	—	—	—
Return, Tax-Adjusted (%). .	14.4	19.1	-8.3	24.7	18.1	—	—	—	—	—

PER SHARE DATA

	1996	1995	1994	1993	1992	1991	1990	1989	1988	1987
Dividends, Net Income ($).	0.43	0.23	0.19	0.09	0.15	—	—	—	—	—
Distrib'ns, Cap Gain ($) . . .	1.07	0.00	0.17	0.51	0.08	—	—	—	—	—
Net Asset Value ($)	16.35	15.17	12.84	14.25	11.77	—	—	—	—	—
Expense Ratio (%).	1.01	1.03	1.15	1.19	1.64	—	—	—	—	—
Yield (%)	2.46	1.51	1.46	0.60	1.26	—	—	—	—	—
Portfolio Turnover (%). . . .	138	119	104	97	693	—	—	—	—	—
Total Assets (Millions $). .	3,442	2,894	2,852	1,795	242	—	—	—	—	—

PORTFOLIO (as of 9/30/96)

Portfolio Manager: Habermann, Vanderheiden, Gray - 1996

Investm't Category: Balanced
- ✔ Domestic
- ✔ Foreign
- ✔ Asset Allocation
- Index
- Sector
- State Specific

Investment Style
- Large-Cap Growth
- Mid-Cap Growth
- Small-Cap Growth
- Large-Cap Value
- Mid-Cap Value
- Small-Cap Value

Portfolio
7.9% cash	21.4% corp bonds
70.7% stocks	0.0% gov't bonds
0.0% preferred	0.0% muni bonds
0.0% conv't/warrants	0.0% other

SHAREHOLDER INFORMATION

Minimum Investment
Initial: $2,500   Subsequent: $250

Minimum IRA Investment
Initial: $500   Subsequent: $250

Maximum Fees
Load: none   12b-1: none
Other: *f*

Distributions
Income: Dec   Capital Gains: Dec

Exchange Options
Number Per Year: 4   Fee: none
Telephone: yes (money market fund available)

Services
IRA, pension, auto exchange, auto invest, auto withdraw

Fidelity Asset Manager: Income (FASIX)

Balanced

82 Devonshire St.
Mail Zone F9A
Boston, MA 02109
800-544-6666, 801-534-1910
www.fidelity.com

PERFORMANCE

fund inception date: 10/1/92

	3yr Annual	5yr Annual	10yr Annual	Bull	Bear
Return (%)	7.4	na	na	26.8	-3.9
Differ from Category (+/-)	-4.3 low	na	na	-18.3 low	1.8 high

Total Risk	Standard Deviation	Category Risk	Risk Index	Beta
low	4.0%	low	0.6	0.37

	1996	1995	1994	1993	1992	1991	1990	1989	1988	1987
Return (%)	7.8	16.6	-1.4	15.3	—	—	—	—	—	—
Differ from Category (+/-)	-6.4	-8.0	0.2	0.9	—	—	—	—	—	—
Return, Tax-Adjusted (%)	5.0	14.5	-3.2	13.1	—	—	—	—	—	—

PER SHARE DATA

	1996	1995	1994	1993	1992	1991	1990	1989	1988	1987
Dividends, Net Income ($)	0.61	0.53	0.49	0.49	—	—	—	—	—	—
Distrib'ns, Cap Gain ($)	0.26	0.00	0.00	0.08	—	—	—	—	—	—
Net Asset Value ($)	11.61	11.60	10.42	11.06	—	—	—	—	—	—
Expense Ratio (%)	0.80	0.79	0.71	0.65	—	—	—	—	—	—
Yield (%)	5.13	4.56	4.70	4.39	—	—	—	—	—	—
Portfolio Turnover (%)	148	157	83	47	—	—	—	—	—	—
Total Assets (Millions $)	589	600	476	292	—	—	—	—	—	—

PORTFOLIO (as of 9/30/96)

Portfolio Manager: Habermann, Vander-heiden, Gray - 1996

Investm't Category: Balanced
✔ Domestic   Index
✔ Foreign   Sector
✔ Asset Allocation State Specific

Investment Style
Large-Cap Growth   Large-Cap Value
Mid-Cap Growth   Mid-Cap Value
Small-Cap Growth   Small-Cap Value

Portfolio
41.3% cash   36.6% corp bonds
22.1% stocks   0.0% gov't bonds
 0.0% preferred   0.0% muni bonds
 0.0% conv't/warrants 0.0% other

SHAREHOLDER INFORMATION

Minimum Investment
Initial: $2,500   Subsequent: $250

Minimum IRA Investment
Initial: $500   Subsequent: $250

Maximum Fees
Load: none   12b-1: none
Other: ƒ

Distributions
Income: monthly   Capital Gains: Sep, Dec

Exchange Options
Number Per Year: 4   Fee: none
Telephone: yes (money market fund available)

Services
IRA, pension, auto exchange, auto invest, auto withdraw

Fidelity Balanced (FBALX)

Balanced

82 Devonshire St.
Mail Zone F9A
Boston, MA 02109
800-544-6666, 801-534-1910
www.fidelity.com

PERFORMANCE

fund inception date: 11/6/86

	3yr Annual	5yr Annual	10yr Annual	Bull	Bear
Return (%)	5.9	8.8	10.5	25.1	-7.5
Differ from Category (+/-)	-5.8 low	-2.6 blw av	-0.3 blw av	-20.0 low	-1.8 blw av

Total Risk	Standard Deviation	Category Risk	Risk Index	Beta
blw av	6.2%	blw av	0.9	0.55

	1996	1995	1994	1993	1992	1991	1990	1989	1988	1987
Return (%)	9.3	14.9	-5.4	19.2	7.9	26.7	-0.5	19.6	15.7	1.9
Differ from Category (+/-)	-4.9	-9.7	-3.8	4.8	-1.0	2.6	0.4	1.5	3.5	-0.8
Return, Tax-Adjusted (%)	7.3	13.0	-6.6	15.8	4.9	23.2	-2.9	15.2	12.9	-0.7

PER SHARE DATA

	1996	1995	1994	1993	1992	1991	1990	1989	1988	1987
Dividends, Net Income ($)	0.65	0.56	0.40	0.60	0.66	0.60	0.68	1.00	0.68	0.60
Distrib'ns, Cap Gain ($)	0.00	0.00	0.00	0.64	0.36	0.45	0.00	0.22	0.00	0.07
Net Asset Value ($)	14.08	13.52	12.29	13.39	12.29	12.35	10.63	11.37	10.55	9.72
Expense Ratio (%)	0.79	0.90	1.01	0.93	0.96	0.98	0.97	1.13	1.30	1.19
Yield (%)	4.61	4.14	3.25	4.27	5.21	4.68	6.39	8.62	6.44	6.12
Portfolio Turnover (%)	247	269	157	162	242	238	223	168	213	161
Total Assets (Millions $)	4,056	4,880	4,999	4,684	1,761	725	293	196	123	121

PORTFOLIO (as of 9/30/96)

Portfolio Manager: Stephen Petersen, Michael Gray - 1996

Investm't Category: Balanced

✔ Domestic	Index
Foreign	Sector
✔ Asset Allocation	State Specific

Investment Style

Large-Cap Growth	Large-Cap Value
Mid-Cap Growth	Mid-Cap Value
Small-Cap Growth	Small-Cap Value

Portfolio

1.1% cash	34.7% corp bonds
58.6% stocks	0.0% gov't bonds
0.0% preferred	0.0% muni bonds
5.6% conv't/warrants	0.0% other

SHAREHOLDER INFORMATION

Minimum Investment
Initial: $2,500   Subsequent: $250

Minimum IRA Investment
Initial: $500   Subsequent: $250

Maximum Fees
Load: none   12b-1: none
Other: *f*

Distributions
Income: quarterly   Capital Gains: Sep, Dec

Exchange Options
Number Per Year: 4   Fee: none
Telephone: yes (money market fund available)

Services
IRA, pension, auto exchange, auto invest, auto withdraw

Fidelity Blue Chip Growth

(FBGRX)

Growth

82 Devonshire St.
Mail Zone F9A
Boston, MA 02109
800-544-6666, 801-534-1910
www.fidelity.com

PERFORMANCE

fund inception date: 12/31/87

	3yr Annual	5yr Annual	10yr Annual	Bull	Bear
Return (%)	17.6	16.5	na	60.3	-2.5
Differ from Category (+/-)	1.9 abv av	2.2 abv av	na	-2.1 av	4.2 high

Total Risk	Standard Deviation	Category Risk	Risk Index	Beta
abv av	10.9%	abv av	1.1	0.92

	1996	1995	1994	1993	1992	1991	1990	1989	1988	1987
Return (%)	15.3	28.3	9.8	24.5	6.1	54.8	3.5	36.2	5.9	—
Differ from Category (+/-)	-4.8	-2.0	10.1	10.5	-5.7	18.8	9.6	10.1	-12.2	—
Return, Tax-Adjusted (%)	12.8	25.4	9.1	19.4	5.0	54.5	3.0	35.2	5.7	—

PER SHARE DATA

	1996	1995	1994	1993	1992	1991	1990	1989	1988	1987
Dividends, Net Income ($)	0.28	0.12	0.00	0.01	0.14	0.08	0.15	0.12	0.03	—
Distrib'ns, Cap Gain ($)	2.25	2.47	0.57	4.12	0.62	0.00	0.00	0.17	0.00	—
Net Asset Value ($)	32.69	30.77	25.95	24.17	22.83	22.25	14.43	14.09	10.56	—
Expense Ratio (%)	0.95	1.02	1.22	1.25	1.27	1.26	1.26	1.56	2.74	—
Yield (%)	0.80	0.36	0.00	0.03	0.59	0.35	1.03	0.84	0.28	—
Portfolio Turnover (%)	206	182	271	319	71	99	68	83	40	—
Total Assets (Millions $)	9,837	7,801	3,287	1,094	565	390	131	64	38	—

PORTFOLIO (as of 9/30/96)

Portfolio Manager: John McDowell - 1996

Investm't Category: Growth
- ✔ Domestic
- ✔ Foreign
-   Asset Allocation
-   Index
-   Sector
-   State Specific

Investment Style
-   Large-Cap Growth
- ✔ Mid-Cap Growth
-   Small-Cap Growth
-   Large-Cap Value
-   Mid-Cap Value
-   Small-Cap Value

Portfolio
6.6% cash	0.0% corp bonds
93.4% stocks	0.0% gov't bonds
0.0% preferred	0.0% muni bonds
0.0% conv't/warrants	0.0% other

SHAREHOLDER INFORMATION

Minimum Investment
Initial: $2,500   Subsequent: $250

Minimum IRA Investment
Initial: $500   Subsequent: $250

Maximum Fees
Load: 3.00% front   12b-1: none
Other: *f*

Distributions
Income: Sep, Dec   Capital Gains: Sep, Dec

Exchange Options
Number Per Year: 4   Fee: none
Telephone: yes (money market fund available)

Services
IRA, pension, auto exchange, auto invest, auto withdraw

Fidelity CA Insured Muni Income (FCXIX)

Tax-Exempt Bond

82 Devonshire St.
Mail Zone F9A
Boston, MA 02109
800-544-6666, 801-534-1910
www.fidelity.com

PERFORMANCE

fund inception date: 9/18/86

	3yr Annual	5yr Annual	10yr Annual	Bull	Bear
Return (%)	3.6	6.7	6.6	20.6	-8.8
Differ from Category (+/-)	-0.6 low	0.3 av	-0.1 blw av	2.2 abv av	-3.4 low

Total Risk	Standard Deviation	Category Risk	Risk Index	Avg Mat
av	7.0%	high	1.3	15.7 yrs

	1996	1995	1994	1993	1992	1991	1990	1989	1988	1987
Return (%)	3.8	19.4	-10.3	13.8	9.1	10.9	7.0	8.7	11.6	-4.5
Differ from Category (+/-)	0.1	4.2	-5.0	2.0	0.8	-0.5	0.6	-0.3	1.6	-3.1
Return, Tax-Adjusted (%)	3.8	19.4	-10.8	13.2	9.1	10.9	7.0	8.7	11.6	-4.5

PER SHARE DATA

	1996	1995	1994	1993	1992	1991	1990	1989	1988	1987
Dividends, Net Income ($)	0.52	0.52	0.56	0.59	0.60	0.59	0.61	0.62	0.60	0.61
Distrib'ns, Cap Gain ($)	0.00	0.00	0.17	0.20	0.00	0.00	0.00	0.00	0.00	0.00
Net Asset Value ($)	10.33	10.47	9.23	11.07	10.45	10.15	9.72	9.68	9.49	9.07
Expense Ratio (%)	0.60	0.59	0.48	0.63	0.66	0.72	0.75	0.83	0.65	0.45
Yield (%)	5.03	4.96	5.95	5.23	5.74	5.81	6.27	6.40	6.32	6.72
Portfolio Turnover (%)	49	32	60	27	19	14	10	32	76	28
Total Assets (Millions $)	211	226	197	311	226	159	103	90	58	37

PORTFOLIO (as of 9/30/96)

Portfolio Manager: Jonathan D. Short - 1995

Investm't Category: Tax-Exempt Bond
- ✔ Domestic
- Foreign
- Asset Allocation
- Index
- Sector
- ✔ State Specific

Investment Style
- Large-Cap Growth
- Mid-Cap Growth
- Small-Cap Growth
- Large-Cap Value
- Mid-Cap Value
- Small-Cap Value

Portfolio
0.3% cash	0.0% corp bonds	
0.0% stocks	0.0% gov't bonds	
0.0% preferred	98.1% muni bonds	
0.0% conv't/warrants	2.2% other	

SHAREHOLDER INFORMATION

Minimum Investment
Initial: $2,500   Subsequent: $250

Minimum IRA Investment
Initial: na   Subsequent: na

Maximum Fees
Load: none   12b-1: none
Other: f

Distributions
Income: monthly   Capital Gains: Apr, Dec

Exchange Options
Number Per Year: 4   Fee: none
Telephone: yes (money market fund available)

Services
auto exchange, auto invest, auto withdraw

Fidelity CA Muni Income

(FCTFX)

Tax-Exempt Bond

82 Devonshire St.
Mail Zone F9A
Boston, MA 02109
800-544-6666, 801-534-1910
www.fidelity.com

PERFORMANCE

fund inception date: 7/3/84

	3yr Annual	5yr Annual	10yr Annual	Bull	Bear
Return (%)	4.3	7.0	6.9	21.8	-7.7
Differ from Category (+/-)	0.1 av	0.6 abv av	0.2 av	3.4 high	-2.3 low

Total Risk	Standard Deviation	Category Risk	Risk Index	Avg Mat
blw av	6.3%	high	1.1	15.0 yrs

	1996	1995	1994	1993	1992	1991	1990	1989	1988	1987
Return (%)	4.7	19.1	-8.9	13.4	8.7	10.1	6.9	9.6	11.7	-3.7
Differ from Category (+/-)	1.0	3.9	-3.6	1.6	0.4	-1.3	0.5	0.6	1.7	-2.3
Return, Tax-Adjusted (%)	4.7	19.1	-9.3	12.7	8.7	10.1	6.9	9.6	11.7	-3.9

PER SHARE DATA

	1996	1995	1994	1993	1992	1991	1990	1989	1988	1987
Dividends, Net Income ($)	0.60	0.62	0.69	0.72	0.74	0.74	0.75	0.76	0.75	0.76
Distrib'ns, Cap Gain ($)	0.00	0.00	0.15	0.27	0.00	0.00	0.00	0.00	0.00	0.06
Net Asset Value ($)	11.77	11.84	10.50	12.42	11.86	11.62	11.26	11.26	10.99	10.54
Expense Ratio (%)	0.58	0.56	0.57	0.60	0.59	0.58	0.60	0.61	0.73	0.68
Yield (%)	5.09	5.23	6.47	5.67	6.23	6.36	6.66	6.74	6.82	7.16
Portfolio Turnover (%)	37	29	44	32	23	15	34	21	52	46
Total Assets (Millions $)	490	507	443	591	548	539	520	563	460	383

PORTFOLIO (as of 9/30/96)

Portfolio Manager: Jonathan D. Short - 1995

Investm't Category: Tax-Exempt Bond
- ✔ Domestic
- Foreign
- Asset Allocation
- Index
- Sector
- ✔ State Specific

Investment Style
- Large-Cap Growth
- Mid-Cap Growth
- Small-Cap Growth
- Large-Cap Value
- Mid-Cap Value
- Small-Cap Value

Portfolio
- 3.4% cash
- 0.0% stocks
- 0.0% preferred
- 0.0% conv't/warrants
- 0.0% corp bonds
- 0.0% gov't bonds
- 95.5% muni bonds
- 1.1% other

SHAREHOLDER INFORMATION

Minimum Investment
Initial: $2,500   Subsequent: $250

Minimum IRA Investment
Initial: na   Subsequent: na

Maximum Fees
Load: none   12b-1: none
Other: *f*

Distributions
Income: monthly   Capital Gains: Apr, Dec

Exchange Options
Number Per Year: 4   Fee: none
Telephone: yes (money market fund available)

Services
auto exchange, auto invest, auto withdraw

Fidelity Canada (FICDX)

International Stock

82 Devonshire St.
Mail Zone F9A
Boston, MA 02109
800-544-6666, 801-534-1910
www.fidelity.com

PERFORMANCE

fund inception date: 11/17/87

	3yr Annual	5yr Annual	10yr Annual	Bull	Bear
Return (%)	6.8	8.2	na	34.3	-13.2
Differ from Category (+/-)	0.5 av	-1.8 blw av	na	10.0 abv av	-6.0 blw av

Total Risk	Standard Deviation	Category Risk	Risk Index	Beta
high	12.2%	abv av	1.2	0.88

	1996	1995	1994	1993	1992	1991	1990	1989	1988	1987
Return (%)	15.9	19.3	-12.0	25.4	-2.9	17.6	-5.5	26.9	19.4	—
Differ from Category (+/-)	1.1	10.2	-8.9	-14.2	0.9	4.4	4.6	4.3	4.5	—
Return, Tax-Adjusted (%)	9.3	19.1	-12.1	25.3	-3.0	15.6	-7.3	25.3	18.5	—

PER SHARE DATA

	1996	1995	1994	1993	1992	1991	1990	1989	1988	1987
Dividends, Net Income ($)	0.13	0.08	0.01	0.00	0.02	0.00	0.06	0.01	0.12	—
Distrib'ns, Cap Gain ($)	4.29	0.00	0.00	0.04	0.00	0.92	0.85	0.68	0.15	—
Net Asset Value ($)	17.62	19.02	16.00	18.19	14.53	14.98	13.53	15.29	12.59	—
Expense Ratio (%)	0.98	1.08	1.57	2.00	2.00	2.01	2.05	2.06	2.02	—
Yield (%)	0.59	0.42	0.06	0.00	0.13	0.00	0.41	0.06	0.94	—
Portfolio Turnover (%)	139	75	59	131	55	68	164	152	401	—
Total Assets (Millions $)	143	174	332	109	26	22	18	24	10	—

PORTFOLIO (as of 9/30/96)

Portfolio Manager: Tom Sweeney - 1996

Investm't Category: International Stock

Domestic	Index
✔ Foreign	Sector
Asset Allocation	State Specific

Investment Style

Large-Cap Growth	Large-Cap Value
Mid-Cap Growth	Mid-Cap Value
Small-Cap Growth	Small-Cap Value

Portfolio

5.6% cash	0.0% corp bonds
94.4% stocks	0.0% gov't bonds
0.0% preferred	0.0% muni bonds
0.0% conv't/warrants	0.0% other

SHAREHOLDER INFORMATION

Minimum Investment
Initial: $2,500   Subsequent: $250

Minimum IRA Investment
Initial: $500   Subsequent: $250

Maximum Fees
Load: 3.00% front   12b-1: none
Other: 1.50% redemption fee (90 days); f

Distributions
Income: Dec   Capital Gains: Dec

Exchange Options
Number Per Year: 4   Fee: none
Telephone: yes (money market fund available)

Services
IRA, pension, auto exchange, auto invest, auto withdraw

Fidelity Capital & Income

(FAGIX)

Corporate High-Yield Bond

82 Devonshire St.
Mail Zone F9A
Boston, MA 02109
800-544-6666, 801-534-1910
www.fidelity.com

PERFORMANCE

fund inception date: 11/1/77

	3yr Annual	5yr Annual	10yr Annual	Bull	Bear
Return (%)	7.4	14.6	10.5	26.7	-5.1
Differ from Category (+/-)	-1.3 blw av	2.5 high	1.2 high	-6.4 blw av	0.3 abv av

Total Risk	Standard Deviation	Category Risk	Risk Index	Avg Mat
blw av	5.1%	abv av	1.1	6.6 yrs

	1996	1995	1994	1993	1992	1991	1990	1989	1988	1987
Return (%).............	11.4	16.7	-4.7	24.9	28.0	29.8	-4.0	-3.1	12.5	1.3
Differ from Category (+/-).	-3.9	-0.8	-1.8	6.0	11.9	2.2	0.9	-4.3	0.0	-0.5
Return, Tax-Adjusted (%)...	7.9	12.7	-7.9	21.0	24.4	25.1	-8.1	-8.1	7.8	-3.8

PER SHARE DATA

	1996	1995	1994	1993	1992	1991	1990	1989	1988	1987
Dividends, Net Income ($).	0.79	0.87	0.79	0.83	0.66	0.73	0.75	1.07	1.00	1.05
Distrib'ns, Cap Gain ($) ...	0.00	0.00	0.00	0.00	0.00	0.00	0.00	0.00	0.00	0.28
Net Asset Value ($)	9.36	9.16	8.63	9.86	8.61	7.28	6.23	7.27	8.56	8.53
Expense Ratio (%)........	0.98	0.96	0.97	0.91	0.80	0.81	0.81	0.77	0.88	0.78
Yield (%)	8.44	9.49	9.15	8.41	7.66	10.02	12.03	14.71	11.68	11.91
Portfolio Turnover (%)....	119	78	100	102	132	108	95	72	68	116
Total Assets (Millions $). .	2,174	2,322	2,039	2,745	1,675	1,155	814	1,288	1,689	1,308

PORTFOLIO (as of 9/30/96)

Portfolio Manager: David L. Glancy - 1996

Investm't Category: Corp. High-Yield Bond
- ✔ Domestic
- ✔ Foreign
-   Asset Allocation

- Index
- Sector
- State Specific

Investment Style
- Large-Cap Growth
- Mid-Cap Growth
- Small-Cap Growth

- Large-Cap Value
- Mid-Cap Value
- Small-Cap Value

Portfolio
20.4% cash	0.0% corp bonds
0.0% stocks	3.7% gov't bonds
24.0% preferred	0.0% muni bonds
48.1% conv't/warrants	3.8% other

SHAREHOLDER INFORMATION

Minimum Investment
Initial: $2,500   Subsequent: $250

Minimum IRA Investment
Initial: $500   Subsequent: $250

Maximum Fees
Load: 1.50% redemption   12b-1: none
Other: redemption fee applies for 1 year; *f*

Distributions
Income: monthly   Capital Gains: Jun, Dec

Exchange Options
Number Per Year: 4   Fee: none
Telephone: yes (money market fund available)

Services
IRA, pension, auto exchange, auto invest, auto withdraw

Fidelity Capital Appreciation (FDCAX)

Growth

82 Devonshire St.
Mail Zone F9A
Boston, MA 02109
800-544-6666, 801-534-1910
www.fidelity.com

PERFORMANCE

fund inception date: 11/26/86

	3yr Annual	5yr Annual	10yr Annual	Bull	Bear
Return (%)	11.9	16.8	15.4	44.5	-8.1
Differ from Category (+/-)	-3.8 low	2.5 abv av	1.5 abv av	-17.9 low	-1.4 blw av

Total Risk	Standard Deviation	Category Risk	Risk Index	Beta
abv av	9.7%	blw av	0.9	0.74

	1996	1995	1994	1993	1992	1991	1990	1989	1988	1987
Return (%)	15.1	18.7	2.5	33.4	16.3	9.9	-15.7	26.9	37.6	19.2
Differ from Category (+/-)	-5.0	-11.6	2.8	19.4	4.5	-26.1	-9.6	0.8	19.5	17.2
Return, Tax-Adjusted (%)	12.2	15.8	-1.0	30.9	14.3	3.8	-16.2	23.8	37.1	16.7

PER SHARE DATA

	1996	1995	1994	1993	1992	1991	1990	1989	1988	1987
Dividends, Net Income ($)	0.12	0.40	0.17	0.10	0.18	0.62	0.17	0.24	0.13	0.02
Distrib'ns, Cap Gain ($)	1.54	1.00	1.85	1.06	0.60	2.13	0.01	1.22	0.00	0.82
Net Asset Value ($)	17.64	16.78	15.31	16.92	13.57	12.34	13.84	16.63	14.29	10.48
Expense Ratio (%)	0.80	1.06	1.17	0.86	0.71	0.83	1.14	1.14	1.36	1.25
Yield (%)	0.62	2.24	0.99	0.55	1.27	4.28	1.22	1.34	0.90	0.17
Portfolio Turnover (%)	205	87	124	120	99	72	56	73	120	203
Total Assets (Millions $)	1,653	1,669	1,623	1,428	988	992	1,414	2,252	1,573	860

PORTFOLIO (as of 9/30/96)

Portfolio Manager: Harry Lange - 1996

Investm't Category: Growth

✔ Domestic	Index
✔ Foreign	Sector
Asset Allocation	State Specific

Investment Style

Large-Cap Growth	Large-Cap Value
Mid-Cap Growth	Mid-Cap Value
✔ Small-Cap Growth	✔ Small-Cap Value

Portfolio

4.3% cash	0.0% corp bonds
95.6% stocks	0.0% gov't bonds
0.0% preferred	0.0% muni bonds
0.1% conv't/warrants	0.0% other

SHAREHOLDER INFORMATION

Minimum Investment
Initial: $2,500   Subsequent: $250

Minimum IRA Investment
Initial: $500   Subsequent: $250

Maximum Fees
Load: none   12b-1: none
Other: *f*

Distributions
Income: Feb, Dec   Capital Gains: Feb, Dec

Exchange Options
Number Per Year: 4   Fee: none
Telephone: yes (money market fund available)

Services
IRA, pension, auto exchange, auto invest, auto withdraw

Fidelity Contrafund

(FCNTX)

Growth

82 Devonshire St.
Mail Zone F9A
Boston, MA 02109
800-544-6666, 801-534-1910
www.fidelity.com

PERFORMANCE

fund inception date: 5/17/67

	3yr Annual	5yr Annual	10yr Annual	Bull	Bear
Return (%)	18.0	18.2	20.2	72.7	-7.8
Differ from Category (+/-)	2.3 abv av	3.9 high	6.3 high	10.3 abv av	-1.1 blw av

Total Risk	Standard Deviation	Category Risk	Risk Index	Beta
abv av	10.4%	av	1.0	0.87

	1996	1995	1994	1993	1992	1991	1990	1989	1988	1987
Return (%)	21.9	36.2	-1.2	21.4	15.8	54.9	3.9	43.1	21.0	-2.0
Differ from Category (+/-)	1.8	5.9	-0.9	7.4	4.0	18.9	10.0	17.0	2.9	-4.0
Return, Tax-Adjusted (%)	18.9	33.1	-1.4	18.8	13.3	52.9	3.6	39.9	19.8	-3.1

PER SHARE DATA

	1996	1995	1994	1993	1992	1991	1990	1989	1988	1987
Dividends, Net Income ($)	0.38	0.09	0.00	0.18	0.20	0.11	0.09	0.25	0.32	0.00
Distrib'ns, Cap Gain ($)	3.45	3.13	0.22	2.25	1.92	1.06	0.00	1.07	0.00	0.43
Net Asset Value ($)	42.15	38.02	30.28	30.84	27.47	25.60	17.35	16.78	12.65	10.72
Expense Ratio (%)	na	0.96	1.03	1.06	0.87	0.89	1.06	0.95	0.98	0.92
Yield (%)	0.83	0.21	0.00	0.54	0.68	0.41	0.51	1.40	2.52	0.00
Portfolio Turnover (%)	na	223	235	255	297	217	320	266	250	196
Total Assets (Millions $)	23,920	14,831	8,682	6,193	1,974	1,002	332	296	105	87

PORTFOLIO (as of 9/30/96)

Portfolio Manager: Will Danoff - 1990

Investm't Category: Growth

- ✔ Domestic
- ✔ Foreign
-   Asset Allocation
-   Index
-   Sector
-   State Specific

Investment Style

Large-Cap Growth	Large-Cap Value
✔ Mid-Cap Growth	✔ Mid-Cap Value
✔ Small-Cap Growth	✔ Small-Cap Value

Portfolio

8.1% cash	2.3% corp bonds
89.2% stocks	0.0% gov't bonds
0.0% preferred	0.0% muni bonds
0.4% conv't/warrants	0.0% other

SHAREHOLDER INFORMATION

Minimum Investment
Initial: $2,500   Subsequent: $250

Minimum IRA Investment
Initial: $500   Subsequent: $250

Maximum Fees
Load: 3.00% front   12b-1: none
Other: f

Distributions
Income: Feb, Dec   Capital Gains: Feb, Dec

Exchange Options
Number Per Year: 4   Fee: none
Telephone: yes (money market fund available)

Services
IRA, pension, auto exchange, auto invest, auto withdraw

Fidelity Convertible Securities (FCVSX)

Growth & Income

82 Devonshire St.
Mail Zone F9A
Boston, MA 02109
800-544-6666, 801-534-1910
www.fidelity.com

PERFORMANCE

fund inception date: 1/5/87

	3yr Annual	5yr Annual	10yr Annual	Bull	Bear
Return (%)	10.5	14.1	na	42.9	-7.9
Differ from Category (+/-)	-4.8 low	0.2 av	na	-16.9 low	-1.5 blw av

Total Risk	Standard Deviation	Category Risk	Risk Index	Beta
av	7.6%	low	0.8	0.65

	1996	1995	1994	1993	1992	1991	1990	1989	1988	1987
Return (%)..............	15.0	19.3	-1.8	17.7	22.0	38.7	-2.9	26.2	15.8	—
Differ from Category (+/-).	-4.7	-10.8	-0.5	3.9	11.3	9.6	3.0	2.7	-1.0	—
Return, Tax-Adjusted (%)..	11.6	15.9	-3.8	13.8	19.2	35.3	-5.1	23.0	12.6	—

PER SHARE DATA

	1996	1995	1994	1993	1992	1991	1990	1989	1988	1987
Dividends, Net Income ($).	0.77	0.76	0.80	0.73	0.67	0.64	0.62	0.77	0.72	—
Distrib'ns, Cap Gain ($) ...	0.89	0.76	0.00	1.09	0.40	0.37	0.00	0.00	0.00	—
Net Asset Value ($)	17.56	16.77	15.36	16.45	15.55	13.67	10.65	11.60	9.83	—
Expense Ratio (%).........	na	0.70	0.85	0.92	0.96	1.17	1.31	1.38	1.60	—
Yield (%)	4.17	4.33	5.20	4.16	4.20	4.55	5.82	6.63	7.32	—
Portfolio Turnover (%).....	na	203	318	312	258	152	223	207	191	—
Total Assets (Millions $).	1,147	1,045	891	1,063	485	133	59	63	40	—

PORTFOLIO (as of 9/30/96)

Portfolio Manager: Bob Bertelson - 1996

Investm't Category: Growth & Income
- ✔ Domestic
- ✔ Foreign
- Asset Allocation
- Index
- Sector
- State Specific

Investment Style
- Large-Cap Growth
- ✔ Mid-Cap Growth
- ✔ Small-Cap Growth
- Large-Cap Value
- ✔ Mid-Cap Value
- ✔ Small-Cap Value

Portfolio
8.6% cash	1.1% corp bonds
12.5% stocks	0.0% gov't bonds
0.0% preferred	0.0% muni bonds
77.8% conv't/warrants	0.0% other

SHAREHOLDER INFORMATION

Minimum Investment
Initial: $2,500   Subsequent: $250

Minimum IRA Investment
Initial: $500   Subsequent: $250

Maximum Fees
Load: none   12b-1: none
Other: f

Distributions
Income: quarterly   Capital Gains: Jan, Dec

Exchange Options
Number Per Year: 4   Fee: none
Telephone: yes (money market fund available)

Services
IRA, pension, auto exchange, auto invest, auto withdraw

Fidelity Disciplined Equity

(FDEQX)

Growth

82 Devonshire St.
Mail Zone F9A
Boston, MA 02109
800-544-6666, 801-534-1910
www.fidelity.com

PERFORMANCE

fund inception date: 12/28/88

	3yr Annual	5yr Annual	10yr Annual	Bull	Bear
Return (%)	15.2	14.5	na	56.2	-6.7
Differ from Category (+/-)	-0.5 av	0.2 av	na	-6.2 blw av	0.0 av

Total Risk	Standard Deviation	Category Risk	Risk Index	Beta
abv av	10.3%	av	1.0	0.93

	1996	1995	1994	1993	1992	1991	1990	1989	1988	1987
Return (%).	15.1	29.0	3.0	13.9	13.2	36.0	-0.8	35.8	—	—
Differ from Category (+/-) .	-5.0	-1.3	3.3	-0.1	1.4	0.0	5.3	9.7	—	—
Return, Tax-Adjusted (%). .	12.6	24.8	1.6	11.7	11.0	32.4	-1.7	34.9	—	—

PER SHARE DATA

	1996	1995	1994	1993	1992	1991	1990	1989	1988	1987
Dividends, Net Income ($).	0.23	0.30	0.25	0.21	0.19	0.23	0.30	0.13	—	—
Distrib'ns, Cap Gain ($) . . .	1.49	2.23	0.52	1.04	0.99	1.32	0.00	0.13	—	—
Net Asset Value ($)	22.04	20.64	17.94	18.18	17.07	16.14	13.11	13.52	—	—
Expense Ratio (%).	0.81	0.93	1.05	1.09	1.16	1.19	1.24	1.94	—	—
Yield (%)	0.97	1.31	1.35	1.09	1.05	1.31	2.28	0.95	—	—
Portfolio Turnover (%). . . .	297	221	143	279	255	210	171	118	—	—
Total Assets (Millions $). .	2,215	2,145	1,160	795	452	175	106	112	—	—

PORTFOLIO (as of 9/30/96)

Portfolio Manager: Brad Lewis - 1988

Investm't Category: Growth

✔ Domestic	Index
✔ Foreign	Sector
Asset Allocation	State Specific

Investment Style

Large-Cap Growth	Large-Cap Value
✔ Mid-Cap Growth	✔ Mid-Cap Value
Small-Cap Growth	Small-Cap Value

Portfolio

1.9% cash	0.0% corp bonds
98.1% stocks	0.0% gov't bonds
0.0% preferred	0.0% muni bonds
0.0% conv't/warrants	0.0% other

SHAREHOLDER INFORMATION

Minimum Investment

Initial: $2,500   Subsequent: $250

Minimum IRA Investment

Initial: $500   Subsequent: $250

Maximum Fees

Load: none   12b-1: none

Other: *f*

Distributions

Income: Dec   Capital Gains: Dec

Exchange Options

Number Per Year: 4   Fee: none

Telephone: yes (money market fund available)

Services

IRA, pension, auto exchange, auto invest, auto withdraw

Fidelity Diversified Int'l

(FDIVX)

International Stock

82 Devonshire St.
Mail Zone F9A
Boston, MA 02109
800-544-6666, 801-534-1910
www.fidelity.com

PERFORMANCE

fund inception date: 12/30/91

	3yr Annual	5yr Annual	10yr Annual	Bull	Bear
Return (%)	12.6	11.0	na	39.7	-4.8
Differ from Category (+/-)	6.3 high	1.0 av	na	15.4 abv av	2.4 abv av

Total Risk	Standard Deviation	Category Risk	Risk Index	Beta
abv av	10.1%	av	1.0	0.74

	1996	1995	1994	1993	1992	1991	1990	1989	1988	1987
Return (%)	20.0	17.9	1.0	36.6	-13.9	—	—	—	—	—
Differ from Category (+/-)	5.2	8.8	4.1	-3.0	-10.1	—	—	—	—	—
Return, Tax-Adjusted (%)	18.7	16.1	-0.1	36.2	-14.3	—	—	—	—	—

PER SHARE DATA

	1996	1995	1994	1993	1992	1991	1990	1989	1988	1987
Dividends, Net Income ($)	0.15	0.22	0.03	0.01	0.10	—	—	—	—	—
Distrib'ns, Cap Gain ($)	0.36	0.41	0.39	0.10	0.00	—	—	—	—	—
Net Asset Value ($)	14.71	12.69	11.30	11.60	8.57	—	—	—	—	—
Expense Ratio (%)	1.27	1.12	1.25	1.47	2.00	—	—	—	—	—
Yield (%)	0.99	1.67	0.25	0.08	1.16	—	—	—	—	—
Portfolio Turnover (%)	94	101	89	56	56	—	—	—	—	—
Total Assets (Millions $)	737	340	306	238	37	—	—	—	—	—

PORTFOLIO (as of 9/30/96)

Portfolio Manager: Greg Fraser - 1991

Investm't Category: International Stock

Domestic	Index
✔ Foreign	Sector
Asset Allocation	State Specific

Investment Style

Large-Cap Growth	Large-Cap Value
Mid-Cap Growth	Mid-Cap Value
Small-Cap Growth	Small-Cap Value

Portfolio

4.8% cash	0.6% corp bonds
94.6% stocks	0.0% gov't bonds
0.0% preferred	0.0% muni bonds
0.0% conv't/warrants	0.0% other

SHAREHOLDER INFORMATION

Minimum Investment
Initial: $2,500   Subsequent: $250

Minimum IRA Investment
Initial: $500   Subsequent: $250

Maximum Fees
Load: none   12b-1: none
Other: *f*

Distributions
Income: Dec   Capital Gains: Dec

Exchange Options
Number Per Year: 4   Fee: none
Telephone: yes (money market fund available)

Services
IRA, pension, auto exchange, auto invest, auto withdraw

Fidelity Dividend Growth

(FDGFX)

Growth

82 Devonshire St.
Mail Zone F9A
Boston, MA 02109
800-544-6666, 801-534-1910
www.fidelity.com

PERFORMANCE

fund inception date: 4/28/93

	3yr Annual	5yr Annual	10yr Annual	Bull	Bear
Return (%)	23.1	na	na	100.8	-9.5
Differ from Category (+/-)	7.4 high	na	na	38.4 high	-2.8 blw av

Total Risk	Standard Deviation	Category Risk	Risk Index	Beta
abv av	11.2%	abv av	1.1	0.99

	1996	1995	1994	1993	1992	1991	1990	1989	1988	1987
Return (%).............	30.1	37.5	4.2	—	—	—	—	—	—	—
Differ from Category (+/-) .	10.0	7.2	4.5	—	—	—	—	—	—	—
Return, Tax-Adjusted (%)..	29.2	34.7	3.6	—	—	—	—	—	—	—

PER SHARE DATA

	1996	1995	1994	1993	1992	1991	1990	1989	1988	1987
Dividends, Net Income ($)	0.09	0.09	0.01	—	—	—	—	—	—	—
Distrib'ns, Cap Gain ($) ...	0.37	1.07	0.24	—	—	—	—	—	—	—
Net Asset Value ($)	20.09	15.84	12.37	—	—	—	—	—	—	—
Expense Ratio (%)........	0.99	1.19	1.40	—	—	—	—	—	—	—
Yield (%)	0.43	0.53	0.07	—	—	—	—	—	—	—
Portfolio Turnover (%)....	129	162	291	—	—	—	—	—	—	—
Total Assets (Millions $)..	2,122	528	102	—	—	—	—	—	—	—

PORTFOLIO (as of 9/30/96)

Portfolio Manager: Steve Wymer - 1995

Investm't Category: Growth

✔ Domestic	Index
Foreign	Sector
Asset Allocation	State Specific

Investment Style

Large-Cap Growth	Large-Cap Value
✔ Mid-Cap Growth	Mid-Cap Value
Small-Cap Growth	Small-Cap Value

Portfolio

5.3% cash	0.0% corp bonds
94.7% stocks	0.0% gov't bonds
0.0% preferred	0.0% muni bonds
0.0% conv't/warrants	0.0% other

SHAREHOLDER INFORMATION

Minimum Investment
Initial: $2,500   Subsequent: $250

Minimum IRA Investment
Initial: $500   Subsequent: $250

Maximum Fees
Load: none   12b-1: none
Other: *f*

Distributions
Income: Sep, Dec   Capital Gains: Sep, Dec

Exchange Options
Number Per Year: 4   Fee: none
Telephone: yes (money market fund available)

Services
IRA, pension, auto exchange, auto invest, auto withdraw

Fidelity Emerging Growth

(FDEGX)

Aggressive Growth

82 Devonshire St.
Mail Zone F9A
Boston, MA 02109
800-544-6666, 801-534-1910
www.fidelity.com

PERFORMANCE

fund inception date: 12/28/90

	3yr Annual	5yr Annual	10yr Annual	Bull	Bear
Return (%)	16.2	15.3	na	80.6	-15.5
Differ from Category (+/-)	0.4 av	0.0 av	na	9.5 abv av	-4.9 blw av

Total Risk	Standard Deviation	Category Risk	Risk Index	Beta
high	17.2%	abv av	1.2	1.16

	1996	1995	1994	1993	1992	1991	1990	1989	1988	1987
Return (%)	15.7	35.9	-0.2	19.8	8.3	67.0	—	—	—	—
Differ from Category (+/-)	-3.4	1.6	-0.2	0.5	-3.4	14.9	—	—	—	—
Return, Tax-Adjusted (%)	14.9	34.5	-0.8	14.1	8.0	65.9	—	—	—	—

PER SHARE DATA

	1996	1995	1994	1993	1992	1991	1990	1989	1988	1987
Dividends, Net Income ($)	0.00	0.00	0.00	0.00	0.02	0.00	—	—	—	—
Distrib'ns, Cap Gain ($)	0.60	0.80	0.31	3.57	0.14	0.39	—	—	—	—
Net Asset Value ($)	25.19	22.32	16.99	17.33	17.58	16.38	—	—	—	—
Expense Ratio (%)	na	1.09	1.02	1.19	1.09	1.31	—	—	—	—
Yield (%)	0.00	0.00	0.00	0.00	0.11	0.00	—	—	—	—
Portfolio Turnover (%)	na	102	180	332	531	326	—	—	—	—
Total Assets (Millions $)	1,939	1,249	635	652	642	724	—	—	—	—

PORTFOLIO (as of 9/30/96)

Portfolio Manager: Lawrence Greenberg - 1993

Investm't Category: Aggressive Growth

✔ Domestic	Index
✔ Foreign	Sector
Asset Allocation	State Specific

Investment Style

Large-Cap Growth	Large-Cap Value
✔ Mid-Cap Growth	Mid-Cap Value
✔ Small-Cap Growth	Small-Cap Value

Portfolio

3.6% cash	0.0% corp bonds
96.4% stocks	0.0% gov't bonds
0.0% preferred	0.0% muni bonds
0.0% conv't/warrants	0.0% other

SHAREHOLDER INFORMATION

Minimum Investment
Initial: $2,500   Subsequent: $250

Minimum IRA Investment
Initial: $500   Subsequent: $250

Maximum Fees
Load: 3.00% front   12b-1: none
Other: 0.75% redemption fee (90 days); *f*

Distributions
Income: Jan, Dec   Capital Gains: Jan, Dec

Exchange Options
Number Per Year: 4   Fee: none
Telephone: yes (money market fund available)

Services
IRA, pension, auto exchange, auto invest, auto withdraw

Fidelity Emerging Markets

(FEMKX)

International Stock

82 Devonshire St.
Mail Zone F9A
Boston, MA 02109
800-544-6666, 801-534-1910
www.fidelity.com

PERFORMANCE

fund inception date: 11/1/90

	3yr Annual	5yr Annual	10yr Annual	Bull	Bear
Return (%)	-4.4	10.9	na	8.4	-17.0
Differ from Category (+/-)	-10.7 low	0.9 av	na	-15.9 blw av	-9.8 low

Total Risk	Standard Deviation	Category Risk	Risk Index	Beta
high	20.3%	high	2.0	1.11

	1996	1995	1994	1993	1992	1991	1990	1989	1988	1987
Return (%).	9.9	-3.2	-18.0	81.7	5.8	6.7	—	—	—	—
Differ from Category (+/-) .	-4.9	-12.3	-14.9	42.1	9.6	-6.5	—	—	—	—
Return, Tax-Adjusted (%). . .	9.2	-3.9	-18.1	81.5	5.0	5.9	—	—	—	—

PER SHARE DATA

	1996	1995	1994	1993	1992	1991	1990	1989	1988	1987
Dividends, Net Income ($).	0.25	0.27	0.04	0.05	0.08	0.08	—	—	—	—
Distrib'ns, Cap Gain ($) . .	0.00	0.00	0.00	0.00	0.15	0.14	—	—	—	—
Net Asset Value ($)	16.62	15.34	16.13	19.70	10.87	10.49	—	—	—	—
Expense Ratio (%).	1.29	1.28	1.52	1.91	2.60	2.60	—	—	—	—
Yield (%)	1.50	1.76	0.24	0.25	0.72	0.75	—	—	—	—
Portfolio Turnover (%). . . .	77	78	107	57	159	45	—	—	—	—
Total Assets (Millions $). .	1,282	1,085	1,508	1,908	14	6	—	—	—	—

PORTFOLIO (as of 9/30/96)

Portfolio Manager: Richard Hazlewood - 1993

Investm't Category: International Stock
Domestic	Index
✔ Foreign	Sector
Asset Allocation	State Specific

Investment Style
Large-Cap Growth	Large-Cap Value
Mid-Cap Growth	Mid-Cap Value
Small-Cap Growth	Small-Cap Value

Portfolio
1.7% cash	0.0% corp bonds
97.7% stocks	0.0% gov't bonds
0.0% preferred	0.0% muni bonds
0.6% conv't/warrants	0.0% other

SHAREHOLDER INFORMATION

Minimum Investment
Initial: $2,500   Subsequent: $250

Minimum IRA Investment
Initial: $500   Subsequent: $250

Maximum Fees
Load: 3.00% front   12b-1: none
Other: 1.50% redemption fee (90 days); *f*

Distributions
Income: Dec   Capital Gains: Dec

Exchange Options
Number Per Year: 4   Fee: none
Telephone: yes (money market fund available)

Services
IRA, pension, auto exchange, auto invest, auto withdraw

Fidelity Equity Income

(FEQIX)

Growth & Income

82 Devonshire St.
Mail Zone F9A
Boston, MA 02109
800-544-6666, 801-534-1910
www.fidelity.com

PERFORMANCE

fund inception date: 5/16/66

	3yr Annual	5yr Annual	10yr Annual	Bull	Bear
Return (%)	16.9	17.3	13.4	61.8	-5.0
Differ from Category (+/-)	1.6 av	3.4 high	0.7 av	2.0 av	1.4 abv av

Total Risk	Standard Deviation	Category Risk	Risk Index	Beta
av	8.8%	blw av	0.9	0.86

	1996	1995	1994	1993	1992	1991	1990	1989	1988	1987
Return (%)	21.0	31.8	0.2	21.3	14.6	29.4	-14.1	18.6	22.4	-1.7
Differ from Category (+/-)	1.3	1.7	1.5	7.5	3.9	0.3	-8.2	-4.9	5.6	-1.9
Return, Tax-Adjusted (%)	18.5	29.3	-2.8	19.6	12.9	27.1	-16.7	14.5	19.6	-8.0

PER SHARE DATA

	1996	1995	1994	1993	1992	1991	1990	1989	1988	1987
Dividends, Net Income ($)	1.02	0.96	0.98	1.14	1.08	1.20	1.55	1.75	1.51	1.51
Distrib'ns, Cap Gain ($)	1.84	1.36	2.22	0.12	0.00	0.00	0.30	1.15	0.00	3.92
Net Asset Value ($)	42.83	37.93	30.70	33.84	29.01	26.31	21.34	26.90	25.20	21.85
Expense Ratio (%)	0.67	0.69	0.66	0.67	0.68	0.70	0.71	0.63	0.66	0.65
Yield (%)	2.28	2.44	2.97	3.35	3.72	4.56	7.16	6.23	5.99	5.85
Portfolio Turnover (%)	39	50	70	84	111	107	92	68	120	110
Total Assets (Millions $)	14,354	10,492	7,412	6,641	4,977	4,413	3,925	5,037	4,064	3,476

PORTFOLIO (as of 9/30/96)

Portfolio Manager: Richard Warden - 1993

Investm't Category: Growth & Income
- ✔ Domestic
- Foreign
- Asset Allocation
- Index
- Sector
- State Specific

Investment Style
- Large-Cap Growth
- Mid-Cap Growth
- Small-Cap Growth
- ✔ Large-Cap Value
- Mid-Cap Value
- Small-Cap Value

Portfolio
- 5.0% cash
- 84.9% stocks
- 0.0% preferred
- 9.2% conv't/warrants
- 0.9% corp bonds
- 0.0% gov't bonds
- 0.0% muni bonds
- 0.0% other

SHAREHOLDER INFORMATION

Minimum Investment
Initial: $2,500   Subsequent: $250

Minimum IRA Investment
Initial: $500   Subsequent: $250

Maximum Fees
Load: none   12b-1: none
Other: f

Distributions
Income: quarterly   Capital Gains: Mar, Dec

Exchange Options
Number Per Year: 4   Fee: none
Telephone: yes (money market fund available)

Services
IRA, pension, auto exchange, auto invest, auto withdraw

Fidelity Equity Income II

(FEQTX)

Growth & Income

82 Devonshire St.
Mail Zone F9A
Boston, MA 02109
800-544-6666, 801-534-1910
www.fidelity.com

PERFORMANCE

fund inception date: 8/21/90

	3yr Annual	5yr Annual	10yr Annual	Bull	Bear
Return (%)	15.6	16.9	na	52.2	-3.0
Differ from Category (+/-)	0.3 blw av	3.0 high	na	-7.6 blw av	3.4 high

Total Risk	Standard Deviation	Category Risk	Risk Index	Beta
av	8.8%	blw av	0.9	0.82

	1996	1995	1994	1993	1992	1991	1990	1989	1988	1987
Return (%)	18.7	26.3	3.1	18.8	19.0	45.1	—	—	—	—
Differ from Category (+/-)	-1.0	-3.8	4.4	5.0	8.3	16.0	—	—	—	—
Return, Tax-Adjusted (%)	16.2	24.6	0.9	16.4	17.2	43.3	—	—	—	—

PER SHARE DATA

	1996	1995	1994	1993	1992	1991	1990	1989	1988	1987
Dividends, Net Income ($)	0.51	0.37	0.39	0.45	0.38	0.34	—	—	—	—
Distrib'ns, Cap Gain ($)	1.13	0.55	0.88	0.73	0.36	0.17	—	—	—	—
Net Asset Value ($)	23.75	21.43	17.72	18.41	16.51	14.52	—	—	—	—
Expense Ratio (%)	na	0.75	0.81	0.88	1.01	1.52	—	—	—	—
Yield (%)	2.04	1.68	2.09	2.35	2.25	2.31	—	—	—	—
Portfolio Turnover (%)	na	45	75	55	89	206	—	—	—	—
Total Assets (Millions $)	15,597	11,977	7,697	5,021	2,180	370	—	—	—	—

PORTFOLIO (as of 9/30/96)

Portfolio Manager: Bettina Doulton - 1996

Investm't Category: Growth & Income
- ✔ Domestic
- ✔ Foreign
-   Asset Allocation
-   Index
-   Sector
-   State Specific

Investment Style
- Large-Cap Growth
- Mid-Cap Growth
- Small-Cap Growth
- ✔ Large-Cap Value
- Mid-Cap Value
- Small-Cap Value

Portfolio
- 9.1% cash
- 84.7% stocks
- 0.0% preferred
- 4.7% conv't/warrants
- 1.5% corp bonds
- 0.0% gov't bonds
- 0.0% muni bonds
- 0.0% other

SHAREHOLDER INFORMATION

Minimum Investment
Initial: $2,500   Subsequent: $250

Minimum IRA Investment
Initial: $500   Subsequent: $250

Maximum Fees
Load: none   12b-1: none
Other: f

Distributions
Income: quarterly   Capital Gains: Jan, Dec

Exchange Options
Number Per Year: 4   Fee: none
Telephone: yes (money market fund available)

Services
IRA, pension, auto exchange, auto invest, auto withdraw

Fidelity Europe (FIEUX)
International Stock

82 Devonshire St.
Mail Zone F9A
Boston, MA 02109
800-544-6666, 801-534-1910
www.fidelity.com

PERFORMANCE

fund inception date: 10/1/86

	3yr Annual	5yr Annual	10yr Annual	Bull	Bear
Return (%)	16.6	14.4	12.1	59.4	-7.3
Differ from Category (+/-)	10.3 high	4.4 high	3.5 high	35.1 high	-0.1 av

Total Risk	Standard Deviation	Category Risk	Risk Index	Beta
av	9.3%	low	0.9	0.60

	1996	1995	1994	1993	1992	1991	1990	1989	1988	1987
Return (%)	25.6	18.8	6.2	27.1	-2.6	4.1	-4.6	32.3	5.8	14.9
Differ from Category (+/-)	10.8	9.7	9.3	-12.5	1.2	-9.1	5.5	9.7	-9.1	2.7
Return, Tax-Adjusted (%)	23.0	17.4	5.6	26.8	-3.4	2.8	-5.5	31.7	4.9	14.8

PER SHARE DATA

	1996	1995	1994	1993	1992	1991	1990	1989	1988	1987
Dividends, Net Income ($)	0.24	0.12	0.20	0.08	0.28	0.51	0.38	0.19	0.28	0.01
Distrib'ns, Cap Gain ($)	1.73	0.81	0.11	0.00	0.00	0.00	0.00	0.00	0.00	0.00
Net Asset Value ($)	26.61	22.82	20.00	19.12	15.10	15.79	15.67	16.81	12.85	12.41
Expense Ratio (%)	1.27	1.18	1.35	1.25	1.22	1.31	1.45	1.89	2.66	1.91
Yield (%)	0.84	0.50	0.99	0.41	1.85	3.22	2.42	1.13	2.17	0.08
Portfolio Turnover (%)	45	38	49	76	95	80	148	160	180	241
Total Assets (Millions $)	749	500	478	494	437	291	366	222	70	108

PORTFOLIO (as of 9/30/96)

Portfolio Manager: Sally Walden - 1992

Investm't Category: International Stock

Domestic	Index
✔ Foreign	Sector
Asset Allocation	State Specific

Investment Style

Large-Cap Growth	Large-Cap Value
Mid-Cap Growth	Mid-Cap Value
Small-Cap Growth	Small-Cap Value

Portfolio

5.9% cash	0.0% corp bonds
94.0% stocks	0.0% gov't bonds
0.0% preferred	0.0% muni bonds
0.1% conv't/warrants	0.0% other

SHAREHOLDER INFORMATION

Minimum Investment
Initial: $2,500   Subsequent: $250

Minimum IRA Investment
Initial: $500   Subsequent: $250

Maximum Fees
Load: 3.00% front   12b-1: none
Other: 1.00% redemption fee (90 days); f

Distributions
Income: Dec   Capital Gains: Dec

Exchange Options
Number Per Year: 4   Fee: none
Telephone: yes (money market fund available)

Services
IRA, pension, auto exchange, auto invest, auto withdraw

Fidelity Europe Capital Appreciation (FECAX)

International Stock

82 Devonshire St.
Mail Zone F9A
Boston, MA 02109
800-544-6666, 801-534-1910
www.fidelity.com

PERFORMANCE

fund inception date: 12/21/93

	3yr Annual	5yr Annual	10yr Annual	Bull	Bear
Return (%)	15.5	na	na	41.6	-4.6
Differ from Category (+/-)	9.2 high	na	na	17.3 high	2.6 abv av

Total Risk	Standard Deviation	Category Risk	Risk Index	Beta
high	12.5%	abv av	1.2	0.72

	1996	1995	1994	1993	1992	1991	1990	1989	1988	1987
Return (%).............	25.8	14.6	6.8	—	—	—	—	—	—	—
Differ from Category (+/-) .	11.0	5.5	9.9	—	—	—	—	—	—	—
Return, Tax-Adjusted (%)..	22.0	13.7	6.8	—	—	—	—	—	—	—

PER SHARE DATA

	1996	1995	1994	1993	1992	1991	1990	1989	1988	1987
Dividends, Net Income ($).	0.23	0.23	0.00	—	—	—	—	—	—	—
Distrib'ns, Cap Gain ($) ...	1.29	0.00	0.00	—	—	—	—	—	—	—
Net Asset Value ($)	13.59	12.06	10.72	—	—	—	—	—	—	—
Expense Ratio (%)........	2.00	1.36	1.54	—	—	—	—	—	—	—
Yield (%)	1.54	1.90	0.00	—	—	—	—	—	—	—
Portfolio Turnover (%)....	155	176	317	—	—	—	—	—	—	—
Total Assets (Millions $)...	185	180	291	—	—	—	—	—	—	—

PORTFOLIO (as of 9/30/96)

Portfolio Manager: Kevin McCarey - 1993

Investm't Category: International Stock

Domestic	Index
✔ Foreign	Sector
Asset Allocation	State Specific

Investment Style

Large-Cap Growth	Large-Cap Value
Mid-Cap Growth	Mid-Cap Value
Small-Cap Growth	Small-Cap Value

Portfolio

6.6% cash	0.0% corp bonds
93.4% stocks	0.0% gov't bonds
0.0% preferred	0.0% muni bonds
0.0% conv't/warrants	0.0% other

SHAREHOLDER INFORMATION

Minimum Investment
Initial: $2,500   Subsequent: $250

Minimum IRA Investment
Initial: $500   Subsequent: $250

Maximum Fees
Load: 3.00% front   12b-1: none
Other: 1.00% redemption fee (90 days); f

Distributions
Income: Dec   Capital Gains: Dec

Exchange Options
Number Per Year: 4   Fee: none
Telephone: yes (money market fund available)

Services
IRA, pension, auto exchange, auto invest, auto withdraw

264   *Guide to Low-Load Mutual Funds*

Fidelity Export (FEXPX)

Growth

82 Devonshire St.
Mail Zone F9A
Boston, MA 02109
800-544-6666, 801-534-1910
www.fidelity.com

PERFORMANCE

fund inception date: 10/4/94

	3yr Annual	5yr Annual	10yr Annual	Bull	Bear
Return (%)	na	na	na	na	na
Differ from Category (+/-)	na	na	na	na	na

Total Risk	Standard Deviation	Category Risk	Risk Index	Beta
na	na	na	na	na

	1996	1995	1994	1993	1992	1991	1990	1989	1988	1987
Return (%)	38.6	32.2	—	—	—	—	—	—	—	—
Differ from Category (+/-)	18.5	1.9	—	—	—	—	—	—	—	—
Return, Tax-Adjusted (%)	36.7	29.9	—	—	—	—	—	—	—	—

PER SHARE DATA

	1996	1995	1994	1993	1992	1991	1990	1989	1988	1987
Dividends, Net Income ($)	0.00	0.00	—	—	—	—	—	—	—	—
Distrib'ns, Cap Gain ($)	0.86	0.84	—	—	—	—	—	—	—	—
Net Asset Value ($)	16.75	12.72	—	—	—	—	—	—	—	—
Expense Ratio (%)	1.03	1.22	—	—	—	—	—	—	—	—
Yield (%)	0.00	0.00	—	—	—	—	—	—	—	—
Portfolio Turnover (%)	313	245	—	—	—	—	—	—	—	—
Total Assets (Millions $)	392	382	—	—	—	—	—	—	—	—

PORTFOLIO (as of 9/30/96)

Portfolio Manager: Arieh Coll - 1994

Investm't Category: Growth
✔ Domestic   Index
✔ Foreign   Sector
   Asset Allocation   State Specific

Investment Style
Large-Cap Growth   Large-Cap Value
Mid-Cap Growth   Mid-Cap Value
Small-Cap Growth   Small-Cap Value

Portfolio
1.2% cash	0.0% corp bonds
98.7% stocks	0.0% gov't bonds
0.0% preferred	0.0% muni bonds
0.1% conv't/warrants	0.0% other

SHAREHOLDER INFORMATION

Minimum Investment
Initial: $2,500   Subsequent: $250

Minimum IRA Investment
Initial: $500   Subsequent: $250

Maximum Fees
Load: 3.00% front   12b-1: none
Other: 0.75% redemption fee (90 days); f

Distributions
Income: Oct, Dec   Capital Gains: Oct, Dec

Exchange Options
Number Per Year: 4   Fee: none
Telephone: yes (money market fund available)

Services
IRA, pension, auto exchange, auto invest, auto withdraw

Fidelity Fifty (FFTYX)

Aggressive Growth

82 Devonshire St.
Mail Zone F9A
Boston, MA 02109
800-544-6666, 801-534-1910
www.fidelity.com

PERFORMANCE

fund inception date: 9/20/93

	3yr Annual	5yr Annual	10yr Annual	Bull	Bear
Return (%)	16.7	na	na	65.7	-7.4
Differ from Category (+/-)	0.9 abv av	na	na	-5.4 av	3.2 abv av

Total Risk	Standard Deviation	Category Risk	Risk Index	Beta
abv av	11.0%	low	0.8	1.02

	1996	1995	1994	1993	1992	1991	1990	1989	1988	1987
Return (%)	15.9	32.1	3.9	—	—	—	—	—	—	—
Differ from Category (+/-)	-3.2	-2.2	3.9	—	—	—	—	—	—	—
Return, Tax-Adjusted (%)	13.8	28.4	3.5	—	—	—	—	—	—	—

PER SHARE DATA

	1996	1995	1994	1993	1992	1991	1990	1989	1988	1987
Dividends, Net Income ($)	0.09	0.13	0.02	—	—	—	—	—	—	—
Distrib'ns, Cap Gain ($)	0.83	1.24	0.10	—	—	—	—	—	—	—
Net Asset Value ($)	14.04	12.97	10.88	—	—	—	—	—	—	—
Expense Ratio (%)	0.99	1.19	1.58	—	—	—	—	—	—	—
Yield (%)	0.60	0.91	0.18	—	—	—	—	—	—	—
Portfolio Turnover (%)	152	180	320	—	—	—	—	—	—	—
Total Assets (Millions $)	155	155	60	—	—	—	—	—	—	—

PORTFOLIO (as of 9/30/96)

Portfolio Manager: Scott Stewart - 1993

Investm't Category: Aggressive Growth
- ✔ Domestic
- ✔ Foreign
- Asset Allocation
- Index
- Sector
- State Specific

Investment Style
- ✔ Large-Cap Growth
- ✔ Mid-Cap Growth
- Small-Cap Growth
- Large-Cap Value
- Mid-Cap Value
- Small-Cap Value

Portfolio
3.9% cash	0.0% corp bonds
96.1% stocks	0.0% gov't bonds
0.0% preferred	0.0% muni bonds
0.0% conv't/warrants	0.0% other

SHAREHOLDER INFORMATION

Minimum Investment
Initial: $2,500   Subsequent: $250

Minimum IRA Investment
Initial: $500   Subsequent: $250

Maximum Fees
Load: 3.00% front   12b-1: none
Other: f

Distributions
Income: Aug, Dec   Capital Gains: Aug, Dec

Exchange Options
Number Per Year: 4   Fee: none
Telephone: yes (money market fund available)

Services
IRA, pension, auto exchange, auto invest, auto withdraw

Fidelity Fund (FFIDX)

Growth & Income

82 Devonshire St.
Mail Zone F9A
Boston, MA 02109
800-544-6666, 801-534-1910
www.fidelity.com

PERFORMANCE
fund inception date: 12/31/30

	3yr Annual	5yr Annual	10yr Annual	Bull	Bear
Return (%)	17.7	15.9	14.4	67.7	-6.7
Differ from Category (+/-)	2.4 abv av	2.0 high	1.7 abv av	7.9 abv av	-0.3 av

Total Risk	Standard Deviation	Category Risk	Risk Index	Beta
av	9.2%	av	1.0	0.89

	1996	1995	1994	1993	1992	1991	1990	1989	1988	1987
Return (%)	19.8	32.8	2.5	18.3	8.4	24.1	-5.1	28.8	17.8	3.2
Differ from Category (+/-)	0.1	2.7	3.8	4.5	-2.3	-5.0	0.8	5.3	1.0	3.0
Return, Tax-Adjusted (%)	16.8	29.7	0.4	13.6	6.5	20.9	-6.8	24.9	16.1	-2.8

PER SHARE DATA

	1996	1995	1994	1993	1992	1991	1990	1989	1988	1987
Dividends, Net Income ($)	0.37	0.42	0.33	0.44	0.48	0.50	0.74	0.68	0.56	0.48
Distrib'ns, Cap Gain ($)	1.82	1.40	0.94	2.54	0.57	1.14	0.00	1.17	0.00	2.72
Net Asset Value ($)	24.70	22.61	18.48	19.27	18.94	18.46	16.29	17.93	15.42	13.58
Expense Ratio (%)	0.60	0.64	0.65	0.66	0.67	0.68	0.66	0.64	0.67	0.67
Yield (%)	1.39	1.74	1.69	2.01	2.46	2.55	4.54	3.56	3.63	2.94
Portfolio Turnover (%)	150	157	207	261	151	267	259	191	175	211
Total Assets (Millions $)	4,553	3,213	1,886	1,546	1,351	1,309	1,065	1,085	895	873

PORTFOLIO (as of 9/30/96)

Portfolio Manager: Beth Terrana - 1993

Investm't Category: Growth & Income
✔ Domestic   Index
✔ Foreign   Sector
  Asset Allocation State Specific

Investment Style
  Large-Cap Growth   ✔ Large-Cap Value
  Mid-Cap Growth   ✔ Mid-Cap Value
  Small-Cap Growth   Small-Cap Value

Portfolio
  7.3% cash   0.3% corp bonds
  90.1% stocks   0.0% gov't bonds
  0.0% preferred   0.0% muni bonds
  2.3% conv't/warrants 0.0% other

SHAREHOLDER INFORMATION

Minimum Investment
Initial: $2,500   Subsequent: $250

Minimum IRA Investment
Initial: $500   Subsequent: $250

Maximum Fees
Load: none   12b-1: none
Other: f

Distributions
Income: quarterly   Capital Gains: Aug, Dec

Exchange Options
Number Per Year: 4   Fee: none
Telephone: yes (money market fund available)

Services
IRA, pension, auto exchange, auto invest, auto withdraw

Fidelity Ginnie Mae

(FGMNX)

Mortgage-Backed Bond

82 Devonshire St.
Mail Zone F9A
Boston, MA 02109
800-544-6666, 801-534-1910
www.fidelity.com

PERFORMANCE

fund inception date: 11/8/85

	3yr Annual	5yr Annual	10yr Annual	Bull	Bear
Return (%)	6.2	6.2	7.7	24.0	-4.5
Differ from Category (+/-)	0.6 abv av	0.2 abv av	0.0 abv av	2.9 high	-0.9 blw av

Total Risk	Standard Deviation	Category Risk	Risk Index	Avg Mat
low	3.9%	abv av	1.0	7.3 yrs

	1996	1995	1994	1993	1992	1991	1990	1989	1988	1987
Return (%)	4.8	16.6	-2.0	6.1	6.6	13.5	10.5	13.8	7.1	1.1
Differ from Category (+/-)	0.4	1.9	-0.3	-0.8	0.4	-0.9	0.7	1.2	-0.3	-0.9
Return, Tax-Adjusted (%)	2.2	13.7	-4.4	3.2	3.9	10.3	7.2	10.4	3.7	-2.1

PER SHARE DATA

	1996	1995	1994	1993	1992	1991	1990	1989	1988	1987
Dividends, Net Income ($)	0.69	0.71	0.63	0.62	0.74	0.83	0.85	0.85	0.84	0.87
Distrib'ns, Cap Gain ($)	0.00	0.00	0.02	0.25	0.00	0.00	0.00	0.00	0.00	0.00
Net Asset Value ($)	10.70	10.89	9.99	10.86	11.07	11.10	10.56	10.38	9.91	10.05
Expense Ratio (%)	0.75	0.75	0.82	0.80	0.80	0.83	0.83	0.85	0.87	0.79
Yield (%)	6.44	6.51	6.29	5.58	6.68	7.47	8.04	8.18	8.47	8.65
Portfolio Turnover (%)	107	210	303	259	114	125	96	291	361	177
Total Assets (Millions $)	802	805	704	887	946	891	719	663	678	741

PORTFOLIO (as of 9/30/96)

Portfolio Manager: Kevin E. Grant - 1995

Investm't Category: Mortgage-Backed Bond

✔ Domestic	Index
✔ Foreign	Sector
Asset Allocation	State Specific

Investment Style

Large-Cap Growth	Large-Cap Value
Mid-Cap Growth	Mid-Cap Value
Small-Cap Growth	Small-Cap Value

Portfolio

1.2% cash	0.0% corp bonds
0.0% stocks	98.8% gov't bonds
0.0% preferred	0.0% muni bonds
0.0% conv't/warrants	0.0% other

SHAREHOLDER INFORMATION

Minimum Investment
Initial: $2,500   Subsequent: $250

Minimum IRA Investment
Initial: $500   Subsequent: $250

Maximum Fees
Load: none   12b-1: none
Other: f

Distributions
Income: monthly   Capital Gains: Sep, Dec

Exchange Options
Number Per Year: 4   Fee: none
Telephone: yes (money market fund available)

Services
IRA, pension, auto exchange, auto invest, auto withdraw

Fidelity Global Balanced

(FGBLX)

International Stock

82 Devonshire St.
Mail Zone F9A
Boston, MA 02109
800-544-6666, 801-534-1910
www.fidelity.com

PERFORMANCE

fund inception date: 2/1/93

	3yr Annual	5yr Annual	10yr Annual	Bull	Bear
Return (%)	2.0	na	na	18.0	-14.1
Differ from Category (+/-)	-4.3 blw av	na	na	-6.3 blw av	-6.9 low

Total Risk	Standard Deviation	Category Risk	Risk Index	Beta
av	8.5%	low	0.8	0.66

	1996	1995	1994	1993	1992	1991	1990	1989	1988	1987
Return (%)	7.7	11.5	-11.5	—	—	—	—	—	—	—
Differ from Category (+/-)	-7.1	2.4	-8.4	—	—	—	—	—	—	—
Return, Tax-Adjusted (%)	6.3	11.3	-11.9	—	—	—	—	—	—	—

PER SHARE DATA

	1996	1995	1994	1993	1992	1991	1990	1989	1988	1987
Dividends, Net Income ($)	0.45	0.05	0.10	—	—	—	—	—	—	—
Distrib'ns, Cap Gain ($)	0.00	0.00	0.00	—	—	—	—	—	—	—
Net Asset Value ($)	13.36	12.84	11.56	—	—	—	—	—	—	—
Expense Ratio (%)	1.36	1.33	1.67	—	—	—	—	—	—	—
Yield (%)	3.36	0.38	0.86	—	—	—	—	—	—	—
Portfolio Turnover (%)	189	242	226	—	—	—	—	—	—	—
Total Assets (Millions $)	81	121	236	—	—	—	—	—	—	—

PORTFOLIO (as of 9/30/96)

Portfolio Manager: Rick Mace - 1996

Investm't Category: International Stock
- ✔ Domestic
- ✔ Foreign
- ✔ Asset Allocation
- Index
- Sector
- State Specific

Investment Style
Large-Cap Growth   Large-Cap Value
Mid-Cap Growth   Mid-Cap Value
Small-Cap Growth   Small-Cap Value

Portfolio
4.7% cash	30.9% corp bonds
62.7% stocks	0.0% gov't bonds
0.0% preferred	0.0% muni bonds
1.7% conv't/warrants	0.0% other

SHAREHOLDER INFORMATION

Minimum Investment
Initial: $2,500   Subsequent: $250

Minimum IRA Investment
Initial: $500   Subsequent: $250

Maximum Fees
Load: none   12b-1: none
Other: f

Distributions
Income: Dec   Capital Gains: Sep, Dec

Exchange Options
Number Per Year: 4   Fee: none
Telephone: yes (money market fund available)

Services
IRA, pension, auto exchange, auto invest, auto withdraw

Fidelity Global Bond

(FGBDX)

International Bond

82 Devonshire St.
Mail Zone F9A
Boston, MA 02109
800-544-6666, 801-534-1910
www.fidelity.com

PERFORMANCE

fund inception date: 12/30/86

	3yr Annual	5yr Annual	10yr Annual	Bull	Bear
Return (%)	-2.7	3.2	7.0	10.3	-17.3
Differ from Category (+/-)	-8.7 low	-3.4 low	-0.3 av	-20.9 low	-7.8 blw av

Total Risk	Standard Deviation	Category Risk	Risk Index	Avg Mat
av	7.4%	abv av	1.1	7.0 yrs

	1996	1995	1994	1993	1992	1991	1990	1989	1988	1987
Return (%).............	3.4	6.6	-16.4	21.9	4.4	12.7	12.2	7.9	3.6	19.1
Differ from Category (+/-) .	-7.9	-9.4	-8.8	6.6	-0.8	-2.3	1.7	4.7	-0.7	8.9
Return, Tax-Adjusted (%)...	1.2	4.3	-18.7	18.3	0.8	9.7	8.4	6.0	0.4	16.3

PER SHARE DATA

	1996	1995	1994	1993	1992	1991	1990	1989	1988	1987
Dividends, Net Income ($).	0.54	0.57	0.69	0.85	1.08	0.72	1.05	0.49	0.90	0.69
Distrib'ns, Cap Gain ($) ...	0.00	0.00	0.02	0.25	0.00	0.18	0.00	0.00	0.00	0.00
Net Asset Value ($)	9.72	9.94	9.88	12.61	11.34	11.90	11.38	11.08	10.72	11.21
Expense Ratio (%).........	na	1.16	1.14	1.17	1.23	1.35	1.40	1.50	1.14	0.95
Yield (%)	5.55	5.73	6.96	6.60	9.52	5.96	9.22	4.42	8.39	6.15
Portfolio Turnover (%).....	na	322	367	198	81	228	154	150	227	297
Total Assets (Millions $)...	128	196	382	681	273	184	134	74	83	105

PORTFOLIO (as of 6/30/95)

Portfolio Manager: I. Spreadbury, C. Thompson - 1996

Investm't Category: International Bond
- ✔ Domestic
- ✔ Foreign
- Asset Allocation
- Index
- Sector
- State Specific

Investment Style
- Large-Cap Growth
- Mid-Cap Growth
- Small-Cap Growth
- Large-Cap Value
- Mid-Cap Value
- Small-Cap Value

Portfolio
0.0% cash	66.6% corp bonds
0.0% stocks	0.0% gov't bonds
0.0% preferred	0.0% muni bonds
0.0% conv't/warrants	33.4% other

SHAREHOLDER INFORMATION

Minimum Investment
Initial: $2,500   Subsequent: $250

Minimum IRA Investment
Initial: $500   Subsequent: $250

Maximum Fees
Load: none   12b-1: none
Other: f

Distributions
Income: monthly   Capital Gains: Feb, Dec

Exchange Options
Number Per Year: 4   Fee: none
Telephone: yes (money market fund available)

Services
IRA, pension, auto exchange, auto invest, auto withdraw

Fidelity Gov't Securities
(FGOVX)
Government Bond

82 Devonshire St.
Mail Zone F9A
Boston, MA 02109
800-544-6666, 801-534-1910
www.fidelity.com

PERFORMANCE

fund inception date: 4/4/79

	3yr Annual	5yr Annual	10yr Annual	Bull	Bear
Return (%)	4.5	6.7	7.8	20.9	-7.1
Differ from Category (+/-)	-0.4 blw av	0.1 abv av	-0.2 av	-1.1 abv av	-0.7 blw av

Total Risk	Standard Deviation	Category Risk	Risk Index	Avg Mat
blw av	5.1%	abv av	1.3	8.2 yrs

	1996	1995	1994	1993	1992	1991	1990	1989	1988	1987
Return (%).	2.0	18.0	-5.3	12.3	7.9	15.9	9.5	12.6	6.3	1.0
Differ from Category (+/-). .	0.5	-1.6	-0.9	0.7	1.2	0.2	3.2	-2.7	-2.0	5.4
Return, Tax-Adjusted (%). .	-0.7	15.3	-7.7	8.8	4.4	12.6	6.0	9.2	2.8	-2.3

PER SHARE DATA

	1996	1995	1994	1993	1992	1991	1990	1989	1988	1987
Dividends, Net Income ($).	0.67	0.61	0.61	0.67	0.73	0.80	0.83	0.78	0.83	0.85
Distrib'ns, Cap Gain ($) . .	0.00	0.00	0.02	0.31	0.25	0.00	0.00	0.00	0.00	0.00
Net Asset Value ($)	9.69	10.17	9.17	10.34	10.10	10.30	9.64	9.61	9.27	9.52
Expense Ratio (%).	0.72	0.71	0.69	0.69	0.70	0.70	0.66	0.73	0.79	0.87
Yield (%)	6.91	5.99	6.63	6.29	7.05	7.76	8.60	8.11	8.95	8.92
Portfolio Turnover (%). . .	124	391	402	323	219	257	302	312	283	253
Total Assets (Millions $). .	972	994	611	753	568	523	464	557	567	678

PORTFOLIO (as of 9/30/96)

Portfolio Manager: Robert Ives - 1995

Investm't Category: Government Bond
✔ Domestic	Index
Foreign	Sector
Asset Allocation	State Specific

Investment Style
Large-Cap Growth	Large-Cap Value
Mid-Cap Growth	Mid-Cap Value
Small-Cap Growth	Small-Cap Value

Portfolio
0.0% cash	0.0% corp bonds
0.0% stocks	100.6% gov't bonds
0.0% preferred	0.0% muni bonds
0.0% conv't/warrants	0.0% other

SHAREHOLDER INFORMATION

Minimum Investment
Initial: $2,500   Subsequent: $250

Minimum IRA Investment
Initial: $500   Subsequent: $250

Maximum Fees
Load: none   12b-1: none
Other: *f*

Distributions
Income: monthly   Capital Gains: Dec

Exchange Options
Number Per Year: 4   Fee: none
Telephone: yes (money market fund available)

Services
IRA, pension, auto exchange, auto invest, auto withdraw

Fidelity Growth & Income Port (FGRIX)

Growth & Income

82 Devonshire St.
Mail Zone F9A
Boston, MA 02109
800-544-6666, 801-534-1910
www.fidelity.com

PERFORMANCE

fund inception date: 12/30/85

	3yr Annual	5yr Annual	10yr Annual	Bull	Bear
Return (%)	18.4	17.2	17.3	69.8	-5.8
Differ from Category (+/-)	3.1 abv av	3.3 high	4.6 high	10.0 abv av	0.6 abv av

Total Risk	Standard Deviation	Category Risk	Risk Index	Beta
av	8.6%	blw av	0.9	0.86

	1996	1995	1994	1993	1992	1991	1990	1989	1988	1987
Return (%)	20.0	35.3	2.2	19.5	11.5	41.8	-6.8	29.6	22.9	5.7
Differ from Category (+/-)	0.3	5.2	3.5	5.7	0.8	12.7	-0.9	6.1	6.1	5.5
Return, Tax-Adjusted (%)	18.1	33.2	-0.1	17.3	7.1	39.6	-8.5	25.2	20.9	1.5

PER SHARE DATA

	1996	1995	1994	1993	1992	1991	1990	1989	1988	1987
Dividends, Net Income ($)	0.46	0.48	0.40	0.52	0.56	0.38	0.57	0.75	0.62	0.45
Distrib'ns, Cap Gain ($)	1.12	0.90	1.24	0.77	2.40	0.64	0.22	1.27	0.00	1.35
Net Asset Value ($)	30.73	27.05	21.09	22.22	19.71	20.49	15.22	17.17	14.85	12.60
Expense Ratio (%)	0.74	0.77	0.82	0.83	0.86	0.87	0.87	0.89	1.02	1.09
Yield (%)	1.44	1.71	1.79	2.26	2.53	1.79	3.69	4.06	4.17	3.22
Portfolio Turnover (%)	41	67	92	87	221	215	108	97	135	165
Total Assets (Millions $)	23,991	14,818	9,344	7,684	4,842	3,355	1,729	1,532	1,145	1,125

PORTFOLIO (as of 9/30/96)

Portfolio Manager: Steven Kaye - 1993

Investm't Category: Growth & Income
- ✔ Domestic
- ✔ Foreign
- Asset Allocation
- Index
- Sector
- State Specific

Investment Style
- Large-Cap Growth
- Mid-Cap Growth
- Small-Cap Growth
- ✔ Large-Cap Value
- Mid-Cap Value
- Small-Cap Value

Portfolio
- 6.9% cash
- 91.2% stocks
- 0.0% preferred
- 0.8% conv't/warrants
- 1.1% corp bonds
- 0.0% gov't bonds
- 0.0% muni bonds
- 0.0% other

SHAREHOLDER INFORMATION

Minimum Investment
Initial: $2,500   Subsequent: $250

Minimum IRA Investment
Initial: $500   Subsequent: $250

Maximum Fees
Load: none   12b-1: none
Other: *f*

Distributions
Income: quarterly   Capital Gains: Sep, Dec

Exchange Options
Number Per Year: 4   Fee: none
Telephone: yes (money market fund available)

Services
IRA, pension, auto exchange, auto invest, auto withdraw

Fidelity Growth Co
(FDGRX)
Aggressive Growth

82 Devonshire St.
Mail Zone F9A
Boston, MA 02109
800-544-6666, 801-534-1910
www.fidelity.com

PERFORMANCE

fund inception date: 1/17/83

	3yr Annual	5yr Annual	10yr Annual	Bull	Bear
Return (%)	16.8	14.8	17.3	71.5	-10.0
Differ from Category (+/-)	1.0 abv av	-0.5 av	2.3 abv av	0.4 av	0.6 av

Total Risk	Standard Deviation	Category Risk	Risk Index	Beta
abv av	11.8%	blw av	0.8	1.03

	1996	1995	1994	1993	1992	1991	1990	1989	1988	1987
Return (%)	16.8	39.6	-2.3	16.1	7.9	48.3	3.5	41.6	16.0	-1.7
Differ from Category (+/-)	-2.3	5.3	-2.3	-3.2	-3.8	-3.8	8.9	13.2	-0.4	0.7
Return, Tax-Adjusted (%)	15.2	37.7	-3.5	13.0	6.2	45.6	3.5	37.4	15.6	-3.4

PER SHARE DATA

	1996	1995	1994	1993	1992	1991	1990	1989	1988	1987
Dividends, Net Income ($)	0.28	0.16	0.22	0.07	0.09	0.08	0.00	0.14	0.11	0.01
Distrib'ns, Cap Gain ($)	1.60	1.57	0.92	2.92	1.48	1.73	0.00	2.00	0.00	0.83
Net Asset Value ($)	40.46	36.29	27.26	29.06	27.64	27.09	19.60	18.92	15.00	13.02
Expense Ratio (%)	na	0.95	1.05	1.07	1.09	1.07	1.14	0.95	1.03	1.02
Yield (%)	0.66	0.42	0.78	0.21	0.30	0.27	0.00	0.66	0.73	0.07
Portfolio Turnover (%)	na	97	135	159	250	174	189	269	257	212
Total Assets (Millions $)	9,602	6,278	2,993	2,542	1,815	1,376	601	298	138	145

PORTFOLIO (as of 9/30/96)

Portfolio Manager: Larry Greenberg - 1996

Investm't Category: Aggressive Growth
- ✔ Domestic
- ✔ Foreign
- Asset Allocation
- Index
- Sector
- State Specific

Investment Style
- Large-Cap Growth
- ✔ Mid-Cap Growth
- Small-Cap Growth
- Large-Cap Value
- Mid-Cap Value
- Small-Cap Value

Portfolio
10.3% cash	0.0% corp bonds
89.7% stocks	0.0% gov't bonds
0.0% preferred	0.0% muni bonds
0.0% conv't/warrants	0.0% other

SHAREHOLDER INFORMATION

Minimum Investment
Initial: $2,500   Subsequent: $250

Minimum IRA Investment
Initial: $500   Subsequent: $250

Maximum Fees
Load: none   12b-1: none
Other: *f*

Distributions
Income: Jan, Dec   Capital Gains: Jan, Dec

Exchange Options
Number Per Year: 4   Fee: none
Telephone: yes (money market fund available)

Services
IRA, pension, auto exchange, auto invest, auto withdraw

Fidelity Hong Kong & China (FHKCX)

International Stock

82 Devonshire St.
Mail Zone F9A
Boston, MA 02109
800-544-6666, 801-534-1910
www.fidelity.com

PERFORMANCE

fund inception date: 11/1/95

	3yr Annual	5yr Annual	10yr Annual	Bull	Bear
Return (%)	na	na	na	na	na
Differ from Category (+/-)	na	na	na	na	na

Total Risk	Standard Deviation	Category Risk	Risk Index	Beta
na	na	na	na	na

	1996	1995	1994	1993	1992	1991	1990	1989	1988	1987
Return (%)	40.9	—	—	—	—	—	—	—	—	—
Differ from Category (+/-)	26.1	—	—	—	—	—	—	—	—	—
Return, Tax-Adjusted (%)	40.1	—	—	—	—	—	—	—	—	—

PER SHARE DATA

	1996	1995	1994	1993	1992	1991	1990	1989	1988	1987
Dividends, Net Income ($)	0.14	—	—	—	—	—	—	—	—	—
Distrib'ns, Cap Gain ($)	0.08	—	—	—	—	—	—	—	—	—
Net Asset Value ($)	14.21	—	—	—	—	—	—	—	—	—
Expense Ratio (%)	1.62	—	—	—	—	—	—	—	—	—
Yield (%)	0.97	—	—	—	—	—	—	—	—	—
Portfolio Turnover (%)	118	—	—	—	—	—	—	—	—	—
Total Assets (Millions $)	167	—	—	—	—	—	—	—	—	—

PORTFOLIO (as of 9/30/96)

Portfolio Manager: Joseph Tse - 1995

Investm't Category: International Stock
- Domestic
- ✔ Foreign
- Asset Allocation
- Index
- Sector
- State Specific

Investment Style
- Large-Cap Growth
- Mid-Cap Growth
- Small-Cap Growth
- Large-Cap Value
- Mid-Cap Value
- Small-Cap Value

Portfolio
- 3.5% cash
- 96.5% stocks
- 0.0% preferred
- 0.0% conv't/warrants
- 0.0% corp bonds
- 0.0% gov't bonds
- 0.0% muni bonds
- 0.0% other

SHAREHOLDER INFORMATION

Minimum Investment
Initial: $2,500   Subsequent: $250

Minimum IRA Investment
Initial: $500   Subsequent: $250

Maximum Fees
Load: 3.00% front   12b-1: none
Other: 1.5% redemption fee (90 days); *f*

Distributions
Income: Dec   Capital Gains: Dec

Exchange Options
Number Per Year: 4   Fee: none
Telephone: yes (money market fund available)

Services
IRA, pension, auto exchange, auto invest, auto withdraw

Fidelity Insured Muni Income (FMUIX)

Tax-Exempt Bond

82 Devonshire St.
Mail Zone F9A
Boston, MA 02109
800-544-6666, 801-534-1910
www.fidelity.com

PERFORMANCE

fund inception date: 11/13/85

	3yr Annual	5yr Annual	10yr Annual	Bull	Bear
Return (%)	4.3	6.8	7.0	21.7	-7.9
Differ from Category (+/-)	0.1 av	0.4 av	0.3 abv av	3.3 high	-2.5 low

Total Risk	Standard Deviation	Category Risk	Risk Index	Avg Mat
blw av	6.6%	high	1.2	13.6 yrs

	1996	1995	1994	1993	1992	1991	1990	1989	1988	1987
Return (%)	3.6	18.6	-7.8	13.8	7.9	11.5	7.0	9.4	11.1	-2.1
Differ from Category (+/-)	-0.1	3.4	-2.5	2.0	-0.4	0.1	0.6	0.4	1.1	-0.7
Return, Tax-Adjusted (%)	3.6	18.6	-8.1	13.1	7.6	11.5	7.0	9.4	11.1	-2.2

PER SHARE DATA

	1996	1995	1994	1993	1992	1991	1990	1989	1988	1987
Dividends, Net Income ($)	0.57	0.59	0.62	0.65	0.68	0.70	0.71	0.71	0.70	0.71
Distrib'ns, Cap Gain ($)	0.00	0.00	0.12	0.28	0.11	0.00	0.00	0.00	0.00	0.01
Net Asset Value ($)	11.89	12.04	10.69	12.37	11.72	11.63	11.09	11.05	10.78	10.36
Expense Ratio (%)	na	0.61	0.58	0.61	0.63	0.65	0.67	0.70	0.70	0.62
Yield (%)	4.79	4.90	5.73	5.13	5.74	6.01	6.40	6.42	6.49	6.84
Portfolio Turnover (%)	na	61	56	78	69	62	66	51	35	57
Total Assets (Millions $)	336	356	318	446	368	301	197	174	152	147

PORTFOLIO (as of 9/30/96)

Portfolio Manager: George A. Fischer - 1995

Investm't Category: Tax-Exempt Bond
- ✔ Domestic
- Foreign
- Asset Allocation
- Index
- Sector
- State Specific

Investment Style
- Large-Cap Growth
- Mid-Cap Growth
- Small-Cap Growth
- Large-Cap Value
- Mid-Cap Value
- Small-Cap Value

Portfolio
1.6%	cash	0.0%	corp bonds
0.0%	stocks	0.0%	gov't bonds
0.0%	preferred	98.4%	muni bonds
0.0%	conv't/warrants	0.0%	other

SHAREHOLDER INFORMATION

Minimum Investment
Initial: $2,500   Subsequent: $250

Minimum IRA Investment
Initial: na   Subsequent: na

Maximum Fees
Load: none   12b-1: none
Other: f

Distributions
Income: monthly   Capital Gains: Feb, Dec

Exchange Options
Number Per Year: 4   Fee: none
Telephone: yes (money market fund available)

Services
auto exchange, auto invest, auto withdraw

Fidelity Interm Bond

(FTHRX)

General Bond

82 Devonshire St.
Mail Zone F9A
Boston, MA 02109
800-544-6666, 801-534-1910
www.fidelity.com

PERFORMANCE

fund inception date: 5/23/75

	3yr Annual	5yr Annual	10yr Annual	Bull	Bear
Return (%)	4.6	6.3	7.4	18.2	-4.3
Differ from Category (+/-)	-0.5 blw av	0.2 av	0.1 av	-2.1 blw av	-0.1 av

Total Risk	Standard Deviation	Category Risk	Risk Index	Avg Mat
low	3.2%	av	0.9	4.7 yrs

	1996	1995	1994	1993	1992	1991	1990	1989	1988	1987
Return (%)	3.6	12.8	-2.1	11.9	6.0	14.4	7.5	11.8	7.2	2.0
Differ from Category (+/-)	-0.3	-2.1	0.2	2.8	-0.5	-0.3	0.2	0.1	-0.4	-0.3
Return, Tax-Adjusted (%)	1.0	10.2	-4.7	8.8	3.0	11.3	4.3	8.2	3.7	-3.8

PER SHARE DATA

	1996	1995	1994	1993	1992	1991	1990	1989	1988	1987
Dividends, Net Income ($)	0.65	0.64	0.64	0.75	0.76	0.76	0.81	0.88	0.87	1.61
Distrib'ns, Cap Gain ($)	0.03	0.00	0.09	0.09	0.06	0.00	0.00	0.00	0.00	0.10
Net Asset Value ($)	10.08	10.41	9.83	10.78	10.41	10.62	10.00	10.10	9.87	10.04
Expense Ratio (%)	0.73	0.68	0.64	0.61	0.63	0.66	0.72	0.62	0.87	0.86
Yield (%)	6.42	6.14	6.45	6.89	7.25	7.15	8.10	8.71	8.81	15.87
Portfolio Turnover (%)	169	75	81	51	80	73	82	101	59	67
Total Assets (Millions $)	3,065	2,821	2,127	1,840	1,454	1,172	806	626	499	367

PORTFOLIO (as of 9/30/96)

Portfolio Manager: Christine J. Thompson - 1995

Investm't Category: General Bond
- ✔ Domestic
- ✔ Foreign
-   Asset Allocation
-   Index
-   Sector
-   State Specific

Investment Style
- Large-Cap Growth
- Mid-Cap Growth
- Small-Cap Growth
- Large-Cap Value
- Mid-Cap Value
- Small-Cap Value

Portfolio
8.5% cash	35.7% corp bonds
0.0% stocks	44.5% gov't bonds
0.0% preferred	0.0% muni bonds
0.0% conv't/warrants	11.3% other

SHAREHOLDER INFORMATION

Minimum Investment
Initial: $2,500   Subsequent: $250

Minimum IRA Investment
Initial: $500   Subsequent: $250

Maximum Fees
Load: none   12b-1: none
Other: *f*

Distributions
Income: monthly   Capital Gains: Jun, Dec

Exchange Options
Number Per Year: 4   Fee: none
Telephone: yes (money market fund available)

Services
IRA, pension, auto exchange, auto invest, auto withdraw

Fidelity Int'l Growth & Income (FIGRX)

International Stock

82 Devonshire St.
Mail Zone F9A
Boston, MA 02109
800-544-6666, 801-534-1910
www.fidelity.com

PERFORMANCE

fund inception date: 12/29/86

	3yr Annual	5yr Annual	10yr Annual	Bull	Bear
Return (%)	7.0	9.9	9.2	24.6	-6.4
Differ from Category (+/-)	0.7 av	-0.1 blw av	0.6 av	0.3 av	0.8 abv av

Total Risk	Standard Deviation	Category Risk	Risk Index	Beta
av	8.7%	low	0.8	0.60

	1996	1995	1994	1993	1992	1991	1990	1989	1988	1987
Return (%)	12.6	12.2	-2.9	35.0	-3.4	8.0	-3.3	19.1	11.5	8.3
Differ from Category (+/-)	-2.2	3.1	0.2	-4.6	0.4	-5.2	6.8	-3.5	-3.4	-3.9
Return, Tax-Adjusted (%)	11.4	10.7	-3.8	34.7	-4.4	7.4	-4.6	18.5	10.7	7.9

PER SHARE DATA

	1996	1995	1994	1993	1992	1991	1990	1989	1988	1987
Dividends, Net Income ($)	0.28	0.60	0.00	0.06	0.32	0.17	0.43	0.16	0.20	0.09
Distrib'ns, Cap Gain ($)	0.37	0.00	0.53	0.05	0.00	0.00	0.00	0.00	0.00	0.00
Net Asset Value ($)	19.55	17.95	16.53	17.57	13.09	13.87	13.00	13.88	11.79	10.75
Expense Ratio (%)	1.14	1.18	1.21	1.52	1.62	1.89	1.98	1.92	2.58	2.72
Yield (%)	1.40	3.34	0.00	0.34	2.44	1.22	3.30	1.15	1.69	0.83
Portfolio Turnover (%)	95	141	173	24	76	117	102	147	112	158
Total Assets (Millions $)	1,063	941	1,272	1,068	65	58	33	33	30	38

PORTFOLIO (as of 9/30/96)

Portfolio Manager: John Hickling - 1996

Investm't Category: International Stock

✔ Domestic   Index
✔ Foreign   Sector
  Asset Allocation   State Specific

Investment Style

Large-Cap Growth   Large-Cap Value
Mid-Cap Growth   Mid-Cap Value
Small-Cap Growth   Small-Cap Value

Portfolio

1.1% cash	21.5% corp bonds
74.3% stocks	0.0% gov't bonds
0.0% preferred	0.0% muni bonds
3.1% conv't/warrants	0.0% other

SHAREHOLDER INFORMATION

Minimum Investment

Initial: $2,500   Subsequent: $250

Minimum IRA Investment

Initial: $500   Subsequent: $250

Maximum Fees

Load: none   12b-1: none
Other: f

Distributions

Income: Dec   Capital Gains: Dec

Exchange Options

Number Per Year: 4   Fee: none
Telephone: yes (money market fund available)

Services

IRA, pension, auto exchange, auto invest, auto withdraw

Fidelity Int'l Value (FIVFX)

International Stock

82 Devonshire St.
Mail Zone F9A
Boston, MA 02109
800-544-6666, 801-534-1910
www.fidelity.com

PERFORMANCE

fund inception date: 11/1/94

	3yr Annual	5yr Annual	10yr Annual	Bull	Bear
Return (%)	na	na	na	na	na
Differ from Category (+/-)	na	na	na	na	na

Total Risk	Standard Deviation	Category Risk	Risk Index	Beta
na	na	na	na	na

	1996	1995	1994	1993	1992	1991	1990	1989	1988	1987
Return (%).	9.5	13.9	—	—	—	—	—	—	—	—
Differ from Category (+/-).	-5.3	4.8	—	—	—	—	—	—	—	—
Return, Tax-Adjusted (%). . .	8.5	13.0	—	—	—	—	—	—	—	—

PER SHARE DATA

	1996	1995	1994	1993	1992	1991	1990	1989	1988	1987
Dividends, Net Income ($).	0.10	0.01	—	—	—	—	—	—	—	—
Distrib'ns, Cap Gain ($) . . .	0.22	0.30	—	—	—	—	—	—	—	—
Net Asset Value ($)	11.55	10.84	—	—	—	—	—	—	—	—
Expense Ratio (%).	1.26	1.72	—	—	—	—	—	—	—	—
Yield (%)	0.84	0.08	—	—	—	—	—	—	—	—
Portfolio Turnover (%).	71	109	—	—	—	—	—	—	—	—
Total Assets (Millions $). . .	275	72	—	—	—	—	—	—	—	—

PORTFOLIO (as of 9/30/96)

Portfolio Manager: Rick Mace - 1994

Investm't Category: International Stock
- Domestic
- ✔ Foreign
- Asset Allocation
- Index
- Sector
- State Specific

Investment Style
- Large-Cap Growth
- Mid-Cap Growth
- Small-Cap Growth
- Large-Cap Value
- Mid-Cap Value
- Small-Cap Value

Portfolio
4.3% cash	0.8% corp bonds
94.1% stocks	0.0% gov't bonds
0.0% preferred	0.0% muni bonds
0.8% conv't/warrants	0.0% other

SHAREHOLDER INFORMATION

Minimum Investment
Initial: $2,500   Subsequent: $250

Minimum IRA Investment
Initial: $500   Subsequent: $250

Maximum Fees
Load: none   12b-1: none
Other: f

Distributions
Income: Dec   Capital Gains: Dec

Exchange Options
Number Per Year: 4   Fee: none
Telephone: yes (money market fund available)

Services
IRA, pension, auto exchange, auto invest, auto withdraw

Guide to Low-Load Mutual Funds

Fidelity Investment Grade Bond (FBNDX)

General Bond

82 Devonshire St.
Mail Zone F9A
Boston, MA 02109
800-544-6666, 801-534-1910
www.fidelity.com

PERFORMANCE

fund inception date: 8/6/71

	3yr Annual	5yr Annual	10yr Annual	Bull	Bear
Return (%)	4.0	7.2	8.1	19.4	-7.2
Differ from Category (+/-)	-1.1 low	1.1 high	0.8 high	-0.9 av	-3.0 low

Total Risk	Standard Deviation	Category Risk	Risk Index	Avg Mat
low	4.7%	abv av	1.2	8.1 yrs

	1996	1995	1994	1993	1992	1991	1990	1989	1988	1987
Return (%).	3.0	15.5	-5.4	16.2	8.3	18.9	6.0	13.0	7.9	0.1
Differ from Category (+/-).	-0.9	0.6	-3.1	7.1	1.8	4.2	-1.3	1.3	0.3	-2.2
Return, Tax-Adjusted (%). . .	0.5	12.7	-8.4	13.1	5.3	15.3	2.5	9.4	4.4	-3.3

PER SHARE DATA

	1996	1995	1994	1993	1992	1991	1990	1989	1988	1987
Dividends, Net Income ($).	0.46	0.46	0.50	0.56	0.55	0.59	0.60	0.60	0.59	0.62
Distrib'ns, Cap Gain ($) . . .	0.00	0.03	0.12	0.00	0.00	0.00	0.00	0.00	0.00	0.00
Net Asset Value ($)	7.12	7.38	6.85	7.89	7.30	7.28	6.67	6.88	6.65	6.73
Expense Ratio (%).	0.77	0.75	0.74	0.68	0.70	0.67	0.70	0.66	0.76	0.69
Yield (%)	6.46	6.20	7.17	7.09	7.53	8.10	8.99	8.72	8.87	9.21
Portfolio Turnover (%). . . .	134	90	61	74	77	101	103	128	118	127
Total Assets (Millions $).	1,469	1,245	995	1,042	1,040	653	410	405	308	311

PORTFOLIO (as of 9/30/96)

Portfolio Manager: Michael Gray - 1987

Investm't Category: General Bond
- ✔ Domestic
- ✔ Foreign
-   Asset Allocation

  Index
  Sector
  State Specific

Investment Style
Large-Cap Growth	Large-Cap Value
Mid-Cap Growth	Mid-Cap Value
Small-Cap Growth	Small-Cap Value

Portfolio
23.8% cash	26.6% corp bonds
0.0% stocks	48.2% gov't bonds
0.0% preferred	0.0% muni bonds
0.0% conv't/warrants	1.4% other

SHAREHOLDER INFORMATION

Minimum Investment
Initial: $2,500   Subsequent: $250

Minimum IRA Investment
Initial: $500   Subsequent: $250

Maximum Fees
Load: none   12b-1: none
Other: *f*

Distributions
Income: monthly   Capital Gains: Jun, Dec

Exchange Options
Number Per Year: 4   Fee: none
Telephone: yes (money market fund available)

Services
IRA, pension, auto exchange, auto invest, auto withdraw

Fidelity Japan (FJAPX)

International Stock

82 Devonshire St.
Mail Zone F9A
Boston, MA 02109
800-544-6666, 801-534-1910
www.fidelity.com

PERFORMANCE

fund inception date: 9/15/92

	3yr Annual	5yr Annual	10yr Annual	Bull	Bear
Return (%)	0.4	na	na	-21.2	14.7
Differ from Category (+/-)	-5.9 low	na	na	-45.5 low	21.9 high

Total Risk	Standard Deviation	Category Risk	Risk Index	Beta
high	15.9%	high	1.5	0.28

	1996	1995	1994	1993	1992	1991	1990	1989	1988	1987
Return (%).............	-11.2	-2.2	16.4	20.4	—	—	—	—	—	—
Differ from Category (+/-)	-26.0	-11.3	19.5	-19.2	—	—	—	—	—	—
Return, Tax-Adjusted (%).	-11.3	-2.2	15.5	19.3	—	—	—	—	—	—

PER SHARE DATA

	1996	1995	1994	1993	1992	1991	1990	1989	1988	1987
Dividends, Net Income ($).	0.01	0.00	0.00	0.00	—	—	—	—	—	—
Distrib'ns, Cap Gain ($) ...	0.00	0.00	0.36	0.39	—	—	—	—	—	—
Net Asset Value ($)	11.42	12.87	13.15	11.61	—	—	—	—	—	—
Expense Ratio (%)........	1.14	1.15	1.42	1.71	—	—	—	—	—	—
Yield (%)	0.08	0.00	0.00	0.00	—	—	—	—	—	—
Portfolio Turnover (%).....	83	86	153	257	—	—	—	—	—	—
Total Assets (Millions $)...	286	378	389	96	—	—	—	—	—	—

PORTFOLIO (as of 9/30/96)

Portfolio Manager: Shigeki Makino - 1994

Investm't Category: International Stock

Domestic	Index
✔ Foreign	Sector
Asset Allocation	State Specific

Investment Style

Large-Cap Growth	Large-Cap Value
Mid-Cap Growth	Mid-Cap Value
Small-Cap Growth	Small-Cap Value

Portfolio

2.1% cash	0.0% corp bonds
97.2% stocks	0.0% gov't bonds
0.0% preferred	0.0% muni bonds
0.7% conv't/warrants	0.0% other

SHAREHOLDER INFORMATION

Minimum Investment
Initial: $2,500   Subsequent: $250

Minimum IRA Investment
Initial: $500   Subsequent: $250

Maximum Fees
Load: 3.00% front   12b-1: none
Other: 1.50% redemption fee (90 days); *f*

Distributions
Income: Dec   Capital Gains: Dec

Exchange Options
Number Per Year: 4   Fee: none
Telephone: yes (money market fund available)

Services
IRA, pension, auto exchange, auto invest, auto withdraw

Fidelity Japan Small Companies (FJSCX)

International Stock

82 Devonshire St.
Mail Zone F9A
Boston, MA 02109
800-544-6666, 801-534-1910
www.fidelity.com

PERFORMANCE

fund inception date: 11/1/95

	3yr Annual	5yr Annual	10yr Annual	Bull	Bear
Return (%)	na	na	na	na	na
Differ from Category (+/-)	na	na	na	na	na

Total Risk	Standard Deviation	Category Risk	Risk Index	Beta
na	na	na	na	na

	1996	1995	1994	1993	1992	1991	1990	1989	1988	1987
Return (%)	-24.6	—	—	—	—	—	—	—	—	—
Differ from Category (+/-)	-39.4	—	—	—	—	—	—	—	—	—
Return, Tax-Adjusted (%)	-24.8	—	—	—	—	—	—	—	—	—

PER SHARE DATA

	1996	1995	1994	1993	1992	1991	1990	1989	1988	1987
Dividends, Net Income ($)	0.00	—	—	—	—	—	—	—	—	—
Distrib'ns, Cap Gain ($)	0.04	—	—	—	—	—	—	—	—	—
Net Asset Value ($)	7.94	—	—	—	—	—	—	—	—	—
Expense Ratio (%)	1.34	—	—	—	—	—	—	—	—	—
Yield (%)	0.00	—	—	—	—	—	—	—	—	—
Portfolio Turnover (%)	66	—	—	—	—	—	—	—	—	—
Total Assets (Millions $)	94	—	—	—	—	—	—	—	—	—

PORTFOLIO (as of 9/30/96)

Portfolio Manager: Simon Fraser - 1995

Investm't Category: International Stock
- Domestic
- ✔ Foreign
- Asset Allocation
- Index
- Sector
- State Specific

Investment Style
- Large-Cap Growth
- Mid-Cap Growth
- Small-Cap Growth
- Large-Cap Value
- Mid-Cap Value
- Small-Cap Value

Portfolio
5.5% cash	0.0% corp bonds
94.1% stocks	0.0% gov't bonds
0.0% preferred	0.0% muni bonds
0.4% conv't/warrants	0.0% other

SHAREHOLDER INFORMATION

Minimum Investment
Initial: $2,500   Subsequent: $250

Minimum IRA Investment
Initial: $500   Subsequent: $250

Maximum Fees
Load: 3.00% front   12b-1: none
Other: 1.50% redemption fee (90 days); f

Distributions
Income: Dec   Capital Gains: Dec

Exchange Options
Number Per Year: 4   Fee: none
Telephone: yes (money market fund available)

Services
IRA, pension, auto exchange, auto invest, auto withdraw

Fidelity Large Cap Stock

(FLCSX)

Growth

82 Devonshire St.
Mail Zone F9A
Boston, MA 02109
800-544-6666, 801-534-1910
www.fidelity.com

PERFORMANCE

fund inception date: 6/22/95

	3yr Annual	5yr Annual	10yr Annual	Bull	Bear
Return (%)	na	na	na	na	na
Differ from Category (+/-)	na	na	na	na	na

Total Risk	Standard Deviation	Category Risk	Risk Index	Beta
na	na	na	na	na

	1996	1995	1994	1993	1992	1991	1990	1989	1988	1987
Return (%)	21.5	—	—	—	—	—	—	—	—	—
Differ from Category (+/-)	1.4	—	—	—	—	—	—	—	—	—
Return, Tax-Adjusted (%)	19.2	—	—	—	—	—	—	—	—	—

PER SHARE DATA

	1996	1995	1994	1993	1992	1991	1990	1989	1988	1987
Dividends, Net Income ($)	0.05	—	—	—	—	—	—	—	—	—
Distrib'ns, Cap Gain ($)	0.80	—	—	—	—	—	—	—	—	—
Net Asset Value ($)	12.51	—	—	—	—	—	—	—	—	—
Expense Ratio (%)	1.31	—	—	—	—	—	—	—	—	—
Yield (%)	0.37	—	—	—	—	—	—	—	—	—
Portfolio Turnover (%)	155	—	—	—	—	—	—	—	—	—
Total Assets (Millions $)	125	—	—	—	—	—	—	—	—	—

PORTFOLIO (as of 9/30/96)

Portfolio Manager: Thomas Sprague - 1996

Investm't Category: Growth
✔ Domestic   Index
✔ Foreign   Sector
  Asset Allocation State Specific

Investment Style
Large-Cap Growth   Large-Cap Value
Mid-Cap Growth   Mid-Cap Value
Small-Cap Growth   Small-Cap Value

Portfolio
5.8% cash   0.0% corp bonds
94.2% stocks   0.0% gov't bonds
0.0% preferred   0.0% muni bonds
0.0% conv't/warrants 0.0% other

SHAREHOLDER INFORMATION

Minimum Investment
Initial: $2,500   Subsequent: $250

Minimum IRA Investment
Initial: $500   Subsequent: $250

Maximum Fees
Load: none   12b-1: none
Other: f

Distributions
Income: Jun, Dec   Capital Gains: Jun, Dec

Exchange Options
Number Per Year: 4   Fee: none
Telephone: yes (money market fund available)

Services
IRA, pension, auto exchange, auto invest, auto
withdraw

Fidelity Latin America

(FLATX)

International Stock

82 Devonshire St.
Mail Zone F9A
Boston, MA 02109
800-544-6666, 801-534-1910
www.fidelity.com

PERFORMANCE

fund inception date: 4/19/93

	3yr Annual	5yr Annual	10yr Annual	Bull	Bear
Return (%)	-5.7	na	na	2.6	-24.4
Differ from Category (+/-)	-12.0 low	na	na	-21.7 low	-17.2 low

Total Risk	Standard Deviation	Category Risk	Risk Index	Beta
high	27.7%	high	2.7	0.84

	1996	1995	1994	1993	1992	1991	1990	1989	1988	1987
Return (%)	30.7	-16.5	-23.2	—	—	—	—	—	—	—
Differ from Category (+/-)	15.9	-25.6	-20.1	—	—	—	—	—	—	—
Return, Tax-Adjusted (%)	29.8	-16.9	-23.2	—	—	—	—	—	—	—

PER SHARE DATA

	1996	1995	1994	1993	1992	1991	1990	1989	1988	1987
Dividends, Net Income ($)	0.23	0.12	0.00	—	—	—	—	—	—	—
Distrib'ns, Cap Gain ($)	0.00	0.00	0.00	—	—	—	—	—	—	—
Net Asset Value ($)	13.11	10.21	12.37	—	—	—	—	—	—	—
Expense Ratio (%)	1.32	1.41	1.48	—	—	—	—	—	—	—
Yield (%)	1.75	1.17	0.00	—	—	—	—	—	—	—
Portfolio Turnover (%)	70	57	77	—	—	—	—	—	—	—
Total Assets (Millions $)	530	473	616	—	—	—	—	—	—	—

PORTFOLIO (as of 9/30/96)

Portfolio Manager: Patti Satterthwaite - 1993

Investm't Category: International Stock

Domestic	Index
✔ Foreign	Sector
Asset Allocation	State Specific

Investment Style

Large-Cap Growth	Large-Cap Value
Mid-Cap Growth	Mid-Cap Value
Small-Cap Growth	Small-Cap Value

Portfolio

9.5% cash	0.0% corp bonds
90.5% stocks	0.0% gov't bonds
0.0% preferred	0.0% muni bonds
0.0% conv't/warrants	0.0% other

SHAREHOLDER INFORMATION

Minimum Investment
Initial: $2,500   Subsequent: $250

Minimum IRA Investment
Initial: $500   Subsequent: $250

Maximum Fees
Load: 3.00% front   12b-1: none
Other: 1.50% redemption fee (90 days); *f*

Distributions
Income: Dec   Capital Gains: Dec

Exchange Options
Number Per Year: 4   Fee: none
Telephone: yes (money market fund available)

Services
IRA, pension, auto exchange, auto invest, auto withdraw

Fidelity Ltd Term Muni Income (FLTMX)

Tax-Exempt Bond

82 Devonshire St.
Mail Zone F9A
Boston, MA 02109
800-544-6666, 801-534-1910
www.fidelity.com

PERFORMANCE

fund inception date: 4/15/77

	3yr Annual	5yr Annual	10yr Annual	Bull	Bear
Return (%)	4.4	6.7	6.8	19.2	-5.4
Differ from Category (+/-)	0.2 abv av	0.3 av	0.1 av	0.8 av	0.0 av

Total Risk	Standard Deviation	Category Risk	Risk Index	Avg Mat
blw av	4.8%	blw av	0.9	8.0 yrs

	1996	1995	1994	1993	1992	1991	1990	1989	1988	1987
Return (%)	4.3	14.8	-4.8	12.2	8.1	11.1	6.9	7.8	8.2	1.1
Differ from Category (+/-)	0.6	-0.4	0.5	0.4	-0.2	-0.3	0.5	-1.2	-1.8	2.5
Return, Tax-Adjusted (%)	4.2	14.8	-4.9	11.5	7.8	10.6	6.7	7.8	8.2	1.1

PER SHARE DATA

	1996	1995	1994	1993	1992	1991	1990	1989	1988	1987
Dividends, Net Income ($)	0.48	0.49	0.51	0.51	0.57	0.60	0.61	0.61	0.59	0.58
Distrib'ns, Cap Gain ($)	0.03	0.00	0.02	0.24	0.10	0.15	0.05	0.00	0.00	0.00
Net Asset Value ($)	9.69	9.80	8.99	9.99	9.60	9.52	9.27	9.31	9.23	9.10
Expense Ratio (%)	na	0.57	0.56	0.57	0.64	0.68	0.67	0.66	0.67	0.74
Yield (%)	4.93	5.00	5.66	4.98	5.87	6.20	6.54	6.55	6.39	6.37
Portfolio Turnover (%)	na	31	30	111	50	42	72	55	30	59
Total Assets (Millions $)	917	941	881	1,195	966	692	466	440	438	458

PORTFOLIO (as of 9/30/96)

Portfolio Manager: David L. Murphy - 1989

Investm't Category: Tax-Exempt Bond
- ✔ Domestic
- Foreign
- Asset Allocation
- Index
- Sector
- State Specific

Investment Style
- Large-Cap Growth
- Mid-Cap Growth
- Small-Cap Growth
- Large-Cap Value
- Mid-Cap Value
- Small-Cap Value

Portfolio
- 0.0% cash
- 0.0% stocks
- 0.0% preferred
- 0.0% conv't/warrants
- 0.0% corp bonds
- 0.0% gov't bonds
- 97.9% muni bonds
- 2.5% other

SHAREHOLDER INFORMATION

Minimum Investment
Initial: $2,500   Subsequent: $250

Minimum IRA Investment
Initial: na   Subsequent: na

Maximum Fees
Load: none   12b-1: none
Other: f

Distributions
Income: monthly   Capital Gains: Feb, Dec

Exchange Options
Number Per Year: 4   Fee: none
Telephone: yes (money market fund available)

Services
auto exchange, auto invest, auto withdraw

Fidelity Low Priced Stock

(FLPSX)

Growth

82 Devonshire St.
Mail Zone F9A
Boston, MA 02109
800-544-6666, 801-534-1910
www.fidelity.com

PERFORMANCE

fund inception date: 12/27/89

	3yr Annual	5yr Annual	10yr Annual	Bull	Bear
Return (%)	18.4	20.8	na	66.7	-5.4
Differ from Category (+/-)	2.7 abv av	6.5 high	na	4.3 abv av	1.3 abv av

Total Risk	Standard Deviation	Category Risk	Risk Index	Beta
av	8.7%	low	0.8	0.65

	1996	1995	1994	1993	1992	1991	1990	1989	1988	1987
Return (%)	26.8	24.8	4.8	20.2	28.9	46.2	-0.7	—	—	—
Differ from Category (+/-)	6.7	-5.5	5.1	6.2	17.1	10.2	5.4	—	—	—
Return, Tax-Adjusted (%)	23.7	22.0	1.2	16.9	27.1	43.7	-2.0	—	—	—

PER SHARE DATA

	1996	1995	1994	1993	1992	1991	1990	1989	1988	1987
Dividends, Net Income ($)	0.24	0.23	0.09	0.16	0.10	0.15	0.14	—	—	—
Distrib'ns, Cap Gain ($)	1.66	1.24	2.04	1.62	0.69	0.60	0.26	—	—	—
Net Asset Value ($)	21.35	18.50	16.00	17.30	15.96	13.05	9.47	—	—	—
Expense Ratio (%)	1.04	1.11	1.13	1.12	1.20	1.36	1.92	—	—	—
Yield (%)	1.04	1.16	0.49	0.84	0.60	1.09	1.43	—	—	—
Portfolio Turnover (%)	79	65	54	47	82	84	126	—	—	—
Total Assets (Millions $)	5,298	3,349	2,354	2,060	2,306	375	88	—	—	—

PORTFOLIO (as of 9/30/96)

Portfolio Manager: Joel Tillinghast - 1989

Investm't Category: Growth

✔ Domestic	Index
✔ Foreign	Sector
Asset Allocation	State Specific

Investment Style

Large-Cap Growth	Large-Cap Value
Mid-Cap Growth	Mid-Cap Value
✔ Small-Cap Growth	✔ Small-Cap Value

Portfolio

18.7% cash	0.0% corp bonds
79.6% stocks	0.0% gov't bonds
0.0% preferred	0.0% muni bonds
1.7% conv't/warrants	0.0% other

SHAREHOLDER INFORMATION

Minimum Investment
Initial: $2,500   Subsequent: $250

Minimum IRA Investment
Initial: $500   Subsequent: $250

Maximum Fees
Load: 3.00% front   12b-1: none
Other: 1.50% redemption fee (90 days); *f*

Distributions
Income: Sep, Dec   Capital Gains: Sep, Dec

Exchange Options
Number Per Year: 4   Fee: none
Telephone: yes (money market fund available)

Services
IRA, pension, auto exchange, auto invest, auto withdraw

Fidelity MA Muni Income

(FDMMX)

Tax-Exempt Bond

82 Devonshire St.
Mail Zone F9A
Boston, MA 02109
800-544-6666, 801-534-1910
www.fidelity.com

PERFORMANCE

fund inception date: 11/10/83

	3yr Annual	5yr Annual	10yr Annual	Bull	Bear
Return (%)	4.6	7.2	7.2	20.1	-5.7
Differ from Category (+/-)	0.4 abv av	0.8 abv av	0.5 abv av	1.7 abv av	-0.3 av

Total Risk	Standard Deviation	Category Risk	Risk Index	Avg Mat
blw av	5.9%	abv av	1.1	15.3 yrs

	1996	1995	1994	1993	1992	1991	1990	1989	1988	1987
Return (%).	3.5	18.0	-6.3	12.9	9.2	11.3	7.3	9.2	10.6	-1.3
Differ from Category (+/-) .	-0.2	2.8	-1.0	1.1	0.9	-0.1	0.9	0.2	0.6	0.1
Return, Tax-Adjusted (%). . .	3.5	18.0	-6.9	12.2	9.0	11.0	7.0	9.2	10.6	-1.4

PER SHARE DATA

	1996	1995	1994	1993	1992	1991	1990	1989	1988	1987
Dividends, Net Income ($).	0.60	0.65	0.68	0.71	0.72	0.75	0.79	0.80	0.80	0.80
Distrib'ns, Cap Gain ($) . . .	0.00	0.00	0.23	0.26	0.07	0.08	0.11	0.00	0.00	0.03
Net Asset Value ($)	11.46	11.67	10.48	12.13	11.64	11.41	11.04	11.16	10.98	10.68
Expense Ratio (%).	0.54	0.55	0.54	0.55	0.57	0.56	0.57	0.56	0.61	0.64
Yield (%)	5.23	5.56	6.34	5.73	6.14	6.52	7.08	7.16	7.28	7.46
Portfolio Turnover (%). . . .	33	11	40	42	18	29	31	26	25	36
Total Assets (Millions $). .	1,146	1,179	993	1,375	1,230	995	717	677	602	537

PORTFOLIO (as of 9/30/96)

Portfolio Manager: Steven Harvey - 1995

Investm't Category: Tax-Exempt Bond
- ✔ Domestic
- Foreign
- Asset Allocation
- Index
- Sector
- ✔ State Specific

Investment Style
- Large-Cap Growth
- Mid-Cap Growth
- Small-Cap Growth
- Large-Cap Value
- Mid-Cap Value
- Small-Cap Value

Portfolio
5.1% cash	0.0% corp bonds
0.0% stocks	0.0% gov't bonds
0.0% preferred	95.0% muni bonds
0.0% conv't/warrants	0.0% other

SHAREHOLDER INFORMATION

Minimum Investment
Initial: $2,500   Subsequent: $250

Minimum IRA Investment
Initial: na   Subsequent: na

Maximum Fees
Load: none   12b-1: none
Other: f

Distributions
Income: monthly   Capital Gains: Dec

Exchange Options
Number Per Year: 4   Fee: none
Telephone: yes (money market fund available)

Services
auto exchange, auto invest, auto withdraw

Fidelity Magellan (FMAGX)

Growth

82 Devonshire St.
Mail Zone F9A
Boston, MA 02109
800-544-6666, 801-534-1910
www.fidelity.com

PERFORMANCE

fund inception date: 5/27/63

	3yr Annual	5yr Annual	10yr Annual	Bull	Bear
Return (%)	14.4	14.8	16.2	59.6	-9.6
Differ from Category (+/-)	-1.3 blw av	0.5 av	2.3 high	-2.8 av	-2.9 blw av

Total Risk	Standard Deviation	Category Risk	Risk Index	Beta
abv av	11.7%	abv av	1.1	1.00

	1996	1995	1994	1993	1992	1991	1990	1989	1988	1987
Return (%)	11.6	36.8	-1.9	24.6	7.0	41.0	-4.6	34.5	22.7	1.0
Differ from Category (+/-)	-8.5	6.5	-1.6	10.6	-4.8	5.0	1.5	8.4	4.6	-1.0
Return, Tax-Adjusted (%)	6.9	34.4	-3.1	21.2	2.6	37.2	-6.3	31.2	21.8	-4.8

PER SHARE DATA

	1996	1995	1994	1993	1992	1991	1990	1989	1988	1987
Dividends, Net Income ($)	1.10	0.59	0.13	0.75	1.25	1.30	0.83	1.24	0.90	0.72
Distrib'ns, Cap Gain ($)	12.85	4.69	2.64	6.50	8.82	5.43	2.42	3.82	0.00	9.02
Net Asset Value ($)	80.65	85.98	66.80	70.85	63.01	68.61	53.93	59.85	48.32	40.10
Expense Ratio (%)	0.92	0.96	0.99	1.00	1.05	1.06	1.03	1.08	1.14	1.08
Yield (%)	1.17	0.65	0.18	0.96	1.74	1.75	1.47	1.94	1.86	1.46
Portfolio Turnover (%)	155	120	132	155	172	135	82	87	101	96
Total Assets (Millions $)	55,851	53,702	36,441	31,705	22,268	19,257	12,325	12,699	8,971	7,800

PORTFOLIO (as of 9/30/96)

Portfolio Manager: Bob Stansky - 1996

Investm't Category: Growth
- ✔ Domestic
- ✔ Foreign
-   Asset Allocation
-   Index
-   Sector
-   State Specific

Investment Style
-   Large-Cap Growth
- ✔ Mid-Cap Growth
-   Small-Cap Growth
-   Large-Cap Value
- ✔ Mid-Cap Value
-   Small-Cap Value

Portfolio

1.2% cash	9.8% corp bonds
88.9% stocks	0.0% gov't bonds
0.0% preferred	0.0% muni bonds
0.1% conv't/warrants	0.0% other

SHAREHOLDER INFORMATION

Minimum Investment
Initial: $2,500   Subsequent: $250

Minimum IRA Investment
Initial: $500   Subsequent: $250

Maximum Fees
Load: 3.00% front   12b-1: none
Other: *f*

Distributions
Income: May, Dec   Capital Gains: May, Dec

Exchange Options
Number Per Year: 4   Fee: none
Telephone: yes (money market fund available)

Services
IRA, pension, auto exchange, auto invest, auto withdraw

Fidelity Market Index

(FSMKX)

Growth & Income

82 Devonshire St.
Mail Zone F9A
Boston, MA 02109
800-544-6666, 801-534-1910
www.fidelity.com

PERFORMANCE

fund inception date: 3/6/90

	3yr Annual	5yr Annual	10yr Annual	Bull	Bear
Return (%)	19.2	14.8	na	75.8	-6.7
Differ from Category (+/-)	3.9 high	0.9 abv av	na	16.0 high	-0.3 av

Total Risk	Standard Deviation	Category Risk	Risk Index	Beta
abv av	9.7%	abv av	1.0	0.99

	1996	1995	1994	1993	1992	1991	1990	1989	1988	1987
Return (%)	22.5	36.9	1.0	9.6	7.3	30.3	—	—	—	—
Differ from Category (+/-)	2.8	6.8	2.3	-4.2	-3.4	1.2	—	—	—	—
Return, Tax-Adjusted (%)	21.0	35.4	0.0	8.4	6.2	28.8	—	—	—	—

PER SHARE DATA

	1996	1995	1994	1993	1992	1991	1990	1989	1988	1987
Dividends, Net Income ($)	0.91	0.96	0.80	0.80	0.81	0.83	—	—	—	—
Distrib'ns, Cap Gain ($)	1.05	0.37	0.00	0.18	0.00	0.07	—	—	—	—
Net Asset Value ($)	53.42	45.32	34.15	34.60	32.49	31.07	—	—	—	—
Expense Ratio (%)	0.45	0.45	0.45	0.44	0.35	0.28	—	—	—	—
Yield (%)	1.67	2.10	2.34	2.30	2.49	2.66	—	—	—	—
Portfolio Turnover (%)	5	2	3	0	1	1	—	—	—	—
Total Assets (Millions $)	1,574	689	306	299	283	202	—	—	—	—

PORTFOLIO (as of 9/30/96)

Portfolio Manager: Jennifer Farrelly - 1994

Investm't Category: Growth & Income
✔ Domestic   ✔ Index
  Foreign   Sector
  Asset Allocation   State Specific

Investment Style
✔ Large-Cap Growth   ✔ Large-Cap Value
  Mid-Cap Growth   Mid-Cap Value
  Small-Cap Growth   Small-Cap Value

Portfolio
  0.0% cash   0.0% corp bonds
100.1% stocks   0.0% gov't bonds
  0.0% preferred   0.0% muni bonds
  0.0% conv't/warrants 0.0% other

SHAREHOLDER INFORMATION

Minimum Investment
Initial: $2,500   Subsequent: $250

Minimum IRA Investment
Initial: $500   Subsequent: $250

Maximum Fees
Load: 0.50% redemption   12b-1: none
Other: redemption fee applies for 3 months; *f*

Distributions
Income: quarterly   Capital Gains: Jun, Dec

Exchange Options
Number Per Year: 4   Fee: none
Telephone: yes (money market fund available)

Services
IRA, pension, auto exchange, auto invest, auto withdraw

Fidelity Michigan Muni Income (FMHTX)

Tax-Exempt Bond

82 Devonshire St.
Mail Zone F9A
Boston, MA 02109
800-544-6666, 801-534-1910
www.fidelity.com

PERFORMANCE

fund inception date: 11/12/85

	3yr Annual	5yr Annual	10yr Annual	Bull	Bear
Return (%)	3.3	6.5	6.9	16.5	-6.7
Differ from Category (+/-)	-0.9 low	0.1 av	0.2 av	-1.9 blw av	-1.3 blw av

Total Risk	Standard Deviation	Category Risk	Risk Index	Avg Mat
blw av	5.9%	abv av	1.1	14.3 yrs

	1996	1995	1994	1993	1992	1991	1990	1989	1988	1987
Return (%)	3.3	15.4	-7.6	13.8	9.5	12.0	5.1	10.2	13.0	-2.9
Differ from Category (+/-)	-0.4	0.2	-2.3	2.0	1.2	0.6	-1.3	1.2	3.0	-1.5
Return, Tax-Adjusted (%)	3.3	15.4	-8.0	13.2	9.4	12.0	5.1	10.2	13.0	-3.0

PER SHARE DATA

	1996	1995	1994	1993	1992	1991	1990	1989	1988	1987
Dividends, Net Income ($)	0.63	0.61	0.68	0.70	0.73	0.74	0.75	0.76	0.75	0.77
Distrib'ns, Cap Gain ($)	0.00	0.00	0.17	0.24	0.02	0.00	0.00	0.00	0.00	0.04
Net Asset Value ($)	11.30	11.56	10.58	12.34	11.71	11.41	10.89	11.10	10.79	10.25
Expense Ratio (%)	na	0.59	0.57	0.59	0.61	0.62	0.64	0.69	0.75	0.72
Yield (%)	5.57	5.27	6.32	5.56	6.22	6.48	6.88	6.84	6.95	7.48
Portfolio Turnover (%)	na	29	18	33	15	12	18	19	24	44
Total Assets (Millions $)	461	491	434	561	460	378	278	233	169	128

PORTFOLIO (as of 9/30/96)

Portfolio Manager: David L. Murphy - 1996

Investm't Category: Tax-Exempt Bond
- ✔ Domestic
- Foreign
- Asset Allocation
- Index
- Sector
- ✔ State Specific

Investment Style
- Large-Cap Growth
- Mid-Cap Growth
- Small-Cap Growth
- Large-Cap Value
- Mid-Cap Value
- Small-Cap Value

Portfolio
4.1% cash	0.0% corp bonds
0.0% stocks	0.0% gov't bonds
0.0% preferred	95.0% muni bonds
0.0% conv't/warrants	0.9% other

SHAREHOLDER INFORMATION

Minimum Investment
Initial: $2,500   Subsequent: $250

Minimum IRA Investment
Initial: na   Subsequent: na

Maximum Fees
Load: none   12b-1: none
Other: f

Distributions
Income: monthly   Capital Gains: Feb, Dec

Exchange Options
Number Per Year: 4   Fee: none
Telephone: yes (money market fund available)

Services
auto exchange, auto invest, auto withdraw

Fidelity Mid Cap Stock

(FMCSX)

Growth

82 Devonshire St.
Mail Zone F9A
Boston, MA 02109
800-544-6666, 801-534-1910
www.fidelity.com

PERFORMANCE

fund inception date: 3/29/94

	3yr Annual	5yr Annual	10yr Annual	Bull	Bear
Return (%)	na	na	na	77.0	na
Differ from Category (+/-)	na	na	na	14.6 high	na

Total Risk	Standard Deviation	Category Risk	Risk Index	Beta
na	na	na	na	na

	1996	1995	1994	1993	1992	1991	1990	1989	1988	1987
Return (%)	18.1	33.9	—	—	—	—	—	—	—	—
Differ from Category (+/-)	-2.0	3.6	—	—	—	—	—	—	—	—
Return, Tax-Adjusted (%)	15.3	31.7	—	—	—	—	—	—	—	—

PER SHARE DATA

	1996	1995	1994	1993	1992	1991	1990	1989	1988	1987
Dividends, Net Income ($)	0.03	0.06	—	—	—	—	—	—	—	—
Distrib'ns, Cap Gain ($)	1.26	0.74	—	—	—	—	—	—	—	—
Net Asset Value ($)	14.64	13.50	—	—	—	—	—	—	—	—
Expense Ratio (%)	1.02	1.63	—	—	—	—	—	—	—	—
Yield (%)	0.18	0.42	—	—	—	—	—	—	—	—
Portfolio Turnover (%)	179	190	—	—	—	—	—	—	—	—
Total Assets (Millions $)	1,738	1,150	—	—	—	—	—	—	—	—

PORTFOLIO (as of 9/30/96)

Portfolio Manager: Jennifer Uhrig - 1994

Investm't Category: Growth

✔ Domestic   Index
✔ Foreign   Sector
   Asset Allocation   State Specific

Investment Style

Large-Cap Growth   Large-Cap Value
Mid-Cap Growth   Mid-Cap Value
Small-Cap Growth   Small-Cap Value

Portfolio

11.0% cash	1.0% corp bonds
87.8% stocks	0.0% gov't bonds
0.0% preferred	0.0% muni bonds
0.2% conv't/warrants	0.0% other

SHAREHOLDER INFORMATION

Minimum Investment
Initial: $2,500   Subsequent: $250

Minimum IRA Investment
Initial: $500   Subsequent: $250

Maximum Fees
Load: none   12b-1: none
Other: f

Distributions
Income: June, Dec   Capital Gains: June, Dec

Exchange Options
Number Per Year: 4   Fee: none
Telephone: yes (money market fund available)

Services
IRA, pension, auto exchange, auto invest, auto withdraw

Fidelity Minnesota Muni Income (FIMIX)

Tax-Exempt Bond

82 Devonshire St.
Mail Zone F9A
Boston, MA 02109
800-544-6666, 801-534-1910
www.fidelity.com

PERFORMANCE

fund inception date: 11/21/85

	3yr Annual	5yr Annual	10yr Annual	Bull	Bear
Return (%)	4.2	6.4	6.5	18.8	-6.0
Differ from Category (+/-)	0.0 av	0.0 blw av	-0.2 blw av	0.4 av	-0.6 av

Total Risk	Standard Deviation	Category Risk	Risk Index	Avg Mat
blw av	5.4%	av	1.0	13.9 yrs

	1996	1995	1994	1993	1992	1991	1990	1989	1988	1987
Return (%)	3.7	15.8	-6.0	12.4	7.6	8.4	7.2	9.2	12.6	-3.9
Differ from Category (+/-)	0.0	0.6	-0.7	0.6	-0.7	-3.0	0.8	0.2	2.6	-2.5
Return, Tax-Adjusted (%)	3.7	15.8	-6.2	12.4	7.6	8.4	7.2	9.2	12.6	-4.0

PER SHARE DATA

	1996	1995	1994	1993	1992	1991	1990	1989	1988	1987
Dividends, Net Income ($)	0.56	0.61	0.63	0.64	0.67	0.68	0.69	0.71	0.71	0.72
Distrib'ns, Cap Gain ($)	0.00	0.00	0.08	0.00	0.00	0.00	0.00	0.00	0.00	0.03
Net Asset Value ($)	10.94	11.10	10.14	11.52	10.85	10.73	10.55	10.52	10.31	9.82
Expense Ratio (%)	na	0.57	0.59	0.61	0.67	0.72	0.76	0.80	0.82	0.79
Yield (%)	5.11	5.49	6.16	5.55	6.17	6.33	6.54	6.74	6.88	7.30
Portfolio Turnover (%)	na	49	26	37	12	14	29	25	31	63
Total Assets (Millions $)	297	314	277	341	278	220	166	130	99	79

PORTFOLIO (as of 9/30/96)

Portfolio Manager: Jonathan D. Short - 1995

Investm't Category: Tax-Exempt Bond
✔ Domestic   Index
  Foreign   Sector
  Asset Allocation ✔ State Specific

Investment Style
  Large-Cap Growth   Large-Cap Value
  Mid-Cap Growth   Mid-Cap Value
  Small-Cap Growth   Small-Cap Value

Portfolio
  0.5% cash   0.0% corp bonds
  0.0% stocks   0.0% gov't bonds
  0.0% preferred   98.9% muni bonds
  0.0% conv't/warrants 0.6% other

SHAREHOLDER INFORMATION

Minimum Investment
Initial: $2,500   Subsequent: $250

Minimum IRA Investment
Initial: na   Subsequent: na

Maximum Fees
Load: none   12b-1: none
Other: f

Distributions
Income: monthly   Capital Gains: Feb, Dec

Exchange Options
Number Per Year: 4   Fee: none
Telephone: yes (money market fund available)

Services
auto exchange, auto invest, auto withdraw

Fidelity Mortgage Securities (FMSFX)

Mortgage-Backed Bond

82 Devonshire St.
Mail Zone F9A
Boston, MA 02109
800-544-6666, 801-534-1910
www.fidelity.com

PERFORMANCE

fund inception date: 12/31/84

	3yr Annual	5yr Annual	10yr Annual	Bull	Bear
Return (%)	7.9	7.2	8.2	25.6	-0.8
Differ from Category (+/-)	2.3 high	1.2 high	0.5 high	4.5 high	2.8 high

Total Risk	Standard Deviation	Category Risk	Risk Index	Avg Mat
low	3.3%	blw av	0.9	6.7 yrs

	1996	1995	1994	1993	1992	1991	1990	1989	1988	1987
Return (%)	5.4	17.0	2.0	6.7	5.4	13.6	10.3	13.6	6.7	2.6
Differ from Category (+/-)	1.0	2.3	3.7	-0.2	-0.8	-0.8	0.5	1.0	-0.7	0.6
Return, Tax-Adjusted (%)	2.6	13.7	-0.5	4.1	2.6	10.4	7.0	10.1	3.4	-0.8

PER SHARE DATA

	1996	1995	1994	1993	1992	1991	1990	1989	1988	1987
Dividends, Net Income ($)	0.70	0.76	0.62	0.63	0.75	0.82	0.83	0.84	0.82	0.90
Distrib'ns, Cap Gain ($)	0.11	0.10	0.05	0.07	0.00	0.00	0.00	0.00	0.00	0.00
Net Asset Value ($)	10.85	11.09	10.26	10.73	10.73	10.91	10.38	10.21	9.77	9.94
Expense Ratio (%)	0.73	0.77	0.79	0.76	0.80	0.82	0.82	0.88	0.90	0.80
Yield (%)	6.38	6.79	6.01	5.83	6.98	7.51	7.99	8.22	8.39	9.05
Portfolio Turnover (%)	221	329	563	278	146	209	110	271	245	160
Total Assets (Millions $)	528	486	349	374	429	436	390	399	442	496

PORTFOLIO (as of 9/30/96)

Portfolio Manager: Kevin E. Grant - 1993

Investm't Category: Mortgage-Backed Bond
- ✔ Domestic   Index
- ✔ Foreign   Sector
-    Asset Allocation   State Specific

Investment Style

Large-Cap Growth	Large-Cap Value
Mid-Cap Growth	Mid-Cap Value
Small-Cap Growth	Small-Cap Value

Portfolio

4.9% cash	0.0% corp bonds
0.0% stocks	95.1% gov't bonds
0.0% preferred	0.0% muni bonds
0.0% conv't/warrants	0.0% other

SHAREHOLDER INFORMATION

Minimum Investment
Initial: $2,500   Subsequent: $250

Minimum IRA Investment
Initial: $250   Subsequent: $250

Maximum Fees
Load: none   12b-1: none
Other: *f*

Distributions
Income: monthly   Capital Gains: Sep, Dec

Exchange Options
Number Per Year: 4   Fee: none
Telephone: yes (money market fund available)

Services
IRA, pension, auto exchange, auto invest, auto withdraw

Fidelity Muni Income

(FHIGX)

Tax-Exempt Bond

82 Devonshire St.
Mail Zone F9A
Boston, MA 02109
800-544-6666, 801-534-1910
www.fidelity.com

PERFORMANCE

fund inception date: 11/30/77

	3yr Annual	5yr Annual	10yr Annual	Bull	Bear
Return (%)	4.1	6.7	7.2	19.4	-6.6
Differ from Category (+/-)	-0.1 blw av	0.3 av	0.5 abv av	1.0 av	-1.2 blw av

Total Risk	Standard Deviation	Category Risk	Risk Index	Avg Mat
blw av	5.9%	abv av	1.1	14.4 yrs

	1996	1995	1994	1993	1992	1991	1990	1989	1988	1987
Return (%)	4.9	16.1	-7.5	13.1	8.3	10.1	8.4	11.3	12.2	-2.9
Differ from Category (+/-)	1.2	0.9	-2.2	1.3	0.0	-1.3	2.0	2.3	2.2	-1.5
Return, Tax-Adjusted (%)	4.8	16.1	-7.5	11.9	7.8	9.7	7.8	10.4	12.1	-3.2

PER SHARE DATA

	1996	1995	1994	1993	1992	1991	1990	1989	1988	1987
Dividends, Net Income ($)	0.64	0.66	0.75	0.76	0.80	0.83	0.85	0.89	0.90	0.93
Distrib'ns, Cap Gain ($)	0.03	0.00	0.00	0.50	0.19	0.16	0.23	0.39	0.01	0.12
Net Asset Value ($)	12.27	12.36	11.25	12.95	12.60	12.58	12.36	12.44	12.36	11.87
Expense Ratio (%)	na	0.57	0.56	0.56	0.57	0.56	0.57	0.58	0.60	0.71
Yield (%)	5.20	5.33	6.66	5.65	6.25	6.51	6.75	6.93	7.27	7.75
Portfolio Turnover (%)	na	50	48	53	47	44	58	71	47	80
Total Assets (Millions $)	1,833	1,794	1,671	2,108	2,060	1,991	1,767	1,716	1,614	1,571

PORTFOLIO (as of 9/30/96)

Portfolio Manager: David L. Murphy - 1995

Investm't Category: Tax-Exempt Bond

✔ Domestic	Index
Foreign	Sector
Asset Allocation	State Specific

Investment Style

Large-Cap Growth	Large-Cap Value
Mid-Cap Growth	Mid-Cap Value
Small-Cap Growth	Small-Cap Value

Portfolio

2.1% cash	0.0% corp bonds
0.0% stocks	0.0% gov't bonds
0.0% preferred	97.7% muni bonds
0.0% conv't/warrants	0.2% other

SHAREHOLDER INFORMATION

Minimum Investment
Initial: $2,500   Subsequent: $250

Minimum IRA Investment
Initial: na   Subsequent: na

Maximum Fees
Load: none   12b-1: none
Other: f

Distributions
Income: monthly   Capital Gains: Jan, Dec

Exchange Options
Number Per Year: 4   Fee: none
Telephone: yes (money market fund available)

Services
auto exchange, auto invest, auto withdraw

Fidelity NY Insured Muni Income (FNTIX)

Tax-Exempt Bond

82 Devonshire St.
Mail Zone F9A
Boston, MA 02109
800-544-6666, 801-534-1910
www.fidelity.com

PERFORMANCE

fund inception date: 10/11/85

	3yr Annual	5yr Annual	10yr Annual	Bull	Bear
Return (%)	4.2	6.7	6.8	20.6	-7.1
Differ from Category (+/-)	0.0 av	0.3 av	0.1 av	2.2 abv av	-1.7 low

Total Risk	Standard Deviation	Category Risk	Risk Index	Avg Mat
blw av	6.6%	high	1.2	12.8 yrs

	1996	1995	1994	1993	1992	1991	1990	1989	1988	1987
Return (%)	3.7	18.4	-8.0	12.8	8.5	12.4	6.1	9.0	11.2	-3.3
Differ from Category (+/-)	0.0	3.2	-2.7	1.0	0.2	1.0	-0.3	0.0	1.2	-1.9
Return, Tax-Adjusted (%)	3.7	18.4	-8.4	12.0	8.5	12.4	6.1	9.0	11.2	-3.3

PER SHARE DATA

	1996	1995	1994	1993	1992	1991	1990	1989	1988	1987
Dividends, Net Income ($)	0.54	0.56	0.63	0.65	0.67	0.68	0.69	0.69	0.68	0.69
Distrib'ns, Cap Gain ($)	0.00	0.00	0.15	0.31	0.00	0.00	0.00	0.00	0.00	0.00
Net Asset Value ($)	11.71	11.83	10.50	12.24	11.73	11.46	10.84	10.89	10.65	10.22
Expense Ratio (%)	0.59	0.58	0.58	0.61	0.62	0.64	0.65	0.65	0.67	0.60
Yield (%)	4.61	4.73	5.91	5.17	5.71	5.93	6.36	6.33	6.38	6.75
Portfolio Turnover (%)	74	41	48	39	17	33	18	31	29	30
Total Assets (Millions $)	324	335	300	409	353	294	227	202	173	159

PORTFOLIO (as of 9/30/96)

Portfolio Manager: Norman Lind - 1994

Investm't Category: Tax-Exempt Bond
✔ Domestic   Index
   Foreign   Sector
   Asset Allocation ✔ State Specific

Investment Style
Large-Cap Growth   Large-Cap Value
Mid-Cap Growth   Mid-Cap Value
Small-Cap Growth   Small-Cap Value

Portfolio
1.1% cash   0.0% corp bonds
0.0% stocks   0.0% gov't bonds
0.0% preferred   98.6% muni bonds
0.0% conv't/warrants 0.3% other

SHAREHOLDER INFORMATION

Minimum Investment
Initial: $2,500   Subsequent: $250

Minimum IRA Investment
Initial: na   Subsequent: na

Maximum Fees
Load: none   12b-1: none
Other: f

Distributions
Income: monthly   Capital Gains: Mar, Dec

Exchange Options
Number Per Year: 4   Fee: none
Telephone: yes (money market fund available)

Services
auto exchange, auto invest, auto withdraw

Fidelity NY Muni Income

(FTFMX)

Tax-Exempt Bond

82 Devonshire St.
Mail Zone F9A
Boston, MA 02109
800-544-6666, 801-534-1910
www.fidelity.com

PERFORMANCE

fund inception date: 7/10/84

	3yr Annual	5yr Annual	10yr Annual	Bull	Bear
Return (%)	4.5	7.0	7.1	21.9	-7.4
Differ from Category (+/-)	0.3 abv av	0.6 abv av	0.4 abv av	3.5 high	-2.0 low

Total Risk	Standard Deviation	Category Risk	Risk Index	Avg Mat
blw av	6.7%	high	1.2	14.3 yrs

	1996	1995	1994	1993	1992	1991	1990	1989	1988	1987
Return (%)	3.7	19.5	-8.1	12.8	8.9	13.3	5.0	9.2	11.9	-2.5
Differ from Category (+/-)	0.0	4.3	-2.8	1.0	0.6	1.9	-1.4	0.2	1.9	-1.1
Return, Tax-Adjusted (%)	3.7	19.5	-8.7	11.7	8.9	13.3	5.0	9.2	11.9	-2.8

PER SHARE DATA

	1996	1995	1994	1993	1992	1991	1990	1989	1988	1987
Dividends, Net Income ($)	0.63	0.63	0.67	0.72	0.77	0.77	0.79	0.80	0.78	0.80
Distrib'ns, Cap Gain ($)	0.00	0.00	0.24	0.46	0.00	0.00	0.00	0.00	0.00	0.10
Net Asset Value ($)	12.33	12.51	11.04	12.97	12.57	12.28	11.56	11.78	11.55	11.06
Expense Ratio (%)	0.58	0.58	0.58	0.61	0.61	0.59	0.61	0.63	0.67	0.60
Yield (%)	5.10	5.03	5.93	5.36	6.12	6.27	6.83	6.79	6.75	7.16
Portfolio Turnover (%)	83	34	70	45	30	45	34	49	64	51
Total Assets (Millions $)	415	434	380	484	438	412	377	417	343	317

PORTFOLIO (as of 9/30/96)

Portfolio Manager: Norman Lind - 1993

Investm't Category: Tax-Exempt Bond
- ✔ Domestic
- Foreign
- Asset Allocation
- Index
- Sector
- ✔ State Specific

Investment Style
- Large-Cap Growth
- Mid-Cap Growth
- Small-Cap Growth
- Large-Cap Value
- Mid-Cap Value
- Small-Cap Value

Portfolio
- 0.4% cash
- 0.0% stocks
- 0.0% preferred
- 0.0% conv't/warrants
- 0.0% corp bonds
- 0.0% gov't bonds
- 97.3% muni bonds
- 2.3% other

SHAREHOLDER INFORMATION

Minimum Investment
Initial: $2,500   Subsequent: $250

Minimum IRA Investment
Initial: na   Subsequent: na

Maximum Fees
Load: none   12b-1: none
Other: *f*

Distributions
Income: monthly   Capital Gains: Mar, Dec

Exchange Options
Number Per Year: 4   Fee: none
Telephone: yes (money market fund available)

Services
auto exchange, auto invest, auto withdraw

Fidelity New Markets Income (FNMIX)

International Bond

82 Devonshire St.
Mail Zone F9A
Boston, MA 02109
800-544-6666, 801-534-1910
www.fidelity.com

PERFORMANCE

fund inception date: 5/4/93

	3yr Annual	5yr Annual	10yr Annual	Bull	Bear
Return (%)	8.4	na	na	68.6	-27.2
Differ from Category (+/-)	2.4 abv av	na	na	37.4 high	-17.7 low

Total Risk	Standard Deviation	Category Risk	Risk Index	Avg Mat
high	20.2%	high	2.9	14.1 yrs

	1996	1995	1994	1993	1992	1991	1990	1989	1988	1987
Return (%).	41.3	7.8	-16.5	—	—	—	—	—	—	—
Differ from Category (+/-)	.30.0	-8.2	-8.9	—	—	—	—	—	—	—
Return, Tax-Adjusted (%). .	.37.5	4.2	-18.7	—	—	—	—	—	—	—

PER SHARE DATA

	1996	1995	1994	1993	1992	1991	1990	1989	1988	1987
Dividends, Net Income ($)	.0.93	0.91	0.56	—	—	—	—	—	—	—
Distrib'ns, Cap Gain ($) . .	.0.00	0.00	0.20	—	—	—	—	—	—	—
Net Asset Value ($)	12.96	9.95	10.20	—	—	—	—	—	—	—
Expense Ratio (%).	.1.12	1.17	1.28	—	—	—	—	—	—	—
Yield (%)	.7.17	9.14	5.38	—	—	—	—	—	—	—
Portfolio Turnover (%). . . .	469	306	409	—	—	—	—	—	—	—
Total Assets (Millions $). . .	302	173	179	—	—	—	—	—	—	—

PORTFOLIO (as of 6/30/96)

Portfolio Manager: John Carlson - 1995

Investm't Category: International Bond
- ✔ Domestic
- ✔ Foreign
- Asset Allocation
- Index
- Sector
- State Specific

Investment Style

Large-Cap Growth	Large-Cap Value
Mid-Cap Growth	Mid-Cap Value
Small-Cap Growth	Small-Cap Value

Portfolio

5.0% cash	8.9% corp bonds
0.0% stocks	83.8% gov't bonds
0.0% preferred	0.0% muni bonds
0.8% conv't/warrants	1.1% other

SHAREHOLDER INFORMATION

Minimum Investment
Initial: $2,500   Subsequent: $250

Minimum IRA Investment
Initial: $500   Subsequent: $250

Maximum Fees
Load: 1.00% redemption   12b-1: none
Other: redemption fee applies for 6 months; *f*

Distributions
Income: monthly   Capital Gains: Feb, Dec

Exchange Options
Number Per Year: 4   Fee: none
Telephone: yes (money market fund available)

Services
IRA, pension, auto exchange, auto invest, auto withdraw

Fidelity New Millennium

(FMILX)

Aggressive Growth

82 Devonshire St.
Mail Zone F9A
Boston, MA 02109
800-544-6666, 801-534-1910
www.fidelity.com

this fund is closed to new investors

PERFORMANCE

fund inception date: 12/28/92

	3yr Annual	5yr Annual	10yr Annual	Bull	Bear
Return (%)	23.6	na	na	104.0	-9.2
Differ from Category (+/-)	7.8 high	na	na	32.9 high	1.4 abv av

Total Risk	Standard Deviation	Category Risk	Risk Index	Beta
high	14.0%	av	1.0	0.99

	1996	1995	1994	1993	1992	1991	1990	1989	1988	1987
Return (%)	23.1	52.1	0.8	24.6	—	—	—	—	—	—
Differ from Category (+/-)	4.0	17.8	0.8	5.3	—	—	—	—	—	—
Return, Tax-Adjusted (%)	22.1	48.8	0.1	23.8	—	—	—	—	—	—

PER SHARE DATA

	1996	1995	1994	1993	1992	1991	1990	1989	1988	1987
Dividends, Net Income ($)	0.00	0.00	0.00	0.01	—	—	—	—	—	—
Distrib'ns, Cap Gain ($)	0.60	1.40	0.28	0.25	—	—	—	—	—	—
Net Asset Value ($)	20.25	16.96	12.11	12.30	—	—	—	—	—	—
Expense Ratio (%)	na	1.20	1.29	1.32	—	—	—	—	—	—
Yield (%)	0.00	0.00	0.00	0.07	—	—	—	—	—	—
Portfolio Turnover (%)	na	176	199	204	—	—	—	—	—	—
Total Assets (Millions $)	1,266	594	319	276	—	—	—	—	—	—

PORTFOLIO (as of 9/30/96)

Portfolio Manager: Neal Miller - 1992

Investm't Category: Aggressive Growth
✔ Domestic   Index
✔ Foreign   Sector
  Asset Allocation   State Specific

Investment Style
  Large-Cap Growth   Large-Cap Value
✔ Mid-Cap Growth   Mid-Cap Value
✔ Small-Cap Growth   Small-Cap Value

Portfolio
  7.2% cash   0.0% corp bonds
  92.8% stocks   0.0% gov't bonds
  0.0% preferred   0.0% muni bonds
  0.0% conv't/warrants 0.0% other

SHAREHOLDER INFORMATION

Minimum Investment
Initial: $2,500   Subsequent: $250

Minimum IRA Investment
Initial: $500   Subsequent: $250

Maximum Fees
Load: 3.00% front   12b-1: none
Other: *f*

Distributions
Income: Jan, Dec   Capital Gains: Jan, Dec

Exchange Options
Number Per Year: 4   Fee: none
Telephone: yes (money market fund available)

Services
IRA, pension, auto exchange, auto invest, auto withdraw

Fidelity OTC Port (FOCPX)

Aggressive Growth

82 Devonshire St.
Mail Zone F9A
Boston, MA 02109
800-544-6666, 801-534-1910
www.fidelity.com

PERFORMANCE

fund inception date: 12/31/84

	3yr Annual	5yr Annual	10yr Annual	Bull	Bear
Return (%)	18.5	15.6	16.9	83.1	-11.6
Differ from Category (+/-)	2.7 abv av	0.3 av	1.9 abv av	12.0 abv av	-1.0 av

Total Risk	Standard Deviation	Category Risk	Risk Index	Beta
high	12.3%	blw av	0.9	0.93

	1996	1995	1994	1993	1992	1991	1990	1989	1988	1987
Return (%)	23.7	38.2	-2.7	8.3	14.9	49.1	-4.8	30.3	22.8	1.5
Differ from Category (+/-)	4.6	3.9	-2.7	-11.0	3.2	-3.0	0.6	1.9	6.4	3.9
Return, Tax-Adjusted (%)	19.6	36.0	-3.1	4.4	11.9	45.0	-5.7	25.3	21.9	-1.9

PER SHARE DATA

	1996	1995	1994	1993	1992	1991	1990	1989	1988	1987
Dividends, Net Income ($)	0.08	0.02	0.21	0.10	0.25	0.12	0.05	0.51	0.30	0.02
Distrib'ns, Cap Gain ($)	4.32	1.80	0.00	3.42	2.24	2.50	0.57	2.41	0.00	1.93
Net Asset Value ($)	32.71	30.33	23.27	24.14	25.65	24.78	18.54	20.14	17.68	14.64
Expense Ratio (%)	0.82	0.81	0.88	1.08	1.17	1.29	1.35	1.32	1.42	1.36
Yield (%)	0.21	0.06	0.90	0.36	0.89	0.43	0.26	2.26	1.69	0.12
Portfolio Turnover (%)	133	62	222	213	245	198	212	118	193	191
Total Assets (Millions $)	3,378	2,350	1,381	1,343	1,256	1,070	618	750	720	764

PORTFOLIO (as of 9/30/96)

Portfolio Manager: Charles Mangum - 1996

Investm't Category: Aggressive Growth
- ✔ Domestic
- Foreign
- Asset Allocation
- Index
- Sector
- State Specific

Investment Style
- Large-Cap Growth
- ✔ Mid-Cap Growth
- Small-Cap Growth
- Large-Cap Value
- Mid-Cap Value
- Small-Cap Value

Portfolio
5.5% cash	0.0% corp bonds
93.0% stocks	0.0% gov't bonds
0.0% preferred	0.0% muni bonds
1.5% conv't/warrants	0.0% other

SHAREHOLDER INFORMATION

Minimum Investment
Initial: $2,500   Subsequent: $250

Minimum IRA Investment
Initial: $500   Subsequent: $250

Maximum Fees
Load: 3.00% front   12b-1: none
Other: *f*

Distributions
Income: Sep, Dec   Capital Gains: Dec

Exchange Options
Number Per Year: 4   Fee: none
Telephone: yes (money market fund available)

Services
IRA, pension, auto exchange, auto invest, auto withdraw

Fidelity Ohio Muni Income

(FOHFX)

Tax-Exempt Bond

82 Devonshire St.
Mail Zone F9A
Boston, MA 02109
800-544-6666, 801-534-1910
www.fidelity.com

PERFORMANCE

fund inception date: 11/15/85

	3yr Annual	5yr Annual	10yr Annual	Bull	Bear
Return (%)	4.6	6.9	7.3	19.8	-5.6
Differ from Category (+/-)	0.4 abv av	0.5 av	0.6 abv av	1.4 abv av	-0.2 av

Total Risk	Standard Deviation	Category Risk	Risk Index	Avg Mat
blw av	5.4%	av	1.0	13.6 yrs

	1996	1995	1994	1993	1992	1991	1990	1989	1988	1987
Return (%)	4.2	16.3	-5.6	12.5	8.6	11.4	7.5	9.9	12.9	-2.4
Differ from Category (+/-)	0.5	1.1	-0.3	0.7	0.3	0.0	1.1	0.9	2.9	-1.0
Return, Tax-Adjusted (%)	4.0	16.3	-6.1	11.8	8.6	11.4	7.5	9.9	12.9	-2.4

PER SHARE DATA

	1996	1995	1994	1993	1992	1991	1990	1989	1988	1987
Dividends, Net Income ($)	0.56	0.61	0.65	0.69	0.71	0.71	0.72	0.72	0.72	0.74
Distrib'ns, Cap Gain ($)	0.07	0.00	0.19	0.25	0.00	0.00	0.00	0.00	0.00	0.00
Net Asset Value ($)	11.43	11.59	10.52	12.02	11.55	11.32	10.84	10.79	10.50	9.97
Expense Ratio (%)	na	0.58	0.57	0.57	0.61	0.64	0.66	0.71	0.73	0.79
Yield (%)	4.86	5.26	6.06	5.62	6.14	6.27	6.64	6.67	6.85	7.42
Portfolio Turnover (%)	na	48	22	41	20	11	12	22	23	36
Total Assets (Millions $)	386	403	349	456	384	326	241	199	152	116

PORTFOLIO (as of 9/30/96)

Portfolio Manager: Steven Harvey - 1994

Investm't Category: Tax-Exempt Bond

✔ Domestic   Index
   Foreign   Sector
   Asset Allocation   ✔ State Specific

Investment Style
   Large-Cap Growth   Large-Cap Value
   Mid-Cap Growth   Mid-Cap Value
   Small-Cap Growth   Small-Cap Value

Portfolio
2.0% cash	0.0% corp bonds
0.0% stocks	0.0% gov't bonds
0.0% preferred	98.0% muni bonds
0.0% conv't/warrants	0.0% other

SHAREHOLDER INFORMATION

Minimum Investment
Initial: $2,500   Subsequent: $250

Minimum IRA Investment
Initial: na   Subsequent: na

Maximum Fees
Load: none   12b-1: none
Other: *f*

Distributions
Income: monthly   Capital Gains: Feb, Dec

Exchange Options
Number Per Year: 4   Fee: none
Telephone: yes (money market fund available)

Services
auto exchange, auto invest, auto withdraw

Fidelity Overseas
(FOSFX)
International Stock

82 Devonshire St.
Mail Zone F9A
Boston, MA 02109
800-544-6666, 801-534-1910
www.fidelity.com

PERFORMANCE   fund inception date: 12/4/84

	3yr Annual	5yr Annual	10yr Annual	Bull	Bear
Return (%)	7.6	9.1	8.9	21.5	-4.1
Differ from Category (+/-)	1.3 av	-0.9 blw av	0.3 av	-2.8 blw av	3.1 abv av

Total Risk	Standard Deviation	Category Risk	Risk Index	Beta
av	9.1%	low	0.9	0.63

	1996	1995	1994	1993	1992	1991	1990	1989	1988	1987
Return (%).............	13.0	9.0	1.2	40.0	-11.5	8.6	-6.7	16.9	8.2	18.3
Differ from Category (+/-).	-1.8	-0.1	4.3	0.4	-7.7	-4.6	3.4	-5.7	-6.7	6.1
Return, Tax-Adjusted (%)..	10.9	8.1	0.7	39.1	-14.5	6.5	-8.6	15.2	7.2	9.1

PER SHARE DATA

	1996	1995	1994	1993	1992	1991	1990	1989	1988	1987
Dividends, Net Income ($).	0.37	0.34	0.00	0.43	0.37	0.44	0.68	0.28	0.57	0.00
Distrib'ns, Cap Gain ($) ...	1.63	0.35	0.47	0.00	2.10	1.15	0.86	1.06	0.00	9.41
Net Asset Value ($)	30.84	29.07	27.30	27.43	19.90	25.26	24.79	28.20	25.30	23.92
Expense Ratio (%)........	1.12	1.05	1.24	1.27	1.52	1.53	1.26	1.06	1.38	1.71
Yield (%)	1.13	1.15	0.00	1.56	1.68	1.66	2.65	0.95	2.25	0.00
Portfolio Turnover (%).....	82	49	49	64	122	132	96	100	115	122
Total Assets (Millions $).	3,252	2,409	2,194	1,519	780	958	974	1,010	1,114	1,363

PORTFOLIO (as of 9/30/96)

Portfolio Manager: Rick Mace - 1996

Investm't Category: International Stock

Domestic	Index
✔ Foreign	Sector
Asset Allocation	State Specific

Investment Style

Large-Cap Growth	Large-Cap Value
Mid-Cap Growth	Mid-Cap Value
Small-Cap Growth	Small-Cap Value

Portfolio

10.8% cash	0.0% corp bonds
88.8% stocks	0.0% gov't bonds
0.0% preferred	0.0% muni bonds
0.4% conv't/warrants	0.0% other

SHAREHOLDER INFORMATION

Minimum Investment
Initial: $2,500   Subsequent: $250

Minimum IRA Investment
Initial: $500   Subsequent: $250

Maximum Fees
Load: none   12b-1: none
Other: *f*

Distributions
Income: Dec   Capital Gains: Dec

Exchange Options
Number Per Year: 4   Fee: none
Telephone: yes (money market fund available)

Services
IRA, pension, auto exchange, auto invest, auto withdraw

Fidelity Pacific Basin

(FPBFX)

International Stock

82 Devonshire St.
Mail Zone F9A
Boston, MA 02109
800-544-6666, 801-534-1910
www.fidelity.com

PERFORMANCE

fund inception date: 10/1/86

	3yr Annual	5yr Annual	10yr Annual	Bull	Bear
Return (%)	-4.0	6.0	5.4	-12.3	-1.6
Differ from Category (+/-)	-10.3 low	-4.0 low	-3.2 low	-36.6 low	5.6 high

Total Risk	Standard Deviation	Category Risk	Risk Index	Beta
high	12.8%	abv av	1.2	0.65

	1996	1995	1994	1993	1992	1991	1990	1989	1988	1987
Return (%)	-2.8	-6.2	-2.9	63.9	-7.7	12.5	-27.3	11.4	10.4	24.9
Differ from Category (+/-)	-17.6	-15.3	0.2	24.3	-3.9	-0.7	-17.2	-11.2	-4.5	12.7
Return, Tax-Adjusted (%)	-3.1	-6.2	-6.0	62.8	-8.1	12.5	-27.7	10.1	10.0	24.3

PER SHARE DATA

	1996	1995	1994	1993	1992	1991	1990	1989	1988	1987
Dividends, Net Income ($)	0.08	0.00	0.02	0.13	0.11	0.00	0.16	0.01	0.09	0.15
Distrib'ns, Cap Gain ($)	0.00	0.00	2.02	0.27	0.00	0.00	0.00	0.63	0.02	0.00
Net Asset Value ($)	14.70	15.20	16.19	18.80	11.74	12.83	11.40	15.87	14.82	13.52
Expense Ratio (%)	1.24	1.32	1.54	1.59	1.84	1.88	1.59	1.40	1.80	2.10
Yield (%)	0.54	0.00	0.10	0.68	0.93	0.00	1.40	0.06	0.60	1.10
Portfolio Turnover (%)	85	65	88	77	105	143	118	133	228	324
Total Assets (Millions $)	500	469	475	526	113	93	71	112	149	168

PORTFOLIO (as of 9/30/96)

Portfolio Manager: Shigeki Makino - 1996

Investm't Category: International Stock

Domestic	Index
✔ Foreign	Sector
Asset Allocation	State Specific

Investment Style

Large-Cap Growth	Large-Cap Value
Mid-Cap Growth	Mid-Cap Value
Small-Cap Growth	Small-Cap Value

Portfolio

1.0% cash	0.0% corp bonds
97.7% stocks	0.0% gov't bonds
0.0% preferred	0.0% muni bonds
1.3% conv't/warrants	0.0% other

SHAREHOLDER INFORMATION

Minimum Investment

Initial: $2,500   Subsequent: $250

Minimum IRA Investment

Initial: $500   Subsequent: $250

Maximum Fees

Load: 3.00% front   12b-1: none
Other: 1.00% redemption fee (90 days); *f*

Distributions

Income: Dec   Capital Gains: Dec

Exchange Options

Number Per Year: 4   Fee: none
Telephone: yes (money market fund available)

Services

IRA, pension, auto exchange, auto invest, auto withdraw

Fidelity Puritan

(FPURX)

Balanced

82 Devonshire St.
Mail Zone F9A
Boston, MA 02109
800-544-6666, 801-534-1910
www.fidelity.com

fund inception date: 4/16/47

	3yr Annual	5yr Annual	10yr Annual	Bull	Bear
Return (%)	12.4	14.8	12.5	41.7	-3.9
Differ from Category (+/-)	0.7 abv av	3.4 high	1.7 high	-3.4 blw av	1.8 high

Total Risk	Standard Deviation	Category Risk	Risk Index	Beta
av	7.2%	abv av	1.1	0.67

	1996	1995	1994	1993	1992	1991	1990	1989	1988	1987
Return (%).............	15.1	21.4	1.7	21.4	15.4	24.4	-6.4	19.5	18.8	-1.8
Differ from Category (+/-)..	0.9	-3.2	3.3	7.0	6.5	0.3	-5.5	1.4	6.6	-4.5
Return, Tax-Adjusted (%)..	11.1	19.2	-1.0	16.8	11.7	21.7	-8.8	15.2	15.6	-6.3

PER SHARE DATA

	1996	1995	1994	1993	1992	1991	1990	1989	1988	1987
Dividends, Net Income ($)	0.62	0.49	0.54	0.72	0.82	0.80	0.80	0.99	0.91	0.94
Distrib'ns, Cap Gain ($) ...	1.54	0.44	0.71	1.36	0.69	0.00	0.00	0.54	0.00	0.77
Net Asset Value ($)	17.24	17.01	14.81	15.75	14.74	14.14	12.05	13.70	12.76	11.53
Expense Ratio (%)........	0.72	0.77	0.79	0.74	0.64	0.66	0.65	0.64	0.72	0.70
Yield (%)	3.30	2.80	3.47	4.20	5.31	5.65	6.63	6.95	7.13	7.64
Portfolio Turnover (%)....	139	76	74	76	102	108	58	77	88	63
Total Assets (Millions $) .	18,868	15,628	11,769	8,988	5,912	5,108	4,356	4,861	4,295	3,959

PORTFOLIO (as of 9/30/96)

Portfolio Manager: Bettina Doulton, Kevin
Grant - 1996

Investm't Category: Balanced

✔ Domestic	Index
✔ Foreign	Sector
Asset Allocation	State Specific

Investment Style

Large-Cap Growth	Large-Cap Value
Mid-Cap Growth	Mid-Cap Value
Small-Cap Growth	Small-Cap Value

Portfolio

7.2% cash	32.4% corp bonds
59.8% stocks	0.0% gov't bonds
0.0% preferred	0.0% muni bonds
0.6% conv't/warrants	0.0% other

SHAREHOLDER INFORMATION

Minimum Investment

Initial: $2,500   Subsequent: $250

Minimum IRA Investment

Initial: $500   Subsequent: $250

Maximum Fees

Load: none   12b-1: none
Other: *f*

Distributions

Income: quarterly   Capital Gains: Sep, Dec

Exchange Options

Number Per Year: 4   Fee: none
Telephone: yes (money market fund available)

Services

IRA, pension, auto exchange, auto invest, auto
withdraw

Fidelity Real Estate Investment Port (FRESX)

Growth & Income

82 Devonshire St.
Mail Zone F9A
Boston, MA 02109
800-544-6666, 801-534-1910
www.fidelity.com

PERFORMANCE

fund inception date: 11/14/86

	3yr Annual	5yr Annual	10yr Annual	Bull	Bear
Return (%)	15.5	15.6	11.8	50.4	1.6
Differ from Category (+/-)	0.2 blw av	1.7 abv av	-0.9 blw av	-9.4 blw av	8.0 high

Total Risk	Standard Deviation	Category Risk	Risk Index	Beta
abv av	11.5%	high	1.2	0.24

	1996	1995	1994	1993	1992	1991	1990	1989	1988	1987
Return (%).	36.2	10.9	2.0	12.5	19.5	39.1	-8.7	13.7	10.3	-7.7
Differ from Category (+/-).	16.5	-19.2	3.3	-1.3	8.8	10.0	-2.8	-9.8	-6.5	-7.9
Return, Tax-Adjusted (%). .	34.1	8.7	0.1	10.6	17.9	36.7	-10.9	11.3	7.5	-10.1

PER SHARE DATA

	1996	1995	1994	1993	1992	1991	1990	1989	1988	1987
Dividends, Net Income ($).	0.72	0.71	0.63	0.60	0.43	0.49	0.51	0.54	0.59	0.60
Distrib'ns, Cap Gain ($) . . .	0.00	0.00	0.00	0.00	0.00	0.00	0.00	0.00	0.00	0.00
Net Asset Value ($)	18.03	13.88	13.20	13.57	12.60	10.94	8.26	9.59	8.92	8.62
Expense Ratio (%).	0.95	1.03	1.13	1.16	1.24	1.47	1.39	1.28	1.50	1.50
Yield (%)	3.99	5.11	4.77	4.42	3.41	4.47	6.17	5.63	6.61	6.96
Portfolio Turnover (%). . . .	85	75	110	82	84	49	70	42	89	6
Total Assets (Millions $).	1,366	708	555	424	150	62	39	53	64	67

PORTFOLIO (as of 9/30/96)

Portfolio Manager: Barry Greenfield - 1986

Investm't Category: Growth & Income
- ✔ Domestic
- Foreign
- Asset Allocation
- Index
- ✔ Sector
- State Specific

Investment Style
- Large-Cap Growth
- Mid-Cap Growth
- Small-Cap Growth
- Large-Cap Value
- Mid-Cap Value
- ✔ Small-Cap Value

Portfolio
- 6.5% cash
- 93.4% stocks
- 0.0% preferred
- 0.1% conv't/warrants
- 0.0% corp bonds
- 0.0% gov't bonds
- 0.0% muni bonds
- 0.0% other

SHAREHOLDER INFORMATION

Minimum Investment
Initial: $2,500   Subsequent: $250

Minimum IRA Investment
Initial: $500   Subsequent: $250

Maximum Fees
Load: 0.75% redemption   12b-1: none
Other: redemption fee applies for 3 months; *f*

Distributions
Income: quarterly   Capital Gains: Mar, Dec

Exchange Options
Number Per Year: 4   Fee: none
Telephone: yes (money market fund available)

Services
IRA, pension, auto exchange, auto invest, auto withdraw

Fidelity Retirement Growth (FDFFX)

Growth

82 Devonshire St.
Mail Zone F9A
Boston, MA 02109
800-544-6666, 801-534-1910
www.fidelity.com

PERFORMANCE

fund inception date: 3/24/83

	3yr Annual	5yr Annual	10yr Annual	Bull	Bear
Return (%)	10.4	12.7	14.6	39.6	-6.2
Differ from Category (+/-)	-5.3 low	-1.6 blw av	0.7 abv av	-22.8 low	0.5 av

Total Risk	Standard Deviation	Category Risk	Risk Index	Beta
av	9.0%	blw av	0.9	0.83

	1996	1995	1994	1993	1992	1991	1990	1989	1988	1987
Return (%)	8.3	24.2	0.0	22.1	10.5	45.5	-10.2	30.4	15.5	9.3
Differ from Category (+/-)	-11.8	-6.1	0.3	8.1	-1.3	9.5	-4.1	4.3	-2.6	7.3
Return, Tax-Adjusted (%)	4.4	20.6	-3.1	18.7	4.7	42.7	-11.5	29.1	14.7	-3.1

PER SHARE DATA

	1996	1995	1994	1993	1992	1991	1990	1989	1988	1987
Dividends, Net Income ($)	0.26	0.35	0.22	0.14	0.16	0.20	0.11	0.38	0.21	0.37
Distrib'ns, Cap Gain ($)	2.15	1.58	1.68	1.75	3.53	1.04	0.56	0.00	0.00	6.68
Net Asset Value ($)	17.29	18.19	16.24	18.14	16.44	18.23	13.45	15.66	12.31	10.84
Expense Ratio (%)	na	0.99	1.07	1.05	1.02	0.83	0.98	0.92	1.09	0.97
Yield (%)	1.33	1.77	1.22	0.70	0.80	1.03	0.78	2.42	1.70	2.11
Portfolio Turnover (%)	na	108	72	101	138	119	127	139	156	171
Total Assets (Millions $)	4,207	4,071	3,184	2,848	2,222	1,835	1,317	1,499	1,219	1,111

PORTFOLIO (as of 9/30/96)

Portfolio Manager: Fergus Shiel - 1996

Investm't Category: Growth
- ✔ Domestic
- ✔ Foreign
- Asset Allocation
- Index
- Sector
- State Specific

Investment Style
- Large-Cap Growth
- ✔ Mid-Cap Growth
- ✔ Small-Cap Growth
- Large-Cap Value
- ✔ Mid-Cap Value
- ✔ Small-Cap Value

Portfolio
- 3.2% cash
- 96.4% stocks
- 0.0% preferred
- 0.4% conv't/warrants
- 0.0% corp bonds
- 0.0% gov't bonds
- 0.0% muni bonds
- 0.0% other

SHAREHOLDER INFORMATION

Minimum Investment
Initial: $500   Subsequent: $250

Minimum IRA Investment
Initial: $500   Subsequent: $250

Maximum Fees
Load: none   12b-1: none
Other: *f*

Distributions
Income: Jan, Dec   Capital Gains: Jan, Dec

Exchange Options
Number Per Year: 4   Fee: none
Telephone: yes (money market fund available)

Services
IRA, pension, auto exchange, auto invest, auto withdraw

Fidelity Sel Air Transportation (FSAIX)

Aggressive Growth

82 Devonshire St.
Mail Zone F9A
Boston, MA 02109
800-544-8888, 801-534-1910
www.fidelity.com

PERFORMANCE

fund inception date: 12/16/85

	3yr Annual	5yr Annual	10yr Annual	Bull	Bear
Return (%)	8.1	12.0	9.9	45.1	-16.2
Differ from Category (+/-)	-7.7 low	-3.3 blw av	-5.1 low	-26.0 low	-5.6 low

Total Risk	Standard Deviation	Category Risk	Risk Index	Beta
high	22.4%	high	1.6	1.55

	1996	1995	1994	1993	1992	1991	1990	1989	1988	1987
Return (%)	1.2	59.5	-21.8	30.8	6.5	37.0	-18.2	26.3	29.0	-20.0
Differ from Category (+/-)	-17.9	25.2	-21.8	11.5	-5.2	-15.1	-12.8	-2.1	12.6	-17.6
Return, Tax-Adjusted (%)	0.8	58.4	-23.6	30.2	5.7	36.2	-18.2	24.6	29.0	-22.8

PER SHARE DATA

	1996	1995	1994	1993	1992	1991	1990	1989	1988	1987
Dividends, Net Income ($)	0.00	0.00	0.00	0.00	0.00	0.00	0.00	0.00	0.00	0.02
Distrib'ns, Cap Gain ($)	0.27	0.46	1.09	0.27	0.36	0.25	0.00	0.56	0.00	1.04
Net Asset Value ($)	19.41	19.40	12.43	17.09	13.27	12.81	9.54	11.66	9.68	7.50
Expense Ratio (%)	1.41	2.50	2.31	2.48	2.51	2.48	2.55	2.52	2.62	1.58
Yield (%)	0.00	0.00	0.00	0.00	0.00	0.00	0.00	0.00	0.00	0.23
Portfolio Turnover (%)	504	200	171	96	261	106	143	115	340	611
Total Assets (Millions $)	131	94	7	15	10	5	3	5	5	2

PORTFOLIO (as of 9/30/96)

Portfolio Manager: Kevin Richardson II - 1996

Investm't Category: Aggressive Growth
- ✔ Domestic
- ✔ Foreign
- Asset Allocation
- Index
- ✔ Sector
- State Specific

Investment Style
- Large-Cap Growth
- Mid-Cap Growth
- Small-Cap Growth
- Large-Cap Value
- ✔ Mid-Cap Value
- Small-Cap Value

Portfolio
11.3% cash	0.0% corp bonds
88.7% stocks	0.0% gov't bonds
0.0% preferred	0.0% muni bonds
0.0% conv't/warrants	0.0% other

SHAREHOLDER INFORMATION

Minimum Investment
Initial: $2,500   Subsequent: $250

Minimum IRA Investment
Initial: $500   Subsequent: $250

Maximum Fees
Load: 3.00% front   12b-1: none
Other: 0.75% fee (less than 30 days), *ff*

Distributions
Income: Apr, Dec   Capital Gains: Apr, Dec

Exchange Options
Number Per Year: no limit   Fee: $7.50
Telephone: yes (money market fund available)

Services
IRA, pension, auto exchange, auto invest, auto withdraw

Fidelity Sel American Gold (FSAGX)

Gold

82 Devonshire St.
Mail Zone F9A
Boston, MA 02109
800-544-8888, 801-534-1910
www.fidelity.com

PERFORMANCE

fund inception date: 12/16/85

	3yr Annual	5yr Annual	10yr Annual	Bull	Bear
Return (%)	4.0	14.3	8.5	25.9	-10.6
Differ from Category (+/-)	3.7 abv av	4.7 abv av	4.2 high	11.0 abv av	-0.4 av

Total Risk	Standard Deviation	Category Risk	Risk Index	Beta
high	25.0%	av	1.0	0.62

	1996	1995	1994	1993	1992	1991	1990	1989	1988	1987
Return (%)	19.9	11.2	-15.5	78.6	-3.1	-6.2	-17.2	22.0	-12.5	40.5
Differ from Category (+/-)	8.7	6.2	-3.4	-9.2	12.2	-1.6	5.1	-2.4	6.6	8.3
Return, Tax-Adjusted (%)	19.2	11.2	-15.5	78.6	-3.1	-6.2	-17.2	22.0	-12.5	39.8

PER SHARE DATA

	1996	1995	1994	1993	1992	1991	1990	1989	1988	1987
Dividends, Net Income ($)	0.00	0.00	0.00	0.00	0.00	0.00	0.00	0.00	0.00	0.06
Distrib'ns, Cap Gain ($)	0.50	0.00	0.00	0.00	0.00	0.00	0.00	0.00	0.00	0.18
Net Asset Value ($)	26.04	22.14	19.91	23.55	13.18	13.60	14.49	17.50	14.34	16.38
Expense Ratio (%)	1.39	1.41	1.49	1.59	1.75	1.75	1.85	2.03	2.33	1.21
Yield (%)	0.00	0.00	0.00	0.00	0.00	0.00	0.00	0.00	0.00	0.36
Portfolio Turnover (%)	56	34	39	30	40	38	68	56	89	78
Total Assets (Millions $)	364	313	314	365	155	153	206	259	191	269

PORTFOLIO (as of 3/31/96)

Portfolio Manager: Lawrence Rakers - 1995

Investm't Category: Gold

✔ Domestic
✔ Foreign
  Asset Allocation

  Index
✔ Sector
  State Specific

Investment Style

Large-Cap Growth   Large-Cap Value
Mid-Cap Growth   Mid-Cap Value
Small-Cap Growth   Small-Cap Value

Portfolio

7.9% cash   0.0% corp bonds
91.6% stocks   0.0% gov't bonds
0.4% preferred   0.0% muni bonds
0.1% conv't/warrants 0.0% other

SHAREHOLDER INFORMATION

Minimum Investment
Initial: $2,500   Subsequent: $250

Minimum IRA Investment
Initial: $500   Subsequent: $250

Maximum Fees
Load: 3.00% front   12b-1: none
Other: 0.75% fee (less than 30 days), *ff*

Distributions
Income: Apr, Dec   Capital Gains: Apr, Dec

Exchange Options
Number Per Year: no limit   Fee: $7.50
Telephone: yes (money market fund available)

Services
IRA, pension, auto exchange, auto invest, auto withdraw

Fidelity Sel Automotive

(FSAVX)

Aggressive Growth

82 Devonshire St.
Mail Zone F9A
Boston, MA 02109
800-544-8888, 801-534-1910
www.fidelity.com

PERFORMANCE

fund inception date: 6/30/86

	3yr Annual	5yr Annual	10yr Annual	Bull	Bear
Return (%)	4.7	17.0	14.1	26.7	-14.3
Differ from Category (+/-)	-11.1 low	1.7 abv av	-0.9 blw av	-44.4 low	-3.7 blw av

Total Risk	Standard Deviation	Category Risk	Risk Index	Beta
high	12.3%	blw av	0.9	0.85

	1996	1995	1994	1993	1992	1991	1990	1989	1988	1987
Return (%)	16.0	13.4	-12.8	35.3	41.5	37.3	-6.8	4.1	20.0	6.5
Differ from Category (+/-)	-3.1	-20.9	-12.8	16.0	29.8	-14.8	-1.4	-24.3	3.6	8.9
Return, Tax-Adjusted (%)	14.7	13.4	-15.5	33.3	40.6	35.4	-7.5	2.7	20.0	4.9

PER SHARE DATA

	1996	1995	1994	1993	1992	1991	1990	1989	1988	1987
Dividends, Net Income ($)	0.17	0.00	0.05	0.05	0.06	0.00	0.18	0.41	0.00	0.04
Distrib'ns, Cap Gain ($)	0.75	0.00	2.25	1.26	0.36	0.70	0.00	0.00	0.00	0.46
Net Asset Value ($)	24.55	21.96	19.36	24.91	19.49	14.07	10.80	11.74	11.67	9.72
Expense Ratio (%)	1.80	1.80	1.68	1.57	2.48	2.25	2.42	2.63	2.49	1.63
Yield (%)	0.67	0.00	0.23	0.19	0.30	0.00	1.66	3.49	0.00	0.39
Portfolio Turnover (%)	61	63	64	140	29	219	121	149	311	284
Total Assets (Millions $)	69	61	64	197	78	2	0	0	2	1

PORTFOLIO (as of 9/30/96)

Portfolio Manager: Douglas B. Chase - 1996

Investm't Category: Aggressive Growth
✔ Domestic   Index
✔ Foreign   ✔ Sector
   Asset Allocation   State Specific

Investment Style
   Large-Cap Growth   Large-Cap Value
   Mid-Cap Growth   Mid-Cap Value
   Small-Cap Growth ✔ Small-Cap Value

Portfolio
43.3% cash   0.0% corp bonds
56.7% stocks   0.0% gov't bonds
0.0% preferred   0.0% muni bonds
0.0% conv't/warrants 0.0% other

SHAREHOLDER INFORMATION

Minimum Investment
Initial: $2,500   Subsequent: $250

Minimum IRA Investment
Initial: $500   Subsequent: $250

Maximum Fees
Load: 3.00% front   12b-1: none
Other: 0.75% fee (less than 30 days), *ff*

Distributions
Income: Apr, Dec   Capital Gains: Apr, Dec

Exchange Options
Number Per Year: no limit   Fee: $7.50
Telephone: yes (money market fund available)

Services
IRA, pension, auto exchange, auto invest, auto
withdraw

Fidelity Sel Biotechnology

(FBIOX)

Aggressive Growth

82 Devonshire St.
Mail Zone F9A
Boston, MA 02109
800-544-8888, 801-534-1910
www.fidelity.com

	3yr Annual	5yr Annual	10yr Annual	Bull	Bear
Return (%)	8.8	3.0	17.0	60.1	-22.3
Differ from Category (+/-)	-7.0 low	-12.3 low	2.0 abv av	-11.0 av	-11.7 low

Total Risk	Standard Deviation	Category Risk	Risk Index	Beta
high	15.3%	abv av	1.1	0.97

	1996	1995	1994	1993	1992	1991	1990	1989	1988	1987
Return (%)	5.5	49.1	-18.2	0.7	-10.4	99.0	44.3	43.9	4.1	-3.4
Differ from Category (+/-)	-13.6	14.8	-18.2	-18.6	-22.1	46.9	49.7	15.5	-12.3	-1.0
Return, Tax-Adjusted (%)	2.2	48.9	-18.2	0.7	-13.4	95.4	42.9	43.2	4.1	-4.2

PER SHARE DATA

	1996	1995	1994	1993	1992	1991	1990	1989	1988	1987
Dividends, Net Income ($)	0.03	0.07	0.00	0.00	0.00	0.02	0.00	0.00	0.00	0.00
Distrib'ns, Cap Gain ($)	4.05	0.00	0.00	0.00	3.89	2.52	0.67	0.24	0.00	0.28
Net Asset Value ($)	32.51	34.83	23.41	28.61	28.41	36.42	19.94	14.30	10.10	9.70
Expense Ratio (%)	1.43	1.59	1.61	1.50	1.50	1.63	2.07	2.21	2.51	1.38
Yield (%)	0.08	0.20	0.00	0.00	0.00	0.05	0.00	0.00	0.00	0.00
Portfolio Turnover (%)	67	77	51	79	160	166	290	80	205	431
Total Assets (Millions $)	568	846	396	557	799	1,146	223	69	39	57

PORTFOLIO (as of 9/30/96)

Portfolio Manager: Karen Firestone - 1992

Investm't Category: Aggressive Growth

✔ Domestic	Index
✔ Foreign	✔ Sector
Asset Allocation	State Specific

Investment Style

✔ Large-Cap Growth	Large-Cap Value
Mid-Cap Growth	Mid-Cap Value
Small-Cap Growth	Small-Cap Value

Portfolio

9.1% cash	0.0% corp bonds
90.9% stocks	0.0% gov't bonds
0.0% preferred	0.0% muni bonds
0.0% conv't/warrants	0.0% other

SHAREHOLDER INFORMATION

Minimum Investment
Initial: $2,500   Subsequent: $250

Minimum IRA Investment
Initial: $500   Subsequent: $250

Maximum Fees
Load: 3.00% front   12b-1: none
Other: 0.75% fee (less than 30 days), *ff*

Distributions
Income: Apr, Dec   Capital Gains: Apr, Dec

Exchange Options
Number Per Year: no limit   Fee: $7.50
Telephone: yes (money market fund available)

Services
IRA, pension, auto exchange, auto invest, auto withdraw

Fidelity Sel Brokerage & Investment (FSLBX)

Aggressive Growth

82 Devonshire St.
Mail Zone F9A
Boston, MA 02109
800-544-8888, 801-534-1910
www.fidelity.com

PERFORMANCE

fund inception date: 7/29/85

	3yr Annual	5yr Annual	10yr Annual	Bull	Bear
Return (%)	12.6	17.5	11.3	57.1	-11.0
Differ from Category (+/-)	-3.2 blw av	2.2 abv av	-3.7 blw av	-14.0 blw av	-0.4 av

Total Risk	Standard Deviation	Category Risk	Risk Index	Beta
high	15.2%	abv av	1.1	1.17

	1996	1995	1994	1993	1992	1991	1990	1989	1988	1987
Return (%)	39.6	23.5	-17.3	49.3	5.1	82.2	-16.2	14.0	18.5	-36.9
Differ from Category (+/-)	20.5	-10.8	-17.3	30.0	-6.6	30.1	-10.8	-14.4	2.1	-34.5
Return, Tax-Adjusted (%)	38.4	20.7	-17.3	46.1	5.1	82.1	-16.7	13.1	17.9	-39.7

PER SHARE DATA

	1996	1995	1994	1993	1992	1991	1990	1989	1988	1987
Dividends, Net Income ($)	0.06	0.04	0.00	0.01	0.00	0.01	0.09	0.16	0.09	0.03
Distrib'ns, Cap Gain ($)	0.65	1.44	0.00	1.47	0.00	0.00	0.00	0.00	0.00	1.14
Net Asset Value ($)	23.17	17.18	15.14	18.30	13.34	12.69	6.97	8.42	7.52	6.42
Expense Ratio (%)	1.61	2.54	1.77	2.21	2.17	2.50	2.50	2.54	2.58	1.67
Yield (%)	0.25	0.21	0.00	0.05	0.00	0.07	1.29	1.90	1.19	0.39
Portfolio Turnover (%)	166	139	295	111	254	62	142	185	447	603
Total Assets (Millions $)	61	26	21	94	20	29	2	2	3	4

PORTFOLIO (as of 9/30/96)

Portfolio Manager: Louis Salemy - 1995

Investm't Category: Aggressive Growth
✔ Domestic   Index
✔ Foreign   ✔ Sector
   Asset Allocation   State Specific

Investment Style
Large-Cap Growth   Large-Cap Value
Mid-Cap Growth   ✔ Mid-Cap Value
Small-Cap Growth   Small-Cap Value

Portfolio
5.0% cash   0.0% corp bonds
95.0% stocks   0.0% gov't bonds
0.0% preferred   0.0% muni bonds
0.0% conv't/warrants 0.0% other

SHAREHOLDER INFORMATION

Minimum Investment
Initial: $2,500   Subsequent: $250

Minimum IRA Investment
Initial: $500   Subsequent: $250

Maximum Fees
Load: 3.00% front   12b-1: none
Other: 0.75% fee (less than 30 days), *ff*

Distributions
Income: Apr, Dec   Capital Gains: Apr, Dec

Exchange Options
Number Per Year: no limit   Fee: $7.50
Telephone: yes (money market fund available)

Services
IRA, pension, auto exchange, auto invest, auto withdraw

Fidelity Sel Chemicals
(FSCHX)
Growth

82 Devonshire St.
Mail Zone F9A
Boston, MA 02109
800-544-8888, 801-534-1910
www.fidelity.com

PERFORMANCE

fund inception date: 7/29/85

	3yr Annual	5yr Annual	10yr Annual	Bull	Bear
Return (%)	19.2	15.7	16.2	53.0	2.6
Differ from Category (+/-)	3.5 high	1.4 abv av	2.3 high	-9.4 blw av	9.3 high

Total Risk	Standard Deviation	Category Risk	Risk Index	Beta
abv av	11.7%	abv av	1.1	0.86

	1996	1995	1994	1993	1992	1991	1990	1989	1988	1987
Return (%).	21.5	21.4	14.7	12.7	8.9	38.6	-4.2	17.3	20.9	14.8
Differ from Category (+/-) . .	1.4	-8.9	15.0	-1.3	-2.9	2.6	1.9	-8.8	2.8	12.8
Return, Tax-Adjusted (%). .	19.2	18.5	13.8	9.4	5.3	37.3	-5.1	15.5	20.9	14.7

PER SHARE DATA

	1996	1995	1994	1993	1992	1991	1990	1989	1988	1987
Dividends, Net Income ($) .	0.12	0.08	0.22	0.23	0.31	0.18	0.10	0.16	0.00	0.00
Distrib'ns, Cap Gain ($) . . .	2.74	3.22	0.60	3.05	3.36	0.71	0.60	1.12	0.00	0.04
Net Asset Value ($)	41.53	36.55	32.91	29.42	29.16	30.20	22.49	24.14	21.70	17.94
Expense Ratio (%)	1.97	1.51	1.93	1.89	2.16	2.50	2.37	2.24	1.93	1.52
Yield (%)	0.27	0.20	0.65	0.70	0.95	0.58	0.43	0.63	0.00	0.00
Portfolio Turnover (%)	87	106	81	214	87	87	99	117	179	170
Total Assets (Millions $) . . .	85	65	167	26	34	24	17	29	79	110

PORTFOLIO (as of 9/30/96)

Portfolio Manager: John D. Avery - 1995

Investm't Category: Growth
✔ Domestic   Index
✔ Foreign   ✔ Sector
   Asset Allocation   State Specific

Investment Style
   Large-Cap Growth   ✔ Large-Cap Value
   Mid-Cap Growth   ✔ Mid-Cap Value
   Small-Cap Growth   ✔ Small-Cap Value

Portfolio
4.1% cash	0.0% corp bonds
95.9% stocks	0.0% gov't bonds
0.0% preferred	0.0% muni bonds
0.0% conv't/warrants	0.0% other

SHAREHOLDER INFORMATION

Minimum Investment
Initial: $2,500   Subsequent: $250

Minimum IRA Investment
Initial: $500   Subsequent: $250

Maximum Fees
Load: 3.00% front   12b-1: none
Other: 0.75% fee (less than 30 days), **ff**

Distributions
Income: Apr, Dec   Capital Gains: Apr, Dec

Exchange Options
Number Per Year: no limit   Fee: $7.50
Telephone: yes (money market fund available)

Services
IRA, pension, auto exchange, auto invest, auto withdraw

Fidelity Sel Computers

(FDCPX)

Aggressive Growth

82 Devonshire St.
Mail Zone F9A
Boston, MA 02109
800-544-8888, 801-534-1910
www.fidelity.com

PERFORMANCE

fund inception date: 7/29/85

	3yr Annual	5yr Annual	10yr Annual	Bull	Bear
Return (%)	33.9	30.4	18.7	140.2	-6.0
Differ from Category (+/-)	18.1 high	15.1 high	3.7 high	69.1 high	4.6 abv av

Total Risk	Standard Deviation	Category Risk	Risk Index	Beta
high	21.5%	high	1.5	1.30

	1996	1995	1994	1993	1992	1991	1990	1989	1988	1987
Return (%)	31.6	51.6	20.4	28.8	21.9	30.7	18.4	6.8	-5.1	-6.4
Differ from Category (+/-)	12.5	17.3	20.4	9.5	10.2	-21.4	23.8	-21.6	-21.5	-4.0
Return, Tax-Adjusted (%)	29.8	46.2	20.4	26.3	21.9	29.4	17.9	6.8	-5.1	-7.2

PER SHARE DATA

	1996	1995	1994	1993	1992	1991	1990	1989	1988	1987
Dividends, Net Income ($)	0.00	0.00	0.00	0.00	0.00	0.27	0.12	0.00	0.00	0.01
Distrib'ns, Cap Gain ($)	2.47	5.61	0.00	1.80	0.00	0.22	0.00	0.00	0.00	0.33
Net Asset Value ($)	48.68	38.99	29.33	24.35	20.44	16.76	13.20	11.25	10.53	11.09
Expense Ratio (%)	1.38	1.69	1.89	1.81	2.17	2.26	2.64	2.56	2.62	1.58
Yield (%)	0.00	0.00	0.00	0.00	0.00	1.59	0.90	0.00	0.00	0.08
Portfolio Turnover (%)	129	189	145	254	568	695	596	466	284	259
Total Assets (Millions $)	662	499	175	61	56	20	24	9	18	34

PORTFOLIO (as of 9/30/96)

Portfolio Manager: Jason Weiner - 1996

Investm't Category: Aggressive Growth
✔ Domestic   Index
✔ Foreign   ✔ Sector
Asset Allocation   State Specific

Investment Style
Large-Cap Growth   Large-Cap Value
✔ Mid-Cap Growth   Mid-Cap Value
✔ Small-Cap Growth Small-Cap Value

Portfolio
2.5% cash   0.0% corp bonds
97.5% stocks   0.0% gov't bonds
0.0% preferred   0.0% muni bonds
0.0% conv't/warrants 0.0% other

SHAREHOLDER INFORMATION

Minimum Investment
Initial: $2,500   Subsequent: $250

Minimum IRA Investment
Initial: $500   Subsequent: $250

Maximum Fees
Load: 3.00% front   12b-1: none
Other: 0.75% fee (less than 30 days), *ff*

Distributions
Income: Apr, Dec   Capital Gains: Apr, Dec

Exchange Options
Number Per Year: no limit   Fee: $7.50
Telephone: yes (money market fund available)

Services
IRA, pension, auto exchange, auto invest, auto withdraw

Fidelity Sel Construction & Housing (FSHOX)

Aggressive Growth

82 Devonshire St.
Mail Zone F9A
Boston, MA 02109
800-544-8888, 801-534-1910
www.fidelity.com

PERFORMANCE
fund inception date: 9/29/86

	3yr Annual	5yr Annual	10yr Annual	Bull	Bear
Return (%)	7.0	14.2	12.5	39.5	-15.0
Differ from Category (+/-)	-8.8 low	-1.1 av	-2.5 blw av	-31.6 low	-4.4 blw av

Total Risk	Standard Deviation	Category Risk	Risk Index	Beta
abv av	11.6%	blw av	0.8	0.91

	1996	1995	1994	1993	1992	1991	1990	1989	1988	1987
Return (%).............	13.2	28.7	-16.0	33.6	18.7	41.3	-9.7	16.5	29.1	-12.5
Differ from Category (+/-) .	-5.9	-5.6	-16.0	14.3	7.0	-10.8	-4.3	-11.9	12.7	-10.1
Return, Tax-Adjusted (%)..	11.6	27.1	-16.8	33.1	18.6	38.7	-13.3	12.3	28.0	-12.9

PER SHARE DATA

	1996	1995	1994	1993	1992	1991	1990	1989	1988	1987
Dividends, Net Income ($).	0.02	0.07	0.00	0.00	0.00	0.00	0.16	0.08	0.06	0.00
Distrib'ns, Cap Gain ($) ...	1.03	0.81	0.52	0.22	0.01	0.88	1.27	1.62	0.27	0.13
Net Asset Value ($)	21.09	19.65	15.95	19.59	14.84	12.51	9.55	11.89	11.65	9.28
Expense Ratio (%)........	1.40	1.74	1.66	2.02	2.50	2.48	2.41	2.56	2.70	1.46
Yield (%)	0.09	0.34	0.00	0.00	0.00	0.00	1.47	0.59	0.50	0.00
Portfolio Turnover (%)....	139	45	35	60	183	137	185	225	330	590
Total Assets (Millions $)...	126	47	17	64	22	3	1	1	1	1

PORTFOLIO (as of 9/30/96)

Portfolio Manager: Peter Saperstone - 1996

Investm't Category: Aggressive Growth
- ✔ Domestic
- ✔ Foreign
-   Asset Allocation
-   Index
- ✔ Sector
-   State Specific

Investment Style

Large-Cap Growth	Large-Cap Value
Mid-Cap Growth	✔ Mid-Cap Value
Small-Cap Growth	✔ Small-Cap Value

Portfolio

4.4% cash	0.0% corp bonds
95.6% stocks	0.0% gov't bonds
0.0% preferred	0.0% muni bonds
0.0% conv't/warrants	0.0% other

SHAREHOLDER INFORMATION

Minimum Investment
Initial: $2,500   Subsequent: $250

Minimum IRA Investment
Initial: $500   Subsequent: $250

Maximum Fees
Load: 3.00% front   12b-1: none
Other: 0.75% fee (less than 30 days), *ff*

Distributions
Income: Apr, Dec   Capital Gains: Apr, Dec

Exchange Options
Number Per Year: no limit   Fee: $7.50
Telephone: yes (money market fund available)

Services
IRA, pension, auto exchange, auto invest, auto withdraw

Fidelity Sel Consumer Industries (FSCPX)

Aggressive Growth

82 Devonshire St.
Mail Zone F9A
Boston, MA 02109
800-544-8888, 801-534-1910
www.fidelity.com

PERFORMANCE

fund inception date: 6/29/90

	3yr Annual	5yr Annual	10yr Annual	Bull	Bear
Return (%)	10.4	12.7	na	54.6	-12.1
Differ from Category (+/-)	-5.4 low	-2.6 blw av	na	-16.5 blw av	-1.5 blw av

Total Risk	Standard Deviation	Category Risk	Risk Index	Beta
high	12.9%	blw av	0.9	1.00

	1996	1995	1994	1993	1992	1991	1990	1989	1988	1987
Return (%)	13.1	28.3	-7.1	24.6	8.5	38.5	—	—	—	—
Differ from Category (+/-)	-6.0	-6.0	-7.1	5.3	-3.2	-13.6	—	—	—	—
Return, Tax-Adjusted (%)	13.1	27.8	-8.2	21.6	6.4	37.8	—	—	—	—

PER SHARE DATA

	1996	1995	1994	1993	1992	1991	1990	1989	1988	1987
Dividends, Net Income ($)	0.00	0.02	0.00	0.00	0.00	0.00	—	—	—	—
Distrib'ns, Cap Gain ($)	0.00	0.21	0.60	1.40	0.97	0.22	—	—	—	—
Net Asset Value ($)	19.62	17.34	13.70	15.41	13.51	13.38	—	—	—	—
Expense Ratio (%)	1.48	2.49	2.48	2.47	2.48	2.43	—	—	—	—
Yield (%)	0.00	0.11	0.00	0.00	0.00	0.00	—	—	—	—
Portfolio Turnover (%)	601	190	169	215	140	108	—	—	—	—
Total Assets (Millions $)	20	70	7	9	8	4	—	—	—	—

PORTFOLIO (as of 9/30/96)

Portfolio Manager: Katherine Collins - 1996

Investm't Category: Aggressive Growth
✔ Domestic   Index
✔ Foreign   ✔ Sector
  Asset Allocation   State Specific

Investment Style
✔ Large-Cap Growth   Large-Cap Value
  Mid-Cap Growth   Mid-Cap Value
  Small-Cap Growth   Small-Cap Value

Portfolio
7.7% cash	0.0% corp bonds
92.3% stocks	0.0% gov't bonds
0.0% preferred	0.0% muni bonds
0.0% conv't/warrants	0.0% other

SHAREHOLDER INFORMATION

Minimum Investment
Initial: $2,500   Subsequent: $250

Minimum IRA Investment
Initial: $500   Subsequent: $250

Maximum Fees
Load: 3.00% front   12b-1: none
Other: 0.75% fee (less than 30 days), *ff*

Distributions
Income: Apr, Dec   Capital Gains: Apr, Dec

Exchange Options
Number Per Year: no limit   Fee: $7.50
Telephone: yes (money market fund available)

Services
IRA, pension, auto exchange, auto invest, auto withdraw

Fidelity Sel Defense & Aerospace (FSDAX)

Aggressive Growth

82 Devonshire St.
Mail Zone F9A
Boston, MA 02109
800-544-8888, 801-534-1910
www.fidelity.com

PERFORMANCE

fund inception date: 5/8/84

	3yr Annual	5yr Annual	10yr Annual	Bull	Bear
Return (%)	23.3	19.2	9.8	89.6	-5.7
Differ from Category (+/-)	7.5 high	3.9 high	-5.2 low	18.5 abv av	4.9 abv av

Total Risk	Standard Deviation	Category Risk	Risk Index	Beta
high	12.8%	blw av	0.9	1.05

	1996	1995	1994	1993	1992	1991	1990	1989	1988	1987
Return (%).............	25.0	47.3	1.7	28.8	0.0	26.9	-4.6	8.8	4.3	-23.2
Differ from Category (+/-)..	5.9	13.0	1.7	9.5	-11.7	-25.2	0.8	-19.6	-12.1	-20.8
Return, Tax-Adjusted (%)..	22.5	44.5	1.2	27.3	0.0	26.6	-5.0	8.8	4.3	-24.1

PER SHARE DATA

	1996	1995	1994	1993	1992	1991	1990	1989	1988	1987
Dividends, Net Income ($).	0.00	0.00	0.00	0.10	0.00	0.06	0.12	0.00	0.00	0.00
Distrib'ns, Cap Gain ($) ...	2.17	1.82	0.27	0.62	0.00	0.00	0.00	0.00	0.00	0.46
Net Asset Value ($)	29.12	25.15	18.32	18.27	14.75	14.75	11.67	12.35	11.35	10.88
Expense Ratio (%)........	1.75	2.49	2.53	2.48	2.46	2.49	2.43	2.53	2.33	1.54
Yield (%)	0.00	0.00	0.00	0.52	0.00	0.40	1.02	0.00	0.00	0.00
Portfolio Turnover (%)....	267	146	324	87	32	162	96	62	162	264
Total Assets (Millions $)....	37	27	3	2	1	1	1	1	1	2

PORTFOLIO (as of 9/30/96)

Portfolio Manager: William Rubin - 1994

Investm't Category: Aggressive Growth
- ✔ Domestic
- ✔ Foreign
-   Asset Allocation
-   Index
- ✔ Sector
-   State Specific

Investment Style
-   Large-Cap Growth
- ✔ Mid-Cap Growth
- ✔ Small-Cap Growth
-   Large-Cap Value
- ✔ Mid-Cap Value
- ✔ Small-Cap Value

Portfolio
1.5% cash	0.0% corp bonds
98.5% stocks	0.0% gov't bonds
0.0% preferred	0.0% muni bonds
0.0% conv't/warrants	0.0% other

SHAREHOLDER INFORMATION

Minimum Investment
Initial: $2,500   Subsequent: $250

Minimum IRA Investment
Initial: $500   Subsequent: $250

Maximum Fees
Load: 3.00% front   12b-1: none
Other: 0.75% fee (less than 30 days), *ff*

Distributions
Income: Apr, Dec   Capital Gains: Apr, Dec

Exchange Options
Number Per Year: no limit   Fee: $7.50
Telephone: yes (money market fund available)

Services
IRA, pension, auto exchange, auto invest, auto withdraw

Fidelity Sel Developing Communications (FSDCX)

Aggressive Growth

82 Devonshire St.
Mail Zone F9A
Boston, MA 02109
800-544-8888, 801-534-1910
www.fidelity.com

PERFORMANCE

fund inception date: 6/29/90

	3yr Annual	5yr Annual	10yr Annual	Bull	Bear
Return (%)	15.6	19.0	na	78.6	-16.6
Differ from Category (+/-)	-0.2 av	3.7 high	na	7.5 abv av	-6.0 low

Total Risk	Standard Deviation	Category Risk	Risk Index	Beta
high	19.9%	high	1.4	1.20

	1996	1995	1994	1993	1992	1991	1990	1989	1988	1987
Return (%)	14.5	17.3	15.1	31.7	17.2	61.3	—	—	—	—
Differ from Category (+/-)	-4.6	-17.0	15.1	12.4	5.5	9.2	—	—	—	—
Return, Tax-Adjusted (%)	14.5	10.3	12.6	29.1	17.1	58.8	—	—	—	—

PER SHARE DATA

	1996	1995	1994	1993	1992	1991	1990	1989	1988	1987
Dividends, Net Income ($)	0.00	0.00	0.00	0.00	0.00	0.00	—	—	—	—
Distrib'ns, Cap Gain ($)	0.00	5.00	1.67	1.47	0.03	0.79	—	—	—	—
Net Asset Value ($)	21.26	18.56	20.24	19.24	15.91	13.60	—	—	—	—
Expense Ratio (%)	1.51	1.56	1.56	1.88	2.50	2.50	—	—	—	—
Yield (%)	0.00	0.00	0.00	0.00	0.00	0.00	—	—	—	—
Portfolio Turnover (%)	249	266	280	77	25	469	—	—	—	—
Total Assets (Millions $)	292	296	276	245	70	19	—	—	—	—

PORTFOLIO (as of 9/30/96)

Portfolio Manager: Minerva Butler - 1996

Investm't Category: Aggressive Growth
- ✔ Domestic
- ✔ Foreign
- Asset Allocation
- Index
- ✔ Sector
- State Specific

Investment Style
- Large-Cap Growth
- ✔ Mid-Cap Growth
- ✔ Small-Cap Growth
- Large-Cap Value
- Mid-Cap Value
- Small-Cap Value

Portfolio
3.7% cash	0.0% corp bonds
96.3% stocks	0.0% gov't bonds
0.0% preferred	0.0% muni bonds
0.0% conv't/warrants	0.0% other

SHAREHOLDER INFORMATION

Minimum Investment
Initial: $2,500   Subsequent: $250

Minimum IRA Investment
Initial: $500   Subsequent: $250

Maximum Fees
Load: 3.00% front   12b-1: none
Other: 0.75% fee (less than 30 days), **ff**

Distributions
Income: Apr, Dec   Capital Gains: Apr, Dec

Exchange Options
Number Per Year: no limit   Fee: $7.50
Telephone: yes (money market fund available)

Services
IRA, pension, auto exchange, auto invest, auto withdraw

Fidelity Sel Electronics

(FSELX)

Aggressive Growth

82 Devonshire St.
Mail Zone F9A
Boston, MA 02109
800-544-8888, 801-534-1910
www.fidelity.com

PERFORMANCE

fund inception date: 7/29/85

	3yr Annual	5yr Annual	10yr Annual	Bull	Bear
Return (%)	41.0	36.4	20.0	169.1	-2.5
Differ from Category (+/-)	25.2 high	21.1 high	5.0 high	98.0 high	8.1 high

Total Risk	Standard Deviation	Category Risk	Risk Index	Beta
high	22.7%	high	1.6	1.34

	1996	1995	1994	1993	1992	1991	1990	1989	1988	1987
Return (%)	41.7	68.9	17.1	32.0	27.4	35.2	5.8	15.6	-8.5	-13.5
Differ from Category (+/-)	22.6	34.6	17.1	12.7	15.7	-16.9	11.2	-12.8	-24.9	-11.1
Return, Tax-Adjusted (%)	41.7	60.9	17.1	26.5	27.4	35.2	5.7	15.6	-8.5	-13.5

PER SHARE DATA

	1996	1995	1994	1993	1992	1991	1990	1989	1988	1987
Dividends, Net Income ($)	0.00	0.00	0.00	0.00	0.00	0.00	0.01	0.00	0.00	0.00
Distrib'ns, Cap Gain ($)	0.00	5.25	0.00	2.75	0.00	0.00	0.00	0.00	0.00	0.00
Net Asset Value ($)	36.48	25.74	18.49	15.78	14.12	11.08	8.19	7.75	6.70	7.32
Expense Ratio (%)	1.22	1.71	1.67	1.69	2.16	2.26	2.57	2.79	2.54	1.61
Yield (%)	0.00	0.00	0.00	0.00	0.00	0.00	0.12	0.00	0.00	0.00
Portfolio Turnover (%)	366	205	163	293	299	268	378	697	686	511
Total Assets (Millions $)	1,407	892	156	45	53	10	13	5	10	17

PORTFOLIO (as of 9/30/96)

Portfolio Manager: Andy Kaplan - 1996

Investm't Category: Aggressive Growth
- ✔ Domestic   Index
- ✔ Foreign   ✔ Sector
-    Asset Allocation   State Specific

Investment Style
-    Large-Cap Growth   Large-Cap Value
- ✔ Mid-Cap Growth   Mid-Cap Value
- ✔ Small-Cap Growth   Small-Cap Value

Portfolio
- 3.5% cash   0.0% corp bonds
- 96.5% stocks   0.0% gov't bonds
- 0.0% preferred   0.0% muni bonds
- 0.0% conv't/warrants   0.0% other

SHAREHOLDER INFORMATION

Minimum Investment
Initial: $2,500   Subsequent: $250

Minimum IRA Investment
Initial: $500   Subsequent: $250

Maximum Fees
Load: 3.00% front   12b-1: none
Other: 0.75% fee (less than 30 days), *ff*

Distributions
Income: Apr, Dec   Capital Gains: Apr, Dec

Exchange Options
Number Per Year: no limit   Fee: $7.50
Telephone: yes (money market fund available)

Services
IRA, pension, auto exchange, auto invest, auto withdraw

Fidelity Sel Energy (FSENX)

Growth

82 Devonshire St.
Mail Zone F9A
Boston, MA 02109
800-544-8888, 801-534-1910
www.fidelity.com

PERFORMANCE

fund inception date: 7/14/81

	3yr Annual	5yr Annual	10yr Annual	Bull	Bear
Return (%)	17.3	13.4	11.3	53.9	-0.5
Differ from Category (+/-)	1.6 abv av	-0.9 blw av	-2.6 low	-8.5 blw av	6.2 high

Total Risk	Standard Deviation	Category Risk	Risk Index	Beta
high	13.2%	high	1.3	0.85

	1996	1995	1994	1993	1992	1991	1990	1989	1988	1987
Return (%)	32.4	21.3	0.4	19.1	-2.4	0.0	-4.5	42.8	15.9	-1.8
Differ from Category (+/-)	12.3	-9.0	0.7	5.1	-14.2	-36.0	1.6	16.7	-2.2	-3.8
Return, Tax-Adjusted (%)	30.1	20.3	-0.8	17.9	-3.2	-0.5	-7.2	42.0	14.7	-2.6

PER SHARE DATA

	1996	1995	1994	1993	1992	1991	1990	1989	1988	1987
Dividends, Net Income ($)	0.13	0.11	0.11	0.03	0.27	0.16	0.15	0.07	0.32	0.03
Distrib'ns, Cap Gain ($)	1.31	0.36	0.51	0.56	0.00	0.02	1.43	0.22	0.00	0.27
Net Asset Value ($)	23.21	18.77	15.87	16.43	14.32	14.95	15.13	17.47	12.44	11.01
Expense Ratio (%)	1.63	1.85	1.66	1.71	1.78	1.79	1.94	1.77	2.09	1.50
Yield (%)	0.53	0.57	0.67	0.17	1.88	1.06	0.90	0.39	2.57	0.26
Portfolio Turnover (%)	97	106	157	72	81	61	74	168	183	226
Total Assets (Millions $)	206	131	96	82	68	72	96	90	75	71

PORTFOLIO (as of 9/30/96)

Portfolio Manager: Stephen DuFour - 1996

Investm't Category: Growth
- ✔ Domestic
- ✔ Foreign
- Asset Allocation
- Index
- ✔ Sector
- State Specific

Investment Style
- Large-Cap Growth
- Mid-Cap Growth
- Small-Cap Growth
- ✔ Large-Cap Value
- Mid-Cap Value
- Small-Cap Value

Portfolio
15.8% cash	0.0% corp bonds
84.2% stocks	0.0% gov't bonds
0.0% preferred	0.0% muni bonds
0.0% conv't/warrants	0.0% other

SHAREHOLDER INFORMATION

Minimum Investment
Initial: $2,500   Subsequent: $250

Minimum IRA Investment
Initial: $500   Subsequent: $250

Maximum Fees
Load: 3.00% front   12b-1: none
Other: 0.75% fee (less than 30 days), *ff*

Distributions
Income: Apr, Dec   Capital Gains: Apr, Dec

Exchange Options
Number Per Year: no limit   Fee: $7.50
Telephone: yes (money market fund available)

Services
IRA, pension, auto exchange, auto invest, auto withdraw

Fidelity Sel Energy Service

(FSESX)

Aggressive Growth

82 Devonshire St.
Mail Zone F9A
Boston, MA 02109
800-544-8888, 801-534-1910
www.fidelity.com

PERFORMANCE

fund inception date: 12/16/85

	3yr Annual	5yr Annual	10yr Annual	Bull	Bear
Return (%)	28.2	21.4	11.1	100.6	4.1
Differ from Category (+/-)	12.4 high	6.1 high	-3.9 low	29.5 high	14.7 high

Total Risk	Standard Deviation	Category Risk	Risk Index	Beta
high	16.8%	abv av	1.2	0.72

	1996	1995	1994	1993	1992	1991	1990	1989	1988	1987
Return (%)	49.0	40.8	0.4	20.9	3.4	-23.5	1.7	59.4	-0.4	-11.8
Differ from Category (+/-)	29.9	6.5	0.4	1.6	-8.3	-75.6	7.1	31.0	-16.8	-9.4
Return, Tax-Adjusted (%)	47.5	39.4	-0.9	20.6	3.4	-23.5	1.6	59.4	-0.4	-11.8

PER SHARE DATA

	1996	1995	1994	1993	1992	1991	1990	1989	1988	1987
Dividends, Net Income ($)	0.01	0.04	0.02	0.05	0.00	0.00	0.02	0.00	0.00	0.00
Distrib'ns, Cap Gain ($)	0.78	0.48	0.48	0.00	0.00	0.00	0.00	0.00	0.00	0.00
Net Asset Value ($)	21.73	15.16	11.14	11.61	9.64	9.32	12.18	11.99	7.52	7.55
Expense Ratio (%)	1.58	1.79	1.65	1.76	2.07	1.82	2.29	2.53	2.71	1.49
Yield (%)	0.04	0.25	0.17	0.43	0.00	0.00	0.16	0.00	0.00	0.00
Portfolio Turnover (%)	223	209	137	236	89	62	128	78	461	575
Total Assets (Millions $)	604	254	50	40	35	28	82	70	29	25

PORTFOLIO (as of 9/30/96)

Portfolio Manager: Robert Ewing - 1996

Investm't Category: Aggressive Growth
- ✔ Domestic
- Index
- ✔ Foreign
- ✔ Sector
- Asset Allocation
- State Specific

Investment Style
- Large-Cap Growth
- ✔ Large-Cap Value
- Mid-Cap Growth
- ✔ Mid-Cap Value
- Small-Cap Growth
- ✔ Small-Cap Value

Portfolio
- 9.2% cash
- 0.3% corp bonds
- 90.5% stocks
- 0.0% gov't bonds
- 0.0% preferred
- 0.0% muni bonds
- 0.0% conv't/warrants
- 0.0% other

SHAREHOLDER INFORMATION

Minimum Investment
Initial: $2,500   Subsequent: $250

Minimum IRA Investment
Initial: $500   Subsequent: $250

Maximum Fees
Load: 3.00% front   12b-1: none
Other: 0.75% fee (less than 30 days), *ff*

Distributions
Income: Apr, Dec   Capital Gains: Apr, Dec

Exchange Options
Number Per Year: no limit   Fee: $7.50
Telephone: yes (money market fund available)

Services
IRA, pension, auto exchange, auto invest, auto withdraw

Fidelity Sel Environmental Services (FSLEX)

Aggressive Growth

82 Devonshire St.
Mail Zone F9A
Boston, MA 02109
800-544-8888, 801-534-1910
www.fidelity.com

PERFORMANCE

fund inception date: 6/29/89

	3yr Annual	5yr Annual	10yr Annual	Bull	Bear
Return (%)	9.6	5.2	na	42.7	-14.9
Differ from Category (+/-)	-6.2 low	-10.1 low	na	-28.4 low	-4.3 blw av

Total Risk	Standard Deviation	Category Risk	Risk Index	Beta
high	15.7%	abv av	1.1	1.17

	1996	1995	1994	1993	1992	1991	1990	1989	1988	1987
Return (%)	15.6	26.0	-9.6	-0.7	-1.4	7.6	-2.5	—	—	—
Differ from Category (+/-)	-3.5	-8.3	-9.6	-20.0	-13.1	-44.5	2.9	—	—	—
Return, Tax-Adjusted (%)	15.5	24.2	-9.6	-0.7	-2.4	6.5	-2.5	—	—	—

PER SHARE DATA

	1996	1995	1994	1993	1992	1991	1990	1989	1988	1987
Dividends, Net Income ($)	0.00	0.00	0.00	0.00	0.00	0.00	0.00	—	—	—
Distrib'ns, Cap Gain ($)	0.02	0.65	0.00	0.00	0.39	0.42	0.00	—	—	—
Net Asset Value ($)	13.99	12.12	10.13	11.20	11.27	11.84	11.42	—	—	—
Expense Ratio (%)	2.32	2.01	2.03	1.99	2.03	2.03	2.25	—	—	—
Yield (%)	0.00	0.00	0.00	0.00	0.00	0.00	0.00	—	—	—
Portfolio Turnover (%)	138	82	191	176	130	122	72	—	—	—
Total Assets (Millions $)	31	27	32	50	68	71	96	—	—	—

PORTFOLIO (as of 9/30/96)

Portfolio Manager: Robert Ewing - 1996

Investm't Category: Aggressive Growth
- ✔ Domestic
- ✔ Foreign
- Asset Allocation
- Index
- ✔ Sector
- State Specific

Investment Style
- Large-Cap Growth
- Mid-Cap Growth
- Small-Cap Growth
- Large-Cap Value
- Mid-Cap Value
- ✔ Small-Cap Value

Portfolio
- 6.0% cash
- 94.0% stocks
- 0.0% preferred
- 0.0% conv't/warrants
- 0.0% corp bonds
- 0.0% gov't bonds
- 0.0% muni bonds
- 0.0% other

SHAREHOLDER INFORMATION

Minimum Investment
Initial: $2,500   Subsequent: $250

Minimum IRA Investment
Initial: $500   Subsequent: $250

Maximum Fees
Load: 3.00% front   12b-1: none
Other: 0.75% fee (less than 30 days), *ff*

Distributions
Income: Apr, Dec   Capital Gains: Apr, Dec

Exchange Options
Number Per Year: no limit   Fee: $7.50
Telephone: yes (money market fund available)

Services
IRA, pension, auto exchange, auto invest, auto withdraw

Fidelity Sel Financial Services (FIDSX)

Growth

82 Devonshire St.
Mail Zone F9A
Boston, MA 02109
800-544-8888, 801-534-1910
www.fidelity.com

PERFORMANCE

fund inception date: 12/10/81

	3yr Annual	5yr Annual	10yr Annual	Bull	Bear
Return (%)	23.3	25.7	15.6	80.7	-2.9
Differ from Category (+/-)	7.6 high	11.4 high	1.7 high	18.3 high	3.8 high

Total Risk	Standard Deviation	Category Risk	Risk Index	Beta
high	13.7%	high	1.3	1.24

	1996	1995	1994	1993	1992	1991	1990	1989	1988	1987
Return (%)	32.1	47.3	-3.7	17.5	42.8	61.6	-24.4	19.3	12.0	-16.6
Differ from Category (+/-)	12.0	17.0	-3.4	3.5	31.0	25.6	-18.3	-6.8	-6.1	-18.6
Return, Tax-Adjusted (%)	29.6	46.3	-6.5	13.1	39.7	61.0	-25.1	18.6	10.6	-18.2

PER SHARE DATA

	1996	1995	1994	1993	1992	1991	1990	1989	1988	1987
Dividends, Net Income ($)	0.63	0.37	0.59	0.20	0.51	0.35	0.52	0.33	0.81	0.12
Distrib'ns, Cap Gain ($)	4.55	0.91	4.13	7.32	3.38	0.00	0.00	0.19	0.00	1.54
Net Asset Value ($)	76.59	62.24	43.12	49.79	48.83	37.14	23.22	31.39	26.73	24.57
Expense Ratio (%)	1.41	1.54	1.63	1.54	1.85	2.49	2.22	1.07	2.47	1.57
Yield (%)	0.77	0.58	1.24	0.35	0.97	0.94	2.23	1.04	3.03	0.45
Portfolio Turnover (%)	125	107	93	100	164	237	308	186	81	40
Total Assets (Millions $)	343	251	94	126	132	53	22	26	26	30

PORTFOLIO (as of 9/30/96)

Portfolio Manager: Louis Salemy - 1994

Investm't Category: Growth
- ✔ Domestic
- ✔ Foreign
-   Asset Allocation
-   Index
- ✔ Sector
-   State Specific

Investment Style
-   Large-Cap Growth
-   Mid-Cap Growth
-   Small-Cap Growth
- ✔ Large-Cap Value
-   Mid-Cap Value
-   Small-Cap Value

Portfolio
5.3% cash	0.0% corp bonds
94.7% stocks	0.0% gov't bonds
0.0% preferred	0.0% muni bonds
0.0% conv't/warrants	0.0% other

SHAREHOLDER INFORMATION

Minimum Investment
Initial: $2,500   Subsequent: $250

Minimum IRA Investment
Initial: $500   Subsequent: $250

Maximum Fees
Load: 3.00% front   12b-1: none
Other: 0.75% fee (less than 30 days), *ff*

Distributions
Income: Apr, Dec   Capital Gains: Apr, Dec

Exchange Options
Number Per Year: no limit   Fee: $7.50
Telephone: yes (money market fund available)

Services
IRA, pension, auto exchange, auto invest, auto withdraw

Fidelity Sel Food & Agriculture (FDFAX)

Aggressive Growth

82 Devonshire St.
Mail Zone F9A
Boston, MA 02109
800-544-8888, 801-534-1910
www.fidelity.com

PERFORMANCE

fund inception date: 7/29/85

	3yr Annual	5yr Annual	10yr Annual	Bull	Bear
Return (%)	17.9	13.6	18.0	70.0	-6.3
Differ from Category (+/-)	2.1 abv av	-1.7 av	3.0 abv av	-1.1 av	4.3 abv av

Total Risk	Standard Deviation	Category Risk	Risk Index	Beta
av	9.3%	low	0.7	0.69

	1996	1995	1994	1993	1992	1991	1990	1989	1988	1987
Return (%)	13.3	36.6	6.0	8.8	6.0	34.0	9.3	38.8	26.7	7.5
Differ from Category (+/-)	-5.8	2.3	6.0	-10.5	-5.7	-18.1	14.7	10.4	10.3	9.9
Return, Tax-Adjusted (%)	11.0	34.3	4.2	6.2	4.4	31.9	7.8	35.4	26.5	6.3

PER SHARE DATA

	1996	1995	1994	1993	1992	1991	1990	1989	1988	1987
Dividends, Net Income ($)	0.24	0.20	0.08	0.08	0.10	0.11	0.27	0.04	0.05	0.03
Distrib'ns, Cap Gain ($)	2.77	2.20	1.85	2.68	1.57	1.59	0.79	2.17	0.00	0.55
Net Asset Value ($)	41.41	39.28	30.60	30.75	30.93	30.86	24.39	23.29	18.42	14.57
Expense Ratio (%)	1.42	1.68	1.64	1.67	1.83	2.22	2.53	2.50	2.45	1.67
Yield (%)	0.54	0.48	0.24	0.23	0.30	0.33	1.07	0.15	0.27	0.19
Portfolio Turnover (%)	124	126	96	515	63	124	267	248	215	608
Total Assets (Millions $)	307	240	85	173	117	122	32	23	21	9

PORTFOLIO (as of 9/30/96)

Portfolio Manager: Scott Offen - 1996

Investm't Category: Aggressive Growth
✔ Domestic   Index
✔ Foreign   ✔ Sector
  Asset Allocation   State Specific

Investment Style
✔ Large-Cap Growth   Large-Cap Value
  Mid-Cap Growth   Mid-Cap Value
  Small-Cap Growth   Small-Cap Value

Portfolio
9.7% cash	0.0% corp bonds
90.3% stocks	0.0% gov't bonds
0.0% preferred	0.0% muni bonds
0.0% conv't/warrants	0.0% other

SHAREHOLDER INFORMATION

Minimum Investment
Initial: $2,500   Subsequent: $250

Minimum IRA Investment
Initial: $500   Subsequent: $250

Maximum Fees
Load: 3.00% front   12b-1: none
Other: 0.75% fee (less than 30 days), *ff*

Distributions
Income: Apr, Dec   Capital Gains: Apr, Dec

Exchange Options
Number Per Year: no limit   Fee: $7.50
Telephone: yes (money market fund available)

Services
IRA, pension, auto exchange, auto invest, auto withdraw

Fidelity Sel Health Care

(FSPHX)

Aggressive Growth

82 Devonshire St.
Mail Zone F9A
Boston, MA 02109
800-544-8888, 801-534-1910
www.fidelity.com

PERFORMANCE

fund inception date: 7/14/81

	3yr Annual	5yr Annual	10yr Annual	Bull	Bear
Return (%)	26.9	11.5	19.7	103.3	-1.4
Differ from Category (+/-)	11.1 high	-3.8 blw av	4.7 high	32.2 high	9.2 high

Total Risk	Standard Deviation	Category Risk	Risk Index	Beta
high	12.0%	blw av	0.8	0.84

	1996	1995	1994	1993	1992	1991	1990	1989	1988	1987
Return (%)..............	15.4	45.8	21.4	2.4	-17.5	83.6	24.3	42.4	8.8	-0.7
Differ from Category (+/-).	-3.7	11.5	21.4	-16.9	-29.2	31.5	29.7	14.0	-7.6	1.7
Return, Tax-Adjusted (%)..	10.5	43.5	18.4	2.3	-20.4	78.6	20.7	41.5	8.4	-1.5

PER SHARE DATA

	1996	1995	1994	1993	1992	1991	1990	1989	1988	1987
Dividends, Net Income ($).	0.65	0.59	0.62	0.07	0.16	0.34	0.20	0.13	0.28	0.00
Distrib'ns, Cap Gain ($) ..	15.95	4.92	5.74	0.00	8.51	8.81	5.67	0.84	0.00	0.92
Net Asset Value ($)	95.40	97.57	70.80	63.62	62.19	85.95	52.98	47.58	34.13	31.62
Expense Ratio (%)........	1.30	1.36	1.64	1.46	1.44	1.53	1.74	1.41	1.64	1.39
Yield (%)	0.58	0.57	0.81	0.11	0.22	0.35	0.34	0.26	0.82	0.00
Portfolio Turnover (%).....	54	151	96	112	154	159	126	114	122	213
Total Assets (Millions $)..	1,263	1,448	796	573	755	1,169	373	222	181	231

PORTFOLIO (as of 9/30/96)

Portfolio Manager: Karen Firestone - 1995

Investm't Category: Aggressive Growth

✔ Domestic	Index
✔ Foreign	✔ Sector
Asset Allocation	State Specific

Investment Style

✔ Large-Cap Growth	Large-Cap Value
Mid-Cap Growth	Mid-Cap Value
Small-Cap Growth	Small-Cap Value

Portfolio

10.5% cash	0.2% corp bonds
88.2% stocks	0.0% gov't bonds
0.0% preferred	0.0% muni bonds
1.1% conv't/warrants	0.0% other

SHAREHOLDER INFORMATION

Minimum Investment

Initial: $2,500   Subsequent: $250

Minimum IRA Investment

Initial: $500   Subsequent: $250

Maximum Fees

Load: 3.00% front   12b-1: none

Other: 0.75% fee (less than 30 days), *ff*

Distributions

Income: Apr, Dec   Capital Gains: Apr, Dec

Exchange Options

Number Per Year: no limit   Fee: $7.50

Telephone: yes (money market fund available)

Services

IRA, pension, auto exchange, auto invest, auto withdraw

Fidelity Sel Home Finance

(FSVLX)

Aggressive Growth

82 Devonshire St.
Mail Zone F9A
Boston, MA 02109
800-544-8888, 801-534-1910
www.fidelity.com

PERFORMANCE

fund inception date: 12/16/85

	3yr Annual	5yr Annual	10yr Annual	Bull	Bear
Return (%)	29.1	34.0	21.8	91.4	7.9
Differ from Category (+/-)	13.3 high	18.7 high	6.8 high	20.3 abv av	18.5 high

Total Risk	Standard Deviation	Category Risk	Risk Index	Beta
high	12.4%	blw av	0.9	0.75

	1996	1995	1994	1993	1992	1991	1990	1989	1988	1987
Return (%)	36.8	53.4	2.6	27.2	57.8	64.6	-15.1	9.3	18.4	-8.0
Differ from Category (+/-)	17.7	19.1	2.6	7.9	46.1	12.5	-9.7	-19.1	2.0	-5.6
Return, Tax-Adjusted (%)	34.5	52.0	-1.8	25.2	57.1	63.9	-15.7	7.6	17.7	-15.7

PER SHARE DATA

	1996	1995	1994	1993	1992	1991	1990	1989	1988	1987
Dividends, Net Income ($)	0.32	0.19	0.12	0.01	0.01	0.14	0.14	0.04	0.13	0.00
Distrib'ns, Cap Gain ($)	2.16	0.73	3.60	1.40	0.28	0.00	0.00	0.49	0.00	3.50
Net Asset Value ($)	40.79	31.82	21.33	24.44	20.35	13.09	8.05	9.65	9.30	7.96
Expense Ratio (%)	1.32	1.45	1.58	1.55	2.08	2.50	2.53	2.56	2.57	1.53
Yield (%)	0.74	0.58	0.48	0.03	0.04	1.06	1.73	0.39	1.39	0.00
Portfolio Turnover (%)	81	124	95	61	134	159	282	216	456	335
Total Assets (Millions $)	981	586	130	159	216	9	5	6	5	9

PORTFOLIO (as of 9/30/96)

Portfolio Manager: William Rubin - 1996

Investm't Category: Aggressive Growth
✔ Domestic
✔ Foreign
  Asset Allocation

  Index
✔ Sector
  State Specific

Investment Style
  Large-Cap Growth
  Mid-Cap Growth
  Small-Cap Growth

✔ Large-Cap Value
✔ Mid-Cap Value
  Small-Cap Value

Portfolio
14.4% cash		0.0% corp bonds
85.0% stocks		0.0% gov't bonds
0.0% preferred		0.0% muni bonds
0.6% conv't/warrants		0.0% other

SHAREHOLDER INFORMATION

Minimum Investment
Initial: $2,500   Subsequent: $250

Minimum IRA Investment
Initial: $500   Subsequent: $250

Maximum Fees
Load: 3.00% front   12b-1: none
Other: 0.75% fee (less than 30 days), *ff*

Distributions
Income: Apr, Dec   Capital Gains: Apr, Dec

Exchange Options
Number Per Year: no limit   Fee: $7.50
Telephone: yes (money market fund available)

Services
IRA, pension, auto exchange, auto invest, auto withdraw

Fidelity Sel Industrial Equipment (FSCGX)

Aggressive Growth

82 Devonshire St.
Mail Zone F9A
Boston, MA 02109
800-544-8888, 801-534-1910
www.fidelity.com

PERFORMANCE

fund inception date: 9/29/86

	3yr Annual	5yr Annual	10yr Annual	Bull	Bear
Return (%)	18.6	21.7	12.3	78.9	-10.8
Differ from Category (+/-)	2.8 abv av	6.4 high	-2.7 blw av	7.8 abv av	-0.2 av

Total Risk	Standard Deviation	Category Risk	Risk Index	Beta
high	13.6%	av	1.0	0.92

	1996	1995	1994	1993	1992	1991	1990	1989	1988	1987
Return (%)	26.7	27.9	3.1	43.3	11.4	26.8	-15.6	17.9	4.8	-9.3
Differ from Category (+/-)	7.6	-6.4	3.1	24.0	-0.3	-25.3	-10.2	-10.5	-11.6	-6.9
Return, Tax-Adjusted (%)	21.9	24.8	2.8	42.4	11.3	26.3	-16.0	17.9	4.8	-10.0

PER SHARE DATA

	1996	1995	1994	1993	1992	1991	1990	1989	1988	1987
Dividends, Net Income ($)	0.04	0.05	0.00	0.01	0.01	0.11	0.09	0.00	0.00	0.00
Distrib'ns, Cap Gain ($)	3.84	2.04	0.17	0.40	0.00	0.00	0.00	0.00	0.00	0.23
Net Asset Value ($)	24.93	22.90	19.57	19.14	13.65	12.26	9.76	11.63	9.86	9.40
Expense Ratio (%)	1.53	1.78	1.68	2.49	2.49	2.52	2.59	2.58	2.65	1.70
Yield (%)	0.13	0.20	0.00	0.05	0.07	0.89	0.92	0.00	0.00	0.00
Portfolio Turnover (%)	115	131	95	407	167	43	132	164	407	514
Total Assets (Millions $)	84	84	104	85	5	1	1	1	3	5

PORTFOLIO (as of 9/30/96)

Portfolio Manager: Paul Antico - 1996

Investm't Category: Aggressive Growth

✔ Domestic	Index
✔ Foreign	✔ Sector
Asset Allocation	State Specific

Investment Style

Large-Cap Growth	Large-Cap Value
✔ Mid-Cap Growth	Mid-Cap Value
Small-Cap Growth	Small-Cap Value

Portfolio

14.0% cash	0.0% corp bonds
86.0% stocks	0.0% gov't bonds
0.0% preferred	0.0% muni bonds
0.0% conv't/warrants	0.0% other

SHAREHOLDER INFORMATION

Minimum Investment
Initial: $2,500   Subsequent: $250

Minimum IRA Investment
Initial: $500   Subsequent: $250

Maximum Fees
Load: 3.00% front   12b-1: none
Other: 0.75% fee (less than 30 days), *ff*

Distributions
Income: Apr, Dec   Capital Gains: Apr, Dec

Exchange Options
Number Per Year: no limit   Fee: $7.50
Telephone: yes (money market fund available)

Services
IRA, pension, auto exchange, auto invest, auto withdraw

Fidelity Sel Industrial Materials (FSDPX)

Aggressive Growth

82 Devonshire St.
Mail Zone F9A
Boston, MA 02109
800-544-8888, 801-534-1910
www.fidelity.com

PERFORMANCE

fund inception date: 9/29/86

	3yr Annual	5yr Annual	10yr Annual	Bull	Bear
Return (%)	12.4	14.1	11.3	33.3	-1.4
Differ from Category (+/-)	-3.4 blw av	-1.2 av	-3.7 low	-37.8 low	9.2 high

Total Risk	Standard Deviation	Category Risk	Risk Index	Beta
high	14.2%	av	1.0	0.81

	1996	1995	1994	1993	1992	1991	1990	1989	1988	1987
Return (%)	14.0	15.3	8.1	21.3	12.2	35.8	-17.2	4.4	10.8	15.6
Differ from Category (+/-)	-5.1	-19.0	8.1	2.0	0.5	-16.3	-11.8	-24.0	-5.6	18.0
Return, Tax-Adjusted (%)	12.1	15.0	7.7	21.1	12.0	35.5	-18.2	4.4	10.1	15.4

PER SHARE DATA

	1996	1995	1994	1993	1992	1991	1990	1989	1988	1987
Dividends, Net Income ($)	0.06	0.15	0.18	0.06	0.07	0.06	0.34	0.00	0.21	0.02
Distrib'ns, Cap Gain ($)	1.57	0.00	0.00	0.00	0.00	0.00	0.00	0.00	0.00	0.01
Net Asset Value ($)	27.04	25.19	21.96	20.47	16.92	15.13	11.19	13.86	13.27	12.17
Expense Ratio (%)	1.61	1.53	2.08	2.02	2.47	2.49	2.59	2.68	2.43	1.56
Yield (%)	0.20	0.59	0.81	0.29	0.41	0.39	3.03	0.00	1.58	0.16
Portfolio Turnover (%)	138	139	185	273	222	148	250	289	455	414
Total Assets (Millions $)	88	112	180	36	22	5	2	4	26	111

PORTFOLIO (as of 9/30/96)

Portfolio Manager: Douglas B. Chase - 1994

Investm't Category: Aggressive Growth

✔ Domestic	Index
✔ Foreign	✔ Sector
Asset Allocation	State Specific

Investment Style

Large-Cap Growth	Large-Cap Value
✔ Mid-Cap Growth	✔ Mid-Cap Value
✔ Small-Cap Growth	✔ Small-Cap Value

Portfolio

9.3% cash	0.0% corp bonds
90.7% stocks	0.0% gov't bonds
0.0% preferred	0.0% muni bonds
0.0% conv't/warrants	0.0% other

SHAREHOLDER INFORMATION

Minimum Investment
Initial: $2,500   Subsequent: $250

Minimum IRA Investment
Initial: $500   Subsequent: $250

Maximum Fees
Load: 3.00% front   12b-1: none
Other: 0.75% fee (less than 30 days), ff

Distributions
Income: Apr, Dec   Capital Gains: Apr, Dec

Exchange Options
Number Per Year: no limit   Fee: $7.50
Telephone: yes (money market fund available)

Services
IRA, pension, auto exchange, auto invest, auto withdraw

Fidelity Sel Insurance

(FSPCX)

Growth

82 Devonshire St.
Mail Zone F9A
Boston, MA 02109
800-544-8888, 801-534-1910
www.fidelity.com

fund inception date: 12/16/85

	3yr Annual	5yr Annual	10yr Annual	Bull	Bear
Return (%)	18.4	17.1	14.4	71.1	-4.2
Differ from Category (+/-)	2.7 abv av	2.8 high	0.5 abv av	8.7 abv av	2.5 abv av

Total Risk	Standard Deviation	Category Risk	Risk Index	Beta
abv av	10.4%	av	1.0	0.85

	1996	1995	1994	1993	1992	1991	1990	1989	1988	1987
Return (%)	23.7	34.8	-0.4	8.1	22.4	36.6	-9.9	37.8	17.4	-12.2
Differ from Category (+/-)	3.6	4.5	-0.1	-5.9	10.6	0.6	-3.8	11.7	-0.7	-14.2
Return, Tax-Adjusted (%)	22.0	33.6	-0.4	5.3	19.7	35.8	-9.9	37.2	17.0	-12.8

PER SHARE DATA

	1996	1995	1994	1993	1992	1991	1990	1989	1988	1987
Dividends, Net Income ($)	0.03	0.07	0.00	0.01	0.03	0.26	0.00	0.15	0.09	0.14
Distrib'ns, Cap Gain ($)	1.45	0.72	0.00	1.96	1.71	0.00	0.00	0.00	0.00	0.00
Net Asset Value ($)	30.67	26.10	19.96	20.03	20.33	18.30	13.60	15.08	11.05	9.49
Expense Ratio (%)	1.74	2.34	1.93	2.49	2.47	2.49	2.50	2.53	2.48	1.63
Yield (%)	0.09	0.26	0.00	0.04	0.13	1.42	0.00	0.99	0.81	1.47
Portfolio Turnover (%)	164	265	101	81	112	98	158	95	174	718
Total Assets (Millions $)	42	32	10	18	22	4	2	5	5	4

PORTFOLIO (as of 9/30/96)

Portfolio Manager: Michael Tempero - 1995

Investm't Category: Growth

✔ Domestic	Index
✔ Foreign	✔ Sector
Asset Allocation	State Specific

Investment Style

Large-Cap Growth	✔ Large-Cap Value
Mid-Cap Growth	✔ Mid-Cap Value
Small-Cap Growth	Small-Cap Value

Portfolio

2.4% cash	0.0% corp bonds
97.6% stocks	0.0% gov't bonds
0.0% preferred	0.0% muni bonds
0.0% conv't/warrants	0.0% other

SHAREHOLDER INFORMATION

Minimum Investment
Initial: $2,500   Subsequent: $250

Minimum IRA Investment
Initial: $500   Subsequent: $250

Maximum Fees
Load: 3.00% front   12b-1: none
Other: 0.75% fee (less than 30 days), *ff*

Distributions
Income: Apr, Dec   Capital Gains: Apr, Dec

Exchange Options
Number Per Year: no limit   Fee: $7.50
Telephone: yes (money market fund available)

Services
IRA, pension, auto exchange, auto invest, auto withdraw

Fidelity Sel Leisure

(FDLSX)

Aggressive Growth

82 Devonshire St.
Mail Zone F9A
Boston, MA 02109
800-544-8888, 801-534-1910
www.fidelity.com

PERFORMANCE

fund inception date: 5/8/84

	3yr Annual	5yr Annual	10yr Annual	Bull	Bear
Return (%)	10.3	16.8	14.6	50.1	-11.6
Differ from Category (+/-)	-5.5 low	1.5 abv av	-0.4 av	-21.0 blw av	-1.0 av

Total Risk	Standard Deviation	Category Risk	Risk Index	Beta
abv av	11.5%	low	0.8	0.86

	1996	1995	1994	1993	1992	1991	1990	1989	1988	1987
Return (%).	13.4	26.9	-6.8	39.5	16.2	32.9	-22.3	31.2	26.0	5.6
Differ from Category (+/-) .	-5.7	-7.4	-6.8	20.2	4.5	-19.2	-16.9	2.8	9.6	8.0
Return, Tax-Adjusted (%). .	11.5	23.0	-9.3	36.8	16.2	32.9	-22.7	28.7	25.4	2.8

PER SHARE DATA

	1996	1995	1994	1993	1992	1991	1990	1989	1988	1987
Dividends, Net Income ($).	0.00	0.00	0.00	0.00	0.00	0.00	0.23	0.07	0.00	0.00
Distrib'ns, Cap Gain ($) . . .	2.83	5.32	3.93	3.26	0.00	0.00	0.00	2.02	0.40	2.02
Net Asset Value ($)	46.06	43.18	38.27	45.22	35.09	30.19	22.71	29.52	24.13	19.49
Expense Ratio (%).	1.63	1.62	1.53	1.90	2.21	2.27	1.96	1.73	1.96	1.55
Yield (%)	0.00	0.00	0.00	0.00	0.00	0.00	1.01	0.22	0.00	0.00
Portfolio Turnover (%). . . .	141	103	170	109	45	75	124	249	229	148
Total Assets (Millions $). . .	111	78	61	117	41	38	37	59	66	52

PORTFOLIO (as of 9/30/96)

Portfolio Manager: Katherine Collins - 1996

Investm't Category: Aggressive Growth
- ✔ Domestic   Index
- ✔ Foreign   ✔ Sector
-     Asset Allocation   State Specific

Investment Style
-     Large-Cap Growth   Large-Cap Value
- ✔ Mid-Cap Growth   ✔ Mid-Cap Value
- ✔ Small-Cap Growth   ✔ Small-Cap Value

Portfolio
9.2%	cash	0.0%	corp bonds
90.6%	stocks	0.0%	gov't bonds
0.0%	preferred	0.0%	muni bonds
0.2%	conv't/warrants	0.0%	other

SHAREHOLDER INFORMATION

Minimum Investment
Initial: $2,500   Subsequent: $250

Minimum IRA Investment
Initial: $500   Subsequent: $250

Maximum Fees
Load: 3.00% front   12b-1: none
Other: 0.75% fee (less than 30 days), *ff*

Distributions
Income: Apr, Dec   Capital Gains: Apr, Dec

Exchange Options
Number Per Year: no limit   Fee: $7.50
Telephone: yes (money market fund available)

Services
IRA, pension, auto exchange, auto invest, auto withdraw

Fidelity Sel Medical Delivery (FSHCX)

Aggressive Growth

82 Devonshire St.
Mail Zone F9A
Boston, MA 02109
800-544-8888, 801-534-1910
www.fidelity.com

PERFORMANCE

fund inception date: 6/30/86

	3yr Annual	5yr Annual	10yr Annual	Bull	Bear
Return (%)	20.7	10.0	18.2	74.1	-4.4
Differ from Category (+/-)	4.9 abv av	-5.3 low	3.2 high	3.0 abv av	6.2 high

Total Risk	Standard Deviation	Category Risk	Risk Index	Beta
high	16.9%	abv av	1.2	1.05

	1996	1995	1994	1993	1992	1991	1990	1989	1988	1987
Return (%)	11.0	32.2	19.8	5.5	-13.2	77.8	16.2	58.0	15.7	-12.1
Differ from Category (+/-)	-8.1	-2.1	19.8	-13.8	-24.9	25.7	21.6	29.6	-0.7	-9.7
Return, Tax-Adjusted (%)	7.4	29.7	18.3	5.5	-15.2	75.2	15.2	56.8	15.7	-13.5

PER SHARE DATA

	1996	1995	1994	1993	1992	1991	1990	1989	1988	1987
Dividends, Net Income ($)	0.00	0.00	0.07	0.00	0.00	0.00	0.00	0.05	0.00	0.02
Distrib'ns, Cap Gain ($)	3.45	1.91	0.88	0.00	1.55	1.24	0.39	0.26	0.00	0.36
Net Asset Value ($)	26.42	26.96	21.87	19.10	18.10	22.76	13.65	12.09	7.85	6.78
Expense Ratio (%)	1.62	1.45	1.79	1.77	1.69	1.94	2.16	2.48	2.48	1.49
Yield (%)	0.00	0.00	0.30	0.00	0.00	0.00	0.00	0.40	0.00	0.28
Portfolio Turnover (%)	132	123	164	155	181	165	253	92	264	221
Total Assets (Millions $)	170	203	247	150	197	200	37	37	3	4

PORTFOLIO (as of 9/30/96)

Portfolio Manager: Deborah Wheeler - 1996

Investm't Category: Aggressive Growth

✔ Domestic   Index
✔ Foreign   ✔ Sector
   Asset Allocation   State Specific

Investment Style

   Large-Cap Growth   Large-Cap Value
✔ Mid-Cap Growth   Mid-Cap Value
✔ Small-Cap Growth   Small-Cap Value

Portfolio

3.3% cash	0.0% corp bonds
96.7% stocks	0.0% gov't bonds
0.0% preferred	0.0% muni bonds
0.0% conv't/warrants	0.0% other

SHAREHOLDER INFORMATION

Minimum Investment
Initial: $2,500   Subsequent: $250

Minimum IRA Investment
Initial: $500   Subsequent: $250

Maximum Fees
Load: 3.00% front   12b-1: none
Other: 0.75% fee (less than 30 days), *ff*

Distributions
Income: Apr, Dec   Capital Gains: Apr, Dec

Exchange Options
Number Per Year: no limit   Fee: $7.50
Telephone: yes (money market fund available)

Services
IRA, pension, auto exchange, auto invest, auto withdraw

Fidelity Sel Multimedia

(FBMPX)

Aggressive Growth

82 Devonshire St.
Mail Zone F9A
Boston, MA 02109
800-544-8888, 801-534-1910
www.fidelity.com

PERFORMANCE

fund inception date: 6/30/86

	3yr Annual	5yr Annual	10yr Annual	Bull	Bear
Return (%)	12.0	18.6	17.0	47.4	-6.1
Differ from Category (+/-)	-3.8 blw av	3.3 abv av	2.0 abv av	-23.7 low	4.5 abv av

Total Risk	Standard Deviation	Category Risk	Risk Index	Beta
high	12.7%	blw av	0.9	0.95

	1996	1995	1994	1993	1992	1991	1990	1989	1988	1987
Return (%)...............	1.0	33.7	3.9	38.0	21.4	37.8	-26.3	32.5	26.8	19.9
Differ from Category (+/-)	-18.1	-0.6	3.9	18.7	9.7	-14.3	-20.9	4.1	10.4	22.3
Return, Tax-Adjusted (%)..	-0.2	30.7	0.1	36.9	20.9	37.8	-26.3	26.9	24.8	17.6

PER SHARE DATA

	1996	1995	1994	1993	1992	1991	1990	1989	1988	1987
Dividends, Net Income ($).	0.00	0.02	0.00	0.00	0.00	0.00	0.00	0.00	0.00	0.01
Distrib'ns, Cap Gain ($) ...	1.07	2.19	3.21	0.65	0.23	0.00	0.00	2.57	0.75	0.78
Net Asset Value ($)	25.37	26.15	21.23	23.84	17.82	14.86	10.78	14.61	12.98	10.87
Expense Ratio (%)........	1.54	2.03	1.63	2.49	2.49	2.53	2.51	2.66	2.48	1.50
Yield (%)	0.00	0.07	0.00	0.00	0.00	0.00	0.00	0.00	0.00	0.08
Portfolio Turnover (%)....	223	107	340	70	111	150	75	437	325	224
Total Assets (Millions $)....	78	89	26	65	16	5	7	13	11	8

PORTFOLIO (as of 9/30/96)

Portfolio Manager: John Porter - 1996

Investm't Category: Aggressive Growth
- ✔ Domestic
- ✔ Foreign
- Asset Allocation
- Index
- ✔ Sector
- State Specific

Investment Style
- Large-Cap Growth
- ✔ Mid-Cap Growth
- ✔ Small-Cap Growth
- Large-Cap Value
- Mid-Cap Value
- Small-Cap Value

Portfolio
3.9% cash	0.0% corp bonds
96.1% stocks	0.0% gov't bonds
0.0% preferred	0.0% muni bonds
0.0% conv't/warrants	0.0% other

SHAREHOLDER INFORMATION

Minimum Investment
Initial: $2,500   Subsequent: $250

Minimum IRA Investment
Initial: $500   Subsequent: $250

Maximum Fees
Load: 3.00% front   12b-1: none
Other: 0.75% fee (less than 30 days), *ff*

Distributions
Income: Apr, Dec   Capital Gains: Apr, Dec

Exchange Options
Number Per Year: no limit   Fee: $7.50
Telephone: yes (money market fund available)

Services
IRA, pension, auto exchange, auto invest, auto withdraw

Fidelity Sel Natural Gas

(FSNGX)

Growth

82 Devonshire St.
Mail Zone F9A
Boston, MA 02109
800-544-8888, 801-534-1910
www.fidelity.com

PERFORMANCE

fund inception date: 4/21/93

	3yr Annual	5yr Annual	10yr Annual	Bull	Bear
Return (%)	17.7	na	na	55.5	-0.2
Differ from Category (+/-)	2.0 abv av	na	na	-6.9 blw av	6.5 high

Total Risk	Standard Deviation	Category Risk	Risk Index	Beta
high	14.9%	high	1.4	0.91

	1996	1995	1994	1993	1992	1991	1990	1989	1988	1987
Return (%)	34.3	30.3	-6.9	—	—	—	—	—	—	—
Differ from Category (+/-)	14.2	0.0	-6.6	—	—	—	—	—	—	—
Return, Tax-Adjusted (%)	33.5	30.0	-7.0	—	—	—	—	—	—	—

PER SHARE DATA

	1996	1995	1994	1993	1992	1991	1990	1989	1988	1987
Dividends, Net Income ($)	0.01	0.05	0.02	—	—	—	—	—	—	—
Distrib'ns, Cap Gain ($)	0.28	0.00	0.00	—	—	—	—	—	—	—
Net Asset Value ($)	14.84	11.29	8.70	—	—	—	—	—	—	—
Expense Ratio (%)	1.67	1.66	1.93	—	—	—	—	—	—	—
Yield (%)	0.06	0.44	0.22	—	—	—	—	—	—	—
Portfolio Turnover (%)	79	177	44	—	—	—	—	—	—	—
Total Assets (Millions $)	165	85	79	—	—	—	—	—	—	—

PORTFOLIO (as of 9/30/96)

Portfolio Manager: Stephen Binder - 1996

Investm't Category: Growth
✔ Domestic   Index
✔ Foreign   ✔ Sector
   Asset Allocation   State Specific

Investment Style
Large-Cap Growth	✔ Large-Cap Value
Mid-Cap Growth	Mid-Cap Value
Small-Cap Growth	Small-Cap Value

Portfolio
4.5% cash	0.0% corp bonds
95.5% stocks	0.0% gov't bonds
0.0% preferred	0.0% muni bonds
0.0% conv't/warrants	0.0% other

SHAREHOLDER INFORMATION

Minimum Investment
Initial: $2,500   Subsequent: $250

Minimum IRA Investment
Initial: $500   Subsequent: $250

Maximum Fees
Load: 3.00% front   12b-1: none
Other: 0.75% fee (less than 30 days), *ff*

Distributions
Income: Apr, Dec   Capital Gains: Apr, Dec

Exchange Options
Number Per Year: no limit   Fee: $7.50
Telephone: yes (money market fund available)

Services
IRA, pension, auto exchange, auto invest, auto withdraw

Fidelity Sel Paper & Forest Products (FSPFX)

Aggressive Growth

82 Devonshire St.
Mail Zone F9A
Boston, MA 02109
800-544-8888, 801-534-1910
www.fidelity.com

PERFORMANCE

fund inception date: 6/30/86

	3yr Annual	5yr Annual	10yr Annual	Bull	Bear
Return (%)	14.2	14.6	10.0	49.3	-10.6
Differ from Category (+/-)	-1.6 av	-0.7 av	-5.0 low	-21.8 blw av	0.0 av

Total Risk	Standard Deviation	Category Risk	Risk Index	Beta
high	17.1%	abv av	1.2	0.89

	1996	1995	1994	1993	1992	1991	1990	1989	1988	1987
Return (%)	7.0	21.9	14.1	18.5	12.0	34.7	-15.2	4.0	6.7	3.9
Differ from Category (+/-)	-12.1	-12.4	14.1	-0.8	0.3	-17.4	-9.8	-24.4	-9.7	6.3
Return, Tax-Adjusted (%)	5.1	18.4	12.2	18.4	11.7	33.5	-15.8	3.5	6.5	1.3

PER SHARE DATA

	1996	1995	1994	1993	1992	1991	1990	1989	1988	1987
Dividends, Net Income ($)	0.10	0.08	0.00	0.01	0.09	0.30	0.17	0.15	0.03	0.04
Distrib'ns, Cap Gain ($)	1.25	2.27	1.17	0.00	0.00	0.00	0.00	0.00	0.00	1.04
Net Asset Value ($)	21.36	21.25	19.36	18.08	15.26	13.70	10.41	12.47	12.13	11.39
Expense Ratio (%)	1.90	1.87	2.07	2.21	2.05	2.49	2.57	2.54	2.52	1.29
Yield (%)	0.44	0.34	0.00	0.05	0.58	2.18	1.63	1.20	0.24	0.32
Portfolio Turnover (%)	78	209	176	222	421	171	221	154	209	466
Total Assets (Millions $)	22	40	76	48	15	11	4	7	14	26

PORTFOLIO (as of 9/30/96)

Portfolio Manager: Lawrence Rakers - 1996

Investm't Category: Aggressive Growth
- ✔ Domestic
- Index
- ✔ Foreign
- ✔ Sector
- Asset Allocation
- State Specific

Investment Style
- Large-Cap Growth
- Large-Cap Value
- Mid-Cap Growth
- Mid-Cap Value
- Small-Cap Growth
- ✔ Small-Cap Value

Portfolio
- 2.7% cash
- 0.2% corp bonds
- 96.7% stocks
- 0.0% gov't bonds
- 0.0% preferred
- 0.0% muni bonds
- 0.4% conv't/warrants
- 0.0% other

SHAREHOLDER INFORMATION

Minimum Investment
Initial: $2,500   Subsequent: $250

Minimum IRA Investment
Initial: $500   Subsequent: $250

Maximum Fees
Load: 3.00% front   12b-1: none
Other: 0.75% fee (less than 30 days), ff

Distributions
Income: Apr, Dec   Capital Gains: Apr, Dec

Exchange Options
Number Per Year: no limit   Fee: $7.50
Telephone: yes (money market fund available)

Services
IRA, pension, auto exchange, auto invest, auto withdraw

Fidelity Sel Precious Metals & Minerals

(FDPMX) *Gold*

82 Devonshire St.
Mail Zone F9A
Boston, MA 02109
800-544-8888, 801-534-1910
www.fidelity.com

PERFORMANCE

fund inception date: 7/14/81

	3yr Annual	5yr Annual	10yr Annual	Bull	Bear
Return (%)	0.2	10.7	6.3	8.6	-3.3
Differ from Category (+/-)	-0.1 av	1.1 av	2.0 high	-6.3 av	6.9 high

Total Risk	Standard Deviation	Category Risk	Risk Index	Beta
high	24.2%	blw av	1.0	0.51

	1996	1995	1994	1993	1992	1991	1990	1989	1988	1987
Return (%)	5.4	-3.4	-1.2	111.6	-21.9	1.5	-21.1	32.1	-23.9	37.5
Differ from Category (+/-)	-5.8	-8.4	10.9	23.8	-6.6	6.1	1.2	7.7	-4.8	5.3
Return, Tax-Adjusted (%)	5.2	-3.6	-1.8	110.6	-22.5	1.1	-21.6	31.4	-25.2	36.9

PER SHARE DATA

	1996	1995	1994	1993	1992	1991	1990	1989	1988	1987
Dividends, Net Income ($)	0.05	0.06	0.23	0.21	0.17	0.10	0.15	0.18	0.46	0.07
Distrib'ns, Cap Gain ($)	0.00	0.00	0.00	0.00	0.00	0.00	0.00	0.00	0.00	0.12
Net Asset Value ($)	17.91	17.03	17.68	18.13	8.67	11.31	11.24	14.44	11.06	15.14
Expense Ratio (%)	1.52	1.46	1.55	1.73	1.81	1.79	1.93	1.88	2.02	1.50
Yield (%)	0.27	0.35	1.30	1.15	1.96	0.88	1.33	1.24	4.15	0.45
Portfolio Turnover (%)	53	43	73	36	44	41	98	72	86	84
Total Assets (Millions $)	271	309	453	500	115	147	189	253	199	343

PORTFOLIO (as of 9/30/96)

Portfolio Manager: Lawrence Rakers - 1996

Investm't Category: Gold
✔ Domestic   Index
✔ Foreign   ✔ Sector
  Asset Allocation   State Specific

Investment Style
  Large-Cap Growth   Large-Cap Value
  Mid-Cap Growth   Mid-Cap Value
  Small-Cap Growth   Small-Cap Value

Portfolio
  2.0% cash   0.0% corp bonds
  97.8% stocks   0.0% gov't bonds
  0.0% preferred   0.0% muni bonds
  0.2% conv't/warrants 0.0% other

SHAREHOLDER INFORMATION

Minimum Investment
Initial: $2,500   Subsequent: $250

Minimum IRA Investment
Initial: $500   Subsequent: $250

Maximum Fees
Load: 3.00% front   12b-1: none
Other: 0.75% fee (less than 30 days), *ff*

Distributions
Income: Apr, Dec   Capital Gains: Apr, Dec

Exchange Options
Number Per Year: no limit   Fee: $7.50
Telephone: yes (money market fund available)

Services
IRA, pension, auto exchange, auto invest, auto withdraw

Fidelity Sel Regional Banks

(FSRBX)

Growth

82 Devonshire St.
Mail Zone F9A
Boston, MA 02109
800-544-8888, 801-534-1910
www.fidelity.com

PERFORMANCE

fund inception date: 6/30/86

	3yr Annual	5yr Annual	10yr Annual	Bull	Bear
Return (%)	25.9	26.9	20.9	83.3	3.0
Differ from Category (+/-)	10.2 high	12.6 high	7.0 high	20.9 high	9.7 high

Total Risk	Standard Deviation	Category Risk	Risk Index	Beta
high	12.2%	high	1.2	1.00

	1996	1995	1994	1993	1992	1991	1990	1989	1988	1987
Return (%).	35.8	46.7	0.2	11.1	48.5	65.7	-20.7	26.6	25.7	-3.1
Differ from Category (+/-)	15.7	16.4	0.5	-2.9	36.7	29.7	-14.6	0.5	7.6	-5.1
Return, Tax-Adjusted (%). .	33.6	44.8	-2.1	5.1	46.5	63.3	-21.3	24.2	23.0	-3.9

PER SHARE DATA

	1996	1995	1994	1993	1992	1991	1990	1989	1988	1987
Dividends, Net Income ($).	0.27	0.25	0.26	0.15	0.11	0.15	0.15	0.11	0.20	0.06
Distrib'ns, Cap Gain ($) . . .	1.40	0.72	1.01	3.92	0.81	0.53	0.00	0.65	0.47	0.15
Net Asset Value ($)	29.29	22.94	16.28	17.49	19.44	13.75	8.74	11.21	9.45	8.05
Expense Ratio (%).	1.40	1.56	1.60	1.49	1.77	2.51	2.55	2.53	2.48	1.63
Yield (%)	0.87	1.05	1.50	0.70	0.54	1.05	1.71	0.92	2.01	0.73
Portfolio Turnover (%). . . .	103	106	74	63	89	110	411	352	291	227
Total Assets (Millions $). . .	551	322	108	113	238	36	9	7	8	4

PORTFOLIO (as of 9/30/96)

Portfolio Manager: John D. Avery - 1996

Investm't Category: Growth
- ✔ Domestic
- ✔ Foreign
- Asset Allocation
- Index
- ✔ Sector
- State Specific

Investment Style
- Large-Cap Growth
- Mid-Cap Growth
- Small-Cap Growth
- ✔ Large-Cap Value
- ✔ Mid-Cap Value
- Small-Cap Value

Portfolio
5.5% cash	0.0% corp bonds
94.5% stocks	0.0% gov't bonds
0.0% preferred	0.0% muni bonds
0.0% conv't/warrants	0.0% other

SHAREHOLDER INFORMATION

Minimum Investment
Initial: $2,500   Subsequent: $250

Minimum IRA Investment
Initial: $500   Subsequent: $250

Maximum Fees
Load: 3.00% front   12b-1: none
Other: 0.75% fee (less than 30 days), *ff*

Distributions
Income: Apr, Dec   Capital Gains: Apr, Dec

Exchange Options
Number Per Year: no limit   Fee: $7.50
Telephone: yes (money market fund available)

Services
IRA, pension, auto exchange, auto invest, auto withdraw

Fidelity Sel Retailing

(FSRPX)

Aggressive Growth

82 Devonshire St.
Mail Zone F9A
Boston, MA 02109
800-544-8888, 801-534-1910
www.fidelity.com

PERFORMANCE
fund inception date: 12/16/85

	3yr Annual	5yr Annual	10yr Annual	Bull	Bear
Return (%)	8.7	12.1	16.7	36.4	-1.4
Differ from Category (+/-)	-7.1 low	-3.2 blw av	1.7 abv av	-34.7 low	9.2 high

Total Risk	Standard Deviation	Category Risk	Risk Index	Beta
high	15.3%	abv av	1.1	0.70

	1996	1995	1994	1993	1992	1991	1990	1989	1988	1987
Return (%)	20.8	11.9	-5.1	13.0	22.0	68.1	-5.1	29.5	38.7	-7.4
Differ from Category (+/-)	1.7	-22.4	-5.1	-6.3	10.3	16.0	0.3	1.1	22.3	-5.0
Return, Tax-Adjusted (%)	20.7	11.9	-5.1	10.0	20.4	67.0	-5.2	23.3	38.0	-10.2

PER SHARE DATA

	1996	1995	1994	1993	1992	1991	1990	1989	1988	1987
Dividends, Net Income ($)	0.00	0.00	0.00	0.00	0.00	0.00	0.00	0.16	0.03	0.23
Distrib'ns, Cap Gain ($)	0.08	0.00	0.00	2.63	1.17	0.50	0.03	2.57	0.18	0.76
Net Asset Value ($)	32.24	26.74	23.88	25.14	24.64	21.28	12.98	13.70	12.74	9.34
Expense Ratio (%)	1.92	1.96	1.83	1.77	1.87	2.54	2.50	2.51	2.47	1.54
Yield (%)	0.00	0.00	0.00	0.00	0.00	0.00	0.00	0.98	0.23	2.27
Portfolio Turnover (%)	235	481	154	171	205	115	212	290	294	596
Total Assets (Millions $)	222	39	35	60	93	29	6	6	14	5

PORTFOLIO (as of 9/30/96)

Portfolio Manager: Erin Sullivan - 1995

Investm't Category: Aggressive Growth
- ✔ Domestic
- ✔ Foreign
-   Asset Allocation

  Index
- ✔ Sector
-   State Specific

Investment Style
Large-Cap Growth	Large-Cap Value
✔ Mid-Cap Growth	Mid-Cap Value
✔ Small-Cap Growth	Small-Cap Value

Portfolio
3.4%	cash	0.0%	corp bonds
96.4%	stocks	0.0%	gov't bonds
0.0%	preferred	0.0%	muni bonds
0.2%	conv't/warrants	0.0%	other

SHAREHOLDER INFORMATION

Minimum Investment
Initial: $2,500   Subsequent: $250

Minimum IRA Investment
Initial: $500   Subsequent: $250

Maximum Fees
Load: 3.00% front   12b-1: none
Other: 0.75% fee (less than 30 days), *ff*

Distributions
Income: Apr, Dec   Capital Gains: Apr, Dec

Exchange Options
Number Per Year: no limit   Fee: $7.50
Telephone: yes (money market fund available)

Services
IRA, pension, auto exchange, auto invest, auto withdraw

Fidelity Sel Software & Computer (FSCSX)

Aggressive Growth

82 Devonshire St.
Mail Zone F9A
Boston, MA 02109
800-544-8888, 801-534-1910
www.fidelity.com

PERFORMANCE

fund inception date: 7/29/85

	3yr Annual	5yr Annual	10yr Annual	Bull	Bear
Return (%)	21.3	26.2	20.2	131.1	-25.4
Differ from Category (+/-)	5.5 high	10.9 high	5.2 high	60.0 high	-14.8 low

Total Risk	Standard Deviation	Category Risk	Risk Index	Beta
high	20.0%	high	1.4	1.29

	1996	1995	1994	1993	1992	1991	1990	1989	1988	1987
Return (%)	21.7	46.0	0.3	32.7	35.5	45.8	0.8	12.0	9.0	9.4
Differ from Category (+/-)	2.6	11.7	0.3	13.4	23.8	-6.3	6.2	-16.4	-7.4	11.8
Return, Tax-Adjusted (%)	19.0	41.2	-0.1	25.8	35.5	41.2	0.8	10.3	9.0	7.8

PER SHARE DATA

	1996	1995	1994	1993	1992	1991	1990	1989	1988	1987
Dividends, Net Income ($)	0.00	0.00	0.00	0.00	0.00	0.00	0.00	0.00	0.00	0.00
Distrib'ns, Cap Gain ($)	3.31	4.59	0.33	6.48	0.00	2.50	0.00	0.86	0.00	0.68
Net Asset Value ($)	39.62	35.46	27.29	27.55	26.43	19.50	15.32	15.19	14.34	13.15
Expense Ratio (%)	1.47	1.50	1.57	1.64	1.98	2.50	2.56	2.63	2.51	1.51
Yield (%)	0.00	0.00	0.00	0.00	0.00	0.00	0.00	0.00	0.00	0.00
Portfolio Turnover (%)	183	164	376	402	348	326	284	434	134	220
Total Assets (Millions $)	428	351	211	164	143	20	11	11	26	32

PORTFOLIO (as of 9/30/96)

Portfolio Manager: John Hurley - 1994

Investm't Category: Aggressive Growth
✔ Domestic	Index
✔ Foreign	✔ Sector
Asset Allocation	State Specific

Investment Style
Large-Cap Growth	Large-Cap Value
✔ Mid-Cap Growth	Mid-Cap Value
✔ Small-Cap Growth	Small-Cap Value

Portfolio
14.1% cash	0.0% corp bonds
85.9% stocks	0.0% gov't bonds
0.0% preferred	0.0% muni bonds
0.0% conv't/warrants	0.0% other

SHAREHOLDER INFORMATION

Minimum Investment
Initial: $2,500   Subsequent: $250

Minimum IRA Investment
Initial: $500   Subsequent: $250

Maximum Fees
Load: 3.00% front   12b-1: none
Other: 0.75% fee (less than 30 days), *ff*

Distributions
Income: Apr, Dec   Capital Gains: Apr, Dec

Exchange Options
Number Per Year: no limit   Fee: $7.50
Telephone: yes (money market fund available)

Services
IRA, pension, auto exchange, auto invest, auto withdraw

Fidelity Sel Technology

(FSPTX)

Aggressive Growth

82 Devonshire St.
Mail Zone F9A
Boston, MA 02109
800-544-8888, 801-534-1910
www.fidelity.com

PERFORMANCE

fund inception date: 7/14/81

	3yr Annual	5yr Annual	10yr Annual	Bull	Bear
Return (%)	22.7	20.9	16.3	97.2	-10.8
Differ from Category (+/-)	6.9 high	5.6 high	1.3 abv av	26.1 high	-0.2 av

Total Risk	Standard Deviation	Category Risk	Risk Index	Beta
high	20.5%	high	1.4	1.38

	1996	1995	1994	1993	1992	1991	1990	1989	1988	1987
Return (%)	15.8	43.6	11.1	28.6	8.7	58.9	10.5	16.9	-2.7	-11.8
Differ from Category (+/-)	-3.3	9.3	11.1	9.3	-3.0	6.8	15.9	-11.5	-19.1	-9.4
Return, Tax-Adjusted (%)	13.7	38.1	10.0	25.3	6.4	58.6	10.5	16.9	-2.7	-13.0

PER SHARE DATA

	1996	1995	1994	1993	1992	1991	1990	1989	1988	1987
Dividends, Net Income ($)	0.00	0.00	0.00	0.13	0.00	0.16	0.00	0.00	0.00	0.00
Distrib'ns, Cap Gain ($)	3.68	8.05	1.50	3.70	2.75	0.00	0.00	0.00	0.00	0.80
Net Asset Value ($)	55.68	51.31	41.36	38.73	33.79	33.92	21.46	19.42	16.60	17.06
Expense Ratio (%)	1.39	1.56	1.54	1.64	1.72	1.83	2.09	1.86	1.76	1.44
Yield (%)	0.00	0.00	0.00	0.30	0.00	0.47	0.00	0.00	0.00	0.00
Portfolio Turnover (%)	112	102	213	259	353	442	327	397	140	73
Total Assets (Millions $)	497	400	227	229	130	124	96	71	148	140

PORTFOLIO (as of 9/30/96)

Portfolio Manager: Adam Hetnarski - 1996

Investm't Category: Aggressive Growth

✔ Domestic	Index
✔ Foreign	✔ Sector
Asset Allocation	State Specific

Investment Style

Large-Cap Growth	Large-Cap Value
✔ Mid-Cap Growth	Mid-Cap Value
✔ Small-Cap Growth	Small-Cap Value

Portfolio

6.6% cash	0.0% corp bonds
93.4% stocks	0.0% gov't bonds
0.0% preferred	0.0% muni bonds
0.0% conv't/warrants	0.0% other

SHAREHOLDER INFORMATION

Minimum Investment
Initial: $2,500   Subsequent: $250

Minimum IRA Investment
Initial: $500   Subsequent: $250

Maximum Fees
Load: 3.00% front   12b-1: none
Other: 0.75% fee (less than 30 days), *ff*

Distributions
Income: Apr, Dec   Capital Gains: Apr, Dec

Exchange Options
Number Per Year: no limit   Fee: $7.50
Telephone: yes (money market fund available)

Services
IRA, pension, auto exchange, auto invest, auto withdraw

Fidelity Sel Telecommunications

(FSTCX) *Growth*

82 Devonshire St.
Mail Zone F9A
Boston, MA 02109
800-544-8888, 801-534-1910
www.fidelity.com

PERFORMANCE

fund inception date: 7/29/85

	3yr Annual	5yr Annual	10yr Annual	Bull	Bear
Return (%)	12.5	16.3	17.8	47.2	-5.2
Differ from Category (+/-)	-3.2 blw av	2.0 abv av	3.9 high	-15.2 low	1.5 abv av

Total Risk	Standard Deviation		Category Risk	Risk Index		Beta
abv av	10.5%		av	1.0		0.77

	1996	1995	1994	1993	1992	1991	1990	1989	1988	1987
Return (%)...............	5.3	29.6	4.3	29.7	15.3	30.8	-16.4	50.8	27.7	15.2
Differ from Category (+/-)	-14.8	-0.7	4.6	15.7	3.5	-5.2	-10.3	24.7	9.6	13.2
Return, Tax-Adjusted (%)...	1.4	27.1	2.9	25.8	14.5	30.3	-17.1	49.0	27.3	14.3

PER SHARE DATA

	1996	1995	1994	1993	1992	1991	1990	1989	1988	1987
Dividends, Net Income ($).	0.27	0.39	0.53	0.20	0.18	0.28	0.43	0.12	0.12	0.02
Distrib'ns, Cap Gain ($) ...	5.87	2.75	1.07	4.18	0.48	0.00	0.00	0.98	0.03	0.36
Net Asset Value ($)	41.16	45.21	37.48	37.54	32.51	28.79	22.23	27.11	18.73	14.78
Expense Ratio (%)........	1.52	1.55	1.53	1.74	1.90	1.97	1.85	2.12	2.48	1.52
Yield (%)	0.57	0.81	1.37	0.47	0.54	0.97	1.93	0.42	0.63	0.13
Portfolio Turnover (%).....	89	107	241	115	20	262	341	224	162	284
Total Assets (Millions $)...	450	451	363	414	111	68	55	114	44	32

PORTFOLIO (as of 9/30/96)

Portfolio Manager: Nicholas Thakore - 1996

Investm't Category: Growth
- ✔ Domestic
- ✔ Foreign
-   Asset Allocation
-   Index
- ✔ Sector
-   State Specific

Investment Style

Large-Cap Growth	Large-Cap Value
Mid-Cap Growth	✔ Mid-Cap Value
Small-Cap Growth	Small-Cap Value

Portfolio

6.8% cash	0.0% corp bonds
93.2% stocks	0.0% gov't bonds
0.0% preferred	0.0% muni bonds
0.0% conv't/warrants	0.0% other

SHAREHOLDER INFORMATION

Minimum Investment
Initial: $2,500   Subsequent: $250

Minimum IRA Investment
Initial: $500   Subsequent: $250

Maximum Fees
Load: 3.00% front   12b-1: none
Other: 0.75% fee (less than 30 days), *ff*

Distributions
Income: Apr, Dec   Capital Gains: Apr, Dec

Exchange Options
Number Per Year: no limit   Fee: $7.50
Telephone: yes (money market fund available)

Services
IRA, pension, auto exchange, auto invest, auto withdraw

Fidelity Sel Transportation (FSRFX)

Aggressive Growth

82 Devonshire St.
Mail Zone F9A
Boston, MA 02109
800-544-8888, 801-534-1910
www.fidelity.com

PERFORMANCE

fund inception date: 9/29/86

	3yr Annual	5yr Annual	10yr Annual	Bull	Bear
Return (%)	9.4	15.9	14.0	28.7	-2.6
Differ from Category (+/-)	-6.4 low	0.6 av	-1.0 blw av	-42.4 low	8.0 high

Total Risk	Standard Deviation	Category Risk	Risk Index	Beta
abv av	11.2%	low	0.8	0.74

	1996	1995	1994	1993	1992	1991	1990	1989	1988	1987
Return (%)	9.5	15.1	3.8	29.3	23.7	54.1	-21.6	28.4	38.4	-17.5
Differ from Category (+/-)	-9.6	-19.2	3.8	10.0	12.0	2.0	-16.2	0.0	22.0	-15.1
Return, Tax-Adjusted (%)	8.5	13.3	0.8	26.1	23.0	53.9	-22.8	22.8	38.4	-17.9

PER SHARE DATA

	1996	1995	1994	1993	1992	1991	1990	1989	1988	1987
Dividends, Net Income ($)	0.00	0.00	0.00	0.00	0.00	0.04	0.00	0.00	0.00	0.00
Distrib'ns, Cap Gain ($)	0.71	1.22	2.19	1.96	0.36	0.00	0.50	2.31	0.00	0.13
Net Asset Value ($)	22.28	21.00	19.29	20.76	17.64	14.55	9.47	12.58	11.63	8.40
Expense Ratio (%)	2.44	2.36	2.39	2.48	2.43	2.39	2.50	2.50	2.41	1.60
Yield (%)	0.00	0.00	0.00	0.00	0.00	0.27	0.00	0.00	0.00	0.00
Portfolio Turnover (%)	175	178	115	116	423	187	156	172	255	218
Total Assets (Millions $)	10	9	11	10	6	2	0	1	3	1

PORTFOLIO (as of 9/30/96)

Portfolio Manager: Steve DuFour - 1994

Investm't Category: Aggressive Growth
- ✔ Domestic
- ✔ Foreign
- Asset Allocation
- Index
- ✔ Sector
- State Specific

Investment Style
- Large-Cap Growth
- ✔ Mid-Cap Growth
- Small-Cap Growth
- Large-Cap Value
- ✔ Mid-Cap Value
- Small-Cap Value

Portfolio

10.7% cash	0.0% corp bonds
89.3% stocks	0.0% gov't bonds
0.0% preferred	0.0% muni bonds
0.0% conv't/warrants	0.0% other

SHAREHOLDER INFORMATION

Minimum Investment
Initial: $2,500   Subsequent: $250

Minimum IRA Investment
Initial: $500   Subsequent: $250

Maximum Fees
Load: 3.00% front   12b-1: none
Other: 0.75% fee (less than 30 days), *ff*

Distributions
Income: Apr, Dec   Capital Gains: Apr, Dec

Exchange Options
Number Per Year: no limit   Fee: $7.50
Telephone: yes (money market fund available)

Services
IRA, pension, auto exchange, auto invest, auto withdraw

Fidelity Sel Utilities Growth (FSUTX)

Growth & Income

82 Devonshire St.
Mail Zone F9A
Boston, MA 02109
800-544-8888, 801-534-1910
www.fidelity.com

PERFORMANCE

fund inception date: 12/10/81

	3yr Annual	5yr Annual	10yr Annual	Bull	Bear
Return (%)	11.4	11.5	11.9	46.8	-7.6
Differ from Category (+/-)	-3.9 blw av	-2.4 low	-0.8 blw av	-13.0 blw av	-1.2 blw av

Total Risk	Standard Deviation	Category Risk	Risk Index	Beta
av	9.0%	blw av	1.0	0.65

	1996	1995	1994	1993	1992	1991	1990	1989	1988	1987
Return (%)..............	11.4	34.3	-7.5	12.5	10.5	21.0	0.5	39.0	16.4	-9.3
Differ from Category (+/-) .	-8.3	4.2	-6.2	-1.3	-0.2	-8.1	6.4	15.5	-0.4	-9.5
Return, Tax-Adjusted (%)...	8.4	33.2	-9.2	7.7	7.8	18.0	-0.7	37.7	14.0	-10.9

PER SHARE DATA

	1996	1995	1994	1993	1992	1991	1990	1989	1988	1987
Dividends, Net Income ($).	0.70	0.84	1.05	1.12	1.33	1.69	0.60	0.81	1.42	0.45
Distrib'ns, Cap Gain ($) ...	3.54	0.00	0.67	4.94	1.70	1.19	0.57	0.00	0.00	0.84
Net Asset Value ($)	43.90	43.59	33.08	37.58	38.80	38.01	34.02	35.05	25.90	23.49
Expense Ratio (%)........	1.38	1.42	1.35	1.42	1.51	1.65	1.67	1.21	1.94	1.45
Yield (%)	1.47	1.92	3.11	2.63	3.28	4.31	1.73	2.31	5.48	1.84
Portfolio Turnover (%).....	65	24	61	34	45	45	75	75	143	161
Total Assets (Millions $)...	249	312	202	275	247	264	167	152	82	77

PORTFOLIO (as of 9/30/96)

Portfolio Manager: John Muresianu - 1992

Investm't Category: Growth & Income

✔ Domestic	Index
✔ Foreign	✔ Sector
Asset Allocation	State Specific

Investment Style

Large-Cap Growth	✔ Large-Cap Value
Mid-Cap Growth	Mid-Cap Value
Small-Cap Growth	Small-Cap Value

Portfolio

1.1% cash	0.0% corp bonds
98.1% stocks	0.0% gov't bonds
0.0% preferred	0.0% muni bonds
0.8% conv't/warrants	0.0% other

SHAREHOLDER INFORMATION

Minimum Investment
Initial: $2,500   Subsequent: $250

Minimum IRA Investment
Initial: $500   Subsequent: $250

Maximum Fees
Load: 3.00% front   12b-1: none
Other: 0.75% fee (less than 30 days), *ff*

Distributions
Income: Apr, Dec   Capital Gains: Apr, Dec

Exchange Options
Number Per Year: no limit   Fee: $7.50
Telephone: yes (money market fund available)

Services
IRA, pension, auto exchange, auto invest, auto withdraw

Fidelity Short—Interm Gov't (FLMGX)

Government Bond

82 Devonshire St.
Mail Zone F9A
Boston, MA 02109
800-544-6666, 801-534-1910
www.fidelity.com

PERFORMANCE

fund inception date: 9/13/91

	3yr Annual	5yr Annual	10yr Annual	Bull	Bear
Return (%)	4.7	4.8	na	17.3	-3.0
Differ from Category (+/-)	-0.2 blw av	-1.8 low	na	-4.7 blw av	3.4 abv av

Total Risk	Standard Deviation	Category Risk	Risk Index	Avg Mat
low	2.6%	blw av	0.6	3.3 yrs

	1996	1995	1994	1993	1992	1991	1990	1989	1988	1987
Return (%).	4.0	11.8	-1.4	5.2	4.7	—	—	—	—	—
Differ from Category (+/-) . .	2.5	-7.8	3.0	-6.4	-2.0	—	—	—	—	—
Return, Tax-Adjusted (%). . .	1.6	9.1	-3.8	2.8	1.9	—	—	—	—	—

PER SHARE DATA

	1996	1995	1994	1993	1992	1991	1990	1989	1988	1987
Dividends, Net Income ($) .	0.58	0.61	0.58	0.58	0.65	—	—	—	—	—
Distrib'ns, Cap Gain ($) . . .	0.00	0.00	0.00	0.00	0.07	—	—	—	—	—
Net Asset Value ($)	9.37	9.58	9.14	9.86	9.93	—	—	—	—	—
Expense Ratio (%).	0.79	0.82	0.95	0.61	0.28	—	—	—	—	—
Yield (%)	6.18	6.36	6.34	5.88	6.50	—	—	—	—	—
Portfolio Turnover (%). . . .	188	266	184	348	419	—	—	—	—	—
Total Assets (Millions $). . .	122	133	151	150	149	—	—	—	—	—

PORTFOLIO (as of 9/30/96)

Portfolio Manager: Curtis Hollingsworth - 1991

Investm't Category: Government Bond

✔ Domestic	Index
Foreign	Sector
Asset Allocation	State Specific

Investment Style

Large-Cap Growth	Large-Cap Value
Mid-Cap Growth	Mid-Cap Value
Small-Cap Growth	Small-Cap Value

Portfolio

1.2% cash	0.0% corp bonds
0.0% stocks	98.8% gov't bonds
0.0% preferred	0.0% muni bonds
0.0% conv't/warrants	0.0% other

SHAREHOLDER INFORMATION

Minimum Investment
Initial: $2,500   Subsequent: $250

Minimum IRA Investment
Initial: $500   Subsequent: $250

Maximum Fees
Load: none   12b-1: none
Other: *f*

Distributions
Income: monthly   Capital Gains: Dec

Exchange Options
Number Per Year: 4   Fee: none
Telephone: yes (money market fund available)

Services
IRA, pension, auto exchange, auto invest, auto withdraw

Fidelity Short-Term Bond

(FSHBX)

Corporate Bond

82 Devonshire St.
Mail Zone F9A
Boston, MA 02109
800-544-6666, 801-534-1910
www.fidelity.com

PERFORMANCE

fund inception date: 9/15/86

	3yr Annual	5yr Annual	10yr Annual	Bull	Bear
Return (%)	3.3	5.2	6.5	14.0	-3.9
Differ from Category (+/-)	-3.0 low	-3.1 low	-1.6 low	-10.8 low	1.2 abv av

Total Risk	Standard Deviation	Category Risk	Risk Index	Avg Mat
low	2.7%	blw av	0.6	2.1 yrs

	1996	1995	1994	1993	1992	1991	1990	1989	1988	1987
Return (%)	4.7	9.8	-4.1	9.1	7.3	14.0	5.7	10.5	5.7	3.9
Differ from Category (+/-)	-0.5	-8.2	-1.0	-2.7	-1.6	-3.2	1.7	1.1	-3.6	1.5
Return, Tax-Adjusted (%)	2.2	7.3	-6.5	6.3	4.1	10.4	2.3	7.0	2.3	0.6

PER SHARE DATA

	1996	1995	1994	1993	1992	1991	1990	1989	1988	1987
Dividends, Net Income ($)	0.56	0.54	0.57	0.66	0.74	0.81	0.80	0.80	0.81	0.83
Distrib'ns, Cap Gain ($)	0.00	0.00	0.00	0.00	0.00	0.00	0.00	0.00	0.00	0.00
Net Asset Value ($)	8.72	8.88	8.60	9.55	9.38	9.45	9.05	9.34	9.21	9.50
Expense Ratio (%)	0.69	0.69	0.80	0.77	0.86	0.83	0.83	0.89	0.88	0.90
Yield (%)	6.42	6.08	6.62	6.91	7.88	8.57	8.83	8.56	8.79	8.73
Portfolio Turnover (%)	151	113	73	63	87	164	148	171	251	149
Total Assets (Millions $)	1,006	1,196	1,514	2,469	1,657	568	224	203	287	246

PORTFOLIO (as of 9/30/96)

Portfolio Manager: Charles Morrison - 1995

Investm't Category: Corporate Bond

✔ Domestic   Index
✔ Foreign   Sector
   Asset Allocation   State Specific

Investment Style

Large-Cap Growth   Large-Cap Value
Mid-Cap Growth   Mid-Cap Value
Small-Cap Growth   Small-Cap Value

Portfolio

0.0%	cash	33.4%	corp bonds
0.0%	stocks	49.0%	gov't bonds
0.0%	preferred	0.0%	muni bonds
0.0%	conv't/warrants	18.0%	other

SHAREHOLDER INFORMATION

Minimum Investment
Initial: $2,500   Subsequent: $250

Minimum IRA Investment
Initial: $500   Subsequent: $250

Maximum Fees
Load: none   12b-1: none
Other: *f*

Distributions
Income: monthly   Capital Gains: Jun, Dec

Exchange Options
Number Per Year: 4   Fee: none
Telephone: yes (money market fund available)

Services
IRA, pension, auto exchange, auto invest, auto withdraw

Fidelity Small Cap Stock

(FDSCX)

Aggressive Growth

82 Devonshire St.
Mail Zone F9A
Boston, MA 02109
800-544-6666, 801-534-1910
www.fidelity.com

PERFORMANCE

fund inception date: 6/28/93

	3yr Annual	5yr Annual	10yr Annual	Bull	Bear
Return (%)	11.6	na	na	53.2	-11.5
Differ from Category (+/-)	-4.2 blw av	na	na	-17.9 blw av	-0.9 av

Total Risk	Standard Deviation	Category Risk	Risk Index	Beta
high	15.6%	abv av	1.1	0.90

	1996	1995	1994	1993	1992	1991	1990	1989	1988	1987
Return (%)	13.6	26.6	-3.4	—	—	—	—	—	—	—
Differ from Category (+/-)	-5.5	-7.7	-3.4	—	—	—	—	—	—	—
Return, Tax-Adjusted (%)	12.4	24.2	-3.5	—	—	—	—	—	—	—

PER SHARE DATA

	1996	1995	1994	1993	1992	1991	1990	1989	1988	1987
Dividends, Net Income ($)	0.01	0.08	0.01	—	—	—	—	—	—	—
Distrib'ns, Cap Gain ($)	0.51	0.77	0.00	—	—	—	—	—	—	—
Net Asset Value ($)	13.56	12.39	10.45	—	—	—	—	—	—	—
Expense Ratio (%)	1.01	0.97	1.20	—	—	—	—	—	—	—
Yield (%)	0.07	0.60	0.09	—	—	—	—	—	—	—
Portfolio Turnover (%)	192	182	210	—	—	—	—	—	—	—
Total Assets (Millions $)	520	438	664	—	—	—	—	—	—	—

PORTFOLIO (as of 9/30/96)

Portfolio Manager: Brad Lewis - 1993

Investm't Category: Aggressive Growth
✔ Domestic   Index
✔ Foreign   Sector
  Asset Allocation   State Specific

Investment Style
  Large-Cap Growth   Large-Cap Value
  Mid-Cap Growth   Mid-Cap Value
✔ Small-Cap Growth   Small-Cap Value

Portfolio
  5.3% cash   0.0% corp bonds
  94.7% stocks   0.0% gov't bonds
  0.0% preferred   0.0% muni bonds
  0.0% conv't/warrants 0.0% other

SHAREHOLDER INFORMATION

Minimum Investment
Initial: $2,500   Subsequent: $250

Minimum IRA Investment
Initial: $500   Subsequent: $250

Maximum Fees
Load: 3.00% front   12b-1: none
Other: 0.75% redemption fee (90 days)

Distributions
Income: June, Dec   Capital Gains: June, Dec

Exchange Options
Number Per Year: 4   Fee: none
Telephone: yes (money market fund available)

Services
IRA, pension, auto exchange, auto invest, auto withdraw

Fidelity Southeast Asia
(FSEAX)
International Stock

82 Devonshire St.
Mail Zone F9A
Boston, MA 02109
800-544-6666, 801-534-1910
www.fidelity.com

PERFORMANCE

fund inception date: 4/19/93

	3yr Annual	5yr Annual	10yr Annual	Bull	Bear
Return (%)	-1.2	na	na	25.7	-16.4
Differ from Category (+/-)	-7.5 low	na	na	1.4 av	-9.2 low

Total Risk	Standard Deviation	Category Risk	Risk Index	Beta
high	20.5%	high	2.0	1.35

	1996	1995	1994	1993	1992	1991	1990	1989	1988	1987
Return (%)	10.1	12.1	-21.8	—	—	—	—	—	—	—
Differ from Category (+/-)	-4.7	3.0	-18.7	—	—	—	—	—	—	—
Return, Tax-Adjusted (%)	8.8	11.3	-21.8	—	—	—	—	—	—	—

PER SHARE DATA

	1996	1995	1994	1993	1992	1991	1990	1989	1988	1987
Dividends, Net Income ($)	0.17	0.23	0.00	—	—	—	—	—	—	—
Distrib'ns, Cap Gain ($)	0.40	0.00	0.00	—	—	—	—	—	—	—
Net Asset Value ($)	15.03	14.17	12.84	—	—	—	—	—	—	—
Expense Ratio (%)	1.12	1.10	1.47	—	—	—	—	—	—	—
Yield (%)	1.10	1.62	0.00	—	—	—	—	—	—	—
Portfolio Turnover (%)	102	94	157	—	—	—	—	—	—	—
Total Assets (Millions $)	795	684	660	—	—	—	—	—	—	—

PORTFOLIO (as of 9/30/96)

Portfolio Manager: Allan Liu - 1993

Investm't Category: International Stock
- Domestic
- ✔ Foreign
- Asset Allocation
- Index
- Sector
- State Specific

Investment Style
- Large-Cap Growth
- Mid-Cap Growth
- Small-Cap Growth
- Large-Cap Value
- Mid-Cap Value
- Small-Cap Value

Portfolio
6.5% cash	0.0% corp bonds
93.5% stocks	0.0% gov't bonds
0.0% preferred	0.0% muni bonds
0.0% conv't/warrants	0.0% other

SHAREHOLDER INFORMATION

Minimum Investment
Initial: $2,500   Subsequent: $250

Minimum IRA Investment
Initial: $500   Subsequent: $250

Maximum Fees
Load: 3.00% front   12b-1: none
Other: 1.50% redemption fee (90 days); f

Distributions
Income: Dec   Capital Gains: Dec

Exchange Options
Number Per Year: 4   Fee: none
Telephone: yes (money market fund available)

Services
IRA, pension, auto exchange, auto invest, auto withdraw

Fidelity Spartan Aggressive Muni (SPAMX)

Tax-Exempt Bond

82 Devonshire St.
Mail Zone F9A
Boston, MA 02109
800-544-8888, 801-534-1910
www.fidelity.com

this fund is closed to new investors

PERFORMANCE

fund inception date: 4/29/93

	3yr Annual	5yr Annual	10yr Annual	Bull	Bear
Return (%)	4.8	na	na	21.0	-6.0
Differ from Category (+/-)	0.6 abv av	na	na	2.6 abv av	-0.6 av

Total Risk	Standard Deviation	Category Risk	Risk Index	Avg Mat
blw av	5.8%	av	1.0	15.1 yrs

	1996	1995	1994	1993	1992	1991	1990	1989	1988	1987
Return (%)	4.1	17.7	-6.2	—	—	—	—	—	—	—
Differ from Category (+/-)	0.4	2.5	-0.9	—	—	—	—	—	—	—
Return, Tax-Adjusted (%)	4.1	17.7	-6.2	—	—	—	—	—	—	—

PER SHARE DATA

	1996	1995	1994	1993	1992	1991	1990	1989	1988	1987
Dividends, Net Income ($)	0.55	0.58	0.60	—	—	—	—	—	—	—
Distrib'ns, Cap Gain ($)	0.00	0.00	0.00	—	—	—	—	—	—	—
Net Asset Value ($)	10.09	10.24	9.23	—	—	—	—	—	—	—
Expense Ratio (%)	0.60	0.60	0.60	—	—	—	—	—	—	—
Yield (%)	5.45	5.66	6.50	—	—	—	—	—	—	—
Portfolio Turnover (%)	45	51	64	—	—	—	—	—	—	—
Total Assets (Millions $)	93	82	57	—	—	—	—	—	—	—

PORTFOLIO (as of 9/30/96)

Portfolio Manager: Tanya M. Roy - 1995

Investm't Category: Tax-Exempt Bond

✔ Domestic   Index
 Foreign   Sector
 Asset Allocation State Specific

Investment Style

Large-Cap Growth   Large-Cap Value
Mid-Cap Growth   Mid-Cap Value
Small-Cap Growth   Small-Cap Value

Portfolio

2.2% cash	0.0% corp bonds
0.0% stocks	0.0% gov't bonds
0.0% preferred	97.8% muni bonds
0.0% conv't/warrants	0.0% other

SHAREHOLDER INFORMATION

Minimum Investment
Initial: $10,000   Subsequent: $1,000

Minimum IRA Investment
Initial: na   Subsequent: na

Maximum Fees
Load: 1.00% redemption   12b-1: none
Other: redemption fee applies for 6 months; *f*

Distributions
Income: monthly   Capital Gains: Oct, Dec

Exchange Options
Number Per Year: 4   Fee: $5
Telephone: yes (money market fund available)

Services
auto exchange, auto invest, auto withdraw

Fidelity Spartan CA Interm Muni Income

(FSCMX) *Tax-Exempt Bond*

82 Devonshire St.
Mail Zone F9A
Boston, MA 02109
800-544-8888, 801-534-1910
www.fidelity.com

PERFORMANCE

fund inception date: 12/30/93

	3yr Annual	5yr Annual	10yr Annual	Bull	Bear
Return (%)	4.7	na	na	19.5	-5.1
Differ from Category (+/-)	0.5 abv av	na	na	1.1 av	0.3 abv av

Total Risk	Standard Deviation	Category Risk	Risk Index	Avg Mat
blw av	4.7%	blw av	0.9	8.5 yrs

	1996	1995	1994	1993	1992	1991	1990	1989	1988	1987
Return (%)	4.6	15.1	-4.7	—	—	—	—	—	—	—
Differ from Category (+/-)	0.9	-0.1	0.6	—	—	—	—	—	—	—
Return, Tax-Adjusted (%)	4.6	15.1	-4.7	—	—	—	—	—	—	—

PER SHARE DATA

	1996	1995	1994	1993	1992	1991	1990	1989	1988	1987
Dividends, Net Income ($)	0.45	0.47	0.46	—	—	—	—	—	—	—
Distrib'ns, Cap Gain ($)	0.00	0.00	0.00	—	—	—	—	—	—	—
Net Asset Value ($)	9.93	9.94	9.07	—	—	—	—	—	—	—
Expense Ratio (%)	0.24	0.05	0.00	—	—	—	—	—	—	—
Yield (%)	4.53	4.72	5.07	—	—	—	—	—	—	—
Portfolio Turnover (%)	35	55	0	—	—	—	—	—	—	—
Total Assets (Millions $)	74	63	38	—	—	—	—	—	—	—

PORTFOLIO (as of 9/30/96)

Portfolio Manager: Jonathan D. Short - 1995

Investm't Category: Tax-Exempt Bond
✔ Domestic   Index
   Foreign   Sector
   Asset Allocation   ✔ State Specific

Investment Style
Large-Cap Growth   Large-Cap Value
Mid-Cap Growth   Mid-Cap Value
Small-Cap Growth   Small-Cap Value

Portfolio
1.2% cash	0.0% corp bonds
0.0% stocks	0.0% gov't bonds
0.0% preferred	98.8% muni bonds
0.0% conv't/warrants	0.0% other

SHAREHOLDER INFORMATION

Minimum Investment
Initial: $10,000   Subsequent: $1,000

Minimum IRA Investment
Initial: na   Subsequent: na

Maximum Fees
Load: none   12b-1: none
Other: f

Distributions
Income: monthly   Capital Gains: Apr, Dec

Exchange Options
Number Per Year: 4   Fee: $5
Telephone: yes (money market fund available)

Services
auto exchange, auto invest, auto withdraw

Fidelity Spartan CA Muni Income (FSCAX)

Tax-Exempt Bond

82 Devonshire St.
Mail Zone F9A
Boston, MA 02109
800-544-8888, 801-534-1910
www.fidelity.com

PERFORMANCE
fund inception date: 11/27/89

	3yr Annual	5yr Annual	10yr Annual	Bull	Bear
Return (%)	4.2	7.0	na	21.6	-7.8
Differ from Category (+/-)	0.0 av	0.6 abv av	na	3.2 high	-2.4 low

Total Risk	Standard Deviation	Category Risk	Risk Index	Avg Mat
blw av	6.3%	high	1.1	16.1 yrs

	1996	1995	1994	1993	1992	1991	1990	1989	1988	1987
Return (%)	4.7	18.9	-9.0	14.0	8.8	11.5	8.1	—	—	—
Differ from Category (+/-)	1.0	3.7	-3.7	2.2	0.5	0.1	1.7	—	—	—
Return, Tax-Adjusted (%)	4.7	18.9	-9.5	12.9	8.6	11.5	8.1	—	—	—

PER SHARE DATA

	1996	1995	1994	1993	1992	1991	1990	1989	1988	1987
Dividends, Net Income ($)	0.55	0.57	0.60	0.63	0.65	0.67	0.71	—	—	—
Distrib'ns, Cap Gain ($)	0.00	0.00	0.18	0.39	0.07	0.00	0.00	—	—	—
Net Asset Value ($)	10.57	10.64	9.46	11.23	10.79	10.61	10.15	—	—	—
Expense Ratio (%)	0.54	0.55	0.52	0.40	0.36	0.19	0.00	—	—	—
Yield (%)	5.20	5.35	6.22	5.42	5.98	6.31	6.99	—	—	—
Portfolio Turnover (%)	38	30	54	26	13	15	5	—	—	—
Total Assets (Millions $)	406	406	371	596	419	436	220	—	—	—

PORTFOLIO (as of 9/30/96)

Portfolio Manager: Diane McLaughlin - 1996

Investm't Category: Tax-Exempt Bond

✔ Domestic	Index
Foreign	Sector
Asset Allocation	✔ State Specific

Investment Style

Large-Cap Growth	Large-Cap Value
Mid-Cap Growth	Mid-Cap Value
Small-Cap Growth	Small-Cap Value

Portfolio

1.6% cash	0.0% corp bonds
0.0% stocks	0.0% gov't bonds
0.0% preferred	96.0% muni bonds
0.0% conv't/warrants	2.4% other

SHAREHOLDER INFORMATION

Minimum Investment
Initial: $10,000   Subsequent: $1,000

Minimum IRA Investment
Initial: na   Subsequent: na

Maximum Fees
Load: 0.50% redemption   12b-1: none
Other: redemption fee applies for 6 months; f

Distributions
Income: monthly   Capital Gains: Apr, Dec

Exchange Options
Number Per Year: 4   Fee: $5
Telephone: yes (money market fund available)

Services
auto exchange, auto invest, auto withdraw

Fidelity Spartan Conn Muni Income (FICNX)

Tax-Exempt Bond

82 Devonshire St.
Mail Zone F9A
Boston, MA 02109
800-544-8888, 801-534-1910
www.fidelity.com

PERFORMANCE

fund inception date: 10/27/87

	3yr Annual	5yr Annual	10yr Annual	Bull	Bear
Return (%)	4.3	6.7	na	19.8	-6.5
Differ from Category (+/-)	0.1 av	0.3 av	na	1.4 abv av	-1.1 blw av

Total Risk	Standard Deviation	Category Risk	Risk Index	Avg Mat
blw av	5.9%	abv av	1.1	13.3 yrs

	1996	1995	1994	1993	1992	1991	1990	1989	1988	1987
Return (%).	4.2	17.1	-7.1	12.9	8.2	10.5	6.6	10.4	10.1	—
Differ from Category (+/-). .	0.5	1.9	-1.8	1.1	-0.1	-0.9	0.2	1.4	0.1	—
Return, Tax-Adjusted (%). . .	4.2	17.1	-7.4	12.0	8.2	10.5	6.4	10.3	10.1	—

PER SHARE DATA

	1996	1995	1994	1993	1992	1991	1990	1989	1988	1987
Dividends, Net Income ($)	0.56	0.61	0.63	0.67	0.69	0.68	0.68	0.70	0.71	—
Distrib'ns, Cap Gain ($) . . .	0.00	0.00	0.11	0.33	0.00	0.00	0.04	0.02	0.00	—
Net Asset Value ($)	11.13	11.24	10.15	11.70	11.28	11.09	10.68	10.72	10.39	—
Expense Ratio (%).	na	0.55	0.55	0.55	0.55	0.55	0.62	0.54	0.11	—
Yield (%)	5.03	5.42	6.14	5.56	6.11	6.13	6.34	6.51	6.83	—
Portfolio Turnover (%).	na	39	11	45	11	6	18	8	11	—
Total Assets (Millions $). . .	333	357	312	448	419	359	251	186	80	—

PORTFOLIO (as of 9/30/96)

Portfolio Manager: Deborah Watson - 1996

Investm't Category: Tax-Exempt Bond
✔ Domestic   Index
  Foreign   Sector
  Asset Allocation ✔ State Specific

Investment Style
  Large-Cap Growth   Large-Cap Value
  Mid-Cap Growth   Mid-Cap Value
  Small-Cap Growth   Small-Cap Value

Portfolio
  3.5% cash   0.0% corp bonds
  0.0% stocks   0.0% gov't bonds
  0.0% preferred   96.5% muni bonds
  0.0% conv't/warrants 0.0% other

SHAREHOLDER INFORMATION

Minimum Investment
Initial: $10,000   Subsequent: $1,000

Minimum IRA Investment
Initial: na   Subsequent: na

Maximum Fees
Load: 0.50% redemption   12b-1: none
Other: redemption fee applies for 6 months; *f*

Distributions
Income: monthly   Capital Gains: Jan, Dec

Exchange Options
Number Per Year: 4   Fee: $5
Telephone: yes (money market fund available)

Services
auto exchange, auto invest, auto withdraw

Fidelity Spartan Florida Muni Income (FFLIX)

Tax-Exempt Bond

82 Devonshire St.
Mail Zone F9A
Boston, MA 02109
800-544-8888, 801-534-1910
www.fidelity.com

PERFORMANCE

fund inception date: 3/16/92

	3yr Annual	5yr Annual	10yr Annual	Bull	Bear
Return (%)	4.7	na	na	21.5	-6.7
Differ from Category (+/-)	0.5 abv av	na	na	3.1 high	-1.3 blw av

Total Risk	Standard Deviation	Category Risk	Risk Index	Avg Mat
blw av	6.3%	high	1.1	14.0 yrs

	1996	1995	1994	1993	1992	1991	1990	1989	1988	1987
Return (%)	3.9	18.6	-6.8	14.8	—	—	—	—	—	—
Differ from Category (+/-)	0.2	3.4	-1.5	3.0	—	—	—	—	—	—
Return, Tax-Adjusted (%)	3.9	18.6	-6.8	14.2	—	—	—	—	—	—

PER SHARE DATA

	1996	1995	1994	1993	1992	1991	1990	1989	1988	1987
Dividends, Net Income ($)	0.54	0.56	0.58	0.61	—	—	—	—	—	—
Distrib'ns, Cap Gain ($)	0.00	0.00	0.00	0.20	—	—	—	—	—	—
Net Asset Value ($)	11.12	11.24	9.99	11.33	—	—	—	—	—	—
Expense Ratio (%)	na	0.55	0.54	0.25	—	—	—	—	—	—
Yield (%)	4.85	4.98	5.80	5.29	—	—	—	—	—	—
Portfolio Turnover (%)	na	65	49	50	—	—	—	—	—	—
Total Assets (Millions $)	390	403	339	450	—	—	—	—	—	—

PORTFOLIO (as of 9/30/96)

Portfolio Manager: Jonathan D. Short - 1996

Investm't Category: Tax-Exempt Bond
- ✔ Domestic
- Foreign
- Asset Allocation
- Index
- Sector
- ✔ State Specific

Investment Style
- Large-Cap Growth
- Mid-Cap Growth
- Small-Cap Growth
- Large-Cap Value
- Mid-Cap Value
- Small-Cap Value

Portfolio
- 0.7% cash
- 0.0% stocks
- 0.0% preferred
- 0.0% conv't/warrants
- 0.0% corp bonds
- 0.0% gov't bonds
- 97.7% muni bonds
- 1.6% other

SHAREHOLDER INFORMATION

Minimum Investment
Initial: $10,000   Subsequent: $1,000

Minimum IRA Investment
Initial: na   Subsequent: na

Maximum Fees
Load: 0.50% redemption   12b-1: none
Other: redemption fee applies for 6 months; *f*

Distributions
Income: monthly   Capital Gains: Jan, Dec

Exchange Options
Number Per Year: no limit   Fee: $5
Telephone: yes (money market fund available)

Services
auto exchange, auto invest, auto withdraw

Fidelity Spartan
Ginnie Mae (SGNMX)

Mortgage-Backed Bond

82 Devonshire St.
Mail Zone F9A
Boston, MA 02109
800-544-8888, 801-534-1910
www.fidelity.com

fund inception date: 12/27/90

	3yr Annual	5yr Annual	10yr Annual	Bull	Bear
Return (%)	6.4	6.4	na	24.4	-4.2
Differ from Category (+/-)	0.8 high	0.4 abv av	na	3.3 high	-0.6 blw av

Total Risk	Standard Deviation	Category Risk	Risk Index	Avg Mat
low	3.9%	abv av	1.0	7.2 yrs

	1996	1995	1994	1993	1992	1991	1990	1989	1988	1987
Return (%).............	4.9	16.6	-1.6	6.2	6.5	13.7	—	—	—	—
Differ from Category (+/-)..	0.5	1.9	0.1	-0.7	0.3	-0.7	—	—	—	—
Return, Tax-Adjusted (%)...	2.3	13.7	-4.1	3.8	2.9	10.3	—	—	—	—

PER SHARE DATA

	1996	1995	1994	1993	1992	1991	1990	1989	1988	1987
Dividends, Net Income ($).	0.65	0.67	0.62	0.56	0.76	0.84	—	—	—	—
Distrib'ns, Cap Gain ($) ...	0.00	0.00	0.00	0.07	0.24	0.02	—	—	—	—
Net Asset Value ($)	9.99	10.16	9.32	10.10	10.11	10.46	—	—	—	—
Expense Ratio (%)........	0.62	0.65	0.65	0.41	0.17	0.25	—	—	—	—
Yield (%)	6.50	6.59	6.65	5.50	7.34	8.01	—	—	—	—
Portfolio Turnover (%)....	115	229	285	241	168	41	—	—	—	—
Total Assets (Millions $)...	446	445	347	579	760	702	—	—	—	—

PORTFOLIO (as of 9/30/96)

Portfolio Manager: Kevin E. Grant - 1995

Investm't Category: Mortgage-Backed Bond
✔ Domestic   Index
✔ Foreign   Sector
  Asset Allocation   State Specific

Investment Style
Large-Cap Growth   Large-Cap Value
Mid-Cap Growth   Mid-Cap Value
Small-Cap Growth   Small-Cap Value

Portfolio
2.4% cash   0.0% corp bonds
0.0% stocks   97.4% gov't bonds
0.0% preferred   0.0% muni bonds
0.0% conv't/warrants 0.2% other

SHAREHOLDER INFORMATION

Minimum Investment
Initial: $10,000   Subsequent: $1,000

Minimum IRA Investment
Initial: $10,000   Subsequent: $1,000

Maximum Fees
Load: none   12b-1: none
Other: f

Distributions
Income: monthly   Capital Gains: Oct, Dec

Exchange Options
Number Per Year: 4   Fee: $5
Telephone: yes (money market fund available)

Services
IRA, pension, auto exchange, auto invest, auto withdraw

Fidelity Spartan Gov't Income (SPGVX)

Government Bond

82 Devonshire St.
Mail Zone F9A
Boston, MA 02109
800-544-8888, 801-534-1910
www.fidelity.com

PERFORMANCE

fund inception date: 12/20/88

	3yr Annual	5yr Annual	10yr Annual	Bull	Bear
Return (%)	5.3	6.0	na	22.7	-6.2
Differ from Category (+/-)	0.4 abv av	-0.6 av	na	0.7 abv av	0.2 av

Total Risk	Standard Deviation	Category Risk	Risk Index	Avg Mat
blw av	4.8%	av	1.2	8.6 yrs

	1996	1995	1994	1993	1992	1991	1990	1989	1988	1987
Return (%)	2.6	18.1	-3.6	7.3	7.1	15.1	9.1	15.2	—	—
Differ from Category (+/-)	1.1	-1.5	0.8	-4.3	0.4	-0.6	2.8	-0.1	—	—
Return, Tax-Adjusted (%)	0.1	15.3	-6.2	4.3	3.3	11.8	5.7	11.4	—	—

PER SHARE DATA

	1996	1995	1994	1993	1992	1991	1990	1989	1988	1987
Dividends, Net Income ($)	0.67	0.66	0.70	0.61	0.76	0.83	0.88	0.93	—	—
Distrib'ns, Cap Gain ($)	0.00	0.00	0.00	0.26	0.42	0.04	0.00	0.03	—	—
Net Asset Value ($)	10.20	10.62	9.59	10.68	10.78	11.21	10.56	10.54	—	—
Expense Ratio (%)	0.65	0.65	0.65	0.65	0.65	0.53	0.16	0.65	—	—
Yield (%)	6.56	6.21	7.29	5.57	6.78	7.37	8.33	8.79	—	—
Portfolio Turnover (%)	114	303	354	170	59	96	68	277	—	—
Total Assets (Millions $)	288	249	231	376	474	522	427	274	—	—

PORTFOLIO (as of 9/30/96)

Portfolio Manager: Robert C. Ives - 1993

Investm't Category: Government Bond
- ✔ Domestic
- Foreign
- Asset Allocation
- Index
- Sector
- State Specific

Investment Style
- Large-Cap Growth
- Mid-Cap Growth
- Small-Cap Growth
- Large-Cap Value
- Mid-Cap Value
- Small-Cap Value

Portfolio
- 1.5% cash
- 0.0% stocks
- 0.0% preferred
- 0.0% conv't/warrants
- 0.0% corp bonds
- 98.5% gov't bonds
- 0.0% muni bonds
- 0.0% other

SHAREHOLDER INFORMATION

Minimum Investment
Initial: $10,000   Subsequent: $1,000

Minimum IRA Investment
Initial: $10,000   Subsequent: $1,000

Maximum Fees
Load: none   12b-1: none
Other: *f*

Distributions
Income: monthly   Capital Gains: Dec

Exchange Options
Number Per Year: 4   Fee: $5
Telephone: yes (money market fund available)

Services
IRA, pension, auto exchange, auto invest, auto withdraw

Fidelity Spartan High Income (SPHIX)

Corporate High-Yield Bond

82 Devonshire St.
Mail Zone F9A
Boston, MA 02109
800-544-8888, 801-534-1910
www.fidelity.com

PERFORMANCE

fund inception date: 8/29/90

	3yr Annual	5yr Annual	10yr Annual	Bull	Bear
Return (%)	11.7	15.6	na	39.5	-3.2
Differ from Category (+/-)	3.0 high	3.5 high	na	6.4 high	2.2 high

Total Risk	Standard Deviation	Category Risk	Risk Index	Avg Mat
low	4.1%	blw av	0.9	6.4 yrs

	1996	1995	1994	1993	1992	1991	1990	1989	1988	1987
Return (%)	14.1	18.5	3.2	21.8	21.5	34.3	—	—	—	—
Differ from Category (+/-)	-1.2	1.0	6.1	2.9	5.4	6.7	—	—	—	—
Return, Tax-Adjusted (%)	10.0	14.1	-0.3	16.0	16.0	27.9	—	—	—	—

PER SHARE DATA

	1996	1995	1994	1993	1992	1991	1990	1989	1988	1987
Dividends, Net Income ($)	1.06	1.17	0.99	1.12	1.25	1.29	—	—	—	—
Distrib'ns, Cap Gain ($)	0.25	0.12	0.08	0.79	0.37	0.32	—	—	—	—
Net Asset Value ($)	12.54	12.21	11.46	12.17	11.65	11.00	—	—	—	—
Expense Ratio (%)	0.80	0.80	0.75	0.70	0.70	0.70	—	—	—	—
Yield (%)	8.28	9.48	8.57	8.64	10.39	11.39	—	—	—	—
Portfolio Turnover (%)	170	172	213	136	99	72	—	—	—	—
Total Assets (Millions $)	1,680	1,080	617	664	435	201	—	—	—	—

PORTFOLIO (as of 9/30/96)

Portfolio Manager: Thomas T. Soviero - 1996

Investm't Category: Corp. High-Yield Bond
✔ Domestic	Index
✔ Foreign	Sector
Asset Allocation	State Specific

Investment Style
Large-Cap Growth	Large-Cap Value
Mid-Cap Growth	Mid-Cap Value
Small-Cap Growth	Small-Cap Value

Portfolio
9.0%	cash	0.0%	corp bonds
6.2%	stocks	0.0%	gov't bonds
18.4%	preferred	0.0%	muni bonds
65.5%	conv't/warrants	0.9%	other

SHAREHOLDER INFORMATION

Minimum Investment
Initial: $10,000   Subsequent: $1,000

Minimum IRA Investment
Initial: $10,000   Subsequent: $1,000

Maximum Fees
Load: 1.00% redemption   12b-1: none
Other: redemption fee applies for 9 months; *f*

Distributions
Income: monthly   Capital Gains: Jun, Dec

Exchange Options
Number Per Year: 4   Fee: $5
Telephone: yes (money market fund available)

Services
IRA, pension, auto exchange, auto invest, auto withdraw

Fidelity Spartan Interm Muni Income (FSIMX)

Tax-Exempt Bond

82 Devonshire St.
Mail Zone F9A
Boston, MA 02109
800-544-8888, 801-534-1910
www.fidelity.com

PERFORMANCE

fund inception date: 4/26/93

	3yr Annual	5yr Annual	10yr Annual	Bull	Bear
Return (%)	4.3	na	na	18.7	-5.3
Differ from Category (+/-)	0.1 av	na	na	0.3 av	0.1 abv av

Total Risk	Standard Deviation	Category Risk	Risk Index	Avg Mat
low	4.7%	blw av	0.8	8.0 yrs

	1996	1995	1994	1993	1992	1991	1990	1989	1988	1987
Return (%)	4.5	14.4	-5.1	—	—	—	—	—	—	—
Differ from Category (+/-)	0.8	-0.8	0.2	—	—	—	—	—	—	—
Return, Tax-Adjusted (%)	4.5	14.4	-5.1	—	—	—	—	—	—	—

PER SHARE DATA

	1996	1995	1994	1993	1992	1991	1990	1989	1988	1987
Dividends, Net Income ($)	0.48	0.48	0.50	—	—	—	—	—	—	—
Distrib'ns, Cap Gain ($)	0.00	0.00	0.00	—	—	—	—	—	—	—
Net Asset Value ($)	10.23	10.26	9.41	—	—	—	—	—	—	—
Expense Ratio (%)	0.50	0.42	0.20	—	—	—	—	—	—	—
Yield (%)	4.69	4.67	5.31	—	—	—	—	—	—	—
Portfolio Turnover (%)	64	44	69	—	—	—	—	—	—	—
Total Assets (Millions $)	215	223	205	—	—	—	—	—	—	—

PORTFOLIO (as of 9/30/96)

Portfolio Manager: Norman Lind - 1995

Investm't Category: Tax-Exempt Bond

✔ Domestic	Index
Foreign	Sector
Asset Allocation	State Specific

Investment Style

Large-Cap Growth	Large-Cap Value
Mid-Cap Growth	Mid-Cap Value
Small-Cap Growth	Small-Cap Value

Portfolio

3.6% cash	0.0% corp bonds
0.0% stocks	0.0% gov't bonds
0.0% preferred	96.4% muni bonds
0.0% conv't/warrants	0.0% other

SHAREHOLDER INFORMATION

Minimum Investment
Initial: $10,000   Subsequent: $1,000

Minimum IRA Investment
Initial: na   Subsequent: na

Maximum Fees
Load: none   12b-1: none
Other: *f*

Distributions
Income: monthly   Capital Gains: Oct, Dec

Exchange Options
Number Per Year: 4   Fee: $5
Telephone: yes (money market fund available)

Services
auto exchange, auto invest, auto withdraw

Fidelity Spartan Investment Grade Bond

(FSIBX) *General Bond*

82 Devonshire St.
Mail Zone F9A
Boston, MA 02109
800-544-8888, 801-534-1910
www.fidelity.com

PERFORMANCE

fund inception date: 9/30/92

	3yr Annual	5yr Annual	10yr Annual	Bull	Bear
Return (%)	5.0	na	na	23.8	-8.3
Differ from Category (+/-)	-0.1 av	na	na	3.5 high	-4.1 low

Total Risk	Standard Deviation	Category Risk	Risk Index	Avg Mat
blw av	5.3%	high	1.4	7.9 yrs

	1996	1995	1994	1993	1992	1991	1990	1989	1988	1987
Return (%)	3.1	18.6	-5.2	15.7	—	—	—	—	—	—
Differ from Category (+/-)	-0.8	3.7	-2.9	6.6	—	—	—	—	—	—
Return, Tax-Adjusted (%)	0.7	15.8	-7.9	12.5	—	—	—	—	—	—

PER SHARE DATA

	1996	1995	1994	1993	1992	1991	1990	1989	1988	1987
Dividends, Net Income ($)	0.63	0.65	0.70	0.78	—	—	—	—	—	—
Distrib'ns, Cap Gain ($)	0.00	0.00	0.03	0.01	—	—	—	—	—	—
Net Asset Value ($)	10.11	10.44	9.40	10.68	—	—	—	—	—	—
Expense Ratio (%)	0.65	0.65	0.65	0.65	—	—	—	—	—	—
Yield (%)	6.23	6.22	7.42	7.29	—	—	—	—	—	—
Portfolio Turnover (%)	169	147	44	55	—	—	—	—	—	—
Total Assets (Millions $)	359	161	118	120	—	—	—	—	—	—

PORTFOLIO (as of 9/30/96)

Portfolio Manager: Michael Gray - 1992

Investm't Category: General Bond
✔ Domestic   Index
✔ Foreign   Sector
  Asset Allocation   State Specific

Investment Style
Large-Cap Growth   Large-Cap Value
Mid-Cap Growth   Mid-Cap Value
Small-Cap Growth   Small-Cap Value

Portfolio
0.3% cash   23.5% corp bonds
0.0% stocks   74.9% gov't bonds
0.0% preferred   0.0% muni bonds
0.0% conv't/warrants 1.3% other

SHAREHOLDER INFORMATION

Minimum Investment
Initial: $10,000   Subsequent: $1,000

Minimum IRA Investment
Initial: $10,000   Subsequent: $1,000

Maximum Fees
Load: none   12b-1: none
Other: *f*

Distributions
Income: monthly   Capital Gains: Nov, Dec

Exchange Options
Number Per Year: 4   Fee: $5
Telephone: yes (money market fund available)

Services
IRA, pension, auto exchange, auto invest, auto withdraw

Fidelity Spartan Ltd Maturity Gov't (FSTGX)

82 Devonshire St.
Mail Zone F9A
Boston, MA 02109
800-544-8888, 801-534-1910
www.fidelity.com

Government Bond

PERFORMANCE

fund inception date: 5/2/88

	3yr Annual	5yr Annual	10yr Annual	Bull	Bear
Return (%)	5.5	5.7	na	19.6	-2.9
Differ from Category (+/-)	0.6 abv av	-0.9 blw av	na	-2.4 av	3.5 abv av

Total Risk	Standard Deviation	Category Risk	Risk Index	Avg Mat
low	2.9%	blw av	0.7	5.0 yrs

	1996	1995	1994	1993	1992	1991	1990	1989	1988	1987
Return (%)	4.1	13.9	-1.0	6.4	5.7	11.9	9.1	10.3	—	—
Differ from Category (+/-)	2.6	-5.7	3.4	-5.2	-1.0	-3.8	2.8	-5.0	—	—
Return, Tax-Adjusted (%)	1.5	11.3	-3.2	3.5	3.2	8.5	5.8	7.0	—	—

PER SHARE DATA

	1996	1995	1994	1993	1992	1991	1990	1989	1988	1987
Dividends, Net Income ($)	0.65	0.61	0.55	0.57	0.60	0.81	0.81	0.81	—	—
Distrib'ns, Cap Gain ($)	0.00	0.00	0.00	0.23	0.05	0.06	0.02	0.00	—	—
Net Asset Value ($)	9.74	10.00	9.35	10.00	10.17	10.25	9.99	9.96	—	—
Expense Ratio (%)	0.62	0.65	0.65	0.65	0.61	0.50	0.83	0.68	—	—
Yield (%)	6.67	6.10	5.88	5.57	5.87	7.85	8.09	8.13	—	—
Portfolio Turnover (%)	105	210	391	324	330	288	270	806	—	—
Total Assets (Millions $)	725	829	830	1,356	1,622	2,085	161	134	—	—

PORTFOLIO (as of 9/30/96)

Portfolio Manager: Curtis Hollingsworth - 1988

Investm't Category: Government Bond

✔ Domestic	Index
✔ Foreign	Sector
Asset Allocation	State Specific

Investment Style

Large-Cap Growth	Large-Cap Value
Mid-Cap Growth	Mid-Cap Value
Small-Cap Growth	Small-Cap Value

Portfolio

2.1% cash	0.0% corp bonds
0.0% stocks	97.9% gov't bonds
0.0% preferred	0.0% muni bonds
0.0% conv't/warrants	0.0% other

SHAREHOLDER INFORMATION

Minimum Investment
Initial: $10,000   Subsequent: $1,000

Minimum IRA Investment
Initial: $10,000   Subsequent: $1,000

Maximum Fees
Load: none   12b-1: none
Other: *f*

Distributions
Income: monthly   Capital Gains: Sep, Dec

Exchange Options
Number Per Year: 4   Fee: $5
Telephone: yes (money market fund available)

Services
IRA, pension, auto exchange, auto invest, auto withdraw

Fidelity Spartan MD Muni Income (SMDMX)

Tax-Exempt Bond

82 Devonshire St.
Mail Zone F9A
Boston, MA 02109
800-544-8888, 801-534-1910
www.fidelity.com

PERFORMANCE

fund inception date: 4/22/93

	3yr Annual	5yr Annual	10yr Annual	Bull	Bear
Return (%)	4.2	na	na	19.7	-6.9
Differ from Category (+/-)	0.0 av	na	na	1.3 av	-1.5 blw av

Total Risk	Standard Deviation	Category Risk	Risk Index	Avg Mat
blw av	6.2%	abv av	1.1	12.9 yrs

	1996	1995	1994	1993	1992	1991	1990	1989	1988	1987
Return (%)	3.8	17.7	-7.6	—	—	—	—	—	—	—
Differ from Category (+/-)	0.1	2.5	-2.3	—	—	—	—	—	—	—
Return, Tax-Adjusted (%)	3.8	17.7	-7.6	—	—	—	—	—	—	—

PER SHARE DATA

	1996	1995	1994	1993	1992	1991	1990	1989	1988	1987
Dividends, Net Income ($)	0.47	0.52	0.55	—	—	—	—	—	—	—
Distrib'ns, Cap Gain ($)	0.00	0.00	0.00	—	—	—	—	—	—	—
Net Asset Value ($)	10.03	10.13	9.07	—	—	—	—	—	—	—
Expense Ratio (%)	0.39	0.15	0.03	—	—	—	—	—	—	—
Yield (%)	4.68	5.13	6.06	—	—	—	—	—	—	—
Portfolio Turnover (%)	74	72	64	—	—	—	—	—	—	—
Total Assets (Millions $)	46	46	35	—	—	—	—	—	—	—

PORTFOLIO (as of 9/30/96)

Portfolio Manager: Steven Harvey - 1993

Investm't Category: Tax-Exempt Bond
- ✔ Domestic
- Foreign
- Asset Allocation
- Index
- Sector
- ✔ State Specific

Investment Style
- Large-Cap Growth
- Mid-Cap Growth
- Small-Cap Growth
- Large-Cap Value
- Mid-Cap Value
- Small-Cap Value

Portfolio
- 4.4% cash
- 0.0% stocks
- 0.0% preferred
- 0.0% conv't/warrants
- 0.0% corp bonds
- 0.0% gov't bonds
- 94.6% muni bonds
- 1.0% other

SHAREHOLDER INFORMATION

Minimum Investment
Initial: $10,000   Subsequent: $1,000

Minimum IRA Investment
Initial: na   Subsequent: na

Maximum Fees
Load: 0.50% redemption   12b-1: none
Other: redemption fee applies for 6 months; *f*

Distributions
Income: monthly   Capital Gains: Dec

Exchange Options
Number Per Year: 4   Fee: $5
Telephone: yes (money market fund available)

Services
auto exchange, auto invest, auto withdraw

Fidelity Spartan Muni Income (FSMIX)

Tax-Exempt Bond

82 Devonshire St.
Mail Zone F9A
Boston, MA 02109
800-544-8888, 801-534-1910
www.fidelity.com

PERFORMANCE

fund inception date: 6/4/90

	3yr Annual	5yr Annual	10yr Annual	Bull	Bear
Return (%)	4.4	7.1	na	21.5	-7.4
Differ from Category (+/-)	0.2 av	0.7 abv av	na	3.1 high	-2.0 low

Total Risk	Standard Deviation	Category Risk	Risk Index	Avg Mat
blw av	6.2%	high	1.1	13.7 yrs

	1996	1995	1994	1993	1992	1991	1990	1989	1988	1987
Return (%).	4.5	18.5	-8.2	14.3	8.3	12.5	—	—	—	—
Differ from Category (+/-) . .	0.8	3.3	-2.9	2.5	0.0	1.1	—	—	—	—
Return, Tax-Adjusted (%). . .	4.5	18.5	-8.5	12.8	8.1	12.4	—	—	—	—

PER SHARE DATA

	1996	1995	1994	1993	1992	1991	1990	1989	1988	1987
Dividends, Net Income ($)	0.52	0.56	0.61	0.64	0.69	0.72	—	—	—	—
Distrib'ns, Cap Gain ($) . . .	0.00	0.00	0.08	0.55	0.07	0.03	—	—	—	—
Net Asset Value ($)	10.44	10.51	9.37	10.93	10.64	10.55	—	—	—	—
Expense Ratio (%).	0.54	0.55	0.55	0.47	0.36	0.23	—	—	—	—
Yield (%)	4.98	5.32	6.45	5.57	6.44	6.80	—	—	—	—
Portfolio Turnover (%).	49	69	48	50	62	78	—	—	—	—
Total Assets (Millions $). . .	570	579	535	862	820	710	—	—	—	—

PORTFOLIO (as of 9/30/96)

Portfolio Manager: David L. Murphy - 1995

Investm't Category: Tax-Exempt Bond

✔ Domestic	Index
Foreign	Sector
Asset Allocation	State Specific

Investment Style

Large-Cap Growth	Large-Cap Value
Mid-Cap Growth	Mid-Cap Value
Small-Cap Growth	Small-Cap Value

Portfolio

2.2% cash	0.0% corp bonds
0.0% stocks	0.0% gov't bonds
0.0% preferred	97.6% muni bonds
0.0% conv't/warrants	0.2% other

SHAREHOLDER INFORMATION

Minimum Investment
Initial: $10,000   Subsequent: $1,000

Minimum IRA Investment
Initial: na   Subsequent: na

Maximum Fees
Load: 0.50% redemption   12b-1: none
Other: redemption fee applies for 6 months; *f*

Distributions
Income: monthly   Capital Gains: Oct, Dec

Exchange Options
Number Per Year: 4   Fee: $5
Telephone: yes (money market fund available)

Services
auto exchange, auto invest, auto withdraw

Fidelity Spartan NJ Muni Income (FNJHX)

Tax-Exempt Bond

82 Devonshire St.
Mail Zone F9A
Boston, MA 02109
800-544-8888, 801-534-1910
www.fidelity.com

PERFORMANCE

fund inception date: 12/31/87

	3yr Annual	5yr Annual	10yr Annual	Bull	Bear
Return (%)	4.2	6.8	na	19.4	-6.3
Differ from Category (+/-)	0.0 av	0.4 av	na	1.0 av	-0.9 blw av

Total Risk	Standard Deviation	Category Risk	Risk Index	Avg Mat
blw av	5.3%	av	1.0	14.1 yrs

	1996	1995	1994	1993	1992	1991	1990	1989	1988	1987
Return (%)	4.0	15.3	-5.8	13.0	8.7	12.3	7.1	10.3	10.8	—
Differ from Category (+/-)	0.3	0.1	-0.5	1.2	0.4	0.9	0.7	1.3	0.8	—
Return, Tax-Adjusted (%)	3.6	15.2	-5.8	12.6	8.2	12.0	7.1	10.3	10.8	—

PER SHARE DATA

	1996	1995	1994	1993	1992	1991	1990	1989	1988	1987
Dividends, Net Income ($)	0.58	0.61	0.63	0.63	0.69	0.69	0.67	0.78	0.74	—
Distrib'ns, Cap Gain ($)	0.16	0.01	0.00	0.15	0.16	0.08	0.00	0.00	0.00	—
Net Asset Value ($)	11.16	11.46	10.51	11.82	11.18	11.10	10.61	10.56	10.314	—
Expense Ratio (%)	na	0.55	0.55	0.55	0.51	0.52	0.65	0.56	0.00	—
Yield (%)	5.12	5.31	5.99	5.26	6.08	6.17	6.31	7.38	7.17	—
Portfolio Turnover (%)	na	36	8	25	33	42	82	90	140	—
Total Assets (Millions $)	356	366	325	429	347	297	209	161	95	—

PORTFOLIO (as of 9/30/96)

Portfolio Manager: Janice Bradburn - 1996

Investm't Category: Tax-Exempt Bond

✔ Domestic	Index
Foreign	Sector
Asset Allocation	✔ State Specific

Investment Style

Large-Cap Growth	Large-Cap Value
Mid-Cap Growth	Mid-Cap Value
Small-Cap Growth	Small-Cap Value

Portfolio

2.9% cash	0.0% corp bonds
0.0% stocks	0.0% gov't bonds
0.0% preferred	96.6% muni bonds
0.0% conv't/warrants	0.5% other

SHAREHOLDER INFORMATION

Minimum Investment
Initial: $10,000   Subsequent: $1,000

Minimum IRA Investment
Initial: na   Subsequent: na

Maximum Fees
Load: 0.50% redemption   12b-1: none
Other: redemption fee applies for 6 months; *f*

Distributions
Income: monthly   Capital Gains: Jan, Dec

Exchange Options
Number Per Year: 4   Fee: $5
Telephone: yes (money market fund available)

Services
auto exchange, auto invest, auto withdraw

Fidelity Spartan NY Interm Muni Income

(FSNMX) *Tax-Exempt Bond*

82 Devonshire St.
Mail Zone F9A
Boston, MA 02109
800-544-8888, 801-534-1910
www.fidelity.com

PERFORMANCE

fund inception date: 12/29/93

	3yr Annual	5yr Annual	10yr Annual	Bull	Bear
Return (%)	4.4	na	na	17.7	-4.4
Differ from Category (+/-)	0.2 av	na	na	-0.7 blw av	1.0 abv av

Total Risk	Standard Deviation	Category Risk	Risk Index	Avg Mat
low	4.7%	blw av	0.8	9.2 yrs

	1996	1995	1994	1993	1992	1991	1990	1989	1988	1987
Return (%)	3.8	14.4	-4.2	—	—	—	—	—	—	—
Differ from Category (+/-)	0.1	-0.8	1.1	—	—	—	—	—	—	—
Return, Tax-Adjusted (%)	3.8	14.4	-4.2	—	—	—	—	—	—	—

PER SHARE DATA

	1996	1995	1994	1993	1992	1991	1990	1989	1988	1987
Dividends, Net Income ($)	0.45	0.47	0.46	—	—	—	—	—	—	—
Distrib'ns, Cap Gain ($)	0.00	0.00	0.00	—	—	—	—	—	—	—
Net Asset Value ($)	9.85	9.93	9.12	—	—	—	—	—	—	—
Expense Ratio (%)	0.22	0.00	0.00	—	—	—	—	—	—	—
Yield (%)	4.56	4.73	5.04	—	—	—	—	—	—	—
Portfolio Turnover (%)	77	33	na	—	—	—	—	—	—	—
Total Assets (Millions $)	55	55	31	—	—	—	—	—	—	—

PORTFOLIO (as of 9/30/96)

Portfolio Manager: Norman Lind - 1995

Investm't Category: Tax-Exempt Bond

✔ Domestic	Index
Foreign	Sector
Asset Allocation	✔ State Specific

Investment Style

Large-Cap Growth	Large-Cap Value
Mid-Cap Growth	Mid-Cap Value
Small-Cap Growth	Small-Cap Value

Portfolio

5.3% cash	0.0% corp bonds
0.0% stocks	0.0% gov't bonds
0.0% preferred	94.7% muni bonds
0.0% conv't/warrants	0.0% other

SHAREHOLDER INFORMATION

Minimum Investment
Initial: $10,000   Subsequent: $1,000

Minimum IRA Investment
Initial: na   Subsequent: na

Maximum Fees
Load: none   12b-1: none
Other: *f*

Distributions
Income: monthly   Capital Gains: Mar, Dec

Exchange Options
Number Per Year: 4   Fee: $5
Telephone: yes (money market fund available)

Services
auto exchange, auto invest, auto withdraw

Fidelity Spartan NY Muni Income (FSNYX)

Tax-Exempt Bond

82 Devonshire St.
Mail Zone F9A
Boston, MA 02109
800-544-8888, 801-534-1910
www.fidelity.com

PERFORMANCE

fund inception date: 2/28/90

	3yr Annual	5yr Annual	10yr Annual	Bull	Bear
Return (%)	4.4	7.1	na	21.9	-7.7
Differ from Category (+/-)	0.2 av	0.7 abv av	na	3.5 high	-2.3 low

Total Risk	Standard Deviation	Category Risk	Risk Index	Avg Mat
blw av	6.7%	high	1.2	14.8 yrs

	1996	1995	1994	1993	1992	1991	1990	1989	1988	1987
Return (%)...............	4.3	19.1	-8.4	13.4	9.4	14.4	—	—	—	—
Differ from Category (+/-)..0.6	0.6	3.9	-3.1	1.6	1.1	3.0	—	—	—	—
Return, Tax-Adjusted (%)...4.3	4.3	19.1	-9.1	12.6	9.1	14.3	—	—	—	—

PER SHARE DATA

	1996	1995	1994	1993	1992	1991	1990	1989	1988	1987
Dividends, Net Income ($)	0.54	0.55	0.60	0.62	0.65	0.68	—	—	—	—
Distrib'ns, Cap Gain ($)...	0.00	0.00	0.28	0.28	0.11	0.02	—	—	—	—
Net Asset Value ($)	10.62	10.72	9.50	11.31	10.80	10.60	—	—	—	—
Expense Ratio (%)........	0.54	0.55	0.55	0.48	0.38	0.19	—	—	—	—
Yield (%)	5.08	5.13	6.13	5.34	5.95	6.40	—	—	—	—
Portfolio Turnover (%).....	82	38	50	35	21	40	—	—	—	—
Total Assets (Millions $)...	316	325	284	443	346	258	—	—	—	—

PORTFOLIO (as of 9/30/96)

Portfolio Manager: Norman Lind - 1993

Investm't Category: Tax-Exempt Bond
- ✔ Domestic
- Foreign
- Asset Allocation
- Index
- Sector
- ✔ State Specific

Investment Style
- Large-Cap Growth
- Mid-Cap Growth
- Small-Cap Growth
- Large-Cap Value
- Mid-Cap Value
- Small-Cap Value

Portfolio
2.3% cash	0.0% corp bonds
0.0% stocks	0.0% gov't bonds
0.0% preferred	97.7% muni bonds
0.0% conv't/warrants	0.0% other

SHAREHOLDER INFORMATION

Minimum Investment
Initial: $10,000   Subsequent: $1,000

Minimum IRA Investment
Initial: na   Subsequent: na

Maximum Fees
Load: 0.50% redemption   12b-1: none
Other: redemption fee applies for 6 months; *f*

Distributions
Income: monthly   Capital Gains: Mar, Dec

Exchange Options
Number Per Year: 4   Fee: $5
Telephone: yes (money market fund available)

Services
auto exchange, auto invest, auto withdraw

Fidelity Spartan Penn Muni Income (FPXTX)

Tax-Exempt Bond

82 Devonshire St.
Mail Zone F9A
Boston, MA 02109
800-544-8888, 801-534-1910
www.fidelity.com

PERFORMANCE

fund inception date: 8/6/86

	3yr Annual	5yr Annual	10yr Annual	Bull	Bear
Return (%)	5.0	7.4	7.4	20.9	-5.4
Differ from Category (+/-)	0.8 high	1.0 high	0.7 abv av	2.5 abv av	0.0 abv av

Total Risk	Standard Deviation	Category Risk	Risk Index	Avg Mat
blw av	5.5%	av	1.0	12.6 yrs

	1996	1995	1994	1993	1992	1991	1990	1989	1988	1987
Return (%)	4.0	17.4	-5.1	13.1	9.1	12.4	7.1	9.8	14.2	-5.8
Differ from Category (+/-)	0.3	2.2	0.2	1.3	0.8	1.0	0.7	0.8	4.2	-4.4
Return, Tax-Adjusted (%)	3.8	17.4	-5.9	12.7	9.1	12.4	7.1	9.8	14.2	-5.8

PER SHARE DATA

	1996	1995	1994	1993	1992	1991	1990	1989	1988	1987
Dividends, Net Income ($)	0.52	0.59	0.65	0.67	0.69	0.70	0.69	0.67	0.66	0.69
Distrib'ns, Cap Gain ($)	0.07	0.00	0.31	0.14	0.00	0.00	0.00	0.00	0.00	0.00
Net Asset Value ($)	10.49	10.67	9.62	11.13	10.59	10.37	9.88	9.90	9.66	9.07
Expense Ratio (%)	na	0.55	0.55	0.55	0.55	0.55	0.60	0.78	0.84	0.63
Yield (%)	4.92	5.52	6.54	5.94	6.51	6.75	6.98	6.76	6.83	7.60
Portfolio Turnover (%)	na	49	26	38	8	6	8	23	31	54
Total Assets (Millions $)	275	287	241	305	241	198	142	103	61	41

PORTFOLIO (as of 9/30/96)

Portfolio Manager: Steven Harvey - 1993

Investm't Category: Tax-Exempt Bond

✔ Domestic	Index
Foreign	Sector
Asset Allocation	✔ State Specific

Investment Style

Large-Cap Growth	Large-Cap Value
Mid-Cap Growth	Mid-Cap Value
Small-Cap Growth	Small-Cap Value

Portfolio

6.1% cash	0.0% corp bonds
0.0% stocks	0.0% gov't bonds
0.0% preferred	93.9% muni bonds
0.0% conv't/warrants	0.0% other

SHAREHOLDER INFORMATION

Minimum Investment
Initial: $10,000   Subsequent: $1,000

Minimum IRA Investment
Initial: na   Subsequent: na

Maximum Fees
Load: 0.50% redemption   12b-1: none
Other: redemption fee applies for 6 months; *f*

Distributions
Income: monthly   Capital Gains: Feb, Dec

Exchange Options
Number Per Year: 4   Fee: $5
Telephone: yes (money market fund available)

Services
auto exchange, auto invest, auto withdraw

Fidelity Spartan Short Interim Gov't (SPSIX)

Government Bond

82 Devonshire St.
Mail Zone F9A
Boston, MA 02109
800-544-8888, 801-534-1910
www.fidelity.com

PERFORMANCE

fund inception date: 12/18/92

	3yr Annual	5yr Annual	10yr Annual	Bull	Bear
Return (%)	5.2	na	na	18.9	-3.0
Differ from Category (+/-)	0.3 av	na	na	-3.1 av	3.4 abv av

Total Risk	Standard Deviation	Category Risk	Risk Index	Avg Mat
low	2.6%	blw av	0.7	3.3 yrs

	1996	1995	1994	1993	1992	1991	1990	1989	1988	1987
Return (%)	4.2	12.2	-0.6	5.6	—	—	—	—	—	—
Differ from Category (+/-)	2.7	-7.4	3.8	-6.0	—	—	—	—	—	—
Return, Tax-Adjusted (%)	1.4	9.2	-3.1	3.0	—	—	—	—	—	—

PER SHARE DATA

	1996	1995	1994	1993	1992	1991	1990	1989	1988	1987
Dividends, Net Income ($)	0.66	0.68	0.62	0.65	—	—	—	—	—	—
Distrib'ns, Cap Gain ($)	0.00	0.00	0.00	0.01	—	—	—	—	—	—
Net Asset Value ($)	9.38	9.65	9.23	9.91	—	—	—	—	—	—
Expense Ratio (%)	0.45	0.10	0.10	0.02	—	—	—	—	—	—
Yield (%)	7.03	7.04	6.71	6.55	—	—	—	—	—	—
Portfolio Turnover (%)	161	282	271	587	—	—	—	—	—	—
Total Assets (Millions $)	73	91	48	67	—	—	—	—	—	—

PORTFOLIO (as of 9/30/96)

Portfolio Manager: Curtis Hollingsworth - 1992

Investm't Category: Government Bond
- ✔ Domestic
- Foreign
- Asset Allocation
- Index
- Sector
- State Specific

Investment Style
- Large-Cap Growth
- Mid-Cap Growth
- Small-Cap Growth
- Large-Cap Value
- Mid-Cap Value
- Small-Cap Value

Portfolio
0.2% cash	0.0% corp bonds
0.0% stocks	99.8% gov't bonds
0.0% preferred	0.0% muni bonds
0.0% conv't/warrants	0.0% other

SHAREHOLDER INFORMATION

Minimum Investment
Initial: $10,000   Subsequent: $1,000

Minimum IRA Investment
Initial: $10,000   Subsequent: $1,000

Maximum Fees
Load: none   12b-1: none
Other: f

Distributions
Income: monthly   Capital Gains: Dec

Exchange Options
Number Per Year: 4   Fee: $5
Telephone: yes (money market fund available)

Services
IRA, pension, auto exchange, auto invest, auto withdraw

Fidelity Spartan Short Interm Muni Inc (FSTFX)

82 Devonshire St.
Mail Zone F9A
Boston, MA 02109
800-544-8888, 801-534-1910
www.fidelity.com

Tax-Exempt Bond

PERFORMANCE

fund inception date: 12/24/86

	3yr Annual	5yr Annual	10yr Annual	Bull	Bear
Return (%)	4.0	5.0	5.1	13.6	-1.7
Differ from Category (+/-)	-0.2 blw av	-1.4 low	-1.6 low	-4.8 low	3.7 high

Total Risk	Standard Deviation	Category Risk	Risk Index	Avg Mat
low	2.1%	low	0.4	3.4 yrs

	1996	1995	1994	1993	1992	1991	1990	1989	1988	1987
Return (%)	3.8	8.4	-0.1	7.1	6.1	8.8	6.4	6.3	4.8	0.2
Differ from Category (+/-)	0.1	-6.8	5.2	-4.7	-2.2	-2.6	0.0	-2.7	-5.2	1.6
Return, Tax-Adjusted (%)	3.8	8.4	-0.1	7.0	6.1	8.8	6.4	6.3	4.8	0.2

PER SHARE DATA

	1996	1995	1994	1993	1992	1991	1990	1989	1988	1987
Dividends, Net Income ($)	0.42	0.42	0.43	0.45	0.49	0.55	0.56	0.53	0.51	0.43
Distrib'ns, Cap Gain ($)	0.00	0.00	0.00	0.01	0.00	0.00	0.00	0.00	0.00	0.00
Net Asset Value ($)	10.00	10.04	9.66	10.11	9.88	9.78	9.52	9.49	9.45	9.51
Expense Ratio (%)	0.54	0.55	0.47	0.55	0.55	0.55	0.60	0.58	0.35	0.60
Yield (%)	4.19	4.18	4.45	4.44	4.95	5.62	5.88	5.58	5.39	4.52
Portfolio Turnover (%)	78	51	44	56	28	59	75	82	96	180
Total Assets (Millions $)	754	904	913	1,188	654	242	58	57	76	59

PORTFOLIO (as of 9/30/96)

Portfolio Manager: Norman Lind - 1995

Investm't Category: Tax-Exempt Bond

✔ Domestic	Index
Foreign	Sector
Asset Allocation	State Specific

Investment Style

Large-Cap Growth	Large-Cap Value
Mid-Cap Growth	Mid-Cap Value
Small-Cap Growth	Small-Cap Value

Portfolio

5.9% cash	0.0% corp bonds
0.0% stocks	0.0% gov't bonds
0.0% preferred	94.1% muni bonds
0.0% conv't/warrants	0.0% other

SHAREHOLDER INFORMATION

Minimum Investment
Initial: $10,000   Subsequent: $1,000

Minimum IRA Investment
Initial: na   Subsequent: na

Maximum Fees
Load: none   12b-1: none
Other: f

Distributions
Income: monthly   Capital Gains: Oct, Dec

Exchange Options
Number Per Year: 4   Fee: $5
Telephone: yes (money market fund available)

Services
auto exchange, auto invest, auto withdraw

Fidelity Spartan Short-Term Bond (FTBDX)

Corporate Bond

82 Devonshire St.
Mail Zone F9A
Boston, MA 02109
800-544-8888, 801-534-1910
www.fidelity.com

PERFORMANCE

fund inception date: 10/1/92

	3yr Annual	5yr Annual	10yr Annual	Bull	Bear
Return (%)	3.2	na	na	13.9	-4.1
Differ from Category (+/-)	-3.1 low	na	na	-10.9 low	1.0 abv av

Total Risk	Standard Deviation	Category Risk	Risk Index	Avg Mat
low	3.0%	blw av	0.7	2.2 yrs

	1996	1995	1994	1993	1992	1991	1990	1989	1988	1987
Return (%)	5.0	9.9	-4.7	9.0	—	—	—	—	—	—
Differ from Category (+/-)	-0.2	-8.1	-1.6	-2.8	—	—	—	—	—	—
Return, Tax-Adjusted (%)	2.4	7.3	-7.1	6.0	—	—	—	—	—	—

PER SHARE DATA

	1996	1995	1994	1993	1992	1991	1990	1989	1988	1987
Dividends, Net Income ($)	0.59	0.58	0.60	0.72	—	—	—	—	—	—
Distrib'ns, Cap Gain ($)	0.00	0.00	0.00	0.01	—	—	—	—	—	—
Net Asset Value ($)	9.05	9.20	8.92	9.97	—	—	—	—	—	—
Expense Ratio (%)	0.65	0.65	0.54	0.20	—	—	—	—	—	—
Yield (%)	6.51	6.30	6.72	7.21	—	—	—	—	—	—
Portfolio Turnover (%)	134	159	97	112	—	—	—	—	—	—
Total Assets (Millions $)	341	479	610	1,506	—	—	—	—	—	—

PORTFOLIO (as of 9/30/96)

Portfolio Manager: Charles Morrison - 1995

Investm't Category: Corporate Bond

✔ Domestic	Index
✔ Foreign	Sector
Asset Allocation	State Specific

Investment Style

Large-Cap Growth	Large-Cap Value
Mid-Cap Growth	Mid-Cap Value
Small-Cap Growth	Small-Cap Value

Portfolio

0.0% cash	35.4% corp bonds
0.0% stocks	30.7% gov't bonds
0.0% preferred	0.0% muni bonds
0.0% conv't/warrants	34.5% other

SHAREHOLDER INFORMATION

Minimum Investment
Initial: $10,000   Subsequent: $1,000

Minimum IRA Investment
Initial: $10,000   Subsequent: $1,000

Maximum Fees
Load: none   12b-1: none
Other: f

Distributions
Income: monthly   Capital Gains: Nov, Dec

Exchange Options
Number Per Year: 4   Fee: $5
Telephone: yes (money market fund available)

Services
IRA, pension, auto exchange, auto invest, auto withdraw

Fidelity Stock Selector

(FDSSX)

Growth

82 Devonshire St.
Mail Zone F9A
Boston, MA 02109
800-544-6666, 801-534-1910
www.fidelity.com

PERFORMANCE

fund inception date: 9/28/90

	3yr Annual	5yr Annual	10yr Annual	Bull	Bear
Return (%)	17.2	16.2	na	63.5	-6.1
Differ from Category (+/-)	1.5 abv av	1.9 abv av	na	1.1 av	0.6 av

Total Risk	Standard Deviation	Category Risk	Risk Index	Beta
high	12.0%	abv av	1.2	0.99

	1996	1995	1994	1993	1992	1991	1990	1989	1988	1987
Return (%)	17.1	36.4	0.7	13.9	15.4	45.9	—	—	—	—
Differ from Category (+/-)	-3.0	6.1	1.0	-0.1	3.6	9.9	—	—	—	—
Return, Tax-Adjusted (%)	14.2	32.7	-0.9	11.6	14.5	44.4	—	—	—	—

PER SHARE DATA

	1996	1995	1994	1993	1992	1991	1990	1989	1988	1987
Dividends, Net Income ($)	0.23	0.20	0.15	0.24	0.10	0.08	—	—	—	—
Distrib'ns, Cap Gain ($)	1.92	2.08	0.81	1.06	0.32	0.47	—	—	—	—
Net Asset Value ($)	23.85	22.19	17.91	18.75	17.61	15.63	—	—	—	—
Expense Ratio (%)	0.84	1.00	1.09	1.10	1.22	1.43	—	—	—	—
Yield (%)	0.89	0.82	0.80	1.21	0.55	0.49	—	—	—	—
Portfolio Turnover (%)	247	220	187	192	268	317	—	—	—	—
Total Assets (Millions $)	1,668	1,262	786	624	353	126	—	—	—	—

PORTFOLIO (as of 9/30/96)

Portfolio Manager: Brad Lewis - 1990

Investm't Category: Growth
✔ Domestic	Index
✔ Foreign	Sector
Asset Allocation	State Specific

Investment Style
Large-Cap Growth	Large-Cap Value
✔ Mid-Cap Growth	Mid-Cap Value
Small-Cap Growth	Small-Cap Value

Portfolio
5.7% cash	0.0% corp bonds
94.3% stocks	0.0% gov't bonds
0.0% preferred	0.0% muni bonds
0.0% conv't/warrants	0.0% other

SHAREHOLDER INFORMATION

Minimum Investment
Initial: $2,500 · Subsequent: $250

Minimum IRA Investment
Initial: $500 · Subsequent: $250

Maximum Fees
Load: none · 12b-1: none
Other: f

Distributions
Income: Dec · Capital Gains: Dec

Exchange Options
Number Per Year: 4 · Fee: none
Telephone: yes (money market fund available)

Services
IRA, pension, auto exchange, auto invest, auto withdraw

Fidelity Trend (FTRNX)

Growth

82 Devonshire St.
Mail Zone F9A
Boston, MA 02109
800-544-6666, 801-534-1910
www.fidelity.com

PERFORMANCE

fund inception date: 6/16/58

	3yr Annual	5yr Annual	10yr Annual	Bull	Bear
Return (%)	10.0	13.1	13.2	44.9	-11.6
Differ from Category (+/-)	-5.7 low	-1.2 blw av	-0.7 blw av	-17.5 low	-4.9 low

Total Risk	Standard Deviation	Category Risk	Risk Index	Beta
abv av	11.3%	abv av	1.1	1.02

	1996	1995	1994	1993	1992	1991	1990	1989	1988	1987
Return (%).	16.9	22.1	-6.7	19.1	16.7	36.2	-12.8	31.6	24.3	-4.2
Differ from Category (+/-). .	-3.2	-8.2	-6.4	5.1	4.9	0.2	-6.7	5.5	6.2	-6.2
Return, Tax-Adjusted (%). .	14.4	16.7	-8.7	16.2	14.5	34.3	-13.1	27.7	22.6	-9.0

PER SHARE DATA

	1996	1995	1994	1993	1992	1991	1990	1989	1988	1987
Dividends, Net Income ($).	0.45	0.39	0.16	0.27	0.44	0.48	0.21	0.63	0.52	0.44
Distrib'ns, Cap Gain ($) . . .	4.01	9.28	3.89	5.05	3.23	1.79	0.14	4.22	1.06	6.20
Net Asset Value ($)	56.81	52.48	50.99	59.08	54.20	49.63	38.25	44.22	37.43	31.40
Expense Ratio (%).	na	0.82	1.04	0.92	0.56	0.53	0.61	0.58	0.47	0.49
Yield (%)	0.73	0.63	0.29	0.42	0.76	0.93	0.54	1.30	1.35	1.17
Portfolio Turnover (%). . . .	na	186	29	50	47	57	48	67	49	128
Total Assets (Millions $). .	1,358	1,274	1,193	1,393	1,115	900	699	883	702	601

PORTFOLIO (as of 9/30/96)

Portfolio Manager: Abigail Johnson - 1996

Investm't Category: Growth

✔ Domestic   Index
✔ Foreign   Sector
   Asset Allocation State Specific

Investment Style

   Large-Cap Growth   Large-Cap Value
✔ Mid-Cap Growth   Mid-Cap Value
   Small-Cap Growth   Small-Cap Value

Portfolio

3.7% cash	0.0% corp bonds
96.2% stocks	0.0% gov't bonds
0.0% preferred	0.0% muni bonds
0.1% conv't/warrants	0.0% other

SHAREHOLDER INFORMATION

Minimum Investment
Initial: $2,500   Subsequent: $250

Minimum IRA Investment
Initial: $500   Subsequent: $250

Maximum Fees
Load: none   12b-1: none
Other: *f*

Distributions
Income: Feb, Dec   Capital Gains: Feb, Dec

Exchange Options
Number Per Year: 4   Fee: none
Telephone: yes (money market fund available)

Services
IRA, pension, auto exchange, auto invest, auto withdraw

Individual Fund Listings   **365**

Fidelity Utilities Income

(FIUIX)

Growth & Income

82 Devonshire St.
Mail Zone F9A
Boston, MA 02109
800-544-6666, 801-534-1910
www.fidelity.com

PERFORMANCE

fund inception date: 11/27/87

	3yr Annual	5yr Annual	10yr Annual	Bull	Bear
Return (%)	11.2	12.0	na	43.3	-7.8
Differ from Category (+/-)	-4.1 low	-1.9 blw av	na	-16.5 low	-1.4 blw av

Total Risk	Standard Deviation	Category Risk	Risk Index	Beta
av	8.8%	blw av	0.9	0.70

	1996	1995	1994	1993	1992	1991	1990	1989	1988	1987
Return (%).............	11.4	30.6	-5.3	15.6	10.9	21.1	1.8	25.9	14.7	—
Differ from Category (+/-) .	-8.3	0.5	-4.0	1.8	0.2	-8.0	7.7	2.4	-2.1	—
Return, Tax-Adjusted (%)...	9.2	28.3	-8.2	13.6	8.3	18.5	-1.1	22.3	12.5	—

PER SHARE DATA

	1996	1995	1994	1993	1992	1991	1990	1989	1988	1987
Dividends, Net Income ($).	0.48	0.54	0.54	0.52	0.60	0.63	0.69	0.76	0.52	—
Distrib'ns, Cap Gain ($) ...	0.54	0.28	0.80	0.22	0.38	0.18	0.30	0.31	0.03	—
Net Asset Value ($)	16.91	16.16	13.06	15.18	13.79	13.38	11.79	12.60	10.93	—
Expense Ratio (%).......	0.77	0.87	0.86	0.87	0.95	0.94	1.02	1.47	2.00	—
Yield (%)	2.75	3.28	3.89	3.37	4.23	4.64	5.70	5.88	4.74	—
Portfolio Turnover (%).....	98	98	47	73	39	43	61	10	na	—
Total Assets (Millions $) .	1,284	1,510	1,079	1,456	962	620	215	165	129	—

PORTFOLIO (as of 9/30/96)

Portfolio Manager: John Muresianu - 1992

Investm't Category: Growth & Income
- ✔ Domestic
- ✔ Foreign
- Asset Allocation
- Index
- ✔ Sector
- State Specific

Investment Style
- Large-Cap Growth
- Mid-Cap Growth
- Small-Cap Growth
- ✔ Large-Cap Value
- Mid-Cap Value
- Small-Cap Value

Portfolio
1.3% cash	0.0% corp bonds
98.0% stocks	0.0% gov't bonds
0.0% preferred	0.0% muni bonds
0.7% conv't/warrants	0.0% other

SHAREHOLDER INFORMATION

Minimum Investment
Initial: $2,500   Subsequent: $250

Minimum IRA Investment
Initial: $500   Subsequent: $250

Maximum Fees
Load: none   12b-1: none
Other: f

Distributions
Income: quarterly   Capital Gains: Mar, Dec

Exchange Options
Number Per Year: 4   Fee: none
Telephone: yes (money market fund available)

Services
IRA, pension, auto exchange, auto invest, auto withdraw

Fidelity Value (FDVLX)

Growth

82 Devonshire St.
Mail Zone F9A
Boston, MA 02109
800-544-6666, 801-534-1910
www.fidelity.com

	3yr Annual	5yr Annual	10yr Annual	Bull	Bear
Return (%)	16.9	18.9	14.2	53.9	-1.3
Differ from Category (+/-)	1.2 abv av	4.6 high	0.3 av	-8.5 blw av	5.4 high

Total Risk	Standard Deviation	Category Risk	Risk Index	Beta
av	8.8%	low	0.9	0.78

	1996	1995	1994	1993	1992	1991	1990	1989	1988	1987
Return (%).	16.8	27.1	7.6	22.9	21.1	26.1	-12.9	22.9	29.0	-8.6
Differ from Category (+/-). .	-3.3	-3.2	7.9	8.9	9.3	-9.9	-6.8	-3.2	10.9	-10.6
Return, Tax-Adjusted (%). .	13.0	25.4	5.8	20.3	20.6	24.7	-14.5	19.3	28.0	-9.4

PER SHARE DATA

	1996	1995	1994	1993	1992	1991	1990	1989	1988	1987
Dividends, Net Income ($).	0.53	0.48	0.17	0.34	0.23	0.85	1.17	0.30	0.48	0.15
Distrib'ns, Cap Gain ($) . . .	5.92	1.73	2.27	2.80	0.15	0.00	0.00	2.85	0.00	0.37
Net Asset Value ($)	51.54	49.64	40.81	40.23	35.35	29.50	24.10	28.99	26.14	20.63
Expense Ratio (%).	0.88	0.96	1.08	1.11	1.00	0.98	1.06	1.13	1.11	1.07
Yield (%)	0.92	0.93	0.39	0.79	0.64	2.88	4.85	0.94	1.83	0.71
Portfolio Turnover (%). . . .	112	125	112	117	81	137	165	386	480	442
Total Assets (Millions $). .	7,285	5,745	3,720	1,716	667	123	97	152	124	85

PORTFOLIO (as of 9/30/96)

Portfolio Manager: Rich Fentin - 1996

Investm't Category: Growth
- ✔ Domestic   Index
- ✔ Foreign   Sector
- Asset Allocation   State Specific

Investment Style

Large-Cap Growth	✔ Large-Cap Value
Mid-Cap Growth	Mid-Cap Value
Small-Cap Growth	Small-Cap Value

Portfolio

5.9% cash	0.0% corp bonds
93.8% stocks	0.0% gov't bonds
0.0% preferred	0.0% muni bonds
0.3% conv't/warrants	0.0% other

SHAREHOLDER INFORMATION

Minimum Investment
Initial: $2,500   Subsequent: $250

Minimum IRA Investment
Initial: $500   Subsequent: $250

Maximum Fees
Load: none   12b-1: none
Other: *f*

Distributions
Income: Dec   Capital Gains: Dec

Exchange Options
Number Per Year: 4   Fee: none
Telephone: yes (money market fund available)

Services
IRA, pension, auto exchange, auto invest, auto withdraw

Fidelity Worldwide

(FWWFX)

International Stock

82 Devonshire St.
Mail Zone F9A
Boston, MA 02109
800-544-6666, 801-534-1910
www.fidelity.com

PERFORMANCE

fund inception date: 5/30/90

	3yr Annual	5yr Annual	10yr Annual	Bull	Bear
Return (%)	9.4	13.6	na	27.5	-4.1
Differ from Category (+/-)	3.1 abv av	3.6 high	na	3.2 av	3.1 abv av

Total Risk	Standard Deviation	Category Risk	Risk Index	Beta
av	8.5%	low	0.8	0.65

	1996	1995	1994	1993	1992	1991	1990	1989	1988	1987
Return (%)	18.7	7.1	2.9	36.5	6.2	7.8	—	—	—	—
Differ from Category (+/-)	3.9	-2.0	6.0	-3.1	10.0	-5.4	—	—	—	—
Return, Tax-Adjusted (%)	17.4	6.6	1.2	35.6	5.1	7.3	—	—	—	—

PER SHARE DATA

	1996	1995	1994	1993	1992	1991	1990	1989	1988	1987
Dividends, Net Income ($)	0.17	0.15	0.07	0.10	0.26	0.10	—	—	—	—
Distrib'ns, Cap Gain ($)	0.38	0.00	0.66	0.15	0.00	0.00	—	—	—	—
Net Asset Value ($)	15.39	13.44	12.68	13.03	9.73	9.41	—	—	—	—
Expense Ratio (%)	1.18	1.16	1.32	1.40	1.51	1.69	—	—	—	—
Yield (%)	1.07	1.11	0.52	0.75	2.67	1.06	—	—	—	—
Portfolio Turnover (%)	49	70	69	57	130	129	—	—	—	—
Total Assets (Millions $)	932	654	703	339	98	100	—	—	—	—

PORTFOLIO (as of 9/30/96)

Portfolio Manager: Penelope Dobkin - 1990

Investm't Category: International Stock

✔ Domestic	Index
✔ Foreign	Sector
Asset Allocation	State Specific

Investment Style

Large-Cap Growth	Large-Cap Value
Mid-Cap Growth	Mid-Cap Value
Small-Cap Growth	Small-Cap Value

Portfolio

9.9% cash	0.0% corp bonds
88.4% stocks	0.0% gov't bonds
0.0% preferred	0.0% muni bonds
1.7% conv't/warrants	0.0% other

SHAREHOLDER INFORMATION

Minimum Investment
Initial: $2,500   Subsequent: $250

Minimum IRA Investment
Initial: $500   Subsequent: $250

Maximum Fees
Load: none   12b-1: none
Other: *f*

Distributions
Income: Dec   Capital Gains: Dec

Exchange Options
Number Per Year: 4   Fee: none
Telephone: yes (money market fund available)

Services
IRA, pension, auto exchange, auto invest, auto withdraw

Fiduciary Capital Growth
(FCGFX)

Growth

225 E. Mason St.
Milwaukee, WI 53202
800-338-1579, 414-226-4555

PERFORMANCE

fund inception date: 12/18/81

	3yr Annual	5yr Annual	10yr Annual	Bull	Bear
Return (%)	14.1	14.3	11.6	59.0	-6.8
Differ from Category (+/-)	-1.6 blw av	0.0 av	-2.3 low	-3.4 av	-0.1 av

Total Risk	Standard Deviation	Category Risk	Risk Index	Beta
av	9.5%	blw av	0.9	0.71

	1996	1995	1994	1993	1992	1991	1990	1989	1988	1987
Return (%)	17.1	26.5	0.3	14.6	14.4	36.2	-11.7	17.9	18.7	-8.9
Differ from Category (+/-)	-3.0	-3.8	0.6	0.6	2.6	0.2	-5.6	-8.2	0.6	-10.9
Return, Tax-Adjusted (%)	13.3	22.9	-2.5	12.5	11.2	33.3	-13.7	17.3	18.6	-14.7

PER SHARE DATA

	1996	1995	1994	1993	1992	1991	1990	1989	1988	1987
Dividends, Net Income ($)	0.14	0.11	0.03	0.05	0.10	0.16	0.23	0.19	0.03	0.14
Distrib'ns, Cap Gain ($)	2.50	2.07	1.88	1.29	1.85	1.22	0.92	0.00	0.00	3.45
Net Asset Value ($)	20.73	20.10	17.76	19.63	18.33	17.87	14.23	17.54	15.04	12.69
Expense Ratio (%)	1.20	1.20	1.20	1.20	1.30	1.50	1.40	1.30	1.30	1.10
Yield (%)	0.60	0.49	0.15	0.23	0.49	0.83	1.51	1.08	0.19	0.86
Portfolio Turnover (%)	43	28	20	33	59	63	55	42	43	83
Total Assets (Millions $)	43	43	39	48	43	35	22	33	40	38

PORTFOLIO (as of 9/30/96)

Portfolio Manager: Ted Kellner, Donald Wilson - 1981

Investm't Category: Growth

✔ Domestic	Index
✔ Foreign	Sector
Asset Allocation	State Specific

Investment Style

Large-Cap Growth	Large-Cap Value
✔ Mid-Cap Growth	Mid-Cap Value
✔ Small-Cap Growth	Small-Cap Value

Portfolio

11.6% cash	0.0% corp bonds
88.4% stocks	0.0% gov't bonds
0.0% preferred	0.0% muni bonds
0.0% conv't/warrants	0.0% other

SHAREHOLDER INFORMATION

Minimum Investment
Initial: $1,000   Subsequent: $100

Minimum IRA Investment
Initial: $1,000   Subsequent: $100

Maximum Fees
Load: none   12b-1: none
Other: none

Distributions
Income: annual   Capital Gains: annual

Exchange Options
Number Per Year: 5   Fee: none
Telephone: none

Services
IRA, pension, auto invest, auto withdraw

First Eagle Fund of America (FEAFX)

Growth

45 Broadway
New York, NY 10006
800-451-3623, 212-698-3000

PERFORMANCE

fund inception date: 4/10/87

	3yr Annual	5yr Annual	10yr Annual	Bull	Bear
Return (%)	19.7	21.4	na	78.7	-9.6
Differ from Category (+/-)	4.0 high	7.1 high	na	16.3 high	-2.9 blw av

Total Risk	Standard Deviation	Category Risk	Risk Index	Beta
abv av	11.6%	abv av	1.1	1.02

	1996	1995	1994	1993	1992	1991	1990	1989	1988	1987
Return (%)	29.3	36.3	-2.6	23.8	24.3	20.9	-17.6	26.6	22.7	—
Differ from Category (+/-)	9.2	6.0	-2.3	9.8	12.5	-15.1	-11.5	0.5	4.6	
Return, Tax-Adjusted (%)	24.1	35.5	-6.4	20.4	21.5	18.6	-18.5	22.8	21.7	

PER SHARE DATA

	1996	1995	1994	1993	1992	1991	1990	1989	1988	1987
Dividends, Net Income ($)	0.00	0.00	0.00	0.00	0.00	0.08	0.28	0.11	0.00	—
Distrib'ns, Cap Gain ($)	3.13	0.35	2.00	1.62	1.17	0.74	0.00	1.40	0.34	—
Net Asset Value ($)	18.30	16.96	12.70	15.04	13.48	11.85	10.51	13.11	11.56	—
Expense Ratio (%)	1.80	1.90	1.90	2.90	3.00	2.00	1.10	2.00	3.30	
Yield (%)	0.00	0.00	0.00	0.00	0.00	0.63	2.66	0.75	0.00	
Portfolio Turnover (%)	93	81	125	141	145	92	72	52	55	
Total Assets (Millions $)	174	132	105	108	85	74	63	91	57	

PORTFOLIO (as of 9/30/96)

Portfolio Manager: Harold Levy, David Cohen - 1987

Investm't Category: Growth

✔ Domestic	Index
✔ Foreign	Sector
Asset Allocation	State Specific

Investment Style

Large-Cap Growth	✔ Large-Cap Value
Mid-Cap Growth	✔ Mid-Cap Value
Small-Cap Growth	Small-Cap Value

Portfolio

0.0% cash	0.0% corp bonds
94.8% stocks	0.0% gov't bonds
1.4% preferred	0.0% muni bonds
1.4% conv't/warrants	2.5% other

SHAREHOLDER INFORMATION

Minimum Investment
Initial: $5,000   Subsequent: $1,000

Minimum IRA Investment
Initial: $2,000   Subsequent: $1

Maximum Fees
Load: none   12b-1: none
Other: none

Distributions
Income: Nov   Capital Gains: Nov

Exchange Options
Number Per Year: none   Fee: na
Telephone: na

Services
IRA, pension

First Eagle Int'l (FEIFX)

International Stock

45 Broadway
New York, NY 10006
800-451-3623, 212-698-3000

	3yr Annual	5yr Annual	10yr Annual	Bull	Bear
Return (%)	na	na	na	32.7	na
Differ from Category (+/-)	na	na	na	8.4 abv av	na

Total Risk	Standard Deviation	Category Risk	Risk Index	Beta
na	na	na	na	na

	1996	1995	1994	1993	1992	1991	1990	1989	1988	1987
Return (%)	15.9	11.6	—	—	—	—	—	—	—	—
Differ from Category (+/-)	1.1	2.5	—	—	—	—	—	—	—	—
Return, Tax-Adjusted (%)	14.9	10.6	—	—	—	—	—	—	—	—

PER SHARE DATA

	1996	1995	1994	1993	1992	1991	1990	1989	1988	1987
Dividends, Net Income ($)	0.00	0.00	—	—	—	—	—	—	—	—
Distrib'ns, Cap Gain ($)	0.47	0.42	—	—	—	—	—	—	—	—
Net Asset Value ($)	15.04	13.38	—	—	—	—	—	—	—	—
Expense Ratio (%)	na	3.10	—	—	—	—	—	—	—	—
Yield (%)	0.00	0.00	—	—	—	—	—	—	—	—
Portfolio Turnover (%)	na	166	—	—	—	—	—	—	—	—
Total Assets (Millions $)	33	22	—	—	—	—	—	—	—	—

PORTFOLIO (as of 9/30/96)

Portfolio Manager: Arthur Lerner, Allan Raphael - 1994

Investm't Category: International Stock
Domestic   Index
✔ Foreign   Sector
Asset Allocation   State Specific

Investment Style
Large-Cap Growth   Large-Cap Value
Mid-Cap Growth   Mid-Cap Value
Small-Cap Growth   Small-Cap Value

Portfolio
8.7% cash	0.0% corp bonds
85.8% stocks	0.0% gov't bonds
2.6% preferred	0.0% muni bonds
0.0% conv't/warrants	0.0% other

SHAREHOLDER INFORMATION

Minimum Investment
Initial: $5,000   Subsequent: $1,000

Minimum IRA Investment
Initial: $2,000   Subsequent: $1,000

Maximum Fees
Load: none   12b-1: 0.25%
Other: none

Distributions
Income: annual   Capital Gains: annual

Exchange Options
Number Per Year: none   Fee: na
Telephone: na

Services
IRA, pension

First Hawaii Muni Bond

(SURFX)

Tax-Exempt Bond

2756 Woodlawn Dr.
#6-201
Honolulu, HI 96822
808-988-8088

PERFORMANCE

fund inception date: 11/30/88

	3yr Annual	5yr Annual	10yr Annual	Bull	Bear
Return (%)	4.2	6.4	na	17.5	-4.3
Differ from Category (+/-)	0.0 av	0.0 blw av	na	-0.9 blw av	1.1 abv av

Total Risk	Standard Deviation	Category Risk	Risk Index	Avg Mat
low	4.3%	blw av	0.8	14.0 yrs

	1996	1995	1994	1993	1992	1991	1990	1989	1988	1987
Return (%)	4.1	14.4	-4.9	10.6	8.7	10.6	6.1	9.2	—	—
Differ from Category (+/-)	0.4	-0.8	0.4	-1.2	0.4	-0.8	-0.3	0.2	—	—
Return, Tax-Adjusted (%)	4.1	14.4	-5.1	10.4	8.6	10.6	5.8	9.2	—	—

PER SHARE DATA

	1996	1995	1994	1993	1992	1991	1990	1989	1988	1987
Dividends, Net Income ($)	0.54	0.55	0.55	0.57	0.61	0.61	0.62	0.65	—	—
Distrib'ns, Cap Gain ($)	0.00	0.00	0.08	0.07	0.01	0.00	0.09	0.00	—	—
Net Asset Value ($)	10.97	11.07	10.18	11.37	10.89	10.61	10.17	10.28	—	—
Expense Ratio (%)	0.98	0.97	0.95	0.95	0.95	0.91	0.83	0.54	—	—
Yield (%)	4.92	4.96	5.36	4.98	5.59	5.74	6.04	6.32	—	—
Portfolio Turnover (%)	15	17	40	28	18	7	47	22	—	—
Total Assets (Millions $)	55	53	46	57	41	28	16	7	—	—

PORTFOLIO (as of 9/30/96)

Portfolio Manager: Louis D'Avanzo - 1991

Investm't Category: Tax-Exempt Bond
- ✔ Domestic
- Foreign
- Asset Allocation
- Index
- Sector
- ✔ State Specific

Investment Style
Large-Cap Growth	Large-Cap Value
Mid-Cap Growth	Mid-Cap Value
Small-Cap Growth	Small-Cap Value

Portfolio
0.0% cash	0.0% corp bonds
0.0% stocks	0.0% gov't bonds
0.0% preferred	100.0% muni bonds
0.0% conv't/warrants	0.0% other

SHAREHOLDER INFORMATION

Minimum Investment
Initial: $1,000   Subsequent: $100

Minimum IRA Investment
Initial: na   Subsequent: na

Maximum Fees
Load: none   12b-1: 0.25%
Other: none

Distributions
Income: monthly   Capital Gains: annual

Exchange Options
Number Per Year: no limit   Fee: none
Telephone: yes (money market fund not available)

Services
auto exchange, auto invest, auto withdraw

Flex Muirfield Fd (FLMFX)

Growth

6000 Memorial Drive
P.O. Box 7177
Dublin, OH 43017
800-325-3539, 614-766-7000
www.flexfunds.com

PERFORMANCE

fund inception date: 8/10/88

	3yr Annual	5yr Annual	10yr Annual	Bull	Bear
Return (%)	10.9	9.5	na	35.7	-0.9
Differ from Category (+/-)	-4.8 low	-4.8 low	na	-26.7 low	5.8 high

Total Risk	Standard Deviation	Category Risk	Risk Index	Beta
av	7.5%	low	0.7	0.53

	1996	1995	1994	1993	1992	1991	1990	1989	1988	1987
Return (%)...............	5.7	25.8	2.7	8.0	6.9	29.8	2.3	13.9	—	—
Differ from Category (+/-)	-14.4	-4.5	3.0	-6.0	-4.9	-6.2	8.4	-12.2	—	—
Return, Tax-Adjusted (%)...	2.6	20.6	1.6	0.8	4.2	27.7	-1.4	12.8	—	—

PER SHARE DATA

	1996	1995	1994	1993	1992	1991	1990	1989	1988	1987
Dividends, Net Income ($)	0.09	0.05	0.13	0.65	0.06	0.27	0.10	0.07	—	—
Distrib'ns, Cap Gain ($)...	0.50	0.92	0.02	0.67	0.52	0.00	0.63	0.10	—	—
Net Asset Value ($)......	5.47	5.73	5.34	5.36	6.25	6.43	5.22	5.84	—	—
Expense Ratio (%).........	na	1.26	1.22	1.26	1.40	1.50	1.52	1.53	—	—
Yield (%)...............	1.50	0.75	2.42	10.77	0.88	4.19	1.70	1.17	—	—
Portfolio Turnover (%).....	na	186	na	na	324	107	649	202	—	—
Total Assets (Millions $)...	127	111	83	73	55	43	29	26	—	—

PORTFOLIO (as of 9/30/96)

Portfolio Manager: Robert Meeder Jr. - 1988

Investm't Category: Growth

✔ Domestic	Index
Foreign	Sector
✔ Asset Allocation	State Specific

Investment Style

Large-Cap Growth	Large-Cap Value
✔ Mid-Cap Growth	Mid-Cap Value
✔ Small-Cap Growth	Small-Cap Value

Portfolio

50.0% cash	0.0% corp bonds
0.0% stocks	0.0% gov't bonds
0.0% preferred	0.0% muni bonds
0.0% conv't/warrants	50.0% other

SHAREHOLDER INFORMATION

Minimum Investment
Initial: $2,500   Subsequent: $100

Minimum IRA Investment
Initial: $500   Subsequent: $100

Maximum Fees
Load: none   12b-1: 0.20%
Other: none

Distributions
Income: quarterly   Capital Gains: annual

Exchange Options
Number Per Year: no limit   Fee: none
Telephone: yes (money market fund available)

Services
IRA, pension, auto invest, auto withdraw

Founders Balanced

(FRINX)

Balanced

Founders Financial Center
2930 E. Third Ave.
Denver, CO 80206
800-525-2440, 303-394-4404
www.founders.com

PERFORMANCE

fund inception date: 2/19/63

	3yr Annual	5yr Annual	10yr Annual	Bull	Bear
Return (%)	14.6	14.2	12.4	52.9	-3.5
Differ from Category (+/-)	2.9 high	2.8 high	1.6 abv av	7.8 high	2.2 high

Total Risk	Standard Deviation	Category Risk	Risk Index	Beta
av	7.0%	abv av	1.0	0.63

	1996	1995	1994	1993	1992	1991	1990	1989	1988	1987
Return (%)	18.7	29.4	-2.0	21.8	6.0	22.8	-5.0	25.2	11.0	1.9
Differ from Category (+/-)	4.5	4.8	-0.4	7.4	-2.9	-1.3	-4.1	7.1	-1.2	-0.8
Return, Tax-Adjusted (%)	16.2	24.2	-2.9	17.6	4.3	19.8	-6.8	21.8	8.7	-0.8

PER SHARE DATA

	1996	1995	1994	1993	1992	1991	1990	1989	1988	1987
Dividends, Net Income ($)	0.26	0.27	0.19	0.20	0.27	0.31	0.35	0.45	0.37	0.40
Distrib'ns, Cap Gain ($)	0.48	1.19	0.00	0.95	0.09	0.33	0.00	0.18	0.00	0.87
Net Asset Value ($)	10.61	9.58	8.56	8.93	8.30	8.19	7.22	7.97	6.89	6.55
Expense Ratio (%)	na	1.23	1.26	1.34	1.88	1.73	1.65	1.52	1.64	1.66
Yield (%)	2.34	2.50	2.21	2.02	3.21	3.63	4.84	5.52	5.37	5.39
Portfolio Turnover (%)	na	286	258	251	96	133	103	85	182	133
Total Assets (Millions $)	395	130	95	72	31	18	13	15	12	13

PORTFOLIO (as of 9/30/96)

Portfolio Manager: Brian Kelly - 1996

Investm't Category: Balanced
- ✔ Domestic
- ✔ Foreign
- Asset Allocation

- Index
- Sector
- State Specific

Investment Style

Large-Cap Growth	Large-Cap Value
Mid-Cap Growth	Mid-Cap Value
Small-Cap Growth	Small-Cap Value

Portfolio

7.6% cash	0.0% corp bonds
63.7% stocks	22.1% gov't bonds
2.8% preferred	0.0% muni bonds
0.0% conv't/warrants	3.7% other

SHAREHOLDER INFORMATION

Minimum Investment
Initial: $1,000   Subsequent: $100

Minimum IRA Investment
Initial: $500   Subsequent: $100

Maximum Fees
Load: none   12b-1: 0.25%
Other: none

Distributions
Income: quarterly   Capital Gains: Dec

Exchange Options
Number Per Year: 4   Fee: none
Telephone: yes (money market fund available)

Services
IRA, pension, auto exchange, auto invest, auto withdraw

Founders Blue Chip

(FRMUX)

Growth & Income

Founders Financial Center
2930 E. Third Ave.
Denver, CO 80206
800-525-2440, 303-394-4404
www.founders.com

PERFORMANCE

	3yr Annual	5yr Annual	10yr Annual	Bull	Bear
Return (%)	17.2	13.0	13.7	67.1	-6.5
Differ from Category (+/-)	1.9 av	-0.9 blw av	1.0 abv av	7.3 abv av	-0.1 av

Total Risk	Standard Deviation	Category Risk	Risk Index	Beta
av	9.4%	av	1.0	0.83

	1996	1995	1994	1993	1992	1991	1990	1989	1988	1987
Return (%)	24.3	29.0	0.5	14.4	-0.3	28.3	0.4	35.5	10.0	1.9
Differ from Category (+/-)	4.6	-1.1	1.8	0.6	-11.0	-0.8	6.3	12.0	-6.8	1.7
Return, Tax-Adjusted (%)	19.7	23.1	-1.1	8.5	-3.1	24.5	-2.5	29.6	7.6	-5.4

PER SHARE DATA

	1996	1995	1994	1993	1992	1991	1990	1989	1988	1987
Dividends, Net Income ($)	0.08	0.08	0.05	0.04	0.08	0.11	0.16	0.30	0.18	0.23
Distrib'ns, Cap Gain ($)	0.98	1.17	0.30	1.38	0.65	0.74	0.51	0.89	0.25	1.70
Net Asset Value ($)	7.23	6.69	6.16	6.49	6.91	7.67	6.67	7.32	6.31	6.14
Expense Ratio (%)	na	1.22	1.21	1.22	1.23	1.10	1.07	0.98	1.00	0.87
Yield (%)	0.97	1.01	0.77	0.50	1.05	1.30	2.22	3.65	2.74	2.93
Portfolio Turnover (%)	na	235	239	212	103	95	82	64	58	56
Total Assets (Millions $)	551	373	312	307	290	290	233	231	173	174

PORTFOLIO (as of 9/30/96)

Portfolio Manager: Brian Kelly - 1996

Investm't Category: Growth & Income

✔ Domestic   Index
✔ Foreign   Sector
   Asset Allocation   State Specific

Investment Style

   Large-Cap Growth   Large-Cap Value
✔ Mid-Cap Growth   ✔ Mid-Cap Value
   Small-Cap Growth   Small-Cap Value

Portfolio

24.0% cash	0.0% corp bonds
62.9% stocks	0.0% gov't bonds
13.1% preferred	0.0% muni bonds
0.0% conv't/warrants	0.0% other

SHAREHOLDER INFORMATION

Minimum Investment
Initial: $1,000   Subsequent: $100

Minimum IRA Investment
Initial: $500   Subsequent: $100

Maximum Fees
Load: none   12b-1: 0.25%
Other: none

Distributions
Income: Dec   Capital Gains: Dec

Exchange Options
Number Per Year: 4   Fee: none
Telephone: yes (money market fund available)

Services
IRA, pension, auto exchange, auto invest, auto withdraw

Founders Discovery

(FDISX)

Aggressive Growth

Founders Financial Center
2930 E. Third Ave.
Denver, CO 80206
800-525-2440, 303-394-4404
www.founders.com

PERFORMANCE
fund inception date: 12/29/89

	3yr Annual	5yr Annual	10yr Annual	Bull	Bear
Return (%)	13.6	13.3	na	75.6	-17.7
Differ from Category (+/-)	-2.2 blw av	-2.0 blw av	na	4.5 abv av	-7.1 low

Total Risk	Standard Deviation	Category Risk	Risk Index	Beta
high	18.2%	high	1.3	0.97

	1996	1995	1994	1993	1992	1991	1990	1989	1988	1987
Return (%)	21.2	31.2	-7.8	10.8	15.1	62.4	13.1	—	—	—
Differ from Category (+/-)	2.1	-3.1	-7.8	-8.5	3.4	10.3	18.5	—	—	—
Return, Tax-Adjusted (%)	18.6	25.0	-7.8	10.0	14.6	60.7	12.7	—	—	—

PER SHARE DATA

	1996	1995	1994	1993	1992	1991	1990	1989	1988	1987
Dividends, Net Income ($)	0.00	0.00	0.00	0.00	0.06	0.00	0.09	—	—	—
Distrib'ns, Cap Gain ($)	1.99	4.34	0.00	0.51	0.17	0.67	0.00	—	—	—
Net Asset Value ($)	24.22	21.70	19.88	21.55	19.93	17.52	11.22	—	—	—
Expense Ratio (%)	na	1.63	1.67	1.65	1.85	1.77	2.03	—	—	—
Yield (%)	0.00	0.00	0.00	0.00	0.29	0.00	0.80	—	—	—
Portfolio Turnover (%)	na	118	72	99	111	165	271	—	—	—
Total Assets (Millions $)	245	218	187	226	150	47	6	—	—	—

PORTFOLIO (as of 9/30/96)

Portfolio Manager: David Kern - 1995

Investm't Category: Aggressive Growth
✔ Domestic   Index
✔ Foreign   Sector
   Asset Allocation   State Specific

Investment Style
Large-Cap Growth   Large-Cap Value
Mid-Cap Growth   Mid-Cap Value
✔ Small-Cap Growth   Small-Cap Value

Portfolio
13.8% cash   0.0% corp bonds
86.3% stocks   0.0% gov't bonds
0.0% preferred   0.0% muni bonds
0.0% conv't/warrants   0.0% other

SHAREHOLDER INFORMATION

Minimum Investment
Initial: $1,000   Subsequent: $100

Minimum IRA Investment
Initial: $500   Subsequent: $100

Maximum Fees
Load: none   12b-1: 0.25%
Other: none

Distributions
Income: Dec   Capital Gains: Dec

Exchange Options
Number Per Year: 4   Fee: none
Telephone: yes (money market fund available)

Services
IRA, pension, auto exchange, auto invest, auto withdraw

Founders Frontier

(FOUNX)

Aggressive Growth

Founders Financial Center
2930 E. Third Ave.
Denver, CO 80206
800-525-2440, 303-394-4404
www.founders.com

PERFORMANCE

fund inception date: 1/22/87

	3yr Annual	5yr Annual	10yr Annual	Bull	Bear
Return (%)	15.0	14.0	na	74.0	-14.7
Differ from Category (+/-)	-0.8 av	-1.3 av	na	2.9 av	-4.1 blw av

Total Risk	Standard Deviation	Category Risk	Risk Index	Beta
high	13.3%	av	0.9	0.88

	1996	1995	1994	1993	1992	1991	1990	1989	1988	1987
Return (%)..............	14.3	37.0	-2.9	16.5	8.9	49.3	-7.5	44.3	29.2	—
Differ from Category (+/-).	-4.8	2.7	-2.9	-2.8	-2.8	-2.8	-2.1	15.9	12.8	—
Return, Tax-Adjusted (%). .	11.5	31.5	-3.6	15.1	7.3	47.7	-8.0	42.4	27.2	—

PER SHARE DATA

	1996	1995	1994	1993	1992	1991	1990	1989	1988	1987
Dividends, Net Income ($).	0.00	0.00	0.00	0.00	0.00	0.01	0.23	0.04	0.00	—
Distrib'ns, Cap Gain ($) . . .	3.04	5.15	0.64	1.20	1.30	0.92	0.00	0.84	0.77	—
Net Asset Value ($)	32.34	31.08	26.50	27.94	25.03	24.21	16.87	18.49	13.45	—
Expense Ratio (%).........	na	1.57	1.62	1.66	1.83	1.68	1.71	1.46	1.89	—
Yield (%)	0.00	0.00	0.00	0.00	0.00	0.03	1.36	0.20	0.00	—
Portfolio Turnover (%).....	na	92	72	109	155	158	207	198	312	—
Total Assets (Millions $). . .	348	322	249	253	145	102	39	49	8	—

PORTFOLIO (as of 9/30/96)

Portfolio Manager: Michael Haines - 1987

Investm't Category: Aggressive Growth

✔ Domestic	Index
✔ Foreign	Sector
Asset Allocation	State Specific

Investment Style

Large-Cap Growth	Large-Cap Value
✔ Mid-Cap Growth	Mid-Cap Value
✔ Small-Cap Growth	Small-Cap Value

Portfolio

8.1% cash	0.0% corp bonds
91.9% stocks	0.0% gov't bonds
0.0% preferred	0.0% muni bonds
0.0% conv't/warrants	0.0% other

SHAREHOLDER INFORMATION

Minimum Investment
Initial: $1,000   Subsequent: $100

Minimum IRA Investment
Initial: $500   Subsequent: $100

Maximum Fees
Load: none   12b-1: 0.25%
Other: none

Distributions
Income: Dec   Capital Gains: Dec

Exchange Options
Number Per Year: 4   Fee: none
Telephone: yes (money market fund available)

Services
IRA, pension, auto exchange, auto invest, auto withdraw

Founders Gov't Securities

(FGVSX)

Government Bond

Founders Financial Center
2930 E. Third Ave.
Denver, CO 80206
800-525-2440, 303-394-4404
www.founders.com

fund inception date: 3/1/88

	3yr Annual	5yr Annual	10yr Annual	Bull	Bear
Return (%)	1.7	3.9	na	12.9	-8.0
Differ from Category (+/-)	-3.2 low	-2.7 low	na	-9.1 low	-1.6 blw av

Total Risk	Standard Deviation	Category Risk	Risk Index	Avg Mat
low	4.5%	av	1.1	6.5 yrs

	1996	1995	1994	1993	1992	1991	1990	1989	1988	1987
Return (%).	2.3	11.1	-7.5	9.2	5.3	14.8	4.4	13.3	—	—
Differ from Category (+/-) . .	0.8	-8.5	-3.1	-2.4	-1.4	-0.9	-1.9	-2.0	—	—
Return, Tax-Adjusted (%). . .	0.3	9.1	-9.5	5.6	2.5	11.9	1.7	10.0	—	—

PER SHARE DATA

	1996	1995	1994	1993	1992	1991	1990	1989	1988	1987
Dividends, Net Income ($).	0.45	0.44	0.50	0.46	0.51	0.59	0.69	0.79	—	—
Distrib'ns, Cap Gain ($) . .	0.00	0.00	0.00	0.64	0.31	0.18	0.00	0.00	—	—
Net Asset Value ($)	9.04	9.29	8.78	10.02	10.19	10.48	9.85	10.13	—	—
Expense Ratio (%).	na	1.30	1.34	1.18	1.18	1.12	1.03	0.65	—	—
Yield (%)	4.97	4.73	5.69	4.31	4.85	5.53	7.00	7.79	—	—
Portfolio Turnover (%). . . .	na	141	379	429	204	261	103	195	—	—
Total Assets (Millions $). . .	16	20	21	28	24	18	7	6	—	—

PORTFOLIO (as of 9/30/96)

Portfolio Manager: committee - 1995

Investm't Category: Government Bond
- ✔ Domestic
- Foreign
- Asset Allocation
- Index
- Sector
- State Specific

Investment Style
- Large-Cap Growth
- Mid-Cap Growth
- Small-Cap Growth
- Large-Cap Value
- Mid-Cap Value
- Small-Cap Value

Portfolio
4.8% cash	0.0% corp bonds
0.0% stocks	79.6% gov't bonds
0.0% preferred	0.0% muni bonds
0.0% conv't/warrants	15.6% other

SHAREHOLDER INFORMATION

Minimum Investment
Initial: $1,000 Subsequent: $100

Minimum IRA Investment
Initial: $500 Subsequent: $100

Maximum Fees
Load: none 12b-1: 0.25%
Other: none

Distributions
Income: monthly Capital Gains: Dec

Exchange Options
Number Per Year: 4 Fee: none
Telephone: yes (money market fund available)

Services
IRA, pension, auto exchange, auto invest, auto withdraw

Founders Growth (FRGRX)

Growth

Founders Financial Center
2930 E. Third Ave.
Denver, CO 80206
800-525-2440, 303-394-4404
www.founders.com

PERFORMANCE

fund inception date: 4/3/63

	3yr Annual	5yr Annual	10yr Annual	Bull	Bear
Return (%)	17.9	16.5	16.5	84.2	-16.2
Differ from Category (+/-)	2.2 abv av	2.2 abv av	2.6 high	21.8 high	-9.5 low

Total Risk	Standard Deviation	Category Risk	Risk Index	Beta
high	13.9%	high	1.3	1.18

	1996	1995	1994	1993	1992	1991	1990	1989	1988	1987
Return (%)	16.5	45.5	-3.4	25.5	4.3	47.3	-10.7	41.7	4.8	10.1
Differ from Category (+/-)	-3.6	15.2	-3.1	11.5	-7.5	11.3	-4.6	15.6	-13.3	8.1
Return, Tax-Adjusted (%)	14.0	40.3	-4.2	23.2	1.3	44.0	-11.3	36.7	3.9	4.0

PER SHARE DATA

	1996	1995	1994	1993	1992	1991	1990	1989	1988	1987
Dividends, Net Income ($)	0.01	0.01	0.00	0.00	0.11	0.06	0.14	0.06	0.15	0.13
Distrib'ns, Cap Gain ($)	1.30	2.13	0.33	0.84	1.04	0.87	0.00	1.27	0.00	1.61
Net Asset Value ($)	15.87	14.77	11.63	12.38	10.54	11.22	8.27	9.41	7.61	7.41
Expense Ratio (%)	na	1.28	1.33	1.32	1.54	1.45	1.45	1.28	1.38	1.25
Yield (%)	0.05	0.05	0.00	0.00	0.94	0.49	1.69	0.56	1.97	1.44
Portfolio Turnover (%)	na	130	172	131	216	161	178	167	179	147
Total Assets (Millions $)	1,051	651	310	343	145	139	87	109	53	68

PORTFOLIO (as of 9/30/96)

Portfolio Manager: Edward Keely - 1993

Investm't Category: Growth

- ✔ Domestic
- ✔ Foreign
- Asset Allocation
- Index
- Sector
- State Specific

Investment Style

- Large-Cap Growth
- ✔ Mid-Cap Growth
- ✔ Small-Cap Growth
- Large-Cap Value
- Mid-Cap Value
- Small-Cap Value

Portfolio

16.0% cash	0.0% corp bonds
84.0% stocks	0.0% gov't bonds
0.0% preferred	0.0% muni bonds
0.0% conv't/warrants	0.0% other

SHAREHOLDER INFORMATION

Minimum Investment
Initial: $1,000   Subsequent: $100

Minimum IRA Investment
Initial: $500   Subsequent: $100

Maximum Fees
Load: none   12b-1: 0.25%
Other: none

Distributions
Income: Dec   Capital Gains: Dec

Exchange Options
Number Per Year: 4   Fee: none
Telephone: yes (money market fund available)

Services
IRA, pension, auto exchange, auto invest, auto withdraw

Founders Passport (FPSSX)

International Stock

Founders Financial Center
2930 E. Third Ave.
Denver, CO 80206
800-525-2440, 303-394-4404
www.founders.com

PERFORMANCE   fund inception date: 11/16/93

	3yr Annual	5yr Annual	10yr Annual	Bull	Bear
Return (%)	10.2	na	na	45.6	-10.7
Differ from Category (+/-)	3.9 abv av	na	na	21.3 high	-3.5 blw av

Total Risk	Standard Deviation	Category Risk	Risk Index	Beta
abv av	10.2%	av	1.0	0.66

	1996	1995	1994	1993	1992	1991	1990	1989	1988	1987
Return (%)	20.0	24.3	-10.4	—	—	—	—	—	—	—
Differ from Category (+/-)	5.2	15.2	-7.3	—	—	—	—	—	—	—
Return, Tax-Adjusted (%)	19.7	24.1	-10.5	—	—	—	—	—	—	—

PER SHARE DATA

	1996	1995	1994	1993	1992	1991	1990	1989	1988	1987
Dividends, Net Income ($)	0.02	0.03	0.01	—	—	—	—	—	—	—
Distrib'ns, Cap Gain ($)	0.08	0.00	0.00	—	—	—	—	—	—	—
Net Asset Value ($)	13.91	11.68	9.42	—	—	—	—	—	—	—
Expense Ratio (%)	na	1.84	1.88	—	—	—	—	—	—	—
Yield (%)	0.14	0.25	0.10	—	—	—	—	—	—	—
Portfolio Turnover (%)	na	37	78	—	—	—	—	—	—	—
Total Assets (Millions $)	178	49	16	—	—	—	—	—	—	—

PORTFOLIO (as of 9/30/96)

Portfolio Manager: Michael Gerding - 1993

Investm't Category: International Stock

Domestic	Index
✔ Foreign	Sector
Asset Allocation	State Specific

Investment Style

Large-Cap Growth	Large-Cap Value
Mid-Cap Growth	Mid-Cap Value
Small-Cap Growth	Small-Cap Value

Portfolio

19.0% cash	0.0% corp bonds
78.1% stocks	0.0% gov't bonds
2.9% preferred	0.0% muni bonds
0.0% conv't/warrants	0.0% other

SHAREHOLDER INFORMATION

Minimum Investment

Initial: $1,000   Subsequent: $100

Minimum IRA Investment

Initial: $500   Subsequent: $100

Maximum Fees

Load: none   12b-1: none
Other: none

Distributions

Income: Dec   Capital Gains: Dec

Exchange Options

Number Per Year: 4   Fee: none
Telephone: yes (money market fund available)

Services

IRA, pension, auto exchange, auto invest, auto withdraw

Founders Special (FRSPX)

Aggressive Growth

Founders Financial Center
2930 E. Third Ave.
Denver, CO 80206
800-525-2440, 303-394-4404
www.founders.com

PERFORMANCE

fund inception date: 9/7/61

	3yr Annual	5yr Annual	10yr Annual	Bull	Bear
Return (%)	11.2	11.6	15.4	56.1	-14.8
Differ from Category (+/-)	-4.6 blw av	-3.7 blw av	0.4 av	-15.0 blw av	-4.2 blw av

Total Risk	Standard Deviation	Category Risk	Risk Index	Beta
high	14.5%	av	1.0	1.13

	1996	1995	1994	1993	1992	1991	1990	1989	1988	1987
Return (%)	15.3	25.6	-5.0	16.0	8.2	63.6	-10.5	39.2	13.1	5.2
Differ from Category (+/-)	-3.8	-8.7	-5.0	-3.3	-3.5	11.5	-5.1	10.8	-3.3	7.6
Return, Tax-Adjusted (%)	13.4	18.6	-6.1	11.2	6.5	60.1	-14.5	34.0	11.2	4.4

PER SHARE DATA

	1996	1995	1994	1993	1992	1991	1990	1989	1988	1987
Dividends, Net Income ($)	0.00	0.00	0.00	0.00	0.00	0.04	0.10	0.14	0.03	0.03
Distrib'ns, Cap Gain ($)	0.46	1.75	0.28	1.33	0.45	0.57	0.80	0.80	0.30	0.71
Net Asset Value ($)	7.66	7.05	7.01	7.67	7.76	7.59	5.03	6.64	5.47	5.14
Expense Ratio (%)	na	1.35	1.36	1.33	1.23	1.15	1.20	1.06	1.12	1.14
Yield (%)	0.00	0.00	0.00	0.00	0.00	0.49	1.71	1.88	0.51	0.51
Portfolio Turnover (%)	na	263	272	285	223	102	146	151	160	210
Total Assets (Millions $)	375	388	300	432	455	224	58	91	63	66

PORTFOLIO (as of 9/30/96)

Portfolio Manager: Ed Keely, Michael Haines - 1996

Investm't Category: Aggressive Growth
- ✔ Domestic
- ✔ Foreign
- Asset Allocation
- Index
- Sector
- State Specific

Investment Style
- Large-Cap Growth
- ✔ Mid-Cap Growth
- Small-Cap Growth
- Large-Cap Value
- Mid-Cap Value
- Small-Cap Value

Portfolio
- 12.4% cash
- 87.6% stocks
- 0.0% preferred
- 0.0% conv't/warrants
- 0.0% corp bonds
- 0.0% gov't bonds
- 0.0% muni bonds
- 0.0% other

SHAREHOLDER INFORMATION

Minimum Investment
Initial: $1,000   Subsequent: $100

Minimum IRA Investment
Initial: $500   Subsequent: $100

Maximum Fees
Load: none   12b-1: 0.25%
Other: none

Distributions
Income: Dec   Capital Gains: Dec

Exchange Options
Number Per Year: 4   Fee: none
Telephone: yes (money market fund available)

Services
IRA, pension, auto exchange, auto invest, auto withdraw

Founders Worldwide Growth (FWWGX)

International Stock

Founders Financial Center
2930 E. Third Ave.
Denver, CO 80206
800-525-2440, 303-394-4404
www.founders.com

PERFORMANCE

fund inception date: 12/29/89

	3yr Annual	5yr Annual	10yr Annual	Bull	Bear
Return (%)	10.3	12.1	na	44.0	-9.9
Differ from Category (+/-)	4.0 high	2.1 abv av	na	19.7 high	-2.7 blw av

Total Risk	Standard Deviation	Category Risk	Risk Index	Beta
abv av	10.3%	av	1.0	0.72

	1996	1995	1994	1993	1992	1991	1990	1989	1988	1987
Return (%)	13.9	20.6	-2.2	29.8	1.5	34.8	6.6	—	—	—
Differ from Category (+/-)	-0.9	11.5	0.9	-9.8	5.3	21.6	16.7	—	—	—
Return, Tax-Adjusted (%)	12.7	19.3	-3.0	28.9	1.5	34.6	5.4	—	—	—

PER SHARE DATA

	1996	1995	1994	1993	1992	1991	1990	1989	1988	1987
Dividends, Net Income ($)	0.07	0.08	0.00	0.00	0.00	0.03	0.28	—	—	—
Distrib'ns, Cap Gain ($)	0.75	0.65	0.45	0.41	0.00	0.03	0.00	—	—	—
Net Asset Value ($)	21.79	19.87	17.09	17.94	14.13	13.92	10.38	—	—	—
Expense Ratio (%)	na	1.65	1.66	1.80	2.06	1.90	2.10	—	—	—
Yield (%)	0.31	0.38	0.00	0.00	0.00	0.21	2.69	—	—	—
Portfolio Turnover (%)	na	54	87	117	152	84	170	—	—	—
Total Assets (Millions $)	338	227	104	84	36	20	5	—	—	—

PORTFOLIO (as of 9/30/96)

Portfolio Manager: Michael Gerding - 1989

Investm't Category: International Stock
- ✔ Domestic
- ✔ Foreign
- Asset Allocation
- Index
- Sector
- State Specific

Investment Style
Large-Cap Growth	Large-Cap Value
Mid-Cap Growth	Mid-Cap Value
Small-Cap Growth	Small-Cap Value

Portfolio
16.3% cash	0.0% corp bonds
79.9% stocks	0.0% gov't bonds
3.7% preferred	0.0% muni bonds
0.0% conv't/warrants	0.0% other

SHAREHOLDER INFORMATION

Minimum Investment
Initial: $1,000   Subsequent: $100

Minimum IRA Investment
Initial: $500   Subsequent: $100

Maximum Fees
Load: none   12b-1: 0.25%
Other: none

Distributions
Income: Dec   Capital Gains: Dec

Exchange Options
Number Per Year: 4   Fee: none
Telephone: yes (money market fund available)

Services
IRA, pension, auto exchange, auto invest, auto withdraw

Fremont Bond (FBDFX)

General Bond

333 Market St.
Suite 2600
San Francisco, CA 94105
800-548-4539, 415-284-8900

PERFORMANCE

fund inception date: 4/30/93

	3yr Annual	5yr Annual	10yr Annual	Bull	Bear
Return (%)	6.9	na	na	27.4	-5.3
Differ from Category (+/-)	1.8 high	na	na	7.1 high	-1.1 blw av

Total Risk	Standard Deviation	Category Risk	Risk Index	Avg Mat
blw av	5.2%	high	1.4	8.1 yrs

	1996	1995	1994	1993	1992	1991	1990	1989	1988	1987
Return (%)	5.2	21.2	-4.1	—	—	—	—	—	—	—
Differ from Category (+/-)	1.3	6.3	-1.8	—	—	—	—	—	—	—
Return, Tax-Adjusted (%)	2.5	17.6	-6.3	—	—	—	—	—	—	—

PER SHARE DATA

	1996	1995	1994	1993	1992	1991	1990	1989	1988	1987
Dividends, Net Income ($)	0.68	0.67	0.55	—	—	—	—	—	—	—
Distrib'ns, Cap Gain ($)	0.00	0.22	0.00	—	—	—	—	—	—	—
Net Asset Value ($)	9.95	10.14	9.15	—	—	—	—	—	—	—
Expense Ratio (%)	na	0.60	0.66	—	—	—	—	—	—	—
Yield (%)	6.83	6.46	6.01	—	—	—	—	—	—	—
Portfolio Turnover (%)	na	21	205	—	—	—	—	—	—	—
Total Assets (Millions $)	73	93	59	—	—	—	—	—	—	—

PORTFOLIO (as of 9/30/96)

Portfolio Manager: William H. Gross - 1994

Investm't Category: General Bond
- ✔ Domestic
- ✔ Foreign
- Asset Allocation
- Index
- Sector
- State Specific

Investment Style
- Large-Cap Growth
- Mid-Cap Growth
- Small-Cap Growth
- Large-Cap Value
- Mid-Cap Value
- Small-Cap Value

Portfolio
1.6% cash	5.8% corp bonds
0.0% stocks	20.7% gov't bonds
0.0% preferred	0.0% muni bonds
0.0% conv't/warrants	71.9% other

SHAREHOLDER INFORMATION

Minimum Investment
Initial: $2,000   Subsequent: $200

Minimum IRA Investment
Initial: $1,000   Subsequent: $1

Maximum Fees
Load: none   12b-1: none
Other: none

Distributions
Income: monthly   Capital Gains: Dec

Exchange Options
Number Per Year: no limit   Fee: none
Telephone: yes (money market fund available)

Services
IRA, pension, auto invest, auto withdraw

Fremont CA Interm Tax-Free (FCATX)

Tax-Exempt Bond

333 Market St.
Suite 2600
San Francisco, CA 94105
800-548-4539, 415-284-8900

PERFORMANCE

fund inception date: 7/2/90

	3yr Annual	5yr Annual	10yr Annual	Bull	Bear
Return (%)	4.2	5.9	na	17.5	-4.8
Differ from Category (+/-)	0.0 av	-0.5 blw av	na	-0.9 blw av	0.6 abv av

Total Risk	Standard Deviation	Category Risk	Risk Index	Avg Mat
low	4.5%	blw av	0.8	7.6 yrs

	1996	1995	1994	1993	1992	1991	1990	1989	1988	1987
Return (%)	3.6	14.8	-4.9	9.9	7.3	10.7	—	—	—	—
Differ from Category (+/-)	-0.1	-0.4	0.4	-1.9	-1.0	-0.7	—	—	—	—
Return, Tax-Adjusted (%)	3.6	14.7	-4.9	9.6	7.2	10.5	—	—	—	—

PER SHARE DATA

	1996	1995	1994	1993	1992	1991	1990	1989	1988	1987
Dividends, Net Income ($)	0.48	0.53	0.52	0.55	0.56	0.60	—	—	—	—
Distrib'ns, Cap Gain ($)	0.00	0.02	0.00	0.08	0.02	0.06	—	—	—	—
Net Asset Value ($)	10.84	10.94	10.03	11.09	10.69	10.53	—	—	—	—
Expense Ratio (%)	na	0.50	0.51	0.50	0.54	0.36	—	—	—	—
Yield (%)	4.42	4.83	5.18	4.92	5.22	5.66	—	—	—	—
Portfolio Turnover (%)	na	18	21	26	18	41	—	—	—	—
Total Assets (Millions $)	60	51	54	62	46	35	—	—	—	—

PORTFOLIO (as of 9/30/96)

Portfolio Manager: William M. Feeney - 1990

Investm't Category: Tax-Exempt Bond
- ✔ Domestic
- Foreign
- Asset Allocation
- Index
- Sector
- ✔ State Specific

Investment Style
- Large-Cap Growth
- Mid-Cap Growth
- Small-Cap Growth
- Large-Cap Value
- Mid-Cap Value
- Small-Cap Value

Portfolio
10.2% cash	0.0% corp bonds
0.0% stocks	0.0% gov't bonds
0.0% preferred	89.8% muni bonds
0.0% conv't/warrants	0.0% other

SHAREHOLDER INFORMATION

Minimum Investment
Initial: $2,000   Subsequent: $200

Minimum IRA Investment
Initial: na   Subsequent: na

Maximum Fees
Load: none   12b-1: none
Other: none

Distributions
Income: monthly   Capital Gains: Dec

Exchange Options
Number Per Year: no limit   Fee: none
Telephone: yes (money market fund available)

Services
auto exchange, auto invest, auto withdraw

Fremont Global (FMAFX)

International Stock

333 Market St.
Suite 2600
San Francisco, CA 94105
800-548-4539, 415-284-8900

PERFORMANCE

fund inception date: 11/18/88

	3yr Annual	5yr Annual	10yr Annual	Bull	Bear
Return (%)	9.2	10.3	na	38.3	-7.2
Differ from Category (+/-)	2.9 abv av	0.3 av	na	14.0 abv av	0.0 av

Total Risk	Standard Deviation	Category Risk	Risk Index	Beta
blw av	6.6%	low	0.6	0.61

	1996	1995	1994	1993	1992	1991	1990	1989	1988	1987
Return (%)	13.9	19.2	-4.2	19.5	5.2	18.6	-1.8	15.9	—	—
Differ from Category (+/-)	-0.9	10.1	-1.1	-20.1	9.0	5.4	8.3	-6.7	—	—
Return, Tax-Adjusted (%)	8.9	16.4	-4.9	18.2	3.3	17.1	-3.8	13.6	—	—

PER SHARE DATA

	1996	1995	1994	1993	1992	1991	1990	1989	1988	1987
Dividends, Net Income ($)	0.49	0.49	0.13	0.33	0.43	0.36	0.52	0.48	—	—
Distrib'ns, Cap Gain ($)	1.80	0.57	0.13	0.06	0.15	0.03	0.02	0.14	—	—
Net Asset Value ($)	13.77	14.16	12.79	13.62	11.74	11.74	10.25	11.02	—	—
Expense Ratio (%)	na	0.88	0.95	0.99	1.09	1.12	1.10	1.02	—	—
Yield (%)	3.14	3.32	1.00	2.41	3.61	3.05	5.06	4.30	—	—
Portfolio Turnover (%)	na	83	52	40	50	81	36	51	—	—
Total Assets (Millions $)	600	502	438	214	109	85	59	49	—	—

PORTFOLIO (as of 9/30/96)

Portfolio Manager: committee - 1988

Investm't Category: International Stock

✔ Domestic	Index
✔ Foreign	Sector
✔ Asset Allocation	State Specific

Investment Style

Large-Cap Growth	Large-Cap Value
Mid-Cap Growth	Mid-Cap Value
Small-Cap Growth	Small-Cap Value

Portfolio

26.8% cash	21.4% corp bonds
51.8% stocks	0.0% gov't bonds
0.0% preferred	0.0% muni bonds
0.0% conv't/warrants	0.0% other

SHAREHOLDER INFORMATION

Minimum Investment
Initial: $2,000   Subsequent: $200

Minimum IRA Investment
Initial: $1,000   Subsequent: $1

Maximum Fees
Load: none   12b-1: none
Other: none

Distributions
Income: quarterly   Capital Gains: Dec

Exchange Options
Number Per Year: no limit   Fee: none
Telephone: yes (money market fund available)

Services
IRA, pension, auto exchange, auto invest, auto withdraw

Fremont Growth (FEQFX)

Growth

333 Market St.
Suite 2600
San Francisco, CA 94105
800-548-4539, 415-284-8900

PERFORMANCE

fund inception date: 5/11/92

	3yr Annual	5yr Annual	10yr Annual	Bull	Bear
Return (%)	18.8	na	na	80.2	-10.0
Differ from Category (+/-)	3.1 abv av	na	na	17.8 high	-3.3 low

Total Risk	Standard Deviation	Category Risk	Risk Index	Beta
abv av	10.5%	av	1.0	1.02

	1996	1995	1994	1993	1992	1991	1990	1989	1988	1987
Return (%).	25.0	33.6	0.4	6.4	—	—	—	—	—	—
Differ from Category (+/-). .	4.9	3.3	0.7	-7.6	—	—	—	—	—	—
Return, Tax-Adjusted (%). .	18.1	31.3	-2.7	5.8	—	—	—	—	—	—

PER SHARE DATA

	1996	1995	1994	1993	1992	1991	1990	1989	1988	1987
Dividends, Net Income ($).	0.13	0.07	0.22	0.16	—	—	—	—	—	—
Distrib'ns, Cap Gain ($) . . .	2.95	0.70	0.90	0.00	—	—	—	—	—	—
Net Asset Value ($)	12.76	12.73	10.11	11.18	—	—	—	—	—	—
Expense Ratio (%).	na	0.97	0.94	0.87	—	—	—	—	—	—
Yield (%)	0.82	0.52	1.99	1.43	—	—	—	—	—	—
Portfolio Turnover (%). . . .	na	108	55	44	—	—	—	—	—	—
Total Assets (Millions $). . . .	97	66	23	42	—	—	—	—	—	—

PORTFOLIO (as of 9/30/96)

Portfolio Manager: Ken Copa, Eugene Sit - 1995

Investm't Category: Growth
- ✔ Domestic
- ✔ Foreign
- Asset Allocation
- Index
- Sector
- State Specific

Investment Style
- ✔ Large-Cap Growth
- Mid-Cap Growth
- Small-Cap Growth
- Large-Cap Value
- Mid-Cap Value
- Small-Cap Value

Portfolio
3.2% cash	0.0% corp bonds
96.8% stocks	0.0% gov't bonds
0.0% preferred	0.0% muni bonds
0.0% conv't/warrants	0.0% other

SHAREHOLDER INFORMATION

Minimum Investment
Initial: $2,000   Subsequent: $200

Minimum IRA Investment
Initial: $1,000   Subsequent: $1

Maximum Fees
Load: none   12b-1: none
Other: none

Distributions
Income: Oct   Capital Gains: Dec

Exchange Options
Number Per Year: no limit   Fee: none
Telephone: yes (money market fund available)

Services
IRA, pension, auto exchange, auto invest, auto withdraw

Fremont Int'l Growth

(FIGFX)

International Stock

333 Market St.
Suite 2600
San Francisco, CA 94105
800-548-4539, 415-284-8900

PERFORMANCE

fund inception date: 3/1/94

	3yr Annual	5yr Annual	10yr Annual	Bull	Bear
Return (%)	na	na	na	23.7	na
Differ from Category (+/-)	na	na	na	-0.6 av	na

Total Risk	Standard Deviation	Category Risk	Risk Index	Beta
na	na	na	na	na

	1996	1995	1994	1993	1992	1991	1990	1989	1988	1987
Return (%)	13.0	7.2	—	—	—	—	—	—	—	—
Differ from Category (+/-)	-1.8	-1.9	—	—	—	—	—	—	—	—
Return, Tax-Adjusted (%)	12.9	6.8	—	—	—	—	—	—	—	—

PER SHARE DATA

	1996	1995	1994	1993	1992	1991	1990	1989	1988	1987
Dividends, Net Income ($)	0.00	0.08	—	—	—	—	—	—	—	—
Distrib'ns, Cap Gain ($)	0.03	0.00	—	—	—	—	—	—	—	—
Net Asset Value ($)	11.10	9.85	—	—	—	—	—	—	—	—
Expense Ratio (%)	na	1.50	—	—	—	—	—	—	—	—
Yield (%)	0.00	0.81	—	—	—	—	—	—	—	—
Portfolio Turnover (%)	na	32	—	—	—	—	—	—	—	—
Total Assets (Millions $)	37	34	—	—	—	—	—	—	—	—

PORTFOLIO (as of 9/30/96)

Portfolio Manager: A. Pang, P. Landini, R. Haddick - 1995

Investm't Category: International Stock

Domestic	Index
✔ Foreign	Sector
Asset Allocation	State Specific

Investment Style

Large-Cap Growth	Large-Cap Value
Mid-Cap Growth	Mid-Cap Value
Small-Cap Growth	Small-Cap Value

Portfolio

1.5% cash	0.0% corp bonds
97.7% stocks	0.0% gov't bonds
0.8% preferred	0.0% muni bonds
0.0% conv't/warrants	0.0% other

SHAREHOLDER INFORMATION

Minimum Investment
Initial: $2,000   Subsequent: $200

Minimum IRA Investment
Initial: $1,000   Subsequent: $1

Maximum Fees
Load: none   12b-1: none
Other: none

Distributions
Income: Oct   Capital Gains: Dec

Exchange Options
Number Per Year: no limit   Fee: none
Telephone: yes (money market fund available)

Services
IRA, pension, auto invest, auto withdraw

Fremont US Micro Cap

(FUSMX)

Aggressive Growth

333 Market St.
Suite 2600
San Francisco, CA 94105
800-548-4539, 415-284-8900

fund inception date: 6/30/94

	3yr Annual	5yr Annual	10yr Annual	Bull	Bear
Return (%)	na	na	na	132.0	na
Differ from Category (+/-)	na	na	na	60.9 high	na

Total Risk	Standard Deviation	Category Risk	Risk Index	Beta
na	na	na	na	na

	1996	1995	1994	1993	1992	1991	1990	1989	1988	1987
Return (%)	48.7	54.0	—	—	—	—	—	—	—	—
Differ from Category (+/-)	29.6	19.7	—	—	—	—	—	—	—	—
Return, Tax-Adjusted (%)	47.0	52.6	—	—	—	—	—	—	—	—

PER SHARE DATA

	1996	1995	1994	1993	1992	1991	1990	1989	1988	1987
Dividends, Net Income ($)	0.00	0.00	—	—	—	—	—	—	—	—
Distrib'ns, Cap Gain ($)	0.91	0.50	—	—	—	—	—	—	—	—
Net Asset Value ($)	21.50	15.10	—	—	—	—	—	—	—	—
Expense Ratio (%)	na	2.04	—	—	—	—	—	—	—	—
Yield (%)	0.00	0.00	—	—	—	—	—	—	—	—
Portfolio Turnover (%)	na	144	—	—	—	—	—	—	—	—
Total Assets (Millions $)	108	9	—	—	—	—	—	—	—	—

PORTFOLIO (as of 9/30/96)

Portfolio Manager: Robert E. Kern - 1994

Investm't Category: Aggressive Growth
✔ Domestic   Index
✔ Foreign   Sector
   Asset Allocation   State Specific

Investment Style
Large-Cap Growth   Large-Cap Value
Mid-Cap Growth   Mid-Cap Value
Small-Cap Growth   Small-Cap Value

Portfolio
26.2% cash   0.0% corp bonds
73.8% stocks   0.0% gov't bonds
0.0% preferred   0.0% muni bonds
0.0% conv't/warrants   0.0% other

SHAREHOLDER INFORMATION

Minimum Investment
Initial: $2,000   Subsequent: $200

Minimum IRA Investment
Initial: $1,000   Subsequent: $1

Maximum Fees
Load: none   12b-1: none
Other: none

Distributions
Income: Oct   Capital Gains: Dec

Exchange Options
Number Per Year: no limit   Fee: none
Telephone: yes (money market fund available)

Services
IRA, pension, auto invest, auto withdraw

Fundamental New York Muni (NYMFX)

Tax-Exempt Bond

90 Washington St.
19th Floor
New York, NY 10006
800-225-6864, 212-635-3005

PERFORMANCE

fund inception date: 4/27/81

	3yr Annual	5yr Annual	10yr Annual	Bull	Bear
Return (%)	-5.3	1.3	3.2	-4.7	-12.2
Differ from Category (+/-)	-9.5 low	-5.1 low	-3.5 low	-23.1 low	-6.8 low

Total Risk	Standard Deviation	Category Risk	Risk Index	Avg Mat
av	7.7%	high	1.4	17.4 yrs

	1996	1995	1994	1993	1992	1991	1990	1989	1988	1987
Return (%)	-7.8	15.5	-20.4	12.5	11.8	15.6	-1.1	9.6	11.2	-7.5
Differ from Category (+/-)	-11.5	0.3	-15.1	0.7	3.5	4.2	-7.5	0.6	1.2	-6.1
Return, Tax-Adjusted (%)	-7.8	15.5	-20.7	9.9	11.8	15.6	-1.1	9.6	11.2	-8.2

PER SHARE DATA

	1996	1995	1994	1993	1992	1991	1990	1989	1988	1987
Dividends, Net Income ($)	0.03	0.03	0.05	0.06	0.06	0.05	0.06	0.07	0.07	0.07
Distrib'ns, Cap Gain ($)	0.00	0.00	0.01	0.11	0.00	0.00	0.00	0.00	0.00	0.03
Net Asset Value ($)	0.87	0.98	0.88	1.18	1.21	1.14	1.04	1.12	1.09	1.05
Expense Ratio (%)	na	3.64	3.21	2.05	1.69	1.78	1.65	1.69	1.74	2.04
Yield (%)	3.44	3.06	5.61	4.65	4.95	4.38	5.76	6.25	6.42	6.48
Portfolio Turnover (%)	na	347	289	404	461	365	483	386	463	549
Total Assets (Millions $)	110	226	213	274	196	184	183	237	229	219

PORTFOLIO (as of 9/30/96)

Portfolio Manager: Lance Brofman - 1982

Investm't Category: Tax-Exempt Bond
- ✔ Domestic
- Foreign
- Asset Allocation
- Index
- Sector
- ✔ State Specific

Investment Style
- Large-Cap Growth
- Mid-Cap Growth
- Small-Cap Growth
- Large-Cap Value
- Mid-Cap Value
- Small-Cap Value

Portfolio
0.0% cash	0.0% corp bonds
0.0% stocks	0.0% gov't bonds
0.0% preferred	100.0% muni bonds
0.0% conv't/warrants	0.0% other

SHAREHOLDER INFORMATION

Minimum Investment
Initial: $1,000   Subsequent: $100

Minimum IRA Investment
Initial: na   Subsequent: na

Maximum Fees
Load: none   12b-1: 0.50%
Other: none

Distributions
Income: monthly   Capital Gains: Dec

Exchange Options
Number Per Year: no limit   Fee: none
Telephone: yes (money market fund available)

Services
auto invest, auto withdraw

GIT Equity Trust: Special Growth

(GTSGX) *Aggressive Growth*

1655 Fort Myer Drive
Suite 1000
Arlington, VA 22209
800-368-3195, 703-528-3600
www.gitfunds.com

PERFORMANCE

fund inception date: 7/21/83

	3yr Annual	5yr Annual	10yr Annual	Bull	Bear
Return (%)	7.8	8.9	9.8	29.4	-4.0
Differ from Category (+/-)	-8.0 low	-6.4 low	-5.2 low	-41.7 low	6.6 high

Total Risk	Standard Deviation	Category Risk	Risk Index	Beta
abv av	9.9%	low	0.7	0.59

	1996	1995	1994	1993	1992	1991	1990	1989	1988	1987
Return (%)	6.9	22.1	-4.0	14.8	6.7	25.7	-15.9	25.1	27.0	-1.4
Differ from Category (+/-)	-12.2	-12.2	-4.0	-4.5	-5.0	-26.4	-10.5	-3.3	10.6	1.0
Return, Tax-Adjusted (%)	-7.8	19.1	-7.9	13.0	6.2	24.8	-16.6	23.0	23.4	-5.5

PER SHARE DATA

	1996	1995	1994	1993	1992	1991	1990	1989	1988	1987
Dividends, Net Income ($)	0.11	0.17	0.09	0.17	0.12	0.20	0.32	0.39	0.57	0.23
Distrib'ns, Cap Gain ($)	10.10	1.65	2.79	0.98	0.13	0.20	0.00	0.57	0.90	1.98
Net Asset Value ($)	10.64	19.63	17.65	21.37	19.64	18.64	15.16	18.40	15.52	13.43
Expense Ratio (%)	1.41	1.30	1.45	1.35	1.39	1.40	1.47	1.50	1.50	1.50
Yield (%)	0.53	0.79	0.44	0.76	0.60	1.06	2.11	2.05	3.47	1.49
Portfolio Turnover (%)	21	4	7	13	24	6	15	27	29	8
Total Assets (Millions $)	15	25	30	36	44	60	37	34	16	13

PORTFOLIO (as of 9/30/96)

Portfolio Manager: Charles Tennes, Frank Burgess - 1995

Investm't Category: Aggressive Growth
- ✔ Domestic
- ✔ Foreign
-   Asset Allocation
-   Index
-   Sector
-   State Specific

Investment Style
- Large-Cap Growth
- Mid-Cap Growth
- Small-Cap Growth
- Large-Cap Value
- Mid-Cap Value
- ✔ Small-Cap Value

Portfolio
23.4% cash	0.0% corp bonds
76.7% stocks	0.0% gov't bonds
0.0% preferred	0.0% muni bonds
0.0% conv't/warrants	0.0% other

SHAREHOLDER INFORMATION

Minimum Investment
Initial: $2,500   Subsequent: $1

Minimum IRA Investment
Initial: $500   Subsequent: $1

Maximum Fees
Load: none   12b-1: none
Other: none

Distributions
Income: Mar, Dec   Capital Gains: Mar, Dec

Exchange Options
Number Per Year: no limit   Fee: none
Telephone: yes (money market fund available)

Services
IRA, pension, auto invest, auto withdraw

GIT Tax-Free Trust: National Port (GTFHX)

Tax-Exempt Bond

1655 Fort Myer Drive
Suite 1000
Arlington, VA 22209
800-368-3195, 703-528-3600
www.gitfunds.com

PERFORMANCE

fund inception date: 12/30/82

	3yr Annual	5yr Annual	10yr Annual	Bull	Bear
Return (%)	2.6	5.5	5.9	17.1	-8.3
Differ from Category (+/-)	-1.6 low	-0.9 low	-0.8 low	-1.3 blw av	-2.9 low

Total Risk	Standard Deviation	Category Risk	Risk Index	Avg Mat
blw av	5.8%	abv av	1.0	16.9 yrs

	1996	1995	1994	1993	1992	1991	1990	1989	1988	1987
Return (%).	2.9	15.3	-8.9	11.8	8.1	10.2	5.4	7.2	8.5	0.1
Differ from Category (+/-).	-0.8	0.1	-3.6	0.0	-0.2	-1.2	-1.0	-1.8	-1.5	1.5
Return, Tax-Adjusted (%). . .	2.9	15.3	-8.9	9.4	7.5	10.2	5.4	7.2	8.5	-0.1

PER SHARE DATA

	1996	1995	1994	1993	1992	1991	1990	1989	1988	1987
Dividends, Net Income ($)	0.44	0.45	0.41	0.51	0.60	0.61	0.68	0.72	0.73	0.79
Distrib'ns, Cap Gain ($) . . .	0.00	0.00	0.00	0.93	0.21	0.00	0.00	0.00	0.00	0.07
Net Asset Value ($)	10.39	10.54	9.55	10.92	11.12	11.06	10.62	10.75	10.72	10.58
Expense Ratio (%).	na	1.18	1.23	1.10	1.17	1.24	1.24	1.19	1.16	0.99
Yield (%)	4.23	4.26	4.29	4.30	5.29	5.51	6.40	6.69	6.80	7.41
Portfolio Turnover (%).	na	56	175	212	114	91	41	58	77	66
Total Assets (Millions $). . . .	29	32	31	41	41	40	41	41	39	39

PORTFOLIO (as of 9/30/96)

Portfolio Manager: T. Daniel Gillespie - 1994

Investm't Category: Tax-Exempt Bond

✔ Domestic | Index
Foreign | Sector
Asset Allocation | State Specific

Investment Style

Large-Cap Growth | Large-Cap Value
Mid-Cap Growth | Mid-Cap Value
Small-Cap Growth | Small-Cap Value

Portfolio

0.0% cash | 0.0% corp bonds
0.0% stocks | 0.0% gov't bonds
0.0% preferred | 100.0% muni bonds
0.0% conv't/warrants | 0.0% other

SHAREHOLDER INFORMATION

Minimum Investment
Initial: $2,500 | Subsequent: $1

Minimum IRA Investment
Initial: na | Subsequent: na

Maximum Fees
Load: none | 12b-1: none
Other: none

Distributions
Income: monthly | Capital Gains: annual

Exchange Options
Number Per Year: no limit | Fee: none
Telephone: yes (money market fund available)

Services
auto invest, auto withdraw

GIT Tax-Free Trust:
Virginia Port (GTVAX)

Tax-Exempt Bond

1655 Fort Myer Drive
Suite 1000
Arlington, VA 22209
800-368-3195, 703-528-3600
www.gitfunds.com

PERFORMANCE

fund inception date: 10/13/87

	3yr Annual	5yr Annual	10yr Annual	Bull	Bear
Return (%)	3.1	5.8	na	18.3	-7.9
Differ from Category (+/-)	-1.1 low	-0.6 low	na	-0.1 av	-2.5 low

Total Risk	Standard Deviation	Category Risk	Risk Index	Avg Mat
blw av	5.8%	abv av	1.0	17.5 yrs

	1996	1995	1994	1993	1992	1991	1990	1989	1988	1987
Return (%).	3.1	16.1	-8.3	12.4	7.5	9.8	5.8	7.3	8.2	—
Differ from Category (+/-) .	-0.6	0.9	-3.0	0.6	-0.8	-1.6	-0.6	-1.7	-1.8	—
Return, Tax-Adjusted (%). . .	3.1	16.1	-8.3	10.9	7.2	9.5	5.8	7.3	7.8	—

PER SHARE DATA

	1996	1995	1994	1993	1992	1991	1990	1989	1988	1987
Dividends, Net Income ($) .	0.50	0.50	0.47	0.55	0.58	0.60	0.61	0.62	0.68	—
Distrib'ns, Cap Gain ($) . . .	0.00	0.00	0.00	0.59	0.11	0.11	0.00	0.00	0.13	—
Net Asset Value ($)	11.31	11.47	10.34	11.78	11.54	11.41	11.08	11.07	10.92	—
Expense Ratio (%).	na	1.14	1.18	1.10	1.13	1.18	1.25	1.22	0.72	—
Yield (%)	4.42	4.35	4.54	4.44	4.97	5.20	5.50	5.60	6.15	—
Portfolio Turnover (%).	na	55	104	80	74	73	11	34	58	—
Total Assets (Millions $). . . .	33	34	32	44	39	32	26	21	18	—

PORTFOLIO (as of 9/30/96)

Portfolio Manager: T. Daniel Gillespie - 1994

Investm't Category: Tax-Exempt Bond

✔ Domestic	Index
Foreign	Sector
Asset Allocation	✔ State Specific

Investment Style

Large-Cap Growth	Large-Cap Value
Mid-Cap Growth	Mid-Cap Value
Small-Cap Growth	Small-Cap Value

Portfolio

1.6% cash	0.0% corp bonds
0.0% stocks	0.0% gov't bonds
0.0% preferred	98.4% muni bonds
0.0% conv't/warrants	0.0% other

SHAREHOLDER INFORMATION

Minimum Investment
Initial: $2,500   Subsequent: $1

Minimum IRA Investment
Initial: na   Subsequent: na

Maximum Fees
Load: none   12b-1: none
Other: none

Distributions
Income: monthly   Capital Gains: annual

Exchange Options
Number Per Year: no limit   Fee: none
Telephone: yes (money market fund available)

Services
auto invest, auto withdraw

Gabelli Asset (GABAX)

Growth

One Corporate Center
Rye, NY 10580
800-422-3554, 914-921-5100
www.gabelli.com

PERFORMANCE

fund inception date: 3/3/86

	3yr Annual	5yr Annual	10yr Annual	Bull	Bear
Return (%)	12.2	14.6	15.6	47.3	-6.6
Differ from Category (+/-)	-3.5 low	0.3 av	1.7 abv av	-15.1 low	0.1 av

Total Risk	Standard Deviation	Category Risk	Risk Index	Beta
av	8.6%	low	0.8	0.81

	1996	1995	1994	1993	1992	1991	1990	1989	1988	1987
Return (%)	13.3	24.9	-0.2	21.8	14.8	18.1	-5.0	26.1	31.1	16.2
Differ from Category (+/-)	-6.8	-5.4	0.1	7.8	3.0	-17.9	1.1	0.0	13.0	14.2
Return, Tax-Adjusted (%)	10.2	22.2	-1.6	20.4	13.4	16.9	-6.8	23.2	27.2	14.8

PER SHARE DATA

	1996	1995	1994	1993	1992	1991	1990	1989	1988	1987
Dividends, Net Income ($)	0.15	0.25	0.26	0.16	0.25	0.38	0.77	0.55	0.37	0.09
Distrib'ns, Cap Gain ($)	2.61	1.74	0.79	0.75	0.50	0.12	0.00	0.72	1.23	0.41
Net Asset Value ($)	26.42	25.75	22.21	23.30	19.88	17.96	15.63	17.26	14.69	12.61
Expense Ratio (%)	na	1.33	1.28	1.31	1.31	1.30	1.20	1.26	1.31	1.26
Yield (%)	0.51	0.90	1.13	0.66	1.22	2.10	4.92	3.05	2.32	0.69
Portfolio Turnover (%)	na	26	18	16	14	20	56	49	47	90
Total Assets (Millions $)	1,120	1,090	940	948	631	485	342	361	143	76

PORTFOLIO (as of 9/30/96)

Portfolio Manager: Mario J. Gabelli - 1986

Investm't Category: Growth
- ✔ Domestic
- ✔ Foreign
- Asset Allocation

- Index
- Sector
- State Specific

Investment Style
Large-Cap Growth	✔ Large-Cap Value
Mid-Cap Growth	✔ Mid-Cap Value
Small-Cap Growth	Small-Cap Value

Portfolio
4.0% cash	0.3% corp bonds
95.3% stocks	0.0% gov't bonds
0.4% preferred	0.0% muni bonds
0.0% conv't/warrants	0.0% other

SHAREHOLDER INFORMATION

Minimum Investment
Initial: $1,000   Subsequent: $1

Minimum IRA Investment
Initial: $1,000   Subsequent: $1

Maximum Fees
Load: none   12b-1: 0.25%
Other: none

Distributions
Income: annual   Capital Gains: annual

Exchange Options
Number Per Year: no limit   Fee: none
Telephone: yes (money market fund available)

Services
IRA, pension, auto invest, auto withdraw

Gabelli Global Telecommunications

(GABTX) *International Stock*

One Corporate Center
Rye, NY 10580
800-422-3554, 914-921-5100
www.gabelli.com

PERFORMANCE

fund inception date: 11/1/93

	3yr Annual	5yr Annual	10yr Annual	Bull	Bear
Return (%)	6.8	na	na	29.2	-8.5
Differ from Category (+/-)	0.5 av	na	na	4.9 abv av	-1.3 blw av

Total Risk	Standard Deviation	Category Risk	Risk Index	Beta
abv av	9.9%	blw av	1.0	0.80

	1996	1995	1994	1993	1992	1991	1990	1989	1988	1987
Return (%)	8.9	16.1	-3.7	—	—	—	—	—	—	—
Differ from Category (+/-)	-5.9	7.0	-0.6	—	—	—	—	—	—	—
Return, Tax-Adjusted (%)	6.7	15.5	-4.1	—	—	—	—	—	—	—

PER SHARE DATA

	1996	1995	1994	1993	1992	1991	1990	1989	1988	1987
Dividends, Net Income ($)	0.04	0.06	0.06	—	—	—	—	—	—	—
Distrib'ns, Cap Gain ($)	0.79	0.11	0.03	—	—	—	—	—	—	—
Net Asset Value ($)	11.28	11.12	9.73	—	—	—	—	—	—	—
Expense Ratio (%)	na	1.75	1.80	—	—	—	—	—	—	—
Yield (%)	0.33	0.53	0.61	—	—	—	—	—	—	—
Portfolio Turnover (%)	na	24	14	—	—	—	—	—	—	—
Total Assets (Millions $)	111	122	137	—	—	—	—	—	—	—

PORTFOLIO (as of 9/30/96)

Portfolio Manager: Mario J. Gabelli - 1993

Investm't Category: International Stock
✔ Domestic   Index
✔ Foreign   ✔ Sector
   Asset Allocation   State Specific

Investment Style
Large-Cap Growth   Large-Cap Value
Mid-Cap Growth   Mid-Cap Value
Small-Cap Growth   Small-Cap Value

Portfolio
0.2% cash   0.0% corp bonds
95.8% stocks   0.0% gov't bonds
2.2% preferred   0.0% muni bonds
1.9% conv't/warrants 0.0% other

SHAREHOLDER INFORMATION

Minimum Investment
Initial: $1,000   Subsequent: $1

Minimum IRA Investment
Initial: $1,000   Subsequent: $1

Maximum Fees
Load: none   12b-1: 0.25%
Other: none

Distributions
Income: annual   Capital Gains: annual

Exchange Options
Number Per Year: no limit   Fee: none
Telephone: yes (money market fund available)

Services
IRA, pension, auto exchange, auto invest, auto withdraw

Gabelli Growth (GABGX)

Growth

One Corporate Center
Rye, NY 10580
800-422-3554, 914-921-5100
www.gabelli.com

PERFORMANCE

fund inception date: 4/10/87

	3yr Annual	5yr Annual	10yr Annual	Bull	Bear
Return (%)	15.2	12.2	na	67.7	-10.1
Differ from Category (+/-)	-0.5 av	-2.1 blw av	na	5.3 abv av	-3.4 low

Total Risk	Standard Deviation	Category Risk	Risk Index	Beta
abv av	10.4%	av	1.0	1.00

	1996	1995	1994	1993	1992	1991	1990	1989	1988	1987
Return (%).............	19.4	32.6	-3.4	11.2	4.4	34.3	-2.0	40.1	39.1	—
Differ from Category (+/-).	-0.7	2.3	-3.1	-2.8	-7.4	-1.7	4.1	14.0	21.0	—
Return, Tax-Adjusted (%)..	16.4	26.9	-6.8	10.1	3.5	33.2	-3.1	38.5	37.3	—

PER SHARE DATA

	1996	1995	1994	1993	1992	1991	1990	1989	1988	1987
Dividends, Net Income ($).	0.02	0.05	0.08	0.09	0.08	0.15	0.39	0.17	0.19	—
Distrib'ns, Cap Gain ($) ...	2.29	3.90	2.70	0.67	0.56	0.41	0.07	0.48	0.33	—
Net Asset Value ($)	24.14	22.16	19.69	23.26	21.59	21.28	16.27	17.07	12.65	—
Expense Ratio (%).........	na	1.44	1.36	1.41	1.41	1.45	1.50	1.85	2.30	—
Yield (%)	0.07	0.19	0.35	0.37	0.36	0.69	2.38	0.96	1.46	—
Portfolio Turnover (%).....	na	140	40	80	46	50	75	48	82	—
Total Assets (Millions $)...	656	526	426	695	624	420	202	110	11	—

PORTFOLIO (as of 9/30/96)

Portfolio Manager: Howard Ward - 1995

Investm't Category: Growth
- ✔ Domestic
- Index
- ✔ Foreign
- Sector
- Asset Allocation
- State Specific

Investment Style
- ✔ Large-Cap Growth
- Large-Cap Value
- Mid-Cap Growth
- Mid-Cap Value
- Small-Cap Growth
- Small-Cap Value

Portfolio

2.5% cash	0.0% corp bonds
97.5% stocks	0.0% gov't bonds
0.0% preferred	0.0% muni bonds
0.0% conv't/warrants	0.0% other

SHAREHOLDER INFORMATION

Minimum Investment
Initial: $1,000   Subsequent: $1

Minimum IRA Investment
Initial: $1,000   Subsequent: $1

Maximum Fees
Load: none   12b-1: 0.25%
Other: none

Distributions
Income: annual   Capital Gains: annual

Exchange Options
Number Per Year: no limit   Fee: none
Telephone: yes (money market fund available)

Services
IRA, pension, auto invest, auto withdraw

Galaxy II: Large Co Index

(ILCIX)

Growth & Income

4400 Computer Drive
Mail Zone B215
Westboro, MA 01581
800-628-0414, 508-871-4091
www.galaxyfunds.com

PERFORMANCE

fund inception date: 10/1/90

	3yr Annual	5yr Annual	10yr Annual	Bull	Bear
Return (%)	19.2	14.7	na	75.7	-6.7
Differ from Category (+/-)	3.9 high	0.8 abv av	na	15.9 high	-0.3 av

Total Risk	Standard Deviation	Category Risk	Risk Index	Beta
abv av	9.6%	abv av	1.0	0.99

	1996	1995	1994	1993	1992	1991	1990	1989	1988	1987
Return (%).	22.5	37.0	0.9	9.6	7.0	29.0	—	—	—	—
Differ from Category (+/-) . .	2.8	6.9	2.2	-4.2	-3.7	-0.1	—	—	—	—
Return, Tax-Adjusted (%). .	21.0	35.3	-0.7	8.5	6.0	27.8	—	—	—	—

PER SHARE DATA

	1996	1995	1994	1993	1992	1991	1990	1989	1988	1987
Dividends, Net Income ($)	0.38	0.38	0.36	0.35	0.32	0.31	—	—	—	—
Distrib'ns, Cap Gain ($) . . .	0.42	0.34	0.33	0.02	0.00	0.00	—	—	—	—
Net Asset Value ($)	22.52	19.05	14.46	15.02	14.06	13.45	—	—	—	—
Expense Ratio (%).	na	0.40	0.40	0.40	0.40	0.40	—	—	—	—
Yield (%)	1.65	1.95	2.43	2.32	2.27	2.30	—	—	—	—
Portfolio Turnover (%).	na	7	3	0	0	0	—	—	—	—
Total Assets (Millions $). . .	358	214	137	149	124	65	—	—	—	—

PORTFOLIO (as of 6/30/96)

Portfolio Manager: Murphy Van Der Velde - 1996

Investm't Category: Growth & Income

✔ Domestic
Foreign
Asset Allocation

✔ Index
Sector
State Specific

Investment Style

✔ Large-Cap Growth
Mid-Cap Growth
Small-Cap Growth

✔ Large-Cap Value
Mid-Cap Value
Small-Cap Value

Portfolio

10.3% cash	0.0% corp bonds
89.2% stocks	0.6% gov't bonds
0.0% preferred	0.0% muni bonds
0.0% conv't/warrants	0.0% other

SHAREHOLDER INFORMATION

Minimum Investment
Initial: $2,500   Subsequent: $100

Minimum IRA Investment
Initial: $500   Subsequent: $100

Maximum Fees
Load: none   12b-1: none
Other: none

Distributions
Income: annual   Capital Gains: Dec

Exchange Options
Number Per Year: no limit   Fee: none
Telephone: yes (money market fund available)

Services
IRA, pension, auto invest, auto withdraw

Galaxy II: Small Co Index

(ISCIX)

Aggressive Growth

4400 Computer Drive
Mail Zone B215
Westboro, MA 01581
800-628-0414, 508-871-4091
www.galaxyfunds.com

PERFORMANCE

fund inception date: 10/1/90

	3yr Annual	5yr Annual	10yr Annual	Bull	Bear
Return (%)	15.3	13.9	na	65.0	-9.3
Differ from Category (+/-)	-0.5 av	-1.4 av	na	-6.1 av	1.3 abv av

Total Risk	Standard Deviation	Category Risk	Risk Index	Beta
abv av	10.4%	low	0.7	0.90

	1996	1995	1994	1993	1992	1991	1990	1989	1988	1987
Return (%)	19.6	33.1	-3.7	11.3	12.2	45.4	—	—	—	—
Differ from Category (+/-)	.0.5	-1.2	-3.7	-8.0	0.5	-6.7	—	—	—	—
Return, Tax-Adjusted (%)	17.0	31.6	-5.6	10.2	11.5	44.4	—	—	—	—

PER SHARE DATA

	1996	1995	1994	1993	1992	1991	1990	1989	1988	1987
Dividends, Net Income ($)	0.33	0.37	0.26	0.24	0.23	0.21	—	—	—	—
Distrib'ns, Cap Gain ($)	1.46	0.33	0.83	0.32	0.05	0.06	—	—	—	—
Net Asset Value ($)	23.38	21.08	16.38	18.16	16.84	15.27	—	—	—	—
Expense Ratio (%)	na	0.40	0.40	0.40	0.40	0.40	—	—	—	—
Yield (%)	1.32	1.72	1.51	1.29	1.36	1.36	—	—	—	—
Portfolio Turnover (%)	na	10	17	4	6	1	—	—	—	—
Total Assets (Millions $)	326	276	230	263	181	67	—	—	—	—

PORTFOLIO (as of 6/30/96)

Portfolio Manager: Murphy Van Der Velde - 1996

Investm't Category: Aggressive Growth
- ✔ Domestic
- ✔ Index
- Foreign
- Sector
- Asset Allocation
- State Specific

Investment Style
- Large-Cap Growth
- Large-Cap Value
- ✔ Mid-Cap Growth
- ✔ Mid-Cap Value
- ✔ Small-Cap Growth
- ✔ Small-Cap Value

Portfolio
10.6% cash	0.0% corp bonds
89.4% stocks	0.0% gov't bonds
0.0% preferred	0.0% muni bonds
0.0% conv't/warrants	0.0% other

SHAREHOLDER INFORMATION

Minimum Investment
Initial: $2,500   Subsequent: $100

Minimum IRA Investment
Initial: $500   Subsequent: $100

Maximum Fees
Load: none   12b-1: none
Other: none

Distributions
Income: annual   Capital Gains: Dec

Exchange Options
Number Per Year: no limit   Fee: none
Telephone: yes (money market fund available)

Services
IRA, pension, auto invest, auto withdraw

Galaxy II: US Treasury Index—Retail (IUTIX)

Government Bond

4400 Computer Drive
Mail Zone B215
Westboro, MA 01581
800-628-0414, 508-871-4091
www.galaxyfunds.com

PERFORMANCE

fund inception date: 6/4/91

	3yr Annual	5yr Annual	10yr Annual	Bull	Bear
Return (%)	5.1	6.4	na	21.4	-5.6
Differ from Category (+/-)	0.2 av	-0.2 abv av	na	-0.6 abv av	0.8 av

Total Risk	Standard Deviation	Category Risk	Risk Index	Avg Mat
low	4.7%	av	1.2	8.3 yrs

	1996	1995	1994	1993	1992	1991	1990	1989	1988	1987
Return (%)	2.2	18.0	-3.8	10.2	6.7	—	—	—	—	—
Differ from Category (+/-)	0.7	-1.6	0.6	-1.4	0.0	—	—	—	—	—
Return, Tax-Adjusted (%)	-0.2	15.2	-6.5	7.1	4.0	—	—	—	—	—

PER SHARE DATA

	1996	1995	1994	1993	1992	1991	1990	1989	1988	1987
Dividends, Net Income ($)	0.64	0.66	0.61	0.58	0.63	—	—	—	—	—
Distrib'ns, Cap Gain ($)	0.00	0.00	0.18	0.33	0.13	—	—	—	—	—
Net Asset Value ($)	10.23	10.66	9.63	10.83	10.68	—	—	—	—	—
Expense Ratio (%)	na	0.40	0.40	0.40	0.40	—	—	—	—	—
Yield (%)	6.25	6.19	6.21	5.19	5.82	—	—	—	—	—
Portfolio Turnover (%)	na	50	74	34	56	—	—	—	—	—
Total Assets (Millions $)	116	128	104	152	142	—	—	—	—	—

PORTFOLIO (as of 6/30/96)

Portfolio Manager: David Lindsay - 1994

Investm't Category: Government Bond
- ✔ Domestic
- ✔ Index
- Foreign
- Sector
- Asset Allocation
- State Specific

Investment Style
- Large-Cap Growth
- Large-Cap Value
- Mid-Cap Growth
- Mid-Cap Value
- Small-Cap Growth
- Small-Cap Value

Portfolio
1.5% cash	0.0% corp bonds
0.0% stocks	98.5% gov't bonds
0.0% preferred	0.0% muni bonds
0.0% conv't/warrants	0.0% other

SHAREHOLDER INFORMATION

Minimum Investment
Initial: $2,500   Subsequent: $100

Minimum IRA Investment
Initial: $500   Subsequent: $100

Maximum Fees
Load: none   12b-1: none
Other: none

Distributions
Income: monthly   Capital Gains: Dec

Exchange Options
Number Per Year: no limit   Fee: none
Telephone: yes (money market fund available)

Services
IRA, pension, auto invest, auto withdraw

Galaxy II: Utility Index

(IUTLX)

Growth & Income

4400 Computer Drive
Mail Zone B215
Westboro, MA 01581
800-628-0414, 508-871-4091
www.galaxyfunds.com

PERFORMANCE

fund inception date: 1/5/93

	3yr Annual	5yr Annual	10yr Annual	Bull	Bear
Return (%)	9.0	na	na	41.1	-8.9
Differ from Category (+/-)	-6.3 low	na	na	-18.7 low	-2.5 low

Total Risk	Standard Deviation	Category Risk	Risk Index	Beta
abv av	10.1%	abv av	1.1	0.71

	1996	1995	1994	1993	1992	1991	1990	1989	1988	1987
Return (%)...............	3.4	37.0	-8.7	—	—	—	—	—	—	—
Differ from Category (+/-)	-16.3	6.9	-7.4	—	—	—	—	—	—	—
Return, Tax-Adjusted (%)...	0.7	35.4	-10.8	—	—	—	—	—	—	—

PER SHARE DATA

	1996	1995	1994	1993	1992	1991	1990	1989	1988	1987
Dividends, Net Income ($)	0.44	0.36	0.58	—	—	—	—	—	—	—
Distrib'ns, Cap Gain ($)...	0.55	0.00	0.00	—	—	—	—	—	—	—
Net Asset Value ($).....	11.88	12.50	9.43	—	—	—	—	—	—	—
Expense Ratio (%).........	na	0.40	0.40	—	—	—	—	—	—	—
Yield (%)...............	3.53	2.88	6.15	—	—	—	—	—	—	—
Portfolio Turnover (%).....	na	5	19	—	—	—	—	—	—	—
Total Assets (Millions $)....	51	58	53	—	—	—	—	—	—	—

PORTFOLIO (as of 6/30/96)

Portfolio Manager: Murphy Van Der Velde - 1996

Investm't Category: Growth & Income
- ✔ Domestic
- Foreign
- Asset Allocation
- ✔ Index
- ✔ Sector
- State Specific

Investment Style
- Large-Cap Growth
- Mid-Cap Growth
- Small-Cap Growth
- ✔ Large-Cap Value
- ✔ Mid-Cap Value
- Small-Cap Value

Portfolio
2.3% cash	0.0% corp bonds
97.7% stocks	0.0% gov't bonds
0.0% preferred	0.0% muni bonds
0.0% conv't/warrants	0.0% other

SHAREHOLDER INFORMATION

Minimum Investment
Initial: $2,500   Subsequent: $100

Minimum IRA Investment
Initial: $500   Subsequent: $100

Maximum Fees
Load: none   12b-1: none
Other: none

Distributions
Income: quarterly   Capital Gains: Dec

Exchange Options
Number Per Year: no limit   Fee: none
Telephone: yes (money market fund available)

Services
IRA, pension, auto invest, auto withdraw

Gateway Index Plus

(GATEX)

Growth & Income

400 Technecenter Drive
Suite 220
Milford, OH 45150
800-354-6339, 513-248-2700

PERFORMANCE

fund inception date: 12/7/77

	3yr Annual	5yr Annual	10yr Annual	Bull	Bear
Return (%)	9.0	7.9	9.8	31.2	-3.0
Differ from Category (+/-)	-6.3 low	-6.0 low	-2.9 low	-28.6 low	3.4 high

Total Risk	Standard Deviation	Category Risk	Risk Index	Beta
low	4.3%	low	0.5	0.36

	1996	1995	1994	1993	1992	1991	1990	1989	1988	1987
Return (%)	10.5	11.0	5.5	7.4	5.1	17.7	10.3	19.4	19.7	-5.7
Differ from Category (+/-)	-9.2	-19.1	6.8	-6.4	-5.6	-11.4	16.2	-4.1	2.9	-5.9
Return, Tax-Adjusted (%)	10.0	10.3	3.1	5.7	3.9	15.7	3.8	17.4	18.9	-10.3

PER SHARE DATA

	1996	1995	1994	1993	1992	1991	1990	1989	1988	1987
Dividends, Net Income ($)	0.20	0.26	0.27	0.28	0.28	0.30	0.41	0.37	0.21	0.33
Distrib'ns, Cap Gain ($)	0.00	0.00	0.97	0.51	0.23	0.51	3.00	0.43	0.00	1.92
Net Asset Value ($)	18.48	16.91	15.48	15.85	15.51	15.24	13.64	15.49	13.67	11.60
Expense Ratio (%)	na	1.19	1.21	1.11	1.11	1.22	1.34	1.40	2.08	1.48
Yield (%)	1.08	1.53	1.64	1.71	1.77	1.90	2.46	2.32	1.53	2.44
Portfolio Turnover (%)	na	5	4	17	15	31	79	30	10	175
Total Assets (Millions $)	192	176	164	207	212	81	38	31	27	27

PORTFOLIO (as of 9/30/96)

Portfolio Manager: Peter Thayer, J. Patrick Rogers - 1977

Investm't Category: Growth & Income
- ✔ Domestic
- Foreign
- Asset Allocation
- Index
- Sector
- State Specific

Investment Style
- ✔ Large-Cap Growth
- Mid-Cap Growth
- Small-Cap Growth
- ✔ Large-Cap Value
- Mid-Cap Value
- Small-Cap Value

Portfolio
- 0.0% cash
- 99.2% stocks
- 0.0% preferred
- 0.0% conv't/warrants
- 0.0% corp bonds
- 0.0% gov't bonds
- 0.0% muni bonds
- 3.8% other

SHAREHOLDER INFORMATION

Minimum Investment
Initial: $1,000   Subsequent: $100

Minimum IRA Investment
Initial: $1,000   Subsequent: $100

Maximum Fees
Load: none   12b-1: none
Other: none

Distributions
Income: quarterly   Capital Gains: Dec

Exchange Options
Number Per Year: no limit   Fee: none
Telephone: yes (money market fund available)

Services
IRA, pension, auto invest, auto withdraw

Gintel (GINLX)

Growth

Greenwich Office Park #6
Greenwich, CT 06830
800-243-5808, 203-622-6400

PERFORMANCE

fund inception date: 6/10/81

	3yr Annual	5yr Annual	10yr Annual	Bull	Bear
Return (%)	12.7	12.7	10.4	65.8	-17.3
Differ from Category (+/-)	-3.0 blw av	-1.6 blw av	-3.5 low	3.4 abv av	-10.6 low

Total Risk	Standard Deviation	Category Risk	Risk Index	Beta
high	13.7%	high	1.3	1.02

	1996	1995	1994	1993	1992	1991	1990	1989	1988	1987
Return (%)	31.0	30.9	-16.5	2.0	24.6	15.5	-6.7	23.8	29.3	-14.3
Differ from Category (+/-)	10.9	0.6	-16.2	-12.0	12.8	-20.5	-0.6	-2.3	11.2	-16.3
Return, Tax-Adjusted (%)	27.0	28.8	-16.9	-1.2	23.7	11.7	-8.1	19.3	29.3	-15.0

PER SHARE DATA

	1996	1995	1994	1993	1992	1991	1990	1989	1988	1987
Dividends, Net Income ($)	0.34	0.00	0.04	0.51	0.12	1.18	0.48	1.44	0.00	0.50
Distrib'ns, Cap Gain ($)	1.68	0.93	0.11	1.13	0.23	0.05	0.00	0.00	0.00	0.83
Net Asset Value ($)	18.10	15.37	12.46	15.11	16.45	13.49	12.75	14.19	12.70	9.82
Expense Ratio (%)	na	2.30	2.40	2.20	1.70	1.40	1.50	1.40	1.60	1.30
Yield (%)	1.71	0.00	0.31	3.14	0.71	8.71	3.76	10.14	0.00	4.69
Portfolio Turnover (%)	na	55	69	50	56	66	75	65	85	111
Total Assets (Millions $)	157	96	88	136	164	77	79	94	84	80

PORTFOLIO (as of 9/30/96)

Portfolio Manager: Robert Gintel - 1981

Investm't Category: Growth

✔ Domestic	Index
✔ Foreign	Sector
Asset Allocation	State Specific

Investment Style

Large-Cap Growth	Large-Cap Value
Mid-Cap Growth	Mid-Cap Value
Small-Cap Growth	✔ Small-Cap Value

Portfolio

17.8% cash	0.0% corp bonds
82.2% stocks	0.0% gov't bonds
0.0% preferred	0.0% muni bonds
0.0% conv't/warrants	0.0% other

SHAREHOLDER INFORMATION

Minimum Investment
Initial: $5,000   Subsequent: $1

Minimum IRA Investment
Initial: $2,000   Subsequent: $1

Maximum Fees
Load: none   12b-1: none
Other: none

Distributions
Income: Dec   Capital Gains: Dec

Exchange Options
Number Per Year: no limit   Fee: none
Telephone: yes (money market fund available)

Services
IRA, pension, auto invest, auto withdraw

Gradison-McDonald Established Value (GETGX)

580 Walnut St.
Cincinnati, OH 45202
800-869-5999, 513-579-5000

Growth

PERFORMANCE
fund inception date: 8/16/83

	3yr Annual	5yr Annual	10yr Annual	Bull	Bear
Return (%)	14.8	15.0	13.0	56.8	-5.6
Differ from Category (+/-)	-0.9 av	0.7 abv av	-0.9 blw av	-5.6 blw av	1.1 abv av

Total Risk	Standard Deviation	Category Risk	Risk Index	Beta
av	8.1%	low	0.8	0.74

	1996	1995	1994	1993	1992	1991	1990	1989	1988	1987
Return (%).	19.3	26.4	0.3	20.7	10.2	22.2	-8.2	16.0	15.1	12.4
Differ from Category (+/-) .	-0.8	-3.9	0.6	6.7	-1.6	-13.8	-2.1	-10.1	-3.0	10.4
Return, Tax-Adjusted (%). .	16.1	24.3	-1.2	18.8	9.1	20.5	-9.7	13.4	13.2	8.3

PER SHARE DATA

	1996	1995	1994	1993	1992	1991	1990	1989	1988	1987
Dividends, Net Income ($).	0.43	0.42	0.34	0.22	0.30	0.45	0.45	0.72	0.49	0.68
Distrib'ns, Cap Gain ($) . . .	2.35	1.01	0.66	1.00	0.27	0.27	0.31	0.50	0.31	1.26
Net Asset Value ($)	28.19	26.00	21.77	22.71	19.87	18.60	15.85	18.07	16.64	15.18
Expense Ratio (%).	1.15	1.20	1.22	1.28	1.31	1.39	1.40	1.45	1.57	1.61
Yield (%)	1.40	1.55	1.51	0.92	1.48	2.38	2.78	3.87	2.89	4.13
Portfolio Turnover (%).	18	24	38	28	68	74	64	50	26	76
Total Assets (Millions $). . .	422	337	260	244	184	170	131	128	82	54

PORTFOLIO (as of 9/30/96)

Portfolio Manager: William Leugers - 1983

Investm't Category: Growth

✔ Domestic	Index
Foreign	Sector
Asset Allocation	State Specific

Investment Style

Large-Cap Growth	Large-Cap Value
✔ Mid-Cap Growth	✔ Mid-Cap Value
Small-Cap Growth	Small-Cap Value

Portfolio

28.0% cash	0.0% corp bonds
72.0% stocks	0.0% gov't bonds
0.0% preferred	0.0% muni bonds
0.0% conv't/warrants	0.0% other

SHAREHOLDER INFORMATION

Minimum Investment
Initial: $1,000   Subsequent: $50

Minimum IRA Investment
Initial: $1,000   Subsequent: $50

Maximum Fees
Load: none   12b-1: 0.45%
Other: none

Distributions
Income: quarterly   Capital Gains: annual

Exchange Options
Number Per Year: no limit   Fee: none
Telephone: yes (money market fund available)

Services
IRA, pension, auto invest, auto withdraw

Gradison-McDonald Opportunity Value

580 Walnut St.
Cincinnati, OH 45202
800-869-5999, 513-579-5000

(GOGFX) *Growth*

PERFORMANCE

fund inception date: 8/16/83

	3yr Annual	5yr Annual	10yr Annual	Bull	Bear
Return (%)	13.9	13.4	12.3	53.5	-4.4
Differ from Category (+/-)	-1.8 blw av	-0.9 av	-1.6 blw av	-8.9 blw av	2.3 abv av

Total Risk	Standard Deviation	Category Risk	Risk Index	Beta
abv av	9.6%	blw av	0.9	0.73

	1996	1995	1994	1993	1992	1991	1990	1989	1988	1987
Return (%)	19.4	26.7	-2.2	11.0	14.3	35.9	-13.1	23.1	23.5	-5.4
Differ from Category (+/-)	-0.7	-3.6	-1.9	-3.0	2.5	-0.1	-7.0	-3.0	5.4	-7.4
Return, Tax-Adjusted (%)	16.4	25.3	-3.2	9.5	12.9	33.5	-13.9	21.4	20.9	-6.2

PER SHARE DATA

	1996	1995	1994	1993	1992	1991	1990	1989	1988	1987
Dividends, Net Income ($)	0.16	0.18	0.12	0.07	0.10	0.27	0.25	0.33	0.18	0.12
Distrib'ns, Cap Gain ($)	2.04	0.57	0.44	0.80	0.64	0.67	0.06	0.26	0.72	0.13
Net Asset Value ($)	23.07	21.23	17.43	18.38	17.37	15.90	12.45	14.67	12.40	10.77
Expense Ratio (%)	1.41	1.37	1.38	1.44	1.49	1.61	1.52	1.84	1.83	1.73
Yield (%)	0.63	0.82	0.67	0.36	0.55	1.62	1.99	2.21	1.37	1.10
Portfolio Turnover (%)	23	31	40	39	64	64	37	36	74	65
Total Assets (Millions $)	112	97	82	83	60	39	23	23	17	14

PORTFOLIO (as of 9/30/96)

Portfolio Manager: William Leugers - 1983

Investm't Category: Growth
- ✔ Domestic
- Foreign
- Asset Allocation
- Index
- Sector
- State Specific

Investment Style
- Large-Cap Growth
- Mid-Cap Growth
- Small-Cap Growth
- Large-Cap Value
- Mid-Cap Value
- ✔ Small-Cap Value

Portfolio
28.0% cash	0.0% corp bonds
72.0% stocks	0.0% gov't bonds
0.0% preferred	0.0% muni bonds
0.0% conv't/warrants	0.0% other

SHAREHOLDER INFORMATION

Minimum Investment
Initial: $1,000   Subsequent: $50

Minimum IRA Investment
Initial: $1,000   Subsequent: $50

Maximum Fees
Load: none   12b-1: 0.46%
Other: none

Distributions
Income: semiannual   Capital Gains: annual

Exchange Options
Number Per Year: no limit   Fee: none
Telephone: yes (money market fund available)

Services
IRA, pension, auto invest, auto withdraw

Greenspring (GRSPX)

Balanced

2330 W. Joppa Road
Suite 110
Lutherville, MD 21093
800-366-3863, 410-823-5353

PERFORMANCE

fund inception date: 7/1/83

	3yr Annual	5yr Annual	10yr Annual	Bull	Bear
Return (%)	14.4	14.8	12.0	46.5	0.1
Differ from Category (+/-)	2.7 high	3.4 high	1.2 abv av	1.4 av	5.8 high

Total Risk	Standard Deviation	Category Risk	Risk Index	Beta
blw av	5.4%	low	0.8	0.35

	1996	1995	1994	1993	1992	1991	1990	1989	1988	1987
Return (%)	22.6	18.7	2.8	14.6	16.5	19.2	-6.5	10.7	15.9	9.1
Differ from Category (+/-)	8.4	-5.9	4.4	0.2	7.6	-4.9	-5.6	-7.4	3.7	6.4
Return, Tax-Adjusted (%)	20.0	16.3	0.4	10.6	13.4	17.2	-8.6	7.7	11.6	1.7

PER SHARE DATA

	1996	1995	1994	1993	1992	1991	1990	1989	1988	1987
Dividends, Net Income ($)	0.59	0.68	0.51	0.39	0.50	0.52	0.68	0.80	1.24	1.64
Distrib'ns, Cap Gain ($)	0.55	0.14	0.45	1.41	0.72	0.06	0.00	0.18	0.04	1.25
Net Asset Value ($)	17.24	15.05	13.39	13.96	13.78	12.91	11.32	12.83	12.49	11.89
Expense Ratio (%)	na	1.06	1.27	1.31	1.48	1.33	1.31	1.27	1.29	1.36
Yield (%)	3.31	4.47	3.68	2.53	3.44	4.00	6.00	6.14	9.89	12.48
Portfolio Turnover (%)	na	65	76	121	100	70	90	106	199	929
Total Assets (Millions $)	86	71	50	29	20	18	18	22	21	18

PORTFOLIO (as of 9/30/96)

Portfolio Manager: Charles Carlson - 1987

Investm't Category: Balanced
- ✔ Domestic
- Foreign
- Asset Allocation
- Index
- Sector
- State Specific

Investment Style
- Large-Cap Growth
- Mid-Cap Growth
- Small-Cap Growth
- Large-Cap Value
- Mid-Cap Value
- Small-Cap Value

Portfolio
- 13.8% cash
- 59.7% stocks
- 5.0% preferred
- 6.7% conv't/warrants
- 13.5% corp bonds
- 1.3% gov't bonds
- 0.0% muni bonds
- 0.0% other

SHAREHOLDER INFORMATION

Minimum Investment
Initial: $2,000   Subsequent: $100

Minimum IRA Investment
Initial: $1,000   Subsequent: $100

Maximum Fees
Load: none   12b-1: none
Other: none

Distributions
Income: annual   Capital Gains: annual

Exchange Options
Number Per Year: none   Fee: na
Telephone: na

Services
IRA, pension, auto invest, auto withdraw

Harbor Bond (HABDX)

General Bond

One Seagate
15th Floor
Toledo, OH 43666
800-422-1050, 419-247-2477

PERFORMANCE

fund inception date: 12/29/87

	3yr Annual	5yr Annual	10yr Annual	Bull	Bear
Return (%)	6.3	8.0	na	26.0	-5.2
Differ from Category (+/-)	1.2 high	1.9 high	na	5.7 high	-1.0 blw av

Total Risk	Standard Deviation	Category Risk	Risk Index	Avg Mat
low	4.6%	abv av	1.2	10.2 yrs

	1996	1995	1994	1993	1992	1991	1990	1989	1988	1987
Return (%)	4.9	19.1	-3.8	12.4	9.1	19.6	7.9	13.6	7.1	—
Differ from Category (+/-)	1.0	4.2	-1.5	3.3	2.6	4.9	0.6	1.9	-0.5	—
Return, Tax-Adjusted (%)	2.4	16.0	-6.0	8.8	5.8	15.6	4.6	10.0	4.2	—

PER SHARE DATA

	1996	1995	1994	1993	1992	1991	1990	1989	1988	1987
Dividends, Net Income ($)	0.70	0.78	0.60	0.64	0.74	0.86	0.84	0.82	0.66	—
Distrib'ns, Cap Gain ($)	0.00	0.00	0.00	0.50	0.24	0.25	0.00	0.09	0.07	—
Net Asset Value ($)	11.24	11.41	10.28	11.31	11.10	11.11	10.29	10.36	9.96	—
Expense Ratio (%)	na	0.70	0.77	0.72	0.77	0.86	1.22	1.21	1.55	—
Yield (%)	6.22	6.83	5.83	5.41	6.52	7.57	8.16	7.84	6.58	—
Portfolio Turnover (%)	na	88	150	119	53	58	91	91	124	—
Total Assets (Millions $)	288	233	167	171	76	41	25	21	15	—

PORTFOLIO (as of 9/30/96)

Portfolio Manager: William H. Gross, Dean Meiling - 1987

Investm't Category: General Bond
✔ Domestic   Index
✔ Foreign   Sector
   Asset Allocation   State Specific

Investment Style
Large-Cap Growth   Large-Cap Value
Mid-Cap Growth   Mid-Cap Value
Small-Cap Growth   Small-Cap Value

Portfolio
18.9% cash   0.0% corp bonds
0.0% stocks   0.0% gov't bonds
0.0% preferred   0.0% muni bonds
0.0% conv't/warrants   81.1% other

SHAREHOLDER INFORMATION

Minimum Investment
Initial: $2,000   Subsequent: $500

Minimum IRA Investment
Initial: $500   Subsequent: $100

Maximum Fees
Load: none   12b-1: none
Other: none

Distributions
Income: quarterly   Capital Gains: Dec

Exchange Options
Number Per Year: no limit   Fee: none
Telephone: yes (money market fund available)

Services
IRA, pension, auto exchange, auto invest, auto withdraw

Harbor Capital Appreciation (HACAX)

Growth

One Seagate
15th Floor
Toledo, OH 43666
800-422-1050, 419-247-2477

PERFORMANCE

fund inception date: 12/29/87

	3yr Annual	5yr Annual	10yr Annual	Bull	Bear
Return (%)	19.5	16.0	na	84.6	-11.1
Differ from Category (+/-)	3.8 high	1.7 abv av	na	22.2 high	-4.4 low

Total Risk	Standard Deviation	Category Risk	Risk Index	Beta
high	14.1%	high	1.4	1.19

	1996	1995	1994	1993	1992	1991	1990	1989	1988	1987
Return (%)	19.8	37.8	3.3	12.1	9.9	54.7	-1.9	24.2	15.3	—
Differ from Category (+/-)	-0.3	7.5	3.6	-1.9	-1.9	18.7	4.2	-1.9	-2.8	—
Return, Tax-Adjusted (%)	18.7	37.2	2.9	10.0	6.3	52.1	-4.3	20.4	13.5	—

PER SHARE DATA

	1996	1995	1994	1993	1992	1991	1990	1989	1988	1987
Dividends, Net Income ($)	0.02	0.02	0.03	0.03	0.01	0.04	0.14	0.20	0.17	—
Distrib'ns, Cap Gain ($)	0.85	0.31	0.17	1.12	2.03	0.97	0.85	1.18	0.38	—
Net Asset Value ($)	26.33	22.69	16.71	16.37	15.65	16.11	11.09	12.31	11.05	—
Expense Ratio (%)	na	0.75	0.81	0.86	0.91	0.89	0.88	0.92	0.99	—
Yield (%)	0.07	0.08	0.17	0.17	0.05	0.23	1.17	1.48	1.48	—
Portfolio Turnover (%)	na	51	72	93	69	90	162	75	48	—
Total Assets (Millions $)	1,748	989	239	149	105	90	62	61	46	—

PORTFOLIO (as of 9/30/96)

Portfolio Manager: Spiros Segalas - 1990

Investm't Category: Growth

✔ Domestic	Index
Foreign	Sector
Asset Allocation	State Specific

Investment Style

Large-Cap Growth	Large-Cap Value
✔ Mid-Cap Growth	Mid-Cap Value
Small-Cap Growth	Small-Cap Value

Portfolio

2.3% cash	0.0% corp bonds
97.7% stocks	0.0% gov't bonds
0.0% preferred	0.0% muni bonds
0.0% conv't/warrants	0.0% other

SHAREHOLDER INFORMATION

Minimum Investment

Initial: $2,000   Subsequent: $500

Minimum IRA Investment

Initial: $500   Subsequent: $100

Maximum Fees

Load: none   12b-1: none
Other: none

Distributions

Income: Dec   Capital Gains: Dec

Exchange Options

Number Per Year: no limit   Fee: none
Telephone: yes (money market fund available)

Services

IRA, auto exchange, auto invest, auto withdraw

Harbor Growth (HAGWX)

Growth

One Seagate
15th Floor
Toledo, OH 43666
800-422-1050, 419-247-2477

fund inception date: 11/19/86

PERFORMANCE

	3yr Annual	5yr Annual	10yr Annual	Bull	Bear
Return (%)	10.7	8.5	11.8	57.6	-13.9
Differ from Category (+/-)	-5.0 low	-5.8 low	-2.1 low	-4.8 av	-7.2 low

Total Risk	Standard Deviation	Category Risk	Risk Index	Beta
high	13.8%	high	1.3	1.02

	1996	1995	1994	1993	1992	1991	1990	1989	1988	1987
Return (%)	11.0	38.1	-11.5	18.3	-6.4	50.4	-6.7	22.9	14.2	2.9
Differ from Category (+/-)	-9.1	7.8	-11.2	4.3	-18.2	14.4	-0.6	-3.2	-3.9	0.9
Return, Tax-Adjusted (%)	3.1	33.7	-12.2	18.2	-9.2	44.3	-9.0	21.3	13.7	0.3

PER SHARE DATA

	1996	1995	1994	1993	1992	1991	1990	1989	1988	1987
Dividends, Net Income ($)	0.00	0.00	0.00	0.01	0.00	0.04	0.08	0.10	0.11	0.10
Distrib'ns, Cap Gain ($)	4.10	1.85	0.32	0.00	1.36	2.30	0.93	0.48	0.00	0.79
Net Asset Value ($)	12.17	14.65	11.97	13.88	11.74	14.02	10.94	12.81	10.91	9.65
Expense Ratio (%)	na	0.93	0.93	0.90	0.90	0.91	0.94	1.03	1.06	1.33
Yield (%)	0.00	0.00	0.00	0.07	0.00	0.24	0.67	0.75	1.00	0.95
Portfolio Turnover (%)	na	87	115	170	83	98	96	104	53	56
Total Assets (Millions $)	115	136	134	192	202	216	142	144	115	101

PORTFOLIO (as of 9/30/96)

Portfolio Manager: Arthur Nicholas, John Marshall - 1993

Investm't Category: Growth

✔ Domestic
  Foreign
  Asset Allocation
  Index
  Sector
  State Specific

Investment Style

  Large-Cap Growth
✔ Mid-Cap Growth
  Small-Cap Growth
  Large-Cap Value
  Mid-Cap Value
  Small-Cap Value

Portfolio

2.7% cash	0.0% corp bonds
97.3% stocks	0.0% gov't bonds
0.0% preferred	0.0% muni bonds
0.0% conv't/warrants	0.0% other

SHAREHOLDER INFORMATION

Minimum Investment
Initial: $2,000   Subsequent: $500

Minimum IRA Investment
Initial: $500   Subsequent: $100

Maximum Fees
Load: none   12b-1: none
Other: none

Distributions
Income: Dec   Capital Gains: Dec

Exchange Options
Number Per Year: no limit   Fee: none
Telephone: yes (money market fund available)

Services
IRA, auto exchange, auto invest, auto withdraw

Harbor Int'l (HAINX)

International Stock

One Seagate
15th Floor
Toledo, OH 43666
800-422-1050, 419-247-2477

this fund is closed to new investors

PERFORMANCE

fund inception date: 12/29/87

	3yr Annual	5yr Annual	10yr Annual	Bull	Bear
Return (%)	13.6	16.3	na	50.8	-8.5
Differ from Category (+/-)	7.3 high	6.3 high	na	26.5 high	-1.3 blw av

Total Risk	Standard Deviation	Category Risk	Risk Index	Beta
abv av	10.9%	av	1.1	0.79

	1996	1995	1994	1993	1992	1991	1990	1989	1988	1987
Return (%)	20.1	16.0	5.4	45.4	-0.1	21.3	-9.8	36.8	37.7	—
Differ from Category (+/-)	5.3	6.9	8.5	5.8	3.7	8.1	0.3	14.2	22.8	—
Return, Tax-Adjusted (%)	18.7	15.2	3.9	44.9	-0.9	20.7	-11.2	34.7	35.2	—

PER SHARE DATA

	1996	1995	1994	1993	1992	1991	1990	1989	1988	1987
Dividends, Net Income ($)	0.41	0.40	0.24	0.21	0.21	0.21	0.33	0.16	0.10	—
Distrib'ns, Cap Gain ($)	0.79	0.12	0.93	0.00	0.17	0.00	0.34	0.72	0.75	—
Net Asset Value ($)	32.20	27.84	24.45	24.32	16.87	17.28	14.42	16.74	12.90	—
Expense Ratio (%)	na	1.04	1.10	1.20	1.28	1.35	1.40	1.15	1.78	—
Yield (%)	1.24	1.43	0.94	0.86	1.23	1.21	2.23	0.91	0.73	—
Portfolio Turnover (%)	na	14	28	15	25	19	28	21	27	—
Total Assets (Millions $)	4,211	3,460	2,953	2,537	728	220	61	35	11	—

PORTFOLIO (as of 6/30/96)

Portfolio Manager: Hakan Castegren - 1987

Investm't Category: International Stock

Domestic	Index
✔ Foreign	Sector
Asset Allocation	State Specific

Investment Style

Large-Cap Growth	Large-Cap Value
Mid-Cap Growth	Mid-Cap Value
Small-Cap Growth	Small-Cap Value

Portfolio

6.6% cash	0.0% corp bonds
93.4% stocks	0.0% gov't bonds
0.0% preferred	0.0% muni bonds
0.0% conv't/warrants	0.0% other

SHAREHOLDER INFORMATION

Minimum Investment
Initial: $2,000   Subsequent: $500

Minimum IRA Investment
Initial: $500   Subsequent: $100

Maximum Fees
Load: none   12b-1: none
Other: none

Distributions
Income: Dec   Capital Gains: Dec

Exchange Options
Number Per Year: no limit   Fee: none
Telephone: yes (money market fund available)

Services
IRA, auto exchange, auto invest, auto withdraw

Harbor Int'l Growth

(HAIGX)

International Stock

One Seagate
15th Floor
Toledo, OH 43666
800-422-1050, 419-247-2477

	3yr Annual	5yr Annual	10yr Annual	Bull	Bear
Return (%)	14.8	na	na	67.7	-14.1
Differ from Category (+/-)	8.5 high	na	na	43.4 high	-6.9 low

Total Risk	Standard Deviation	Category Risk	Risk Index	Beta
high	14.5%	high	1.4	1.03

	1996	1995	1994	1993	1992	1991	1990	1989	1988	1987
Return (%)	32.0	24.2	-7.8	—	—	—	—	—	—	—
Differ from Category (+/-)	17.2	15.1	-4.7	—	—	—	—	—	—	—
Return, Tax-Adjusted (%)	30.9	23.7	-8.1	—	—	—	—	—	—	—

PER SHARE DATA

	1996	1995	1994	1993	1992	1991	1990	1989	1988	1987
Dividends, Net Income ($)	0.07	0.12	0.06	—	—	—	—	—	—	—
Distrib'ns, Cap Gain ($)	0.36	0.00	0.00	—	—	—	—	—	—	—
Net Asset Value ($)	16.24	12.64	10.27	—	—	—	—	—	—	—
Expense Ratio (%)	na	1.21	1.32	—	—	—	—	—	—	—
Yield (%)	0.42	0.94	0.58	—	—	—	—	—	—	—
Portfolio Turnover (%)	na	74	41	—	—	—	—	—	—	—
Total Assets (Millions $)	566	147	69	—	—	—	—	—	—	—

PORTFOLIO (as of 9/30/96)

Portfolio Manager: Howard Moss, Blair Boyer - 1993

Investm't Category: International Stock
- Domestic
- ✔ Foreign
- Asset Allocation
- Index
- Sector
- State Specific

Investment Style
- Large-Cap Growth
- Mid-Cap Growth
- Small-Cap Growth
- Large-Cap Value
- Mid-Cap Value
- Small-Cap Value

Portfolio
5.8% cash	0.0% corp bonds
94.2% stocks	0.0% gov't bonds
0.0% preferred	0.0% muni bonds
0.0% conv't/warrants	0.0% other

SHAREHOLDER INFORMATION

Minimum Investment
Initial: $2,000   Subsequent: $500

Minimum IRA Investment
Initial: $500   Subsequent: $100

Maximum Fees
Load: none   12b-1: none
Other: none

Distributions
Income: Dec   Capital Gains: Dec

Exchange Options
Number Per Year: no limit   Fee: none
Telephone: yes (money market fund available)

Services
IRA, auto exchange, auto invest, auto withdraw

Harbor Short Duration

(HASDX)

General Bond

One Seagate
15th Floor
Toledo, OH 43666
800-422-1050, 419-247-2477

PERFORMANCE

fund inception date: 1/2/92

	3yr Annual	5yr Annual	10yr Annual	Bull	Bear
Return (%)	5.4	na	na	16.8	0.0
Differ from Category (+/-)	0.3 abv av	na	na	-3.5 blw av	4.2 high

Total Risk	Standard Deviation	Category Risk	Risk Index	Avg Mat
low	1.3%	low	0.4	1.2 yrs

	1996	1995	1994	1993	1992	1991	1990	1989	1988	1987
Return (%)	6.3	7.4	2.7	4.4	—	—	—	—	—	—
Differ from Category (+/-)	2.4	-7.5	5.0	-4.7	—	—	—	—	—	—
Return, Tax-Adjusted (%)	3.1	4.8	-0.7	-0.2	—	—	—	—	—	—

PER SHARE DATA

	1996	1995	1994	1993	1992	1991	1990	1989	1988	1987
Dividends, Net Income ($)	0.69	0.56	0.78	1.15	—	—	—	—	—	—
Distrib'ns, Cap Gain ($)	0.00	0.00	0.00	0.00	—	—	—	—	—	—
Net Asset Value ($)	8.62	8.78	8.71	9.25	—	—	—	—	—	—
Expense Ratio (%)	1.84	0.38	0.38	0.43	—	—	—	—	—	—
Yield (%)	8.00	6.37	8.95	12.43	—	—	—	—	—	—
Portfolio Turnover (%)	1,041	725	895	1,212	—	—	—	—	—	—
Total Assets (Millions $)	164	121	101	118	—	—	—	—	—	—

PORTFOLIO (as of 9/30/96)

Portfolio Manager: Stewart Russell - 1994

Investm't Category: General Bond

✔ Domestic	Index
Foreign	Sector
Asset Allocation	State Specific

Investment Style

Large-Cap Growth	Large-Cap Value
Mid-Cap Growth	Mid-Cap Value
Small-Cap Growth	Small-Cap Value

Portfolio

21.2% cash	0.0% corp bonds
0.0% stocks	66.2% gov't bonds
0.0% preferred	0.0% muni bonds
12.5% conv't/warrants	0.0% other

SHAREHOLDER INFORMATION

Minimum Investment
Initial: $2,000   Subsequent: $500

Minimum IRA Investment
Initial: $500   Subsequent: $100

Maximum Fees
Load: none   12b-1: none
Other: none

Distributions
Income: monthly   Capital Gains: Dec

Exchange Options
Number Per Year: no limit   Fee: none
Telephone: yes (money market fund available)

Services
IRA, auto exchange, auto invest, auto withdraw

Harbor Value (HAVLX)

Growth & Income

One Seagate
15th Floor
Toledo, OH 43666
800-422-1050, 419-247-2477

PERFORMANCE

fund inception date: 12/29/87

	3yr Annual	5yr Annual	10yr Annual	Bull	Bear
Return (%)	17.8	13.7	na	66.6	-5.2
Differ from Category (+/-)	2.5 abv av	-0.2 blw av	na	6.8 abv av	1.2 abv av

Total Risk	Standard Deviation	Category Risk	Risk Index	Beta
av	9.0%	blw av	1.0	0.86

	1996	1995	1994	1993	1992	1991	1990	1989	1988	1987
Return (%)	20.0	35.3	0.6	8.3	7.4	21.2	-5.7	29.8	19.7	—
Differ from Category (+/-)	0.3	5.2	1.9	-5.5	-3.3	-7.9	0.2	6.3	2.9	—
Return, Tax-Adjusted (%)	14.9	30.9	-2.7	5.1	5.9	18.7	-8.2	26.0	17.0	—

PER SHARE DATA

	1996	1995	1994	1993	1992	1991	1990	1989	1988	1987
Dividends, Net Income ($)	0.40	0.40	0.35	0.32	0.37	0.46	0.51	0.50	0.35	—
Distrib'ns, Cap Gain ($)	2.00	1.26	1.06	1.09	0.14	0.34	0.43	0.79	0.44	—
Net Asset Value ($)	14.79	14.34	11.88	13.21	13.50	13.06	11.46	13.14	11.16	—
Expense Ratio (%)	na	0.90	1.04	0.88	0.84	0.93	1.01	1.02	1.40	—
Yield (%)	2.38	2.56	2.70	2.23	2.71	3.43	4.28	3.58	3.01	—
Portfolio Turnover (%)	na	135	150	50	20	33	31	40	44	—
Total Assets (Millions $)	119	91	56	59	66	42	26	24	11	—

PORTFOLIO (as of 9/30/96)

Portfolio Manager: Gregory DePrince, David Tierney - 1994

Investm't Category: Growth & Income
- ✔ Domestic
- Foreign
- Asset Allocation
- Index
- Sector
- State Specific

Investment Style
- Large-Cap Growth
- Mid-Cap Growth
- Small-Cap Growth
- ✔ Large-Cap Value
- Mid-Cap Value
- Small-Cap Value

Portfolio
4.3% cash	0.0% corp bonds
95.7% stocks	0.0% gov't bonds
0.0% preferred	0.0% muni bonds
0.0% conv't/warrants	0.0% other

SHAREHOLDER INFORMATION

Minimum Investment
Initial: $2,000   Subsequent: $500

Minimum IRA Investment
Initial: $500   Subsequent: $100

Maximum Fees
Load: none   12b-1: none
Other: none

Distributions
Income: quarterly   Capital Gains: Dec

Exchange Options
Number Per Year: no limit   Fee: none
Telephone: yes (money market fund available)

Services
IRA, auto exchange, auto invest, auto withdraw

Heartland Small Cap
Contrarian (HRSMX)

790 N. Milwaukee St.
Milwaukee, WI 53202
800-432-7856, 414-347-7777

Aggressive Growth

fund inception date: 4/27/95

PERFORMANCE

	3yr Annual	5yr Annual	10yr Annual	Bull	Bear
Return (%)	na	na	na	na	na
Differ from Category (+/-)	na	na	na	na	na

Total Risk	Standard Deviation	Category Risk	Risk Index	Beta
na	na	na	na	na

	1996	1995	1994	1993	1992	1991	1990	1989	1988	1987
Return (%)	18.8	—	—	—	—	—	—	—	—	—
Differ from Category (+/-)	-0.3	—	—	—	—	—	—	—	—	—
Return, Tax-Adjusted (%)	17.3	—	—	—	—	—	—	—	—	—

PER SHARE DATA

	1996	1995	1994	1993	1992	1991	1990	1989	1988	1987
Dividends, Net Income ($)	0.02	—	—	—	—	—	—	—	—	—
Distrib'ns, Cap Gain ($)	0.58	—	—	—	—	—	—	—	—	—
Net Asset Value ($)	13.40	—	—	—	—	—	—	—	—	—
Expense Ratio (%)	na	—	—	—	—	—	—	—	—	—
Yield (%)	0.14	—	—	—	—	—	—	—	—	—
Portfolio Turnover (%)	na	—	—	—	—	—	—	—	—	—
Total Assets (Millions $)	255	—	—	—	—	—	—	—	—	—

PORTFOLIO (as of 9/30/96)

Portfolio Manager: William J. Nasgovitz - 1995

Investm't Category: Aggressive Growth
- ✔ Domestic
- ✔ Foreign
- Asset Allocation
- Index
- Sector
- State Specific

Investment Style
- Large-Cap Growth
- Mid-Cap Growth
- Small-Cap Growth
- Large-Cap Value
- Mid-Cap Value
- Small-Cap Value

Portfolio
11.9% cash	0.0% corp bonds
87.0% stocks	0.0% gov't bonds
1.1% preferred	0.0% muni bonds
0.0% conv't/warrants	0.0% other

SHAREHOLDER INFORMATION

Minimum Investment
Initial: $1,000   Subsequent: $100

Minimum IRA Investment
Initial: $500   Subsequent: $50

Maximum Fees
Load: none   12b-1: 0.25%
Other: none

Distributions
Income: annual   Capital Gains: annual

Exchange Options
Number Per Year: 4   Fee: none
Telephone: yes (money market fund available)

Services
IRA, pension, auto invest, auto withdraw

Heartland US Gov't Securities (HRUSX)

General Bond

790 N. Milwaukee St.
Milwaukee, WI 53202
800-432-7856, 414-347-7777

PERFORMANCE

fund inception date: 4/9/87

	3yr Annual	5yr Annual	10yr Annual	Bull	Bear
Return (%)	3.1	7.2	na	19.8	-10.4
Differ from Category (+/-)	-2.0 low	1.1 high	na	-0.5 av	-6.2 low

Total Risk	Standard Deviation	Category Risk	Risk Index	Avg Mat
blw av	6.3%	high	1.7	na

	1996	1995	1994	1993	1992	1991	1990	1989	1988	1987
Return (%)	2.0	18.9	-9.7	17.8	10.0	16.9	9.9	11.3	6.4	—
Differ from Category (+/-)	-1.9	4.0	-7.4	8.7	3.5	2.2	2.6	-0.4	-1.2	—
Return, Tax-Adjusted (%)	-0.4	16.2	-12.0	13.8	6.4	13.2	6.7	7.9	3.1	—

PER SHARE DATA

	1996	1995	1994	1993	1992	1991	1990	1989	1988	1987
Dividends, Net Income ($)	0.59	0.59	0.59	0.55	0.66	0.69	0.73	0.77	0.75	—
Distrib'ns, Cap Gain ($)	0.00	0.00	0.00	0.61	0.33	0.25	0.00	0.00	0.00	—
Net Asset Value ($)	9.54	9.96	8.91	10.50	9.93	9.97	9.39	9.25	9.04	—
Expense Ratio (%)	na	1.07	1.07	1.06	0.92	0.92	0.86	0.89	0.95	—
Yield (%)	6.18	5.92	6.62	4.95	6.43	6.75	7.77	8.32	8.29	—
Portfolio Turnover (%)	na	97	95	200	149	185	127	142	136	—
Total Assets (Millions $)	53	66	64	66	27	29	16	11	12	—

PORTFOLIO (as of 9/30/96)

Portfolio Manager: Patrick J. Retzer - 1988

Investm't Category: General Bond

✔ Domestic   Index
  Foreign   Sector
  Asset Allocation   State Specific

Investment Style

  Large-Cap Growth   Large-Cap Value
  Mid-Cap Growth   Mid-Cap Value
  Small-Cap Growth   Small-Cap Value

Portfolio

2.7% cash	0.0% corp bonds
0.0% stocks	72.3% gov't bonds
0.0% preferred	0.0% muni bonds
0.0% conv't/warrants	25.0% other

SHAREHOLDER INFORMATION

Minimum Investment
Initial: $1,000   Subsequent: $100

Minimum IRA Investment
Initial: $500   Subsequent: $100

Maximum Fees
Load: none   12b-1: 0.25%
Other: none

Distributions
Income: monthly   Capital Gains: annual

Exchange Options
Number Per Year: 4   Fee: none
Telephone: yes (money market fund available)

Services
IRA, pension, auto invest, auto withdraw

Heartland Value (HRTVX)

Aggressive Growth

790 N. Milwaukee St.
Milwaukee, WI 53202
800-432-7856, 414-347-7777

this fund is closed to new investors

fund inception date: 12/28/84

	3yr Annual	5yr Annual	10yr Annual	Bull	Bear
Return (%)	16.8	22.0	15.2	56.8	-4.6
Differ from Category (+/-)	1.0 abv av	6.7 high	0.2 av	-14.3 blw av	6.0 high

Total Risk	Standard Deviation	Category Risk	Risk Index	Beta
abv av	9.7%	low	0.7	0.60

	1996	1995	1994	1993	1992	1991	1990	1989	1988	1987
Return (%)	20.9	29.8	1.7	18.7	42.4	49.3	-17.1	6.5	27.0	-8.5
Differ from Category (+/-)	1.8	-4.5	1.7	-0.6	30.7	-2.8	-11.7	-21.9	10.6	-6.1
Return, Tax-Adjusted (%)	18.7	27.8	0.6	17.3	38.0	47.2	-17.4	3.5	25.5	-11.0

PER SHARE DATA

	1996	1995	1994	1993	1992	1991	1990	1989	1988	1987
Dividends, Net Income ($)	0.06	0.13	0.00	0.00	0.00	0.00	0.02	0.13	0.13	0.14
Distrib'ns, Cap Gain ($)	2.07	1.39	0.87	1.02	2.47	0.84	0.11	1.33	0.43	1.03
Net Asset Value ($)	31.65	27.95	22.72	23.22	20.41	16.06	11.32	13.82	14.35	11.74
Expense Ratio (%)	na	1.29	1.39	1.51	1.48	1.69	1.74	1.65	1.71	1.51
Yield (%)	0.17	0.44	0.00	0.00	0.00	0.00	0.17	0.85	0.87	1.09
Portfolio Turnover (%)	na	31	35	51	76	79	76	88	50	78
Total Assets (Millions $)	1,607	1,190	338	186	43	29	19	30	28	27

PORTFOLIO (as of 9/30/96)

Portfolio Manager: William J. Nasgovitz - 1984

Investm't Category: Aggressive Growth
✔ Domestic   Index
✔ Foreign   Sector
  Asset Allocation   State Specific

Investment Style
  Large-Cap Growth   Large-Cap Value
  Mid-Cap Growth   Mid-Cap Value
  Small-Cap Growth ✔ Small-Cap Value

Portfolio
  7.6% cash   0.0% corp bonds
  88.4% stocks   3.2% gov't bonds
  0.0% preferred   0.0% muni bonds
  0.3% conv't/warrants 0.5% other

SHAREHOLDER INFORMATION

Minimum Investment
Initial: $1,000   Subsequent: $100

Minimum IRA Investment
Initial: $500   Subsequent: $100

Maximum Fees
Load: none   12b-1: 0.25%
Other: none

Distributions
Income: annual   Capital Gains: annual

Exchange Options
Number Per Year: 4   Fee: none
Telephone: yes (money market fund available)

Services
IRA, pension, auto invest, auto withdraw

Heartland Wisconsin Tax-Free (HRWIX)

790 N. Milwaukee St.
Milwaukee, WI 53202
800-432-7856, 414-347-7777

Tax-Exempt Bond

PERFORMANCE

fund inception date: 4/3/92

	3yr Annual	5yr Annual	10yr Annual	Bull	Bear
Return (%)	4.5	na	na	20.4	-6.3
Differ from Category (+/-)	0.3 abv av	na	na	2.0 abv av	-0.9 blw av

Total Risk	Standard Deviation	Category Risk	Risk Index	Avg Mat
blw av	6.2%	abv av	1.1	19.1 yrs

	1996	1995	1994	1993	1992	1991	1990	1989	1988	1987
Return (%)	3.8	17.7	-6.5	10.5	—	—	—	—	—	—
Differ from Category (+/-)	0.1	2.5	-1.2	-1.3	—	—	—	—	—	—
Return, Tax-Adjusted (%)	3.8	17.7	-6.5	10.5	—	—	—	—	—	—

PER SHARE DATA

	1996	1995	1994	1993	1992	1991	1990	1989	1988	1987
Dividends, Net Income ($)	0.51	0.51	0.50	0.49	—	—	—	—	—	—
Distrib'ns, Cap Gain ($)	0.00	0.00	0.00	0.00	—	—	—	—	—	—
Net Asset Value ($)	10.16	10.30	9.21	10.38	—	—	—	—	—	—
Expense Ratio (%)	na	0.84	0.85	0.84	—	—	—	—	—	—
Yield (%)	5.01	4.95	5.42	4.72	—	—	—	—	—	—
Portfolio Turnover (%)	na	10	21	6	—	—	—	—	—	—
Total Assets (Millions $)	125	118	101	99	—	—	—	—	—	—

PORTFOLIO (as of 9/30/96)

Portfolio Manager: Patrick J. Retzer - 1992

Investm't Category: Tax-Exempt Bond
- ✔ Domestic
- Foreign
- Asset Allocation
- Index
- Sector
- ✔ State Specific

Investment Style
- Large-Cap Growth
- Mid-Cap Growth
- Small-Cap Growth
- Large-Cap Value
- Mid-Cap Value
- Small-Cap Value

Portfolio
- 0.7% cash
- 0.0% stocks
- 0.0% preferred
- 0.0% conv't/warrants
- 0.0% corp bonds
- 0.0% gov't bonds
- 99.4% muni bonds
- 0.0% other

SHAREHOLDER INFORMATION

Minimum Investment
Initial: $1,000   Subsequent: $1

Minimum IRA Investment
Initial: na   Subsequent: na

Maximum Fees
Load: none   12b-1: none
Other: none

Distributions
Income: monthly   Capital Gains: annual

Exchange Options
Number Per Year: 4   Fee: none
Telephone: yes (money market fund available)

Services
auto invest, auto withdraw

Homestead Short-Term Bond (HOSBX)

4301 Wilson Blvd.
Arlington, VA 22203
800-258-3030, 703-907-6039

Corporate Bond

PERFORMANCE

fund inception date: 11/5/91

	3yr Annual	5yr Annual	10yr Annual	Bull	Bear
Return (%)	5.2	na	na	17.5	-1.6
Differ from Category (+/-)	-1.1 blw av	na	na	-7.3 blw av	3.5 high

Total Risk	Standard Deviation	Category Risk	Risk Index	Avg Mat
low	2.0%	low	0.4	2.9 yrs

	1996	1995	1994	1993	1992	1991	1990	1989	1988	1987
Return (%)	5.1	10.7	0.0	6.6	—	—	—	—	—	—
Differ from Category (+/-)	-0.1	-7.3	3.1	-5.2	—	—	—	—	—	—
Return, Tax-Adjusted (%)	2.8	8.5	-1.9	4.7	—	—	—	—	—	—

PER SHARE DATA

	1996	1995	1994	1993	1992	1991	1990	1989	1988	1987
Dividends, Net Income ($)	0.29	0.27	0.24	0.24	—	—	—	—	—	—
Distrib'ns, Cap Gain ($)	0.00	0.00	0.00	0.00	—	—	—	—	—	—
Net Asset Value ($)	5.15	5.19	4.95	5.19	—	—	—	—	—	—
Expense Ratio (%)	na	0.75	0.75	0.75	—	—	—	—	—	—
Yield (%)	5.63	5.20	4.84	4.62	—	—	—	—	—	—
Portfolio Turnover (%)	na	35	13	14	—	—	—	—	—	—
Total Assets (Millions $)	79	61	52	36	—	—	—	—	—	—

PORTFOLIO (as of 9/30/96)

Portfolio Manager: Douglas G. Kern - 1991

Investm't Category: Corporate Bond
- ✔ Domestic
- Foreign
- Asset Allocation
- Index
- Sector
- State Specific

Investment Style
- Large-Cap Growth
- Mid-Cap Growth
- Small-Cap Growth
- Large-Cap Value
- Mid-Cap Value
- Small-Cap Value

Portfolio
3.3% cash	43.8% corp bonds
0.0% stocks	52.9% gov't bonds
0.0% preferred	0.0% muni bonds
0.0% conv't/warrants	0.0% other

SHAREHOLDER INFORMATION

Minimum Investment
Initial: $1,000   Subsequent: $100

Minimum IRA Investment
Initial: $200   Subsequent: $100

Maximum Fees
Load: none   12b-1: none
Other: none

Distributions
Income: monthly   Capital Gains: annual

Exchange Options
Number Per Year: 4   Fee: none
Telephone: yes (money market fund available)

Services
IRA, pension, auto invest, auto withdraw

Homestead Value

(HOVLX)

Growth & Income

4301 Wilson Blvd.
Arlington, VA 22203
800-258-3030, 703-907-6039

PERFORMANCE

fund inception date: 11/19/90

	3yr Annual	5yr Annual	10yr Annual	Bull	Bear
Return (%)	17.3	16.5	na	59.4	-2.3
Differ from Category (+/-)	2.0 abv av	2.6 high	na	-0.4 av	4.1 high

Total Risk	Standard Deviation	Category Risk	Risk Index	Beta
av	9.2%	av	1.0	0.85

	1996	1995	1994	1993	1992	1991	1990	1989	1988	1987
Return (%)	17.9	33.7	2.4	18.8	11.6	17.1	—	—	—	—
Differ from Category (+/-)	-1.8	3.6	3.7	5.0	0.9	-12.0	—	—	—	—
Return, Tax-Adjusted (%)	16.5	31.6	1.4	17.9	10.6	15.5	—	—	—	—

PER SHARE DATA

	1996	1995	1994	1993	1992	1991	1990	1989	1988	1987
Dividends, Net Income ($)	0.38	0.40	0.28	0.22	0.24	0.38	—	—	—	—
Distrib'ns, Cap Gain ($)	0.35	0.52	0.11	0.07	0.07	0.01	—	—	—	—
Net Asset Value ($)	20.99	18.44	14.50	14.54	12.49	11.48	—	—	—	—
Expense Ratio (%)	na	0.84	1.15	1.25	1.25	1.25	—	—	—	—
Yield (%)	1.78	2.10	1.91	1.50	1.91	3.30	—	—	—	—
Portfolio Turnover (%)	na	10	4	2	5	26	—	—	—	—
Total Assets (Millions $)	237	141	90	52	19	10	—	—	—	—

PORTFOLIO (as of 9/30/96)

Portfolio Manager: Stuart E. Teach - 1990

Investm't Category: Growth & Income
- ✔ Domestic
- Foreign
- Asset Allocation
- Index
- Sector
- State Specific

Investment Style
- Large-Cap Growth
- Mid-Cap Growth
- Small-Cap Growth
- ✔ Large-Cap Value
- ✔ Mid-Cap Value
- Small-Cap Value

Portfolio
10.3% cash	0.0% corp bonds
89.1% stocks	0.0% gov't bonds
0.6% preferred	0.0% muni bonds
0.0% conv't/warrants	0.0% other

SHAREHOLDER INFORMATION

Minimum Investment
Initial: $1,000   Subsequent: $100

Minimum IRA Investment
Initial: $200   Subsequent: $100

Maximum Fees
Load: none   12b-1: none
Other: none

Distributions
Income: semiannual   Capital Gains: annual

Exchange Options
Number Per Year: 4   Fee: none
Telephone: yes (money market fund available)

Services
IRA, pension, auto invest, auto withdraw

Hotchkis & Wiley Balanced Income

(HWBAX) *Balanced*

800 W. Sixth St.
Suite 540
Los Angeles, CA 90017
800-346-7301, 213-362-8900

PERFORMANCE

fund inception date: 8/12/85

	3yr Annual	5yr Annual	10yr Annual	Bull	Bear
Return (%)	12.0	11.5	11.2	42.9	-3.9
Differ from Category (+/-)	0.3 av	0.1 av	0.4 abv av	-2.2 av	1.8 high

Total Risk	Standard Deviation	Category Risk	Risk Index	Beta
blw av	5.8%	blw av	0.9	0.54

	1996	1995	1994	1993	1992	1991	1990	1989	1988	1987
Return (%).	11.7	24.7	0.8	12.5	9.4	20.5	-0.5	17.8	14.6	3.9
Differ from Category (+/-).	-2.5	0.1	2.4	-1.9	0.5	-3.6	0.4	-0.3	2.4	1.2
Return, Tax-Adjusted (%). . .	8.7	22.1	-2.2	9.1	6.6	17.5	-3.5	13.6	12.4	0.2

PER SHARE DATA

	1996	1995	1994	1993	1992	1991	1990	1989	1988	1987
Dividends, Net Income ($)	0.89	0.98	0.81	0.90	0.72	0.79	0.85	0.93	0.73	0.79
Distrib'ns, Cap Gain ($) . . .	0.65	0.02	0.59	0.66	0.51	0.36	0.40	0.86	0.00	0.75
Net Asset Value ($)	18.33	17.83	15.16	16.44	16.02	15.79	14.10	15.44	14.67	13.46
Expense Ratio (%).	1.00	1.00	1.00	1.00	1.00	1.00	1.00	1.00	1.00	1.00
Yield (%)	4.68	5.49	5.14	5.26	4.35	4.89	5.86	5.70	4.97	5.55
Portfolio Turnover (%).	92	51	97	155	36	75	78	97	112	81
Total Assets (Millions $). . . .	70	39	34	33	20	14	9	8	6	3

PORTFOLIO (as of 9/30/96)

Portfolio Manager: Michael Sanchez - 1996

Investm't Category: Balanced
- ✔ Domestic
- ✔ Foreign
- ✔ Asset Allocation
- Index
- Sector
- State Specific

Investment Style

Large-Cap Growth	Large-Cap Value
Mid-Cap Growth	Mid-Cap Value
Small-Cap Growth	Small-Cap Value

Portfolio

1.0% cash	0.0% corp bonds
44.1% stocks	25.1% gov't bonds
0.0% preferred	0.0% muni bonds
0.0% conv't/warrants	29.8% other

SHAREHOLDER INFORMATION

Minimum Investment
Initial: $5,000   Subsequent: $1

Minimum IRA Investment
Initial: $1,000   Subsequent: $1

Maximum Fees
Load: none   12b-1: none
Other: none

Distributions
Income: quarterly   Capital Gains: annual

Exchange Options
Number Per Year: no limit   Fee: none
Telephone: yes (money market fund not available)

Services
IRA

Hotchkis & Wiley
Equity Income (HWEQX)

Growth & Income

800 W. Sixth St.
Suite 540
Los Angeles, CA 90017
800-346-7301, 213-362-8900

PERFORMANCE

fund inception date: 6/30/87

	3yr Annual	5yr Annual	10yr Annual	Bull	Bear
Return (%)	15.0	14.9	na	59.2	-8.6
Differ from Category (+/-)	-0.3 blw av	1.0 abv av	na	-0.6 av	-2.2 blw av

Total Risk	Standard Deviation	Category Risk	Risk Index	Beta
abv av	10.4%	high	1.1	1.00

	1996	1995	1994	1993	1992	1991	1990	1989	1988	1987
Return (%).	17.3	34.4	-3.5	15.7	13.9	34.6	-18.1	23.6	21.1	—
Differ from Category (+/-).	-2.4	4.3	-2.2	1.9	3.2	5.5	-12.2	0.1	4.3	—
Return, Tax-Adjusted (%). .	13.2	31.0	-5.3	13.4	12.1	33.0	-20.4	21.0	18.9	—

PER SHARE DATA

	1996	1995	1994	1993	1992	1991	1990	1989	1988	1987
Dividends, Net Income ($)	0.57	0.47	0.44	0.45	0.45	0.41	0.56	0.59	0.55	—
Distrib'ns, Cap Gain ($) . . .	1.81	1.06	0.36	0.53	0.23	0.00	0.30	0.25	0.02	—
Net Asset Value ($)	18.75	18.04	14.61	15.97	14.66	13.48	10.34	13.65	11.75	—
Expense Ratio (%).	0.98	0.96	1.00	1.00	1.00	1.00	1.00	1.00	1.00	—
Yield (%)	2.77	2.46	2.93	2.72	3.02	3.04	5.26	4.24	4.67	—
Portfolio Turnover (%).	24	50	36	25	32	39	39	9	20	—
Total Assets (Millions $). . .	209	162	106	82	65	78	51	53	31	—

PORTFOLIO (as of 9/30/96)

Portfolio Manager: Gail Bardin - 1994

Investm't Category: Growth & Income
- ✔ Domestic
- ✔ Foreign
- Asset Allocation
- Index
- Sector
- State Specific

Investment Style
- Large-Cap Growth
- Mid-Cap Growth
- Small-Cap Growth
- ✔ Large-Cap Value
- Mid-Cap Value
- Small-Cap Value

Portfolio
0.0% cash	0.0% corp bonds
98.9% stocks	0.0% gov't bonds
1.1% preferred	0.0% muni bonds
0.0% conv't/warrants	0.0% other

SHAREHOLDER INFORMATION

Minimum Investment
Initial: $5,000   Subsequent: $1

Minimum IRA Investment
Initial: $1,000   Subsequent: $1

Maximum Fees
Load: none   12b-1: none
Other: none

Distributions
Income: quarterly   Capital Gains: annual

Exchange Options
Number Per Year: no limit   Fee: none
Telephone: yes (money market fund not available)

Services
IRA

Hotchkis & Wiley Int'l

(HWINX)

International Stock

800 W. Sixth St.
Suite 540
Los Angeles, CA 90017
800-346-7301, 213-362-8900

PERFORMANCE

fund inception date: 10/1/90

	3yr Annual	5yr Annual	10yr Annual	Bull	Bear
Return (%)	11.2	14.3	na	45.3	-8.2
Differ from Category (+/-)	4.9 high	4.3 high	na	21.0 high	-1.0 blw av

Total Risk	Standard Deviation	Category Risk	Risk Index	Beta
av	9.1%	low	0.9	0.74

	1996	1995	1994	1993	1992	1991	1990	1989	1988	1987
Return (%)	18.2	19.8	-3.0	45.7	-2.7	20.3	—	—	—	—
Differ from Category (+/-)	3.4	10.7	0.1	6.1	1.1	7.1	—	—	—	—
Return, Tax-Adjusted (%)	17.1	18.5	-4.4	45.3	-4.0	15.8	—	—	—	—

PER SHARE DATA

	1996	1995	1994	1993	1992	1991	1990	1989	1988	1987
Dividends, Net Income ($)	0.38	0.40	0.31	0.00	0.21	0.50	—	—	—	—
Distrib'ns, Cap Gain ($)	0.16	0.18	0.45	0.15	0.31	1.29	—	—	—	—
Net Asset Value ($)	22.19	19.25	16.58	17.88	12.37	13.23	—	—	—	—
Expense Ratio (%)	1.00	1.00	1.00	1.00	1.00	1.00	—	—	—	—
Yield (%)	1.70	2.05	1.82	0.00	1.65	3.44	—	—	—	—
Portfolio Turnover (%)	12	24	23	24	88	224	—	—	—	—
Total Assets (Millions $)	474	97	27	10	4	1	—	—	—	—

PORTFOLIO (as of 9/30/96)

Portfolio Manager: D. Bouwer, S. Ketterer, H. Hartford - 1990

Investm't Category: International Stock

Domestic	Index
✔ Foreign	Sector
Asset Allocation	State Specific

Investment Style

Large-Cap Growth	Large-Cap Value
Mid-Cap Growth	Mid-Cap Value
Small-Cap Growth	Small-Cap Value

Portfolio

5.7% cash	0.0% corp bonds
94.3% stocks	0.0% gov't bonds
0.0% preferred	0.0% muni bonds
0.0% conv't/warrants	0.0% other

SHAREHOLDER INFORMATION

Minimum Investment
Initial: $5,000   Subsequent: $1

Minimum IRA Investment
Initial: $1,000   Subsequent: $1

Maximum Fees
Load: none   12b-1: none
Other: none

Distributions
Income: semiannual   Capital Gains: annual

Exchange Options
Number Per Year: no limit   Fee: none
Telephone: yes (money market fund not available)

Services
IRA

Hotchkis & Wiley
Low Duration (HWLDX)

General Bond

800 W. Sixth St.
Suite 540
Los Angeles, CA 90017
800-346-7301, 213-362-8900

PERFORMANCE

fund inception date: 5/19/93

	3yr Annual	5yr Annual	10yr Annual	Bull	Bear
Return (%)	8.0	na	na	23.2	1.7
Differ from Category (+/-)	2.9 high	na	na	2.9 abv av	5.9 high

Total Risk	Standard Deviation	Category Risk	Risk Index	Avg Mat
low	1.6%	low	0.4	2.9 yrs

	1996	1995	1994	1993	1992	1991	1990	1989	1988	1987
Return (%)	6.2	12.7	5.2	—	—	—	—	—	—	—
Differ from Category (+/-)	2.3	-2.2	7.5	—	—	—	—	—	—	—
Return, Tax-Adjusted (%)	3.5	9.5	2.4	—	—	—	—	—	—	—

PER SHARE DATA

	1996	1995	1994	1993	1992	1991	1990	1989	1988	1987
Dividends, Net Income ($)	0.67	0.75	0.69	—	—	—	—	—	—	—
Distrib'ns, Cap Gain ($)	0.01	0.04	0.01	—	—	—	—	—	—	—
Net Asset Value ($)	10.18	10.25	9.84	—	—	—	—	—	—	—
Expense Ratio (%)	0.58	0.58	0.58	—	—	—	—	—	—	—
Yield (%)	6.57	7.28	7.00	—	—	—	—	—	—	—
Portfolio Turnover (%)	50	71	254	—	—	—	—	—	—	—
Total Assets (Millions $)	168	157	70	—	—	—	—	—	—	—

PORTFOLIO (as of 9/30/96)

Portfolio Manager: Roger DeBard, Michael Sanchez - 1996

Investm't Category: General Bond
- ✔ Domestic
- ✔ Foreign
- Asset Allocation
- Index
- Sector
- State Specific

Investment Style
- Large-Cap Growth
- Mid-Cap Growth
- Small-Cap Growth
- Large-Cap Value
- Mid-Cap Value
- Small-Cap Value

Portfolio
- 11.5% cash
- 0.0% stocks
- 0.0% preferred
- 0.0% conv't/warrants
- 27.5% corp bonds
- 35.0% gov't bonds
- 0.0% muni bonds
- 25.9% other

SHAREHOLDER INFORMATION

Minimum Investment
Initial: $5,000   Subsequent: $1

Minimum IRA Investment
Initial: $1,000   Subsequent: $1

Maximum Fees
Load: none   12b-1: none
Other: none

Distributions
Income: monthly   Capital Gains: annual

Exchange Options
Number Per Year: no limit   Fee: none
Telephone: yes (money market fund not available)

Services
IRA

Hotchkis & Wiley
Total Return

800 W. Sixth St.
Suite 540
Los Angeles, CA 90017
800-346-7301, 213-362-8900

(HWTRX) *General Bond*

PERFORMANCE

fund inception date: 12/6/94

	3yr Annual	5yr Annual	10yr Annual	Bull	Bear
Return (%)	na	na	na	na	na
Differ from Category (+/-)	na	na	na	na	na

Total Risk	Standard Deviation	Category Risk	Risk Index	Avg Mat
na	na	na	na	6.9 yrs

	1996	1995	1994	1993	1992	1991	1990	1989	1988	1987
Return (%)	4.3	21.4	—	—	—	—	—	—	—	—
Differ from Category (+/-)	0.4	6.5	—	—	—	—	—	—	—	—
Return, Tax-Adjusted (%)	1.3	18.1	—	—	—	—	—	—	—	—

PER SHARE DATA

	1996	1995	1994	1993	1992	1991	1990	1989	1988	1987
Dividends, Net Income ($)	0.92	0.90	—	—	—	—	—	—	—	—
Distrib'ns, Cap Gain ($)	0.11	0.12	—	—	—	—	—	—	—	—
Net Asset Value ($)	12.97	13.46	—	—	—	—	—	—	—	—
Expense Ratio (%)	0.68	0.80	—	—	—	—	—	—	—	—
Yield (%)	7.03	6.62	—	—	—	—	—	—	—	—
Portfolio Turnover (%)	51	68	—	—	—	—	—	—	—	—
Total Assets (Millions $)	25	32	—	—	—	—	—	—	—	—

PORTFOLIO (as of 9/30/96)

Portfolio Manager: Roger Debard, Michael Sanchez - 1996

Investm't Category: General Bond
- ✔ Domestic
- ✔ Foreign
-   Asset Allocation
-   Index
-   Sector
-   State Specific

Investment Style
Large-Cap Growth   Large-Cap Value
Mid-Cap Growth   Mid-Cap Value
Small-Cap Growth   Small-Cap Value

Portfolio
3.8% cash	47.4% corp bonds
0.0% stocks	14.6% gov't bonds
0.0% preferred	0.0% muni bonds
0.0% conv't/warrants	34.3% other

SHAREHOLDER INFORMATION

Minimum Investment
Initial: $5,000   Subsequent: $1

Minimum IRA Investment
Initial: $1,000   Subsequent: $1

Maximum Fees
Load: none   12b-1: none
Other: none

Distributions
Income: monthly   Capital Gains: annual

Exchange Options
Number Per Year: no limit   Fee: none
Telephone: yes (money market fund available)

Services
IRA

IAI Balanced (IABLX)

Balanced

3700 First Bank Place
P.O. Box 357
Minneapolis, MN 55440
800-945-3863, 612-376-2600
www.iaifunds.com

PERFORMANCE

fund inception date: 4/6/92

	3yr Annual	5yr Annual	10yr Annual	Bull	Bear
Return (%)	10.2	na	na	42.8	-8.6
Differ from Category (+/-)	-1.5 blw av	na	na	-2.3 av	-2.9 low

Total Risk	Standard Deviation	Category Risk	Risk Index	Beta
av	7.5%	abv av	1.1	0.62

	1996	1995	1994	1993	1992	1991	1990	1989	1988	1987
Return (%)	14.7	18.5	-1.5	4.9	—	—	—	—	—	—
Differ from Category (+/-)	0.5	-6.1	0.1	-9.5	—	—	—	—	—	—
Return, Tax-Adjusted (%)	8.2	17.3	-3.7	3.4	—	—	—	—	—	—

PER SHARE DATA

	1996	1995	1994	1993	1992	1991	1990	1989	1988	1987
Dividends, Net Income ($)	0.49	0.30	0.32	0.25	—	—	—	—	—	—
Distrib'ns, Cap Gain ($)	1.96	0.00	0.37	0.20	—	—	—	—	—	—
Net Asset Value ($)	10.64	11.48	9.95	10.83	—	—	—	—	—	—
Expense Ratio (%)	1.25	1.25	1.25	1.25	—	—	—	—	—	—
Yield (%)	3.88	2.61	3.10	2.26	—	—	—	—	—	—
Portfolio Turnover (%)	193	256	211	83	—	—	—	—	—	—
Total Assets (Millions $)	32	41	42	64	—	—	—	—	—	—

PORTFOLIO (as of 9/30/96)

Portfolio Manager: L. Hill, Don Hoelting - 1995

Investm't Category: Balanced
- ✔ Domestic
- Foreign
- ✔ Asset Allocation
- Index
- Sector
- State Specific

Investment Style
- Large-Cap Growth
- Mid-Cap Growth
- Small-Cap Growth
- Large-Cap Value
- Mid-Cap Value
- Small-Cap Value

Portfolio
1.3% cash	45.7% corp bonds
51.0% stocks	0.0% gov't bonds
1.8% preferred	0.0% muni bonds
0.3% conv't/warrants	0.0% other

SHAREHOLDER INFORMATION

Minimum Investment
Initial: $5,000   Subsequent: $100

Minimum IRA Investment
Initial: $2,000   Subsequent: $100

Maximum Fees
Load: none   12b-1: none
Other: none

Distributions
Income: semiannual   Capital Gains: annual

Exchange Options
Number Per Year: 4   Fee: none
Telephone: yes (money market fund available)

Services
IRA, pension, auto exchange, auto invest, auto withdraw

IAI Bond (IAIBX)

General Bond

3700 First Bank Place
P.O. Box 357
Minneapolis, MN 55440
800-945-3863, 612-376-2600
www.iaifunds.com

fund inception date: 8/9/77

PERFORMANCE

	3yr Annual	5yr Annual	10yr Annual	Bull	Bear
Return (%)	4.7	6.6	8.1	21.9	-7.9
Differ from Category (+/-)	-0.4 blw av	0.5 av	0.8 abv av	1.6 abv av	-3.7 low

Total Risk	Standard Deviation	Category Risk	Risk Index	Avg Mat
blw av	4.9%	high	1.3	14.9 yrs

	1996	1995	1994	1993	1992	1991	1990	1989	1988	1987
Return (%)	4.1	16.2	-5.0	12.3	6.7	17.3	7.0	15.9	6.3	2.0
Differ from Category (+/-)	0.2	1.3	-2.7	3.2	0.2	2.6	-0.3	4.2	-1.3	-0.3
Return, Tax-Adjusted (%)	1.9	12.9	-7.4	7.5	2.0	14.1	4.0	12.8	3.3	-2.0

PER SHARE DATA

	1996	1995	1994	1993	1992	1991	1990	1989	1988	1987
Dividends, Net Income ($)	0.50	0.72	0.49	0.63	0.74	0.74	0.76	0.71	0.71	0.97
Distrib'ns, Cap Gain ($)	0.00	0.00	0.13	0.81	0.76	0.09	0.00	0.02	0.00	0.09
Net Asset Value ($)	9.16	9.30	8.66	9.76	9.99	10.82	10.00	10.10	9.39	9.51
Expense Ratio (%)	na	1.09	1.09	1.10	1.10	0.88	0.90	0.90	0.80	0.70
Yield (%)	5.45	7.74	5.57	5.96	6.88	6.78	7.60	7.01	7.56	10.10
Portfolio Turnover (%)	na	424	333	160	126	43	78	115	20	35
Total Assets (Millions $)	86	78	80	110	114	113	102	67	48	39

PORTFOLIO (as of 9/30/96)

Portfolio Manager: L. Hill, S. Bettin, L. Douglas - 1984

Investm't Category: General Bond
- ✔ Domestic
- ✔ Foreign
-   Asset Allocation
-   Index
-   Sector
-   State Specific

Investment Style
- Large-Cap Growth
- Mid-Cap Growth
- Small-Cap Growth
- Large-Cap Value
- Mid-Cap Value
- Small-Cap Value

Portfolio
2.8% cash	93.6% corp bonds
0.0% stocks	0.0% gov't bonds
3.6% preferred	0.0% muni bonds
0.0% conv't/warrants	0.0% other

SHAREHOLDER INFORMATION

Minimum Investment
Initial: $5,000   Subsequent: $100

Minimum IRA Investment
Initial: $2,000   Subsequent: $100

Maximum Fees
Load: none   12b-1: none
Other: none

Distributions
Income: monthly   Capital Gains: annual

Exchange Options
Number Per Year: 4   Fee: none
Telephone: yes (money market fund available)

Services
IRA, pension, auto exchange, auto invest, auto withdraw

IAI Emerging Growth

(IAEGX)

Aggressive Growth

3700 First Bank Place
P.O. Box 357
Minneapolis, MN 55440
800-945-3863, 612-376-2600
www.iaifunds.com

this fund is closed to new investors

fund inception date: 8/5/91

PERFORMANCE

	3yr Annual	5yr Annual	10yr Annual	Bull	Bear
Return (%)	17.0	17.6	na	92.1	-18.3
Differ from Category (+/-)	1.2 abv av	2.3 abv av	na	21.0 abv av	-7.7 low

Total Risk	Standard Deviation	Category Risk	Risk Index	Beta
high	20.8%	high	1.5	1.09

	1996	1995	1994	1993	1992	1991	1990	1989	1988	1987
Return (%)	6.9	49.5	0.1	14.7	22.4	—	—	—	—	—
Differ from Category (+/-)	-12.2	15.2	0.1	-4.6	10.7	—	—	—	—	—
Return, Tax-Adjusted (%)	2.4	48.7	-1.2	14.0	20.6	—	—	—	—	—

PER SHARE DATA

	1996	1995	1994	1993	1992	1991	1990	1989	1988	1987
Dividends, Net Income ($)	0.00	0.00	0.00	0.00	0.00	—	—	—	—	—
Distrib'ns, Cap Gain ($)	3.50	0.42	0.72	0.34	0.75	—	—	—	—	—
Net Asset Value ($)	19.96	21.84	14.90	15.74	14.03	—	—	—	—	—
Expense Ratio (%)	1.24	1.25	1.25	1.25	1.25	—	—	—	—	—
Yield (%)	0.00	0.00	0.00	0.00	0.00	—	—	—	—	—
Portfolio Turnover (%)	62	58	76	96	127	—	—	—	—	—
Total Assets (Millions $)	663	608	317	227	100	—	—	—	—	—

PORTFOLIO (as of 9/30/96)

Portfolio Manager: Rick Leggott - 1991

Investm't Category: Aggressive Growth
- ✔ Domestic
- ✔ Foreign
- Asset Allocation
- Index
- Sector
- State Specific

Investment Style
- Large-Cap Growth
- Mid-Cap Growth
- ✔ Small-Cap Growth
- Large-Cap Value
- Mid-Cap Value
- Small-Cap Value

Portfolio
- 7.6% cash
- 89.4% stocks
- 0.0% preferred
- 0.0% conv't/warrants
- 0.0% corp bonds
- 0.0% gov't bonds
- 0.0% muni bonds
- 3.0% other

SHAREHOLDER INFORMATION

Minimum Investment
Initial: $5,000   Subsequent: $100

Minimum IRA Investment
Initial: $2,000   Subsequent: $100

Maximum Fees
Load: none   12b-1: none
Other: none

Distributions
Income: semiannual   Capital Gains: annual

Exchange Options
Number Per Year: 4   Fee: none
Telephone: yes (money market fund available)

Services
IRA, pension, auto exchange, auto invest, auto withdraw

IAI Gov't (IAGVX)

General Bond

3700 First Bank Place
P.O. Box 357
Minneapolis, MN 55440
800-945-3863, 612-376-2600
www.iaifunds.com

PERFORMANCE   fund inception date: 8/5/91

	3yr Annual	5yr Annual	10yr Annual	Bull	Bear
Return (%)	3.9	5.1	na	16.1	-4.2
Differ from Category (+/-)	-1.2 low	-1.0 blw av	na	-4.2 blw av	0.0 av

Total Risk	Standard Deviation	Category Risk	Risk Index	Avg Mat
low	3.3%	av	0.9	5.2 yrs

	1996	1995	1994	1993	1992	1991	1990	1989	1988	1987
Return (%)...............	2.9	11.5	-2.3	8.5	5.6	—	—	—	—	—
Differ from Category (+/-)	-1.0	-3.4	0.0	-0.6	-0.9	—	—	—	—	—
Return, Tax-Adjusted (%)...	0.6	9.1	-4.2	5.7	2.5	—	—	—	—	—

PER SHARE DATA

	1996	1995	1994	1993	1992	1991	1990	1989	1988	1987
Dividends, Net Income ($)	0.58	0.58	0.46	0.55	0.58	—	—	—	—	—
Distrib'ns, Cap Gain ($) ...	0.00	0.00	0.02	0.21	0.34	—	—	—	—	—
Net Asset Value ($)	9.78	10.09	9.60	10.33	10.23	—	—	—	—	—
Expense Ratio (%)........	na	1.10	1.10	1.10	1.10	—	—	—	—	—
Yield (%)	5.93	5.74	4.78	5.21	5.48	—	—	—	—	—
Portfolio Turnover (%).....	na	284	641	236	170	—	—	—	—	—
Total Assets (Millions $)....	29	47	39	42	42	—	—	—	—	—

PORTFOLIO (as of 9/30/96)

Portfolio Manager: Scott Bettin, Steve Coleman - 1991

Investm't Category: General Bond
✔ Domestic   Index
  Foreign   Sector
  Asset Allocation State Specific

Investment Style
  Large-Cap Growth   Large-Cap Value
  Mid-Cap Growth   Mid-Cap Value
  Small-Cap Growth   Small-Cap Value

Portfolio
  9.4% cash   0.0% corp bonds
  0.0% stocks   90.6% gov't bonds
  0.0% preferred   0.0% muni bonds
  0.0% conv't/warrants 0.0% other

SHAREHOLDER INFORMATION

Minimum Investment
Initial: $5,000   Subsequent: $100

Minimum IRA Investment
Initial: $2,000   Subsequent: $100

Maximum Fees
Load: none   12b-1: none
Other: none

Distributions
Income: monthly   Capital Gains: annual

Exchange Options
Number Per Year: 4   Fee: none
Telephone: yes (money market fund available)

Services
IRA, pension, auto exchange, auto invest, auto withdraw

IAI Growth & Income

(IASKX)

Growth & Income

3700 First Bank Place
P.O. Box 357
Minneapolis, MN 55440
800-945-3863, 612-376-2600
www.iaifunds.com

PERFORMANCE   fund inception date: 8/16/71

	3yr Annual	5yr Annual	10yr Annual	Bull	Bear
Return (%)	13.3	10.7	12.3	55.0	-7.8
Differ from Category (+/-)	-2.0 blw av	-3.2 low	-0.4 av	-4.8 blw av	-1.4 blw av

Total Risk	Standard Deviation	Category Risk	Risk Index	Beta
av	9.1%	av	1.0	0.85

	1996	1995	1994	1993	1992	1991	1990	1989	1988	1987
Return (%)	20.2	27.1	-4.8	9.9	3.9	26.6	-6.7	29.8	8.4	15.5
Differ from Category (+/-)	0.5	-3.0	-3.5	-3.9	-6.8	-2.5	-0.8	6.3	-8.4	15.3
Return, Tax-Adjusted (%)	15.3	22.7	-6.4	6.5	2.4	24.1	-10.5	23.4	5.7	11.8

PER SHARE DATA

	1996	1995	1994	1993	1992	1991	1990	1989	1988	1987
Dividends, Net Income ($)	0.19	0.13	0.10	0.06	0.08	0.14	0.29	0.42	0.22	0.36
Distrib'ns, Cap Gain ($)	2.25	1.84	0.64	1.68	0.68	0.94	1.69	2.76	1.10	1.34
Net Asset Value ($)	15.01	14.60	13.06	14.51	14.85	15.10	12.84	15.79	14.70	14.79
Expense Ratio (%)	1.25	1.25	1.25	1.25	1.25	1.05	1.00	0.90	0.80	0.80
Yield (%)	1.10	0.79	0.72	0.37	0.51	0.87	1.99	2.26	1.39	2.23
Portfolio Turnover (%)	89	79	205	175	210	69	66	48	36	68
Total Assets (Millions $)	94	85	104	130	135	115	77	73	72	83

PORTFOLIO (as of 9/30/96)

Portfolio Manager: Don Hoelting - 1996

Investm't Category: Growth & Income
- ✔ Domestic
- ✔ Foreign
- Asset Allocation
- Index
- Sector
- State Specific

Investment Style
- ✔ Large-Cap Growth
- ✔ Mid-Cap Growth
- Small-Cap Growth
- ✔ Large-Cap Value
- ✔ Mid-Cap Value
- Small-Cap Value

Portfolio
4.3% cash	0.0% corp bonds
87.5% stocks	0.0% gov't bonds
0.0% preferred	0.0% muni bonds
0.0% conv't/warrants	8.2% other

SHAREHOLDER INFORMATION

Minimum Investment
Initial: $5,000   Subsequent: $100

Minimum IRA Investment
Initial: $2,000   Subsequent: $100

Maximum Fees
Load: none   12b-1: none
Other: none

Distributions
Income: semiannual   Capital Gains: annual

Exchange Options
Number Per Year: 4   Fee: none
Telephone: yes (money market fund available)

Services
IRA, pension, auto exchange, auto invest, auto withdraw

IAI Int'l (IAINX)

International Stock

3700 First Bank Place
P.O. Box 357
Minneapolis, MN 55440
800-945-3863, 612-376-2600
www.iaifunds.com

PERFORMANCE

fund inception date: 4/3/87

	3yr Annual	5yr Annual	10yr Annual	Bull	Bear
Return (%)	5.9	9.2	na	16.8	-3.7
Differ from Category (+/-)	-0.4 blw av	-0.8 blw av	na	-7.5 blw av	3.5 abv av

Total Risk	Standard Deviation	Category Risk	Risk Index	Beta
abv av	9.8%	blw av	1.0	0.67

	1996	1995	1994	1993	1992	1991	1990	1989	1988	1987
Return (%)	8.4	9.0	0.4	39.4	-6.4	16.5	-13.1	18.3	18.0	—
Differ from Category (+/-)	-6.4	-0.1	3.5	-0.2	-2.6	3.3	-3.0	-4.3	3.1	—
Return, Tax-Adjusted (%)	4.9	5.9	-1.5	37.9	-7.6	14.7	-13.5	15.6	17.5	—

PER SHARE DATA

	1996	1995	1994	1993	1992	1991	1990	1989	1988	1987
Dividends, Net Income ($)	0.28	0.52	0.00	0.34	0.03	0.21	0.00	0.29	0.10	—
Distrib'ns, Cap Gain ($)	1.16	0.65	0.88	0.04	0.41	0.33	0.14	0.63	0.00	—
Net Asset Value ($)	12.35	12.75	12.79	13.61	10.08	11.22	10.15	11.84	10.85	—
Expense Ratio (%)	1.66	1.72	1.74	1.91	2.00	1.73	1.90	2.10	2.13	—
Yield (%)	2.07	3.88	0.00	2.49	0.28	1.81	0.00	2.32	0.92	—
Portfolio Turnover (%)	39	27	50	28	35	41	33	71	53	—
Total Assets (Millions $)	122	142	149	121	49	36	32	28	17	—

PORTFOLIO (as of 9/30/96)

Portfolio Manager: Roy Gillson - 1990

Investm't Category: International Stock

Domestic	Index
✔ Foreign	Sector
Asset Allocation	State Specific

Investment Style

Large-Cap Growth	Large-Cap Value
Mid-Cap Growth	Mid-Cap Value
Small-Cap Growth	Small-Cap Value

Portfolio

3.2% cash	0.0% corp bonds
96.5% stocks	0.0% gov't bonds
0.3% preferred	0.0% muni bonds
0.0% conv't/warrants	0.0% other

SHAREHOLDER INFORMATION

Minimum Investment
Initial: $5,000   Subsequent: $1,000

Minimum IRA Investment
Initial: $2,000   Subsequent: $100

Maximum Fees
Load: none   12b-1: none
Other: none

Distributions
Income: semiannual   Capital Gains: annual

Exchange Options
Number Per Year: 4   Fee: none
Telephone: yes (money market fund available)

Services
IRA, pension, auto exchange, auto invest, auto withdraw

IAI Midcap Growth

(IAMCX)

Growth

3700 First Bank Place
P.O. Box 357
Minneapolis, MN 55440
800-945-3863, 612-376-2600
www.iaifunds.com

PERFORMANCE

fund inception date: 4/6/92

	3yr Annual	5yr Annual	10yr Annual	Bull	Bear
Return (%)	15.8	na	na	62.4	-5.5
Differ from Category (+/-)	0.1 av	na	na	0.0 av	1.2 abv av

Total Risk	Standard Deviation	Category Risk	Risk Index	Beta
abv av	11.5%	abv av	1.1	0.84

	1996	1995	1994	1993	1992	1991	1990	1989	1988	1987
Return (%)	16.5	26.0	5.6	22.8	—	—	—	—	—	—
Differ from Category (+/-)	-3.6	-4.3	5.9	8.8	—	—	—	—	—	—
Return, Tax-Adjusted (%)	13.7	23.8	4.2	22.4	—	—	—	—	—	—

PER SHARE DATA

	1996	1995	1994	1993	1992	1991	1990	1989	1988	1987
Dividends, Net Income ($)	0.00	0.00	0.07	0.00	—	—	—	—	—	—
Distrib'ns, Cap Gain ($)	1.62	1.09	0.55	0.15	—	—	—	—	—	—
Net Asset Value ($)	17.62	16.54	14.05	13.93	—	—	—	—	—	—
Expense Ratio (%)	1.25	1.25	1.25	1.25	—	—	—	—	—	—
Yield (%)	0.00	0.00	0.47	0.00	—	—	—	—	—	—
Portfolio Turnover (%)	29	51	49	57	—	—	—	—	—	—
Total Assets (Millions $)	144	114	84	43	—	—	—	—	—	—

PORTFOLIO (as of 9/30/96)

Portfolio Manager: Suzanne Zak - 1993

Investm't Category: Growth

✔ Domestic	Index
✔ Foreign	Sector
Asset Allocation	State Specific

Investment Style

Large-Cap Growth	Large-Cap Value
✔ Mid-Cap Growth	Mid-Cap Value
✔ Small-Cap Growth	Small-Cap Value

Portfolio

5.9% cash	0.0% corp bonds
92.5% stocks	0.0% gov't bonds
0.0% preferred	0.0% muni bonds
0.0% conv't/warrants	1.6% other

SHAREHOLDER INFORMATION

Minimum Investment
Initial: $5,000   Subsequent: $100

Minimum IRA Investment
Initial: $2,000   Subsequent: $100

Maximum Fees
Load: none   12b-1: none
Other: none

Distributions
Income: semiannual   Capital Gains: annual

Exchange Options
Number Per Year: 4   Fee: none
Telephone: yes (money market fund available)

Services
IRA, pension, auto exchange, auto invest, auto withdraw

Individual Fund Listings   **429**

IAI Regional (IARGX)

Growth

3700 First Bank Place
P.O. Box 357
Minneapolis, MN 55440
800-945-3863, 612-376-2600
www.iaifunds.com

PERFORMANCE   fund inception date: 5/20/80

	3yr Annual	5yr Annual	10yr Annual	Bull	Bear
Return (%)	15.6	11.7	14.4	62.7	-7.5
Differ from Category (+/-)	-0.1 av	-2.6 blw av	0.5 abv av	0.3 av	-0.8 blw av

Total Risk	Standard Deviation	Category Risk	Risk Index	Beta
abv av	9.8%	av	0.9	0.80

	1996	1995	1994	1993	1992	1991	1990	1989	1988	1987
Return (%)	15.7	32.6	0.6	8.9	3.5	35.3	-0.4	31.2	18.5	5.3
Differ from Category (+/-)	-4.4	2.3	0.9	-5.1	-8.3	-0.7	5.7	5.1	0.4	3.3
Return, Tax-Adjusted (%)	10.8	28.4	-1.4	6.2	2.4	31.5	-2.3	23.9	16.8	-0.5

PER SHARE DATA

	1996	1995	1994	1993	1992	1991	1990	1989	1988	1987
Dividends, Net Income ($)	0.10	0.19	0.19	0.17	0.22	0.24	0.33	0.50	0.27	0.39
Distrib'ns, Cap Gain ($)	3.98	2.70	1.19	1.83	0.51	2.07	0.82	3.97	0.56	3.21
Net Asset Value ($)	23.19	23.68	20.15	21.45	21.58	21.62	17.79	18.98	17.99	15.89
Expense Ratio (%)	1.25	1.23	1.25	1.25	1.25	1.01	1.00	1.00	0.80	0.80
Yield (%)	0.36	0.72	0.89	0.73	0.99	1.01	1.77	2.17	1.45	2.04
Portfolio Turnover (%)	89	150	163	139	141	169	116	94	85	133
Total Assets (Millions $)	563	577	514	650	628	454	210	121	92	81

PORTFOLIO (as of 9/30/96)

Portfolio Manager: Mark Hoonsbeen - 1994

Investm't Category: Growth
- ✔ Domestic
-    Foreign
-    Asset Allocation
-    Index
-    Sector
-    State Specific

Investment Style
- Large-Cap Growth
- ✔ Mid-Cap Growth
- ✔ Small-Cap Growth
- Large-Cap Value
- ✔ Mid-Cap Value
- ✔ Small-Cap Value

Portfolio
13.1% cash	0.0% corp bonds
80.2% stocks	0.0% gov't bonds
0.0% preferred	0.0% muni bonds
0.0% conv't/warrants	6.7% other

SHAREHOLDER INFORMATION

Minimum Investment
Initial: $5,000   Subsequent: $100

Minimum IRA Investment
Initial: $2,000   Subsequent: $100

Maximum Fees
Load: none   12b-1: none
Other: none

Distributions
Income: semiannual   Capital Gains: annual

Exchange Options
Number Per Year: 4   Fee: none
Telephone: yes (money market fund available)

Services
IRA, pension, auto exchange, auto invest, auto withdraw

IAI Reserve (IARVX)

General Bond

3700 First Bank Place
P.O. Box 357
Minneapolis, MN 55440
800-945-3863, 612-376-2600
www.iaifunds.com

PERFORMANCE

fund inception date: 1/31/86

	3yr Annual	5yr Annual	10yr Annual	Bull	Bear
Return (%)	4.6	4.1	5.8	13.7	0.3
Differ from Category (+/-)	-0.5 blw av	-2.0 low	-1.5 low	-6.6 low	4.5 high

Total Risk	Standard Deviation	Category Risk	Risk Index	Avg Mat
low	1.0%	low	0.3	1.5 yrs

	1996	1995	1994	1993	1992	1991	1990	1989	1988	1987
Return (%)	4.4	6.9	2.7	3.3	3.2	7.9	8.3	8.7	6.7	5.8
Differ from Category (+/-)	0.5	-8.0	5.0	-5.8	-3.3	-6.8	1.0	-3.0	-0.9	3.5
Return, Tax-Adjusted (%)	2.2	4.7	0.9	1.8	1.4	5.4	5.2	5.6	3.9	3.1

PER SHARE DATA

	1996	1995	1994	1993	1992	1991	1990	1989	1988	1987
Dividends, Net Income ($)	0.53	0.54	0.45	0.37	0.39	0.59	0.79	0.78	0.69	0.69
Distrib'ns, Cap Gain ($)	0.00	0.00	0.00	0.01	0.08	0.07	0.00	0.00	0.00	0.00
Net Asset Value ($)	9.86	9.97	9.85	10.04	10.09	10.24	10.13	10.11	10.04	10.07
Expense Ratio (%)	0.85	0.85	0.85	0.85	0.85	0.85	0.85	0.80	0.80	0.80
Yield (%)	5.37	5.41	4.56	3.68	3.83	5.72	7.79	7.71	6.87	6.85
Portfolio Turnover (%)	261	170	235	538	218	87	63	64	0	30
Total Assets (Millions $)	65	61	78	91	106	98	90	101	70	46

PORTFOLIO (as of 9/30/96)

Portfolio Manager: Tim Palmer, L. Douglas - 1991

Investm't Category: General Bond
✔ Domestic	Index
✔ Foreign	Sector
Asset Allocation	State Specific

Investment Style
Large-Cap Growth	Large-Cap Value
Mid-Cap Growth	Mid-Cap Value
Small-Cap Growth	Small-Cap Value

Portfolio
40.0% cash	59.6% corp bonds
0.0% stocks	0.0% gov't bonds
0.0% preferred	0.0% muni bonds
0.0% conv't/warrants	0.4% other

SHAREHOLDER INFORMATION

Minimum Investment
Initial: $5,000   Subsequent: $1,000

Minimum IRA Investment
Initial: $2,000   Subsequent: $100

Maximum Fees
Load: none   12b-1: none
Other: none

Distributions
Income: monthly   Capital Gains: annual

Exchange Options
Number Per Year: 4   Fee: none
Telephone: yes (money market fund available)

Services
IRA, pension, auto exchange, auto invest, auto withdraw

IAI Value (IAAPX)

Growth

3700 First Bank Place
P.O. Box 357
Minneapolis, MN 55440
800-945-3863, 612-376-2600
www.iaifunds.com

PERFORMANCE

fund inception date: 10/12/83

	3yr Annual	5yr Annual	10yr Annual	Bull	Bear
Return (%)	11.2	13.4	13.2	44.4	-5.9
Differ from Category (+/-)	-4.5 low	-0.9 av	-0.7 av	-18.0 low	0.8 av

Total Risk	Standard Deviation	Category Risk	Risk Index	Beta
abv av	9.7%	blw av	0.9	0.64

	1996	1995	1994	1993	1992	1991	1990	1989	1988	1987
Return (%)	21.8	24.3	-9.1	22.0	11.9	19.7	-11.5	22.5	24.3	14.0
Differ from Category (+/-)	1.7	-6.0	-8.8	8.0	0.1	-16.3	-5.4	-3.6	6.2	12.0
Return, Tax-Adjusted (%)	18.0	21.5	-11.2	18.1	11.6	17.6	-17.1	17.3	23.7	8.7

PER SHARE DATA

	1996	1995	1994	1993	1992	1991	1990	1989	1988	1987
Dividends, Net Income ($)	0.11	0.00	0.02	0.13	0.00	0.15	0.17	0.17	0.09	0.16
Distrib'ns, Cap Gain ($)	1.41	1.00	0.84	1.36	0.10	0.44	2.24	1.97	0.08	1.67
Net Asset Value ($)	12.57	11.63	10.18	12.11	11.18	10.09	8.94	12.60	12.08	9.87
Expense Ratio (%)	1.25	1.25	1.25	1.25	1.25	1.10	1.00	1.00	1.00	1.00
Yield (%)	0.78	0.00	0.18	0.96	0.00	1.42	1.52	1.16	0.74	1.38
Portfolio Turnover (%)	73	102	191	118	125	57	70	53	63	86
Total Assets (Millions $)	33	41	34	32	26	22	18	28	25	19

PORTFOLIO (as of 9/30/96)

Portfolio Manager: Douglas Platt, Don Hoelting - 1991

Investm't Category: Growth
- ✔ Domestic
- ✔ Foreign
- Asset Allocation
- Index
- Sector
- State Specific

Investment Style
- Large-Cap Growth
- ✔ Mid-Cap Growth
- Small-Cap Growth
- Large-Cap Value
- ✔ Mid-Cap Value
- Small-Cap Value

Portfolio
19.4% cash	0.0% corp bonds
73.9% stocks	0.0% gov't bonds
0.0% preferred	0.0% muni bonds
0.0% conv't/warrants	6.7% other

SHAREHOLDER INFORMATION

Minimum Investment
Initial: $5,000   Subsequent: $100

Minimum IRA Investment
Initial: $2,000   Subsequent: $100

Maximum Fees
Load: none   12b-1: none
Other: none

Distributions
Income: semiannual   Capital Gains: annual

Exchange Options
Number Per Year: 4   Fee: none
Telephone: yes (money market fund available)

Services
IRA, pension, auto exchange, auto invest, auto withdraw

432   *Guide to Low-Load Mutual Funds*

INVESCO Diversified Fds: Small Co (IDSCX)

Aggressive Growth

P.O. Box 173706
Denver, CO 80217
800-525-8085, 303-930-6300
www.invesco.com

PERFORMANCE

fund inception date: 12/1/93

	3yr Annual	5yr Annual	10yr Annual	Bull	Bear
Return (%)	11.9	na	na	48.1	-6.8
Differ from Category (+/-)	-3.9 blw av	na	na	-23.0 blw av	3.8 abv av

Total Risk	Standard Deviation	Category Risk	Risk Index	Beta
abv av	10.1%	low	0.7	0.71

	1996	1995	1994	1993	1992	1991	1990	1989	1988	1987
Return (%)	12.4	27.0	-1.8	—	—	—	—	—	—	—
Differ from Category (+/-)	-6.7	-7.3	-1.8	—	—	—	—	—	—	—
Return, Tax-Adjusted (%)	9.1	25.9	-1.8	—	—	—	—	—	—	—

PER SHARE DATA

	1996	1995	1994	1993	1992	1991	1990	1989	1988	1987
Dividends, Net Income ($)	0.05	0.07	0.00	—	—	—	—	—	—	—
Distrib'ns, Cap Gain ($)	1.35	0.26	0.00	—	—	—	—	—	—	—
Net Asset Value ($)	12.42	12.32	9.96	—	—	—	—	—	—	—
Expense Ratio (%)	1.09	1.00	1.00	—	—	—	—	—	—	—
Yield (%)	0.36	0.55	0.00	—	—	—	—	—	—	—
Portfolio Turnover (%)	156	73	55	—	—	—	—	—	—	—
Total Assets (Millions $)	54	58	16	—	—	—	—	—	—	—

PORTFOLIO (as of 9/30/96)

Portfolio Manager: Bob Slotpole - 1994

Investm't Category: Aggressive Growth
- ✔ Domestic
- ✔ Foreign
- Asset Allocation
- Index
- Sector
- State Specific

Investment Style
Large-Cap Growth	Large-Cap Value
Mid-Cap Growth	Mid-Cap Value
✔ Small-Cap Growth	✔ Small-Cap Value

Portfolio
0.0% cash	0.0% corp bonds
100.0% stocks	0.0% gov't bonds
0.0% preferred	0.0% muni bonds
0.0% conv't/warrants	0.0% other

SHAREHOLDER INFORMATION

Minimum Investment
Initial: $1,000   Subsequent: $50

Minimum IRA Investment
Initial: $1   Subsequent: $1

Maximum Fees
Load: none   12b-1: none
Other: none

Distributions
Income: annual   Capital Gains: Dec

Exchange Options
Number Per Year: 4   Fee: none
Telephone: yes (money market fund available)

Services
IRA, pension, auto exchange, auto invest, auto withdraw

INVESCO Dynamics

(FIDYX)

Aggressive Growth

P.O. Box 173706
Denver, CO 80217
800-525-8085, 303-930-6300
www.invesco.com

PERFORMANCE   fund inception date: 9/15/67

	3yr Annual	5yr Annual	10yr Annual	Bull	Bear
Return (%)	15.9	16.0	16.4	69.6	-11.0
Differ from Category (+/-)	0.1 av	0.7 abv av	1.4 abv av	-1.5 av	-0.4 av

Total Risk	Standard Deviation	Category Risk	Risk Index	Beta
abv av	11.5%	blw av	0.8	0.92

	1996	1995	1994	1993	1992	1991	1990	1989	1988	1987
Return (%).	15.6	37.5	-2.0	19.1	13.1	67.0	-6.4	22.6	9.1	3.8
Differ from Category (+/-).	-3.5	3.2	-2.0	-0.2	1.4	14.9	-1.0	-5.8	-7.3	6.2
Return, Tax-Adjusted (%). .	12.4	32.7	-7.0	17.1	12.3	62.2	-7.1	20.7	8.5	-1.8

PER SHARE DATA

	1996	1995	1994	1993	1992	1991	1990	1989	1988	1987
Dividends, Net Income ($).	0.01	0.03	0.00	0.00	0.00	0.00	0.12	0.11	0.08	0.02
Distrib'ns, Cap Gain ($) . . .	1.36	1.70	2.29	0.80	0.28	1.20	0.00	0.28	0.00	1.36
Net Asset Value ($)	12.89	12.34	10.24	12.83	11.50	10.47	7.09	7.70	6.61	6.14
Expense Ratio (%).	1.14	1.20	1.17	1.20	1.18	1.15	0.98	0.98	1.02	0.92
Yield (%)	0.07	0.21	0.00	0.00	0.00	0.00	1.69	1.37	1.21	0.26
Portfolio Turnover (%). . . .	196	176	169	144	174	243	225	237	199	234
Total Assets (Millions $). . .	883	624	338	319	273	141	57	93	91	76

PORTFOLIO (as of 9/30/96)

Portfolio Manager: Timothy J. Miller - 1993

Investm't Category: Aggressive Growth
- ✔ Domestic   Index
- ✔ Foreign   Sector
-   Asset Allocation State Specific

Investment Style
-   Large-Cap Growth   Large-Cap Value
- ✔ Mid-Cap Growth   Mid-Cap Value
-   Small-Cap Growth   Small-Cap Value

Portfolio
2.9% cash	0.0% corp bonds
96.3% stocks	0.0% gov't bonds
0.8% preferred	0.0% muni bonds
0.0% conv't/warrants	0.0% other

SHAREHOLDER INFORMATION

Minimum Investment
Initial: $1,000   Subsequent: $50

Minimum IRA Investment
Initial: $250   Subsequent: $50

Maximum Fees
Load: none   12b-1: 0.25%
Other: none

Distributions
Income: annual   Capital Gains: Dec

Exchange Options
Number Per Year: 4   Fee: none
Telephone: yes (money market fund available)

Services
IRA, pension, auto exchange, auto invest, auto withdraw

INVESCO Emerging Growth (FIEGX)

Aggressive Growth

P.O. Box 173706
Denver, CO 80217
800-525-8085, 303-930-6300
www.invesco.com

PERFORMANCE

fund inception date: 1/2/92

	3yr Annual	5yr Annual	10yr Annual	Bull	Bear
Return (%)	11.7	16.7	na	48.5	-6.8
Differ from Category (+/-)	-4.1 blw av	1.4 abv av	na	-22.6 blw av	3.8 abv av

Total Risk	Standard Deviation	Category Risk	Risk Index	Beta
high	16.5%	abv av	1.2	0.76

	1996	1995	1994	1993	1992	1991	1990	1989	1988	1987
Return (%)	11.6	30.0	-3.8	23.3	25.7	—	—	—	—	—
Differ from Category (+/-)	-7.5	-4.3	-3.8	4.0	14.0	—	—	—	—	—
Return, Tax-Adjusted (%)	10.3	29.3	-9.6	23.3	25.7	—	—	—	—	—

PER SHARE DATA

	1996	1995	1994	1993	1992	1991	1990	1989	1988	1987
Dividends, Net Income ($)	0.00	0.04	0.00	0.00	0.00	—	—	—	—	—
Distrib'ns, Cap Gain ($)	0.53	0.17	2.48	0.00	0.00	—	—	—	—	—
Net Asset Value ($)	12.52	11.69	9.17	12.11	9.82	—	—	—	—	—
Expense Ratio (%)	1.48	1.49	1.37	1.54	1.93	—	—	—	—	—
Yield (%)	0.00	0.33	0.00	0.00	0.00	—	—	—	—	—
Portfolio Turnover (%)	221	228	196	153	50	—	—	—	—	—
Total Assets (Millions $)	270	212	179	223	123	—	—	—	—	—

PORTFOLIO (as of 9/30/96)

Portfolio Manager: John Schroer, Paul Rasplicka - 1995

Investm't Category: Aggressive Growth
- ✔ Domestic
- ✔ Foreign
- Asset Allocation
- Index
- Sector
- State Specific

Investment Style
- Large-Cap Growth
- Mid-Cap Growth
- ✔ Small-Cap Growth
- Large-Cap Value
- Mid-Cap Value
- Small-Cap Value

Portfolio
9.5%	cash	0.0%	corp bonds
90.5%	stocks	0.0%	gov't bonds
0.0%	preferred	0.0%	muni bonds
0.0%	conv't/warrants	0.0%	other

SHAREHOLDER INFORMATION

Minimum Investment
Initial: $1,000   Subsequent: $50

Minimum IRA Investment
Initial: $250   Subsequent: $50

Maximum Fees
Load: none   12b-1: 0.25%
Other: none

Distributions
Income: annual   Capital Gains: Dec

Exchange Options
Number Per Year: 4   Fee: none
Telephone: yes (money market fund available)

Services
IRA, pension, auto exchange, auto invest, auto withdraw

INVESCO European Small Co (IVECX)

International Stock

P.O. Box 173706
Denver, CO 80217
800-525-8085, 303-930-6300
www.invesco.com

PERFORMANCE

fund inception date: 2/15/95

	3yr Annual	5yr Annual	10yr Annual	Bull	Bear
Return (%)	na	na	na	na	na
Differ from Category (+/-)	na	na	na	na	na

Total Risk	Standard Deviation	Category Risk	Risk Index	Beta
na	na	na	na	na

	1996	1995	1994	1993	1992	1991	1990	1989	1988	1987
Return (%)	31.0	—	—	—	—	—	—	—	—	—
Differ from Category (+/-)	16.2	—	—	—	—	—	—	—	—	—
Return, Tax-Adjusted (%)	29.6	—	—	—	—	—	—	—	—	—

PER SHARE DATA

	1996	1995	1994	1993	1992	1991	1990	1989	1988	1987
Dividends, Net Income ($)	0.07	—	—	—	—	—	—	—	—	—
Distrib'ns, Cap Gain ($)	0.53	—	—	—	—	—	—	—	—	—
Net Asset Value ($)	16.03	—	—	—	—	—	—	—	—	—
Expense Ratio (%)	1.68	—	—	—	—	—	—	—	—	—
Yield (%)	0.42	—	—	—	—	—	—	—	—	—
Portfolio Turnover (%)	141	—	—	—	—	—	—	—	—	—
Total Assets (Millions $)	126	—	—	—	—	—	—	—	—	—

PORTFOLIO (as of 9/30/96)

Portfolio Manager: Claire Griffiths, Andy Crossley - 1995

Investm't Category: International Stock
Domestic	Index
✔ Foreign	Sector
Asset Allocation	State Specific

Investment Style
Large-Cap Growth	Large-Cap Value
Mid-Cap Growth	Mid-Cap Value
Small-Cap Growth	Small-Cap Value

Portfolio
4.3% cash	0.0% corp bonds
89.0% stocks	0.0% gov't bonds
6.6% preferred	0.0% muni bonds
0.0% conv't/warrants	0.0% other

SHAREHOLDER INFORMATION

Minimum Investment
Initial: $1,000   Subsequent: $50

Minimum IRA Investment
Initial: $250   Subsequent: $50

Maximum Fees
Load: none   12b-1: 0.25%
Other: none

Distributions
Income: annual   Capital Gains: Dec

Exchange Options
Number Per Year: 4   Fee: none
Telephone: yes (money market fund available)

Services
IRA, pension, auto exchange, auto invest, auto withdraw

INVESCO Growth (FLRFX)

Growth

P.O. Box 173706
Denver, CO 80217
800-525-8085, 303-930-6300
www.invesco.com

PERFORMANCE

fund inception date: 1/8/35

	3yr Annual	5yr Annual	10yr Annual	Bull	Bear
Return (%)	12.6	11.6	12.9	57.1	-12.1
Differ from Category (+/-)	-3.1 blw av	-2.7 blw av	-1.0 blw av	-5.3 blw av	-5.4 low

Total Risk	Standard Deviation	Category Risk	Risk Index	Beta
abv av	10.5%	av	1.0	0.98

	1996	1995	1994	1993	1992	1991	1990	1989	1988	1987
Return (%)	20.9	29.5	-8.9	17.9	2.9	42.1	-1.3	31.2	5.8	-0.1
Differ from Category (+/-)	0.8	-0.8	-8.6	3.9	-8.9	6.1	4.8	5.1	-12.3	-2.1
Return, Tax-Adjusted (%)	16.4	23.8	-11.7	15.2	-0.1	38.4	-2.4	30.0	4.9	-5.3

PER SHARE DATA

	1996	1995	1994	1993	1992	1991	1990	1989	1988	1987
Dividends, Net Income ($)	0.02	0.05	0.03	0.03	0.04	0.07	0.11	0.10	0.07	0.07
Distrib'ns, Cap Gain ($)	0.76	0.84	0.50	0.44	0.54	0.47	0.02	0.00	0.00	0.63
Net Asset Value ($)	5.19	4.95	4.52	5.54	5.12	5.59	4.36	4.55	3.55	3.42
Expense Ratio (%)	1.05	1.06	1.03	1.04	1.04	1.00	0.78	0.82	0.81	0.77
Yield (%)	0.33	0.86	0.59	0.50	0.70	1.15	2.51	2.19	1.97	1.72
Portfolio Turnover (%)	207	111	63	77	77	69	86	90	116	250
Total Assets (Millions $)	703	535	444	510	449	455	340	369	317	351

PORTFOLIO (as of 9/30/96)

Portfolio Manager: Timothy J. Miller - 1996

Investm't Category: Growth
- ✔ Domestic
- Foreign
- Asset Allocation
- Index
- Sector
- State Specific

Investment Style
- Large-Cap Growth
- ✔ Mid-Cap Growth
- Small-Cap Growth
- Large-Cap Value
- Mid-Cap Value
- Small-Cap Value

Portfolio
2.9% cash	0.0% corp bonds
96.3% stocks	0.0% gov't bonds
0.8% preferred	0.0% muni bonds
0.0% conv't/warrants	0.0% other

SHAREHOLDER INFORMATION

Minimum Investment
Initial: $1,000   Subsequent: $50

Minimum IRA Investment
Initial: $250   Subsequent: $50

Maximum Fees
Load: none   12b-1: 0.25%
Other: none

Distributions
Income: quarterly   Capital Gains: Dec

Exchange Options
Number Per Year: 4   Fee: none
Telephone: yes (money market fund available)

Services
IRA, pension, auto exchange, auto invest, auto withdraw

INVESCO Income— High Yield Port (FHYPX)

Corporate High-Yield Bond

P.O. Box 173706
Denver, CO 80217
800-525-8085, 303-930-6300
www.invesco.com

PERFORMANCE
fund inception date: 3/1/84

	3yr Annual	5yr Annual	10yr Annual	Bull	Bear
Return (%)	8.4	11.1	9.3	33.7	-6.2
Differ from Category (+/-)	-0.3 av	-1.0 av	0.0 abv av	0.6 abv av	-0.8 blw av

Total Risk	Standard Deviation	Category Risk	Risk Index	Avg Mat
blw av	5.1%	high	1.1	7.8 yrs

	1996	1995	1994	1993	1992	1991	1990	1989	1988	1987
Return (%)	13.9	17.9	-5.0	15.7	14.6	23.5	-4.6	3.6	13.4	3.6
Differ from Category (+/-)	-1.4	0.4	-2.1	-3.2	-1.5	-4.1	0.3	2.4	0.9	1.8
Return, Tax-Adjusted (%)	10.2	13.9	-8.6	12.2	10.9	19.0	-9.3	-1.3	8.6	-0.9

PER SHARE DATA

	1996	1995	1994	1993	1992	1991	1990	1989	1988	1987
Dividends, Net Income ($)	0.60	0.64	0.65	0.60	0.62	0.68	0.84	0.95	0.93	0.94
Distrib'ns, Cap Gain ($)	0.03	0.00	0.03	0.00	0.00	0.00	0.00	0.00	0.00	0.00
Net Asset Value ($)	7.10	6.83	6.38	7.43	6.97	6.66	6.00	7.16	7.82	7.75
Expense Ratio (%)	0.99	1.00	0.97	0.97	1.00	1.05	0.94	0.83	0.82	0.86
Yield (%)	8.41	9.37	10.14	8.07	8.89	10.21	13.99	13.26	11.89	12.12
Portfolio Turnover (%)	266	201	195	45	120	64	28	53	42	89
Total Assets (Millions $)	414	343	210	306	212	99	40	49	60	37

PORTFOLIO (as of 9/30/96)

Portfolio Manager: Jerry Paul - 1994

Investm't Category: Corp. High-Yield Bond
- ✔ Domestic
- Foreign
- Asset Allocation
- Index
- Sector
- State Specific

Investment Style
- Large-Cap Growth
- Mid-Cap Growth
- Small-Cap Growth
- Large-Cap Value
- Mid-Cap Value
- Small-Cap Value

Portfolio
6.1% cash	84.6% corp bonds
0.0% stocks	0.0% gov't bonds
4.6% preferred	0.0% muni bonds
1.0% conv't/warrants	3.7% other

SHAREHOLDER INFORMATION

Minimum Investment
Initial: $1,000   Subsequent: $50

Minimum IRA Investment
Initial: $250   Subsequent: $50

Maximum Fees
Load: none   12b-1: 0.25%
Other: none

Distributions
Income: monthly   Capital Gains: Dec

Exchange Options
Number Per Year: 4   Fee: none
Telephone: yes (money market fund available)

Services
IRA, pension, auto exchange, auto invest, auto withdraw

INVESCO Income—
Select Income (FBDSX)

Corporate Bond

P.O. Box 173706
Denver, CO 80217
800-525-8085, 303-930-6300
www.invesco.com

PERFORMANCE

fund inception date: 8/20/76

	3yr Annual	5yr Annual	10yr Annual	Bull	Bear
Return (%)	7.6	8.9	8.4	28.5	-4.2
Differ from Category (+/-)	1.3 abv av	0.6 abv av	0.3 abv av	3.7 abv av	0.9 abv av

Total Risk	Standard Deviation	Category Risk	Risk Index	Avg Mat
low	4.4%	av	1.0	10.2 yrs

	1996	1995	1994	1993	1992	1991	1990	1989	1988	1987
Return (%)	4.7	20.6	-1.2	11.3	10.3	18.6	4.9	8.1	10.3	-1.6
Differ from Category (+/-)	-0.5	2.6	1.9	-0.5	1.4	1.4	0.9	-1.3	1.0	-4.0
Return, Tax-Adjusted (%)	1.9	17.4	-4.0	7.5	6.7	15.1	1.2	4.1	6.5	-5.2

PER SHARE DATA

	1996	1995	1994	1993	1992	1991	1990	1989	1988	1987
Dividends, Net Income ($)	0.46	0.46	0.45	0.49	0.52	0.52	0.58	0.63	0.60	0.63
Distrib'ns, Cap Gain ($)	0.02	0.02	0.00	0.18	0.09	0.00	0.00	0.00	0.00	0.00
Net Asset Value ($)	6.55	6.74	6.03	6.57	6.53	6.50	5.96	6.26	6.39	6.36
Expense Ratio (%)	1.01	1.00	1.11	1.15	1.14	1.15	1.01	0.99	1.00	0.99
Yield (%)	7.00	6.80	7.46	7.25	7.85	8.00	9.73	10.06	9.38	9.90
Portfolio Turnover (%)	210	181	135	105	178	117	38	121	143	131
Total Assets (Millions $)	271	261	136	157	123	93	46	32	29	19

PORTFOLIO (as of 9/30/96)

Portfolio Manager: Jerry Paul - 1994

Investm't Category: Corporate Bond

✔ Domestic   Index
   Foreign   Sector
   Asset Allocation   State Specific

Investment Style
Large-Cap Growth   Large-Cap Value
Mid-Cap Growth   Mid-Cap Value
Small-Cap Growth   Small-Cap Value

Portfolio
3.0% cash	63.1% corp bonds
0.0% stocks	32.0% gov't bonds
0.0% preferred	0.0% muni bonds
1.9% conv't/warrants	0.0% other

SHAREHOLDER INFORMATION

Minimum Investment
Initial: $1,000   Subsequent: $50

Minimum IRA Investment
Initial: $250   Subsequent: $50

Maximum Fees
Load: none   12b-1: 0.25%
Other: none

Distributions
Income: monthly   Capital Gains: Dec

Exchange Options
Number Per Year: 4   Fee: none
Telephone: yes (money market fund available)

Services
IRA, pension, auto exchange, auto invest, auto withdraw

INVESCO Income—
US Gov't Securities

P.O. Box 173706
Denver, CO 80217
800-525-8085, 303-930-6300
www.invesco.com

(FBDGX) *General Bond*

PERFORMANCE

fund inception date: 1/2/86

	3yr Annual	5yr Annual	10yr Annual	Bull	Bear
Return (%)	4.4	5.8	6.4	23.1	-9.0
Differ from Category (+/-)	-0.7 blw av	-0.3 blw av	-0.9 blw av	2.8 abv av	-4.8 low

Total Risk	Standard Deviation	Category Risk	Risk Index	Avg Mat
blw av	6.7%	high	1.8	21.0 yrs

	1996	1995	1994	1993	1992	1991	1990	1989	1988	1987
Return (%)	0.4	22.1	-7.2	10.2	5.7	15.4	7.2	12.4	6.2	-5.1
Differ from Category (+/-)	-3.5	7.2	-4.9	1.1	-0.8	0.7	-0.1	0.7	-1.4	-7.4
Return, Tax-Adjusted (%)	-1.8	19.5	-9.4	7.4	3.3	12.6	4.2	9.2	3.1	-7.8

PER SHARE DATA

	1996	1995	1994	1993	1992	1991	1990	1989	1988	1987
Dividends, Net Income ($)	0.43	0.44	0.42	0.42	0.45	0.49	0.53	0.55	0.53	0.52
Distrib'ns, Cap Gain ($)	0.00	0.00	0.00	0.16	0.00	0.00	0.00	0.00	0.00	0.00
Net Asset Value ($)	7.42	7.83	6.81	7.79	7.61	7.65	7.09	7.14	6.87	6.98
Expense Ratio (%)	1.02	1.00	1.32	1.40	1.27	1.27	1.07	1.04	1.19	1.29
Yield (%)	5.79	5.61	6.16	5.28	5.91	6.40	7.47	7.70	7.71	7.44
Portfolio Turnover (%)	212	99	95	na	115	67	38	159	221	284
Total Assets (Millions $)	59	45	31	34	35	29	21	19	9	7

PORTFOLIO (as of 9/30/96)

Portfolio Manager: Richard Hinderlie - 1994

Investm't Category: General Bond
- ✔ Domestic
- Foreign
- Asset Allocation
- Index
- Sector
- State Specific

Investment Style
- Large-Cap Growth
- Mid-Cap Growth
- Small-Cap Growth
- Large-Cap Value
- Mid-Cap Value
- Small-Cap Value

Portfolio
16.1% cash	0.0% corp bonds
0.0% stocks	83.9% gov't bonds
0.0% preferred	0.0% muni bonds
0.0% conv't/warrants	0.0% other

SHAREHOLDER INFORMATION

Minimum Investment
Initial: $1,000   Subsequent: $50

Minimum IRA Investment
Initial: $250   Subsequent: $50

Maximum Fees
Load: none   12b-1: 0.25%
Other: none

Distributions
Income: monthly   Capital Gains: Dec

Exchange Options
Number Per Year: 4   Fee: none
Telephone: yes (money market fund available)

Services
IRA, pension, auto exchange, auto invest, auto withdraw

INVESCO Industrial Income (FIIIX)

Balanced

P.O. Box 173706
Denver, CO 80217
800-525-8085, 303-930-6300
www.invesco.com

PERFORMANCE

fund inception date: 3/20/59

	3yr Annual	5yr Annual	10yr Annual	Bull	Bear
Return (%)	12.6	10.9	14.7	47.9	-6.5
Differ from Category (+/-)	0.9 abv av	-0.5 av	3.9 high	2.8 abv av	-0.8 blw av

Total Risk	Standard Deviation	Category Risk	Risk Index	Beta
av	7.5%	abv av	1.1	0.74

	1996	1995	1994	1993	1992	1991	1990	1989	1988	1987
Return (%)	16.7	27.3	-3.9	16.6	0.9	46.2	0.9	31.8	15.3	4.9
Differ from Category (+/-)	2.5	2.7	-2.3	2.2	-8.0	22.1	1.8	13.7	3.1	2.2
Return, Tax-Adjusted (%)	13.3	25.1	-6.6	13.7	-1.0	43.2	-2.0	27.2	13.3	0.0

PER SHARE DATA

	1996	1995	1994	1993	1992	1991	1990	1989	1988	1987
Dividends, Net Income ($)	0.39	0.40	0.41	0.43	0.29	0.31	0.37	0.41	0.36	0.36
Distrib'ns, Cap Gain ($)	0.95	0.23	0.53	0.54	0.38	0.46	0.41	0.73	0.00	0.89
Net Asset Value ($)	13.46	12.72	10.52	11.93	11.10	11.70	8.62	9.32	7.98	7.24
Expense Ratio (%)	0.93	0.94	0.92	0.96	0.98	0.94	0.76	0.78	0.78	0.74
Yield (%)	2.70	3.08	3.71	3.44	2.52	2.54	4.09	4.07	4.51	4.42
Portfolio Turnover (%)	63	54	56	121	119	104	132	124	148	195
Total Assets (Millions $)	4,412	4,256	3,695	3,905	2,751	1,596	549	448	372	357

PORTFOLIO (as of 9/30/96)

Portfolio Manager: Charles Mayer, Jerry Paul - 1993

Investm't Category: Balanced

✔ Domestic	Index
✔ Foreign	Sector
✔ Asset Allocation	State Specific

Investment Style

Large-Cap Growth	Large-Cap Value
Mid-Cap Growth	Mid-Cap Value
Small-Cap Growth	Small-Cap Value

Portfolio

2.8% cash	9.5% corp bonds
79.1% stocks	8.0% gov't bonds
0.3% preferred	0.0% muni bonds
0.3% conv't/warrants	0.0% other

SHAREHOLDER INFORMATION

Minimum Investment
Initial: $1,000   Subsequent: $50

Minimum IRA Investment
Initial: $250   Subsequent: $50

Maximum Fees
Load: none   12b-1: 0.25%
Other: none

Distributions
Income: quarterly   Capital Gains: Dec

Exchange Options
Number Per Year: 4   Fee: none
Telephone: yes (money market fund available)

Services
IRA, pension, auto exchange, auto invest, auto withdraw

INVESCO Int'l Fds:
European (FEURX)
International Stock

P.O. Box 173706
Denver, CO 80217
800-525-8085, 303-930-6300
www.invesco.com

PERFORMANCE   fund inception date: 6/2/86

	3yr Annual	5yr Annual	10yr Annual	Bull	Bear
Return (%)	14.4	11.5	9.4	56.0	-9.1
Differ from Category (+/-)	8.1 high	1.5 abv av	0.8 abv av	31.7 high	-1.9 blw av

Total Risk	Standard Deviation	Category Risk	Risk Index	Beta
abv av	11.3%	abv av	1.1	0.74

	1996	1995	1994	1993	1992	1991	1990	1989	1988	1987
Return (%)............	29.6	19.1	-3.1	24.5	-7.7	8.0	0.7	24.2	10.5	-4.6
Differ from Category (+/-) .	14.8	10.0	0.0	-15.1	-3.9	-5.2	10.8	1.6	-4.4	-16.8
Return, Tax-Adjusted (%). .	27.0	15.5	-3.6	24.0	-8.4	6.7	-0.3	23.6	10.1	-4.9

PER SHARE DATA

	1996	1995	1994	1993	1992	1991	1990	1989	1988	1987
Dividends, Net Income ($).	0.05	0.24	0.15	0.13	0.19	0.36	0.26	0.13	0.08	0.05
Distrib'ns, Cap Gain ($) ...	1.13	1.21	0.00	0.00	0.00	0.00	0.00	0.00	0.00	0.00
Net Asset Value ($)	15.86	13.19	12.29	12.83	10.41	11.49	10.99	11.17	9.11	8.31
Expense Ratio (%).........	na	1.40	1.20	1.28	1.29	1.43	1.29	1.78	1.88	1.50
Yield (%)	0.29	1.66	1.22	1.01	1.82	3.13	2.36	1.16	0.87	0.60
Portfolio Turnover (%).....	na	96	70	44	87	61	20	118	75	131
Total Assets (Millions $)...	307	221	245	308	124	79	72	21	6	8

PORTFOLIO (as of 9/30/96)

Portfolio Manager: committee - 1990

Investm't Category: International Stock
Domestic	Index
✔ Foreign	Sector
Asset Allocation	State Specific

Investment Style
Large-Cap Growth	Large-Cap Value
Mid-Cap Growth	Mid-Cap Value
Small-Cap Growth	Small-Cap Value

Portfolio
2.7% cash	0.0% corp bonds
89.6% stocks	0.0% gov't bonds
6.7% preferred	0.0% muni bonds
1.0% conv't/warrants	0.0% other

SHAREHOLDER INFORMATION

Minimum Investment
Initial: $1,000   Subsequent: $50

Minimum IRA Investment
Initial: $250   Subsequent: $50

Maximum Fees
Load: none   12b-1: none
Other: none

Distributions
Income: annual   Capital Gains: Dec

Exchange Options
Number Per Year: 4   Fee: none
Telephone: yes (money market fund available)

Services
IRA, pension, auto exchange, auto invest, auto withdraw

INVESCO Int'l Fds:
Int'l Growth (FSIGX)

International Stock

P.O. Box 173706
Denver, CO 80217
800-525-8085, 303-930-6300
www.invesco.com

PERFORMANCE

fund inception date: 9/22/87

	3yr Annual	5yr Annual	10yr Annual	Bull	Bear
Return (%)	6.8	6.4	na	18.4	-3.9
Differ from Category (+/-)	0.5 av	-3.6 low	na	-5.9 blw av	3.3 abv av

Total Risk	Standard Deviation	Category Risk	Risk Index	Beta
abv av	9.9%	blw av	1.0	0.67

	1996	1995	1994	1993	1992	1991	1990	1989	1988	1987
Return (%)	11.9	8.2	0.5	27.8	-12.6	7.2	-14.7	16.1	16.6	—
Differ from Category (+/-)	-2.9	-0.9	3.6	-11.8	-8.8	-6.0	-4.6	-6.5	1.7	—
Return, Tax-Adjusted (%)	10.2	6.6	-1.2	27.6	-13.0	6.7	-14.9	14.6	16.3	—

PER SHARE DATA

	1996	1995	1994	1993	1992	1991	1990	1989	1988	1987
Dividends, Net Income ($)	0.09	0.18	0.07	0.06	0.12	0.17	0.02	0.16	0.09	—
Distrib'ns, Cap Gain ($)	0.79	0.56	0.86	0.00	0.00	0.00	0.05	0.50	0.00	—
Net Asset Value ($)	16.63	15.68	15.17	16.01	12.57	14.51	13.69	16.13	14.48	—
Expense Ratio (%)	na	1.81	1.50	1.43	1.36	1.48	1.48	1.24	1.26	—
Yield (%)	0.51	1.10	0.43	0.37	0.95	1.17	0.14	0.96	0.62	—
Portfolio Turnover (%)	na	62	87	46	50	71	78	35	73	—
Total Assets (Millions $)	94	85	108	113	35	42	39	40	12	—

PORTFOLIO (as of 9/30/96)

Portfolio Manager: Francesco Bertoni - 1995

Investm't Category: International Stock
Domestic	Index
✔ Foreign	Sector
Asset Allocation	State Specific

Investment Style
Large-Cap Growth	Large-Cap Value
Mid-Cap Growth	Mid-Cap Value
Small-Cap Growth	Small-Cap Value

Portfolio
10.9% cash	0.0% corp bonds
84.3% stocks	0.0% gov't bonds
4.0% preferred	0.0% muni bonds
0.8% conv't/warrants	0.0% other

SHAREHOLDER INFORMATION

Minimum Investment
Initial: $1,000   Subsequent: $50

Minimum IRA Investment
Initial: $250   Subsequent: $50

Maximum Fees
Load: none   12b-1: none
Other: none

Distributions
Income: annual   Capital Gains: Dec

Exchange Options
Number Per Year: 4   Fee: none
Telephone: yes (money market fund available)

Services
IRA, pension, auto exchange, auto invest, auto withdraw

INVESCO Int'l Fds: Pacific Basin (FPBSX)

International Stock

P.O. Box 173706
Denver, CO 80217
800-525-8085, 303-930-6300
www.invesco.com

PERFORMANCE

fund inception date: 1/19/84

	3yr Annual	5yr Annual	10yr Annual	Bull	Bear
Return (%)	2.4	5.8	6.3	-0.5	2.2
Differ from Category (+/-)	-3.9 blw av	-4.2 low	-2.3 blw av	-24.8 low	9.4 high

Total Risk	Standard Deviation	Category Risk	Risk Index	Beta
high	12.2%	abv av	1.2	0.74

	1996	1995	1994	1993	1992	1991	1990	1989	1988	1987
Return (%)	-1.2	4.0	4.6	42.6	-13.6	13.2	-24.5	20.1	23.1	9.7
Differ from Category (+/-)	-16.0	-5.1	7.7	3.0	-9.8	0.0	-14.4	-2.5	8.2	-2.5
Return, Tax-Adjusted (%)	-2.8	3.3	1.2	41.6	-13.8	12.8	-25.3	20.0	23.1	2.6

PER SHARE DATA

	1996	1995	1994	1993	1992	1991	1990	1989	1988	1987
Dividends, Net Income ($)	0.00	0.09	0.04	0.04	0.06	0.10	0.09	0.02	0.00	0.07
Distrib'ns, Cap Gain ($)	0.82	0.18	1.79	0.32	0.00	0.00	0.28	0.00	0.00	3.11
Net Asset Value ($)	13.43	14.44	14.15	15.27	10.96	12.75	11.35	15.49	12.91	10.48
Expense Ratio (%)	na	1.52	1.24	1.22	1.78	1.87	1.79	1.62	1.62	1.26
Yield (%)	0.00	0.61	0.25	0.25	0.54	0.78	0.77	0.12	0.00	0.51
Portfolio Turnover (%)	na	56	70	30	123	89	93	86	69	155
Total Assets (Millions $)	174	193	252	274	22	19	14	26	29	28

PORTFOLIO (as of 9/30/96)

Portfolio Manager: committee - 1994

Investm't Category: International Stock

Domestic	Index
✔ Foreign	Sector
Asset Allocation	State Specific

Investment Style

Large-Cap Growth	Large-Cap Value
Mid-Cap Growth	Mid-Cap Value
Small-Cap Growth	Small-Cap Value

Portfolio

2.5% cash	0.0% corp bonds
97.0% stocks	0.0% gov't bonds
0.0% preferred	0.0% muni bonds
0.5% conv't/warrants	0.0% other

SHAREHOLDER INFORMATION

Minimum Investment
Initial: $1,000   Subsequent: $50

Minimum IRA Investment
Initial: $250   Subsequent: $50

Maximum Fees
Load: none   12b-1: none
Other: none

Distributions
Income: annual   Capital Gains: Dec

Exchange Options
Number Per Year: 4   Fee: none
Telephone: yes (money market fund available)

Services
IRA, pension, auto exchange, auto invest, auto withdraw

INVESCO Latin American Growth (IVSLX)

International Stock

P.O. Box 173706
Denver, CO 80217
800-525-8085, 303-930-6300
www.invesco.com

PERFORMANCE

fund inception date: 2/15/95

	3yr Annual	5yr Annual	10yr Annual	Bull	Bear
Return (%)	na	na	na	na	na
Differ from Category (+/-)	na	na	na	na	na

Total Risk	Standard Deviation	Category Risk	Risk Index	Beta
na	na	na	na	na

	1996	1995	1994	1993	1992	1991	1990	1989	1988	1987
Return (%)	25.8	—	—	—	—	—	—	—	—	—
Differ from Category (+/-)	11.0	—	—	—	—	—	—	—	—	—
Return, Tax-Adjusted (%)	24.5	—	—	—	—	—	—	—	—	—

PER SHARE DATA

	1996	1995	1994	1993	1992	1991	1990	1989	1988	1987
Dividends, Net Income ($)	0.10	—	—	—	—	—	—	—	—	—
Distrib'ns, Cap Gain ($)	0.36	—	—	—	—	—	—	—	—	—
Net Asset Value ($)	13.26	—	—	—	—	—	—	—	—	—
Expense Ratio (%)	2.14	—	—	—	—	—	—	—	—	—
Yield (%)	0.73	—	—	—	—	—	—	—	—	—
Portfolio Turnover (%)	29	—	—	—	—	—	—	—	—	—
Total Assets (Millions $)	28	—	—	—	—	—	—	—	—	—

PORTFOLIO (as of 9/30/96)

Portfolio Manager: Peter Jarvis, Jane Lyon - 1995

Investm't Category: International Stock
- Domestic
- ✔ Foreign
- Asset Allocation
- Index
- Sector
- State Specific

Investment Style
- Large-Cap Growth
- Mid-Cap Growth
- Small-Cap Growth
- Large-Cap Value
- Mid-Cap Value
- Small-Cap Value

Portfolio
3.6% cash	0.0% corp bonds
63.6% stocks	0.0% gov't bonds
32.7% preferred	0.0% muni bonds
0.0% conv't/warrants	0.0% other

SHAREHOLDER INFORMATION

Minimum Investment
Initial: $1,000   Subsequent: $50

Minimum IRA Investment
Initial: $250   Subsequent: $50

Maximum Fees
Load: 1.00% redemption   12b-1: 0.25%
Other: redemption and exchange fees apply to shares held less than 3 months

Distributions
Income: annual   Capital Gains: Dec

Exchange Options
Number Per Year: 4   Fee: 1%
Telephone: yes (money market fund available)

Services
IRA, pension, auto exchange, auto invest, auto withdraw

INVESCO Multiple Asset: Balanced (IMABX)

Balanced

P.O. Box 173706
Denver, CO 80217
800-525-8085, 303-930-6300
www.invesco.com

PERFORMANCE

fund inception date: 12/1/93

	3yr Annual	5yr Annual	10yr Annual	Bull	Bear
Return (%)	19.0	na	na	64.9	-1.4
Differ from Category (+/-)	7.3 high	na	na	19.8 high	4.3 high

Total Risk	Standard Deviation	Category Risk	Risk Index	Beta
blw av	6.7%	av	1.0	0.41

	1996	1995	1994	1993	1992	1991	1990	1989	1988	1987
Return (%).............	14.6	36.4	7.7	—	—	—	—	—	—	—
Differ from Category (+/-)..	0.4	11.8	9.3	—	—	—	—	—	—	—
Return, Tax-Adjusted (%)..	11.5	33.0	6.8	—	—	—	—	—	—	—

PER SHARE DATA

	1996	1995	1994	1993	1992	1991	1990	1989	1988	1987
Dividends, Net Income ($).	0.39	0.30	0.05	—	—	—	—	—	—	—
Distrib'ns, Cap Gain ($) ...	0.87	0.84	0.24	—	—	—	—	—	—	—
Net Asset Value ($)	13.82	13.19	10.54	—	—	—	—	—	—	—
Expense Ratio (%)........	1.25	1.25	1.25	—	—	—	—	—	—	—
Yield (%)	2.65	2.13	0.46	—	—	—	—	—	—	—
Portfolio Turnover (%)....	259	255	61	—	—	—	—	—	—	—
Total Assets (Millions $)...	140	87	12	—	—	—	—	—	—	—

PORTFOLIO (as of 9/30/96)

Portfolio Manager: Jerry Paul, Charles Mayer - 1994

Investm't Category: Balanced

✔ Domestic
  Foreign
  Asset Allocation

  Index
  Sector
  State Specific

Investment Style

Large-Cap Growth
Mid-Cap Growth
Small-Cap Growth

Large-Cap Value
Mid-Cap Value
Small-Cap Value

Portfolio

11.2% cash	2.3% corp bonds
56.1% stocks	29.0% gov't bonds
1.5% preferred	0.0% muni bonds
0.0% conv't/warrants	0.0% other

SHAREHOLDER INFORMATION

Minimum Investment
Initial: $1,000   Subsequent: $50

Minimum IRA Investment
Initial: $250   Subsequent: $50

Maximum Fees
Load: none   12b-1: 0.25%
Other: none

Distributions
Income: quarterly   Capital Gains: Dec

Exchange Options
Number Per Year: 4   Fee: none
Telephone: yes (money market fund available)

Services
IRA, pension, auto exchange, auto invest, auto withdraw

INVESCO Strat Port— Environmental (FSEVX)

Aggressive Growth

P.O. Box 173706
Denver, CO 80217
800-525-8085, 303-930-6300
www.invesco.com

PERFORMANCE

fund inception date: 1/2/91

	3yr Annual	5yr Annual	10yr Annual	Bull	Bear
Return (%)	14.0	2.8	na	69.3	-16.2
Differ from Category (+/-)	-1.8 av	-12.5 low	na	-1.8 av	-5.6 low

Total Risk	Standard Deviation	Category Risk	Risk Index	Beta
high	13.9%	av	1.0	1.01

	1996	1995	1994	1993	1992	1991	1990	1989	1988	1987
Return (%).	18.7	41.0	-11.4	-4.7	-18.8	—	—	—	—	—
Differ from Category (+/-) .	-0.4	6.7	-11.4	-24.0	-30.5	—	—	—	—	—
Return, Tax-Adjusted (%). .	16.8	40.5	-11.7	-4.7	-18.8	—	—	—	—	—

PER SHARE DATA

	1996	1995	1994	1993	1992	1991	1990	1989	1988	1987
Dividends, Net Income ($).	0.05	0.07	0.05	0.00	0.00	—	—	—	—	—
Distrib'ns, Cap Gain ($) . . .	0.53	0.00	0.00	0.00	0.00	—	—	—	—	—
Net Asset Value ($)	9.95	8.89	6.36	7.24	7.60	—	—	—	—	—
Expense Ratio (%).	na	1.57	1.29	1.62	1.85	—	—	—	—	—
Yield (%)	0.47	0.78	0.78	0.00	0.00	—	—	—	—	—
Portfolio Turnover (%).	na	195	211	155	113	—	—	—	—	—
Total Assets (Millions $). . . .	26	30	22	59	20	—	—	—	—	—

PORTFOLIO (as of 9/30/96)

Portfolio Manager: Jeffrey G. Morris - 1995

Investm't Category: Aggressive Growth
- ✔ Domestic
- ✔ Foreign
- Asset Allocation
- Index
- ✔ Sector
- State Specific

Investment Style
- Large-Cap Growth
- Mid-Cap Growth
- Small-Cap Growth
- Large-Cap Value
- Mid-Cap Value
- ✔ Small-Cap Value

Portfolio
24.2% cash	0.0% corp bonds	
75.8% stocks	0.0% gov't bonds	
0.0% preferred	0.0% muni bonds	
0.0% conv't/warrants	0.0% other	

SHAREHOLDER INFORMATION

Minimum Investment
Initial: $1,000   Subsequent: $50

Minimum IRA Investment
Initial: $250   Subsequent: $50

Maximum Fees
Load: none   12b-1: none
Other: none

Distributions
Income: annual   Capital Gains: Dec

Exchange Options
Number Per Year: 4   Fee: none
Telephone: yes (money market fund available)

Services
IRA, pension, auto exchange, auto invest, auto withdraw

INVESCO Strat Port— Energy (FSTEX)

Aggressive Growth

P.O. Box 173706
Denver, CO 80217
800-525-8085, 303-930-6300
www.invesco.com

PERFORMANCE

fund inception date: 1/19/84

	3yr Annual	5yr Annual	10yr Annual	Bull	Bear
Return (%)	15.5	9.3	8.1	50.4	-1.3
Differ from Category (+/-)	-0.3 av	-6.0 low	-6.9 low	-20.7 blw av	9.3 high

Total Risk	Standard Deviation	Category Risk	Risk Index	Beta
high	13.6%	av	1.0	0.75

	1996	1995	1994	1993	1992	1991	1990	1989	1988	1987
Return (%)	38.8	19.7	-7.3	16.7	-13.3	-3.5	-16.5	43.5	14.9	4.9
Differ from Category (+/-)	19.7	-14.6	-7.3	-2.6	-25.0	-55.6	-11.1	15.1	-1.5	7.3
Return, Tax-Adjusted (%)	35.7	19.3	-7.5	16.2	-13.4	-4.0	-16.9	42.4	14.2	2.1

PER SHARE DATA

	1996	1995	1994	1993	1992	1991	1990	1989	1988	1987
Dividends, Net Income ($)	0.03	0.09	0.05	0.10	0.02	0.11	0.11	0.24	0.14	0.14
Distrib'ns, Cap Gain ($)	1.21	0.00	0.00	0.00	0.00	0.00	0.00	0.00	0.00	0.64
Net Asset Value ($)	14.46	11.36	9.57	10.37	8.97	10.36	10.84	13.10	9.32	8.23
Expense Ratio (%)	na	1.53	1.35	1.18	1.73	1.69	1.42	1.75	1.90	1.30
Yield (%)	0.19	0.79	0.52	0.96	0.22	1.06	1.01	1.83	1.50	1.57
Portfolio Turnover (%)	na	300	123	190	370	337	321	109	177	452
Total Assets (Millions $)	271	98	46	49	12	10	14	16	5	6

PORTFOLIO (as of 9/30/96)

Portfolio Manager: Thomas R. Samuelson - 1995

Investm't Category: Aggressive Growth
- ✔ Domestic   Index
- ✔ Foreign   ✔ Sector
- Asset Allocation   State Specific

Investment Style
- Large-Cap Growth   ✔ Large-Cap Value
- Mid-Cap Growth   ✔ Mid-Cap Value
- Small-Cap Growth   ✔ Small-Cap Value

Portfolio
13.8% cash	0.0% corp bonds
81.7% stocks	0.0% gov't bonds
3.7% preferred	0.0% muni bonds
0.9% conv't/warrants	0.0% other

SHAREHOLDER INFORMATION

Minimum Investment
Initial: $1,000   Subsequent: $50

Minimum IRA Investment
Initial: $250   Subsequent: $50

Maximum Fees
Load: none   12b-1: none
Other: none

Distributions
Income: annual   Capital Gains: Dec

Exchange Options
Number Per Year: 4   Fee: none
Telephone: yes (money market fund available)

Services
IRA, pension, auto exchange, auto invest, auto withdraw

INVESCO Strat Port— Financial Svcs (FSFSX)

Growth

P.O. Box 173706
Denver, CO 80217
800-525-8085, 303-930-6300
www.invesco.com

PERFORMANCE

fund inception date: 6/2/86

	3yr Annual	5yr Annual	10yr Annual	Bull	Bear
Return (%)	19.6	20.8	19.4	78.5	-7.2
Differ from Category (+/-)	3.9 high	6.5 high	5.5 high	16.1 high	-0.5 av

Total Risk	Standard Deviation	Category Risk	Risk Index	Beta
abv av	11.6%	abv av	1.1	1.02

	1996	1995	1994	1993	1992	1991	1990	1989	1988	1987
Return (%)	30.2	39.8	-5.9	18.4	26.7	73.9	-7.2	36.9	17.1	-11.1
Differ from Category (+/-)	10.1	9.5	-5.6	4.4	14.9	37.9	-1.1	10.8	-1.0	-13.1
Return, Tax-Adjusted (%)	26.2	36.8	-6.8	10.9	24.4	73.0	-7.3	33.3	16.3	-12.0

PER SHARE DATA

	1996	1995	1994	1993	1992	1991	1990	1989	1988	1987
Dividends, Net Income ($)	0.53	0.28	0.34	0.21	0.18	0.11	0.00	0.09	0.12	0.07
Distrib'ns, Cap Gain ($)	1.93	1.14	0.00	4.30	0.90	0.10	0.02	0.80	0.00	0.12
Net Asset Value ($)	22.22	19.02	14.64	15.91	17.24	14.57	8.50	9.19	7.38	6.40
Expense Ratio (%)	na	1.26	1.18	1.03	1.07	1.13	2.50	2.50	1.95	1.50
Yield (%)	2.19	1.38	2.32	1.03	0.99	0.74	0.00	0.90	1.62	1.07
Portfolio Turnover (%)	na	171	88	236	208	249	528	217	175	284
Total Assets (Millions $)	700	432	236	339	246	90	3	1	1	1

PORTFOLIO (as of 9/30/96)

Portfolio Manager: Dan Leonard - 1996

Investm't Category: Growth
- ✔ Domestic
- ✔ Foreign
- Asset Allocation
- Index
- ✔ Sector
- State Specific

Investment Style
- Large-Cap Growth
- Mid-Cap Growth
- Small-Cap Growth
- ✔ Large-Cap Value
- ✔ Mid-Cap Value
- Small-Cap Value

Portfolio
4.1% cash	0.0% corp bonds
96.0% stocks	0.0% gov't bonds
0.0% preferred	0.0% muni bonds
0.0% conv't/warrants	0.0% other

SHAREHOLDER INFORMATION

Minimum Investment
Initial: $1,000   Subsequent: $50

Minimum IRA Investment
Initial: $250   Subsequent: $50

Maximum Fees
Load: none   12b-1: none
Other: none

Distributions
Income: annual   Capital Gains: Dec

Exchange Options
Number Per Year: 4   Fee: none
Telephone: yes (money market fund available)

Services
IRA, pension, auto exchange, auto invest, auto withdraw

INVESCO Strat Port— Gold (FGLDX)

P.O. Box 173706
Denver, CO 80217
800-525-8085, 303-930-6300
www.invesco.com

Gold

PERFORMANCE

fund inception date: 1/19/84

	3yr Annual	5yr Annual	10yr Annual	Bull	Bear
Return (%)	4.5	12.6	3.8	34.7	-17.7
Differ from Category (+/-)	4.2 abv av	3.0 abv av	-0.5 av	19.8 high	-7.5 low

Total Risk	Standard Deviation	Category Risk	Risk Index	Beta
high	29.0%	high	1.2	0.64

	1996	1995	1994	1993	1992	1991	1990	1989	1988	1987
Return (%)	40.6	12.7	-27.9	72.6	-8.3	-7.2	-23.1	21.3	-20.1	15.9
Differ from Category (+/-)	29.4	7.7	-15.8	-15.2	7.0	-2.6	-0.8	-3.1	-1.0	-16.3
Return, Tax-Adjusted (%)	25.1	12.7	-27.9	72.6	-8.3	-7.2	-23.1	21.1	-20.5	15.2

PER SHARE DATA

	1996	1995	1994	1993	1992	1991	1990	1989	1988	1987
Dividends, Net Income ($)	2.14	0.00	0.00	0.00	0.00	0.00	0.00	0.02	0.06	0.06
Distrib'ns, Cap Gain ($)	0.00	0.00	0.00	0.00	0.00	0.00	0.00	0.00	0.00	0.04
Net Asset Value ($)	5.56	5.48	4.87	6.75	3.91	4.26	4.59	5.97	4.94	6.25
Expense Ratio (%)	na	1.32	1.07	1.03	1.41	1.47	1.32	1.63	1.58	1.15
Yield (%)	na	0.00	0.00	0.00	0.00	0.00	0.00	0.33	1.21	0.95
Portfolio Turnover (%)	na	72	97	142	101	43	107	77	47	124
Total Assets (Millions $)	266	163	222	315	55	35	42	54	31	41

PORTFOLIO (as of 9/30/96)

Portfolio Manager: Daniel B. Leonard - 1989

Investm't Category: Gold
- ✔ Domestic
- ✔ Foreign
- Asset Allocation
- Index
- ✔ Sector
- State Specific

Investment Style
Large-Cap Growth	Large-Cap Value
Mid-Cap Growth	Mid-Cap Value
Small-Cap Growth	Small-Cap Value

Portfolio
0.0% cash	0.0% corp bonds
95.6% stocks	0.0% gov't bonds
5.2% preferred	0.0% muni bonds
3.1% conv't/warrants	0.0% other

SHAREHOLDER INFORMATION

Minimum Investment
Initial: $1,000   Subsequent: $50

Minimum IRA Investment
Initial: $250   Subsequent: $50

Maximum Fees
Load: none   12b-1: none
Other: none

Distributions
Income: annual   Capital Gains: Dec

Exchange Options
Number Per Year: 4   Fee: none
Telephone: yes (money market fund available)

Services
IRA, pension, auto exchange, auto invest, auto withdraw

INVESCO Strat Port— Health Science (FHLSX)

Aggressive Growth

P.O. Box 173706
Denver, CO 80217
800-525-8085, 303-930-6300
www.invesco.com

PERFORMANCE

fund inception date: 1/19/84

	3yr Annual	5yr Annual	10yr Annual	Bull	Bear
Return (%)	21.3	7.1	21.0	100.5	-14.9
Differ from Category (+/-)	5.5 high	-8.2 low	6.0 high	29.4 high	-4.3 blw av

Total Risk	Standard Deviation	Category Risk	Risk Index	Beta
high	14.9%	av	1.0	0.94

	1996	1995	1994	1993	1992	1991	1990	1989	1988	1987
Return (%)	11.4	58.8	0.9	-8.5	-13.8	91.7	25.7	59.4	16.0	7.0
Differ from Category (+/-)	-7.7	24.5	0.9	-27.8	-25.5	39.6	31.1	31.0	-0.4	9.4
Return, Tax-Adjusted (%)	6.7	55.6	0.9	-8.5	-14.2	87.7	25.0	55.3	16.0	4.9

PER SHARE DATA

	1996	1995	1994	1993	1992	1991	1990	1989	1988	1987
Dividends, Net Income ($)	0.07	0.00	0.00	0.00	0.10	0.10	0.17	0.10	0.00	0.00
Distrib'ns, Cap Gain ($)	8.59	4.00	0.00	0.00	0.44	3.47	0.21	1.94	0.00	0.92
Net Asset Value ($)	49.36	52.35	35.47	35.14	38.38	45.17	25.63	20.76	14.39	12.40
Expense Ratio (%)	na	1.15	1.19	1.16	1.00	1.03	1.12	1.42	1.65	1.42
Yield (%)	0.12	0.00	0.00	0.00	0.25	0.20	0.65	0.44	0.00	0.00
Portfolio Turnover (%)	na	107	80	87	91	100	242	272	280	364
Total Assets (Millions $)	932	1,040	488	566	792	1,069	160	36	9	10

PORTFOLIO (as of 9/30/96)

Portfolio Manager: John Schroer, Carol Werthers - 1994

Investm't Category: Aggressive Growth
✔ Domestic   Index
✔ Foreign   ✔ Sector
   Asset Allocation   State Specific

Investment Style
   Large-Cap Growth   Large-Cap Value
   Mid-Cap Growth   Mid-Cap Value
✔ Small-Cap Growth   Small-Cap Value

Portfolio
   4.7% cash   0.0% corp bonds
   92.8% stocks   0.0% gov't bonds
   1.5% preferred   0.0% muni bonds
   1.1% conv't/warrants   0.0% other

SHAREHOLDER INFORMATION

Minimum Investment
Initial: $1,000   Subsequent: $50

Minimum IRA Investment
Initial: $250   Subsequent: $50

Maximum Fees
Load: none   12b-1: none
Other: none

Distributions
Income: annual   Capital Gains: Dec

Exchange Options
Number Per Year: 4   Fee: none
Telephone: yes (money market fund available)

Services
IRA, pension, auto exchange, auto invest, auto withdraw

INVESCO Strat Port— Leisure (FLISX)

Aggressive Growth

P.O. Box 173706
Denver, CO 80217
800-525-8085, 303-930-6300
www.invesco.com

PERFORMANCE

fund inception date: 1/19/84

	3yr Annual	5yr Annual	10yr Annual	Bull	Bear
Return (%)	6.2	14.9	17.2	34.3	-8.8
Differ from Category (+/-)	-9.6 low	-0.4 av	2.2 abv av	-36.8 low	1.8 abv av

Total Risk	Standard Deviation	Category Risk	Risk Index	Beta
abv av	10.1%	low	0.7	0.66

	1996	1995	1994	1993	1992	1991	1990	1989	1988	1987
Return (%)	9.0	15.7	-5.0	35.7	23.4	52.7	-11.0	38.2	28.5	0.7
Differ from Category (+/-)	-10.1	-18.6	-5.0	16.4	11.7	0.6	-5.6	9.8	12.1	3.1
Return, Tax-Adjusted (%)	8.0	11.4	-6.1	32.8	21.6	47.7	-12.4	32.8	28.5	-3.1

PER SHARE DATA

	1996	1995	1994	1993	1992	1991	1990	1989	1988	1987
Dividends, Net Income ($)	0.04	0.08	0.00	0.00	0.00	0.00	0.03	0.20	0.00	0.00
Distrib'ns, Cap Gain ($)	0.63	3.14	0.91	1.89	0.98	2.12	0.67	1.99	0.00	1.43
Net Asset Value ($)	22.58	21.33	21.21	23.28	18.55	15.94	11.93	14.34	11.94	9.29
Expense Ratio (%)	na	1.29	1.17	1.14	1.51	1.86	1.84	1.38	1.89	1.50
Yield (%)	0.17	0.32	0.00	0.00	0.00	0.00	0.23	1.22	0.00	0.00
Portfolio Turnover (%)	na	119	116	116	148	122	89	119	136	376
Total Assets (Millions $)	252	262	262	304	79	17	7	8	4	2

PORTFOLIO (as of 9/30/96)

Portfolio Manager: Mark Greenberg - 1996

Investm't Category: Aggressive Growth
- ✔ Domestic
- ✔ Foreign
-   Asset Allocation
-   Index
- ✔ Sector
-   State Specific

Investment Style
-   Large-Cap Growth
- ✔ Mid-Cap Growth
- ✔ Small-Cap Growth
-   Large-Cap Value
-   Mid-Cap Value
-   Small-Cap Value

Portfolio
5.4% cash	1.6% corp bonds
90.4% stocks	0.0% gov't bonds
2.5% preferred	0.0% muni bonds
0.0% conv't/warrants	0.0% other

SHAREHOLDER INFORMATION

Minimum Investment
Initial: $1,000   Subsequent: $50

Minimum IRA Investment
Initial: $250   Subsequent: $50

Maximum Fees
Load: none   12b-1: none
Other: none

Distributions
Income: annual   Capital Gains: Dec

Exchange Options
Number Per Year: 4   Fee: none
Telephone: yes (money market fund available)

Services
IRA, pension, auto exchange, auto invest, auto withdraw

INVESCO Strat Port— Technology (FTCHX)

Aggressive Growth

P.O. Box 173706
Denver, CO 80217
800-525-8085, 303-930-6300
www.invesco.com

PERFORMANCE

fund inception date: 1/19/84

	3yr Annual	5yr Annual	10yr Annual	Bull	Bear
Return (%)	23.1	20.6	20.4	103.8	-10.5
Differ from Category (+/-)	7.3 high	5.3 high	5.4 high	32.7 high	0.1 av

Total Risk	Standard Deviation	Category Risk	Risk Index	Beta
high	14.7%	av	1.0	0.99

	1996	1995	1994	1993	1992	1991	1990	1989	1988	1987
Return (%)	21.7	45.7	5.2	15.0	18.8	76.8	8.5	21.4	14.2	-5.3
Differ from Category (+/-)	2.6	11.4	5.2	-4.3	7.1	24.7	13.9	-7.0	-2.2	-2.9
Return, Tax-Adjusted (%)	17.2	38.8	4.2	11.1	18.8	67.9	8.5	21.4	14.2	-5.3

PER SHARE DATA

	1996	1995	1994	1993	1992	1991	1990	1989	1988	1987
Dividends, Net Income ($)	0.07	0.00	0.00	0.00	0.00	0.00	0.00	0.00	0.00	0.00
Distrib'ns, Cap Gain ($)	4.49	5.85	0.79	3.22	0.00	4.38	0.00	0.00	0.00	0.00
Net Asset Value ($)	30.99	29.19	24.04	23.59	23.31	19.62	13.78	12.69	10.45	9.15
Expense Ratio (%)	na	1.12	1.17	1.13	1.12	1.19	1.25	1.59	1.72	1.47
Yield (%)	0.19	0.00	0.00	0.00	0.00	0.00	0.00	0.00	0.00	0.00
Portfolio Turnover (%)	na	191	145	184	169	307	345	259	356	556
Total Assets (Millions $)	857	576	310	253	256	106	26	10	14	14

PORTFOLIO (as of 9/30/96)

Portfolio Manager: Daniel Leonard, Gerard Hallaren - 1985

Investm't Category: Aggressive Growth
✔ Domestic	Index
✔ Foreign	✔ Sector
Asset Allocation	State Specific

Investment Style
Large-Cap Growth	Large-Cap Value
✔ Mid-Cap Growth	Mid-Cap Value
✔ Small-Cap Growth	Small-Cap Value

Portfolio
19.0% cash	0.0% corp bonds
80.9% stocks	0.0% gov't bonds
0.2% preferred	0.0% muni bonds
0.0% conv't/warrants	0.0% other

SHAREHOLDER INFORMATION

Minimum Investment
Initial: $1,000   Subsequent: $50

Minimum IRA Investment
Initial: $250   Subsequent: $50

Maximum Fees
Load: none   12b-1: none
Other: none

Distributions
Income: annual   Capital Gains: Dec

Exchange Options
Number Per Year: 4   Fee: none
Telephone: yes (money market fund available)

Services
IRA, pension, auto exchange, auto invest, auto withdraw

INVESCO Strat Port— Utilities (FSTUX)

Growth & Income

P.O. Box 173706
Denver, CO 80217
800-525-8085, 303-930-6300
www.invesco.com

PERFORMANCE

fund inception date: 6/2/86

	3yr Annual	5yr Annual	10yr Annual	Bull	Bear
Return (%)	8.3	11.2	10.8	40.2	-10.2
Differ from Category (+/-)	-7.0 low	-2.7 low	-1.9 blw av	-19.6 low	-3.8 low

Total Risk	Standard Deviation	Category Risk	Risk Index	Beta
av	7.3%	low	0.8	0.56

	1996	1995	1994	1993	1992	1991	1990	1989	1988	1987
Return (%).	12.7	25.2	-10.0	21.2	10.7	27.9	-10.1	31.4	14.2	-5.0
Differ from Category (+/-) .	-7.0	-4.9	-8.7	7.4	0.0	-1.2	-4.2	7.9	-2.6	-5.2
Return, Tax-Adjusted (%). . .	9.3	23.4	-11.2	14.9	7.7	26.3	-11.5	27.3	12.2	-7.2

PER SHARE DATA

	1996	1995	1994	1993	1992	1991	1990	1989	1988	1987
Dividends, Net Income ($).	0.34	0.41	0.31	0.26	0.25	0.34	0.34	0.37	0.38	0.47
Distrib'ns, Cap Gain ($) . . .	0.87	0.00	0.00	2.00	0.77	0.00	0.00	0.71	0.00	0.00
Net Asset Value ($)	11.38	11.21	9.32	10.68	10.69	10.64	8.62	9.96	8.47	7.76
Expense Ratio (%).	na	1.18	1.13	1.06	1.13	1.21	1.26	1.35	1.39	1.39
Yield (%)	2.77	3.65	3.32	2.05	2.18	3.19	3.94	3.46	4.48	6.05
Portfolio Turnover (%).	na	185	180	202	226	151	264	220	164	84
Total Assets (Millions $). . .	153	150	122	174	108	85	32	35	18	17

PORTFOLIO (as of 9/30/96)

Portfolio Manager: Jeffrey G. Morris - 1996

Investm't Category: Growth & Income
✔ Domestic
  Foreign
  Asset Allocation
  Index
✔ Sector
  State Specific

Investment Style
  Large-Cap Growth
  Mid-Cap Growth
  Small-Cap Growth
✔ Large-Cap Value
✔ Mid-Cap Value
  Small-Cap Value

Portfolio
24.2% cash
75.8% stocks
 0.0% preferred
 0.0% conv't/warrants
 0.0% corp bonds
 0.0% gov't bonds
 0.0% muni bonds
 0.0% other

SHAREHOLDER INFORMATION

Minimum Investment
Initial: $1,000   Subsequent: $50

Minimum IRA Investment
Initial: $250   Subsequent: $50

Maximum Fees
Load: none   12b-1: none
Other: none

Distributions
Income: na   Capital Gains: Dec

Exchange Options
Number Per Year: 4   Fee: none
Telephone: yes (money market fund available)

Services
IRA, pension, auto exchange, auto invest, auto withdraw

INVESCO Tax-Free Long Term Bond (FTIFX)

Tax-Exempt Bond

P.O. Box 173706
Denver, CO 80217
800-525-8085, 303-930-6300
www.invesco.com

PERFORMANCE

fund inception date: 8/14/81

	3yr Annual	5yr Annual	10yr Annual	Bull	Bear
Return (%)	3.7	6.4	7.3	17.9	-6.1
Differ from Category (+/-)	-0.5 blw av	0.0 blw av	0.6 abv av	-0.5 blw av	-0.7 av

Total Risk	Standard Deviation	Category Risk	Risk Index	Avg Mat
blw av	5.4%	av	1.0	20.3 yrs

	1996	1995	1994	1993	1992	1991	1990	1989	1988	1987
Return (%)	2.3	15.6	-5.6	12.0	8.7	12.5	7.1	11.6	15.1	-4.1
Differ from Category (+/-)	-1.4	0.4	-0.3	0.2	0.4	1.1	0.7	2.6	5.1	-2.7
Return, Tax-Adjusted (%)	1.9	15.2	-6.2	11.3	8.1	12.2	7.1	11.6	15.1	-5.0

PER SHARE DATA

	1996	1995	1994	1993	1992	1991	1990	1989	1988	1987
Dividends, Net Income ($)	0.69	0.78	0.81	0.85	0.90	0.93	0.98	1.00	1.00	1.02
Distrib'ns, Cap Gain ($)	0.22	0.19	0.30	0.38	0.33	0.16	0.00	0.00	0.00	0.47
Net Asset Value ($)	15.19	15.76	14.52	16.54	15.90	15.81	15.09	15.05	14.42	13.46
Expense Ratio (%)	0.91	0.92	1.00	1.03	1.02	0.93	0.75	0.74	0.77	0.70
Yield (%)	4.47	4.89	5.46	5.02	5.54	5.82	6.49	6.64	6.93	7.32
Portfolio Turnover (%)	146	99	28	30	28	25	27	27	41	98
Total Assets (Millions $)	243	261	254	337	293	247	190	164	121	103

PORTFOLIO (as of 9/30/96)

Portfolio Manager: James S. Grabovac - 1995

Investm't Category: Tax-Exempt Bond

✔ Domestic	Index
Foreign	Sector
Asset Allocation	State Specific

Investment Style

Large-Cap Growth	Large-Cap Value
Mid-Cap Growth	Mid-Cap Value
Small-Cap Growth	Small-Cap Value

Portfolio

19.0% cash	0.0% corp bonds
0.0% stocks	0.0% gov't bonds
0.0% preferred	81.0% muni bonds
0.0% conv't/warrants	0.0% other

SHAREHOLDER INFORMATION

Minimum Investment
Initial: $1,000   Subsequent: $50

Minimum IRA Investment
Initial: na   Subsequent: na

Maximum Fees
Load: none   12b-1: 0.25%
Other: none

Distributions
Income: monthly   Capital Gains: Dec

Exchange Options
Number Per Year: 4   Fee: none
Telephone: yes (money market fund available)

Services
auto exchange, auto invest, auto withdraw

INVESCO Value Trust:
Total Return (FSFLX)

Balanced

P.O. Box 173706
Denver, CO 80217
800-525-8085, 303-930-6300
www.invesco.com

PERFORMANCE

fund inception date: 9/22/87

	3yr Annual	5yr Annual	10yr Annual	Bull	Bear
Return (%)	13.9	12.8	na	51.1	-4.8
Differ from Category (+/-)	2.2 abv av	1.4 abv av	na	6.0 abv av	0.9 abv av

Total Risk	Standard Deviation	Category Risk	Risk Index	Beta
blw av	6.8%	av	1.0	0.68

	1996	1995	1994	1993	1992	1991	1990	1989	1988	1987
Return (%)	12.3	28.6	2.5	12.3	9.8	24.9	-0.4	19.0	11.5	—
Differ from Category (+/-)	-1.9	4.0	4.1	-2.1	0.9	0.8	0.5	0.9	-0.7	—
Return, Tax-Adjusted (%)	11.0	26.8	1.2	10.1	7.9	21.8	-2.5	16.4	9.8	—

PER SHARE DATA

	1996	1995	1994	1993	1992	1991	1990	1989	1988	1987
Dividends, Net Income ($)	0.65	0.73	0.56	0.69	0.65	0.71	0.74	0.77	0.52	—
Distrib'ns, Cap Gain ($)	0.08	0.12	0.04	0.32	0.18	0.55	0.05	0.13	0.02	—
Net Asset Value ($)	24.30	22.34	18.10	18.26	17.18	16.43	14.21	15.08	13.46	—
Expense Ratio (%)	0.89	0.95	0.96	0.93	0.88	0.92	1.00	1.00	1.00	—
Yield (%)	2.66	3.25	3.08	3.71	3.74	4.18	5.18	5.06	3.85	—
Portfolio Turnover (%)	10	30	12	na	13	49	24	28	13	—
Total Assets (Millions $)	1,208	768	293	240	137	82	54	44	28	—

PORTFOLIO (as of 9/30/96)

Portfolio Manager: Edward Mitchell - 1987

Investm't Category: Balanced
- ✔ Domestic
- ✔ Foreign
- ✔ Asset Allocation

Index
Sector
State Specific

Investment Style

Large-Cap Growth	Large-Cap Value
Mid-Cap Growth	Mid-Cap Value
Small-Cap Growth	Small-Cap Value

Portfolio
4.0% cash	2.2% corp bonds
62.6% stocks	31.3% gov't bonds
0.0% preferred	0.0% muni bonds
0.0% conv't/warrants	0.0% other

SHAREHOLDER INFORMATION

Minimum Investment
Initial: $1,000   Subsequent: $50

Minimum IRA Investment
Initial: $250   Subsequent: $50

Maximum Fees
Load: none   12b-1: none
Other: none

Distributions
Income: quarterly   Capital Gains: Dec

Exchange Options
Number Per Year: 4   Fee: none
Telephone: yes (money market fund available)

Services
IRA, pension, auto exchange, auto invest, auto withdraw

INVESCO Value: Interm Gov't Bond (FIGBX)

Government Bond

P.O. Box 173706
Denver, CO 80217
800-525-8085, 303-930-6300
www.invesco.com

PERFORMANCE

fund inception date: 5/19/86

	3yr Annual	5yr Annual	10yr Annual	Bull	Bear
Return (%)	5.1	6.0	7.0	18.7	-2.7
Differ from Category (+/-)	0.2 av	-0.6 av	-1.0 blw av	-3.3 blw av	3.7 abv av

Total Risk	Standard Deviation	Category Risk	Risk Index	Avg Mat
low	3.7%	av	0.9	3.4 yrs

	1996	1995	1994	1993	1992	1991	1990	1989	1988	1987
Return (%)	1.3	16.8	-1.7	8.8	6.0	14.1	9.1	10.5	5.4	1.2
Differ from Category (+/-)	-0.2	-2.8	2.7	-2.8	-0.7	-1.6	2.8	-4.8	-2.9	5.6
Return, Tax-Adjusted (%)	-0.9	14.3	-3.9	5.8	3.1	11.1	5.8	7.1	2.3	-1.4

PER SHARE DATA

	1996	1995	1994	1993	1992	1991	1990	1989	1988	1987
Dividends, Net Income ($)	0.70	0.73	0.69	0.72	0.90	0.89	0.99	1.02	0.95	0.83
Distrib'ns, Cap Gain ($)	0.00	0.00	0.00	0.34	0.04	0.00	0.00	0.00	0.00	0.00
Net Asset Value ($)	12.46	13.01	11.81	12.72	12.68	12.89	12.13	12.07	11.89	12.19
Expense Ratio (%)	1.15	1.20	1.07	0.96	0.97	0.93	0.85	0.85	0.85	0.94
Yield (%)	5.61	5.61	5.84	5.51	7.07	6.90	8.16	8.45	7.98	6.80
Portfolio Turnover (%)	63	92	49	34	93	51	31	52	6	28
Total Assets (Millions $)	45	40	31	40	29	24	18	19	18	14

PORTFOLIO (as of 9/30/96)

Portfolio Manager: James O. Baker - 1993

Investm't Category: Government Bond
✔ Domestic
✔ Foreign
Asset Allocation

Index
Sector
State Specific

Investment Style
Large-Cap Growth   Large-Cap Value
Mid-Cap Growth   Mid-Cap Value
Small-Cap Growth   Small-Cap Value

Portfolio
7.7% cash   0.0% corp bonds
0.0% stocks   92.3% gov't bonds
0.0% preferred   0.0% muni bonds
0.0% conv't/warrants 0.0% other

SHAREHOLDER INFORMATION

Minimum Investment
Initial: $1,000   Subsequent: $50

Minimum IRA Investment
Initial: $250   Subsequent: $50

Maximum Fees
Load: none   12b-1: none
Other: none

Distributions
Income: monthly   Capital Gains: Dec

Exchange Options
Number Per Year: 4   Fee: none
Telephone: yes (money market fund available)

Services
IRA, pension, auto exchange, auto invest, auto withdraw

INVESCO Value:
Value Equity (FSEQX)

Growth & Income

P.O. Box 173706
Denver, CO 80217
800-525-8085, 303-930-6300
www.invesco.com

PERFORMANCE

fund inception date: 5/16/86

	3yr Annual	5yr Annual	10yr Annual	Bull	Bear
Return (%)	17.2	13.2	13.5	64.6	-5.4
Differ from Category (+/-)	1.9 av	-0.7 blw av	0.8 abv av	4.8 av	1.0 abv av

Total Risk	Standard Deviation	Category Risk	Risk Index	Beta
av	9.0%	blw av	1.0	0.91

	1996	1995	1994	1993	1992	1991	1990	1989	1988	1987
Return (%).............	18.4	30.6	4.0	10.4	4.9	35.8	-6.2	21.3	16.9	5.9
Differ from Category (+/-).	-1.3	0.5	5.3	-3.4	-5.8	6.7	-0.3	-2.2	0.1	5.7
Return, Tax-Adjusted (%)..	16.8	29.0	1.4	8.1	3.8	30.9	-7.5	18.2	14.8	2.9

PER SHARE DATA

	1996	1995	1994	1993	1992	1991	1990	1989	1988	1987
Dividends, Net Income ($).	0.43	0.39	0.30	0.36	0.34	0.39	0.47	0.48	0.42	0.49
Distrib'ns, Cap Gain ($) ...	0.56	0.37	1.17	0.87	0.12	1.84	0.01	0.83	0.32	0.64
Net Asset Value ($)	23.74	20.90	16.63	17.41	16.91	16.57	13.88	15.30	13.72	12.39
Expense Ratio (%)........	1.01	0.97	1.01	1.00	0.91	0.98	1.00	1.00	1.00	1.00
Yield (%)	1.76	1.83	1.68	1.96	1.99	2.11	3.38	2.97	2.99	3.76
Portfolio Turnover (%).....	27	34	53	35	37	64	23	30	16	20
Total Assets (Millions $) ...	255	174	108	108	78	39	29	36	26	14

PORTFOLIO (as of 9/30/96)

Portfolio Manager: Mike Harhai - 1993

Investm't Category: Growth & Income
- ✔ Domestic
- ✔ Foreign
- Asset Allocation
- Index
- Sector
- State Specific

Investment Style
- ✔ Large-Cap Growth
- Mid-Cap Growth
- Small-Cap Growth
- ✔ Large-Cap Value
- Mid-Cap Value
- Small-Cap Value

Portfolio
6.8% cash	0.0% corp bonds
93.2% stocks	0.0% gov't bonds
0.0% preferred	0.0% muni bonds
0.0% conv't/warrants	0.0% other

SHAREHOLDER INFORMATION

Minimum Investment
Initial: $1,000   Subsequent: $50

Minimum IRA Investment
Initial: $250   Subsequent: $50

Maximum Fees
Load: none   12b-1: none
Other: none

Distributions
Income: quarterly   Capital Gains: Dec

Exchange Options
Number Per Year: 4   Fee: none
Telephone: yes (money market fund available)

Services
IRA, pension, auto exchange, auto invest, auto withdraw

Guide to Low-Load Mutual Funds

INVESCO Worldwide Communications (ISWCX)

International Stock

P.O. Box 173706
Denver, CO 80217
800-525-8085, 303-930-6300
www.invesco.com

PERFORMANCE

fund inception date: 8/1/94

	3yr Annual	5yr Annual	10yr Annual	Bull	Bear
Return (%)	na	na	na	na	na
Differ from Category (+/-)	na	na	na	na	na

Total Risk	Standard Deviation	Category Risk	Risk Index	Beta
na	na	na	na	na

	1996	1995	1994	1993	1992	1991	1990	1989	1988	1987
Return (%)	16.8	27.3	—	—	—	—	—	—	—	—
Differ from Category (+/-)	2.0	18.2	—	—	—	—	—	—	—	—
Return, Tax-Adjusted (%)	13.9	23.3	—	—	—	—	—	—	—	—

PER SHARE DATA

	1996	1995	1994	1993	1992	1991	1990	1989	1988	1987
Dividends, Net Income ($)	0.13	0.16	—	—	—	—	—	—	—	—
Distrib'ns, Cap Gain ($)	1.01	1.24	—	—	—	—	—	—	—	—
Net Asset Value ($)	12.63	11.83	—	—	—	—	—	—	—	—
Expense Ratio (%)	1.66	1.95	—	—	—	—	—	—	—	—
Yield (%)	0.95	1.22	—	—	—	—	—	—	—	—
Portfolio Turnover (%)	157	215	—	—	—	—	—	—	—	—
Total Assets (Millions $)	55	31	—	—	—	—	—	—	—	—

PORTFOLIO (as of 9/30/96)

Portfolio Manager: Jeffrey G. Morris - 1996

Investm't Category: International Stock

✔ Domestic	Index
✔ Foreign	✔ Sector
Asset Allocation	State Specific

Investment Style

Large-Cap Growth	Large-Cap Value
Mid-Cap Growth	Mid-Cap Value
Small-Cap Growth	Small-Cap Value

Portfolio

24.2% cash	0.0% corp bonds
75.8% stocks	0.0% gov't bonds
0.0% preferred	0.0% muni bonds
0.0% conv't/warrants	0.0% other

SHAREHOLDER INFORMATION

Minimum Investment
Initial: $1,000   Subsequent: $50

Minimum IRA Investment
Initial: $250   Subsequent: $50

Maximum Fees
Load: none   12b-1: 0.25%
Other: none

Distributions
Income: annual   Capital Gains: Dec

Exchange Options
Number Per Year: 4   Fee: none
Telephone: yes (money market fund available)

Services
IRA, pension, auto exchange, auto invest, auto withdraw

Janus Balanced (JABAX)

Balanced

100 Fillmore St.
Suite 300
Denver, CO 80206
800-525-3713, 303-333-3863
www.janusfunds.com

PERFORMANCE

fund inception date: 9/1/92

	3yr Annual	5yr Annual	10yr Annual	Bull	Bear
Return (%)	13.6	na	na	48.1	-2.5
Differ from Category (+/-)	1.9 abv av	na	na	3.0 abv av	3.2 high

Total Risk	Standard Deviation	Category Risk	Risk Index	Beta
blw av	5.4%	low	0.8	0.48

	1996	1995	1994	1993	1992	1991	1990	1989	1988	1987
Return (%)	15.3	27.3	0.0	10.5	—	—	—	—	—	—
Differ from Category (+/-)	1.1	2.7	1.6	-3.9	—	—	—	—	—	—
Return, Tax-Adjusted (%)	11.6	23.6	-1.9	9.7	—	—	—	—	—	—

PER SHARE DATA

	1996	1995	1994	1993	1992	1991	1990	1989	1988	1987
Dividends, Net Income ($)	0.31	1.06	0.56	0.22	—	—	—	—	—	—
Distrib'ns, Cap Gain ($)	1.34	0.00	0.00	0.00	—	—	—	—	—	—
Net Asset Value ($)	14.14	13.72	11.63	12.19	—	—	—	—	—	—
Expense Ratio (%)	na	1.35	1.42	1.70	—	—	—	—	—	—
Yield (%)	2.00	na	na	1.80	—	—	—	—	—	—
Portfolio Turnover (%)	na	185	167	131	—	—	—	—	—	—
Total Assets (Millions $)	224	138	93	77	—	—	—	—	—	—

PORTFOLIO (as of 9/30/96)

Portfolio Manager: Blaine P. Rollins - 1996

Investm't Category: Balanced

✔ Domestic	Index
Foreign	Sector
Asset Allocation	State Specific

Investment Style

Large-Cap Growth	Large-Cap Value
Mid-Cap Growth	Mid-Cap Value
Small-Cap Growth	Small-Cap Value

Portfolio

9.1% cash	17.9% corp bonds
50.9% stocks	20.0% gov't bonds
0.9% preferred	0.0% muni bonds
1.4% conv't/warrants	0.0% other

SHAREHOLDER INFORMATION

Minimum Investment
Initial: $2,500   Subsequent: $100

Minimum IRA Investment
Initial: $500   Subsequent: $100

Maximum Fees
Load: none   12b-1: none
Other: none

Distributions
Income: quarterly   Capital Gains: Dec

Exchange Options
Number Per Year: no limit   Fee: $5 (first 4 free)
Telephone: yes (money market fund available)

Services
IRA, pension, auto exchange, auto invest, auto withdraw

Janus Enterprise (JAENX)

Aggressive Growth

100 Fillmore St.
Suite 300
Denver, CO 80206
800-525-3713, 303-333-3863
www.janusfunds.com

PERFORMANCE

fund inception date: 9/1/92

	3yr Annual	5yr Annual	10yr Annual	Bull	Bear
Return (%)	15.6	na	na	65.7	-6.6
Differ from Category (+/-)	-0.2 av	na	na	-5.4 av	4.0 abv av

Total Risk	Standard Deviation	Category Risk	Risk Index	Beta
high	14.5%	av	1.0	0.78

	1996	1995	1994	1993	1992	1991	1990	1989	1988	1987
Return (%)	11.6	27.2	8.9	15.6	—	—	—	—	—	—
Differ from Category (+/-)	-7.5	-7.1	8.9	-3.7	—	—	—	—	—	—
Return, Tax-Adjusted (%)	10.3	24.1	7.5	14.8	—	—	—	—	—	—

PER SHARE DATA

	1996	1995	1994	1993	1992	1991	1990	1989	1988	1987
Dividends, Net Income ($)	0.00	1.63	0.51	0.01	—	—	—	—	—	—
Distrib'ns, Cap Gain ($)	1.27	0.16	0.37	0.54	—	—	—	—	—	—
Net Asset Value ($)	29.34	27.44	22.98	21.92	—	—	—	—	—	—
Expense Ratio (%)	na	1.26	1.25	1.36	—	—	—	—	—	—
Yield (%)	0.00	na	na	0.04	—	—	—	—	—	—
Portfolio Turnover (%)	na	194	193	201	—	—	—	—	—	—
Total Assets (Millions $)	735	498	354	258	—	—	—	—	—	—

PORTFOLIO (as of 9/30/96)

Portfolio Manager: James P. Goff - 1992

Investm't Category: Aggressive Growth
- ✔ Domestic
- ✔ Foreign
-   Asset Allocation
-   Index
-   Sector
-   State Specific

Investment Style
Large-Cap Growth	Large-Cap Value
Mid-Cap Growth	Mid-Cap Value
✔ Small-Cap Growth	Small-Cap Value

Portfolio
7.2% cash	0.0% corp bonds
91.5% stocks	0.0% gov't bonds
0.0% preferred	0.0% muni bonds
1.3% conv't/warrants	0.0% other

SHAREHOLDER INFORMATION

Minimum Investment
Initial: $2,500   Subsequent: $100

Minimum IRA Investment
Initial: $500   Subsequent: $100

Maximum Fees
Load: none   12b-1: none
Other: none

Distributions
Income: Dec   Capital Gains: Dec

Exchange Options
Number Per Year: no limit Fee: $5 (first 4 free)
Telephone: yes (money market fund available)

Services
IRA, pension, auto exchange, auto invest, auto withdraw

Janus Federal Tax-Exempt (JATEX)

Tax-Exempt Bond

100 Fillmore St.
Suite 300
Denver, CO 80206
800-525-3713, 303-333-3863
www.janusfunds.com

PERFORMANCE

fund inception date: 5/3/93

	3yr Annual	5yr Annual	10yr Annual	Bull	Bear
Return (%)	3.8	na	na	19.1	-7.3
Differ from Category (+/-)	-0.4 blw av	na	na	0.7 av	-1.9 low

Total Risk	Standard Deviation	Category Risk	Risk Index	Avg Mat
blw av	5.9%	abv av	1.1	16.7 yrs

	1996	1995	1994	1993	1992	1991	1990	1989	1988	1987
Return (%)	4.7	15.8	-7.8	—	—	—	—	—	—	—
Differ from Category (+/-)	1.0	0.6	-2.5	—	—	—	—	—	—	—
Return, Tax-Adjusted (%)	4.7	15.8	-7.8	—	—	—	—	—	—	—

PER SHARE DATA

	1996	1995	1994	1993	1992	1991	1990	1989	1988	1987
Dividends, Net Income ($)	0.36	0.36	0.36	—	—	—	—	—	—	—
Distrib'ns, Cap Gain ($)	0.00	0.00	0.00	—	—	—	—	—	—	—
Net Asset Value ($)	6.98	7.02	6.39	—	—	—	—	—	—	—
Expense Ratio (%)	na	0.70	0.65	—	—	—	—	—	—	—
Yield (%)	5.15	5.12	5.63	—	—	—	—	—	—	—
Portfolio Turnover (%)	na	164	160	—	—	—	—	—	—	—
Total Assets (Millions $)	47	32	24	—	—	—	—	—	—	—

PORTFOLIO (as of 9/30/96)

Portfolio Manager: Darrell Watters - 1996

Investm't Category: Tax-Exempt Bond

✔ Domestic   Index
   Foreign   Sector
   Asset Allocation   State Specific

Investment Style

Large-Cap Growth   Large-Cap Value
Mid-Cap Growth   Mid-Cap Value
Small-Cap Growth   Small-Cap Value

Portfolio

0.0%	cash	0.0%	corp bonds
0.0%	stocks	0.0%	gov't bonds
0.0%	preferred	101.3%	muni bonds
0.0%	conv't/warrants	2.3%	other

SHAREHOLDER INFORMATION

Minimum Investment
Initial: $2,500   Subsequent: $100

Minimum IRA Investment
Initial: na   Subsequent: na

Maximum Fees
Load: none   12b-1: none
Other: none

Distributions
Income: monthly   Capital Gains: Dec

Exchange Options
Number Per Year: no limit   Fee: $5 (first 4 free)
Telephone: yes (money market fund available)

Services
auto exchange, auto invest, auto withdraw

Janus Flexible Income

(JAFIX)

Corporate Bond

100 Fillmore St.
Suite 300
Denver, CO 80206
800-525-3713, 303-333-3863
www.janusfunds.com

PERFORMANCE

fund inception date: 7/7/87

	3yr Annual	5yr Annual	10yr Annual	Bull	Bear
Return (%)	7.9	10.2	na	29.0	-5.0
Differ from Category (+/-)	1.6 high	1.9 high	na	4.2 abv av	0.1 av

Total Risk	Standard Deviation	Category Risk	Risk Index	Avg Mat
blw av	4.9%	abv av	1.1	7.5 yrs

	1996	1995	1994	1993	1992	1991	1990	1989	1988	1987
Return (%)	6.8	21.1	-3.0	15.6	11.8	25.9	-4.7	4.1	10.7	—
Differ from Category (+/-)	1.6	3.1	0.1	3.8	2.9	8.7	-8.7	-5.3	1.4	—
Return, Tax-Adjusted (%)	3.8	17.8	-5.9	11.7	8.2	21.4	-8.6	0.0	6.9	—

PER SHARE DATA

	1996	1995	1994	1993	1992	1991	1990	1989	1988	1987
Dividends, Net Income ($)	0.73	0.72	0.71	0.75	0.79	0.89	0.90	0.97	0.93	—
Distrib'ns, Cap Gain ($)	0.01	0.00	0.00	0.22	0.02	0.00	0.00	0.07	0.00	—
Net Asset Value ($)	9.69	9.81	8.75	9.74	9.31	9.09	8.00	9.35	9.99	—
Expense Ratio (%)	na	0.96	0.93	1.00	1.00	1.00	1.00	1.00	1.00	—
Yield (%)	7.52	7.33	8.11	7.53	8.46	9.79	11.25	10.29	9.30	—
Portfolio Turnover (%)	na	250	137	201	210	88	96	75	76	—
Total Assets (Millions $)	622	620	353	469	207	71	13	18	9	—

PORTFOLIO (as of 9/30/96)

Portfolio Manager: Ronald V. Speaker - 1991

Investm't Category: Corporate Bond

✔ Domestic	Index
✔ Foreign	Sector
Asset Allocation	State Specific

Investment Style

Large-Cap Growth	Large-Cap Value
Mid-Cap Growth	Mid-Cap Value
Small-Cap Growth	Small-Cap Value

Portfolio

6.9% cash	83.5% corp bonds
0.0% stocks	6.0% gov't bonds
2.3% preferred	0.0% muni bonds
1.3% conv't/warrants	0.0% other

SHAREHOLDER INFORMATION

Minimum Investment
Initial: $2,500   Subsequent: $100

Minimum IRA Investment
Initial: $500   Subsequent: $100

Maximum Fees
Load: none   12b-1: none
Other: none

Distributions
Income: monthly   Capital Gains: Dec

Exchange Options
Number Per Year: no limit   Fee: $5 (first 4 free)
Telephone: yes (money market fund available)

Services
IRA, pension, auto exchange, auto invest, auto withdraw

Janus Fund (JANSX)

Growth

100 Fillmore St.
Suite 300
Denver, CO 80206
800-525-3713, 303-333-3863
www.janusfunds.com

PERFORMANCE

	3yr Annual	5yr Annual	10yr Annual	Bull	Bear
Return (%)	15.2	12.6	16.4	59.0	-6.6
Differ from Category (+/-)	-0.5 av	-1.7 blw av	2.5 high	-3.4 av	0.1 av

Total Risk	Standard Deviation	Category Risk	Risk Index	Beta
av	8.6%	low	0.8	0.79

	1996	1995	1994	1993	1992	1991	1990	1989	1988	1987
Return (%).	19.6	29.4	-1.2	10.9	6.8	42.7	-0.8	46.3	16.5	4.1
Differ from Category (+/-) .	-0.5	-0.9	-0.9	-3.1	-5.0	6.7	5.3	20.2	-1.6	2.1
Return, Tax-Adjusted (%). .	15.7	27.0	-1.8	8.6	4.8	40.3	-1.7	39.5	14.3	-2.7

PER SHARE DATA

	1996	1995	1994	1993	1992	1991	1990	1989	1988	1987
Dividends, Net Income ($).	0.20	0.77	0.00	0.38	0.29	0.18	0.30	0.19	0.56	0.98
Distrib'ns, Cap Gain ($) . . .	2.91	0.49	0.38	0.94	0.90	0.90	0.00	2.50	0.00	1.60
Net Asset Value ($)	24.45	23.04	18.78	19.39	18.68	18.60	13.79	14.21	11.55	10.39
Expense Ratio (%).	na	0.87	0.91	0.92	0.97	0.98	1.02	0.92	0.98	1.01
Yield (%)	0.73	na	0.00	1.86	1.48	0.92	2.17	1.13	4.84	na
Portfolio Turnover (%).	na	118	139	127	153	132	307	205	175	214
Total Assets (Millions $) .	16,096	12,466	9,400	9,199	5,831	2,992	1,156	704	377	377

PORTFOLIO (as of 9/30/96)

Portfolio Manager: James P. Craig III - 1986

Investm't Category: Growth
- ✔ Domestic
- ✔ Foreign
- Asset Allocation

- Index
- Sector
- State Specific

Investment Style
- ✔ Large-Cap Growth
- Mid-Cap Growth
- Small-Cap Growth

- ✔ Large-Cap Value
- Mid-Cap Value
- Small-Cap Value

Portfolio
17.0%	cash	0.0%	corp bonds
83.0%	stocks	0.0%	gov't bonds
0.0%	preferred	0.0%	muni bonds
0.0%	conv't/warrants	0.0%	other

SHAREHOLDER INFORMATION

Minimum Investment
Initial: $2,500   Subsequent: $100

Minimum IRA Investment
Initial: $500   Subsequent: $100

Maximum Fees
Load: none   12b-1: none
Other: none

Distributions
Income: Dec   Capital Gains: Dec

Exchange Options
Number Per Year: no limit   Fee: $5 (first 4 free)
Telephone: yes (money market fund available)

Services
IRA, pension, auto exchange, auto invest, auto withdraw

Janus Growth & Income
(JAGIX)
Growth & Income

100 Fillmore St.
Suite 300
Denver, CO 80206
800-525-3713, 303-333-3863
www.janusfunds.com

PERFORMANCE

fund inception date: 5/15/91

	3yr Annual	5yr Annual	10yr Annual	Bull	Bear
Return (%)	17.7	12.9	na	74.7	-10.3
Differ from Category (+/-)	2.4 abv av	-1.0 blw av	na	14.9 high	-3.9 low

Total Risk	Standard Deviation	Category Risk	Risk Index	Beta
abv av	11.8%	high	1.3	1.10

	1996	1995	1994	1993	1992	1991	1990	1989	1988	1987
Return (%)	26.0	36.3	-4.9	6.6	5.3	—	—	—	—	—
Differ from Category (+/-)	6.3	6.2	-3.6	-7.2	-5.4	—	—	—	—	—
Return, Tax-Adjusted (%)	22.6	30.9	-5.2	5.5	4.8	—	—	—	—	—

PER SHARE DATA

	1996	1995	1994	1993	1992	1991	1990	1989	1988	1987
Dividends, Net Income ($)	0.11	1.01	0.09	0.16	0.15	—	—	—	—	—
Distrib'ns, Cap Gain ($)	1.86	1.23	0.00	0.33	0.00	—	—	—	—	—
Net Asset Value ($)	19.05	16.67	13.88	14.69	14.24	—	—	—	—	—
Expense Ratio (%)	na	1.19	1.22	1.28	1.52	—	—	—	—	—
Yield (%)	0.52	na	na	1.06	1.05	—	—	—	—	—
Portfolio Turnover (%)	na	195	123	138	120	—	—	—	—	—
Total Assets (Millions $)	1,125	632	456	513	310	—	—	—	—	—

PORTFOLIO (as of 9/30/96)

Portfolio Manager: Thomas F. Marsico - 1991

Investm't Category: Growth & Income
- ✔ Domestic
- ✔ Foreign
-   Asset Allocation
-   Index
-   Sector
-   State Specific

Investment Style
- ✔ Large-Cap Growth
- ✔ Mid-Cap Growth
-   Small-Cap Growth
- ✔ Large-Cap Value
- ✔ Mid-Cap Value
-   Small-Cap Value

Portfolio
5.3% cash	1.3% corp bonds
84.8% stocks	0.0% gov't bonds
7.0% preferred	0.0% muni bonds
1.7% conv't/warrants	0.0% other

SHAREHOLDER INFORMATION

Minimum Investment
Initial: $2,500   Subsequent: $100

Minimum IRA Investment
Initial: $500   Subsequent: $100

Maximum Fees
Load: none   12b-1: none
Other: none

Distributions
Income: quarterly   Capital Gains: Dec

Exchange Options
Number Per Year: no limit   Fee: $5 (first 4 free)
Telephone: yes (money market fund available)

Services
IRA, pension, auto exchange, auto invest, auto withdraw

Janus High Yield (JAHYX)
Corporate High-Yield Bond

100 Fillmore St.
Suite 300
Denver, CO 80206
800-525-3713, 303-333-3863
www.janusfunds.com

PERFORMANCE

fund inception date: 12/29/95

	3yr Annual	5yr Annual	10yr Annual	Bull	Bear
Return (%)	na	na	na	na	na
Differ from Category (+/-)	na	na	na	na	na

Total Risk	Standard Deviation	Category Risk	Risk Index	Avg Mat
na	na	na	na	6.9 yrs

	1996	1995	1994	1993	1992	1991	1990	1989	1988	1987
Return (%)	24.0	—	—	—	—	—	—	—	—	—
Differ from Category (+/-)	8.7	—	—	—	—	—	—	—	—	—
Return, Tax-Adjusted (%)	19.8	—	—	—	—	—	—	—	—	—

PER SHARE DATA

	1996	1995	1994	1993	1992	1991	1990	1989	1988	1987
Dividends, Net Income ($)	0.97	—	—	—	—	—	—	—	—	—
Distrib'ns, Cap Gain ($)	0.11	—	—	—	—	—	—	—	—	—
Net Asset Value ($)	11.23	—	—	—	—	—	—	—	—	—
Expense Ratio (%)	na	—	—	—	—	—	—	—	—	—
Yield (%)	8.55	—	—	—	—	—	—	—	—	—
Portfolio Turnover (%)	na	—	—	—	—	—	—	—	—	—
Total Assets (Millions $)	229	—	—	—	—	—	—	—	—	—

PORTFOLIO (as of 9/30/96)

Portfolio Manager: Ronald V. Speaker - 1995

Investm't Category: Corp. High-Yield Bond

✔ Domestic   Index
✔ Foreign   Sector
  Asset Allocation State Specific

Investment Style

Large-Cap Growth	Large-Cap Value
Mid-Cap Growth	Mid-Cap Value
Small-Cap Growth	Small-Cap Value

Portfolio

15.2% cash	82.1% corp bonds
0.2% stocks	0.0% gov't bonds
0.3% preferred	0.0% muni bonds
2.3% conv't/warrants	0.0% other

SHAREHOLDER INFORMATION

Minimum Investment
Initial: $2,500   Subsequent: $100

Minimum IRA Investment
Initial: $500   Subsequent: $100

Maximum Fees
Load: none   12b-1: none
Other: none

Distributions
Income: monthly   Capital Gains: Dec

Exchange Options
Number Per Year: no limit   Fee: $5 (first 4 free)
Telephone: yes (money market fund available)

Services
IRA, pension, auto exchange, auto invest, auto withdraw

Janus Interm Gov't Sec

(JAIGX)

Government Bond

100 Fillmore St.
Suite 300
Denver, CO 80206
800-525-3713, 303-333-3863
www.janusfunds.com

fund inception date: 7/26/91

PERFORMANCE

	3yr Annual	5yr Annual	10yr Annual	Bull	Bear
Return (%)	3.5	3.5	na	14.1	-3.7
Differ from Category (+/-)	-1.4 low	-3.1 low	na	-7.9 low	2.7 av

Total Risk	Standard Deviation	Category Risk	Risk Index	Avg Mat
low	3.5%	av	0.9	3.4 yrs

	1996	1995	1994	1993	1992	1991	1990	1989	1988	1987
Return (%)	0.5	13.1	-2.4	2.4	4.8	—	—	—	—	—
Differ from Category (+/-)	-1.0	-6.5	2.0	-9.2	-1.9	—	—	—	—	—
Return, Tax-Adjusted (%)	-1.6	10.6	-4.5	0.8	2.2	—	—	—	—	—

PER SHARE DATA

	1996	1995	1994	1993	1992	1991	1990	1989	1988	1987
Dividends, Net Income ($)	0.26	0.29	0.26	0.21	0.26	—	—	—	—	—
Distrib'ns, Cap Gain ($)	0.00	0.00	0.00	0.00	0.11	—	—	—	—	—
Net Asset Value ($)	4.81	5.05	4.74	5.13	5.22	—	—	—	—	—
Expense Ratio (%)	na	0.65	0.65	0.91	1.00	—	—	—	—	—
Yield (%)	5.40	5.74	5.48	4.09	4.87	—	—	—	—	—
Portfolio Turnover (%)	na	252	304	371	270	—	—	—	—	—
Total Assets (Millions $)	23	39	34	57	61	—	—	—	—	—

PORTFOLIO (as of 9/30/96)

Portfolio Manager: Sandy Rufenacht - 1996

Investm't Category: Government Bond
✔ Domestic   Index
  Foreign   Sector
  Asset Allocation State Specific

Investment Style
Large-Cap Growth   Large-Cap Value
Mid-Cap Growth   Mid-Cap Value
Small-Cap Growth   Small-Cap Value

Portfolio
1.9% cash	0.0% corp bonds
0.0% stocks	98.1% gov't bonds
0.0% preferred	0.0% muni bonds
0.0% conv't/warrants	0.0% other

SHAREHOLDER INFORMATION

Minimum Investment
Initial: $2,500   Subsequent: $100

Minimum IRA Investment
Initial: $500   Subsequent: $100

Maximum Fees
Load: none   12b-1: none
Other: none

Distributions
Income: monthly   Capital Gains: Dec

Exchange Options
Number Per Year: no limit   Fee: $5 (first 4 free)
Telephone: yes (money market fund available)

Services
IRA, pension, auto exchange, auto invest, auto withdraw

Janus Mercury (JAMRX)

Growth

100 Fillmore St.
Suite 300
Denver, CO 80206
800-525-3713, 303-333-3863
www.janusfunds.com

PERFORMANCE

fund inception date: 5/3/93

	3yr Annual	5yr Annual	10yr Annual	Bull	Bear
Return (%)	21.9	na	na	83.6	-6.3
Differ from Category (+/-)	6.2 high	na	na	21.2 high	0.4 av

Total Risk	Standard Deviation	Category Risk	Risk Index	Beta
high	12.8%	high	1.2	0.85

	1996	1995	1994	1993	1992	1991	1990	1989	1988	1987
Return (%)	17.6	33.0	15.8	—	—	—	—	—	—	—
Differ from Category (+/-)	-2.5	2.7	16.1	—	—	—	—	—	—	—
Return, Tax-Adjusted (%)	13.4	27.2	15.0	—	—	—	—	—	—	—

PER SHARE DATA

	1996	1995	1994	1993	1992	1991	1990	1989	1988	1987
Dividends, Net Income ($)	0.07	1.75	0.16	—	—	—	—	—	—	—
Distrib'ns, Cap Gain ($)	2.28	0.30	0.10	—	—	—	—	—	—	—
Net Asset Value ($)	16.52	16.04	13.61	—	—	—	—	—	—	—
Expense Ratio (%)	na	1.14	1.33	—	—	—	—	—	—	—
Yield (%)	0.37	na	na	—	—	—	—	—	—	—
Portfolio Turnover (%)	na	201	283	—	—	—	—	—	—	—
Total Assets (Millions $)	2,080	1,596	690	—	—	—	—	—	—	—

PORTFOLIO (as of 9/30/96)

Portfolio Manager: Warren B. Lammert - 1993

Investm't Category: Growth
✔ Domestic   Index
✔ Foreign   Sector
   Asset Allocation   State Specific

Investment Style
   Large-Cap Growth   Large-Cap Value
✔ Mid-Cap Growth   Mid-Cap Value
   Small-Cap Growth   Small-Cap Value

Portfolio
13.0% cash   0.0% corp bonds
86.8% stocks   0.0% gov't bonds
 0.2% preferred   0.0% muni bonds
 0.0% conv't/warrants 0.0% other

SHAREHOLDER INFORMATION

Minimum Investment
Initial: $2,500   Subsequent: $100

Minimum IRA Investment
Initial: $500   Subsequent: $100

Maximum Fees
Load: none   12b-1: none
Other: none

Distributions
Income: Dec   Capital Gains: Dec

Exchange Options
Number Per Year: no limit   Fee: $5 (first 4 free)
Telephone: yes (money market fund available)

Services
IRA, pension, auto exchange, auto invest, auto withdraw

Janus Olympus (JAOLX)

Aggressive Growth

100 Fillmore St.
Suite 300
Denver, CO 80206
800-525-3713, 303-333-3863
www.janusfunds.com

PERFORMANCE

fund inception date: 12/29/95

	3yr Annual	5yr Annual	10yr Annual	Bull	Bear
Return (%)	na	na	na	na	na
Differ from Category (+/-)	na	na	na	na	na

Total Risk	Standard Deviation	Category Risk	Risk Index	Beta
na	na	na	na	na

	1996	1995	1994	1993	1992	1991	1990	1989	1988	1987
Return (%)	21.7	—	—	—	—	—	—	—	—	—
Differ from Category (+/-)	2.6	—	—	—	—	—	—	—	—	—
Return, Tax-Adjusted (%)	21.3	—	—	—	—	—	—	—	—	—

PER SHARE DATA

	1996	1995	1994	1993	1992	1991	1990	1989	1988	1987
Dividends, Net Income ($)	0.12	—	—	—	—	—	—	—	—	—
Distrib'ns, Cap Gain ($)	0.00	—	—	—	—	—	—	—	—	—
Net Asset Value ($)	14.48	—	—	—	—	—	—	—	—	—
Expense Ratio (%)	na	—	—	—	—	—	—	—	—	—
Yield (%)	0.82	—	—	—	—	—	—	—	—	—
Portfolio Turnover (%)	na	—	—	—	—	—	—	—	—	—
Total Assets (Millions $)	430	—	—	—	—	—	—	—	—	—

PORTFOLIO (as of 9/30/96)

Portfolio Manager: Scott W. Schoelzel - 1995

Investm't Category: Aggressive Growth
- ✔ Domestic
- ✔ Foreign
- Asset Allocation
- Index
- Sector
- State Specific

Investment Style
- Large-Cap Growth
- Mid-Cap Growth
- Small-Cap Growth
- Large-Cap Value
- Mid-Cap Value
- Small-Cap Value

Portfolio

19.7% cash	0.0% corp bonds	
80.3% stocks	0.0% gov't bonds	
0.0% preferred	0.0% muni bonds	
0.0% conv't/warrants	0.0% other	

SHAREHOLDER INFORMATION

Minimum Investment
Initial: $2,500   Subsequent: $100

Minimum IRA Investment
Initial: $500   Subsequent: $100

Maximum Fees
Load: none   12b-1: none
Other: none

Distributions
Income: Dec   Capital Gains: Dec

Exchange Options
Number Per Year: no limit   Fee: $5 (first 4 free)
Telephone: yes (money market fund available)

Services
IRA, pension, auto exchange, auto invest, auto withdraw

Janus Overseas (JAOSX)

International Stock

100 Fillmore St.
Suite 300
Denver, CO 80206
800-525-3713, 303-333-3863
www.janusfunds.com

PERFORMANCE
fund inception date: 5/2/94

	3yr Annual	5yr Annual	10yr Annual	Bull	Bear
Return (%)	na	na	na	61.2	na
Differ from Category (+/-)	na	na	na	36.9 high	na

Total Risk	Standard Deviation	Category Risk	Risk Index	Beta
na	na	na	na	na

	1996	1995	1994	1993	1992	1991	1990	1989	1988	1987
Return (%)	28.8	22.0	—	—	—	—	—	—	—	—
Differ from Category (+/-)	14.0	12.9	—	—	—	—	—	—	—	—
Return, Tax-Adjusted (%)	28.0	21.2	—	—	—	—	—	—	—	—

PER SHARE DATA

	1996	1995	1994	1993	1992	1991	1990	1989	1988	1987
Dividends, Net Income ($)	0.04	0.16	—	—	—	—	—	—	—	—
Distrib'ns, Cap Gain ($)	0.25	0.05	—	—	—	—	—	—	—	—
Net Asset Value ($)	15.22	12.05	—	—	—	—	—	—	—	—
Expense Ratio (%)	na	1.76	—	—	—	—	—	—	—	—
Yield (%)	0.25	na	—	—	—	—	—	—	—	—
Portfolio Turnover (%)	na	188	—	—	—	—	—	—	—	—
Total Assets (Millions $)	886	129	—	—	—	—	—	—	—	—

PORTFOLIO (as of 9/30/96)

Portfolio Manager: Helen Young Hayes - 1994

Investm't Category: International Stock

Domestic	Index
✔ Foreign	Sector
Asset Allocation	State Specific

Investment Style

Large-Cap Growth	Large-Cap Value
Mid-Cap Growth	Mid-Cap Value
Small-Cap Growth	Small-Cap Value

Portfolio

18.9% cash	0.0% corp bonds
79.8% stocks	0.0% gov't bonds
1.3% preferred	0.0% muni bonds
0.0% conv't/warrants	0.0% other

SHAREHOLDER INFORMATION

Minimum Investment
Initial: $2,500   Subsequent: $100

Minimum IRA Investment
Initial: $500   Subsequent: $100

Maximum Fees
Load: none   12b-1: none
Other: none

Distributions
Income: Dec   Capital Gains: Dec

Exchange Options
Number Per Year: no limit   Fee: $5 (first 4 free)
Telephone: yes (money market fund available)

Services
IRA, pension, auto exchange, auto invest, auto withdraw

Janus Short-Term Bond

(JASBX)

Corporate Bond

100 Fillmore St.
Suite 300
Denver, CO 80206
800-525-3713, 303-333-3863
www.janusfunds.com

PERFORMANCE

fund inception date: 9/1/92

	3yr Annual	5yr Annual	10yr Annual	Bull	Bear
Return (%)	4.7	na	na	15.5	-1.6
Differ from Category (+/-)	-1.6 blw av	na	na	-9.3 low	3.5 high

Total Risk	Standard Deviation	Category Risk	Risk Index	Avg Mat
low	2.1%	low	0.5	2.2 yrs

	1996	1995	1994	1993	1992	1991	1990	1989	1988	1987
Return (%)	6.1	7.9	0.3	6.1	—	—	—	—	—	—
Differ from Category (+/-)	0.9	-10.1	3.4	-5.7	—	—	—	—	—	—
Return, Tax-Adjusted (%)	3.8	5.5	-2.1	4.1	—	—	—	—	—	—

PER SHARE DATA

	1996	1995	1994	1993	1992	1991	1990	1989	1988	1987
Dividends, Net Income ($)	0.16	0.17	0.18	0.14	—	—	—	—	—	—
Distrib'ns, Cap Gain ($)	0.00	0.00	0.00	0.01	—	—	—	—	—	—
Net Asset Value ($)	2.88	2.87	2.83	3.00	—	—	—	—	—	—
Expense Ratio (%)	na	0.66	0.65	0.83	—	—	—	—	—	—
Yield (%)	5.55	5.92	6.36	4.65	—	—	—	—	—	—
Portfolio Turnover (%)	na	337	346	372	—	—	—	—	—	—
Total Assets (Millions $)	42	46	45	53	—	—	—	—	—	—

PORTFOLIO (as of 9/30/96)

Portfolio Manager: Sandy Rufenacht - 1996

Investm't Category: Corporate Bond

✔ Domestic	Index
Foreign	Sector
Asset Allocation	State Specific

Investment Style

Large-Cap Growth	Large-Cap Value
Mid-Cap Growth	Mid-Cap Value
Small-Cap Growth	Small-Cap Value

Portfolio

31.7% cash	68.3% corp bonds
0.0% stocks	0.0% gov't bonds
0.0% preferred	0.0% muni bonds
0.0% conv't/warrants	0.0% other

SHAREHOLDER INFORMATION

Minimum Investment
Initial: $2,500   Subsequent: $100

Minimum IRA Investment
Initial: $500   Subsequent: $100

Maximum Fees
Load: none   12b-1: none
Other: none

Distributions
Income: monthly   Capital Gains: Dec

Exchange Options
Number Per Year: no limit   Fee: $5 (first 4 free)
Telephone: yes (money market fund available)

Services
IRA, pension, auto exchange, auto invest, auto withdraw

Janus Twenty (JAVLX)

Aggressive Growth

100 Fillmore St.
Suite 300
Denver, CO 80206
800-525-3713, 303-333-3863
www.janusfunds.com

PERFORMANCE   fund inception date: 4/26/85

	3yr Annual	5yr Annual	10yr Annual	Bull	Bear
Return (%)	17.5	11.3	16.5	80.3	-13.6
Differ from Category (+/-)	1.7 abv av	-4.0 blw av	1.5 abv av	9.2 abv av	-3.0 blw av

Total Risk	Standard Deviation	Category Risk	Risk Index	Beta
high	12.7%	blw av	0.9	1.18

	1996	1995	1994	1993	1992	1991	1990	1989	1988	1987
Return (%)	27.8	36.2	-6.8	3.4	1.9	69.2	0.5	50.8	19.0	-11.7
Differ from Category (+/-)	8.7	1.9	-6.8	-15.9	-9.8	17.1	5.9	22.4	2.6	-9.3
Return, Tax-Adjusted (%)	21.7	28.5	-6.9	2.4	1.3	68.3	0.0	49.5	15.5	-15.8

PER SHARE DATA

	1996	1995	1994	1993	1992	1991	1990	1989	1988	1987
Dividends, Net Income ($)	0.18	2.27	0.06	0.25	0.18	0.02	0.18	0.01	0.80	0.40
Distrib'ns, Cap Gain ($)	5.31	2.98	0.00	0.45	0.19	0.42	0.00	0.42	0.00	1.17
Net Asset Value ($)	27.47	25.67	22.71	24.42	24.29	24.19	14.56	14.66	10.01	9.08
Expense Ratio (%)	na	1.00	1.02	1.05	1.01	1.07	1.32	1.88	1.70	1.79
Yield (%)	0.54	na	na	1.00	0.73	0.08	1.23	0.06	7.99	3.90
Portfolio Turnover (%)	na	147	102	99	83	163	228	220	317	202
Total Assets (Millions $)	4,312	3,057	2,504	3,575	3,137	1,348	244	67	7	13

PORTFOLIO (as of 9/30/96)

Portfolio Manager: Thomas F. Marsico - 1988

Investm't Category: Aggressive Growth
✔ Domestic   Index
✔ Foreign   Sector
  Asset Allocation State Specific

Investment Style
✔ Large-Cap Growth   Large-Cap Value
  Mid-Cap Growth   Mid-Cap Value
  Small-Cap Growth   Small-Cap Value

Portfolio
  2.2% cash   1.4% corp bonds
 95.3% stocks   0.0% gov't bonds
  1.2% preferred   0.0% muni bonds
  0.0% conv't/warrants 0.0% other

SHAREHOLDER INFORMATION

Minimum Investment
Initial: $2,500   Subsequent: $100

Minimum IRA Investment
Initial: $500   Subsequent: $100

Maximum Fees
Load: none   12b-1: none
Other: none

Distributions
Income: Dec   Capital Gains: Dec

Exchange Options
Number Per Year: no limit   Fee: $5 (first 4 free)
Telephone: yes (money market fund available)

Services
IRA, pension, auto exchange, auto invest, auto withdraw

Janus Venture (JAVTX)

Aggressive Growth

100 Fillmore St.
Suite 300
Denver, CO 80206
800-525-3713, 303-333-3863
www.janusfunds.com

this fund is closed to new investors

PERFORMANCE

fund inception date: 4/26/85

	3yr Annual	5yr Annual	10yr Annual	Bull	Bear
Return (%)	12.9	11.0	15.8	52.8	-7.8
Differ from Category (+/-)	-2.9 blw av	-4.3 low	0.8 av	-18.3 blw av	2.8 abv av

Total Risk	Standard Deviation	Category Risk	Risk Index	Beta
high	14.1%	av	1.0	0.85

	1996	1995	1994	1993	1992	1991	1990	1989	1988	1987
Return (%)	8.0	26.4	5.4	9.0	7.4	47.8	-0.4	38.7	19.6	5.1
Differ from Category (+/-)	-11.1	-7.9	5.4	-10.3	-4.3	-4.3	5.0	10.3	3.2	7.5
Return, Tax-Adjusted (%)	5.2	21.2	3.7	6.1	6.0	44.7	-1.3	35.7	17.1	0.6

PER SHARE DATA

	1996	1995	1994	1993	1992	1991	1990	1989	1988	1987
Dividends, Net Income ($)	0.00	3.60	0.02	0.52	1.16	0.24	0.10	0.44	1.52	0.14
Distrib'ns, Cap Gain ($)	5.27	3.85	2.83	4.36	0.71	3.43	0.89	2.35	0.00	4.17
Net Asset Value ($)	53.06	54.10	48.68	48.88	49.30	47.63	34.71	35.85	27.85	24.55
Expense Ratio (%)	na	0.92	0.96	0.97	1.00	1.04	1.16	1.28	1.41	1.44
Yield (%)	0.00	na	na	0.97	2.31	0.47	0.28	1.15	5.45	0.48
Portfolio Turnover (%)	na	113	114	139	166	167	184	219	299	250
Total Assets (Millions $)	1,728	1,790	1,496	1,778	1,706	1,464	276	104	34	30

PORTFOLIO (as of 9/30/96)

Portfolio Manager: Warren B. Lammert, James P. Goff - 1993

Investm't Category: Aggressive Growth
- ✔ Domestic
- ✔ Foreign
- Asset Allocation
- Index
- Sector
- State Specific

Investment Style
- Large-Cap Growth
- Mid-Cap Growth
- ✔ Small-Cap Growth
- Large-Cap Value
- Mid-Cap Value
- Small-Cap Value

Portfolio
5.7% cash	0.0% corp bonds
92.5% stocks	0.0% gov't bonds
1.6% preferred	0.0% muni bonds
0.2% conv't/warrants	0.0% other

SHAREHOLDER INFORMATION

Minimum Investment
Initial: $2,500   Subsequent: $100

Minimum IRA Investment
Initial: $500   Subsequent: $100

Maximum Fees
Load: none   12b-1: none
Other: none

Distributions
Income: Dec   Capital Gains: Dec

Exchange Options
Number Per Year: no limit   Fee: $5 (first 4 free)
Telephone: yes (money market fund available)

Services
IRA, pension, auto exchange, auto invest, auto withdraw

Janus Worldwide (JAWWX)

International Stock

100 Fillmore St.
Suite 300
Denver, CO 80206
800-525-3713, 303-333-3863
www.janusfunds.com

PERFORMANCE

fund inception date: 5/15/91

	3yr Annual	5yr Annual	10yr Annual	Bull	Bear
Return (%)	16.8	17.4	na	62.8	-7.2
Differ from Category (+/-)	10.5 high	7.4 high	na	38.5 high	0.0 av

Total Risk	Standard Deviation	Category Risk	Risk Index	Beta
abv av	10.0%	blw av	1.0	0.69

	1996	1995	1994	1993	1992	1991	1990	1989	1988	1987
Return (%)	26.4	21.8	3.6	28.4	9.0	—	—	—	—	—
Differ from Category (+/-)	11.6	12.7	6.7	-11.2	12.8	—	—	—	—	—
Return, Tax-Adjusted (%)	24.1	20.1	1.6	27.3	8.5	—	—	—	—	—

PER SHARE DATA

	1996	1995	1994	1993	1992	1991	1990	1989	1988	1987
Dividends, Net Income ($)	0.15	0.26	0.53	0.27	0.22	—	—	—	—	—
Distrib'ns, Cap Gain ($)	2.04	1.06	1.00	0.37	0.00	—	—	—	—	—
Net Asset Value ($)	33.69	28.40	24.39	25.03	20.00	—	—	—	—	—
Expense Ratio (%)	na	1.24	1.12	1.32	1.73	—	—	—	—	—
Yield (%)	0.41	na	na	1.06	1.09	—	—	—	—	—
Portfolio Turnover (%)	na	142	158	124	147	—	—	—	—	—
Total Assets (Millions $)	4,897	1,975	1,542	935	208	—	—	—	—	—

PORTFOLIO (as of 9/30/96)

Portfolio Manager: Helen Young Hayes - 1991

Investm't Category: International Stock
✔ Domestic   Index
✔ Foreign   Sector
   Asset Allocation   State Specific

Investment Style
Large-Cap Growth   Large-Cap Value
Mid-Cap Growth   Mid-Cap Value
Small-Cap Growth   Small-Cap Value

Portfolio
11.2% cash   0.0% corp bonds
87.3% stocks   0.0% gov't bonds
1.5% preferred   0.0% muni bonds
0.0% conv't/warrants 0.0% other

SHAREHOLDER INFORMATION

Minimum Investment
Initial: $2,500   Subsequent: $100

Minimum IRA Investment
Initial: $500   Subsequent: $100

Maximum Fees
Load: none   12b-1: none
Other: none

Distributions
Income: Dec   Capital Gains: Dec

Exchange Options
Number Per Year: no limit   Fee: $5 (first 4 free)
Telephone: yes (money market fund available)

Services
IRA, pension, auto exchange, auto invest, auto withdraw

Japan Fund (SJPNX)

International Stock

Two International Place
Boston, MA 02110
800-225-2470, 617-295-1000
www.funds.scudder.com

PERFORMANCE

fund inception date: 3/30/62

	3yr Annual	5yr Annual	10yr Annual	Bull	Bear
Return (%)	-3.8	-1.8	3.4	-27.6	8.5
Differ from Category (+/-)	-10.1 low	-11.8 low	-5.2 low	-51.9 low	15.7 high

Total Risk	Standard Deviation	Category Risk	Risk Index	Beta
high	18.2%	high	1.8	0.23

	1996	1995	1994	1993	1992	1991	1990	1989	1988	1987
Return (%).............	-11.0	-9.1	10.0	23.6	-16.8	3.1	-16.4	11.6	19.4	33.0
Differ from Category (+/-)	-25.8	-18.2	13.1	-16.0	-13.0	-10.1	-6.3	-11.0	4.5	20.8
Return, Tax-Adjusted (%).	-11.4	-9.4	7.6	21.1	-16.8	2.0	-18.9	5.2	12.9	20.0

PER SHARE DATA

	1996	1995	1994	1993	1992	1991	1990	1989	1988	1987
Dividends, Net Income ($).	0.08	0.00	0.00	0.28	0.00	0.00	0.20	0.08	0.02	0.19
Distrib'ns, Cap Gain ($)...	0.00	0.11	0.85	0.39	0.00	0.41	0.99	3.59	3.88	9.08
Net Asset Value ($)......	8.33	9.44	10.51	10.33	8.90	10.69	10.76	14.27	16.24	16.97
Expense Ratio (%).........	na	1.21	1.08	1.25	1.42	1.26	1.05	1.02	1.01	0.90
Yield (%)	0.96	0.00	0.00	2.61	0.00	0.00	1.70	0.44	0.09	0.72
Portfolio Turnover (%).....	na	69	74	81	47	46	53	60	39	34
Total Assets (Millions $)...	413	550	585	471	409	334	313	400	403	349

PORTFOLIO (as of 9/30/96)

Portfolio Manager: Seung Kwak - 1988

Investm't Category: International Stock
- Domestic
- ✔ Foreign
- Asset Allocation
- Index
- Sector
- State Specific

Investment Style
- Large-Cap Growth
- Mid-Cap Growth
- Small-Cap Growth
- Large-Cap Value
- Mid-Cap Value
- Small-Cap Value

Portfolio
- 4.2% cash
- 90.0% stocks
- 0.0% preferred
- 5.8% conv't/warrants
- 0.0% corp bonds
- 0.0% gov't bonds
- 0.0% muni bonds
- 0.0% other

SHAREHOLDER INFORMATION

Minimum Investment
Initial: $1,000   Subsequent: $100

Minimum IRA Investment
Initial: $500   Subsequent: $50

Maximum Fees
Load: none   12b-1: none
Other: *f*

Distributions
Income: Dec   Capital Gains: Dec

Exchange Options
Number Per Year: no limit   Fee: none
Telephone: yes (money market fund available)

Services
IRA, pension, auto exchange, auto invest, auto withdraw

Jurika & Voyles Balanced /J
(JVBAX)
Balanced

1999 Harrison St.
Suite 700
Oakland, CA 94612
800-584-6878, 610-254-1000

PERFORMANCE

fund inception date: 3/9/92

	3yr Annual	5yr Annual	10yr Annual	Bull	Bear
Return (%)	12.3	na	na	44.8	-4.4
Differ from Category (+/-)	0.6 av	na	na	-0.3 av	1.3 abv av

Total Risk	Standard Deviation	Category Risk	Risk Index	Beta
av	8.0%	high	1.2	0.65

	1996	1995	1994	1993	1992	1991	1990	1989	1988	1987
Return (%)	15.4	25.4	-2.2	17.0	—	—	—	—	—	—
Differ from Category (+/-)	1.2	0.8	-0.6	2.6	—	—	—	—	—	—
Return, Tax-Adjusted (%)	11.5	22.8	-4.0	16.0	—	—	—	—	—	—

PER SHARE DATA

	1996	1995	1994	1993	1992	1991	1990	1989	1988	1987
Dividends, Net Income ($)	0.36	0.40	0.25	0.16	—	—	—	—	—	—
Distrib'ns, Cap Gain ($)	1.41	0.53	0.48	0.17	—	—	—	—	—	—
Net Asset Value ($)	14.43	14.07	11.98	13.00	—	—	—	—	—	—
Expense Ratio (%)	1.35	1.33	1.63	1.47	—	—	—	—	—	—
Yield (%)	2.27	2.73	2.00	1.21	—	—	—	—	—	—
Portfolio Turnover (%)	69	54	na	44	—	—	—	—	—	—
Total Assets (Millions $)	51	42	32	24	—	—	—	—	—	—

PORTFOLIO (as of 9/30/96)

Portfolio Manager: Bill Jurika, Glenn Voyles - 1992

Investm't Category: Balanced
✔ Domestic   Index
   Foreign   Sector
✔ Asset Allocation State Specific

Investment Style
Large-Cap Growth   Large-Cap Value
Mid-Cap Growth   Mid-Cap Value
Small-Cap Growth   Small-Cap Value

Portfolio
16.0% cash   0.0% corp bonds
56.0% stocks   0.0% gov't bonds
0.0% preferred   0.0% muni bonds
28.0% conv't/warrants 0.0% other

SHAREHOLDER INFORMATION

Minimum Investment
Initial: $250,000   Subsequent: $1,000

Minimum IRA Investment
Initial: $250,000   Subsequent: $1,000

Maximum Fees
Load: none   12b-1: none
Other: none

Distributions
Income: quarterly   Capital Gains: Dec

Exchange Options
Number Per Year: no limit   Fee: none
Telephone: yes (money market fund available)

Services
IRA, pension, auto invest, auto withdraw

Kaufmann (KAUFX)

Aggressive Growth

140 E. 45th St.
43rd Floor
New York, NY 10017
800-666-9181, 212-922-0123
www.kaufmann.com

PERFORMANCE

fund inception date: 2/21/86

	3yr Annual	5yr Annual	10yr Annual	Bull	Bear
Return (%)	21.7	18.8	19.3	94.4	-10.4
Differ from Category (+/-)	5.9 high	3.5 abv av	4.3 high	23.3 high	0.2 av

Total Risk	Standard Deviation	Category Risk	Risk Index	Beta
high	14.9%	av	1.0	0.90

	1996	1995	1994	1993	1992	1991	1990	1989	1988	1987
Return (%)	20.9	36.8	8.9	18.1	11.3	79.4	-6.2	46.8	58.5	-37.2
Differ from Category (+/-)	1.8	2.5	8.9	-1.2	-0.4	27.3	-0.8	18.4	42.1	-34.8
Return, Tax-Adjusted (%)	19.4	36.1	8.9	17.8	11.3	77.9	-6.2	46.8	58.5	-37.6

PER SHARE DATA

	1996	1995	1994	1993	1992	1991	1990	1989	1988	1987
Dividends, Net Income ($)	0.00	0.00	0.00	0.00	0.00	0.00	0.00	0.00	0.00	0.01
Distrib'ns, Cap Gain ($)	0.26	0.09	0.00	0.03	0.00	0.08	0.00	0.00	0.00	0.00
Net Asset Value ($)	5.84	5.05	3.76	3.45	2.95	2.65	1.53	1.63	1.11	0.70
Expense Ratio (%)	na	2.16	2.29	2.53	2.94	3.64	3.45	2.36	2.00	2.00
Yield (%)	0.00	0.00	0.00	0.00	0.00	0.00	0.00	0.00	0.00	1.42
Portfolio Turnover (%)	na	60	47	55	51	128	195	202	343	228
Total Assets (Millions $)	5,274	3,159	1,583	965	313	140	39	36	5	1

PORTFOLIO (as of 3/31/96)

Portfolio Manager: Hans P. Utsch,
Lawrence Auriana - 1986

Investm't Category: Aggressive Growth
- ✔ Domestic
- ✔ Foreign
- Asset Allocation
- Index
- Sector
- State Specific

Investment Style
- Large-Cap Growth
- Mid-Cap Growth
- ✔ Small-Cap Growth
- Large-Cap Value
- Mid-Cap Value
- Small-Cap Value

Portfolio
- 12.0% cash
- 84.0% stocks
- 0.0% preferred
- 0.0% conv't/warrants
- 0.0% corp bonds
- 0.0% gov't bonds
- 0.0% muni bonds
- 4.0% other

SHAREHOLDER INFORMATION

Minimum Investment
Initial: $1,500   Subsequent: $100

Minimum IRA Investment
Initial: $500   Subsequent: $50

Maximum Fees
Load: 0.20% redemption   12b-1: 1.00%
Other: none

Distributions
Income: Dec   Capital Gains: Dec

Exchange Options
Number Per Year: no limit   Fee: none
Telephone: yes (money market fund available)

Services
IRA, pension, auto invest, auto withdraw

KEY Capital Growth

(SFCGX)

Aggressive Growth

45 Rockefeller Plaza
33rd Floor
New York, NY 10111
800-422-7273, 212-903-1200

PERFORMANCE

fund inception date: 11/1/93

	3yr Annual	5yr Annual	10yr Annual	Bull	Bear
Return (%)	9.7	na	na	41.9	-9.8
Differ from Category (+/-)	-6.1 low	na	na	-29.2 low	0.8 av

Total Risk	Standard Deviation	Category Risk	Risk Index	Beta
high	15.3%	abv av	1.1	0.93

	1996	1995	1994	1993	1992	1991	1990	1989	1988	1987
Return (%)	3.5	33.6	-4.5	—	—	—	—	—	—	—
Differ from Category (+/-)	-15.6	-0.7	-4.5	—	—	—	—	—	—	—
Return, Tax-Adjusted (%)	3.5	32.5	-4.5	—	—	—	—	—	—	—

PER SHARE DATA

	1996	1995	1994	1993	1992	1991	1990	1989	1988	1987
Dividends, Net Income ($)	0.00	0.00	0.00	—	—	—	—	—	—	—
Distrib'ns, Cap Gain ($)	0.00	0.29	0.00	—	—	—	—	—	—	—
Net Asset Value ($)	10.03	9.69	7.48	—	—	—	—	—	—	—
Expense Ratio (%)	na	1.20	1.22	—	—	—	—	—	—	—
Yield (%)	0.00	0.00	0.00	—	—	—	—	—	—	—
Portfolio Turnover (%)	na	97	80	—	—	—	—	—	—	—
Total Assets (Millions $)	36	33	4	—	—	—	—	—	—	—

PORTFOLIO (as of 9/30/96)

Portfolio Manager: Charles Crane, Annette Geddes - 1993

Investm't Category: Aggressive Growth
- ✔ Domestic   Index
- ✔ Foreign   Sector
-   Asset Allocation   State Specific

Investment Style
-   Large-Cap Growth   Large-Cap Value
- ✔ Mid-Cap Growth   Mid-Cap Value
- ✔ Small-Cap Growth   Small-Cap Value

Portfolio
3.7% cash	0.0% corp bonds
96.3% stocks	0.0% gov't bonds
0.0% preferred	0.0% muni bonds
0.0% conv't/warrants	0.0% other

SHAREHOLDER INFORMATION

Minimum Investment
Initial: $500   Subsequent: $25

Minimum IRA Investment
Initial: $250   Subsequent: $1

Maximum Fees
Load: none   12b-1: 0.25%
Other: none

Distributions
Income: Jun, Dec   Capital Gains: Dec

Exchange Options
Number Per Year: no limit   Fee: none
Telephone: yes (money market fund available)

Services
IRA, pension, auto invest, auto withdraw

KEY Convertible Securities (SBFCX)

Growth & Income

45 Rockefeller Plaza
33rd Floor
New York, NY 10111
800-422-7273, 212-903-1200

PERFORMANCE

fund inception date: 4/14/88

	3yr Annual	5yr Annual	10yr Annual	Bull	Bear
Return (%)	11.4	13.1	na	44.9	-5.4
Differ from Category (+/-)	-3.9 blw av	-0.8 blw av	na	-14.9 blw av	1.0 abv av

Total Risk	Standard Deviation	Category Risk	Risk Index	Beta
blw av	6.5%	low	0.7	0.51

	1996	1995	1994	1993	1992	1991	1990	1989	1988	1987
Return (%)	19.1	24.3	-6.5	20.0	11.2	27.7	-5.2	18.9	—	—
Differ from Category (+/-)	-0.6	-5.8	-5.2	6.2	0.5	-1.4	0.7	-4.6	—	—
Return, Tax-Adjusted (%)	15.5	21.1	-9.5	17.0	8.0	24.1	-8.7	15.0	—	—

PER SHARE DATA

	1996	1995	1994	1993	1992	1991	1990	1989	1988	1987
Dividends, Net Income ($)	0.64	0.60	0.60	0.64	0.68	0.74	0.90	0.82	—	—
Distrib'ns, Cap Gain ($)	0.62	0.34	0.43	0.24	0.23	0.10	0.03	0.19	—	—
Net Asset Value ($)	12.90	11.94	10.41	12.21	10.93	10.67	9.06	10.52	—	—
Expense Ratio (%)	na	1.31	1.30	1.24	1.32	1.37	1.52	1.15	—	—
Yield (%)	4.73	4.88	5.53	5.14	6.09	6.87	9.90	7.65	—	—
Portfolio Turnover (%)	na	52	49	30	42	53	32	76	—	—
Total Assets (Millions $)	81	70	59	62	47	29	15	12	—	—

PORTFOLIO (as of 9/30/96)

Portfolio Manager: L. Benzak, R. Janus, J. Kaesberg - 1988

Investm't Category: Growth & Income
- ✔ Domestic
- Foreign
- Asset Allocation
- Index
- Sector
- State Specific

Investment Style
- Large-Cap Growth
- Mid-Cap Growth
- Small-Cap Growth
- ✔ Large-Cap Value
- ✔ Mid-Cap Value
- Small-Cap Value

Portfolio
- 5.8% cash
- 10.1% stocks
- 49.2% preferred
- 32.6% conv't/warrants
- 2.3% corp bonds
- 0.0% gov't bonds
- 0.0% muni bonds
- 0.0% other

SHAREHOLDER INFORMATION

Minimum Investment
Initial: $500   Subsequent: $25

Minimum IRA Investment
Initial: $250   Subsequent: $1

Maximum Fees
Load: none   12b-1: 0.25%
Other: none

Distributions
Income: quarterly   Capital Gains: Dec

Exchange Options
Number Per Year: no limit   Fee: none
Telephone: yes (money market fund available)

Services
IRA, pension, auto invest, auto withdraw

KEY Fund (SBFFX)

Growth

45 Rockefeller Plaza
33rd Floor
New York, NY 10111
800-422-7273, 212-903-1200

PERFORMANCE

fund inception date: 10/17/83

	3yr Annual	5yr Annual	10yr Annual	Bull	Bear
Return (%)	14.6	14.1	13.0	57.1	-6.2
Differ from Category (+/-)	-1.1 blw av	-0.2 av	-0.9 blw av	-5.3 blw av	0.5 av

Total Risk	Standard Deviation	Category Risk	Risk Index	Beta
av	8.6%	low	0.8	0.78

	1996	1995	1994	1993	1992	1991	1990	1989	1988	1987
Return (%)	20.4	32.6	-5.7	20.4	6.6	19.0	-2.7	34.0	17.2	-3.2
Differ from Category (+/-)	0.3	2.3	-5.4	6.4	-5.2	-17.0	3.4	7.9	-0.9	-5.2
Return, Tax-Adjusted (%)	15.4	28.0	-7.7	15.6	3.7	14.4	-4.9	31.2	15.6	-5.5

PER SHARE DATA

	1996	1995	1994	1993	1992	1991	1990	1989	1988	1987
Dividends, Net Income ($)	0.07	0.13	0.21	0.30	0.40	0.56	0.59	0.51	0.42	0.45
Distrib'ns, Cap Gain ($)	2.75	2.04	0.79	2.11	1.00	1.60	0.41	0.57	0.06	0.40
Net Asset Value ($)	16.54	16.08	13.82	15.71	15.07	15.46	14.83	16.26	12.97	11.49
Expense Ratio (%)	na	1.26	1.23	1.15	1.16	1.15	1.15	1.20	1.16	1.10
Yield (%)	0.36	0.71	1.43	1.68	2.48	3.28	3.87	3.03	3.22	3.78
Portfolio Turnover (%)	na	59	83	70	45	50	42	44	47	66
Total Assets (Millions $)	118	116	107	120	102	107	92	98	78	84

PORTFOLIO (as of 9/30/96)

Portfolio Manager: Louis Benzak, C. Grisanti - 1983

Investm't Category: Growth

✔ Domestic	Index
Foreign	Sector
Asset Allocation	State Specific

Investment Style

Large-Cap Growth	✔ Large-Cap Value
Mid-Cap Growth	✔ Mid-Cap Value
Small-Cap Growth	Small-Cap Value

Portfolio

5.5% cash	0.0% corp bonds
94.5% stocks	0.0% gov't bonds
0.0% preferred	0.0% muni bonds
0.0% conv't/warrants	0.0% other

SHAREHOLDER INFORMATION

Minimum Investment
Initial: $500   Subsequent: $25

Minimum IRA Investment
Initial: $250   Subsequent: $1

Maximum Fees
Load: none   12b-1: 0.25%
Other: none

Distributions
Income: Jun, Dec   Capital Gains: Dec

Exchange Options
Number Per Year: no limit   Fee: none
Telephone: yes (money market fund available)

Services
IRA, pension, auto invest, auto withdraw

L. Roy Papp Stock

(LRPSX)

Growth

4400 N. 32nd St.
Suite 280
Phoenix, AZ 85018
800-421-4004, 602-956-1115

PERFORMANCE

fund inception date: 11/29/89

	3yr Annual	5yr Annual	10yr Annual	Bull	Bear
Return (%)	16.8	12.9	na	68.6	-7.1
Differ from Category (+/-)	1.1 av	-1.4 blw av	na	6.2 abv av	-0.4 av

Total Risk	Standard Deviation	Category Risk	Risk Index	Beta
abv av	10.1%	av	1.0	0.87

	1996	1995	1994	1993	1992	1991	1990	1989	1988	1987
Return (%)	21.8	32.9	-1.5	1.6	13.5	33.8	2.5	—	—	—
Differ from Category (+/-)	1.7	2.6	-1.2	-12.4	1.7	-2.2	8.6	—	—	—
Return, Tax-Adjusted (%)	20.7	32.5	-1.9	1.0	12.7	32.3	1.7	—	—	—

PER SHARE DATA

	1996	1995	1994	1993	1992	1991	1990	1989	1988	1987
Dividends, Net Income ($)	0.00	0.07	0.13	0.13	0.13	0.13	0.12	—	—	—
Distrib'ns, Cap Gain ($)	0.75	0.07	0.00	0.09	0.16	0.34	0.10	—	—	—
Net Asset Value ($)	22.70	19.29	14.63	14.98	14.96	13.45	10.42	—	—	—
Expense Ratio (%)	na	1.17	1.19	1.25	1.25	1.25	1.25	—	—	—
Yield (%)	0.00	0.36	0.88	0.86	0.85	0.94	1.14	—	—	—
Portfolio Turnover (%)	na	22	20	15	11	4	28	—	—	—
Total Assets (Millions $)	54	44	36	39	22	13	6	—	—	—

PORTFOLIO (as of 9/30/96)

Portfolio Manager: L. Roy Papp, Rosellen C. Papp - 1989

Investm't Category: Growth

✔ Domestic	Index
Foreign	Sector
Asset Allocation	State Specific

Investment Style

✔ Large-Cap Growth	Large-Cap Value
Mid-Cap Growth	Mid-Cap Value
Small-Cap Growth	Small-Cap Value

Portfolio

1.1% cash	0.0% corp bonds
98.9% stocks	0.0% gov't bonds
0.0% preferred	0.0% muni bonds
0.0% conv't/warrants	0.0% other

SHAREHOLDER INFORMATION

Minimum Investment
Initial: $5,000   Subsequent: $1,000

Minimum IRA Investment
Initial: $1,000   Subsequent: $1,000

Maximum Fees
Load: none   12b-1: none
Other: none

Distributions
Income: Jun, Dec   Capital Gains: Dec

Exchange Options
Number Per Year: none   Fee: na
Telephone: na

Services
IRA

Legg Mason American Leading Cos (LMALX)

Growth & Income

7 E. Redwood
10th Floor
Baltimore, MD 21202
800-822-5544, 410-539-0000

PERFORMANCE

fund inception date: 9/1/93

	3yr Annual	5yr Annual	10yr Annual	Bull	Bear
Return (%)	14.7	na	na	56.9	-5.9
Differ from Category (+/-)	-0.6 blw av	na	na	-2.9 blw av	0.5 abv av

Total Risk	Standard Deviation	Category Risk	Risk Index	Beta
abv av	9.6%	av	1.0	0.92

	1996	1995	1994	1993	1992	1991	1990	1989	1988	1987
Return (%)	28.3	22.9	-4.2	—	—	—	—	—	—	—
Differ from Category (+/-)	8.6	-7.2	-2.9	—	—	—	—	—	—	—
Return, Tax-Adjusted (%)	27.0	22.4	-4.7	—	—	—	—	—	—	—

PER SHARE DATA

	1996	1995	1994	1993	1992	1991	1990	1989	1988	1987
Dividends, Net Income ($)	0.02	0.10	0.11	—	—	—	—	—	—	—
Distrib'ns, Cap Gain ($)	0.47	0.00	0.00	—	—	—	—	—	—	—
Net Asset Value ($)	14.40	11.61	9.53	—	—	—	—	—	—	—
Expense Ratio (%)	1.95	1.95	1.95	—	—	—	—	—	—	—
Yield (%)	0.13	0.86	1.15	—	—	—	—	—	—	—
Portfolio Turnover (%)	43	30	21	—	—	—	—	—	—	—
Total Assets (Millions $)	91	71	56	—	—	—	—	—	—	—

PORTFOLIO (as of 9/30/96)

Portfolio Manager: J. Eric Leo - 1993

Investm't Category: Growth & Income
- ✔ Domestic
- ✔ Foreign
-   Asset Allocation
-   Index
-   Sector
-   State Specific

Investment Style
- ✔ Large-Cap Growth
-   Mid-Cap Growth
-   Small-Cap Growth
- ✔ Large-Cap Value
-   Mid-Cap Value
-   Small-Cap Value

Portfolio
5.0% cash	0.0% corp bonds
95.0% stocks	0.0% gov't bonds
0.0% preferred	0.0% muni bonds
0.0% conv't/warrants	0.0% other

SHAREHOLDER INFORMATION

Minimum Investment
Initial: $1,000   Subsequent: $100

Minimum IRA Investment
Initial: $1,000   Subsequent: $100

Maximum Fees
Load: none   12b-1: 1.00%
Other: none

Distributions
Income: Dec   Capital Gains: Dec

Exchange Options
Number Per Year: 4   Fee: none
Telephone: yes (money market fund available)

Services
IRA, pension, auto exchange, auto invest, auto withdraw

Legg Mason Global Gov't Trust/Prim (LMGGX)

International Bond

7 E. Redwood
10th Floor
Baltimore, MD 21202
800-822-5544, 410-539-0000

	3yr Annual	5yr Annual	10yr Annual	Bull	Bear
Return (%)	8.8	na	na	32.2	-3.0
Differ from Category (+/-)	2.8 high	na	na	1.0 abv av	6.5 high

Total Risk	Standard Deviation	Category Risk	Risk Index	Avg Mat
blw av	5.3%	av	0.8	7.7 yrs

	1996	1995	1994	1993	1992	1991	1990	1989	1988	1987
Return (%)	8.2	21.0	-1.7	—	—	—	—	—	—	—
Differ from Category (+/-)	-3.1	5.0	5.9	—	—	—	—	—	—	—
Return, Tax-Adjusted (%)	5.5	16.2	-4.0	—	—	—	—	—	—	—

PER SHARE DATA

	1996	1995	1994	1993	1992	1991	1990	1989	1988	1987
Dividends, Net Income ($)	0.62	1.15	0.58	—	—	—	—	—	—	—
Distrib'ns, Cap Gain ($)	0.10	0.00	0.00	—	—	—	—	—	—	—
Net Asset Value ($)	10.41	10.32	9.52	—	—	—	—	—	—	—
Expense Ratio (%)	na	1.80	1.30	—	—	—	—	—	—	—
Yield (%)	5.89	11.14	6.09	—	—	—	—	—	—	—
Portfolio Turnover (%)	na	163	127	—	—	—	—	—	—	—
Total Assets (Millions $)	162	146	145	—	—	—	—	—	—	—

PORTFOLIO (as of 9/30/96)

Portfolio Manager: Keith Gardner - 1993

Investm't Category: International Bond
- ✔ Domestic
- ✔ Foreign
- Asset Allocation
- Index
- Sector
- State Specific

Investment Style
Large-Cap Growth	Large-Cap Value
Mid-Cap Growth	Mid-Cap Value
Small-Cap Growth	Small-Cap Value

Portfolio
8.2% cash	17.0% corp bonds
0.0% stocks	65.7% gov't bonds
0.0% preferred	0.0% muni bonds
0.0% conv't/warrants	9.2% other

SHAREHOLDER INFORMATION

Minimum Investment
Initial: $1,000   Subsequent: $100

Minimum IRA Investment
Initial: $1,000   Subsequent: $100

Maximum Fees
Load: none   12b-1: 0.75%
Other: none

Distributions
Income: monthly   Capital Gains: Dec

Exchange Options
Number Per Year: 4   Fee: none
Telephone: yes (money market fund available)

Services
IRA, pension, auto exchange, auto invest, auto withdraw

Legg Mason High Yield

(LMHYX)

Corporate High-Yield Bond

7 E. Redwood
10th Floor
Baltimore, MD 21202
800-822-5544, 410-539-0000

PERFORMANCE

fund inception date: 2/1/94

	3yr Annual	5yr Annual	10yr Annual	Bull	Bear
Return (%)	na	na	na	35.2	na
Differ from Category (+/-)	na	na	na	2.1 abv av	na

Total Risk	Standard Deviation	Category Risk	Risk Index	Avg Mat
na	na	na	na	6.6 yrs

	1996	1995	1994	1993	1992	1991	1990	1989	1988	1987
Return (%)	14.9	18.0	—	—	—	—	—	—	—	—
Differ from Category (+/-)	-0.4	0.5	—	—	—	—	—	—	—	—
Return, Tax-Adjusted (%)	11.2	14.2	—	—	—	—	—	—	—	—

PER SHARE DATA

	1996	1995	1994	1993	1992	1991	1990	1989	1988	1987
Dividends, Net Income ($)	1.34	1.28	—	—	—	—	—	—	—	—
Distrib'ns, Cap Gain ($)	0.00	0.00	—	—	—	—	—	—	—	—
Net Asset Value ($)	15.37	14.62	—	—	—	—	—	—	—	—
Expense Ratio (%)	na	1.50	—	—	—	—	—	—	—	—
Yield (%)	8.71	8.75	—	—	—	—	—	—	—	—
Portfolio Turnover (%)	na	47	—	—	—	—	—	—	—	—
Total Assets (Millions $)	220	107	—	—	—	—	—	—	—	—

PORTFOLIO (as of 9/30/96)

Portfolio Manager: Trudi Whitehead - 1994

Investm't Category: Corp. High-Yield Bond

✔ Domestic   Index
✔ Foreign   Sector
  Asset Allocation   State Specific

Investment Style

Large-Cap Growth	Large-Cap Value
Mid-Cap Growth	Mid-Cap Value
Small-Cap Growth	Small-Cap Value

Portfolio

1.9% cash	94.1% corp bonds
0.8% stocks	0.0% gov't bonds
2.9% preferred	0.0% muni bonds
0.3% conv't/warrants	0.0% other

SHAREHOLDER INFORMATION

Minimum Investment
Initial: $1,000   Subsequent: $100

Minimum IRA Investment
Initial: $1,000   Subsequent: $100

Maximum Fees
Load: none   12b-1: 0.50%
Other: none

Distributions
Income: monthly   Capital Gains: Dec

Exchange Options
Number Per Year: 4   Fee: none
Telephone: yes (money market fund available)

Services
IRA, pension, auto exchange, auto invest, auto withdraw

Legg Mason Int'l Equity Trust/Prim (LMGEX)

International Stock

7 E. Redwood
10th Floor
Baltimore, MD 21202
800-822-5544, 410-539-0000

PERFORMANCE

fund inception date: 2/17/95

	3yr Annual	5yr Annual	10yr Annual	Bull	Bear
Return (%)	na	na	na	na	na
Differ from Category (+/-)	na	na	na	na	na

Total Risk	Standard Deviation	Category Risk	Risk Index	Beta
na	na	na	na	na

	1996	1995	1994	1993	1992	1991	1990	1989	1988	1987
Return (%)	16.5	—	—	—	—	—	—	—	—	—
Differ from Category (+/-)	1.7	—	—	—	—	—	—	—	—	—
Return, Tax-Adjusted (%)	15.5	—	—	—	—	—	—	—	—	—

PER SHARE DATA

	1996	1995	1994	1993	1992	1991	1990	1989	1988	1987
Dividends, Net Income ($)	0.04	—	—	—	—	—	—	—	—	—
Distrib'ns, Cap Gain ($)	0.32	—	—	—	—	—	—	—	—	—
Net Asset Value ($)	12.10	—	—	—	—	—	—	—	—	—
Expense Ratio (%)	na	—	—	—	—	—	—	—	—	—
Yield (%)	0.32	—	—	—	—	—	—	—	—	—
Portfolio Turnover (%)	na	—	—	—	—	—	—	—	—	—
Total Assets (Millions $)	158	—	—	—	—	—	—	—	—	—

PORTFOLIO (as of 9/30/96)

Portfolio Manager: Charles Lovejoy, S. McCarthy - 1995

Investm't Category: International Stock

Domestic	Index
✔ Foreign	Sector
Asset Allocation	State Specific

Investment Style

Large-Cap Growth	Large-Cap Value
Mid-Cap Growth	Mid-Cap Value
Small-Cap Growth	Small-Cap Value

Portfolio

3.0% cash	0.0% corp bonds
95.9% stocks	0.0% gov't bonds
1.2% preferred	0.0% muni bonds
0.0% conv't/warrants	0.0% other

SHAREHOLDER INFORMATION

Minimum Investment
Initial: $1,000   Subsequent: $100

Minimum IRA Investment
Initial: $1,000   Subsequent: $100

Maximum Fees
Load: none   12b-1: 1.00%
Other: none

Distributions
Income: Dec   Capital Gains: Dec

Exchange Options
Number Per Year: 4   Fee: none
Telephone: yes (money market fund available)

Services
IRA, pension, auto invest, auto withdraw

Legg Mason Invest Grade /Prim (LMIGX)

7 E. Redwood
10th Floor
Baltimore, MD 21202
800-822-5544, 410-539-0000

General Bond

PERFORMANCE

fund inception date: 8/7/87

	3yr Annual	5yr Annual	10yr Annual	Bull	Bear
Return (%)	6.0	7.2	na	25.8	-6.7
Differ from Category (+/-)	0.9 high	1.1 abv av	na	5.5 high	-2.5 low

Total Risk	Standard Deviation	Category Risk	Risk Index	Avg Mat
blw av	5.0%	high	1.3	9.1 yrs

	1996	1995	1994	1993	1992	1991	1990	1989	1988	1987
Return (%)	4.3	20.1	-4.9	11.2	6.7	15.9	5.7	12.9	7.6	—
Differ from Category (+/-)	0.4	5.2	-2.6	2.1	0.2	1.2	-1.6	1.2	0.0	—
Return, Tax-Adjusted (%)	1.8	17.3	-7.3	6.6	4.1	12.8	2.3	9.6	4.4	—

PER SHARE DATA

	1996	1995	1994	1993	1992	1991	1990	1989	1988	1987
Dividends, Net Income ($)	0.64	0.64	0.59	0.62	0.66	0.75	0.83	0.82	0.77	—
Distrib'ns, Cap Gain ($)	0.00	0.00	0.04	0.85	0.04	0.03	0.04	0.00	0.02	—
Net Asset Value ($)	10.22	10.44	9.27	10.40	10.71	10.71	9.97	10.29	9.88	—
Expense Ratio (%)	na	0.88	0.85	0.85	0.85	0.71	0.50	0.80	1.00	—
Yield (%)	6.26	6.13	6.33	5.51	6.13	6.98	8.29	7.96	7.77	—
Portfolio Turnover (%)	na	221	200	348	317	213	55	92	146	—
Total Assets (Millions $)	92	85	66	68	47	36	22	13	9	—

PORTFOLIO (as of 9/30/96)

Portfolio Manager: Kent S. Engle - 1987

Investm't Category: General Bond
- ✔ Domestic
- ✔ Foreign
- Asset Allocation
- Index
- Sector
- State Specific

Investment Style
Large-Cap Growth	Large-Cap Value
Mid-Cap Growth	Mid-Cap Value
Small-Cap Growth	Small-Cap Value

Portfolio
2.8% cash	28.2% corp bonds
0.0% stocks	59.7% gov't bonds
1.2% preferred	0.0% muni bonds
0.0% conv't/warrants	8.2% other

SHAREHOLDER INFORMATION

Minimum Investment
Initial: $1,000   Subsequent: $100

Minimum IRA Investment
Initial: $1,000   Subsequent: $100

Maximum Fees
Load: none   12b-1: 0.50%
Other: none

Distributions
Income: monthly   Capital Gains: Dec

Exchange Options
Number Per Year: 4   Fee: none
Telephone: yes (money market fund available)

Services
IRA, pension, auto exchange, auto invest, auto withdraw

Legg Mason Special Investment Trust/Prim

7 E. Redwood
10th Floor
Baltimore, MD 21202
800-822-5544, 410-539-0000

(LMASX) *Aggressive Growth*

PERFORMANCE

fund inception date: 12/30/85

	3yr Annual	5yr Annual	10yr Annual	Bull	Bear
Return (%)	11.0	14.4	14.5	51.9	-15.1
Differ from Category (+/-)	-4.8 blw av	-0.9 av	-0.5 av	-19.2 blw av	-4.5 blw av

Total Risk	Standard Deviation	Category Risk	Risk Index	Beta
high	14.5%	av	1.0	1.09

	1996	1995	1994	1993	1992	1991	1990	1989	1988	1987
Return (%)	28.6	22.5	-13.1	24.1	15.3	39.4	0.5	32.0	19.6	-10.4
Differ from Category (+/-)	9.5	-11.8	-13.1	4.8	3.6	-12.7	5.9	3.6	3.2	-8.0
Return, Tax-Adjusted (%)	26.8	21.7	-13.4	23.8	13.2	39.1	-3.0	31.6	19.5	-13.1

PER SHARE DATA

	1996	1995	1994	1993	1992	1991	1990	1989	1988	1987
Dividends, Net Income ($)	0.00	0.03	0.00	0.03	0.11	0.03	0.27	0.08	0.01	0.08
Distrib'ns, Cap Gain ($)	1.41	0.44	0.23	0.14	1.10	0.08	1.32	0.00	0.00	0.89
Net Asset Value ($)	27.83	22.81	19.03	22.14	17.98	16.78	12.12	13.63	10.38	8.68
Expense Ratio (%)	1.96	1.93	1.94	2.00	2.10	2.30	2.30	2.50	2.50	2.50
Yield (%)	0.00	0.12	0.00	0.13	0.57	0.17	2.00	0.58	0.09	0.83
Portfolio Turnover (%)	35	27	16	32	57	76	116	122	159	77
Total Assets (Millions $)	928	713	605	510	287	163	76	63	40	41

PORTFOLIO (as of 6/30/96)

Portfolio Manager: William H. Miller III - 1985

Investm't Category: Aggressive Growth
✔ Domestic   Index
✔ Foreign   Sector
   Asset Allocation   State Specific

Investment Style
Large-Cap Growth   Large-Cap Value
Mid-Cap Growth   Mid-Cap Value
Small-Cap Growth   ✔ Small-Cap Value

Portfolio
3.6% cash   0.0% corp bonds
94.4% stocks   0.0% gov't bonds
0.2% preferred   0.0% muni bonds
0.0% conv't/warrants 1.8% other

SHAREHOLDER INFORMATION

Minimum Investment
Initial: $1,000   Subsequent: $100

Minimum IRA Investment
Initial: $1,000   Subsequent: $100

Maximum Fees
Load: none   12b-1: 1.00%
Other: none

Distributions
Income: Dec   Capital Gains: Dec

Exchange Options
Number Per Year: 4   Fee: none
Telephone: yes (money market fund available)

Services
IRA, pension, auto exchange, auto invest, auto withdraw

Legg Mason Total Return Trust/Prim (LMTRX)

Growth & Income

7 E. Redwood
10th Floor
Baltimore, MD 21202
800-822-5544, 410-539-0000

PERFORMANCE
fund inception date: 11/21/85

	3yr Annual	5yr Annual	10yr Annual	Bull	Bear
Return (%)	16.6	15.6	12.1	64.1	-6.9
Differ from Category (+/-)	1.3 av	1.7 abv av	-0.6 av	4.3 av	-0.5 av

Total Risk	Standard Deviation	Category Risk	Risk Index	Beta
abv av	10.4%	high	1.1	0.88

	1996	1995	1994	1993	1992	1991	1990	1989	1988	1987
Return (%)	31.1	30.3	-7.2	14.0	14.3	40.4	-16.9	16.3	21.7	-7.8
Differ from Category (+/-)	11.4	0.2	-5.9	0.2	3.6	11.3	-11.0	-7.2	4.9	-8.0
Return, Tax-Adjusted (%)	29.0	28.6	-9.2	12.0	13.2	39.5	-18.2	14.8	21.0	-12.7

PER SHARE DATA

	1996	1995	1994	1993	1992	1991	1990	1989	1988	1987
Dividends, Net Income ($)	0.42	0.51	0.28	0.41	0.30	0.18	0.28	0.21	0.13	0.28
Distrib'ns, Cap Gain ($)	0.55	0.00	0.60	0.34	0.00	0.00	0.07	0.18	0.00	1.34
Net Asset Value ($)	19.01	15.29	12.15	14.00	12.98	11.64	8.43	10.54	9.40	7.83
Expense Ratio (%)	1.95	1.93	1.94	1.95	2.30	2.50	2.40	2.40	2.30	2.40
Yield (%)	2.14	3.33	2.19	2.85	2.31	1.54	3.29	1.95	1.38	3.05
Portfolio Turnover (%)	34	61	46	40	38	62	39	26	50	83
Total Assets (Millions $)	340	242	193	175	110	40	18	29	30	36

PORTFOLIO (as of 9/30/96)

Portfolio Manager: William H. Miller III - 1990

Investm't Category: Growth & Income
- ✔ Domestic
- ✔ Foreign
-   Asset Allocation
-   Index
-   Sector
-   State Specific

Investment Style
Large-Cap Growth	✔ Large-Cap Value
Mid-Cap Growth	Mid-Cap Value
Small-Cap Growth	Small-Cap Value

Portfolio
5.5% cash	0.0% corp bonds
84.1% stocks	5.5% gov't bonds
4.9% preferred	0.0% muni bonds
0.0% conv't/warrants	0.0% other

SHAREHOLDER INFORMATION

Minimum Investment
Initial: $1,000   Subsequent: $100

Minimum IRA Investment
Initial: $1,000   Subsequent: $100

Maximum Fees
Load: none   12b-1: 1.00%
Other: none

Distributions
Income: quarterly   Capital Gains: Dec

Exchange Options
Number Per Year: 4   Fee: none
Telephone: yes (money market fund available)

Services
IRA, pension, auto exchange, auto invest, auto withdraw

Legg Mason US Gov't Interm/Prim (LGINX)

7 E. Redwood
10th Floor
Baltimore, MD 21202
800-822-5544, 410-539-0000

General Bond

PERFORMANCE

fund inception date: 8/7/87

	3yr Annual	5yr Annual	10yr Annual	Bull	Bear
Return (%)	5.2	5.7	na	19.4	-2.6
Differ from Category (+/-)	0.1 av	-0.4 blw av	na	-0.9 av	1.6 abv av

Total Risk	Standard Deviation	Category Risk	Risk Index	Avg Mat
low	3.0%	blw av	0.8	5.7 yrs

	1996	1995	1994	1993	1992	1991	1990	1989	1988	1987
Return (%)	4.4	13.8	-2.0	6.6	6.2	14.3	9.0	12.7	6.4	—
Differ from Category (+/-)	0.5	-1.1	0.3	-2.5	-0.3	-0.4	1.7	1.0	-1.2	—
Return, Tax-Adjusted (%)	2.1	11.5	-4.0	3.4	3.7	10.9	5.9	9.5	3.4	—

PER SHARE DATA

	1996	1995	1994	1993	1992	1991	1990	1989	1988	1987
Dividends, Net Income ($)	0.60	0.56	0.51	0.54	0.60	0.71	0.78	0.79	0.75	—
Distrib'ns, Cap Gain ($)	0.00	0.00	0.00	0.44	0.10	0.22	0.00	0.00	0.00	—
Net Asset Value ($)	10.31	10.47	9.72	10.43	10.72	10.77	10.29	10.20	9.79	—
Expense Ratio (%)	na	0.90	0.90	0.90	0.90	0.80	0.60	0.80	1.00	—
Yield (%)	5.81	5.34	5.24	4.96	5.54	6.46	7.58	7.74	7.66	—
Portfolio Turnover (%)	na	289	315	490	513	643	67	57	133	—
Total Assets (Millions $)	222	231	235	299	307	211	74	43	26	—

PORTFOLIO (as of 6/30/96)

Portfolio Manager: Carl L. Eichstaedt - 1994

Investm't Category: General Bond
- ✔ Domestic
- Foreign
- Asset Allocation
- Index
- Sector
- State Specific

Investment Style
- Large-Cap Growth
- Mid-Cap Growth
- Small-Cap Growth
- Large-Cap Value
- Mid-Cap Value
- Small-Cap Value

Portfolio
10.8% cash	5.2% corp bonds
0.0% stocks	79.1% gov't bonds
0.0% preferred	0.0% muni bonds
0.0% conv't/warrants	5.0% other

SHAREHOLDER INFORMATION

Minimum Investment
Initial: $1,000   Subsequent: $100

Minimum IRA Investment
Initial: $1,000   Subsequent: $100

Maximum Fees
Load: none   12b-1: 0.50%
Other: none

Distributions
Income: monthly   Capital Gains: Dec

Exchange Options
Number Per Year: 4   Fee: none
Telephone: yes (money market fund available)

Services
IRA, pension, auto exchange, auto invest, auto withdraw

Legg Mason Value Trust/Prim (LMVTX)

Growth

7 E. Redwood
10th Floor
Baltimore, MD 21202
800-822-5544, 410-539-0000

PERFORMANCE

fund inception date: 4/16/82

	3yr Annual	5yr Annual	10yr Annual	Bull	Bear
Return (%)	25.4	19.6	14.3	104.2	-9.0
Differ from Category (+/-)	9.7 high	5.3 high	0.4 av	41.8 high	-2.3 blw av

Total Risk	Standard Deviation	Category Risk	Risk Index	Beta
high	12.2%	high	1.2	1.17

	1996	1995	1994	1993	1992	1991	1990	1989	1988	1987
Return (%)	38.4	40.7	1.3	11.2	11.4	34.7	-17.0	20.1	25.7	-7.4
Differ from Category (+/-)	18.3	10.4	1.6	-2.8	-0.4	-1.3	-10.9	-6.0	7.6	-9.4
Return, Tax-Adjusted (%)	36.4	38.5	1.1	10.4	10.9	33.9	-18.1	17.5	25.0	-9.3

PER SHARE DATA

	1996	1995	1994	1993	1992	1991	1990	1989	1988	1987
Dividends, Net Income ($)	0.16	0.17	0.05	0.23	0.16	0.22	0.36	0.33	0.18	0.25
Distrib'ns, Cap Gain ($)	1.53	1.24	0.04	0.15	0.00	0.00	0.03	0.73	0.00	1.39
Net Asset Value ($)	32.99	25.19	19.04	18.87	17.32	15.70	11.84	14.69	13.14	10.60
Expense Ratio (%)	1.82	1.81	1.82	1.86	1.90	1.90	1.86	1.96	1.97	2.00
Yield (%)	0.46	0.64	0.26	1.20	0.92	1.40	3.03	2.14	1.36	2.08
Portfolio Turnover (%)	19	20	25	21	39	39	31	30	48	43
Total Assets (Millions $)	1,977	1,340	967	914	842	747	636	823	678	606

PORTFOLIO (as of 9/30/96)

Portfolio Manager: William H. Miller III - 1982

Investm't Category: Growth
- ✔ Domestic
- ✔ Foreign
- Asset Allocation
- Index
- Sector
- State Specific

Investment Style
Large-Cap Growth	✔ Large-Cap Value
Mid-Cap Growth	Mid-Cap Value
Small-Cap Growth	Small-Cap Value

Portfolio
4.6% cash	0.0% corp bonds
91.2% stocks	3.7% gov't bonds
0.4% preferred	0.0% muni bonds
0.0% conv't/warrants	0.0% other

SHAREHOLDER INFORMATION

Minimum Investment
Initial: $1,000   Subsequent: $100

Minimum IRA Investment
Initial: $1,000   Subsequent: $100

Maximum Fees
Load: none   12b-1: 0.95%
Other: none

Distributions
Income: quarterly   Capital Gains: Dec

Exchange Options
Number Per Year: 4   Fee: none
Telephone: yes (money market fund available)

Services
IRA, pension, auto exchange, auto invest, auto withdraw

Lexington GNMA Income
(LEXNX)

Park 80 W. Plaza Two
Saddle Brook, NJ 07663
800-526-0056, 201-845-7300

Mortgage-Backed Bond

PERFORMANCE

fund inception date: 10/17/73

	3yr Annual	5yr Annual	10yr Annual	Bull	Bear
Return (%)	6.2	6.3	8.0	23.9	-4.2
Differ from Category (+/-)	0.6 abv av	0.3 abv av	0.3 abv av	2.8 high	-0.6 blw av

Total Risk	Standard Deviation	Category Risk	Risk Index	Avg Mat
low	3.6%	av	1.0	2.5 yrs

	1996	1995	1994	1993	1992	1991	1990	1989	1988	1987
Return (%)	5.6	15.9	-2.1	8.0	5.1	15.7	9.2	15.5	6.8	1.6
Differ from Category (+/-)	1.2	1.2	-0.4	1.1	-1.1	1.3	-0.6	2.9	-0.6	-0.4
Return, Tax-Adjusted (%)	3.1	12.8	-4.7	5.2	2.2	12.5	5.8	11.8	3.4	-2.0

PER SHARE DATA

	1996	1995	1994	1993	1992	1991	1990	1989	1988	1987
Dividends, Net Income ($)	0.51	0.58	0.54	0.58	0.60	0.63	0.66	0.68	0.64	0.72
Distrib'ns, Cap Gain ($)	0.00	0.00	0.00	0.00	0.00	0.00	0.00	0.00	0.00	0.03
Net Asset Value ($)	8.12	8.19	7.60	8.32	8.26	8.45	7.90	7.88	7.45	7.58
Expense Ratio (%)	na	1.01	0.98	1.02	1.01	1.02	1.04	1.03	1.07	0.98
Yield (%)	6.28	7.08	7.10	6.97	7.26	7.45	8.35	8.62	8.59	9.46
Portfolio Turnover (%)	na	30	37	52	180	139	113	103	233	89
Total Assets (Millions $)	132	130	132	149	132	122	97	96	97	106

PORTFOLIO (as of 9/30/96)

Portfolio Manager: Denis Jamison, committee - 1981

Investm't Category: Mortgage-Backed Bond
✔ Domestic   Index
  Foreign   Sector
  Asset Allocation   State Specific

Investment Style
  Large-Cap Growth   Large-Cap Value
  Mid-Cap Growth   Mid-Cap Value
  Small-Cap Growth   Small-Cap Value

Portfolio
  0.0% cash   0.0% corp bonds
  0.0% stocks   100.0% gov't bonds
  0.0% preferred   0.0% muni bonds
  0.0% conv't/warrants 0.0% other

SHAREHOLDER INFORMATION

Minimum Investment
Initial: $1,000   Subsequent: $50

Minimum IRA Investment
Initial: $250   Subsequent: $50

Maximum Fees
Load: none   12b-1: none
Other: none

Distributions
Income: monthly   Capital Gains: Dec

Exchange Options
Number Per Year: no limit   Fee: none
Telephone: yes (money market fund available)

Services
IRA, pension, auto exchange, auto invest, auto withdraw

Lexington Global (LXGLX)

International Stock

Park 80 W. Plaza Two
Saddle Brook, NJ 07663
800-526-0056, 201-845-7300

	3yr Annual	5yr Annual	10yr Annual	Bull	Bear
Return (%)	9.4	10.7	na	27.8	-3.5
Differ from Category (+/-)	3.1 abv av	0.7 av	na	3.5 abv av	3.7 high

Total Risk	Standard Deviation	Category Risk	Risk Index	Beta
av	9.3%	blw av	0.9	0.63

	1996	1995	1994	1993	1992	1991	1990	1989	1988	1987
Return (%)	16.4	10.6	1.8	31.8	-3.6	15.5	-16.8	25.1	16.3	—
Differ from Category (+/-)	1.6	1.5	4.9	-7.8	0.2	2.3	-6.7	2.5	1.4	—
Return, Tax-Adjusted (%)	11.5	7.5	-3.6	28.9	-3.9	14.5	-17.9	23.0	14.0	—

PER SHARE DATA

	1996	1995	1994	1993	1992	1991	1990	1989	1988	1987
Dividends, Net Income ($)	0.16	0.42	0.00	0.05	0.07	0.15	0.13	0.02	0.51	—
Distrib'ns, Cap Gain ($)	1.72	0.62	2.58	1.05	0.00	0.13	0.30	0.77	0.07	—
Net Asset Value ($)	11.28	11.32	11.17	13.51	11.09	11.57	10.26	12.83	10.89	—
Expense Ratio (%)	na	1.67	1.61	1.49	1.52	1.57	1.59	1.64	1.80	—
Yield (%)	1.23	3.51	0.00	0.34	0.63	1.28	1.23	0.14	4.65	—
Portfolio Turnover (%)	na	166	83	84	81	76	82	114	97	—
Total Assets (Millions $)	37	53	67	87	50	53	50	56	38	—

PORTFOLIO (as of 9/30/96)

Portfolio Manager: R. Saler, P. Schwartz, A. Wapnick - 1994

Investm't Category: International Stock
✔ Domestic   Index
✔ Foreign   Sector
   Asset Allocation   State Specific

Investment Style
Large-Cap Growth   Large-Cap Value
Mid-Cap Growth   Mid-Cap Value
Small-Cap Growth   Small-Cap Value

Portfolio
11.2% cash	0.0% corp bonds
88.9% stocks	0.0% gov't bonds
0.0% preferred	0.0% muni bonds
0.0% conv't/warrants	0.0% other

SHAREHOLDER INFORMATION

Minimum Investment
Initial: $1,000   Subsequent: $50

Minimum IRA Investment
Initial: $250   Subsequent: $50

Maximum Fees
Load: none   12b-1: none
Other: none

Distributions
Income: Dec   Capital Gains: Dec

Exchange Options
Number Per Year: no limit   Fee: none
Telephone: yes (money market fund available)

Services
IRA, pension, auto exchange, auto invest, auto withdraw

Lexington Goldfund
(LEXMX)
Gold

Park 80 W. Plaza Two
Saddle Brook, NJ 07663
800-526-0056, 201-845-7300

PERFORMANCE

fund inception date: 5/3/79

	3yr Annual	5yr Annual	10yr Annual	Bull	Bear
Return (%)	-0.7	7.8	5.2	10.2	-9.8
Differ from Category (+/-)	-1.0 av	-1.8 blw av	0.9 av	-4.7 av	0.4 abv av

Total Risk	Standard Deviation	Category Risk	Risk Index	Beta
high	22.5%	low	0.9	0.54

	1996	1995	1994	1993	1992	1991	1990	1989	1988	1987
Return (%)	7.8	-1.9	-7.3	86.9	-20.6	-6.2	-20.7	23.6	-15.2	46.5
Differ from Category (+/-)	-3.4	-6.9	4.8	-0.9	-5.3	-1.6	1.6	-0.8	3.9	14.3
Return, Tax-Adjusted (%)	2.7	-2.0	-7.5	86.7	-20.8	-6.6	-21.0	23.2	-15.6	44.0

PER SHARE DATA

	1996	1995	1994	1993	1992	1991	1990	1989	1988	1987
Dividends, Net Income ($)	0.79	0.01	0.02	0.01	0.02	0.04	0.04	0.05	0.05	0.05
Distrib'ns, Cap Gain ($)	0.00	0.00	0.00	0.00	0.00	0.00	0.00	0.00	0.00	0.32
Net Asset Value ($)	5.97	6.24	6.37	6.90	3.70	4.68	5.03	6.39	5.21	6.20
Expense Ratio (%)	na	1.70	1.54	1.63	1.69	1.43	1.36	1.42	1.61	1.29
Yield (%)	na	0.16	0.31	0.14	0.54	0.85	0.79	0.78	0.95	0.76
Portfolio Turnover (%)	na	40	23	28	13	22	12	16	20	14
Total Assets (Millions $)	112	136	158	159	71	96	106	155	92	103

PORTFOLIO (as of 9/30/96)

Portfolio Manager: Robert Radsch CFA - 1994

Investm't Category: Gold
- ✔ Domestic
- ✔ Foreign
- Asset Allocation
- Index
- ✔ Sector
- State Specific

Investment Style
- Large-Cap Growth
- Mid-Cap Growth
- Small-Cap Growth
- Large-Cap Value
- Mid-Cap Value
- Small-Cap Value

Portfolio

2.7%	cash	0.0%	corp bonds
85.8%	stocks	0.0%	gov't bonds
0.0%	preferred	0.0%	muni bonds
0.0%	conv't/warrants	11.5%	other

SHAREHOLDER INFORMATION

Minimum Investment
Initial: $1,000   Subsequent: $50

Minimum IRA Investment
Initial: $250   Subsequent: $50

Maximum Fees
Load: none   12b-1: 0.25%
Other: none

Distributions
Income: Aug, Dec   Capital Gains: Dec

Exchange Options
Number Per Year: no limit   Fee: none
Telephone: yes (money market fund available)

Services
IRA, pension, auto exchange, auto invest, auto withdraw

Lexington Growth & Income (LEXRX)

Park 80 W. Plaza Two
Saddle Brook, NJ 07663
800-526-0056, 201-845-7300

Growth & Income

PERFORMANCE

fund inception date: 2/11/59

	3yr Annual	5yr Annual	10yr Annual	Bull	Bear
Return (%)	14.5	13.8	11.5	55.9	-7.2
Differ from Category (+/-)	-0.8 blw av	-0.1 blw av	-1.2 blw av	-3.9 blw av	-0.8 blw av

Total Risk	Standard Deviation	Category Risk	Risk Index	Beta
abv av	9.7%	abv av	1.0	0.90

	1996	1995	1994	1993	1992	1991	1990	1989	1988	1987
Return (%).	26.4	22.5	-3.2	13.2	12.3	24.8	-10.3	27.5	9.4	0.0
Differ from Category (+/-). .	6.7	-7.6	-1.9	-0.6	1.6	-4.3	-4.4	4.0	-7.4	-0.2
Return, Tax-Adjusted (%). .	24.0	18.7	-5.6	9.2	8.3	21.8	-11.1	22.8	8.0	-9.5

PER SHARE DATA

	1996	1995	1994	1993	1992	1991	1990	1989	1988	1987
Dividends, Net Income ($).	0.13	0.21	0.16	0.20	0.32	0.35	0.30	0.60	0.45	1.10
Distrib'ns, Cap Gain ($) . . .	1.16	1.64	1.13	2.02	1.84	1.02	0.00	1.54	0.00	4.93
Net Asset Value ($)	18.56	15.71	14.36	16.16	16.25	16.39	14.24	16.19	14.39	13.57
Expense Ratio (%).	na	1.09	1.15	1.29	1.20	1.13	1.04	1.02	1.10	0.96
Yield (%)	0.65	1.21	1.03	1.10	1.76	2.01	2.10	3.38	3.12	5.94
Portfolio Turnover (%). . . .	na	159	63	93	88	80	67	64	81	95
Total Assets (Millions $). . .	223	138	124	134	125	121	104	128	111	112

PORTFOLIO (as of 9/30/96)

Portfolio Manager: Alan Wapnick, committee - 1994

Investm't Category: Growth & Income
- ✔ Domestic
- ✔ Foreign
-   Asset Allocation
-   Index
-   Sector
-   State Specific

Investment Style
Large-Cap Growth	✔ Large-Cap Value
Mid-Cap Growth	Mid-Cap Value
Small-Cap Growth	Small-Cap Value

Portfolio
7.8% cash	0.0% corp bonds
92.2% stocks	0.0% gov't bonds
0.0% preferred	0.0% muni bonds
0.0% conv't/warrants	0.0% other

SHAREHOLDER INFORMATION

Minimum Investment
Initial: $1,000   Subsequent: $50

Minimum IRA Investment
Initial: $250   Subsequent: $50

Maximum Fees
Load: none   12b-1: 0.25%
Other: none

Distributions
Income: quarterly   Capital Gains: Dec

Exchange Options
Number Per Year: no limit   Fee: none
Telephone: yes (money market fund available)

Services
IRA, pension, auto exchange, auto invest, auto withdraw

Lexington Ramirez Global Income (LEBDX)

Park 80 W. Plaza Two
Saddle Brook, NJ 07663
800-526-0056, 201-845-7300

International Bond

PERFORMANCE

fund inception date: 7/10/86

	3yr Annual	5yr Annual	10yr Annual	Bull	Bear
Return (%)	8.3	8.4	7.6	34.9	-6.9
Differ from Category (+/-)	2.3 abv av	1.8 high	0.3 abv av	3.7 high	2.6 av

Total Risk	Standard Deviation	Category Risk	Risk Index	Avg Mat
blw av	5.9%	av	0.8	7.9 yrs

	1996	1995	1994	1993	1992	1991	1990	1989	1988	1987
Return (%)	13.3	20.1	-6.6	10.9	6.5	10.0	6.6	7.3	10.3	0.1
Differ from Category (+/-)	2.0	4.1	1.0	-4.4	1.3	-5.0	-3.9	4.1	6.0	-10.1
Return, Tax-Adjusted (%)	10.0	16.2	-8.2	8.8	4.1	7.3	3.8	4.8	7.7	-3.2

PER SHARE DATA

	1996	1995	1994	1993	1992	1991	1990	1989	1988	1987
Dividends, Net Income ($)	0.86	0.95	0.44	0.55	0.61	0.67	0.71	0.63	0.63	0.87
Distrib'ns, Cap Gain ($)	0.03	0.00	0.00	0.00	0.00	0.00	0.00	0.00	0.00	0.00
Net Asset Value ($)	11.22	10.75	9.80	10.95	10.39	10.35	10.05	10.12	10.03	9.69
Expense Ratio (%)	na	2.75	1.50	1.44	1.50	1.12	1.08	1.72	1.33	0.00
Yield (%)	7.64	8.83	4.48	5.02	5.87	6.47	7.06	6.22	6.28	8.97
Portfolio Turnover (%)	na	164	10	31	31	29	45	47	67	67
Total Assets (Millions $)	29	10	10	14	13	12	10	12	13	11

PORTFOLIO (as of 9/30/96)

Portfolio Manager: D. Jamison, M. Forini Ramirez - 1986

Investm't Category: International Bond
- ✔ Domestic
- ✔ Foreign
- Asset Allocation
- Index
- Sector
- State Specific

Investment Style
Large-Cap Growth   Large-Cap Value
Mid-Cap Growth   Mid-Cap Value
Small-Cap Growth   Small-Cap Value

Portfolio
27.0% cash	0.0% corp bonds
0.0% stocks	0.0% gov't bonds
0.0% preferred	0.0% muni bonds
0.0% conv't/warrants	73.0% other

SHAREHOLDER INFORMATION

Minimum Investment
Initial: $1,000   Subsequent: $50

Minimum IRA Investment
Initial: $250   Subsequent: $50

Maximum Fees
Load: none   12b-1: 0.25%
Other: none

Distributions
Income: quarterly   Capital Gains: Dec

Exchange Options
Number Per Year: no limit   Fee: none
Telephone: yes (money market fund available)

Services
IRA, pension, auto exchange, auto invest, auto withdraw

Lexington Worldwide Emerging Mkts (LEXGX)

Park 80 W. Plaza Two
Saddle Brook, NJ 07663
800-526-0056, 201-845-7300

International Stock

PERFORMANCE

fund inception date: 7/1/69

	3yr Annual	5yr Annual	10yr Annual	Bull	Bear
Return (%)	-4.6	8.0	8.3	0.6	-15.3
Differ from Category (+/-)	-10.9 low	-2.0 blw av	-0.3 blw av	-23.7 low	-8.1 low

Total Risk	Standard Deviation	Category Risk	Risk Index	Beta
high	16.1%	high	1.6	0.82

	1996	1995	1994	1993	1992	1991	1990	1989	1988	1987
Return (%)	7.3	-6.0	-13.9	63.3	3.7	24.1	-14.5	28.1	10.4	0.2
Differ from Category (+/-)	-7.5	-15.1	-10.8	23.7	7.5	10.9	-4.4	5.5	-4.5	-12.0
Return, Tax-Adjusted (%)	7.3	-6.3	-15.1	62.7	1.3	18.7	-16.6	26.6	9.8	-10.2

PER SHARE DATA

	1996	1995	1994	1993	1992	1991	1990	1989	1988	1987
Dividends, Net Income ($)	0.00	0.08	0.00	0.00	0.11	0.11	0.27	0.21	0.12	0.75
Distrib'ns, Cap Gain ($)	0.00	0.00	0.56	0.17	0.60	1.48	0.40	0.17	0.00	3.30
Net Asset Value ($)	11.49	10.70	11.47	13.96	8.66	9.03	8.56	10.79	8.72	8.00
Expense Ratio (%)	na	1.88	1.65	1.64	1.89	1.97	1.42	1.36	1.33	1.34
Yield (%)	0.00	0.74	0.00	0.00	1.18	1.04	3.01	1.91	1.37	6.63
Portfolio Turnover (%)	na	92	79	38	91	112	52	59	48	83
Total Assets (Millions $)	265	260	288	227	30	24	22	29	26	25

PORTFOLIO (as of 9/30/96)

Portfolio Manager: Richard Saler, committee - 1994

Investm't Category: International Stock
- ✔ Domestic
- ✔ Foreign
-   Asset Allocation
-   Index
-   Sector
-   State Specific

Investment Style
Large-Cap Growth   Large-Cap Value
Mid-Cap Growth   Mid-Cap Value
Small-Cap Growth   Small-Cap Value

Portfolio
5.5% cash	0.0% corp bonds
94.5% stocks	0.0% gov't bonds
0.0% preferred	0.0% muni bonds
0.0% conv't/warrants	0.0% other

SHAREHOLDER INFORMATION

Minimum Investment
Initial: $1,000   Subsequent: $50

Minimum IRA Investment
Initial: $250   Subsequent: $50

Maximum Fees
Load: none   12b-1: none
Other: none

Distributions
Income: Dec   Capital Gains: Dec

Exchange Options
Number Per Year: no limit   Fee: none
Telephone: yes (money market fund available)

Services
IRA, pension, auto exchange, auto invest, auto withdraw

Lindner Bulwark (LDNBX)

Aggressive Growth

7711 Carondelet Ave.
Suite 700
P.O. Box 11208
St. Louis, MO 63105
800-995-7777, 314-727-5305

PERFORMANCE

fund inception date: 2/11/94

	3yr Annual	5yr Annual	10yr Annual	Bull	Bear
Return (%)	na	na	na	19.9	na
Differ from Category (+/-)	na	na	na	-51.2 low	na

Total Risk	Standard Deviation	Category Risk	Risk Index	Beta
na	na	na	na	na

	1996	1995	1994	1993	1992	1991	1990	1989	1988	1987
Return (%)	28.7	-11.1	—	—	—	—	—	—	—	—
Differ from Category (+/-)	9.6	-45.4	—	—	—	—	—	—	—	—
Return, Tax-Adjusted (%)	27.8	-12.9	—	—	—	—	—	—	—	—

PER SHARE DATA

	1996	1995	1994	1993	1992	1991	1990	1989	1988	1987
Dividends, Net Income ($)	0.14	0.30	—	—	—	—	—	—	—	—
Distrib'ns, Cap Gain ($)	0.00	0.03	—	—	—	—	—	—	—	—
Net Asset Value ($)	7.97	6.30	—	—	—	—	—	—	—	—
Expense Ratio (%)	1.24	1.27	—	—	—	—	—	—	—	—
Yield (%)	1.75	4.73	—	—	—	—	—	—	—	—
Portfolio Turnover (%)	139	34	—	—	—	—	—	—	—	—
Total Assets (Millions $)	76	24	—	—	—	—	—	—	—	—

PORTFOLIO (as of 9/30/96)

Portfolio Manager: Lawrence Callahan - 1994

Investm't Category: Aggressive Growth
✔ Domestic   Index
✔ Foreign   Sector
  Asset Allocation   State Specific

Investment Style
Large-Cap Growth   Large-Cap Value
Mid-Cap Growth   Mid-Cap Value
Small-Cap Growth   Small-Cap Value

Portfolio
60.3% cash   1.2% corp bonds
21.6% stocks   0.0% gov't bonds
 1.4% preferred   0.0% muni bonds
12.7% conv't/warrants 2.9% other

SHAREHOLDER INFORMATION

Minimum Investment
Initial: $3,000   Subsequent: $100

Minimum IRA Investment
Initial: $250   Subsequent: $100

Maximum Fees
Load: none   12b-1: none
Other: none

Distributions
Income: Sep   Capital Gains: Sep

Exchange Options
Number Per Year: no limit   Fee: none
Telephone: yes (money market fund available)

Services
IRA, pension, auto invest, auto withdraw

Lindner Dividend (LDDVX)

Balanced

7711 Carondelet Ave.
Suite 700
P.O. Box 11208
St. Louis, MO 63105
800-995-7777, 314-727-5305

PERFORMANCE

fund inception date: 6/22/76

	3yr Annual	5yr Annual	10yr Annual	Bull	Bear
Return (%)	9.4	12.7	11.2	34.6	-5.0
Differ from Category (+/-)	-2.3 blw av	1.3 abv av	0.4 av	-10.5 low	0.7 av

Total Risk	Standard Deviation	Category Risk	Risk Index	Beta
blw av	6.0%	blw av	0.9	0.53

	1996	1995	1994	1993	1992	1991	1990	1989	1988	1987
Return (%).	11.5	21.5	-3.4	14.9	21.1	27.3	-6.6	11.8	24.2	-4.1
Differ from Category (+/-). .	-2.7	-3.1	-1.8	0.5	12.2	3.2	-5.7	-6.3	12.0	-6.8
Return, Tax-Adjusted (%). . .	8.1	18.2	-6.8	11.6	17.7	23.3	-9.9	7.9	20.6	-8.6

PER SHARE DATA

	1996	1995	1994	1993	1992	1991	1990	1989	1988	1987
Dividends, Net Income ($).	1.72	1.83	1.90	1.74	1.86	1.99	1.86	2.19	1.76	1.87
Distrib'ns, Cap Gain ($) . .	0.78	0.23	0.57	0.58	0.10	0.00	0.02	0.00	0.06	1.15
Net Asset Value ($)	27.50	26.96	23.97	27.32	25.84	23.06	19.77	23.11	22.67	19.87
Expense Ratio (%).	0.60	0.21	0.64	0.74	0.80	0.87	0.87	0.97	1.04	1.00
Yield (%)	6.08	6.73	7.74	6.23	7.17	8.62	9.39	9.47	7.74	8.89
Portfolio Turnover (%). . . .	30	11	43	13	24	3	5	2	17	56
Total Assets (Millions $).	2,308	2,088	1,605	1,374	711	234	149	136	83	45

PORTFOLIO (as of 9/30/96)

Portfolio Manager: Eric E. Ryback - 1982

Investm't Category: Balanced

✔ Domestic	Index
Foreign	Sector
Asset Allocation	State Specific

Investment Style

Large-Cap Growth	Large-Cap Value
Mid-Cap Growth	Mid-Cap Value
Small-Cap Growth	Small-Cap Value

Portfolio

3.3% cash	19.6% corp bonds
62.4% stocks	0.0% gov't bonds
5.6% preferred	0.0% muni bonds
9.3% conv't/warrants	0.0% other

SHAREHOLDER INFORMATION

Minimum Investment
Initial: $2,000   Subsequent: $100

Minimum IRA Investment
Initial: $250   Subsequent: $100

Maximum Fees
Load: none   12b-1: none
Other: none

Distributions
Income: quarterly   Capital Gains: Sep

Exchange Options
Number Per Year: no limit   Fee: none
Telephone: yes (money market account available)

Services
IRA, auto invest, auto withdraw

Lindner Growth (LDNRX)

Growth & Income

7711 Carondelet Ave.
Suite 700
P.O. Box 11208
St. Louis, MO 63105
800-995-7777, 314-727-5305

PERFORMANCE

fund inception date: 9/30/69

	3yr Annual	5yr Annual	10yr Annual	Bull	Bear
Return (%)	12.9	14.2	12.9	49.2	-7.1
Differ from Category (+/-)	-2.4 blw av	0.3 av	0.2 av	-10.6 blw av	-0.7 blw av

Total Risk	Standard Deviation	Category Risk	Risk Index	Beta
abv av	9.6%	abv av	1.0	0.66

	1996	1995	1994	1993	1992	1991	1990	1989	1988	1987
Return (%).	21.0	19.8	-0.7	19.8	12.7	23.4	-11.4	21.2	20.3	8.8
Differ from Category (+/-). .	1.3	-10.3	0.6	6.0	2.0	-5.7	-5.5	-2.3	3.5	8.6
Return, Tax-Adjusted (%). .	16.5	17.1	-3.5	18.1	11.3	21.7	-14.2	17.7	18.1	3.5

PER SHARE DATA

	1996	1995	1994	1993	1992	1991	1990	1989	1988	1987
Dividends, Net Income ($).	0.39	0.46	0.33	0.45	0.52	0.66	0.85	0.90	0.70	1.01
Distrib'ns, Cap Gain ($) . . .	3.10	1.34	1.84	0.53	0.15	0.00	0.70	0.84	0.16	1.57
Net Asset Value ($)	24.60	23.23	20.89	23.22	20.22	18.55	15.58	19.21	17.31	15.12
Expense Ratio (%).	0.63	0.54	0.65	0.80	0.80	0.83	0.74	0.92	1.07	0.89
Yield (%)	1.40	1.87	1.45	1.89	2.55	3.55	5.22	4.48	4.00	6.05
Portfolio Turnover (%). . . .	39	24	37	18	11	13	19	18	21	39
Total Assets (Millions $). .	1,493	1,407	1,503	1,469	1,073	836	650	595	425	350

PORTFOLIO (as of 9/30/96)

Portfolio Manager: Robert A. Lange - 1977

Investm't Category: Growth & Income
✔ Domestic   Index
✔ Foreign   Sector
  Asset Allocation   State Specific

Investment Style
  Large-Cap Growth   Large-Cap Value
  Mid-Cap Growth   Mid-Cap Value
  Small-Cap Growth ✔ Small-Cap Value

Portfolio
  4.4% cash   3.6% corp bonds
  90.5% stocks   0.0% gov't bonds
  0.0% preferred   0.0% muni bonds
  1.5% conv't/warrants 0.0% other

SHAREHOLDER INFORMATION

Minimum Investment
Initial: $2,000   Subsequent: $100

Minimum IRA Investment
Initial: $250   Subsequent: $100

Maximum Fees
Load: none   12b-1: none
Other: none

Distributions
Income: Sep   Capital Gains: Sep

Exchange Options
Number Per Year: no limit   Fee: none
Telephone: yes (money market account available)

Services
IRA, pension, auto invest, auto withdraw

Lindner Utility (LDUTX)

Growth & Income

7711 Carondelet Ave.
Suite 700
P.O. Box 11208
St. Louis, MO 63105
800-995-7777, 314-727-5305

PERFORMANCE

fund inception date: 11/8/93

	3yr Annual	5yr Annual	10yr Annual	Bull	Bear
Return (%)	14.7	na	na	59.7	-9.5
Differ from Category (+/-)	-0.6 blw av	na	na	-0.1 av	-3.1 low

Total Risk	Standard Deviation	Category Risk	Risk Index	Beta
high	13.1%	high	1.4	0.81

	1996	1995	1994	1993	1992	1991	1990	1989	1988	1987
Return (%)	23.1	23.8	-1.0	—	—	—	—	—	—	—
Differ from Category (+/-)	3.4	-6.3	0.3	—	—	—	—	—	—	—
Return, Tax-Adjusted (%)	21.8	22.0	-1.8	—	—	—	—	—	—	—

PER SHARE DATA

	1996	1995	1994	1993	1992	1991	1990	1989	1988	1987
Dividends, Net Income ($)	0.38	0.45	0.15	—	—	—	—	—	—	—
Distrib'ns, Cap Gain ($)	0.01	0.00	0.08	—	—	—	—	—	—	—
Net Asset Value ($)	14.64	12.22	10.27	—	—	—	—	—	—	—
Expense Ratio (%)	0.95	1.04	1.30	—	—	—	—	—	—	—
Yield (%)	2.59	3.68	1.44	—	—	—	—	—	—	—
Portfolio Turnover (%)	98	190	44	—	—	—	—	—	—	—
Total Assets (Millions $)	34	22	43	—	—	—	—	—	—	—

PORTFOLIO (as of 9/30/96)

Portfolio Manager: Eric E. Ryback - 1993

Investm't Category: Growth & Income
- ✔ Domestic
- ✔ Foreign
- Asset Allocation
- Index
- ✔ Sector
- State Specific

Investment Style
- Large-Cap Growth
- Mid-Cap Growth
- Small-Cap Growth
- Large-Cap Value
- Mid-Cap Value
- ✔ Small-Cap Value

Portfolio
1.2% cash	4.5% corp bonds
86.7% stocks	0.0% gov't bonds
3.7% preferred	0.0% muni bonds
3.9% conv't/warrants	0.0% other

SHAREHOLDER INFORMATION

Minimum Investment
Initial: $3,000   Subsequent: $100

Minimum IRA Investment
Initial: $250   Subsequent: $100

Maximum Fees
Load: none   12b-1: none
Other: none

Distributions
Income: quarterly   Capital Gains: Sep

Exchange Options
Number Per Year: no limit   Fee: none
Telephone: yes (money market account available)

Services
IRA, auto invest, auto withdraw

Longleaf Partners (LLPFX)

Growth

6075 Poplar Ave.
Suite 900
Memphis, TN 38119
800-445-9469, 901-761-2474

this fund is closed to new investors

PERFORMANCE

fund inception date: 3/24/87

	3yr Annual	5yr Annual	10yr Annual	Bull	Bear
Return (%)	18.9	19.8	na	54.5	5.9
Differ from Category (+/-)	3.2 high	5.5 high	na	-7.9 blw av	12.6 high

Total Risk	Standard Deviation	Category Risk	Risk Index	Beta
av	8.6%	low	0.8	0.70

	1996	1995	1994	1993	1992	1991	1990	1989	1988	1987
Return (%)	21.0	27.4	8.9	22.2	20.4	39.1	-16.4	23.2	35.2	—
Differ from Category (+/-)	0.9	-2.9	9.2	8.2	8.6	3.1	-10.3	-2.9	17.1	—
Return, Tax-Adjusted (%)	17.1	26.1	6.6	20.1	17.4	36.7	-17.4	19.0	34.9	—

PER SHARE DATA

	1996	1995	1994	1993	1992	1991	1990	1989	1988	1987
Dividends, Net Income ($)	0.38	0.24	0.16	0.09	0.07	0.05	0.14	0.14	0.06	—
Distrib'ns, Cap Gain ($)	2.38	0.44	1.13	0.95	1.29	0.78	0.23	1.53	0.00	—
Net Asset Value ($)	22.85	21.15	17.13	16.92	14.70	13.34	10.21	12.62	11.60	—
Expense Ratio (%)	na	1.01	1.17	1.26	1.29	1.30	1.32	1.35	1.50	—
Yield (%)	1.50	1.11	0.87	0.50	0.43	0.35	1.34	0.98	0.51	—
Portfolio Turnover (%)	na	12	27	19	29	45	52	58	93	—
Total Assets (Millions $)	2,376	1,876	753	397	243	177	129	148	74	—

PORTFOLIO (as of 9/30/96)

Portfolio Manager: O. Mason Hawkins, G. Staley Cates - 1987

Investm't Category: Growth
✔ Domestic
✔ Foreign
  Asset Allocation
  Index
  Sector
  State Specific

Investment Style
✔ Large-Cap Growth   ✔ Large-Cap Value
✔ Mid-Cap Growth   ✔ Mid-Cap Value
  Small-Cap Growth   Small-Cap Value

Portfolio
18.6%	cash	0.0%	corp bonds
81.8%	stocks	0.0%	gov't bonds
0.0%	preferred	0.0%	muni bonds
0.0%	conv't/warrants	0.0%	other

SHAREHOLDER INFORMATION

Minimum Investment
Initial: $10,000   Subsequent: $1

Minimum IRA Investment
Initial: $10,000   Subsequent: $1

Maximum Fees
Load: none   12b-1: none
Other: none

Distributions
Income: Dec   Capital Gains: Dec

Exchange Options
Number Per Year: no limit   Fee: none
Telephone: none

Services
IRA, pension, auto invest, auto withdraw

Longleaf Partners Small Cap (LLSCX)

Growth

6075 Poplar Ave.
Suite 900
Memphis, TN 38119
800-445-9469, 901-761-2474

PERFORMANCE

fund inception date: 12/28/88

	3yr Annual	5yr Annual	10yr Annual	Bull	Bear
Return (%)	17.1	15.5	na	64.4	-5.0
Differ from Category (+/-)	1.4 abv av	1.2 abv av	na	2.0 abv av	1.7 abv av

Total Risk	Standard Deviation	Category Risk	Risk Index	Beta
av	8.1%	low	0.8	0.47

	1996	1995	1994	1993	1992	1991	1990	1989	1988	1987
Return (%)	30.6	18.5	3.7	19.8	6.8	26.2	-30.1	33.8	—	—
Differ from Category (+/-)	10.5	-11.8	4.0	5.8	-5.0	-9.8	-24.0	7.7	—	—
Return, Tax-Adjusted (%)	28.6	15.7	2.2	19.4	6.8	25.9	-31.7	32.2	—	—

PER SHARE DATA

	1996	1995	1994	1993	1992	1991	1990	1989	1988	1987
Dividends, Net Income ($)	0.02	0.11	0.00	0.00	0.00	0.06	0.36	0.14	—	—
Distrib'ns, Cap Gain ($)	1.00	1.16	0.70	0.16	0.00	0.00	0.22	0.36	—	—
Net Asset Value ($)	17.86	14.46	13.28	13.49	11.40	10.67	8.50	12.87	—	—
Expense Ratio (%)	na	1.30	1.38	1.45	1.45	1.43	1.43	1.50	—	—
Yield (%)	0.10	0.70	0.00	0.00	0.00	0.56	4.12	1.05	—	—
Portfolio Turnover (%)	na	32	19	14	26	65	15	20	—	—
Total Assets (Millions $)	229	135	99	85	62	60	47	52	—	—

PORTFOLIO (as of 9/30/96)

Portfolio Manager: O. Mason Hawkins, G. Staley Cates - 1988

Investm't Category: Growth
✔ Domestic   Index
✔ Foreign   Sector
  Asset Allocation State Specific

Investment Style

Large-Cap Growth	Large-Cap Value
Mid-Cap Growth	Mid-Cap Value
✔ Small-Cap Growth	✔ Small-Cap Value

Portfolio

7.2% cash	0.0% corp bonds
93.1% stocks	0.0% gov't bonds
0.0% preferred	0.0% muni bonds
0.0% conv't/warrants	0.0% other

SHAREHOLDER INFORMATION

Minimum Investment
Initial: $10,000   Subsequent: $1

Minimum IRA Investment
Initial: $10,000   Subsequent: $1

Maximum Fees
Load: none   12b-1: none
Other: none

Distributions
Income: Dec   Capital Gains: Dec

Exchange Options
Number Per Year: no limit   Fee: none
Telephone: none

Services
IRA, pension, auto invest, auto withdraw

Loomis Sayles Bond

(LSBDX)

Corporate Bond

One Financial Center
Boston, MA 02111
800-633-3330, 617-482-2450

PERFORMANCE

fund inception date: 5/10/91

	3yr Annual	5yr Annual	10yr Annual	Bull	Bear
Return (%)	11.7	14.2	na	45.9	-8.0
Differ from Category (+/-)	5.4 high	5.9 high	na	21.1 high	-2.9 blw av

Total Risk	Standard Deviation	Category Risk	Risk Index	Avg Mat
av	7.3%	high	1.6	19.1 yrs

	1996	1995	1994	1993	1992	1991	1990	1989	1988	1987
Return (%)	10.2	31.9	-4.1	22.2	14.2	—	—	—	—	—
Differ from Category (+/-)	5.0	13.9	-1.0	10.4	5.3	—	—	—	—	—
Return, Tax-Adjusted (%)	6.8	28.4	-7.1	17.9	9.7	—	—	—	—	—

PER SHARE DATA

	1996	1995	1994	1993	1992	1991	1990	1989	1988	1987
Dividends, Net Income ($)	0.86	0.82	0.86	0.80	0.76	—	—	—	—	—
Distrib'ns, Cap Gain ($)	0.25	0.08	0.00	0.45	0.54	—	—	—	—	—
Net Asset Value ($)	12.38	12.29	10.05	11.37	10.36	—	—	—	—	—
Expense Ratio (%)	na	0.79	0.84	0.94	1.00	—	—	—	—	—
Yield (%)	6.80	6.62	8.55	6.76	6.97	—	—	—	—	—
Portfolio Turnover (%)	na	35	87	170	101	—	—	—	—	—
Total Assets (Millions $)	535	252	82	64	18	—	—	—	—	—

PORTFOLIO (as of 9/30/96)

Portfolio Manager: Daniel J. Fuss - 1991

Investm't Category: Corporate Bond
- ✔ Domestic
- ✔ Foreign
-   Asset Allocation

    Index
    Sector
    State Specific

Investment Style

Large-Cap Growth   Large-Cap Value
Mid-Cap Growth   Mid-Cap Value
Small-Cap Growth   Small-Cap Value

Portfolio

0.1% cash	83.1% corp bonds
0.0% stocks	0.0% gov't bonds
3.0% preferred	0.0% muni bonds
13.8% conv't/warrants	0.0% other

SHAREHOLDER INFORMATION

Minimum Investment
Initial: $2,500   Subsequent: $50

Minimum IRA Investment
Initial: $250   Subsequent: $50

Maximum Fees
Load: none   12b-1: none
Other: none

Distributions
Income: quarterly   Capital Gains: Dec

Exchange Options
Number Per Year: 4   Fee: none
Telephone: yes (money market fund available)

Services
IRA, auto invest, auto withdraw

Loomis Sayles Global Bond (LSGBX)

One Financial Center
Boston, MA 02111
800-633-3330, 617-482-2450

International Bond

PERFORMANCE

fund inception date: 5/16/91

	3yr Annual	5yr Annual	10yr Annual	Bull	Bear
Return (%)	9.1	8.4	na	44.1	-11.5
Differ from Category (+/-)	3.1 high	1.8 high	na	12.9 high	-2.0 blw av

Total Risk	Standard Deviation	Category Risk	Risk Index	Avg Mat
av	7.7%	high	1.1	14.6 yrs

	1996	1995	1994	1993	1992	1991	1990	1989	1988	1987
Return (%)	15.0	23.9	-8.8	14.6	0.8	—	—	—	—	—
Differ from Category (+/-)	3.7	7.9	-1.2	-0.7	-4.4	—	—	—	—	—
Return, Tax-Adjusted (%)	12.4	20.7	-9.9	12.0	-2.9	—	—	—	—	—

PER SHARE DATA

	1996	1995	1994	1993	1992	1991	1990	1989	1988	1987
Dividends, Net Income ($)	0.74	0.77	0.28	0.49	0.77	—	—	—	—	—
Distrib'ns, Cap Gain ($)	0.00	0.00	0.00	0.26	0.39	—	—	—	—	—
Net Asset Value ($)	12.35	11.39	9.82	11.06	10.32	—	—	—	—	—
Expense Ratio (%)	na	1.50	1.30	1.50	1.50	—	—	—	—	—
Yield (%)	5.99	6.76	2.85	4.32	7.18	—	—	—	—	—
Portfolio Turnover (%)	na	148	153	150	72	—	—	—	—	—
Total Assets (Millions $)	26	10	25	21	10	—	—	—	—	—

PORTFOLIO (as of 9/30/96)

Portfolio Manager: E. John de Beer - 1991

Investm't Category: International Bond
✔ Domestic   Index
✔ Foreign   Sector
    Asset Allocation   State Specific

Investment Style
Large-Cap Growth   Large-Cap Value
Mid-Cap Growth   Mid-Cap Value
Small-Cap Growth   Small-Cap Value

Portfolio
4.4% cash   13.9% corp bonds
0.0% stocks   10.1% gov't bonds
0.0% preferred   0.0% muni bonds
9.1% conv't/warrants   62.5% other

SHAREHOLDER INFORMATION

Minimum Investment
Initial: $2,500   Subsequent: $50

Minimum IRA Investment
Initial: $250   Subsequent: $50

Maximum Fees
Load: none   12b-1: none
Other: none

Distributions
Income: Dec   Capital Gains: Dec

Exchange Options
Number Per Year: 4   Fee: none
Telephone: yes (money market fund available)

Services
IRA, auto invest, auto withdraw

Loomis Sayles Growth

(LSGRX)

Growth

One Financial Center
Boston, MA 02111
800-633-3330, 617-482-2450

	3yr Annual	5yr Annual	10yr Annual	Bull	Bear
Return (%)	14.7	11.3	na	63.6	-10.9
Differ from Category (+/-)	-1.0 av	-3.0 low	na	1.2 av	-4.2 low

Total Risk	Standard Deviation	Category Risk	Risk Index	Beta
high	12.1%	high	1.2	1.03

	1996	1995	1994	1993	1992	1991	1990	1989	1988	1987
Return (%)	19.8	30.9	-3.7	9.2	3.8	—	—	—	—	—
Differ from Category (+/-)	-0.3	0.6	-3.4	-4.8	-8.0	—	—	—	—	—
Return, Tax-Adjusted (%)	10.9	28.4	-3.8	7.8	3.8	—	—	—	—	—

PER SHARE DATA

	1996	1995	1994	1993	1992	1991	1990	1989	1988	1987
Dividends, Net Income ($)	0.00	0.00	0.00	0.00	0.00	—	—	—	—	—
Distrib'ns, Cap Gain ($)	4.84	1.08	0.04	0.60	0.00	—	—	—	—	—
Net Asset Value ($)	13.44	15.27	12.50	13.02	12.47	—	—	—	—	—
Expense Ratio (%)	na	1.08	1.16	1.20	1.50	—	—	—	—	—
Yield (%)	0.00	0.00	0.00	0.00	0.00	—	—	—	—	—
Portfolio Turnover (%)	na	48	46	64	98	—	—	—	—	—
Total Assets (Millions $)	38	45	36	32	24	—	—	—	—	—

PORTFOLIO (as of 9/30/96)

Portfolio Manager: Jerome Castellini - 1991

Investm't Category: Growth
- ✔ Domestic   Index
- ✔ Foreign   Sector
-    Asset Allocation State Specific

Investment Style
-    Large-Cap Growth   Large-Cap Value
- ✔ Mid-Cap Growth   Mid-Cap Value
-    Small-Cap Growth   Small-Cap Value

Portfolio
0.9% cash	0.0% corp bonds
99.1% stocks	0.0% gov't bonds
0.0% preferred	0.0% muni bonds
0.0% conv't/warrants	0.0% other

SHAREHOLDER INFORMATION

Minimum Investment
Initial: $2,500   Subsequent: $50

Minimum IRA Investment
Initial: $250   Subsequent: $50

Maximum Fees
Load: none   12b-1: none
Other: none

Distributions
Income: Dec   Capital Gains: Dec

Exchange Options
Number Per Year: 4   Fee: none
Telephone: yes (money market fund available)

Services
IRA, auto invest, auto withdraw

Loomis Sayles Growth & Income (LSGIX)

One Financial Center
Boston, MA 02111
800-633-3330, 617-482-2450

Growth & Income

PERFORMANCE

fund inception date: 5/16/91

	3yr Annual	5yr Annual	10yr Annual	Bull	Bear
Return (%)	17.5	15.6	na	64.7	-5.1
Differ from Category (+/-)	2.2 abv av	1.7 abv av	na	4.9 av	1.3 abv av

Total Risk	Standard Deviation	Category Risk	Risk Index	Beta
abv av	9.9%	abv av	1.1	0.97

	1996	1995	1994	1993	1992	1991	1990	1989	1988	1987
Return (%)	21.1	35.2	-0.9	11.8	14.0	—	—	—	—	—
Differ from Category (+/-)	1.4	5.1	0.4	-2.0	3.3	—	—	—	—	—
Return, Tax-Adjusted (%)	17.0	31.7	-2.4	10.7	12.5	—	—	—	—	—

PER SHARE DATA

	1996	1995	1994	1993	1992	1991	1990	1989	1988	1987
Dividends, Net Income ($)	0.21	0.22	0.15	0.12	0.12	—	—	—	—	—
Distrib'ns, Cap Gain ($)	1.80	1.15	0.43	0.28	0.36	—	—	—	—	—
Net Asset Value ($)	15.60	14.57	11.80	12.49	11.53	—	—	—	—	—
Expense Ratio (%)	na	1.20	1.33	1.50	1.50	—	—	—	—	—
Yield (%)	1.20	1.39	1.22	0.93	1.00	—	—	—	—	—
Portfolio Turnover (%)	na	60	48	53	67	—	—	—	—	—
Total Assets (Millions $)	43	36	25	20	12	—	—	—	—	—

PORTFOLIO (as of 9/30/96)

Portfolio Manager: Jeffrey Wardlow - 1991

Investm't Category: Growth & Income
- ✔ Domestic
- ✔ Foreign
-   Asset Allocation

  Index
  Sector
  State Specific

Investment Style
Large-Cap Growth	✔ Large-Cap Value
Mid-Cap Growth	Mid-Cap Value
Small-Cap Growth	Small-Cap Value

Portfolio
5.8% cash	0.0% corp bonds
94.2% stocks	0.0% gov't bonds
0.0% preferred	0.0% muni bonds
0.0% conv't/warrants	0.0% other

SHAREHOLDER INFORMATION

Minimum Investment
Initial: $2,500   Subsequent: $50

Minimum IRA Investment
Initial: $250   Subsequent: $50

Maximum Fees
Load: none   12b-1: none
Other: none

Distributions
Income: Dec   Capital Gains: Dec

Exchange Options
Number Per Year: 4   Fee: none
Telephone: yes (money market fund available)

Services
IRA, auto invest, auto withdraw

Loomis Sayles Int'l Equity

(LSIEX)

International Stock

One Financial Center
Boston, MA 02111
800-633-3330, 617-482-2450

PERFORMANCE

fund inception date: 5/10/91

	3yr Annual	5yr Annual	10yr Annual	Bull	Bear
Return (%)	8.1	10.6	na	28.3	-7.8
Differ from Category (+/-)	1.8 av	0.6 av	na	4.0 abv av	-0.6 av

Total Risk	Standard Deviation	Category Risk	Risk Index	Beta
av	8.5%	low	0.8	0.59

	1996	1995	1994	1993	1992	1991	1990	1989	1988	1987
Return (%)	18.3	8.7	-1.8	38.5	-5.1	—	—	—	—	—
Differ from Category (+/-)	3.5	-0.4	1.3	-1.1	-1.3	—	—	—	—	—
Return, Tax-Adjusted (%)	16.7	6.2	-4.3	37.0	-5.5	—	—	—	—	—

PER SHARE DATA

	1996	1995	1994	1993	1992	1991	1990	1989	1988	1987
Dividends, Net Income ($)	0.08	0.14	0.14	0.10	0.09	—	—	—	—	—
Distrib'ns, Cap Gain ($)	0.53	0.82	0.92	0.35	0.01	—	—	—	—	—
Net Asset Value ($)	13.16	11.65	11.61	12.90	9.64	—	—	—	—	—
Expense Ratio (%)	na	1.45	1.46	1.50	1.50	—	—	—	—	—
Yield (%)	0.58	1.12	1.11	0.75	0.93	—	—	—	—	—
Portfolio Turnover (%)	na	133	116	128	101	—	—	—	—	—
Total Assets (Millions $)	90	79	71	56	15	—	—	—	—	—

PORTFOLIO (as of 9/30/96)

Portfolio Manager: Paul Drexcer - 1996

Investm't Category: International Stock

Domestic	Index
✔ Foreign	Sector
Asset Allocation	State Specific

Investment Style

Large-Cap Growth	Large-Cap Value
Mid-Cap Growth	Mid-Cap Value
Small-Cap Growth	Small-Cap Value

Portfolio

1.3% cash	0.0% corp bonds
98.7% stocks	0.0% gov't bonds
0.0% preferred	0.0% muni bonds
0.0% conv't/warrants	0.0% other

SHAREHOLDER INFORMATION

Minimum Investment
Initial: $2,500   Subsequent: $50

Minimum IRA Investment
Initial: $250   Subsequent: $50

Maximum Fees
Load: none   12b-1: none
Other: none

Distributions
Income: Dec   Capital Gains: Dec

Exchange Options
Number Per Year: 4   Fee: none
Telephone: yes (money market fund available)

Services
IRA, auto invest, auto withdraw

Loomis Sayles Small Cap

(LSSCX)

Aggressive Growth

One Financial Center
Boston, MA 02111
800-633-3330, 617-482-2450

PERFORMANCE

fund inception date: 5/13/91

	3yr Annual	5yr Annual	10yr Annual	Bull	Bear
Return (%)	16.4	17.3	na	75.4	-11.8
Differ from Category (+/-)	0.6 abv av	2.0 abv av	na	4.3 abv av	-1.2 av

Total Risk	Standard Deviation	Category Risk	Risk Index	Beta
abv av	11.5%	blw av	0.8	0.78

	1996	1995	1994	1993	1992	1991	1990	1989	1988	1987
Return (%)	30.3	32.1	-8.4	24.6	13.1	—	—	—	—	—
Differ from Category (+/-)	11.2	-2.2	-8.4	5.3	1.4	—	—	—	—	—
Return, Tax-Adjusted (%)	25.6	28.5	-8.6	20.4	10.3	—	—	—	—	—

PER SHARE DATA

	1996	1995	1994	1993	1992	1991	1990	1989	1988	1987
Dividends, Net Income ($)	0.10	0.04	0.00	0.00	0.00	—	—	—	—	—
Distrib'ns, Cap Gain ($)	2.41	1.58	0.10	1.90	1.22	—	—	—	—	—
Net Asset Value ($)	17.39	15.33	12.85	14.13	12.88	—	—	—	—	—
Expense Ratio (%)	na	1.25	1.27	1.35	1.50	—	—	—	—	—
Yield (%)	0.50	0.23	0.00	0.00	0.00	—	—	—	—	—
Portfolio Turnover (%)	na	155	87	106	109	—	—	—	—	—
Total Assets (Millions $)	142	90	74	67	39	—	—	—	—	—

PORTFOLIO (as of 9/30/96)

Portfolio Manager: Jeff Petherik, Mary Champagne - 1993

Investm't Category: Aggressive Growth
- ✔ Domestic
- Foreign
- Asset Allocation
- Index
- Sector
- State Specific

Investment Style
- Large-Cap Growth
- Mid-Cap Growth
- ✔ Small-Cap Growth
- Large-Cap Value
- Mid-Cap Value
- ✔ Small-Cap Value

Portfolio
13.2% cash	0.0% corp bonds
86.8% stocks	0.0% gov't bonds
0.0% preferred	0.0% muni bonds
0.0% conv't/warrants	0.0% other

SHAREHOLDER INFORMATION

Minimum Investment
Initial: $2,500   Subsequent: $50

Minimum IRA Investment
Initial: $250   Subsequent: $50

Maximum Fees
Load: none   12b-1: none
Other: none

Distributions
Income: Dec   Capital Gains: Dec

Exchange Options
Number Per Year: 4   Fee: none
Telephone: yes (money market fund available)

Services
IRA, auto invest, auto withdraw

MSB (MSBFX)

Growth

111 E. Wacker Drive
26th Floor
Chicago, IL 60601
212-797-2730

PERFORMANCE

fund inception date: 12/31/64

	3yr Annual	5yr Annual	10yr Annual	Bull	Bear
Return (%)	14.1	14.7	12.2	54.4	-6.3
Differ from Category (+/-)	-1.6 blw av	0.4 av	-1.7 blw av	-8.0 blw av	0.4 av

Total Risk	Standard Deviation	Category Risk	Risk Index	Beta
av	9.4%	blw av	0.9	0.84

	1996	1995	1994	1993	1992	1991	1990	1989	1988	1987
Return (%)	21.1	24.8	-1.7	20.6	10.6	16.9	-7.4	28.0	9.7	4.6
Differ from Category (+/-)	1.0	-5.5	-1.4	6.6	-1.2	-19.1	-1.3	1.9	-8.4	2.6
Return, Tax-Adjusted (%)	17.1	18.4	-7.3	16.7	9.4	12.2	-10.8	22.5	5.4	-1.4

PER SHARE DATA

	1996	1995	1994	1993	1992	1991	1990	1989	1988	1987
Dividends, Net Income ($)	0.13	0.08	0.45	0.17	0.28	0.21	0.40	0.25	0.37	0.33
Distrib'ns, Cap Gain ($)	1.75	2.93	2.67	1.92	0.22	2.11	1.58	2.86	2.11	3.88
Net Asset Value ($)	14.60	13.64	13.39	16.79	15.67	14.62	14.54	17.82	16.40	17.23
Expense Ratio (%)	na	1.69	1.28	1.12	1.13	1.86	1.39	1.20	1.19	0.98
Yield (%)	0.79	0.48	2.80	0.90	1.76	1.25	2.48	1.20	1.99	1.56
Portfolio Turnover (%)	na	68	62	26	13	17	31	29	19	37
Total Assets (Millions $)	38	28	35	45	40	41	42	51	49	48

PORTFOLIO (as of 9/30/96)

Portfolio Manager: John McCabe, Mark Trautman - 1993

Investm't Category: Growth
- ✔ Domestic
- Foreign
- Asset Allocation
- Index
- Sector
- State Specific

Investment Style
- ✔ Large-Cap Growth
- ✔ Mid-Cap Growth
- Small-Cap Growth
- ✔ Large-Cap Value
- ✔ Mid-Cap Value
- Small-Cap Value

Portfolio
7.8%	cash	0.0%	corp bonds
92.2%	stocks	0.0%	gov't bonds
0.0%	preferred	0.0%	muni bonds
0.0%	conv't/warrants	0.0%	other

SHAREHOLDER INFORMATION

Minimum Investment
Initial: $50   Subsequent: $25

Minimum IRA Investment
Initial: $50   Subsequent: $25

Maximum Fees
Load: none   12b-1: none
Other: none

Distributions
Income: quarterly   Capital Gains: annual

Exchange Options
Number Per Year: none   Fee: na
Telephone: na

Services
IRA, pension, auto invest, auto withdraw

Mairs & Power Growth

(MPGFX)

Growth

W-2062 First Nat'l Bank Bldg.
332 Minnesota St.
St. Paul, MN 55101
800-304-7404, 612-222-8478

PERFORMANCE

fund inception date: 1/1/58

	3yr Annual	5yr Annual	10yr Annual	Bull	Bear
Return (%)	25.8	19.3	17.2	101.6	-2.8
Differ from Category (+/-)	10.1 high	5.0 high	3.3 high	39.2 high	3.9 high

Total Risk	Standard Deviation	Category Risk	Risk Index	Beta
abv av	10.9%	abv av	1.1	1.01

	1996	1995	1994	1993	1992	1991	1990	1989	1988	1987
Return (%).............	26.4	49.3	5.6	12.8	7.8	42.0	3.6	28.0	10.2	-2.6
Differ from Category (+/-)..	6.3	19.0	5.9	-1.2	-4.0	6.0	9.7	1.9	-7.9	-4.6
Return, Tax-Adjusted (%)..	25.2	47.6	4.2	11.3	6.4	39.6	2.2	24.9	7.8	-6.0

PER SHARE DATA

	1996	1995	1994	1993	1992	1991	1990	1989	1988	1987
Dividends, Net Income ($).	0.75	0.56	0.65	0.43	0.40	0.39	0.42	0.43	0.41	0.48
Distrib'ns, Cap Gain ($) ...	1.35	1.51	0.98	1.22	1.15	1.58	0.70	1.83	1.21	2.29
Net Asset Value ($)	69.48	56.64	39.37	38.84	35.91	34.78	25.94	26.11	22.21	21.63
Expense Ratio (%).........	na	0.99	0.99	0.98	1.00	1.09	1.05	1.07	1.11	1.04
Yield (%)	1.05	0.96	1.61	1.07	1.07	1.07	1.57	1.53	1.75	2.00
Portfolio Turnover (%).....	na	3	5	4	4	5	5	2	4	3
Total Assets (Millions $)...	148	70	41	39	34	31	22	22	22	19

PORTFOLIO (as of 9/30/96)

Portfolio Manager: George A. Mairs III - 1980

Investm't Category: Growth
- ✔ Domestic
- Foreign
- Asset Allocation
- Index
- Sector
- State Specific

Investment Style
- ✔ Large-Cap Growth
- ✔ Mid-Cap Growth
- Small-Cap Growth
- ✔ Large-Cap Value
- ✔ Mid-Cap Value
- Small-Cap Value

Portfolio
5.6%	cash	0.0% corp bonds
94.4%	stocks	0.0% gov't bonds
0.0%	preferred	0.0% muni bonds
0.0%	conv't/warrants	0.0% other

SHAREHOLDER INFORMATION

Minimum Investment
Initial: $2,500   Subsequent: $100

Minimum IRA Investment
Initial: $1,000   Subsequent: $100

Maximum Fees
Load: none   12b-1: none
Other: none

Distributions
Income: Jun, Dec   Capital Gains: annual

Exchange Options
Number Per Year: none   Fee: na
Telephone: na

Services
IRA, pension, auto withdraw

Markman Moderate Growth (MMMGX)

Growth & Income

6600 France Ave. S.
Suite 565
Edina, MN 55435
612-920-4848

PERFORMANCE

fund inception date: 1/26/95

	3yr Annual	5yr Annual	10yr Annual	Bull	Bear
Return (%)	na	na	na	na	na
Differ from Category (+/-)	na	na	na	na	na

Total Risk	Standard Deviation	Category Risk	Risk Index	Beta
na	na	na	na	na

	1996	1995	1994	1993	1992	1991	1990	1989	1988	1987
Return (%)	11.1	—	—	—	—	—	—	—	—	—
Differ from Category (+/-)	-8.6	—	—	—	—	—	—	—	—	—
Return, Tax-Adjusted (%)	8.1	—	—	—	—	—	—	—	—	—

PER SHARE DATA

	1996	1995	1994	1993	1992	1991	1990	1989	1988	1987
Dividends, Net Income ($)	0.31	—	—	—	—	—	—	—	—	—
Distrib'ns, Cap Gain ($)	0.76	—	—	—	—	—	—	—	—	—
Net Asset Value ($)	11.49	—	—	—	—	—	—	—	—	—
Expense Ratio (%)	na	—	—	—	—	—	—	—	—	—
Yield (%)	2.53	—	—	—	—	—	—	—	—	—
Portfolio Turnover (%)	na	—	—	—	—	—	—	—	—	—
Total Assets (Millions $)	81	—	—	—	—	—	—	—	—	—

PORTFOLIO (as of 9/30/96)

Portfolio Manager: Robert Markman - 1995

Investm't Category: Growth & Income
- ✔ Domestic
- ✔ Foreign
-   Asset Allocation
-   Index
- ✔ Sector
-   State Specific

Investment Style
- Large-Cap Growth
- Mid-Cap Growth
- Small-Cap Growth
- Large-Cap Value
- Mid-Cap Value
- Small-Cap Value

Portfolio
0.0% cash	0.0% corp bonds
100.0% stocks	0.0% gov't bonds
0.0% preferred	0.0% muni bonds
0.0% conv't/warrants	0.0% other

SHAREHOLDER INFORMATION

Minimum Investment
Initial: $25,000   Subsequent: $500

Minimum IRA Investment
Initial: $25,000   Subsequent: $500

Maximum Fees
Load: none   12b-1: 0.25%
Other: none

Distributions
Income: annual   Capital Gains: annual

Exchange Options
Number Per Year: no limit   Fee: none
Telephone: yes

Services
IRA, pension, auto invest, auto withdraw

Marshall Equity Income

(MREIX)

Growth & Income

Federated Investors Tower
1001 Liberty Ave.
Pittsburgh, PA 15222
800-236-8560, 414-287-8500

PERFORMANCE

fund inception date: 9/30/93

	3yr Annual	5yr Annual	10yr Annual	Bull	Bear
Return (%)	16.9	na	na	66.9	-6.0
Differ from Category (+/-)	1.6 av	na	na	7.1 abv av	0.4 av

Total Risk	Standard Deviation	Category Risk	Risk Index	Beta
av	7.9%	low	0.9	0.77

	1996	1995	1994	1993	1992	1991	1990	1989	1988	1987
Return (%)	21.1	34.2	-1.7	—	—	—	—	—	—	—
Differ from Category (+/-)	1.4	4.1	-0.4	—	—	—	—	—	—	—
Return, Tax-Adjusted (%)	18.0	32.1	-3.0	—	—	—	—	—	—	—

PER SHARE DATA

	1996	1995	1994	1993	1992	1991	1990	1989	1988	1987
Dividends, Net Income ($)	0.34	0.34	0.31	—	—	—	—	—	—	—
Distrib'ns, Cap Gain ($)	0.85	0.20	0.00	—	—	—	—	—	—	—
Net Asset Value ($)	13.55	12.20	9.53	—	—	—	—	—	—	—
Expense Ratio (%)	na	1.01	1.01	—	—	—	—	—	—	—
Yield (%)	2.36	2.74	3.25	—	—	—	—	—	—	—
Portfolio Turnover (%)	na	43	na	—	—	—	—	—	—	—
Total Assets (Millions $)	216	132	60	—	—	—	—	—	—	—

PORTFOLIO (as of 9/30/96)

Portfolio Manager: Bruce Hutson - 1993

Investm't Category: Growth & Income
- ✔ Domestic
- Foreign
- Asset Allocation
- Index
- Sector
- State Specific

Investment Style
- Large-Cap Growth
- Mid-Cap Growth
- Small-Cap Growth
- ✔ Large-Cap Value
- Mid-Cap Value
- Small-Cap Value

Portfolio
18.6% cash	0.0% corp bonds
80.5% stocks	0.1% gov't bonds
0.8% preferred	0.0% muni bonds
0.0% conv't/warrants	0.0% other

SHAREHOLDER INFORMATION

Minimum Investment
Initial: $1,000   Subsequent: $50

Minimum IRA Investment
Initial: $1,000   Subsequent: $50

Maximum Fees
Load: none   12b-1: none
Other: none

Distributions
Income: quarterly   Capital Gains: annual

Exchange Options
Number Per Year: no limit   Fee: none
Telephone: yes (money market fund available)

Services
IRA, pension, auto exchange, auto invest, auto withdraw

Marshall Gov't Income
(MRGIX)
Mortgage-Backed Bond

Federated Investors Tower
1001 Liberty Ave.
Pittsburgh, PA 15222
800-236-8560, 414-287-8500

PERFORMANCE

fund inception date: 12/11/92

	3yr Annual	5yr Annual	10yr Annual	Bull	Bear
Return (%)	5.4	na	na	21.3	-4.1
Differ from Category (+/-)	-0.2 blw av	na	na	0.2 av	-0.5 av

Total Risk	Standard Deviation	Category Risk	Risk Index	Avg Mat
low	4.1%	high	1.1	7.8 yrs

	1996	1995	1994	1993	1992	1991	1990	1989	1988	1987
Return (%)	3.0	16.9	-2.8	5.9	—	—	—	—	—	—
Differ from Category (+/-)	-1.4	2.2	-1.1	-1.0	—	—	—	—	—	—
Return, Tax-Adjusted (%)	0.5	14.1	-5.3	2.8	—	—	—	—	—	—

PER SHARE DATA

	1996	1995	1994	1993	1992	1991	1990	1989	1988	1987
Dividends, Net Income ($)	0.61	0.61	0.60	0.67	—	—	—	—	—	—
Distrib'ns, Cap Gain ($)	0.00	0.00	0.00	0.14	—	—	—	—	—	—
Net Asset Value ($)	9.45	9.79	8.93	9.80	—	—	—	—	—	—
Expense Ratio (%)	na	0.86	0.86	0.85	—	—	—	—	—	—
Yield (%)	6.45	6.23	6.71	6.74	—	—	—	—	—	—
Portfolio Turnover (%)	na	360	175	na	—	—	—	—	—	—
Total Assets (Millions $)	155	114	78	50	—	—	—	—	—	—

PORTFOLIO (as of 9/30/96)

Portfolio Manager: Larry Pavelec - 1992

Investm't Category: Mortgage-Backed Bond
- ✔ Domestic
- Foreign
- Asset Allocation
- Index
- Sector
- State Specific

Investment Style
- Large-Cap Growth
- Mid-Cap Growth
- Small-Cap Growth
- Large-Cap Value
- Mid-Cap Value
- Small-Cap Value

Portfolio
0.0% cash	0.0% corp bonds
0.0% stocks	100.0% gov't bonds
0.0% preferred	0.0% muni bonds
0.0% conv't/warrants	0.0% other

SHAREHOLDER INFORMATION

Minimum Investment
Initial: $1,000   Subsequent: $50

Minimum IRA Investment
Initial: $250   Subsequent: $50

Maximum Fees
Load: none   12b-1: none
Other: none

Distributions
Income: monthly   Capital Gains: annual

Exchange Options
Number Per Year: no limit   Fee: none
Telephone: yes (money market fund available)

Services
IRA, pension, auto exchange, auto invest, auto withdraw

Marshall Interm Bond

(MAIBX)

General Bond

Federated Investors Tower
1001 Liberty Ave.
Pittsburgh, PA 15222
800-236-8560, 414-287-8500

PERFORMANCE

fund inception date: 11/20/92

	3yr Annual	5yr Annual	10yr Annual	Bull	Bear
Return (%)	4.6	na	na	18.5	-4.3
Differ from Category (+/-)	-0.5 blw av	na	na	-1.8 blw av	-0.1 av

Total Risk	Standard Deviation	Category Risk	Risk Index	Avg Mat
low	3.7%	av	1.0	4.1 yrs

	1996	1995	1994	1993	1992	1991	1990	1989	1988	1987
Return (%)	2.4	15.4	-3.1	6.8	—	—	—	—	—	—
Differ from Category (+/-)	-1.5	0.5	-0.8	-2.3	—	—	—	—	—	—
Return, Tax-Adjusted (%)	0.0	12.7	-5.5	3.8	—	—	—	—	—	—

PER SHARE DATA

	1996	1995	1994	1993	1992	1991	1990	1989	1988	1987
Dividends, Net Income ($)	0.57	0.60	0.59	0.62	—	—	—	—	—	—
Distrib'ns, Cap Gain ($)	0.00	0.00	0.00	0.17	—	—	—	—	—	—
Net Asset Value ($)	9.44	9.79	9.04	9.93	—	—	—	—	—	—
Expense Ratio (%)	na	0.71	0.71	0.70	—	—	—	—	—	—
Yield (%)	6.03	6.12	6.52	6.13	—	—	—	—	—	—
Portfolio Turnover (%)	na	232	228	na	—	—	—	—	—	—
Total Assets (Millions $)	429	357	326	312	—	—	—	—	—	—

PORTFOLIO (as of 9/30/96)

Portfolio Manager: Mark Pittman - 1995

Investm't Category: General Bond
- ✔ Domestic
- Foreign
- Asset Allocation
- Index
- Sector
- State Specific

Investment Style
- Large-Cap Growth
- Mid-Cap Growth
- Small-Cap Growth
- Large-Cap Value
- Mid-Cap Value
- Small-Cap Value

Portfolio
0.0% cash	58.1% corp bonds
0.0% stocks	41.9% gov't bonds
0.0% preferred	0.0% muni bonds
0.0% conv't/warrants	0.0% other

SHAREHOLDER INFORMATION

Minimum Investment
Initial: $1,000   Subsequent: $50

Minimum IRA Investment
Initial: $250   Subsequent: $50

Maximum Fees
Load: none   12b-1: none
Other: none

Distributions
Income: monthly   Capital Gains: annual

Exchange Options
Number Per Year: no limit   Fee: none
Telephone: yes (money market fund available)

Services
IRA, pension, auto exchange, auto invest, auto withdraw

Marshall Mid Cap Stock

(MRMSX)

Aggressive Growth

Federated Investors Tower
1001 Liberty Ave.
Pittsburgh, PA 15222
800-236-8560, 414-287-8500

PERFORMANCE

fund inception date: 9/30/93

	3yr Annual	5yr Annual	10yr Annual	Bull	Bear
Return (%)	15.0	na	na	73.2	-13.6
Differ from Category (+/-)	-0.8 av	na	na	2.1 av	-3.0 blw av

Total Risk	Standard Deviation	Category Risk	Risk Index	Beta
high	15.1%	av	1.1	1.15

	1996	1995	1994	1993	1992	1991	1990	1989	1988	1987
Return (%)	20.6	33.7	-5.7	—	—	—	—	—	—	—
Differ from Category (+/-)	1.5	-0.6	-5.7	—	—	—	—	—	—	—
Return, Tax-Adjusted (%)	17.7	31.0	-5.7	—	—	—	—	—	—	—

PER SHARE DATA

	1996	1995	1994	1993	1992	1991	1990	1989	1988	1987
Dividends, Net Income ($)	0.00	0.00	0.00	—	—	—	—	—	—	—
Distrib'ns, Cap Gain ($)	1.21	0.91	0.00	—	—	—	—	—	—	—
Net Asset Value ($)	13.10	11.84	9.55	—	—	—	—	—	—	—
Expense Ratio (%)	na	1.01	1.01	—	—	—	—	—	—	—
Yield (%)	0.00	0.00	0.00	—	—	—	—	—	—	—
Portfolio Turnover (%)	na	157	na	—	—	—	—	—	—	—
Total Assets (Millions $)	159	108	69	—	—	—	—	—	—	—

PORTFOLIO (as of 9/30/96)

Portfolio Manager: Steve Hayward - 1993

Investm't Category: Aggressive Growth

✔ Domestic	Index
Foreign	Sector
Asset Allocation	State Specific

Investment Style

Large-Cap Growth	Large-Cap Value
✔ Mid-Cap Growth	Mid-Cap Value
✔ Small-Cap Growth	Small-Cap Value

Portfolio

2.9% cash	0.0% corp bonds
97.0% stocks	0.1% gov't bonds
0.0% preferred	0.0% muni bonds
0.0% conv't/warrants	0.0% other

SHAREHOLDER INFORMATION

Minimum Investment
Initial: $1,000   Subsequent: $50

Minimum IRA Investment
Initial: $1,000   Subsequent: $50

Maximum Fees
Load: none   12b-1: none
Other: none

Distributions
Income: quarterly   Capital Gains: annual

Exchange Options
Number Per Year: no limit   Fee: none
Telephone: yes (money market fund available)

Services
IRA, pension, auto exchange, auto invest, auto withdraw

Marshall Short-Term Income (MSINX)

General Bond

Federated Investors Tower
1001 Liberty Ave.
Pittsburgh, PA 15222
800-236-8560, 414-287-8500

PERFORMANCE

fund inception date: 10/30/92

	3yr Annual	5yr Annual	10yr Annual	Bull	Bear
Return (%)	5.2	na	na	15.8	-0.1
Differ from Category (+/-)	0.1 av	na	na	-4.5 low	4.1 high

Total Risk	Standard Deviation	Category Risk	Risk Index	Avg Mat
low	1.3%	low	0.4	1.9 yrs

	1996	1995	1994	1993	1992	1991	1990	1989	1988	1987
Return (%).	4.9	8.9	1.8	3.6	—	—	—	—	—	—
Differ from Category (+/-). .	1.0	-6.0	4.1	-5.5	—	—	—	—	—	—
Return, Tax-Adjusted (%). . .	2.4	6.4	-0.1	1.7	—	—	—	—	—	—

PER SHARE DATA

	1996	1995	1994	1993	1992	1991	1990	1989	1988	1987
Dividends, Net Income ($)	0.61	0.59	0.47	0.47	—	—	—	—	—	—
Distrib'ns, Cap Gain ($) . . .	0.00	0.00	0.00	0.00	—	—	—	—	—	—
Net Asset Value ($)	9.65	9.80	9.56	9.86	—	—	—	—	—	—
Expense Ratio (%).	na	0.51	0.50	0.50	—	—	—	—	—	—
Yield (%)	6.32	6.02	4.91	4.76	—	—	—	—	—	—
Portfolio Turnover (%).	na	194	185	na	—	—	—	—	—	—
Total Assets (Millions $). . .	102	87	92	82	—	—	—	—	—	—

PORTFOLIO (as of 9/30/96)

Portfolio Manager: Mark Pittman - 1992

Investm't Category: General Bond

- ✔ Domestic
- Foreign
- Asset Allocation
- Index
- Sector
- State Specific

Investment Style

- Large-Cap Growth
- Mid-Cap Growth
- Small-Cap Growth
- Large-Cap Value
- Mid-Cap Value
- Small-Cap Value

Portfolio

9.0% cash	11.0% corp bonds
0.0% stocks	34.4% gov't bonds
0.0% preferred	0.0% muni bonds
0.0% conv't/warrants	45.6% other

SHAREHOLDER INFORMATION

Minimum Investment
Initial: $1,000   Subsequent: $50

Minimum IRA Investment
Initial: $1   Subsequent: $1

Maximum Fees
Load: none   12b-1: none
Other: none

Distributions
Income: monthly   Capital Gains: annual

Exchange Options
Number Per Year: no limit   Fee: none
Telephone: yes (money market fund available)

Services
IRA, pension, auto exchange, auto invest, auto withdraw

Marshall Stock (MASTX)

Growth

Federated Investors Tower
1001 Liberty Ave.
Pittsburgh, PA 15222
800-236-8560, 414-287-8500

fund inception date: 11/20/92

PERFORMANCE

	3yr Annual	5yr Annual	10yr Annual	Bull	Bear
Return (%)	11.9	na	na	53.4	-10.1
Differ from Category (+/-)	-3.8 low	na	na	-9.0 blw av	-3.4 low

Total Risk	Standard Deviation	Category Risk	Risk Index	Beta
abv av	9.6%	blw av	0.9	0.92

	1996	1995	1994	1993	1992	1991	1990	1989	1988	1987
Return (%)	11.7	33.1	-5.8	1.1	—	—	—	—	—	—
Differ from Category (+/-)	-8.4	2.8	-5.5	-12.9	—	—	—	—	—	—
Return, Tax-Adjusted (%)	7.5	30.7	-6.1	0.6	—	—	—	—	—	—

PER SHARE DATA

	1996	1995	1994	1993	1992	1991	1990	1989	1988	1987
Dividends, Net Income ($)	0.15	0.10	0.07	0.11	—	—	—	—	—	—
Distrib'ns, Cap Gain ($)	1.58	0.66	0.00	0.00	—	—	—	—	—	—
Net Asset Value ($)	11.81	12.11	9.68	10.35	—	—	—	—	—	—
Expense Ratio (%)	na	0.98	0.99	0.94	—	—	—	—	—	—
Yield (%)	1.12	0.78	0.72	1.06	—	—	—	—	—	—
Portfolio Turnover (%)	na	79	86	na	—	—	—	—	—	—
Total Assets (Millions $)	244	273	226	265	—	—	—	—	—	—

PORTFOLIO (as of 9/30/96)

Portfolio Manager: O. Connor, Frazier, Kuehn - 1995

Investm't Category: Growth
- ✔ Domestic
- Foreign
- Asset Allocation
- Index
- Sector
- State Specific

Investment Style
- ✔ Large-Cap Growth
- Mid-Cap Growth
- Small-Cap Growth
- ✔ Large-Cap Value
- Mid-Cap Value
- Small-Cap Value

Portfolio
0.8% cash	0.0% corp bonds
99.2% stocks	0.0% gov't bonds
0.0% preferred	0.0% muni bonds
0.0% conv't/warrants	0.0% other

SHAREHOLDER INFORMATION

Minimum Investment
Initial: $1,000   Subsequent: $50

Minimum IRA Investment
Initial: $250   Subsequent: $50

Maximum Fees
Load: none   12b-1: none
Other: none

Distributions
Income: quarterly   Capital Gains: annual

Exchange Options
Number Per Year: no limit   Fee: none
Telephone: yes (money market fund available)

Services
IRA, pension, auto exchange, auto invest, auto withdraw

Marshall Value Equity

(MRVEX)

Growth

Federated Investors Tower
1001 Liberty Ave.
Pittsburgh, PA 15222
800-236-8560, 414-287-8500

PERFORMANCE

fund inception date: 9/30/93

	3yr Annual	5yr Annual	10yr Annual	Bull	Bear
Return (%)	13.3	na	na	47.3	-4.0
Differ from Category (+/-)	-2.4 blw av	na	na	-15.1 low	2.7 abv av

Total Risk	Standard Deviation	Category Risk	Risk Index	Beta
av	9.1%	blw av	0.9	0.81

	1996	1995	1994	1993	1992	1991	1990	1989	1988	1987
Return (%)	13.9	25.3	2.0	—	—	—	—	—	—	—
Differ from Category (+/-)	-6.2	-5.0	2.3	—	—	—	—	—	—	—
Return, Tax-Adjusted (%)	8.7	22.0	1.1	—	—	—	—	—	—	—

PER SHARE DATA

	1996	1995	1994	1993	1992	1991	1990	1989	1988	1987
Dividends, Net Income ($)	0.18	0.21	0.15	—	—	—	—	—	—	—
Distrib'ns, Cap Gain ($)	1.88	0.87	0.11	—	—	—	—	—	—	—
Net Asset Value ($)	11.09	11.59	10.13	—	—	—	—	—	—	—
Expense Ratio (%)	na	0.96	1.00	—	—	—	—	—	—	—
Yield (%)	1.38	1.68	1.46	—	—	—	—	—	—	—
Portfolio Turnover (%)	na	78	na	—	—	—	—	—	—	—
Total Assets (Millions $)	180	204	195	—	—	—	—	—	—	—

PORTFOLIO (as of 9/30/96)

Portfolio Manager: Gerry Sandel - 1993

Investm't Category: Growth

✔ Domestic	Index
Foreign	Sector
Asset Allocation	State Specific

Investment Style

Large-Cap Growth	✔ Large-Cap Value
Mid-Cap Growth	✔ Mid-Cap Value
Small-Cap Growth	Small-Cap Value

Portfolio

15.2% cash	0.0% corp bonds
84.8% stocks	0.0% gov't bonds
0.0% preferred	0.0% muni bonds
0.0% conv't/warrants	0.0% other

SHAREHOLDER INFORMATION

Minimum Investment
Initial: $1,000   Subsequent: $50

Minimum IRA Investment
Initial: $1,000   Subsequent: $50

Maximum Fees
Load: none   12b-1: none
Other: none

Distributions
Income: quarterly   Capital Gains: annual

Exchange Options
Number Per Year: no limit   Fee: none
Telephone: yes (money market fund available)

Services
IRA, pension, auto exchange, auto invest, auto withdraw

Mathers (MATRX)
Growth

100 Corporate N.
Suite 201
Bannockburn, IL 60015
800-962-3863, 847-295-7400

PERFORMANCE

fund inception date: 8/19/65

	3yr Annual	5yr Annual	10yr Annual	Bull	Bear
Return (%)	0.2	1.1	7.4	5.6	-3.7
Differ from Category (+/-)	-15.5 low	-13.2 low	-6.5 low	-56.8 low	3.0 high

Total Risk	Standard Deviation	Category Risk	Risk Index	Beta
blw av	5.8%	low	0.6	0.15

	1996	1995	1994	1993	1992	1991	1990	1989	1988	1987
Return (%)	-0.1	7.0	-5.9	2.1	3.1	9.4	10.4	10.4	13.7	27.0
Differ from Category (+/-)	-20.2	-23.3	-5.6	-11.9	-8.7	-26.6	16.5	-15.7	-4.4	25.0
Return, Tax-Adjusted (%)	-1.5	4.8	-7.7	1.4	1.7	6.4	7.6	4.8	11.8	15.0

PER SHARE DATA

	1996	1995	1994	1993	1992	1991	1990	1989	1988	1987
Dividends, Net Income ($)	0.47	0.71	0.67	0.23	0.50	0.74	0.84	0.97	0.33	0.88
Distrib'ns, Cap Gain ($)	0.00	0.03	0.00	0.00	0.00	0.55	0.24	1.73	0.50	5.97
Net Asset Value ($)	13.27	13.75	13.55	15.11	15.02	15.06	14.95	14.52	15.60	14.46
Expense Ratio (%)	na	0.98	0.93	0.89	0.88	0.94	0.98	1.01	0.98	0.82
Yield (%)	3.54	5.15	4.94	1.52	3.32	4.74	5.52	5.96	2.04	4.30
Portfolio Turnover (%)	na	58	211	136	212	80	190	303	148	202
Total Assets (Millions $)	175	232	293	435	554	516	299	214	200	151

PORTFOLIO (as of 9/30/96)

Portfolio Manager: Henry G. Van der Eb Jr. - 1975

Investm't Category: Growth
- ✔ Domestic
- ✔ Foreign
- Asset Allocation
- Index
- Sector
- State Specific

Investment Style
- Large-Cap Growth
- Mid-Cap Growth
- Small-Cap Growth
- Large-Cap Value
- Mid-Cap Value
- ✔ Small-Cap Value

Portfolio
11.9% cash	0.0% corp bonds
0.0% stocks	46.0% gov't bonds
42.1% preferred	0.0% muni bonds
0.0% conv't/warrants	0.0% other

SHAREHOLDER INFORMATION

Minimum Investment
Initial: $1,000   Subsequent: $200

Minimum IRA Investment
Initial: $200   Subsequent: $1

Maximum Fees
Load: none   12b-1: none
Other: none

Distributions
Income: Dec   Capital Gains: Dec

Exchange Options
Number Per Year: none   Fee: na
Telephone: na

Services
IRA, pension, auto invest, auto withdraw

Maxus Equity (MXSEX)

Growth & Income

Cambridge Court at Eton Sq.
28601 Chagrin Blvd., Ste. 500
Cleveland, OH 44122
800-446-2987, 216-292-3434

PERFORMANCE

fund inception date: 10/2/89

	3yr Annual	5yr Annual	10yr Annual	Bull	Bear
Return (%)	13.6	15.7	na	51.0	-5.3
Differ from Category (+/-)	-1.7 blw av	1.8 abv av	na	-8.8 blw av	1.1 abv av

Total Risk	Standard Deviation	Category Risk	Risk Index	Beta
av	8.0%	low	0.9	0.69

	1996	1995	1994	1993	1992	1991	1990	1989	1988	1987
Return (%)	19.2	22.3	0.6	24.5	13.5	36.4	-10.9	—	—	—
Differ from Category (+/-)	-0.5	-7.8	1.9	10.7	2.8	7.3	-5.0	—	—	—
Return, Tax-Adjusted (%)	16.4	19.3	-1.1	20.6	11.7	34.1	-10.9	—	—	—

PER SHARE DATA

	1996	1995	1994	1993	1992	1991	1990	1989	1988	1987
Dividends, Net Income ($)	0.26	0.26	0.22	0.10	0.08	0.49	0.00	—	—	—
Distrib'ns, Cap Gain ($)	1.06	1.01	0.51	1.56	0.58	0.00	0.00	—	—	—
Net Asset Value ($)	16.00	14.56	12.95	13.60	12.28	11.41	8.73	—	—	—
Expense Ratio (%)	na	1.08	2.00	2.61	2.89	3.94	5.25	—	—	—
Yield (%)	1.52	1.66	1.63	0.65	0.62	4.29	0.00	—	—	—
Portfolio Turnover (%)	na	201	184	175	187	189	221	—	—	—
Total Assets (Millions $)	39	31	17	11	5	3	1	—	—	—

PORTFOLIO (as of 9/30/96)

Portfolio Manager: Richard Barone - 1989

Investm't Category: Growth & Income
- ✔ Domestic
- Foreign
- ✔ Asset Allocation
- Index
- Sector
- State Specific

Investment Style
- Large-Cap Growth
- ✔ Mid-Cap Growth
- Small-Cap Growth
- Large-Cap Value
- Mid-Cap Value
- Small-Cap Value

Portfolio
9.6% cash	0.0% corp bonds
71.1% stocks	10.7% gov't bonds
7.2% preferred	0.0% muni bonds
1.3% conv't/warrants	0.0% other

SHAREHOLDER INFORMATION

Minimum Investment
Initial: $1,000   Subsequent: $100

Minimum IRA Investment
Initial: $1,000   Subsequent: $100

Maximum Fees
Load: none   12b-1: 0.50%
Other: none

Distributions
Income: annual   Capital Gains: annual

Exchange Options
Number Per Year: no limit   Fee: none
Telephone: yes (money market fund not available)

Services
IRA, pension, auto exchange, auto withdraw

Maxus Income (MXSFX)

Balanced

Cambridge Court at Eton Sq.
28601 Chagrin Blvd., Ste. 500
Cleveland, OH 44122
800-446-2987, 216-292-3434

PERFORMANCE

fund inception date: 3/11/85

	3yr Annual	5yr Annual	10yr Annual	Bull	Bear
Return (%)	6.6	7.2	7.9	26.0	-4.7
Differ from Category (+/-)	-5.1 low	-4.2 low	-2.9 low	-19.1 low	1.0 abv av

Total Risk	Standard Deviation	Category Risk	Risk Index	Beta
low	4.3%	low	0.6	0.21

	1996	1995	1994	1993	1992	1991	1990	1989	1988	1987
Return (%)	9.2	16.1	-4.5	8.7	7.8	19.2	1.7	11.4	7.6	3.5
Differ from Category (+/-)	-5.0	-8.5	-2.9	-5.7	-1.1	-4.9	2.6	-6.7	-4.6	0.8
Return, Tax-Adjusted (%)	6.6	13.1	-7.2	5.7	4.5	15.9	-1.1	6.8	5.2	-1.3

PER SHARE DATA

	1996	1995	1994	1993	1992	1991	1990	1989	1988	1987
Dividends, Net Income ($)	0.69	0.72	0.72	0.67	0.78	0.81	0.74	1.22	0.61	1.23
Distrib'ns, Cap Gain ($)	0.00	0.00	0.00	0.20	0.16	0.00	0.00	0.00	0.00	0.19
Net Asset Value ($)	10.78	10.54	9.73	10.94	10.88	10.98	9.94	10.51	10.57	10.39
Expense Ratio (%)	na	1.90	1.81	1.90	1.94	2.00	2.00	2.00	2.00	2.01
Yield (%)	6.40	6.83	7.39	6.01	7.06	7.37	7.44	11.60	5.77	11.62
Portfolio Turnover (%)	na	121	138	88	91	108	155	145	139	168
Total Assets (Millions $)	35	37	33	36	28	18	13	12	11	10

PORTFOLIO (as of 9/30/96)

Portfolio Manager: Richard Barone - 1985

Investm't Category: Balanced

✔ Domestic	Index
Foreign	Sector
✔ Asset Allocation	State Specific

Investment Style

Large-Cap Growth	Large-Cap Value
Mid-Cap Growth	Mid-Cap Value
Small-Cap Growth	Small-Cap Value

Portfolio

2.5% cash	2.1% corp bonds
32.8% stocks	22.4% gov't bonds
25.1% preferred	0.0% muni bonds
15.2% conv't/warrants	0.0% other

SHAREHOLDER INFORMATION

Minimum Investment
Initial: $1,000   Subsequent: $100

Minimum IRA Investment
Initial: $1,000   Subsequent: $100

Maximum Fees
Load: none   12b-1: 0.50%
Other: none

Distributions
Income: annual   Capital Gains: annual

Exchange Options
Number Per Year: no limit   Fee: none
Telephone: yes (money market fund not available)

Services
IRA, pension, auto exchange, auto withdraw

Megatrend (MEGAX)

Balanced

7900 Callaghan Road
San Antonio, TX 78229
210-308-1234
www.usfunds.com

PERFORMANCE

fund inception date: 10/22/91

	3yr Annual	5yr Annual	10yr Annual	Bull	Bear
Return (%)	11.5	8.7	na	42.5	-5.0
Differ from Category (+/-)	-0.2 av	-2.7 low	na	-2.6 blw av	0.7 abv av

Total Risk	Standard Deviation	Category Risk	Risk Index	Beta
av	7.4%	abv av	1.1	0.64

	1996	1995	1994	1993	1992	1991	1990	1989	1988	1987
Return (%)	15.3	24.2	-3.1	2.8	6.2	—	—	—	—	—
Differ from Category (+/-)	1.1	-0.4	-1.5	-11.6	-2.7	—	—	—	—	—
Return, Tax-Adjusted (%)	11.1	22.6	-4.3	1.7	5.3	—	—	—	—	—

PER SHARE DATA

	1996	1995	1994	1993	1992	1991	1990	1989	1988	1987
Dividends, Net Income ($)	0.20	0.26	0.22	0.16	0.14	—	—	—	—	—
Distrib'ns, Cap Gain ($)	1.49	0.20	0.13	0.18	0.10	—	—	—	—	—
Net Asset Value ($)	12.01	11.99	10.04	10.73	10.78	—	—	—	—	—
Expense Ratio (%)	1.50	1.50	1.50	1.50	1.47	—	—	—	—	—
Yield (%)	1.48	2.13	2.16	1.46	1.28	—	—	—	—	—
Portfolio Turnover (%)	115	163	143	83	75	—	—	—	—	—
Total Assets (Millions $)	25	30	38	54	46	—	—	—	—	—

PORTFOLIO (as of 9/30/96)

Portfolio Manager: Stephen Leeb - 1991

Investm't Category: Balanced

✔ Domestic	Index
Foreign	Sector
Asset Allocation	State Specific

Investment Style

Large-Cap Growth	Large-Cap Value
Mid-Cap Growth	Mid-Cap Value
Small-Cap Growth	Small-Cap Value

Portfolio

15.3% cash	0.0% corp bonds
84.7% stocks	0.0% gov't bonds
0.0% preferred	0.0% muni bonds
0.0% conv't/warrants	0.0% other

SHAREHOLDER INFORMATION

Minimum Investment
Initial: $5,000   Subsequent: $100

Minimum IRA Investment
Initial: $1   Subsequent: $1

Maximum Fees
Load: none   12b-1: 0.25%
Other: *f*

Distributions
Income: semiannual   Capital Gains: annual

Exchange Options
Number Per Year: no limit   Fee: $5 (first 12 free)
Telephone: yes (money market fund available)

Services
IRA, pension, auto invest, auto withdraw

Merger (MERFX)

Aggressive Growth

100 Summit Lake Drive
Valhalla, NY 10595
800-343-8959, 914-741-5600

this fund is closed to new investors

PERFORMANCE

fund inception date: 7/20/82

	3yr Annual	5yr Annual	10yr Annual	Bull	Bear
Return (%)	10.3	10.7	7.1	29.6	2.5
Differ from Category (+/-)	-5.5 low	-4.6 low	-7.9 low	-41.5 low	13.1 high

Total Risk	Standard Deviation	Category Risk	Risk Index	Beta
low	2.5%	low	0.2	0.13

	1996	1995	1994	1993	1992	1991	1990	1989	1988	1987
Return (%)	9.9	14.1	7.1	17.6	5.3	16.8	1.0	9.5	18.2	-21.9
Differ from Category (+/-)	-9.2	-20.2	7.1	-1.7	-6.4	-35.3	6.4	-18.9	1.8	-19.5
Return, Tax-Adjusted (%)	6.9	12.1	5.5	15.0	3.8	14.9	-0.9	6.7	17.6	-22.6

PER SHARE DATA

	1996	1995	1994	1993	1992	1991	1990	1989	1988	1987
Dividends, Net Income ($)	0.18	0.07	0.00	0.00	0.00	0.03	0.00	0.03	0.14	0.00
Distrib'ns, Cap Gain ($)	1.23	0.82	0.70	1.09	0.63	0.67	0.77	1.09	0.00	0.31
Net Asset Value ($)	14.11	14.13	13.17	12.96	11.95	11.95	10.83	11.49	11.53	9.87
Expense Ratio (%)	na	1.41	1.58	2.19	2.75	3.05	3.26	2.80	2.57	2.41
Yield (%)	1.17	0.46	0.00	0.00	0.00	0.23	0.00	0.23	1.21	0.00
Portfolio Turnover (%)	na	418	390	186	231	311	357	430	187	323
Total Assets (Millions $)	489	245	171	27	11	10	9	10	8	9

PORTFOLIO (as of 9/30/96)

Portfolio Manager: Fred Green, Bonnie Smith - 1989

Investm't Category: Aggressive Growth
- ✔ Domestic
- Foreign
- Asset Allocation
- Index
- Sector
- State Specific

Investment Style
- Large-Cap Growth
- ✔ Mid-Cap Growth
- Small-Cap Growth
- Large-Cap Value
- ✔ Mid-Cap Value
- Small-Cap Value

Portfolio
13.9% cash	13.9% corp bonds
45.9% stocks	0.0% gov't bonds
0.2% preferred	0.0% muni bonds
0.0% conv't/warrants	26.1% other

SHAREHOLDER INFORMATION

Minimum Investment
Initial: $2,000   Subsequent: $1

Minimum IRA Investment
Initial: $2,000   Subsequent: $1

Maximum Fees
Load: none   12b-1: 0.25%
Other: none

Distributions
Income: annual   Capital Gains: annual

Exchange Options
Number Per Year: none   Fee: na
Telephone: na

Services
IRA, pension, auto invest, auto withdraw

Meridian (MERDX)

Growth

60 E. Sir Francis Drake Blvd.
Wood Island, Suite 306
Larkspur, CA 94939
800-446-6662, 415-461-6237

PERFORMANCE

fund inception date: 8/2/84

	3yr Annual	5yr Annual	10yr Annual	Bull	Bear
Return (%)	11.0	12.3	14.3	45.9	-6.6
Differ from Category (+/-)	-4.7 low	-2.0 blw av	0.4 av	-16.5 low	0.1 av

Total Risk	Standard Deviation	Category Risk	Risk Index	Beta
abv av	9.6%	blw av	0.9	0.59

	1996	1995	1994	1993	1992	1991	1990	1989	1988	1987
Return (%)	11.1	22.4	0.5	13.0	15.5	56.8	4.6	19.5	18.0	-7.9
Differ from Category (+/-)	-9.0	-7.9	0.8	-1.0	3.7	20.8	10.7	-6.6	-0.1	-9.9
Return, Tax-Adjusted (%)	8.0	21.3	-0.6	12.4	14.6	53.3	2.3	16.8	18.0	-10.5

PER SHARE DATA

	1996	1995	1994	1993	1992	1991	1990	1989	1988	1987
Dividends, Net Income ($)	0.36	0.30	0.17	0.02	0.03	0.09	0.11	0.47	0.00	0.02
Distrib'ns, Cap Gain ($)	2.75	0.53	0.70	0.43	0.56	1.69	1.04	0.64	0.00	1.22
Net Asset Value ($)	30.08	29.90	25.12	25.87	23.29	20.75	14.55	15.09	13.59	11.51
Expense Ratio (%)	0.96	1.06	1.22	1.47	1.75	1.68	2.08	2.01	1.85	1.72
Yield (%)	1.09	0.98	0.65	0.07	0.12	0.40	0.70	2.98	0.00	0.15
Portfolio Turnover (%)	34	29	43	61	61	85	66	62	58	88
Total Assets (Millions $)	385	395	256	160	34	16	9	9	8	11

PORTFOLIO (as of 9/30/96)

Portfolio Manager: Richard F. Aster Jr. - 1984

Investm't Category: Growth
- ✔ Domestic
- Foreign
- Asset Allocation
- Index
- Sector
- State Specific

Investment Style
- Large-Cap Growth
- ✔ Mid-Cap Growth
- ✔ Small-Cap Growth
- Large-Cap Value
- Mid-Cap Value
- Small-Cap Value

Portfolio
29.9% cash	0.0% corp bonds
70.1% stocks	0.0% gov't bonds
0.0% preferred	0.0% muni bonds
0.0% conv't/warrants	0.0% other

SHAREHOLDER INFORMATION

Minimum Investment
Initial: $1,000   Subsequent: $50

Minimum IRA Investment
Initial: $1,000   Subsequent: $50

Maximum Fees
Load: none   12b-1: none
Other: none

Distributions
Income: annual   Capital Gains: annual

Exchange Options
Number Per Year: no limit   Fee: none
Telephone: yes (money market fund not available)

Services
IRA, auto invest, auto withdraw

Midas (EMGSX)
Gold

111 Hanover Square
10th Floor
New York, NY 10005
800-847-4200, 212-363-1100

PERFORMANCE

fund inception date: 1/8/86

	3yr Annual	5yr Annual	10yr Annual	Bull	Bear
Return (%)	11.1	20.4	10.8	50.9	-10.7
Differ from Category (+/-)	10.8 high	10.8 high	6.5 high	36.0 high	-0.5 av

Total Risk	Standard Deviation	Category Risk	Risk Index	Beta
high	28.3%	high	1.1	0.81

	1996	1995	1994	1993	1992	1991	1990	1989	1988	1987
Return (%).	21.2	36.7	-17.1	98.7	-7.2	-0.2	-17.0	21.8	-19.0	34.7
Differ from Category (+/-) .	10.0	31.7	-5.0	10.9	8.1	4.4	5.3	-2.6	0.1	2.5
Return, Tax-Adjusted (%). .	21.2	34.3	-17.9	92.6	-7.4	-0.7	-17.0	21.8	-19.0	33.2

PER SHARE DATA

	1996	1995	1994	1993	1992	1991	1990	1989	1988	1987
Dividends, Net Income ($).	0.00	0.00	0.00	0.00	0.01	0.03	0.00	0.00	0.00	0.05
Distrib'ns, Cap Gain ($) . .	0.00	0.28	0.11	0.51	0.00	0.00	0.00	0.00	0.00	0.33
Net Asset Value ($)	5.15	4.25	3.32	4.15	2.35	2.55	2.59	3.12	2.56	3.16
Expense Ratio (%).	na	2.26	2.15	2.18	2.25	2.25	2.25	2.20	1.82	1.79
Yield (%)	0.00	0.00	0.00	0.00	0.42	1.17	0.00	0.00	0.00	1.43
Portfolio Turnover (%). . . .	na	47	53	63	72	77	58	24	8	27
Total Assets (Millions $). . .	217	15	7	10	4	6	7	11	12	17

PORTFOLIO (as of 9/30/96)

Portfolio Manager: Kjeld R. Thygesen - 1995

Investm't Category: Gold

✔ Domestic	Index
✔ Foreign	Sector
Asset Allocation	State Specific

Investment Style

Large-Cap Growth	Large-Cap Value
Mid-Cap Growth	Mid-Cap Value
Small-Cap Growth	Small-Cap Value

Portfolio

0.0% cash	0.0% corp bonds
99.0% stocks	0.0% gov't bonds
0.0% preferred	0.0% muni bonds
3.0% conv't/warrants	0.0% other

SHAREHOLDER INFORMATION

Minimum Investment
Initial: $500   Subsequent: $50

Minimum IRA Investment
Initial: $100   Subsequent: $50

Maximum Fees
Load: 1.00% redemption   12b-1: 0.25%
Other: redemption fee applies for 1 month

Distributions
Income: Dec   Capital Gains: Dec

Exchange Options
Number Per Year: none   Fee: na
Telephone: na

Services
IRA, pension, auto invest, auto withdraw

Monetta (MONTX)

Growth

1776-A S. Naperville Road
Suite 207
Wheaton, IL 60187
800-666-3882, 630-462-9800

PERFORMANCE

fund inception date: 5/6/86

	3yr Annual	5yr Annual	10yr Annual	Bull	Bear
Return (%)	6.8	5.2	12.4	32.4	-9.5
Differ from Category (+/-)	-8.9 low	-9.1 low	-1.5 blw av	-30.0 low	-2.8 blw av

Total Risk	Standard Deviation	Category Risk	Risk Index	Beta
high	14.6%	high	1.4	0.87

	1996	1995	1994	1993	1992	1991	1990	1989	1988	1987
Return (%)	1.6	28.0	-6.3	0.4	5.4	55.8	11.3	15.2	23.0	1.5
Differ from Category (+/-)	-18.5	-2.3	-6.0	-13.6	-6.4	19.8	17.4	-10.9	4.9	-0.5
Return, Tax-Adjusted (%)	1.6	22.1	-6.5	-0.6	4.3	52.2	9.3	12.1	17.2	0.9

PER SHARE DATA

	1996	1995	1994	1993	1992	1991	1990	1989	1988	1987
Dividends, Net Income ($)	0.00	0.02	0.05	0.00	0.02	0.05	0.10	0.22	0.07	0.14
Distrib'ns, Cap Gain ($)	0.00	3.00	0.00	0.53	0.57	1.30	0.58	0.76	1.90	0.00
Net Asset Value ($)	15.84	15.59	14.52	15.54	15.99	15.73	10.96	10.44	9.93	9.68
Expense Ratio (%)	na	1.36	1.35	1.38	1.45	1.42	1.50	1.57	1.50	2.31
Yield (%)	0.00	0.10	0.34	0.00	0.12	0.29	0.86	1.96	0.59	1.44
Portfolio Turnover (%)	na	272	191	226	127	154	207	258	170	333
Total Assets (Millions $)	228	362	364	524	408	56	6	3	2	2

PORTFOLIO (as of 12/31/96)

Portfolio Manager: Robert S. Bacarella - 1986

Investm't Category: Growth

✔ Domestic   Index
   Foreign   Sector
   Asset Allocation   State Specific

Investment Style

   Large-Cap Growth   Large-Cap Value
✔ Mid-Cap Growth   Mid-Cap Value
✔ Small-Cap Growth   Small-Cap Value

Portfolio

0.0% cash	0.0% corp bonds
0.0% stocks	0.0% gov't bonds
0.0% preferred	0.0% muni bonds
0.0% conv't/warrants	0.0% other

SHAREHOLDER INFORMATION

Minimum Investment
Initial: $1,000   Subsequent: $50

Minimum IRA Investment
Initial: $250   Subsequent: $50

Maximum Fees
Load: none   12b-1: none
Other: none

Distributions
Income: Dec   Capital Gains: Dec

Exchange Options
Number Per Year: no limit   Fee: $5 (telephone)
Telephone: yes (money market fund available)

Services
IRA, pension, auto exchange, auto invest, auto withdraw

Montgomery Asset Allocation—R (MNAAX)

Balanced

600 Montgomery St.
17th Floor
San Francisco, CA 94111
800-572-3863, 415-627-2485
www.xperts.montgomery.com/1

PERFORMANCE

fund inception date: 3/31/94

	3yr Annual	5yr Annual	10yr Annual	Bull	Bear
Return (%)	na	na	na	75.6	na
Differ from Category (+/-)	na	na	na	30.5 high	na

Total Risk	Standard Deviation	Category Risk	Risk Index	Beta
na	na	na	na	na

	1996	1995	1994	1993	1992	1991	1990	1989	1988	1987
Return (%)	12.8	32.6	—	—	—	—	—	—	—	—
Differ from Category (+/-)	-1.4	8.0	—	—	—	—	—	—	—	—
Return, Tax-Adjusted (%)	9.3	30.8	—	—	—	—	—	—	—	—

PER SHARE DATA

	1996	1995	1994	1993	1992	1991	1990	1989	1988	1987
Dividends, Net Income ($)	0.39	0.25	—	—	—	—	—	—	—	—
Distrib'ns, Cap Gain ($)	1.66	0.55	—	—	—	—	—	—	—	—
Net Asset Value ($)	18.09	17.86	—	—	—	—	—	—	—	—
Expense Ratio (%)	na	1.31	—	—	—	—	—	—	—	—
Yield (%)	1.97	1.35	—	—	—	—	—	—	—	—
Portfolio Turnover (%)	na	95	—	—	—	—	—	—	—	—
Total Assets (Millions $)	146	120	—	—	—	—	—	—	—	—

PORTFOLIO (as of 9/30/96)

Portfolio Manager: Stevens, Honour, Pratt - 1994

Investm't Category: Balanced
✔ Domestic   Index
  Foreign   Sector
✔ Asset Allocation   State Specific

Investment Style
  Large-Cap Growth   Large-Cap Value
  Mid-Cap Growth   Mid-Cap Value
  Small-Cap Growth   Small-Cap Value

Portfolio
  4.4% cash   4.4% corp bonds
  44.5% stocks   45.8% gov't bonds
  0.0% preferred   0.0% muni bonds
  0.0% conv't/warrants 1.0% other

SHAREHOLDER INFORMATION

Minimum Investment
Initial: $1,000   Subsequent: $100

Minimum IRA Investment
Initial: $1,000   Subsequent: $100

Maximum Fees
Load: none   12b-1: none
Other: none

Distributions
Income: annual   Capital Gains: annual

Exchange Options
Number Per Year: 4   Fee: none
Telephone: yes (money market fund available)

Services
IRA, pension, auto exchange, auto invest, auto withdraw

Montgomery Emerging Markets—R (MNEMX)

International Stock

600 Montgomery St.
17th Floor
San Francisco, CA 94111
800-572-3863, 415-627-2485
www.xperts.montgomery.com/1

PERFORMANCE

fund inception date: 3/2/92

	3yr Annual	5yr Annual	10yr Annual	Bull	Bear
Return (%)	-1.9	na	na	7.5	-13.3
Differ from Category (+/-)	-8.2 low	na	na	-16.8 blw av	-6.1 low

Total Risk	Standard Deviation	Category Risk	Risk Index	Beta
high	14.7%	high	1.4	0.75

	1996	1995	1994	1993	1992	1991	1990	1989	1988	1987
Return (%)	12.3	-9.1	-7.6	58.6	—	—	—	—	—	—
Differ from Category (+/-)	-2.5	-18.2	-4.5	19.0	—	—	—	—	—	—
Return, Tax-Adjusted (%)	12.1	-9.1	-9.1	57.8	—	—	—	—	—	—

PER SHARE DATA

	1996	1995	1994	1993	1992	1991	1990	1989	1988	1987
Dividends, Net Income ($)	0.06	0.00	0.00	0.01	—	—	—	—	—	—
Distrib'ns, Cap Gain ($)	0.00	0.00	0.79	0.25	—	—	—	—	—	—
Net Asset Value ($)	13.87	12.41	13.65	15.58	—	—	—	—	—	—
Expense Ratio (%)	1.72	1.80	1.85	1.90	—	—	—	—	—	—
Yield (%)	0.43	0.00	0.00	0.06	—	—	—	—	—	—
Portfolio Turnover (%)	109	92	63	21	—	—	—	—	—	—
Total Assets (Millions $)	906	855	878	610	—	—	—	—	—	—

PORTFOLIO (as of 9/30/96)

Portfolio Manager: Jiménez, Sudweeks - 1992

Investm't Category: International Stock

Domestic	Index
✔ Foreign	Sector
Asset Allocation	State Specific

Investment Style

Large-Cap Growth	Large-Cap Value
Mid-Cap Growth	Mid-Cap Value
Small-Cap Growth	Small-Cap Value

Portfolio

5.4% cash	0.0% corp bonds
70.8% stocks	0.0% gov't bonds
19.3% preferred	0.0% muni bonds
2.6% conv't/warrants	2.0% other

SHAREHOLDER INFORMATION

Minimum Investment
Initial: $1,000   Subsequent: $100

Minimum IRA Investment
Initial: $1,000   Subsequent: $100

Maximum Fees
Load: none   12b-1: none
Other: none

Distributions
Income: annual   Capital Gains: annual

Exchange Options
Number Per Year: 4   Fee: none
Telephone: yes (money market fund available)

Services
IRA, pension, auto exchange, auto invest, auto withdraw

Montgomery Global Communications

(MNGCX) *International Stock*

600 Montgomery St.
17th Floor
San Francisco, CA 94111
800-572-3863, 415-627-2485
www.xperts.montgomery.com/1

PERFORMANCE

fund inception date: 6/1/93

	3yr Annual	5yr Annual	10yr Annual	Bull	Bear
Return (%)	3.0	na	na	24.6	-15.8
Differ from Category (+/-)	-3.3 blw av	na	na	0.3 av	-8.6 low

Total Risk	Standard Deviation	Category Risk	Risk Index	Beta
high	14.2%	abv av	1.4	1.09

	1996	1995	1994	1993	1992	1991	1990	1989	1988	1987
Return (%)	8.0	16.8	-13.5	—	—	—	—	—	—	—
Differ from Category (+/-)	-6.8	7.7	-10.4	—	—	—	—	—	—	—
Return, Tax-Adjusted (%)	6.4	16.8	-13.6	—	—	—	—	—	—	—

PER SHARE DATA

	1996	1995	1994	1993	1992	1991	1990	1989	1988	1987
Dividends, Net Income ($)	0.00	0.00	0.00	—	—	—	—	—	—	—
Distrib'ns, Cap Gain ($)	0.90	0.00	0.03	—	—	—	—	—	—	—
Net Asset Value ($)	16.74	16.34	13.98	—	—	—	—	—	—	—
Expense Ratio (%)	1.90	1.91	1.94	—	—	—	—	—	—	—
Yield (%)	0.00	0.00	0.00	—	—	—	—	—	—	—
Portfolio Turnover (%)	103	50	29	—	—	—	—	—	—	—
Total Assets (Millions $)	176	219	216	—	—	—	—	—	—	—

PORTFOLIO (as of 9/30/96)

Portfolio Manager: Oscar A. Castro, John D. Boich - 1993

Investm't Category: International Stock

✔ Domestic
✔ Foreign
Asset Allocation

Index
✔ Sector
State Specific

Investment Style

Large-Cap Growth
Mid-Cap Growth
Small-Cap Growth

Large-Cap Value
Mid-Cap Value
Small-Cap Value

Portfolio

17.5% cash
82.5% stocks
0.0% preferred
0.0% conv't/warrants

0.0% corp bonds
0.0% gov't bonds
0.0% muni bonds
0.0% other

SHAREHOLDER INFORMATION

Minimum Investment
Initial: $1,000   Subsequent: $100

Minimum IRA Investment
Initial: $1,000   Subsequent: $100

Maximum Fees
Load: none   12b-1: none
Other: none

Distributions
Income: annual   Capital Gains: annual

Exchange Options
Number Per Year: 4   Fee: none
Telephone: yes (money market fund available)

Services
IRA, pension, auto exchange, auto invest, auto withdraw

Montgomery Global Opportunities (MNGOX)

International Stock

600 Montgomery St.
17th Floor
San Francisco, CA 94111
800-572-3863, 415-627-2485
www.xperts.montgomery.com/1

PERFORMANCE

fund inception date: 9/30/93

	3yr Annual	5yr Annual	10yr Annual	Bull	Bear
Return (%)	8.8	na	na	42.0	-14.1
Differ from Category (+/-)	2.5 abv av	na	na	17.7 high	-6.9 low

Total Risk	Standard Deviation	Category Risk	Risk Index	Beta
high	13.1%	abv av	1.3	1.04

	1996	1995	1994	1993	1992	1991	1990	1989	1988	1987
Return (%)	20.1	17.2	-8.5	—	—	—	—	—	—	—
Differ from Category (+/-)	5.3	8.1	-5.4	—	—	—	—	—	—	—
Return, Tax-Adjusted (%)	18.5	16.9	-9.5	—	—	—	—	—	—	—

PER SHARE DATA

	1996	1995	1994	1993	1992	1991	1990	1989	1988	1987
Dividends, Net Income ($)	0.00	0.07	0.00	—	—	—	—	—	—	—
Distrib'ns, Cap Gain ($)	0.82	0.00	0.49	—	—	—	—	—	—	—
Net Asset Value ($)	16.73	14.62	12.53	—	—	—	—	—	—	—
Expense Ratio (%)	1.90	1.91	1.99	—	—	—	—	—	—	—
Yield (%)	0.00	0.47	0.00	—	—	—	—	—	—	—
Portfolio Turnover (%)	163	118	na	—	—	—	—	—	—	—
Total Assets (Millions $)	30	16	13	—	—	—	—	—	—	—

PORTFOLIO (as of 9/30/96)

Portfolio Manager: Oscar A. Castro, John D. Boich - 1993

Investm't Category: International Stock
- ✔ Domestic
- ✔ Foreign
- Asset Allocation
- Index
- Sector
- State Specific

Investment Style
- Large-Cap Growth
- Mid-Cap Growth
- Small-Cap Growth
- Large-Cap Value
- Mid-Cap Value
- Small-Cap Value

Portfolio
3.1% cash	0.0% corp bonds
95.7% stocks	0.0% gov't bonds
1.2% preferred	0.0% muni bonds
0.0% conv't/warrants	0.0% other

SHAREHOLDER INFORMATION

Minimum Investment
Initial: $1,000   Subsequent: $100

Minimum IRA Investment
Initial: $1,000   Subsequent: $100

Maximum Fees
Load: none   12b-1: none
Other: none

Distributions
Income: annual   Capital Gains: annual

Exchange Options
Number Per Year: 4   Fee: none
Telephone: yes (money market fund available)

Services
IRA, pension, auto exchange, auto invest, auto withdraw

Montgomery Growth—R (MNGFX)

Growth

600 Montgomery St.
17th Floor
San Francisco, CA 94111
800-572-3863, 415-627-2485
www.xperts.montgomery.com/1

PERFORMANCE

fund inception date: 9/30/93

	3yr Annual	5yr Annual	10yr Annual	Bull	Bear
Return (%)	21.5	na	na	66.2	2.4
Differ from Category (+/-)	5.8 high	na	na	3.8 abv av	9.1 high

Total Risk	Standard Deviation	Category Risk	Risk Index	Beta
av	9.2%	blw av	0.9	0.69

	1996	1995	1994	1993	1992	1991	1990	1989	1988	1987
Return (%)	20.2	23.6	20.9	—	—	—	—	—	—	—
Differ from Category (+/-)	0.1	-6.7	21.2	—	—	—	—	—	—	—
Return, Tax-Adjusted (%)	15.8	20.6	20.5	—	—	—	—	—	—	—

PER SHARE DATA

	1996	1995	1994	1993	1992	1991	1990	1989	1988	1987
Dividends, Net Income ($)	0.15	0.16	0.07	—	—	—	—	—	—	—
Distrib'ns, Cap Gain ($)	2.76	1.53	0.07	—	—	—	—	—	—	—
Net Asset Value ($)	20.15	19.20	16.93	—	—	—	—	—	—	—
Expense Ratio (%)	1.35	1.50	1.49	—	—	—	—	—	—	—
Yield (%)	0.65	0.77	0.41	—	—	—	—	—	—	—
Portfolio Turnover (%)	118	128	110	—	—	—	—	—	—	—
Total Assets (Millions $)	1,023	859	592	—	—	—	—	—	—	—

PORTFOLIO (as of 9/30/96)

Portfolio Manager: Roger W. Honour - 1993

Investm't Category: Growth
- ✔ Domestic
- Foreign
- Asset Allocation
- Index
- Sector
- State Specific

Investment Style
- Large-Cap Growth
- Mid-Cap Growth
- ✔ Small-Cap Growth
- Large-Cap Value
- Mid-Cap Value
- Small-Cap Value

Portfolio
17.1% cash	0.0% corp bonds
82.9% stocks	0.0% gov't bonds
0.0% preferred	0.0% muni bonds
0.0% conv't/warrants	0.0% other

SHAREHOLDER INFORMATION

Minimum Investment
Initial: $1,000   Subsequent: $100

Minimum IRA Investment
Initial: $1,000   Subsequent: $100

Maximum Fees
Load: none   12b-1: none
Other: none

Distributions
Income: annual   Capital Gains: annual

Exchange Options
Number Per Year: 4   Fee: none
Telephone: yes (money market fund available)

Services
IRA, pension, auto exchange, auto invest, auto withdraw

Montgomery Int'l Small Cap (MNISX)

International Stock

600 Montgomery St.
17th Floor
San Francisco, CA 94111
800-572-3863, 415-627-2485
www.xperts.montgomery.com/1

PERFORMANCE

fund inception date: 9/30/93

	3yr Annual	5yr Annual	10yr Annual	Bull	Bear
Return (%)	3.6	na	na	26.1	-17.4
Differ from Category (+/-)	-2.7 blw av	na	na	1.8 av	-10.2 low

Total Risk	Standard Deviation	Category Risk	Risk Index	Beta
high	11.9%	abv av	1.2	0.83

	1996	1995	1994	1993	1992	1991	1990	1989	1988	1987
Return (%)	14.9	11.7	-13.3	—	—	—	—	—	—	—
Differ from Category (+/-)	0.1	2.6	-10.2	—	—	—	—	—	—	—
Return, Tax-Adjusted (%)	14.9	11.6	-13.3	—	—	—	—	—	—	—

PER SHARE DATA

	1996	1995	1994	1993	1992	1991	1990	1989	1988	1987
Dividends, Net Income ($)	0.00	0.02	0.00	—	—	—	—	—	—	—
Distrib'ns, Cap Gain ($)	0.00	0.00	0.00	—	—	—	—	—	—	—
Net Asset Value ($)	15.13	13.16	11.80	—	—	—	—	—	—	—
Expense Ratio (%)	1.90	1.91	1.99	—	—	—	—	—	—	—
Yield (%)	0.00	0.15	0.00	—	—	—	—	—	—	—
Portfolio Turnover (%)	177	156	123	—	—	—	—	—	—	—
Total Assets (Millions $)	42	34	29	—	—	—	—	—	—	—

PORTFOLIO (as of 9/30/96)

Portfolio Manager: Oscar A. Castro, John D. Boich - 1993

Investm't Category: International Stock
- Domestic
- ✔ Foreign
- Asset Allocation
- Index
- Sector
- State Specific

Investment Style
- Large-Cap Growth
- Mid-Cap Growth
- Small-Cap Growth
- Large-Cap Value
- Mid-Cap Value
- Small-Cap Value

Portfolio
9.5% cash	0.0% corp bonds
90.5% stocks	0.0% gov't bonds
0.0% preferred	0.0% muni bonds
0.0% conv't/warrants	0.0% other

SHAREHOLDER INFORMATION

Minimum Investment
Initial: $1,000   Subsequent: $100

Minimum IRA Investment
Initial: $1,000   Subsequent: $100

Maximum Fees
Load: none   12b-1: none
Other: none

Distributions
Income: annual   Capital Gains: annual

Exchange Options
Number Per Year: 4   Fee: none
Telephone: yes (money market fund available)

Services
IRA, pension, auto exchange, auto invest, auto withdraw

Montgomery
Micro Cap (MNMCX)
Aggressive Growth

600 Montgomery St.
17th Floor
San Francisco, CA 94111
800-572-3863, 415-627-2485
www.xperts.montgomery.com/1

this fund is closed to new investors

PERFORMANCE

fund inception date: 12/30/94

	3yr Annual	5yr Annual	10yr Annual	Bull	Bear
Return (%)	na	na	na	na	na
Differ from Category (+/-)	na	na	na	na	na

Total Risk	Standard Deviation	Category Risk	Risk Index	Beta
na	na	na	na	na

	1996	1995	1994	1993	1992	1991	1990	1989	1988	1987
Return (%)	19.1	28.6	—	—	—	—	—	—	—	—
Differ from Category (+/-)	0.0	-5.7	—	—	—	—	—	—	—	—
Return, Tax-Adjusted (%)	16.8	28.1	—	—	—	—	—	—	—	—

PER SHARE DATA

	1996	1995	1994	1993	1992	1991	1990	1989	1988	1987
Dividends, Net Income ($)	0.00	0.08	—	—	—	—	—	—	—	—
Distrib'ns, Cap Gain ($)	1.22	0.06	—	—	—	—	—	—	—	—
Net Asset Value ($)	16.91	15.28	—	—	—	—	—	—	—	—
Expense Ratio (%)	1.75	1.75	—	—	—	—	—	—	—	—
Yield (%)	0.00	0.52	—	—	—	—	—	—	—	—
Portfolio Turnover (%)	88	44	—	—	—	—	—	—	—	—
Total Assets (Millions $)	293	272	—	—	—	—	—	—	—	—

PORTFOLIO (as of 9/30/96)

Portfolio Manager: Honour, Pratt, Carmen - 1994

Investm't Category: Aggressive Growth
✔ Domestic   Index
✔ Foreign   Sector
  Asset Allocation State Specific

Investment Style
Large-Cap Growth   Large-Cap Value
Mid-Cap Growth   Mid-Cap Value
Small-Cap Growth   Small-Cap Value

Portfolio
12.3% cash   0.0% corp bonds
87.7% stocks   0.0% gov't bonds
0.0% preferred   0.0% muni bonds
0.0% conv't/warrants 0.0% other

SHAREHOLDER INFORMATION

Minimum Investment
Initial: $5,000   Subsequent: $500

Minimum IRA Investment
Initial: $5,000   Subsequent: $500

Maximum Fees
Load: none   12b-1: none
Other: none

Distributions
Income: annual   Capital Gains: annual

Exchange Options
Number Per Year: 4   Fee: none
Telephone: yes (money market fund available)

Services
IRA, pension, auto exchange, auto invest, auto withdraw

Montgomery Select 50—R (MNSFX)

600 Montgomery St.
17th Floor
San Francisco, CA 94111
800-572-3863, 415-627-2485
www.xperts.montgomery.com/1

International Stock

PERFORMANCE

fund inception date: 10/2/95

	3yr Annual	5yr Annual	10yr Annual	Bull	Bear
Return (%)	na	na	na	na	na
Differ from Category (+/-)	na	na	na	na	na

Total Risk	Standard Deviation	Category Risk	Risk Index	Beta
na	na	na	na	na

	1996	1995	1994	1993	1992	1991	1990	1989	1988	1987
Return (%)	20.4	—	—	—	—	—	—	—	—	—
Differ from Category (+/-)	5.6	—	—	—	—	—	—	—	—	—
Return, Tax-Adjusted (%)	19.1	—	—	—	—	—	—	—	—	—

PER SHARE DATA

	1996	1995	1994	1993	1992	1991	1990	1989	1988	1987
Dividends, Net Income ($)	0.01	—	—	—	—	—	—	—	—	—
Distrib'ns, Cap Gain ($)	0.60	—	—	—	—	—	—	—	—	—
Net Asset Value ($)	16.03	—	—	—	—	—	—	—	—	—
Expense Ratio (%)	na	—	—	—	—	—	—	—	—	—
Yield (%)	0.06	—	—	—	—	—	—	—	—	—
Portfolio Turnover (%)	na	—	—	—	—	—	—	—	—	—
Total Assets (Millions $)	90	—	—	—	—	—	—	—	—	—

PORTFOLIO (as of 9/30/96)

Portfolio Manager: Kevin T. Hamilton - 1995

Investm't Category: International Stock
- ✔ Domestic
- ✔ Foreign
- Asset Allocation
- Index
- Sector
- State Specific

Investment Style
Large-Cap Growth	Large-Cap Value
Mid-Cap Growth	Mid-Cap Value
Small-Cap Growth	Small-Cap Value

Portfolio
7.7% cash	0.0% corp bonds
92.3% stocks	0.0% gov't bonds
0.0% preferred	0.0% muni bonds
0.0% conv't/warrants	0.0% other

SHAREHOLDER INFORMATION

Minimum Investment
Initial: $1,000   Subsequent: $100

Minimum IRA Investment
Initial: $1,000   Subsequent: $100

Maximum Fees
Load: none   12b-1: none
Other: none

Distributions
Income: annual   Capital Gains: annual

Exchange Options
Number Per Year: 4   Fee: none
Telephone: yes (money market fund available)

Services
IRA, pension, auto exchange, auto invest, auto withdraw

Montgomery Short Gov't Bond (MNSGX)

Mortgage-Backed Bond

600 Montgomery St.
17th Floor
San Francisco, CA 94111
800-572-3863, 415-627-2485
www.xperts.montgomery.com/1

PERFORMANCE

fund inception date: 12/18/92

	3yr Annual	5yr Annual	10yr Annual	Bull	Bear
Return (%)	5.8	na	na	18.8	-1.1
Differ from Category (+/-)	0.2 av	na	na	-2.3 blw av	2.5 high

Total Risk	Standard Deviation	Category Risk	Risk Index	Avg Mat
low	2.0%	low	0.5	2.0 yrs

	1996	1995	1994	1993	1992	1991	1990	1989	1988	1987
Return (%)	5.1	11.5	1.1	8.0	—	—	—	—	—	—
Differ from Category (+/-)	0.7	-3.2	2.8	1.1	—	—	—	—	—	—
Return, Tax-Adjusted (%)	2.8	8.9	-1.2	5.3	—	—	—	—	—	—

PER SHARE DATA

	1996	1995	1994	1993	1992	1991	1990	1989	1988	1987
Dividends, Net Income ($)	0.57	0.62	0.58	0.64	—	—	—	—	—	—
Distrib'ns, Cap Gain ($)	0.00	0.00	0.00	0.06	—	—	—	—	—	—
Net Asset Value ($)	10.00	10.08	9.63	10.10	—	—	—	—	—	—
Expense Ratio (%)	na	1.38	0.71	0.22	—	—	—	—	—	—
Yield (%)	5.69	6.15	6.02	6.29	—	—	—	—	—	—
Portfolio Turnover (%)	na	284	603	213	—	—	—	—	—	—
Total Assets (Millions $)	37	17	19	24	—	—	—	—	—	—

PORTFOLIO (as of 12/31/96)

Portfolio Manager: William C. Stevens - 1992

Investm't Category: Mortgage-Backed Bond
- ✔ Domestic
- Foreign
- Asset Allocation
- Index
- Sector
- State Specific

Investment Style
- Large-Cap Growth
- Mid-Cap Growth
- Small-Cap Growth
- Large-Cap Value
- Mid-Cap Value
- Small-Cap Value

Portfolio
0.0% cash	3.0% corp bonds
0.0% stocks	97.0% gov't bonds
0.0% preferred	0.0% muni bonds
0.0% conv't/warrants	0.0% other

SHAREHOLDER INFORMATION

Minimum Investment
Initial: $1,000   Subsequent: $100

Minimum IRA Investment
Initial: $1,000   Subsequent: $100

Maximum Fees
Load: none   12b-1: none
Other: none

Distributions
Income: monthly   Capital Gains: annual

Exchange Options
Number Per Year: 4   Fee: none
Telephone: yes (money market fund available)

Services
IRA, pension, auto exchange, auto invest, auto withdraw

Montgomery Small Cap
(MNSCX)
Aggressive Growth

600 Montgomery St.
17th Floor
San Francisco, CA 94111
800-572-3863, 415-627-2485
www.xperts.montgomery.com/1

this fund is closed to new investors

PERFORMANCE

fund inception date: 7/13/90

	3yr Annual	5yr Annual	10yr Annual	Bull	Bear
Return (%)	13.0	14.4	na	68.4	-17.0
Differ from Category (+/-)	-2.8 blw av	-0.9 av	na	-2.7 av	-6.4 low

Total Risk	Standard Deviation	Category Risk	Risk Index	Beta
high	14.3%	av	1.0	0.96

	1996	1995	1994	1993	1992	1991	1990	1989	1988	1987
Return (%)	18.6	35.1	-10.0	24.3	9.5	98.7	—	—	—	—
Differ from Category (+/-)	-0.5	0.8	-10.0	5.0	-2.2	46.6	—	—	—	—
Return, Tax-Adjusted (%)	13.5	31.7	-11.6	21.5	9.5	88.1	—	—	—	—

PER SHARE DATA

	1996	1995	1994	1993	1992	1991	1990	1989	1988	1987
Dividends, Net Income ($)	0.00	0.00	0.00	0.00	0.00	0.00	—	—	—	—
Distrib'ns, Cap Gain ($)	3.28	1.78	0.97	1.51	0.00	3.52	—	—	—	—
Net Asset Value ($)	18.40	18.28	14.96	17.67	15.54	14.18	—	—	—	—
Expense Ratio (%)	1.24	1.37	1.35	1.40	1.50	1.45	—	—	—	—
Yield (%)	0.00	0.00	0.00	0.00	0.00	0.00	—	—	—	—
Portfolio Turnover (%)	80	85	95	130	81	194	—	—	—	—
Total Assets (Millions $)	274	236	202	259	207	74	—	—	—	—

PORTFOLIO (as of 9/30/96)

Portfolio Manager: Roberts, Philpott, Kidwell - 1990

Investm't Category: Aggressive Growth
- ✔ Domestic
- Foreign
- Asset Allocation
- Index
- Sector
- State Specific

Investment Style
- Large-Cap Growth
- Mid-Cap Growth
- ✔ Small-Cap Growth
- Large-Cap Value
- Mid-Cap Value
- ✔ Small-Cap Value

Portfolio
- 2.7% cash
- 96.9% stocks
- 0.0% preferred
- 0.4% conv't/warrants
- 0.0% corp bonds
- 0.0% gov't bonds
- 0.0% muni bonds
- 0.0% other

SHAREHOLDER INFORMATION

Minimum Investment
Initial: $1,000   Subsequent: $100

Minimum IRA Investment
Initial: $1,000   Subsequent: $100

Maximum Fees
Load: none   12b-1: none
Other: none

Distributions
Income: annual   Capital Gains: annual

Exchange Options
Number Per Year: 4   Fee: none
Telephone: yes (money market fund available)

Services
IRA, pension, auto exchange, auto invest, auto withdraw

Montgomery Small Cap Opportunities (MNSOX)

Aggressive Growth

600 Montgomery St.
17th Floor
San Francisco, CA 94111
800-572-3863, 415-627-2485
www.xperts.montgomery.com/1

PERFORMANCE

fund inception date: 12/29/95

	3yr Annual	5yr Annual	10yr Annual	Bull	Bear
Return (%)	na	na	na	na	na
Differ from Category (+/-)	na	na	na	na	na

Total Risk	Standard Deviation	Category Risk	Risk Index	Beta
na	na	na	na	na

	1996	1995	1994	1993	1992	1991	1990	1989	1988	1987
Return (%)	37.2	—	—	—	—	—	—	—	—	—
Differ from Category (+/-)	18.1	—	—	—	—	—	—	—	—	—
Return, Tax-Adjusted (%)	37.2	—	—	—	—	—	—	—	—	—

PER SHARE DATA

	1996	1995	1994	1993	1992	1991	1990	1989	1988	1987
Dividends, Net Income ($)	0.00	—	—	—	—	—	—	—	—	—
Distrib'ns, Cap Gain ($)	0.00	—	—	—	—	—	—	—	—	—
Net Asset Value ($)	16.47	—	—	—	—	—	—	—	—	—
Expense Ratio (%)	1.50	—	—	—	—	—	—	—	—	—
Yield (%)	0.00	—	—	—	—	—	—	—	—	—
Portfolio Turnover (%)	81	—	—	—	—	—	—	—	—	—
Total Assets (Millions $)	174	—	—	—	—	—	—	—	—	—

PORTFOLIO (as of 9/30/96)

Portfolio Manager: Honour, Pratt, Carmen - 1995

Investm't Category: Aggressive Growth
✔ Domestic   Index
✔ Foreign   Sector
  Asset Allocation State Specific

Investment Style
Large-Cap Growth   Large-Cap Value
Mid-Cap Growth   Mid-Cap Value
Small-Cap Growth   Small-Cap Value

Portfolio
4.6% cash	0.0% corp bonds
95.4% stocks	0.0% gov't bonds
0.0% preferred	0.0% muni bonds
0.0% conv't/warrants	0.0% other

SHAREHOLDER INFORMATION

Minimum Investment
Initial: $1,000   Subsequent: $100

Minimum IRA Investment
Initial: $1,000   Subsequent: $100

Maximum Fees
Load: none   12b-1: none
Other: none

Distributions
Income: annual   Capital Gains: annual

Exchange Options
Number Per Year: 4   Fee: none
Telephone: yes (money market fund available)

Services
IRA, pension, auto exchange, auto invest, auto withdraw

Neuberger & Berman
Focus (NBSSX)
Growth

605 Third Ave.
2nd Floor
New York, NY 10158
800-877-9700, 212-476-8800
www.nbfunds.com

PERFORMANCE   fund inception date: 10/19/55

	3yr Annual	5yr Annual	10yr Annual	Bull	Bear
Return (%)	16.8	17.5	14.9	62.0	-5.1
Differ from Category (+/-)	1.1 av	3.2 high	1.0 abv av	-0.4 av	1.6 abv av

Total Risk	Standard Deviation	Category Risk	Risk Index	Beta
high	12.8%	high	1.2	1.15

	1996	1995	1994	1993	1992	1991	1990	1989	1988	1987
Return (%)	16.2	36.1	0.8	16.3	21.0	24.6	-6.0	29.7	16.4	0.6
Differ from Category (+/-)	-3.9	5.8	1.1	2.3	9.2	-11.4	0.1	3.6	-1.7	-1.4
Return, Tax-Adjusted (%)	14.4	34.1	-1.4	13.6	17.4	22.3	-7.3	24.3	14.1	-5.8

PER SHARE DATA

	1996	1995	1994	1993	1992	1991	1990	1989	1988	1987
Dividends, Net Income ($)	0.22	0.11	0.20	0.25	0.28	0.36	0.35	0.47	0.51	0.59
Distrib'ns, Cap Gain ($)	1.43	1.35	1.48	1.70	2.13	0.87	0.38	2.57	0.54	3.35
Net Asset Value ($)	30.82	27.93	21.58	23.06	21.50	19.97	17.06	18.93	16.96	15.49
Expense Ratio (%)	0.89	0.87	0.85	0.92	0.91	0.93	0.92	0.99	1.01	0.86
Yield (%)	0.68	0.37	0.86	1.00	1.18	1.72	2.00	2.18	2.91	3.13
Portfolio Turnover (%)	39	36	52	52	77	60	66	60	66	88
Total Assets (Millions $)	1,212	1,027	603	591	497	421	371	437	375	359

PORTFOLIO (as of 9/30/96)

Portfolio Manager: K. Simons, L. Marx, K. Risen - 1988

Investm't Category: Growth
- ✔ Domestic
- ✔ Foreign
-   Asset Allocation
-   Index
-   Sector
-   State Specific

Investment Style
- Large-Cap Growth
- ✔ Mid-Cap Growth
- Small-Cap Growth
- Large-Cap Value
- ✔ Mid-Cap Value
- Small-Cap Value

Portfolio
0.0% cash	0.0% corp bonds
98.3% stocks	1.6% gov't bonds
0.0% preferred	0.0% muni bonds
0.1% conv't/warrants	0.0% other

SHAREHOLDER INFORMATION

Minimum Investment
Initial: $1,000   Subsequent: $100

Minimum IRA Investment
Initial: $250   Subsequent: $100

Maximum Fees
Load: none   12b-1: none
Other: none

Distributions
Income: Dec   Capital Gains: Dec

Exchange Options
Number Per Year: no limit   Fee: none
Telephone: yes (money market fund available)

Services
IRA, pension, auto exchange, auto invest, auto withdraw

538   *Guide to Low-Load Mutual Funds*

Neuberger & Berman Genesis (NBGNX)

Growth

605 Third Ave.
2nd Floor
New York, NY 10158
800-877-9700, 212-476-8800
www.nbfunds.com

PERFORMANCE

fund inception date: 9/26/88

	3yr Annual	5yr Annual	10yr Annual	Bull	Bear
Return (%)	17.5	16.4	na	70.3	-5.3
Differ from Category (+/-)	1.8 abv av	2.1 abv av	na	7.9 abv av	1.4 abv av

Total Risk	Standard Deviation	Category Risk	Risk Index	Beta
abv av	9.7%	blw av	0.9	0.66

	1996	1995	1994	1993	1992	1991	1990	1989	1988	1987
Return (%)	29.8	27.3	-1.9	13.8	15.6	41.5	-16.3	17.2	—	—
Differ from Category (+/-)	9.7	-3.0	-1.6	-0.2	3.8	5.5	-10.2	-8.9	—	—
Return, Tax-Adjusted (%)	29.3	25.3	-3.0	11.0	15.6	40.9	-16.6	16.3	—	—

PER SHARE DATA

	1996	1995	1994	1993	1992	1991	1990	1989	1988	1987
Dividends, Net Income ($)	0.00	0.00	0.00	0.01	0.00	0.01	0.04	0.02	—	—
Distrib'ns, Cap Gain ($)	0.15	0.55	0.31	0.75	0.00	0.09	0.00	0.12	—	—
Net Asset Value ($)	12.03	9.38	7.80	8.26	7.92	6.85	4.91	5.91	—	—
Expense Ratio (%)	1.28	1.35	1.36	1.65	2.00	2.00	2.00	2.00	—	—
Yield (%)	0.00	0.00	0.00	0.11	0.00	0.14	0.81	0.33	—	—
Portfolio Turnover (%)	21	37	63	54	23	46	37	10	—	—
Total Assets (Millions $)	278	118	108	124	87	42	17	20	—	—

PORTFOLIO (as of 9/30/96)

Portfolio Manager: Judy Vale - 1994

Investm't Category: Growth

✔ Domestic	Index
✔ Foreign	Sector
Asset Allocation	State Specific

Investment Style

Large-Cap Growth	Large-Cap Value
Mid-Cap Growth	Mid-Cap Value
Small-Cap Growth	✔ Small-Cap Value

Portfolio

2.5% cash	0.0% corp bonds
94.8% stocks	2.7% gov't bonds
0.0% preferred	0.0% muni bonds
0.0% conv't/warrants	0.0% other

SHAREHOLDER INFORMATION

Minimum Investment
Initial: $1,000   Subsequent: $100

Minimum IRA Investment
Initial: $250   Subsequent: $100

Maximum Fees
Load: none   12b-1: none
Other: none

Distributions
Income: Dec   Capital Gains: Dec

Exchange Options
Number Per Year: no limit   Fee: none
Telephone: yes (money market fund available)

Services
IRA, pension, auto exchange, auto invest, auto withdraw

Neuberger & Berman Guardian (NGUAX)

Growth & Income

605 Third Ave.
2nd Floor
New York, NY 10158
800-877-9700, 212-476-8800
www.nbfunds.com

PERFORMANCE

fund inception date: 6/1/50

	3yr Annual	5yr Annual	10yr Annual	Bull	Bear
Return (%)	16.1	16.3	15.4	59.0	-4.5
Differ from Category (+/-)	0.8 av	2.4 high	2.7 high	-0.8 blw av	1.9 abv av

Total Risk	Standard Deviation	Category Risk	Risk Index	Beta
abv av	11.0%	high	1.2	1.01

	1996	1995	1994	1993	1992	1991	1990	1989	1988	1987
Return (%)	17.8	32.1	0.6	14.4	19.0	34.3	-4.8	21.5	28.0	-1.1
Differ from Category (+/-)	-1.9	2.0	1.9	0.6	8.3	5.2	1.1	-2.0	11.2	-1.3
Return, Tax-Adjusted (%)	15.8	30.3	-0.3	13.0	17.1	31.1	-6.2	17.6	23.5	-2.7

PER SHARE DATA

	1996	1995	1994	1993	1992	1991	1990	1989	1988	1987
Dividends, Net Income ($)	0.27	0.28	0.25	0.30	0.25	0.31	0.35	0.35	0.35	0.49
Distrib'ns, Cap Gain ($)	1.24	0.76	0.23	0.40	0.66	0.90	0.16	1.18	1.22	1.40
Net Asset Value ($)	25.63	23.03	18.23	18.60	16.87	14.97	12.08	13.22	12.17	10.74
Expense Ratio (%)	0.82	0.80	0.80	0.81	0.82	0.84	0.86	0.84	0.84	0.74
Yield (%)	1.00	1.17	1.35	1.57	1.42	1.95	2.86	2.42	2.61	4.03
Portfolio Turnover (%)	37	26	24	27	41	59	58	52	73	91
Total Assets (Millions $)	5,607	4,389	2,423	1,973	1,038	682	519	570	530	442

PORTFOLIO (as of 9/30/96)

Portfolio Manager: K. Simons, L. Marx, K. Risen - 1981

Investm't Category: Growth & Income
- ✔ Domestic
- ✔ Foreign
- Asset Allocation
- Index
- Sector
- State Specific

Investment Style
- Large-Cap Growth
- ✔ Mid-Cap Growth
- Small-Cap Growth
- Large-Cap Value
- ✔ Mid-Cap Value
- Small-Cap Value

Portfolio
- 3.9% cash
- 94.9% stocks
- 0.7% preferred
- 0.3% conv't/warrants
- 0.0% corp bonds
- 0.2% gov't bonds
- 0.0% muni bonds
- 0.0% other

SHAREHOLDER INFORMATION

Minimum Investment
Initial: $1,000   Subsequent: $100

Minimum IRA Investment
Initial: $250   Subsequent: $100

Maximum Fees
Load: none   12b-1: none
Other: none

Distributions
Income: quarterly   Capital Gains: Dec

Exchange Options
Number Per Year: no limit   Fee: none
Telephone: yes (money market fund available)

Services
IRA, pension, auto exchange, auto invest, auto withdraw

Neuberger & Berman Int'l (NBISX)

International Stock

605 Third Ave.
2nd Floor
New York, NY 10158
800-877-9700, 212-476-8800
www.nbfunds.com

PERFORMANCE

fund inception date: 6/15/94

	3yr Annual	5yr Annual	10yr Annual	Bull	Bear
Return (%)	na	na	na	33.4	na
Differ from Category (+/-)	na	na	na	9.1 abv av	na

Total Risk	Standard Deviation	Category Risk	Risk Index	Beta
na	na	na	na	na

	1996	1995	1994	1993	1992	1991	1990	1989	1988	1987
Return (%)	23.6	7.8	—	—	—	—	—	—	—	—
Differ from Category (+/-)	8.8	-1.3	—	—	—	—	—	—	—	—
Return, Tax-Adjusted (%)	23.5	7.6	—	—	—	—	—	—	—	—

PER SHARE DATA

	1996	1995	1994	1993	1992	1991	1990	1989	1988	1987
Dividends, Net Income ($)	0.02	0.04	—	—	—	—	—	—	—	—
Distrib'ns, Cap Gain ($)	0.00	0.00	—	—	—	—	—	—	—	—
Net Asset Value ($)	13.14	10.64	—	—	—	—	—	—	—	—
Expense Ratio (%)	1.70	1.70	—	—	—	—	—	—	—	—
Yield (%)	0.15	0.37	—	—	—	—	—	—	—	—
Portfolio Turnover (%)	45	41	—	—	—	—	—	—	—	—
Total Assets (Millions $)	69	33	—	—	—	—	—	—	—	—

PORTFOLIO (as of 9/30/96)

Portfolio Manager: Felix Rovelli, Robert Cresci - 1994

Investm't Category: International Stock
Domestic	Index
✔ Foreign	Sector
Asset Allocation	State Specific

Investment Style
Large-Cap Growth	Large-Cap Value
Mid-Cap Growth	Mid-Cap Value
Small-Cap Growth	Small-Cap Value

Portfolio
0.0% cash	0.0% corp bonds
89.6% stocks	6.7% gov't bonds
3.4% preferred	0.0% muni bonds
0.6% conv't/warrants	0.0% other

SHAREHOLDER INFORMATION

Minimum Investment
Initial: $1,000   Subsequent: $100

Minimum IRA Investment
Initial: $250   Subsequent: $100

Maximum Fees
Load: none   12b-1: none
Other: none

Distributions
Income: Dec   Capital Gains: Dec

Exchange Options
Number Per Year: no limit   Fee: none
Telephone: yes (money market fund available)

Services
IRA, pension, auto exchange, auto invest, auto withdraw

Neuberger & Berman Ltd Maturity Bond (NLMBX)

General Bond

605 Third Ave.
2nd Floor
New York, NY 10158
800-877-9700, 212-476-8800
www.nbfunds.com

PERFORMANCE

fund inception date: 6/9/86

	3yr Annual	5yr Annual	10yr Annual	Bull	Bear
Return (%)	4.8	5.2	6.8	16.7	-2.2
Differ from Category (+/-)	-0.3 blw av	-0.9 blw av	-0.5 blw av	-3.6 blw av	2.0 abv av

Total Risk	Standard Deviation	Category Risk	Risk Index	Avg Mat
low	2.2%	blw av	0.6	3.1 yrs

	1996	1995	1994	1993	1992	1991	1990	1989	1988	1987
Return (%)	4.5	10.5	-0.4	6.7	5.1	11.8	8.7	11.1	6.7	3.5
Differ from Category (+/-)	0.6	-4.4	1.9	-2.4	-1.4	-2.9	1.4	-0.6	-0.9	1.2
Return, Tax-Adjusted (%)	2.1	8.0	-2.6	4.3	2.6	9.0	5.5	7.7	3.7	0.8

PER SHARE DATA

	1996	1995	1994	1993	1992	1991	1990	1989	1988	1987
Dividends, Net Income ($)	0.60	0.61	0.56	0.56	0.61	0.69	0.79	0.82	0.73	0.67
Distrib'ns, Cap Gain ($)	0.00	0.00	0.00	0.06	0.05	0.00	0.00	0.00	0.00	0.00
Net Asset Value ($)	9.98	10.15	9.76	10.36	10.30	10.44	10.00	9.96	9.74	9.83
Expense Ratio (%)	na	0.70	0.69	0.65	0.65	0.65	0.65	0.65	0.50	0.50
Yield (%)	6.01	6.00	5.73	5.37	5.89	6.60	7.90	8.23	7.49	6.81
Portfolio Turnover (%)	na	88	102	114	113	88	88	121	158	41
Total Assets (Millions $)	242	303	292	349	272	174	116	112	123	94

PORTFOLIO (as of 9/30/96)

Portfolio Manager: Thomas Wolfe - 1995

Investm't Category: General Bond
✔ Domestic   Index
  Foreign   Sector
  Asset Allocation   State Specific

Investment Style
Large-Cap Growth   Large-Cap Value
Mid-Cap Growth   Mid-Cap Value
Small-Cap Growth   Small-Cap Value

Portfolio
5.6% cash   39.5% corp bonds
0.0% stocks   24.0% gov't bonds
0.0% preferred   0.0% muni bonds
0.0% conv't/warrants 30.9% other

SHAREHOLDER INFORMATION

Minimum Investment
Initial: $2,000   Subsequent: $100

Minimum IRA Investment
Initial: $250   Subsequent: $100

Maximum Fees
Load: none   12b-1: none
Other: none

Distributions
Income: monthly   Capital Gains: Dec

Exchange Options
Number Per Year: no limit   Fee: none
Telephone: yes (money market fund available)

Services
IRA, pension, auto exchange, auto invest, auto withdraw

Neuberger & Berman Manhattan (NMANX)

Growth

605 Third Ave.
2nd Floor
New York, NY 10158
800-877-9700, 212-476-8800
www.nbfunds.com

fund inception date: 2/15/66

	3yr Annual	5yr Annual	10yr Annual	Bull	Bear
Return (%)	11.5	12.4	12.7	51.6	-10.6
Differ from Category (+/-)	-4.2 low	-1.9 blw av	-1.2 blw av	-10.8 blw av	-3.9 low

Total Risk	Standard Deviation	Category Risk	Risk Index	Beta
high	15.0%	high	1.5	1.25

	1996	1995	1994	1993	1992	1991	1990	1989	1988	1987
Return (%)	9.8	30.9	-3.7	10.0	17.7	30.8	-8.1	29.0	18.3	0.0
Differ from Category (+/-)	-10.3	0.6	-3.4	-4.0	5.9	-5.2	-2.0	2.9	0.2	-2.0
Return, Tax-Adjusted (%)	5.9	28.2	-5.5	5.1	13.4	29.1	-9.2	24.9	17.3	-4.2

PER SHARE DATA

	1996	1995	1994	1993	1992	1991	1990	1989	1988	1987
Dividends, Net Income ($)	0.00	0.00	0.01	0.02	0.05	0.11	0.16	0.18	0.16	0.26
Distrib'ns, Cap Gain ($)	1.66	0.96	0.70	2.06	1.68	0.40	0.15	1.05	0.04	0.95
Net Asset Value ($)	11.68	12.14	10.00	11.11	11.99	11.65	9.29	10.44	9.04	7.81
Expense Ratio (%)	0.98	0.98	0.96	1.04	1.07	1.09	1.14	1.12	1.18	1.00
Yield (%)	0.00	0.00	0.09	0.15	0.36	0.91	1.69	1.56	1.76	2.96
Portfolio Turnover (%)	53	44	50	76	83	78	91	77	70	111
Total Assets (Millions $)	545	594	462	524	514	463	368	404	341	327

PORTFOLIO (as of 9/30/96)

Portfolio Manager: Mark Goldstein, Susan Switzer - 1992

Investm't Category: Growth
- ✔ Domestic
- ✔ Foreign
- Asset Allocation
- Index
- Sector
- State Specific

Investment Style
- Large-Cap Growth
- ✔ Mid-Cap Growth
- Small-Cap Growth
- Large-Cap Value
- Mid-Cap Value
- Small-Cap Value

Portfolio
- 0.0% cash
- 99.4% stocks
- 0.0% preferred
- 0.0% conv't/warrants
- 0.0% corp bonds
- 3.9% gov't bonds
- 0.0% muni bonds
- 0.0% other

SHAREHOLDER INFORMATION

Minimum Investment
Initial: $1,000   Subsequent: $100

Minimum IRA Investment
Initial: $250   Subsequent: $100

Maximum Fees
Load: none   12b-1: none
Other: none

Distributions
Income: Dec   Capital Gains: Dec

Exchange Options
Number Per Year: no limit   Fee: none
Telephone: yes (money market fund available)

Services
IRA, pension, auto exchange, auto invest, auto withdraw

Neuberger & Berman Muni Securities Trust

605 Third Ave.
2nd Floor
New York, NY 10158
800-877-9700, 212-476-8800
www.nbfunds.com

(NBMUX) *Tax-Exempt Bond*

PERFORMANCE   fund inception date: 7/9/87

	3yr Annual	5yr Annual	10yr Annual	Bull	Bear
Return (%)	3.8	5.5	na	15.2	-3.8
Differ from Category (+/-)	-0.4 blw av	-0.9 low	na	-3.2 low	1.6 high

Total Risk	Standard Deviation	Category Risk	Risk Index	Avg Mat
low	3.8%	low	0.7	7.7 yrs

	1996	1995	1994	1993	1992	1991	1990	1989	1988	1987
Return (%)	3.5	12.7	-4.0	9.5	6.9	9.0	6.8	8.2	6.7	—
Differ from Category (+/-)	-0.2	-2.5	1.3	-2.3	-1.4	-2.4	0.4	-0.8	-3.3	—
Return, Tax-Adjusted (%)	3.5	12.7	-4.0	9.1	6.6	9.0	6.8	8.2	6.7	—

PER SHARE DATA

	1996	1995	1994	1993	1992	1991	1990	1989	1988	1987
Dividends, Net Income ($)	0.46	0.46	0.45	0.46	0.53	0.57	0.63	0.63	0.59	—
Distrib'ns, Cap Gain ($)	0.00	0.00	0.00	0.13	0.09	0.00	0.00	0.00	0.00	—
Net Asset Value ($)	10.83	10.92	10.12	11.01	10.61	10.53	10.21	10.17	10.00	—
Expense Ratio (%)	na	0.65	0.65	0.62	0.50	0.50	0.50	0.50	0.50	—
Yield (%)	4.24	4.21	4.44	4.12	4.95	5.41	6.17	6.19	5.90	—
Portfolio Turnover (%)	na	66	127	35	46	10	42	17	23	—
Total Assets (Millions $)	38	43	40	105	40	24	14	12	9	—

PORTFOLIO (as of 9/30/96)

Portfolio Manager: Clara Del Villar - 1991

Investm't Category: Tax-Exempt Bond
- ✔ Domestic
- Foreign
- Asset Allocation
- Index
- Sector
- State Specific

Investment Style
- Large-Cap Growth
- Mid-Cap Growth
- Small-Cap Growth
- Large-Cap Value
- Mid-Cap Value
- Small-Cap Value

Portfolio
4.1% cash	0.0% corp bonds
0.0% stocks	0.0% gov't bonds
0.0% preferred	95.9% muni bonds
0.0% conv't/warrants	0.0% other

SHAREHOLDER INFORMATION

Minimum Investment
Initial: $2,000   Subsequent: $100

Minimum IRA Investment
Initial: na   Subsequent: na

Maximum Fees
Load: none   12b-1: none
Other: none

Distributions
Income: monthly   Capital Gains: Dec

Exchange Options
Number Per Year: no limit   Fee: none
Telephone: yes (money market fund available)

Services
auto exchange, auto invest, auto withdraw

Neuberger & Berman Partners (NPRTX)

Growth

605 Third Ave.
2nd Floor
New York, NY 10158
800-877-9700, 212-476-8800
www.nbfunds.com

PERFORMANCE

fund inception date: 7/16/68

	3yr Annual	5yr Annual	10yr Annual	Bull	Bear
Return (%)	18.8	18.0	14.7	77.2	-8.0
Differ from Category (+/-)	3.1 abv av	3.7 high	0.8 abv av	14.8 high	-1.3 blw av

Total Risk	Standard Deviation	Category Risk	Risk Index	Beta
abv av	11.4%	abv av	1.1	1.07

	1996	1995	1994	1993	1992	1991	1990	1989	1988	1987
Return (%).	26.4	35.2	-1.9	16.4	17.5	22.3	-5.2	22.7	15.4	4.3
Differ from Category (+/-). .	6.3	4.9	-1.6	2.4	5.7	-13.7	0.9	-3.4	-2.7	2.3
Return, Tax-Adjusted (%). .	22.7	30.6	-4.3	13.0	14.3	20.0	-7.4	18.0	13.6	-1.8

PER SHARE DATA

	1996	1995	1994	1993	1992	1991	1990	1989	1988	1987
Dividends, Net Income ($).	0.22	0.20	0.11	0.11	0.19	0.34	0.74	0.76	0.65	0.70
Distrib'ns, Cap Gain ($) . . .	2.61	2.70	1.60	2.20	1.79	0.78	0.34	1.68	0.00	2.79
Net Asset Value ($)	25.19	22.14	18.52	20.62	19.69	18.44	16.02	18.06	16.72	15.06
Expense Ratio (%).	0.84	0.83	0.81	0.86	0.86	0.88	0.91	0.97	0.95	0.86
Yield (%)	0.79	0.80	0.54	0.48	0.88	1.76	4.52	3.85	3.88	3.92
Portfolio Turnover (%). . . .	96	98	75	82	97	161	136	157	210	169
Total Assets (Millions $). .	2,221	1,656	1,245	1,127	974	889	727	764	695	637

PORTFOLIO (as of 9/30/96)

Portfolio Manager: Mike Kassen, Robert Gendelman - 1990

Investm't Category: Growth
- ✔ Domestic
- ✔ Foreign
- Asset Allocation
- Index
- Sector
- State Specific

Investment Style
- Large-Cap Growth
- Mid-Cap Growth
- Small-Cap Growth
- ✔ Large-Cap Value
- ✔ Mid-Cap Value
- Small-Cap Value

Portfolio
- 0.0% cash
- 94.8% stocks
- 0.4% preferred
- 0.0% conv't/warrants
- 0.0% corp bonds
- 5.6% gov't bonds
- 0.0% muni bonds
- 0.0% other

SHAREHOLDER INFORMATION

Minimum Investment
Initial: $1,000   Subsequent: $100

Minimum IRA Investment
Initial: $250   Subsequent: $100

Maximum Fees
Load: none   12b-1: none
Other: none

Distributions
Income: Dec   Capital Gains: Dec

Exchange Options
Number Per Year: no limit   Fee: none
Telephone: yes (money market fund available)

Services
IRA, pension, auto exchange, auto invest, auto withdraw

Neuberger & Berman
Ultra Short Bond (NBMMX)

General Bond

605 Third Ave.
2nd Floor
New York, NY 10158
800-877-9700, 212-476-8800
www.nbfunds.com

PERFORMANCE

fund inception date: 11/7/86

	3yr Annual	5yr Annual	10yr Annual	Bull	Bear
Return (%)	4.6	4.1	5.8	14.0	-0.1
Differ from Category (+/-)	-0.5 blw av	-2.0 low	-1.5 low	-6.3 low	4.1 high

Total Risk	Standard Deviation	Category Risk	Risk Index	Avg Mat
low	0.9%	low	0.3	1.2 yrs

	1996	1995	1994	1993	1992	1991	1990	1989	1988	1987
Return (%)	4.8	6.8	2.2	3.2	3.6	7.4	8.3	9.3	6.8	5.5
Differ from Category (+/-)	0.9	-8.1	4.5	-5.9	-2.9	-7.3	1.0	-2.4	-0.8	3.2
Return, Tax-Adjusted (%)	2.6	4.5	0.7	1.6	1.5	4.7	5.1	5.6	3.9	3.0

PER SHARE DATA

	1996	1995	1994	1993	1992	1991	1990	1989	1988	1987
Dividends, Net Income ($)	0.52	0.53	0.36	0.38	0.51	0.66	0.77	0.91	0.70	0.63
Distrib'ns, Cap Gain ($)	0.00	0.00	0.00	0.00	0.00	0.00	0.00	0.00	0.00	0.00
Net Asset Value ($)	9.47	9.55	9.45	9.61	9.69	9.86	9.82	9.80	9.83	9.88
Expense Ratio (%)	na	0.65	0.65	0.65	0.65	0.65	0.65	0.65	0.50	0.50
Yield (%)	5.49	5.54	3.80	3.95	5.26	6.69	7.84	9.28	7.12	6.37
Portfolio Turnover (%)	na	148	94	115	66	89	120	85	121	39
Total Assets (Millions $)	86	96	90	105	102	93	85	105	96	125

PORTFOLIO (as of 9/30/96)

Portfolio Manager: Josephine Mahaney - 1993

Investm't Category: General Bond
✔ Domestic   Index
   Foreign   Sector
   Asset Allocation   State Specific

Investment Style
   Large-Cap Growth   Large-Cap Value
   Mid-Cap Growth   Mid-Cap Value
   Small-Cap Growth   Small-Cap Value

Portfolio
29.0%	cash	4.2%	corp bonds
0.0%	stocks	47.7%	gov't bonds
0.0%	preferred	0.0%	muni bonds
0.0%	conv't/warrants	19.1%	other

SHAREHOLDER INFORMATION

Minimum Investment
Initial: $2,000   Subsequent: $100

Minimum IRA Investment
Initial: $250   Subsequent: $100

Maximum Fees
Load: none   12b-1: none
Other: none

Distributions
Income: monthly   Capital Gains: Dec

Exchange Options
Number Per Year: no limit   Fee: none
Telephone: yes (money market fund available)

Services
IRA, pension, auto exchange, auto invest, auto withdraw

Nicholas (NICSX)
Growth

700 N. Water St.
Suite 1010
Milwaukee, WI 53202
800-227-5987, 414-272-6133

PERFORMANCE
fund inception date: 7/14/69

	3yr Annual	5yr Annual	10yr Annual	Bull	Bear
Return (%)	16.3	13.4	13.9	64.1	-5.5
Differ from Category (+/-)	0.6 av	-0.9 blw av	0.0 av	1.7 abv av	1.2 abv av

Total Risk	Standard Deviation	Category Risk	Risk Index	Beta
av	9.3%	blw av	0.9	0.88

	1996	1995	1994	1993	1992	1991	1990	1989	1988	1987
Return (%)	19.7	35.3	-2.9	5.8	12.6	41.9	-4.9	24.5	17.9	-0.8
Differ from Category (+/-)	-0.4	5.0	-2.6	-8.2	0.8	5.9	1.2	-1.6	-0.2	-2.8
Return, Tax-Adjusted (%)	16.9	32.4	-5.2	4.6	10.8	40.5	-5.9	22.4	16.0	-6.2

PER SHARE DATA

	1996	1995	1994	1993	1992	1991	1990	1989	1988	1987
Dividends, Net Income ($)	0.56	0.62	0.70	0.81	0.71	0.67	0.79	0.92	1.02	1.84
Distrib'ns, Cap Gain ($)	5.17	4.03	3.31	1.04	2.00	0.82	0.22	1.05	0.45	4.03
Net Asset Value ($)	65.94	60.03	48.03	53.64	52.47	49.17	35.76	38.61	32.63	28.94
Expense Ratio (%)	0.74	0.77	0.78	0.76	0.78	0.81	0.82	0.86	0.86	0.86
Yield (%)	0.78	0.96	1.36	1.48	1.30	1.34	2.19	2.31	3.08	5.58
Portfolio Turnover (%)	25	29	33	10	15	22	21	24	32	27
Total Assets (Millions $)	3,827	3,505	2,820	3,179	2,772	2,103	1,379	1,385	1,107	1,028

PORTFOLIO (as of 6/30/96)

Portfolio Manager: Albert O. Nicholas - 1969

Investm't Category: Growth
- ✔ Domestic
- Foreign
- Asset Allocation
- Index
- Sector
- State Specific

Investment Style
- Large-Cap Growth
- Mid-Cap Growth
- Small-Cap Growth
- ✔ Large-Cap Value
- ✔ Mid-Cap Value
- Small-Cap Value

Portfolio
5.5% cash	0.0% corp bonds
93.8% stocks	0.0% gov't bonds
0.0% preferred	0.0% muni bonds
0.7% conv't/warrants	0.0% other

SHAREHOLDER INFORMATION

Minimum Investment
Initial: $500   Subsequent: $100

Minimum IRA Investment
Initial: $500   Subsequent: $100

Maximum Fees
Load: none   12b-1: none
Other: none

Distributions
Income: annual   Capital Gains: annual

Exchange Options
Number Per Year: no limit   Fee: $5 (telephone)
Telephone: yes; 4/yr (money market fund available)

Services
IRA, pension, auto exchange, auto invest, auto withdraw

Nicholas II (NCTWX)

Growth

700 N. Water St.
Suite 1010
Milwaukee, WI 53202
800-227-5987, 414-272-6133

PERFORMANCE

fund inception date: 10/17/83

	3yr Annual	5yr Annual	10yr Annual	Bull	Bear
Return (%)	15.7	12.5	13.3	60.2	-4.3
Differ from Category (+/-)	0.0 av	-1.8 blw av	-0.6 av	-2.2 av	2.4 abv av

Total Risk	Standard Deviation	Category Risk	Risk Index	Beta
abv av	10.6%	av	1.0	0.74

	1996	1995	1994	1993	1992	1991	1990	1989	1988	1987
Return (%)	19.3	28.5	1.0	6.4	9.3	39.5	-6.3	17.6	17.2	7.7
Differ from Category (+/-)	-0.8	-1.8	1.3	-7.6	-2.5	3.5	-0.2	-8.5	-0.9	5.7
Return, Tax-Adjusted (%)	16.0	25.3	-1.4	4.5	8.0	38.3	-7.2	15.8	16.2	4.6

PER SHARE DATA

	1996	1995	1994	1993	1992	1991	1990	1989	1988	1987
Dividends, Net Income ($)	0.22	0.27	0.31	0.27	0.23	0.24	0.34	0.31	0.33	0.33
Distrib'ns, Cap Gain ($)	3.02	2.40	1.79	1.40	0.80	0.40	0.14	0.66	0.08	1.30
Net Asset Value ($)	30.99	28.73	24.46	26.32	26.32	25.02	18.42	20.16	17.98	15.69
Expense Ratio (%)	0.62	0.66	0.67	0.67	0.66	0.70	0.71	0.74	0.77	0.74
Yield (%)	0.64	0.86	1.18	0.97	0.84	0.94	1.83	1.48	1.82	1.94
Portfolio Turnover (%)	24	19	17	27	11	12	19	8	18	26
Total Assets (Millions $)	792	693	603	703	742	557	355	404	361	339

PORTFOLIO (as of 9/30/96)

Portfolio Manager: David O. Nicholas - 1993

Investm't Category: Growth

✔ Domestic	Index
Foreign	Sector
Asset Allocation	State Specific

Investment Style

Large-Cap Growth	Large-Cap Value
✔ Mid-Cap Growth	✔ Mid-Cap Value
✔ Small-Cap Growth	✔ Small-Cap Value

Portfolio

4.2% cash	0.0% corp bonds
95.7% stocks	0.0% gov't bonds
0.0% preferred	0.0% muni bonds
0.1% conv't/warrants	0.0% other

SHAREHOLDER INFORMATION

Minimum Investment
Initial: $1,000   Subsequent: $100

Minimum IRA Investment
Initial: $1,000   Subsequent: $100

Maximum Fees
Load: none   12b-1: none
Other: none

Distributions
Income: Dec   Capital Gains: Dec

Exchange Options
Number Per Year: no limit   Fee: $5 (telephone)
Telephone: yes; 4/yr (money market fund available)

Services
IRA, pension, auto exchange, auto invest, auto withdraw

Nicholas Income (NCINX)

Corporate High-Yield Bond

700 N. Water St.
Suite 1010
Milwaukee, WI 53202
800-227-5987, 414-272-6133

PERFORMANCE

fund inception date: 11/10/24

	3yr Annual	5yr Annual	10yr Annual	Bull	Bear
Return (%)	9.2	10.1	8.9	32.4	-3.3
Differ from Category (+/-)	0.5 abv av	-2.0 low	-0.4 blw av	-0.7 av	2.1 high

Total Risk	Standard Deviation	Category Risk	Risk Index	Avg Mat
low	3.7%	low	0.8	6.5 yrs

	1996	1995	1994	1993	1992	1991	1990	1989	1988	1987
Return (%)	12.3	16.1	-0.2	12.9	10.3	23.0	-1.1	3.9	11.5	2.5
Differ from Category (+/-)	-3.0	-1.4	2.7	-6.0	-5.8	-4.6	3.8	2.7	-1.0	0.7
Return, Tax-Adjusted (%)	8.9	12.5	-3.6	9.6	6.8	18.5	-5.6	-0.2	7.4	-2.1

PER SHARE DATA

	1996	1995	1994	1993	1992	1991	1990	1989	1988	1987
Dividends, Net Income ($)	0.29	0.29	0.30	0.28	0.29	0.34	0.39	0.38	0.37	0.46
Distrib'ns, Cap Gain ($)	0.00	0.00	0.00	0.00	0.00	0.00	0.00	0.00	0.00	0.00
Net Asset Value ($)	3.53	3.42	3.21	3.52	3.38	3.34	3.01	3.44	3.68	3.64
Expense Ratio (%)	na	0.58	0.59	0.62	0.69	0.76	0.77	0.81	0.83	0.86
Yield (%)	8.21	8.47	9.34	7.95	8.57	10.17	12.95	11.04	10.05	12.63
Portfolio Turnover (%)	na	29	29	39	56	28	40	40	12	48
Total Assets (Millions $)	180	162	140	158	119	79	60	75	78	69

PORTFOLIO (as of 9/30/96)

Portfolio Manager: Albert O. Nicholas - 1977

Investm't Category: Corp. High-Yield Bond
✔ Domestic   Index
  Foreign   Sector
  Asset Allocation   State Specific

Investment Style
  Large-Cap Growth   Large-Cap Value
  Mid-Cap Growth   Mid-Cap Value
  Small-Cap Growth   Small-Cap Value

Portfolio
  8.8% cash   81.3% corp bonds
  9.6% stocks   0.0% gov't bonds
  0.0% preferred   0.0% muni bonds
  0.3% conv't/warrants 0.0% other

SHAREHOLDER INFORMATION

Minimum Investment
Initial: $500   Subsequent: $100

Minimum IRA Investment
Initial: $500   Subsequent: $100

Maximum Fees
Load: none   12b-1: none
Other: none

Distributions
Income: quarterly   Capital Gains: Dec

Exchange Options
Number Per Year: no limit   Fee: $5 (telephone)
Telephone: yes; 4/yr (money market fund available)

Services
IRA, pension, auto exchange, auto invest, auto withdraw

Nicholas Ltd Edition

(NCLEX)

Growth

700 N. Water St.
Suite 1010
Milwaukee, WI 53202
800-227-5987, 414-272-6133

	3yr Annual	5yr Annual	10yr Annual	Bull	Bear
Return (%)	15.4	14.3	na	62.8	-6.9
Differ from Category (+/-)	-0.3 av	0.0 av	na	0.4 av	-0.2 av

Total Risk	Standard Deviation	Category Risk	Risk Index	Beta
abv av	10.7%	abv av	1.0	0.63

	1996	1995	1994	1993	1992	1991	1990	1989	1988	1987
Return (%)	21.8	30.1	-3.1	9.0	16.7	43.2	-1.8	17.3	27.2	—
Differ from Category (+/-)	1.7	-0.2	-2.8	-5.0	4.9	7.2	4.3	-8.8	9.1	—
Return, Tax-Adjusted (%)	17.6	24.9	-4.7	6.3	15.1	42.2	-2.5	15.2	26.0	—

PER SHARE DATA

	1996	1995	1994	1993	1992	1991	1990	1989	1988	1987
Dividends, Net Income ($)	0.52	0.30	0.10	0.08	0.08	0.12	0.12	0.14	0.09	—
Distrib'ns, Cap Gain ($)	2.09	2.71	0.90	1.67	0.82	0.24	0.12	0.61	0.25	—
Net Asset Value ($)	20.74	19.22	17.09	18.68	18.77	16.86	12.03	12.49	11.29	—
Expense Ratio (%)	na	0.90	0.90	0.88	0.92	0.94	1.07	1.12	1.32	—
Yield (%)	2.27	1.36	0.55	0.39	0.40	0.70	0.98	1.06	0.77	—
Portfolio Turnover (%)	na	35	16	24	24	13	15	31	31	—
Total Assets (Millions $)	266	169	142	180	190	175	70	54	33	—

PORTFOLIO (as of 3/31/96)

Portfolio Manager: David O. Nicholas - 1993

Investm't Category: Growth

✔ Domestic	Index
Foreign	Sector
Asset Allocation	State Specific

Investment Style

Large-Cap Growth	Large-Cap Value
Mid-Cap Growth	Mid-Cap Value
✔ Small-Cap Growth	✔ Small-Cap Value

Portfolio

2.7% cash	0.0% corp bonds
96.6% stocks	0.0% gov't bonds
0.0% preferred	0.0% muni bonds
0.7% conv't/warrants	0.0% other

SHAREHOLDER INFORMATION

Minimum Investment

Initial: $2,000   Subsequent: $100

Minimum IRA Investment

Initial: $2,000   Subsequent: $100

Maximum Fees

Load: none   12b-1: none
Other: none

Distributions

Income: Dec   Capital Gains: Dec

Exchange Options

Number Per Year: no limit   Fee: $5 (telephone)
Telephone: yes; 4/yr (money market fund available)

Services

IRA, pension, auto exchange, auto invest, auto withdraw

Nomura Pacific Basin

(NPBFX)

International Stock

180 Maiden Lane
New York, NY 10038
800-833-0018, 212-509-9037

PERFORMANCE

fund inception date: 7/8/85

	3yr Annual	5yr Annual	10yr Annual	Bull	Bear
Return (%)	3.6	6.4	9.4	0.1	2.2
Differ from Category (+/-)	-2.7 blw av	-3.6 low	0.8 av	-24.2 low	9.4 high

Total Risk	Standard Deviation	Category Risk	Risk Index	Beta
high	12.3%	abv av	1.2	0.73

	1996	1995	1994	1993	1992	1991	1990	1989	1988	1987
Return (%)	3.0	3.5	4.2	40.4	-12.7	11.7	-15.4	22.7	16.3	33.4
Differ from Category (+/-)	-11.8	-5.6	7.3	0.8	-8.9	-1.5	-5.3	0.1	1.4	21.2
Return, Tax-Adjusted (%)	-0.3	2.5	0.5	39.5	-12.8	9.5	-19.7	16.7	14.2	19.4

PER SHARE DATA

	1996	1995	1994	1993	1992	1991	1990	1989	1988	1987
Dividends, Net Income ($)	0.28	0.00	0.00	0.28	0.02	0.52	0.45	0.10	0.05	0.08
Distrib'ns, Cap Gain ($)	1.47	0.57	2.25	0.00	0.01	0.34	2.29	3.97	1.21	10.46
Net Asset Value ($)	14.70	15.95	15.97	17.47	12.64	14.51	13.75	19.27	19.39	17.75
Expense Ratio (%)	1.78	1.38	1.39	1.51	1.46	1.42	1.32	1.25	1.22	1.45
Yield (%)	1.73	0.00	0.00	1.60	0.15	3.50	2.80	0.43	0.24	0.28
Portfolio Turnover (%)	45	49	76	55	41	76	46	37	61	46
Total Assets (Millions $)	31	37	55	56	42	51	48	70	78	74

PORTFOLIO (as of 9/30/96)

Portfolio Manager: Iwao Komatsu - 1995

Investm't Category: International Stock

Domestic	Index
✔ Foreign	Sector
Asset Allocation	State Specific

Investment Style

Large-Cap Growth	Large-Cap Value
Mid-Cap Growth	Mid-Cap Value
Small-Cap Growth	Small-Cap Value

Portfolio

1.3% cash	0.0% corp bonds
98.7% stocks	0.0% gov't bonds
0.0% preferred	0.0% muni bonds
0.0% conv't/warrants	0.0% other

SHAREHOLDER INFORMATION

Minimum Investment
Initial: $1,000   Subsequent: $1

Minimum IRA Investment
Initial: $1,000   Subsequent: $1

Maximum Fees
Load: none   12b-1: none
Other: none

Distributions
Income: May, Dec   Capital Gains: Dec

Exchange Options
Number Per Year: none   Fee: na
Telephone: na

Services
IRA

Northeast Investors Growth (NTHFX)

Growth

50 Congress St.
Suite 1000
Boston, MA 02109
800-225-6704, 617-523-3588

fund inception date: 10/27/80

PERFORMANCE

	3yr Annual	5yr Annual	10yr Annual	Bull	Bear
Return (%)	19.3	11.5	13.2	78.8	-6.7
Differ from Category (+/-)	3.6 high	-2.8 low	-0.7 av	16.4 high	0.0 av

Total Risk	Standard Deviation	Category Risk	Risk Index	Beta
abv av	10.5%	av	1.0	1.01

	1996	1995	1994	1993	1992	1991	1990	1989	1988	1987
Return (%)	24.6	36.4	-0.1	2.3	-0.8	36.9	1.5	32.7	12.9	-3.6
Differ from Category (+/-)	4.5	6.1	0.2	-11.7	-12.6	0.9	7.6	6.6	-5.2	-5.6
Return, Tax-Adjusted (%)	21.8	34.5	-1.0	-2.3	-2.5	35.6	0.6	31.6	11.5	-5.0

PER SHARE DATA

	1996	1995	1994	1993	1992	1991	1990	1989	1988	1987
Dividends, Net Income ($)	0.16	0.21	0.19	0.19	0.20	0.36	0.26	0.28	0.26	0.31
Distrib'ns, Cap Gain ($)	2.95	1.32	0.50	4.46	1.57	0.55	0.33	0.29	0.46	0.43
Net Asset Value ($)	36.45	31.78	24.40	25.11	29.11	31.12	23.45	23.68	18.28	16.84
Expense Ratio (%)	na	1.37	1.53	1.45	1.42	1.50	1.74	1.77	1.74	1.60
Yield (%)	0.40	0.63	0.76	0.64	0.65	1.13	1.09	1.16	1.38	1.79
Portfolio Turnover (%)	na	26	25	35	29	16	37	23	16	36
Total Assets (Millions $)	61	48	35	38	42	40	27	27	19	21

PORTFOLIO (as of 9/30/96)

Portfolio Manager: William Oates Jr. - 1980

Investm't Category: Growth

✔ Domestic	Index
Foreign	Sector
Asset Allocation	State Specific

Investment Style

✔ Large-Cap Growth	✔ Large-Cap Value
Mid-Cap Growth	Mid-Cap Value
Small-Cap Growth	Small-Cap Value

Portfolio

1.0% cash	0.0% corp bonds
99.0% stocks	0.0% gov't bonds
0.0% preferred	0.0% muni bonds
0.0% conv't/warrants	0.0% other

SHAREHOLDER INFORMATION

Minimum Investment
Initial: $1,000   Subsequent: $1

Minimum IRA Investment
Initial: $500   Subsequent: $1

Maximum Fees
Load: none   12b-1: none
Other: none

Distributions
Income: annual   Capital Gains: annual

Exchange Options
Number Per Year: no limit   Fee: none
Telephone: yes (money market fund not available)

Services
IRA, pension, auto exchange, auto invest, auto withdraw

Northeast Investors Trust

(NTHEX)

Balanced

50 Congress St.
Suite 1000
Boston, MA 02109
800-225-6704, 617-523-3588

PERFORMANCE

fund inception date: 3/1/50

	3yr Annual	5yr Annual	10yr Annual	Bull	Bear
Return (%)	12.9	15.8	10.6	39.3	-2.3
Differ from Category (+/-)	1.2 abv av	4.4 high	-0.2 blw av	-5.8 blw av	3.4 high

Total Risk	Standard Deviation	Category Risk	Risk Index	Beta
blw av	5.7%	low	0.8	0.34

	1996	1995	1994	1993	1992	1991	1990	1989	1988	1987
Return (%)	20.1	17.2	2.2	23.5	17.4	26.3	-9.2	0.0	14.0	0.1
Differ from Category (+/-)	5.9	-7.4	3.8	9.1	8.5	2.2	-8.3	-18.1	1.8	-2.6
Return, Tax-Adjusted (%)	16.2	13.0	-1.6	19.2	12.4	19.9	-14.6	-5.0	8.8	-5.5

PER SHARE DATA

	1996	1995	1994	1993	1992	1991	1990	1989	1988	1987
Dividends, Net Income ($)	1.00	0.99	0.98	1.00	1.11	1.30	1.40	1.49	1.54	1.92
Distrib'ns, Cap Gain ($)	0.00	0.00	0.00	0.00	0.00	0.00	0.00	0.00	0.00	0.00
Net Asset Value ($)	11.12	10.16	9.55	10.29	9.21	8.83	8.14	10.43	11.89	11.83
Expense Ratio (%)	0.66	0.67	0.70	0.73	0.79	0.88	0.78	0.72	0.75	0.76
Yield (%)	8.99	9.74	10.26	9.71	12.05	14.72	17.19	14.28	12.95	16.22
Portfolio Turnover (%)	32	40	73	75	59	34	21	32	17	52
Total Assets (Millions $)	1,303	805	554	548	399	304	243	339	408	337

PORTFOLIO (as of 9/30/96)

Portfolio Manager: Ernest Monrad - 1960

Investm't Category: Balanced

✔ Domestic	Index
Foreign	Sector
✔ Asset Allocation	State Specific

Investment Style

Large-Cap Growth	Large-Cap Value
Mid-Cap Growth	Mid-Cap Value
Small-Cap Growth	Small-Cap Value

Portfolio

4.1% cash	76.0% corp bonds
14.0% stocks	0.0% gov't bonds
2.9% preferred	0.0% muni bonds
2.9% conv't/warrants	0.0% other

SHAREHOLDER INFORMATION

Minimum Investment

Initial: $1,000   Subsequent: $1

Minimum IRA Investment

Initial: $500   Subsequent: $1

Maximum Fees

Load: none   12b-1: none
Other: none

Distributions

Income: quarterly   Capital Gains: annual

Exchange Options

Number Per Year: no limit   Fee: none
Telephone: yes (money market fund not available)

Services

IRA, pension, auto exchange, auto invest, auto withdraw

Northern Fixed Income

50 S. LaSalle St.
Chicago, IL 60675
800-595-9111, 312-630-6000

(NOFIX)

General Bond

PERFORMANCE
fund inception date: 4/4/94

	3yr Annual	5yr Annual	10yr Annual	Bull	Bear
Return (%)	na	na	na	24.0	na
Differ from Category (+/-)	na	na	na	3.7 high	na

Total Risk	Standard Deviation	Category Risk	Risk Index	Avg Mat
na	na	na	na	12.0 yrs

	1996	1995	1994	1993	1992	1991	1990	1989	1988	1987
Return (%).	2.5	18.7	—	—	—	—	—	—	—	—
Differ from Category (+/-) .	-1.4	3.8	—	—	—	—	—	—	—	—
Return, Tax-Adjusted (%). .	0.1	15.6	—	—	—	—	—	—	—	—

PER SHARE DATA

	1996	1995	1994	1993	1992	1991	1990	1989	1988	1987
Dividends, Net Income ($).	0.56	0.61	—	—	—	—	—	—	—	—
Distrib'ns, Cap Gain ($) . . .	0.11	0.17	—	—	—	—	—	—	—	—
Net Asset Value ($)	10.10	10.53	—	—	—	—	—	—	—	—
Expense Ratio (%).	0.90	0.90	—	—	—	—	—	—	—	—
Yield (%)	5.48	5.70	—	—	—	—	—	—	—	—
Portfolio Turnover (%). . . .	116	55	—	—	—	—	—	—	—	—
Total Assets (Millions $). . .	113	95	—	—	—	—	—	—	—	—

PORTFOLIO (as of 9/30/96)

Portfolio Manager: Michael Lannan - 1994

Investm't Category: General Bond

✔ Domestic	Index
✔ Foreign	Sector
Asset Allocation	State Specific

Investment Style

Large-Cap Growth	Large-Cap Value
Mid-Cap Growth	Mid-Cap Value
Small-Cap Growth	Small-Cap Value

Portfolio

7.8% cash	42.8% corp bonds
0.0% stocks	48.5% gov't bonds
0.0% preferred	0.0% muni bonds
0.0% conv't/warrants	0.9% other

SHAREHOLDER INFORMATION

Minimum Investment
Initial: $2,500   Subsequent: $50

Minimum IRA Investment
Initial: $500   Subsequent: $50

Maximum Fees
Load: none   12b-1: 0.25%
Other: none

Distributions
Income: monthly   Capital Gains: annual

Exchange Options
Number Per Year: 8   Fee: none
Telephone: yes (money market fund available)

Services
IRA, pension, auto invest, auto withdraw

Northern Growth Equity
(NOGEX)
Growth

50 S. LaSalle St.
Chicago, IL 60675
800-595-9111, 312-630-6000

PERFORMANCE

fund inception date: 4/4/94

	3yr Annual	5yr Annual	10yr Annual	Bull	Bear
Return (%)	na	na	na	51.8	na
Differ from Category (+/-)	na	na	na	-10.6 blw av	na

Total Risk	Standard Deviation	Category Risk	Risk Index	Beta
na	na	na	na	na

	1996	1995	1994	1993	1992	1991	1990	1989	1988	1987
Return (%)	17.8	26.1	—	—	—	—	—	—	—	—
Differ from Category (+/-)	-2.3	-4.2	—	—	—	—	—	—	—	—
Return, Tax-Adjusted (%)	16.0	25.6	—	—	—	—	—	—	—	—

PER SHARE DATA

	1996	1995	1994	1993	1992	1991	1990	1989	1988	1987
Dividends, Net Income ($)	0.06	0.08	—	—	—	—	—	—	—	—
Distrib'ns, Cap Gain ($)	0.71	0.04	—	—	—	—	—	—	—	—
Net Asset Value ($)	14.11	12.62	—	—	—	—	—	—	—	—
Expense Ratio (%)	1.00	1.00	—	—	—	—	—	—	—	—
Yield (%)	0.40	0.63	—	—	—	—	—	—	—	—
Portfolio Turnover (%)	73	82	—	—	—	—	—	—	—	—
Total Assets (Millions $)	297	192	—	—	—	—	—	—	—	—

PORTFOLIO (as of 9/30/96)

Portfolio Manager: Theodore Breckel - 1994

Investm't Category: Growth
- ✔ Domestic
- ✔ Foreign
-   Asset Allocation

  Index
  Sector
  State Specific

Investment Style

Large-Cap Growth	Large-Cap Value
Mid-Cap Growth	Mid-Cap Value
Small-Cap Growth	Small-Cap Value

Portfolio

6.3% cash	0.0% corp bonds
93.5% stocks	0.0% gov't bonds
0.0% preferred	0.0% muni bonds
0.0% conv't/warrants	0.2% other

SHAREHOLDER INFORMATION

Minimum Investment
Initial: $2,500   Subsequent: $50

Minimum IRA Investment
Initial: $500   Subsequent: $50

Maximum Fees
Load: none   12b-1: 0.25%
Other: none

Distributions
Income: quarterly   Capital Gains: annual

Exchange Options
Number Per Year: 8   Fee: none
Telephone: yes (money market fund available)

Services
IRA, pension, auto invest, auto withdraw

Northern Income Equity

(NOIEX)

Growth & Income

50 S. LaSalle St.
Chicago, IL 60675
800-595-9111, 312-630-6000

PERFORMANCE

fund inception date: 4/4/94

	3yr Annual	5yr Annual	10yr Annual	Bull	Bear
Return (%)	na	na	na	41.6	na
Differ from Category (+/-)	na	na	na	-18.2 low	na

Total Risk	Standard Deviation	Category Risk	Risk Index	Beta
na	na	na	na	na

	1996	1995	1994	1993	1992	1991	1990	1989	1988	1987
Return (%)	19.9	19.0	—	—	—	—	—	—	—	—
Differ from Category (+/-)	0.2	-11.1	—	—	—	—	—	—	—	—
Return, Tax-Adjusted (%)	15.9	17.7	—	—	—	—	—	—	—	—

PER SHARE DATA

	1996	1995	1994	1993	1992	1991	1990	1989	1988	1987
Dividends, Net Income ($)	0.41	0.31	—	—	—	—	—	—	—	—
Distrib'ns, Cap Gain ($)	0.97	0.00	—	—	—	—	—	—	—	—
Net Asset Value ($)	11.77	11.00	—	—	—	—	—	—	—	—
Expense Ratio (%)	1.00	1.00	—	—	—	—	—	—	—	—
Yield (%)	3.21	2.81	—	—	—	—	—	—	—	—
Portfolio Turnover (%)	67	45	—	—	—	—	—	—	—	—
Total Assets (Millions $)	70	48	—	—	—	—	—	—	—	—

PORTFOLIO (as of 9/30/96)

Portfolio Manager: Theodore T. Southworth - 1995

Investm't Category: Growth & Income

✔ Domestic	Index
✔ Foreign	Sector
Asset Allocation	State Specific

Investment Style

Large-Cap Growth	Large-Cap Value
Mid-Cap Growth	Mid-Cap Value
Small-Cap Growth	Small-Cap Value

Portfolio

6.4% cash	0.0% corp bonds
19.8% stocks	0.0% gov't bonds
30.0% preferred	0.0% muni bonds
43.8% conv't/warrants	0.0% other

SHAREHOLDER INFORMATION

Minimum Investment

Initial: $2,500   Subsequent: $50

Minimum IRA Investment

Initial: $500   Subsequent: $50

Maximum Fees

Load: none   12b-1: 0.25%
Other: none

Distributions

Income: monthly   Capital Gains: annual

Exchange Options

Number Per Year: 8   Fee: none
Telephone: yes (money market fund available)

Services

IRA, pension, auto invest, auto withdraw

Northern Interm Tax-Exempt (NOITX)

Tax-Exempt Bond

50 S. LaSalle St.
Chicago, IL 60675
800-595-9111, 312-630-6000

PERFORMANCE

fund inception date: 4/4/94

	3yr Annual	5yr Annual	10yr Annual	Bull	Bear
Return (%)	na	na	na	14.9	na
Differ from Category (+/-)	na	na	na	-3.5 low	na

Total Risk	Standard Deviation	Category Risk	Risk Index	Avg Mat
na	na	na	na	5.3 yrs

	1996	1995	1994	1993	1992	1991	1990	1989	1988	1987
Return (%)	3.3	11.9	—	—	—	—	—	—	—	—
Differ from Category (+/-)	-0.4	-3.3	—	—	—	—	—	—	—	—
Return, Tax-Adjusted (%)	3.0	11.6	—	—	—	—	—	—	—	—

PER SHARE DATA

	1996	1995	1994	1993	1992	1991	1990	1989	1988	1987
Dividends, Net Income ($)	0.40	0.40	—	—	—	—	—	—	—	—
Distrib'ns, Cap Gain ($)	0.09	0.07	—	—	—	—	—	—	—	—
Net Asset Value ($)	10.19	10.35	—	—	—	—	—	—	—	—
Expense Ratio (%)	0.85	0.85	—	—	—	—	—	—	—	—
Yield (%)	3.89	3.83	—	—	—	—	—	—	—	—
Portfolio Turnover (%)	137	78	—	—	—	—	—	—	—	—
Total Assets (Millions $)	255	238	—	—	—	—	—	—	—	—

PORTFOLIO (as of 9/30/96)

Portfolio Manager: Eric Boeckmann - 1994

Investm't Category: Tax-Exempt Bond
- ✔ Domestic
- Foreign
- Asset Allocation
- Index
- Sector
- State Specific

Investment Style
- Large-Cap Growth
- Mid-Cap Growth
- Small-Cap Growth
- Large-Cap Value
- Mid-Cap Value
- Small-Cap Value

Portfolio
1.2% cash	0.0% corp bonds
0.0% stocks	0.0% gov't bonds
0.0% preferred	98.8% muni bonds
0.0% conv't/warrants	0.0% other

SHAREHOLDER INFORMATION

Minimum Investment
Initial: $2,500   Subsequent: $50

Minimum IRA Investment
Initial: na   Subsequent: na

Maximum Fees
Load: none   12b-1: 0.25%
Other: none

Distributions
Income: monthly   Capital Gains: annual

Exchange Options
Number Per Year: 8   Fee: none
Telephone: yes (money market fund available)

Services
auto invest, auto withdraw

Northern Int'l Growth Equity (NOIGX)

50 S. LaSalle St.
Chicago, IL 60675
800-595-9111, 312-630-6000

International Stock

PERFORMANCE

fund inception date: 4/4/94

	3yr Annual	5yr Annual	10yr Annual	Bull	Bear
Return (%)	na	na	na	5.2	na
Differ from Category (+/-)	na	na	na	-19.1 low	na

Total Risk	Standard Deviation	Category Risk	Risk Index	Beta
na	na	na	na	na

	1996	1995	1994	1993	1992	1991	1990	1989	1988	1987
Return (%)	5.0	2.0	—	—	—	—	—	—	—	—
Differ from Category (+/-)	-9.8	-7.1	—	—	—	—	—	—	—	—
Return, Tax-Adjusted (%)	3.7	1.2	—	—	—	—	—	—	—	—

PER SHARE DATA

	1996	1995	1994	1993	1992	1991	1990	1989	1988	1987
Dividends, Net Income ($)	0.06	0.19	—	—	—	—	—	—	—	—
Distrib'ns, Cap Gain ($)	0.37	0.00	—	—	—	—	—	—	—	—
Net Asset Value ($)	10.07	10.02	—	—	—	—	—	—	—	—
Expense Ratio (%)	1.25	1.25	—	—	—	—	—	—	—	—
Yield (%)	0.57	1.89	—	—	—	—	—	—	—	—
Portfolio Turnover (%)	216	158	—	—	—	—	—	—	—	—
Total Assets (Millions $)	185	161	—	—	—	—	—	—	—	—

PORTFOLIO (as of 9/30/96)

Portfolio Manager: Robert LaFleur - 1994

Investm't Category: International Stock

Domestic	Index
✔ Foreign	Sector
Asset Allocation	State Specific

Investment Style

Large-Cap Growth	Large-Cap Value
Mid-Cap Growth	Mid-Cap Value
Small-Cap Growth	Small-Cap Value

Portfolio

3.8% cash	0.0% corp bonds
88.9% stocks	0.0% gov't bonds
2.9% preferred	0.0% muni bonds
0.0% conv't/warrants	4.4% other

SHAREHOLDER INFORMATION

Minimum Investment
Initial: $2,500   Subsequent: $50

Minimum IRA Investment
Initial: $500   Subsequent: $50

Maximum Fees
Load: none   12b-1: 0.25%
Other: none

Distributions
Income: annual   Capital Gains: annual

Exchange Options
Number Per Year: 8   Fee: none
Telephone: yes (money market fund available)

Services
IRA, pension, auto invest, auto withdraw

Northern Int'l Select Equity (NINEX)

50 S. LaSalle St.
Chicago, IL 60675
800-595-9111, 312-630-6000

International Stock

PERFORMANCE

fund inception date: 4/5/94

	3yr Annual	5yr Annual	10yr Annual	Bull	Bear
Return (%)	na	na	na	2.5	na
Differ from Category (+/-)	na	na	na	-21.8 low	na

Total Risk	Standard Deviation	Category Risk	Risk Index	Beta
na	na	na	na	na

	1996	1995	1994	1993	1992	1991	1990	1989	1988	1987
Return (%)	2.8	-0.9	—	—	—	—	—	—	—	—
Differ from Category (+/-)	-12.0	-10.0	—	—	—	—	—	—	—	—
Return, Tax-Adjusted (%)	2.3	-1.1	—	—	—	—	—	—	—	—

PER SHARE DATA

	1996	1995	1994	1993	1992	1991	1990	1989	1988	1987
Dividends, Net Income ($)	0.06	0.04	—	—	—	—	—	—	—	—
Distrib'ns, Cap Gain ($)	0.08	0.00	—	—	—	—	—	—	—	—
Net Asset Value ($)	10.22	10.08	—	—	—	—	—	—	—	—
Expense Ratio (%)	1.25	1.25	—	—	—	—	—	—	—	—
Yield (%)	0.58	0.39	—	—	—	—	—	—	—	—
Portfolio Turnover (%)	176	97	—	—	—	—	—	—	—	—
Total Assets (Millions $)	114	80	—	—	—	—	—	—	—	—

PORTFOLIO (as of 9/30/96)

Portfolio Manager: Robert LaFleur - 1994

Investm't Category: International Stock

Domestic	Index
✔ Foreign	Sector
Asset Allocation	State Specific

Investment Style

Large-Cap Growth	Large-Cap Value
Mid-Cap Growth	Mid-Cap Value
Small-Cap Growth	Small-Cap Value

Portfolio

7.7% cash	0.0% corp bonds
85.8% stocks	0.0% gov't bonds
3.8% preferred	0.0% muni bonds
0.0% conv't/warrants	2.7% other

SHAREHOLDER INFORMATION

Minimum Investment
Initial: $2,500   Subsequent: $50

Minimum IRA Investment
Initial: $500   Subsequent: $50

Maximum Fees
Load: none   12b-1: 0.25%
Other: none

Distributions
Income: annual   Capital Gains: annual

Exchange Options
Number Per Year: 8   Fee: none
Telephone: yes (money market fund available)

Services
IRA, pension, auto invest, auto withdraw

Northern Select Equity
(NOEQX)
Aggressive Growth

50 S. LaSalle St.
Chicago, IL 60675
800-595-9111, 312-630-6000

	3yr Annual	5yr Annual	10yr Annual	Bull	Bear
Return (%)	na	na	na	63.9	na
Differ from Category (+/-)	na	na	na	-7.2 av	na

Total Risk	Standard Deviation		Category Risk	Risk Index	Beta
na	na		na	na	na

	1996	1995	1994	1993	1992	1991	1990	1989	1988	1987
Return (%)	21.5	28.9	—	—	—	—	—	—	—	—
Differ from Category (+/-)	2.4	-5.4	—	—	—	—	—	—	—	—
Return, Tax-Adjusted (%)	20.1	27.8	—	—	—	—	—	—	—	—

PER SHARE DATA

	1996	1995	1994	1993	1992	1991	1990	1989	1988	1987
Dividends, Net Income ($)	0.01	0.02	—	—	—	—	—	—	—	—
Distrib'ns, Cap Gain ($)	0.61	0.36	—	—	—	—	—	—	—	—
Net Asset Value ($)	14.65	12.57	—	—	—	—	—	—	—	—
Expense Ratio (%)	1.00	1.00	—	—	—	—	—	—	—	—
Yield (%)	0.06	0.15	—	—	—	—	—	—	—	—
Portfolio Turnover (%)	137	49	—	—	—	—	—	—	—	—
Total Assets (Millions $)	54	27	—	—	—	—	—	—	—	—

PORTFOLIO (as of 9/30/96)

Portfolio Manager: Robert Streed - 1994

Investm't Category: Aggressive Growth
- ✔ Domestic
- ✔ Foreign
-   Asset Allocation

  Index
  Sector
  State Specific

Investment Style

Large-Cap Growth	Large-Cap Value
Mid-Cap Growth	Mid-Cap Value
Small-Cap Growth	Small-Cap Value

Portfolio

1.2% cash	0.0% corp bonds
98.6% stocks	0.0% gov't bonds
0.0% preferred	0.0% muni bonds
0.0% conv't/warrants	0.2% other

SHAREHOLDER INFORMATION

Minimum Investment
Initial: $2,500   Subsequent: $50

Minimum IRA Investment
Initial: $500   Subsequent: $50

Maximum Fees
Load: none   12b-1: 0.25%
Other: none

Distributions
Income: annual   Capital Gains: annual

Exchange Options
Number Per Year: 8   Fee: none
Telephone: yes (money market fund available)

Services
IRA, pension, auto invest, auto withdraw

Northern Small Cap
(NOSGX)
Aggressive Growth

50 S. LaSalle St.
Chicago, IL 60675
800-595-9111, 312-630-6000

PERFORMANCE

fund inception date: 4/4/94

	3yr Annual	5yr Annual	10yr Annual	Bull	Bear
Return (%)	na	na	na	45.6	na
Differ from Category (+/-)	na	na	na	-25.5 low	na

Total Risk	Standard Deviation	Category Risk	Risk Index	Beta
na	na	na	na	na

	1996	1995	1994	1993	1992	1991	1990	1989	1988	1987
Return (%).............	18.9	22.5	—	—	—	—	—	—	—	—
Differ from Category (+/-).	-0.2	-11.8	—	—	—	—	—	—	—	—
Return, Tax-Adjusted (%)..	17.0	20.3	—	—	—	—	—	—	—	—

PER SHARE DATA

	1996	1995	1994	1993	1992	1991	1990	1989	1988	1987
Dividends, Net Income ($).	0.05	0.06	—	—	—	—	—	—	—	—
Distrib'ns, Cap Gain ($) ...	0.65	0.66	—	—	—	—	—	—	—	—
Net Asset Value ($)	12.33	10.97	—	—	—	—	—	—	—	—
Expense Ratio (%)........	1.00	1.00	—	—	—	—	—	—	—	—
Yield (%)	0.38	0.51	—	—	—	—	—	—	—	—
Portfolio Turnover (%).....	46	82	—	—	—	—	—	—	—	—
Total Assets (Millions $)...	176	142	—	—	—	—	—	—	—	—

PORTFOLIO (as of 9/30/96)

Portfolio Manager: Susan French - 1994

Investm't Category: Aggressive Growth
- ✔ Domestic
- ✔ Foreign
-   Asset Allocation
-   Index
-   Sector
-   State Specific

Investment Style
Large-Cap Growth	Large-Cap Value
Mid-Cap Growth	Mid-Cap Value
Small-Cap Growth	Small-Cap Value

Portfolio
4.2% cash	0.0% corp bonds
94.5% stocks	0.0% gov't bonds
0.0% preferred	0.0% muni bonds
0.0% conv't/warrants	1.4% other

SHAREHOLDER INFORMATION

Minimum Investment
Initial: $2,500   Subsequent: $50

Minimum IRA Investment
Initial: $500   Subsequent: $50

Maximum Fees
Load: none   12b-1: 0.25%
Other: none

Distributions
Income: annual   Capital Gains: annual

Exchange Options
Number Per Year: 8   Fee: none
Telephone: yes (money market fund available)

Services
IRA, pension, auto invest, auto withdraw

Northern Tax-Exempt

(NOTEX)

Tax-Exempt Bond

50 S. LaSalle St.
Chicago, IL 60675
800-595-9111, 312-630-6000

	3yr Annual	5yr Annual	10yr Annual	Bull	Bear
Return (%)	na	na	na	19.5	na
Differ from Category (+/-)	na	na	na	1.1 av	na

Total Risk	Standard Deviation	Category Risk	Risk Index	Avg Mat
na	na	na	na	14.2 yrs

	1996	1995	1994	1993	1992	1991	1990	1989	1988	1987
Return (%)	2.8	17.3	—	—	—	—	—	—	—	—
Differ from Category (+/-)	-0.9	2.1	—	—	—	—	—	—	—	—
Return, Tax-Adjusted (%)	2.6	17.2	—	—	—	—	—	—	—	—

PER SHARE DATA

	1996	1995	1994	1993	1992	1991	1990	1989	1988	1987
Dividends, Net Income ($)	0.50	0.47	—	—	—	—	—	—	—	—
Distrib'ns, Cap Gain ($)	0.05	0.02	—	—	—	—	—	—	—	—
Net Asset Value ($)	10.43	10.70	—	—	—	—	—	—	—	—
Expense Ratio (%)	0.85	0.85	—	—	—	—	—	—	—	—
Yield (%)	4.77	4.38	—	—	—	—	—	—	—	—
Portfolio Turnover (%)	60	54	—	—	—	—	—	—	—	—
Total Assets (Millions $)	133	125	—	—	—	—	—	—	—	—

PORTFOLIO (as of 9/30/96)

Portfolio Manager: Peter Flood - 1994

Investm't Category: Tax-Exempt Bond
- ✔ Domestic
- Foreign
- Asset Allocation
- Index
- Sector
- State Specific

Investment Style
- Large-Cap Growth
- Mid-Cap Growth
- Small-Cap Growth
- Large-Cap Value
- Mid-Cap Value
- Small-Cap Value

Portfolio
2.4% cash	0.0% corp bonds
0.0% stocks	0.0% gov't bonds
0.0% preferred	97.6% muni bonds
0.0% conv't/warrants	0.0% other

SHAREHOLDER INFORMATION

Minimum Investment
Initial: $2,500   Subsequent: $50

Minimum IRA Investment
Initial: na   Subsequent: na

Maximum Fees
Load: none   12b-1: 0.25%
Other: none

Distributions
Income: monthly   Capital Gains: annual

Exchange Options
Number Per Year: 8   Fee: none
Telephone: yes (money market fund available)

Services
auto invest, auto withdraw

Northern US Gov't
(NOUGX)
Government Bond

50 S. LaSalle St.
Chicago, IL 60675
800-595-9111, 312-630-6000

PERFORMANCE
fund inception date: 4/4/94

	3yr Annual	5yr Annual	10yr Annual	Bull	Bear
Return (%)	na	na	na	16.8	na
Differ from Category (+/-)	na	na	na	-5.2 blw av	na

Total Risk	Standard Deviation		Category Risk	Risk Index	Avg Mat
na	na		na	na	3.9 yrs

	1996	1995	1994	1993	1992	1991	1990	1989	1988	1987
Return (%)	3.0	12.6	—	—	—	—	—	—	—	—
Differ from Category (+/-)	1.5	-7.0	—	—	—	—	—	—	—	—
Return, Tax-Adjusted (%)	0.9	10.5	—	—	—	—	—	—	—	—

PER SHARE DATA

	1996	1995	1994	1993	1992	1991	1990	1989	1988	1987
Dividends, Net Income ($)	0.50	0.51	—	—	—	—	—	—	—	—
Distrib'ns, Cap Gain ($)	0.06	0.00	—	—	—	—	—	—	—	—
Net Asset Value ($)	10.03	10.30	—	—	—	—	—	—	—	—
Expense Ratio (%)	0.90	0.90	—	—	—	—	—	—	—	—
Yield (%)	4.95	4.95	—	—	—	—	—	—	—	—
Portfolio Turnover (%)	112	42	—	—	—	—	—	—	—	—
Total Assets (Millions $)	170	143	—	—	—	—	—	—	—	—

PORTFOLIO (as of 9/30/96)

Portfolio Manager: Monty Memler - 1994

Investm't Category: Government Bond
- ✔ Domestic
- Foreign
- Asset Allocation
- Index
- Sector
- State Specific

Investment Style
- Large-Cap Growth
- Mid-Cap Growth
- Small-Cap Growth
- Large-Cap Value
- Mid-Cap Value
- Small-Cap Value

Portfolio
- 4.1% cash
- 0.0% stocks
- 0.0% preferred
- 0.0% conv't/warrants
- 0.0% corp bonds
- 94.9% gov't bonds
- 0.0% muni bonds
- 1.0% other

SHAREHOLDER INFORMATION

Minimum Investment
Initial: $2,500   Subsequent: $50

Minimum IRA Investment
Initial: $500   Subsequent: $50

Maximum Fees
Load: none   12b-1: 0.25%
Other: none

Distributions
Income: monthly   Capital Gains: annual

Exchange Options
Number Per Year: 8   Fee: none
Telephone: yes (money market fund available)

Services
IRA, pension, auto invest, auto withdraw

Oakmark (OAKMX)

Growth

Two N. LaSalle St.
Suite 500
Chicago, IL 60602
800-625-6275, 312-621-0600

fund inception date: 8/5/91

	3yr Annual	5yr Annual	10yr Annual	Bull	Bear
Return (%)	17.2	25.6	na	63.6	-2.8
Differ from Category (+/-)	1.5 abv av	11.3 high	na	1.2 av	3.9 high

Total Risk	Standard Deviation	Category Risk	Risk Index	Beta
av	9.2%	blw av	0.9	0.84

	1996	1995	1994	1993	1992	1991	1990	1989	1988	1987
Return (%).............	16.2	34.4	3.3	30.5	48.8	—	—	—	—	—
Differ from Category (+/-) .	-3.9	4.1	3.6	16.5	37.0	—	—	—	—	—
Return, Tax-Adjusted (%)..	13.9	32.8	1.2	28.8	48.2	—	—	—	—	—

PER SHARE DATA

	1996	1995	1994	1993	1992	1991	1990	1989	1988	1987
Dividends, Net Income ($).	0.34	0.28	0.23	0.23	0.03	—	—	—	—	—
Distrib'ns, Cap Gain ($) ...	1.86	0.84	1.46	0.77	0.21	—	—	—	—	—
Net Asset Value ($)	32.35	29.75	22.97	23.93	19.13	—	—	—	—	—
Expense Ratio (%)........	1.18	1.17	1.22	1.32	1.70	—	—	—	—	—
Yield (%)	0.99	0.91	0.94	0.93	0.15	—	—	—	—	—
Portfolio Turnover (%).....	23	18	29	18	34	—	—	—	—	—
Total Assets (Millions $)..	4,196	3,301	1,626	1,214	328	—	—	—	—	—

PORTFOLIO (as of 9/30/96)

Portfolio Manager: Robert Sanborn - 1991

Investm't Category: Growth
- ✔ Domestic
- ✔ Foreign
- Asset Allocation
- Index
- Sector
- State Specific

Investment Style
- ✔ Large-Cap Growth
- Mid-Cap Growth
- Small-Cap Growth
- Large-Cap Value
- Mid-Cap Value
- Small-Cap Value

Portfolio
9.3% cash	0.0% corp bonds
91.1% stocks	0.0% gov't bonds
0.0% preferred	0.0% muni bonds
0.0% conv't/warrants	0.0% other

SHAREHOLDER INFORMATION

Minimum Investment
Initial: $2,500   Subsequent: $100

Minimum IRA Investment
Initial: $1,000   Subsequent: $100

Maximum Fees
Load: none   12b-1: none
Other: none

Distributions
Income: annual   Capital Gains: annual

Exchange Options
Number Per Year: 6   Fee: $5
Telephone: yes (money market fund available)

Services
IRA, pension, auto exchange, auto invest, auto withdraw

Oakmark Int'l (OAKIX)

International Stock

Two N. LaSalle St.
Suite 500
Chicago, IL 60602
800-625-6275, 312-621-0600

PERFORMANCE

fund inception date: 9/30/92

	3yr Annual	5yr Annual	10yr Annual	Bull	Bear
Return (%)	8.0	na	na	35.5	-13.0
Differ from Category (+/-)	1.7 av	na	na	11.2 abv av	-5.8 blw av

Total Risk	Standard Deviation	Category Risk	Risk Index	Beta
high	12.5%	abv av	1.2	0.78

	1996	1995	1994	1993	1992	1991	1990	1989	1988	1987
Return (%)	28.0	8.3	-9.1	53.5	—	—	—	—	—	—
Differ from Category (+/-)	13.2	-0.8	-6.0	13.9	—	—	—	—	—	—
Return, Tax-Adjusted (%)	27.4	5.9	-11.1	52.7	—	—	—	—	—	—

PER SHARE DATA

	1996	1995	1994	1993	1992	1991	1990	1989	1988	1987
Dividends, Net Income ($)	0.16	0.00	0.00	0.08	—	—	—	—	—	—
Distrib'ns, Cap Gain ($)	0.00	1.04	1.05	0.15	—	—	—	—	—	—
Net Asset Value ($)	15.68	12.38	12.41	14.79	—	—	—	—	—	—
Expense Ratio (%)	1.32	1.40	1.37	1.26	—	—	—	—	—	—
Yield (%)	1.02	0.00	0.00	0.53	—	—	—	—	—	—
Portfolio Turnover (%)	42	27	55	21	—	—	—	—	—	—
Total Assets (Millions $)	1,193	785	1,079	1,108	—	—	—	—	—	—

PORTFOLIO (as of 9/30/96)

Portfolio Manager: David Herro, Michael Welsh - 1992

Investm't Category: International Stock
- Domestic
- ✔ Foreign
- Asset Allocation
- Index
- Sector
- State Specific

Investment Style
- Large-Cap Growth
- Mid-Cap Growth
- Small-Cap Growth
- Large-Cap Value
- Mid-Cap Value
- Small-Cap Value

Portfolio
- 4.7% cash
- 95.3% stocks
- 0.0% preferred
- 0.0% conv't/warrants
- 0.0% corp bonds
- 0.0% gov't bonds
- 0.0% muni bonds
- 0.0% other

SHAREHOLDER INFORMATION

Minimum Investment
Initial: $2,500   Subsequent: $100

Minimum IRA Investment
Initial: $1,000   Subsequent: $100

Maximum Fees
Load: none   12b-1: none
Other: none

Distributions
Income: annual   Capital Gains: annual

Exchange Options
Number Per Year: 6   Fee: $5
Telephone: yes (money market fund available)

Services
IRA, pension, auto exchange, auto invest, auto withdraw

Oakmark Small Cap

(OAKSX)

Aggressive Growth

Two N. LaSalle St.
Suite 500
Chicago, IL 60602
800-625-6275, 312-621-0600

PERFORMANCE

fund inception date: 11/1/95

	3yr Annual	5yr Annual	10yr Annual	Bull	Bear
Return (%)	na	na	na	na	na
Differ from Category (+/-)	na	na	na	na	na

Total Risk	Standard Deviation	Category Risk	Risk Index	Beta
na	na	na	na	na

	1996	1995	1994	1993	1992	1991	1990	1989	1988	1987
Return (%)	39.7	—	—	—	—	—	—	—	—	—
Differ from Category (+/-)	20.6	—	—	—	—	—	—	—	—	—
Return, Tax-Adjusted (%)	39.7	—	—	—	—	—	—	—	—	—

PER SHARE DATA

	1996	1995	1994	1993	1992	1991	1990	1989	1988	1987
Dividends, Net Income ($)	0.00	—	—	—	—	—	—	—	—	—
Distrib'ns, Cap Gain ($)	0.00	—	—	—	—	—	—	—	—	—
Net Asset Value ($)	14.44	—	—	—	—	—	—	—	—	—
Expense Ratio (%)	1.61	—	—	—	—	—	—	—	—	—
Yield (%)	0.00	—	—	—	—	—	—	—	—	—
Portfolio Turnover (%)	23	—	—	—	—	—	—	—	—	—
Total Assets (Millions $)	245	—	—	—	—	—	—	—	—	—

PORTFOLIO (as of 9/30/96)

Portfolio Manager: Steve Reid - 1995

Investm't Category: Aggressive Growth

✔ Domestic	Index
✔ Foreign	Sector
Asset Allocation	State Specific

Investment Style

Large-Cap Growth	Large-Cap Value
Mid-Cap Growth	Mid-Cap Value
Small-Cap Growth	Small-Cap Value

Portfolio

5.8% cash	1.0% corp bonds
93.2% stocks	0.0% gov't bonds
0.0% preferred	0.0% muni bonds
0.0% conv't/warrants	0.0% other

SHAREHOLDER INFORMATION

Minimum Investment
Initial: $1,000   Subsequent: $100

Minimum IRA Investment
Initial: $1,000   Subsequent: $100

Maximum Fees
Load: 2.00% redemption   12b-1: none
Other: redemption fee applies for 6 months

Distributions
Income: annual   Capital Gains: annual

Exchange Options
Number Per Year: 6   Fee: none
Telephone: yes (money market fund available)

Services
IRA, pension, auto exchange, auto invest, auto withdraw

Oberweis Emerging Growth Port (OBEGX)

Aggressive Growth

951 Ice Cream Drive
Suite 200
North Aurora, IL 60542
800-323-6166, 708-801-6000

PERFORMANCE

fund inception date: 1/7/87

	3yr Annual	5yr Annual	10yr Annual	Bull	Bear
Return (%)	19.2	16.1	na	107.0	-19.7
Differ from Category (+/-)	3.4 abv av	0.8 abv av	na	35.9 high	-9.1 low

Total Risk	Standard Deviation	Category Risk	Risk Index	Beta
high	22.6%	high	1.6	1.25

	1996	1995	1994	1993	1992	1991	1990	1989	1988	1987
Return (%).............	23.1	42.5	-3.6	9.7	13.7	87.0	0.4	24.9	5.6	—
Differ from Category (+/-)..	4.0	8.2	-3.6	-9.6	2.0	34.9	5.8	-3.5	-10.8	—
Return, Tax-Adjusted (%)..	20.5	40.6	-3.6	8.7	13.7	77.1	0.4	24.9	5.6	—

PER SHARE DATA

	1996	1995	1994	1993	1992	1991	1990	1989	1988	1987
Dividends, Net Income ($).	0.00	0.00	0.00	0.00	0.00	0.00	0.00	0.00	0.00	—
Distrib'ns, Cap Gain ($)...	2.64	1.42	0.00	0.74	0.00	4.27	0.00	0.00	0.00	—
Net Asset Value ($).....	33.06	29.09	21.41	22.19	20.90	18.38	12.11	12.06	9.65	—
Expense Ratio (%).........	na	1.73	1.78	1.80	1.99	2.13	2.15	2.00	2.46	—
Yield (%)...............	0.00	0.00	0.00	0.00	0.00	0.00	0.00	0.00	0.00	—
Portfolio Turnover (%).....	na	79	66	70	63	114	63	112	67	—
Total Assets (Millions $)...	182	134	90	101	53	19	11	12	15	—

PORTFOLIO (as of 9/30/96)

Portfolio Manager: James D. Oberweis - 1987

Investm't Category: Aggressive Growth
✔ Domestic   Index
Foreign   Sector
Asset Allocation   State Specific

Investment Style
Large-Cap Growth   Large-Cap Value
Mid-Cap Growth   Mid-Cap Value
✔ Small-Cap Growth Small-Cap Value

Portfolio
3.3% cash   0.0% corp bonds
93.4% stocks   0.0% gov't bonds
0.0% preferred   0.0% muni bonds
3.3% conv't/warrants 0.0% other

SHAREHOLDER INFORMATION

Minimum Investment
Initial: $1,000   Subsequent: $100

Minimum IRA Investment
Initial: $1,000   Subsequent: $100

Maximum Fees
Load: none   12b-1: 0.25%
Other: none

Distributions
Income: Dec   Capital Gains: Dec

Exchange Options
Number Per Year: no limit   Fee: none
Telephone: yes

Services
IRA, pension, auto invest, auto withdraw

PBHG Core Growth

(PBCRX)

Aggressive Growth

680 E. Swedesford Road
Wayne, PA 19087
800-433-0051, 610-254-1000
www.pbhgfunds.com

PERFORMANCE

fund inception date: 12/29/95

	3yr Annual	5yr Annual	10yr Annual	Bull	Bear
Return (%)	na	na	na	na	na
Differ from Category (+/-)	na	na	na	na	na

Total Risk	Standard Deviation	Category Risk	Risk Index	Beta
na	na	na	na	na

	1996	1995	1994	1993	1992	1991	1990	1989	1988	1987
Return (%)	32.8	—	—	—	—	—	—	—	—	—
Differ from Category (+/-)	13.7	—	—	—	—	—	—	—	—	—
Return, Tax-Adjusted (%)	32.8	—	—	—	—	—	—	—	—	—

PER SHARE DATA

	1996	1995	1994	1993	1992	1991	1990	1989	1988	1987
Dividends, Net Income ($)	0.00	—	—	—	—	—	—	—	—	—
Distrib'ns, Cap Gain ($)	0.00	—	—	—	—	—	—	—	—	—
Net Asset Value ($)	13.28	—	—	—	—	—	—	—	—	—
Expense Ratio (%)	na	—	—	—	—	—	—	—	—	—
Yield (%)	0.00	—	—	—	—	—	—	—	—	—
Portfolio Turnover (%)	na	—	—	—	—	—	—	—	—	—
Total Assets (Millions $)	489	—	—	—	—	—	—	—	—	—

PORTFOLIO (as of 9/30/96)

Portfolio Manager: McCall, Pilgrim, Baxter - 1995

Investm't Category: Aggressive Growth
✔ Domestic	Index
✔ Foreign	Sector
Asset Allocation	State Specific

Investment Style
Large-Cap Growth	Large-Cap Value
Mid-Cap Growth	Mid-Cap Value
Small-Cap Growth	Small-Cap Value

Portfolio
12.6% cash	0.0% corp bonds
87.4% stocks	0.0% gov't bonds
0.0% preferred	0.0% muni bonds
0.0% conv't/warrants	0.0% other

SHAREHOLDER INFORMATION

Minimum Investment
Initial: $2,500   Subsequent: $1

Minimum IRA Investment
Initial: $2,000   Subsequent: $1

Maximum Fees
Load: none   12b-1: none
Other: none

Distributions
Income: annual   Capital Gains: annual

Exchange Options
Number Per Year: 4   Fee: none
Telephone: yes (money market fund available)

Services
IRA, pension, auto invest, auto withdraw

PBHG Emerging Growth
(PBEGX)
Aggressive Growth

680 E. Swedesford Road
Wayne, PA 19087
800-433-0051, 610-254-1000
www.pbhgfunds.com

PERFORMANCE

fund inception date: 6/14/93

	3yr Annual	5yr Annual	10yr Annual	Bull	Bear
Return (%)	29.0	na	na	134.7	-12.0
Differ from Category (+/-)	13.2 high	na	na	63.6 high	-1.4 blw av

Total Risk	Standard Deviation	Category Risk	Risk Index	Beta
high	20.5%	high	1.4	0.97

	1996	1995	1994	1993	1992	1991	1990	1989	1988	1987
Return (%)	17.0	48.4	23.7	—	—	—	—	—	—	—
Differ from Category (+/-)	-2.1	14.1	23.7	—	—	—	—	—	—	—
Return, Tax-Adjusted (%)	15.9	46.5	23.6	—	—	—	—	—	—	—

PER SHARE DATA

	1996	1995	1994	1993	1992	1991	1990	1989	1988	1987
Dividends, Net Income ($)	0.00	0.00	0.00	—	—	—	—	—	—	—
Distrib'ns, Cap Gain ($)	0.82	0.98	0.03	—	—	—	—	—	—	—
Net Asset Value ($)	24.23	21.39	15.10	—	—	—	—	—	—	—
Expense Ratio (%)	1.47	1.50	1.45	—	—	—	—	—	—	—
Yield (%)	0.00	0.00	0.00	—	—	—	—	—	—	—
Portfolio Turnover (%)	97	27	95	—	—	—	—	—	—	—
Total Assets (Millions $)	1,479	635	177	—	—	—	—	—	—	—

PORTFOLIO (as of 9/30/96)

Portfolio Manager: Gary L. Pilgrim - 1993

Investm't Category: Aggressive Growth
- ✔ Domestic
- ✔ Foreign
- Asset Allocation
- Index
- Sector
- State Specific

Investment Style
- Large-Cap Growth
- Mid-Cap Growth
- ✔ Small-Cap Growth
- Large-Cap Value
- Mid-Cap Value
- Small-Cap Value

Portfolio
- 12.2% cash
- 87.8% stocks
- 0.0% preferred
- 0.0% conv't/warrants
- 0.0% corp bonds
- 0.0% gov't bonds
- 0.0% muni bonds
- 0.0% other

SHAREHOLDER INFORMATION

Minimum Investment
Initial: $2,500   Subsequent: $1

Minimum IRA Investment
Initial: $2,000   Subsequent: $1

Maximum Fees
Load: none   12b-1: none
Other: none

Distributions
Income: annual   Capital Gains: annual

Exchange Options
Number Per Year: 4   Fee: none
Telephone: yes (money market fund available)

Services
IRA, pension, auto invest, auto withdraw

PBHG Growth (PBHGX)

Aggressive Growth

680 E. Swedesford Road
Wayne, PA 19087
800-433-0051, 610-254-1000
www.pbhgfunds.com

PERFORMANCE

fund inception date: 12/19/85

	3yr Annual	5yr Annual	10yr Annual	Bull	Bear
Return (%)	20.0	26.6	21.2	105.0	-18.9
Differ from Category (+/-)	4.2 abv av	11.3 high	6.2 high	33.9 high	-8.3 low

Total Risk	Standard Deviation	Category Risk	Risk Index	Beta
high	19.5%	high	1.4	1.06

	1996	1995	1994	1993	1992	1991	1990	1989	1988	1987
Return (%)	9.8	50.3	4.7	46.7	28.3	51.6	-9.8	29.4	6.8	11.6
Differ from Category (+/-)	-9.3	16.0	4.7	27.4	16.6	-0.5	-4.4	1.0	-9.6	14.0
Return, Tax-Adjusted (%)	9.8	50.3	4.6	45.9	21.7	43.8	-11.9	21.7	6.7	1.9

PER SHARE DATA

	1996	1995	1994	1993	1992	1991	1990	1989	1988	1987
Dividends, Net Income ($)	0.00	0.00	0.00	0.19	0.00	0.00	0.00	0.04	0.00	0.00
Distrib'ns, Cap Gain ($)	0.00	0.00	0.01	0.00	2.45	2.43	0.79	2.81	0.02	4.24
Net Asset Value ($)	26.27	23.92	15.91	15.20	10.50	10.53	8.74	10.71	10.51	9.86
Expense Ratio (%)	1.48	1.50	1.55	2.39	1.52	1.50	1.32	1.19	1.21	1.31
Yield (%)	0.00	0.00	0.00	1.25	0.00	0.00	0.00	0.29	0.00	0.00
Portfolio Turnover (%)	44	118	94	209	114	228	219	175	208	213
Total Assets (Millions $)	6,011	2,028	745	121	2	8	12	18	24	26

PORTFOLIO (as of 9/30/96)

Portfolio Manager: Gary L. Pilgrim - 1985

Investm't Category: Aggressive Growth

✔ Domestic	Index
✔ Foreign	Sector
Asset Allocation	State Specific

Investment Style

Large-Cap Growth	Large-Cap Value
Mid-Cap Growth	Mid-Cap Value
✔ Small-Cap Growth	Small-Cap Value

Portfolio

9.0% cash	0.0% corp bonds
91.0% stocks	0.0% gov't bonds
0.0% preferred	0.0% muni bonds
0.0% conv't/warrants	0.0% other

SHAREHOLDER INFORMATION

Minimum Investment
Initial: $2,500   Subsequent: $1

Minimum IRA Investment
Initial: $2,000   Subsequent: $1

Maximum Fees
Load: none   12b-1: none
Other: none

Distributions
Income: annual   Capital Gains: annual

Exchange Options
Number Per Year: 4   Fee: none
Telephone: yes (money market fund available)

Services
IRA, pension, auto invest, auto withdraw

PBHG Large Cap Growth
(PBHLX)
Growth

680 E. Swedesford Road
Wayne, PA 19087
800-433-0051, 610-254-1000
www.pbhgfunds.com

PERFORMANCE

fund inception date: 4/5/95

	3yr Annual	5yr Annual	10yr Annual	Bull	Bear
Return (%)	na	na	na	na	na
Differ from Category (+/-)	na	na	na	na	na

Total Risk	Standard Deviation	Category Risk	Risk Index	Beta
na	na	na	na	na

	1996	1995	1994	1993	1992	1991	1990	1989	1988	1987
Return (%)	23.3	—	—	—	—	—	—	—	—	—
Differ from Category (+/-)	3.2	—	—	—	—	—	—	—	—	—
Return, Tax-Adjusted (%)	23.2	—	—	—	—	—	—	—	—	—

PER SHARE DATA

	1996	1995	1994	1993	1992	1991	1990	1989	1988	1987
Dividends, Net Income ($)	0.00	—	—	—	—	—	—	—	—	—
Distrib'ns, Cap Gain ($)	0.01	—	—	—	—	—	—	—	—	—
Net Asset Value ($)	15.99	—	—	—	—	—	—	—	—	—
Expense Ratio (%)	1.50	—	—	—	—	—	—	—	—	—
Yield (%)	0.00	—	—	—	—	—	—	—	—	—
Portfolio Turnover (%)	116	—	—	—	—	—	—	—	—	—
Total Assets (Millions $)	167	—	—	—	—	—	—	—	—	—

PORTFOLIO (as of 9/30/96)

Portfolio Manager: Gary L. Pilgrim, James McCall - 1995

Investm't Category: Growth
- ✔ Domestic
- ✔ Foreign
- Asset Allocation
- Index
- Sector
- State Specific

Investment Style
- Large-Cap Growth
- Mid-Cap Growth
- Small-Cap Growth
- Large-Cap Value
- Mid-Cap Value
- Small-Cap Value

Portfolio
12.5% cash	0.0% corp bonds
87.5% stocks	0.0% gov't bonds
0.0% preferred	0.0% muni bonds
0.0% conv't/warrants	0.0% other

SHAREHOLDER INFORMATION

Minimum Investment
Initial: $2,500   Subsequent: $1

Minimum IRA Investment
Initial: $2,000   Subsequent: $1

Maximum Fees
Load: none   12b-1: none
Other: none

Distributions
Income: annual   Capital Gains: annual

Exchange Options
Number Per Year: 4   Fee: none
Telephone: yes (money market fund available)

Services
IRA, pension, auto invest, auto withdraw

PBHG Select Equity

(PBHEX)

Aggressive Growth

680 E. Swedesford Road
Wayne, PA 19087
800-433-0051, 610-254-1000
www.pbhgfunds.com

this fund is closed to new investors

PERFORMANCE

fund inception date: 4/5/95

	3yr Annual	5yr Annual	10yr Annual	Bull	Bear
Return (%)	na	na	na	na	na
Differ from Category (+/-)	na	na	na	na	na

Total Risk	Standard Deviation	Category Risk	Risk Index	Beta
na	na	na	na	na

	1996	1995	1994	1993	1992	1991	1990	1989	1988	1987
Return (%)	27.9	—	—	—	—	—	—	—	—	—
Differ from Category (+/-)	8.8	—	—	—	—	—	—	—	—	—
Return, Tax-Adjusted (%)	27.5	—	—	—	—	—	—	—	—	—

PER SHARE DATA

	1996	1995	1994	1993	1992	1991	1990	1989	1988	1987
Dividends, Net Income ($)	0.00	—	—	—	—	—	—	—	—	—
Distrib'ns, Cap Gain ($)	0.20	—	—	—	—	—	—	—	—	—
Net Asset Value ($)	19.59	—	—	—	—	—	—	—	—	—
Expense Ratio (%)	1.50	—	—	—	—	—	—	—	—	—
Yield (%)	0.00	—	—	—	—	—	—	—	—	—
Portfolio Turnover (%)	206	—	—	—	—	—	—	—	—	—
Total Assets (Millions $)	615	—	—	—	—	—	—	—	—	—

PORTFOLIO (as of 9/30/96)

Portfolio Manager: Gary L. Pilgrim, James McCall - 1995

Investm't Category: Aggressive Growth

✔ Domestic   Index
✔ Foreign   Sector
   Asset Allocation   State Specific

Investment Style

Large-Cap Growth   Large-Cap Value
Mid-Cap Growth   Mid-Cap Value
Small-Cap Growth   Small-Cap Value

Portfolio

12.5% cash	0.0% corp bonds
87.5% stocks	0.0% gov't bonds
0.0% preferred	0.0% muni bonds
0.0% conv't/warrants	0.0% other

SHAREHOLDER INFORMATION

Minimum Investment
Initial: $2,500   Subsequent: $1

Minimum IRA Investment
Initial: $2,000   Subsequent: $1

Maximum Fees
Load: none   12b-1: none
Other: none

Distributions
Income: annual   Capital Gains: annual

Exchange Options
Number Per Year: 4   Fee: none
Telephone: yes (money market fund available)

Services
IRA, pension, auto invest, auto withdraw

PBHG Technology & Communications (PBTCX)

Aggressive Growth

680 E. Swedesford Road
Wayne, PA 19087
800-433-0051, 610-254-1000
www.pbhgfunds.com

PERFORMANCE

fund inception date: 9/29/95

	3yr Annual	5yr Annual	10yr Annual	Bull	Bear
Return (%)	na	na	na	na	na
Differ from Category (+/-)	na	na	na	na	na

Total Risk	Standard Deviation	Category Risk	Risk Index	Beta
na	na	na	na	na

	1996	1995	1994	1993	1992	1991	1990	1989	1988	1987
Return (%)	54.4	—	—	—	—	—	—	—	—	—
Differ from Category (+/-)	35.3	—	—	—	—	—	—	—	—	—
Return, Tax-Adjusted (%)	53.5	—	—	—	—	—	—	—	—	—

PER SHARE DATA

	1996	1995	1994	1993	1992	1991	1990	1989	1988	1987
Dividends, Net Income ($)	0.00	—	—	—	—	—	—	—	—	—
Distrib'ns, Cap Gain ($)	0.35	—	—	—	—	—	—	—	—	—
Net Asset Value ($)	17.56	—	—	—	—	—	—	—	—	—
Expense Ratio (%)	na	—	—	—	—	—	—	—	—	—
Yield (%)	0.00	—	—	—	—	—	—	—	—	—
Portfolio Turnover (%)	na	—	—	—	—	—	—	—	—	—
Total Assets (Millions $)	472	—	—	—	—	—	—	—	—	—

PORTFOLIO (as of 9/30/96)

Portfolio Manager: John Force, James Smith - 1995

Investm't Category: Aggressive Growth
- ✔ Domestic
- ✔ Foreign
- Asset Allocation
- Index
- ✔ Sector
- State Specific

Investment Style
- Large-Cap Growth
- Mid-Cap Growth
- Small-Cap Growth
- Large-Cap Value
- Mid-Cap Value
- Small-Cap Value

Portfolio
- 15.0% cash
- 85.0% stocks
- 0.0% preferred
- 0.0% conv't/warrants
- 0.0% corp bonds
- 0.0% gov't bonds
- 0.0% muni bonds
- 0.0% other

SHAREHOLDER INFORMATION

Minimum Investment
Initial: $2,500   Subsequent: $1

Minimum IRA Investment
Initial: $2,000   Subsequent: $1

Maximum Fees
Load: none   12b-1: none
Other: none

Distributions
Income: annual   Capital Gains: annual

Exchange Options
Number Per Year: 4   Fee: none
Telephone: yes (money market fund available)

Services
IRA, pension, auto invest, auto withdraw

Pax World (PAXWX)

Balanced

222 State St.
Portsmouth, NH 03801
800-767-1729, 603-431-8022
www.greenmoney.com/pax

PERFORMANCE

fund inception date: 8/10/71

	3yr Annual	5yr Annual	10yr Annual	Bull	Bear
Return (%)	13.5	7.8	10.7	51.0	-3.8
Differ from Category (+/-)	1.8 abv av	-3.6 low	-0.1 av	5.9 abv av	1.9 high

Total Risk	Standard Deviation	Category Risk	Risk Index	Beta
blw av	6.7%	av	1.0	0.56

	1996	1995	1994	1993	1992	1991	1990	1989	1988	1987
Return (%).............	10.3	29.1	2.6	-1.1	0.6	20.7	10.4	24.9	11.5	2.5
Differ from Category (+/-).	-3.9	4.5	4.2	-15.5	-8.3	-3.4	11.3	6.8	-0.7	-0.2
Return, Tax-Adjusted (%)...	7.4	26.4	1.1	-2.7	-1.5	16.4	7.0	22.2	8.5	-2.4

PER SHARE DATA

	1996	1995	1994	1993	1992	1991	1990	1989	1988	1987
Dividends, Net Income ($).	0.55	0.79	0.50	0.50	0.67	0.76	0.61	0.62	0.61	0.75
Distrib'ns, Cap Gain ($) ...	0.89	0.14	0.00	0.07	0.13	1.04	0.83	0.24	0.37	1.24
Net Asset Value ($)	16.56	16.33	13.39	13.55	14.27	14.99	13.97	13.98	11.92	11.58
Expense Ratio (%).........	na	0.97	0.98	0.94	1.00	1.20	1.20	1.10	1.10	1.10
Yield (%)	3.15	4.79	3.73	3.67	4.65	4.74	4.12	4.36	4.96	5.85
Portfolio Turnover (%).....	na	28	25	22	17	26	39	37	58	124
Total Assets (Millions $)...	536	476	388	464	468	270	119	93	73	65

PORTFOLIO (as of 9/30/96)

Portfolio Manager: Anthony S. Brown - 1971

Investm't Category: Balanced

✔ Domestic	Index
Foreign	Sector
Asset Allocation	State Specific

Investment Style

Large-Cap Growth	Large-Cap Value
Mid-Cap Growth	Mid-Cap Value
Small-Cap Growth	Small-Cap Value

Portfolio

10.6% cash	0.0% corp bonds
56.9% stocks	32.6% gov't bonds
0.0% preferred	0.0% muni bonds
0.0% conv't/warrants	0.0% other

SHAREHOLDER INFORMATION

Minimum Investment
Initial: $250   Subsequent: $50

Minimum IRA Investment
Initial: $250   Subsequent: $50

Maximum Fees
Load: none   12b-1: 0.25%
Other: none

Distributions
Income: annual   Capital Gains: annual

Exchange Options
Number Per Year: none   Fee: na
Telephone: na

Services
IRA, pension, auto invest, auto withdraw

Payden & Rygel Global Fixed Income—A (PYGFX)

International Bond

333 S. Grand Ave.
32nd Floor
Los Angeles, CA 90071
800-572-9336, 213-625-1900

PERFORMANCE

fund inception date: 9/1/92

	3yr Annual	5yr Annual	10yr Annual	Bull	Bear
Return (%)	6.5	na	na	27.1	-5.5
Differ from Category (+/-)	0.5 av	na	na	-4.1 av	4.0 abv av

Total Risk	Standard Deviation	Category Risk	Risk Index	Avg Mat
low	4.3%	low	0.6	6.6

	1996	1995	1994	1993	1992	1991	1990	1989	1988	1987
Return (%)	5.7	17.9	-3.1	13.1	—	—	—	—	—	—
Differ from Category (+/-)	-5.6	1.9	4.5	-2.2	—	—	—	—	—	—
Return, Tax-Adjusted (%)	2.8	14.3	-4.6	10.4	—	—	—	—	—	—

PER SHARE DATA

	1996	1995	1994	1993	1992	1991	1990	1989	1988	1987
Dividends, Net Income ($)	0.76	0.88	0.38	0.50	—	—	—	—	—	—
Distrib'ns, Cap Gain ($)	0.00	0.00	0.00	0.24	—	—	—	—	—	—
Net Asset Value ($)	10.30	10.50	9.70	10.40	—	—	—	—	—	—
Expense Ratio (%)	0.53	0.50	0.55	0.70	—	—	—	—	—	—
Yield (%)	7.37	8.38	3.91	4.69	—	—	—	—	—	—
Portfolio Turnover (%)	175	226	348	253	—	—	—	—	—	—
Total Assets (Millions $)	663	583	421	285	—	—	—	—	—	—

PORTFOLIO (as of 9/30/96)

Portfolio Manager: committee - 1992

Investm't Category: International Bond
- ✔ Domestic
- ✔ Foreign
- Asset Allocation
- Index
- Sector
- State Specific

Investment Style

Large-Cap Growth	Large-Cap Value
Mid-Cap Growth	Mid-Cap Value
Small-Cap Growth	Small-Cap Value

Portfolio

1.0% cash	0.0% corp bonds
0.0% stocks	34.0% gov't bonds
0.0% preferred	0.0% muni bonds
0.0% conv't/warrants	65.0% other

SHAREHOLDER INFORMATION

Minimum Investment
Initial: $5,000   Subsequent: $1,000

Minimum IRA Investment
Initial: $5,000   Subsequent: $1,000

Maximum Fees
Load: none   12b-1: none
Other: none

Distributions
Income: monthly   Capital Gains: annual

Exchange Options
Number Per Year: no limit   Fee: none
Telephone: yes

Services
IRA, pension

Permanent Portfolio

(PRPFX)

Balanced

625 Second St.
Suite 102
Petaluma, CA 94952
800-531-5142, 512-453-7558

PERFORMANCE

fund inception date: 12/1/82

	3yr Annual	5yr Annual	10yr Annual	Bull	Bear
Return (%)	4.4	6.1	5.5	18.7	-5.6
Differ from Category (+/-)	-7.3 low	-5.3 low	-5.3 low	-26.4 low	0.1 av

Total Risk	Standard Deviation	Category Risk	Risk Index	Beta
blw av	4.7%	low	0.7	0.36

	1996	1995	1994	1993	1992	1991	1990	1989	1988	1987
Return (%)	1.6	15.4	-2.9	15.5	2.5	8.0	-3.9	6.3	1.2	13.1
Differ from Category (+/-)	-12.6	-9.2	-1.3	1.1	-6.4	-16.1	-3.0	-11.8	-11.0	10.4
Return, Tax-Adjusted (%)	0.5	14.4	-3.5	14.8	1.7	5.5	-5.1	6.3	1.1	12.8

PER SHARE DATA

	1996	1995	1994	1993	1992	1991	1990	1989	1988	1987
Dividends, Net Income ($)	0.42	0.38	0.22	0.24	0.28	0.91	0.48	0.00	0.00	0.00
Distrib'ns, Cap Gain ($)	0.09	0.00	0.00	0.00	0.00	0.00	0.00	0.00	0.02	0.12
Net Asset Value ($)	18.53	18.73	16.55	17.27	15.16	15.07	14.81	15.91	14.96	14.79
Expense Ratio (%)	1.35	1.32	1.21	1.25	1.27	1.36	1.17	1.17	1.15	1.17
Yield (%)	2.25	2.02	1.32	1.38	1.84	6.03	3.24	0.00	0.00	0.00
Portfolio Turnover (%)	9	31	49	70	8	32	61	24	22	31
Total Assets (Millions $)	75	75	72	83	65	71	80	97	98	89

PORTFOLIO (as of 9/30/96)

Portfolio Manager: Terry Coxon - 1982

Investm't Category: Balanced

✔ Domestic	Index
✔ Foreign	Sector
✔ Asset Allocation	State Specific

Investment Style

Large-Cap Growth	Large-Cap Value
Mid-Cap Growth	Mid-Cap Value
Small-Cap Growth	Small-Cap Value

Portfolio

12.8% cash	0.0% corp bonds
30.3% stocks	21.4% gov't bonds
0.0% preferred	0.0% muni bonds
1.0% conv't/warrants	34.5% other

SHAREHOLDER INFORMATION

Minimum Investment
Initial: $1,000   Subsequent: $100

Minimum IRA Investment
Initial: $1,000   Subsequent: $100

Maximum Fees
Load: none   12b-1: none
Other: f

Distributions
Income: annual   Capital Gains: annual

Exchange Options
Number Per Year: no limit   Fee: $5
Telephone: yes (money market fund available)

Services
IRA, auto withdraw

Permanent Treasury Bill Portfolio (PRTBX)

Government Bond

625 Second St.
Suite 102
Petaluma, CA 94952
800-531-5142, 512-453-7558

PERFORMANCE

fund inception date: 9/21/87

	3yr Annual	5yr Annual	10yr Annual	Bull	Bear
Return (%)	4.1	3.5	na	11.6	1.0
Differ from Category (+/-)	-0.8 low	-3.1 low	na	-10.4 low	7.4 high

Total Risk	Standard Deviation	Category Risk	Risk Index	Avg Mat
low	0.2%	low	0.1	0.2 yrs

	1996	1995	1994	1993	1992	1991	1990	1989	1988	1987
Return (%)	4.2	4.9	3.3	2.2	2.8	5.2	7.3	8.1	6.3	—
Differ from Category (+/-)	2.7	-14.7	7.7	-9.4	-3.9	-10.5	1.0	-7.2	-2.0	—
Return, Tax-Adjusted (%)	2.3	3.7	2.8	1.5	1.3	4.3	7.0	8.1	6.2	—

PER SHARE DATA

	1996	1995	1994	1993	1992	1991	1990	1989	1988	1987
Dividends, Net Income ($)	3.14	1.84	0.67	1.08	2.41	1.30	0.43	0.00	0.03	—
Distrib'ns, Cap Gain ($)	0.00	0.00	0.00	0.00	0.00	0.00	0.00	0.00	0.00	—
Net Asset Value ($)	67.33	67.58	66.16	64.67	64.29	64.86	62.85	58.96	54.53	—
Expense Ratio (%)	0.82	0.82	0.72	0.73	0.73	0.83	0.54	0.54	0.50	—
Yield (%)	4.66	2.72	1.01	1.67	3.74	2.00	0.68	0.00	0.05	—
Portfolio Turnover (%)	na	—	—	—	—	—	—	—	—	—
Total Assets (Millions $)	108	115	122	134	167	312	191	54	29	—

PORTFOLIO (as of 9/30/96)

Portfolio Manager: Terry Coxon - 1987

Investm't Category: Government Bond

✔ Domestic	Index
Foreign	Sector
Asset Allocation	State Specific

Investment Style

Large-Cap Growth	Large-Cap Value
Mid-Cap Growth	Mid-Cap Value
Small-Cap Growth	Small-Cap Value

Portfolio

100.0% cash	0.0% corp bonds
0.0% stocks	0.0% gov't bonds
0.0% preferred	0.0% muni bonds
0.0% conv't/warrants	0.0% other

SHAREHOLDER INFORMATION

Minimum Investment
Initial: $1,000   Subsequent: $100

Minimum IRA Investment
Initial: $1,000   Subsequent: $100

Maximum Fees
Load: none   12b-1: none
Other: *f*

Distributions
Income: annual   Capital Gains: annual

Exchange Options
Number Per Year: no limit   Fee: $5
Telephone: yes (money market fund available)

Services
IRA, auto withdraw

Philadelphia (PHILX)

Growth & Income

1200 N. Federal Highway
Suite 424
Boca Raton, FL 33432
800-749-9933, 407-395-2155
www.netrunner.net/~philfund

PERFORMANCE

fund inception date: 1/1/29

	3yr Annual	5yr Annual	10yr Annual	Bull	Bear
Return (%)	9.5	13.1	10.6	44.7	-8.8
Differ from Category (+/-)	-5.8 low	-0.8 blw av	-2.1 blw av	-15.1 blw av	-2.4 low

Total Risk	Standard Deviation	Category Risk	Risk Index	Beta
av	7.9%	low	0.9	0.68

	1996	1995	1994	1993	1992	1991	1990	1989	1988	1987
Return (%)	12.7	27.3	-8.6	18.2	19.7	5.7	-11.5	32.6	15.2	3.8
Differ from Category (+/-)	-7.0	-2.8	-7.3	4.4	9.0	-23.4	-5.6	9.1	-1.6	3.6
Return, Tax-Adjusted (%)	11.9	22.9	-9.2	14.6	18.7	5.0	-12.7	27.1	13.6	-4.4

PER SHARE DATA

	1996	1995	1994	1993	1992	1991	1990	1989	1988	1987
Dividends, Net Income ($)	0.12	0.13	0.09	0.13	0.08	0.09	0.18	0.14	0.09	0.14
Distrib'ns, Cap Gain ($)	0.03	0.79	0.02	0.66	0.07	0.00	0.00	0.89	0.15	1.76
Net Asset Value ($)	7.82	7.08	6.29	7.01	6.61	5.66	5.44	6.34	5.57	5.05
Expense Ratio (%)	na	1.62	1.67	1.60	1.79	1.61	1.19	0.95	0.90	0.87
Yield (%)	1.52	1.65	1.42	1.69	1.19	1.59	3.30	1.93	1.57	2.05
Portfolio Turnover (%)	na	59	28	24	39	49	43	9	16	152
Total Assets (Millions $)	97	91	80	94	87	84	89	96	91	91

PORTFOLIO (as of 9/30/96)

Portfolio Manager: Donald Baxter - 1987

Investm't Category: Growth & Income
✔ Domestic	Index
✔ Foreign	Sector
Asset Allocation	State Specific

Investment Style
✔ Large-Cap Growth	Large-Cap Value
Mid-Cap Growth	Mid-Cap Value
Small-Cap Growth	Small-Cap Value

Portfolio
12.1% cash	0.0% corp bonds
80.1% stocks	7.8% gov't bonds
0.0% preferred	0.0% muni bonds
0.0% conv't/warrants	0.0% other

SHAREHOLDER INFORMATION

Minimum Investment
Initial: $1,000   Subsequent: $1

Minimum IRA Investment
Initial: $1,000   Subsequent: $1

Maximum Fees
Load: none   12b-1: 0.50%
Other: none

Distributions
Income: quarterly   Capital Gains: Dec

Exchange Options
Number Per Year: none   Fee: na
Telephone: na

Services
IRA, pension, auto invest, auto withdraw

Preferred Asset Allocation
(PFAAX)
Balanced

100 N.E. Adams St.
Peoria, IL 61629
800-662-4769, 309-675-5123

PERFORMANCE

fund inception date: 7/1/92

	3yr Annual	5yr Annual	10yr Annual	Bull	Bear
Return (%)	14.1	na	na	57.6	-8.4
Differ from Category (+/-)	2.4 high	na	na	12.5 high	-2.7 low

Total Risk	Standard Deviation	Category Risk	Risk Index	Beta
av	8.1%	high	1.2	0.79

	1996	1995	1994	1993	1992	1991	1990	1989	1988	1987
Return (%)	15.0	32.8	-2.6	10.5	—	—	—	—	—	—
Differ from Category (+/-)	0.8	8.2	-1.0	-3.9	—	—	—	—	—	—
Return, Tax-Adjusted (%)	12.5	29.1	-4.0	8.7	—	—	—	—	—	—

PER SHARE DATA

	1996	1995	1994	1993	1992	1991	1990	1989	1988	1987
Dividends, Net Income ($)	0.41	0.39	0.33	0.31	—	—	—	—	—	—
Distrib'ns, Cap Gain ($)	0.52	0.81	0.08	0.21	—	—	—	—	—	—
Net Asset Value ($)	13.37	12.45	10.32	11.02	—	—	—	—	—	—
Expense Ratio (%)	1.04	1.11	1.25	1.27	—	—	—	—	—	—
Yield (%)	2.95	2.94	3.17	2.76	—	—	—	—	—	—
Portfolio Turnover (%)	38	18	24	34	—	—	—	—	—	—
Total Assets (Millions $)	108	82	61	53	—	—	—	—	—	—

PORTFOLIO (as of 9/30/96)

Portfolio Manager: Thomas Hazuka - 1992

Investm't Category: Balanced

✔ Domestic	Index
✔ Foreign	Sector
✔ Asset Allocation	State Specific

Investment Style

Large-Cap Growth	Large-Cap Value
Mid-Cap Growth	Mid-Cap Value
Small-Cap Growth	Small-Cap Value

Portfolio

22.9% cash	0.0% corp bonds
45.7% stocks	31.4% gov't bonds
0.0% preferred	0.0% muni bonds
0.0% conv't/warrants	0.0% other

SHAREHOLDER INFORMATION

Minimum Investment
Initial: $1,000   Subsequent: $50

Minimum IRA Investment
Initial: $250   Subsequent: $50

Maximum Fees
Load: none   12b-1: none
Other: none

Distributions
Income: quarterly   Capital Gains: annual

Exchange Options
Number Per Year: 3   Fee: none
Telephone: yes (money market fund available)

Services
IRA, pension, auto invest, auto withdraw

Preferred Fixed Income

(PFXIX)

General Bond

100 N.E. Adams St.
Peoria, IL 61629
800-662-4769, 309-675-5123

PERFORMANCE   fund inception date: 7/1/92

	3yr Annual	5yr Annual	10yr Annual	Bull	Bear
Return (%)	5.7	na	na	21.8	-4.2
Differ from Category (+/-)	0.6 abv av	na	na	1.5 abv av	0.0 av

Total Risk	Standard Deviation	Category Risk	Risk Index	Avg Mat
low	4.3%	abv av	1.1	12.7 yrs

	1996	1995	1994	1993	1992	1991	1990	1989	1988	1987
Return (%)	2.9	17.6	-2.4	10.2	—	—	—	—	—	—
Differ from Category (+/-)	-1.0	2.7	-0.1	1.1	—	—	—	—	—	—
Return, Tax-Adjusted (%)	0.6	15.0	-4.4	7.5	—	—	—	—	—	—

PER SHARE DATA

	1996	1995	1994	1993	1992	1991	1990	1989	1988	1987
Dividends, Net Income ($)	0.59	0.59	0.51	0.47	—	—	—	—	—	—
Distrib'ns, Cap Gain ($)	0.03	0.05	0.00	0.30	—	—	—	—	—	—
Net Asset Value ($)	10.24	10.58	9.58	10.34	—	—	—	—	—	—
Expense Ratio (%)	0.93	0.95	0.97	1.05	—	—	—	—	—	—
Yield (%)	5.74	5.55	5.32	4.41	—	—	—	—	—	—
Portfolio Turnover (%)	313	330	254	316	—	—	—	—	—	—
Total Assets (Millions $)	132	65	46	40	—	—	—	—	—	—

PORTFOLIO (as of 9/30/96)

Portfolio Manager: Paul Zemsky - 1994

Investm't Category: General Bond

✔ Domestic	Index
✔ Foreign	Sector
Asset Allocation	State Specific

Investment Style

Large-Cap Growth	Large-Cap Value
Mid-Cap Growth	Mid-Cap Value
Small-Cap Growth	Small-Cap Value

Portfolio

1.7% cash	21.8% corp bonds
0.0% stocks	76.5% gov't bonds
0.0% preferred	0.0% muni bonds
0.0% conv't/warrants	0.0% other

SHAREHOLDER INFORMATION

Minimum Investment
Initial: $1,000   Subsequent: $50

Minimum IRA Investment
Initial: $250   Subsequent: $50

Maximum Fees
Load: none   12b-1: none
Other: none

Distributions
Income: monthly   Capital Gains: annual

Exchange Options
Number Per Year: 3   Fee: none
Telephone: yes (money market fund available)

Services
IRA, pension, auto invest, auto withdraw

Preferred Growth (PFGRX)

Growth

100 N.E. Adams St.
Peoria, IL 61629
800-662-4769, 309-675-5123

PERFORMANCE

fund inception date: 7/1/92

	3yr Annual	5yr Annual	10yr Annual	Bull	Bear
Return (%)	14.6	na	na	67.1	-13.2
Differ from Category (+/-)	-1.1 blw av	na	na	4.7 abv av	-6.5 low

Total Risk	Standard Deviation	Category Risk	Risk Index	Beta
high	14.3%	high	1.4	1.16

	1996	1995	1994	1993	1992	1991	1990	1989	1988	1987
Return (%)	18.7	28.3	-1.2	16.0	—	—	—	—	—	—
Differ from Category (+/-)	-1.4	-2.0	-0.9	2.0	—	—	—	—	—	—
Return, Tax-Adjusted (%)	13.9	27.2	-1.4	16.0	—	—	—	—	—	—

PER SHARE DATA

	1996	1995	1994	1993	1992	1991	1990	1989	1988	1987
Dividends, Net Income ($)	0.00	0.00	0.02	0.00	—	—	—	—	—	—
Distrib'ns, Cap Gain ($)	2.86	0.53	0.05	0.00	—	—	—	—	—	—
Net Asset Value ($)	17.23	16.90	13.59	13.82	—	—	—	—	—	—
Expense Ratio (%)	0.86	0.87	0.91	1.00	—	—	—	—	—	—
Yield (%)	0.00	0.00	0.14	0.00	—	—	—	—	—	—
Portfolio Turnover (%)	75	55	51	58	—	—	—	—	—	—
Total Assets (Millions $)	391	390	241	143	—	—	—	—	—	—

PORTFOLIO (as of 9/30/96)

Portfolio Manager: L. Wang - 1992

Investm't Category: Growth
- ✔ Domestic
- ✔ Foreign
- Asset Allocation
- Index
- Sector
- State Specific

Investment Style
- Large-Cap Growth
- ✔ Mid-Cap Growth
- Small-Cap Growth
- Large-Cap Value
- Mid-Cap Value
- Small-Cap Value

Portfolio
2.2% cash	0.0% corp bonds
97.8% stocks	0.0% gov't bonds
0.0% preferred	0.0% muni bonds
0.0% conv't/warrants	0.0% other

SHAREHOLDER INFORMATION

Minimum Investment
Initial: $1,000   Subsequent: $50

Minimum IRA Investment
Initial: $250   Subsequent: $50

Maximum Fees
Load: none   12b-1: none
Other: none

Distributions
Income: annual   Capital Gains: annual

Exchange Options
Number Per Year: 3   Fee: none
Telephone: yes (money market fund available)

Services
IRA, pension, auto invest, auto withdraw

Preferred Int'l (PFIFX)

International Stock

100 N.E. Adams St.
Peoria, IL 61629
800-662-4769, 309-675-5123

PERFORMANCE

fund inception date: 7/1/92

	3yr Annual	5yr Annual	10yr Annual	Bull	Bear
Return (%)	9.0	na	na	26.7	-6.9
Differ from Category (+/-)	2.7 abv av	na	na	2.4 av	0.3 av

Total Risk	Standard Deviation	Category Risk	Risk Index	Beta
abv av	11.3%	abv av	1.1	0.68

	1996	1995	1994	1993	1992	1991	1990	1989	1988	1987
Return (%)	17.2	9.9	0.6	41.5	—	—	—	—	—	—
Differ from Category (+/-)	2.4	0.8	3.7	1.9	—	—	—	—	—	—
Return, Tax-Adjusted (%)	15.5	9.3	-0.1	41.0	—	—	—	—	—	—

PER SHARE DATA

	1996	1995	1994	1993	1992	1991	1990	1989	1988	1987
Dividends, Net Income ($)	0.34	0.16	0.12	0.07	—	—	—	—	—	—
Distrib'ns, Cap Gain ($)	0.25	0.01	0.11	0.05	—	—	—	—	—	—
Net Asset Value ($)	14.10	12.55	11.58	11.75	—	—	—	—	—	—
Expense Ratio (%)	1.31	1.32	1.38	1.60	—	—	—	—	—	—
Yield (%)	2.36	1.27	1.02	0.59	—	—	—	—	—	—
Portfolio Turnover (%)	19	29	27	16	—	—	—	—	—	—
Total Assets (Millions $)	199	136	107	65	—	—	—	—	—	—

PORTFOLIO (as of 9/30/96)

Portfolio Manager: P. Spano - 1992

Investm't Category: International Stock

Domestic	Index
✔ Foreign	Sector
Asset Allocation	State Specific

Investment Style

Large-Cap Growth	Large-Cap Value
Mid-Cap Growth	Mid-Cap Value
Small-Cap Growth	Small-Cap Value

Portfolio

5.6% cash	0.0% corp bonds
94.4% stocks	0.0% gov't bonds
0.0% preferred	0.0% muni bonds
0.0% conv't/warrants	0.0% other

SHAREHOLDER INFORMATION

Minimum Investment
Initial: $1,000   Subsequent: $50

Minimum IRA Investment
Initial: $250   Subsequent: $50

Maximum Fees
Load: none   12b-1: none
Other: none

Distributions
Income: annual   Capital Gains: annual

Exchange Options
Number Per Year: 3   Fee: none
Telephone: yes (money market fund available)

Services
IRA, pension, auto invest, auto withdraw

Preferred Short-Term Gov't Securities (PFSGX)

General Bond

100 N.E. Adams St.
Peoria, IL 61629
800-662-4769, 309-675-5123

PERFORMANCE

fund inception date: 7/1/92

	3yr Annual	5yr Annual	10yr Annual	Bull	Bear
Return (%)	4.2	na	na	14.5	-1.7
Differ from Category (+/-)	-0.9 low	na	na	-5.8 low	2.5 abv av

Total Risk	Standard Deviation	Category Risk	Risk Index	Avg Mat
low	1.8%	blw av	0.5	2.2 yrs

	1996	1995	1994	1993	1992	1991	1990	1989	1988	1987
Return (%)	4.7	9.0	-0.7	5.5	—	—	—	—	—	—
Differ from Category (+/-)	0.8	-5.9	1.6	-3.6	—	—	—	—	—	—
Return, Tax-Adjusted (%)	2.6	6.7	-2.4	3.9	—	—	—	—	—	—

PER SHARE DATA

	1996	1995	1994	1993	1992	1991	1990	1989	1988	1987
Dividends, Net Income ($)	0.52	0.54	0.42	0.38	—	—	—	—	—	—
Distrib'ns, Cap Gain ($)	0.00	0.00	0.00	0.02	—	—	—	—	—	—
Net Asset Value ($)	9.80	9.87	9.57	10.06	—	—	—	—	—	—
Expense Ratio (%)	0.66	0.71	0.74	0.78	—	—	—	—	—	—
Yield (%)	5.30	5.47	4.38	3.76	—	—	—	—	—	—
Portfolio Turnover (%)	79	256	134	268	—	—	—	—	—	—
Total Assets (Millions $)	54	32	29	29	—	—	—	—	—	—

PORTFOLIO (as of 9/30/96)

Portfolio Manager: J.S. Orr - 1995

Investm't Category: General Bond

✔ Domestic   Index
  Foreign   Sector
  Asset Allocation State Specific

Investment Style

Large-Cap Growth   Large-Cap Value
Mid-Cap Growth   Mid-Cap Value
Small-Cap Growth   Small-Cap Value

Portfolio

1.5% cash	0.0% corp bonds
0.0% stocks	73.2% gov't bonds
0.0% preferred	0.0% muni bonds
0.0% conv't/warrants	25.3% other

SHAREHOLDER INFORMATION

Minimum Investment
Initial: $1,000   Subsequent: $50

Minimum IRA Investment
Initial: $250   Subsequent: $50

Maximum Fees
Load: none   12b-1: none
Other: none

Distributions
Income: monthly   Capital Gains: annual

Exchange Options
Number Per Year: 3   Fee: none
Telephone: yes (money market fund available)

Services
IRA, pension, auto invest, auto withdraw

Preferred Small Cap
(PSMCX)

Aggressive Growth

100 N.E. Adams St.
Peoria, IL 61629
800-662-4769, 309-675-5123

PERFORMANCE

fund inception date: 11/1/95

	3yr Annual	5yr Annual	10yr Annual	Bull	Bear
Return (%)	na	na	na	na	na
Differ from Category (+/-)	na	na	na	na	na

Total Risk	Standard Deviation	Category Risk	Risk Index	Beta
na	na	na	na	na

	1996	1995	1994	1993	1992	1991	1990	1989	1988	1987
Return (%)	20.4	—	—	—	—	—	—	—	—	—
Differ from Category (+/-)	1.3	—	—	—	—	—	—	—	—	—
Return, Tax-Adjusted (%)	19.9	—	—	—	—	—	—	—	—	—

PER SHARE DATA

	1996	1995	1994	1993	1992	1991	1990	1989	1988	1987
Dividends, Net Income ($)	0.02	—	—	—	—	—	—	—	—	—
Distrib'ns, Cap Gain ($)	0.15	—	—	—	—	—	—	—	—	—
Net Asset Value ($)	12.45	—	—	—	—	—	—	—	—	—
Expense Ratio (%)	na	—	—	—	—	—	—	—	—	—
Yield (%)	0.15	—	—	—	—	—	—	—	—	—
Portfolio Turnover (%)	na	—	—	—	—	—	—	—	—	—
Total Assets (Millions $)	65	—	—	—	—	—	—	—	—	—

PORTFOLIO (as of 9/30/96)

Portfolio Manager: Todd Sheridan - 1995

Investm't Category: Aggressive Growth
- ✔ Domestic
- ✔ Foreign
-   Asset Allocation
-   Index
-   Sector
-   State Specific

Investment Style
- Large-Cap Growth
- Mid-Cap Growth
- Small-Cap Growth
- Large-Cap Value
- Mid-Cap Value
- Small-Cap Value

Portfolio
2.4% cash	0.0% corp bonds
97.6% stocks	0.0% gov't bonds
0.0% preferred	0.0% muni bonds
0.0% conv't/warrants	0.0% other

SHAREHOLDER INFORMATION

Minimum Investment
Initial: $1,000   Subsequent: $50

Minimum IRA Investment
Initial: $250   Subsequent: $50

Maximum Fees
Load: none   12b-1: none
Other: none

Distributions
Income: annual   Capital Gains: annual

Exchange Options
Number Per Year: 3   Fee: none
Telephone: yes (money market fund available)

Services
IRA, pension, auto invest, auto withdraw

Preferred Value (PFVLX)

Growth & Income

100 N.E. Adams St.
Peoria, IL 61629
800-662-4769, 309-675-5123

PERFORMANCE

fund inception date: 7/1/92

	3yr Annual	5yr Annual	10yr Annual	Bull	Bear
Return (%)	20.1	na	na	76.9	-4.6
Differ from Category (+/-)	4.8 high	na	na	17.1 high	1.8 abv av

Total Risk	Standard Deviation	Category Risk	Risk Index	Beta
av	9.3%	av	1.0	0.88

	1996	1995	1994	1993	1992	1991	1990	1989	1988	1987
Return (%)	25.2	37.7	0.4	8.8	—	—	—	—	—	—
Differ from Category (+/-)	5.5	7.6	1.7	-5.0	—	—	—	—	—	—
Return, Tax-Adjusted (%)	23.5	36.2	-0.7	7.9	—	—	—	—	—	—

PER SHARE DATA

	1996	1995	1994	1993	1992	1991	1990	1989	1988	1987
Dividends, Net Income ($)	0.20	0.20	0.20	0.16	—	—	—	—	—	—
Distrib'ns, Cap Gain ($)	0.60	0.29	0.14	0.11	—	—	—	—	—	—
Net Asset Value ($)	18.02	15.02	11.27	11.56	—	—	—	—	—	—
Expense Ratio (%)	0.85	0.89	0.93	0.96	—	—	—	—	—	—
Yield (%)	1.07	1.30	1.75	1.37	—	—	—	—	—	—
Portfolio Turnover (%)	17	29	11	17	—	—	—	—	—	—
Total Assets (Millions $)	307	229	148	123	—	—	—	—	—	—

PORTFOLIO (as of 9/30/96)

Portfolio Manager: John Lindenthal - 1992

Investm't Category: Growth & Income
- ✔ Domestic
- ✔ Foreign
- Asset Allocation
- Index
- Sector
- State Specific

Investment Style
- Large-Cap Growth
- Mid-Cap Growth
- Small-Cap Growth
- ✔ Large-Cap Value
- ✔ Mid-Cap Value
- Small-Cap Value

Portfolio
8.0% cash	0.0% corp bonds
92.0% stocks	0.0% gov't bonds
0.0% preferred	0.0% muni bonds
0.0% conv't/warrants	0.0% other

SHAREHOLDER INFORMATION

Minimum Investment
Initial: $1,000   Subsequent: $50

Minimum IRA Investment
Initial: $250   Subsequent: $50

Maximum Fees
Load: none   12b-1: none
Other: none

Distributions
Income: annual   Capital Gains: annual

Exchange Options
Number Per Year: 3   Fee: none
Telephone: yes (money market fund available)

Services
IRA, pension, auto invest, auto withdraw

Rainier Investment: Small/Mid Cap Equity

601 Union St.
Suite 2801
Seattle, WA 98101
800-248-6314, 206-464-0400

(RIMSX) *Aggressive Growth*

PERFORMANCE

fund inception date: 5/9/94

	3yr Annual	5yr Annual	10yr Annual	Bull	Bear
Return (%)	na	na	na	93.6	na
Differ from Category (+/-)	na	na	na	22.5 abv av	na

Total Risk	Standard Deviation	Category Risk	Risk Index	Beta
na	na	na	na	na

	1996	1995	1994	1993	1992	1991	1990	1989	1988	1987
Return (%)	22.5	47.4	—	—	—	—	—	—	—	—
Differ from Category (+/-)	3.4	13.1	—	—	—	—	—	—	—	—
Return, Tax-Adjusted (%)	19.4	44.5	—	—	—	—	—	—	—	—

PER SHARE DATA

	1996	1995	1994	1993	1992	1991	1990	1989	1988	1987
Dividends, Net Income ($)	0.05	0.06	—	—	—	—	—	—	—	—
Distrib'ns, Cap Gain ($)	1.77	1.15	—	—	—	—	—	—	—	—
Net Asset Value ($)	18.78	16.94	—	—	—	—	—	—	—	—
Expense Ratio (%)	1.48	1.48	—	—	—	—	—	—	—	—
Yield (%)	0.24	0.33	—	—	—	—	—	—	—	—
Portfolio Turnover (%)	151	152	—	—	—	—	—	—	—	—
Total Assets (Millions $)	122	53	—	—	—	—	—	—	—	—

PORTFOLIO (as of 9/30/96)

Portfolio Manager: James Margard CFA - 1994

Investm't Category: Aggressive Growth
- ✔ Domestic
- Foreign
- Asset Allocation
- Index
- Sector
- State Specific

Investment Style
- Large-Cap Growth
- Mid-Cap Growth
- Small-Cap Growth
- Large-Cap Value
- Mid-Cap Value
- Small-Cap Value

Portfolio
- 5.4% cash
- 94.6% stocks
- 0.0% preferred
- 0.0% conv't/warrants
- 0.0% corp bonds
- 0.0% gov't bonds
- 0.0% muni bonds
- 0.0% other

SHAREHOLDER INFORMATION

Minimum Investment
Initial: $25,000   Subsequent: $1,000

Minimum IRA Investment
Initial: $25,000   Subsequent: $1,000

Maximum Fees
Load: none   12b-1: 0.25%
Other: none

Distributions
Income: semiannual   Capital Gains: annual

Exchange Options
Number Per Year: 4   Fee: none
Telephone: yes (money market fund available)

Services
IRA, pension, auto withdraw

Reich & Tang Equity

(RCHTX)

Growth

600 Fifth Ave.
8th Floor
New York, NY 10020
800-221-3079, 212-830-5271

PERFORMANCE

fund inception date: 1/4/85

	3yr Annual	5yr Annual	10yr Annual	Bull	Bear
Return (%)	15.0	15.0	13.5	55.5	-4.5
Differ from Category (+/-)	-0.7 av	0.7 abv av	-0.4 av	-6.9 blw av	2.2 abv av

Total Risk	Standard Deviation	Category Risk	Risk Index	Beta
av	9.2%	blw av	0.9	0.74

	1996	1995	1994	1993	1992	1991	1990	1989	1988	1987
Return (%)	16.8	28.1	1.6	13.8	16.3	23.0	-5.9	17.9	22.8	5.1
Differ from Category (+/-)	-3.3	-2.2	1.9	-0.2	4.5	-13.0	0.2	-8.2	4.7	3.1
Return, Tax-Adjusted (%)	12.5	24.3	-2.6	10.9	13.8	21.8	-7.0	12.8	18.2	0.5

PER SHARE DATA

	1996	1995	1994	1993	1992	1991	1990	1989	1988	1987
Dividends, Net Income ($)	0.15	0.21	0.24	0.20	0.22	0.36	0.36	0.45	0.44	0.40
Distrib'ns, Cap Gain ($)	2.46	1.76	2.27	1.43	1.03	0.03	0.00	1.93	1.53	1.78
Net Asset Value ($)	18.10	17.73	15.39	17.61	16.92	15.64	13.05	14.24	14.11	13.11
Expense Ratio (%)	na	1.15	1.17	1.15	1.15	1.14	1.12	1.10	1.11	1.11
Yield (%)	0.72	1.07	1.35	1.05	1.22	2.29	2.75	2.78	2.81	2.68
Portfolio Turnover (%)	na	27	25	26	27	43	27	48	27	43
Total Assets (Millions $)	115	111	91	105	92	83	96	112	102	101

PORTFOLIO (as of 9/30/96)

Portfolio Manager: Robert F. Hoerle, Steven Wilson - 1985

Investm't Category: Growth

✔ Domestic	Index
✔ Foreign	Sector
Asset Allocation	State Specific

Investment Style

Large-Cap Growth	Large-Cap Value
✔ Mid-Cap Growth	✔ Mid-Cap Value
Small-Cap Growth	Small-Cap Value

Portfolio

4.6% cash	0.0% corp bonds
95.4% stocks	0.0% gov't bonds
0.0% preferred	0.0% muni bonds
0.0% conv't/warrants	0.0% other

SHAREHOLDER INFORMATION

Minimum Investment
Initial: $5,000   Subsequent: $1

Minimum IRA Investment
Initial: $250   Subsequent: $1

Maximum Fees
Load: none   12b-1: 0.5%
Other: none

Distributions
Income: quarterly   Capital Gains: annual

Exchange Options
Number Per Year: no limit   Fee: none
Telephone: yes (money market fund available)

Services
IRA, pension, auto withdraw

Reynolds Blue Chip Growth (RBCGX)

Growth & Income

Wood Island, Third Floor
80 E. Sir Francis Drake Blvd.
Larkspur, CA 94939
800-338-1579, 415-461-7860

PERFORMANCE

fund inception date: 8/12/88

	3yr Annual	5yr Annual	10yr Annual	Bull	Bear
Return (%)	19.2	9.9	na	84.3	-10.3
Differ from Category (+/-)	3.9 high	-4.0 low	na	24.5 high	-3.9 low

Total Risk	Standard Deviation	Category Risk	Risk Index	Beta
high	12.3%	high	1.3	1.11

	1996	1995	1994	1993	1992	1991	1990	1989	1988	1987
Return (%).	28.2	32.9	-0.6	-5.3	0.1	35.8	0.0	20.6	—	—
Differ from Category (+/-) . .	8.5	2.8	0.7	-19.1	-10.6	6.7	5.9	-2.9	—	—
Return, Tax-Adjusted (%). .	27.7	32.7	-1.1	-5.7	-0.1	35.4	-0.5	19.8	—	—

PER SHARE DATA

	1996	1995	1994	1993	1992	1991	1990	1989	1988	1987
Dividends, Net Income ($) .	0.00	0.03	0.06	0.13	0.08	0.09	0.14	0.15	—	—
Distrib'ns, Cap Gain ($) . . .	0.34	0.02	0.16	0.00	0.00	0.00	0.00	0.04	—	—
Net Asset Value ($)	24.27	19.22	14.50	14.82	15.78	15.85	11.74	11.88	—	—
Expense Ratio (%)	1.50	1.50	1.50	1.40	1.50	1.70	2.10	2.00	—	—
Yield (%)	0.00	0.15	0.40	0.87	0.50	0.56	1.19	1.25	—	—
Portfolio Turnover (%)	21	49	43	38	0	1	66	33	—	—
Total Assets (Millions $)	35	31	23	37	44	34	13	6	—	—

PORTFOLIO (as of 9/30/96)

Portfolio Manager: Frederick Reynolds - 1988

Investm't Category: Growth & Income
✔ Domestic   Index
  Foreign   Sector
  Asset Allocation   State Specific

Investment Style
✔ Large-Cap Growth   Large-Cap Value
  Mid-Cap Growth   Mid-Cap Value
  Small-Cap Growth   Small-Cap Value

Portfolio
  0.6% cash   0.0% corp bonds
  99.3% stocks   0.0% gov't bonds
  0.1% preferred   0.0% muni bonds
  0.0% conv't/warrants 0.0% other

SHAREHOLDER INFORMATION

Minimum Investment
Initial: $1,000   Subsequent: $100

Minimum IRA Investment
Initial: $1,000   Subsequent: $100

Maximum Fees
Load: none   12b-1: none
Other: none

Distributions
Income: annual   Capital Gains: annual

Exchange Options
Number Per Year: no limit   Fee: none
Telephone: yes (money market fund available)

Services
IRA, pension, auto exchange, auto invest, auto withdraw

Rightime Fund (RTFDX)

Growth

Lincoln Investment Mgmt.
218 Glenside Ave.
Wyncote, PA 19095
800-242-1421, 215-887-8111

PERFORMANCE

fund inception date: 9/17/85

	3yr Annual	5yr Annual	10yr Annual	Bull	Bear
Return (%)	11.5	9.2	10.4	39.1	-0.3
Differ from Category (+/-)	-4.2 low	-5.1 low	-3.5 low	-23.3 low	6.4 high

Total Risk	Standard Deviation	Category Risk	Risk Index	Beta
blw av	5.9%	low	0.6	0.28

	1996	1995	1994	1993	1992	1991	1990	1989	1988	1987
Return (%)	8.5	26.8	0.8	8.0	3.6	30.1	1.1	11.8	-1.4	19.1
Differ from Category (+/-)	-11.6	-3.5	1.1	-6.0	-8.2	-5.9	7.2	-14.3	-19.5	17.1
Return, Tax-Adjusted (%)	2.0	24.9	-3.4	6.5	1.6	25.6	-0.9	11.3	-2.3	14.4

PER SHARE DATA

	1996	1995	1994	1993	1992	1991	1990	1989	1988	1987
Dividends, Net Income ($)	0.42	0.73	0.43	0.00	0.05	0.17	0.61	0.35	0.14	0.67
Distrib'ns, Cap Gain ($)	7.95	0.94	4.62	1.72	2.38	4.68	1.46	0.00	0.78	3.97
Net Asset Value ($)	31.67	37.07	30.53	35.32	34.29	35.43	31.09	32.79	29.64	30.97
Expense Ratio (%)	na	2.47	2.51	2.52	2.56	2.67	2.67	2.58	2.58	2.55
Yield (%)	1.06	1.92	1.22	0.00	0.13	0.42	1.87	1.06	0.46	1.91
Portfolio Turnover (%)	na	9	11	2	73	136	383	168	187	166
Total Assets (Millions $)	171	162	143	166	179	173	138	166	218	218

PORTFOLIO (as of 9/30/96)

Portfolio Manager: Rights, Soslow, Houser - 1987

Investm't Category: Growth
✔ Domestic	Index
Foreign	Sector
Asset Allocation	State Specific

Investment Style
Large-Cap Growth	Large-Cap Value
✔ Mid-Cap Growth	Mid-Cap Value
✔ Small-Cap Growth	Small-Cap Value

Portfolio
50.0% cash	0.0% corp bonds
0.0% stocks	0.0% gov't bonds
0.0% preferred	0.0% muni bonds
0.0% conv't/warrants	50.0% other

SHAREHOLDER INFORMATION

Minimum Investment
Initial: $2,000   Subsequent: $100

Minimum IRA Investment
Initial: $1   Subsequent: $1

Maximum Fees
Load: none   12b-1: 0.75%
Other: none

Distributions
Income: Dec   Capital Gains: Dec

Exchange Options
Number Per Year: no limit   Fee: none
Telephone: yes (money market fund available)

Services
IRA, pension, auto withdraw

Robertson Stephens Contrarian (RSCOX)

International Stock

555 California St.
San Francisco, CA 94104
800-766-3863, 415-781-9700
www.rsim.com

PERFORMANCE

fund inception date: 6/30/93

	3yr Annual	5yr Annual	10yr Annual	Bull	Bear
Return (%)	14.5	na	na	44.8	1.1
Differ from Category (+/-)	8.2 high	na	na	20.5 high	8.3 high

Total Risk	Standard Deviation	Category Risk	Risk Index	Beta
high	14.7%	high	1.4	0.05

	1996	1995	1994	1993	1992	1991	1990	1989	1988	1987
Return (%).	21.6	30.8	-5.6	—	—	—	—	—	—	—
Differ from Category (+/-). .	6.8	21.7	-2.5	—	—	—	—	—	—	—
Return, Tax-Adjusted (%). .	21.2	30.8	-6.3	—	—	—	—	—	—	—

PER SHARE DATA

	1996	1995	1994	1993	1992	1991	1990	1989	1988	1987
Dividends, Net Income ($).	0.00	0.00	0.00	—	—	—	—	—	—	—
Distrib'ns, Cap Gain ($) . . .	0.19	0.00	0.25	—	—	—	—	—	—	—
Net Asset Value ($)	16.57	13.78	10.53	—	—	—	—	—	—	—
Expense Ratio (%).	na	2.54	na	—	—	—	—	—	—	—
Yield (%)	0.00	0.00	0.00	—	—	—	—	—	—	—
Portfolio Turnover (%). . . .	na	29	na	—	—	—	—	—	—	—
Total Assets (Millions $). .	1,069	508	485	—	—	—	—	—	—	—

PORTFOLIO (as of 9/30/96)

Portfolio Manager: Paul H. Stephens - 1993

Investm't Category: International Stock

✔ Domestic	Index
✔ Foreign	Sector
Asset Allocation	State Specific

Investment Style

Large-Cap Growth	Large-Cap Value
Mid-Cap Growth	Mid-Cap Value
Small-Cap Growth	Small-Cap Value

Portfolio

6.4% cash	0.0% corp bonds
25.5% stocks	0.0% gov't bonds
2.9% preferred	0.0% muni bonds
0.6% conv't/warrants	64.7% other

SHAREHOLDER INFORMATION

Minimum Investment
Initial: $5,000   Subsequent: $100

Minimum IRA Investment
Initial: $1,000   Subsequent: $1

Maximum Fees
Load: none   12b-1: 0.75%
Other: none

Distributions
Income: annual   Capital Gains: annual

Exchange Options
Number Per Year: 4   Fee: none
Telephone: yes (money market fund available)

Services
IRA, pension, auto invest, auto withdraw

Robertson Stephens Developing Century

(RSDCX) *International Stock*

555 California St.
San Francisco, CA 94104
800-766-3863, 415-781-9700
www.rsim.com

PERFORMANCE
fund inception date: 5/2/94

	3yr Annual	5yr Annual	10yr Annual	Bull	Bear
Return (%)	na	na	na	-1.2	na
Differ from Category (+/-)	na	na	na	-25.5 low	na

Total Risk	Standard Deviation	Category Risk	Risk Index	Beta
na	na	na	na	na

	1996	1995	1994	1993	1992	1991	1990	1989	1988	1987
Return (%)	21.0	-14.5	—	—	—	—	—	—	—	—
Differ from Category (+/-)	6.2	-23.6	—	—	—	—	—	—	—	—
Return, Tax-Adjusted (%)	20.9	-14.5	—	—	—	—	—	—	—	—

PER SHARE DATA

	1996	1995	1994	1993	1992	1991	1990	1989	1988	1987
Dividends, Net Income ($)	0.02	0.00	—	—	—	—	—	—	—	—
Distrib'ns, Cap Gain ($)	0.00	0.00	—	—	—	—	—	—	—	—
Net Asset Value ($)	9.68	8.02	—	—	—	—	—	—	—	—
Expense Ratio (%)	na	1.83	—	—	—	—	—	—	—	—
Yield (%)	0.20	0.00	—	—	—	—	—	—	—	—
Portfolio Turnover (%)	na	103	—	—	—	—	—	—	—	—
Total Assets (Millions $)	50	14	—	—	—	—	—	—	—	—

PORTFOLIO (as of 12/31/96)

Portfolio Manager: Michael C. Hoffman - 1994

Investm't Category: International Stock
Domestic	Index
✔ Foreign	Sector
Asset Allocation	State Specific

Investment Style
Large-Cap Growth	Large-Cap Value
Mid-Cap Growth	Mid-Cap Value
Small-Cap Growth	Small-Cap Value

Portfolio
7.7% cash	0.0% corp bonds
88.8% stocks	0.0% gov't bonds
0.0% preferred	0.0% muni bonds
0.0% conv't/warrants	3.5% other

SHAREHOLDER INFORMATION

Minimum Investment
Initial: $5,000   Subsequent: $100

Minimum IRA Investment
Initial: $1,000   Subsequent: $1

Maximum Fees
Load: none   12b-1: 0.25%
Other: none

Distributions
Income: annual   Capital Gains: annual

Exchange Options
Number Per Year: 4   Fee: none
Telephone: yes (money market fund available)

Services
IRA, pension, auto invest, auto withdraw

Robertson Stephens Emerging Growth (RSEGX)

555 California St.
San Francisco, CA 94104
800-766-3863, 415-781-9700
www.rsim.com

Aggressive Growth

PERFORMANCE

fund inception date: 11/30/87

	3yr Annual	5yr Annual	10yr Annual	Bull	Bear
Return (%)	16.4	10.5	na	68.2	-11.4
Differ from Category (+/-)	0.6 av	-4.8 low	na	-2.9 av	-0.8 av

Total Risk	Standard Deviation	Category Risk	Risk Index	Beta
high	19.7%	high	1.4	1.00

	1996	1995	1994	1993	1992	1991	1990	1989	1988	1987
Return (%)	21.5	20.3	7.9	7.2	-2.5	58.5	9.5	44.4	14.0	—
Differ from Category (+/-)	2.4	-14.0	7.9	-12.1	-14.2	6.4	14.9	16.0	-2.4	—
Return, Tax-Adjusted (%)	16.8	17.7	4.6	7.2	-3.1	56.3	7.4	39.4	14.0	—

PER SHARE DATA

	1996	1995	1994	1993	1992	1991	1990	1989	1988	1987
Dividends, Net Income ($)	0.00	0.00	0.00	0.00	0.20	0.00	0.00	0.00	0.00	—
Distrib'ns, Cap Gain ($)	3.19	1.58	2.10	0.00	0.07	0.90	0.85	1.60	0.00	—
Net Asset Value ($)	20.07	19.21	17.32	17.98	16.77	17.48	11.67	11.46	9.09	—
Expense Ratio (%)	na	1.64	1.60	1.54	1.49	1.59	1.88	2.15	2.85	—
Yield (%)	0.00	0.00	0.00	0.00	1.18	0.00	0.00	0.00	0.00	—
Portfolio Turnover (%)	na	147	274	43	124	147	272	236	139	—
Total Assets (Millions $)	197	158	176	169	277	141	22	12	7	—

PORTFOLIO (as of 9/30/96)

Portfolio Manager: Jim Callinan - 1996

Investm't Category: Aggressive Growth

✔ Domestic	Index
Foreign	Sector
Asset Allocation	State Specific

Investment Style

Large-Cap Growth	Large-Cap Value
Mid-Cap Growth	Mid-Cap Value
✔ Small-Cap Growth	Small-Cap Value

Portfolio

6.7% cash	0.0% corp bonds
91.9% stocks	0.0% gov't bonds
0.0% preferred	0.0% muni bonds
0.6% conv't/warrants	0.9% other

SHAREHOLDER INFORMATION

Minimum Investment

Initial: $5,000   Subsequent: $100

Minimum IRA Investment

Initial: $1,000   Subsequent: $1

Maximum Fees

Load: none   12b-1: 0.25%
Other: none

Distributions

Income: annual   Capital Gains: annual

Exchange Options

Number Per Year: 4   Fee: none
Telephone: yes (money market fund not available)

Services

IRA, pension, auto invest, auto withdraw

Robertson Stephens Glbl Low Priced Stk (RSLPX)

555 California St.
San Francisco, CA 94104
800-766-3863, 415-781-9700
www.rsim.com

International Stock

PERFORMANCE

fund inception date: 11/15/95

	3yr Annual	5yr Annual	10yr Annual	Bull	Bear
Return (%)	na	na	na	na	na
Differ from Category (+/-)	na	na	na	na	na

Total Risk	Standard Deviation	Category Risk	Risk Index	Beta
na	na	na	na	na

	1996	1995	1994	1993	1992	1991	1990	1989	1988	1987
Return (%)	29.3	—	—	—	—	—	—	—	—	—
Differ from Category (+/-)	14.5	—	—	—	—	—	—	—	—	—
Return, Tax-Adjusted (%)	29.3	—	—	—	—	—	—	—	—	—

PER SHARE DATA

	1996	1995	1994	1993	1992	1991	1990	1989	1988	1987
Dividends, Net Income ($)	0.00	—	—	—	—	—	—	—	—	—
Distrib'ns, Cap Gain ($)	0.00	—	—	—	—	—	—	—	—	—
Net Asset Value ($)	13.52	—	—	—	—	—	—	—	—	—
Expense Ratio (%)	na	—	—	—	—	—	—	—	—	—
Yield (%)	0.00	—	—	—	—	—	—	—	—	—
Portfolio Turnover (%)	na	—	—	—	—	—	—	—	—	—
Total Assets (Millions $)	31	—	—	—	—	—	—	—	—	—

PORTFOLIO (as of 9/30/96)

Portfolio Manager: M. Hannah Sullivan - 1995

Investm't Category: International Stock
✔ Domestic   Index
✔ Foreign   Sector
   Asset Allocation State Specific

Investment Style
Large-Cap Growth   Large-Cap Value
Mid-Cap Growth   Mid-Cap Value
Small-Cap Growth   Small-Cap Value

Portfolio
15.5% cash   0.0% corp bonds
33.9% stocks   0.0% gov't bonds
3.0% preferred   0.0% muni bonds
0.0% conv't/warrants 47.7% other

SHAREHOLDER INFORMATION

Minimum Investment
Initial: $5,000   Subsequent: $100

Minimum IRA Investment
Initial: $1,000   Subsequent: $1

Maximum Fees
Load: none   12b-1: 0.25%
Other: none

Distributions
Income: annual   Capital Gains: annual

Exchange Options
Number Per Year: 4   Fee: none
Telephone: yes (money market fund available)

Services
IRA, pension, auto invest, auto withdraw

Robertson Stephens Glbl Natrl Res (RSNRX)

555 California St.
San Francisco, CA 94104
800-766-3863, 415-781-9700
www.rsim.com

International Stock

PERFORMANCE

fund inception date: 11/15/95

	3yr Annual	5yr Annual	10yr Annual	Bull	Bear
Return (%)	na	na	na	na	na
Differ from Category (+/-)	na	na	na	na	na

Total Risk	Standard Deviation	Category Risk	Risk Index	Beta
na	na	na	na	na

	1996	1995	1994	1993	1992	1991	1990	1989	1988	1987
Return (%)	41.2	—	—	—	—	—	—	—	—	—
Differ from Category (+/-)	26.4	—	—	—	—	—	—	—	—	—
Return, Tax-Adjusted (%)	41.2	—	—	—	—	—	—	—	—	—

PER SHARE DATA

	1996	1995	1994	1993	1992	1991	1990	1989	1988	1987
Dividends, Net Income ($)	0.00	—	—	—	—	—	—	—	—	—
Distrib'ns, Cap Gain ($)	0.00	—	—	—	—	—	—	—	—	—
Net Asset Value ($)	14.29	—	—	—	—	—	—	—	—	—
Expense Ratio (%)	na	—	—	—	—	—	—	—	—	—
Yield (%)	0.00	—	—	—	—	—	—	—	—	—
Portfolio Turnover (%)	na	—	—	—	—	—	—	—	—	—
Total Assets (Millions $)	119	—	—	—	—	—	—	—	—	—

PORTFOLIO (as of 9/30/96)

Portfolio Manager: Andrew P. Pilara - 1995

Investm't Category: International Stock
✔ Domestic   Index
✔ Foreign   ✔ Sector
   Asset Allocation   State Specific

Investment Style
Large-Cap Growth   Large-Cap Value
Mid-Cap Growth   Mid-Cap Value
Small-Cap Growth   Small-Cap Value

Portfolio
13.2% cash   0.0% corp bonds
33.2% stocks   6.1% gov't bonds
1.7% preferred   0.0% muni bonds
2.0% conv't/warrants 43.7% other

SHAREHOLDER INFORMATION

Minimum Investment
Initial: $5,000   Subsequent: $100

Minimum IRA Investment
Initial: $1,000   Subsequent: $1

Maximum Fees
Load: none   12b-1: 0.25%
Other: none

Distributions
Income: annual   Capital Gains: annual

Exchange Options
Number Per Year: 4   Fee: none
Telephone: yes (money market fund available

Services
IRA, pension, auto invest, auto withdraw

Robertson Stephens Information Age (RSIFX)

Aggressive Growth

555 California St.
San Francisco, CA 94104
800-766-3863, 415-781-9700
www.rsim.com

PERFORMANCE

fund inception date: 11/15/95

	3yr Annual	5yr Annual	10yr Annual	Bull	Bear
Return (%)	na	na	na	na	na
Differ from Category (+/-)	na	na	na	na	na

Total Risk	Standard Deviation	Category Risk	Risk Index	Beta
na	na	na	na	na

	1996	1995	1994	1993	1992	1991	1990	1989	1988	1987
Return (%)	26.7	—	—	—	—	—	—	—	—	—
Differ from Category (+/-)	7.6	—	—	—	—	—	—	—	—	—
Return, Tax-Adjusted (%)	25.5	—	—	—	—	—	—	—	—	—

PER SHARE DATA

	1996	1995	1994	1993	1992	1991	1990	1989	1988	1987
Dividends, Net Income ($)	0.27	—	—	—	—	—	—	—	—	—
Distrib'ns, Cap Gain ($)	0.00	—	—	—	—	—	—	—	—	—
Net Asset Value ($)	11.51	—	—	—	—	—	—	—	—	—
Expense Ratio (%)	na	—	—	—	—	—	—	—	—	—
Yield (%)	2.34	—	—	—	—	—	—	—	—	—
Portfolio Turnover (%)	na	—	—	—	—	—	—	—	—	—
Total Assets (Millions $)	100	—	—	—	—	—	—	—	—	—

PORTFOLIO (as of 9/30/96)

Portfolio Manager: Ronald E. Elijah - 1995

Investm't Category: Aggressive Growth

✔ Domestic
✔ Foreign
  Asset Allocation
  Index
✔ Sector
  State Specific

Investment Style

Large-Cap Growth	Large-Cap Value
Mid-Cap Growth	Mid-Cap Value
Small-Cap Growth	Small-Cap Value

Portfolio

5.7% cash	0.0% corp bonds
92.4% stocks	0.0% gov't bonds
0.0% preferred	0.0% muni bonds
0.0% conv't/warrants	0.0% other

SHAREHOLDER INFORMATION

Minimum Investment
Initial: $5,000   Subsequent: $100

Minimum IRA Investment
Initial: $1,000   Subsequent: $1

Maximum Fees
Load: none   12b-1: 0.25%
Other: none

Distributions
Income: annual   Capital Gains: annual

Exchange Options
Number Per Year: 4   Fee: none
Telephone: yes (money market fund available)

Services
IRA, pension, auto invest, auto withdraw

Robertson Stephens Value + Growth (RSVPX)

555 California St.
San Francisco, CA 94104
800-766-3863, 415-781-9700
www.rsim.com

Aggressive Growth

PERFORMANCE

fund inception date: 5/12/92

	3yr Annual	5yr Annual	10yr Annual	Bull	Bear
Return (%)	26.0	na	na	101.9	-5.7
Differ from Category (+/-)	10.2 high	na	na	30.8 high	4.9 high

Total Risk	Standard Deviation	Category Risk	Risk Index	Beta
high	19.4%	high	1.4	1.15

	1996	1995	1994	1993	1992	1991	1990	1989	1988	1987
Return (%)	14.0	42.6	23.1	21.5	—	—	—	—	—	—
Differ from Category (+/-)	-5.1	8.3	23.1	2.2	—	—	—	—	—	—
Return, Tax-Adjusted (%)	11.8	42.6	22.6	20.6	—	—	—	—	—	—

PER SHARE DATA

	1996	1995	1994	1993	1992	1991	1990	1989	1988	1987
Dividends, Net Income ($)	0.00	0.00	0.00	0.00	—	—	—	—	—	—
Distrib'ns, Cap Gain ($)	1.73	0.00	0.19	0.32	—	—	—	—	—	—
Net Asset Value ($)	24.15	22.66	15.88	13.06	—	—	—	—	—	—
Expense Ratio (%)	na	1.45	1.55	1.33	—	—	—	—	—	—
Yield (%)	0.00	0.00	0.00	0.00	—	—	—	—	—	—
Portfolio Turnover (%)	na	104	250	210	—	—	—	—	—	—
Total Assets (Millions $)	660	1,144	132	23	—	—	—	—	—	—

PORTFOLIO (as of 9/30/96)

Portfolio Manager: Ronald E. Elijah - 1992

Investm't Category: Aggressive Growth

✔ Domestic	Index
Foreign	Sector
Asset Allocation	State Specific

Investment Style

Large-Cap Growth	Large-Cap Value
✔ Mid-Cap Growth	Mid-Cap Value
Small-Cap Growth	Small-Cap Value

Portfolio

0.5% cash	0.0% corp bonds
99.4% stocks	0.0% gov't bonds
0.0% preferred	0.0% muni bonds
0.0% conv't/warrants	0.1% other

SHAREHOLDER INFORMATION

Minimum Investment
Initial: $5,000   Subsequent: $100

Minimum IRA Investment
Initial: $1,000   Subsequent: $1

Maximum Fees
Load: none   12b-1: 0.25%
Other: none

Distributions
Income: annual   Capital Gains: annual

Exchange Options
Number Per Year: 4   Fee: none
Telephone: yes (money market fund not available)

Services
IRA, pension, auto invest, auto withdraw

Royce: Equity Income

(RYEQX)

Growth & Income

1414 Avenue of the Americas
New York, NY 10019
800-221-4268, 212-355-7311
www.roycefunds.com

PERFORMANCE

fund inception date: 12/29/89

	3yr Annual	5yr Annual	10yr Annual	Bull	Bear
Return (%)	9.4	12.1	na	35.2	-4.3
Differ from Category (+/-)	-5.9 low	-1.8 blw av	na	-24.6 low	2.1 high

Total Risk	Standard Deviation	Category Risk	Risk Index	Beta
blw av	6.3%	low	0.7	0.43

	1996	1995	1994	1993	1992	1991	1990	1989	1988	1987
Return (%).	16.4	16.3	-3.3	13.0	19.3	30.3	-15.4	—	—	—
Differ from Category (+/-). .	-3.3	-13.8	-2.0	-0.8	8.6	1.2	-9.5	—	—	—
Return, Tax-Adjusted (%). .	11.5	14.4	-5.1	9.3	16.6	27.5	-17.2	—	—	—

PER SHARE DATA

	1996	1995	1994	1993	1992	1991	1990	1989	1988	1987
Dividends, Net Income ($).	0.20	0.21	0.18	0.21	0.22	0.22	0.22	—	—	—
Distrib'ns, Cap Gain ($) . . .	0.70	0.04	0.09	0.41	0.16	0.09	0.00	—	—	—
Net Asset Value ($)	5.71	5.70	5.12	5.58	5.49	4.93	4.03	—	—	—
Expense Ratio (%).	na	1.24	1.27	1.00	0.99	0.99	1.00	—	—	—
Yield (%)	3.12	3.65	3.45	3.50	3.89	4.38	5.45	—	—	—
Portfolio Turnover (%).	na	29	47	100	59	72	28	—	—	—
Total Assets (Millions $). . . .	36	56	77	84	54	41	19	—	—	—

PORTFOLIO (as of 9/30/96)

Portfolio Manager: Royce, Fockler, George - 1972

Investm't Category: Growth & Income
- ✔ Domestic
- Foreign
- Asset Allocation
- Index
- Sector
- State Specific

Investment Style
- Large-Cap Growth
- Mid-Cap Growth
- Small-Cap Growth
- Large-Cap Value
- Mid-Cap Value
- ✔ Small-Cap Value

Portfolio
9.1% cash	0.0% corp bonds
76.7% stocks	0.0% gov't bonds
3.3% preferred	0.0% muni bonds
10.9% conv't/warrants	0.0% other

SHAREHOLDER INFORMATION

Minimum Investment
Initial: $2,000   Subsequent: $50

Minimum IRA Investment
Initial: $500   Subsequent: $50

Maximum Fees
Load: 1.00% redemption   12b-1: none
Other: redemption fee applies for 1 year

Distributions
Income: quarterly   Capital Gains: Dec

Exchange Options
Number Per Year: no limit   Fee: none
Telephone: yes

Services
IRA, pension, auto invest, auto withdraw

Royce: Micro-Cap

(RYOTX)

Aggressive Growth

1414 Avenue of the Americas
New York, NY 10019
800-221-4268, 212-355-7311
www.roycefunds.com

Royce: Penn Mutual

(PENNX)

Growth

1414 Avenue of the Americas
New York, NY 10019
800-221-4268, 212-355-7311
www.roycefunds.com

PERFORMANCE

fund inception date: 10/3/68

	3yr Annual	5yr Annual	10yr Annual	Bull	Bear
Return (%)	9.9	11.4	11.4	37.4	-5.1
Differ from Category (+/-)	-5.8 low	-2.9 low	-2.5 low	-25.0 low	1.6 abv av

Total Risk	Standard Deviation	Category Risk	Risk Index	Beta
av	7.4%	low	0.7	0.51

	1996	1995	1994	1993	1992	1991	1990	1989	1988	1987
Return (%)	12.8	18.7	-0.8	11.2	16.1	31.8	-11.6	16.6	24.5	1.3
Differ from Category (+/-)	-7.3	-11.6	-0.5	-2.8	4.3	-4.2	-5.5	-9.5	6.4	-0.7
Return, Tax-Adjusted (%)	7.0	14.4	-3.8	8.9	14.1	29.9	-13.1	13.4	22.1	-5.8

PER SHARE DATA

	1996	1995	1994	1993	1992	1991	1990	1989	1988	1987
Dividends, Net Income ($)	0.11	0.11	0.11	0.11	0.10	0.12	0.16	0.22	0.12	0.33
Distrib'ns, Cap Gain ($)	1.44	0.97	0.73	0.48	0.37	0.21	0.12	0.41	0.28	1.30
Net Asset Value ($)	7.11	7.71	7.41	8.31	8.00	7.29	5.78	6.85	6.41	5.47
Expense Ratio (%)	na	0.98	0.98	0.98	0.91	0.95	0.96	0.97	1.01	0.99
Yield (%)	1.28	1.26	1.35	1.25	1.19	1.60	2.71	3.03	1.79	4.87
Portfolio Turnover (%)	na	10	17	24	22	29	15	23	24	23
Total Assets (Millions $)	490	637	771	1,022	1,102	789	548	550	436	279

PORTFOLIO (as of 9/30/96)

Portfolio Manager: Royce, Fockler, George - 1972

Investm't Category: Growth
- ✔ Domestic
- Foreign
- Asset Allocation
- Index
- Sector
- State Specific

Investment Style
- Large-Cap Growth
- Mid-Cap Growth
- Small-Cap Growth
- Large-Cap Value
- Mid-Cap Value
- ✔ Small-Cap Value

Portfolio
- 5.0% cash
- 94.9% stocks
- 0.1% preferred
- 0.0% conv't/warrants
- 0.0% corp bonds
- 0.0% gov't bonds
- 0.0% muni bonds
- 0.0% other

SHAREHOLDER INFORMATION

Minimum Investment
Initial: $2,000   Subsequent: $50

Minimum IRA Investment
Initial: $500   Subsequent: $50

Maximum Fees
Load: 1.00% redemption   12b-1: none
Other: redemption fee applies for 1 year

Distributions
Income: Dec   Capital Gains: Dec

Exchange Options
Number Per Year: no limit   Fee: none
Telephone: yes

Services
IRA, pension, auto invest, auto withdraw

Royce: Premier (RYPRX)

Growth

1414 Avenue of the Americas
New York, NY 10019
800-221-4268, 212-355-7311
www.roycefunds.com

PERFORMANCE

fund inception date: 12/31/91

	3yr Annual	5yr Annual	10yr Annual	Bull	Bear
Return (%)	12.8	14.6	na	44.1	-1.6
Differ from Category (+/-)	-2.9 blw av	0.3 av	na	-18.3 low	5.1 high

Total Risk	Standard Deviation	Category Risk	Risk Index	Beta
blw av	6.7%	low	0.6	0.44

	1996	1995	1994	1993	1992	1991	1990	1989	1988	1987
Return (%).............	18.1	17.8	3.2	19.0	15.8	—	—	—	—	—
Differ from Category (+/-) .	-2.0	-12.5	3.5	5.0	4.0	—	—	—	—	—
Return, Tax-Adjusted (%)..	15.6	15.4	2.4	18.1	14.2	—	—	—	—	—

PER SHARE DATA

	1996	1995	1994	1993	1992	1991	1990	1989	1988	1987
Dividends, Net Income ($).	0.10	0.09	0.05	0.02	0.02	—	—	—	—	—
Distrib'ns, Cap Gain ($) ...	0.49	0.41	0.09	0.14	0.25	—	—	—	—	—
Net Asset Value ($)	7.81	7.12	6.48	6.41	5.52	—	—	—	—	—
Expense Ratio (%)........	na	1.25	1.38	1.50	1.77	—	—	—	—	—
Yield (%)	1.20	1.19	0.76	0.30	0.34	—	—	—	—	—
Portfolio Turnover (%).....	na	39	38	85	116	—	—	—	—	—
Total Assets (Millions $)...	294	302	202	47	2	—	—	—	—	—

PORTFOLIO (as of 9/30/96)

Portfolio Manager: Royce, Fockler, George - 1972

Investm't Category: Growth
- ✔ Domestic
- ✔ Foreign
- Asset Allocation
- Index
- Sector
- State Specific

Investment Style
- Large-Cap Growth
- Mid-Cap Growth
- Small-Cap Growth
- Large-Cap Value
- Mid-Cap Value
- ✔ Small-Cap Value

Portfolio
11.7% cash	0.0% corp bonds
88.3% stocks	0.0% gov't bonds
0.0% preferred	0.0% muni bonds
0.0% conv't/warrants	0.0% other

SHAREHOLDER INFORMATION

Minimum Investment
Initial: $2,000   Subsequent: $50

Minimum IRA Investment
Initial: $500   Subsequent: $50

Maximum Fees
Load: 1.00% redemption   12b-1: none
Other: redemption fee applies for 1 year

Distributions
Income: Dec   Capital Gains: Dec

Exchange Options
Number Per Year: no limit   Fee: none
Telephone: yes

Services
IRA, pension, auto invest, auto withdraw

Rushmore Fund for Tax-Free Invest: MD

4922 Fairmont Ave.
Bethesda, MD 20814
800-621-7874, 301-657-1500

(RSXLX) *Tax-Exempt Bond*

PERFORMANCE

fund inception date: 9/12/83

	3yr Annual	5yr Annual	10yr Annual	Bull	Bear
Return (%)	3.6	6.1	6.0	16.6	-5.7
Differ from Category (+/-)	-0.6 low	-0.3 blw av	-0.7 low	-1.8 blw av	-0.3 av

Total Risk	Standard Deviation	Category Risk	Risk Index	Avg Mat
blw av	4.9%	blw av	0.9	16.0 yrs

	1996	1995	1994	1993	1992	1991	1990	1989	1988	1987
Return (%)	2.8	14.2	-5.3	11.9	7.9	10.2	2.8	6.6	9.6	1.1
Differ from Category (+/-)	-0.9	-1.0	0.0	0.1	-0.4	-1.2	-3.6	-2.4	-0.4	2.5
Return, Tax-Adjusted (%)	2.8	14.2	-5.3	11.9	7.9	10.2	2.8	6.6	9.6	1.1

PER SHARE DATA

	1996	1995	1994	1993	1992	1991	1990	1989	1988	1987
Dividends, Net Income ($)	0.48	0.55	0.56	0.56	0.59	0.59	0.61	0.68	0.70	0.73
Distrib'ns, Cap Gain ($)	0.00	0.00	0.00	0.00	0.00	0.00	0.00	0.00	0.00	0.00
Net Asset Value ($)	10.79	10.98	10.12	11.27	10.60	10.39	9.99	10.33	10.34	10.09
Expense Ratio (%)	na	0.77	0.55	0.50	0.50	0.62	0.93	0.92	0.93	0.93
Yield (%)	4.44	5.00	5.53	4.96	5.56	5.67	6.10	6.58	6.76	7.23
Portfolio Turnover (%)	na	37	38	30	21	61	244	173	102	84
Total Assets (Millions $)	47	49	44	57	43	23	9	11	9	9

PORTFOLIO (as of 9/30/96)

Portfolio Manager: committee - 1983

Investm't Category: Tax-Exempt Bond
- ✔ Domestic
- Foreign
- Asset Allocation
- Index
- Sector
- ✔ State Specific

Investment Style
- Large-Cap Growth
- Mid-Cap Growth
- Small-Cap Growth
- Large-Cap Value
- Mid-Cap Value
- Small-Cap Value

Portfolio
4.6% cash	0.0% corp bonds
0.0% stocks	0.0% gov't bonds
0.0% preferred	95.4% muni bonds
0.0% conv't/warrants	0.0% other

SHAREHOLDER INFORMATION

Minimum Investment
Initial: $2,500   Subsequent: $1

Minimum IRA Investment
Initial: na   Subsequent: na

Maximum Fees
Load: none   12b-1: none
Other: none

Distributions
Income: monthly   Capital Gains: annual

Exchange Options
Number Per Year: no limit   Fee: none
Telephone: yes (money market fund available)

Services
auto exchange, auto invest, auto withdraw

Rushmore Fund for Tax-Free Invest: VA

4922 Fairmont Ave.
Bethesda, MD 20814
800-621-7874, 301-657-1500

(RSXIX) *Tax-Exempt Bond*

PERFORMANCE

fund inception date: 9/12/83

	3yr Annual	5yr Annual	10yr Annual	Bull	Bear
Return (%)	3.9	6.2	6.0	17.3	-5.7
Differ from Category (+/-)	-0.3 blw av	-0.2 blw av	-0.7 low	-1.1 blw av	-0.3 av

Total Risk	Standard Deviation	Category Risk	Risk Index	Avg Mat
blw av	5.0%	blw av	0.9	17.4 yrs

	1996	1995	1994	1993	1992	1991	1990	1989	1988	1987
Return (%).	2.9	14.9	-5.1	11.7	7.9	10.8	4.4	7.9	7.5	-1.2
Differ from Category (+/-) .	-0.8	-0.3	0.2	-0.1	-0.4	-0.6	-2.0	-1.1	-2.5	0.2
Return, Tax-Adjusted (%). . .	2.9	14.9	-5.1	11.7	7.9	10.8	4.4	7.9	7.5	-1.2

PER SHARE DATA

	1996	1995	1994	1993	1992	1991	1990	1989	1988	1987
Dividends, Net Income ($).	0.53	0.56	0.58	0.58	0.61	0.61	0.57	0.59	0.60	0.63
Distrib'ns, Cap Gain ($) . . .	0.00	0.00	0.00	0.00	0.00	0.00	0.00	0.00	0.00	0.00
Net Asset Value ($)	11.09	11.31	10.36	11.51	10.84	10.63	10.17	10.31	10.12	9.98
Expense Ratio (%).	na	0.77	0.55	0.50	0.50	0.61	0.93	0.94	0.93	0.92
Yield (%)	4.77	4.95	5.59	5.03	5.62	5.73	5.60	5.72	5.92	6.31
Portfolio Turnover (%).	na	55	33	43	50	74	202	150	78	125
Total Assets (Millions $). . . .	33	33	27	34	25	16	7	6	7	8

PORTFOLIO (as of 9/30/96)

Portfolio Manager: committee - 1983

Investm't Category: Tax-Exempt Bond
- ✔ Domestic
- Foreign
- Asset Allocation
- Index
- Sector
- ✔ State Specific

Investment Style
- Large-Cap Growth
- Mid-Cap Growth
- Small-Cap Growth
- Large-Cap Value
- Mid-Cap Value
- Small-Cap Value

Portfolio
2.0%	cash	0.0%	corp bonds
0.0%	stocks	0.0%	gov't bonds
0.0%	preferred	98.0%	muni bonds
0.0%	conv't/warrants	0.0%	other

SHAREHOLDER INFORMATION

Minimum Investment
Initial: $2,500   Subsequent: $1

Minimum IRA Investment
Initial: na   Subsequent: na

Maximum Fees
Load: none   12b-1: none
Other: none

Distributions
Income: monthly   Capital Gains: annual

Exchange Options
Number Per Year: no limit   Fee: none
Telephone: yes (money market fund available)

Services
auto exchange, auto invest, auto withdraw

SAFECO CA Tax-Free Income (SFCAX)

Tax-Exempt Bond

Safeco Tower S-1
P.O. Box 34890
Seattle, WA 98124
800-624-5711, 206-545-7319
networth.galt.com/safeco

PERFORMANCE

fund inception date: 8/1/83

	3yr Annual	5yr Annual	10yr Annual	Bull	Bear
Return (%)	5.5	7.5	7.6	25.6	-8.0
Differ from Category (+/-)	1.3 high	1.1 high	0.9 high	7.2 high	-2.6 low

Total Risk	Standard Deviation	Category Risk	Risk Index	Avg Mat
av	8.2%	high	1.5	24.1 yrs

	1996	1995	1994	1993	1992	1991	1990	1989	1988	1987
Return (%)	2.5	26.1	-9.2	13.2	7.9	12.5	6.9	9.9	12.7	-2.1
Differ from Category (+/-)	-1.2	10.9	-3.9	1.4	-0.4	1.1	0.5	0.9	2.7	-0.7
Return, Tax-Adjusted (%)	2.2	26.1	-9.5	12.4	7.5	12.3	6.7	9.4	12.7	-3.2

PER SHARE DATA

	1996	1995	1994	1993	1992	1991	1990	1989	1988	1987
Dividends, Net Income ($)	0.61	0.62	0.63	0.66	0.68	0.70	0.71	0.72	0.74	0.76
Distrib'ns, Cap Gain ($)	0.11	0.00	0.09	0.34	0.13	0.07	0.06	0.18	0.00	0.43
Net Asset Value ($)	12.22	12.66	10.58	12.43	11.90	11.81	11.23	11.26	11.11	10.55
Expense Ratio (%)	0.68	0.70	0.68	0.66	0.67	0.67	0.68	0.71	0.72	0.70
Yield (%)	4.94	4.89	5.90	5.16	5.65	5.89	6.28	6.29	6.66	6.92
Portfolio Turnover (%)	16	44	32	23	39	23	71	77	67	45
Total Assets (Millions $)	73	72	58	84	78	69	54	46	34	27

PORTFOLIO (as of 9/30/96)

Portfolio Manager: Stephen Bauer - 1983

Investm't Category: Tax-Exempt Bond
- ✔ Domestic
- Foreign
- Asset Allocation
- Index
- Sector
- ✔ State Specific

Investment Style
- Large-Cap Growth
- Mid-Cap Growth
- Small-Cap Growth
- Large-Cap Value
- Mid-Cap Value
- Small-Cap Value

Portfolio
3.2% cash	0.0% corp bonds
0.0% stocks	0.0% gov't bonds
0.0% preferred	94.9% muni bonds
0.0% conv't/warrants	1.9% other

SHAREHOLDER INFORMATION

Minimum Investment
Initial: $1,000   Subsequent: $100

Minimum IRA Investment
Initial: na   Subsequent: na

Maximum Fees
Load: none   12b-1: none
Other: none

Distributions
Income: monthly   Capital Gains: Mar, Dec

Exchange Options
Number Per Year: no limit   Fee: none
Telephone: yes (money market fund available)

Services
auto exchange, auto invest, auto withdraw

SAFECO Equity (SAFQX)

Growth & Income

Safeco Tower S-1
P.O. Box 34890
Seattle, WA 98124
800-624-5711, 206-545-7319
networth.galt.com/safeco

PERFORMANCE

fund inception date: 3/14/32

	3yr Annual	5yr Annual	10yr Annual	Bull	Bear
Return (%)	19.8	19.7	16.6	69.1	-4.1
Differ from Category (+/-)	4.5 high	5.8 high	3.9 high	9.3 abv av	2.3 high

Total Risk	Standard Deviation	Category Risk	Risk Index	Beta
av	9.5%	av	1.0	0.87

	1996	1995	1994	1993	1992	1991	1990	1989	1988	1987
Return (%)	25.0	25.2	9.9	30.9	9.2	27.9	-8.6	35.7	25.2	-4.9
Differ from Category (+/-)	5.3	-4.9	11.2	17.1	-1.5	-1.2	-2.7	12.2	8.4	-5.1
Return, Tax-Adjusted (%)	20.4	21.3	7.9	28.1	7.4	25.0	-10.4	31.8	23.6	-11.2

PER SHARE DATA

	1996	1995	1994	1993	1992	1991	1990	1989	1988	1987
Dividends, Net Income ($)	0.25	0.34	0.26	0.17	0.13	0.17	0.19	0.39	0.20	0.24
Distrib'ns, Cap Gain ($)	2.14	1.40	0.53	0.81	0.48	0.67	0.38	0.63	0.12	1.78
Net Asset Value ($)	16.60	15.33	13.68	13.18	10.87	10.59	8.97	10.48	8.55	7.09
Expense Ratio (%)	na	0.84	0.85	0.94	0.96	0.98	0.97	0.96	1.00	0.97
Yield (%)	1.33	2.03	1.82	1.21	1.14	1.50	2.03	3.51	2.30	2.70
Portfolio Turnover (%)	na	56	33	37	40	45	51	64	88	85
Total Assets (Millions $)	860	604	449	193	84	75	55	59	43	41

PORTFOLIO (as of 9/30/96)

Portfolio Manager: Richard Meagley - 1995

Investm't Category: Growth & Income
- ✔ Domestic
- Foreign
- Asset Allocation
- Index
- Sector
- State Specific

Investment Style
- ✔ Large-Cap Growth
- Mid-Cap Growth
- Small-Cap Growth
- ✔ Large-Cap Value
- Mid-Cap Value
- Small-Cap Value

Portfolio
0.0% cash	0.0% corp bonds
97.0% stocks	6.3% gov't bonds
0.0% preferred	0.0% muni bonds
0.0% conv't/warrants	0.0% other

SHAREHOLDER INFORMATION

Minimum Investment
Initial: $1,000   Subsequent: $100

Minimum IRA Investment
Initial: $250   Subsequent: $100

Maximum Fees
Load: none   12b-1: none
Other: none

Distributions
Income: quarterly   Capital Gains: Sep, Dec

Exchange Options
Number Per Year: no limit   Fee: none
Telephone: yes (money market fund available)

Services
IRA, pension, auto exchange, auto invest, auto withdraw

Guide to Low-Load Mutual Funds

SAFECO GNMA (SFUSX)

Mortgage-Backed Bond

Safeco Tower S-1
P.O. Box 34890
Seattle, WA 98124
800-624-5711, 206-545-7319
networth.galt.com/safeco

PERFORMANCE

fund inception date: 5/31/86

	3yr Annual	5yr Annual	10yr Annual	Bull	Bear
Return (%)	4.7	5.6	7.2	20.3	-5.6
Differ from Category (+/-)	-0.9 low	-0.4 blw av	-0.5 low	-0.8 av	-2.0 low

Total Risk	Standard Deviation	Category Risk	Risk Index	Avg Mat
low	4.3%	high	1.1	24.0 yrs

	1996	1995	1994	1993	1992	1991	1990	1989	1988	1987
Return (%)	3.9	15.4	-4.3	7.0	6.6	14.8	8.7	12.9	7.8	0.8
Differ from Category (+/-)	-0.5	0.7	-2.6	0.1	0.4	0.4	-1.1	0.3	0.4	-1.2
Return, Tax-Adjusted (%)	1.4	12.7	-6.7	4.4	3.7	11.5	5.4	9.5	4.0	-2.5

PER SHARE DATA

	1996	1995	1994	1993	1992	1991	1990	1989	1988	1987
Dividends, Net Income ($)	0.60	0.60	0.59	0.64	0.72	0.76	0.77	0.77	0.87	0.81
Distrib'ns, Cap Gain ($)	0.00	0.00	0.00	0.00	0.00	0.00	0.00	0.00	0.00	0.00
Net Asset Value ($)	9.36	9.60	8.87	9.88	9.84	9.93	9.37	9.37	9.03	9.21
Expense Ratio (%)	na	1.01	0.95	0.93	0.94	0.97	0.99	1.02	1.06	1.05
Yield (%)	6.41	6.25	6.65	6.47	7.31	7.65	8.21	8.21	9.63	8.79
Portfolio Turnover (%)	na	131	55	70	25	44	90	77	110	101
Total Assets (Millions $)	40	43	41	60	56	48	30	28	27	22

PORTFOLIO (as of 9/30/96)

Portfolio Manager: Paul Stevenson - 1988

Investm't Category: Mortgage-Backed Bond
- ✔ Domestic
- Foreign
- Asset Allocation
- Index
- Sector
- State Specific

Investment Style
- Large-Cap Growth
- Mid-Cap Growth
- Small-Cap Growth
- Large-Cap Value
- Mid-Cap Value
- Small-Cap Value

Portfolio
0.4% cash	0.0% corp bonds
0.0% stocks	99.6% gov't bonds
0.0% preferred	0.0% muni bonds
0.0% conv't/warrants	0.0% other

SHAREHOLDER INFORMATION

Minimum Investment
Initial: $1,000   Subsequent: $100

Minimum IRA Investment
Initial: $250   Subsequent: $100

Maximum Fees
Load: none   12b-1: none
Other: none

Distributions
Income: monthly   Capital Gains: Sep, Dec

Exchange Options
Number Per Year: no limit   Fee: none
Telephone: yes (money market fund available)

Services
IRA, pension, auto exchange, auto invest, auto withdraw

SAFECO Growth (SAFGX)

Aggressive Growth

Safeco Tower S-1
P.O. Box 34890
Seattle, WA 98124
800-624-5711, 206-545-7319
networth.galt.com/safeco

PERFORMANCE

fund inception date: 1/18/68

	3yr Annual	5yr Annual	10yr Annual	Bull	Bear
Return (%)	15.0	12.5	14.5	66.6	-13.3
Differ from Category (+/-)	-0.8 av	-2.8 blw av	-0.5 av	-4.5 av	-2.7 blw av

Total Risk	Standard Deviation	Category Risk	Risk Index	Beta
high	13.7%	av	1.0	1.03

	1996	1995	1994	1993	1992	1991	1990	1989	1988	1987
Return (%)	22.8	26.1	-1.7	22.1	-3.1	62.6	-15.0	19.1	22.1	7.0
Differ from Category (+/-)	.3.7	-8.2	-1.7	2.8	-14.8	10.5	-9.6	-9.3	5.7	9.4
Return, Tax-Adjusted (%)	18.2	16.9	-4.8	20.9	-4.1	59.8	-18.4	16.3	19.1	3.5

PER SHARE DATA

	1996	1995	1994	1993	1992	1991	1990	1989	1988	1987
Dividends, Net Income ($)	0.00	0.06	0.00	0.00	0.00	0.04	0.08	0.42	0.43	0.32
Distrib'ns, Cap Gain ($)	2.66	5.67	2.15	0.70	0.61	1.14	1.88	0.90	0.81	1.25
Net Asset Value ($)	16.97	16.20	17.55	20.06	17.00	18.31	12.01	16.61	15.04	13.36
Expense Ratio (%)	na	0.98	0.95	0.91	0.91	0.90	1.01	0.94	0.98	0.92
Yield (%)	0.00	0.27	0.00	0.00	0.00	0.20	0.57	2.39	2.71	2.19
Portfolio Turnover (%)	na	110	71	57	85	50	90	11	19	24
Total Assets (Millions $)	184	181	150	163	171	172	65	78	71	64

PORTFOLIO (as of 9/30/96)

Portfolio Manager: Thomas Maguire - 1989

Investm't Category: Aggressive Growth
- ✔ Domestic
- Foreign
- Asset Allocation
- Index
- Sector
- State Specific

Investment Style
- Large-Cap Growth
- ✔ Mid-Cap Growth
- ✔ Small-Cap Growth
- Large-Cap Value
- ✔ Mid-Cap Value
- ✔ Small-Cap Value

Portfolio
0.9% cash	0.0% corp bonds
99.8% stocks	0.0% gov't bonds
0.0% preferred	0.0% muni bonds
0.0% conv't/warrants	0.0% other

SHAREHOLDER INFORMATION

Minimum Investment
Initial: $1,000   Subsequent: $100

Minimum IRA Investment
Initial: $250   Subsequent: $100

Maximum Fees
Load: none   12b-1: none
Other: none

Distributions
Income: quarterly   Capital Gains: Sep, Dec

Exchange Options
Number Per Year: no limit   Fee: none
Telephone: yes (money market fund available)

Services
IRA, pension, auto exchange, auto invest, auto withdraw

SAFECO High Yield Bond

(SAFHX)

Corporate High-Yield Bond

Safeco Tower S-1
P.O. Box 34890
Seattle, WA 98124
800-624-5711, 206-545-7319
networth.galt.com/safeco

PERFORMANCE

fund inception date: 9/7/88

	3yr Annual	5yr Annual	10yr Annual	Bull	Bear
Return (%)	7.6	10.6	na	26.7	-3.5
Differ from Category (+/-)	-1.1 blw av	-1.5 blw av	na	-6.4 low	1.9 abv av

Total Risk	Standard Deviation	Category Risk	Risk Index	Avg Mat
low	3.8%	blw av	0.8	9.9 yrs

	1996	1995	1994	1993	1992	1991	1990	1989	1988	1987
Return (%)	10.3	15.5	-2.3	16.9	13.8	24.2	-3.6	1.9	—	—
Differ from Category (+/-)	-5.0	-2.0	0.6	-2.0	-2.3	-3.4	1.3	0.7	—	—
Return, Tax-Adjusted (%)	6.8	11.9	-5.9	13.0	9.6	19.7	-8.2	-2.6	—	—

PER SHARE DATA

	1996	1995	1994	1993	1992	1991	1990	1989	1988	1987
Dividends, Net Income ($)	0.77	0.75	0.84	0.85	0.88	0.85	1.03	1.11	—	—
Distrib'ns, Cap Gain ($)	0.00	0.00	0.00	0.00	0.00	0.00	0.00	0.00	—	—
Net Asset Value ($)	8.82	8.73	8.25	9.30	8.73	8.48	7.58	8.91	—	—
Expense Ratio (%)	na	1.01	1.03	1.09	1.05	1.11	1.15	1.11	—	—
Yield (%)	8.73	8.59	10.18	9.13	10.08	10.02	13.58	12.45	—	—
Portfolio Turnover (%)	na	38	63	50	40	32	18	12	—	—
Total Assets (Millions $)	53	40	25	34	18	11	7	7	—	—

PORTFOLIO (as of 9/30/96)

Portfolio Manager: Kurt Havnaer - 1995

Investm't Category: Corp. High-Yield Bond

✔ Domestic   Index
  Foreign   Sector
  Asset Allocation   State Specific

Investment Style

Large-Cap Growth   Large-Cap Value
Mid-Cap Growth   Mid-Cap Value
Small-Cap Growth   Small-Cap Value

Portfolio

9.5% cash	89.7% corp bonds
0.0% stocks	0.0% gov't bonds
0.0% preferred	0.0% muni bonds
0.0% conv't/warrants	0.8% other

SHAREHOLDER INFORMATION

Minimum Investment
Initial: $1,000   Subsequent: $100

Minimum IRA Investment
Initial: $250   Subsequent: $100

Maximum Fees
Load: none   12b-1: none
Other: none

Distributions
Income: monthly   Capital Gains: Sep, Dec

Exchange Options
Number Per Year: no limit   Fee: none
Telephone: yes (money market fund available)

Services
IRA, pension, auto exchange, auto invest, auto withdraw

SAFECO Income (SAFIX)

Balanced

Safeco Tower S-1
P.O. Box 34890
Seattle, WA 98124
800-624-5711, 206-545-7319
networth.galt.com/safeco

PERFORMANCE

	3yr Annual	5yr Annual	10yr Annual	Bull	Bear
Return (%)	16.9	14.9	11.3	64.5	-5.9
Differ from Category (+/-)	5.2 high	3.5 high	0.5 abv av	19.4 high	-0.2 av

Total Risk	Standard Deviation	Category Risk	Risk Index	Beta
av	7.8%	high	1.2	0.76

	1996	1995	1994	1993	1992	1991	1990	1989	1988	1987
Return (%).............	23.9	30.3	-1.1	12.5	11.4	23.2	-10.8	19.2	18.9	-6.0
Differ from Category (+/-).	9.7	5.7	0.5	-1.9	2.5	-0.9	-9.9	1.1	6.7	-8.7
Return, Tax-Adjusted (%)..	19.1	26.7	-3.3	10.6	9.3	20.7	-13.1	16.7	16.4	-10.1

PER SHARE DATA

	1996	1995	1994	1993	1992	1991	1990	1989	1988	1987
Dividends, Net Income ($)	0.67	0.82	0.80	0.78	0.78	0.80	0.85	0.81	0.78	0.99
Distrib'ns, Cap Gain ($) ...	2.38	0.91	0.23	0.00	0.04	0.05	0.09	0.08	0.00	0.83
Net Asset Value ($)	21.13	19.70	16.54	17.77	16.50	15.58	13.37	16.03	14.23	12.64
Expense Ratio (%).........	na	0.87	0.86	0.90	0.90	0.93	0.92	0.92	0.97	0.94
Yield (%)	2.84	3.97	4.77	4.38	4.71	5.11	6.31	5.02	5.48	7.34
Portfolio Turnover (%).....	na	31	19	20	20	22	19	16	34	33
Total Assets (Millions $)...	290	226	180	200	185	181	174	226	216	219

PORTFOLIO (as of 6/30/96)

Portfolio Manager: Thomas E. Rath - 1994

Investm't Category: Balanced
✔ Domestic	Index
Foreign	Sector
Asset Allocation	State Specific

Investment Style
Large-Cap Growth	Large-Cap Value
Mid-Cap Growth	Mid-Cap Value
Small-Cap Growth	Small-Cap Value

Portfolio
1.8% cash	0.0% corp bonds
65.8% stocks	0.0% gov't bonds
14.9% preferred	0.0% muni bonds
17.5% conv't/warrants	0.0% other

SHAREHOLDER INFORMATION

Minimum Investment
Initial: $1,000   Subsequent: $100

Minimum IRA Investment
Initial: $250   Subsequent: $100

Maximum Fees
Load: none   12b-1: none
Other: none

Distributions
Income: quarterly   Capital Gains: Sep, Dec

Exchange Options
Number Per Year: no limit   Fee: none
Telephone: yes (money market fund available)

Services
IRA, pension, auto exchange, auto invest, auto withdraw

SAFECO Muni Bond
(SFCOX)
Tax-Exempt Bond

Safeco Tower S-1
P.O. Box 34890
Seattle, WA 98124
800-624-5711, 206-545-7319
networth.galt.com/safeco

PERFORMANCE

fund inception date: 11/18/81

	3yr Annual	5yr Annual	10yr Annual	Bull	Bear
Return (%)	4.6	7.0	7.8	22.6	-7.8
Differ from Category (+/-)	0.4 abv av	0.6 abv av	1.1 high	4.2 high	-2.4 low

Total Risk	Standard Deviation	Category Risk	Risk Index	Avg Mat
av	7.2%	high	1.3	23.8 yrs

	1996	1995	1994	1993	1992	1991	1990	1989	1988	1987
Return (%)	3.1	20.9	-8.3	12.6	8.7	13.7	6.6	10.0	13.8	0.1
Differ from Category (+/-)	-0.6	5.7	-3.0	0.8	0.4	2.3	0.2	1.0	3.8	1.5
Return, Tax-Adjusted (%)	3.1	20.9	-8.4	11.9	8.3	13.5	6.5	9.0	13.1	-0.8

PER SHARE DATA

	1996	1995	1994	1993	1992	1991	1990	1989	1988	1987
Dividends, Net Income ($)	0.75	0.70	0.76	0.78	0.82	0.85	0.86	0.89	0.94	0.96
Distrib'ns, Cap Gain ($)	0.00	0.00	0.03	0.30	0.18	0.06	0.04	0.44	0.28	0.40
Net Asset Value ($)	13.98	14.31	12.46	14.43	13.82	13.68	12.88	12.97	13.05	12.60
Expense Ratio (%)	0.54	0.56	0.52	0.53	0.54	0.56	0.57	0.60	0.61	0.59
Yield (%)	5.36	4.89	6.08	5.29	5.85	6.18	6.65	6.63	7.05	7.38
Portfolio Turnover (%)	12	26	22	31	25	39	66	136	72	23
Total Assets (Millions $)	491	521	434	572	528	422	311	281	222	174

PORTFOLIO (as of 9/30/96)

Portfolio Manager: Stephen Bauer - 1981

Investm't Category: Tax-Exempt Bond
- ✔ Domestic
- Foreign
- Asset Allocation
- Index
- Sector
- State Specific

Investment Style
- Large-Cap Growth
- Mid-Cap Growth
- Small-Cap Growth
- Large-Cap Value
- Mid-Cap Value
- Small-Cap Value

Portfolio
0.0% cash	0.0% corp bonds
0.0% stocks	0.0% gov't bonds
0.0% preferred	98.5% muni bonds
0.0% conv't/warrants	1.5% other

SHAREHOLDER INFORMATION

Minimum Investment
Initial: $1,000   Subsequent: $100

Minimum IRA Investment
Initial: na   Subsequent: na

Maximum Fees
Load: none   12b-1: none
Other: none

Distributions
Income: monthly   Capital Gains: Mar, Dec

Exchange Options
Number Per Year: no limit   Fee: none
Telephone: yes (money market fund available)

Services
auto exchange, auto invest, auto withdraw

SAFECO Northwest
(SFNWX)
Growth

Safeco Tower S-1
P.O. Box 34890
Seattle, WA 98124
800-624-5711, 206-545-7319
networth.galt.com/safeco

PERFORMANCE

fund inception date: 2/7/91

	3yr Annual	5yr Annual	10yr Annual	Bull	Bear
Return (%)	10.8	9.4	na	38.0	-3.1
Differ from Category (+/-)	-4.9 low	-4.9 low	na	-24.4 low	3.6 high

Total Risk	Standard Deviation	Category Risk	Risk Index	Beta
av	9.1%	blw av	0.9	0.56

	1996	1995	1994	1993	1992	1991	1990	1989	1988	1987
Return (%).	15.0	20.1	-1.6	1.0	14.0	—	—	—	—	—
Differ from Category (+/-) .	-5.1	-10.2	-1.3	-13.0	2.2	—	—	—	—	—
Return, Tax-Adjusted (%). .	11.7	17.9	-2.0	0.3	13.0	—	—	—	—	—

PER SHARE DATA

	1996	1995	1994	1993	1992	1991	1990	1989	1988	1987
Dividends, Net Income ($).	0.00	0.04	0.03	0.03	0.06	—	—	—	—	—
Distrib'ns, Cap Gain ($) . . .	1.60	0.87	0.10	0.23	0.31	—	—	—	—	—
Net Asset Value ($)	14.07	13.66	12.12	12.45	12.59	—	—	—	—	—
Expense Ratio (%).	na	1.09	1.06	1.11	1.11	—	—	—	—	—
Yield (%)	0.00	0.27	0.24	0.23	0.46	—	—	—	—	—
Portfolio Turnover (%).	na	19	18	14	33	—	—	—	—	—
Total Assets (Millions $). . . .	43	38	34	39	40	—	—	—	—	—

PORTFOLIO (as of 9/30/96)

Portfolio Manager: Charles Driggs - 1992

Investm't Category: Growth
- ✔ Domestic
- Foreign
- Asset Allocation
- Index
- Sector
- State Specific

Investment Style
- Large-Cap Growth
- ✔ Mid-Cap Growth
- ✔ Small-Cap Growth
- Large-Cap Value
- ✔ Mid-Cap Value
- ✔ Small-Cap Value

Portfolio
5.0% cash	0.0% corp bonds
95.0% stocks	0.0% gov't bonds
0.0% preferred	0.0% muni bonds
0.0% conv't/warrants	0.0% other

SHAREHOLDER INFORMATION

Minimum Investment
Initial: $1,000   Subsequent: $100

Minimum IRA Investment
Initial: $250   Subsequent: $100

Maximum Fees
Load: none   12b-1: none
Other: none

Distributions
Income: quarterly   Capital Gains: Sep, Dec

Exchange Options
Number Per Year: no limit   Fee: none
Telephone: yes (money market fund available)

Services
IRA, pension, auto exchange, auto invest, auto withdraw

SSgA: Emerging Markets
(SSEMX)

909 A St.
5th Floor
Tacoma, WA 98402
800-647-7327, 206-572-9500

International Stock

PERFORMANCE

fund inception date: 3/1/94

	3yr Annual	5yr Annual	10yr Annual	Bull	Bear
Return (%)	na	na	na	24.2	na
Differ from Category (+/-)	na	na	na	-0.1 av	na

Total Risk	Standard Deviation	Category Risk	Risk Index	Beta
na	na	na	na	na

	1996	1995	1994	1993	1992	1991	1990	1989	1988	1987
Return (%)	14.8	-7.9	—	—	—	—	—	—	—	—
Differ from Category (+/-)	0.0	-17.0	—	—	—	—	—	—	—	—
Return, Tax-Adjusted (%)	14.2	-8.6	—	—	—	—	—	—	—	—

PER SHARE DATA

	1996	1995	1994	1993	1992	1991	1990	1989	1988	1987
Dividends, Net Income ($)	0.10	0.11	—	—	—	—	—	—	—	—
Distrib'ns, Cap Gain ($)	0.05	0.10	—	—	—	—	—	—	—	—
Net Asset Value ($)	10.98	9.70	—	—	—	—	—	—	—	—
Expense Ratio (%)	1.28	1.50	—	—	—	—	—	—	—	—
Yield (%)	0.90	1.12	—	—	—	—	—	—	—	—
Portfolio Turnover (%)	4	19	—	—	—	—	—	—	—	—
Total Assets (Millions $)	145	80	—	—	—	—	—	—	—	—

PORTFOLIO (as of 9/30/96)

Portfolio Manager: Robert Furdak, committee - 1994

Investm't Category: International Stock
- ✔ Domestic
- ✔ Foreign
- Asset Allocation
- Index
- Sector
- State Specific

Investment Style
- Large-Cap Growth
- Mid-Cap Growth
- Small-Cap Growth
- Large-Cap Value
- Mid-Cap Value
- Small-Cap Value

Portfolio
1.7% cash	0.0% corp bonds	
84.7% stocks	0.0% gov't bonds	
13.6% preferred	0.0% muni bonds	
0.0% conv't/warrants	0.0% other	

SHAREHOLDER INFORMATION

Minimum Investment
Initial: $1,000   Subsequent: $1

Minimum IRA Investment
Initial: $1   Subsequent: $1

Maximum Fees
Load: none   12b-1: 0.25%
Other: none

Distributions
Income: annual   Capital Gains: Oct

Exchange Options
Number Per Year: no limit   Fee: none
Telephone: yes (money market fund available)

Services
IRA

SSgA: Growth & Income
(SSGWX)

Growth & Income

909 A St.
5th Floor
Tacoma, WA 98402
800-647-7327, 206-572-9500

PERFORMANCE

fund inception date: 9/1/93

	3yr Annual	5yr Annual	10yr Annual	Bull	Bear
Return (%)	15.9	na	na	61.7	-6.8
Differ from Category (+/-)	0.6 av	na	na	1.9 av	-0.4 av

Total Risk	Standard Deviation	Category Risk	Risk Index	Beta
abv av	9.7%	abv av	1.1	0.94

	1996	1995	1994	1993	1992	1991	1990	1989	1988	1987
Return (%)	21.4	28.6	-0.3	—	—	—	—	—	—	—
Differ from Category (+/-)	1.7	-1.5	1.0	—	—	—	—	—	—	—
Return, Tax-Adjusted (%)	19.9	27.8	-1.0	—	—	—	—	—	—	—

PER SHARE DATA

	1996	1995	1994	1993	1992	1991	1990	1989	1988	1987
Dividends, Net Income ($)	0.14	0.17	0.17	—	—	—	—	—	—	—
Distrib'ns, Cap Gain ($)	0.44	0.04	0.00	—	—	—	—	—	—	—
Net Asset Value ($)	14.54	12.49	9.89	—	—	—	—	—	—	—
Expense Ratio (%)	0.95	0.95	0.95	—	—	—	—	—	—	—
Yield (%)	0.93	1.35	1.71	—	—	—	—	—	—	—
Portfolio Turnover (%)	38	39	36	—	—	—	—	—	—	—
Total Assets (Millions $)	73	49	26	—	—	—	—	—	—	—

PORTFOLIO (as of 9/30/96)

Portfolio Manager: Brenton Dickson, committee - 1993

Investm't Category: Growth & Income
- ✔ Domestic
- Foreign
- Asset Allocation
- Index
- Sector
- State Specific

Investment Style
- ✔ Large-Cap Growth
- Mid-Cap Growth
- Small-Cap Growth
- ✔ Large-Cap Value
- Mid-Cap Value
- Small-Cap Value

Portfolio
4.8% cash	0.0% corp bonds
95.2% stocks	0.0% gov't bonds
0.0% preferred	0.0% muni bonds
0.0% conv't/warrants	0.0% other

SHAREHOLDER INFORMATION

Minimum Investment
Initial: $1,000   Subsequent: $1

Minimum IRA Investment
Initial: $1   Subsequent: $1

Maximum Fees
Load: none   12b-1: 0.25%
Other: none

Distributions
Income: quarterly   Capital Gains: Oct

Exchange Options
Number Per Year: no limit   Fee: none
Telephone: yes (money market fund availabe)

Services
IRA

SSgA: Interm (SSINX)

General Bond

909 A St.
5th Floor
Tacoma, WA 98402
800-647-7327, 206-572-9500

PERFORMANCE

fund inception date: 9/1/93

	3yr Annual	5yr Annual	10yr Annual	Bull	Bear
Return (%)	4.9	na	na	21.2	-5.7
Differ from Category (+/-)	-0.2 av	na	na	0.9 av	-1.5 blw av

Total Risk	Standard Deviation	Category Risk	Risk Index	Avg Mat
low	4.1%	av	1.1	4.2 yrs

	1996	1995	1994	1993	1992	1991	1990	1989	1988	1987
Return (%).	3.6	16.6	-4.5	—	—	—	—	—	—	—
Differ from Category (+/-) .	-0.3	1.7	-2.2	—	—	—	—	—	—	—
Return, Tax-Adjusted (%). . .	1.4	14.1	-6.5	—	—	—	—	—	—	—

PER SHARE DATA

	1996	1995	1994	1993	1992	1991	1990	1989	1988	1987
Dividends, Net Income ($).	0.54	0.54	0.49	—	—	—	—	—	—	—
Distrib'ns, Cap Gain ($) . . .	0.00	0.00	0.00	—	—	—	—	—	—	—
Net Asset Value ($)	9.60	9.80	8.89	—	—	—	—	—	—	—
Expense Ratio (%).	0.60	0.60	na	—	—	—	—	—	—	—
Yield (%)	5.62	5.51	5.51	—	—	—	—	—	—	—
Portfolio Turnover (%). . . .	221	26	na	—	—	—	—	—	—	—
Total Assets (Millions $). . . .	48	44	19	—	—	—	—	—	—	—

PORTFOLIO (as of 9/30/96)

Portfolio Manager: John Kirby - 1996

Investm't Category: General Bond
- ✔ Domestic
- ✔ Foreign
- Asset Allocation
- Index
- Sector
- State Specific

Investment Style
- Large-Cap Growth
- Mid-Cap Growth
- Small-Cap Growth
- Large-Cap Value
- Mid-Cap Value
- Small-Cap Value

Portfolio
3.0% cash	48.0% corp bonds
0.0% stocks	23.5% gov't bonds
0.0% preferred	0.0% muni bonds
0.0% conv't/warrants	25.5% other

SHAREHOLDER INFORMATION

Minimum Investment
Initial: $1,000   Subsequent: $1

Minimum IRA Investment
Initial: $1   Subsequent: $1

Maximum Fees
Load: none   12b-1: 0.25%
Other: none

Distributions
Income: quarterly   Capital Gains: Oct

Exchange Options
Number Per Year: no limit   Fee: none
Telephone: yes (money market fund available)

Services
IRA

SSgA: Matrix Equity

(SSMTX)

Growth & Income

909 A St.
5th Floor
Tacoma, WA 98402
800-647-7327, 206-572-9500

PERFORMANCE

fund inception date: 5/4/92

	3yr Annual	5yr Annual	10yr Annual	Bull	Bear
Return (%)	16.4	na	na	66.1	-7.3
Differ from Category (+/-)	1.1 av	na	na	6.3 abv av	-0.9 blw av

Total Risk	Standard Deviation	Category Risk	Risk Index	Beta
av	9.5%	av	1.0	0.94

	1996	1995	1994	1993	1992	1991	1990	1989	1988	1987
Return (%)	23.6	28.1	-0.4	16.2	—	—	—	—	—	—
Differ from Category (+/-)	3.9	-2.0	0.9	2.4	—	—	—	—	—	—
Return, Tax-Adjusted (%)	20.4	23.7	-1.4	15.0	—	—	—	—	—	—

PER SHARE DATA

	1996	1995	1994	1993	1992	1991	1990	1989	1988	1987
Dividends, Net Income ($)	0.24	0.25	0.26	0.18	—	—	—	—	—	—
Distrib'ns, Cap Gain ($)	1.13	1.43	0.05	0.18	—	—	—	—	—	—
Net Asset Value ($)	14.73	13.08	11.56	11.93	—	—	—	—	—	—
Expense Ratio (%)	0.66	0.68	0.58	0.60	—	—	—	—	—	—
Yield (%)	1.51	1.72	2.23	1.48	—	—	—	—	—	—
Portfolio Turnover (%)	150	129	127	58	—	—	—	—	—	—
Total Assets (Millions $)	319	211	138	89	—	—	—	—	—	—

PORTFOLIO (as of 9/30/96)

Portfolio Manager: Doug Holmes, committee - 1992

Investm't Category: Growth & Income
- ✔ Domestic
- Foreign
- Asset Allocation
- Index
- Sector
- State Specific

Investment Style
- ✔ Large-Cap Growth
- Mid-Cap Growth
- Small-Cap Growth
- ✔ Large-Cap Value
- Mid-Cap Value
- Small-Cap Value

Portfolio

0.9% cash	0.0% corp bonds
99.1% stocks	0.0% gov't bonds
0.0% preferred	0.0% muni bonds
0.0% conv't/warrants	0.0% other

SHAREHOLDER INFORMATION

Minimum Investment
Initial: $1,000   Subsequent: $1

Minimum IRA Investment
Initial: $1   Subsequent: $1

Maximum Fees
Load: none   12b-1: 0.25%
Other: none

Distributions
Income: quarterly   Capital Gains: Oct

Exchange Options
Number Per Year: no limit   Fee: none
Telephone: yes (money market fund available)

Services
IRA

SSgA: S&P 500 Index
(SVSPX)
Growth & Income

909 A St.
5th Floor
Tacoma, WA 98402
800-647-7327, 206-572-9500

PERFORMANCE

fund inception date: 12/30/92

	3yr Annual	5yr Annual	10yr Annual	Bull	Bear
Return (%)	19.4	na	na	76.1	-6.7
Differ from Category (+/-)	4.1 high	na	na	16.3 high	-0.3 av

Total Risk	Standard Deviation	Category Risk	Risk Index	Beta
abv av	9.6%	abv av	1.0	0.99

	1996	1995	1994	1993	1992	1991	1990	1989	1988	1987
Return (%)	22.6	37.0	1.3	9.6	—	—	—	—	—	—
Differ from Category (+/-)	2.9	6.9	2.6	-4.2	—	—	—	—	—	—
Return, Tax-Adjusted (%)	20.3	34.7	0.1	8.5	—	—	—	—	—	—

PER SHARE DATA

	1996	1995	1994	1993	1992	1991	1990	1989	1988	1987
Dividends, Net Income ($)	0.31	0.31	0.29	0.19	—	—	—	—	—	—
Distrib'ns, Cap Gain ($)	0.67	0.39	0.02	0.12	—	—	—	—	—	—
Net Asset Value ($)	15.57	13.55	10.44	10.63	—	—	—	—	—	—
Expense Ratio (%)	0.18	0.19	0.15	0.15	—	—	—	—	—	—
Yield (%)	1.90	2.22	2.77	1.76	—	—	—	—	—	—
Portfolio Turnover (%)	28	38	7	48	—	—	—	—	—	—
Total Assets (Millions $)	876	532	302	309	—	—	—	—	—	—

PORTFOLIO (as of 9/30/96)

Portfolio Manager: James May, committee - 1995

Investm't Category: Growth & Income
✔ Domestic   ✔ Index
  Foreign   Sector
  Asset Allocation   State Specific

Investment Style
✔ Large-Cap Growth   ✔ Large-Cap Value
  Mid-Cap Growth   Mid-Cap Value
  Small-Cap Growth   Small-Cap Value

Portfolio
0.0% cash   0.0% corp bonds
100.0% stocks   0.0% gov't bonds
0.0% preferred   0.0% muni bonds
0.0% conv't/warrants   0.0% other

SHAREHOLDER INFORMATION

Minimum Investment
Initial: $1,000   Subsequent: $1

Minimum IRA Investment
Initial: $1   Subsequent: $1

Maximum Fees
Load: none   12b-1: 0.25%
Other: none

Distributions
Income: quarterly   Capital Gains: Oct

Exchange Options
Number Per Year: no limit   Fee: none
Telephone: yes (money market fund available)

Services
IRA

SSgA: Small Cap (SVSCX)

Aggressive Growth

909 A St.
5th Floor
Tacoma, WA 98402
800-647-7327, 206-572-9500

PERFORMANCE

fund inception date: 7/1/92

	3yr Annual	5yr Annual	10yr Annual	Bull	Bear
Return (%)	21.8	na	na	95.5	-9.6
Differ from Category (+/-)	6.0 high	na	na	24.4 high	1.0 av

Total Risk	Standard Deviation	Category Risk	Risk Index	Beta
abv av	11.4%	low	0.8	0.87

	1996	1995	1994	1993	1992	1991	1990	1989	1988	1987
Return (%)	28.7	41.8	-1.0	12.9	—	—	—	—	—	—
Differ from Category (+/-)	9.6	7.5	-1.0	-6.4	—	—	—	—	—	—
Return, Tax-Adjusted (%)	26.3	41.1	-3.3	10.6	—	—	—	—	—	—

PER SHARE DATA

	1996	1995	1994	1993	1992	1991	1990	1989	1988	1987
Dividends, Net Income ($)	0.03	0.05	0.23	0.22	—	—	—	—	—	—
Distrib'ns, Cap Gain ($)	1.22	0.19	0.63	0.60	—	—	—	—	—	—
Net Asset Value ($)	18.30	15.25	10.94	11.92	—	—	—	—	—	—
Expense Ratio (%)	1.00	0.97	0.30	0.25	—	—	—	—	—	—
Yield (%)	0.15	0.32	1.98	1.75	—	—	—	—	—	—
Portfolio Turnover (%)	76	192	45	81	—	—	—	—	—	—
Total Assets (Millions $)	71	29	4	37	—	—	—	—	—	—

PORTFOLIO (as of 9/30/96)

Portfolio Manager: Doug Holmes, committee - 1992

Investm't Category: Aggressive Growth
✔ Domestic	Index
Foreign	Sector
Asset Allocation	State Specific

Investment Style
Large-Cap Growth	Large-Cap Value
Mid-Cap Growth	Mid-Cap Value
✔ Small-Cap Growth	✔ Small-Cap Value

Portfolio
6.6% cash	0.0% corp bonds
93.4% stocks	0.0% gov't bonds
0.0% preferred	0.0% muni bonds
0.0% conv't/warrants	0.0% other

SHAREHOLDER INFORMATION

Minimum Investment
Initial: $1,000   Subsequent: $1

Minimum IRA Investment
Initial: $1   Subsequent: $1

Maximum Fees
Load: none   12b-1: 0.25%
Other: none

Distributions
Income: quarterly   Capital Gains: Oct

Exchange Options
Number Per Year: no limit   Fee: none
Telephone: yes (money market fund availble)

Services
IRA

SSgA: Yield Plus (SSYPX)

General Bond

909 A St.
5th Floor
Tacoma, WA 98402
800-647-7327, 206-572-9500

PERFORMANCE

	3yr Annual	5yr Annual	10yr Annual	Bull	Bear
Return (%)	5.3	na	na	15.1	1.2
Differ from Category (+/-)	0.2 av	na	na	-5.2 low	5.4 high

Total Risk	Standard Deviation	Category Risk	Risk Index	Avg Mat
low	0.3%	low	0.1	0.4 yrs

	1996	1995	1994	1993	1992	1991	1990	1989	1988	1987
Return (%)	5.4	6.5	4.1	3.4	—	—	—	—	—	—
Differ from Category (+/-)	1.5	-8.4	6.4	-5.7	—	—	—	—	—	—
Return, Tax-Adjusted (%)	3.2	4.1	2.3	2.0	—	—	—	—	—	—

PER SHARE DATA

	1996	1995	1994	1993	1992	1991	1990	1989	1988	1987
Dividends, Net Income ($)	0.54	0.58	0.43	0.34	—	—	—	—	—	—
Distrib'ns, Cap Gain ($)	0.00	0.00	0.00	0.00	—	—	—	—	—	—
Net Asset Value ($)	10.00	10.01	9.96	10.00	—	—	—	—	—	—
Expense Ratio (%)	0.36	0.38	0.35	0.38	—	—	—	—	—	—
Yield (%)	5.40	5.79	4.31	3.40	—	—	—	—	—	—
Portfolio Turnover (%)	97	199	142	137	—	—	—	—	—	—
Total Assets (Millions $)	1,039	1,380	1,209	1,234	—	—	—	—	—	—

PORTFOLIO (as of 9/30/96)

Portfolio Manager: Susan R. Bonfeld, committee - 1996

Investm't Category: General Bond
- ✔ Domestic
- ✔ Foreign
- Asset Allocation
- Index
- Sector
- State Specific

Investment Style
- Large-Cap Growth
- Mid-Cap Growth
- Small-Cap Growth
- Large-Cap Value
- Mid-Cap Value
- Small-Cap Value

Portfolio
24.2% cash	38.1% corp bonds
0.0% stocks	1.2% gov't bonds
0.0% preferred	0.0% muni bonds
0.0% conv't/warrants	36.5% other

SHAREHOLDER INFORMATION

Minimum Investment
Initial: $1,000   Subsequent: $1

Minimum IRA Investment
Initial: $1   Subsequent: $1

Maximum Fees
Load: none   12b-1: 0.25%
Other: none

Distributions
Income: monthly   Capital Gains: annual

Exchange Options
Number Per Year: no limit   Fee: none
Telephone: yes (money market fund available)

Services
IRA

Schroder Capital Int'l—Inv

(SCIEX)

P.O. Box 7148
Portland, ME 04112
800-963-6786, 207-879-1900

International Stock

PERFORMANCE   fund inception date: 12/20/85

	3yr Annual	5yr Annual	10yr Annual	Bull	Bear
Return (%)	6.9	11.3	9.1	21.7	-5.0
Differ from Category (+/-)	0.6 av	1.3 abv av	0.5 av	-2.6 av	2.2 abv av

Total Risk	Standard Deviation	Category Risk	Risk Index	Beta
abv av	10.0%	blw av	1.0	0.67

	1996	1995	1994	1993	1992	1991	1990	1989	1988	1987
Return (%)	9.9	11.5	-0.3	45.7	-4.1	4.5	-11.4	22.1	19.4	3.7
Differ from Category (+/-)	-4.9	2.4	2.8	6.1	-0.3	-8.7	-1.3	-0.5	4.5	-8.5
Return, Tax-Adjusted (%)	5.0	7.2	-3.6	45.5	-4.4	3.8	-14.1	20.8	19.2	1.1

PER SHARE DATA

	1996	1995	1994	1993	1992	1991	1990	1989	1988	1987
Dividends, Net Income ($)	0.45	0.47	0.00	0.07	0.11	0.23	0.73	0.44	0.04	0.00
Distrib'ns, Cap Gain ($)	2.62	2.31	2.54	0.00	0.00	0.05	0.75	0.08	0.04	1.33
Net Asset Value ($)	17.57	18.86	19.44	21.94	15.11	15.86	15.44	19.10	16.07	13.52
Expense Ratio (%)	na	0.91	0.90	0.91	0.93	1.07	1.12	1.12	1.30	1.64
Yield (%)	2.22	2.22	0.00	0.31	0.72	1.44	4.50	2.29	0.24	0.00
Portfolio Turnover (%)	na	61	25	56	49	51	56	72	86	85
Total Assets (Millions $)	209	205	174	358	172	115	60	60	35	27

PORTFOLIO (as of 9/30/96)

Portfolio Manager: Mark J. Smith - 1989

Investm't Category: International Stock

Domestic	Index
✔ Foreign	Sector
Asset Allocation	State Specific

Investment Style

Large-Cap Growth	Large-Cap Value
Mid-Cap Growth	Mid-Cap Value
Small-Cap Growth	Small-Cap Value

Portfolio

1.3% cash	0.0% corp bonds
93.6% stocks	0.0% gov't bonds
2.2% preferred	0.0% muni bonds
0.1% conv't/warrants	2.9% other

SHAREHOLDER INFORMATION

Minimum Investment
Initial: $10,000   Subsequent: $2,500

Minimum IRA Investment
Initial: $2,000   Subsequent: $250

Maximum Fees
Load: none   12b-1: 0.50%
Other: *f*

Distributions
Income: annual   Capital Gains: annual

Exchange Options
Number Per Year: none   Fee: na
Telephone: na

Services
IRA

Schwab 1000 (SNXFX)

Growth & Income

The Schwab Building
101 Montgomery St.
San Francisco, CA 94104
800-266-5623
www.schwab.com

PERFORMANCE

fund inception date: 4/2/91

	3yr Annual	5yr Annual	10yr Annual	Bull	Bear
Return (%)	18.3	14.5	na	73.6	-7.3
Differ from Category (+/-)	3.0 abv av	0.6 av	na	13.8 high	-0.9 blw av

Total Risk	Standard Deviation	Category Risk	Risk Index	Beta
abv av	9.5%	av	1.0	0.98

	1996	1995	1994	1993	1992	1991	1990	1989	1988	1987
Return (%)	21.5	36.6	-0.2	9.6	8.5	—	—	—	—	—
Differ from Category (+/-)	1.8	6.5	1.1	-4.2	-2.2	—	—	—	—	—
Return, Tax-Adjusted (%)	20.9	35.8	-1.1	8.7	7.6	—	—	—	—	—

PER SHARE DATA

	1996	1995	1994	1993	1992	1991	1990	1989	1988	1987
Dividends, Net Income ($)	0.25	0.23	0.26	0.25	0.24	—	—	—	—	—
Distrib'ns, Cap Gain ($)	0.00	0.00	0.00	0.00	0.00	—	—	—	—	—
Net Asset Value ($)	20.34	16.94	12.57	12.85	11.96	—	—	—	—	—
Expense Ratio (%)	0.49	0.54	0.51	0.45	0.35	—	—	—	—	—
Yield (%)	1.22	1.35	2.06	1.94	2.00	—	—	—	—	—
Portfolio Turnover (%)	2	2	3	1	1	—	—	—	—	—
Total Assets (Millions $)	1,922	1,063	553	529	370	—	—	—	—	—

PORTFOLIO (as of 9/30/96)

Portfolio Manager: Geri Hom - 1995

Investm't Category: Growth & Income
- ✔ Domestic
- ✔ Index
- Foreign
- Sector
- Asset Allocation
- State Specific

Investment Style
- ✔ Large-Cap Growth
- ✔ Large-Cap Value
- Mid-Cap Growth
- Mid-Cap Value
- Small-Cap Growth
- Small-Cap Value

Portfolio
0.3%	cash	0.0%	corp bonds
99.7%	stocks	0.0%	gov't bonds
0.0%	preferred	0.0%	muni bonds
0.0%	conv't/warrants	0.0%	other

SHAREHOLDER INFORMATION

Minimum Investment
Initial: $1,000   Subsequent: $100

Minimum IRA Investment
Initial: $500   Subsequent: $100

Maximum Fees
Load: 0.50% redemption   12b-1: none
Other: redemption fee applies for 6 months

Distributions
Income: Dec   Capital Gains: Dec

Exchange Options
Number Per Year: no limit   Fee: none
Telephone: yes (money market fund available)

Services
IRA, pension, auto invest

Schwab Asset Director: Balanced Growth (SWBGX)

Balanced

The Schwab Building
101 Montgomery St.
San Francisco, CA 94104
800-266-5623
www.schwab.com

PERFORMANCE

fund inception date: 11/17/95

	3yr Annual	5yr Annual	10yr Annual	Bull	Bear
Return (%)	na	na	na	na	na
Differ from Category (+/-)	na	na	na	na	na

Total Risk	Standard Deviation		Category Risk	Risk Index	Beta
na	na		na	na	na

	1996	1995	1994	1993	1992	1991	1990	1989	1988	1987
Return (%)	11.1	—	—	—	—	—	—	—	—	—
Differ from Category (+/-)	-3.1	—	—	—	—	—	—	—	—	—
Return, Tax-Adjusted (%)	10.2	—	—	—	—	—	—	—	—	—

PER SHARE DATA

	1996	1995	1994	1993	1992	1991	1990	1989	1988	1987
Dividends, Net Income ($)	0.23	—	—	—	—	—	—	—	—	—
Distrib'ns, Cap Gain ($)	0.00	—	—	—	—	—	—	—	—	—
Net Asset Value ($)	11.15	—	—	—	—	—	—	—	—	—
Expense Ratio (%)	na	—	—	—	—	—	—	—	—	—
Yield (%)	2.06	—	—	—	—	—	—	—	—	—
Portfolio Turnover (%)	na	—	—	—	—	—	—	—	—	—
Total Assets (Millions $)	97	—	—	—	—	—	—	—	—	—

PORTFOLIO (as of 9/30/96)

Portfolio Manager: Hom, Regan, Ward - 1995

Investm't Category: Balanced
✔ Domestic   Index
✔ Foreign   Sector
✔ Asset Allocation State Specific

Investment Style
Large-Cap Growth   Large-Cap Value
Mid-Cap Growth   Mid-Cap Value
Small-Cap Growth   Small-Cap Value

Portfolio
6.0% cash   0.0% corp bonds
57.0% stocks   37.0% gov't bonds
0.0% preferred   0.0% muni bonds
0.0% conv't/warrants 0.0% other

SHAREHOLDER INFORMATION

Minimum Investment
Initial: $1,000   Subsequent: $100

Minimum IRA Investment
Initial: $500   Subsequent: $100

Maximum Fees
Load: none   12b-1: none
Other: none

Distributions
Income: Dec   Capital Gains: Dec

Exchange Options
Number Per Year: no limit   Fee: none
Telephone: yes (money market fund available)

Services
IRA, pension, auto invest

Schwab Asset Director: High Growth (SWHGX)

Balanced

The Schwab Building
101 Montgomery St.
San Francisco, CA 94104
800-266-5623
www.schwab.com

PERFORMANCE

fund inception date: 11/17/95

	3yr Annual	5yr Annual	10yr Annual	Bull	Bear
Return (%)	na	na	na	na	na
Differ from Category (+/-)	na	na	na	na	na

Total Risk	Standard Deviation	Category Risk	Risk Index	Beta
na	na	na	na	na

	1996	1995	1994	1993	1992	1991	1990	1989	1988	1987
Return (%)	14.4	—	—	—	—	—	—	—	—	—
Differ from Category (+/-)	0.2	—	—	—	—	—	—	—	—	—
Return, Tax-Adjusted (%)	13.6	—	—	—	—	—	—	—	—	—

PER SHARE DATA

	1996	1995	1994	1993	1992	1991	1990	1989	1988	1987
Dividends, Net Income ($)	0.19	—	—	—	—	—	—	—	—	—
Distrib'ns, Cap Gain ($)	0.00	—	—	—	—	—	—	—	—	—
Net Asset Value ($)	11.56	—	—	—	—	—	—	—	—	—
Expense Ratio (%)	na	—	—	—	—	—	—	—	—	—
Yield (%)	1.64	—	—	—	—	—	—	—	—	—
Portfolio Turnover (%)	na	—	—	—	—	—	—	—	—	—
Total Assets (Millions $)	112	—	—	—	—	—	—	—	—	—

PORTFOLIO (as of 9/30/96)

Portfolio Manager: Hom, Regan, Ward - 1995

Investm't Category: Balanced

✔ Domestic Index
✔ Foreign Sector
✔ Asset Allocation State Specific

Investment Style
Large-Cap Growth Large-Cap Value
Mid-Cap Growth Mid-Cap Value
Small-Cap Growth Small-Cap Value

Portfolio

5.0% cash	0.0% corp bonds
76.0% stocks	19.0% gov't bonds
0.0% preferred	0.0% muni bonds
0.0% conv't/warrants	0.0% other

SHAREHOLDER INFORMATION

Minimum Investment
Initial: $1,000   Subsequent: $100

Minimum IRA Investment
Initial: $500   Subsequent: $100

Maximum Fees
Load: none   12b-1: none
Other: none

Distributions
Income: Dec   Capital Gains: Dec

Exchange Options
Number Per Year: no limit   Fee: none
Telephone: yes (money market fund available)

Services
IRA, pension, auto invest

Schwab CA Long-Term Tx Fr Bond (SWCAX)

Tax-Exempt Bond

The Schwab Building
101 Montgomery St.
San Francisco, CA 94104
800-266-5623
www.schwab.com

PERFORMANCE

fund inception date: 2/24/92

	3yr Annual	5yr Annual	10yr Annual	Bull	Bear
Return (%)	4.4	na	na	21.6	-7.3
Differ from Category (+/-)	0.2 av	na	na	3.2 high	-1.9 low

Total Risk	Standard Deviation	Category Risk	Risk Index	Avg Mat
blw av	6.6%	high	1.2	18.8 yrs

	1996	1995	1994	1993	1992	1991	1990	1989	1988	1987
Return (%)	4.3	19.8	-9.0	12.8	—	—	—	—	—	—
Differ from Category (+/-)	0.6	4.6	-3.7	1.0	—	—	—	—	—	—
Return, Tax-Adjusted (%)	4.3	19.8	-9.0	12.4	—	—	—	—	—	—

PER SHARE DATA

	1996	1995	1994	1993	1992	1991	1990	1989	1988	1987
Dividends, Net Income ($)	0.56	0.56	0.55	0.56	—	—	—	—	—	—
Distrib'ns, Cap Gain ($)	0.00	0.00	0.00	0.12	—	—	—	—	—	—
Net Asset Value ($)	10.90	11.01	9.69	11.23	—	—	—	—	—	—
Expense Ratio (%)	0.49	0.58	0.60	0.60	—	—	—	—	—	—
Yield (%)	5.13	5.08	5.67	4.93	—	—	—	—	—	—
Portfolio Turnover (%)	36	46	48	47	—	—	—	—	—	—
Total Assets (Millions $)	108	97	87	131	—	—	—	—	—	—

PORTFOLIO (as of 9/30/96)

Portfolio Manager: Joanne Keighley - 1992

Investm't Category: Tax-Exempt Bond
- ✔ Domestic
- Foreign
- Asset Allocation
- Index
- Sector
- ✔ State Specific

Investment Style
- Large-Cap Growth
- Mid-Cap Growth
- Small-Cap Growth
- Large-Cap Value
- Mid-Cap Value
- Small-Cap Value

Portfolio
4.0% cash	0.0% corp bonds
0.0% stocks	0.0% gov't bonds
0.0% preferred	96.0% muni bonds
0.0% conv't/warrants	0.0% other

SHAREHOLDER INFORMATION

Minimum Investment
Initial: $1,000   Subsequent: $100

Minimum IRA Investment
Initial: na   Subsequent: na

Maximum Fees
Load: none   12b-1: none
Other: none

Distributions
Income: monthly   Capital Gains: Dec

Exchange Options
Number Per Year: no limit   Fee: none
Telephone: yes (money market fund available)

Services
auto invest

Schwab CA Short Interm Tx Fr Bond (SWCSX)

Tax-Exempt Bond

The Schwab Building
101 Montgomery St.
San Francisco, CA 94104
800-266-5623
www.schwab.com

PERFORMANCE

fund inception date: 4/20/93

	3yr Annual	5yr Annual	10yr Annual	Bull	Bear
Return (%)	3.9	na	na	14.4	-2.5
Differ from Category (+/-)	-0.3 blw av	na	na	-4.0 low	2.9 high

Total Risk	Standard Deviation	Category Risk	Risk Index	Avg Mat
low	2.6%	low	0.5	3.4 yrs

	1996	1995	1994	1993	1992	1991	1990	1989	1988	1987
Return (%)	3.9	10.4	-2.1	—	—	—	—	—	—	—
Differ from Category (+/-)	0.2	-4.8	3.2	—	—	—	—	—	—	—
Return, Tax-Adjusted (%)	3.9	10.4	-2.1	—	—	—	—	—	—	—

PER SHARE DATA

	1996	1995	1994	1993	1992	1991	1990	1989	1988	1987
Dividends, Net Income ($)	0.42	0.42	0.38	—	—	—	—	—	—	—
Distrib'ns, Cap Gain ($)	0.00	0.00	0.00	—	—	—	—	—	—	—
Net Asset Value ($)	10.12	10.16	9.60	—	—	—	—	—	—	—
Expense Ratio (%)	0.49	0.50	0.48	—	—	—	—	—	—	—
Yield (%)	4.15	4.13	3.95	—	—	—	—	—	—	—
Portfolio Turnover (%)	20	62	35	—	—	—	—	—	—	—
Total Assets (Millions $)	48	42	40	—	—	—	—	—	—	—

PORTFOLIO (as of 9/30/96)

Portfolio Manager: Joanne Keighley - 1993

Investm't Category: Tax-Exempt Bond
- ✔ Domestic
- Foreign
- Asset Allocation
- Index
- Sector
- ✔ State Specific

Investment Style
- Large-Cap Growth
- Mid-Cap Growth
- Small-Cap Growth
- Large-Cap Value
- Mid-Cap Value
- Small-Cap Value

Portfolio
1.4% cash	0.0% corp bonds
0.0% stocks	0.0% gov't bonds
0.0% preferred	98.6% muni bonds
0.0% conv't/warrants	0.0% other

SHAREHOLDER INFORMATION

Minimum Investment
Initial: $1,000   Subsequent: $100

Minimum IRA Investment
Initial: na   Subsequent: na

Maximum Fees
Load: none   12b-1: none
Other: none

Distributions
Income: monthly   Capital Gains: Dec

Exchange Options
Number Per Year: no limit   Fee: none
Telephone: yes (money market fund available)

Services
auto invest

Schwab Capital Trust: Int'l Index (SWINX)

International Stock

The Schwab Building
101 Montgomery St.
San Francisco, CA 94104
800-266-5623
www.schwab.com

PERFORMANCE

fund inception date: 9/9/93

	3yr Annual	5yr Annual	10yr Annual	Bull	Bear
Return (%)	8.9	na	na	24.5	-2.7
Differ from Category (+/-)	2.6 abv av	na	na	0.2 av	4.5 high

Total Risk	Standard Deviation	Category Risk	Risk Index	Beta
abv av	9.7%	blw av	0.9	0.66

	1996	1995	1994	1993	1992	1991	1990	1989	1988	1987
Return (%)	9.1	14.2	3.8	—	—	—	—	—	—	—
Differ from Category (+/-)	-5.7	5.1	6.9	—	—	—	—	—	—	—
Return, Tax-Adjusted (%)	8.5	13.7	3.3	—	—	—	—	—	—	—

PER SHARE DATA

	1996	1995	1994	1993	1992	1991	1990	1989	1988	1987
Dividends, Net Income ($)	0.16	0.12	0.11	—	—	—	—	—	—	—
Distrib'ns, Cap Gain ($)	0.00	0.00	0.00	—	—	—	—	—	—	—
Net Asset Value ($)	12.54	11.65	10.31	—	—	—	—	—	—	—
Expense Ratio (%)	na	0.85	0.90	—	—	—	—	—	—	—
Yield (%)	1.27	1.03	1.06	—	—	—	—	—	—	—
Portfolio Turnover (%)	na	0	6	—	—	—	—	—	—	—
Total Assets (Millions $)	259	195	138	—	—	—	—	—	—	—

PORTFOLIO (as of 9/30/96)

Portfolio Manager: Geri Hom - 1995

Investm't Category: International Stock
- Domestic
- ✔ Foreign
- Asset Allocation
- ✔ Index
- Sector
- State Specific

Investment Style
- Large-Cap Growth
- Mid-Cap Growth
- Small-Cap Growth
- Large-Cap Value
- Mid-Cap Value
- Small-Cap Value

Portfolio
0.5% cash	0.0% corp bonds
99.5% stocks	0.0% gov't bonds
0.0% preferred	0.0% muni bonds
0.0% conv't/warrants	0.0% other

SHAREHOLDER INFORMATION

Minimum Investment
Initial: $1,000   Subsequent: $100

Minimum IRA Investment
Initial: $500   Subsequent: $100

Maximum Fees
Load: 0.75% redemption   12b-1: none
Other: redemption fee applies for 6 months

Distributions
Income: Dec   Capital Gains: Dec

Exchange Options
Number Per Year: no limit   Fee: none
Telephone: yes (money market fund available)

Services
IRA, pension, auto invest

Schwab Capital Trust: Small Cap Index (SWSMX)

Aggressive Growth

The Schwab Building
101 Montgomery St.
San Francisco, CA 94104
800-266-5623
www.schwab.com

PERFORMANCE

fund inception date: 12/3/93

	3yr Annual	5yr Annual	10yr Annual	Bull	Bear
Return (%)	12.6	na	na	55.4	-10.3
Differ from Category (+/-)	-3.2 blw av	na	na	-15.7 blw av	0.3 av

Total Risk	Standard Deviation	Category Risk	Risk Index	Beta
high	12.2%	blw av	0.9	0.88

	1996	1995	1994	1993	1992	1991	1990	1989	1988	1987
Return (%)	15.4	27.6	-3.1	—	—	—	—	—	—	—
Differ from Category (+/-)	-3.7	-6.7	-3.1	—	—	—	—	—	—	—
Return, Tax-Adjusted (%)	15.2	27.3	-3.3	—	—	—	—	—	—	—

PER SHARE DATA

	1996	1995	1994	1993	1992	1991	1990	1989	1988	1987
Dividends, Net Income ($)	0.06	0.06	0.05	—	—	—	—	—	—	—
Distrib'ns, Cap Gain ($)	0.00	0.00	0.00	—	—	—	—	—	—	—
Net Asset Value ($)	14.27	12.41	9.77	—	—	—	—	—	—	—
Expense Ratio (%)	na	0.68	0.67	—	—	—	—	—	—	—
Yield (%)	0.42	0.48	0.51	—	—	—	—	—	—	—
Portfolio Turnover (%)	na	24	16	—	—	—	—	—	—	—
Total Assets (Millions $)	220	138	70	—	—	—	—	—	—	—

PORTFOLIO (as of 9/30/96)

Portfolio Manager: Geri Hom - 1995

Investm't Category: Aggressive Growth

✔ Domestic	✔ Index
Foreign	Sector
Asset Allocation	State Specific

Investment Style

Large-Cap Growth	Large-Cap Value
Mid-Cap Growth	Mid-Cap Value
✔ Small-Cap Growth	✔ Small-Cap Value

Portfolio

0.3% cash	0.0% corp bonds
99.7% stocks	0.0% gov't bonds
0.0% preferred	0.0% muni bonds
0.0% conv't/warrants	0.0% other

SHAREHOLDER INFORMATION

Minimum Investment

Initial: $1,000   Subsequent: $100

Minimum IRA Investment

Initial: $500   Subsequent: $100

Maximum Fees

Load: 0.50% redemption   12b-1: none
Other: redemption fee applies for 6 months

Distributions

Income: Dec   Capital Gains: Dec

Exchange Options

Number Per Year: no limit   Fee: none
Telephone: yes (money market fund available)

Services

IRA, pension, auto invest

Schwab Long-Term Tax-Free Bond (SWNTX)

Tax-Exempt Bond

The Schwab Building
101 Montgomery St.
San Francisco, CA 94104
800-266-5623
www.schwab.com

PERFORMANCE

fund inception date: 9/11/92

	3yr Annual	5yr Annual	10yr Annual	Bull	Bear
Return (%)	4.5	na	na	20.7	-6.2
Differ from Category (+/-)	0.3 abv av	na	na	2.3 abv av	-0.8 blw av

Total Risk	Standard Deviation	Category Risk	Risk Index	Avg Mat
blw av	6.2%	abv av	1.1	19.2 yrs

	1996	1995	1994	1993	1992	1991	1990	1989	1988	1987
Return (%)	4.1	18.1	-7.1	13.6	—	—	—	—	—	—
Differ from Category (+/-)	0.4	2.9	-1.8	1.8	—	—	—	—	—	—
Return, Tax-Adjusted (%)	4.1	18.1	-7.1	13.3	—	—	—	—	—	—

PER SHARE DATA

	1996	1995	1994	1993	1992	1991	1990	1989	1988	1987
Dividends, Net Income ($)	0.51	0.52	0.51	0.54	—	—	—	—	—	—
Distrib'ns, Cap Gain ($)	0.00	0.00	0.00	0.08	—	—	—	—	—	—
Net Asset Value ($)	10.41	10.51	9.37	10.62	—	—	—	—	—	—
Expense Ratio (%)	0.49	0.54	0.51	0.45	—	—	—	—	—	—
Yield (%)	4.89	4.94	5.44	5.04	—	—	—	—	—	—
Portfolio Turnover (%)	50	70	62	90	—	—	—	—	—	—
Total Assets (Millions $)	43	43	36	49	—	—	—	—	—	—

PORTFOLIO (as of 9/30/96)

Portfolio Manager: Joanne Keighley - 1992

Investm't Category: Tax-Exempt Bond
- ✔ Domestic
- Foreign
- Asset Allocation
- Index
- Sector
- State Specific

Investment Style
- Large-Cap Growth
- Mid-Cap Growth
- Small-Cap Growth
- Large-Cap Value
- Mid-Cap Value
- Small-Cap Value

Portfolio
- 6.0% cash
- 0.0% stocks
- 0.0% preferred
- 0.0% conv't/warrants
- 0.0% corp bonds
- 0.0% gov't bonds
- 94.0% muni bonds
- 0.0% other

SHAREHOLDER INFORMATION

Minimum Investment
Initial: $1,000   Subsequent: $100

Minimum IRA Investment
Initial: na   Subsequent: na

Maximum Fees
Load: none   12b-1: none
Other: none

Distributions
Income: monthly   Capital Gains: Dec

Exchange Options
Number Per Year: no limit   Fee: none
Telephone: yes (money market fund available)

Services
auto invest

Schwab Short/Interm Gov't Bond (SWBDX)

Government Bond

The Schwab Building
101 Montgomery St.
San Francisco, CA 94104
800-266-5623
www.schwab.com

PERFORMANCE

fund inception date: 11/5/91

	3yr Annual	5yr Annual	10yr Annual	Bull	Bear
Return (%)	3.8	5.0	na	15.8	-3.9
Differ from Category (+/-)	-1.1 low	-1.6 blw av	na	-6.2 low	2.5 av

Total Risk	Standard Deviation	Category Risk	Risk Index	Avg Mat
low	2.5%	blw av	0.6	2.6 yrs

	1996	1995	1994	1993	1992	1991	1990	1989	1988	1987
Return (%)	4.0	10.9	-2.8	7.8	6.0	—	—	—	—	—
Differ from Category (+/-)	2.5	-8.7	1.6	-3.8	-0.7	—	—	—	—	—
Return, Tax-Adjusted (%)	1.6	8.4	-4.9	5.3	3.6	—	—	—	—	—

PER SHARE DATA

	1996	1995	1994	1993	1992	1991	1990	1989	1988	1987
Dividends, Net Income ($)	0.59	0.60	0.54	0.55	0.59	—	—	—	—	—
Distrib'ns, Cap Gain ($)	0.00	0.00	0.00	0.12	0.02	—	—	—	—	—
Net Asset Value ($)	9.75	9.96	9.55	10.38	10.26	—	—	—	—	—
Expense Ratio (%)	0.49	0.58	0.60	0.60	0.43	—	—	—	—	—
Yield (%)	6.05	6.02	5.65	5.23	5.73	—	—	—	—	—
Portfolio Turnover (%)	80	203	91	107	185	—	—	—	—	—
Total Assets (Millions $)	134	156	159	271	226	—	—	—	—	—

PORTFOLIO (as of 9/30/96)

Portfolio Manager: Andrea Regan - 1991

Investm't Category: Government Bond
- ✔ Domestic
- Foreign
- Asset Allocation
- Index
- Sector
- State Specific

Investment Style
- Large-Cap Growth
- Mid-Cap Growth
- Small-Cap Growth
- Large-Cap Value
- Mid-Cap Value
- Small-Cap Value

Portfolio
- 1.3% cash
- 0.0% stocks
- 0.0% preferred
- 0.0% conv't/warrants
- 0.0% corp bonds
- 98.7% gov't bonds
- 0.0% muni bonds
- 0.0% other

SHAREHOLDER INFORMATION

Minimum Investment
Initial: $1,000   Subsequent: $100

Minimum IRA Investment
Initial: $500   Subsequent: $100

Maximum Fees
Load: none   12b-1: none
Other: none

Distributions
Income: monthly   Capital Gains: Dec

Exchange Options
Number Per Year: no limit   Fee: none
Telephone: yes (money market fund available)

Services
IRA, pension, auto invest

Schwab Short/Interm Tax-Free Bond (SWITX)

Tax-Exempt Bond

The Schwab Building
101 Montgomery St.
San Francisco, CA 94104
800-266-5623
www.schwab.com

PERFORMANCE

fund inception date: 4/21/93

	3yr Annual	5yr Annual	10yr Annual	Bull	Bear
Return (%)	3.8	na	na	13.5	-2.4
Differ from Category (+/-)	-0.4 blw av	na	na	-4.9 low	3.0 high

Total Risk	Standard Deviation	Category Risk	Risk Index	Avg Mat
low	2.5%	low	0.4	3.5 yrs

	1996	1995	1994	1993	1992	1991	1990	1989	1988	1987
Return (%)	3.5	9.2	-1.2	—	—	—	—	—	—	—
Differ from Category (+/-)	-0.2	-6.0	4.1	—	—	—	—	—	—	—
Return, Tax-Adjusted (%)	3.5	9.2	-1.2	—	—	—	—	—	—	—

PER SHARE DATA

	1996	1995	1994	1993	1992	1991	1990	1989	1988	1987
Dividends, Net Income ($)	0.41	0.40	0.37	—	—	—	—	—	—	—
Distrib'ns, Cap Gain ($)	0.00	0.00	0.00	—	—	—	—	—	—	—
Net Asset Value ($)	10.13	10.19	9.71	—	—	—	—	—	—	—
Expense Ratio (%)	0.49	0.49	0.48	—	—	—	—	—	—	—
Yield (%)	4.04	3.92	3.81	—	—	—	—	—	—	—
Portfolio Turnover (%)	44	35	19	—	—	—	—	—	—	—
Total Assets (Millions $)	54	52	55	—	—	—	—	—	—	—

PORTFOLIO (as of 9/30/96)

Portfolio Manager: Joanne Keighley - 1993

Investm't Category: Tax-Exempt Bond
- ✔ Domestic
- Foreign
- Asset Allocation
- Index
- Sector
- State Specific

Investment Style
- Large-Cap Growth
- Mid-Cap Growth
- Small-Cap Growth
- Large-Cap Value
- Mid-Cap Value
- Small-Cap Value

Portfolio
3.2% cash	0.0% corp bonds
0.0% stocks	0.0% gov't bonds
0.0% preferred	96.8% muni bonds
0.0% conv't/warrants	0.0% other

SHAREHOLDER INFORMATION

Minimum Investment
Initial: $1,000   Subsequent: $100

Minimum IRA Investment
Initial: na   Subsequent: na

Maximum Fees
Load: none   12b-1: none
Other: none

Distributions
Income: monthly   Capital Gains: Dec

Exchange Options
Number Per Year: no limit   Fee: none
Telephone: yes (money market fund available)

Services
auto invest

Schwartz Value (RCMFX)
Growth

3707 W. Maple Road
Bloomfield Hills, MI 48301
810-644-2701

PERFORMANCE

fund inception date: 12/31/82

	3yr Annual	5yr Annual	10yr Annual	Bull	Bear
Return (%)	8.8	13.7	12.2	38.1	-9.4
Differ from Category (+/-)	-6.9 low	-0.6 av	-1.7 blw av	-24.3 low	-2.7 blw av

Total Risk	Standard Deviation	Category Risk	Risk Index	Beta
av	8.7%	low	0.8	0.53

	1996	1995	1994	1993	1992	1991	1990	1989	1988	1987
Return (%)	18.2	16.8	-6.8	20.5	22.6	32.8	-2.8	8.4	19.8	-0.5
Differ from Category (+/-)	-1.9	-13.5	-6.5	6.5	10.8	-3.2	3.3	-17.7	1.7	-2.5
Return, Tax-Adjusted (%)	15.2	14.4	-8.8	16.4	20.7	31.2	-4.9	5.3	19.8	-0.5

PER SHARE DATA

	1996	1995	1994	1993	1992	1991	1990	1989	1988	1987
Dividends, Net Income ($)	0.00	0.00	0.00	0.00	0.00	0.00	0.00	0.00	0.00	0.00
Distrib'ns, Cap Gain ($)	2.06	1.51	1.43	2.88	1.17	0.80	1.14	1.78	0.00	0.00
Net Asset Value ($)	21.19	19.66	18.12	20.97	20.15	17.57	14.05	15.57	16.09	13.43
Expense Ratio (%)	na	2.00	2.01	1.95	1.75	1.71	2.95	1.89	na	na
Yield (%)	0.00	0.00	0.00	0.00	0.00	0.00	0.00	0.00	0.00	0.00
Portfolio Turnover (%)	na	70	78	92	70	62	76	36	na	na
Total Assets (Millions $)	55	53	45	40	26	20	17	22	20	20

PORTFOLIO (as of 6/30/96)

Portfolio Manager: George Schwartz - 1993

Investm't Category: Growth
- ✔ Domestic
- Foreign
- Asset Allocation
- Index
- Sector
- State Specific

Investment Style
Large-Cap Growth	Large-Cap Value
Mid-Cap Growth	Mid-Cap Value
Small-Cap Growth	✔ Small-Cap Value

Portfolio
4.6% cash	0.0% corp bonds
88.7% stocks	3.7% gov't bonds
0.4% preferred	0.0% muni bonds
0.0% conv't/warrants	2.6% other

SHAREHOLDER INFORMATION

Minimum Investment
Initial: $25,000   Subsequent: $1

Minimum IRA Investment
Initial: $1   Subsequent: $1

Maximum Fees
Load: none   12b-1: none
Other: none

Distributions
Income: Dec   Capital Gains: Dec

Exchange Options
Number Per Year: none   Fee: na
Telephone: na

Services
IRA

Scout Bond (UMBBX)

General Bond

Trust Operations, 10th Floor
928 Grand
Kansas City, MO 64141
816-860-3714

PERFORMANCE

fund inception date: 11/18/82

	3yr Annual	5yr Annual	10yr Annual	Bull	Bear
Return (%)	4.5	5.7	6.9	18.4	-4.4
Differ from Category (+/-)	-0.6 blw av	-0.4 blw av	-0.4 av	-1.9 blw av	-0.2 av

Total Risk	Standard Deviation	Category Risk	Risk Index	Avg Mat
low	3.4%	av	0.9	3.7 yrs

	1996	1995	1994	1993	1992	1991	1990	1989	1988	1987
Return (%)	3.5	14.0	-3.1	8.3	6.6	13.2	8.0	11.3	5.8	2.9
Differ from Category (+/-)	-0.4	-0.9	-0.8	-0.8	0.1	-1.5	0.7	-0.4	-1.8	0.6
Return, Tax-Adjusted (%)	1.3	11.6	-5.3	5.9	4.0	10.5	5.0	8.1	2.6	-1.5

PER SHARE DATA

	1996	1995	1994	1993	1992	1991	1990	1989	1988	1987
Dividends, Net Income ($)	0.62	0.62	0.63	0.63	0.71	0.71	0.78	0.82	0.80	1.24
Distrib'ns, Cap Gain ($)	0.00	0.00	0.00	0.03	0.00	0.00	0.00	0.00	0.03	0.01
Net Asset Value ($)	11.02	11.26	10.46	11.44	11.20	11.19	10.54	10.50	10.19	10.42
Expense Ratio (%)	0.86	0.86	0.87	0.87	0.87	0.87	0.88	0.88	0.87	0.87
Yield (%)	5.62	5.50	6.02	5.49	6.33	6.34	7.40	7.80	7.82	11.88
Portfolio Turnover (%)	12	2	9	19	24	21	13	8	7	12
Total Assets (Millions $)	81	78	75	89	70	55	34	30	28	28

PORTFOLIO (as of 9/30/96)

Portfolio Manager: George W. Root - 1982

Investm't Category: General Bond
- ✔ Domestic
- Foreign
- Asset Allocation
- Index
- Sector
- State Specific

Investment Style

Large-Cap Growth	Large-Cap Value
Mid-Cap Growth	Mid-Cap Value
Small-Cap Growth	Small-Cap Value

Portfolio

5.3% cash	43.1% corp bonds
0.0% stocks	51.6% gov't bonds
0.0% preferred	0.0% muni bonds
0.0% conv't/warrants	0.0% other

SHAREHOLDER INFORMATION

Minimum Investment
Initial: $1,000   Subsequent: $100

Minimum IRA Investment
Initial: $250   Subsequent: $50

Maximum Fees
Load: none   12b-1: none
Other: none

Distributions
Income: monthly   Capital Gains: Jun

Exchange Options
Number Per Year: no limit   Fee: none
Telephone: yes (money market fund available)

Services
IRA, pension, auto invest, auto withdraw

Scout Regional (UMBHX)

Growth

Trust Operations, 10th Floor
928 Grand
Kansas City, MO 64141
816-860-3714

PERFORMANCE

fund inception date: 10/31/86

	3yr Annual	5yr Annual	10yr Annual	Bull	Bear
Return (%)	10.7	9.8	6.2	37.6	-3.1
Differ from Category (+/-)	-5.0 low	-4.5 low	-7.7 low	-24.8 low	3.6 high

Total Risk	Standard Deviation	Category Risk	Risk Index	Beta
av	7.1%	low	0.7	0.49

	1996	1995	1994	1993	1992	1991	1990	1989	1988	1987
Return (%).	12.5	19.9	0.7	5.9	10.9	13.0	-1.0	3.0	-5.1	4.9
Differ from Category (+/-) .	-7.6	-10.4	1.0	-8.1	-0.9	-23.0	5.1	-23.1	-23.2	2.9
Return, Tax-Adjusted (%). .	.9.7	16.9	-0.6	5.3	10.3	11.5	-4.0	0.2	-8.0	2.4

PER SHARE DATA

	1996	1995	1994	1993	1992	1991	1990	1989	1988	1987
Dividends, Net Income ($).	0.20	0.19	0.19	0.13	0.11	0.28	0.63	0.60	0.71	0.61
Distrib'ns, Cap Gain ($) . .	.0.71	0.70	0.15	0.00	0.00	0.00	0.00	0.00	0.00	0.00
Net Asset Value ($)	10.43	10.11	9.20	9.49	9.09	8.30	7.61	8.32	8.67	9.87
Expense Ratio (%).	na	0.89	0.91	0.92	1.06	1.04	1.12	1.06	1.04	1.13
Yield (%)	1.79	1.75	2.03	1.36	1.21	3.37	8.27	7.21	8.18	6.18
Portfolio Turnover (%). . . .	na	37	27	17	7	0	0	8	12	14
Total Assets (Millions $). . .	46	35	28	25	8	1	0	2	3	5

PORTFOLIO (as of 9/30/96)

Portfolio Manager: David B. Anderson - 1986

Investm't Category: Growth
- ✔ Domestic
- Foreign
- Asset Allocation
- Index
- Sector
- State Specific

Investment Style
- Large-Cap Growth
- Mid-Cap Growth
- ✔ Small-Cap Growth
- Large-Cap Value
- Mid-Cap Value
- ✔ Small-Cap Value

Portfolio
22.2%	cash	0.0%	corp bonds
77.0%	stocks	0.0%	gov't bonds
0.0%	preferred	0.0%	muni bonds
0.8%	conv't/warrants	0.0%	other

SHAREHOLDER INFORMATION

Minimum Investment
Initial: $1,000   Subsequent: $100

Minimum IRA Investment
Initial: $250   Subsequent: $50

Maximum Fees
Load: none   12b-1: none
Other: none

Distributions
Income: Jun, Dec   Capital Gains: Jun

Exchange Options
Number Per Year: no limit   Fee: none
Telephone: yes (money market fund available)

Services
IRA, pension, auto invest, auto withdraw

Scout Stock (UMBSX)

Growth & Income

Trust Operations, 10th Floor
928 Grand
Kansas City, MO 64141
816-860-3714

PERFORMANCE

fund inception date: 11/18/82

	3yr Annual	5yr Annual	10yr Annual	Bull	Bear
Return (%)	11.3	10.3	11.0	39.1	-3.6
Differ from Category (+/-)	-4.0 blw av	-3.6 low	-1.7 blw av	-20.7 low	2.8 high

Total Risk	Standard Deviation	Category Risk	Risk Index	Beta
av	7.3%	low	0.8	0.67

	1996	1995	1994	1993	1992	1991	1990	1989	1988	1987
Return (%)	12.2	19.6	2.7	10.6	7.1	24.7	-2.4	19.0	13.8	5.5
Differ from Category (+/-)	-7.5	-10.5	4.0	-3.2	-3.6	-4.4	3.5	-4.5	-3.0	5.3
Return, Tax-Adjusted (%)	9.5	16.2	-0.5	8.3	5.5	23.2	-4.5	16.0	11.2	1.1

PER SHARE DATA

	1996	1995	1994	1993	1992	1991	1990	1989	1988	1987
Dividends, Net Income ($)	0.43	0.51	0.46	0.33	0.38	0.47	0.58	0.58	0.47	0.62
Distrib'ns, Cap Gain ($)	0.91	1.08	1.19	0.82	0.31	0.00	0.21	0.52	0.40	1.12
Net Asset Value ($)	16.97	16.34	15.01	16.24	15.77	15.40	12.76	13.87	12.62	11.87
Expense Ratio (%)	0.85	0.86	0.87	0.87	0.86	0.85	0.88	0.87	0.86	0.87
Yield (%)	2.40	2.92	2.83	1.93	2.36	3.05	4.47	4.03	3.60	4.77
Portfolio Turnover (%)	28	52	22	21	12	8	9	17	33	50
Total Assets (Millions $)	182	146	120	113	85	65	45	45	40	39

PORTFOLIO (as of 9/30/96)

Portfolio Manager: David B. Anderson - 1982

Investm't Category: Growth & Income
- ✔ Domestic
- Foreign
- Asset Allocation
- Index
- Sector
- State Specific

Investment Style
- Large-Cap Growth
- Mid-Cap Growth
- Small-Cap Growth
- ✔ Large-Cap Value
- Mid-Cap Value
- Small-Cap Value

Portfolio
- 26.2% cash
- 71.0% stocks
- 0.4% preferred
- 1.6% conv't/warrants
- 0.0% corp bonds
- 0.0% gov't bonds
- 0.0% muni bonds
- 0.8% other

SHAREHOLDER INFORMATION

Minimum Investment
Initial: $1,000   Subsequent: $100

Minimum IRA Investment
Initial: $250   Subsequent: $50

Maximum Fees
Load: none   12b-1: none
Other: none

Distributions
Income: Jun, Dec   Capital Gains: Jun

Exchange Options
Number Per Year: no limit   Fee: none
Telephone: yes (money market fund available)

Services
IRA, pension, auto invest, auto withdraw

Scout Worldwide

(UMBWX)

International Stock

Trust Operations, 10th Floor
928 Grand
Kansas City, MO 64141
816-860-3714

PERFORMANCE
fund inception date: 9/14/93

	3yr Annual	5yr Annual	10yr Annual	Bull	Bear
Return (%)	12.1	na	na	40.6	-4.0
Differ from Category (+/-)	5.8 high	na	na	16.3 high	3.2 abv av

Total Risk	Standard Deviation	Category Risk	Risk Index	Beta
av	7.8%	low	0.8	0.63

	1996	1995	1994	1993	1992	1991	1990	1989	1988	1987
Return (%).	18.3	14.6	3.8	—	—	—	—	—	—	—
Differ from Category (+/-). .	3.5	5.5	6.9	—	—	—	—	—	—	—
Return, Tax-Adjusted (%). .	17.3	13.4	2.9	—	—	—	—	—	—	—

PER SHARE DATA

	1996	1995	1994	1993	1992	1991	1990	1989	1988	1987
Dividends, Net Income ($).	0.23	0.22	0.22	—	—	—	—	—	—	—
Distrib'ns, Cap Gain ($) . .	0.10	0.12	0.02	—	—	—	—	—	—	—
Net Asset Value ($)	13.94	12.08	10.84	—	—	—	—	—	—	—
Expense Ratio (%).	na	0.85	0.85	—	—	—	—	—	—	—
Yield (%)	1.63	1.80	2.02	—	—	—	—	—	—	—
Portfolio Turnover (%). . . .	na	27	24	—	—	—	—	—	—	—
Total Assets (Millions $). . .	38	23	17	—	—	—	—	—	—	—

PORTFOLIO (as of 9/30/96)

Portfolio Manager: James L. Moffett - 1993

Investm't Category: International Stock
- ✔ Domestic
- ✔ Foreign
- Asset Allocation
- Index
- Sector
- State Specific

Investment Style
- Large-Cap Growth
- Mid-Cap Growth
- Small-Cap Growth
- Large-Cap Value
- Mid-Cap Value
- Small-Cap Value

Portfolio

20.4% cash	0.0% corp bonds
79.6% stocks	0.0% gov't bonds
0.0% preferred	0.0% muni bonds
0.0% conv't/warrants	0.0% other

SHAREHOLDER INFORMATION

Minimum Investment
Initial: $1,000   Subsequent: $100

Minimum IRA Investment
Initial: $250   Subsequent: $50

Maximum Fees
Load: none   12b-1: none
Other: none

Distributions
Income: Jun, Dec   Capital Gains: Jun

Exchange Options
Number Per Year: no limit   Fee: none
Telephone: yes (money market fund available)

Services
IRA, pension, auto invest, auto withdraw

Scudder CA Tax-Free

(SCTFX)

Tax-Exempt Bond

Two International Place
Boston, MA 02110
800-225-2470, 617-295-1000
www.funds.scudder.com

PERFORMANCE

fund inception date: 7/22/83

	3yr Annual	5yr Annual	10yr Annual	Bull	Bear
Return (%)	4.5	7.2	7.6	21.1	-7.0
Differ from Category (+/-)	0.3 abv av	0.8 high	0.9 high	2.7 abv av	-1.6 low

Total Risk	Standard Deviation	Category Risk	Risk Index	Avg Mat
blw av	6.2%	high	1.1	13.0 yrs

	1996	1995	1994	1993	1992	1991	1990	1989	1988	1987
Return (%).	3.5	18.9	-7.3	13.8	9.3	12.6	6.3	10.3	11.8	-1.2
Differ from Category (+/-) .	-0.2	3.7	-2.0	2.0	1.0	1.2	-0.1	1.3	1.8	0.2
Return, Tax-Adjusted (%). . .	3.5	18.9	-7.6	12.0	8.0	11.8	6.0	9.8	11.8	-1.9

PER SHARE DATA

	1996	1995	1994	1993	1992	1991	1990	1989	1988	1987
Dividends, Net Income ($).	0.51	0.50	0.50	0.55	0.59	0.62	0.63	0.65	0.68	0.75
Distrib'ns, Cap Gain ($) . . .	0.00	0.00	0.08	0.68	0.48	0.27	0.09	0.18	0.00	0.26
Net Asset Value ($)	10.57	10.73	9.48	10.85	10.66	10.77	10.41	10.50	10.31	9.86
Expense Ratio (%).	0.77	0.80	0.78	0.79	0.81	0.84	0.83	0.89	0.88	0.84
Yield (%)	4.82	4.65	5.23	4.77	5.29	5.61	6.00	6.08	6.59	7.41
Portfolio Turnover (%).	49	87	126	208	143	171	70	159	52	68
Total Assets (Millions $). . .	299	307	274	352	282	239	206	192	166	149

PORTFOLIO (as of 9/30/96)

Portfolio Manager: Jeremy L. Ragus, Donald Carleton - 1990

Investm't Category: Tax-Exempt Bond
✔ Domestic   Index
  Foreign   Sector
  Asset Allocation ✔ State Specific

Investment Style
  Large-Cap Growth   Large-Cap Value
  Mid-Cap Growth   Mid-Cap Value
  Small-Cap Growth   Small-Cap Value

Portfolio
  1.0% cash   0.0% corp bonds
  0.0% stocks   0.0% gov't bonds
  0.0% preferred   99.0% muni bonds
  0.0% conv't/warrants 0.0% other

SHAREHOLDER INFORMATION

Minimum Investment
Initial: $2,500   Subsequent: $100

Minimum IRA Investment
Initial: na   Subsequent: na

Maximum Fees
Load: none   12b-1: none
Other: f

Distributions
Income: monthly   Capital Gains: Nov

Exchange Options
Number Per Year: call fund   Fee: none
Telephone: yes (money market fund available)

Services
auto exchange, auto invest, auto withdraw

Scudder Development

(SCDVX)

Aggressive Growth

Two International Place
Boston, MA 02110
800-225-2470, 617-295-1000
www.funds.scudder.com

PERFORMANCE

fund inception date: 1/18/71

	3yr Annual	5yr Annual	10yr Annual	Bull	Bear
Return (%)	16.2	10.8	14.7	90.6	-18.7
Differ from Category (+/-)	0.4 av	-4.5 low	-0.3 av	19.5 abv av	-8.1 low

Total Risk	Standard Deviation	Category Risk	Risk Index	Beta
high	18.8%	high	1.3	1.18

	1996	1995	1994	1993	1992	1991	1990	1989	1988	1987
Return (%)	10.0	50.6	-5.4	8.8	-1.9	71.8	1.4	23.2	11.0	-1.5
Differ from Category (+/-)	-9.1	16.3	-5.4	-10.5	-13.6	19.7	6.8	-5.2	-5.4	0.9
Return, Tax-Adjusted (%)	6.8	46.6	-7.2	6.2	-3.3	70.5	-0.2	20.0	10.3	-4.1

PER SHARE DATA

	1996	1995	1994	1993	1992	1991	1990	1989	1988	1987
Dividends, Net Income ($)	0.00	0.00	0.00	0.00	0.00	0.00	0.00	0.00	0.00	0.00
Distrib'ns, Cap Gain ($)	4.48	4.20	2.12	3.07	1.70	0.96	1.23	2.27	0.42	1.89
Net Asset Value ($)	39.79	40.12	29.54	33.51	33.62	36.23	21.73	22.69	20.32	18.69
Expense Ratio (%)	1.24	1.32	1.27	1.30	1.30	1.29	1.34	1.32	1.30	1.27
Yield (%)	0.00	0.00	0.00	0.00	0.00	0.00	0.00	0.00	0.00	0.00
Portfolio Turnover (%)	58	41	48	49	54	71	40	32	39	24
Total Assets (Millions $)	979	877	601	765	923	892	310	282	292	270

PORTFOLIO (as of 9/30/96)

Portfolio Manager: Roy C. McKay, Peter Chin - 1988

Investm't Category: Aggressive Growth
- ✔ Domestic
- ✔ Foreign
- Asset Allocation
- Index
- Sector
- State Specific

Investment Style
- Large-Cap Growth
- Mid-Cap Growth
- ✔ Small-Cap Growth
- Large-Cap Value
- Mid-Cap Value
- Small-Cap Value

Portfolio
2.2% cash	0.0% corp bonds
97.0% stocks	0.0% gov't bonds
0.4% preferred	0.0% muni bonds
0.4% conv't/warrants	0.0% other

SHAREHOLDER INFORMATION

Minimum Investment
Initial: $2,500   Subsequent: $100

Minimum IRA Investment
Initial: $1,000   Subsequent: $50

Maximum Fees
Load: none   12b-1: none
Other: *f*

Distributions
Income: Dec   Capital Gains: Dec

Exchange Options
Number Per Year: call fund   Fee: none
Telephone: yes (money market fund available)

Services
IRA, pension, auto exchange, auto invest, auto withdraw

Scudder Emerging Markets Income (SCEMX)

International Bond

Two International Place
Boston, MA 02110
800-225-2470, 617-295-1000
www.funds.scudder.com

PERFORMANCE

fund inception date: 12/31/93

	3yr Annual	5yr Annual	10yr Annual	Bull	Bear
Return (%)	13.9	na	na	65.2	-11.1
Differ from Category (+/-)	7.9 high	na	na	34.0 high	-1.6 av

Total Risk	Standard Deviation	Category Risk	Risk Index	Avg Mat
high	13.5%	high	1.9	15.5 yrs

	1996	1995	1994	1993	1992	1991	1990	1989	1988	1987
Return (%)	34.5	19.4	-8.1	—	—	—	—	—	—	—
Differ from Category (+/-)	23.2	3.4	-0.5	—	—	—	—	—	—	—
Return, Tax-Adjusted (%)	27.1	15.0	-10.7	—	—	—	—	—	—	—

PER SHARE DATA

	1996	1995	1994	1993	1992	1991	1990	1989	1988	1987
Dividends, Net Income ($)	1.20	1.13	0.76	—	—	—	—	—	—	—
Distrib'ns, Cap Gain ($)	1.18	0.00	0.00	—	—	—	—	—	—	—
Net Asset Value ($)	12.28	11.00	10.27	—	—	—	—	—	—	—
Expense Ratio (%)	na	1.50	1.50	—	—	—	—	—	—	—
Yield (%)	8.91	10.27	7.40	—	—	—	—	—	—	—
Portfolio Turnover (%)	na	302	180	—	—	—	—	—	—	—
Total Assets (Millions $)	323	188	89	—	—	—	—	—	—	—

PORTFOLIO (as of 9/30/96)

Portfolio Manager: Susan E. Gray, M. Isabel Saltzman - 1996

Investm't Category: International Bond
- Domestic
- ✔ Foreign
- Asset Allocation
- Index
- Sector
- State Specific

Investment Style
Large-Cap Growth   Large-Cap Value
Mid-Cap Growth   Mid-Cap Value
Small-Cap Growth   Small-Cap Value

Portfolio
2.0% cash	0.0% corp bonds
0.0% stocks	3.0% gov't bonds
0.0% preferred	0.0% muni bonds
0.0% conv't/warrants	95.0% other

SHAREHOLDER INFORMATION

Minimum Investment
Initial: $2,500   Subsequent: $100

Minimum IRA Investment
Initial: $1,000   Subsequent: $50

Maximum Fees
Load: none   12b-1: none
Other: f

Distributions
Income: quarterly   Capital Gains: Dec

Exchange Options
Number Per Year: call fund   Fee: none
Telephone: yes (money market fund available)

Services
IRA, pension, auto exchange, auto invest, auto withdraw

Scudder Equity Trust: Capital Growth (SCDUX)

Growth

Two International Place
Boston, MA 02110
800-225-2470, 617-295-1000
www.funds.scudder.com

PERFORMANCE

fund inception date: 6/26/56

	3yr Annual	5yr Annual	10yr Annual	Bull	Bear
Return (%)	12.3	12.7	14.0	62.3	-12.4
Differ from Category (+/-)	-3.4 blw av	-1.6 blw av	0.1 av	-0.1 av	-5.7 low

Total Risk	Standard Deviation		Category Risk	Risk Index		Beta
abv av	10.5%		av	1.0		0.97

	1996	1995	1994	1993	1992	1991	1990	1989	1988	1987
Return (%)	19.5	31.6	-9.9	20.0	7.0	42.9	-17.0	33.8	29.7	-0.8
Differ from Category (+/-)	-0.6	1.3	-9.6	6.0	-4.8	6.9	-10.9	7.7	11.6	-2.8
Return, Tax-Adjusted (%)	15.8	26.1	-10.9	16.3	5.0	40.4	-19.7	30.8	27.8	-5.2

PER SHARE DATA

	1996	1995	1994	1993	1992	1991	1990	1989	1988	1987
Dividends, Net Income ($)	0.16	0.08	0.00	0.00	0.10	0.22	0.37	0.16	0.07	0.19
Distrib'ns, Cap Gain ($)	2.48	3.50	0.72	2.62	1.25	0.98	1.35	1.45	0.78	2.13
Net Asset Value ($)	22.11	20.67	18.43	21.26	19.91	19.86	14.81	19.91	16.13	13.14
Expense Ratio (%)	na	0.98	0.97	0.96	0.98	1.04	0.94	0.88	0.95	0.88
Yield (%)	0.65	0.33	0.00	0.00	0.47	1.05	2.28	0.74	0.41	1.24
Portfolio Turnover (%)	na	153	75	92	92	93	88	56	49	58
Total Assets (Millions $)	1,810	1,565	1,291	1,427	1,244	1,152	806	993	499	350

PORTFOLIO (as of 9/30/96)

Portfolio Manager: Kathleen Millard, Lois Friedman - 1995

Investm't Category: Growth
- ✔ Domestic
- ✔ Foreign
- Asset Allocation
- Index
- Sector
- State Specific

Investment Style
- ✔ Large-Cap Growth
- Mid-Cap Growth
- Small-Cap Growth
- Large-Cap Value
- Mid-Cap Value
- Small-Cap Value

Portfolio
1.6% cash	0.0% corp bonds
97.9% stocks	0.0% gov't bonds
0.5% preferred	0.0% muni bonds
0.0% conv't/warrants	0.0% other

SHAREHOLDER INFORMATION

Minimum Investment
Initial: $2,500   Subsequent: $100

Minimum IRA Investment
Initial: $1,000   Subsequent: $50

Maximum Fees
Load: none   12b-1: none
Other: *f*

Distributions
Income: Dec   Capital Gains: Dec

Exchange Options
Number Per Year: call fund   Fee: none
Telephone: yes (money market fund available)

Services
IRA, pension, auto exchange, auto invest, auto withdraw

Scudder Equity Trust: Value (SCVAX)

Growth

Two International Place
Boston, MA 02110
800-225-2470, 617-295-1000
www.funds.scudder.com

PERFORMANCE

fund inception date: 12/31/92

	3yr Annual	5yr Annual	10yr Annual	Bull	Bear
Return (%)	17.6	na	na	68.0	-5.4
Differ from Category (+/-)	1.9 abv av	na	na	5.6 abv av	1.3 abv av

Total Risk	Standard Deviation	Category Risk	Risk Index	Beta
av	9.0%	blw av	0.9	0.83

	1996	1995	1994	1993	1992	1991	1990	1989	1988	1987
Return (%).	22.9	30.1	1.6	11.6	—	—	—	—	—	—
Differ from Category (+/-) . .	2.8	-0.2	1.9	-2.4	—	—	—	—	—	—
Return, Tax-Adjusted (%). .	20.0	27.9	0.9	10.2	—	—	—	—	—	—

PER SHARE DATA

	1996	1995	1994	1993	1992	1991	1990	1989	1988	1987
Dividends, Net Income ($).	0.07	0.04	0.11	0.11	—	—	—	—	—	—
Distrib'ns, Cap Gain ($) . . .	1.48	0.91	0.12	0.43	—	—	—	—	—	—
Net Asset Value ($)	17.81	15.73	12.82	12.85	—	—	—	—	—	—
Expense Ratio (%).	na	1.25	1.25	1.25	—	—	—	—	—	—
Yield (%)	0.36	0.24	0.85	0.82	—	—	—	—	—	—
Portfolio Turnover (%).	na	98	74	60	—	—	—	—	—	—
Total Assets (Millions $). . .	103	73	34	33	—	—	—	—	—	—

PORTFOLIO (as of 9/30/96)

Portfolio Manager: Donald E. Hall, William Wallace - 1992

Investm't Category: Growth
- ✔ Domestic
- Index
- ✔ Foreign
- Sector
- Asset Allocation
- State Specific

Investment Style
Large-Cap Growth	✔ Large-Cap Value
Mid-Cap Growth	✔ Mid-Cap Value
Small-Cap Growth	Small-Cap Value

Portfolio
7.4% cash	0.0% corp bonds
92.4% stocks	0.0% gov't bonds
0.0% preferred	0.0% muni bonds
0.2% conv't/warrants	0.0% other

SHAREHOLDER INFORMATION

Minimum Investment
Initial: $2,500   Subsequent: $100

Minimum IRA Investment
Initial: $1,000   Subsequent: $50

Maximum Fees
Load: none   12b-1: none
Other: *f*

Distributions
Income: Dec   Capital Gains: Dec

Exchange Options
Number Per Year: call fund   Fee: none
Telephone: yes (money market fund available)

Services
IRA, pension, auto exchange, auto invest, auto withdraw

Scudder GNMA (SGMSX)

Mortgage-Backed Bond

Two International Place
Boston, MA 02110
800-225-2470, 617-295-1000
www.funds.scudder.com

PERFORMANCE

fund inception date: 7/5/85

	3yr Annual	5yr Annual	10yr Annual	Bull	Bear
Return (%)	5.5	5.9	7.6	22.9	-5.7
Differ from Category (+/-)	-0.1 av	-0.1 blw av	-0.1 av	1.8 abv av	-2.1 low

Total Risk	Standard Deviation	Category Risk	Risk Index	Avg Mat
low	4.3%	high	1.2	8.2 yrs

	1996	1995	1994	1993	1992	1991	1990	1989	1988	1987
Return (%)	4.2	16.5	-3.2	5.9	6.9	15.0	10.1	12.8	6.8	2.2
Differ from Category (+/-)	-0.2	1.8	-1.5	-1.0	0.7	0.6	0.3	0.2	-0.6	0.2
Return, Tax-Adjusted (%)	1.7	13.7	-5.7	2.8	3.6	11.7	6.7	9.2	3.2	-1.4

PER SHARE DATA

	1996	1995	1994	1993	1992	1991	1990	1989	1988	1987
Dividends, Net Income ($)	0.92	0.94	0.93	1.20	1.29	1.21	1.23	1.26	1.30	1.38
Distrib'ns, Cap Gain ($)	0.00	0.00	0.00	0.00	0.00	0.00	0.00	0.00	0.00	0.00
Net Asset Value ($)	14.59	14.92	13.66	15.06	15.36	15.62	14.72	14.56	14.09	14.43
Expense Ratio (%)	0.94	0.96	0.95	0.93	0.99	1.04	1.05	1.04	1.04	1.05
Yield (%)	6.30	6.30	6.80	7.96	8.39	7.74	8.35	8.65	9.22	9.56
Portfolio Turnover (%)	157	112	220	87	147	52	71	128	92	59
Total Assets (Millions $)	413	436	417	610	511	328	252	259	247	234

PORTFOLIO (as of 9/30/96)

Portfolio Manager: David H. Glen, Mark
Boyadjian - 1985

Investm't Category: Mortgage-Backed Bond
✔ Domestic   Index
   Foreign   Sector
   Asset Allocation   State Specific

Investment Style
Large-Cap Growth   Large-Cap Value
Mid-Cap Growth   Mid-Cap Value
Small-Cap Growth   Small-Cap Value

Portfolio
7.3%	cash	0.0%	corp bonds
0.0%	stocks	92.8%	gov't bonds
0.0%	preferred	0.0%	muni bonds
0.0%	conv't/warrants	0.0%	other

SHAREHOLDER INFORMATION

Minimum Investment
Initial: $2,500   Subsequent: $100

Minimum IRA Investment
Initial: $1,000   Subsequent: $50

Maximum Fees
Load: none   12b-1: none
Other: *f*

Distributions
Income: monthly   Capital Gains: Nov

Exchange Options
Number Per Year: call fund   Fee: none
Telephone: yes (money market fund available)

Services
IRA, pension, auto exchange, auto invest, auto
withdraw

Scudder Global (SCOBX)
International Stock

Two International Place
Boston, MA 02110
800-225-2470, 617-295-1000
www.funds.scudder.com

PERFORMANCE

fund inception date: 7/23/86

	3yr Annual	5yr Annual	10yr Annual	Bull	Bear
Return (%)	9.4	12.4	12.7	35.7	-7.7
Differ from Category (+/-)	3.1 abv av	2.4 abv av	4.1 high	11.4 abv av	-0.5 av

Total Risk	Standard Deviation	Category Risk	Risk Index	Beta
av	8.9%	low	0.9	0.73

	1996	1995	1994	1993	1992	1991	1990	1989	1988	1987
Return (%).	13.6	20.5	-4.3	31.1	4.4	17.0	-6.5	37.4	19.1	3.0
Differ from Category (+/-) .	-1.2	11.4	-1.2	-8.5	8.2	3.8	3.6	14.8	4.2	-9.2
Return, Tax-Adjusted (%). .	11.6	19.0	-4.9	30.2	3.5	15.1	-8.6	35.8	18.4	2.2

PER SHARE DATA

	1996	1995	1994	1993	1992	1991	1990	1989	1988	1987
Dividends, Net Income ($).	0.28	0.25	0.11	0.23	0.16	0.31	0.62	0.11	0.22	0.06
Distrib'ns, Cap Gain ($) . . .	1.53	0.84	0.34	0.26	0.34	0.66	0.57	0.64	0.00	0.24
Net Asset Value ($)	28.80	27.01	23.33	24.80	19.31	18.96	17.06	19.48	14.74	12.56
Expense Ratio (%).	1.34	1.38	1.45	1.48	1.59	1.70	1.81	1.98	1.71	1.84
Yield (%)	0.92	0.89	0.46	0.91	0.81	1.58	3.51	0.54	1.49	0.46
Portfolio Turnover (%). . . .	29	44	59	64	45	85	38	31	54	32
Total Assets (Millions $).	1,413	1,271	1,117	963	400	298	237	145	74	72

PORTFOLIO (as of 9/30/96)

Portfolio Manager: Holzer, Bratt, Ho - 1986

Investm't Category: International Stock

✔ Domestic	Index
✔ Foreign	Sector
Asset Allocation	State Specific

Investment Style

Large-Cap Growth	Large-Cap Value
Mid-Cap Growth	Mid-Cap Value
Small-Cap Growth	Small-Cap Value

Portfolio

9.2% cash	0.0% corp bonds
86.0% stocks	0.0% gov't bonds
4.9% preferred	0.0% muni bonds
0.0% conv't/warrants	0.0% other

SHAREHOLDER INFORMATION

Minimum Investment
Initial: $2,500   Subsequent: $100

Minimum IRA Investment
Initial: $1,000   Subsequent: $50

Maximum Fees
Load: none   12b-1: none
Other: *f*

Distributions
Income: Dec   Capital Gains: Dec

Exchange Options
Number Per Year: call fund   Fee: none
Telephone: yes (money market fund available)

Services
IRA, pension, auto exchange, auto invest, auto withdraw

Scudder Global Bond

(SSTGX)

International Bond

Two International Place
Boston, MA 02110
800-225-2470, 617-295-1000
www.funds.scudder.com

PERFORMANCE

fund inception date: 3/1/91

	3yr Annual	5yr Annual	10yr Annual	Bull	Bear
Return (%)	3.1	4.3	na	11.3	-1.4
Differ from Category (+/-)	-2.9 blw av	-2.3 blw av	na	-19.9 low	8.1 high

Total Risk	Standard Deviation	Category Risk	Risk Index	Avg Mat
low	3.0%	low	0.4	9.9 yrs

	1996	1995	1994	1993	1992	1991	1990	1989	1988	1987
Return (%)	3.1	7.7	-1.2	6.7	5.4	—	—	—	—	—
Differ from Category (+/-)	-8.2	-8.3	6.4	-8.6	0.2	—	—	—	—	—
Return, Tax-Adjusted (%)	0.7	4.7	-4.2	3.5	1.9	—	—	—	—	—

PER SHARE DATA

	1996	1995	1994	1993	1992	1991	1990	1989	1988	1987
Dividends, Net Income ($)	0.63	0.79	0.86	0.93	1.05	—	—	—	—	—
Distrib'ns, Cap Gain ($)	0.00	0.00	0.00	0.00	0.02	—	—	—	—	—
Net Asset Value ($)	10.20	10.53	10.54	11.53	11.70	—	—	—	—	—
Expense Ratio (%)	na	1.00	1.00	1.00	1.00	—	—	—	—	—
Yield (%)	6.17	7.50	8.15	8.06	8.95	—	—	—	—	—
Portfolio Turnover (%)	na	182	272	259	274	—	—	—	—	—
Total Assets (Millions $)	213	334	496	939	1,109	—	—	—	—	—

PORTFOLIO (as of 9/30/96)

Portfolio Manager: Adam Greshin, Margaret Hadzima - 1995

Investm't Category: International Bond
✔ Domestic   Index
✔ Foreign   Sector
    Asset Allocation   State Specific

Investment Style
Large-Cap Growth   Large-Cap Value
Mid-Cap Growth   Mid-Cap Value
Small-Cap Growth   Small-Cap Value

Portfolio
4.0% cash	9.0% corp bonds
0.0% stocks	14.0% gov't bonds
0.0% preferred	0.0% muni bonds
0.0% conv't/warrants	73.0% other

SHAREHOLDER INFORMATION

Minimum Investment
Initial: $2,500   Subsequent: $100

Minimum IRA Investment
Initial: $1,000   Subsequent: $50

Maximum Fees
Load: none   12b-1: none
Other: f

Distributions
Income: monthly   Capital Gains: Dec

Exchange Options
Number Per Year: call fund   Fee: none
Telephone: yes (money market fund available)

Services
IRA, pension, auto exchange, auto invest, auto withdraw

Scudder Global Discovery

(SGSCX)

International Stock

Two International Place
Boston, MA 02110
800-225-2470, 617-295-1000
www.funds.scudder.com

PERFORMANCE

fund inception date: 9/3/91

	3yr Annual	5yr Annual	10yr Annual	Bull	Bear
Return (%)	9.7	12.7	na	40.5	-7.8
Differ from Category (+/-)	3.4 abv av	2.7 high	na	16.2 high	-0.6 blw av

Total Risk	Standard Deviation	Category Risk	Risk Index	Beta
abv av	10.6%	av	1.0	0.68

	1996	1995	1994	1993	1992	1991	1990	1989	1988	1987
Return (%)	21.4	17.8	-7.7	38.1	-0.1	—	—	—	—	—
Differ from Category (+/-)	6.6	8.7	-4.6	-1.5	3.7	—	—	—	—	—
Return, Tax-Adjusted (%)	19.7	16.4	-7.9	37.2	-0.6	—	—	—	—	—

PER SHARE DATA

	1996	1995	1994	1993	1992	1991	1990	1989	1988	1987
Dividends, Net Income ($)	0.13	0.20	0.00	0.17	0.07	—	—	—	—	—
Distrib'ns, Cap Gain ($)	0.86	0.43	0.08	0.15	0.12	—	—	—	—	—
Net Asset Value ($)	19.95	17.25	15.18	16.53	12.20	—	—	—	—	—
Expense Ratio (%)	na	1.69	1.70	1.50	1.50	—	—	—	—	—
Yield (%)	0.62	1.13	0.00	1.01	0.56	—	—	—	—	—
Portfolio Turnover (%)	na	43	45	54	23	—	—	—	—	—
Total Assets (Millions $)	361	253	235	219	58	—	—	—	—	—

PORTFOLIO (as of 9/30/96)

Portfolio Manager: Moran, Allan, Hodges, Gregory - 1991

Investm't Category: International Stock
- ✔ Domestic
- ✔ Foreign
-   Asset Allocation
-   Index
-   Sector
-   State Specific

Investment Style
- Large-Cap Growth
- Mid-Cap Growth
- Small-Cap Growth
- Large-Cap Value
- Mid-Cap Value
- Small-Cap Value

Portfolio
9.2% cash	0.0% corp bonds
86.0% stocks	0.0% gov't bonds
4.9% preferred	0.0% muni bonds
0.0% conv't/warrants	0.0% other

SHAREHOLDER INFORMATION

Minimum Investment
Initial: $2,500   Subsequent: $100

Minimum IRA Investment
Initial: $1,000   Subsequent: $50

Maximum Fees
Load: none   12b-1: none
Other: f

Distributions
Income: Dec   Capital Gains: Dec

Exchange Options
Number Per Year: call fund   Fee: none
Telephone: yes (money market fund available)

Services
IRA, pension, auto exchange, auto invest, auto withdraw

Scudder Gold (SCGDX)

Gold

Two International Place
Boston, MA 02110
800-225-2470, 617-295-1000
www.funds.scudder.com

PERFORMANCE

fund inception date: 8/12/88

	3yr Annual	5yr Annual	10yr Annual	Bull	Bear
Return (%)	11.4	14.9	na	46.2	-8.9
Differ from Category (+/-)	11.1 high	5.3 high	na	31.3 high	1.3 abv av

Total Risk	Standard Deviation	Category Risk	Risk Index	Beta
high	23.8%	blw av	1.0	0.55

	1996	1995	1994	1993	1992	1991	1990	1989	1988	1987
Return (%)	32.1	13.1	-7.4	59.3	-9.1	-7.0	-16.7	10.6	—	—
Differ from Category (+/-)	20.9	8.1	4.7	-28.5	6.2	-2.4	5.6	-13.8	—	—
Return, Tax-Adjusted (%)	23.2	7.9	-9.1	58.1	-9.1	-7.0	-16.7	10.2	—	—

PER SHARE DATA

	1996	1995	1994	1993	1992	1991	1990	1989	1988	1987
Dividends, Net Income ($)	2.39	1.08	0.24	0.24	0.00	0.00	0.00	0.06	—	—
Distrib'ns, Cap Gain ($)	0.26	0.63	0.46	0.00	0.00	0.00	0.00	0.04	—	—
Net Asset Value ($)	12.68	11.53	11.71	13.35	8.55	9.40	10.10	12.12	—	—
Expense Ratio (%)	1.50	1.65	1.69	2.17	2.54	2.54	2.60	3.00	—	—
Yield (%)	na	na	1.97	1.79	0.00	0.00	0.00	0.49	—	—
Portfolio Turnover (%)	29	42	50	59	58	71	81	35	—	—
Total Assets (Millions $)	196	117	129	110	31	22	29	22	—	—

PORTFOLIO (as of 9/30/96)

Portfolio Manager: Douglas D. Donald, Clay L. Hoes - 1988

Investm't Category: Gold
- ✔ Domestic
- ✔ Foreign
- Asset Allocation
- Index
- ✔ Sector
- State Specific

Investment Style
- Large-Cap Growth
- Mid-Cap Growth
- Small-Cap Growth
- Large-Cap Value
- Mid-Cap Value
- Small-Cap Value

Portfolio
1.6% cash	0.0% corp bonds
75.8% stocks	0.0% gov't bonds
0.0% preferred	0.0% muni bonds
3.1% conv't/warrants	19.5% other

SHAREHOLDER INFORMATION

Minimum Investment
Initial: $2,500   Subsequent: $100

Minimum IRA Investment
Initial: $1,000   Subsequent: $50

Maximum Fees
Load: none   12b-1: none
Other: *f*

Distributions
Income: Dec   Capital Gains: Dec

Exchange Options
Number Per Year: call fund   Fee: none
Telephone: yes (money market fund available)

Services
IRA, pension, auto exchange, auto invest, auto withdraw

Scudder Greater Europe Growth (SCGEX)

International Stock

Two International Place
Boston, MA 02110
800-225-2470, 617-295-1000
www.funds.scudder.com

PERFORMANCE

fund inception date: 10/10/94

	3yr Annual	5yr Annual	10yr Annual	Bull	Bear
Return (%)	na	na	na	na	na
Differ from Category (+/-)	na	na	na	na	na

Total Risk	Standard Deviation	Category Risk	Risk Index	Beta
na	na	na	na	na

	1996	1995	1994	1993	1992	1991	1990	1989	1988	1987
Return (%)	30.8	23.6	—	—	—	—	—	—	—	—
Differ from Category (+/-)	16.0	14.5	—	—	—	—	—	—	—	—
Return, Tax-Adjusted (%)	30.3	22.9	—	—	—	—	—	—	—	—

PER SHARE DATA

	1996	1995	1994	1993	1992	1991	1990	1989	1988	1987
Dividends, Net Income ($)	0.06	0.10	—	—	—	—	—	—	—	—
Distrib'ns, Cap Gain ($)	0.14	0.14	—	—	—	—	—	—	—	—
Net Asset Value ($)	18.08	13.97	—	—	—	—	—	—	—	—
Expense Ratio (%)	na	1.50	—	—	—	—	—	—	—	—
Yield (%)	0.32	0.70	—	—	—	—	—	—	—	—
Portfolio Turnover (%)	na	27	—	—	—	—	—	—	—	—
Total Assets (Millions $)	145	43	—	—	—	—	—	—	—	—

PORTFOLIO (as of 9/30/96)

Portfolio Manager: Franklin, Bratt, Gregory - 1994

Investm't Category: International Stock
- Domestic
- ✔ Foreign
- Asset Allocation
- Index
- Sector
- State Specific

Investment Style
- Large-Cap Growth
- Mid-Cap Growth
- Small-Cap Growth
- Large-Cap Value
- Mid-Cap Value
- Small-Cap Value

Portfolio
6.2% cash	0.0% corp bonds
91.6% stocks	0.0% gov't bonds
2.2% preferred	0.0% muni bonds
0.0% conv't/warrants	0.0% other

SHAREHOLDER INFORMATION

Minimum Investment
Initial: $2,500   Subsequent: $100

Minimum IRA Investment
Initial: $1,000   Subsequent: $50

Maximum Fees
Load: none   12b-1: none
Other: f

Distributions
Income: Dec   Capital Gains: Dec

Exchange Options
Number Per Year: call fund   Fee: none
Telephone: yes (money market fund available)

Services
IRA, pension, auto invest, auto withdraw

Scudder Growth & Income (SCDGX)

Growth & Income

Two International Place
Boston, MA 02110
800-225-2470, 617-295-1000
www.funds.scudder.com

PERFORMANCE

fund inception date: 11/13/84

	3yr Annual	5yr Annual	10yr Annual	Bull	Bear
Return (%)	18.0	15.8	14.3	64.9	-4.5
Differ from Category (+/-)	2.7 abv av	1.9 abv av	1.6 abv av	5.1 av	1.9 high

Total Risk	Standard Deviation	Category Risk	Risk Index	Beta
av	9.0%	blw av	1.0	0.87

	1996	1995	1994	1993	1992	1991	1990	1989	1988	1987
Return (%)	22.1	31.1	2.5	15.5	9.5	28.1	-2.4	26.4	11.9	3.5
Differ from Category (+/-)	2.4	1.0	3.8	1.7	-1.2	-1.0	3.5	2.9	-4.9	3.3
Return, Tax-Adjusted (%)	19.8	28.9	-0.2	12.6	7.3	26.3	-5.0	20.5	10.0	-3.2

PER SHARE DATA

	1996	1995	1994	1993	1992	1991	1990	1989	1988	1987
Dividends, Net Income ($)	0.56	0.55	0.50	0.45	0.52	0.55	0.67	0.69	0.59	0.67
Distrib'ns, Cap Gain ($)	0.86	0.48	0.90	1.01	0.50	0.00	0.34	1.77	0.00	2.64
Net Asset Value ($)	23.23	20.23	16.27	17.24	16.20	15.76	12.77	14.14	13.17	12.31
Expense Ratio (%)	na	0.80	0.86	0.86	0.94	0.97	0.95	0.87	0.92	0.89
Yield (%)	2.32	2.65	2.91	2.46	3.11	3.48	5.11	4.33	4.47	4.48
Portfolio Turnover (%)	na	26	42	36	28	45	65	77	48	60
Total Assets (Millions $)	4,218	3,067	1,994	1,631	1,168	723	490	490	400	329

PORTFOLIO (as of 9/30/96)

Portfolio Manager: Robert T. Hoffman - 1991

Investm't Category: Growth & Income
- ✔ Domestic
- ✔ Foreign
-   Asset Allocation
-   Index
-   Sector
-   State Specific

Investment Style
- Large-Cap Growth
- Mid-Cap Growth
- Small-Cap Growth
- ✔ Large-Cap Value
- Mid-Cap Value
- Small-Cap Value

Portfolio
- 3.6% cash
- 93.4% stocks
- 2.8% preferred
- 0.0% conv't/warrants
- 0.2% corp bonds
- 0.0% gov't bonds
- 0.0% muni bonds
- 0.0% other

SHAREHOLDER INFORMATION

Minimum Investment
Initial: $2,500   Subsequent: $100

Minimum IRA Investment
Initial: $1,000   Subsequent: $50

Maximum Fees
Load: none   12b-1: none
Other: *f*

Distributions
Income: quarterly   Capital Gains: Dec

Exchange Options
Number Per Year: call fund   Fee: none
Telephone: yes (money market fund available)

Services
IRA, pension, auto exchange, auto invest, auto withdraw

Scudder Int'l (SCINX)

International Stock

Two International Place
Boston, MA 02110
800-225-2470, 617-295-1000
www.funds.scudder.com

PERFORMANCE

fund inception date: 6/14/54

	3yr Annual	5yr Annual	10yr Annual	Bull	Bear
Return (%)	7.6	10.6	9.8	25.7	-5.3
Differ from Category (+/-)	1.3 av	0.6 av	1.2 abv av	1.4 av	1.9 abv av

Total Risk	Standard Deviation	Category Risk	Risk Index	Beta
abv av	9.9%	blw av	1.0	0.71

	1996	1995	1994	1993	1992	1991	1990	1989	1988	1987
Return (%)...............	14.5	12.2	-3.0	36.5	-2.7	11.7	-9.0	27.0	18.8	0.8
Differ from Category (+/-) .	-0.3	3.1	0.1	-3.1	1.1	-1.5	1.1	4.4	3.9	-11.4
Return, Tax-Adjusted (%). .	12.5	10.9	-4.6	35.7	-4.4	11.3	-11.3	23.8	15.8	-6.7

PER SHARE DATA

	1996	1995	1994	1993	1992	1991	1990	1989	1988	1987
Dividends, Net Income ($).	1.28	0.40	0.00	0.39	0.83	0.00	0.74	0.43	0.18	0.99
Distrib'ns, Cap Gain ($) ...	1.19	1.18	2.42	0.38	0.86	0.40	1.98	3.15	2.99	9.21
Net Asset Value ($)	47.56	43.72	40.37	44.10	32.93	35.53	32.15	38.20	33.10	30.60
Expense Ratio (%)........	1.14	1.19	1.21	1.26	1.30	1.24	1.18	1.22	1.21	1.09
Yield (%)	2.62	0.89	0.00	0.87	2.45	0.00	2.16	1.03	0.49	2.48
Portfolio Turnover (%).....	45	46	39	29	50	70	49	48	55	67
Total Assets (Millions $). .	2,637	2,352	2,271	2,069	1,048	965	802	767	537	471

PORTFOLIO (as of 9/30/96)

Portfolio Manager: Carol L. Franklin - 1989

Investm't Category: International Stock
Domestic	Index
✔ Foreign	Sector
Asset Allocation	State Specific

Investment Style
Large-Cap Growth	Large-Cap Value
Mid-Cap Growth	Mid-Cap Value
Small-Cap Growth	Small-Cap Value

Portfolio
4.2% cash	0.0% corp bonds
91.7% stocks	0.0% gov't bonds
2.6% preferred	0.0% muni bonds
1.5% conv't/warrants	0.0% other

SHAREHOLDER INFORMATION

Minimum Investment
Initial: $2,500   Subsequent: $100

Minimum IRA Investment
Initial: $1,000   Subsequent: $50

Maximum Fees
Load: none   12b-1: none
Other: f

Distributions
Income: Dec   Capital Gains: Dec

Exchange Options
Number Per Year: call fund   Fee: none
Telephone: yes (money market fund available)

Services
IRA, pension, auto exchange, auto invest, auto withdraw

Scudder Int'l Bond (SCIBX)

International Bond

Two International Place
Boston, MA 02110
800-225-2470, 617-295-1000
www.funds.scudder.com

PERFORMANCE

fund inception date: 7/6/88

	3yr Annual	5yr Annual	10yr Annual	Bull	Bear
Return (%)	0.8	5.0	na	11.6	-9.2
Differ from Category (+/-)	-5.2 low	-1.6 blw av	na	-19.6 low	0.3 av

Total Risk	Standard Deviation	Category Risk	Risk Index	Avg Mat
blw av	4.8%	blw av	0.7	9.0 yrs

	1996	1995	1994	1993	1992	1991	1990	1989	1988	1987
Return (%)	3.5	8.5	-8.7	15.8	7.6	22.2	21.1	7.2	—	—
Differ from Category (+/-)	-7.8	-7.5	-1.1	0.5	2.4	7.2	10.6	4.0	—	—
Return, Tax-Adjusted (%)	1.2	5.5	-11.6	12.1	3.2	16.8	16.6	3.8	—	—

PER SHARE DATA

	1996	1995	1994	1993	1992	1991	1990	1989	1988	1987
Dividends, Net Income ($)	0.64	0.84	0.98	0.92	1.06	1.16	1.15	1.04	—	—
Distrib'ns, Cap Gain ($)	0.00	0.00	0.00	0.38	0.61	0.81	0.28	0.00	—	—
Net Asset Value ($)	11.20	11.46	11.38	13.50	12.83	13.53	12.90	11.97	—	—
Expense Ratio (%)	na	1.30	1.27	1.25	1.25	1.25	1.25	1.00	—	—
Yield (%)	5.71	7.32	8.61	6.62	7.88	8.08	8.72	8.68	—	—
Portfolio Turnover (%)	na	318	232	249	148	260	216	104	—	—
Total Assets (Millions $)	397	736	1,086	1,364	741	296	190	31	—	—

PORTFOLIO (as of 9/30/96)

Portfolio Manager: Adam Greshin, C. Steward - 1995

Investm't Category: International Bond

✔ Domestic   Index
✔ Foreign   Sector
  Asset Allocation   State Specific

Investment Style

Large-Cap Growth   Large-Cap Value
Mid-Cap Growth   Mid-Cap Value
Small-Cap Growth   Small-Cap Value

Portfolio

3.0% cash	0.0% corp bonds
0.0% stocks	1.0% gov't bonds
0.0% preferred	0.0% muni bonds
0.0% conv't/warrants	96.0% other

SHAREHOLDER INFORMATION

Minimum Investment
Initial: $2,500   Subsequent: $100

Minimum IRA Investment
Initial: $1,000   Subsequent: $50

Maximum Fees
Load: none   12b-1: none
Other: *f*

Distributions
Income: monthly   Capital Gains: Nov

Exchange Options
Number Per Year: call fund   Fee: none
Telephone: yes (money market fund available)

Services
IRA, pension, auto exchange, auto invest, auto withdraw

Scudder Int'l: Latin America (SLAFX)

Two International Place
Boston, MA 02110
800-225-2470, 617-295-1000
www.funds.scudder.com

International Stock

PERFORMANCE

fund inception date: 12/8/92

	3yr Annual	5yr Annual	10yr Annual	Bull	Bear
Return (%)	1.5	na	na	14.2	-18.4
Differ from Category (+/-)	-4.8 blw av	na	na	-10.1 blw av	-11.2 low

Total Risk	Standard Deviation	Category Risk	Risk Index	Beta
high	24.3%	high	2.4	0.81

	1996	1995	1994	1993	1992	1991	1990	1989	1988	1987
Return (%)	28.3	-9.9	-9.5	74.3	—	—	—	—	—	—
Differ from Category (+/-)	13.5	-19.0	-6.4	34.7	—	—	—	—	—	—
Return, Tax-Adjusted (%)	27.6	-10.3	-10.5	74.0	—	—	—	—	—	—

PER SHARE DATA

	1996	1995	1994	1993	1992	1991	1990	1989	1988	1987
Dividends, Net Income ($)	0.26	0.15	0.00	0.05	—	—	—	—	—	—
Distrib'ns, Cap Gain ($)	0.00	0.00	0.73	0.05	—	—	—	—	—	—
Net Asset Value ($)	21.40	16.88	18.88	21.68	—	—	—	—	—	—
Expense Ratio (%)	na	2.08	2.01	2.00	—	—	—	—	—	—
Yield (%)	1.21	0.88	0.00	0.23	—	—	—	—	—	—
Portfolio Turnover (%)	na	39	22	5	—	—	—	—	—	—
Total Assets (Millions $)	617	514	649	409	—	—	—	—	—	—

PORTFOLIO (as of 9/30/96)

Portfolio Manager: E.B. Games Jr., T. Kenney, P. Rogers - 1992

Investm't Category: International Stock
- Domestic
- Index
- ✔ Foreign
- Sector
- Asset Allocation
- State Specific

Investment Style
- Large-Cap Growth
- Large-Cap Value
- Mid-Cap Growth
- Mid-Cap Value
- Small-Cap Growth
- Small-Cap Value

Portfolio
0.2% cash	0.0% corp bonds
99.8% stocks	0.0% gov't bonds
0.0% preferred	0.0% muni bonds
0.0% conv't/warrants	0.0% other

SHAREHOLDER INFORMATION

Minimum Investment
Initial: $2,500   Subsequent: $100

Minimum IRA Investment
Initial: $1,000   Subsequent: $50

Maximum Fees
Load: none   12b-1: none
Other: *f*

Distributions
Income: Dec   Capital Gains: Dec

Exchange Options
Number Per Year: call fund   Fee: none
Telephone: yes (money market fund available)

Services
IRA, pension, auto exchange, auto invest, auto withdraw

Scudder Int'l: Pacific Opport Fd (SCOPX)

International Stock

Two International Place
Boston, MA 02110
800-225-2470, 617-295-1000
www.funds.scudder.com

PERFORMANCE

fund inception date: 12/8/92

	3yr Annual	5yr Annual	10yr Annual	Bull	Bear
Return (%)	-3.7	na	na	7.2	-14.3
Differ from Category (+/-)	-10.0 low	na	na	-17.1 blw av	-7.1 low

Total Risk	Standard Deviation	Category Risk	Risk Index	Beta
high	15.0%	high	1.5	1.05

	1996	1995	1994	1993	1992	1991	1990	1989	1988	1987
Return (%)	6.4	1.2	-17.2	60.0	—	—	—	—	—	—
Differ from Category (+/-)	-8.4	-7.9	-14.1	20.4	—	—	—	—	—	—
Return, Tax-Adjusted (%)	6.3	0.9	-17.4	59.7	—	—	—	—	—	—

PER SHARE DATA

	1996	1995	1994	1993	1992	1991	1990	1989	1988	1987
Dividends, Net Income ($)	0.01	0.10	0.09	0.08	—	—	—	—	—	—
Distrib'ns, Cap Gain ($)	0.00	0.00	0.00	0.01	—	—	—	—	—	—
Net Asset Value ($)	16.82	15.81	15.71	19.07	—	—	—	—	—	—
Expense Ratio (%)	na	1.74	1.81	1.75	—	—	—	—	—	—
Yield (%)	0.05	0.63	0.57	0.41	—	—	—	—	—	—
Portfolio Turnover (%)	na	64	38	10	—	—	—	—	—	—
Total Assets (Millions $)	353	377	422	453	—	—	—	—	—	—

PORTFOLIO (as of 9/30/96)

Portfolio Manager: E. Allan, N. Bratt, J.E. Cornell - 1994

Investm't Category: International Stock
- Domestic
- ✔ Foreign
- Asset Allocation
- Index
- Sector
- State Specific

Investment Style
- Large-Cap Growth
- Mid-Cap Growth
- Small-Cap Growth
- Large-Cap Value
- Mid-Cap Value
- Small-Cap Value

Portfolio
4.2% cash	0.0% corp bonds	
90.2% stocks	0.0% gov't bonds	
0.0% preferred	0.0% muni bonds	
5.6% conv't/warrants	0.0% other	

SHAREHOLDER INFORMATION

Minimum Investment
Initial: $2,500   Subsequent: $100

Minimum IRA Investment
Initial: $1,000   Subsequent: $50

Maximum Fees
Load: none   12b-1: none
Other: *f*

Distributions
Income: Dec   Capital Gains: Dec

Exchange Options
Number Per Year: call fund   Fee: none
Telephone: yes (money market fund available)

Services
IRA, pension, auto exchange, auto invest, auto withdraw

Scudder Ltd Term Tax-Free (SCLTX)

Tax-Exempt Bond

Two International Place
Boston, MA 02110
800-225-2470, 617-295-1000
www.funds.scudder.com

PERFORMANCE

fund inception date: 2/15/94

	3yr Annual	5yr Annual	10yr Annual	Bull	Bear
Return (%)	na	na	na	13.9	na
Differ from Category (+/-)	na	na	na	-4.5 low	na

Total Risk	Standard Deviation	Category Risk	Risk Index	Avg Mat
na	na	na	na	4.0 yrs

	1996	1995	1994	1993	1992	1991	1990	1989	1988	1987
Return (%)	3.9	9.3	—	—	—	—	—	—	—	—
Differ from Category (+/-)	0.2	-5.9	—	—	—	—	—	—	—	—
Return, Tax-Adjusted (%)	3.8	9.3	—	—	—	—	—	—	—	—

PER SHARE DATA

	1996	1995	1994	1993	1992	1991	1990	1989	1988	1987
Dividends, Net Income ($)	0.52	0.55	—	—	—	—	—	—	—	—
Distrib'ns, Cap Gain ($)	0.02	0.00	—	—	—	—	—	—	—	—
Net Asset Value ($)	11.99	12.07	—	—	—	—	—	—	—	—
Expense Ratio (%)	na	0.23	—	—	—	—	—	—	—	—
Yield (%)	4.32	4.55	—	—	—	—	—	—	—	—
Portfolio Turnover (%)	na	37	—	—	—	—	—	—	—	—
Total Assets (Millions $)	124	119	—	—	—	—	—	—	—	—

PORTFOLIO (as of 9/30/96)

Portfolio Manager: M. Ashton Patton, D.C. Carleton - 1994

Investm't Category: Tax-Exempt Bond

✔ Domestic	Index
Foreign	Sector
Asset Allocation	State Specific

Investment Style

Large-Cap Growth	Large-Cap Value
Mid-Cap Growth	Mid-Cap Value
Small-Cap Growth	Small-Cap Value

Portfolio

21.0%	cash	0.0% corp bonds
0.0%	stocks	0.0% gov't bonds
0.0%	preferred	79.0% muni bonds
0.0%	conv't/warrants	0.0% other

SHAREHOLDER INFORMATION

Minimum Investment
Initial: $2,500   Subsequent: $100

Minimum IRA Investment
Initial: na   Subsequent: na

Maximum Fees
Load: none   12b-1: none
Other: *f*

Distributions
Income: monthly   Capital Gains: Nov

Exchange Options
Number Per Year: call fund   Fee: none
Telephone: yes (money market fund available)

Services
auto exchange, auto invest, auto withdraw

Scudder MA Ltd Tax Free

(SMLFX)

Tax-Exempt Bond

Two International Place
Boston, MA 02110
800-225-2470, 617-295-1000
www.funds.scudder.com

PERFORMANCE

fund inception date: 2/15/94

	3yr Annual	5yr Annual	10yr Annual	Bull	Bear
Return (%)	na	na	na	14.1	na
Differ from Category (+/-)	na	na	na	-4.3 low	na

Total Risk	Standard Deviation	Category Risk	Risk Index	Avg Mat
na	na	na	na	4.0 yrs

	1996	1995	1994	1993	1992	1991	1990	1989	1988	1987
Return (%)	3.3	9.4	—	—	—	—	—	—	—	—
Differ from Category (+/-)	-0.4	-5.8	—	—	—	—	—	—	—	—
Return, Tax-Adjusted (%)	3.3	9.4	—	—	—	—	—	—	—	—

PER SHARE DATA

	1996	1995	1994	1993	1992	1991	1990	1989	1988	1987
Dividends, Net Income ($)	0.49	0.53	—	—	—	—	—	—	—	—
Distrib'ns, Cap Gain ($)	0.00	0.00	—	—	—	—	—	—	—	—
Net Asset Value ($)	12.02	12.12	—	—	—	—	—	—	—	—
Expense Ratio (%)	na	0.90	—	—	—	—	—	—	—	—
Yield (%)	4.07	4.37	—	—	—	—	—	—	—	—
Portfolio Turnover (%)	na	27	—	—	—	—	—	—	—	—
Total Assets (Millions $)	66	55	—	—	—	—	—	—	—	—

PORTFOLIO (as of 6/30/96)

Portfolio Manager: Philip G. Condon - 1994

Investm't Category: Tax-Exempt Bond
- ✔ Domestic
- Foreign
- Asset Allocation
- Index
- Sector
- ✔ State Specific

Investment Style
- Large-Cap Growth
- Mid-Cap Growth
- Small-Cap Growth
- Large-Cap Value
- Mid-Cap Value
- Small-Cap Value

Portfolio
20.0% cash	0.0% corp bonds
0.0% stocks	0.0% gov't bonds
0.0% preferred	80.0% muni bonds
0.0% conv't/warrants	0.0% other

SHAREHOLDER INFORMATION

Minimum Investment
Initial: $2,500   Subsequent: $100

Minimum IRA Investment
Initial: na   Subsequent: na

Maximum Fees
Load: none   12b-1: none
Other: *f*

Distributions
Income: monthly   Capital Gains: Nov

Exchange Options
Number Per Year: call fund   Fee: none
Telephone: yes (money market fund available)

Services
auto exchange, auto invest, auto withdraw

Scudder MA Tax-Free

(SCMAX)

Tax-Exempt Bond

Two International Place
Boston, MA 02110
800-225-2470, 617-295-1000
www.funds.scudder.com

PERFORMANCE

fund inception date: 5/28/87

	3yr Annual	5yr Annual	10yr Annual	Bull	Bear
Return (%)	4.8	7.8	na	21.3	-6.6
Differ from Category (+/-)	0.6 abv av	1.4 high	na	2.9 high	-1.2 blw av

Total Risk	Standard Deviation	Category Risk	Risk Index	Avg Mat
blw av	6.0%	abv av	1.1	9.9 yrs

	1996	1995	1994	1993	1992	1991	1990	1989	1988	1987
Return (%)	4.0	17.8	-6.2	14.2	10.8	12.2	6.3	9.8	12.3	—
Differ from Category (+/-)	0.3	2.6	-0.9	2.4	2.5	0.8	-0.1	0.8	2.3	—
Return, Tax-Adjusted (%)	4.0	17.8	-6.3	13.9	10.4	12.0	6.3	9.5	11.8	—

PER SHARE DATA

	1996	1995	1994	1993	1992	1991	1990	1989	1988	1987
Dividends, Net Income ($)	0.70	0.71	0.76	0.82	0.83	0.80	0.82	0.83	0.89	—
Distrib'ns, Cap Gain ($)	0.00	0.00	0.01	0.12	0.16	0.08	0.00	0.10	0.20	—
Net Asset Value ($)	13.90	14.06	12.57	14.21	13.31	12.96	12.39	12.46	12.24	—
Expense Ratio (%)	0.75	0.47	0.07	0.00	0.48	0.60	0.60	0.51	0.50	—
Yield (%)	5.03	5.04	6.04	5.72	6.16	6.13	6.61	6.60	7.15	—
Portfolio Turnover (%)	20	10	17	29	23	27	46	111	96	—
Total Assets (Millions $)	330	322	277	375	218	100	60	46	27	—

PORTFOLIO (as of 9/30/96)

Portfolio Manager: Philip G. Condon - 1989

Investm't Category: Tax-Exempt Bond

✔ Domestic	Index
Foreign	Sector
Asset Allocation	✔ State Specific

Investment Style

Large-Cap Growth	Large-Cap Value
Mid-Cap Growth	Mid-Cap Value
Small-Cap Growth	Small-Cap Value

Portfolio

1.2% cash	0.0% corp bonds
0.0% stocks	0.0% gov't bonds
0.0% preferred	98.9% muni bonds
0.0% conv't/warrants	0.0% other

SHAREHOLDER INFORMATION

Minimum Investment
Initial: $2,500   Subsequent: $100

Minimum IRA Investment
Initial: na   Subsequent: na

Maximum Fees
Load: none   12b-1: none
Other: f

Distributions
Income: monthly   Capital Gains: Nov

Exchange Options
Number Per Year: call fund   Fee: none
Telephone: yes (money market fund available)

Services
auto exchange, auto invest, auto withdraw

Scudder Muni Trust: High Yield Tax-Free

Two International Place
Boston, MA 02110
800-225-2470, 617-295-1000
www.funds.scudder.com

(SHYTX) *Tax-Exempt Bond*

PERFORMANCE

fund inception date: 1/22/87

	3yr Annual	5yr Annual	10yr Annual	Bull	Bear
Return (%)	4.5	7.5	na	20.8	-7.0
Differ from Category (+/-)	0.3 abv av	1.1 high	na	2.4 abv av	-1.6 blw av

Total Risk	Standard Deviation	Category Risk	Risk Index	Avg Mat
blw av	6.2%	high	1.1	11.0 yrs

	1996	1995	1994	1993	1992	1991	1990	1989	1988	1987
Return (%)	4.4	19.2	-8.4	13.8	10.8	13.4	6.0	10.3	13.4	—
Differ from Category (+/-)	0.7	4.0	-3.1	2.0	2.5	2.0	-0.4	1.3	3.4	—
Return, Tax-Adjusted (%)	4.4	19.2	-8.4	13.1	10.1	12.8	5.9	10.1	13.4	—

PER SHARE DATA

	1996	1995	1994	1993	1992	1991	1990	1989	1988	1987
Dividends, Net Income ($)	0.66	0.71	0.66	0.67	0.72	0.75	0.76	0.75	0.82	—
Distrib'ns, Cap Gain ($)	0.00	0.00	0.00	0.28	0.26	0.20	0.04	0.06	0.00	—
Net Asset Value ($)	12.04	12.19	10.86	12.55	11.90	11.67	11.19	11.35	11.06	—
Expense Ratio (%)	na	0.80	0.80	0.92	0.98	1.00	1.00	1.00	0.67	—
Yield (%)	5.48	5.82	6.07	5.22	5.92	6.31	6.76	6.57	7.41	—
Portfolio Turnover (%)	na	27	34	56	57	46	33	76	37	—
Total Assets (Millions $)	297	302	259	315	203	159	128	113	73	—

PORTFOLIO (as of 9/30/96)

Portfolio Manager: Philip G. Condon - 1987

Investm't Category: Tax-Exempt Bond
- ✔ Domestic
- Foreign
- Asset Allocation
- Index
- Sector
- State Specific

Investment Style
- Large-Cap Growth
- Mid-Cap Growth
- Small-Cap Growth
- Large-Cap Value
- Mid-Cap Value
- Small-Cap Value

Portfolio
4.0% cash	0.0% corp bonds
0.0% stocks	0.0% gov't bonds
0.0% preferred	96.0% muni bonds
0.0% conv't/warrants	0.0% other

SHAREHOLDER INFORMATION

Minimum Investment
Initial: $2,500   Subsequent: $100

Minimum IRA Investment
Initial: na   Subsequent: na

Maximum Fees
Load: none   12b-1: none
Other: *f*

Distributions
Income: monthly   Capital Gains: Nov

Exchange Options
Number Per Year: call fund   Fee: none
Telephone: yes (money market fund available)

Services
auto exchange, auto invest, auto withdraw

Scudder Muni Trust: Managed Muni Bond

Two International Place
Boston, MA 02110
800-225-2470, 617-295-1000
www.funds.scudder.com

(SCMBX) *Tax-Exempt Bond*

	3yr Annual	5yr Annual	10yr Annual	Bull	Bear
Return (%)	4.6	7.1	7.8	21.2	-6.6
Differ from Category (+/-)	0.4 abv av	0.7 abv av	1.1 high	2.8 abv av	-1.2 blw av

Total Risk	Standard Deviation	Category Risk	Risk Index	Avg Mat
blw av	5.8%	abv av	1.0	10.4 yrs

	1996	1995	1994	1993	1992	1991	1990	1989	1988	1987
Return (%)	4.1	17.1	-6.1	13.3	8.9	12.2	6.7	11.1	12.2	0.9
Differ from Category (+/-)	0.4	1.9	-0.8	1.5	0.6	0.8	0.3	2.1	2.2	2.3
Return, Tax-Adjusted (%)	4.1	17.1	-6.2	12.4	7.8	11.8	6.4	9.8	12.1	0.5

PER SHARE DATA

	1996	1995	1994	1993	1992	1991	1990	1989	1988	1987
Dividends, Net Income ($)	0.45	0.47	0.45	0.47	0.50	0.52	0.55	0.58	0.60	0.66
Distrib'ns, Cap Gain ($)	0.00	0.00	0.02	0.28	0.33	0.11	0.08	0.39	0.01	0.10
Net Asset Value ($)	8.84	8.94	8.07	9.09	8.72	8.80	8.45	8.54	8.60	8.24
Expense Ratio (%)	na	0.63	0.63	0.63	0.63	0.64	0.61	0.62	0.61	0.63
Yield (%)	5.09	5.25	5.56	5.01	5.52	5.83	6.44	6.49	6.96	7.91
Portfolio Turnover (%)	na	17	33	53	60	32	72	90	76	73
Total Assets (Millions $)	748	773	708	908	827	794	719	689	631	585

PORTFOLIO (as of 9/30/96)

Portfolio Manager: D.C. Carleton, P.G.
Condon - 1986

Investm't Category: Tax-Exempt Bond
✔ Domestic   Index
   Foreign   Sector
   Asset Allocation   State Specific

Investment Style
Large-Cap Growth   Large-Cap Value
Mid-Cap Growth   Mid-Cap Value
Small-Cap Growth   Small-Cap Value

Portfolio
9.0%	cash	0.0%	corp bonds
0.0%	stocks	0.0%	gov't bonds
0.0%	preferred	91.0%	muni bonds
0.0%	conv't/warrants	0.0%	other

SHAREHOLDER INFORMATION

Minimum Investment
Initial: $2,500   Subsequent: $100

Minimum IRA Investment
Initial: na   Subsequent: na

Maximum Fees
Load: none   12b-1: none
Other: *f*

Distributions
Income: monthly   Capital Gains: Nov

Exchange Options
Number Per Year: call fund   Fee: none
Telephone: yes (money market fund available)

Services
auto exchange, auto invest, auto withdraw

Scudder Muni Trust: Med-Term Tax-Free

(SCMTX) *Tax-Exempt Bond*

Two International Place
Boston, MA 02110
800-225-2470, 617-295-1000
www.funds.scudder.com

PERFORMANCE

fund inception date: 4/12/83

	3yr Annual	5yr Annual	10yr Annual	Bull	Bear
Return (%)	4.6	6.7	6.6	18.2	-4.0
Differ from Category (+/-)	0.4 abv av	0.3 av	-0.1 blw av	-0.2 av	1.4 abv av

Total Risk	Standard Deviation	Category Risk	Risk Index	Avg Mat
low	4.1%	blw av	0.7	6.8 yrs

	1996	1995	1994	1993	1992	1991	1990	1989	1988	1987
Return (%)	4.0	14.3	-3.5	10.9	8.9	12.1	6.2	5.9	4.9	3.7
Differ from Category (+/-)	0.3	-0.9	1.8	-0.9	0.6	0.7	-0.2	-3.1	-5.1	5.1
Return, Tax-Adjusted (%)	3.9	14.1	-3.6	10.7	8.8	12.1	6.2	5.9	4.9	3.5

PER SHARE DATA

	1996	1995	1994	1993	1992	1991	1990	1989	1988	1987
Dividends, Net Income ($)	0.52	0.53	0.55	0.60	0.64	0.66	0.54	0.56	0.53	0.59
Distrib'ns, Cap Gain ($)	0.02	0.05	0.02	0.06	0.03	0.00	0.00	0.00	0.00	0.05
Net Asset Value ($)	11.15	11.26	10.39	11.36	10.86	10.62	10.11	10.04	10.02	10.07
Expense Ratio (%)	na	0.70	0.63	0.14	0.00	0.00	0.97	0.91	0.79	0.80
Yield (%)	4.65	4.68	5.28	5.25	5.87	6.21	5.34	5.57	5.28	5.83
Portfolio Turnover (%)	na	36	33	37	22	14	117	16	31	33
Total Assets (Millions $)	658	709	703	1,012	649	267	26	54	98	125

PORTFOLIO (as of 9/30/96)

Portfolio Manager: Donald C. Carleton, M. Patton - 1986

Investm't Category: Tax-Exempt Bond

✔ Domestic	Index
Foreign	Sector
Asset Allocation	State Specific

Investment Style

Large-Cap Growth	Large-Cap Value
Mid-Cap Growth	Mid-Cap Value
Small-Cap Growth	Small-Cap Value

Portfolio

7.7% cash	0.0% corp bonds
0.0% stocks	0.0% gov't bonds
0.0% preferred	92.3% muni bonds
0.0% conv't/warrants	0.0% other

SHAREHOLDER INFORMATION

Minimum Investment
Initial: $2,500   Subsequent: $100

Minimum IRA Investment
Initial: na   Subsequent: na

Maximum Fees
Load: none   12b-1: none
Other: *f*

Distributions
Income: monthly   Capital Gains: Nov

Exchange Options
Number Per Year: call fund   Fee: none
Telephone: yes (money market fund available)

Services
auto exchange, auto invest, auto withdraw

Scudder NY Tax-Free

(SCYTX)

Tax-Exempt Bond

Two International Place
Boston, MA 02110
800-225-2470, 617-295-1000
www.funds.scudder.com

PERFORMANCE

fund inception date: 7/22/83

	3yr Annual	5yr Annual	10yr Annual	Bull	Bear
Return (%)	4.1	7.0	7.4	19.6	-7.0
Differ from Category (+/-)	-0.1 blw av	0.6 abv av	0.7 abv av	1.2 av	-1.6 low

Total Risk	Standard Deviation	Category Risk	Risk Index	Avg Mat
blw av	6.5%	high	1.2	11.7 yrs

	1996	1995	1994	1993	1992	1991	1990	1989	1988	1987
Return (%)	3.2	17.9	-7.2	12.9	10.2	14.4	4.2	10.0	10.8	-0.2
Differ from Category (+/-)	-0.5	2.7	-1.9	1.1	1.9	3.0	-2.2	1.0	0.8	1.2
Return, Tax-Adjusted (%)	3.1	17.9	-7.4	11.0	8.7	13.7	4.2	9.7	10.8	-0.7

PER SHARE DATA

	1996	1995	1994	1993	1992	1991	1990	1989	1988	1987
Dividends, Net Income ($)	0.53	0.52	0.51	0.56	0.61	0.65	0.67	0.70	0.72	0.79
Distrib'ns, Cap Gain ($)	0.01	0.00	0.05	0.73	0.60	0.25	0.00	0.09	0.00	0.19
Net Asset Value ($)	10.81	11.01	9.81	11.17	11.08	11.21	10.65	10.88	10.64	10.28
Expense Ratio (%)	0.82	0.82	0.82	0.82	0.87	0.91	0.89	0.89	0.95	0.88
Yield (%)	4.89	4.72	5.17	4.70	5.22	5.67	6.29	6.38	6.76	7.54
Portfolio Turnover (%)	80	83	158	201	168	225	114	132	44	72
Total Assets (Millions $)	190	197	182	229	184	158	140	134	120	113

PORTFOLIO (as of 9/30/96)

Portfolio Manager: Jeremy L. Ragus, Donald Carleton - 1990

Investm't Category: Tax-Exempt Bond

✔ Domestic	Index
Foreign	Sector
Asset Allocation	✔ State Specific

Investment Style

Large-Cap Growth	Large-Cap Value
Mid-Cap Growth	Mid-Cap Value
Small-Cap Growth	Small-Cap Value

Portfolio

1.0% cash	0.0% corp bonds
0.0% stocks	0.0% gov't bonds
0.0% preferred	99.0% muni bonds
0.0% conv't/warrants	0.0% other

SHAREHOLDER INFORMATION

Minimum Investment
Initial: $2,500   Subsequent: $100

Minimum IRA Investment
Initial: na   Subsequent: na

Maximum Fees
Load: none   12b-1: none
Other: *f*

Distributions
Income: monthly   Capital Gains: Nov

Exchange Options
Number Per Year: call fund   Fee: none
Telephone: yes (money market fund available)

Services
auto exchange, auto invest, auto withdraw

Scudder Ohio Tax-Free
(SCOHX)
Tax-Exempt Bond

Two International Place
Boston, MA 02110
800-225-2470, 617-295-1000
www.funds.scudder.com

PERFORMANCE
fund inception date: 5/28/87

	3yr Annual	5yr Annual	10yr Annual	Bull	Bear
Return (%)	4.8	7.1	na	21.0	-6.0
Differ from Category (+/-)	0.6 high	0.7 abv av	na	2.6 abv av	-0.6 av

Total Risk	Standard Deviation	Category Risk	Risk Index	Avg Mat
blw av	5.7%	av	1.0	9.7 yrs

	1996	1995	1994	1993	1992	1991	1990	1989	1988	1987
Return (%)	4.1	17.2	-5.6	12.2	8.8	11.8	6.6	9.5	12.7	—
Differ from Category (+/-)	0.4	2.0	-0.3	0.4	0.5	0.4	0.2	0.5	2.7	—
Return, Tax-Adjusted (%)	4.0	16.9	-5.7	12.0	8.3	11.7	6.4	9.3	12.6	—

PER SHARE DATA

	1996	1995	1994	1993	1992	1991	1990	1989	1988	1987
Dividends, Net Income ($)	0.68	0.69	0.70	0.70	0.72	0.75	0.79	0.82	0.82	—
Distrib'ns, Cap Gain ($)	0.03	0.11	0.04	0.09	0.19	0.02	0.06	0.06	0.02	—
Net Asset Value ($)	13.15	13.34	12.11	13.59	12.85	12.69	12.09	12.17	11.95	—
Expense Ratio (%)	0.50	0.50	0.50	0.50	0.50	0.50	0.50	0.50	0.50	—
Yield (%)	5.15	5.13	5.76	5.11	5.52	5.90	6.50	6.70	6.85	—
Portfolio Turnover (%)	19	19	12	34	13	23	16	36	106	—
Total Assets (Millions $)	87	83	72	84	62	49	34	22	9	—

PORTFOLIO (as of 9/30/96)

Portfolio Manager: Donald C. Carleton, P.
Condon - 1995

Investm't Category: Tax-Exempt Bond
✔ Domestic   Index
   Foreign   Sector
   Asset Allocation   ✔ State Specific

Investment Style
Large-Cap Growth   Large-Cap Value
Mid-Cap Growth   Mid-Cap Value
Small-Cap Growth   Small-Cap Value

Portfolio
1.0% cash	0.0% corp bonds
0.0% stocks	0.0% gov't bonds
0.0% preferred	99.0% muni bonds
0.0% conv't/warrants	0.0% other

SHAREHOLDER INFORMATION

Minimum Investment
Initial: $2,500   Subsequent: $100

Minimum IRA Investment
Initial: na   Subsequent: na

Maximum Fees
Load: none   12b-1: none
Other: f

Distributions
Income: monthly   Capital Gains: Nov

Exchange Options
Number Per Year: call fund   Fee: none
Telephone: yes (money market fund available)

Services
auto exchange, auto invest, auto withdraw

Scudder Penn Tax-Free

(SCPAX)

Tax-Exempt Bond

Two International Place
Boston, MA 02110
800-225-2470, 617-295-1000
www.funds.scudder.com

PERFORMANCE

fund inception date: 5/28/87

	3yr Annual	5yr Annual	10yr Annual	Bull	Bear
Return (%)	4.5	7.1	na	20.2	-6.2
Differ from Category (+/-)	0.3 abv av	0.7 abv av	na	1.8 abv av	-0.8 blw av

Total Risk	Standard Deviation	Category Risk	Risk Index	Avg Mat
blw av	5.7%	av	1.0	10.1 yrs

	1996	1995	1994	1993	1992	1991	1990	1989	1988	1987
Return (%)	3.5	17.3	-5.9	13.1	9.0	12.4	5.8	10.1	13.4	—
Differ from Category (+/-)	-0.2	2.1	-0.6	1.3	0.7	1.0	-0.6	1.1	3.4	—
Return, Tax-Adjusted (%)	3.4	17.1	-6.0	12.9	8.6	12.2	5.8	10.0	13.2	—

PER SHARE DATA

	1996	1995	1994	1993	1992	1991	1990	1989	1988	1987
Dividends, Net Income ($)	0.70	0.71	0.74	0.74	0.83	0.78	0.82	0.84	0.84	—
Distrib'ns, Cap Gain ($)	0.02	0.07	0.02	0.08	0.14	0.07	0.00	0.01	0.06	—
Net Asset Value ($)	13.46	13.73	12.41	13.99	13.14	12.98	12.35	12.48	12.14	—
Expense Ratio (%)	0.50	0.50	0.50	0.50	0.50	0.50	0.50	0.50	0.50	—
Yield (%)	5.19	5.14	5.95	5.25	6.24	5.97	6.63	6.72	6.88	—
Portfolio Turnover (%)	11	26	17	29	11	8	2	14	98	—
Total Assets (Millions $)	77	77	67	76	56	38	24	16	8	—

PORTFOLIO (as of 9/30/96)

Portfolio Manager: Donald C. Carleton, P.G. Condon - 1995

Investm't Category: Tax-Exempt Bond
- ✔ Domestic
- Foreign
- Asset Allocation
- Index
- Sector
- ✔ State Specific

Investment Style
- Large-Cap Growth
- Mid-Cap Growth
- Small-Cap Growth
- Large-Cap Value
- Mid-Cap Value
- Small-Cap Value

Portfolio
6.0% cash	0.0% corp bonds
0.0% stocks	0.0% gov't bonds
0.0% preferred	94.0% muni bonds
0.0% conv't/warrants	0.0% other

SHAREHOLDER INFORMATION

Minimum Investment
Initial: $2,500   Subsequent: $100

Minimum IRA Investment
Initial: na   Subsequent: na

Maximum Fees
Load: none   12b-1: none
Other: *f*

Distributions
Income: monthly   Capital Gains: Nov

Exchange Options
Number Per Year: call fund   Fee: none
Telephone: yes (money market fund available)

Services
auto exchange, auto invest, auto withdraw

Scudder Portfolio Trust: Balanced (SCBAX)

Balanced

Two International Place
Boston, MA 02110
800-225-2470, 617-295-1000
www.funds.scudder.com

PERFORMANCE

fund inception date: 1/4/93

	3yr Annual	5yr Annual	10yr Annual	Bull	Bear
Return (%)	11.2	na	na	45.7	-8.0
Differ from Category (+/-)	-0.5 av	na	na	0.6 av	-2.3 low

Total Risk	Standard Deviation	Category Risk	Risk Index	Beta
av	7.8%	high	1.2	0.78

	1996	1995	1994	1993	1992	1991	1990	1989	1988	1987
Return (%)	11.5	26.4	-2.4	—	—	—	—	—	—	—
Differ from Category (+/-)	-2.7	1.8	-0.8	—	—	—	—	—	—	—
Return, Tax-Adjusted (%)	8.9	24.7	-3.4	—	—	—	—	—	—	—

PER SHARE DATA

	1996	1995	1994	1993	1992	1991	1990	1989	1988	1987
Dividends, Net Income ($)	0.34	0.32	0.30	—	—	—	—	—	—	—
Distrib'ns, Cap Gain ($)	0.79	0.24	0.00	—	—	—	—	—	—	—
Net Asset Value ($)	14.60	14.12	11.63	—	—	—	—	—	—	—
Expense Ratio (%)	na	1.00	1.00	—	—	—	—	—	—	—
Yield (%)	2.20	2.22	2.57	—	—	—	—	—	—	—
Portfolio Turnover (%)	na	103	105	—	—	—	—	—	—	—
Total Assets (Millions $)	116	90	66	—	—	—	—	—	—	—

PORTFOLIO (as of 9/30/96)

Portfolio Manager: Malter, Hutchinson, Shields - 1995

Investm't Category: Balanced
- ✔ Domestic
- ✔ Foreign
-   Asset Allocation

- Index
- Sector
- State Specific

Investment Style

Large-Cap Growth	Large-Cap Value
Mid-Cap Growth	Mid-Cap Value
Small-Cap Growth	Small-Cap Value

Portfolio

4.0% cash	10.0% corp bonds
59.0% stocks	25.0% gov't bonds
0.0% preferred	0.0% muni bonds
0.0% conv't/warrants	2.0% other

SHAREHOLDER INFORMATION

Minimum Investment
Initial: $2,500   Subsequent: $100

Minimum IRA Investment
Initial: $1,000   Subsequent: $50

Maximum Fees
Load: none   12b-1: none
Other: f

Distributions
Income: quarterly   Capital Gains: Dec

Exchange Options
Number Per Year: call fund   Fee: none
Telephone: yes (money market fund available)

Services
IRA, pension, auto exchange, auto invest, auto withdraw

Scudder Portfolio Trust: Income (SCSBX)

Two International Place
Boston, MA 02110
800-225-2470, 617-295-1000
www.funds.scudder.com

General Bond

PERFORMANCE

fund inception date: 4/24/92

	3yr Annual	5yr Annual	10yr Annual	Bull	Bear
Return (%)	5.3	7.0	8.2	24.1	-7.6
Differ from Category (+/-)	0.2 abv av	0.9 abv av	0.9 high	3.8 high	-3.4 low

Total Risk	Standard Deviation	Category Risk	Risk Index	Avg Mat
blw av	5.0%	high	1.3	10.0 yrs

	1996	1995	1994	1993	1992	1991	1990	1989	1988	1987
Return (%)	3.4	18.5	-4.5	12.6	6.7	17.3	8.3	12.7	8.9	0.7
Differ from Category (+/-)	-0.5	3.6	-2.2	3.5	0.2	2.6	1.0	1.0	1.3	-1.6
Return, Tax-Adjusted (%)	0.8	15.5	-6.8	8.8	3.2	14.1	4.9	9.3	5.4	-2.6

PER SHARE DATA

	1996	1995	1994	1993	1992	1991	1990	1989	1988	1987
Dividends, Net Income ($)	0.81	0.86	0.76	0.87	0.93	0.94	1.09	1.06	1.07	1.09
Distrib'ns, Cap Gain ($)	0.09	0.08	0.02	0.56	0.39	0.11	0.00	0.00	0.00	0.00
Net Asset Value ($)	13.15	13.61	12.32	13.72	13.48	13.91	12.82	12.89	12.41	12.40
Expense Ratio (%)	na	0.99	0.97	0.92	0.93	0.97	0.95	0.93	0.94	0.94
Yield (%)	6.11	6.28	6.15	6.09	6.70	6.70	8.50	8.22	8.62	8.79
Portfolio Turnover (%)	na	128	60	130	121	110	48	63	20	34
Total Assets (Millions $)	586	579	464	508	456	404	301	271	244	243

PORTFOLIO (as of 9/30/96)

Portfolio Manager: William M. Hutchinson - 1986

Investm't Category: General Bond

✔ Domestic	Index
Foreign	Sector
Asset Allocation	State Specific

Investment Style

Large-Cap Growth	Large-Cap Value
Mid-Cap Growth	Mid-Cap Value
Small-Cap Growth	Small-Cap Value

Portfolio

17.0% cash	34.0% corp bonds
0.0% stocks	42.0% gov't bonds
0.0% preferred	0.0% muni bonds
0.0% conv't/warrants	7.0% other

SHAREHOLDER INFORMATION

Minimum Investment

Initial: $2,500   Subsequent: $100

Minimum IRA Investment

Initial: $1,000   Subsequent: $50

Maximum Fees

Load: none   12b-1: none
Other: *f*

Distributions

Income: quarterly   Capital Gains: Nov

Exchange Options

Number Per Year: call fund   Fee: none
Telephone: yes (money market fund available)

Services

IRA, pension, auto exchange, auto invest, auto withdraw

Scudder Quality Growth
(SCQGX)
Growth

Two International Place
Boston, MA 02110
800-225-2470, 617-295-1000
www.funds.scudder.com

PERFORMANCE

fund inception date: 5/20/91

	3yr Annual	5yr Annual	10yr Annual	Bull	Bear
Return (%)	15.6	10.5	na	62.9	-7.9
Differ from Category (+/-)	-0.1 av	-3.8 low	na	0.5 av	-1.2 blw av

Total Risk	Standard Deviation	Category Risk	Risk Index	Beta
abv av	10.6%	abv av	1.0	1.04

	1996	1995	1994	1993	1992	1991	1990	1989	1988	1987
Return (%)	18.2	32.4	-1.4	-0.1	6.6	—	—	—	—	—
Differ from Category (+/-)	-1.9	2.1	-1.1	-14.1	-5.2	—	—	—	—	—
Return, Tax-Adjusted (%)	15.5	30.8	-3.7	-0.7	6.5	—	—	—	—	—

PER SHARE DATA

	1996	1995	1994	1993	1992	1991	1990	1989	1988	1987
Dividends, Net Income ($)	0.00	0.14	0.15	0.07	0.02	—	—	—	—	—
Distrib'ns, Cap Gain ($)	1.77	0.60	1.09	0.23	0.00	—	—	—	—	—
Net Asset Value ($)	20.04	18.43	14.47	15.92	16.23	—	—	—	—	—
Expense Ratio (%)	na	1.17	1.25	1.20	1.25	—	—	—	—	—
Yield (%)	0.00	0.73	0.96	0.43	0.12	—	—	—	—	—
Portfolio Turnover (%)	na	91	119	111	27	—	—	—	—	—
Total Assets (Millions $)	227	185	112	123	130	—	—	—	—	—

PORTFOLIO (as of 9/30/96)

Portfolio Manager: Valerie F. Malter, M.K. Shields - 1995

Investm't Category: Growth
✔ Domestic
✔ Foreign
  Asset Allocation
  Index
  Sector
  State Specific

Investment Style
✔ Large-Cap Growth
  Mid-Cap Growth
  Small-Cap Growth
  Large-Cap Value
  Mid-Cap Value
  Small-Cap Value

Portfolio
3.7% cash	0.0% corp bonds
96.3% stocks	0.0% gov't bonds
0.0% preferred	0.0% muni bonds
0.0% conv't/warrants	0.0% other

SHAREHOLDER INFORMATION

Minimum Investment
Initial: $2,500   Subsequent: $100

Minimum IRA Investment
Initial: $1,000   Subsequent: $50

Maximum Fees
Load: none   12b-1: none
Other: f

Distributions
Income: Dec   Capital Gains: Dec

Exchange Options
Number Per Year: call fund   Fee: none
Telephone: yes (money market fund available)

Services
IRA, pension, auto exchange, auto invest, auto withdraw

Scudder Short-Term Bond (SCSTX)

General Bond

Two International Place
Boston, MA 02110
800-225-2470, 617-295-1000
www.funds.scudder.com

PERFORMANCE

fund inception date: 4/2/84

	3yr Annual	5yr Annual	10yr Annual	Bull	Bear
Return (%)	3.7	4.9	6.9	14.3	-3.0
Differ from Category (+/-)	-1.4 low	-1.2 blw av	-0.4 blw av	-6.0 low	1.2 abv av

Total Risk	Standard Deviation	Category Risk	Risk Index	Avg Mat
low	2.7%	blw av	0.7	2.5 yrs

	1996	1995	1994	1993	1992	1991	1990	1989	1988	1987
Return (%)	3.8	10.7	-2.9	8.1	5.5	14.2	9.8	13.2	6.3	1.4
Differ from Category (+/-)	-0.1	-4.2	-0.6	-1.0	-1.0	-0.5	2.5	1.5	-1.3	-0.9
Return, Tax-Adjusted (%)	1.3	8.1	-5.4	5.2	2.4	10.5	6.1	10.0	3.7	-1.3

PER SHARE DATA

	1996	1995	1994	1993	1992	1991	1990	1989	1988	1987
Dividends, Net Income ($)	0.71	0.70	0.75	0.80	0.95	1.08	1.08	0.82	0.73	0.74
Distrib'ns, Cap Gain ($)	0.00	0.00	0.00	0.07	0.00	0.00	0.00	0.08	0.00	0.10
Net Asset Value ($)	11.05	11.35	10.92	12.01	11.93	12.24	11.72	11.71	11.19	11.23
Expense Ratio (%)	na	0.75	0.73	0.68	0.75	0.44	0.16	0.36	1.50	1.45
Yield (%)	6.42	6.16	6.86	6.62	7.96	8.82	9.21	6.95	6.52	6.53
Portfolio Turnover (%)	na	101	65	66	84	41	53	40	24	29
Total Assets (Millions $)	1,538	1,818	2,138	3,196	2,854	2,234	340	70	10	9

PORTFOLIO (as of 9/30/96)

Portfolio Manager: T.M. Poor, C.L. Gootkind, S. Dolan - 1989

Investm't Category: General Bond
✔ Domestic   Index
✔ Foreign   Sector
  Asset Allocation State Specific

Investment Style
Large-Cap Growth   Large-Cap Value
Mid-Cap Growth   Mid-Cap Value
Small-Cap Growth   Small-Cap Value

Portfolio
10.2% cash   18.4% corp bonds
0.0% stocks   30.4% gov't bonds
0.0% preferred   0.0% muni bonds
0.0% conv't/warrants 41.1% other

SHAREHOLDER INFORMATION

Minimum Investment
Initial: $2,500   Subsequent: $100

Minimum IRA Investment
Initial: $1,000   Subsequent: $50

Maximum Fees
Load: none   12b-1: none
Other: f

Distributions
Income: monthly   Capital Gains: Nov

Exchange Options
Number Per Year: call fund   Fee: none
Telephone: yes (money market fund available)

Services
IRA, pension, auto exchange, auto invest, auto withdraw

Scudder Small Company Value (SCSUX)

Aggressive Growth

Two International Place
Boston, MA 02110
800-225-2470, 617-295-1000
www.funds.scudder.com

PERFORMANCE

fund inception date: 10/6/95

	3yr Annual	5yr Annual	10yr Annual	Bull	Bear
Return (%)	na	na	na	na	na
Differ from Category (+/-)	na	na	na	na	na

Total Risk	Standard Deviation	Category Risk	Risk Index	Beta
na	na	na	na	na

	1996	1995	1994	1993	1992	1991	1990	1989	1988	1987
Return (%)	23.8	—	—	—	—	—	—	—	—	—
Differ from Category (+/-)	4.7	—	—	—	—	—	—	—	—	—
Return, Tax-Adjusted (%)	23.7	—	—	—	—	—	—	—	—	—

PER SHARE DATA

	1996	1995	1994	1993	1992	1991	1990	1989	1988	1987
Dividends, Net Income ($)	0.03	—	—	—	—	—	—	—	—	—
Distrib'ns, Cap Gain ($)	0.00	—	—	—	—	—	—	—	—	—
Net Asset Value ($)	15.44	—	—	—	—	—	—	—	—	—
Expense Ratio (%)	na	—	—	—	—	—	—	—	—	—
Yield (%)	0.19	—	—	—	—	—	—	—	—	—
Portfolio Turnover (%)	na	—	—	—	—	—	—	—	—	—
Total Assets (Millions $)	50	—	—	—	—	—	—	—	—	—

PORTFOLIO (as of 9/30/96)

Portfolio Manager: P. Fortuna, Mac Eysenbach - 1995

Investm't Category: Aggressive Growth

✔ Domestic
  Foreign
  Asset Allocation

  Index
  Sector
  State Specific

Investment Style

Large-Cap Growth
Mid-Cap Growth
Small-Cap Growth

Large-Cap Value
Mid-Cap Value
Small-Cap Value

Portfolio

2.9% cash
97.1% stocks
0.0% preferred
0.0% conv't/warrants

0.0% corp bonds
0.0% gov't bonds
0.0% muni bonds
0.0% other

SHAREHOLDER INFORMATION

Minimum Investment
Initial: $2,500   Subsequent: $100

Minimum IRA Investment
Initial: $1,000   Subsequent: $50

Maximum Fees
Load: 1.00% redemption   12b-1: none
Other: redemption fee applies for 1 year; f

Distributions
Income: Dec   Capital Gains: Dec

Exchange Options
Number Per Year: call fund   Fee: none
Telephone: yes (money market fund available)

Services
IRA, pension, auto exchange, auto invest, auto withdraw

Scudder Zero Coupon 2000 (SGZTX)

Two International Place
Boston, MA 02110
800-225-2470, 617-295-1000
www.funds.scudder.com

Government Bond

PERFORMANCE

fund inception date: 2/4/86

	3yr Annual	5yr Annual	10yr Annual	Bull	Bear
Return (%)	3.3	6.7	7.9	19.3	-9.4
Differ from Category (+/-)	-1.6 low	0.1 abv av	-0.1 av	-2.7 av	-3.0 blw av

Total Risk	Standard Deviation	Category Risk	Risk Index	Avg Mat
blw av	6.0%	abv av	1.5	4.4 yrs

	1996	1995	1994	1993	1992	1991	1990	1989	1988	1987
Return (%)	0.6	19.0	-8.0	16.0	8.1	20.0	4.5	20.3	11.7	-8.1
Differ from Category (+/-)	-0.9	-0.6	-3.6	4.4	1.4	4.3	-1.8	5.0	3.4	-3.7
Return, Tax-Adjusted (%)	-1.6	16.7	-10.3	11.4	2.6	16.9	1.7	18.3	9.2	-12.2

PER SHARE DATA

	1996	1995	1994	1993	1992	1991	1990	1989	1988	1987
Dividends, Net Income ($)	0.68	0.62	0.31	0.82	0.93	0.94	0.83	0.52	0.63	1.22
Distrib'ns, Cap Gain ($)	0.00	0.00	0.59	0.88	1.38	0.00	0.08	0.02	0.00	0.10
Net Asset Value ($)	11.77	12.38	10.95	12.85	12.55	13.76	12.27	12.61	10.92	10.34
Expense Ratio (%)	na	1.48	1.00	1.00	1.00	1.00	1.00	1.00	1.00	1.00
Yield (%)	5.77	5.00	2.68	5.97	6.67	6.83	6.72	4.11	5.76	11.68
Portfolio Turnover (%)	na	86	89	102	119	91	99	87	149	37
Total Assets (Millions $)	25	29	24	31	29	34	33	31	4	2

PORTFOLIO (as of 9/30/96)

Portfolio Manager: R. Heisler, R. Ross, S. Wohler - 1994

Investm't Category: Government Bond

✔ Domestic	Index
Foreign	Sector
Asset Allocation	State Specific

Investment Style

Large-Cap Growth	Large-Cap Value
Mid-Cap Growth	Mid-Cap Value
Small-Cap Growth	Small-Cap Value

Portfolio

0.0% cash	0.0% corp bonds
0.0% stocks	100.0% gov't bonds
0.0% preferred	0.0% muni bonds
0.0% conv't/warrants	0.0% other

SHAREHOLDER INFORMATION

Minimum Investment

Initial: $2,500   Subsequent: $100

Minimum IRA Investment

Initial: $1,000   Subsequent: $50

Maximum Fees

Load: none   12b-1: none

Other: f

Distributions

Income: Nov   Capital Gains: Nov

Exchange Options

Number Per Year: call fund   Fee: none

Telephone: yes (money market fund available)

Services

IRA, pension, auto exchange, auto invest, auto withdraw

Selected American Shares

(SLASX)

Growth & Income

124 E. Marcy St.
P.O. Box 1688
Santa Fe, NM 87504
800-243-1575, 505-983-4335

PERFORMANCE

fund inception date: 1/30/33

	3yr Annual	5yr Annual	10yr Annual	Bull	Bear
Return (%)	20.4	14.2	14.9	81.9	-7.7
Differ from Category (+/-)	5.1 high	0.3 av	2.2 high	22.1 high	-1.3 blw av

Total Risk	Standard Deviation	Category Risk	Risk Index	Beta
abv av	10.8%	high	1.2	1.04

	1996	1995	1994	1993	1992	1991	1990	1989	1988	1987
Return (%)	30.7	38.0	-3.3	5.4	5.8	46.2	-4.0	20.0	22.0	0.2
Differ from Category (+/-)	11.0	7.9	-2.0	-8.4	-4.9	17.1	1.9	-3.5	5.2	0.0
Return, Tax-Adjusted (%)	28.2	37.0	-5.5	-0.5	2.0	45.4	-5.4	14.3	21.0	-3.2

PER SHARE DATA

	1996	1995	1994	1993	1992	1991	1990	1989	1988	1987
Dividends, Net Income ($)	0.18	0.22	0.22	0.26	0.19	0.24	0.43	0.45	0.26	0.42
Distrib'ns, Cap Gain ($)	1.30	0.15	0.82	3.22	2.19	0.00	0.04	2.10	0.00	0.92
Net Asset Value ($)	21.53	17.68	13.09	14.60	17.13	18.43	12.79	13.81	13.67	11.43
Expense Ratio (%)	na	1.09	1.26	1.01	1.17	1.19	1.35	1.08	1.11	1.11
Yield (%)	0.78	1.23	1.58	1.45	0.98	1.30	3.35	2.82	1.90	3.40
Portfolio Turnover (%)	na	27	23	79	50	21	48	46	35	45
Total Assets (Millions $)	1,389	924	502	451	587	711	400	360	285	264

PORTFOLIO (as of 9/30/96)

Portfolio Manager: Shelby Davis, Christopher Davis - 1993

Investm't Category: Growth & Income

✔ Domestic
Foreign
Asset Allocation
Index
Sector
State Specific

Investment Style

Large-Cap Growth
Mid-Cap Growth
Small-Cap Growth
✔ Large-Cap Value
Mid-Cap Value
Small-Cap Value

Portfolio

0.7% cash	0.0% corp bonds
96.1% stocks	0.0% gov't bonds
2.6% preferred	0.0% muni bonds
1.0% conv't/warrants	0.0% other

SHAREHOLDER INFORMATION

Minimum Investment
Initial: $1,000   Subsequent: $100

Minimum IRA Investment
Initial: $250   Subsequent: $100

Maximum Fees
Load: none   12b-1: 0.25%
Other: none

Distributions
Income: annual   Capital Gains: annual

Exchange Options
Number Per Year: 4   Fee: none
Telephone: yes (money market fund available)

Services
IRA, pension, auto invest, auto withdraw

Selected Special Shares

(SLSSX)

Growth

124 E. Marcy St.
P.O. Box 1688
Santa Fe, NM 87504
800-243-1575, 505-983-4335

PERFORMANCE

fund inception date: 5/1/39

	3yr Annual	5yr Annual	10yr Annual	Bull	Bear
Return (%)	13.5	11.9	12.2	56.5	-8.0
Differ from Category (+/-)	-2.2 blw av	-2.4 blw av	-1.7 blw av	-5.9 blw av	-1.3 blw av

Total Risk	Standard Deviation	Category Risk	Risk Index	Beta
high	12.2%	high	1.2	0.87

	1996	1995	1994	1993	1992	1991	1990	1989	1988	1987
Return (%)	11.8	34.2	-2.6	10.8	8.4	25.5	-6.9	28.9	19.5	0.5
Differ from Category (+/-)	-8.3	3.9	-2.3	-3.2	-3.4	-10.5	-0.8	2.8	1.4	-1.5
Return, Tax-Adjusted (%)	8.7	30.2	-5.2	7.3	6.6	21.4	-7.8	25.3	15.9	-1.3

PER SHARE DATA

	1996	1995	1994	1993	1992	1991	1990	1989	1988	1987
Dividends, Net Income ($)	0.00	0.00	0.00	0.00	0.06	0.49	0.19	0.18	0.10	0.31
Distrib'ns, Cap Gain ($)	1.18	1.26	0.93	1.30	0.54	0.61	0.03	0.82	0.87	0.70
Net Asset Value ($)	10.89	10.80	9.02	10.21	10.41	10.17	9.04	9.95	8.52	7.96
Expense Ratio (%)	na	1.48	1.41	1.24	1.41	1.39	1.41	1.22	1.24	1.10
Yield (%)	0.00	0.00	0.00	0.00	0.54	4.54	2.09	1.67	1.06	3.58
Portfolio Turnover (%)	na	127	99	100	41	74	87	45	71	89
Total Assets (Millions $)	64	59	45	53	57	60	50	50	35	35

PORTFOLIO (as of 9/30/96)

Portfolio Manager: Elizabeth Bramwell - 1994

Investm't Category: Growth

✔ Domestic	Index
Foreign	Sector
Asset Allocation	State Specific

Investment Style

Large-Cap Growth	Large-Cap Value
✔ Mid-Cap Growth	Mid-Cap Value
✔ Small-Cap Growth	Small-Cap Value

Portfolio

1.5% cash	0.0% corp bonds
98.5% stocks	0.0% gov't bonds
0.0% preferred	0.0% muni bonds
0.0% conv't/warrants	0.0% other

SHAREHOLDER INFORMATION

Minimum Investment
Initial: $1,000   Subsequent: $100

Minimum IRA Investment
Initial: $250   Subsequent: $100

Maximum Fees
Load: none   12b-1: 0.25%
Other: none

Distributions
Income: annual   Capital Gains: annual

Exchange Options
Number Per Year: 4   Fee: none
Telephone: yes (money market fund available)

Services
IRA, pension, auto invest, auto withdraw

Sentry (SNTRX)
Growth

1800 N. Point Drive
Stevens Point, WI 54481
800-533-7827, 715-346-7048

PERFORMANCE

fund inception date: 5/22/70

	3yr Annual	5yr Annual	10yr Annual	Bull	Bear
Return (%)	15.7	12.0	12.6	56.9	-2.2
Differ from Category (+/-)	0.0 av	-2.3 blw av	-1.3 blw av	-5.5 blw av	4.5 high

Total Risk	Standard Deviation	Category Risk	Risk Index	Beta
av	8.8%	low	0.9	0.73

	1996	1995	1994	1993	1992	1991	1990	1989	1988	1987
Return (%)	22.8	27.7	-1.2	5.9	7.4	28.8	5.2	24.0	16.9	-5.5
Differ from Category (+/-)	2.7	-2.6	-0.9	-8.1	-4.4	-7.2	11.3	-2.1	-1.2	-7.5
Return, Tax-Adjusted (%)	20.8	24.9	-3.1	3.5	6.0	25.0	2.7	20.8	15.2	-9.7

PER SHARE DATA

	1996	1995	1994	1993	1992	1991	1990	1989	1988	1987
Dividends, Net Income ($)	0.16	0.18	0.17	0.21	0.26	0.38	0.35	0.38	0.22	0.30
Distrib'ns, Cap Gain ($)	0.91	1.11	0.76	0.98	0.36	1.13	0.65	0.73	0.30	1.47
Net Asset Value ($)	18.84	16.24	13.75	14.85	15.15	14.68	12.60	12.93	11.33	10.14
Expense Ratio (%)	na	0.86	0.86	0.87	0.88	0.84	0.69	0.65	0.66	0.67
Yield (%)	0.81	1.03	1.17	1.32	1.67	2.40	2.64	2.78	1.89	2.58
Portfolio Turnover (%)	na	26	16	22	13	3	30	15	19	35
Total Assets (Millions $)	103	88	75	76	72	64	49	47	41	38

PORTFOLIO (as of 9/30/96)

Portfolio Manager: Keith Ringberg - 1977

Investm't Category: Growth
- ✔ Domestic
- Foreign
- Asset Allocation
- Index
- Sector
- State Specific

Investment Style
- ✔ Large-Cap Growth
- Mid-Cap Growth
- Small-Cap Growth
- ✔ Large-Cap Value
- Mid-Cap Value
- Small-Cap Value

Portfolio
5.4% cash	0.0% corp bonds
94.6% stocks	0.0% gov't bonds
0.0% preferred	0.0% muni bonds
0.0% conv't/warrants	0.0% other

SHAREHOLDER INFORMATION

Minimum Investment
Initial: $500   Subsequent: $50

Minimum IRA Investment
Initial: $500   Subsequent: $50

Maximum Fees
Load: none   12b-1: none
Other: none

Distributions
Income: annual   Capital Gains: annual

Exchange Options
Number Per Year: none   Fee: na
Telephone: na

Services
IRA, auto invest, auto withdraw

Sequoia (SEQUX)

Growth & Income

767 Fifth Ave.
Suite 4701
New York, NY 10153
800-686-6884, 212-832-5280

this fund is closed to new investors

PERFORMANCE

fund inception date: 7/20/70

	3yr Annual	5yr Annual	10yr Annual	Bull	Bear
Return (%)	21.1	16.5	16.0	76.3	-1.1
Differ from Category (+/-)	5.8 high	2.6 high	3.3 high	16.5 high	5.3 high

Total Risk	Standard Deviation	Category Risk	Risk Index	Beta
abv av	11.2%	high	1.2	0.78

	1996	1995	1994	1993	1992	1991	1990	1989	1988	1987
Return (%)	21.7	41.3	3.3	10.7	9.3	40.0	-3.8	27.9	11.0	7.4
Differ from Category (+/-)	2.0	11.2	4.6	-3.1	-1.4	10.9	2.1	4.4	-5.8	7.2
Return, Tax-Adjusted (%)	19.3	41.0	2.6	6.6	8.2	36.3	-6.1	25.5	7.9	4.0

PER SHARE DATA

	1996	1995	1994	1993	1992	1991	1990	1989	1988	1987
Dividends, Net Income ($)	0.38	0.39	0.41	0.65	0.93	1.36	1.38	1.28	1.38	2.21
Distrib'ns, Cap Gain ($)	6.10	0.00	0.66	7.19	0.62	3.58	1.78	1.43	2.23	1.59
Net Asset Value ($)	88.44	78.13	55.59	54.84	56.66	53.31	41.94	46.86	38.81	38.43
Expense Ratio (%)	na	1.00	1.00	1.00	1.00	1.00	1.00	1.00	1.00	1.00
Yield (%)	0.40	0.49	0.72	1.04	1.62	2.39	3.15	2.65	3.36	5.52
Portfolio Turnover (%)	na	15	32	24	28	36	29	44	39	43
Total Assets (Millions $)	2,677	2,185	1,548	1,512	1,389	1,251	870	924	714	720

PORTFOLIO (as of 9/30/96)

Portfolio Manager: W. Ruane, R. Cunniff - 1970

Investm't Category: Growth & Income
- ✔ Domestic
- ✔ Foreign
- Asset Allocation
- Index
- Sector
- State Specific

Investment Style
- Large-Cap Growth
- Mid-Cap Growth
- Small-Cap Growth
- ✔ Large-Cap Value
- Mid-Cap Value
- Small-Cap Value

Portfolio
14.5% cash	0.0% corp bonds
85.5% stocks	0.0% gov't bonds
0.0% preferred	0.0% muni bonds
0.0% conv't/warrants	0.0% other

SHAREHOLDER INFORMATION

Minimum Investment
Initial: na   Subsequent: $50

Minimum IRA Investment
Initial: na   Subsequent: na

Maximum Fees
Load: none   12b-1: none
Other: none

Distributions
Income: Feb, Jun, Dec   Capital Gains: Feb, Dec

Exchange Options
Number Per Year: none   Fee: na
Telephone: na

Services
IRA, auto withdraw

Sit Int'l Growth (SNGRX)

International Stock

4600 Norwest Center
90 S. Seventh St.
Minneapolis, MN 55402
800-332-5580, 612-334-5888
www.sitfunds.com

PERFORMANCE

fund inception date: 11/1/91

	3yr Annual	5yr Annual	10yr Annual	Bull	Bear
Return (%)	5.3	12.2	na	22.9	-9.2
Differ from Category (+/-)	-1.0 blw av	2.2 abv av	na	-1.4 av	-2.0 blw av

Total Risk	Standard Deviation	Category Risk	Risk Index	Beta
abv av	10.9%	av	1.1	0.73

	1996	1995	1994	1993	1992	1991	1990	1989	1988	1987
Return (%)	10.3	9.3	-3.0	48.3	2.6	—	—	—	—	—
Differ from Category (+/-)	-4.5	0.2	0.1	8.7	6.4	—	—	—	—	—
Return, Tax-Adjusted (%)	9.5	7.5	-3.6	47.8	2.5	—	—	—	—	—

PER SHARE DATA

	1996	1995	1994	1993	1992	1991	1990	1989	1988	1987
Dividends, Net Income ($)	0.01	0.08	0.03	0.09	0.02	—	—	—	—	—
Distrib'ns, Cap Gain ($)	0.41	0.84	0.26	0.05	0.00	—	—	—	—	—
Net Asset Value ($)	16.45	15.31	14.88	15.66	10.66	—	—	—	—	—
Expense Ratio (%)	1.50	1.50	1.65	1.85	1.85	—	—	—	—	—
Yield (%)	0.05	0.49	0.19	0.57	0.18	—	—	—	—	—
Portfolio Turnover (%)	38	40	42	52	19	—	—	—	—	—
Total Assets (Millions $)	87	73	65	64	26	—	—	—	—	—

PORTFOLIO (as of 6/30/96)

Portfolio Manager: Andrew B. Kim - 1991

Investm't Category: International Stock

Domestic	Index
✔ Foreign	Sector
Asset Allocation	State Specific

Investment Style

Large-Cap Growth	Large-Cap Value
Mid-Cap Growth	Mid-Cap Value
Small-Cap Growth	Small-Cap Value

Portfolio

6.9% cash	0.0% corp bonds
92.2% stocks	0.0% gov't bonds
0.0% preferred	0.0% muni bonds
0.9% conv't/warrants	0.0% other

SHAREHOLDER INFORMATION

Minimum Investment
Initial: $2,000   Subsequent: $100

Minimum IRA Investment
Initial: $1   Subsequent: $1

Maximum Fees
Load: none   12b-1: none
Other: none

Distributions
Income: annual   Capital Gains: annual

Exchange Options
Number Per Year: 4   Fee: none
Telephone: yes (money market fund available)

Services
IRA, pension, auto exchange, auto invest, auto withdraw

Sit Large Cap Growth

(SNIGX)

Growth & Income

4600 Norwest Center
90 S. Seventh St.
Minneapolis, MN 55402
800-332-5580, 612-334-5888
www.sitfunds.com

PERFORMANCE

fund inception date: 10/19/81

	3yr Annual	5yr Annual	10yr Annual	Bull	Bear
Return (%)	18.5	12.5	13.0	73.5	-6.9
Differ from Category (+/-)	3.2 abv av	-1.4 blw av	0.3 av	13.7 high	-0.5 av

Total Risk	Standard Deviation	Category Risk	Risk Index	Beta
abv av	11.0%	high	1.2	1.01

	1996	1995	1994	1993	1992	1991	1990	1989	1988	1987
Return (%)	23.0	31.6	2.8	3.1	4.9	32.7	-2.4	31.9	5.3	5.3
Differ from Category (+/-)	3.3	1.5	4.1	-10.7	-5.8	3.6	3.5	8.4	-11.5	5.1
Return, Tax-Adjusted (%)	20.6	28.9	1.0	1.1	3.7	30.9	-4.5	29.3	4.2	2.1

PER SHARE DATA

	1996	1995	1994	1993	1992	1991	1990	1989	1988	1987
Dividends, Net Income ($)	0.04	0.05	0.09	0.27	0.38	0.52	0.70	0.51	0.45	0.61
Distrib'ns, Cap Gain ($)	2.41	2.24	1.40	1.38	0.54	0.54	0.62	0.91	0.00	1.13
Net Asset Value ($)	33.68	29.39	24.09	24.92	25.79	25.49	20.06	21.90	17.69	17.22
Expense Ratio (%)	1.00	1.00	1.10	1.42	1.50	1.50	1.50	1.50	1.50	1.50
Yield (%)	0.11	0.15	0.35	1.02	1.44	1.99	3.38	2.23	2.54	3.32
Portfolio Turnover (%)	49	67	73	47	73	70	55	82	67	61
Total Assets (Millions $)	62	46	36	37	37	30	17	15	11	10

PORTFOLIO (as of 6/30/96)

Portfolio Manager: Peter Mitchelson, Ron Sit - 1982

Investm't Category: Growth & Income
- ✔ Domestic
-   Foreign
-   Asset Allocation
-   Index
-   Sector
-   State Specific

Investment Style
- ✔ Large-Cap Growth
-   Mid-Cap Growth
-   Small-Cap Growth
-   Large-Cap Value
-   Mid-Cap Value
-   Small-Cap Value

Portfolio
6.2% cash	0.0% corp bonds
93.8% stocks	0.0% gov't bonds
0.0% preferred	0.0% muni bonds
0.0% conv't/warrants	0.0% other

SHAREHOLDER INFORMATION

Minimum Investment
Initial: $2,000   Subsequent: $100

Minimum IRA Investment
Initial: $1   Subsequent: $1

Maximum Fees
Load: none   12b-1: none
Other: none

Distributions
Income: annual   Capital Gains: annual

Exchange Options
Number Per Year: 4   Fee: none
Telephone: yes (money market fund available)

Services
IRA, pension, auto exchange, auto invest, auto withdraw

Sit Mid Cap Growth

(NBNGX)

Aggressive Growth

4600 Norwest Center
90 S. Seventh St.
Minneapolis, MN 55402
800-332-5580, 612-334-5888
www.sitfunds.com

PERFORMANCE

fund inception date: 10/19/81

	3yr Annual	5yr Annual	10yr Annual	Bull	Bear
Return (%)	17.4	11.4	15.8	85.2	-16.1
Differ from Category (+/-)	1.6 abv av	-3.9 blw av	0.8 av	14.1 abv av	-5.5 low

Total Risk	Standard Deviation	Category Risk	Risk Index	Beta
high	15.5%	abv av	1.1	1.13

	1996	1995	1994	1993	1992	1991	1990	1989	1988	1987
Return (%)	21.8	33.6	-0.5	8.5	-2.2	65.4	-2.1	35.1	9.7	5.4
Differ from Category (+/-)	2.7	-0.7	-0.5	-10.8	-13.9	13.3	3.3	6.7	-6.7	7.8
Return, Tax-Adjusted (%)	16.5	30.0	-2.9	7.7	-2.4	65.0	-3.8	33.0	7.9	4.5

PER SHARE DATA

	1996	1995	1994	1993	1992	1991	1990	1989	1988	1987
Dividends, Net Income ($)	0.00	0.00	0.00	0.01	0.04	0.05	0.07	0.08	0.09	0.00
Distrib'ns, Cap Gain ($)	2.62	1.45	1.04	0.29	0.02	0.03	0.38	0.36	0.25	0.73
Net Asset Value ($)	14.27	13.86	11.51	12.66	11.96	12.29	7.48	8.11	6.33	6.09
Expense Ratio (%)	0.77	0.83	0.82	0.80	0.83	1.03	1.10	1.19	1.21	1.20
Yield (%)	0.00	0.00	0.00	0.07	0.33	0.40	0.89	0.94	1.36	0.00
Portfolio Turnover (%)	50	75	46	45	25	37	55	88	78	81
Total Assets (Millions $)	398	377	303	332	334	208	68	58	49	39

PORTFOLIO (as of 6/30/96)

Portfolio Manager: Eugene C. Sit - 1982

Investm't Category: Aggressive Growth

✔ Domestic	Index
Foreign	Sector
Asset Allocation	State Specific

Investment Style

Large-Cap Growth	Large-Cap Value
✔ Mid-Cap Growth	Mid-Cap Value
✔ Small-Cap Growth	Small-Cap Value

Portfolio

5.9% cash	0.0% corp bonds
94.1% stocks	0.0% gov't bonds
0.0% preferred	0.0% muni bonds
0.0% conv't/warrants	0.0% other

SHAREHOLDER INFORMATION

Minimum Investment
Initial: $2,000   Subsequent: $100

Minimum IRA Investment
Initial: $1   Subsequent: $1

Maximum Fees
Load: none   12b-1: none
Other: none

Distributions
Income: annual   Capital Gains: annual

Exchange Options
Number Per Year: 4   Fee: none
Telephone: yes (money market fund available)

Services
IRA, pension, auto exchange, auto invest, auto withdraw

Sit Minnesota Tax-Free Income (SMTFX)

Tax-Exempt Bond

4600 Norwest Center
90 S. Seventh St.
Minneapolis, MN 55402
800-332-5580, 612-334-5888
www.sitfunds.com

PERFORMANCE

fund inception date: 12/1/93

	3yr Annual	5yr Annual	10yr Annual	Bull	Bear
Return (%)	6.0	na	na	19.6	-1.2
Differ from Category (+/-)	1.8 high	na	na	1.2 av	4.2 high

Total Risk	Standard Deviation	Category Risk	Risk Index	Avg Mat
low	3.3%	low	0.6	18.9 yrs

	1996	1995	1994	1993	1992	1991	1990	1989	1988	1987
Return (%)	5.8	11.8	0.6	—	—	—	—	—	—	—
Differ from Category (+/-)	2.1	-3.4	5.9	—	—	—	—	—	—	—
Return, Tax-Adjusted (%)	5.8	11.8	0.6	—	—	—	—	—	—	—

PER SHARE DATA

	1996	1995	1994	1993	1992	1991	1990	1989	1988	1987
Dividends, Net Income ($)	0.57	0.56	0.55	—	—	—	—	—	—	—
Distrib'ns, Cap Gain ($)	0.00	0.00	0.00	—	—	—	—	—	—	—
Net Asset Value ($)	10.24	10.23	9.67	—	—	—	—	—	—	—
Expense Ratio (%)	0.80	0.80	0.80	—	—	—	—	—	—	—
Yield (%)	5.56	5.47	5.68	—	—	—	—	—	—	—
Portfolio Turnover (%)	15	34	12	—	—	—	—	—	—	—
Total Assets (Millions $)	79	62	37	—	—	—	—	—	—	—

PORTFOLIO (as of 6/30/96)

Portfolio Manager: Michael Brilley, Debra Sit - 1993

Investm't Category: Tax-Exempt Bond
- ✔ Domestic
- Foreign
- Asset Allocation
- Index
- Sector
- ✔ State Specific

Investment Style
- Large-Cap Growth
- Mid-Cap Growth
- Small-Cap Growth
- Large-Cap Value
- Mid-Cap Value
- Small-Cap Value

Portfolio
2.7% cash	0.0% corp bonds
0.0% stocks	0.0% gov't bonds
0.0% preferred	97.3% muni bonds
0.0% conv't/warrants	0.0% other

SHAREHOLDER INFORMATION

Minimum Investment
Initial: $2,000   Subsequent: $100

Minimum IRA Investment
Initial: na   Subsequent: na

Maximum Fees
Load: none   12b-1: none
Other: none

Distributions
Income: monthly   Capital Gains: annual

Exchange Options
Number Per Year: 4   Fee: none
Telephone: yes (money market funds available)

Services
auto exchange, auto invest, auto withdraw

Sit Small Cap Growth

(SSMGX)

Aggressive Growth

4600 Norwest Center
90 S. Seventh St.
Minneapolis, MN 55402
800-332-5580, 612-334-5888
www.sitfunds.com

PERFORMANCE

fund inception date: 7/1/94

	3yr Annual	5yr Annual	10yr Annual	Bull	Bear
Return (%)	na	na	na	na	na
Differ from Category (+/-)	na	na	na	na	na

Total Risk	Standard Deviation	Category Risk	Risk Index	Beta
na	na	na	na	na

	1996	1995	1994	1993	1992	1991	1990	1989	1988	1987
Return (%).	14.9	52.1	—	—	—	—	—	—	—	—
Differ from Category (+/-).	-4.2	17.8	—	—	—	—	—	—	—	—
Return, Tax-Adjusted (%). .	13.5	51.7	—	—	—	—	—	—	—	—

PER SHARE DATA

	1996	1995	1994	1993	1992	1991	1990	1989	1988	1987
Dividends, Net Income ($).	0.00	0.00	—	—	—	—	—	—	—	—
Distrib'ns, Cap Gain ($) . . .	0.80	0.14	—	—	—	—	—	—	—	—
Net Asset Value ($)	18.43	16.74	—	—	—	—	—	—	—	—
Expense Ratio (%).	1.50	1.50	—	—	—	—	—	—	—	—
Yield (%)	0.00	0.00	—	—	—	—	—	—	—	—
Portfolio Turnover (%).	69	49	—	—	—	—	—	—	—	—
Total Assets (Millions $). . . .	58	31	—	—	—	—	—	—	—	—

PORTFOLIO (as of 6/30/96)

Portfolio Manager: Eugene C. Sit - 1994

Investm't Category: Aggressive Growth

✔ Domestic
   Foreign
   Asset Allocation

   Index
   Sector
   State Specific

Investment Style
   Large-Cap Growth
   Mid-Cap Growth
   Small-Cap Growth

   Large-Cap Value
   Mid-Cap Value
   Small-Cap Value

Portfolio

6.6% cash	0.0% corp bonds
92.6% stocks	0.0% gov't bonds
0.0% preferred	0.0% muni bonds
0.0% conv't/warrants	0.0% other

SHAREHOLDER INFORMATION

Minimum Investment
Initial: $2,000   Subsequent: $100

Minimum IRA Investment
Initial: $1   Subsequent: $1

Maximum Fees
Load: none   12b-1: none
Other: none

Distributions
Income: annual   Capital Gains: annual

Exchange Options
Number Per Year: 4   Fee: none
Telephone: yes (money market fund available)

Services
IRA, pension, auto exchange, auto invest, auto withdraw

Sit Tax-Free Income
(SNTIX)
Tax-Exempt Bond

4600 Norwest Center
90 S. Seventh St.
Minneapolis, MN 55402
800-332-5580, 612-334-5888
www.sitfunds.com

PERFORMANCE

fund inception date: 9/29/88

	3yr Annual	5yr Annual	10yr Annual	Bull	Bear
Return (%)	5.8	7.1	na	20.1	-2.5
Differ from Category (+/-)	1.6 high	0.7 abv av	na	1.7 abv av	2.9 high

Total Risk	Standard Deviation	Category Risk	Risk Index	Avg Mat
low	3.4%	low	0.6	16.1 yrs

	1996	1995	1994	1993	1992	1991	1990	1989	1988	1987
Return (%)	5.6	12.8	-0.7	10.4	7.7	9.2	7.2	8.3	—	—
Differ from Category (+/-)	1.9	-2.4	4.6	-1.4	-0.6	-2.2	0.8	-0.7	—	—
Return, Tax-Adjusted (%)	5.6	12.8	-0.8	10.1	7.5	9.2	7.2	8.3	—	—

PER SHARE DATA

	1996	1995	1994	1993	1992	1991	1990	1989	1988	1987
Dividends, Net Income ($)	0.56	0.55	0.56	0.58	0.64	0.70	0.78	0.77	—	—
Distrib'ns, Cap Gain ($)	0.00	0.00	0.02	0.08	0.04	0.00	0.00	0.00	—	—
Net Asset Value ($)	10.05	10.06	9.43	10.08	9.76	9.72	9.57	9.68	—	—
Expense Ratio (%)	0.80	0.79	0.77	0.80	0.80	0.80	0.80	0.80	—	—
Yield (%)	5.57	5.46	5.92	5.70	6.53	7.20	8.15	7.95	—	—
Portfolio Turnover (%)	25	13	47	58	80	74	87	132	—	—
Total Assets (Millions $)	309	281	243	340	278	133	47	20	—	—

PORTFOLIO (as of 6/30/96)

Portfolio Manager: Michael Brilley, Debra Sit - 1988

Investm't Category: Tax-Exempt Bond

✔ Domestic	Index
Foreign	Sector
Asset Allocation	State Specific

Investment Style

Large-Cap Growth	Large-Cap Value
Mid-Cap Growth	Mid-Cap Value
Small-Cap Growth	Small-Cap Value

Portfolio

5.3% cash	0.0% corp bonds
0.0% stocks	0.0% gov't bonds
0.0% preferred	94.7% muni bonds
0.0% conv't/warrants	0.0% other

SHAREHOLDER INFORMATION

Minimum Investment
Initial: $2,000   Subsequent: $100

Minimum IRA Investment
Initial: na   Subsequent: na

Maximum Fees
Load: none   12b-1: none
Other: none

Distributions
Income: monthly   Capital Gains: annual

Exchange Options
Number Per Year: 4   Fee: none
Telephone: yes (money market fund available)

Services
auto exchange, auto invest, auto withdraw

Sit US Gov't Securities
(SNGVX)
Mortgage-Backed Bond

4600 Norwest Center
90 S. Seventh St.
Minneapolis, MN 55402
800-332-5580, 612-334-5888
www.sitfunds.com

PERFORMANCE
fund inception date: 6/2/87

	3yr Annual	5yr Annual	10yr Annual	Bull	Bear
Return (%)	6.0	6.1	na	18.9	-0.6
Differ from Category (+/-)	0.4 av	0.1 av	na	-2.2 blw av	3.0 high

Total Risk	Standard Deviation	Category Risk	Risk Index	Avg Mat
low	1.9%	low	0.5	13.7 yrs

	1996	1995	1994	1993	1992	1991	1990	1989	1988	1987
Return (%)	4.9	11.5	1.7	7.3	5.4	12.8	10.8	11.0	7.8	—
Differ from Category (+/-)	0.5	-3.2	3.4	0.4	-0.8	-1.6	1.0	-1.6	0.4	—
Return, Tax-Adjusted (%)	2.4	8.7	-0.7	4.6	2.4	9.3	7.8	7.6	4.5	—

PER SHARE DATA

	1996	1995	1994	1993	1992	1991	1990	1989	1988	1987
Dividends, Net Income ($)	0.65	0.70	0.64	0.67	0.70	0.79	0.77	0.84	0.83	—
Distrib'ns, Cap Gain ($)	0.00	0.00	0.00	0.05	0.15	0.17	0.00	0.00	0.00	—
Net Asset Value ($)	10.45	10.60	10.17	10.63	10.60	10.89	10.56	10.27	10.05	—
Expense Ratio (%)	0.80	0.80	0.86	0.89	0.80	0.90	1.25	1.25	1.25	—
Yield (%)	6.22	6.60	6.29	6.27	6.51	7.14	7.29	8.17	8.25	—
Portfolio Turnover (%)	51	38	73	76	134	118	126	139	136	—
Total Assets (Millions $)	60	48	36	39	30	35	15	12	13	—

PORTFOLIO (as of 6/30/96)

Portfolio Manager: Michael Brilley - 1987

Investm't Category: Mortgage-Backed Bond
- ✔ Domestic
- Foreign
- Asset Allocation
- Index
- Sector
- State Specific

Investment Style
- Large-Cap Growth
- Mid-Cap Growth
- Small-Cap Growth
- Large-Cap Value
- Mid-Cap Value
- Small-Cap Value

Portfolio
3.2%	cash	0.0%	corp bonds
0.0%	stocks	96.8%	gov't bonds
0.0%	preferred	0.0%	muni bonds
0.0%	conv't/warrants	0.0%	other

SHAREHOLDER INFORMATION

Minimum Investment
Initial: $2,000   Subsequent: $100

Minimum IRA Investment
Initial: $1   Subsequent: $1

Maximum Fees
Load: none   12b-1: none
Other: none

Distributions
Income: monthly   Capital Gains: annual

Exchange Options
Number Per Year: 4   Fee: none
Telephone: yes (money market fund available)

Services
IRA, pension, auto exchange, auto invest, auto withdraw

Skyline: Special Equities II
(SPEQX)
Growth

311 S. Wacker Drive
Suite 4500
Chicago, IL 60606
800-458-5222, 312-595-6035

PERFORMANCE

fund inception date: 2/9/93

	3yr Annual	5yr Annual	10yr Annual	Bull	Bear
Return (%)	14.6	na	na	56.2	-6.1
Differ from Category (+/-)	-1.1 av	na	na	-6.2 blw av	0.6 av

Total Risk	Standard Deviation	Category Risk	Risk Index	Beta
abv av	11.2%	abv av	1.1	0.78

	1996	1995	1994	1993	1992	1991	1990	1989	1988	1987
Return (%).	26.5	20.9	-1.6	—	—	—	—	—	—	—
Differ from Category (+/-) . .	6.4	-9.4	-1.3	—	—	—	—	—	—	—
Return, Tax-Adjusted (%). .	20.8	18.2	-2.9	—	—	—	—	—	—	—

PER SHARE DATA

	1996	1995	1994	1993	1992	1991	1990	1989	1988	1987
Dividends, Net Income ($).	0.01	0.05	0.01	—	—	—	—	—	—	—
Distrib'ns, Cap Gain ($) . . .	2.25	0.90	0.46	—	—	—	—	—	—	—
Net Asset Value ($)	11.94	11.29	10.14	—	—	—	—	—	—	—
Expense Ratio (%).	na	1.52	1.51	—	—	—	—	—	—	—
Yield (%)	0.07	0.41	0.09	—	—	—	—	—	—	—
Portfolio Turnover (%).	na	102	82	—	—	—	—	—	—	—
Total Assets (Millions $). . .	101	88	100	—	—	—	—	—	—	—

PORTFOLIO (as of 9/30/96)

Portfolio Manager: Kenneth S. Kailin - 1993

Investm't Category: Growth

✔ Domestic	Index
Foreign	Sector
Asset Allocation	State Specific

Investment Style

Large-Cap Growth	Large-Cap Value
Mid-Cap Growth	Mid-Cap Value
✔ Small-Cap Growth	✔ Small-Cap Value

Portfolio

5.0% cash	0.0% corp bonds
95.0% stocks	0.0% gov't bonds
0.0% preferred	0.0% muni bonds
0.0% conv't/warrants	0.0% other

SHAREHOLDER INFORMATION

Minimum Investment
Initial: $1,000   Subsequent: $100

Minimum IRA Investment
Initial: $1,000   Subsequent: $100

Maximum Fees
Load: none   12b-1: none
Other: none

Distributions
Income: annual   Capital Gains: annual

Exchange Options
Number Per Year: none   Fee: none
Telephone: yes (money market fund available)

Services
IRA, pension, auto exchange, auto invest, auto withdraw

Skyline: Special Equities Port (SKSEX)

Aggressive Growth

311 S. Wacker Drive
Suite 4500
Chicago, IL 60606
800-458-5222, 312-595-6035

PERFORMANCE

fund inception date: 4/23/87

	3yr Annual	5yr Annual	10yr Annual	Bull	Bear
Return (%)	13.6	20.7	na	53.0	-8.3
Differ from Category (+/-)	-2.2 blw av	5.4 high	na	-18.1 blw av	2.3 abv av

Total Risk	Standard Deviation	Category Risk	Risk Index	Beta
abv av	11.1%	low	0.8	0.61

	1996	1995	1994	1993	1992	1991	1990	1989	1988	1987
Return (%)	30.3	13.8	-1.2	22.8	42.4	47.3	-9.3	24.0	29.7	—
Differ from Category (+/-)	11.2	-20.5	-1.2	3.5	30.7	-4.8	-3.9	-4.4	13.3	—
Return, Tax-Adjusted (%)	24.2	12.0	-4.3	17.6	40.4	40.7	-9.7	20.3	29.5	—

PER SHARE DATA

	1996	1995	1994	1993	1992	1991	1990	1989	1988	1987
Dividends, Net Income ($)	0.00	0.00	0.00	0.00	0.00	0.01	0.10	0.13	0.04	—
Distrib'ns, Cap Gain ($)	3.61	1.00	1.93	3.14	0.90	2.39	0.00	1.15	0.00	—
Net Asset Value ($)	18.16	16.79	15.64	17.83	17.12	12.67	10.32	11.49	10.32	—
Expense Ratio (%)	na	1.51	1.49	1.48	1.51	1.55	1.59	1.60	1.70	—
Yield (%)	0.00	0.00	0.00	0.00	0.00	0.06	0.96	1.02	0.38	—
Portfolio Turnover (%)	na	97	82	104	87	104	98	90	68	—
Total Assets (Millions $)	188	175	202	227	172	37	22	20	11	—

PORTFOLIO (as of 9/30/96)

Portfolio Manager: William Dutton - 1987

Investm't Category: Aggressive Growth
- ✔ Domestic
- Foreign
- Asset Allocation
- Index
- Sector
- State Specific

Investment Style
- Large-Cap Growth
- Mid-Cap Growth
- Small-Cap Growth
- Large-Cap Value
- Mid-Cap Value
- ✔ Small-Cap Value

Portfolio
7.4% cash	0.0% corp bonds
93.1% stocks	0.0% gov't bonds
0.0% preferred	0.0% muni bonds
0.0% conv't/warrants	0.0% other

SHAREHOLDER INFORMATION

Minimum Investment
Initial: $1,000   Subsequent: $100

Minimum IRA Investment
Initial: $1,000   Subsequent: $100

Maximum Fees
Load: none   12b-1: none
Other: none

Distributions
Income: annual   Capital Gains: annual

Exchange Options
Number Per Year: no limit   Fee: none
Telephone: yes (money market fund available)

Services
IRA, pension, auto invest, auto withdraw

Smith Breeden Interm Duration US Gov't (SBIDX)

Mortgage-Backed Bond

100 Europa Drive
Suite 200
Chapel Hill, NC 27514
800-221-3138, 919-967-7221

PERFORMANCE

fund inception date: 3/31/92

	3yr Annual	5yr Annual	10yr Annual	Bull	Bear
Return (%)	6.3	na	na	23.7	-4.2
Differ from Category (+/-)	0.7 high	na	na	2.6 abv av	-0.6 blw av

Total Risk	Standard Deviation	Category Risk	Risk Index	Avg Mat
low	4.1%	abv av	1.1	26.3 yrs

	1996	1995	1994	1993	1992	1991	1990	1989	1988	1987
Return (%)	5.0	16.4	-1.7	11.1	—	—	—	—	—	—
Differ from Category (+/-)	0.6	1.7	0.0	4.2	—	—	—	—	—	—
Return, Tax-Adjusted (%)	1.9	13.3	-4.3	6.8	—	—	—	—	—	—

PER SHARE DATA

	1996	1995	1994	1993	1992	1991	1990	1989	1988	1987
Dividends, Net Income ($)	0.61	0.65	0.58	1.10	—	—	—	—	—	—
Distrib'ns, Cap Gain ($)	0.25	0.10	0.13	0.01	—	—	—	—	—	—
Net Asset Value ($)	9.86	10.23	9.47	10.36	—	—	—	—	—	—
Expense Ratio (%)	0.90	0.90	0.00	0.31	—	—	—	—	—	—
Yield (%)	6.03	6.29	6.04	10.60	—	—	—	—	—	—
Portfolio Turnover (%)	193	557	84	42	—	—	—	—	—	—
Total Assets (Millions $)	38	37	33	4	—	—	—	—	—	—

PORTFOLIO (as of 9/30/96)

Portfolio Manager: Daniel C. Dektar - 1992

Investm't Category: Mortgage-Backed Bond
✔ Domestic   Index
  Foreign   Sector
  Asset Allocation State Specific

Investment Style
Large-Cap Growth   Large-Cap Value
Mid-Cap Growth   Mid-Cap Value
Small-Cap Growth   Small-Cap Value

Portfolio
0.0% cash   0.0% corp bonds
0.0% stocks   124.6% gov't bonds
0.0% preferred   0.0% muni bonds
0.0% conv't/warrants 0.0% other

SHAREHOLDER INFORMATION

Minimum Investment
Initial: $500   Subsequent: $50

Minimum IRA Investment
Initial: $500   Subsequent: $50

Maximum Fees
Load: none   12b-1: 0.25%
Other: none

Distributions
Income: annual   Capital Gains: annual

Exchange Options
Number Per Year: 5   Fee: none
Telephone: yes (money market fund available)

Services
IRA, pension, auto invest, auto withdraw

Smith Breeden Short Duration US Gov't Series

100 Europa Drive
Suite 200
Chapel Hill, NC 27514
800-221-3138, 919-967-7221

(SBSHX) *Mortgage-Backed Bond*

PERFORMANCE

fund inception date: 3/31/92

	3yr Annual	5yr Annual	10yr Annual	Bull	Bear
Return (%)	5.5	na	na	16.6	0.0
Differ from Category (+/-)	-0.1 av	na	na	-4.5 low	3.6 high

Total Risk	Standard Deviation	Category Risk	Risk Index	Avg Mat
low	1.4%	low	0.4	26.0 yrs

	1996	1995	1994	1993	1992	1991	1990	1989	1988	1987
Return (%)	6.2	6.1	4.1	4.6	—	—	—	—	—	—
Differ from Category (+/-)	1.8	-8.6	5.8	-2.3	—	—	—	—	—	—
Return, Tax-Adjusted (%)	4.0	3.4	1.8	2.6	—	—	—	—	—	—

PER SHARE DATA

	1996	1995	1994	1993	1992	1991	1990	1989	1988	1987
Dividends, Net Income ($)	0.54	0.66	0.57	0.49	—	—	—	—	—	—
Distrib'ns, Cap Gain ($)	0.00	0.00	0.00	0.00	—	—	—	—	—	—
Net Asset Value ($)	9.81	9.76	9.84	10.01	—	—	—	—	—	—
Expense Ratio (%)	0.78	0.78	0.29	0.27	—	—	—	—	—	—
Yield (%)	5.50	6.76	5.79	4.89	—	—	—	—	—	—
Portfolio Turnover (%)	225	47	112	3	—	—	—	—	—	—
Total Assets (Millions $)	199	235	195	130	—	—	—	—	—	—

PORTFOLIO (as of 9/30/96)

Portfolio Manager: Daniel C. Dektar - 1992

Investm't Category: Mortgage-Backed Bond
- ✔ Domestic
- Foreign
- Asset Allocation
- Index
- Sector
- State Specific

Investment Style
- Large-Cap Growth
- Mid-Cap Growth
- Small-Cap Growth
- Large-Cap Value
- Mid-Cap Value
- Small-Cap Value

Portfolio
0.0% cash	0.0% corp bonds	
0.0% stocks	119.7% gov't bonds	
0.0% preferred	0.0% muni bonds	
0.0% conv't/warrants	2.3% other	

SHAREHOLDER INFORMATION

Minimum Investment
Initial: $500   Subsequent: $50

Minimum IRA Investment
Initial: $500   Subsequent: $50

Maximum Fees
Load: none   12b-1: 0.25%
Other: none

Distributions
Income: annual   Capital Gains: annual

Exchange Options
Number Per Year: 5   Fee: none
Telephone: yes (money market fund available)

Services
IRA, pension, auto invest, auto withdraw

Sound Shore (SSHFX)

Growth

P.O. Box 7148
Portland, ME 04112
800-953-6786, 800-754-8758

PERFORMANCE **fund inception date: 5/3/85**

	3yr Annual	5yr Annual	10yr Annual	Bull	Bear
Return (%)	20.1	18.6	14.7	76.3	-5.0
Differ from Category (+/-)	4.4 high	4.3 high	0.8 abv av	13.9 abv av	1.7 abv av

Total Risk	Standard Deviation	Category Risk	Risk Index	Beta
av	9.1%	blw av	0.9	0.82

	1996	1995	1994	1993	1992	1991	1990	1989	1988	1987
Return (%)	33.2	29.8	0.2	11.9	21.1	32.2	-10.7	22.4	21.1	-3.8
Differ from Category (+/-)	13.1	-0.5	0.5	-2.1	9.3	-3.8	-4.6	-3.7	3.0	-5.8
Return, Tax-Adjusted (%)	29.3	26.2	-1.8	8.9	17.0	31.0	-12.2	18.2	17.6	-6.9

PER SHARE DATA

	1996	1995	1994	1993	1992	1991	1990	1989	1988	1987
Dividends, Net Income ($)	0.12	0.21	0.21	0.14	0.17	0.28	0.52	0.34	0.17	0.18
Distrib'ns, Cap Gain ($)	2.35	1.67	0.86	1.53	1.95	0.09	0.00	1.41	1.17	1.21
Net Asset Value ($)	21.71	18.16	15.46	16.50	16.24	15.17	11.77	13.73	12.67	11.58
Expense Ratio (%)	na	1.15	1.22	1.27	1.37	1.30	1.33	1.24	1.40	1.45
Yield (%)	0.49	1.05	1.28	0.77	0.93	1.83	4.41	2.24	1.22	1.40
Portfolio Turnover (%)	na	53	75	90	88	100	105	91	134	91
Total Assets (Millions $)	116	67	56	58	35	31	27	42	28	22

PORTFOLIO (as of 9/30/96)

Portfolio Manager: T. Gibbs Kane Jr., H. Burn - 1985

Investm't Category: Growth
- ✔ Domestic
- Foreign
- Asset Allocation
- Index
- Sector
- State Specific

Investment Style
- Large-Cap Growth
- ✔ Mid-Cap Growth
- Small-Cap Growth
- Large-Cap Value
- ✔ Mid-Cap Value
- Small-Cap Value

Portfolio
5.5% cash	0.0% corp bonds
94.5% stocks	0.0% gov't bonds
0.0% preferred	0.0% muni bonds
0.0% conv't/warrants	0.0% other

SHAREHOLDER INFORMATION

Minimum Investment
Initial: $10,000   Subsequent: $1

Minimum IRA Investment
Initial: $250   Subsequent: $1

Maximum Fees
Load: none   12b-1: none
Other: none

Distributions
Income: Jun, Dec   Capital Gains: Dec

Exchange Options
Number Per Year: no limit   Fee: none
Telephone: yes (money market fund available)

Services
IRA, pension, auto withdraw

680 *Guide to Low-Load Mutual Funds*

SteinRoe Balanced (SRFBX)

Balanced

P.O. Box 1162
Chicago, IL 60690
800-338-2550, 312-368-7800
www.steinroe.com

PERFORMANCE

fund inception date: 8/25/49

	3yr Annual	5yr Annual	10yr Annual	Bull	Bear
Return (%)	11.2	10.7	10.7	43.9	-7.0
Differ from Category (+/-)	-0.5 blw av	-0.7 blw av	-0.1 av	-1.2 av	-1.3 blw av

Total Risk	Standard Deviation	Category Risk	Risk Index	Beta
blw av	6.8%	av	1.0	0.63

	1996	1995	1994	1993	1992	1991	1990	1989	1988	1987
Return (%)	17.0	22.6	-4.2	12.3	7.8	29.5	-18	20.3	7.8	0.7
Differ from Category (+/-)	2.8	-2.0	-2.6	-2.1	-1.1	5.4	-0.9	2.2	-4.4	-2.0
Return, Tax-Adjusted (%)	13.3	19.8	-6.3	9.6	4.1	26.3	-4.4	16.8	4.8	-3.5

PER SHARE DATA

	1996	1995	1994	1993	1992	1991	1990	1989	1988	1987
Dividends, Net Income ($)	0.99	1.17	1.18	1.22	1.29	1.32	1.06	1.40	1.31	1.62
Distrib'ns, Cap Gain ($)	2.26	0.70	0.27	0.71	1.66	0.61	0.73	0.73	0.49	1.45
Net Asset Value ($)	29.18	27.80	24.30	26.85	25.69	26.62	22.16	24.41	22.15	22.25
Expense Ratio (%)	1.05	0.87	0.83	0.81	0.85	0.87	0.88	0.90	0.87	0.80
Yield (%)	3.14	4.10	4.80	4.42	4.71	4.84	4.63	5.56	5.78	6.83
Portfolio Turnover (%)	87	45	29	53	59	71	75	93	85	86
Total Assets (Millions $)	266	227	215	226	180	156	128	142	130	140

PORTFOLIO (as of 9/30/96)

Portfolio Manager: Harvey B. Hirschhorn - 1996

Investm't Category: Balanced
✔ Domestic   Index
✔ Foreign   Sector
✔ Asset Allocation State Specific

Investment Style
Large-Cap Growth   Large-Cap Value
Mid-Cap Growth   Mid-Cap Value
Small-Cap Growth   Small-Cap Value

Portfolio
8.0%	cash	7.0%	corp bonds
48.0%	stocks	24.0%	gov't bonds
2.0%	preferred	0.0%	muni bonds
11.0%	conv't/warrants	0.0%	other

SHAREHOLDER INFORMATION

Minimum Investment
Initial: $2,500   Subsequent: $100

Minimum IRA Investment
Initial: $500   Subsequent: $50

Maximum Fees
Load: none   12b-1: none
Other: none

Distributions
Income: quarterly   Capital Gains: annual

Exchange Options
Number Per Year: no limit   Fee: none
Telephone: yes; 4/yr (money market fund available)

Services
IRA, pension, auto exchange, auto invest, auto withdraw

SteinRoe Capital Opportunities (SRFCX)

P.O. Box 1162
Chicago, IL 60690
800-338-2550, 312-368-7800
www.steinroe.com

Aggressive Growth

this fund is closed to new investors

PERFORMANCE

fund inception date: 3/31/69

	3yr Annual	5yr Annual	10yr Annual	Bull	Bear
Return (%)	21.9	18.8	14.6	104.7	-11.7
Differ from Category (+/-)	6.1 high	3.5 abv av	-0.4 av	33.6 high	-1.1 av

Total Risk	Standard Deviation	Category Risk	Risk Index	Beta
high	16.8%	abv av	1.2	1.02

	1996	1995	1994	1993	1992	1991	1990	1989	1988	1987
Return (%)	20.3	50.7	0.0	27.5	2.4	62.7	-29.1	36.8	-3.9	9.3
Differ from Category (+/-)	1.2	16.4	0.0	8.2	-9.3	10.6	-23.7	8.4	-20.3	11.7
Return, Tax-Adjusted (%)	20.3	48.9	-0.1	27.5	2.2	62.2	-29.6	29.5	-4.2	5.7

PER SHARE DATA

	1996	1995	1994	1993	1992	1991	1990	1989	1988	1987
Dividends, Net Income ($)	0.00	0.01	0.01	0.00	0.04	0.09	0.08	0.05	0.04	0.04
Distrib'ns, Cap Gain ($)	0.00	0.99	0.00	0.00	0.00	0.00	0.08	2.53	0.05	3.36
Net Asset Value ($)	28.11	23.35	16.19	16.20	12.71	12.45	7.71	11.10	10.10	10.62
Expense Ratio (%)	1.22	1.05	0.97	1.06	1.06	1.18	1.14	1.09	1.01	0.95
Yield (%)	0.00	0.04	0.06	0.00	0.31	0.72	1.02	0.36	0.39	0.28
Portfolio Turnover (%)	22	60	46	55	46	53	171	245	164	133
Total Assets (Millions $)	1,544	332	172	166	129	152	89	246	151	171

PORTFOLIO (as of 9/30/96)

Portfolio Manager: Gloria Santella, Eric Maddix - 1991

Investm't Category: Aggressive Growth
- ✔ Domestic
- ✔ Foreign
-   Asset Allocation

  Index
  Sector
  State Specific

Investment Style
-   Large-Cap Growth
- ✔ Mid-Cap Growth
- ✔ Small-Cap Growth

  Large-Cap Value
  Mid-Cap Value
  Small-Cap Value

Portfolio

12.0% cash	0.0% corp bonds
87.0% stocks	0.0% gov't bonds
0.0% preferred	0.0% muni bonds
1.0% conv't/warrants	0.0% other

SHAREHOLDER INFORMATION

Minimum Investment
Initial: $2,500   Subsequent: $100

Minimum IRA Investment
Initial: $500   Subsequent: $50

Maximum Fees
Load: none   12b-1: none
Other: none

Distributions
Income: annual   Capital Gains: annual

Exchange Options
Number Per Year: no limit   Fee: none
Telephone: yes; 4/yr (money market fund available)

Services
IRA, pension, auto exchange, auto invest, auto withdraw

SteinRoe Gov't Income

(SRGPX)

General Bond

P.O. Box 1162
Chicago, IL 60690
800-338-2550, 312-368-7800
www.steinroe.com

PERFORMANCE

fund inception date: 3/5/86

	3yr Annual	5yr Annual	10yr Annual	Bull	Bear
Return (%)	5.1	5.7	7.3	21.2	-5.5
Differ from Category (+/-)	0.0 av	-0.4 blw av	0.0 av	0.9 abv av	-1.3 blw av

Total Risk	Standard Deviation	Category Risk	Risk Index	Avg Mat
low	4.4%	abv av	1.2	14.2 yrs

	1996	1995	1994	1993	1992	1991	1990	1989	1988	1987
Return (%)	2.6	16.9	-3.2	7.2	6.1	14.9	8.4	13.3	6.8	1.6
Differ from Category (+/-)	-1.3	2.0	-0.9	-1.9	-0.4	0.2	1.1	1.6	-0.8	-0.7
Return, Tax-Adjusted (%)	0.2	14.2	-5.5	4.4	2.8	12.0	5.3	10.0	3.6	-2.0

PER SHARE DATA

	1996	1995	1994	1993	1992	1991	1990	1989	1988	1987
Dividends, Net Income ($)	0.61	0.61	0.58	0.58	0.69	0.72	0.76	0.78	0.75	0.88
Distrib'ns, Cap Gain ($)	0.00	0.00	0.00	0.20	0.25	0.00	0.00	0.00	0.00	0.05
Net Asset Value ($)	9.80	10.17	9.26	10.16	10.22	10.55	9.86	9.84	9.42	9.54
Expense Ratio (%)	1.00	1.00	0.98	0.95	0.99	1.00	1.00	1.00	1.00	1.00
Yield (%)	6.22	5.99	6.26	5.59	6.59	6.82	7.70	7.92	7.96	9.17
Portfolio Turnover (%)	73	225	167	170	139	136	181	239	237	205
Total Assets (Millions $)	39	36	44	56	58	83	50	40	28	24

PORTFOLIO (as of 9/30/96)

Portfolio Manager: Michael Kennedy,
Steven Luetger - 1988

Investm't Category: General Bond

✔ Domestic Index
  Foreign Sector
  Asset Allocation State Specific

Investment Style

  Large-Cap Growth Large-Cap Value
  Mid-Cap Growth Mid-Cap Value
  Small-Cap Growth Small-Cap Value

Portfolio

9.0% cash	7.0% corp bonds
0.0% stocks	84.0% gov't bonds
0.0% preferred	0.0% muni bonds
0.0% conv't/warrants	0.0% other

SHAREHOLDER INFORMATION

Minimum Investment
Initial: $2,500   Subsequent: $100

Minimum IRA Investment
Initial: $500   Subsequent: $100

Maximum Fees
Load: none   12b-1: none
Other: none

Distributions
Income: monthly   Capital Gains: Dec

Exchange Options
Number Per Year: no limit   Fee: none
Telephone: yes; 4/yr (money market fund available)

Services
IRA, pension, auto exchange, auto invest, auto
withdraw

SteinRoe Growth & Income (SRPEX)

Growth & Income

P.O. Box 1162
Chicago, IL 60690
800-338-2550, 312-368-7800
www.steinroe.com

PERFORMANCE

fund inception date: 3/24/87

	3yr Annual	5yr Annual	10yr Annual	Bull	Bear
Return (%)	16.5	14.4	na	63.1	-5.0
Differ from Category (+/-)	1.2 av	0.5 av	na	3.3 av	1.4 abv av

Total Risk	Standard Deviation	Category Risk	Risk Index	Beta
av	7.6%	low	0.8	0.74

	1996	1995	1994	1993	1992	1991	1990	1989	1988	1987
Return (%)	21.8	30.1	-0.2	12.8	10.0	32.4	-1.8	30.9	9.0	—
Differ from Category (+/-)	2.1	0.0	1.1	-1.0	-0.7	3.3	4.1	7.4	-7.8	—
Return, Tax-Adjusted (%)	20.0	26.3	-1.9	10.9	7.9	30.6	-3.7	29.8	8.1	—

PER SHARE DATA

	1996	1995	1994	1993	1992	1991	1990	1989	1988	1987
Dividends, Net Income ($)	0.27	0.28	0.18	0.16	0.16	0.23	0.28	0.23	0.18	—
Distrib'ns, Cap Gain ($)	0.64	1.43	0.59	0.70	0.75	0.35	0.36	0.00	0.00	—
Net Asset Value ($)	18.73	16.17	13.78	14.58	13.71	13.32	10.54	11.39	8.89	—
Expense Ratio (%)	1.18	0.96	0.90	0.88	0.97	1.00	1.08	1.24	1.47	—
Yield (%)	1.39	1.59	1.25	1.04	1.10	1.68	2.56	2.01	2.02	—
Portfolio Turnover (%)	13	70	85	50	40	48	51	63	105	—
Total Assets (Millions $)	240	151	121	108	77	62	46	33	23	—

PORTFOLIO (as of 9/30/96)

Portfolio Manager: Dan Cantor, Jeff Kinzel - 1996

Investm't Category: Growth & Income
- ✔ Domestic
- ✔ Foreign
-   Asset Allocation
-   Index
-   Sector
-   State Specific

Investment Style
- ✔ Large-Cap Growth
-   Mid-Cap Growth
-   Small-Cap Growth
- ✔ Large-Cap Value
-   Mid-Cap Value
-   Small-Cap Value

Portfolio
18.0% cash	0.0% corp bonds
80.0% stocks	2.0% gov't bonds
0.0% preferred	0.0% muni bonds
0.0% conv't/warrants	0.0% other

SHAREHOLDER INFORMATION

Minimum Investment
Initial: $2,500   Subsequent: $100

Minimum IRA Investment
Initial: $500   Subsequent: $50

Maximum Fees
Load: none   12b-1: none
Other: none

Distributions
Income: quarterly   Capital Gains: annual

Exchange Options
Number Per Year: no limit   Fee: none
Telephone: yes; 4/yr (money market fund available)

Services
IRA, pension, auto exchange, auto invest, auto withdraw

SteinRoe Growth Stock

(SRFSX)

Growth

P.O. Box 1162
Chicago, IL 60690
800-338-2550, 312-368-7800
www.steinroe.com

PERFORMANCE

fund inception date: 7/1/58

	3yr Annual	5yr Annual	10yr Annual	Bull	Bear
Return (%)	16.4	11.9	14.0	72.5	-11.1
Differ from Category (+/-)	0.7 av	-2.4 blw av	0.1 av	10.1 abv av	-4.4 low

Total Risk	Standard Deviation	Category Risk	Risk Index	Beta
abv av	10.6%	av	1.0	1.02

	1996	1995	1994	1993	1992	1991	1990	1989	1988	1987
Return (%).	20.9	35.6	-3.8	2.8	8.2	46.0	0.9	35.4	0.6	5.5
Differ from Category (+/-). .	0.8	5.3	-3.5	-11.2	-3.6	10.0	7.0	9.3	-17.5	3.5
Return, Tax-Adjusted (%). .	18.2	32.2	-7.5	0.6	6.8	43.5	-1.4	34.4	-0.3	0.3

PER SHARE DATA

	1996	1995	1994	1993	1992	1991	1990	1989	1988	1987
Dividends, Net Income ($)	0.07	0.09	0.14	0.15	0.15	0.27	0.42	0.36	0.27	0.29
Distrib'ns, Cap Gain ($) . . .	2.23	2.33	3.01	1.73	0.94	1.17	0.91	0.00	0.05	2.71
Net Asset Value ($)	27.90	25.05	20.29	24.39	25.59	24.67	17.97	19.14	14.43	14.67
Expense Ratio (%).	1.08	0.99	0.94	0.93	0.92	0.79	0.73	0.77	0.76	0.65
Yield (%)	0.23	0.32	0.60	0.57	0.56	1.04	2.22	1.88	1.86	1.66
Portfolio Turnover (%).	39	36	27	29	23	34	40	47	84	143
Total Assets (Millions $). . .	465	375	302	369	426	344	225	204	174	232

PORTFOLIO (as of 9/30/96)

Portfolio Manager: Erik Gustafson, David Brady - 1994

Investm't Category: Growth
- ✔ Domestic
- ✔ Foreign
- Asset Allocation
- Index
- Sector
- State Specific

Investment Style
- ✔ Large-Cap Growth
- Mid-Cap Growth
- Small-Cap Growth
- Large-Cap Value
- Mid-Cap Value
- Small-Cap Value

Portfolio

11.0% cash	0.0% corp bonds
88.0% stocks	0.0% gov't bonds
1.0% preferred	0.0% muni bonds
0.0% conv't/warrants	0.0% other

SHAREHOLDER INFORMATION

Minimum Investment
Initial: $2,500   Subsequent: $100

Minimum IRA Investment
Initial: $500   Subsequent: $50

Maximum Fees
Load: none   12b-1: none
Other: none

Distributions
Income: annual   Capital Gains: annual

Exchange Options
Number Per Year: no limit   Fee: none
Telephone: yes; 4/yr (money market fund available)

Services
IRA, pension, auto exchange, auto invest, auto withdraw

SteinRoe Income (SRHBX)

Corporate Bond

P.O. Box 1162
Chicago, IL 60690
800-338-2550, 312-368-7800
www.steinroe.com

PERFORMANCE

fund inception date: 3/5/86

	3yr Annual	5yr Annual	10yr Annual	Bull	Bear
Return (%)	6.4	8.3	8.9	26.4	-5.9
Differ from Category (+/-)	0.1 abv av	0.0 av	0.8 high	1.6 abv av	-0.8 av

Total Risk	Standard Deviation	Category Risk	Risk Index	Avg Mat
low	4.7%	av	1.0	7.2 yrs

	1996	1995	1994	1993	1992	1991	1990	1989	1988	1987
Return (%)	4.8	19.7	-3.9	13.3	9.1	17.1	6.1	7.1	11.5	6.5
Differ from Category (+/-)	-0.4	1.7	-0.8	1.5	0.2	-0.1	2.1	-2.3	2.2	4.1
Return, Tax-Adjusted (%)	2.0	16.5	-6.6	10.3	5.9	13.6	2.4	3.1	7.5	1.6

PER SHARE DATA

	1996	1995	1994	1993	1992	1991	1990	1989	1988	1987
Dividends, Net Income ($)	0.70	0.71	0.69	0.71	0.76	0.77	0.84	0.95	0.94	1.21
Distrib'ns, Cap Gain ($)	0.00	0.00	0.00	0.00	0.00	0.00	0.00	0.00	0.00	0.00
Net Asset Value ($)	9.83	10.08	9.06	10.14	9.60	9.53	8.85	9.17	9.47	9.37
Expense Ratio (%)	0.82	0.82	0.82	0.82	0.90	0.95	0.93	0.90	0.91	0.96
Yield (%)	7.12	7.04	7.61	7.00	7.91	8.07	9.49	10.35	9.92	12.91
Portfolio Turnover (%)	135	64	53	39	76	77	90	94	158	153
Total Assets (Millions $)	340	207	152	161	117	105	88	94	102	94

PORTFOLIO (as of 9/30/96)

Portfolio Manager: Ann H. Benjamin, Stephen Lockman - 1990

Investm't Category: Corporate Bond
- ✔ Domestic
- ✔ Foreign
- Asset Allocation
- Index
- Sector
- State Specific

Investment Style
Large-Cap Growth   Large-Cap Value
Mid-Cap Growth   Mid-Cap Value
Small-Cap Growth   Small-Cap Value

Portfolio
5.0%	cash	90.0%	corp bonds
0.0%	stocks	5.0%	gov't bonds
0.0%	preferred	0.0%	muni bonds
0.0%	conv't/warrants	0.0%	other

SHAREHOLDER INFORMATION

Minimum Investment
Initial: $2,500   Subsequent: $100

Minimum IRA Investment
Initial: $500   Subsequent: $100

Maximum Fees
Load: none   12b-1: none
Other: none

Distributions
Income: monthly   Capital Gains: annual

Exchange Options
Number Per Year: no limit   Fee: none
Telephone: yes; 4/yr (money market fund available)

Services
IRA, pension, auto exchange, auto invest, auto withdraw

SteinRoe Int'l (SRITX)
International Stock

P.O. Box 1162
Chicago, IL 60690
800-338-2550, 312-368-7800
www.steinroe.com

PERFORMANCE

fund inception date: 3/1/94

	3yr Annual	5yr Annual	10yr Annual	Bull	Bear
Return (%)	na	na	na	13.7	na
Differ from Category (+/-)	na	na	na	-10.6 blw av	na

Total Risk	Standard Deviation	Category Risk	Risk Index	Beta
na	na	na	na	na

	1996	1995	1994	1993	1992	1991	1990	1989	1988	1987
Return (%).	8.3	3.8	—	—	—	—	—	—	—	—
Differ from Category (+/-) .	-6.5	-5.3	—	—	—	—	—	—	—	—
Return, Tax-Adjusted (%). . .	7.6	3.3	—	—	—	—	—	—	—	—

PER SHARE DATA

	1996	1995	1994	1993	1992	1991	1990	1989	1988	1987
Dividends, Net Income ($).	0.07	0.12	—	—	—	—	—	—	—	—
Distrib'ns, Cap Gain ($) . . .	0.14	0.00	—	—	—	—	—	—	—	—
Net Asset Value ($)	10.76	10.14	—	—	—	—	—	—	—	—
Expense Ratio (%).	1.51	1.59	—	—	—	—	—	—	—	—
Yield (%)	0.64	1.18	—	—	—	—	—	—	—	—
Portfolio Turnover (%). . . .	42	59	—	—	—	—	—	—	—	—
Total Assets (Millions $). . .	140	91	—	—	—	—	—	—	—	—

PORTFOLIO (as of 9/30/96)

Portfolio Manager: Bruno Bertocci, David Harris - 1994

Investm't Category: International Stock

Domestic	Index
✔ Foreign	Sector
Asset Allocation	State Specific

Investment Style

Large-Cap Growth	Large-Cap Value
Mid-Cap Growth	Mid-Cap Value
Small-Cap Growth	Small-Cap Value

Portfolio

2.0% cash	0.0% corp bonds
98.0% stocks	0.0% gov't bonds
0.0% preferred	0.0% muni bonds
0.0% conv't/warrants	0.0% other

SHAREHOLDER INFORMATION

Minimum Investment
Initial: $2,500   Subsequent: $100

Minimum IRA Investment
Initial: $500   Subsequent: $50

Maximum Fees
Load: none   12b-1: none
Other: none

Distributions
Income: annual   Capital Gains: annual

Exchange Options
Number Per Year: no limit   Fee: none
Telephone: yes; 4/yr (money market fund available)

Services
IRA, pension, auto exchange, auto invest, auto withdraw

SteinRoe Interm Bond

(SRBFX)

General Bond

P.O. Box 1162
Chicago, IL 60690
800-338-2550, 312-368-7800
www.steinroe.com

PERFORMANCE

fund inception date: 12/5/78

	3yr Annual	5yr Annual	10yr Annual	Bull	Bear
Return (%)	5.9	6.9	7.8	22.8	-4.6
Differ from Category (+/-)	0.8 high	0.8 abv av	0.5 abv av	2.5 abv av	-0.4 av

Total Risk	Standard Deviation	Category Risk	Risk Index	Avg Mat
low	4.1%	av	1.1	9.9 yrs

	1996	1995	1994	1993	1992	1991	1990	1989	1988	1987
Return (%)	4.5	16.8	-2.6	9.1	7.6	15.0	7.1	12.5	7.2	2.5
Differ from Category (+/-)	0.6	1.9	-0.3	0.0	1.1	0.3	-0.2	0.8	-0.4	0.2
Return, Tax-Adjusted (%)	1.8	13.9	-5.1	5.7	4.6	11.8	3.7	9.0	3.9	-1.7

PER SHARE DATA

	1996	1995	1994	1993	1992	1991	1990	1989	1988	1987
Dividends, Net Income ($)	0.60	0.58	0.56	0.59	0.68	0.68	0.72	0.73	0.70	0.87
Distrib'ns, Cap Gain ($)	0.00	0.00	0.00	0.23	0.00	0.00	0.00	0.00	0.00	0.13
Net Asset Value ($)	8.72	8.94	8.19	8.98	9.00	9.02	8.48	8.63	8.35	8.46
Expense Ratio (%)	0.70	0.70	0.70	0.67	0.70	0.73	0.74	0.73	0.73	0.68
Yield (%)	6.88	6.48	6.83	6.40	7.55	7.53	8.49	8.45	8.38	10.12
Portfolio Turnover (%)	202	162	206	214	202	239	296	197	273	230
Total Assets (Millions $)	319	312	281	326	273	220	168	166	164	164

PORTFOLIO (as of 9/30/96)

Portfolio Manager: Michael Kennedy,
Steven Luetger - 1988

Investm't Category: General Bond
- ✔ Domestic
- ✔ Foreign
-   Asset Allocation
-   Index
-   Sector
-   State Specific

Investment Style

Large-Cap Growth	Large-Cap Value
Mid-Cap Growth	Mid-Cap Value
Small-Cap Growth	Small-Cap Value

Portfolio

8.0% cash	55.0% corp bonds
0.0% stocks	32.0% gov't bonds
0.0% preferred	0.0% muni bonds
0.0% conv't/warrants	5.0% other

SHAREHOLDER INFORMATION

Minimum Investment
Initial: $2,500   Subsequent: $100

Minimum IRA Investment
Initial: $500   Subsequent: $100

Maximum Fees
Load: none   12b-1: none
Other: none

Distributions
Income: monthly   Capital Gains: annual

Exchange Options
Number Per Year: no limit   Fee: none
Telephone: yes; 4/yr (money market fund available)

Services
IRA, pension, auto exchange, auto invest, auto withdraw

SteinRoe Muni Trust: High Yield Muni (SRMFX)

P.O. Box 1162
Chicago, IL 60690
800-338-2550, 312-368-7800
www.steinroe.com

Tax-Exempt Bond

PERFORMANCE

fund inception date: 3/5/84

	3yr Annual	5yr Annual	10yr Annual	Bull	Bear
Return (%)	5.6	6.5	7.6	22.0	-4.2
Differ from Category (+/-)	1.4 high	0.1 av	0.9 high	3.6 high	1.2 abv av

Total Risk	Standard Deviation	Category Risk	Risk Index	Avg Mat
blw av	5.1%	blw av	0.9	17.8 yrs

	1996	1995	1994	1993	1992	1991	1990	1989	1988	1987
Return (%)..............	4.5	17.6	-4.1	10.6	5.3	9.8	7.6	11.4	13.6	1.6
Differ from Category (+/-)..	0.8	2.4	1.2	-1.2	-3.0	-1.6	1.2	2.4	3.6	3.0
Return, Tax-Adjusted (%)...	4.5	17.6	-4.1	10.0	4.8	9.3	7.2	10.9	13.5	1.3

PER SHARE DATA

	1996	1995	1994	1993	1992	1991	1990	1989	1988	1987
Dividends, Net Income ($).	0.70	0.66	0.65	0.68	0.74	0.81	0.84	0.86	0.88	1.07
Distrib'ns, Cap Gain ($) ...	0.00	0.00	0.00	0.23	0.17	0.18	0.16	0.20	0.03	0.10
Net Asset Value ($)	11.61	11.81	10.64	11.76	11.49	11.80	11.68	11.82	11.61	11.06
Expense Ratio (%)........	0.85	0.86	0.76	0.73	0.69	0.71	0.71	0.73	0.76	0.73
Yield (%)	6.02	5.58	6.10	5.67	6.34	6.76	7.09	7.15	7.56	9.58
Portfolio Turnover (%).....	34	23	36	75	88	195	261	208	53	110
Total Assets (Millions $)...	297	282	266	348	366	399	333	285	243	181

PORTFOLIO (as of 9/30/96)

Portfolio Manager: M. Jane McCart - 1995

Investm't Category: Tax-Exempt Bond

✔ Domestic	Index
Foreign	Sector
Asset Allocation	State Specific

Investment Style

Large-Cap Growth	Large-Cap Value
Mid-Cap Growth	Mid-Cap Value
Small-Cap Growth	Small-Cap Value

Portfolio

6.0% cash	0.0% corp bonds
0.0% stocks	0.0% gov't bonds
0.0% preferred	94.0% muni bonds
0.0% conv't/warrants	0.0% other

SHAREHOLDER INFORMATION

Minimum Investment
Initial: $2,500   Subsequent: $100

Minimum IRA Investment
Initial: na   Subsequent: na

Maximum Fees
Load: none   12b-1: none
Other: none

Distributions
Income: monthly   Capital Gains: annual

Exchange Options
Number Per Year: no limit   Fee: none
Telephone: yes; 4/yr (money market fund available)

Services
auto exchange, auto invest, auto withdraw

SteinRoe Muni Trust: Interm Muni (SRIMX)

Tax-Exempt Bond

P.O. Box 1162
Chicago, IL 60690
800-338-2550, 312-368-7800
www.steinroe.com

PERFORMANCE

fund inception date: 10/9/85

	3yr Annual	5yr Annual	10yr Annual	Bull	Bear
Return (%)	4.3	6.3	6.7	17.4	-4.2
Differ from Category (+/-)	0.1 av	-0.1 blw av	0.0 blw av	-1.0 blw av	1.2 abv av

Total Risk	Standard Deviation	Category Risk	Risk Index	Avg Mat
low	4.0%	blw av	0.7	8.7 yrs

	1996	1995	1994	1993	1992	1991	1990	1989	1988	1987
Return (%)	4.1	12.9	-3.4	11.0	7.6	10.6	7.5	8.1	6.1	3.2
Differ from Category (+/-)	0.4	-2.3	1.9	-0.8	-0.7	-0.8	1.1	-0.9	-3.9	4.6
Return, Tax-Adjusted (%)	3.9	12.9	-3.4	10.5	7.2	10.1	7.4	8.0	6.1	3.1

PER SHARE DATA

	1996	1995	1994	1993	1992	1991	1990	1989	1988	1987
Dividends, Net Income ($)	0.54	0.54	0.53	0.53	0.55	0.59	0.63	0.62	0.59	0.71
Distrib'ns, Cap Gain ($)	0.06	0.00	0.00	0.18	0.12	0.16	0.03	0.03	0.00	0.01
Net Asset Value ($)	11.36	11.51	10.70	11.62	11.13	10.99	10.65	10.55	10.39	10.37
Expense Ratio (%)	0.70	0.74	0.71	0.72	0.79	0.80	0.80	0.80	0.80	0.80
Yield (%)	4.72	4.69	4.95	4.49	4.88	5.29	5.89	5.86	5.67	6.84
Portfolio Turnover (%)	66	67	55	96	109	96	141	83	22	49
Total Assets (Millions $)	204	217	215	258	201	148	104	96	91	96

PORTFOLIO (as of 9/30/96)

Portfolio Manager: Joanne Costopoulos - 1991

Investm't Category: Tax-Exempt Bond
✔ Domestic	Index
Foreign	Sector
Asset Allocation	State Specific

Investment Style
Large-Cap Growth	Large-Cap Value
Mid-Cap Growth	Mid-Cap Value
Small-Cap Growth	Small-Cap Value

Portfolio
3.0% cash	0.0% corp bonds
0.0% stocks	0.0% gov't bonds
0.0% preferred	97.0% muni bonds
0.0% conv't/warrants	0.0% other

SHAREHOLDER INFORMATION

Minimum Investment
Initial: $2,500   Subsequent: $100

Minimum IRA Investment
Initial: na   Subsequent: na

Maximum Fees
Load: none   12b-1: none
Other: none

Distributions
Income: monthly   Capital Gains: annual

Exchange Options
Number Per Year: no limit   Fee: none
Telephone: yes; 4/yr (money market fund available)

Services
auto exchange, auto invest, auto withdraw

SteinRoe Muni Trust: Managed Muni (SRMMX)

Tax-Exempt Bond

P.O. Box 1162
Chicago, IL 60690
800-338-2550, 312-368-7800
www.steinroe.com

PERFORMANCE

fund inception date: 2/23/77

	3yr Annual	5yr Annual	10yr Annual	Bull	Bear
Return (%)	4.6	6.6	7.4	20.0	-5.6
Differ from Category (+/-)	0.4 abv av	0.2 av	0.7 abv av	1.6 abv av	-0.2 av

Total Risk	Standard Deviation	Category Risk	Risk Index	Avg Mat
blw av	5.3%	av	0.9	16.8 yrs

	1996	1995	1994	1993	1992	1991	1990	1989	1988	1987
Return (%)	3.7	16.6	-5.4	11.2	8.2	11.8	7.0	10.6	10.8	0.9
Differ from Category (+/-)	0.0	1.4	-0.1	-0.6	-0.1	0.4	0.6	1.6	0.8	2.3
Return, Tax-Adjusted (%)	3.7	16.6	-5.4	10.7	7.7	11.1	6.8	9.8	10.7	0.5

PER SHARE DATA

	1996	1995	1994	1993	1992	1991	1990	1989	1988	1987
Dividends, Net Income ($)	0.48	0.49	0.50	0.50	0.53	0.55	0.57	0.60	0.60	0.65
Distrib'ns, Cap Gain ($)	0.00	0.00	0.00	0.16	0.15	0.20	0.05	0.25	0.02	0.13
Net Asset Value ($)	9.07	9.22	8.36	9.36	9.04	9.01	8.76	8.80	8.76	8.50
Expense Ratio (%)	0.72	0.65	0.65	0.64	0.64	0.66	0.66	0.65	0.65	0.65
Yield (%)	5.29	5.31	5.98	5.25	5.76	5.97	6.46	6.62	6.83	7.53
Portfolio Turnover (%)	40	33	36	63	94	203	95	102	28	113
Total Assets (Millions $)	623	637	604	781	741	713	613	553	475	458

PORTFOLIO (as of 9/30/96)

Portfolio Manager: M. Jane McCart - 1991

Investm't Category: Tax-Exempt Bond
- ✔ Domestic
- Foreign
- Asset Allocation
- Index
- Sector
- State Specific

Investment Style
- Large-Cap Growth
- Mid-Cap Growth
- Small-Cap Growth
- Large-Cap Value
- Mid-Cap Value
- Small-Cap Value

Portfolio
4.0% cash	0.0% corp bonds
0.0% stocks	0.0% gov't bonds
0.0% preferred	96.0% muni bonds
0.0% conv't/warrants	0.0% other

SHAREHOLDER INFORMATION

Minimum Investment
Initial: $2,500   Subsequent: $100

Minimum IRA Investment
Initial: na   Subsequent: na

Maximum Fees
Load: none   12b-1: none
Other: none

Distributions
Income: monthly   Capital Gains: annual

Exchange Options
Number Per Year: no limit   Fee: none
Telephone: yes; 4/yr (money market fund available)

Services
auto exchange, auto invest, auto withdraw

SteinRoe Special (SRSPX)

Aggressive Growth

P.O. Box 1162
Chicago, IL 60690
800-338-2550, 312-368-7800
www.steinroe.com

PERFORMANCE   fund inception date: 5/22/68

	3yr Annual	5yr Annual	10yr Annual	Bull	Bear
Return (%)	10.8	13.3	15.1	47.1	-8.1
Differ from Category (+/-)	-5.0 low	-2.0 blw av	0.1 av	-24.0 low	2.5 abv av

Total Risk	Standard Deviation	Category Risk	Risk Index	Beta
av	8.9%	low	0.6	0.68

	1996	1995	1994	1993	1992	1991	1990	1989	1988	1987
Return (%)	18.8	18.7	-3.4	20.4	14.0	34.0	-5.9	37.8	20.2	4.2
Differ from Category (+/-)	-0.3	-15.6	-3.4	1.1	2.3	-18.1	-0.5	9.4	3.8	6.6
Return, Tax-Adjusted (%)	16.3	16.0	-5.2	17.7	12.0	32.5	-8.7	32.9	19.4	-3.6

PER SHARE DATA

	1996	1995	1994	1993	1992	1991	1990	1989	1988	1987
Dividends, Net Income ($)	0.00	0.10	0.14	0.21	0.18	0.36	0.34	0.39	0.22	0.57
Distrib'ns, Cap Gain ($)	2.10	1.91	1.31	1.77	1.16	0.30	1.31	2.08	0.05	3.89
Net Asset Value ($)	26.01	23.72	21.72	24.00	21.63	20.16	15.58	18.31	15.14	12.83
Expense Ratio (%)	1.18	1.02	0.96	0.97	0.99	1.04	1.02	0.96	0.99	0.96
Yield (%)	0.00	0.39	0.60	0.81	0.78	1.75	2.01	1.91	1.44	3.40
Portfolio Turnover (%)	32	41	58	42	40	50	70	85	42	103
Total Assets (Millions $)	1,159	1,133	1,167	1,167	718	590	388	320	229	187

PORTFOLIO (as of 9/30/96)

Portfolio Manager: E. Bruce Dunn, Richard Peterson - 1991

Investm't Category: Aggressive Growth

✔ Domestic   Index
✔ Foreign   Sector
  Asset Allocation State Specific

Investment Style

  Large-Cap Growth   Large-Cap Value
✔ Mid-Cap Growth   Mid-Cap Value
✔ Small-Cap Growth   Small-Cap Value

Portfolio

10.0%	cash	0.0%	corp bonds
90.0%	stocks	0.0%	gov't bonds
0.0%	preferred	0.0%	muni bonds
0.0%	conv't/warrants	0.0%	other

SHAREHOLDER INFORMATION

Minimum Investment
Initial: $2,500   Subsequent: $100

Minimum IRA Investment
Initial: $500   Subsequent: $50

Maximum Fees
Load: none   12b-1: none
Other: none

Distributions
Income: annual   Capital Gains: annual

Exchange Options
Number Per Year: no limit   Fee: none
Telephone: yes; 4/yr (money market fund available)

Services
IRA, pension, auto exchange, auto invest, auto withdraw

SteinRoe Special Venture
(SRSVX)
Aggressive Growth

P.O. Box 1162
Chicago, IL 60690
800-338-2550, 312-368-7800
www.steinroe.com

PERFORMANCE

fund inception date: 10/17/94

	3yr Annual	5yr Annual	10yr Annual	Bull	Bear
Return (%)	na	na	na	na	na
Differ from Category (+/-)	na	na	na	na	na

Total Risk	Standard Deviation	Category Risk	Risk Index	Beta
na	na	na	na	na

	1996	1995	1994	1993	1992	1991	1990	1989	1988	1987
Return (%)	28.6	27.1	—	—	—	—	—	—	—	—
Differ from Category (+/-)	9.5	-7.2	—	—	—	—	—	—	—	—
Return, Tax-Adjusted (%)	25.2	25.5	—	—	—	—	—	—	—	—

PER SHARE DATA

	1996	1995	1994	1993	1992	1991	1990	1989	1988	1987
Dividends, Net Income ($)	0.00	0.00	—	—	—	—	—	—	—	—
Distrib'ns, Cap Gain ($)	1.52	0.56	—	—	—	—	—	—	—	—
Net Asset Value ($)	14.70	12.65	—	—	—	—	—	—	—	—
Expense Ratio (%)	1.25	1.25	—	—	—	—	—	—	—	—
Yield (%)	0.00	0.00	—	—	—	—	—	—	—	—
Portfolio Turnover (%)	72	84	—	—	—	—	—	—	—	—
Total Assets (Millions $)	148	70	—	—	—	—	—	—	—	—

PORTFOLIO (as of 9/30/96)

Portfolio Manager: E. Bruce Dunn, Richard Peterson - 1994

Investm't Category: Aggressive Growth
- ✔ Domestic
- Foreign
- Asset Allocation
- Index
- Sector
- State Specific

Investment Style
- Large-Cap Growth
- Mid-Cap Growth
- Small-Cap Growth
- Large-Cap Value
- Mid-Cap Value
- Small-Cap Value

Portfolio
- 5.0% cash
- 95.0% stocks
- 0.0% preferred
- 0.0% conv't/warrants
- 0.0% corp bonds
- 0.0% gov't bonds
- 0.0% muni bonds
- 0.0% other

SHAREHOLDER INFORMATION

Minimum Investment
Initial: $2,500   Subsequent: $100

Minimum IRA Investment
Initial: $500   Subsequent: $100

Maximum Fees
Load: none   12b-1: none
Other: none

Distributions
Income: annual   Capital Gains: annual

Exchange Options
Number Per Year: no limit   Fee: none
Telephone: yes; 4/yr (money market fund available)

Services
IRA, pension, auto exchange, auto invest, auto withdraw

SteinRoe Young Investor

(SRYIX)

Growth

P.O. Box 1162
Chicago, IL 60690
800-338-2550, 312-368-7800
www.steinroe.com

PERFORMANCE   fund inception date: 4/29/94

	3yr Annual	5yr Annual	10yr Annual	Bull	Bear
Return (%)	na	na	na	108.0	na
Differ from Category (+/-)	na	na	na	45.6 high	na

Total Risk	Standard Deviation	Category Risk	Risk Index	Beta
na	na	na	na	na

	1996	1995	1994	1993	1992	1991	1990	1989	1988	1987
Return (%)	35.0	39.7	—	—	—	—	—	—	—	—
Differ from Category (+/-)	14.9	9.4	—	—	—	—	—	—	—	—
Return, Tax-Adjusted (%)	33.7	38.2	—	—	—	—	—	—	—	—

PER SHARE DATA

	1996	1995	1994	1993	1992	1991	1990	1989	1988	1987
Dividends, Net Income ($)	0.01	0.04	—	—	—	—	—	—	—	—
Distrib'ns, Cap Gain ($)	0.62	0.50	—	—	—	—	—	—	—	—
Net Asset Value ($)	18.71	14.34	—	—	—	—	—	—	—	—
Expense Ratio (%)	1.21	0.99	—	—	—	—	—	—	—	—
Yield (%)	0.05	0.26	—	—	—	—	—	—	—	—
Portfolio Turnover (%)	98	55	—	—	—	—	—	—	—	—
Total Assets (Millions $)	256	41	—	—	—	—	—	—	—	—

PORTFOLIO (as of 9/30/96)

Portfolio Manager: Erik Gustafson, David Brady - 1995

Investm't Category: Growth
- ✔ Domestic
- ✔ Foreign
- Asset Allocation
- Index
- Sector
- State Specific

Investment Style
- Large-Cap Growth
- Mid-Cap Growth
- Small-Cap Growth
- Large-Cap Value
- Mid-Cap Value
- Small-Cap Value

Portfolio
11.0% cash	0.0% corp bonds
88.0% stocks	0.0% gov't bonds
1.0% preferred	0.0% muni bonds
0.0% conv't/warrants	0.0% other

SHAREHOLDER INFORMATION

Minimum Investment
Initial: $2,500   Subsequent: $50

Minimum IRA Investment
Initial: $500   Subsequent: $50

Maximum Fees
Load: none   12b-1: none
Other: none

Distributions
Income: annual   Capital Gains: annual

Exchange Options
Number Per Year: no limit   Fee: none
Telephone: yes; 4/yr (money market fund available)

Services
IRA, pension, auto exchange, auto invest, auto withdraw

694   *Guide to Low-Load Mutual Funds*

Stonebridge Growth

(NAIDX)

Growth

5990 Greenwood Plaza Blvd.
Suite 325
Englewood, CO 80111
800-367-7814, 303-220-8500

PERFORMANCE

fund inception date: 3/18/60

	3yr Annual	5yr Annual	10yr Annual	Bull	Bear
Return (%)	12.7	7.6	10.9	50.3	-6.7
Differ from Category (+/-)	-3.0 blw av	-6.7 low	-3.0 low	-12.1 blw av	0.0 av

Total Risk	Standard Deviation	Category Risk	Risk Index	Beta
av	8.3%	low	0.8	0.76

	1996	1995	1994	1993	1992	1991	1990	1989	1988	1987
Return (%)	18.4	21.3	-0.3	1.3	-0.6	31.9	3.1	24.4	12.6	2.5
Differ from Category (+/-)	-1.7	-9.0	0.0	-12.7	-12.4	-4.1	9.2	-1.7	-5.5	0.5
Return, Tax-Adjusted (%)	14.5	19.4	-2.1	0.4	-4.5	28.7	1.6	20.0	10.8	-0.6

PER SHARE DATA

	1996	1995	1994	1993	1992	1991	1990	1989	1988	1987
Dividends, Net Income ($)	0.27	0.17	0.07	0.06	0.14	0.21	0.22	0.20	0.13	0.10
Distrib'ns, Cap Gain ($)	1.51	0.55	0.68	0.30	1.88	1.10	0.33	1.47	0.50	1.14
Net Asset Value ($)	14.50	13.73	11.92	12.71	12.90	15.01	12.37	12.53	11.41	10.69
Expense Ratio (%)	na	1.49	0.81	1.60	1.50	1.48	1.70	1.69	1.70	1.65
Yield (%)	1.68	1.19	0.55	0.46	0.94	1.30	1.73	1.42	1.09	0.84
Portfolio Turnover (%)	na	38	20	56	45	22	64	83	32	68
Total Assets (Millions $)	39	34	30	33	34	33	30	27	26	23

PORTFOLIO (as of 9/30/96)

Portfolio Manager: Richard C. Barrett - 1984

Investm't Category: Growth
- ✔ Domestic
- ✔ Foreign
-   Asset Allocation
-   Index
-   Sector
-   State Specific

Investment Style
-   Large-Cap Growth
- ✔ Mid-Cap Growth
-   Small-Cap Growth
-   Large-Cap Value
-   Mid-Cap Value
-   Small-Cap Value

Portfolio
1.3% cash	0.0% corp bonds
89.1% stocks	9.7% gov't bonds
0.0% preferred	0.0% muni bonds
0.0% conv't/warrants	0.0% other

SHAREHOLDER INFORMATION

Minimum Investment
Initial: $250   Subsequent: $25

Minimum IRA Investment
Initial: na   Subsequent: na

Maximum Fees
Load: none   12b-1: none
Other: none

Distributions
Income: Dec   Capital Gains: Dec

Exchange Options
Number Per Year: none   Fee: na
Telephone: na

Services
auto withdraw

Stratton Growth (STRGX)

Growth & Income

610 W. Germantown Pike
Suite 300
Plymouth Meeting, PA 19462
800-441-6580, 610-941-0255

PERFORMANCE

fund inception date: 9/30/72

	3yr Annual	5yr Annual	10yr Annual	Bull	Bear
Return (%)	18.9	13.8	12.2	64.2	-0.5
Differ from Category (+/-)	3.6 high	-0.1 av	-0.5 av	4.4 av	5.9 high

Total Risk	Standard Deviation	Category Risk	Risk Index	Beta
av	8.9%	blw av	1.0	0.77

	1996	1995	1994	1993	1992	1991	1990	1989	1988	1987
Return (%)	14.1	37.6	7.1	6.4	6.7	22.1	-6.8	23.7	22.5	-3.9
Differ from Category (+/-)	-5.6	7.5	8.4	-7.4	-4.0	-7.0	-0.9	0.2	5.7	-4.1
Return, Tax-Adjusted (%)	11.8	35.1	4.2	4.1	4.4	19.7	-9.1	18.5	18.8	-7.5

PER SHARE DATA

	1996	1995	1994	1993	1992	1991	1990	1989	1988	1987
Dividends, Net Income ($)	0.57	0.54	0.54	0.51	0.56	0.72	0.82	0.71	0.53	0.70
Distrib'ns, Cap Gain ($)	1.21	0.94	1.27	0.90	0.81	0.43	0.46	2.49	1.49	1.53
Net Asset Value ($)	27.00	25.33	19.61	20.05	20.19	20.27	17.63	20.24	19.06	17.23
Expense Ratio (%)	1.16	1.31	1.34	1.39	1.35	1.41	1.38	1.41	1.48	1.50
Yield (%)	2.02	2.05	2.58	2.43	2.66	3.47	4.53	3.12	2.57	3.73
Portfolio Turnover (%)	15	42	49	35	60	57	55	50	34	23
Total Assets (Millions $)	45	39	26	24	25	26	22	23	17	15

PORTFOLIO (as of 9/30/96)

Portfolio Manager: J. Stratton, J. Affleck - 1972

Investm't Category: Growth & Income
- ✔ Domestic
- Foreign
- Asset Allocation
- Index
- Sector
- State Specific

Investment Style
- Large-Cap Growth
- Mid-Cap Growth
- Small-Cap Growth
- ✔ Large-Cap Value
- Mid-Cap Value
- Small-Cap Value

Portfolio
10.1% cash	0.0% corp bonds
89.9% stocks	0.0% gov't bonds
0.0% preferred	0.0% muni bonds
0.0% conv't/warrants	0.0% other

SHAREHOLDER INFORMATION

Minimum Investment
Initial: $2,000   Subsequent: $100

Minimum IRA Investment
Initial: $1   Subsequent: $1

Maximum Fees
Load: none   12b-1: none
Other: none

Distributions
Income: semiannual   Capital Gains: semiannual

Exchange Options
Number Per Year: no limit   Fee: none
Telephone: yes (money market fund not available)

Services
IRA, pension, auto exchange, auto invest, auto withdraw

Stratton Monthly Dividend Shares (STMDX)

Growth & Income

610 W. Germantown Pike
Suite 300
Plymouth Meeting, PA 19462
800-441-6580, 610-941-0255

PERFORMANCE

fund inception date: 4/13/72

	3yr Annual	5yr Annual	10yr Annual	Bull	Bear
Return (%)	5.6	6.7	7.6	36.4	-12.8
Differ from Category (+/-)	-9.7 low	-7.2 low	-5.1 low	-23.4 low	-6.4 low

Total Risk	Standard Deviation	Category Risk	Risk Index	Beta
av	9.3%	av	1.0	0.42

	1996	1995	1994	1993	1992	1991	1990	1989	1988	1987
Return (%)	8.5	23.4	-12.2	6.6	10.4	35.0	-3.9	18.7	9.7	-11.5
Differ from Category (+/-)	-11.2	-6.7	-10.9	-7.2	-0.3	5.9	2.0	-4.8	-7.1	-11.7
Return, Tax-Adjusted (%)	5.7	20.2	-14.9	3.9	7.6	31.5	-7.3	15.2	6.1	-15.0

PER SHARE DATA

	1996	1995	1994	1993	1992	1991	1990	1989	1988	1987
Dividends, Net Income ($)	1.92	1.92	1.92	1.95	1.94	1.95	2.20	2.04	2.08	2.09
Distrib'ns, Cap Gain ($)	0.00	0.00	0.00	0.00	0.00	0.00	0.00	0.00	0.00	0.65
Net Asset Value ($)	27.43	27.19	23.78	29.17	29.16	28.31	22.66	25.88	23.63	23.44
Expense Ratio (%)	0.99	1.08	0.99	1.10	1.23	1.27	1.25	1.21	1.21	1.24
Yield (%)	6.99	7.06	8.07	6.68	6.65	6.88	9.70	7.88	8.80	8.67
Portfolio Turnover (%)	53	39	19	35	44	14	39	15	24	15
Total Assets (Millions $)	101	128	121	176	88	43	30	34	32	33

PORTFOLIO (as of 9/30/96)

Portfolio Manager: J. Stratton, G. Heffernan - 1980

Investm't Category: Growth & Income

✔ Domestic
  Index
  Foreign
  Sector
  Asset Allocation
  State Specific

Investment Style

  Large-Cap Growth   ✔ Large-Cap Value
  Mid-Cap Growth   ✔ Mid-Cap Value
  Small-Cap Growth   Small-Cap Value

Portfolio

7.5% cash	0.0% corp bonds
86.6% stocks	0.0% gov't bonds
0.0% preferred	0.0% muni bonds
5.9% conv't/warrants	0.0% other

SHAREHOLDER INFORMATION

Minimum Investment
Initial: $2,000   Subsequent: $100

Minimum IRA Investment
Initial: $1   Subsequent: $1

Maximum Fees
Load: none   12b-1: none
Other: none

Distributions
Income: monthly   Capital Gains: Dec

Exchange Options
Number Per Year: no limit   Fee: none
Telephone: yes (money market fund not available)

Services
IRA, pension, auto exchange, auto invest, auto withdraw

Strong Advantage

(STADX)

General Bond

100 Heritage Reserve
P.O. Box 2936
Milwaukee, WI 53201
800-368-1030, 414-359-3400
www.strong-funds.com

PERFORMANCE

fund inception date: 11/25/88

	3yr Annual	5yr Annual	10yr Annual	Bull	Bear
Return (%)	5.8	6.7	na	17.4	0.5
Differ from Category (+/-)	0.7 abv av	0.6 abv av	na	-2.9 blw av	4.7 high

Total Risk	Standard Deviation	Category Risk	Risk Index	Avg Mat
low	0.7%	low	0.2	0.4 yrs

	1996	1995	1994	1993	1992	1991	1990	1989	1988	1987
Return (%)	6.6	7.5	3.5	7.8	8.4	10.6	6.6	9.3	—	—
Differ from Category (+/-)	2.7	-7.4	5.8	-1.3	1.9	-4.1	-0.7	-2.4	—	—
Return, Tax-Adjusted (%)	4.1	4.8	1.3	5.4	5.6	7.5	3.3	5.2	—	—

PER SHARE DATA

	1996	1995	1994	1993	1992	1991	1990	1989	1988	1987
Dividends, Net Income ($)	0.61	0.66	0.54	0.59	0.70	0.75	0.82	1.02	—	—
Distrib'ns, Cap Gain ($)	0.00	0.00	0.01	0.00	0.00	0.00	0.00	0.00	—	—
Net Asset Value ($)	10.07	10.04	9.98	10.19	10.01	9.90	9.67	9.87	—	—
Expense Ratio (%)	na	0.80	0.80	0.90	1.00	1.20	1.20	1.10	—	—
Yield (%)	6.05	6.57	5.40	5.78	6.99	7.57	8.47	10.33	—	—
Portfolio Turnover (%)	na	183	221	304	316	503	274	211	—	—
Total Assets (Millions $)	1,394	989	910	415	272	143	119	142	—	—

PORTFOLIO (as of 6/30/96)

Portfolio Manager: Jeffrey A. Koch - 1991

Investm't Category: General Bond
- ✔ Domestic
- Index
- ✔ Foreign
- Sector
- Asset Allocation
- State Specific

Investment Style

Large-Cap Growth	Large-Cap Value
Mid-Cap Growth	Mid-Cap Value
Small-Cap Growth	Small-Cap Value

Portfolio

5.8% cash	62.3% corp bonds
0.0% stocks	22.6% gov't bonds
0.0% preferred	0.0% muni bonds
0.0% conv't/warrants	9.3% other

SHAREHOLDER INFORMATION

Minimum Investment
Initial: $2,500   Subsequent: $50

Minimum IRA Investment
Initial: $1,000   Subsequent: $50

Maximum Fees
Load: none   12b-1: none
Other: none

Distributions
Income: monthly   Capital Gains: annual

Exchange Options
Number Per Year: 5   Fee: none
Telephone: yes (money market fund available)

Services
IRA, pension, auto exchange, auto invest, auto withdraw

Strong American Utilities

(SAMUX) *Growth & Income*

100 Heritage Reserve
P.O. Box 2936
Milwaukee, WI 53201
800-368-1030, 414-359-3400
www.strong-funds.com

PERFORMANCE

fund inception date: 7/1/93

	3yr Annual	5yr Annual	10yr Annual	Bull	Bear
Return (%)	13.0	na	na	50.7	-5.3
Differ from Category (+/-)	-2.3 blw av	na	na	-9.1 blw av	1.1 abv av

Total Risk	Standard Deviation	Category Risk	Risk Index	Beta
av	9.2%	av	1.0	0.61

	1996	1995	1994	1993	1992	1991	1990	1989	1988	1987
Return (%)	8.3	36.9	-2.7	—	—	—	—	—	—	—
Differ from Category (+/-)	-11.4	6.8	-1.4	—	—	—	—	—	—	—
Return, Tax-Adjusted (%)	5.5	35.5	-4.5	—	—	—	—	—	—	—

PER SHARE DATA

	1996	1995	1994	1993	1992	1991	1990	1989	1988	1987
Dividends, Net Income ($)	0.40	0.32	0.46	—	—	—	—	—	—	—
Distrib'ns, Cap Gain ($)	0.67	0.00	0.00	—	—	—	—	—	—	—
Net Asset Value ($)	12.54	12.58	9.46	—	—	—	—	—	—	—
Expense Ratio (%)	na	1.20	0.50	—	—	—	—	—	—	—
Yield (%)	3.02	2.54	4.86	—	—	—	—	—	—	—
Portfolio Turnover (%)	na	56	105	—	—	—	—	—	—	—
Total Assets (Millions $)	134	118	37	—	—	—	—	—	—	—

PORTFOLIO (as of 9/30/96)

Portfolio Manager: William H. Reaves, committee - 1993

Investm't Category: Growth & Income
- ✔ Domestic
- Foreign
- Asset Allocation
- Index
- ✔ Sector
- State Specific

Investment Style
- Large-Cap Growth
- Mid-Cap Growth
- Small-Cap Growth
- ✔ Large-Cap Value
- Mid-Cap Value
- Small-Cap Value

Portfolio
4.8% cash	0.0% corp bonds
95.2% stocks	0.0% gov't bonds
0.0% preferred	0.0% muni bonds
0.0% conv't/warrants	0.0% other

SHAREHOLDER INFORMATION

Minimum Investment
Initial: $1,000   Subsequent: $50

Minimum IRA Investment
Initial: $250   Subsequent: $50

Maximum Fees
Load: none   12b-1: none
Other: none

Distributions
Income: quarterly   Capital Gains: annual

Exchange Options
Number Per Year: 5   Fee: none
Telephone: yes (money market fund available)

Services
IRA, pension, auto exchange, auto invest, auto withdraw

Strong Asia Pacific
(SASPX)
International Stock

100 Heritage Reserve
P.O. Box 2936
Milwaukee, WI 53201
800-368-1030, 414-359-3400
www.strong-funds.com

PERFORMANCE

fund inception date: 12/31/93

	3yr Annual	5yr Annual	10yr Annual	Bull	Bear
Return (%)	0.8	na	na	4.1	-7.9
Differ from Category (+/-)	-5.5 low	na	na	-20.2 low	-0.7 blw av

Total Risk	Standard Deviation	Category Risk	Risk Index	Beta
high	12.3%	abv av	1.2	0.77

	1996	1995	1994	1993	1992	1991	1990	1989	1988	1987
Return (%)	2.1	5.9	-5.3	—	—	—	—	—	—	—
Differ from Category (+/-)	-12.7	-3.2	-2.2	—	—	—	—	—	—	—
Return, Tax-Adjusted (%)	1.0	4.7	-5.7	—	—	—	—	—	—	—

PER SHARE DATA

	1996	1995	1994	1993	1992	1991	1990	1989	1988	1987
Dividends, Net Income ($)	0.17	0.28	0.00	—	—	—	—	—	—	—
Distrib'ns, Cap Gain ($)	0.11	0.00	0.11	—	—	—	—	—	—	—
Net Asset Value ($)	9.54	9.62	9.35	—	—	—	—	—	—	—
Expense Ratio (%)	na	2.00	2.00	—	—	—	—	—	—	—
Yield (%)	1.76	2.91	0.00	—	—	—	—	—	—	—
Portfolio Turnover (%)	na	104	103	—	—	—	—	—	—	—
Total Assets (Millions $)	74	57	57	—	—	—	—	—	—	—

PORTFOLIO (as of 9/30/96)

Portfolio Manager: Anthony L.T. Cragg - 1993

Investm't Category: International Stock
- Domestic
- ✔ Foreign
- Asset Allocation
- Index
- Sector
- State Specific

Investment Style
- Large-Cap Growth
- Mid-Cap Growth
- Small-Cap Growth
- Large-Cap Value
- Mid-Cap Value
- Small-Cap Value

Portfolio
- 0.0% cash
- 87.7% stocks
- 1.1% preferred
- 0.0% conv't/warrants
- 0.3% corp bonds
- 1.6% gov't bonds
- 0.0% muni bonds
- 9.3% other

SHAREHOLDER INFORMATION

Minimum Investment
Initial: $1,000   Subsequent: $50

Minimum IRA Investment
Initial: $250   Subsequent: $50

Maximum Fees
Load: none   12b-1: none
Other: none

Distributions
Income: quarterly   Capital Gains: annual

Exchange Options
Number Per Year: 5   Fee: none
Telephone: yes (money market fund available)

Services
IRA, pension, auto exchange, auto invest, auto withdraw

Strong Asset Allocation
(STAAX)
Balanced

100 Heritage Reserve
P.O. Box 2936
Milwaukee, WI 53201
800-368-1030, 414-359-3400
www.strong-funds.com

PERFORMANCE

fund inception date: 12/30/81

	3yr Annual	5yr Annual	10yr Annual	Bull	Bear
Return (%)	9.8	9.4	8.8	38.1	-5.8
Differ from Category (+/-)	-1.9 blw av	-2.0 blw av	-2.0 low	-7.0 blw av	-0.1 av

Total Risk	Standard Deviation	Category Risk	Risk Index	Beta
blw av	6.2%	blw av	0.9	0.53

	1996	1995	1994	1993	1992	1991	1990	1989	1988	1987
Return (%)	10.4	21.9	-1.6	14.5	3.2	19.6	2.7	11.2	9.1	-0.3
Differ from Category (+/-)	-3.8	-2.7	0.0	0.1	-5.7	-4.5	3.6	-6.9	-3.1	-3.0
Return, Tax-Adjusted (%)	6.4	18.2	-3.3	10.8	0.1	17.1	-0.3	8.8	5.6	-7.3

PER SHARE DATA

	1996	1995	1994	1993	1992	1991	1990	1989	1988	1987
Dividends, Net Income ($)	0.86	0.81	0.69	0.82	0.86	0.96	1.38	0.96	1.37	1.78
Distrib'ns, Cap Gain ($)	1.54	1.17	0.16	1.23	0.93	0.19	0.00	0.13	0.23	2.95
Net Asset Value ($)	19.40	19.78	17.91	19.06	18.49	19.68	17.50	18.41	17.57	17.60
Expense Ratio (%)	na	1.20	1.20	1.20	1.20	1.30	1.30	1.30	1.20	1.10
Yield (%)	4.10	3.86	3.81	4.04	4.42	4.83	7.88	5.17	7.69	8.66
Portfolio Turnover (%)	na	326	359	348	320	418	320	207	426	337
Total Assets (Millions $)	271	268	248	254	208	214	203	240	256	272

PORTFOLIO (as of 6/30/96)

Portfolio Manager: Bradley C. Tank, committee - 1993

Investm't Category: Balanced
- ✔ Domestic
- ✔ Foreign
- ✔ Asset Allocation

Index
Sector
State Specific

Investment Style

Large-Cap Growth
Mid-Cap Growth
Small-Cap Growth

Large-Cap Value
Mid-Cap Value
Small-Cap Value

Portfolio

6.0% cash	20.3% corp bonds
51.1% stocks	2.7% gov't bonds
3.6% preferred	0.0% muni bonds
0.7% conv't/warrants	15.6% other

SHAREHOLDER INFORMATION

Minimum Investment
Initial: $250   Subsequent: $50

Minimum IRA Investment
Initial: $250   Subsequent: $50

Maximum Fees
Load: none   12b-1: none
Other: none

Distributions
Income: quarterly   Capital Gains: annual

Exchange Options
Number Per Year: 5   Fee: none
Telephone: yes (money market fund available)

Services
IRA, pension, auto exchange, auto invest, auto withdraw

Strong Common Stock

(STCSX)

Aggressive Growth

100 Heritage Reserve
P.O. Box 2936
Milwaukee, WI 53201
800-368-1030, 414-359-3400
www.strong-funds.com

this fund is closed to new investors

PERFORMANCE

fund inception date: 12/29/89

	3yr Annual	5yr Annual	10yr Annual	Bull	Bear
Return (%)	16.6	19.1	na	63.8	-5.2
Differ from Category (+/-)	0.8 abv av	3.8 high	na	-7.3 av	5.4 high

Total Risk	Standard Deviation	Category Risk	Risk Index	Beta
abv av	9.8%	low	0.7	0.83

	1996	1995	1994	1993	1992	1991	1990	1989	1988	1987
Return (%)	20.4	32.4	-0.5	25.1	20.7	57.0	1.0	—	—	—
Differ from Category (+/-)	1.3	-1.9	-0.5	5.8	9.0	4.9	6.4	—	—	—
Return, Tax-Adjusted (%)	15.4	28.4	-2.3	23.4	19.6	49.7	0.6	—	—	—

PER SHARE DATA

	1996	1995	1994	1993	1992	1991	1990	1989	1988	1987
Dividends, Net Income ($)	0.11	0.11	0.04	0.03	0.22	0.00	0.08	—	—	—
Distrib'ns, Cap Gain ($)	3.35	2.21	1.06	0.86	0.15	2.58	0.00	—	—	—
Net Asset Value ($)	20.24	19.77	16.74	17.94	15.07	12.84	10.02	—	—	—
Expense Ratio (%)	na	1.20	1.30	1.40	1.40	2.00	2.00	—	—	—
Yield (%)	0.46	0.50	0.22	0.15	1.44	0.00	0.79	—	—	—
Portfolio Turnover (%)	na	91	83	80	292	2,461	291	—	—	—
Total Assets (Millions $)	1,250	1,061	790	762	179	48	2	—	—	—

PORTFOLIO (as of 9/30/96)

Portfolio Manager: Richard T. Weiss, Marina Carlson - 1991

Investm't Category: Aggressive Growth
- ✔ Domestic
- ✔ Foreign
- Asset Allocation
- Index
- Sector
- State Specific

Investment Style
- Large-Cap Growth
- ✔ Mid-Cap Growth
- ✔ Small-Cap Growth
- Large-Cap Value
- ✔ Mid-Cap Value
- ✔ Small-Cap Value

Portfolio
12.0% cash	0.0% corp bonds
88.0% stocks	0.0% gov't bonds
0.0% preferred	0.0% muni bonds
0.0% conv't/warrants	0.0% other

SHAREHOLDER INFORMATION

Minimum Investment
Initial: $1,000   Subsequent: $50

Minimum IRA Investment
Initial: $250   Subsequent: $50

Maximum Fees
Load: none   12b-1: none
Other: none

Distributions
Income: quarterly   Capital Gains: annual

Exchange Options
Number Per Year: 5   Fee: none
Telephone: yes (money market fund available)

Services
IRA, pension, auto exchange, auto invest, auto withdraw

Strong Corporate Bond

(STCBX)

Corporate Bond

100 Heritage Reserve
P.O. Box 2936
Milwaukee, WI 53201
800-368-1030, 414-359-3400
www.strong-funds.com

PERFORMANCE

fund inception date: 12/12/85

	3yr Annual	5yr Annual	10yr Annual	Bull	Bear
Return (%)	9.3	10.7	7.7	36.0	-6.1
Differ from Category (+/-)	3.0 high	2.4 high	-0.4 av	11.2 high	-1.0 blw av

Total Risk	Standard Deviation	Category Risk	Risk Index	Avg Mat
blw av	5.6%	high	1.2	13.9 yrs

	1996	1995	1994	1993	1992	1991	1990	1989	1988	1987
Return (%)	5.5	25.3	-1.4	16.7	9.3	14.8	-6.3	0.3	12.4	4.4
Differ from Category (+/-)	0.3	7.3	1.7	4.9	0.4	-2.4	-10.3	-9.1	3.1	2.0
Return, Tax-Adjusted (%)	2.8	22.0	-4.3	13.7	5.8	11.4	-10.3	-4.4	8.4	-0.5

PER SHARE DATA

	1996	1995	1994	1993	1992	1991	1990	1989	1988	1987
Dividends, Net Income ($)	0.72	0.76	0.73	0.69	0.81	0.76	1.05	1.40	1.16	1.52
Distrib'ns, Cap Gain ($)	0.00	0.00	0.00	0.00	0.00	0.00	0.00	0.00	0.00	0.04
Net Asset Value ($)	10.73	10.89	9.36	10.24	9.40	9.37	8.87	10.57	11.88	11.64
Expense Ratio (%)	na	1.00	1.10	1.10	1.30	1.50	1.40	1.20	1.20	1.10
Yield (%)	6.71	6.97	7.79	6.73	8.61	8.11	11.83	13.24	9.76	13.01
Portfolio Turnover (%)	na	621	603	666	557	392	294	207	400	245
Total Assets (Millions $)	305	259	123	123	102	92	92	195	202	137

PORTFOLIO (as of 6/30/96)

Portfolio Manager: Jeffrey A. Koch, John Bender - 1992

Investm't Category: Corporate Bond
✔ Domestic   Index
✔ Foreign   Sector
   Asset Allocation   State Specific

Investment Style
Large-Cap Growth   Large-Cap Value
Mid-Cap Growth   Mid-Cap Value
Small-Cap Growth   Small-Cap Value

Portfolio
1.6% cash   81.7% corp bonds
0.0% stocks   7.7% gov't bonds
5.0% preferred   0.0% muni bonds
0.4% conv't/warrants 3.6% other

SHAREHOLDER INFORMATION

Minimum Investment
Initial: $2,500   Subsequent: $50

Minimum IRA Investment
Initial: $1,000   Subsequent: $50

Maximum Fees
Load: none   12b-1: none
Other: none

Distributions
Income: monthly   Capital Gains: annual

Exchange Options
Number Per Year: 5   Fee: none
Telephone: yes (money market fund available)

Services
IRA, pension, auto exchange, auto invest, auto withdraw

Strong Discovery

(STDIX)

Growth

100 Heritage Reserve
P.O. Box 2936
Milwaukee, WI 53201
800-368-1030, 414-359-3400
www.strong-funds.com

PERFORMANCE

fund inception date: 12/31/87

	3yr Annual	5yr Annual	10yr Annual	Bull	Bear
Return (%)	8.8	9.9	na	44.8	-13.9
Differ from Category (+/-)	-6.9 low	-4.4 low	na	-17.6 low	-7.2 low

Total Risk	Standard Deviation	Category Risk	Risk Index	Beta
high	13.9%	high	1.3	1.06

	1996	1995	1994	1993	1992	1991	1990	1989	1988	1987
Return (%)	1.4	34.8	-5.7	22.2	1.9	67.6	-2.8	23.9	24.4	—
Differ from Category (+/-)	-18.7	4.5	-5.4	8.2	-9.9	31.6	3.3	-2.2	6.3	—
Return, Tax-Adjusted (%)	-1.8	30.9	-8.3	19.3	-1.8	59.1	-3.8	21.2	20.5	—

PER SHARE DATA

	1996	1995	1994	1993	1992	1991	1990	1989	1988	1987
Dividends, Net Income ($)	1.11	0.10	0.69	0.49	1.49	0.83	0.30	0.27	0.97	—
Distrib'ns, Cap Gain ($)	0.59	2.04	0.68	0.92	0.15	2.59	0.00	0.71	0.02	—
Net Asset Value ($)	17.45	18.96	15.67	18.05	16.01	17.49	12.51	13.18	11.44	—
Expense Ratio (%)	na	1.40	1.50	1.50	1.50	1.60	1.90	1.90	2.00	—
Yield (%)	6.15	0.47	4.22	2.58	9.22	4.13	2.39	1.94	8.46	—
Portfolio Turnover (%)	na	516	408	668	1,259	1,060	494	550	442	—
Total Assets (Millions $)	525	599	388	301	193	162	56	57	13	—

PORTFOLIO (as of 9/30/96)

Portfolio Manager: R.S. Strong, C.A. Pacquelet - 1987

Investm't Category: Growth

✔ Domestic — Index
✔ Foreign — Sector
 Asset Allocation — State Specific

Investment Style

 Large-Cap Growth — Large-Cap Value
 Mid-Cap Growth — Mid-Cap Value
✔ Small-Cap Growth — Small-Cap Value

Portfolio

5.8% cash	0.0% corp bonds
94.1% stocks	0.0% gov't bonds
0.0% preferred	0.0% muni bonds
0.1% conv't/warrants	0.0% other

SHAREHOLDER INFORMATION

Minimum Investment
Initial: $1,000   Subsequent: $50

Minimum IRA Investment
Initial: $250   Subsequent: $50

Maximum Fees
Load: none   12b-1: none
Other: none

Distributions
Income: quarterly   Capital Gains: annual

Exchange Options
Number Per Year: 5   Fee: none
Telephone: yes (money market fund available)

Services
IRA, pension, auto exchange, auto invest, auto withdraw

Strong Gov't Securities
(STVSX)
General Bond

100 Heritage Reserve
P.O. Box 2936
Milwaukee, WI 53201
800-368-1030, 414-359-3400
www.strong-funds.com

PERFORMANCE
fund inception date: 10/29/86

	3yr Annual	5yr Annual	10yr Annual	Bull	Bear
Return (%)	5.9	7.9	8.8	24.5	-5.8
Differ from Category (+/-)	0.8 high	1.8 high	1.5 high	4.2 high	-1.6 blw av

Total Risk	Standard Deviation	Category Risk	Risk Index	Avg Mat
blw av	4.8%	high	1.3	8.2 yrs

	1996	1995	1994	1993	1992	1991	1990	1989	1988	1987
Return (%).............	2.8	19.9	-3.4	12.7	9.2	16.6	8.7	9.8	10.5	3.4
Differ from Category (+/-)	-1.1	5.0	-1.1	3.6	2.7	1.9	1.4	-1.9	2.9	1.1
Return, Tax-Adjusted (%)...	0.4	17.1	-5.8	9.1	5.0	13.1	5.5	6.5	7.5	0.8

PER SHARE DATA

	1996	1995	1994	1993	1992	1991	1990	1989	1988	1987
Dividends, Net Income ($)	0.63	0.66	0.62	0.65	0.80	0.76	0.77	0.79	0.67	0.65
Distrib'ns, Cap Gain ($) ...	0.00	0.00	0.00	0.41	0.48	0.16	0.04	0.05	0.09	0.00
Net Asset Value ($)	10.48	10.83	9.63	10.61	10.39	10.77	10.10	10.08	9.98	9.75
Expense Ratio (%).........	na	0.90	0.90	0.80	0.70	0.80	1.30	1.30	0.40	1.00
Yield (%)	6.01	6.09	6.43	5.89	7.35	6.95	7.59	7.79	6.65	6.66
Portfolio Turnover (%).....	na	409	479	520	629	293	254	422	1,728	715
Total Assets (Millions $)...	657	504	276	221	82	51	41	35	25	11

PORTFOLIO (as of 9/30/96)

Portfolio Manager: Bradley C. Tank - 1990

Investm't Category: General Bond
✔ Domestic
✔ Foreign
  Asset Allocation

  Index
  Sector
  State Specific

Investment Style
Large-Cap Growth   Large-Cap Value
Mid-Cap Growth   Mid-Cap Value
Small-Cap Growth   Small-Cap Value

Portfolio
0.6% cash   10.3% corp bonds
0.0% stocks   79.6% gov't bonds
3.9% preferred   0.6% muni bonds
0.0% conv't/warrants 5.0% other

SHAREHOLDER INFORMATION

Minimum Investment
Initial: $2,500   Subsequent: $50

Minimum IRA Investment
Initial: $1,000   Subsequent: $50

Maximum Fees
Load: none   12b-1: none
Other: none

Distributions
Income: monthly   Capital Gains: annual

Exchange Options
Number Per Year: 5   Fee: none
Telephone: yes (money market fund available)

Services
IRA, pension, auto exchange, auto invest, auto withdraw

Strong Growth (SGROX)

Growth

100 Heritage Reserve
P.O. Box 2936
Milwaukee, WI 53201
800-368-1030, 414-359-3400
www.strong-funds.com

PERFORMANCE

fund inception date: 12/31/93

	3yr Annual	5yr Annual	10yr Annual	Bull	Bear
Return (%)	25.4	na	na	85.8	0.0
Differ from Category (+/-)	9.7 high	na	na	23.4 high	6.7 high

Total Risk	Standard Deviation	Category Risk	Risk Index	Beta
high	14.4%	high	1.4	0.93

	1996	1995	1994	1993	1992	1991	1990	1989	1988	1987
Return (%)	19.5	41.0	17.2	—	—	—	—	—	—	—
Differ from Category (+/-)	-0.6	10.7	17.5	—	—	—	—	—	—	—
Return, Tax-Adjusted (%)	18.6	39.8	16.8	—	—	—	—	—	—	—

PER SHARE DATA

	1996	1995	1994	1993	1992	1991	1990	1989	1988	1987
Dividends, Net Income ($)	0.02	0.02	0.10	—	—	—	—	—	—	—
Distrib'ns, Cap Gain ($)	0.45	0.45	0.00	—	—	—	—	—	—	—
Net Asset Value ($)	18.50	15.88	11.61	—	—	—	—	—	—	—
Expense Ratio (%)	na	1.40	1.60	—	—	—	—	—	—	—
Yield (%)	0.10	0.12	0.86	—	—	—	—	—	—	—
Portfolio Turnover (%)	na	321	386	—	—	—	—	—	—	—
Total Assets (Millions $)	1,351	642	106	—	—	—	—	—	—	—

PORTFOLIO (as of 9/30/96)

Portfolio Manager: Ronald C. Ognar - 1993

Investm't Category: Growth

✔ Domestic	Index
✔ Foreign	Sector
Asset Allocation	State Specific

Investment Style

Large-Cap Growth	Large-Cap Value
✔ Mid-Cap Growth	Mid-Cap Value
✔ Small-Cap Growth	Small-Cap Value

Portfolio

2.8% cash	0.2% corp bonds
96.8% stocks	0.0% gov't bonds
0.1% preferred	0.0% muni bonds
0.1% conv't/warrants	0.0% other

SHAREHOLDER INFORMATION

Minimum Investment
Initial: $1,000   Subsequent: $50

Minimum IRA Investment
Initial: $250   Subsequent: $50

Maximum Fees
Load: none   12b-1: none
Other: none

Distributions
Income: quarterly   Capital Gains: annual

Exchange Options
Number Per Year: 5   Fee: none
Telephone: yes (money market fund available)

Services
IRA, pension, auto exchange, auto invest, auto withdraw

Strong High Yield Bond

(STHYX)

Corporate High-Yield Bond

100 Heritage Reserve
P.O. Box 2936
Milwaukee, WI 53201
800-368-1030, 414-359-3400
www.strong-funds.com

PERFORMANCE

fund inception date: 12/28/95

	3yr Annual	5yr Annual	10yr Annual	Bull	Bear
Return (%)	na	na	na	na	na
Differ from Category (+/-)	na	na	na	na	na

Total Risk	Standard Deviation	Category Risk	Risk Index	Avg Mat
na	na	na	na	6.5 yrs

	1996	1995	1994	1993	1992	1991	1990	1989	1988	1987
Return (%)	26.8	—	—	—	—	—	—	—	—	—
Differ from Category (+/-)	11.5	—	—	—	—	—	—	—	—	—
Return, Tax-Adjusted (%)	22.4	—	—	—	—	—	—	—	—	—

PER SHARE DATA

	1996	1995	1994	1993	1992	1991	1990	1989	1988	1987
Dividends, Net Income ($)	1.02	—	—	—	—	—	—	—	—	—
Distrib'ns, Cap Gain ($)	0.13	—	—	—	—	—	—	—	—	—
Net Asset Value ($)	11.45	—	—	—	—	—	—	—	—	—
Expense Ratio (%)	na	—	—	—	—	—	—	—	—	—
Yield (%)	8.80	—	—	—	—	—	—	—	—	—
Portfolio Turnover (%)	na	—	—	—	—	—	—	—	—	—
Total Assets (Millions $)	250	—	—	—	—	—	—	—	—	—

PORTFOLIO (as of 6/30/96)

Portfolio Manager: Jeffrey A. Koch - 1995

Investm't Category: Corp. High-Yield Bond
- ✔ Domestic   Index
- ✔ Foreign   Sector
-    Asset Allocation   State Specific

Investment Style

Large-Cap Growth	Large-Cap Value
Mid-Cap Growth	Mid-Cap Value
Small-Cap Growth	Small-Cap Value

Portfolio

7.6% cash	2.3% corp bonds
0.2% stocks	0.0% gov't bonds
4.0% preferred	0.0% muni bonds
75.3% conv't/warrants	10.6% other

SHAREHOLDER INFORMATION

Minimum Investment
Initial: $2,500   Subsequent: $50

Minimum IRA Investment
Initial: $1,000   Subsequent: $50

Maximum Fees
Load: none   12b-1: none
Other: none

Distributions
Income: monthly   Capital Gains: annual

Exchange Options
Number Per Year: 5   Fee: none
Telephone: yes (money market fund available)

Services
IRA, pension, auto exchange, auto invest, auto withdraw

Strong High Yield Muni Bond (SHYLX)

Tax-Exempt Bond

100 Heritage Reserve
P.O. Box 2936
Milwaukee, WI 53201
800-368-1030, 414-359-3400
www.strong-funds.com

PERFORMANCE

fund inception date: 10/1/93

	3yr Annual	5yr Annual	10yr Annual	Bull	Bear
Return (%)	6.0	na	na	20.4	-2.4
Differ from Category (+/-)	1.8 high	na	na	2.0 abv av	3.0 high

Total Risk	Standard Deviation	Category Risk	Risk Index	Avg Mat
low	4.2%	blw av	0.8	18.9 yrs

	1996	1995	1994	1993	1992	1991	1990	1989	1988	1987
Return (%)	5.1	14.6	-1.0	—	—	—	—	—	—	—
Differ from Category (+/-)	1.4	-0.6	4.3	—	—	—	—	—	—	—
Return, Tax-Adjusted (%)	5.1	14.6	-1.0	—	—	—	—	—	—	—

PER SHARE DATA

	1996	1995	1994	1993	1992	1991	1990	1989	1988	1987
Dividends, Net Income ($)	0.64	0.69	0.71	—	—	—	—	—	—	—
Distrib'ns, Cap Gain ($)	0.00	0.00	0.00	—	—	—	—	—	—	—
Net Asset Value ($)	9.74	9.91	9.29	—	—	—	—	—	—	—
Expense Ratio (%)	na	0.40	0.00	—	—	—	—	—	—	—
Yield (%)	6.57	6.96	7.64	—	—	—	—	—	—	—
Portfolio Turnover (%)	na	113	198	—	—	—	—	—	—	—
Total Assets (Millions $)	251	266	107	—	—	—	—	—	—	—

PORTFOLIO (as of 6/30/96)

Portfolio Manager: Mary Kay Bourbulas - 1993

Investm't Category: Tax-Exempt Bond

✔ Domestic
Foreign
Asset Allocation
Index
Sector
State Specific

Investment Style
Large-Cap Growth
Mid-Cap Growth
Small-Cap Growth
Large-Cap Value
Mid-Cap Value
Small-Cap Value

Portfolio
4.9% cash
0.0% stocks
0.0% preferred
0.0% conv't/warrants
0.0% corp bonds
0.0% gov't bonds
95.1% muni bonds
0.0% other

SHAREHOLDER INFORMATION

Minimum Investment
Initial: $2,500   Subsequent: $50

Minimum IRA Investment
Initial: na   Subsequent: na

Maximum Fees
Load: none   12b-1: none
Other: none

Distributions
Income: monthly   Capital Gains: annual

Exchange Options
Number Per Year: 5   Fee: none
Telephone: yes (money market fund available)

Services
auto exchange, auto invest, auto withdraw

Strong Int'l Bond (SIBUX)

International Bond

100 Heritage Reserve
P.O. Box 2936
Milwaukee, WI 53201
800-368-1030, 414-359-3400
www.strong-funds.com

PERFORMANCE

fund inception date: 3/31/94

	3yr Annual	5yr Annual	10yr Annual	Bull	Bear
Return (%)	na	na	na	32.2	na
Differ from Category (+/-)	na	na	na	1.0 abv av	na

Total Risk	Standard Deviation	Category Risk	Risk Index	Avg Mat
na	na	na	na	7.3 yrs

	1996	1995	1994	1993	1992	1991	1990	1989	1988	1987
Return (%)	7.9	19.0	—	—	—	—	—	—	—	—
Differ from Category (+/-)	-3.4	3.0	—	—	—	—	—	—	—	—
Return, Tax-Adjusted (%)	6.4	15.2	—	—	—	—	—	—	—	—

PER SHARE DATA

	1996	1995	1994	1993	1992	1991	1990	1989	1988	1987
Dividends, Net Income ($)	0.40	0.94	—	—	—	—	—	—	—	—
Distrib'ns, Cap Gain ($)	0.01	0.06	—	—	—	—	—	—	—	—
Net Asset Value ($)	11.77	11.30	—	—	—	—	—	—	—	—
Expense Ratio (%)	na	0.00	—	—	—	—	—	—	—	—
Yield (%)	3.39	8.27	—	—	—	—	—	—	—	—
Portfolio Turnover (%)	na	473	—	—	—	—	—	—	—	—
Total Assets (Millions $)	33	24	—	—	—	—	—	—	—	—

PORTFOLIO (as of 6/30/96)

Portfolio Manager: Shirish T. Malekar - 1994

Investm't Category: International Bond

Domestic	Index
✔ Foreign	Sector
Asset Allocation	State Specific

Investment Style

Large-Cap Growth	Large-Cap Value
Mid-Cap Growth	Mid-Cap Value
Small-Cap Growth	Small-Cap Value

Portfolio

19.3% cash	0.8% corp bonds
0.0% stocks	71.8% gov't bonds
0.0% preferred	0.0% muni bonds
0.0% conv't/warrants	8.1% other

SHAREHOLDER INFORMATION

Minimum Investment
Initial: $1,000   Subsequent: $50

Minimum IRA Investment
Initial: $250   Subsequent: $50

Maximum Fees
Load: none   12b-1: none
Other: none

Distributions
Income: quarterly   Capital Gains: annual

Exchange Options
Number Per Year: 5   Fee: none
Telephone: yes (money market fund available)

Services
IRA, pension, auto exchange, auto invest, auto withdraw

Strong Int'l Stock (STISX)

International Stock

100 Heritage Reserve
P.O. Box 2936
Milwaukee, WI 53201
800-368-1030, 414-359-3400
www.strong-funds.com

PERFORMANCE

fund inception date: 3/4/92

	3yr Annual	5yr Annual	10yr Annual	Bull	Bear
Return (%)	4.7	na	na	15.4	-5.8
Differ from Category (+/-)	-1.6 blw av	na	na	-8.9 blw av	1.4 abv av

Total Risk	Standard Deviation	Category Risk	Risk Index	Beta
abv av	11.0%	abv av	1.1	0.69

	1996	1995	1994	1993	1992	1991	1990	1989	1988	1987
Return (%)	8.1	7.8	-1.6	47.7	—	—	—	—	—	—
Differ from Category (+/-)	-6.7	-1.3	1.5	8.1	—	—	—	—	—	—
Return, Tax-Adjusted (%)	5.4	6.7	-4.2	46.9	—	—	—	—	—	—

PER SHARE DATA

	1996	1995	1994	1993	1992	1991	1990	1989	1988	1987
Dividends, Net Income ($)	0.33	0.35	0.00	0.02	—	—	—	—	—	—
Distrib'ns, Cap Gain ($)	0.80	0.00	1.30	0.22	—	—	—	—	—	—
Net Asset Value ($)	13.23	13.28	12.65	14.18	—	—	—	—	—	—
Expense Ratio (%)	na	1.80	1.70	1.90	—	—	—	—	—	—
Yield (%)	2.35	2.63	0.00	0.13	—	—	—	—	—	—
Portfolio Turnover (%)	na	102	137	140	—	—	—	—	—	—
Total Assets (Millions $)	308	214	257	128	—	—	—	—	—	—

PORTFOLIO (as of 9/30/96)

Portfolio Manager: Anthony L.T. Cragg - 1993

Investm't Category: International Stock
- Domestic
- ✔ Foreign
- Asset Allocation
- Index
- Sector
- State Specific

Investment Style
- Large-Cap Growth
- Mid-Cap Growth
- Small-Cap Growth
- Large-Cap Value
- Mid-Cap Value
- Small-Cap Value

Portfolio
0.0%	cash	1.0% corp bonds
86.5%	stocks	1.9% gov't bonds
2.4%	preferred	0.0% muni bonds
0.0%	conv't/warrants	8.2% other

SHAREHOLDER INFORMATION

Minimum Investment
Initial: $1,000   Subsequent: $50

Minimum IRA Investment
Initial: $250   Subsequent: $50

Maximum Fees
Load: none   12b-1: none
Other: none

Distributions
Income: quarterly   Capital Gains: annual

Exchange Options
Number Per Year: 5   Fee: none
Telephone: yes (money market fund available)

Services
IRA, pension, auto exchange, auto invest, auto withdraw

Strong Muni Advantage

(SMUAX)

Tax-Exempt Bond

100 Heritage Reserve
P.O. Box 2936
Milwaukee, WI 53201
800-368-1030, 414-359-3400
www.strong-funds.com

PERFORMANCE

fund inception date: 11/30/95

	3yr Annual	5yr Annual	10yr Annual	Bull	Bear
Return (%)	na	na	na	na	na
Differ from Category (+/-)	na	na	na	na	na

Total Risk	Standard Deviation	Category Risk	Risk Index	Avg Mat
na	na	na	na	0.9 yrs

	1996	1995	1994	1993	1992	1991	1990	1989	1988	1987
Return (%)	4.8	—	—	—	—	—	—	—	—	—
Differ from Category (+/-)	1.1	—	—	—	—	—	—	—	—	—
Return, Tax-Adjusted (%)	4.8	—	—	—	—	—	—	—	—	—

PER SHARE DATA

	1996	1995	1994	1993	1992	1991	1990	1989	1988	1987
Dividends, Net Income ($)	0.24	—	—	—	—	—	—	—	—	—
Distrib'ns, Cap Gain ($)	0.00	—	—	—	—	—	—	—	—	—
Net Asset Value ($)	5.01	—	—	—	—	—	—	—	—	—
Expense Ratio (%)	na	—	—	—	—	—	—	—	—	—
Yield (%)	4.79	—	—	—	—	—	—	—	—	—
Portfolio Turnover (%)	na	—	—	—	—	—	—	—	—	—
Total Assets (Millions $)	516	—	—	—	—	—	—	—	—	—

PORTFOLIO (as of 6/30/96)

Portfolio Manager: Steven D. Harrop - 1995

Investm't Category: Tax-Exempt Bond
✔ Domestic   Index
  Foreign   Sector
  Asset Allocation   State Specific

Investment Style
  Large-Cap Growth   Large-Cap Value
  Mid-Cap Growth   Mid-Cap Value
  Small-Cap Growth   Small-Cap Value

Portfolio
57.0%	cash	0.0%	corp bonds
0.0%	stocks	0.0%	gov't bonds
0.0%	preferred	43.0%	muni bonds
0.0%	conv't/warrants	0.0%	other

SHAREHOLDER INFORMATION

Minimum Investment
Initial: $2,500   Subsequent: $50

Minimum IRA Investment
Initial: na   Subsequent: na

Maximum Fees
Load: none   12b-1: none
Other: none

Distributions
Income: monthly   Capital Gains: annual

Exchange Options
Number Per Year: 5   Fee: none
Telephone: yes (money market fund available)

Services
auto exchange, auto invest, auto withdraw

Strong Muni Bond

(SXFIX)

Tax-Exempt Bond

100 Heritage Reserve
P.O. Box 2936
Milwaukee, WI 53201
800-368-1030, 414-359-3400
www.strong-funds.com

PERFORMANCE   fund inception date: 10/23/86

	3yr Annual	5yr Annual	10yr Annual	Bull	Bear
Return (%)	2.8	6.4	6.2	13.9	-5.4
Differ from Category (+/-)	-1.4 low	0.0 blw av	-0.5 low	-4.5 low	0.0 abv av

Total Risk	Standard Deviation	Category Risk	Risk Index	Avg Mat
blw av	5.2%	av	0.9	16.7 yrs

	1996	1995	1994	1993	1992	1991	1990	1989	1988	1987
Return (%)	2.4	11.3	-4.6	11.7	12.1	13.2	4.6	7.0	7.5	-1.7
Differ from Category (+/-)	-1.3	-3.9	0.7	-0.1	3.8	1.8	-1.8	-2.0	-2.5	-0.3
Return, Tax-Adjusted (%)	2.4	11.3	-4.6	10.8	11.3	13.2	4.6	7.0	7.5	-1.7

PER SHARE DATA

	1996	1995	1994	1993	1992	1991	1990	1989	1988	1987
Dividends, Net Income ($)	0.49	0.73	0.55	0.58	0.65	0.64	0.66	0.52	0.49	0.67
Distrib'ns, Cap Gain ($)	0.00	0.00	0.00	0.31	0.25	0.00	0.00	0.00	0.00	0.00
Net Asset Value ($)	9.24	9.52	9.23	10.25	10.00	9.76	9.22	9.47	9.35	9.16
Expense Ratio (%)	na	0.80	0.80	0.70	0.10	0.10	0.30	1.70	1.30	1.00
Yield (%)	5.30	7.66	5.95	5.49	6.34	6.55	7.15	5.49	5.24	7.31
Portfolio Turnover (%)	na	513	311	156	324	465	586	243	344	284
Total Assets (Millions $)	242	246	279	398	289	115	31	18	18	19

PORTFOLIO (as of 6/30/96)

Portfolio Manager: Steven D. Harrop - 1996

Investm't Category: Tax-Exempt Bond

✔ Domestic	Index
Foreign	Sector
Asset Allocation	State Specific

Investment Style

Large-Cap Growth	Large-Cap Value
Mid-Cap Growth	Mid-Cap Value
Small-Cap Growth	Small-Cap Value

Portfolio

4.8% cash	0.0% corp bonds
0.0% stocks	0.0% gov't bonds
0.0% preferred	95.2% muni bonds
0.0% conv't/warrants	0.0% other

SHAREHOLDER INFORMATION

Minimum Investment

Initial: $2,500   Subsequent: $50

Minimum IRA Investment

Initial: na   Subsequent: na

Maximum Fees

Load: none   12b-1: none
Other: none

Distributions

Income: monthly   Capital Gains: annual

Exchange Options

Number Per Year: 5   Fee: none
Telephone: yes (money market fund available)

Services

auto exchange, auto invest, auto withdraw

Strong Opportunity

(SOPFX)

Growth

100 Heritage Reserve
P.O. Box 2936
Milwaukee, WI 53201
800-368-1030, 414-359-3400
www.strong-funds.com

PERFORMANCE

fund inception date: 12/31/85

	3yr Annual	5yr Annual	10yr Annual	Bull	Bear
Return (%)	15.7	17.1	14.8	54.7	-3.0
Differ from Category (+/-)	0.0 av	2.8 high	0.9 abv av	-7.7 blw av	3.7 high

Total Risk	Standard Deviation	Category Risk	Risk Index	Beta
abv av	9.7%	blw av	0.9	0.84

	1996	1995	1994	1993	1992	1991	1990	1989	1988	1987
Return (%)	18.1	27.2	3.1	21.1	17.3	31.6	-11.4	18.4	16.4	11.8
Differ from Category (+/-)	-2.0	-3.1	3.4	7.1	5.5	-4.4	-5.3	-7.7	-1.7	9.8
Return, Tax-Adjusted (%)	14.5	25.2	1.6	19.2	17.0	31.1	-13.0	16.5	12.6	8.0

PER SHARE DATA

	1996	1995	1994	1993	1992	1991	1990	1989	1988	1987
Dividends, Net Income ($)	0.25	0.21	0.13	0.06	0.05	0.19	0.74	0.67	1.37	0.23
Distrib'ns, Cap Gain ($)	3.82	1.62	1.27	1.56	0.15	0.00	0.04	0.15	0.18	1.80
Net Asset Value ($)	35.26	33.35	27.71	28.23	24.70	21.24	16.29	19.21	16.90	15.87
Expense Ratio (%)	na	1.30	1.40	1.40	1.50	1.70	1.70	1.60	1.60	1.50
Yield (%)	0.63	0.60	0.44	0.20	0.20	0.89	4.53	3.46	8.02	1.30
Portfolio Turnover (%)	na	92	59	109	139	271	275	306	352	371
Total Assets (Millions $)	1,775	1,327	805	443	193	159	131	205	157	153

PORTFOLIO (as of 9/30/96)

Portfolio Manager: Richard T. Weiss, Marina Carlson - 1991

Investm't Category: Growth
✔ Domestic   Index
✔ Foreign   Sector
   Asset Allocation State Specific

Investment Style
   Large-Cap Growth   Large-Cap Value
✔ Mid-Cap Growth   ✔ Mid-Cap Value
   Small-Cap Growth   Small-Cap Value

Portfolio
14.4% cash   0.0% corp bonds
85.3% stocks   0.0% gov't bonds
 0.0% preferred   0.0% muni bonds
 0.3% conv't/warrants 0.0% other

SHAREHOLDER INFORMATION

Minimum Investment
Initial: $1,000   Subsequent: $50

Minimum IRA Investment
Initial: $250   Subsequent: $50

Maximum Fees
Load: none   12b-1: none
Other: none

Distributions
Income: quarterly   Capital Gains: Dec

Exchange Options
Number Per Year: 5   Fee: none
Telephone: yes (money market fund available)

Services
IRA, pension, auto exchange, auto invest, auto withdraw

Strong Schafer Value

(SCHVX)

Growth

100 Heritage Reserve
P.O. Box 2936
Milwaukee, WI 53201
800-368-1030, 414-359-3400
www.strong-funds.com

PERFORMANCE

fund inception date: 10/22/85

	3yr Annual	5yr Annual	10yr Annual	Bull	Bear
Return (%)	16.5	18.4	16.2	63.6	-6.6
Differ from Category (+/-)	0.8 av	4.1 high	2.3 high	1.2 av	0.1 av

Total Risk	Standard Deviation	Category Risk	Risk Index	Beta
abv av	9.9%	av	1.0	0.90

	1996	1995	1994	1993	1992	1991	1990	1989	1988	1987
Return (%)	23.2	34.1	-4.3	23.9	18.6	40.9	-10.1	30.0	17.9	-0.4
Differ from Category (+/-)	3.1	3.8	-4.0	9.9	6.8	4.9	-4.0	3.9	-0.2	-2.4
Return, Tax-Adjusted (%)	21.8	32.5	-6.0	22.6	14.9	33.9	-12.5	27.3	16.0	-0.4

PER SHARE DATA

	1996	1995	1994	1993	1992	1991	1990	1989	1988	1987
Dividends, Net Income ($)	0.44	0.38	0.33	0.19	0.39	0.52	0.57	1.26	0.22	0.00
Distrib'ns, Cap Gain ($)	1.42	1.27	1.64	1.08	3.27	5.48	1.73	0.60	1.18	0.00
Net Asset Value ($)	51.02	42.92	33.23	36.78	30.70	28.98	24.91	30.28	24.86	22.42
Expense Ratio (%)	na	1.28	1.48	1.74	2.08	2.00	2.00	2.09	1.82	1.96
Yield (%)	0.83	0.85	0.94	0.50	1.14	1.50	2.13	4.08	0.84	0.00
Portfolio Turnover (%)	na	33	28	33	53	55	36	42	43	47
Total Assets (Millions $)	496	186	72	25	13	10	10	13	11	13

PORTFOLIO (as of 9/30/96)

Portfolio Manager: David K. Schafer - 1985

Investm't Category: Growth
✔ Domestic   Index
✔ Foreign   Sector
   Asset Allocation   State Specific

Investment Style
   Large-Cap Growth   Large-Cap Value
   Mid-Cap Growth   ✔ Mid-Cap Value
   Small-Cap Growth   Small-Cap Value

Portfolio
1.9% cash	0.0% corp bonds
98.1% stocks	0.0% gov't bonds
0.0% preferred	0.0% muni bonds
0.0% conv't/warrants	0.0% other

SHAREHOLDER INFORMATION

Minimum Investment
Initial: $2,500   Subsequent: $50

Minimum IRA Investment
Initial: $250   Subsequent: $1

Maximum Fees
Load: none   12b-1: none
Other: *f*

Distributions
Income: annual   Capital Gains: annual

Exchange Options
Number Per Year: 5   Fee: none
Telephone: yes (money market fund available)

Services
IRA, pension, auto exchange, auto invest, auto withdraw

Strong Short-Term Bond (SSTBX)

General Bond

100 Heritage Reserve
P.O. Box 2936
Milwaukee, WI 53201
800-368-1030, 414-359-3400
www.strong-funds.com

PERFORMANCE

fund inception date: 8/31/87

	3yr Annual	5yr Annual	10yr Annual	Bull	Bear
Return (%)	5.5	6.5	na	19.9	-3.0
Differ from Category (+/-)	0.4 abv av	0.4 av	na	-0.4 av	1.2 abv av

Total Risk	Standard Deviation	Category Risk	Risk Index	Avg Mat
low	2.5%	blw av	0.7	2.3 yrs

	1996	1995	1994	1993	1992	1991	1990	1989	1988	1987
Return (%)	6.7	11.9	-1.7	9.3	6.6	14.6	5.2	8.2	10.1	—
Differ from Category (+/-)	2.8	-3.0	0.6	0.2	0.1	-0.1	-2.1	-3.5	2.5	—
Return, Tax-Adjusted (%)	3.9	9.0	-4.2	6.6	3.5	11.5	1.9	4.2	6.5	—

PER SHARE DATA

	1996	1995	1994	1993	1992	1991	1990	1989	1988	1987
Dividends, Net Income ($)	0.68	0.67	0.64	0.66	0.78	0.74	0.81	1.00	0.85	—
Distrib'ns, Cap Gain ($)	0.00	0.00	0.00	0.00	0.00	0.00	0.00	0.02	0.06	—
Net Asset Value ($)	9.79	9.84	9.42	10.23	9.99	10.12	9.53	9.86	10.09	—
Expense Ratio (%)	na	0.90	0.90	0.80	0.60	1.00	1.30	1.10	1.00	—
Yield (%)	6.94	6.80	6.79	6.45	7.80	7.31	8.49	10.12	8.37	—
Portfolio Turnover (%)	na	317	249	445	353	398	314	177	461	—
Total Assets (Millions $)	1,172	1,104	1,041	1,531	756	164	80	130	102	—

PORTFOLIO (as of 6/30/96)

Portfolio Manager: B.C. Tank, L.J. Fitlerer - 1990

Investm't Category: General Bond
- ✔ Domestic
- ✔ Foreign
- Asset Allocation
- Index
- Sector
- State Specific

Investment Style
- Large-Cap Growth
- Mid-Cap Growth
- Small-Cap Growth
- Large-Cap Value
- Mid-Cap Value
- Small-Cap Value

Portfolio
2.2% cash	40.5% corp bonds
0.0% stocks	18.6% gov't bonds
4.6% preferred	0.0% muni bonds
1.9% conv't/warrants	32.2% other

SHAREHOLDER INFORMATION

Minimum Investment
Initial: $2,500   Subsequent: $50

Minimum IRA Investment
Initial: $1,000   Subsequent: $50

Maximum Fees
Load: none   12b-1: none
Other: none

Distributions
Income: monthly   Capital Gains: annual

Exchange Options
Number Per Year: 5   Fee: none
Telephone: yes (money market fund available)

Services
IRA, pension, auto exchange, auto invest, auto withdraw

Strong Short-Term Global Bond (STGBX)

International Bond

100 Heritage Reserve
P.O. Box 2936
Milwaukee, WI 53201
800-368-1030, 414-359-3400
www.strong-funds.com

PERFORMANCE

fund inception date: 3/31/94

	3yr Annual	5yr Annual	10yr Annual	Bull	Bear
Return (%)	na	na	na	25.4	na
Differ from Category (+/-)	na	na	na	-5.8 blw av	na

Total Risk	Standard Deviation	Category Risk	Risk Index	Avg Mat
na	na	na	na	1.9 yrs

	1996	1995	1994	1993	1992	1991	1990	1989	1988	1987
Return (%)	10.0	10.4	—	—	—	—	—	—	—	—
Differ from Category (+/-)	-1.3	-5.6	—	—	—	—	—	—	—	—
Return, Tax-Adjusted (%)	7.2	7.4	—	—	—	—	—	—	—	—

PER SHARE DATA

	1996	1995	1994	1993	1992	1991	1990	1989	1988	1987
Dividends, Net Income ($)	0.72	0.76	—	—	—	—	—	—	—	—
Distrib'ns, Cap Gain ($)	0.00	0.00	—	—	—	—	—	—	—	—
Net Asset Value ($)	10.71	10.42	—	—	—	—	—	—	—	—
Expense Ratio (%)	na	0.00	—	—	—	—	—	—	—	—
Yield (%)	6.72	7.29	—	—	—	—	—	—	—	—
Portfolio Turnover (%)	na	437	—	—	—	—	—	—	—	—
Total Assets (Millions $)	74	25	—	—	—	—	—	—	—	—

PORTFOLIO (as of 6/30/96)

Portfolio Manager: Shirish T. Malekar - 1994

Investm't Category: International Bond

✔ Domestic	Index
✔ Foreign	Sector
Asset Allocation	State Specific

Investment Style

Large-Cap Growth	Large-Cap Value
Mid-Cap Growth	Mid-Cap Value
Small-Cap Growth	Small-Cap Value

Portfolio

30.5% cash	9.6% corp bonds
0.0% stocks	53.5% gov't bonds
0.0% preferred	0.0% muni bonds
0.0% conv't/warrants	6.4% other

SHAREHOLDER INFORMATION

Minimum Investment
Initial: $1,000   Subsequent: $50

Minimum IRA Investment
Initial: $250   Subsequent: $50

Maximum Fees
Load: none   12b-1: none
Other: none

Distributions
Income: quarterly   Capital Gains: annual

Exchange Options
Number Per Year: no limit   Fee: none
Telephone: yes (money market fund available)

Services
IRA, pension, auto exchange, auto invest, auto withdraw

Strong Short-Term Muni Bond (STSMX)

Tax-Exempt Bond

100 Heritage Reserve
P.O. Box 2936
Milwaukee, WI 53201
800-368-1030, 414-359-3400
www.strong-funds.com

PERFORMANCE

fund inception date: 12/31/91

	3yr Annual	5yr Annual	10yr Annual	Bull	Bear
Return (%)	2.8	4.4	na	9.8	-1.8
Differ from Category (+/-)	-1.4 low	-2.0 low	na	-8.6 low	3.6 high

Total Risk	Standard Deviation	Category Risk	Risk Index	Avg Mat
low	2.4%	low	0.4	3.0 yrs

	1996	1995	1994	1993	1992	1991	1990	1989	1988	1987
Return (%)	4.8	5.3	-1.7	6.7	7.1	—	—	—	—	—
Differ from Category (+/-)	1.1	-9.9	3.6	-5.1	-1.2	—	—	—	—	—
Return, Tax-Adjusted (%)	4.8	5.3	-1.8	6.5	7.0	—	—	—	—	—

PER SHARE DATA

	1996	1995	1994	1993	1992	1991	1990	1989	1988	1987
Dividends, Net Income ($)	0.49	0.47	0.45	0.44	0.48	—	—	—	—	—
Distrib'ns, Cap Gain ($)	0.00	0.00	0.01	0.07	0.01	—	—	—	—	—
Net Asset Value ($)	9.74	9.77	9.73	10.36	10.20	—	—	—	—	—
Expense Ratio (%)	na	0.80	0.70	0.60	0.20	—	—	—	—	—
Yield (%)	5.03	4.81	4.62	4.21	4.70	—	—	—	—	—
Portfolio Turnover (%)	na	226	273	141	140	—	—	—	—	—
Total Assets (Millions $)	147	132	161	216	110	—	—	—	—	—

PORTFOLIO (as of 6/30/96)

Portfolio Manager: Steven D. Harrop - 1995

Investm't Category: Tax-Exempt Bond
- ✔ Domestic
- Foreign
- Asset Allocation
- Index
- Sector
- State Specific

Investment Style
- Large-Cap Growth
- Mid-Cap Growth
- Small-Cap Growth
- Large-Cap Value
- Mid-Cap Value
- Small-Cap Value

Portfolio
4.7% cash	0.0% corp bonds
0.0% stocks	0.0% gov't bonds
0.0% preferred	95.3% muni bonds
0.0% conv't/warrants	0.0% other

SHAREHOLDER INFORMATION

Minimum Investment
Initial: $2,500   Subsequent: $50

Minimum IRA Investment
Initial: na   Subsequent: na

Maximum Fees
Load: none   12b-1: none
Other: none

Distributions
Income: monthly   Capital Gains: annual

Exchange Options
Number Per Year: 5   Fee: none
Telephone: yes (money market fund available)

Services
auto exchange, auto invest, auto withdraw

Strong Small Cap

(SCAPX)

Aggressive Growth

100 Heritage Reserve
P.O. Box 2936
Milwaukee, WI 53201
800-368-1030, 414-359-3400
www.strong-funds.com

PERFORMANCE

fund inception date: 12/29/95

	3yr Annual	5yr Annual	10yr Annual	Bull	Bear
Return (%)	na	na	na	na	na
Differ from Category (+/-)	na	na	na	na	na

Total Risk	Standard Deviation	Category Risk	Risk Index	Beta
na	na	na	na	na

	1996	1995	1994	1993	1992	1991	1990	1989	1988	1987
Return (%)	22.6	—	—	—	—	—	—	—	—	—
Differ from Category (+/-)	3.5	—	—	—	—	—	—	—	—	—
Return, Tax-Adjusted (%)	21.8	—	—	—	—	—	—	—	—	—

PER SHARE DATA

	1996	1995	1994	1993	1992	1991	1990	1989	1988	1987
Dividends, Net Income ($)	0.18	—	—	—	—	—	—	—	—	—
Distrib'ns, Cap Gain ($)	0.00	—	—	—	—	—	—	—	—	—
Net Asset Value ($)	12.08	—	—	—	—	—	—	—	—	—
Expense Ratio (%)	na	—	—	—	—	—	—	—	—	—
Yield (%)	1.49	—	—	—	—	—	—	—	—	—
Portfolio Turnover (%)	na	—	—	—	—	—	—	—	—	—
Total Assets (Millions $)	136	—	—	—	—	—	—	—	—	—

PORTFOLIO (as of 9/30/96)

Portfolio Manager: Mary Lisanti - 1996

Investm't Category: Aggressive Growth

✔ Domestic	Index
✔ Foreign	Sector
Asset Allocation	State Specific

Investment Style

Large-Cap Growth	Large-Cap Value
Mid-Cap Growth	Mid-Cap Value
Small-Cap Growth	Small-Cap Value

Portfolio

11.4% cash	0.0% corp bonds
88.6% stocks	0.0% gov't bonds
0.0% preferred	0.0% muni bonds
0.0% conv't/warrants	0.0% other

SHAREHOLDER INFORMATION

Minimum Investment
Initial: $2,500   Subsequent: $250

Minimum IRA Investment
Initial: $250   Subsequent: $50

Maximum Fees
Load: none   12b-1: none
Other: none

Distributions
Income: quarterly   Capital Gains: annual

Exchange Options
Number Per Year: 5   Fee: none
Telephone: yes (money market fund available)

Services
IRA, pension, auto exchange, auto invest, auto withdraw

Strong Total Return

(STRFX)

Growth & Income

100 Heritage Reserve
P.O. Box 2936
Milwaukee, WI 53201
800-368-1030, 414-359-3400
www.strong-funds.com

PERFORMANCE

fund inception date: 12/30/81

	3yr Annual	5yr Annual	10yr Annual	Bull	Bear
Return (%)	12.6	11.9	10.6	50.4	-9.0
Differ from Category (+/-)	-2.7 blw av	-2.0 blw av	-2.1 low	-9.4 blw av	-2.6 low

Total Risk	Standard Deviation	Category Risk	Risk Index	Beta
abv av	10.5%	high	1.1	0.99

	1996	1995	1994	1993	1992	1991	1990	1989	1988	1987
Return (%).............	14.0	26.9	-1.4	22.5	0.5	33.5	-7.1	2.6	15.5	6.0
Differ from Category (+/-).	-5.7	-3.2	-0.1	8.7	-10.2	4.4	-1.2	-20.9	-1.3	5.8
Return, Tax-Adjusted (%)...	8.7	24.8	-2.0	21.7	0.1	32.9	-9.7	-0.9	10.8	-1.2

PER SHARE DATA

	1996	1995	1994	1993	1992	1991	1990	1989	1988	1987
Dividends, Net Income ($)	0.43	0.36	0.34	0.33	0.17	0.22	1.14	1.31	1.96	1.65
Distrib'ns, Cap Gain ($) ...	4.76	1.21	0.00	0.05	0.00	0.00	0.00	0.50	0.25	3.17
Net Asset Value ($)	27.23	28.38	23.62	24.30	20.17	20.24	15.34	17.72	18.96	18.37
Expense Ratio (%).........	na	1.10	1.20	1.20	1.30	1.40	1.40	1.20	1.20	1.10
Yield (%)	1.34	1.21	1.43	1.35	0.84	1.08	7.43	7.18	10.20	7.66
Portfolio Turnover (%).....	na	298	290	271	372	426	312	305	281	224
Total Assets (Millions $)...	791	708	606	630	587	691	646	1,065	1,005	802

PORTFOLIO (as of 9/30/96)

Portfolio Manager: Laura J. Sloate, Jeffrey B. Cohen - 1993

Investm't Category: Growth & Income
- ✔ Domestic
- ✔ Foreign
-   Asset Allocation
-   Index
-   Sector
-   State Specific

Investment Style
-   Large-Cap Growth
- ✔ Mid-Cap Growth
-   Small-Cap Growth
-   Large-Cap Value
-   Mid-Cap Value
-   Small-Cap Value

Portfolio
2.9% cash	0.0% corp bonds
89.0% stocks	0.0% gov't bonds
1.6% preferred	0.0% muni bonds
6.5% conv't/warrants	0.0% other

SHAREHOLDER INFORMATION

Minimum Investment
Initial: $250   Subsequent: $50

Minimum IRA Investment
Initial: $250   Subsequent: $50

Maximum Fees
Load: none   12b-1: none
Other: none

Distributions
Income: quarterly   Capital Gains: annual

Exchange Options
Number Per Year: 5   Fee: none
Telephone: yes (money market fund available)

Services
IRA, pension, auto exchange, auto invest, auto withdraw

Strong Value (STVAX)

Growth

100 Heritage Reserve
P.O. Box 2936
Milwaukee, WI 53201
800-368-1030, 414-359-3400
www.strong-funds.com

PERFORMANCE

fund inception date: 12/29/95

	3yr Annual	5yr Annual	10yr Annual	Bull	Bear
Return (%)	na	na	na	na	na
Differ from Category (+/-)	na	na	na	na	na

Total Risk	Standard Deviation	Category Risk	Risk Index	Beta
na	na	na	na	na

	1996	1995	1994	1993	1992	1991	1990	1989	1988	1987
Return (%)	16.8	—	—	—	—	—	—	—	—	—
Differ from Category (+/-)	-3.3	—	—	—	—	—	—	—	—	—
Return, Tax-Adjusted (%)	16.3	—	—	—	—	—	—	—	—	—

PER SHARE DATA

	1996	1995	1994	1993	1992	1991	1990	1989	1988	1987
Dividends, Net Income ($)	0.12	—	—	—	—	—	—	—	—	—
Distrib'ns, Cap Gain ($)	0.00	—	—	—	—	—	—	—	—	—
Net Asset Value ($)	11.55	—	—	—	—	—	—	—	—	—
Expense Ratio (%)	na	—	—	—	—	—	—	—	—	—
Yield (%)	1.03	—	—	—	—	—	—	—	—	—
Portfolio Turnover (%)	na	—	—	—	—	—	—	—	—	—
Total Assets (Millions $)	54	—	—	—	—	—	—	—	—	—

PORTFOLIO (as of 9/30/96)

Portfolio Manager: Laura J. Sloate, Jeffrey B. Cohen - 1995

Investm't Category: Growth
- ✔ Domestic
- Foreign
- Asset Allocation
- Index
- Sector
- State Specific

Investment Style
- Large-Cap Growth
- Mid-Cap Growth
- Small-Cap Growth
- Large-Cap Value
- Mid-Cap Value
- Small-Cap Value

Portfolio
31.0%	cash	0.0%	corp bonds
66.6%	stocks	0.0%	gov't bonds
2.4%	preferred	0.0%	muni bonds
0.0%	conv't/warrants	0.0%	other

SHAREHOLDER INFORMATION

Minimum Investment
Initial: $2,500   Subsequent: $50

Minimum IRA Investment
Initial: $250   Subsequent: $50

Maximum Fees
Load: none   12b-1: none
Other: none

Distributions
Income: quarterly   Capital Gains: annual

Exchange Options
Number Per Year: 5   Fee: none
Telephone: yes (money market fund available)

Services
IRA, pension, auto exchange, auto invest, auto withdraw

T. Rowe Price Balanced

(RPBAX)

Balanced

Public Relations Department
100 E. Pratt St.
Baltimore, MD 21202
800-225-5132, 410-547-2000
www.troweprice.com

PERFORMANCE

fund inception date: 12/31/39

	3yr Annual	5yr Annual	10yr Annual	Bull	Bear
Return (%)	11.9	11.4	11.0	47.5	-6.7
Differ from Category (+/-)	0.2 av	0.0 av	0.2 av	2.4 abv av	-1.0 blw av

Total Risk	Standard Deviation	Category Risk	Risk Index	Beta
blw av	6.4%	blw av	1.0	0.64

	1996	1995	1994	1993	1992	1991	1990	1989	1988	1987
Return (%)	14.5	24.8	-2.1	13.8	7.7	21.9	7.2	20.5	8.9	-3.4
Differ from Category (+/-)	0.3	0.2	-0.5	-0.6	-1.2	-2.2	8.1	2.4	-3.3	-6.1
Return, Tax-Adjusted (%)	12.7	22.7	-4.0	11.9	4.3	18.0	4.6	17.5	6.7	-12.0

PER SHARE DATA

	1996	1995	1994	1993	1992	1991	1990	1989	1988	1987
Dividends, Net Income ($)	0.50	0.47	0.43	0.44	0.50	0.61	0.66	0.68	0.48	0.78
Distrib'ns, Cap Gain ($)	0.13	0.17	0.20	0.11	0.66	0.56	0.00	0.00	0.00	2.83
Net Asset Value ($)	14.48	13.22	11.14	12.02	11.07	11.42	10.37	10.32	9.15	8.85
Expense Ratio (%)	na	0.95	1.00	1.00	1.03	1.10	0.94	1.15	1.25	1.18
Yield (%)	3.42	3.51	3.79	3.62	4.26	5.09	6.36	6.58	5.24	6.67
Portfolio Turnover (%)	na	12	33	8	208	240	127	219	251	324
Total Assets (Millions $)	885	608	392	340	250	175	156	167	163	172

PORTFOLIO (as of 9/30/96)

Portfolio Manager: Richard Whitney, Edmund Notzon - 1991

Investm't Category: Balanced
- ✔ Domestic
- ✔ Foreign
- Asset Allocation
- Index
- Sector
- State Specific

Investment Style
- Large-Cap Growth
- Mid-Cap Growth
- Small-Cap Growth
- Large-Cap Value
- Mid-Cap Value
- Small-Cap Value

Portfolio
- 6.0% cash
- 54.2% stocks
- 0.7% preferred
- 0.1% conv't/warrants
- 16.6% corp bonds
- 22.4% gov't bonds
- 0.0% muni bonds
- 0.0% other

SHAREHOLDER INFORMATION

Minimum Investment
Initial: $2,500   Subsequent: $100

Minimum IRA Investment
Initial: $1,000   Subsequent: $50

Maximum Fees
Load: none   12b-1: none
Other: f

Distributions
Income: quarterly   Capital Gains: Dec

Exchange Options
Number Per Year: 6   Fee: none
Telephone: yes (money market fund available)

Services
IRA, pension, auto exchange, auto invest, auto withdraw

T. Rowe Price Blue Chip Growth (TRBCX)

Growth & Income

Public Relations Department
100 E. Pratt St.
Baltimore, MD 21202
800-225-5132, 410-547-2000
www.troweprice.com

PERFORMANCE

fund inception date: 6/30/93

	3yr Annual	5yr Annual	10yr Annual	Bull	Bear
Return (%)	21.0	na	na	84.1	-5.7
Differ from Category (+/-)	5.7 high	na	na	24.3 high	0.7 abv av

Total Risk	Standard Deviation	Category Risk	Risk Index	Beta
av	9.2%	av	1.0	0.90

	1996	1995	1994	1993	1992	1991	1990	1989	1988	1987
Return (%)	27.7	37.8	0.8	—	—	—	—	—	—	—
Differ from Category (+/-)	8.0	7.7	2.1	—	—	—	—	—	—	—
Return, Tax-Adjusted (%)	27.1	37.0	0.1	—	—	—	—	—	—	—

PER SHARE DATA

	1996	1995	1994	1993	1992	1991	1990	1989	1988	1987
Dividends, Net Income ($)	0.14	0.15	0.11	—	—	—	—	—	—	—
Distrib'ns, Cap Gain ($)	0.08	0.08	0.11	—	—	—	—	—	—	—
Net Asset Value ($)	19.06	15.09	11.11	—	—	—	—	—	—	—
Expense Ratio (%)	na	1.25	1.25	—	—	—	—	—	—	—
Yield (%)	0.73	0.98	0.98	—	—	—	—	—	—	—
Portfolio Turnover (%)	na	38	75	—	—	—	—	—	—	—
Total Assets (Millions $)	515	146	38	—	—	—	—	—	—	—

PORTFOLIO (as of 9/30/96)

Portfolio Manager: Thomas Broadus Jr. - 1993

Investm't Category: Growth & Income
- ✔ Domestic
- ✔ Foreign
- Asset Allocation
- Index
- Sector
- State Specific

Investment Style
- ✔ Large-Cap Growth
- Mid-Cap Growth
- Small-Cap Growth
- ✔ Large-Cap Value
- Mid-Cap Value
- Small-Cap Value

Portfolio
- 12.8% cash
- 87.2% stocks
- 0.0% preferred
- 0.0% conv't/warrants
- 0.0% corp bonds
- 0.0% gov't bonds
- 0.0% muni bonds
- 0.0% other

SHAREHOLDER INFORMATION

Minimum Investment
Initial: $2,500   Subsequent: $100

Minimum IRA Investment
Initial: $1,000   Subsequent: $50

Maximum Fees
Load: none   12b-1: none
Other: *f*

Distributions
Income: annual   Capital Gains: Dec

Exchange Options
Number Per Year: 6   Fee: none
Telephone: yes (money market fund available)

Services
IRA, pension, auto exchange, auto invest, auto withdraw

T. Rowe Price CA Tax-Free Bond (PRXCX)

Tax-Exempt Bond

Public Relations Department
100 E. Pratt St.
Baltimore, MD 21202
800-225-5132, 410-547-2000
www.troweprice.com

PERFORMANCE

fund inception date: 9/15/86

	3yr Annual	5yr Annual	10yr Annual	Bull	Bear
Return (%)	4.9	7.2	6.4	21.8	-6.2
Differ from Category (+/-)	0.7 high	0.8 abv av	-0.3 blw av	3.4 high	-0.8 av

Total Risk	Standard Deviation	Category Risk	Risk Index	Avg Mat
blw av	5.7%	av	1.0	17.1 yrs

	1996	1995	1994	1993	1992	1991	1990	1989	1988	1987
Return (%)	4.5	17.3	-5.8	12.4	8.9	12.1	5.8	8.4	9.5	-6.8
Differ from Category (+/-)	0.8	2.1	-0.5	0.6	0.6	0.7	-0.6	-0.6	-0.5	-5.4
Return, Tax-Adjusted (%)	4.5	17.3	-5.9	11.7	8.9	12.1	5.8	8.4	9.5	-6.8

PER SHARE DATA

	1996	1995	1994	1993	1992	1991	1990	1989	1988	1987
Dividends, Net Income ($)	0.54	0.55	0.54	0.55	0.58	0.58	0.59	0.58	0.57	0.57
Distrib'ns, Cap Gain ($)	0.00	0.00	0.02	0.23	0.00	0.00	0.00	0.00	0.00	0.00
Net Asset Value ($)	10.48	10.57	9.51	10.68	10.22	9.94	9.42	9.48	9.30	9.03
Expense Ratio (%)	0.63	0.55	0.60	0.60	0.60	0.73	0.93	1.00	1.00	0.85
Yield (%)	5.15	5.20	5.66	5.04	5.67	5.83	6.26	6.11	6.12	6.31
Portfolio Turnover (%)	61	78	73	57	80	193	88	77	152	88
Total Assets (Millions $)	156	146	122	154	132	108	80	64	40	31

PORTFOLIO (as of 9/30/96)

Portfolio Manager: Mary J. Miller - 1990

Investm't Category: Tax-Exempt Bond
- ✔ Domestic
- Foreign
- Asset Allocation
- Index
- Sector
- ✔ State Specific

Investment Style
- Large-Cap Growth
- Mid-Cap Growth
- Small-Cap Growth
- Large-Cap Value
- Mid-Cap Value
- Small-Cap Value

Portfolio
5.6% cash	0.0% corp bonds
0.0% stocks	0.0% gov't bonds
0.0% preferred	94.4% muni bonds
0.0% conv't/warrants	0.0% other

SHAREHOLDER INFORMATION

Minimum Investment
Initial: $2,500   Subsequent: $100

Minimum IRA Investment
Initial: na   Subsequent: na

Maximum Fees
Load: none   12b-1: none
Other: f

Distributions
Income: monthly   Capital Gains: Dec

Exchange Options
Number Per Year: 6   Fee: none
Telephone: yes (money market fund available)

Services
auto exchange, auto invest, auto withdraw

T. Rowe Price Capital Appreciation (PRWCX)

Growth

Public Relations Department
100 E. Pratt St.
Baltimore, MD 21202
800-225-5132, 410-547-2000
www.troweprice.com

PERFORMANCE

fund inception date: 6/30/86

	3yr Annual	5yr Annual	10yr Annual	Bull	Bear
Return (%)	14.1	13.4	13.3	49.4	-3.2
Differ from Category (+/-)	-1.6 blw av	-0.9 blw av	-0.6 av	-13.0 blw av	3.5 high

Total Risk	Standard Deviation	Category Risk	Risk Index	Beta
blw av	5.5%	low	0.5	0.52

	1996	1995	1994	1993	1992	1991	1990	1989	1988	1987
Return (%)	16.8	22.5	3.7	15.6	9.3	21.5	-1.3	21.4	21.2	5.8
Differ from Category (+/-)	-3.3	-7.8	4.0	1.6	-2.5	-14.5	4.8	-4.7	3.1	3.8
Return, Tax-Adjusted (%)	13.2	19.3	1.0	14.1	7.0	17.9	-3.6	16.0	18.8	-0.8

PER SHARE DATA

	1996	1995	1994	1993	1992	1991	1990	1989	1988	1987
Dividends, Net Income ($)	0.60	0.44	0.35	0.18	0.50	0.43	0.39	0.45	0.28	0.48
Distrib'ns, Cap Gain ($)	0.90	0.72	0.69	0.33	0.16	0.64	0.31	1.36	0.37	1.85
Net Asset Value ($)	14.47	13.67	12.10	12.66	11.39	11.02	9.98	10.82	10.42	9.15
Expense Ratio (%)	na	0.97	1.10	1.09	1.08	1.20	1.25	1.50	1.50	1.20
Yield (%)	3.90	3.05	2.73	1.38	4.32	3.68	3.79	3.69	2.59	4.36
Portfolio Turnover (%)	na	47	43	39	30	51	50	99	166	291
Total Assets (Millions $)	978	864	653	536	359	215	141	133	99	63

PORTFOLIO (as of 9/30/96)

Portfolio Manager: Richard P. Howard - 1989

Investm't Category: Growth
- ✔ Domestic
- ✔ Foreign
- Asset Allocation
- Index
- Sector
- State Specific

Investment Style
- ✔ Large-Cap Growth
- Mid-Cap Growth
- Small-Cap Growth
- ✔ Large-Cap Value
- Mid-Cap Value
- Small-Cap Value

Portfolio
14.5% cash	0.0% corp bonds
50.5% stocks	5.0% gov't bonds
2.8% preferred	0.0% muni bonds
27.2% conv't/warrants	0.0% other

SHAREHOLDER INFORMATION

Minimum Investment
Initial: $2,500   Subsequent: $100

Minimum IRA Investment
Initial: $1,000   Subsequent: $50

Maximum Fees
Load: none   12b-1: none
Other: *f*

Distributions
Income: annual   Capital Gains: Dec

Exchange Options
Number Per Year: 6   Fee: none
Telephone: yes (money market fund available)

Services
IRA, pension, auto exchange, auto invest, auto withdraw

T. Rowe Price Capital Opportunity (PRCOX)

Aggressive Growth

Public Relations Department
100 E. Pratt St.
Baltimore, MD 21202
800-225-5132, 410-547-2000
www.troweprice.com

PERFORMANCE

fund inception date: 11/30/94

	3yr Annual	5yr Annual	10yr Annual	Bull	Bear
Return (%)	na	na	na	na	na
Differ from Category (+/-)	na	na	na	na	na

Total Risk	Standard Deviation	Category Risk	Risk Index	Beta
na	na	na	na	na

	1996	1995	1994	1993	1992	1991	1990	1989	1988	1987
Return (%)	16.7	46.5	—	—	—	—	—	—	—	—
Differ from Category (+/-)	-2.4	12.2	—	—	—	—	—	—	—	—
Return, Tax-Adjusted (%)	15.2	43.4	—	—	—	—	—	—	—	—

PER SHARE DATA

	1996	1995	1994	1993	1992	1991	1990	1989	1988	1987
Dividends, Net Income ($)	0.00	0.01	—	—	—	—	—	—	—	—
Distrib'ns, Cap Gain ($)	0.74	1.12	—	—	—	—	—	—	—	—
Net Asset Value ($)	15.75	14.13	—	—	—	—	—	—	—	—
Expense Ratio (%)	na	1.35	—	—	—	—	—	—	—	—
Yield (%)	0.00	0.06	—	—	—	—	—	—	—	—
Portfolio Turnover (%)	na	136	—	—	—	—	—	—	—	—
Total Assets (Millions $)	128	61	—	—	—	—	—	—	—	—

PORTFOLIO (as of 9/30/96)

Portfolio Manager: John F. Wakeman - 1994

Investm't Category: Aggressive Growth

✔ Domestic   Index
✔ Foreign   Sector
  Asset Allocation State Specific

Investment Style

Large-Cap Growth   Large-Cap Value
Mid-Cap Growth   Mid-Cap Value
Small-Cap Growth   Small-Cap Value

Portfolio

10.8% cash	0.0% corp bonds
89.2% stocks	0.0% gov't bonds
0.0% preferred	0.0% muni bonds
0.0% conv't/warrants	0.0% other

SHAREHOLDER INFORMATION

Minimum Investment
Initial: $2,500   Subsequent: $100

Minimum IRA Investment
Initial: $1,000   Subsequent: $50

Maximum Fees
Load: none   12b-1: none
Other: f

Distributions
Income: annual   Capital Gains: Dec

Exchange Options
Number Per Year: 6   Fee: none
Telephone: yes (money market fund available)

Services
IRA, pension, auto exchange, auto invest, auto withdraw

T. Rowe Price Dividend Growth (PRDGX)

Growth & Income

Public Relations Department
100 E. Pratt St.
Baltimore, MD 21202
800-225-5132, 410-547-2000
www.troweprice.com

PERFORMANCE

fund inception date: 12/31/92

	3yr Annual	5yr Annual	10yr Annual	Bull	Bear
Return (%)	19.0	na	na	72.4	-4.4
Differ from Category (+/-)	3.7 high	na	na	12.6 high	2.0 high

Total Risk	Standard Deviation	Category Risk	Risk Index	Beta
av	7.1%	low	0.8	0.69

	1996	1995	1994	1993	1992	1991	1990	1989	1988	1987
Return (%)	25.3	31.7	2.1	19.4	—	—	—	—	—	—
Differ from Category (+/-)	5.6	1.6	3.4	5.6	—	—	—	—	—	—
Return, Tax-Adjusted (%)	23.2	29.5	0.0	17.8	—	—	—	—	—	—

PER SHARE DATA

	1996	1995	1994	1993	1992	1991	1990	1989	1988	1987
Dividends, Net Income ($)	0.36	0.36	0.34	0.28	—	—	—	—	—	—
Distrib'ns, Cap Gain ($)	0.51	0.33	0.34	0.15	—	—	—	—	—	—
Net Asset Value ($)	16.37	13.81	11.04	11.48	—	—	—	—	—	—
Expense Ratio (%)	na	1.10	1.00	1.00	—	—	—	—	—	—
Yield (%)	2.13	2.54	2.98	2.40	—	—	—	—	—	—
Portfolio Turnover (%)	na	56	71	51	—	—	—	—	—	—
Total Assets (Millions $)	200	84	53	40	—	—	—	—	—	—

PORTFOLIO (as of 9/30/96)

Portfolio Manager: William J. Stromberg - 1992

Investm't Category: Growth & Income
- ✔ Domestic
- ✔ Foreign
- Asset Allocation
- Index
- Sector
- State Specific

Investment Style
- Large-Cap Growth
- Mid-Cap Growth
- Small-Cap Growth
- ✔ Large-Cap Value
- Mid-Cap Value
- Small-Cap Value

Portfolio
- 11.6% cash
- 81.5% stocks
- 1.5% preferred
- 2.5% conv't/warrants
- 1.2% corp bonds
- 1.7% gov't bonds
- 0.0% muni bonds
- 0.0% other

SHAREHOLDER INFORMATION

Minimum Investment
Initial: $2,500   Subsequent: $100

Minimum IRA Investment
Initial: $1,000   Subsequent: $50

Maximum Fees
Load: none   12b-1: none
Other: f

Distributions
Income: quarterly   Capital Gains: Dec

Exchange Options
Number Per Year: 6   Fee: none
Telephone: yes (money market fund available)

Services
IRA, pension, auto exchange, auto invest, auto withdraw

T. Rowe Price Equity Income (PRFDX)

Growth & Income

Public Relations Department
100 E. Pratt St.
Baltimore, MD 21202
800-225-5132, 410-547-2000
www.troweprice.com

PERFORMANCE

fund inception date: 10/31/85

	3yr Annual	5yr Annual	10yr Annual	Bull	Bear
Return (%)	18.8	17.0	14.4	69.3	-3.8
Differ from Category (+/-)	3.5 high	3.1 high	1.7 abv av	9.5 abv av	2.6 high

Total Risk	Standard Deviation	Category Risk	Risk Index	Beta
av	7.4%	low	0.8	0.74

	1996	1995	1994	1993	1992	1991	1990	1989	1988	1987
Return (%)	20.3	33.3	4.5	14.8	14.1	25.2	-6.8	13.6	27.6	3.5
Differ from Category (+/-)	0.6	3.2	5.8	1.0	3.4	-3.9	-0.9	-9.9	10.8	3.3
Return, Tax-Adjusted (%)	17.8	30.7	1.7	12.1	11.6	23.0	-9.1	10.5	24.4	-2.0

PER SHARE DATA

	1996	1995	1994	1993	1992	1991	1990	1989	1988	1987
Dividends, Net Income ($)	0.65	0.65	0.59	0.54	0.63	0.61	0.65	0.76	0.62	0.82
Distrib'ns, Cap Gain ($)	0.84	0.54	0.81	0.72	0.39	0.10	0.19	0.39	0.38	1.35
Net Asset Value ($)	22.54	20.01	15.98	16.65	15.63	14.62	12.27	14.06	13.39	11.29
Expense Ratio (%)	na	0.85	0.88	0.91	0.97	1.05	1.13	1.11	1.30	1.10
Yield (%)	2.78	3.16	3.51	3.10	3.93	4.14	5.21	5.25	4.50	6.48
Portfolio Turnover (%)	na	21	36	31	30	34	24	34	36	80
Total Assets (Millions $)	7,733	5,214	3,203	2,851	2,091	1,335	862	968	497	185

PORTFOLIO (as of 9/30/96)

Portfolio Manager: Brian C. Rogers - 1995

Investm't Category: Growth & Income
✔ Domestic   Index
✔ Foreign   Sector
   Asset Allocation   State Specific

Investment Style
   Large-Cap Growth   ✔ Large-Cap Value
   Mid-Cap Growth   Mid-Cap Value
   Small-Cap Growth   Small-Cap Value

Portfolio

10.3% cash	1.2% corp bonds
83.6% stocks	3.4% gov't bonds
0.2% preferred	0.0% muni bonds
1.3% conv't/warrants	0.0% other

SHAREHOLDER INFORMATION

Minimum Investment
Initial: $2,500   Subsequent: $100

Minimum IRA Investment
Initial: $1,000   Subsequent: $50

Maximum Fees
Load: none   12b-1: none
Other: *f*

Distributions
Income: quarterly   Capital Gains: Dec

Exchange Options
Number Per Year: 6   Fee: none
Telephone: yes (money market fund available)

Services
IRA, pension, auto exchange, auto invest, auto withdraw

T. Rowe Price Equity Index (PREIX)

Growth & Income

Public Relations Department
100 E. Pratt St.
Baltimore, MD 21202
800-225-5132, 410-547-2000
www.troweprice.com

PERFORMANCE

fund inception date: 3/30/90

	3yr Annual	5yr Annual	10yr Annual	Bull	Bear
Return (%)	19.3	14.7	na	76.2	-6.7
Differ from Category (+/-)	4.0 high	0.8 abv av	na	16.4 high	-0.3 av

Total Risk	Standard Deviation	Category Risk	Risk Index	Beta
abv av	9.6%	abv av	1.0	0.99

	1996	1995	1994	1993	1992	1991	1990	1989	1988	1987
Return (%)	22.6	37.1	1.0	9.4	7.1	29.2	—	—	—	—
Differ from Category (+/-)	2.9	7.0	2.3	-4.4	-3.6	0.1	—	—	—	—
Return, Tax-Adjusted (%)	21.1	35.2	-0.4	8.3	6.0	27.5	—	—	—	—

PER SHARE DATA

	1996	1995	1994	1993	1992	1991	1990	1989	1988	1987
Dividends, Net Income ($)	0.38	0.40	0.36	0.32	0.30	0.34	—	—	—	—
Distrib'ns, Cap Gain ($)	0.34	0.30	0.16	0.01	0.01	0.08	—	—	—	—
Net Asset Value ($)	20.34	17.21	13.09	13.48	12.63	12.10	—	—	—	—
Expense Ratio (%)	na	0.45	0.45	0.45	0.45	0.45	—	—	—	—
Yield (%)	1.83	2.28	2.71	2.37	2.37	2.79	—	—	—	—
Portfolio Turnover (%)	na	1	1	0	0	5	—	—	—	—
Total Assets (Millions $)	819	457	270	166	128	22	—	—	—	—

PORTFOLIO (as of 9/30/96)

Portfolio Manager: Richard Whitney - 1990

Investm't Category: Growth & Income
- ✔ Domestic
- Foreign
- Asset Allocation
- ✔ Index
- Sector
- State Specific

Investment Style
- ✔ Large-Cap Growth
- Mid-Cap Growth
- Small-Cap Growth
- ✔ Large-Cap Value
- Mid-Cap Value
- Small-Cap Value

Portfolio
- 6.4% cash
- 93.7% stocks
- 0.0% preferred
- 0.0% conv't/warrants
- 0.0% corp bonds
- 0.0% gov't bonds
- 0.0% muni bonds
- 0.0% other

SHAREHOLDER INFORMATION

Minimum Investment
Initial: $2,500   Subsequent: $100

Minimum IRA Investment
Initial: $1,000   Subsequent: $50

Maximum Fees
Load: 0.50% redemption   12b-1: none
Other: redemption fee applies for 6 months; f

Distributions
Income: quarterly   Capital Gains: Dec

Exchange Options
Number Per Year: 6   Fee: none
Telephone: yes (money market fund available)

Services
IRA, pension, auto exchange, auto invest, auto withdraw

T. Rowe Price FL Ins Interm Tax-Free (FLTFX)

Tax-Exempt Bond

Public Relations Department
100 E. Pratt St.
Baltimore, MD 21202
800-225-5132, 410-547-2000
www.troweprice.com

PERFORMANCE

fund inception date: 3/31/93

	3yr Annual	5yr Annual	10yr Annual	Bull	Bear
Return (%)	4.5	na	na	17.5	-3.8
Differ from Category (+/-)	0.3 abv av	na	na	-0.9 blw av	1.6 high

Total Risk	Standard Deviation	Category Risk	Risk Index	Avg Mat
low	3.9%	low	0.7	7.6 yrs

	1996	1995	1994	1993	1992	1991	1990	1989	1988	1987
Return (%)	3.6	13.1	-2.7	—	—	—	—	—	—	—
Differ from Category (+/-)	-0.1	-2.1	2.6	—	—	—	—	—	—	—
Return, Tax-Adjusted (%)	3.5	13.1	-2.8	—	—	—	—	—	—	—

PER SHARE DATA

	1996	1995	1994	1993	1992	1991	1990	1989	1988	1987
Dividends, Net Income ($)	0.45	0.46	0.42	—	—	—	—	—	—	—
Distrib'ns, Cap Gain ($)	0.02	0.00	0.02	—	—	—	—	—	—	—
Net Asset Value ($)	10.51	10.61	9.81	—	—	—	—	—	—	—
Expense Ratio (%)	0.60	0.60	0.60	—	—	—	—	—	—	—
Yield (%)	4.27	4.33	4.27	—	—	—	—	—	—	—
Portfolio Turnover (%)	98	141	71	—	—	—	—	—	—	—
Total Assets (Millions $)	70	72	51	—	—	—	—	—	—	—

PORTFOLIO (as of 9/30/96)

Portfolio Manager: William T. Reynolds - 1993

Investm't Category: Tax-Exempt Bond
- ✔ Domestic
- Foreign
- Asset Allocation
- Index
- Sector
- ✔ State Specific

Investment Style
- Large-Cap Growth
- Mid-Cap Growth
- Small-Cap Growth
- Large-Cap Value
- Mid-Cap Value
- Small-Cap Value

Portfolio

2.0% cash	0.0% corp bonds
0.0% stocks	0.0% gov't bonds
0.0% preferred	98.1% muni bonds
0.0% conv't/warrants	0.0% other

SHAREHOLDER INFORMATION

Minimum Investment
Initial: $2,500   Subsequent: $100

Minimum IRA Investment
Initial: na   Subsequent: na

Maximum Fees
Load: none   12b-1: none
Other: f

Distributions
Income: monthly   Capital Gains: Dec

Exchange Options
Number Per Year: 6   Fee: none
Telephone: yes (money market fund available)

Services
auto exchange, auto invest, auto withdraw

T. Rowe Price GA
Tax-Free Bond (GTFBX)

Tax-Exempt Bond

Public Relations Department
100 E. Pratt St.
Baltimore, MD 21202
800-225-5132, 410-547-2000
www.troweprice.com

PERFORMANCE

fund inception date: 3/31/93

	3yr Annual	5yr Annual	10yr Annual	Bull	Bear
Return (%)	4.8	na	na	21.8	-6.9
Differ from Category (+/-)	0.6 abv av	na	na	3.4 high	-1.5 blw av

Total Risk	Standard Deviation	Category Risk	Risk Index	Avg Mat
blw av	6.1%	abv av	1.1	16.4 yrs

	1996	1995	1994	1993	1992	1991	1990	1989	1988	1987
Return (%)	3.9	17.7	-6.0	—	—	—	—	—	—	—
Differ from Category (+/-)	0.2	2.5	-0.7	—	—	—	—	—	—	—
Return, Tax-Adjusted (%)	3.9	17.7	-6.2	—	—	—	—	—	—	—

PER SHARE DATA

	1996	1995	1994	1993	1992	1991	1990	1989	1988	1987
Dividends, Net Income ($)	0.51	0.52	0.50	—	—	—	—	—	—	—
Distrib'ns, Cap Gain ($)	0.00	0.00	0.05	—	—	—	—	—	—	—
Net Asset Value ($)	10.43	10.55	9.43	—	—	—	—	—	—	—
Expense Ratio (%)	0.65	0.65	0.65	—	—	—	—	—	—	—
Yield (%)	4.88	4.92	5.27	—	—	—	—	—	—	—
Portfolio Turnover (%)	71	72	154	—	—	—	—	—	—	—
Total Assets (Millions $)	37	31	20	—	—	—	—	—	—	—

PORTFOLIO (as of 9/30/96)

Portfolio Manager: Mary J. Miller - 1993

Investm't Category: Tax-Exempt Bond
- ✔ Domestic
- Foreign
- Asset Allocation
- Index
- Sector
- ✔ State Specific

Investment Style
- Large-Cap Growth
- Mid-Cap Growth
- Small-Cap Growth
- Large-Cap Value
- Mid-Cap Value
- Small-Cap Value

Portfolio
4.0% cash	0.0% corp bonds
0.0% stocks	0.0% gov't bonds
0.0% preferred	96.1% muni bonds
0.0% conv't/warrants	0.0% other

SHAREHOLDER INFORMATION

Minimum Investment
Initial: $2,500   Subsequent: $100

Minimum IRA Investment
Initial: na   Subsequent: na

Maximum Fees
Load: none   12b-1: none
Other: f

Distributions
Income: monthly   Capital Gains: Dec

Exchange Options
Number Per Year: 6   Fee: none
Telephone: yes (money market fund available)

Services
auto exchange, auto invest, auto withdraw

T. Rowe Price GNMA
(PRGMX)
Mortgage-Backed Bond

Public Relations Department
100 E. Pratt St.
Baltimore, MD 21202
800-225-5132, 410-547-2000
www.troweprice.com

PERFORMANCE
fund inception date: 11/26/85

	3yr Annual	5yr Annual	10yr Annual	Bull	Bear
Return (%)	6.1	6.1	7.6	23.8	-4.4
Differ from Category (+/-)	0.5 abv av	0.1 av	-0.1 av	2.7 abv av	-0.8 blw av

Total Risk	Standard Deviation	Category Risk	Risk Index	Avg Mat
low	4.3%	high	1.1	8.1 yrs

	1996	1995	1994	1993	1992	1991	1990	1989	1988	1987
Return (%)	3.1	17.8	-1.7	6.1	6.4	15.0	10.0	14.0	5.9	0.8
Differ from Category (+/-)	-1.3	3.1	0.0	-0.8	0.2	0.6	0.2	1.4	-1.5	-1.2
Return, Tax-Adjusted (%)	0.4	14.8	-4.5	3.3	3.3	11.6	6.4	10.3	2.0	-2.8

PER SHARE DATA

	1996	1995	1994	1993	1992	1991	1990	1989	1988	1987
Dividends, Net Income ($)	0.65	0.67	0.67	0.69	0.76	0.80	0.83	0.84	0.91	0.90
Distrib'ns, Cap Gain ($)	0.00	0.00	0.00	0.00	0.00	0.00	0.00	0.00	0.00	0.02
Net Asset Value ($)	9.37	9.74	8.88	9.72	9.82	9.97	9.42	9.37	9.01	9.38
Expense Ratio (%)	0.74	0.76	0.77	0.79	0.86	0.85	0.90	0.94	0.99	1.00
Yield (%)	6.93	6.87	7.54	7.09	7.73	8.02	8.81	8.96	10.09	9.57
Portfolio Turnover (%)	113	121	92	94	66	92	171	135	193	226
Total Assets (Millions $)	941	896	752	918	863	734	452	387	358	332

PORTFOLIO (as of 9/30/96)

Portfolio Manager: Peter Van Dyke - 1987

Investm't Category: Mortgage-Backed Bond
- ✔ Domestic
- Foreign
- Asset Allocation
- Index
- Sector
- State Specific

Investment Style
- Large-Cap Growth
- Mid-Cap Growth
- Small-Cap Growth
- Large-Cap Value
- Mid-Cap Value
- Small-Cap Value

Portfolio
0.0% cash	0.0% corp bonds
0.0% stocks	104.3% gov't bonds
0.0% preferred	0.0% muni bonds
0.0% conv't/warrants	0.0% other

SHAREHOLDER INFORMATION

Minimum Investment
Initial: $2,500   Subsequent: $100

Minimum IRA Investment
Initial: $1,000   Subsequent: $50

Maximum Fees
Load: none   12b-1: none
Other: f

Distributions
Income: monthly   Capital Gains: Dec

Exchange Options
Number Per Year: 6   Fee: none
Telephone: yes (money market fund available)

Services
IRA, pension, auto exchange, auto invest, auto withdraw

T. Rowe Price Growth & Income (PRGIX)

Growth & Income

Public Relations Department
100 E. Pratt St.
Baltimore, MD 21202
800-225-5132, 410-547-2000
www.troweprice.com

PERFORMANCE

fund inception date: 12/21/82

	3yr Annual	5yr Annual	10yr Annual	Bull	Bear
Return (%)	17.9	16.4	13.5	69.2	-5.9
Differ from Category (+/-)	2.6 abv av	2.5 high	0.8 abv av	9.4 abv av	0.5 abv av

Total Risk	Standard Deviation	Category Risk	Risk Index	Beta
av	8.0%	low	0.9	0.79

	1996	1995	1994	1993	1992	1991	1990	1989	1988	1987
Return (%)	25.6	30.9	-0.2	12.9	15.3	31.5	-11.2	19.2	25.1	-4.3
Differ from Category (+/-)	5.9	0.8	1.1	-0.9	4.6	2.4	-5.3	-4.3	8.3	-4.5
Return, Tax-Adjusted (%)	23.2	28.3	-2.1	10.8	13.3	29.5	-12.9	15.3	22.0	-9.3

PER SHARE DATA

	1996	1995	1994	1993	1992	1991	1990	1989	1988	1987
Dividends, Net Income ($)	0.51	0.59	0.49	0.47	0.60	0.56	0.56	0.64	0.49	0.88
Distrib'ns, Cap Gain ($)	0.90	0.60	0.42	0.48	0.15	0.00	0.01	0.79	0.47	1.04
Net Asset Value ($)	22.63	19.18	15.63	16.57	15.53	14.16	11.22	13.25	12.32	10.63
Expense Ratio (%)	na	0.84	0.81	0.83	0.85	0.93	0.97	0.96	1.04	1.03
Yield (%)	2.16	2.98	3.05	2.75	3.82	3.95	4.98	4.55	3.83	7.54
Portfolio Turnover (%)	na	26	25	22	30	48	35	57	50	114
Total Assets (Millions $)	2,480	1,748	1,228	1,167	839	655	474	553	444	365

PORTFOLIO (as of 9/30/96)

Portfolio Manager: Stephen W. Boesel - 1987

Investm't Category: Growth & Income
- ✔ Domestic
- ✔ Foreign
- Asset Allocation
- Index
- Sector
- State Specific

Investment Style
- Large-Cap Growth
- Mid-Cap Growth
- Small-Cap Growth
- ✔ Large-Cap Value
- Mid-Cap Value
- Small-Cap Value

Portfolio
7.5% cash	0.0% corp bonds
85.3% stocks	2.2% gov't bonds
0.1% preferred	0.0% muni bonds
4.9% conv't/warrants	0.0% other

SHAREHOLDER INFORMATION

Minimum Investment
Initial: $2,500   Subsequent: $100

Minimum IRA Investment
Initial: $1,000   Subsequent: $50

Maximum Fees
Load: none   12b-1: none
Other: f

Distributions
Income: quarterly   Capital Gains: Dec

Exchange Options
Number Per Year: 6   Fee: none
Telephone: yes (money market fund available)

Services
IRA, pension, auto exchange, auto invest, auto withdraw

T. Rowe Price Growth Stock (PRGFX)

Growth

Public Relations Department
100 E. Pratt St.
Baltimore, MD 21202
800-225-5132, 410-547-2000
www.troweprice.com

PERFORMANCE

fund inception date: 4/11/50

	3yr Annual	5yr Annual	10yr Annual	Bull	Bear
Return (%)	17.1	14.5	13.2	66.9	-7.2
Differ from Category (+/-)	1.4 abv av	0.2 av	-0.7 av	4.5 abv av	-0.5 av

Total Risk	Standard Deviation	Category Risk	Risk Index	Beta
av	9.1%	blw av	0.9	0.89

	1996	1995	1994	1993	1992	1991	1990	1989	1988	1987
Return (%)	21.7	30.9	0.8	15.5	5.9	33.7	-4.3	25.4	6.0	3.6
Differ from Category (+/-)	1.6	0.6	1.1	1.5	-5.9	-2.3	1.8	-0.7	-12.1	1.6
Return, Tax-Adjusted (%)	18.9	28.9	-1.9	13.7	3.9	31.8	-6.1	21.4	4.6	-2.3

PER SHARE DATA

	1996	1995	1994	1993	1992	1991	1990	1989	1988	1987
Dividends, Net Income ($)	0.19	0.23	0.18	0.14	0.18	0.25	0.43	0.34	0.32	0.63
Distrib'ns, Cap Gain ($)	2.06	0.97	1.66	0.99	1.03	0.62	0.43	1.58	0.26	2.66
Net Asset Value ($)	26.18	23.35	18.75	20.42	18.66	18.75	14.71	16.27	14.55	14.27
Expense Ratio (%)	na	0.80	0.81	0.82	0.83	0.85	0.76	0.69	0.77	0.67
Yield (%)	0.67	0.94	0.88	0.65	0.91	1.29	2.84	1.90	2.16	3.72
Portfolio Turnover (%)	na	42	54	35	27	32	30	39	41	51
Total Assets (Millions $)	3,473	2,761	2,067	1,975	1,946	1,846	1,396	1,516	1,296	1,267

PORTFOLIO (as of 9/30/96)

Portfolio Manager: John D. Gillespie, M.
David Testa - 1993

Investm't Category: Growth
✔ Domestic   Index
✔ Foreign   Sector
  Asset Allocation   State Specific

Investment Style
✔ Large-Cap Growth   ✔ Large-Cap Value
✔ Mid-Cap Growth   ✔ Mid-Cap Value
  Small-Cap Growth   Small-Cap Value

Portfolio

3.9%	cash	0.0%	corp bonds
95.5%	stocks	0.0%	gov't bonds
0.5%	preferred	0.0%	muni bonds
0.1%	conv't/warrants	0.0%	other

SHAREHOLDER INFORMATION

Minimum Investment
Initial: $2,500   Subsequent: $100

Minimum IRA Investment
Initial: $1,000   Subsequent: $50

Maximum Fees
Load: none   12b-1: none
Other: *f*

Distributions
Income: annual   Capital Gains: Dec

Exchange Options
Number Per Year: 6   Fee: none
Telephone: yes (money market fund available)

Services
IRA, pension, auto exchange, auto invest, auto withdraw

T. Rowe Price Health Sciences (PRHSX)

Aggressive Growth

Public Relations Department
100 E. Pratt St.
Baltimore, MD 21202
800-225-5132, 410-547-2000
www.troweprice.com

PERFORMANCE

fund inception date: 12/29/95

	3yr Annual	5yr Annual	10yr Annual	Bull	Bear
Return (%)	na	na	na	na	na
Differ from Category (+/-)	na	na	na	na	na

Total Risk	Standard Deviation	Category Risk	Risk Index	Beta
na	na	na	na	na

	1996	1995	1994	1993	1992	1991	1990	1989	1988	1987
Return (%)	26.7	—	—	—	—	—	—	—	—	—
Differ from Category (+/-)	7.6	—	—	—	—	—	—	—	—	—
Return, Tax-Adjusted (%)	25.5	—	—	—	—	—	—	—	—	—

PER SHARE DATA

	1996	1995	1994	1993	1992	1991	1990	1989	1988	1987
Dividends, Net Income ($)	0.00	—	—	—	—	—	—	—	—	—
Distrib'ns, Cap Gain ($)	0.40	—	—	—	—	—	—	—	—	—
Net Asset Value ($)	12.27	—	—	—	—	—	—	—	—	—
Expense Ratio (%)	na	—	—	—	—	—	—	—	—	—
Yield (%)	0.00	—	—	—	—	—	—	—	—	—
Portfolio Turnover (%)	na	—	—	—	—	—	—	—	—	—
Total Assets (Millions $)	183	—	—	—	—	—	—	—	—	—

PORTFOLIO (as of 9/30/96)

Portfolio Manager: Joseph Klein - 1995

Investm't Category: Aggressive Growth
- ✔ Domestic
-   Index
-   Foreign
- ✔ Sector
-   Asset Allocation
-   State Specific

Investment Style
- Large-Cap Growth
- Large-Cap Value
- Mid-Cap Growth
- Mid-Cap Value
- Small-Cap Growth
- Small-Cap Value

Portfolio
8.0% cash	0.0% corp bonds
92.0% stocks	0.0% gov't bonds
0.0% preferred	0.0% muni bonds
0.0% conv't/warrants	0.0% other

SHAREHOLDER INFORMATION

Minimum Investment
Initial: $2,500   Subsequent: $100

Minimum IRA Investment
Initial: $2,000   Subsequent: $100

Maximum Fees
Load: none   12b-1: none
Other: f

Distributions
Income: annual   Capital Gains: Dec

Exchange Options
Number Per Year: 6   Fee: none
Telephone: yes (money market fund available)

Services
IRA, pension, auto exchange, auto invest, auto withdraw

T. Rowe Price High Yield

(PRHYX)

Corporate High-Yield Bond

Public Relations Department
100 E. Pratt St.
Baltimore, MD 21202
800-225-5132, 410-547-2000
www.troweprice.com

PERFORMANCE

fund inception date: 12/31/84

	3yr Annual	5yr Annual	10yr Annual	Bull	Bear
Return (%)	5.9	10.6	8.7	28.4	-9.4
Differ from Category (+/-)	-2.8 low	-1.5 blw av	-0.6 low	-4.7 blw av	-4.0 low

Total Risk	Standard Deviation	Category Risk	Risk Index	Avg Mat
blw av	5.4%	high	1.2	8.2 yrs

	1996	1995	1994	1993	1992	1991	1990	1989	1988	1987
Return (%)............	11.5	15.7	-8.0	21.8	14.7	30.8	-11.0	-1.5	17.9	3.0
Differ from Category (+/-)	-3.8	-1.8	-5.1	2.9	-1.4	3.2	-6.1	-2.7	5.4	1.2
Return, Tax-Adjusted (%)...	7.8	11.9	-11.3	17.9	10.6	25.6	-16.0	-6.4	12.8	-2.0

PER SHARE DATA

	1996	1995	1994	1993	1992	1991	1990	1989	1988	1987
Dividends, Net Income ($)	0.75	0.74	0.75	0.81	0.82	0.89	1.11	1.26	1.25	1.26
Distrib'ns, Cap Gain ($) ...	0.00	0.00	0.00	0.00	0.00	0.00	0.00	0.00	0.00	0.14
Net Asset Value ($)	8.34	8.19	7.75	9.22	8.29	7.98	6.86	8.88	10.25	9.82
Expense Ratio (%)........	0.85	0.88	0.85	0.89	0.97	1.03	1.02	0.95	0.99	0.99
Yield (%)	8.99	9.03	9.67	8.78	9.89	11.15	16.18	14.18	12.19	12.65
Portfolio Turnover (%).....	91	74	107	104	59	83	66	80	138	166
Total Assets (Millions $). .	1,317	1,226	1,040	1,631	1,204	968	478	774	1,119	703

PORTFOLIO (as of 9/30/96)

Portfolio Manager: Mark J. Vaselkiv - 1996

Investm't Category: Corp. High-Yield Bond
✔ Domestic   Index
✔ Foreign   Sector
    Asset Allocation   State Specific

Investment Style
    Large-Cap Growth   Large-Cap Value
    Mid-Cap Growth   Mid-Cap Value
    Small-Cap Growth   Small-Cap Value

Portfolio
4.1% cash	91.0% corp bonds
3.9% stocks	0.0% gov't bonds
0.8% preferred	0.0% muni bonds
0.2% conv't/warrants	0.0% other

SHAREHOLDER INFORMATION

Minimum Investment
Initial: $2,500   Subsequent: $100

Minimum IRA Investment
Initial: $1,000   Subsequent: $50

Maximum Fees
Load: 1.00% redemption   12b-1: none
Other: redemption fee applies for 1 year; *f*

Distributions
Income: monthly   Capital Gains: Dec

Exchange Options
Number Per Year: 6   Fee: none
Telephone: yes (money market fund available)

Services
IRA, pension, auto exchange, auto invest, auto withdraw

T. Rowe Price Int'l: Bond

(RPIBX)

International Bond

Public Relations Department
100 E. Pratt St.
Baltimore, MD 21202
800-638-5660, 410-547-2308
www.troweprice.com

PERFORMANCE

fund inception date: 9/10/86

	3yr Annual	5yr Annual	10yr Annual	Bull	Bear
Return (%)	8.1	9.2	10.0	29.4	-3.3
Differ from Category (+/-)	2.1 abv av	2.6 high	2.7 high	-1.8 av	6.2 high

Total Risk	Standard Deviation	Category Risk	Risk Index	Avg Mat
blw av	7.0%	av	1.0	7.4 yrs

	1996	1995	1994	1993	1992	1991	1990	1989	1988	1987
Return (%)	7.1	20.3	-1.9	20.0	2.3	17.7	16.0	-3.2	-1.3	28.1
Differ from Category (+/-)	-4.2	4.3	5.7	4.7	-2.9	2.7	5.5	-6.4	-5.6	17.9
Return, Tax-Adjusted (%)	4.5	17.3	-4.8	15.8	-1.3	14.5	11.8	-6.1	-5.1	23.9

PER SHARE DATA

	1996	1995	1994	1993	1992	1991	1990	1989	1988	1987
Dividends, Net Income ($)	0.60	0.62	0.59	0.68	0.83	0.77	0.83	0.74	0.91	1.01
Distrib'ns, Cap Gain ($)	0.11	0.12	0.21	0.46	0.15	0.00	0.17	0.00	0.26	0.05
Net Asset Value ($)	10.46	10.46	9.34	10.34	9.61	10.35	9.53	9.15	10.25	11.60
Expense Ratio (%)	na	0.90	0.98	0.99	1.08	1.24	1.15	1.23	1.20	1.25
Yield (%)	5.67	5.86	6.17	6.29	8.50	7.43	8.55	8.08	8.65	8.66
Portfolio Turnover (%)	na	238	345	395	358	296	211	293	368	284
Total Assets (Millions $)	992	1,015	738	745	516	413	430	303	405	400

PORTFOLIO (as of 9/30/96)

Portfolio Manager: Peter Askew, Chris Rothery - 1994

Investm't Category: International Bond

Domestic	Index
✔ Foreign	Sector
Asset Allocation	State Specific

Investment Style

Large-Cap Growth	Large-Cap Value
Mid-Cap Growth	Mid-Cap Value
Small-Cap Growth	Small-Cap Value

Portfolio

5.3% cash	16.0% corp bonds
0.0% stocks	78.7% gov't bonds
0.0% preferred	0.0% muni bonds
0.0% conv't/warrants	0.0% other

SHAREHOLDER INFORMATION

Minimum Investment
Initial: $2,500   Subsequent: $100

Minimum IRA Investment
Initial: $1,000   Subsequent: $50

Maximum Fees
Load: none   12b-1: none
Other: f

Distributions
Income: monthly   Capital Gains: Dec

Exchange Options
Number Per Year: 6   Fee: none
Telephone: yes (money market fund available)

Services
IRA, pension, auto exchange, auto invest, auto withdraw

T. Rowe Price Int'l: Discovery (PRIDX)

International Stock

Public Relations Department
100 E. Pratt St.
Baltimore, MD 21202
800-638-5660, 410-547-2308
www.troweprice.com

PERFORMANCE

fund inception date: 12/30/88

	3yr Annual	5yr Annual	10yr Annual	Bull	Bear
Return (%)	0.2	6.5	na	3.0	-6.6
Differ from Category (+/-)	-6.1 low	-3.5 blw av	na	-21.3 low	0.6 av

Total Risk	Standard Deviation	Category Risk	Risk Index	Beta
abv av	10.5%	av	1.0	0.52

	1996	1995	1994	1993	1992	1991	1990	1989	1988	1987
Return (%)	13.8	-4.4	-7.7	49.8	-9.1	11.6	-12.9	41.7	—	—
Differ from Category (+/-)	-1.0	-13.5	-4.6	10.2	-5.3	-1.6	-2.8	19.1	—	—
Return, Tax-Adjusted (%)	13.4	-4.7	-9.3	49.5	-9.5	11.1	-13.9	40.9	—	—

PER SHARE DATA

	1996	1995	1994	1993	1992	1991	1990	1989	1988	1987
Dividends, Net Income ($)	0.07	0.10	0.06	0.07	0.13	0.13	0.15	0.13	—	—
Distrib'ns, Cap Gain ($)	0.06	0.02	0.87	0.02	0.00	0.00	0.27	0.10	—	—
Net Asset Value ($)	16.22	14.36	15.14	17.41	11.68	12.99	11.75	13.94	—	—
Expense Ratio (%)	na	1.50	1.50	1.50	1.50	1.50	1.50	1.50	—	—
Yield (%)	0.42	0.69	0.37	0.40	1.11	1.00	1.24	0.92	—	—
Portfolio Turnover (%)	na	43	57	72	38	56	44	38	—	—
Total Assets (Millions $)	326	302	437	392	166	166	136	61	—	—

PORTFOLIO (as of 9/30/96)

Portfolio Manager: Martin G. Wade - 1988

Investm't Category: International Stock

Domestic	Index
✔ Foreign	Sector
Asset Allocation	State Specific

Investment Style

Large-Cap Growth	Large-Cap Value
Mid-Cap Growth	Mid-Cap Value
Small-Cap Growth	Small-Cap Value

Portfolio

8.2% cash	0.2% corp bonds
84.7% stocks	0.0% gov't bonds
5.9% preferred	0.0% muni bonds
1.0% conv't/warrants	0.0% other

SHAREHOLDER INFORMATION

Minimum Investment
Initial: $2,500   Subsequent: $100

Minimum IRA Investment
Initial: $1,000   Subsequent: $50

Maximum Fees
Load: 2.00% redemption   12b-1: none
Other: redemption fee applies for 1 year; *f*

Distributions
Income: annual   Capital Gains: Dec

Exchange Options
Number Per Year: 6   Fee: none
Telephone: yes (money market fund available)

Services
IRA, pension, auto exchange, auto invest, auto withdraw

Individual Fund Listings   737

T. Rowe Price Int'l: Emerging Mkts Stock

(PRMSX) *International Stock*

Public Relations Department
100 E. Pratt St.
Baltimore, MD 21202
800-638-5660, 410-547-2308
www.troweprice.com

PERFORMANCE

fund inception date: 3/31/95

	3yr Annual	5yr Annual	10yr Annual	Bull	Bear
Return (%)	na	na	na	na	na
Differ from Category (+/-)	na	na	na	na	na

Total Risk	Standard Deviation	Category Risk	Risk Index	Beta
na	na	na	na	na

	1996	1995	1994	1993	1992	1991	1990	1989	1988	1987
Return (%)	11.8	—	—	—	—	—	—	—	—	—
Differ from Category (+/-)	-3.0	—	—	—	—	—	—	—	—	—
Return, Tax-Adjusted (%)	10.8	—	—	—	—	—	—	—	—	—

PER SHARE DATA

	1996	1995	1994	1993	1992	1991	1990	1989	1988	1987
Dividends, Net Income ($)	0.04	—	—	—	—	—	—	—	—	—
Distrib'ns, Cap Gain ($)	0.30	—	—	—	—	—	—	—	—	—
Net Asset Value ($)	11.69	—	—	—	—	—	—	—	—	—
Expense Ratio (%)	na	—	—	—	—	—	—	—	—	—
Yield (%)	0.33	—	—	—	—	—	—	—	—	—
Portfolio Turnover (%)	na	—	—	—	—	—	—	—	—	—
Total Assets (Millions $)	71	—	—	—	—	—	—	—	—	—

PORTFOLIO (as of 9/30/96)

Portfolio Manager: Martin G. Wade - 1995

Investm't Category: International Stock
- Domestic
- ✔ Foreign
- Asset Allocation
- Index
- Sector
- State Specific

Investment Style
- Large-Cap Growth
- Mid-Cap Growth
- Small-Cap Growth
- Large-Cap Value
- Mid-Cap Value
- Small-Cap Value

Portfolio
8.2% cash	0.0% corp bonds
78.2% stocks	0.0% gov't bonds
12.8% preferred	0.0% muni bonds
0.8% conv't/warrants	0.0% other

SHAREHOLDER INFORMATION

Minimum Investment
Initial: $2,500   Subsequent: $100

Minimum IRA Investment
Initial: $1,000   Subsequent: $50

Maximum Fees
Load: 2.00% redemption   12b-1: none
Other: redemption fee applies for 1 year; *f*

Distributions
Income: annual   Capital Gains: Dec

Exchange Options
Number Per Year: 6   Fee: none
Telephone: yes (money market fund available)

Services
IRA, pension, auto exchange, auto invest, auto withdraw

Guide to Low-Load Mutual Funds

T. Rowe Price Int'l: European Stock

(PRESX) *International Stock*

Public Relations Department
100 E. Pratt St.
Baltimore, MD 21202
800-638-5660, 410-547-2308
www.troweprice.com

PERFORMANCE

fund inception date: 2/28/90

	3yr Annual	5yr Annual	10yr Annual	Bull	Bear
Return (%)	16.8	13.9	na	61.2	-6.9
Differ from Category (+/-)	10.5 high	3.9 high	na	36.9 high	0.3 av

Total Risk	Standard Deviation	Category Risk	Risk Index	Beta
av	9.3%	blw av	0.9	0.64

	1996	1995	1994	1993	1992	1991	1990	1989	1988	1987
Return (%)	25.8	21.8	4.0	27.2	-5.6	7.3	—	—	—	—
Differ from Category (+/-)	11.0	12.7	7.1	-12.4	-1.8	-5.9	—	—	—	—
Return, Tax-Adjusted (%)	24.6	20.5	3.4	27.0	-6.3	6.9	—	—	—	—

PER SHARE DATA

	1996	1995	1994	1993	1992	1991	1990	1989	1988	1987
Dividends, Net Income ($)	0.26	0.21	0.12	0.04	0.17	0.08	—	—	—	—
Distrib'ns, Cap Gain ($)	0.20	0.25	0.05	0.01	0.00	0.00	—	—	—	—
Net Asset Value ($)	17.62	14.37	12.17	11.86	9.36	10.09	—	—	—	—
Expense Ratio (%)	na	1.20	1.25	1.35	1.48	1.71	—	—	—	—
Yield (%)	1.45	1.43	0.98	0.33	1.81	0.79	—	—	—	—
Portfolio Turnover (%)	na	17	24	21	52	58	—	—	—	—
Total Assets (Millions $)	744	531	366	289	173	103	—	—	—	—

PORTFOLIO (as of 9/30/96)

Portfolio Manager: Martin G. Wade - 1990

Investm't Category: International Stock

Domestic	Index
✔ Foreign	Sector
Asset Allocation	State Specific

Investment Style

Large-Cap Growth	Large-Cap Value
Mid-Cap Growth	Mid-Cap Value
Small-Cap Growth	Small-Cap Value

Portfolio

5.7% cash	0.0% corp bonds
93.4% stocks	0.0% gov't bonds
0.8% preferred	0.0% muni bonds
0.1% conv't/warrants	0.0% other

SHAREHOLDER INFORMATION

Minimum Investment
Initial: $2,500   Subsequent: $100

Minimum IRA Investment
Initial: $1,000   Subsequent: $50

Maximum Fees
Load: none   12b-1: none
Other: *f*

Distributions
Income: annual   Capital Gains: Dec

Exchange Options
Number Per Year: 6   Fee: none
Telephone: yes (money market fund available)

Services
IRA, pension, auto exchange, auto invest, auto withdraw

T. Rowe Price Int'l: Global Gov't Bd (RPGGX)

International Bond

Public Relations Department
100 E. Pratt St.
Baltimore, MD 21202
800-638-5660, 410-547-2308
www.troweprice.com

PERFORMANCE

fund inception date: 12/28/90

	3yr Annual	5yr Annual	10yr Annual	Bull	Bear
Return (%)	6.8	6.9	na	26.0	-3.8
Differ from Category (+/-)	0.8 av	0.3 av	na	-5.2 blw av	5.7 abv av

Total Risk	Standard Deviation	Category Risk	Risk Index	Avg Mat
blw av	4.8%	blw av	0.7	7.1 yrs

	1996	1995	1994	1993	1992	1991	1990	1989	1988	1987
Return (%)	6.5	18.1	-3.1	10.7	3.6	11.3	—	—	—	—
Differ from Category (+/-)	-4.8	2.1	4.5	-4.6	-1.6	-3.7	—	—	—	—
Return, Tax-Adjusted (%)	4.3	15.5	-5.3	7.6	0.6	8.2	—	—	—	—

PER SHARE DATA

	1996	1995	1994	1993	1992	1991	1990	1989	1988	1987
Dividends, Net Income ($)	0.55	0.59	0.53	0.56	0.75	0.77	—	—	—	—
Distrib'ns, Cap Gain ($)	0.00	0.00	0.02	0.28	0.01	0.00	—	—	—	—
Net Asset Value ($)	10.35	10.26	9.22	10.08	9.89	10.30	—	—	—	—
Expense Ratio (%)	na	1.20	1.20	1.20	1.20	1.20	—	—	—	—
Yield (%)	5.31	5.75	5.73	5.40	7.57	7.47	—	—	—	—
Portfolio Turnover (%)	na	290	254	134	237	94	—	—	—	—
Total Assets (Millions $)	57	28	36	48	53	39	—	—	—	—

PORTFOLIO (as of 9/30/96)

Portfolio Manager: Peter Askew, Chris Rothery - 1994

Investm't Category: International Bond

✔ Domestic   Index
✔ Foreign   Sector
    Asset Allocation   State Specific

Investment Style

Large-Cap Growth   Large-Cap Value
Mid-Cap Growth   Mid-Cap Value
Small-Cap Growth   Small-Cap Value

Portfolio

8.7% cash	5.7% corp bonds
0.0% stocks	85.6% gov't bonds
0.0% preferred	0.0% muni bonds
0.0% conv't/warrants	0.0% other

SHAREHOLDER INFORMATION

Minimum Investment
Initial: $2,500   Subsequent: $100

Minimum IRA Investment
Initial: $1,000   Subsequent: $50

Maximum Fees
Load: none   12b-1: none
Other: ƒ

Distributions
Income: monthly   Capital Gains: Dec

Exchange Options
Number Per Year: 6   Fee: none
Telephone: yes (money market fund available)

Services
IRA, pension, auto exchange, auto invest, auto withdraw

T. Rowe Price Int'l: Japan

(PRJPX)

International Stock

Public Relations Department
100 E. Pratt St.
Baltimore, MD 21202
800-638-5660, 410-547-2308
www.troweprice.com

PERFORMANCE

fund inception date: 12/27/91

	3yr Annual	5yr Annual	10yr Annual	Bull	Bear
Return (%)	-0.3	0.7	na	-22.1	12.7
Differ from Category (+/-)	-6.6 low	-9.3 low	na	-46.4 low	19.9 high

Total Risk	Standard Deviation	Category Risk	Risk Index	Beta
high	16.8%	high	1.6	0.27

	1996	1995	1994	1993	1992	1991	1990	1989	1988	1987
Return (%)	-11.0	-3.2	15.0	20.6	-13.5	—	—	—	—	—
Differ from Category (+/-)	-25.8	-12.3	18.1	-19.0	-9.7	—	—	—	—	—
Return, Tax-Adjusted (%)	-11.0	-3.2	12.6	17.8	-13.5	—	—	—	—	—

PER SHARE DATA

	1996	1995	1994	1993	1992	1991	1990	1989	1988	1987
Dividends, Net Income ($)	0.00	0.00	0.00	0.00	0.00	—	—	—	—	—
Distrib'ns, Cap Gain ($)	0.00	0.00	0.81	0.85	0.00	—	—	—	—	—
Net Asset Value ($)	8.83	9.92	10.24	9.61	8.66	—	—	—	—	—
Expense Ratio (%)	na	1.50	1.50	1.50	1.50	—	—	—	—	—
Yield (%)	0.00	0.00	0.00	0.00	0.00	—	—	—	—	—
Portfolio Turnover (%)	na	62	61	61	42	—	—	—	—	—
Total Assets (Millions $)	165	207	169	70	45	—	—	—	—	—

PORTFOLIO (as of 9/30/96)

Portfolio Manager: Martin G. Wade - 1991

Investm't Category: International Stock

Domestic	Index
✓ Foreign	Sector
Asset Allocation	State Specific

Investment Style

Large-Cap Growth	Large-Cap Value
Mid-Cap Growth	Mid-Cap Value
Small-Cap Growth	Small-Cap Value

Portfolio

2.3% cash	0.0% corp bonds
97.7% stocks	0.0% gov't bonds
0.0% preferred	0.0% muni bonds
0.0% conv't/warrants	0.0% other

SHAREHOLDER INFORMATION

Minimum Investment
Initial: $2,500   Subsequent: $100

Minimum IRA Investment
Initial: $1,000   Subsequent: $50

Maximum Fees
Load: none   12b-1: none
Other: f

Distributions
Income: annual   Capital Gains: Dec

Exchange Options
Number Per Year: 6   Fee: none
Telephone: yes (money market fund available)

Services
IRA, pension, auto exchange, auto invest, auto withdraw

T. Rowe Price Int'l: Latin America (PRLAX)

International Stock

Public Relations Department
100 E. Pratt St.
Baltimore, MD 21202
800-638-5660, 410-547-2308
www.troweprice.com

PERFORMANCE

fund inception date: 12/29/93

	3yr Annual	5yr Annual	10yr Annual	Bull	Bear
Return (%)	-5.6	na	na	-0.6	-22.5
Differ from Category (+/-)	-11.9 low	na	na	-24.9 low	-15.3 low

Total Risk	Standard Deviation	Category Risk	Risk Index	Beta
high	25.1%	high	2.4	0.75

	1996	1995	1994	1993	1992	1991	1990	1989	1988	1987
Return (%)	23.3	-18.8	-16.0	—	—	—	—	—	—	—
Differ from Category (+/-)	8.5	-27.9	-12.9	—	—	—	—	—	—	—
Return, Tax-Adjusted (%)	22.5	-19.1	-16.0	—	—	—	—	—	—	—

PER SHARE DATA

	1996	1995	1994	1993	1992	1991	1990	1989	1988	1987
Dividends, Net Income ($)	0.11	0.06	0.00	—	—	—	—	—	—	—
Distrib'ns, Cap Gain ($)	0.03	0.00	0.00	—	—	—	—	—	—	—
Net Asset Value ($)	8.26	6.81	8.45	—	—	—	—	—	—	—
Expense Ratio (%)	na	1.82	1.99	—	—	—	—	—	—	—
Yield (%)	1.32	0.88	0.00	—	—	—	—	—	—	—
Portfolio Turnover (%)	na	18	12	—	—	—	—	—	—	—
Total Assets (Millions $)	208	149	163	—	—	—	—	—	—	—

PORTFOLIO (as of 9/30/96)

Portfolio Manager: Martin G. Wade - 1993

Investm't Category: International Stock
- Domestic
- ✔ Foreign
- Asset Allocation
- Index
- Sector
- State Specific

Investment Style
Large-Cap Growth	Large-Cap Value
Mid-Cap Growth	Mid-Cap Value
Small-Cap Growth	Small-Cap Value

Portfolio
4.5% cash	0.2% corp bonds
56.8% stocks	0.0% gov't bonds
38.5% preferred	0.0% muni bonds
0.0% conv't/warrants	0.0% other

SHAREHOLDER INFORMATION

Minimum Investment
Initial: $2,500   Subsequent: $100

Minimum IRA Investment
Initial: $1,000   Subsequent: $50

Maximum Fees
Load: 2.00% redemption   12b-1: none
Other: redemption applies for 1 year; f

Distributions
Income: annual   Capital Gains: Dec

Exchange Options
Number Per Year: 6   Fee: none
Telephone: yes (money market fund available)

Services
IRA, pension, auto exchange, auto invest, auto withdraw

T. Rowe Price Int'l: New Asia (PRASX)

International Stock

Public Relations Department
100 E. Pratt St.
Baltimore, MD 21202
800-638-5660, 410-547-2308
www.troweprice.com

PERFORMANCE

fund inception date: 9/28/90

	3yr Annual	5yr Annual	10yr Annual	Bull	Bear
Return (%)	-1.7	13.6	na	18.2	-15.4
Differ from Category (+/-)	-8.0 low	3.6 high	na	-6.1 blw av	-8.2 low

Total Risk	Standard Deviation	Category Risk	Risk Index	Beta
high	18.7%	high	1.8	1.20

	1996	1995	1994	1993	1992	1991	1990	1989	1988	1987
Return (%)	13.5	3.7	-19.2	78.7	11.2	19.3	—	—	—	—
Differ from Category (+/-)	-1.3	-5.4	-16.1	39.1	15.0	6.1	—	—	—	—
Return, Tax-Adjusted (%)	13.1	3.2	-21.7	77.6	9.9	18.5	—	—	—	—

PER SHARE DATA

	1996	1995	1994	1993	1992	1991	1990	1989	1988	1987
Dividends, Net Income ($)	0.06	0.09	0.07	0.03	0.10	0.10	—	—	—	—
Distrib'ns, Cap Gain ($)	0.01	0.00	0.89	0.19	0.13	0.00	—	—	—	—
Net Asset Value ($)	9.26	8.22	8.01	11.10	6.34	5.91	—	—	—	—
Expense Ratio (%)	na	1.15	1.22	1.29	1.51	1.75	—	—	—	—
Yield (%)	0.64	1.09	0.78	0.26	1.54	1.69	—	—	—	—
Portfolio Turnover (%)	na	63	63	40	36	49	—	—	—	—
Total Assets (Millions $)	2,221	1,880	1,987	2,247	314	102	—	—	—	—

PORTFOLIO (as of 9/30/96)

Portfolio Manager: Martin G. Wade - 1990

Investm't Category: International Stock

Domestic	Index
✔ Foreign	Sector
Asset Allocation	State Specific

Investment Style

Large-Cap Growth	Large-Cap Value
Mid-Cap Growth	Mid-Cap Value
Small-Cap Growth	Small-Cap Value

Portfolio

4.8% cash	0.0% corp bonds
93.0% stocks	0.0% gov't bonds
0.4% preferred	0.0% muni bonds
1.8% conv't/warrants	0.0% other

SHAREHOLDER INFORMATION

Minimum Investment
Initial: $2,500   Subsequent: $100

Minimum IRA Investment
Initial: $1,000   Subsequent: $50

Maximum Fees
Load: none   12b-1: none
Other: f

Distributions
Income: annual   Capital Gains: Dec

Exchange Options
Number Per Year: 6   Fee: none
Telephone: yes (money market fund available)

Services
IRA, pension, auto exchange, auto invest, auto withdraw

T. Rowe Price Int'l: Stock

(PRITX)

International Stock

Public Relations Department
100 E. Pratt St.
Baltimore, MD 21202
800-638-5660, 410-547-2308
www.troweprice.com

PERFORMANCE

fund inception date: 5/9/80

	3yr Annual	5yr Annual	10yr Annual	Bull	Bear
Return (%)	8.6	11.6	11.1	30.2	-6.4
Differ from Category (+/-)	2.3 abv av	1.6 abv av	2.5 high	5.9 abv av	0.8 abv av

Total Risk	Standard Deviation	Category Risk	Risk Index	Beta
abv av	10.0%	av	1.0	0.70

	1996	1995	1994	1993	1992	1991	1990	1989	1988	1987
Return (%)	15.9	11.3	-0.8	40.1	-3.5	15.8	-8.9	23.7	17.9	7.9
Differ from Category (+/-)	1.1	2.2	2.3	0.5	0.3	2.6	1.2	1.1	3.0	-4.3
Return, Tax-Adjusted (%)	14.8	10.1	-2.7	39.0	-4.7	13.5	-10.6	20.9	14.1	2.1

PER SHARE DATA

	1996	1995	1994	1993	1992	1991	1990	1989	1988	1987
Dividends, Net Income ($)	0.18	0.18	0.12	0.09	0.16	0.15	0.16	0.16	0.16	0.23
Distrib'ns, Cap Gain ($)	0.20	0.20	0.62	0.20	0.16	0.49	0.36	0.67	0.93	4.97
Net Asset Value ($)	13.80	12.23	11.32	12.16	8.89	9.54	8.81	10.24	8.97	8.54
Expense Ratio (%)	na	0.91	0.97	1.01	1.05	1.10	1.09	1.10	1.16	1.14
Yield (%)	1.28	1.44	1.00	0.72	1.76	1.49	1.74	1.46	1.61	1.70
Portfolio Turnover (%)	na	17	22	29	38	45	47	48	42	77
Total Assets (Millions $)	9,239	6,703	5,786	4,296	1,949	1,476	1,030	970	629	642

PORTFOLIO (as of 9/30/96)

Portfolio Manager: Martin G. Wade - 1980

Investm't Category: International Stock

Domestic	Index
✔ Foreign	Sector
Asset Allocation	State Specific

Investment Style

Large-Cap Growth	Large-Cap Value
Mid-Cap Growth	Mid-Cap Value
Small-Cap Growth	Small-Cap Value

Portfolio

5.8% cash	0.0% corp bonds
90.4% stocks	0.0% gov't bonds
3.4% preferred	0.0% muni bonds
0.4% conv't/warrants	0.0% other

SHAREHOLDER INFORMATION

Minimum Investment
Initial: $2,500   Subsequent: $100

Minimum IRA Investment
Initial: $1,000   Subsequent: $50

Maximum Fees
Load: none   12b-1: none
Other: *f*

Distributions
Income: annual   Capital Gains: Dec

Exchange Options
Number Per Year: 6   Fee: none
Telephone: yes (money market fund available)

Services
IRA, pension, auto exchange, auto invest, auto withdraw

T. Rowe Price MD Sh Term Tax Free

(PRMDX) *Tax-Exempt Bond*

Public Relations Department
100 E. Pratt St.
Baltimore, MD 21202
800-225-5132, 410-547-2000
www.troweprice.com

PERFORMANCE

fund inception date: 1/29/93

	3yr Annual	5yr Annual	10yr Annual	Bull	Bear
Return (%)	3.8	na	na	12.2	-0.9
Differ from Category (+/-)	-0.4 blw av	na	na	-6.2 low	4.5 high

Total Risk	Standard Deviation	Category Risk	Risk Index	Avg Mat
low	1.4%	low	0.3	2.0 yrs

	1996	1995	1994	1993	1992	1991	1990	1989	1988	1987
Return (%)	3.4	7.5	0.6	—	—	—	—	—	—	—
Differ from Category (+/-)	-0.3	-7.7	5.9	—	—	—	—	—	—	—
Return, Tax-Adjusted (%)	3.4	7.5	0.6	—	—	—	—	—	—	—

PER SHARE DATA

	1996	1995	1994	1993	1992	1991	1990	1989	1988	1987
Dividends, Net Income ($)	0.20	0.21	0.17	—	—	—	—	—	—	—
Distrib'ns, Cap Gain ($)	0.00	0.00	0.00	—	—	—	—	—	—	—
Net Asset Value ($)	5.11	5.14	4.98	—	—	—	—	—	—	—
Expense Ratio (%)	0.65	0.65	0.65	—	—	—	—	—	—	—
Yield (%)	3.91	4.08	3.41	—	—	—	—	—	—	—
Portfolio Turnover (%)	39	105	20	—	—	—	—	—	—	—
Total Assets (Millions $)	95	83	76	—	—	—	—	—	—	—

PORTFOLIO (as of 9/30/96)

Portfolio Manager: Charles B. Hill - 1995

Investm't Category: Tax-Exempt Bond

✔ Domestic   Index
   Foreign   Sector
   Asset Allocation   ✔ State Specific

Investment Style
   Large-Cap Growth   Large-Cap Value
   Mid-Cap Growth   Mid-Cap Value
   Small-Cap Growth   Small-Cap Value

Portfolio
20.3%	cash	0.0%	corp bonds
0.0%	stocks	0.0%	gov't bonds
0.0%	preferred	79.7%	muni bonds
0.0%	conv't/warrants	0.0%	other

SHAREHOLDER INFORMATION

Minimum Investment
Initial: $2,500   Subsequent: $100

Minimum IRA Investment
Initial: na   Subsequent: na

Maximum Fees
Load: none   12b-1: none
Other: *f*

Distributions
Income: monthly   Capital Gains: Dec

Exchange Options
Number Per Year: 6   Fee: none
Telephone: yes (money market fund available)

Services
auto exchange, auto invest, auto withdraw

T. Rowe Price MD Tax-Free Bond (MDXBX)

Tax-Exempt Bond

Public Relations Department
100 E. Pratt St.
Baltimore, MD 21202
800-225-5132, 410-547-2000
www.troweprice.com

PERFORMANCE
fund inception date: 3/31/87

	3yr Annual	5yr Annual	10yr Annual	Bull	Bear
Return (%)	4.7	7.0	na	20.2	-5.9
Differ from Category (+/-)	0.5 abv av	0.6 abv av	na	1.8 abv av	-0.5 av

Total Risk	Standard Deviation	Category Risk	Risk Index	Avg Mat
blw av	5.2%	av	0.9	16.7 yrs

	1996	1995	1994	1993	1992	1991	1990	1989	1988	1987
Return (%).	3.7	16.4	-5.1	12.6	8.5	11.2	6.2	9.5	8.8	—
Differ from Category (+/-) . .	0.0	1.2	0.2	0.8	0.2	-0.2	-0.2	0.5	-1.2	—
Return, Tax-Adjusted (%). . .	3.7	16.4	-5.2	12.3	8.3	11.0	6.2	9.4	8.8	—

PER SHARE DATA

	1996	1995	1994	1993	1992	1991	1990	1989	1988	1987
Dividends, Net Income ($).	0.55	0.56	0.56	0.56	0.57	0.59	0.59	0.59	0.56	—
Distrib'ns, Cap Gain ($) . . .	0.00	0.00	0.02	0.10	0.05	0.05	0.00	0.03	0.00	—
Net Asset Value ($)	10.35	10.53	9.56	10.67	10.08	9.89	9.50	9.53	9.29	—
Expense Ratio (%).	0.54	0.57	0.57	0.61	0.64	0.68	0.85	0.92	0.85	—
Yield (%)	5.31	5.31	5.84	5.19	5.62	5.93	6.21	6.17	6.02	—
Portfolio Turnover (%). . . .	23	28	24	23	21	52	58	64	178	—
Total Assets (Millions $). . .	813	799	675	825	651	452	283	183	99	—

PORTFOLIO (as of 9/30/96)

Portfolio Manager: Mary J. Miller - 1990

Investm't Category: Tax-Exempt Bond
- ✔ Domestic
- Foreign
- Asset Allocation
- Index
- Sector
- ✔ State Specific

Investment Style
- Large-Cap Growth
- Mid-Cap Growth
- Small-Cap Growth
- Large-Cap Value
- Mid-Cap Value
- Small-Cap Value

Portfolio
2.0%	cash	0.0%	corp bonds
0.0%	stocks	0.0%	gov't bonds
0.0%	preferred	98.0%	muni bonds
0.0%	conv't/warrants	0.0%	other

SHAREHOLDER INFORMATION

Minimum Investment
Initial: $2,500   Subsequent: $100

Minimum IRA Investment
Initial: na   Subsequent: na

Maximum Fees
Load: none   12b-1: none
Other: f

Distributions
Income: monthly   Capital Gains: Dec

Exchange Options
Number Per Year: 6   Fee: none
Telephone: yes (money market fund available)

Services
auto exchange, auto invest, auto withdraw

T. Rowe Price Mid-Cap Growth (RPMGX)

Growth

Public Relations Department
100 E. Pratt St.
Baltimore, MD 21202
800-225-5132, 410-547-2000
www.troweprice.com

PERFORMANCE

fund inception date: 6/30/92

	3yr Annual	5yr Annual	10yr Annual	Bull	Bear
Return (%)	20.8	na	na	87.3	-7.1
Differ from Category (+/-)	5.1 high	na	na	24.9 high	-0.4 av

Total Risk	Standard Deviation	Category Risk	Risk Index	Beta
abv av	11.1%	abv av	1.1	0.80

	1996	1995	1994	1993	1992	1991	1990	1989	1988	1987
Return (%).	24.8	40.9	0.2	26.2	—	—	—	—	—	—
Differ from Category (+/-) . .	4.7	10.6	0.5	12.2	—	—	—	—	—	—
Return, Tax-Adjusted (%). .	23.8	39.4	-0.5	25.5	—	—	—	—	—	—

PER SHARE DATA

	1996	1995	1994	1993	1992	1991	1990	1989	1988	1987
Dividends, Net Income ($).	0.00	0.00	0.00	0.00	—	—	—	—	—	—
Distrib'ns, Cap Gain ($) . . .	0.69	0.79	0.37	0.30	—	—	—	—	—	—
Net Asset Value ($)	24.43	20.13	14.85	15.18	—	—	—	—	—	—
Expense Ratio (%).	na	1.25	1.25	1.25	—	—	—	—	—	—
Yield (%)	0.00	0.00	0.00	0.00	—	—	—	—	—	—
Portfolio Turnover (%).	na	57	48	62	—	—	—	—	—	—
Total Assets (Millions $). . .	976	263	100	65	—	—	—	—	—	—

PORTFOLIO (as of 9/30/96)

Portfolio Manager: Brian Berghuis - 1992

Investm't Category: Growth

✔ Domestic	Index
✔ Foreign	Sector
Asset Allocation	State Specific

Investment Style

Large-Cap Growth	Large-Cap Value
✔ Mid-Cap Growth	Mid-Cap Value
✔ Small-Cap Growth	Small-Cap Value

Portfolio

8.0% cash	0.0% corp bonds
92.0% stocks	0.0% gov't bonds
0.0% preferred	0.0% muni bonds
0.0% conv't/warrants	0.0% other

SHAREHOLDER INFORMATION

Minimum Investment
Initial: $2,500   Subsequent: $100

Minimum IRA Investment
Initial: $1,000   Subsequent: $50

Maximum Fees
Load: none   12b-1: none
Other: *f*

Distributions
Income: annual   Capital Gains: Dec

Exchange Options
Number Per Year: 6   Fee: none
Telephone: yes (money market fund available)

Services
IRA, pension, auto exchange, auto invest, auto withdraw

T. Rowe Price NJ Tax-Free Bond (NJTFX)

Tax-Exempt Bond

Public Relations Department
100 E. Pratt St.
Baltimore, MD 21202
800-225-5132, 410-547-2000
www.troweprice.com

PERFORMANCE

fund inception date: 4/30/91

	3yr Annual	5yr Annual	10yr Annual	Bull	Bear
Return (%)	4.2	7.2	na	20.1	-6.7
Differ from Category (+/-)	0.0 av	0.8 abv av	na	1.7 abv av	-1.3 blw av

Total Risk	Standard Deviation	Category Risk	Risk Index	Avg Mat
blw av	5.6%	av	1.0	18.5 yrs

	1996	1995	1994	1993	1992	1991	1990	1989	1988	1987
Return (%)	3.2	16.9	-6.1	13.9	9.6	—	—	—	—	—
Differ from Category (+/-)	-0.5	1.7	-0.8	2.1	1.3	—	—	—	—	—
Return, Tax-Adjusted (%)	3.2	16.9	-6.2	13.5	9.4	—	—	—	—	—

PER SHARE DATA

	1996	1995	1994	1993	1992	1991	1990	1989	1988	1987
Dividends, Net Income ($)	0.56	0.58	0.56	0.55	0.58	—	—	—	—	—
Distrib'ns, Cap Gain ($)	0.00	0.00	0.01	0.14	0.07	—	—	—	—	—
Net Asset Value ($)	11.08	11.30	10.19	11.45	10.69	—	—	—	—	—
Expense Ratio (%)	0.65	0.65	0.65	0.65	0.65	—	—	—	—	—
Yield (%)	5.05	5.13	5.49	4.74	5.39	—	—	—	—	—
Portfolio Turnover (%)	98	139	68	103	152	—	—	—	—	—
Total Assets (Millions $)	78	70	53	61	31	—	—	—	—	—

PORTFOLIO (as of 9/30/96)

Portfolio Manager: W.T. Reynolds, W.F. Snider - 1991

Investm't Category: Tax-Exempt Bond
- ✔ Domestic
- Foreign
- Asset Allocation
- Index
- Sector
- ✔ State Specific

Investment Style
Large-Cap Growth	Large-Cap Value
Mid-Cap Growth	Mid-Cap Value
Small-Cap Growth	Small-Cap Value

Portfolio
4.0% cash	0.0% corp bonds
0.0% stocks	0.0% gov't bonds
0.0% preferred	96.0% muni bonds
0.0% conv't/warrants	0.0% other

SHAREHOLDER INFORMATION

Minimum Investment
Initial: $2,500   Subsequent: $100

Minimum IRA Investment
Initial: na   Subsequent: na

Maximum Fees
Load: none   12b-1: none
Other: f

Distributions
Income: monthly   Capital Gains: Dec

Exchange Options
Number Per Year: 6   Fee: none
Telephone: yes (money market fund available)

Services
auto exchange, auto invest, auto withdraw

T. Rowe Price NY Tax-Free Bond (PRNYX)

Tax-Exempt Bond

Public Relations Department
100 E. Pratt St.
Baltimore, MD 21202
800-225-5132, 410-547-2000
www.troweprice.com

PERFORMANCE

fund inception date: 8/28/86

	3yr Annual	5yr Annual	10yr Annual	Bull	Bear
Return (%)	4.6	7.4	7.0	20.5	-6.2
Differ from Category (+/-)	0.4 abv av	1.0 high	0.3 av	2.1 abv av	-0.8 blw av

Total Risk	Standard Deviation	Category Risk	Risk Index	Avg Mat
blw av	5.6%	av	1.0	18.3 yrs

	1996	1995	1994	1993	1992	1991	1990	1989	1988	1987
Return (%)	3.7	17.2	-5.9	13.3	10.3	12.4	5.2	8.0	10.4	-2.5
Differ from Category (+/-)	0.0	2.0	-0.6	1.5	2.0	1.0	-1.2	-1.0	0.4	-1.1
Return, Tax-Adjusted (%)	3.7	17.2	-6.1	12.8	10.3	12.4	5.2	8.0	10.4	-2.5

PER SHARE DATA

	1996	1995	1994	1993	1992	1991	1990	1989	1988	1987
Dividends, Net Income ($)	0.57	0.57	0.58	0.59	0.62	0.62	0.62	0.62	0.60	0.60
Distrib'ns, Cap Gain ($)	0.00	0.00	0.08	0.16	0.00	0.00	0.00	0.00	0.00	0.00
Net Asset Value ($)	10.81	10.99	9.90	11.21	10.59	10.19	9.65	9.78	9.65	9.31
Expense Ratio (%)	0.65	0.60	0.60	0.60	0.60	0.73	0.96	1.00	1.00	0.85
Yield (%)	5.27	5.18	5.81	5.18	5.85	6.08	6.42	6.33	6.21	6.44
Portfolio Turnover (%)	116	134	84	41	49	62	72	89	147	126
Total Assets (Millions $)	142	134	110	135	100	72	53	47	35	25

PORTFOLIO (as of 9/30/96)

Portfolio Manager: Reynolds, Snider - 1986

Investm't Category: Tax-Exempt Bond

✔ Domestic	Index
Foreign	Sector
Asset Allocation	✔ State Specific

Investment Style

Large-Cap Growth	Large-Cap Value
Mid-Cap Growth	Mid-Cap Value
Small-Cap Growth	Small-Cap Value

Portfolio

4.7% cash	0.0% corp bonds
0.0% stocks	0.0% gov't bonds
0.0% preferred	95.4% muni bonds
0.0% conv't/warrants	0.0% other

SHAREHOLDER INFORMATION

Minimum Investment
Initial: $2,500   Subsequent: $100

Minimum IRA Investment
Initial: na   Subsequent: na

Maximum Fees
Load: none   12b-1: none
Other: *f*

Distributions
Income: monthly   Capital Gains: Dec

Exchange Options
Number Per Year: 6   Fee: none
Telephone: yes (money market fund available)

Services
auto exchange, auto invest, auto withdraw

T. Rowe Price New America Growth (PRWAX)

Growth

Public Relations Department
100 E. Pratt St.
Baltimore, MD 21202
800-225-5132, 410-547-2000
www.troweprice.com

fund inception date: 9/30/85

	3yr Annual	5yr Annual	10yr Annual	Bull	Bear
Return (%)	17.0	15.6	15.8	78.0	-10.6
Differ from Category (+/-)	1.3 abv av	1.3 abv av	1.9 high	15.6 high	-3.9 low

Total Risk	Standard Deviation	Category Risk	Risk Index	Beta
high	12.7%	high	1.2	0.98

	1996	1995	1994	1993	1992	1991	1990	1989	1988	1987
Return (%).	20.0	44.3	-7.5	17.4	9.8	61.9	-12.3	38.4	18.4	-9.4
Differ from Category (+/-).	-0.1	14.0	-7.2	3.4	-2.0	25.9	-6.2	12.3	0.3	-11.4
Return, Tax-Adjusted (%). .	17.2	42.3	-8.1	16.1	9.5	60.2	-12.7	37.8	18.4	-12.6

PER SHARE DATA

	1996	1995	1994	1993	1992	1991	1990	1989	1988	1987
Dividends, Net Income ($)	0.00	0.00	0.00	0.00	0.00	0.00	0.17	0.00	0.00	0.06
Distrib'ns, Cap Gain ($) . . .	3.49	1.75	0.53	1.12	0.18	0.87	0.00	0.23	0.00	1.39
Net Asset Value ($)	38.37	34.91	25.42	28.04	24.86	22.79	14.66	16.90	12.38	10.45
Expense Ratio (%).	na	1.07	1.14	1.23	1.25	1.25	1.25	1.50	1.50	1.23
Yield (%)	0.00	0.00	0.00	0.00	0.00	0.00	1.15	0.00	0.00	0.50
Portfolio Turnover (%). . . .	na	56	31	43	26	42	42	40	45	72
Total Assets (Millions $). .	1,464	1,028	646	619	480	231	95	134	66	62

PORTFOLIO (as of 9/30/96)

Portfolio Manager: John LaPorte - 1985

Investm't Category: Growth

✔ Domestic	Index
Foreign	Sector
Asset Allocation	State Specific

Investment Style

Large-Cap Growth	Large-Cap Value
✔ Mid-Cap Growth	Mid-Cap Value
Small-Cap Growth	Small-Cap Value

Portfolio

3.5% cash	0.0% corp bonds
96.5% stocks	0.0% gov't bonds
0.0% preferred	0.0% muni bonds
0.0% conv't/warrants	0.0% other

SHAREHOLDER INFORMATION

Minimum Investment

Initial: $2,500   Subsequent: $100

Minimum IRA Investment

Initial: $1,000   Subsequent: $50

Maximum Fees

Load: none   12b-1: none

Other: *f*

Distributions

Income: annual   Capital Gains: Dec

Exchange Options

Number Per Year: 6   Fee: none

Telephone: yes (money market fund available)

Services

IRA, pension, auto exchange, auto invest, auto withdraw

750   *Guide to Low-Load Mutual Funds*

T. Rowe Price New Era

(PRNEX)

Growth

Public Relations Department
100 E. Pratt St.
Baltimore, MD 21202
800-225-5132, 410-547-2000
www.troweprice.com

PERFORMANCE

fund inception date: 5/28/69

	3yr Annual	5yr Annual	10yr Annual	Bull	Bear
Return (%)	16.4	13.1	12.1	56.9	-3.3
Differ from Category (+/-)	0.7 av	-1.2 blw av	-1.8 low	-5.5 blw av	3.4 high

Total Risk	Standard Deviation	Category Risk	Risk Index	Beta
av	9.4%	blw av	0.9	0.69

	1996	1995	1994	1993	1992	1991	1990	1989	1988	1987
Return (%).............	24.2	20.7	5.1	15.3	2.0	14.7	-8.8	24.2	10.3	17.8
Differ from Category (+/-).	.4.1	-9.6	5.4	1.3	-9.8	-21.3	-2.7	-1.9	-7.8	15.8
Return, Tax-Adjusted (%)..	21.4	18.0	3.1	12.9	-0.3	12.4	-10.9	21.4	8.1	12.8

PER SHARE DATA

	1996	1995	1994	1993	1992	1991	1990	1989	1988	1987
Dividends, Net Income ($).	0.38	0.48	0.38	0.38	0.45	0.55	0.62	0.56	0.53	0.98
Distrib'ns, Cap Gain ($)...	1.71	1.20	0.87	1.03	0.94	0.73	0.71	1.05	0.61	1.77
Net Asset Value ($).....	26.06	22.65	20.15	20.35	18.88	19.86	18.48	21.73	18.79	18.08
Expense Ratio (%).........	na	0.79	0.80	0.80	0.81	0.85	0.83	0.83	0.89	0.82
Yield (%)...............	1.36	2.01	1.80	1.77	2.27	2.67	3.23	2.45	2.73	4.93
Portfolio Turnover (%).....	na	22	24	24	17	9	9	19	16	30
Total Assets (Millions $).	1,466	1,090	979	752	699	756	707	826	727	756

PORTFOLIO (as of 9/30/96)

Portfolio Manager: George A. Roche - 1979

Investm't Category: Growth
- ✔ Domestic
- ✔ Foreign
- Asset Allocation
- Index
- ✔ Sector
- State Specific

Investment Style
- Large-Cap Growth
- Mid-Cap Growth
- Small-Cap Growth
- ✔ Large-Cap Value
- Mid-Cap Value
- Small-Cap Value

Portfolio
7.7% cash	0.0% corp bonds
91.9% stocks	0.0% gov't bonds
0.4% preferred	0.0% muni bonds
0.0% conv't/warrants	0.0% other

SHAREHOLDER INFORMATION

Minimum Investment
Initial: $2,500   Subsequent: $100

Minimum IRA Investment
Initial: $1,000   Subsequent: $50

Maximum Fees
Load: none   12b-1: none
Other: *f*

Distributions
Income: annual   Capital Gains: Dec

Exchange Options
Number Per Year: 6   Fee: none
Telephone: yes (money market fund available)

Services
IRA, pension, auto exchange, auto invest, auto withdraw

T. Rowe Price New Horizons (PRNHX)

Aggressive Growth

Public Relations Department
100 E. Pratt St.
Baltimore, MD 21202
800-225-5132, 410-547-2000
www.troweprice.com

this fund is closed to new investors

PERFORMANCE

fund inception date: 1/2/61

	3yr Annual	5yr Annual	10yr Annual	Bull	Bear
Return (%)	22.1	19.7	16.2	102.2	-12.0
Differ from Category (+/-)	6.3 high	4.4 high	1.2 abv av	31.1 high	-1.4 blw av

Total Risk	Standard Deviation	Category Risk	Risk Index	Beta
high	14.5%	av	1.0	0.98

	1996	1995	1994	1993	1992	1991	1990	1989	1988	1987
Return (%).............	17.0	55.4	0.3	22.0	10.5	52.3	-9.7	26.1	14.0	-7.3
Differ from Category (+/-).	-2.1	21.1	0.3	2.7	-1.2	0.2	-4.3	-2.3	-2.4	-4.9
Return, Tax-Adjusted (%)..	14.0	50.8	-2.2	17.1	7.3	51.0	-11.2	23.2	13.6	-11.9

PER SHARE DATA

	1996	1995	1994	1993	1992	1991	1990	1989	1988	1987
Dividends, Net Income ($)	0.00	0.00	0.00	0.00	0.00	0.05	0.09	0.07	0.07	0.06
Distrib'ns, Cap Gain ($) ...	2.19	2.41	1.43	2.70	1.76	0.39	0.53	1.01	0.03	1.93
Net Asset Value ($)	21.77	20.50	14.76	16.16	15.53	15.68	10.61	12.43	10.74	9.51
Expense Ratio (%).........	na	0.90	0.93	0.93	0.93	0.92	0.82	0.79	0.84	0.78
Yield (%)	0.00	0.00	0.00	0.00	0.00	0.31	0.80	0.52	0.64	0.52
Portfolio Turnover (%).....	na	55	44	49	50	33	38	45	43	50
Total Assets (Millions $)..	4,393	2,854	1,648	1,627	1,547	1,470	855	1,043	915	855

PORTFOLIO (as of 9/30/96)

Portfolio Manager: John LaPorte - 1987

Investm't Category: Aggressive Growth
- ✔ Domestic
- ✔ Foreign
- Asset Allocation
- Index
- Sector
- State Specific

Investment Style
- Large-Cap Growth
- ✔ Mid-Cap Growth
- ✔ Small-Cap Growth
- Large-Cap Value
- Mid-Cap Value
- Small-Cap Value

Portfolio
6.5% cash	0.0% corp bonds
93.5% stocks	0.0% gov't bonds
0.0% preferred	0.0% muni bonds
0.0% conv't/warrants	0.0% other

SHAREHOLDER INFORMATION

Minimum Investment
Initial: $2,500   Subsequent: $100

Minimum IRA Investment
Initial: $1,000   Subsequent: $50

Maximum Fees
Load: none   12b-1: none
Other: *f*

Distributions
Income: annual   Capital Gains: Dec

Exchange Options
Number Per Year: 6   Fee: none
Telephone: yes (money market fund available)

Services
IRA, pension, auto exchange, auto invest, auto withdraw

T. Rowe Price New Income (PRCIX)

General Bond

Public Relations Department
100 E. Pratt St.
Baltimore, MD 21202
800-225-5132, 410-547-2000
www.troweprice.com

PERFORMANCE

fund inception date: 10/15/73

	3yr Annual	5yr Annual	10yr Annual	Bull	Bear
Return (%)	5.8	6.3	7.7	22.5	-4.4
Differ from Category (+/-)	0.7 abv av	0.2 av	0.4 av	2.2 abv av	-0.2 av

Total Risk	Standard Deviation	Category Risk	Risk Index	Avg Mat
low	4.5%	abv av	1.2	9.3 yrs

	1996	1995	1994	1993	1992	1991	1990	1989	1988	1987
Return (%)	2.3	18.3	-2.3	9.5	4.9	15.5	8.7	12.2	7.5	2.0
Differ from Category (+/-)	-1.6	3.4	0.0	0.4	-1.6	0.8	1.4	0.5	-0.1	-0.3
Return, Tax-Adjusted (%)	-0.3	15.4	-5.0	6.9	2.3	12.3	5.4	8.6	3.7	-1.3

PER SHARE DATA

	1996	1995	1994	1993	1992	1991	1990	1989	1988	1987
Dividends, Net Income ($)	0.59	0.60	0.57	0.53	0.59	0.67	0.70	0.76	0.80	0.74
Distrib'ns, Cap Gain ($)	0.00	0.00	0.07	0.07	0.00	0.01	0.00	0.00	0.00	0.00
Net Asset Value ($)	8.89	9.28	8.39	9.24	9.00	9.16	8.58	8.59	8.37	8.55
Expense Ratio (%)	0.75	0.78	0.82	0.84	0.87	0.88	0.86	0.91	0.80	0.65
Yield (%)	6.63	6.46	6.73	5.69	6.55	7.30	8.15	8.84	9.55	8.65
Portfolio Turnover (%)	35	54	58	86	50	21	51	92	158	125
Total Assets (Millions $)	1,710	1,668	1,367	1,562	1,461	1,400	1,092	1,043	845	789

PORTFOLIO (as of 9/30/96)

Portfolio Manager: Charles P. Smith - 1986

Investm't Category: General Bond
- ✔ Domestic
- ✔ Foreign
- Asset Allocation
- Index
- Sector
- State Specific

Investment Style
- Large-Cap Growth
- Mid-Cap Growth
- Small-Cap Growth
- Large-Cap Value
- Mid-Cap Value
- Small-Cap Value

Portfolio
- 1.5% cash
- 0.0% stocks
- 0.0% preferred
- 0.0% conv't/warrants
- 20.7% corp bonds
- 75.8% gov't bonds
- 0.0% muni bonds
- 2.0% other

SHAREHOLDER INFORMATION

Minimum Investment
Initial: $2,500   Subsequent: $100

Minimum IRA Investment
Initial: $1,000   Subsequent: $50

Maximum Fees
Load: none   12b-1: none
Other: *f*

Distributions
Income: monthly   Capital Gains: Dec

Exchange Options
Number Per Year: 6   Fee: none
Telephone: yes (money market fund available)

Services
IRA, pension, auto exchange, auto invest, auto withdraw

T. Rowe Price OTC

(OTCFX)

Aggressive Growth

Public Relations Department
100 E. Pratt St.
Baltimore, MD 21202
800-225-5132, 410-547-2000
www.troweprice.com

PERFORMANCE

fund inception date: 6/1/56

	3yr Annual	5yr Annual	10yr Annual	Bull	Bear
Return (%)	17.4	16.9	12.3	68.8	-5.4
Differ from Category (+/-)	1.6 abv av	1.6 abv av	-2.7 blw av	-2.3 av	5.2 high

Total Risk	Standard Deviation	Category Risk	Risk Index	Beta
abv av	10.0%	low	0.7	0.60

	1996	1995	1994	1993	1992	1991	1990	1989	1988	1987
Return (%)	21.0	33.8	0.0	18.4	13.9	38.6	-20.5	19.1	27.1	-12.6
Differ from Category (+/-)	1.9	-0.5	0.0	-0.9	2.2	-13.5	-15.1	-9.3	10.7	-10.2
Return, Tax-Adjusted (%)	18.0	29.3	-3.0	15.3	6.0	36.8	-20.9	17.8	21.4	-15.9

PER SHARE DATA

	1996	1995	1994	1993	1992	1991	1990	1989	1988	1987
Dividends, Net Income ($)	0.09	0.12	0.03	0.00	0.07	0.09	0.08	0.12	0.13	0.32
Distrib'ns, Cap Gain ($)	1.58	2.00	1.56	1.58	4.63	0.68	0.10	0.48	2.50	1.51
Net Asset Value ($)	18.07	16.32	13.80	15.39	14.37	16.86	12.72	16.23	14.14	13.19
Expense Ratio (%)	na	1.11	1.11	1.20	1.32	1.34	1.47	1.45	1.55	1.00
Yield (%)	0.45	0.65	0.19	0.00	0.36	0.51	0.62	0.71	0.78	2.17
Portfolio Turnover (%)	na	57	41	40	31	31	35	33	27	49
Total Assets (Millions $)	401	278	196	204	186	268	215	316	292	210

PORTFOLIO (as of 9/30/96)

Portfolio Manager: Gregory A. McCrickard - 1992

Investm't Category: Aggressive Growth
✔ Domestic	Index
✔ Foreign	Sector
Asset Allocation	State Specific

Investment Style
Large-Cap Growth	Large-Cap Value
Mid-Cap Growth	Mid-Cap Value
✔ Small-Cap Growth	✔ Small-Cap Value

Portfolio
10.7% cash	0.0% corp bonds
88.4% stocks	0.0% gov't bonds
0.2% preferred	0.0% muni bonds
0.7% conv't/warrants	0.0% other

SHAREHOLDER INFORMATION

Minimum Investment
Initial: $2,500   Subsequent: $100

Minimum IRA Investment
Initial: $1,000   Subsequent: $50

Maximum Fees
Load: none   12b-1: none
Other: *f*

Distributions
Income: annual   Capital Gains: Dec

Exchange Options
Number Per Year: 3   Fee: none
Telephone: yes (money market fund available)

Services
IRA, pension, auto exchange, auto invest, auto withdraw

T. Rowe Price Personal Strat Fds: Bal (TRPBX)

Balanced

Public Relations Department
100 E. Pratt St.
Baltimore, MD 21202
800-638-5660, 410-547-2308
www.troweprice.com

PERFORMANCE

fund inception date: 7/29/94

	3yr Annual	5yr Annual	10yr Annual	Bull	Bear
Return (%)	na	na	na	na	na
Differ from Category (+/-)	na	na	na	na	na

Total Risk	Standard Deviation	Category Risk	Risk Index	Beta
na	na	na	na	na

	1996	1995	1994	1993	1992	1991	1990	1989	1988	1987
Return (%)	14.2	28.1	—	—	—	—	—	—	—	—
Differ from Category (+/-)	0.0	3.5	—	—	—	—	—	—	—	—
Return, Tax-Adjusted (%)	12.2	26.3	—	—	—	—	—	—	—	—

PER SHARE DATA

	1996	1995	1994	1993	1992	1991	1990	1989	1988	1987
Dividends, Net Income ($)	0.39	0.38	—	—	—	—	—	—	—	—
Distrib'ns, Cap Gain ($)	0.32	0.07	—	—	—	—	—	—	—	—
Net Asset Value ($)	13.29	12.29	—	—	—	—	—	—	—	—
Expense Ratio (%)	na	1.05	—	—	—	—	—	—	—	—
Yield (%)	2.86	3.07	—	—	—	—	—	—	—	—
Portfolio Turnover (%)	na	25	—	—	—	—	—	—	—	—
Total Assets (Millions $)	167	18	—	—	—	—	—	—	—	—

PORTFOLIO (as of 9/30/96)

Portfolio Manager: Peter Van Dyke - 1994

Investm't Category: Balanced

✔ Domestic	Index
✔ Foreign	Sector
✔ Asset Allocation	State Specific

Investment Style

Large-Cap Growth	Large-Cap Value
Mid-Cap Growth	Mid-Cap Value
Small-Cap Growth	Small-Cap Value

Portfolio

3.8% cash	17.3% corp bonds
60.0% stocks	15.3% gov't bonds
0.0% preferred	0.0% muni bonds
0.0% conv't/warrants	3.6% other

SHAREHOLDER INFORMATION

Minimum Investment

Initial: $2,500   Subsequent: $100

Minimum IRA Investment

Initial: $1,000   Subsequent: $50

Maximum Fees

Load: none   12b-1: none

Other: f

Distributions

Income: quarterly   Capital Gains: Dec

Exchange Options

Number Per Year: 6   Fee: none

Telephone: yes (money market fund available)

Services

IRA, pension, auto exchange, auto invest, auto withdraw

T. Rowe Price Personal Strat Fds: Inc (PRSIX)

Balanced

Public Relations Department
100 E. Pratt St.
Baltimore, MD 21202
800-638-5660, 410-547-2308
www.troweprice.com

PERFORMANCE   fund inception date: 7/29/94

	3yr Annual	5yr Annual	10yr Annual	Bull	Bear
Return (%)	na	na	na	na	na
Differ from Category (+/-)	na	na	na	na	na

Total Risk	Standard Deviation	Category Risk	Risk Index	Beta
na	na	na	na	na

	1996	1995	1994	1993	1992	1991	1990	1989	1988	1987
Return (%)	11.7	24.7	—	—	—	—	—	—	—	—
Differ from Category (+/-)	-2.5	0.1	—	—	—	—	—	—	—	—
Return, Tax-Adjusted (%)	7.7	22.4	—	—	—	—	—	—	—	—

PER SHARE DATA

	1996	1995	1994	1993	1992	1991	1990	1989	1988	1987
Dividends, Net Income ($)	0.47	0.48	—	—	—	—	—	—	—	—
Distrib'ns, Cap Gain ($)	0.98	0.10	—	—	—	—	—	—	—	—
Net Asset Value ($)	11.56	11.70	—	—	—	—	—	—	—	—
Expense Ratio (%)	na	0.95	—	—	—	—	—	—	—	—
Yield (%)	3.74	4.06	—	—	—	—	—	—	—	—
Portfolio Turnover (%)	na	50	—	—	—	—	—	—	—	—
Total Assets (Millions $)	33	25	—	—	—	—	—	—	—	—

PORTFOLIO (as of 9/30/96)

Portfolio Manager: Peter Van Dyke - 1994

Investm't Category: Balanced

✔ Domestic	Index
✔ Foreign	Sector
✔ Asset Allocation	State Specific

Investment Style

Large-Cap Growth	Large-Cap Value
Mid-Cap Growth	Mid-Cap Value
Small-Cap Growth	Small-Cap Value

Portfolio

11.7%	cash	23.0%	corp bonds
40.2%	stocks	20.1%	gov't bonds
0.0%	preferred	0.0%	muni bonds
0.0%	conv't/warrants	5.0%	other

SHAREHOLDER INFORMATION

Minimum Investment
Initial: $2,500   Subsequent: $100

Minimum IRA Investment
Initial: $1,000   Subsequent: $50

Maximum Fees
Load: none   12b-1: none
Other: *f*

Distributions
Income: quarterly   Capital Gains: Dec

Exchange Options
Number Per Year: 6   Fee: none
Telephone: yes (money market fund available)

Services
IRA, pension, auto exchange, auto invest, auto withdraw

756   *Guide to Low-Load Mutual Funds*

T. Rowe Price Science & Technology (PRSCX)

Aggressive Growth

Public Relations Department
100 E. Pratt St.
Baltimore, MD 21202
800-225-5132, 410-547-2000
www.troweprice.com

PERFORMANCE

fund inception date: 9/30/87

	3yr Annual	5yr Annual	10yr Annual	Bull	Bear
Return (%)	27.1	24.8	na	127.4	-12.6
Differ from Category (+/-)	11.3 high	9.5 high	na	56.3 high	-2.0 blw av

Total Risk	Standard Deviation	Category Risk	Risk Index	Beta
high	17.8%	abv av	1.3	1.07

	1996	1995	1994	1993	1992	1991	1990	1989	1988	1987
Return (%)	14.2	55.5	15.7	24.2	18.7	60.1	-1.4	40.6	13.2	—
Differ from Category (+/-)	-4.9	21.2	15.7	4.9	7.0	8.0	4.0	12.2	-3.2	—
Return, Tax-Adjusted (%)	10.7	49.6	15.2	20.1	16.6	58.7	-2.4	35.7	11.3	—

PER SHARE DATA

	1996	1995	1994	1993	1992	1991	1990	1989	1988	1987
Dividends, Net Income ($)	0.00	0.00	0.00	0.00	0.00	0.00	0.09	0.06	0.07	—
Distrib'ns, Cap Gain ($)	3.60	4.54	0.30	2.50	1.12	0.48	0.24	1.39	0.44	—
Net Asset Value ($)	29.71	29.12	21.64	18.95	17.33	15.57	10.05	10.53	8.57	—
Expense Ratio (%)	na	1.01	1.11	1.25	1.25	1.25	1.25	1.20	1.20	—
Yield (%)	0.00	0.00	0.00	0.00	0.00	0.00	0.87	0.50	0.77	—
Portfolio Turnover (%)	na	130	113	163	144	148	183	203	92	—
Total Assets (Millions $)	3,438	2,285	915	501	281	166	61	23	12	—

PORTFOLIO (as of 9/30/96)

Portfolio Manager: Charles Morris - 1991

Investm't Category: Aggressive Growth
- ✔ Domestic
- ✔ Foreign
- Asset Allocation
- Index
- ✔ Sector
- State Specific

Investment Style
- Large-Cap Growth
- ✔ Mid-Cap Growth
- ✔ Small-Cap Growth
- Large-Cap Value
- Mid-Cap Value
- Small-Cap Value

Portfolio
21.3% cash	0.0% corp bonds
78.7% stocks	0.0% gov't bonds
0.0% preferred	0.0% muni bonds
0.0% conv't/warrants	0.0% other

SHAREHOLDER INFORMATION

Minimum Investment
Initial: $2,500   Subsequent: $100

Minimum IRA Investment
Initial: $1,000   Subsequent: $50

Maximum Fees
Load: none   12b-1: none
Other: f

Distributions
Income: annual   Capital Gains: Dec

Exchange Options
Number Per Year: 6   Fee: none
Telephone: yes (money market fund available)

Services
IRA, pension, auto exchange, auto invest, auto withdraw

T. Rowe Price Short-Term Bond (PRWBX)

General Bond

Public Relations Department
100 E. Pratt St.
Baltimore, MD 21202
800-225-5132, 410-547-2000
www.troweprice.com

PERFORMANCE

	3yr Annual	5yr Annual	10yr Annual	Bull	Bear
Return (%)	3.4	4.3	6.2	12.5	-2.6
Differ from Category (+/-)	-1.7 low	-1.8 low	-1.1 low	-7.8 low	1.6 abv av

Total Risk	Standard Deviation	Category Risk	Risk Index	Avg Mat
low	2.2%	blw av	0.6	2.3 yrs

	1996	1995	1994	1993	1992	1991	1990	1989	1988	1987
Return (%)	3.9	9.7	-3.0	6.6	5.0	11.2	8.6	9.9	5.5	5.2
Differ from Category (+/-)	0.0	-5.2	-0.7	-2.5	-1.5	-3.5	1.3	-1.8	-2.1	2.9
Return, Tax-Adjusted (%)	1.6	7.2	-5.2	4.1	2.4	8.4	5.3	6.6	2.3	2.3

PER SHARE DATA

	1996	1995	1994	1993	1992	1991	1990	1989	1988	1987
Dividends, Net Income ($)	0.27	0.29	0.27	0.31	0.33	0.35	0.39	0.41	0.40	0.38
Distrib'ns, Cap Gain ($)	0.00	0.00	0.00	0.00	0.00	0.00	0.03	0.00	0.00	0.00
Net Asset Value ($)	4.67	4.77	4.63	5.05	5.04	5.13	4.95	4.97	4.92	5.06
Expense Ratio (%)	0.72	0.79	0.74	0.76	0.88	0.93	0.95	0.94	0.91	0.94
Yield (%)	5.78	6.07	5.83	6.13	6.54	6.82	7.83	8.24	8.13	7.50
Portfolio Turnover (%)	118	136	90	68	381	980	161	309	203	7
Total Assets (Millions $)	455	464	474	681	543	401	215	216	262	234

PORTFOLIO (as of 9/30/96)

Portfolio Manager: Edward A. Weise - 1995

Investm't Category: General Bond
✔ Domestic   Index
✔ Foreign   Sector
   Asset Allocation   State Specific

Investment Style
Large-Cap Growth   Large-Cap Value
Mid-Cap Growth   Mid-Cap Value
Small-Cap Growth   Small-Cap Value

Portfolio
8.0% cash	38.0% corp bonds
0.0% stocks	47.0% gov't bonds
0.0% preferred	0.0% muni bonds
0.0% conv't/warrants	7.0% other

SHAREHOLDER INFORMATION

Minimum Investment
Initial: $2,500   Subsequent: $100

Minimum IRA Investment
Initial: $1,000   Subsequent: $50

Maximum Fees
Load: none   12b-1: none
Other: *f*

Distributions
Income: monthly   Capital Gains: Dec

Exchange Options
Number Per Year: 6   Fee: none
Telephone: yes (money market fund available)

Services
IRA, pension, auto exchange, auto invest, auto withdraw

T. Rowe Price Short-Term US Gov't (PRARX)

General Bond

Public Relations Department
100 E. Pratt St.
Baltimore, MD 21202
800-225-5132, 410-547-2000
www.troweprice.com

PERFORMANCE

fund inception date: 9/30/91

	3yr Annual	5yr Annual	10yr Annual	Bull	Bear
Return (%)	4.8	4.2	na	15.6	-1.1
Differ from Category (+/-)	-0.3 blw av	-1.9 low	na	-4.7 low	3.1 high

Total Risk	Standard Deviation	Category Risk	Risk Index	Avg Mat
low	2.2%	blw av	0.6	2.8 yrs

	1996	1995	1994	1993	1992	1991	1990	1989	1988	1987
Return (%)	4.2	11.1	-0.7	2.7	3.9	—	—	—	—	—
Differ from Category (+/-)	0.3	-3.8	1.6	-6.4	-2.6	—	—	—	—	—
Return, Tax-Adjusted (%)	1.9	8.7	-2.7	0.8	1.3	—	—	—	—	—

PER SHARE DATA

	1996	1995	1994	1993	1992	1991	1990	1989	1988	1987
Dividends, Net Income ($)	0.27	0.27	0.23	0.23	0.32	—	—	—	—	—
Distrib'ns, Cap Gain ($)	0.00	0.00	0.00	0.00	0.00	—	—	—	—	—
Net Asset Value ($)	4.64	4.72	4.51	4.77	4.87	—	—	—	—	—
Expense Ratio (%)	0.70	0.59	0.40	0.25	0.00	—	—	—	—	—
Yield (%)	5.81	5.72	5.09	4.82	6.57	—	—	—	—	—
Portfolio Turnover (%)	152	100	70	110	98	—	—	—	—	—
Total Assets (Millions $)	97	105	120	250	558	—	—	—	—	—

PORTFOLIO (as of 9/30/96)

Portfolio Manager: Peter Van Dyke - 1993

Investm't Category: General Bond
- ✔ Domestic
- Foreign
- Asset Allocation
- Index
- Sector
- State Specific

Investment Style
- Large-Cap Growth
- Mid-Cap Growth
- Small-Cap Growth
- Large-Cap Value
- Mid-Cap Value
- Small-Cap Value

Portfolio

15.1% cash	17.4% corp bonds
0.0% stocks	67.5% gov't bonds
0.0% preferred	0.0% muni bonds
0.0% conv't/warrants	0.0% other

SHAREHOLDER INFORMATION

Minimum Investment
Initial: $2,500   Subsequent: $100

Minimum IRA Investment
Initial: $1,000   Subsequent: $50

Maximum Fees
Load: none   12b-1: none
Other: f

Distributions
Income: monthly   Capital Gains: Dec

Exchange Options
Number Per Year: 6   Fee: none
Telephone: yes (money market fund available)

Services
IRA, pension, auto exchange, auto invest, auto withdraw

T. Rowe Price Small Cap Value (PRSVX)

Growth

Public Relations Department
100 E. Pratt St.
Baltimore, MD 21202
800-225-5132, 410-547-2000
www.troweprice.com

this fund is closed to new investors

PERFORMANCE

fund inception date: 6/30/88

	3yr Annual	5yr Annual	10yr Annual	Bull	Bear
Return (%)	16.6	18.8	na	62.1	-3.7
Differ from Category (+/-)	0.9 av	4.5 high	na	-0.3 av	3.0 abv av

Total Risk	Standard Deviation	Category Risk	Risk Index	Beta
av	7.9%	low	0.8	0.48

	1996	1995	1994	1993	1992	1991	1990	1989	1988	1987
Return (%)	24.6	29.2	-1.4	23.3	20.8	34.1	-11.3	18.0	—	—
Differ from Category (+/-)	4.5	-1.1	-1.1	9.3	9.0	-1.9	-5.2	-8.1	—	—
Return, Tax-Adjusted (%)	22.6	27.3	-3.6	22.1	20.0	32.3	-12.7	14.5	—	—

PER SHARE DATA

	1996	1995	1994	1993	1992	1991	1990	1989	1988	1987
Dividends, Net Income ($)	0.23	0.18	0.14	0.10	0.10	0.12	0.24	0.14	—	—
Distrib'ns, Cap Gain ($)	0.80	0.61	0.92	0.35	0.15	0.34	0.12	0.90	—	—
Net Asset Value ($)	19.56	16.53	13.40	14.68	12.28	10.37	8.09	9.53	—	—
Expense Ratio (%)	na	0.98	0.97	1.05	1.25	1.25	1.25	1.25	—	—
Yield (%)	1.12	1.05	0.97	0.66	0.80	1.12	2.92	1.34	—	—
Portfolio Turnover (%)	na	18	21	11	12	31	33	43	—	—
Total Assets (Millions $)	1,352	936	408	452	264	53	26	32	—	—

PORTFOLIO (as of 9/30/96)

Portfolio Manager: Preston G. Athey - 1988

Investm't Category: Growth
- ✔ Domestic
- ✔ Foreign
-   Asset Allocation
-   Index
-   Sector
-   State Specific

Investment Style
Large-Cap Growth	Large-Cap Value
Mid-Cap Growth	Mid-Cap Value
Small-Cap Growth	✔ Small-Cap Value

Portfolio
12.9% cash	0.0% corp bonds
83.9% stocks	0.0% gov't bonds
1.8% preferred	0.0% muni bonds
1.4% conv't/warrants	0.0% other

SHAREHOLDER INFORMATION

Minimum Investment
Initial: $2,500   Subsequent: $100

Minimum IRA Investment
Initial: $1,000   Subsequent: $50

Maximum Fees
Load: 1.00% redemption   12b-1: none
Other: redemption fee applies for 1 year; *f*

Distributions
Income: annual   Capital Gains: Dec

Exchange Options
Number Per Year: 6   Fee: none
Telephone: yes (money market fund available)

Services
IRA, pension, auto exchange, auto invest, auto withdraw

T. Rowe Price Spectrum: Growth (PRSGX)

Growth & Income

Public Relations Department
100 E. Pratt St.
Baltimore, MD 21202
800-225-5132, 410-547-2000
www.troweprice.com

PERFORMANCE

fund inception date: 6/29/90

	3yr Annual	5yr Annual	10yr Annual	Bull	Bear
Return (%)	16.6	15.5	na	64.6	-6.9
Differ from Category (+/-)	1.3 av	1.6 abv av	na	4.8 av	-0.5 av

Total Risk	Standard Deviation	Category Risk	Risk Index	Beta
av	8.7%	blw av	0.9	0.81

	1996	1995	1994	1993	1992	1991	1990	1989	1988	1987
Return (%)	20.5	29.9	1.3	20.9	7.2	29.8	—	—	—	—
Differ from Category (+/-)	0.8	-0.2	2.6	7.1	-3.5	0.7	—	—	—	—
Return, Tax-Adjusted (%)	17.9	27.2	-1.0	18.3	4.9	27.7	—	—	—	—

PER SHARE DATA

	1996	1995	1994	1993	1992	1991	1990	1989	1988	1987
Dividends, Net Income ($)	0.20	0.21	0.17	0.16	0.20	0.21	—	—	—	—
Distrib'ns, Cap Gain ($)	0.93	0.76	0.73	0.72	0.55	0.32	—	—	—	—
Net Asset Value ($)	15.13	13.49	11.13	11.87	10.54	10.53	—	—	—	—
Expense Ratio (%)	na	0.00	0.00	0.00	0.00	0.00	—	—	—	—
Yield (%)	1.24	1.47	1.43	1.27	1.80	1.93	—	—	—	—
Portfolio Turnover (%)	na	7	20	7	8	15	—	—	—	—
Total Assets (Millions $)	2,100	1,358	879	584	355	148	—	—	—	—

PORTFOLIO (as of 9/30/96)

Portfolio Manager: Peter Van Dyke - 1990

Investm't Category: Growth & Income
- ✔ Domestic
- ✔ Foreign
- Asset Allocation
- Index
- Sector
- State Specific

Investment Style
- Large-Cap Growth
- ✔ Mid-Cap Growth
- Small-Cap Growth
- Large-Cap Value
- Mid-Cap Value
- Small-Cap Value

Portfolio
0.0% cash	0.0% corp bonds
100.0% stocks	0.0% gov't bonds
0.0% preferred	0.0% muni bonds
0.0% conv't/warrants	0.0% other

SHAREHOLDER INFORMATION

Minimum Investment
Initial: $2,500   Subsequent: $100

Minimum IRA Investment
Initial: $1,000   Subsequent: $50

Maximum Fees
Load: none   12b-1: none
Other: f

Distributions
Income: annual   Capital Gains: Dec

Exchange Options
Number Per Year: 6   Fee: none
Telephone: yes (money market fund available)

Services
IRA, pension, auto exchange, auto invest, auto withdraw

T. Rowe Price Spectrum: Income (RPSIX)

Balanced

Public Relations Department
100 E. Pratt St.
Baltimore, MD 21202
800-225-5132, 410-547-2000
www.troweprice.com

PERFORMANCE

fund inception date: 6/29/90

	3yr Annual	5yr Annual	10yr Annual	Bull	Bear
Return (%)	8.0	8.8	na	30.5	-4.9
Differ from Category (+/-)	-3.7 low	-2.6 low	na	-14.6 low	0.8 abv av

Total Risk	Standard Deviation	Category Risk	Risk Index	Beta
low	4.1%	low	0.6	0.34

	1996	1995	1994	1993	1992	1991	1990	1989	1988	1987
Return (%)	7.6	19.4	-2.0	12.3	7.8	19.6	—	—	—	—
Differ from Category (+/-)	-6.6	-5.2	-0.4	-2.1	-1.1	-4.5	—	—	—	—
Return, Tax-Adjusted (%)	4.7	16.4	-4.7	9.2	4.7	16.1	—	—	—	—

PER SHARE DATA

	1996	1995	1994	1993	1992	1991	1990	1989	1988	1987
Dividends, Net Income ($)	0.71	0.71	0.68	0.69	0.76	0.82	—	—	—	—
Distrib'ns, Cap Gain ($)	0.15	0.06	0.10	0.19	0.08	0.06	—	—	—	—
Net Asset Value ($)	11.20	11.24	10.11	11.11	10.70	10.73	—	—	—	—
Expense Ratio (%)	na	0.00	0.00	0.00	0.00	0.00	—	—	—	—
Yield (%)	6.25	6.28	6.66	6.10	7.05	7.59	—	—	—	—
Portfolio Turnover (%)	na	20	23	14	14	19	—	—	—	—
Total Assets (Millions $)	1,353	986	624	587	376	147	—	—	—	—

PORTFOLIO (as of 9/30/96)

Portfolio Manager: Peter Van Dyke - 1990

Investm't Category: Balanced

✔ Domestic	Index
✔ Foreign	Sector
✔ Asset Allocation	State Specific

Investment Style

Large-Cap Growth	Large-Cap Value
Mid-Cap Growth	Mid-Cap Value
Small-Cap Growth	Small-Cap Value

Portfolio

9.8% cash	24.9% corp bonds
14.6% stocks	43.9% gov't bonds
0.0% preferred	0.0% muni bonds
0.2% conv't/warrants	6.5% other

SHAREHOLDER INFORMATION

Minimum Investment
Initial: $2,500   Subsequent: $100

Minimum IRA Investment
Initial: $1,000   Subsequent: $50

Maximum Fees
Load: none   12b-1: none
Other: *f*

Distributions
Income: monthly   Capital Gains: Dec

Exchange Options
Number Per Year: 6   Fee: none
Telephone: yes (money market fund available)

Services
IRA, pension, auto exchange, auto invest, auto withdraw

T. Rowe Price Summit Fds: Ltd Term Bond

(PRSBX) *General Bond*

Public Relations Department
100 E. Pratt St.
Baltimore, MD 21202
800-225-5132, 410-547-2000
www.troweprice.com

PERFORMANCE

fund inception date: 10/29/93

	3yr Annual	5yr Annual	10yr Annual	Bull	Bear
Return (%)	3.4	na	na	15.8	-4.9
Differ from Category (+/-)	-1.7 low	na	na	-4.5 low	-0.7 av

Total Risk	Standard Deviation	Category Risk	Risk Index	Avg Mat
low	2.7%	blw av	0.7	3.5 yrs

	1996	1995	1994	1993	1992	1991	1990	1989	1988	1987
Return (%)	3.9	10.1	-3.2	—	—	—	—	—	—	—
Differ from Category (+/-)	0.0	-4.8	-0.9	—	—	—	—	—	—	—
Return, Tax-Adjusted (%)	1.4	7.4	-5.8	—	—	—	—	—	—	—

PER SHARE DATA

	1996	1995	1994	1993	1992	1991	1990	1989	1988	1987
Dividends, Net Income ($)	0.29	0.31	0.33	—	—	—	—	—	—	—
Distrib'ns, Cap Gain ($)	0.00	0.00	0.00	—	—	—	—	—	—	—
Net Asset Value ($)	4.58	4.70	4.56	—	—	—	—	—	—	—
Expense Ratio (%)	na	0.55	0.55	—	—	—	—	—	—	—
Yield (%)	6.33	6.59	7.23	—	—	—	—	—	—	—
Portfolio Turnover (%)	na	84	296	—	—	—	—	—	—	—
Total Assets (Millions $)	26	27	17	—	—	—	—	—	—	—

PORTFOLIO (as of 9/30/96)

Portfolio Manager: Edward A. Wiese - 1995

Investm't Category: General Bond
- ✔ Domestic
- Foreign
- Asset Allocation
- Index
- Sector
- State Specific

Investment Style
- Large-Cap Growth
- Mid-Cap Growth
- Small-Cap Growth
- Large-Cap Value
- Mid-Cap Value
- Small-Cap Value

Portfolio
3.0% cash	45.0% corp bonds
0.0% stocks	47.0% gov't bonds
0.0% preferred	0.0% muni bonds
0.0% conv't/warrants	5.0% other

SHAREHOLDER INFORMATION

Minimum Investment
Initial: $25,000   Subsequent: $1,000

Minimum IRA Investment
Initial: $25,000   Subsequent: $100

Maximum Fees
Load: none   12b-1: none
Other: *f*

Distributions
Income: monthly   Capital Gains: Dec

Exchange Options
Number Per Year: 6   Fee: none
Telephone: yes (money market fund available)

Services
IRA, pension, auto exchange, auto invest, auto withdraw

T. Rowe Price Summit Fds: Muni Interm

(PRSMX) *Tax-Exempt Bond*

Public Relations Department
100 E. Pratt St.
Baltimore, MD 21202
800-225-5132, 410-547-2000
www.troweprice.com

PERFORMANCE

fund inception date: 10/29/93

	3yr Annual	5yr Annual	10yr Annual	Bull	Bear
Return (%)	5.3	na	na	18.8	-3.0
Differ from Category (+/-)	1.1 high	na	na	0.4 av	2.4 high

Total Risk	Standard Deviation	Category Risk	Risk Index	Avg Mat
low	3.7%	low	0.7	8.7 yrs

	1996	1995	1994	1993	1992	1991	1990	1989	1988	1987
Return (%)	4.6	13.7	-1.7	—	—	—	—	—	—	—
Differ from Category (+/-)	0.9	-1.5	3.6	—	—	—	—	—	—	—
Return, Tax-Adjusted (%)	4.6	13.7	-1.7	—	—	—	—	—	—	—

PER SHARE DATA

	1996	1995	1994	1993	1992	1991	1990	1989	1988	1987
Dividends, Net Income ($)	0.48	0.48	0.44	—	—	—	—	—	—	—
Distrib'ns, Cap Gain ($)	0.00	0.00	0.00	—	—	—	—	—	—	—
Net Asset Value ($)	10.26	10.28	9.49	—	—	—	—	—	—	—
Expense Ratio (%)	na	0.50	0.50	—	—	—	—	—	—	—
Yield (%)	4.67	4.66	4.63	—	—	—	—	—	—	—
Portfolio Turnover (%)	na	86	158	—	—	—	—	—	—	—
Total Assets (Millions $)	30	22	16	—	—	—	—	—	—	—

PORTFOLIO (as of 9/30/96)

Portfolio Manager: Charles B. Hill - 1994

Investm't Category: Tax-Exempt Bond

- ✔ Domestic
- Foreign
- Asset Allocation
- Index
- Sector
- State Specific

Investment Style

- Large-Cap Growth
- Mid-Cap Growth
- Small-Cap Growth
- Large-Cap Value
- Mid-Cap Value
- Small-Cap Value

Portfolio

4.9% cash	0.0% corp bonds
0.0% stocks	0.0% gov't bonds
0.0% preferred	95.1% muni bonds
0.0% conv't/warrants	0.0% other

SHAREHOLDER INFORMATION

Minimum Investment
Initial: $25,000   Subsequent: $1,000

Minimum IRA Investment
Initial: na   Subsequent: na

Maximum Fees
Load: none   12b-1: none
Other: *f*

Distributions
Income: monthly   Capital Gains: Dec

Exchange Options
Number Per Year: 6   Fee: none
Telephone: yes (money market fund available)

Services
auto exchange, auto invest, auto withdraw

T. Rowe Price Tax-Free High Yield (PRFHX)

Tax-Exempt Bond

Public Relations Department
100 E. Pratt St.
Baltimore, MD 21202
800-225-5132, 410-547-2000
www.troweprice.com

PERFORMANCE

fund inception date: 3/1/85

	3yr Annual	5yr Annual	10yr Annual	Bull	Bear
Return (%)	5.3	7.6	7.8	21.4	-4.8
Differ from Category (+/-)	1.1 high	1.2 high	1.1 high	3.0 high	0.6 abv av

Total Risk	Standard Deviation	Category Risk	Risk Index	Avg Mat
low	4.7%	blw av	0.9	19.0 yrs

	1996	1995	1994	1993	1992	1991	1990	1989	1988	1987
Return (%)	4.9	16.5	-4.4	12.9	9.5	11.7	7.1	10.5	11.1	0.2
Differ from Category (+/-)	1.2	1.3	0.9	1.1	1.2	0.3	0.7	1.5	1.1	1.6
Return, Tax-Adjusted (%)	4.9	16.5	-4.5	12.3	9.2	11.4	7.0	10.3	11.1	-0.4

PER SHARE DATA

	1996	1995	1994	1993	1992	1991	1990	1989	1988	1987
Dividends, Net Income ($)	0.70	0.72	0.72	0.74	0.79	0.81	0.82	0.84	0.82	0.84
Distrib'ns, Cap Gain ($)	0.00	0.00	0.04	0.23	0.10	0.10	0.03	0.06	0.00	0.25
Net Asset Value ($)	12.12	12.24	11.16	12.46	11.93	11.74	11.37	11.45	11.21	10.86
Expense Ratio (%)	0.75	0.79	0.79	0.81	0.83	0.85	0.88	0.92	0.96	0.98
Yield (%)	5.77	5.88	6.42	5.83	6.56	6.84	7.19	7.29	7.31	7.56
Portfolio Turnover (%)	39	59	59	34	51	51	72	62	128	111
Total Assets (Millions $)	1,044	982	802	957	761	622	490	431	310	249

PORTFOLIO (as of 9/30/96)

Portfolio Manager: C. Stephen Wolfe - 1994

Investm't Category: Tax-Exempt Bond

✔ Domestic	Index
Foreign	Sector
Asset Allocation	State Specific

Investment Style

Large-Cap Growth	Large-Cap Value
Mid-Cap Growth	Mid-Cap Value
Small-Cap Growth	Small-Cap Value

Portfolio

6.1% cash	0.0% corp bonds
0.0% stocks	0.0% gov't bonds
0.0% preferred	93.9% muni bonds
0.0% conv't/warrants	0.0% other

SHAREHOLDER INFORMATION

Minimum Investment

Initial: $2,500   Subsequent: $100

Minimum IRA Investment

Initial: na   Subsequent: na

Maximum Fees

Load: none   12b-1: none
Other: *f*

Distributions

Income: monthly   Capital Gains: Dec

Exchange Options

Number Per Year: 6   Fee: none
Telephone: yes (money market fund available)

Services

auto exchange, auto invest, auto withdraw

T. Rowe Price Tax-Free Income (PRTAX)

Tax-Exempt Bond

Public Relations Department
100 E. Pratt St.
Baltimore, MD 21202
800-225-5132, 410-547-2000
www.troweprice.com

PERFORMANCE

fund inception date: 10/26/76

	3yr Annual	5yr Annual	10yr Annual	Bull	Bear
Return (%)	4.7	7.2	6.6	21.0	-6.2
Differ from Category (+/-)	0.5 abv av	0.8 abv av	-0.1 blw av	2.6 abv av	-0.8 blw av

Total Risk	Standard Deviation	Category Risk	Risk Index	Avg Mat
blw av	5.7%	av	1.0	16.8 yrs

	1996	1995	1994	1993	1992	1991	1990	1989	1988	1987
Return (%)	3.2	17.6	-5.5	12.7	9.3	12.1	5.8	9.1	7.9	-4.3
Differ from Category (+/-)	-0.5	2.4	-0.2	0.9	1.0	0.7	-0.6	0.1	-2.1	-2.9
Return, Tax-Adjusted (%)	3.2	17.6	-5.7	12.1	9.3	12.1	5.8	9.1	7.9	-5.9

PER SHARE DATA

	1996	1995	1994	1993	1992	1991	1990	1989	1988	1987
Dividends, Net Income ($)	0.51	0.52	0.52	0.53	0.56	0.56	0.57	0.59	0.58	0.59
Distrib'ns, Cap Gain ($)	0.00	0.00	0.04	0.18	0.00	0.00	0.00	0.00	0.00	0.54
Net Asset Value ($)	9.59	9.80	8.80	9.90	9.44	9.17	8.71	8.79	8.62	8.55
Expense Ratio (%)	0.58	0.59	0.59	0.61	0.62	0.63	0.64	0.66	0.65	0.61
Yield (%)	5.31	5.30	5.88	5.25	5.93	6.10	6.54	6.71	6.72	6.49
Portfolio Turnover (%)	48	49	71	76	58	80	141	116	181	237
Total Assets (Millions $)	1,365	1,358	1,253	1,504	1,349	1,251	1,106	1,112	1,017	1,021

PORTFOLIO (as of 9/30/96)

Portfolio Manager: William T. Reynolds - 1990

Investm't Category: Tax-Exempt Bond
- ✔ Domestic
- Foreign
- Asset Allocation
- Index
- Sector
- State Specific

Investment Style
- Large-Cap Growth
- Mid-Cap Growth
- Small-Cap Growth
- Large-Cap Value
- Mid-Cap Value
- Small-Cap Value

Portfolio
5.1% cash	0.0% corp bonds
0.0% stocks	0.0% gov't bonds
0.0% preferred	94.9% muni bonds
0.0% conv't/warrants	0.0% other

SHAREHOLDER INFORMATION

Minimum Investment
Initial: $2,500   Subsequent: $100

Minimum IRA Investment
Initial: na   Subsequent: na

Maximum Fees
Load: none   12b-1: none
Other: f

Distributions
Income: monthly   Capital Gains: Dec

Exchange Options
Number Per Year: 6   Fee: none
Telephone: yes (money market fund available)

Services
auto exchange, auto invest, auto withdraw

T. Rowe Price Tax-Free Ins Interm Bond

(PTIBX) *Tax-Exempt Bond*

Public Relations Department
100 E. Pratt St.
Baltimore, MD 21202
800-225-5132, 410-547-2000
www.troweprice.com

PERFORMANCE

fund inception date: 11/30/92

	3yr Annual	5yr Annual	10yr Annual	Bull	Bear
Return (%)	4.6	na	na	17.6	-3.6
Differ from Category (+/-)	0.4 abv av	na	na	-0.8 blw av	1.8 high

Total Risk	Standard Deviation	Category Risk	Risk Index	Avg Mat
low	3.8%	low	0.7	7.3 yrs

	1996	1995	1994	1993	1992	1991	1990	1989	1988	1987
Return (%)	4.1	13.0	-2.7	12.6	—	—	—	—	—	—
Differ from Category (+/-)	0.4	-2.2	2.6	0.8	—	—	—	—	—	—
Return, Tax-Adjusted (%)	4.1	13.0	-2.8	12.4	—	—	—	—	—	—

PER SHARE DATA

	1996	1995	1994	1993	1992	1991	1990	1989	1988	1987
Dividends, Net Income ($)	0.47	0.48	0.45	0.48	—	—	—	—	—	—
Distrib'ns, Cap Gain ($)	0.00	0.00	0.03	0.06	—	—	—	—	—	—
Net Asset Value ($)	10.79	10.83	10.03	10.80	—	—	—	—	—	—
Expense Ratio (%)	0.65	0.65	0.33	0.00	—	—	—	—	—	—
Yield (%)	4.35	4.43	4.47	4.41	—	—	—	—	—	—
Portfolio Turnover (%)	63	170	74	65	—	—	—	—	—	—
Total Assets (Millions $)	97	91	79	97	—	—	—	—	—	—

PORTFOLIO (as of 9/30/96)

Portfolio Manager: Charles B. Hill - 1994

Investm't Category: Tax-Exempt Bond
- ✔ Domestic
- Foreign
- Asset Allocation
- Index
- Sector
- State Specific

Investment Style
- Large-Cap Growth
- Mid-Cap Growth
- Small-Cap Growth
- Large-Cap Value
- Mid-Cap Value
- Small-Cap Value

Portfolio
0.0% cash	0.0% corp bonds
0.0% stocks	0.0% gov't bonds
0.0% preferred	100.6% muni bonds
0.0% conv't/warrants	0.0% other

SHAREHOLDER INFORMATION

Minimum Investment
Initial: $2,500   Subsequent: $100

Minimum IRA Investment
Initial: na   Subsequent: na

Maximum Fees
Load: none   12b-1: none
Other: f

Distributions
Income: monthly   Capital Gains: Dec

Exchange Options
Number Per Year: 6   Fee: none
Telephone: yes (money market fund available)

Services
auto exchange, auto invest, auto withdraw

T. Rowe Price Tax-Free Short Interm (PRFSX)

Tax-Exempt Bond

Public Relations Department
100 E. Pratt St.
Baltimore, MD 21202
800-225-5132, 410-547-2000
www.troweprice.com

PERFORMANCE

fund inception date: 12/23/83

	3yr Annual	5yr Annual	10yr Annual	Bull	Bear
Return (%)	4.1	4.9	5.2	13.5	-1.2
Differ from Category (+/-)	-0.1 blw av	-1.5 low	-1.5 low	-4.9 low	4.2 high

Total Risk	Standard Deviation	Category Risk	Risk Index	Avg Mat
low	1.7%	low	0.3	3.1 yrs

	1996	1995	1994	1993	1992	1991	1990	1989	1988	1987
Return (%).	4.0	8.1	0.3	6.3	6.0	7.8	6.0	6.8	4.9	2.2
Differ from Category (+/-). .	0.3	-7.1	5.6	-5.5	-2.3	-3.6	-0.4	-2.2	-5.1	3.6
Return, Tax-Adjusted (%). . .	4.0	8.1	0.3	6.3	6.0	7.8	6.0	6.8	4.9	2.0

PER SHARE DATA

	1996	1995	1994	1993	1992	1991	1990	1989	1988	1987
Dividends, Net Income ($).	0.22	0.23	0.21	0.22	0.24	0.28	0.28	0.29	0.27	0.27
Distrib'ns, Cap Gain ($) . . .	0.00	0.00	0.00	0.00	0.00	0.00	0.00	0.00	0.00	0.02
Net Asset Value ($)	5.34	5.36	5.18	5.38	5.28	5.22	5.11	5.10	5.06	5.09
Expense Ratio (%).	0.57	0.59	0.60	0.63	0.67	0.74	0.75	0.74	0.74	0.73
Yield (%)	4.11	4.29	4.05	4.08	4.54	5.36	5.47	5.68	5.33	5.28
Portfolio Turnover (%).	69	93	51	38	81	190	191	53	225	120
Total Assets (Millions $). . .	444	450	451	535	424	306	227	220	266	275

PORTFOLIO (as of 9/30/96)

Portfolio Manager: Charles B. Hill - 1995

Investm't Category: Tax-Exempt Bond
✔ Domestic   Index
   Foreign   Sector
   Asset Allocation   State Specific

Investment Style
Large-Cap Growth   Large-Cap Value
Mid-Cap Growth   Mid-Cap Value
Small-Cap Growth   Small-Cap Value

Portfolio
14.7% cash   0.0% corp bonds
0.0% stocks   0.0% gov't bonds
0.0% preferred   85.3% muni bonds
0.0% conv't/warrants   0.0% other

SHAREHOLDER INFORMATION

Minimum Investment
Initial: $2,500   Subsequent: $100

Minimum IRA Investment
Initial: na   Subsequent: na

Maximum Fees
Load: none   12b-1: none
Other: f

Distributions
Income: monthly   Capital Gains: Dec

Exchange Options
Number Per Year: 6   Fee: none
Telephone: yes (money market fund available)

Services
auto exchange, auto invest, auto withdraw

T. Rowe Price US Treasury Interm (PRTIX)

Government Bond

Public Relations Department
100 E. Pratt St.
Baltimore, MD 21202
800-225-5132, 410-547-2000
www.troweprice.com

PERFORMANCE

fund inception date: 9/28/89

	3yr Annual	5yr Annual	10yr Annual	Bull	Bear
Return (%)	5.0	5.8	na	18.7	-3.3
Differ from Category (+/-)	0.1 av	-0.8 av	na	-3.3 av	3.1 abv av

Total Risk	Standard Deviation	Category Risk	Risk Index	Avg Mat
low	3.7%	av	0.9	4.4 yrs

	1996	1995	1994	1993	1992	1991	1990	1989	1988	1987
Return (%)	2.3	15.8	-2.3	7.9	6.2	14.7	8.9	—	—	—
Differ from Category (+/-)	0.8	-3.8	2.1	-3.7	-0.5	-1.0	2.6	—	—	—
Return, Tax-Adjusted (%)	0.0	13.2	-4.7	5.6	3.1	11.8	5.7	—	—	—

PER SHARE DATA

	1996	1995	1994	1993	1992	1991	1990	1989	1988	1987
Dividends, Net Income ($)	0.31	0.32	0.30	0.29	0.32	0.35	0.40	—	—	—
Distrib'ns, Cap Gain ($)	0.00	0.00	0.02	0.01	0.13	0.03	0.00	—	—	—
Net Asset Value ($)	5.18	5.38	4.94	5.38	5.27	5.41	5.08	—	—	—
Expense Ratio (%)	0.65	0.69	0.79	0.80	0.80	0.80	0.80	—	—	—
Yield (%)	5.98	5.94	6.04	5.38	5.92	6.43	7.87	—	—	—
Portfolio Turnover (%)	40	81	20	23	91	175	195	—	—	—
Total Assets (Millions $)	188	183	163	171	151	126	57	—	—	—

PORTFOLIO (as of 9/30/96)

Portfolio Manager: Charles P. Smith - 1989

Investm't Category: Government Bond
✔ Domestic   Index
   Foreign   Sector
   Asset Allocation   State Specific

Investment Style
Large-Cap Growth   Large-Cap Value
Mid-Cap Growth   Mid-Cap Value
Small-Cap Growth   Small-Cap Value

Portfolio

1.5% cash	0.0% corp bonds
0.0% stocks	98.5% gov't bonds
0.0% preferred	0.0% muni bonds
0.0% conv't/warrants	0.0% other

SHAREHOLDER INFORMATION

Minimum Investment
Initial: $2,500   Subsequent: $100

Minimum IRA Investment
Initial: $1,000   Subsequent: $50

Maximum Fees
Load: none   12b-1: none
Other: f

Distributions
Income: monthly   Capital Gains: Dec

Exchange Options
Number Per Year: 6   Fee: none
Telephone: yes (money market fund available)

Services
IRA, pension, auto exchange, auto invest, auto withdraw

T. Rowe Price US Treasury Long-Term

(PRULX) *Government Bond*

Public Relations Department
100 E. Pratt St.
Baltimore, MD 21202
800-225-5132, 410-547-2000
www.troweprice.com

PERFORMANCE

fund inception date: 9/28/89

	3yr Annual	5yr Annual	10yr Annual	Bull	Bear
Return (%)	5.7	7.1	na	26.6	-8.4
Differ from Category (+/-)	0.8 high	0.5 abv av	na	4.6 high	-2.0 blw av

Total Risk	Standard Deviation	Category Risk	Risk Index	Avg Mat
av	8.4%	high	2.1	21.8 yrs

	1996	1995	1994	1993	1992	1991	1990	1989	1988	1987
Return (%)	-2.4	28.5	-5.8	12.9	5.8	16.2	6.6	—	—	—
Differ from Category (+/-)	-3.9	8.9	-1.4	1.3	-0.9	0.5	0.3	—	—	—
Return, Tax-Adjusted (%)	-4.6	25.7	-8.4	9.5	2.4	13.1	3.4	—	—	—

PER SHARE DATA

	1996	1995	1994	1993	1992	1991	1990	1989	1988	1987
Dividends, Net Income ($)	0.63	0.65	0.68	0.67	0.72	0.77	0.81	—	—	—
Distrib'ns, Cap Gain ($)	0.00	0.00	0.01	0.28	0.28	0.00	0.00	—	—	—
Net Asset Value ($)	10.43	11.36	9.41	10.71	10.36	10.78	10.01	—	—	—
Expense Ratio (%)	0.80	0.80	0.80	0.80	0.80	0.80	0.80	—	—	—
Yield (%)	6.04	5.72	7.21	6.09	6.76	7.14	8.09	—	—	—
Portfolio Turnover (%)	58	99	59	165	162	159	316	—	—	—
Total Assets (Millions $)	75	71	58	57	62	59	44	—	—	—

PORTFOLIO (as of 9/30/96)

Portfolio Manager: Peter Van Dyke - 1989

Investm't Category: Government Bond

✔ Domestic   Index
   Foreign   Sector
   Asset Allocation   State Specific

Investment Style

   Large-Cap Growth   Large-Cap Value
   Mid-Cap Growth   Mid-Cap Value
   Small-Cap Growth   Small-Cap Value

Portfolio

1.6%	cash	0.0%	corp bonds
0.0%	stocks	98.4%	gov't bonds
0.0%	preferred	0.0%	muni bonds
0.0%	conv't/warrants	0.0%	other

SHAREHOLDER INFORMATION

Minimum Investment
Initial: $2,500   Subsequent: $100

Minimum IRA Investment
Initial: $1,000   Subsequent: $50

Maximum Fees
Load: none   12b-1: none
Other: *f*

Distributions
Income: monthly   Capital Gains: Dec

Exchange Options
Number Per Year: 6   Fee: none
Telephone: yes (money market fund available)

Services
IRA, pension, auto exchange, auto invest, auto withdraw

T. Rowe Price VA
Tax-Free Bond (PRVAX)

Tax-Exempt Bond

Public Relations Department
100 E. Pratt St.
Baltimore, MD 21202
800-225-5132, 410-547-2000
www.troweprice.com

PERFORMANCE

fund inception date: 4/30/91

	3yr Annual	5yr Annual	10yr Annual	Bull	Bear
Return (%)	4.9	7.2	na	21.2	-6.1
Differ from Category (+/-)	0.7 high	0.8 high	na	2.8 high	-0.7 av

Total Risk	Standard Deviation	Category Risk	Risk Index	Avg Mat
blw av	5.6%	av	1.0	17.4 yrs

	1996	1995	1994	1993	1992	1991	1990	1989	1988	1987
Return (%)	4.1	16.8	-5.1	12.5	9.1	—	—	—	—	—
Differ from Category (+/-)	0.4	1.6	0.2	0.7	0.8	—	—	—	—	—
Return, Tax-Adjusted (%)	4.1	16.8	-5.2	12.1	9.0	—	—	—	—	—

PER SHARE DATA

	1996	1995	1994	1993	1992	1991	1990	1989	1988	1987
Dividends, Net Income ($)	0.57	0.57	0.56	0.56	0.57	—	—	—	—	—
Distrib'ns, Cap Gain ($)	0.00	0.00	0.01	0.15	0.03	—	—	—	—	—
Net Asset Value ($)	11.06	11.19	10.10	11.24	10.65	—	—	—	—	—
Expense Ratio (%)	0.65	0.65	0.65	0.65	0.65	—	—	—	—	—
Yield (%)	5.15	5.09	5.53	4.91	5.33	—	—	—	—	—
Portfolio Turnover (%)	93	89	61	68	76	—	—	—	—	—
Total Assets (Millions $)	189	177	143	164	92	—	—	—	—	—

PORTFOLIO (as of 9/30/96)

Portfolio Manager: Mary J. Miller - 1991

Investm't Category: Tax-Exempt Bond
✔ Domestic	Index
Foreign	Sector
Asset Allocation	✔ State Specific

Investment Style
Large-Cap Growth	Large-Cap Value
Mid-Cap Growth	Mid-Cap Value
Small-Cap Growth	Small-Cap Value

Portfolio
5.3% cash	0.0% corp bonds
0.0% stocks	0.0% gov't bonds
0.0% preferred	94.7% muni bonds
0.0% conv't/warrants	0.0% other

SHAREHOLDER INFORMATION

Minimum Investment
Initial: $2,500   Subsequent: $100

Minimum IRA Investment
Initial: na   Subsequent: na

Maximum Fees
Load: none   12b-1: none
Other: *f*

Distributions
Income: monthly   Capital Gains: Dec

Exchange Options
Number Per Year: 6   Fee: none
Telephone: yes (money market fund available)

Services
auto exchange, auto invest, auto withdraw

T. Rowe Price Value

(TRVLX)

Growth

Public Relations Department
100 E. Pratt St.
Baltimore, MD 21202
800-225-5132, 410-547-2000
www.troweprice.com

PERFORMANCE   fund inception date: 9/30/94

	3yr Annual	5yr Annual	10yr Annual	Bull	Bear
Return (%)	na	na	na	na	na
Differ from Category (+/-)	na	na	na	na	na

Total Risk	Standard Deviation	Category Risk	Risk Index	Beta
na	na	na	na	na

	1996	1995	1994	1993	1992	1991	1990	1989	1988	1987
Return (%)	28.5	39.8	—	—	—	—	—	—	—	—
Differ from Category (+/-)	8.4	9.5	—	—	—	—	—	—	—	—
Return, Tax-Adjusted (%)	25.7	36.5	—	—	—	—	—	—	—	—

PER SHARE DATA

	1996	1995	1994	1993	1992	1991	1990	1989	1988	1987
Dividends, Net Income ($)	0.26	0.26	—	—	—	—	—	—	—	—
Distrib'ns, Cap Gain ($)	0.91	0.82	—	—	—	—	—	—	—	—
Net Asset Value ($)	15.76	13.21	—	—	—	—	—	—	—	—
Expense Ratio (%)	na	1.10	—	—	—	—	—	—	—	—
Yield (%)	1.55	1.85	—	—	—	—	—	—	—	—
Portfolio Turnover (%)	na	89	—	—	—	—	—	—	—	—
Total Assets (Millions $)	182	46	—	—	—	—	—	—	—	—

PORTFOLIO (as of 9/30/96)

Portfolio Manager: Brian C. Rogers - 1994

Investm't Category: Growth

✔ Domestic	Index
Foreign	Sector
Asset Allocation	State Specific

Investment Style

Large-Cap Growth	Large-Cap Value
Mid-Cap Growth	Mid-Cap Value
Small-Cap Growth	Small-Cap Value

Portfolio

7.5% cash	0.0% corp bonds
92.5% stocks	0.0% gov't bonds
0.0% preferred	0.0% muni bonds
0.0% conv't/warrants	0.0% other

SHAREHOLDER INFORMATION

Minimum Investment
Initial: $2,500   Subsequent: $100

Minimum IRA Investment
Initial: $1,000   Subsequent: $50

Maximum Fees
Load: none   12b-1: none
Other: *f*

Distributions
Income: quarterly   Capital Gains: Dec

Exchange Options
Number Per Year: 6   Fee: none
Telephone: yes (money market fund available)

Services
IRA, pension, auto exchange, auto invest, auto withdraw

772   *Guide to Low-Load Mutual Funds*

Third Avenue Value

(TAVFX)

Balanced

767 Third Ave.
Fifth Floor
New York, NY 10017
800-443-1021, 212-906-0268
www.mjwhitman.com/
third.htm

PERFORMANCE

fund inception date: 10/9/90

	3yr Annual	5yr Annual	10yr Annual	Bull	Bear
Return (%)	16.5	18.8	na	64.6	-4.3
Differ from Category (+/-)	4.8 high	7.4 high	na	19.5 high	1.4 abv av

Total Risk	Standard Deviation	Category Risk	Risk Index	Beta
av	8.1%	high	1.2	0.66

	1996	1995	1994	1993	1992	1991	1990	1989	1988	1987
Return (%)..............	21.9	31.7	-1.5	23.6	21.2	34.1	—	—	—	—
Differ from Category (+/-)..	7.7	7.1	0.1	9.2	12.3	10.0	—	—	—	—
Return, Tax-Adjusted (%)..	20.6	30.5	-2.3	22.4	20.0	28.7	—	—	—	—

PER SHARE DATA

	1996	1995	1994	1993	1992	1991	1990	1989	1988	1987
Dividends, Net Income ($).	0.57	0.40	0.24	0.26	0.20	0.14	—	—	—	—
Distrib'ns, Cap Gain ($) ...	0.14	0.14	0.14	0.24	0.24	1.89	—	—	—	—
Net Asset Value ($)	25.86	21.80	16.97	17.62	14.67	12.47	—	—	—	—
Expense Ratio (%).........	na	1.25	1.16	1.42	2.32	2.50	—	—	—	—
Yield (%)	2.19	1.82	1.40	1.45	1.34	0.97	—	—	—	—
Portfolio Turnover (%).....	na	15	5	17	31	67	—	—	—	—
Total Assets (Millions $)...	621	328	180	137	38	18	—	—	—	—

PORTFOLIO (as of 9/30/96)

Portfolio Manager: Martin J. Whitman - 1990

Investm't Category: Balanced

✔ Domestic   Index
   Foreign   Sector
   Asset Allocation   State Specific

Investment Style

Large-Cap Growth   Large-Cap Value
Mid-Cap Growth   Mid-Cap Value
Small-Cap Growth   Small-Cap Value

Portfolio

25.4% cash	9.2% corp bonds
60.3% stocks	0.0% gov't bonds
0.2% preferred	0.0% muni bonds
0.0% conv't/warrants	4.9% other

SHAREHOLDER INFORMATION

Minimum Investment
Initial: $1,000   Subsequent: $1,000

Minimum IRA Investment
Initial: $500   Subsequent: $200

Maximum Fees
Load: none   12b-1: none
Other: none

Distributions
Income: Dec   Capital Gains: Dec

Exchange Options
Number Per Year: no limit   Fee: none
Telephone: yes (money market fund available)

Services
IRA, pension, auto invest, auto withdraw

Turner Growth Equity

(TRGEX)

Growth

680 E. Swedesford Road
Wayne, PA 19087
800-932-7781, 610-254-1000

PERFORMANCE

fund inception date: 3/11/92

	3yr Annual	5yr Annual	10yr Annual	Bull	Bear
Return (%)	13.1	na	na	61.0	-11.8
Differ from Category (+/-)	-2.6 blw av	na	na	-1.4 av	-5.1 low

Total Risk	Standard Deviation	Category Risk	Risk Index	Beta
high	12.2%	high	1.2	1.07

	1996	1995	1994	1993	1992	1991	1990	1989	1988	1987
Return (%).............	19.2	30.3	-6.8	15.3	—	—	—	—	—	—
Differ from Category (+/-) .	-0.9	0.0	-6.5	1.3	—	—	—	—	—	—
Return, Tax-Adjusted (%). .	10.3	27.8	-7.2	15.0	—	—	—	—	—	—

PER SHARE DATA

	1996	1995	1994	1993	1992	1991	1990	1989	1988	1987
Dividends, Net Income ($).	0.00	0.13	0.10	0.08	—	—	—	—	—	—
Distrib'ns, Cap Gain ($) . . .	4.59	0.84	0.00	0.00	—	—	—	—	—	—
Net Asset Value ($)	12.76	14.53	11.92	12.89	—	—	—	—	—	—
Expense Ratio (%)........	0.94	0.94	0.95	1.00	—	—	—	—	—	—
Yield (%)	0.00	0.84	0.83	0.62	—	—	—	—	—	—
Portfolio Turnover (%)....	147	177	164	88	—	—	—	—	—	—
Total Assets (Millions $)....	95	105	112	71	—	—	—	—	—	—

PORTFOLIO (as of 9/30/96)

Portfolio Manager: Robert Turner - 1992

Investm't Category: Growth

✔ Domestic	Index
Foreign	Sector
Asset Allocation	State Specific

Investment Style

✔ Large-Cap Growth	Large-Cap Value
Mid-Cap Growth	Mid-Cap Value
Small-Cap Growth	Small-Cap Value

Portfolio

0.7% cash	0.0% corp bonds
99.3% stocks	0.0% gov't bonds
0.0% preferred	0.0% muni bonds
0.0% conv't/warrants	0.0% other

SHAREHOLDER INFORMATION

Minimum Investment
Initial: $100,000   Subsequent: $10,000

Minimum IRA Investment
Initial: $1   Subsequent: $1

Maximum Fees
Load: none   12b-1: none
Other: none

Distributions
Income: quarterly   Capital Gains: annual

Exchange Options
Number Per Year: no limit   Fee: none
Telephone: yes (money market fund not available)

Services
IRA

Turner Small Cap
(TSCEX)
Aggressive Growth

680 E. Swedesford Road
Wayne, PA 19087
800-224-6312, 610-254-1000

PERFORMANCE

fund inception date: 2/4/94

	3yr Annual	5yr Annual	10yr Annual	Bull	Bear
Return (%)	na	na	na	157.1	na
Differ from Category (+/-)	na	na	na	86.0 high	na

Total Risk	Standard Deviation	Category Risk	Risk Index	Beta
na	na	na	na	na

	1996	1995	1994	1993	1992	1991	1990	1989	1988	1987
Return (%)	28.8	68.1	—	—	—	—	—	—	—	—
Differ from Category (+/-)	9.7	33.8	—	—	—	—	—	—	—	—
Return, Tax-Adjusted (%)	27.9	65.4	—	—	—	—	—	—	—	—

PER SHARE DATA

	1996	1995	1994	1993	1992	1991	1990	1989	1988	1987
Dividends, Net Income ($)	0.00	0.00	—	—	—	—	—	—	—	—
Distrib'ns, Cap Gain ($)	1.01	1.03	—	—	—	—	—	—	—	—
Net Asset Value ($)	21.86	17.37	—	—	—	—	—	—	—	—
Expense Ratio (%)	1.25	1.25	—	—	—	—	—	—	—	—
Yield (%)	0.00	0.00	—	—	—	—	—	—	—	—
Portfolio Turnover (%)	149	183	—	—	—	—	—	—	—	—
Total Assets (Millions $)	70	16	—	—	—	—	—	—	—	—

PORTFOLIO (as of 9/30/96)

Portfolio Manager: William H. Chenoweth - 1994

Investm't Category: Aggressive Growth
- ✔ Domestic
- Foreign
- Asset Allocation
- Index
- Sector
- State Specific

Investment Style
- Large-Cap Growth
- Mid-Cap Growth
- Small-Cap Growth
- Large-Cap Value
- Mid-Cap Value
- Small-Cap Value

Portfolio
6.2% cash	0.0% corp bonds
93.8% stocks	0.0% gov't bonds
0.0% preferred	0.0% muni bonds
0.0% conv't/warrants	0.0% other

SHAREHOLDER INFORMATION

Minimum Investment
Initial: $100,000   Subsequent: $10,000

Minimum IRA Investment
Initial: $1   Subsequent: $1

Maximum Fees
Load: none   12b-1: none
Other: none

Distributions
Income: annual   Capital Gains: annual

Exchange Options
Number Per Year: no limit   Fee: none
Telephone: yes (money market fund not available)

Services
IRA

Tweedy Browne
American Value (TWEBX)

Growth

52 Vanderbilt Ave.
New York, NY 10017
800-432-4789, 212-916-0600

PERFORMANCE

fund inception date: 12/8/93

	3yr Annual	5yr Annual	10yr Annual	Bull	Bear
Return (%)	18.2	na	na	67.5	-3.0
Differ from Category (+/-)	2.5 abv av	na	na	5.1 abv av	3.7 high

Total Risk	Standard Deviation	Category Risk	Risk Index	Beta
av	8.0%	low	0.8	0.69

	1996	1995	1994	1993	1992	1991	1990	1989	1988	1987
Return (%)	22.1	36.2	-0.6	—	—	—	—	—	—	—
Differ from Category (+/-)	2.0	5.9	-0.3	—	—	—	—	—	—	—
Return, Tax-Adjusted (%)	20.7	35.7	-0.9	—	—	—	—	—	—	—

PER SHARE DATA

	1996	1995	1994	1993	1992	1991	1990	1989	1988	1987
Dividends, Net Income ($)	0.17	0.10	0.06	—	—	—	—	—	—	—
Distrib'ns, Cap Gain ($)	0.38	0.02	0.00	—	—	—	—	—	—	—
Net Asset Value ($)	15.64	13.25	9.82	—	—	—	—	—	—	—
Expense Ratio (%)	1.39	1.74	2.26	—	—	—	—	—	—	—
Yield (%)	1.06	0.75	0.61	—	—	—	—	—	—	—
Portfolio Turnover (%)	9	4	0	—	—	—	—	—	—	—
Total Assets (Millions $)	272	168	35	—	—	—	—	—	—	—

PORTFOLIO (as of 9/30/96)

Portfolio Manager: C. Browne, W. Browne, Clarke, Spears - 1993

Investm't Category: Growth
✔ Domestic   Index
✔ Foreign   Sector
  Asset Allocation State Specific

Investment Style
  Large-Cap Growth   ✔ Large-Cap Value
  Mid-Cap Growth   ✔ Mid-Cap Value
  Small-Cap Growth   Small-Cap Value

Portfolio
  6.8% cash   0.0% corp bonds
  93.2% stocks   0.0% gov't bonds
  0.0% preferred   0.0% muni bonds
  0.0% conv't/warrants 0.0% other

SHAREHOLDER INFORMATION

Minimum Investment
Initial: $2,500   Subsequent: $500

Minimum IRA Investment
Initial: $500   Subsequent: $1

Maximum Fees
Load: none   12b-1: none
Other: none

Distributions
Income: Dec   Capital Gains: Dec

Exchange Options
Number Per Year: no limit   Fee: none
Telephone: yes (money market fund not available)

Services
IRA, pension, auto invest, auto withdraw

Tweedy Browne Global Value (TBGVX)

52 Vanderbilt Ave.
New York, NY 10017
800-432-4789, 212-916-0600

International Stock

PERFORMANCE   fund inception date: 6/15/93

	3yr Annual	5yr Annual	10yr Annual	Bull	Bear
Return (%)	11.5	na	na	31.2	-3.0
Differ from Category (+/-)	5.2 high	na	na	6.9 abv av	4.2 high

Total Risk	Standard Deviation	Category Risk	Risk Index	Beta
av	8.6%	low	0.8	0.54

	1996	1995	1994	1993	1992	1991	1990	1989	1988	1987
Return (%)	20.2	10.7	4.3	—	—	—	—	—	—	—
Differ from Category (+/-)	5.4	1.6	7.4	—	—	—	—	—	—	—
Return, Tax-Adjusted (%)	17.3	10.2	3.9	—	—	—	—	—	—	—

PER SHARE DATA

	1996	1995	1994	1993	1992	1991	1990	1989	1988	1987
Dividends, Net Income ($)	0.55	0.00	0.00	—	—	—	—	—	—	—
Distrib'ns, Cap Gain ($)	0.56	0.20	0.16	—	—	—	—	—	—	—
Net Asset Value ($)	14.45	12.95	11.88	—	—	—	—	—	—	—
Expense Ratio (%)	1.60	1.65	1.73	—	—	—	—	—	—	—
Yield (%)	3.66	0.00	0.00	—	—	—	—	—	—	—
Portfolio Turnover (%)	17	16	na	—	—	—	—	—	—	—
Total Assets (Millions $)	1,200	801	565	—	—	—	—	—	—	—

PORTFOLIO (as of 9/30/96)

Portfolio Manager: C. Browne, W. Browne, Clarke, Spears - 1993

Investm't Category: International Stock

✔ Domestic	Index
✔ Foreign	Sector
Asset Allocation	State Specific

Investment Style

Large-Cap Growth	Large-Cap Value
Mid-Cap Growth	Mid-Cap Value
Small-Cap Growth	Small-Cap Value

Portfolio

10.0% cash	0.0% corp bonds
89.2% stocks	0.0% gov't bonds
0.8% preferred	0.0% muni bonds
0.0% conv't/warrants	0.0% other

SHAREHOLDER INFORMATION

Minimum Investment
Initial: $2,500   Subsequent: $500

Minimum IRA Investment
Initial: $500   Subsequent: $1

Maximum Fees
Load: none   12b-1: none
Other: none

Distributions
Income: Dec   Capital Gains: Dec

Exchange Options
Number Per Year: no limit   Fee: none
Telephone: yes (money market fund not available)

Services
IRA, pension, auto invest, auto withdraw

Twentieth Century Giftrust (TWGTX)

Aggressive Growth

4500 Main St., 14th Floor
P.O. Box 418210
Kansas City, MO 64141
800-345-2021, 816-531-5575
www.americancentury.com

PERFORMANCE

fund inception date: 11/25/83

	3yr Annual	5yr Annual	10yr Annual	Bull	Bear
Return (%)	18.4	20.8	21.7	83.6	-11.2
Differ from Category (+/-)	2.6 abv av	5.5 high	6.7 high	12.5 abv av	-0.6 av

Total Risk	Standard Deviation	Category Risk	Risk Index	Beta
high	23.5%	high	1.6	1.03

	1996	1995	1994	1993	1992	1991	1990	1989	1988	1987
Return (%)	5.7	38.3	13.5	31.4	17.9	84.9	-17.0	50.2	11.0	8.6
Differ from Category (+/-)	-13.4	4.0	13.5	12.1	6.2	32.8	-11.6	21.8	-5.4	11.0
Return, Tax-Adjusted (%)	4.7	35.1	11.7	27.8	15.0	82.4	-17.1	46.5	10.1	5.0

PER SHARE DATA

	1996	1995	1994	1993	1992	1991	1990	1989	1988	1987
Dividends, Net Income ($)	0.00	0.00	0.00	0.00	0.00	0.00	0.00	0.00	0.00	0.00
Distrib'ns, Cap Gain ($)	0.78	2.09	1.08	1.91	1.43	0.69	0.02	0.92	0.20	0.85
Net Asset Value ($)	24.39	23.81	18.77	17.53	14.86	13.85	7.88	9.52	6.97	6.47
Expense Ratio (%)	na	0.98	1.00	1.00	1.00	1.00	1.00	1.00	1.00	1.00
Yield (%)	0.00	0.00	0.00	0.00	0.00	0.00	0.00	0.00	0.00	0.00
Portfolio Turnover (%)	na	105	115	143	134	143	137	160	157	130
Total Assets (Millions $)	846	603	274	164	97	64	28	24	14	11

PORTFOLIO (as of 6/30/96)

Portfolio Manager: committee - 1983

Investm't Category: Aggressive Growth

✔ Domestic   Index
✔ Foreign   Sector
   Asset Allocation   State Specific

Investment Style

   Large-Cap Growth   Large-Cap Value
   Mid-Cap Growth   Mid-Cap Value
✔ Small-Cap Growth   Small-Cap Value

Portfolio

2.8% cash	0.0% corp bonds
97.2% stocks	0.0% gov't bonds
0.0% preferred	0.0% muni bonds
0.0% conv't/warrants	0.0% other

SHAREHOLDER INFORMATION

Minimum Investment
Initial: $500   Subsequent: $50

Minimum IRA Investment
Initial: na   Subsequent: na

Maximum Fees
Load: none   12b-1: none
Other: f

Distributions
Income: Dec   Capital Gains: Dec

Exchange Options
Number Per Year: none   Fee: na
Telephone: na

Services
auto invest

Twentieth Century Growth (TWCGX)

Aggressive Growth

4500 Main St., 14th Floor
P.O. Box 418210
Kansas City, MO 64141
800-345-2021, 816-531-5575
www.americancentury.com

PERFORMANCE

fund inception date: 12/31/58

	3yr Annual	5yr Annual	10yr Annual	Bull	Bear
Return (%)	10.8	6.2	13.8	42.9	-8.6
Differ from Category (+/-)	-5.0 low	-9.1 low	-1.2 blw av	-28.2 low	2.0 abv av

Total Risk	Standard Deviation	Category Risk	Risk Index	Beta
high	12.8%	blw av	0.9	1.04

	1996	1995	1994	1993	1992	1991	1990	1989	1988	1987
Return (%)	15.0	20.3	-1.5	3.7	-4.3	69.0	-3.9	43.1	2.7	13.1
Differ from Category (+/-)	-4.1	-14.0	-1.5	-15.6	-16.0	16.9	1.5	14.7	-13.7	15.5
Return, Tax-Adjusted (%)	14.2	15.6	-5.7	0.4	-4.7	68.9	-5.7	41.5	1.6	5.8

PER SHARE DATA

	1996	1995	1994	1993	1992	1991	1990	1989	1988	1987
Dividends, Net Income ($)	0.18	0.06	0.05	0.05	0.00	0.01	0.11	0.07	0.32	0.13
Distrib'ns, Cap Gain ($)	0.24	3.05	3.22	2.76	0.36	0.00	0.89	0.59	0.00	3.46
Net Asset Value ($)	21.88	19.39	18.74	22.40	24.36	25.83	15.29	16.95	12.31	12.30
Expense Ratio (%)	na	1.00	1.00	1.00	1.00	1.00	1.00	1.00	1.00	1.00
Yield (%)	0.81	0.26	0.22	0.19	0.00	0.03	0.67	0.39	2.59	0.82
Portfolio Turnover (%)	na	141	100	94	53	69	118	98	143	114
Total Assets (Millions $)	4,909	4,849	4,158	4,552	4,853	3,879	1,914	1,642	1,193	1,231

PORTFOLIO (as of 6/30/96)

Portfolio Manager: committee - 1958

Investm't Category: Aggressive Growth
- ✔ Domestic
- ✔ Foreign
- Asset Allocation
- Index
- Sector
- State Specific

Investment Style
- Large-Cap Growth
- ✔ Mid-Cap Growth
- Small-Cap Growth
- Large-Cap Value
- Mid-Cap Value
- Small-Cap Value

Portfolio
1.3% cash	0.0% corp bonds
98.7% stocks	0.0% gov't bonds
0.0% preferred	0.0% muni bonds
0.0% conv't/warrants	0.0% other

SHAREHOLDER INFORMATION

Minimum Investment
Initial: $2,500   Subsequent: $50

Minimum IRA Investment
Initial: $1,000   Subsequent: $50

Maximum Fees
Load: none   12b-1: none
Other: none

Distributions
Income: Dec   Capital Gains: Dec

Exchange Options
Number Per Year: 6   Fee: none
Telephone: yes (money market fund available)

Services
IRA, pension, auto exchange, auto invest, auto withdraw

Twentieth Century Heritage (TWHIX)

Growth

4500 Main St., 14th Floor
P.O. Box 418210
Kansas City, MO 64141
800-345-2021, 816-531-5575
www.americancentury.com

PERFORMANCE

fund inception date: 11/10/87

	3yr Annual	5yr Annual	10yr Annual	Bull	Bear
Return (%)	11.0	12.6	na	48.7	-10.6
Differ from Category (+/-)	-4.7 low	-1.7 blw av	na	-13.7 low	-3.9 low

Total Risk	Standard Deviation	Category Risk	Risk Index	Beta
high	12.3%	high	1.2	0.97

	1996	1995	1994	1993	1992	1991	1990	1989	1988	1987
Return (%)	15.3	26.6	-6.4	20.4	10.1	35.9	-9.2	35.0	16.4	—
Differ from Category (+/-)	-4.8	-3.7	-6.1	6.4	-1.7	-0.1	-3.1	8.9	-1.7	—
Return, Tax-Adjusted (%)	13.2	24.6	-8.0	18.6	7.6	35.2	-9.8	31.5	15.9	—

PER SHARE DATA

	1996	1995	1994	1993	1992	1991	1990	1989	1988	1987
Dividends, Net Income ($)	0.09	0.04	0.03	0.06	0.09	0.11	0.11	0.06	0.06	—
Distrib'ns, Cap Gain ($)	0.70	0.61	0.54	0.50	0.67	0.00	0.00	0.69	0.00	—
Net Asset Value ($)	12.07	11.17	9.35	10.61	9.31	9.17	6.83	7.64	6.22	—
Expense Ratio (%)	na	0.99	1.00	1.00	1.00	1.00	1.00	1.00	1.00	—
Yield (%)	0.70	0.33	0.30	0.54	0.90	1.19	1.61	0.72	0.96	—
Portfolio Turnover (%)	na	121	136	116	119	146	127	159	130	—
Total Assets (Millions $)	1,132	1,026	851	724	424	292	210	144	58	—

PORTFOLIO (as of 6/30/96)

Portfolio Manager: committee - 1987

Investm't Category: Growth
- ✔ Domestic
- ✔ Foreign
- Asset Allocation
- Index
- Sector
- State Specific

Investment Style
- Large-Cap Growth
- ✔ Mid-Cap Growth
- Small-Cap Growth
- Large-Cap Value
- Mid-Cap Value
- Small-Cap Value

Portfolio
- 0.3% cash
- 98.1% stocks
- 0.0% preferred
- 0.0% conv't/warrants
- 0.0% corp bonds
- 0.0% gov't bonds
- 0.0% muni bonds
- 1.6% other

SHAREHOLDER INFORMATION

Minimum Investment
Initial: $2,500   Subsequent: $50

Minimum IRA Investment
Initial: $1,000   Subsequent: $50

Maximum Fees
Load: none   12b-1: none
Other: none

Distributions
Income: Dec   Capital Gains: Dec

Exchange Options
Number Per Year: 6   Fee: none
Telephone: yes (money market fund available)

Services
IRA, pension, auto exchange, auto invest, auto withdraw

Twentieth Century Int'l Discovery (TWEGX)

International Stock

4500 Main St., 14th Floor
P.O. Box 418210
Kansas City, MO 64141
800-345-2021, 816-531-5575
www.americancentury.com

PERFORMANCE

fund inception date: 4/1/94

	3yr Annual	5yr Annual	10yr Annual	Bull	Bear
Return (%)	na	na	na	44.1	na
Differ from Category (+/-)	na	na	na	19.8 high	na

Total Risk	Standard Deviation	Category Risk	Risk Index	Beta
na	na	na	na	na

	1996	1995	1994	1993	1992	1991	1990	1989	1988	1987
Return (%)	31.1	9.8	—	—	—	—	—	—	—	—
Differ from Category (+/-)	16.3	0.7	—	—	—	—	—	—	—	—
Return, Tax-Adjusted (%)	29.5	9.5	—	—	—	—	—	—	—	—

PER SHARE DATA

	1996	1995	1994	1993	1992	1991	1990	1989	1988	1987
Dividends, Net Income ($)	0.01	0.03	—	—	—	—	—	—	—	—
Distrib'ns, Cap Gain ($)	0.32	0.00	—	—	—	—	—	—	—	—
Net Asset Value ($)	7.36	5.88	—	—	—	—	—	—	—	—
Expense Ratio (%)	2.00	2.00	—	—	—	—	—	—	—	—
Yield (%)	0.13	0.51	—	—	—	—	—	—	—	—
Portfolio Turnover (%)	na	168	—	—	—	—	—	—	—	—
Total Assets (Millions $)	375	121	—	—	—	—	—	—	—	—

PORTFOLIO (as of 5/31/96)

Portfolio Manager: Henrik Strabo - 1994

Investm't Category: International Stock
- Domestic
- ✔ Foreign
- Asset Allocation
- Index
- Sector
- State Specific

Investment Style
- Large-Cap Growth
- Mid-Cap Growth
- Small-Cap Growth
- Large-Cap Value
- Mid-Cap Value
- Small-Cap Value

Portfolio
4.3% cash	0.0% corp bonds
90.3% stocks	0.0% gov't bonds
5.4% preferred	0.0% muni bonds
0.0% conv't/warrants	0.0% other

SHAREHOLDER INFORMATION

Minimum Investment
Initial: $10,000   Subsequent: $50

Minimum IRA Investment
Initial: $10,000   Subsequent: $50

Maximum Fees
Load: none   12b-1: none
Other: none

Distributions
Income: Dec   Capital Gains: Dec

Exchange Options
Number Per Year: 6   Fee: none
Telephone: yes (money market fund available)

Services
IRA, pension, auto exchange, auto invest, auto withdraw

Twentieth Century Int'l Growth (TWIEX)

International Stock

4500 Main St., 14th Floor
P.O. Box 418210
Kansas City, MO 64141
800-345-2021, 816-531-5575
www.americancentury.com

PERFORMANCE

fund inception date: 5/9/91

	3yr Annual	5yr Annual	10yr Annual	Bull	Bear
Return (%)	6.8	12.7	na	24.8	-5.8
Differ from Category (+/-)	0.5 av	2.7 abv av	na	0.5 av	1.4 abv av

Total Risk	Standard Deviation	Category Risk	Risk Index	Beta
abv av	10.0%	av	1.0	0.65

	1996	1995	1994	1993	1992	1991	1990	1989	1988	1987
Return (%)	14.4	11.8	-4.8	42.6	4.8	—	—	—	—	—
Differ from Category (+/-)	-0.4	2.7	-1.7	3.0	8.6	—	—	—	—	—
Return, Tax-Adjusted (%)	11.1	11.8	-6.2	40.6	3.4	—	—	—	—	—

PER SHARE DATA

	1996	1995	1994	1993	1992	1991	1990	1989	1988	1987
Dividends, Net Income ($)	0.00	0.00	0.00	0.00	0.19	—	—	—	—	—
Distrib'ns, Cap Gain ($)	0.91	0.00	0.37	0.40	0.00	—	—	—	—	—
Net Asset Value ($)	7.96	7.78	6.96	7.70	5.69	—	—	—	—	—
Expense Ratio (%)	na	1.77	1.84	1.90	1.91	—	—	—	—	—
Yield (%)	0.00	0.00	0.00	0.00	3.33	—	—	—	—	—
Portfolio Turnover (%)	na	169	242	255	180	—	—	—	—	—
Total Assets (Millions $)	1,346	1,258	1,272	944	222	—	—	—	—	—

PORTFOLIO (as of 6/30/96)

Portfolio Manager: Henrik Strabo - 1994

Investm't Category: International Stock

Domestic	Index
✔ Foreign	Sector
Asset Allocation	State Specific

Investment Style

Large-Cap Growth	Large-Cap Value
Mid-Cap Growth	Mid-Cap Value
Small-Cap Growth	Small-Cap Value

Portfolio

2.9%	cash	0.0% corp bonds
96.1%	stocks	0.0% gov't bonds
1.0%	preferred	0.0% muni bonds
0.0%	conv't/warrants	0.0% other

SHAREHOLDER INFORMATION

Minimum Investment
Initial: $2,500   Subsequent: $50

Minimum IRA Investment
Initial: $50   Subsequent: $50

Maximum Fees
Load: none   12b-1: none
Other: none

Distributions
Income: Dec   Capital Gains: Dec

Exchange Options
Number Per Year: 6   Fee: none
Telephone: yes (money market fund available)

Services
IRA, pension, auto exchange, auto invest, auto withdraw

Twentieth Century Select
(TWCIX)
Growth

4500 Main St., 14th Floor
P.O. Box 418210
Kansas City, MO 64141
800-345-2021, 816-531-5575
www.americancentury.com

PERFORMANCE

fund inception date: 10/31/58

	3yr Annual	5yr Annual	10yr Annual	Bull	Bear
Return (%)	10.3	8.0	11.6	47.0	-12.4
Differ from Category (+/-)	-5.4 low	-6.3 low	-2.3 low	-15.4 low	-5.7 low

Total Risk	Standard Deviation	Category Risk	Risk Index	Beta
abv av	10.8%	abv av	1.0	1.00

	1996	1995	1994	1993	1992	1991	1990	1989	1988	1987
Return (%)	19.2	22.6	-8.1	14.6	-4.5	31.5	-0.5	39.5	5.6	5.7
Differ from Category (+/-)	-0.9	-7.7	-7.8	0.6	-16.3	-4.5	5.6	13.4	-12.5	3.7
Return, Tax-Adjusted (%)	15.9	18.3	-10.5	10.9	-5.9	29.2	-2.4	37.8	4.5	-1.1

PER SHARE DATA

	1996	1995	1994	1993	1992	1991	1990	1989	1988	1987
Dividends, Net Income ($)	0.32	0.26	0.28	0.43	0.49	0.65	0.65	1.11	0.70	0.86
Distrib'ns, Cap Gain ($)	3.68	4.65	2.87	4.46	1.32	1.82	1.55	0.00	0.00	6.36
Net Asset Value ($)	38.53	35.62	33.10	39.46	38.72	42.40	34.14	36.51	26.98	26.22
Expense Ratio (%)	na	1.00	1.00	1.00	1.00	1.00	1.00	1.00	1.00	1.00
Yield (%)	0.75	0.64	0.77	0.97	1.22	1.46	1.82	3.04	2.59	2.63
Portfolio Turnover (%)	na	106	126	82	95	84	83	93	140	123
Total Assets (Millions $)	4,226	3,982	3,995	4,939	4,691	4,634	3,196	2,858	2,265	2,393

PORTFOLIO (as of 6/30/96)

Portfolio Manager: committee - 1958

Investm't Category: Growth
- ✔ Domestic
- ✔ Foreign
-   Asset Allocation
-   Index
-   Sector
-   State Specific

Investment Style
- ✔ Large-Cap Growth
- ✔ Mid-Cap Growth
-   Small-Cap Growth
- ✔ Large-Cap Value
- ✔ Mid-Cap Value
-   Small-Cap Value

Portfolio
2.8% cash	0.0% corp bonds
97.2% stocks	0.0% gov't bonds
0.0% preferred	0.0% muni bonds
0.0% conv't/warrants	0.0% other

SHAREHOLDER INFORMATION

Minimum Investment
Initial: $2,500   Subsequent: $50

Minimum IRA Investment
Initial: $1,000   Subsequent: $50

Maximum Fees
Load: none   12b-1: none
Other: none

Distributions
Income: Dec   Capital Gains: Dec

Exchange Options
Number Per Year: 6   Fee: none
Telephone: yes (money market fund available)

Services
IRA, pension, auto exchange, auto invest, auto withdraw

Twentieth Century Ultra

(TWCUX)

Aggressive Growth

4500 Main St., 14th Floor
P.O. Box 418210
Kansas City, MO 64141
800-345-2021, 816-531-5575
www.americancentury.com

	3yr Annual	5yr Annual	10yr Annual	Bull	Bear
Return (%)	14.7	13.2	20.1	67.8	-15.1
Differ from Category (+/-)	-1.1 av	-2.1 blw av	5.1 high	-3.3 av	-4.5 blw av

Total Risk	Standard Deviation	Category Risk	Risk Index	Beta
high	16.3%	abv av	1.1	1.25

	1996	1995	1994	1993	1992	1991	1990	1989	1988	1987
Return (%).............	13.8	37.6	-3.7	21.8	1.2	86.4	9.3	36.9	13.3	6.6
Differ from Category (+/-).	-5.3	3.3	-3.7	2.5	-10.5	34.3	14.7	8.5	-3.1	9.0
Return, Tax-Adjusted (%)..	11.9	35.7	-4.6	21.8	1.2	86.4	9.2	32.1	13.3	-3.7

PER SHARE DATA

	1996	1995	1994	1993	1992	1991	1990	1989	1988	1987
Dividends, Net Income ($).	0.00	0.00	0.00	0.00	0.00	0.00	0.00	0.19	0.00	0.00
Distrib'ns, Cap Gain ($) ...	1.68	1.29	0.64	0.00	0.00	0.00	0.02	0.94	0.00	3.25
Net Asset Value ($)	28.09	26.11	19.95	21.39	17.56	17.34	9.30	8.53	7.06	6.23
Expense Ratio (%).........	na	1.00	1.00	1.00	1.00	1.00	1.00	1.00	1.00	1.00
Yield (%)	0.00	0.00	0.00	0.00	0.00	0.00	0.00	2.00	0.00	0.00
Portfolio Turnover (%).....	na	87	78	53	59	42	141	132	140	137
Total Assets (Millions $) .	19,530	14,551	9,850	8,362	5,299	2,939	458	345	255	247

PORTFOLIO (as of 6/30/96)

Portfolio Manager: committee - 1981

Investm't Category: Aggressive Growth
- ✔ Domestic
- ✔ Foreign
-    Asset Allocation
-    Index
-    Sector
-    State Specific

Investment Style
-    Large-Cap Growth
- ✔ Mid-Cap Growth
-    Small-Cap Growth
-    Large-Cap Value
-    Mid-Cap Value
-    Small-Cap Value

Portfolio
0.6% cash	0.0% corp bonds
99.4% stocks	0.0% gov't bonds
0.0% preferred	0.0% muni bonds
0.0% conv't/warrants	0.0% other

SHAREHOLDER INFORMATION

Minimum Investment
Initial: $2,500   Subsequent: $50

Minimum IRA Investment
Initial: $1,000   Subsequent: $50

Maximum Fees
Load: none   12b-1: none
Other: none

Distributions
Income: Dec   Capital Gains: Dec

Exchange Options
Number Per Year: 6   Fee: none
Telephone: yes (money market fund available)

Services
IRA, pension, auto exchange, auto invest, auto withdraw

Twentieth Century Vista
(TWCVX)
Aggressive Growth

4500 Main St., 14th Floor
P.O. Box 418210
Kansas City, MO 64141
800-345-2021, 816-531-5575
www.americancentury.com

PERFORMANCE — fund inception date: 11/25/83

	3yr Annual	5yr Annual	10yr Annual	Bull	Bear
Return (%)	18.0	11.1	15.1	93.5	-17.6
Differ from Category (+/-)	2.2 abv av	-4.2 low	0.1 av	22.4 abv av	-7.0 low

Total Risk	Standard Deviation	Category Risk	Risk Index	Beta
high	20.9%	high	1.5	1.14

	1996	1995	1994	1993	1992	1991	1990	1989	1988	1987
Return (%)	7.5	46.1	4.6	5.4	-2.2	73.6	-15.8	52.1	2.4	6.0
Differ from Category (+/-)	-11.6	11.8	4.6	-13.9	-13.9	21.5	-10.4	23.7	-14.0	8.4
Return, Tax-Adjusted (%)	5.2	43.4	4.5	1.2	-3.7	73.6	-15.8	48.8	2.3	3.8

PER SHARE DATA

	1996	1995	1994	1993	1992	1991	1990	1989	1988	1987
Dividends, Net Income ($)	0.00	0.00	0.00	0.00	0.00	0.00	0.00	0.00	0.01	0.00
Distrib'ns, Cap Gain ($)	1.18	1.02	0.02	1.67	0.64	0.00	0.00	0.69	0.00	0.46
Net Asset Value ($)	14.51	14.60	10.72	10.27	11.35	12.28	7.07	8.39	5.97	5.84
Expense Ratio (%)	na	0.98	1.00	1.00	1.00	1.00	1.00	1.00	1.00	1.00
Yield (%)	0.00	0.00	0.00	0.00	0.00	0.00	0.00	0.00	0.16	0.00
Portfolio Turnover (%)	na	89	111	133	87	92	103	125	145	123
Total Assets (Millions $)	2,209	1,774	820	795	935	766	389	291	201	216

PORTFOLIO (as of 6/30/96)

Portfolio Manager: committee - 1983

Investm't Category: Aggressive Growth
- ✔ Domestic
- ✔ Foreign
-   Asset Allocation
-   Index
-   Sector
-   State Specific

Investment Style
Large-Cap Growth	Large-Cap Value
Mid-Cap Growth	Mid-Cap Value
✔ Small-Cap Growth	Small-Cap Value

Portfolio
4.8% cash	0.0% corp bonds
95.2% stocks	0.0% gov't bonds
0.0% preferred	0.0% muni bonds
0.0% conv't/warrants	0.0% other

SHAREHOLDER INFORMATION

Minimum Investment
Initial: $2,500   Subsequent: $50

Minimum IRA Investment
Initial: $1,000   Subsequent: $50

Maximum Fees
Load: none   12b-1: none
Other: none

Distributions
Income: Dec   Capital Gains: Dec

Exchange Options
Number Per Year: 6   Fee: none
Telephone: yes (money market fund available)

Services
IRA, pension, auto exchange, auto invest, auto withdraw

US Gov't Securities
(CAUSX)
Government Bond

44 Montgomery St.
Suite 2100
San Francisco, CA 94104
800-225-8778, 415-398-2727
www.caltrust.com

PERFORMANCE
fund inception date: 12/4/85

	3yr Annual	5yr Annual	10yr Annual	Bull	Bear
Return (%)	4.5	7.4	8.4	22.8	-9.0
Differ from Category (+/-)	-0.4 low	0.8 abv av	0.4 av	0.8 abv av	-2.6 blw av

Total Risk	Standard Deviation	Category Risk	Risk Index	Avg Mat
av	7.3%	abv av	1.8	22.4 yrs

	1996	1995	1994	1993	1992	1991	1990	1989	1988	1987
Return (%).	-0.5	23.3	-7.0	15.7	8.3	17.4	8.5	13.4	7.2	1.2
Differ from Category (+/-). .	-2.0	3.7	-2.6	4.1	1.6	1.7	2.2	-1.9	-1.1	5.6
Return, Tax-Adjusted (%). .	-3.2	20.5	-9.4	12.9	5.4	14.0	5.1	9.7	3.5	-2.5

PER SHARE DATA

	1996	1995	1994	1993	1992	1991	1990	1989	1988	1987
Dividends, Net Income ($).	0.66	0.68	0.66	0.70	0.71	0.82	0.81	0.85	0.87	0.95
Distrib'ns, Cap Gain ($) . . .	0.14	0.00	0.00	0.05	0.05	0.00	0.00	0.00	0.00	0.00
Net Asset Value ($)	10.50	11.38	9.84	11.29	10.43	10.38	9.61	9.64	9.29	9.49
Expense Ratio (%).	na	0.64	0.62	0.52	0.38	0.60	0.60	0.61	0.59	0.34
Yield (%)	6.20	5.97	6.70	6.17	6.77	7.89	8.42	8.81	9.36	10.01
Portfolio Turnover (%).	na	169	129	52	122	53	78	78	110	115
Total Assets (Millions $). . . .	30	31	26	35	24	25	12	9	10	12

PORTFOLIO (as of 9/30/96)

Portfolio Manager: Phillip McClanahan - 1985

Investm't Category: Government Bond
✔ Domestic	Index
Foreign	Sector
Asset Allocation	State Specific

Investment Style
Large-Cap Growth	Large-Cap Value
Mid-Cap Growth	Mid-Cap Value
Small-Cap Growth	Small-Cap Value

Portfolio
0.0% cash	0.0% corp bonds
0.0% stocks	100.0% gov't bonds
0.0% preferred	0.0% muni bonds
0.0% conv't/warrants	0.0% other

SHAREHOLDER INFORMATION

Minimum Investment
Initial: $10,000   Subsequent: $250

Minimum IRA Investment
Initial: $1   Subsequent: $1

Maximum Fees
Load: none   12b-1: none
Other: none

Distributions
Income: monthly   Capital Gains: Oct

Exchange Options
Number Per Year: no limit   Fee: none
Telephone: yes (money market fund available)

Services
IRA, pension, auto invest, auto withdraw

USAA Aggressive Growth
(USAUX)

Aggressive Growth

USAA Building
San Antonio, TX 78288
800-531-8722, 210-456-7211

PERFORMANCE

fund inception date: 10/19/81

	3yr Annual	5yr Annual	10yr Annual	Bull	Bear
Return (%)	20.2	11.4	13.1	105.1	-16.7
Differ from Category (+/-)	4.4 abv av	-3.9 blw av	-1.9 blw av	34.0 high	-6.1 low

Total Risk	Standard Deviation	Category Risk	Risk Index	Beta
high	19.9%	high	1.4	1.12

	1996	1995	1994	1993	1992	1991	1990	1989	1988	1987
Return (%)	16.4	50.4	-0.9	8.1	-8.6	71.6	-12.0	16.5	14.2	-1.0
Differ from Category (+/-)	-2.7	16.1	-0.9	-11.2	-20.3	19.5	-6.6	-11.9	-2.2	1.4
Return, Tax-Adjusted (%)	15.7	47.9	-3.1	6.3	-11.1	71.5	-12.3	11.5	12.9	-4.4

PER SHARE DATA

	1996	1995	1994	1993	1992	1991	1990	1989	1988	1987
Dividends, Net Income ($)	0.00	0.00	0.00	0.02	0.00	0.01	0.10	0.19	0.14	0.12
Distrib'ns, Cap Gain ($)	0.57	1.61	1.55	1.25	2.14	0.00	0.00	2.62	0.47	1.86
Net Asset Value ($)	29.81	26.09	18.46	20.22	19.93	24.42	14.23	16.28	16.34	14.85
Expense Ratio (%)	0.74	0.86	0.83	0.86	0.82	0.87	0.94	0.91	1.00	0.97
Yield (%)	0.00	0.00	0.00	0.09	0.00	0.04	0.70	1.00	0.83	0.71
Portfolio Turnover (%)	43	138	na	113	74	50	78	98	68	35
Total Assets (Millions $)	712	442	283	288	289	271	135	149	137	118

PORTFOLIO (as of 9/30/96)

Portfolio Manager: John Cabell, Eric Efron - 1995

Investm't Category: Aggressive Growth
- ✔ Domestic
- Foreign
- Asset Allocation
- Index
- Sector
- State Specific

Investment Style
- Large-Cap Growth
- Mid-Cap Growth
- ✔ Small-Cap Growth
- Large-Cap Value
- Mid-Cap Value
- Small-Cap Value

Portfolio
2.0% cash	0.0% corp bonds
98.0% stocks	0.0% gov't bonds
0.0% preferred	0.0% muni bonds
0.0% conv't/warrants	0.0% other

SHAREHOLDER INFORMATION

Minimum Investment
Initial: $3,000   Subsequent: $50

Minimum IRA Investment
Initial: $250   Subsequent: $50

Maximum Fees
Load: none   12b-1: none
Other: none

Distributions
Income: annual   Capital Gains: annual

Exchange Options
Number Per Year: 6   Fee: none
Telephone: yes (money market fund available)

Services
IRA, pension, auto exchange, auto invest, auto withdraw

USAA Florida Tax Free Income (UFLTX)

USAA Building
San Antonio, TX 78288
800-531-8722, 210-456-7211

Tax-Exempt Bond

PERFORMANCE
fund inception date: 10/1/93

	3yr Annual	5yr Annual	10yr Annual	Bull	Bear
Return (%)	3.7	na	na	21.1	-8.9
Differ from Category (+/-)	-0.5 low	na	na	2.7 abv av	-3.5 low

Total Risk	Standard Deviation	Category Risk	Risk Index	Avg Mat
av	7.3%	high	1.3	21.4 yrs

	1996	1995	1994	1993	1992	1991	1990	1989	1988	1987
Return (%)	4.3	18.9	-10.1	—	—	—	—	—	—	—
Differ from Category (+/-)	0.6	3.7	-4.8	—	—	—	—	—	—	—
Return, Tax-Adjusted (%)	4.3	18.9	-10.1	—	—	—	—	—	—	—

PER SHARE DATA

	1996	1995	1994	1993	1992	1991	1990	1989	1988	1987
Dividends, Net Income ($)	0.51	0.51	0.48	—	—	—	—	—	—	—
Distrib'ns, Cap Gain ($)	0.00	0.00	0.00	—	—	—	—	—	—	—
Net Asset Value ($)	9.45	9.57	8.51	—	—	—	—	—	—	—
Expense Ratio (%)	0.50	0.50	0.50	—	—	—	—	—	—	—
Yield (%)	5.39	5.32	5.64	—	—	—	—	—	—	—
Portfolio Turnover (%)	88	183	284	—	—	—	—	—	—	—
Total Assets (Millions $)	85	68	37	—	—	—	—	—	—	—

PORTFOLIO (as of 9/30/96)

Portfolio Manager: Robert R. Pariseau - 1995

Investm't Category: Tax-Exempt Bond
- ✔ Domestic
- Foreign
- Asset Allocation
- Index
- Sector
- ✔ State Specific

Investment Style
- Large-Cap Growth
- Mid-Cap Growth
- Small-Cap Growth
- Large-Cap Value
- Mid-Cap Value
- Small-Cap Value

Portfolio
4.0% cash	0.0% corp bonds
0.0% stocks	0.0% gov't bonds
0.0% preferred	96.0% muni bonds
0.0% conv't/warrants	0.0% other

SHAREHOLDER INFORMATION

Minimum Investment
Initial: $3,000   Subsequent: $50

Minimum IRA Investment
Initial: na   Subsequent: na

Maximum Fees
Load: none   12b-1: none
Other: none

Distributions
Income: monthly   Capital Gains: annual

Exchange Options
Number Per Year: 6   Fee: none
Telephone: yes (money market fund available)

Services
auto exchange, auto invest, auto withdraw

USAA Growth (USAAX)

Growth

USAA Building
San Antonio, TX 78288
800-531-8722, 210-456-7211

PERFORMANCE

fund inception date: 4/5/71

	3yr Annual	5yr Annual	10yr Annual	Bull	Bear
Return (%)	17.1	13.7	13.2	66.5	-5.2
Differ from Category (+/-)	1.4 abv av	-0.6 av	-0.7 av	4.1 abv av	1.5 abv av

Total Risk	Standard Deviation	Category Risk	Risk Index	Beta
high	12.2%	high	1.2	0.89

	1996	1995	1994	1993	1992	1991	1990	1989	1988	1987
Return (%)	17.8	32.1	3.3	7.4	9.9	27.8	-0.1	27.3	6.5	5.3
Differ from Category (+/-)	-2.3	1.8	3.6	-6.6	-1.9	-8.2	6.0	1.2	-11.6	3.3
Return, Tax-Adjusted (%)	12.4	29.6	-1.3	4.0	8.7	26.6	-1.4	25.7	5.3	-3.1

PER SHARE DATA

	1996	1995	1994	1993	1992	1991	1990	1989	1988	1987
Dividends, Net Income ($)	0.34	0.29	0.27	0.16	0.32	0.41	0.46	0.46	0.34	0.37
Distrib'ns, Cap Gain ($)	3.21	0.97	2.50	1.99	0.27	0.00	0.00	0.00	0.00	3.88
Net Asset Value ($)	18.84	19.31	15.63	17.69	18.51	17.40	13.96	14.45	11.72	11.32
Expense Ratio (%)	1.01	1.04	1.04	1.07	1.07	1.11	1.18	1.19	1.22	1.09
Yield (%)	1.54	1.42	1.48	0.81	1.70	2.35	3.29	3.18	2.90	2.43
Portfolio Turnover (%)	62	69	na	96	39	37	56	95	109	124
Total Assets (Millions $)	1,335	1,067	677	617	503	365	243	235	211	211

PORTFOLIO (as of 9/30/96)

Portfolio Manager: David G. Parsons - 1994

Investm't Category: Growth
- ✔ Domestic
- Foreign
- Asset Allocation
- Index
- Sector
- State Specific

Investment Style
- Large-Cap Growth
- Mid-Cap Growth
- Small-Cap Growth
- ✔ Large-Cap Value
- ✔ Mid-Cap Value
- Small-Cap Value

Portfolio
3.0% cash	0.0% corp bonds
97.0% stocks	0.0% gov't bonds
0.0% preferred	0.0% muni bonds
0.0% conv't/warrants	0.0% other

SHAREHOLDER INFORMATION

Minimum Investment
Initial: $3,000   Subsequent: $50

Minimum IRA Investment
Initial: $250   Subsequent: $50

Maximum Fees
Load: none   12b-1: none
Other: none

Distributions
Income: annual   Capital Gains: annual

Exchange Options
Number Per Year: 6   Fee: none
Telephone: yes (money market fund available)

Services
IRA, pension, auto exchange, auto invest, auto withdraw

USAA Growth & Income
(USGRX)
Growth & Income

USAA Building
San Antonio, TX 78288
800-531-8722, 210-456-7211

PERFORMANCE   fund inception date: 6/1/93

	3yr Annual	5yr Annual	10yr Annual	Bull	Bear
Return (%)	17.9	na	na	69.1	-6.6
Differ from Category (+/-)	2.6 abv av	na	na	9.3 abv av	-0.2 av

Total Risk	Standard Deviation	Category Risk	Risk Index	Beta
av	9.4%	av	1.0	0.91

	1996	1995	1994	1993	1992	1991	1990	1989	1988	1987
Return (%)	23.0	31.5	1.2	—	—	—	—	—	—	—
Differ from Category (+/-)	3.3	1.4	2.5	—	—	—	—	—	—	—
Return, Tax-Adjusted (%)	21.3	30.2	0.0	—	—	—	—	—	—	—

PER SHARE DATA

	1996	1995	1994	1993	1992	1991	1990	1989	1988	1987
Dividends, Net Income ($)	0.22	0.23	0.22	—	—	—	—	—	—	—
Distrib'ns, Cap Gain ($)	0.44	0.13	0.11	—	—	—	—	—	—	—
Net Asset Value ($)	15.26	13.00	10.18	—	—	—	—	—	—	—
Expense Ratio (%)	0.95	1.01	1.12	—	—	—	—	—	—	—
Yield (%)	1.40	1.75	2.13	—	—	—	—	—	—	—
Portfolio Turnover (%)	16	19	na	—	—	—	—	—	—	—
Total Assets (Millions $)	499	267	150	—	—	—	—	—	—	—

PORTFOLIO (as of 9/30/96)

Portfolio Manager: R. David Ullom - 1993

Investm't Category: Growth & Income
- ✔ Domestic
- Foreign
- Asset Allocation
- Index
- Sector
- State Specific

Investment Style
- Large-Cap Growth
- Mid-Cap Growth
- Small-Cap Growth
- ✔ Large-Cap Value
- Mid-Cap Value
- Small-Cap Value

Portfolio
2.0% cash	0.0% corp bonds
98.0% stocks	0.0% gov't bonds
0.0% preferred	0.0% muni bonds
0.0% conv't/warrants	0.0% other

SHAREHOLDER INFORMATION

Minimum Investment
Initial: $3,000   Subsequent: $50

Minimum IRA Investment
Initial: $250   Subsequent: $50

Maximum Fees
Load: none   12b-1: none
Other: none

Distributions
Income: quarterly   Capital Gains: annual

Exchange Options
Number Per Year: 6   Fee: none
Telephone: yes (money market fund available)

Services
IRA, pension, auto exchange, auto invest, auto withdraw

USAA Income (USAIX)

Balanced

USAA Building
San Antonio, TX 78288
800-531-8722, 210-456-7211

PERFORMANCE
fund inception date: 3/4/74

	3yr Annual	5yr Annual	10yr Annual	Bull	Bear
Return (%)	6.1	7.3	9.2	28.5	-7.8
Differ from Category (+/-)	-5.6 low	-4.1 low	-1.6 blw av	-16.6 low	-2.1 low

Total Risk	Standard Deviation	Category Risk	Risk Index	Beta
blw av	6.7%	blw av	1.0	0.41

	1996	1995	1994	1993	1992	1991	1990	1989	1988	1987
Return (%).	1.3	24.4	-5.3	9.9	8.3	19.3	7.6	16.2	9.9	3.4
Differ from Category (+/-)	-12.9	-0.2	-3.7	-4.5	-0.6	-4.8	8.5	-1.9	-2.3	0.7
Return, Tax-Adjusted (%). .	-1.3	21.4	-8.0	6.5	5.3	15.9	4.0	12.4	6.0	-1.0

PER SHARE DATA

	1996	1995	1994	1993	1992	1991	1990	1989	1988	1987
Dividends, Net Income ($).	0.83	0.84	0.86	0.88	0.94	0.96	1.03	1.03	1.07	1.12
Distrib'ns, Cap Gain ($) . . .	0.00	0.00	0.00	0.25	0.00	0.01	0.00	0.03	0.00	0.26
Net Asset Value ($)	12.31	13.00	11.19	12.71	12.61	12.55	11.41	11.61	10.96	10.97
Expense Ratio (%).	0.40	0.41	0.41	0.41	0.42	0.47	0.53	0.57	0.61	0.61
Yield (%)	6.74	6.46	7.68	6.79	7.45	7.64	9.02	8.84	9.76	9.97
Portfolio Turnover (%).	81	30	na	44	22	15	12	14	11	36
Total Assets (Millions $). .	1,784	1,893	1,611	1,945	1,452	1,004	481	356	288	255

PORTFOLIO (as of 9/30/96)

Portfolio Manager: John W. Saunders Jr. - 1985

Investm't Category: Balanced
✔ Domestic	Index
Foreign	Sector
Asset Allocation	State Specific

Investment Style
Large-Cap Growth	Large-Cap Value
Mid-Cap Growth	Mid-Cap Value
Small-Cap Growth	Small-Cap Value

Portfolio
1.0% cash	0.0% corp bonds
11.0% stocks	86.0% gov't bonds
0.0% preferred	0.0% muni bonds
1.0% conv't/warrants	1.0% other

SHAREHOLDER INFORMATION

Minimum Investment
Initial: $3,000   Subsequent: $50

Minimum IRA Investment
Initial: $250   Subsequent: $50

Maximum Fees
Load: none   12b-1: none
Other: none

Distributions
Income: monthly   Capital Gains: annual

Exchange Options
Number Per Year: 6   Fee: none
Telephone: yes (money market fund available)

Services
IRA, pension, auto exchange, auto invest, auto withdraw

USAA Income Stock
(USISX)

Growth & Income

USAA Building
San Antonio, TX 78288
800-531-8722, 210-456-7211

PERFORMANCE

fund inception date: 5/4/87

	3yr Annual	5yr Annual	10yr Annual	Bull	Bear
Return (%)	14.6	12.6	na	56.7	-6.7
Differ from Category (+/-)	-0.7 blw av	-1.3 blw av	na	-3.1 blw av	-0.3 av

Total Risk	Standard Deviation	Category Risk	Risk Index	Beta
av	8.1%	low	0.9	0.77

	1996	1995	1994	1993	1992	1991	1990	1989	1988	1987
Return (%).	17.8	28.6	-0.8	11.5	7.7	27.3	-1.5	27.1	19.4	—
Differ from Category (+/-) .	-1.9	-1.5	0.5	-2.3	-3.0	-1.8	4.4	3.6	2.6	—
Return, Tax-Adjusted (%). .	14.5	25.6	-3.4	9.0	5.4	24.8	-3.7	23.3	17.2	—

PER SHARE DATA

	1996	1995	1994	1993	1992	1991	1990	1989	1988	1987
Dividends, Net Income ($).	0.78	0.77	0.75	0.71	0.70	0.68	0.65	0.56	0.48	—
Distrib'ns, Cap Gain ($) . .	0.74	0.27	0.22	0.19	0.09	0.00	0.00	0.57	0.00	—
Net Asset Value ($)	16.83	15.67	13.06	14.13	13.48	13.27	11.01	11.85	10.28	—
Expense Ratio (%).	0.72	0.75	0.73	0.70	0.74	0.83	1.00	1.00	1.00	—
Yield (%)	4.43	4.83	5.64	4.95	5.15	5.12	5.90	4.50	4.66	—
Portfolio Turnover (%). . . .	32	34	na	26	16	27	49	72	28	—
Total Assets (Millions $). .	1,915	1,585	1,171	1,129	592	243	92	65	33	—

PORTFOLIO (as of 9/30/96)

Portfolio Manager: Harry W. Miller - 1989

Investm't Category: Growth & Income

✔ Domestic	Index
Foreign	Sector
Asset Allocation	State Specific

Investment Style

Large-Cap Growth	✔ Large-Cap Value
Mid-Cap Growth	Mid-Cap Value
Small-Cap Growth	Small-Cap Value

Portfolio

4.0% cash	0.0% corp bonds
79.0% stocks	0.0% gov't bonds
0.0% preferred	0.0% muni bonds
17.0% conv't/warrants	0.0% other

SHAREHOLDER INFORMATION

Minimum Investment
Initial: $3,000   Subsequent: $50

Minimum IRA Investment
Initial: $250   Subsequent: $50

Maximum Fees
Load: none   12b-1: none
Other: none

Distributions
Income: quarterly   Capital Gains: annual

Exchange Options
Number Per Year: 6   Fee: none
Telephone: yes (money market fund available)

Services
IRA, pension, auto exchange, auto invest, auto
withdraw

USAA Invest Trust: Cornerstone Strategy

USAA Building
San Antonio, TX 78288
800-531-8722, 210-456-7211

(USCRX) *Balanced*

PERFORMANCE

fund inception date: 8/15/84

	3yr Annual	5yr Annual	10yr Annual	Bull	Bear
Return (%)	11.3	12.6	10.6	41.5	-5.3
Differ from Category (+/-)	-0.4 av	1.2 abv av	-0.2 blw av	-3.6 blw av	0.4 av

Total Risk	Standard Deviation	Category Risk	Risk Index	Beta
av	7.2%	abv av	1.1	0.59

	1996	1995	1994	1993	1992	1991	1990	1989	1988	1987
Return (%)	17.8	18.3	-1.1	23.7	6.3	16.2	-9.2	21.9	8.3	8.9
Differ from Category (+/-)	3.6	-6.3	0.5	9.3	-2.6	-7.9	-8.3	3.8	-3.9	6.2
Return, Tax-Adjusted (%)	15.5	16.4	-3.8	22.1	4.9	14.8	-10.6	20.2	6.6	7.9

PER SHARE DATA

	1996	1995	1994	1993	1992	1991	1990	1989	1988	1987
Dividends, Net Income ($)	0.77	0.74	0.57	0.59	0.63	0.59	0.65	0.71	0.66	0.36
Distrib'ns, Cap Gain ($)	0.83	0.33	1.38	0.28	0.00	0.00	0.00	0.00	0.00	0.02
Net Asset Value ($)	26.59	24.03	21.24	23.46	19.69	19.12	16.98	19.44	16.54	15.87
Expense Ratio (%)	1.15	1.13	1.11	1.18	1.18	1.18	1.21	1.21	1.21	1.07
Yield (%)	2.80	3.03	2.51	2.48	3.19	3.08	3.82	3.65	3.99	2.26
Portfolio Turnover (%)	36	33	na	45	33	28	41	33	28	15
Total Assets (Millions $)	1,151	949	841	762	578	603	551	549	519	587

PORTFOLIO (as of 9/30/96)

Portfolio Manager: committee - 1990

Investm't Category: Balanced
- ✔ Domestic
- ✔ Foreign
- ✔ Asset Allocation
- Index
- Sector
- State Specific

Investment Style
- Large-Cap Growth
- Mid-Cap Growth
- Small-Cap Growth
- Large-Cap Value
- Mid-Cap Value
- Small-Cap Value

Portfolio
7.0% cash	0.0% corp bonds
74.0% stocks	18.0% gov't bonds
1.0% preferred	0.0% muni bonds
0.0% conv't/warrants	0.0% other

SHAREHOLDER INFORMATION

Minimum Investment
Initial: $3,000   Subsequent: $50

Minimum IRA Investment
Initial: $250   Subsequent: $50

Maximum Fees
Load: none   12b-1: none
Other: none

Distributions
Income: annual   Capital Gains: annual

Exchange Options
Number Per Year: 6   Fee: none
Telephone: yes (money market fund available)

Services
IRA, pension, auto exchange, auto invest, auto withdraw

USAA Invest Trust: Emerging Markets (USEMX)

International Stock

USAA Building
San Antonio, TX 78288
800-531-8722, 210-456-7211

PERFORMANCE

fund inception date: 11/7/94

	3yr Annual	5yr Annual	10yr Annual	Bull	Bear
Return (%)	na	na	na	na	na
Differ from Category (+/-)	na	na	na	na	na

Total Risk	Standard Deviation	Category Risk	Risk Index	Beta
na	na	na	na	na

	1996	1995	1994	1993	1992	1991	1990	1989	1988	1987
Return (%)	16.5	3.6	—	—	—	—	—	—	—	—
Differ from Category (+/-)	1.7	-5.5	—	—	—	—	—	—	—	—
Return, Tax-Adjusted (%)	14.9	2.8	—	—	—	—	—	—	—	—

PER SHARE DATA

	1996	1995	1994	1993	1992	1991	1990	1989	1988	1987
Dividends, Net Income ($)	0.00	0.01	—	—	—	—	—	—	—	—
Distrib'ns, Cap Gain ($)	0.50	0.22	—	—	—	—	—	—	—	—
Net Asset Value ($)	10.29	9.26	—	—	—	—	—	—	—	—
Expense Ratio (%)	2.27	2.40	—	—	—	—	—	—	—	—
Yield (%)	0.00	0.10	—	—	—	—	—	—	—	—
Portfolio Turnover (%)	87	46	—	—	—	—	—	—	—	—
Total Assets (Millions $)	54	25	—	—	—	—	—	—	—	—

PORTFOLIO (as of 9/30/96)

Portfolio Manager: W. Travis Selmier II - 1994

Investm't Category: International Stock

Domestic	Index
✔ Foreign	Sector
Asset Allocation	State Specific

Investment Style

Large-Cap Growth	Large-Cap Value
Mid-Cap Growth	Mid-Cap Value
Small-Cap Growth	Small-Cap Value

Portfolio

3.0%	cash	0.0%	corp bonds
91.0%	stocks	0.0%	gov't bonds
6.0%	preferred	0.0%	muni bonds
0.0%	conv't/warrants	0.0%	other

SHAREHOLDER INFORMATION

Minimum Investment
Initial: $3,000   Subsequent: $50

Minimum IRA Investment
Initial: $250   Subsequent: $50

Maximum Fees
Load: none   12b-1: none
Other: none

Distributions
Income: annual   Capital Gains: annual

Exchange Options
Number Per Year: 6   Fee: none
Telephone: yes (money market fund available)

Services
IRA, pension, auto exchange, auto invest, auto withdraw

USAA Invest Trust: GNMA (USGNX)

USAA Building
San Antonio, TX 78288
800-531-8722, 210-456-7211

Mortgage-Backed Bond

PERFORMANCE

fund inception date: 2/1/91

	3yr Annual	5yr Annual	10yr Annual	Bull	Bear
Return (%)	6.3	6.4	na	21.7	-1.9
Differ from Category (+/-)	0.7 abv av	0.4 abv av	na	0.6 av	1.7 abv av

Total Risk	Standard Deviation	Category Risk	Risk Index	Avg Mat
low	3.8%	av	1.0	9.2 yrs

	1996	1995	1994	1993	1992	1991	1990	1989	1988	1987
Return (%)	2.9	16.7	-0.1	7.1	6.0	—	—	—	—	—
Differ from Category (+/-)	-1.5	2.0	1.6	0.2	-0.2	—	—	—	—	—
Return, Tax-Adjusted (%)	0.2	13.7	-2.8	4.1	2.9	—	—	—	—	—

PER SHARE DATA

	1996	1995	1994	1993	1992	1991	1990	1989	1988	1987
Dividends, Net Income ($)	0.69	0.72	0.70	0.78	0.80	—	—	—	—	—
Distrib'ns, Cap Gain ($)	0.00	0.00	0.00	0.00	0.00	—	—	—	—	—
Net Asset Value ($)	9.99	10.40	9.57	10.28	10.34	—	—	—	—	—
Expense Ratio (%)	0.32	0.32	0.31	0.32	0.38	—	—	—	—	—
Yield (%)	6.90	6.92	7.31	7.58	7.73	—	—	—	—	—
Portfolio Turnover (%)	127	93	na	81	36	—	—	—	—	—
Total Assets (Millions $)	311	297	244	277	232	—	—	—	—	—

PORTFOLIO (as of 9/30/96)

Portfolio Manager: Kenneth E. Willmann - 1995

Investm't Category: Mortgage-Backed Bond
- ✔ Domestic
- Foreign
- Asset Allocation
- Index
- Sector
- State Specific

Investment Style
- Large-Cap Growth
- Mid-Cap Growth
- Small-Cap Growth
- Large-Cap Value
- Mid-Cap Value
- Small-Cap Value

Portfolio
0.0%	cash	0.0%	corp bonds
0.0%	stocks	100.0%	gov't bonds
0.0%	preferred	0.0%	muni bonds
0.0%	conv't/warrants	0.0%	other

SHAREHOLDER INFORMATION

Minimum Investment
Initial: $3,000   Subsequent: $50

Minimum IRA Investment
Initial: $250   Subsequent: $50

Maximum Fees
Load: none   12b-1: none
Other: none

Distributions
Income: monthly   Capital Gains: annual

Exchange Options
Number Per Year: 6   Fee: none
Telephone: yes (money market fund available)

Services
IRA, pension, auto exchange, auto invest, auto withdraw

USAA Invest Trust: Gold
(USAGX)

Gold

USAA Building
San Antonio, TX 78288
800-531-8722, 210-456-7211

PERFORMANCE

fund inception date: 8/15/84

	3yr Annual	5yr Annual	10yr Annual	Bull	Bear
Return (%)	-2.0	6.5	0.9	6.0	-11.5
Differ from Category (+/-)	-2.3 blw av	-3.1 blw av	-3.4 blw av	-8.9 blw av	-1.3 blw av

Total Risk	Standard Deviation	Category Risk	Risk Index	Beta
high	24.2%	av	1.0	0.63

	1996	1995	1994	1993	1992	1991	1990	1989	1988	1987
Return (%)	0.0	4.0	-9.4	58.3	-8.0	-4.5	-26.6	18.1	-17.2	16.2
Differ from Category (+/-)	-11.2	-1.0	2.7	-29.5	7.3	0.1	-4.3	-6.3	1.9	-16.0
Return, Tax-Adjusted (%)	0.0	4.0	-9.5	58.2	-8.3	-5.0	-26.9	17.3	-17.8	14.4

PER SHARE DATA

	1996	1995	1994	1993	1992	1991	1990	1989	1988	1987
Dividends, Net Income ($)	0.00	0.00	0.01	0.01	0.04	0.08	0.06	0.15	0.13	0.05
Distrib'ns, Cap Gain ($)	0.00	0.00	0.00	0.00	0.00	0.00	0.00	0.00	0.00	0.51
Net Asset Value ($)	8.93	8.93	8.59	9.49	6.00	6.56	6.95	9.55	8.21	10.06
Expense Ratio (%)	1.33	1.28	1.26	1.41	1.43	1.45	1.43	1.34	1.42	1.14
Yield (%)	0.00	0.00	0.11	0.10	0.66	1.21	0.86	1.57	1.58	0.47
Portfolio Turnover (%)	16	34	na	81	19	13	42	17	27	54
Total Assets (Millions $)	130	143	158	181	109	118	141	177	176	215

PORTFOLIO (as of 9/30/96)

Portfolio Manager: Mark Johnson - 1994

Investm't Category: Gold
- ✔ Domestic
- ✔ Foreign
-   Asset Allocation

-   Index
- ✔ Sector
-   State Specific

Investment Style

Large-Cap Growth	Large-Cap Value
Mid-Cap Growth	Mid-Cap Value
Small-Cap Growth	Small-Cap Value

Portfolio

2.0% cash	0.0% corp bonds
98.0% stocks	0.0% gov't bonds
0.0% preferred	0.0% muni bonds
0.0% conv't/warrants	0.0% other

SHAREHOLDER INFORMATION

Minimum Investment
Initial: $3,000   Subsequent: $50

Minimum IRA Investment
Initial: $250   Subsequent: $50

Maximum Fees
Load: none   12b-1: none
Other: none

Distributions
Income: annual   Capital Gains: annual

Exchange Options
Number Per Year: 6   Fee: none
Telephone: yes (money market fund available)

Services
IRA, pension, auto exchange, auto invest, auto withdraw

796   *Guide to Low-Load Mutual Funds*

USAA Invest Trust: Growth & Tax Strategy

USAA Building
San Antonio, TX 78288
800-531-8722, 210-456-7211

(USBLX) *Balanced*

PERFORMANCE

fund inception date: 1/11/89

	3yr Annual	5yr Annual	10yr Annual	Bull	Bear
Return (%)	9.9	9.6	na	36.2	-4.5
Differ from Category (+/-)	-1.8 blw av	-1.8 blw av	na	-8.9 blw av	1.2 abv av

Total Risk	Standard Deviation	Category Risk	Risk Index	Beta
blw av	5.6%	low	0.8	0.52

	1996	1995	1994	1993	1992	1991	1990	1989	1988	1987
Return (%).	11.1	22.7	-2.7	13.7	4.9	14.6	1.3	—	—	—
Differ from Category (+/-). .	-3.1	-1.9	-1.1	-0.7	-4.0	-9.5	2.2	—	—	—
Return, Tax-Adjusted (%). . .	8.9	20.9	-4.8	11.3	3.3	12.7	-0.7	—	—	—

PER SHARE DATA

	1996	1995	1994	1993	1992	1991	1990	1989	1988	1987
Dividends, Net Income ($).	0.51	0.50	0.47	0.45	0.46	0.51	0.54	—	—	—
Distrib'ns, Cap Gain ($) . . .	0.35	0.03	0.27	0.37	0.01	0.00	0.00	—	—	—
Net Asset Value ($)	14.31	13.70	11.64	12.71	11.92	11.82	10.78	—	—	—
Expense Ratio (%).	0.82	0.80	0.84	0.86	0.92	1.00	1.00	—	—	—
Yield (%)	3.47	3.64	3.94	3.44	3.85	4.31	5.00	—	—	—
Portfolio Turnover (%). . . .	202	314	na	98	107	81	106	—	—	—
Total Assets (Millions $). . .	173	149	124	127	91	61	39	—	—	—

PORTFOLIO (as of 9/30/96)

Portfolio Manager: committee - 1989

Investm't Category: Balanced
✔ Domestic   Index
  Foreign   Sector
✔ Asset Allocation   State Specific

Investment Style
  Large-Cap Growth   Large-Cap Value
  Mid-Cap Growth   Mid-Cap Value
  Small-Cap Growth   Small-Cap Value

Portfolio
13.0%	cash	0.0%	corp bonds
43.0%	stocks	0.0%	gov't bonds
0.0%	preferred	44.0%	muni bonds
0.0%	conv't/warrants	0.0%	other

SHAREHOLDER INFORMATION

Minimum Investment
Initial: $3,000   Subsequent: $50

Minimum IRA Investment
Initial: $250   Subsequent: $50

Maximum Fees
Load: none   12b-1: none
Other: none

Distributions
Income: quarterly   Capital Gains: annual

Exchange Options
Number Per Year: 6   Fee: none
Telephone: yes (money market fund available)

Services
IRA, pension, auto exchange, auto invest, auto withdraw

Individual Fund Listings   **797**

USAA Invest Trust: Growth Strategy (USGSX)

USAA Building
San Antonio, TX 78288
800-531-8722, 210-456-7211

Balanced

PERFORMANCE

fund inception date: 9/1/95

	3yr Annual	5yr Annual	10yr Annual	Bull	Bear
Return (%)	na	na	na	na	na
Differ from Category (+/-)	na	na	na	na	na

Total Risk	Standard Deviation	Category Risk	Risk Index	Beta
na	na	na	na	na

	1996	1995	1994	1993	1992	1991	1990	1989	1988	1987
Return (%)	22.1	—	—	—	—	—	—	—	—	—
Differ from Category (+/-)	7.9	—	—	—	—	—	—	—	—	—
Return, Tax-Adjusted (%)	20.4	—	—	—	—	—	—	—	—	—

PER SHARE DATA

	1996	1995	1994	1993	1992	1991	1990	1989	1988	1987
Dividends, Net Income ($)	0.12	—	—	—	—	—	—	—	—	—
Distrib'ns, Cap Gain ($)	0.44	—	—	—	—	—	—	—	—	—
Net Asset Value ($)	12.38	—	—	—	—	—	—	—	—	—
Expense Ratio (%)	na	—	—	—	—	—	—	—	—	—
Yield (%)	0.93	—	—	—	—	—	—	—	—	—
Portfolio Turnover (%)	na	—	—	—	—	—	—	—	—	—
Total Assets (Millions $)	133	—	—	—	—	—	—	—	—	—

PORTFOLIO (as of 9/30/96)

Portfolio Manager: committee - 1995

Investm't Category: Balanced
- ✔ Domestic
- ✔ Foreign
- ✔ Asset Allocation
- Index
- Sector
- State Specific

Investment Style
Large-Cap Growth	Large-Cap Value
Mid-Cap Growth	Mid-Cap Value
Small-Cap Growth	Small-Cap Value

Portfolio
2.0% cash	14.0% corp bonds
76.0% stocks	5.0% gov't bonds
1.0% preferred	0.0% muni bonds
0.0% conv't/warrants	2.0% other

SHAREHOLDER INFORMATION

Minimum Investment
Initial: $3,000   Subsequent: $50

Minimum IRA Investment
Initial: $250   Subsequent: $50

Maximum Fees
Load: none   12b-1: none
Other: none

Distributions
Income: annual   Capital Gains: annual

Exchange Options
Number Per Year: 6   Fee: none
Telephone: yes (money market fund available)

Services
IRA, pension, auto exchange, auto invest, auto withdraw

USAA Invest Trust: Int'l
(USIFX)

International Stock

USAA Building
San Antonio, TX 78288
800-531-8722, 210-456-7211

PERFORMANCE
fund inception date: 7/11/88

	3yr Annual	5yr Annual	10yr Annual	Bull	Bear
Return (%)	9.8	13.0	na	31.6	-5.0
Differ from Category (+/-)	3.5 abv av	3.0 high	na	7.3 abv av	2.2 abv av

Total Risk	Standard Deviation	Category Risk	Risk Index	Beta
abv av	10.5%	av	1.0	0.70

	1996	1995	1994	1993	1992	1991	1990	1989	1988	1987
Return (%)	19.1	8.2	2.6	39.8	-0.2	13.4	-9.4	17.3	—	—
Differ from Category (+/-)	4.3	-0.9	5.7	0.2	3.6	0.2	0.7	-5.3	—	—
Return, Tax-Adjusted (%)	17.8	7.9	0.9	38.9	-0.7	13.0	-9.8	16.0	—	—

PER SHARE DATA

	1996	1995	1994	1993	1992	1991	1990	1989	1988	1987
Dividends, Net Income ($)	0.19	0.06	0.00	0.00	0.13	0.09	0.06	0.02	—	—
Distrib'ns, Cap Gain ($)	0.50	0.08	0.97	0.35	0.00	0.00	0.05	0.45	—	—
Net Asset Value ($)	19.15	16.69	15.56	16.10	11.79	11.94	10.61	11.82	—	—
Expense Ratio (%)	1.19	1.17	1.31	1.50	1.69	1.82	2.09	2.30	—	—
Yield (%)	0.96	0.35	0.00	0.00	1.10	0.75	0.56	0.16	—	—
Portfolio Turnover (%)	70	64	na	52	34	64	70	95	—	—
Total Assets (Millions $)	504	351	337	131	43	31	23	16	—	—

PORTFOLIO (as of 9/30/96)

Portfolio Manager: Peebles, Sebastian, Selmier - 1988

Investm't Category: International Stock

Domestic	Index
✔ Foreign	Sector
Asset Allocation	State Specific

Investment Style

Large-Cap Growth	Large-Cap Value
Mid-Cap Growth	Mid-Cap Value
Small-Cap Growth	Small-Cap Value

Portfolio

6.0% cash	0.0% corp bonds
90.0% stocks	0.0% gov't bonds
4.0% preferred	0.0% muni bonds
0.0% conv't/warrants	0.0% other

SHAREHOLDER INFORMATION

Minimum Investment
Initial: $3,000   Subsequent: $50

Minimum IRA Investment
Initial: $250   Subsequent: $50

Maximum Fees
Load: none   12b-1: none
Other: none

Distributions
Income: annual   Capital Gains: annual

Exchange Options
Number Per Year: 6   Fee: none
Telephone: yes (money market fund available)

Services
IRA, pension, auto exchange, auto invest, auto withdraw

USAA Invest Trust: World Growth (USAWX)

International Stock

USAA Building
San Antonio, TX 78288
800-531-8722, 210-456-7211

PERFORMANCE

fund inception date: 10/1/92

	3yr Annual	5yr Annual	10yr Annual	Bull	Bear
Return (%)	10.5	na	na	37.1	-6.6
Differ from Category (+/-)	4.2 high	na	na	12.8 abv av	0.6 av

Total Risk	Standard Deviation	Category Risk	Risk Index	Beta
abv av	10.1%	av	1.0	0.77

	1996	1995	1994	1993	1992	1991	1990	1989	1988	1987
Return (%)	19.0	12.8	0.6	24.0	—	—	—	—	—	—
Differ from Category (+/-)	4.2	3.7	3.7	-15.6	—	—	—	—	—	—
Return, Tax-Adjusted (%)	16.7	12.0	-0.1	23.8	—	—	—	—	—	—

PER SHARE DATA

	1996	1995	1994	1993	1992	1991	1990	1989	1988	1987
Dividends, Net Income ($)	0.13	0.08	0.00	0.01	—	—	—	—	—	—
Distrib'ns, Cap Gain ($)	0.91	0.23	0.28	0.05	—	—	—	—	—	—
Net Asset Value ($)	15.30	13.78	12.50	12.70	—	—	—	—	—	—
Expense Ratio (%)	1.27	1.28	1.28	1.70	—	—	—	—	—	—
Yield (%)	0.80	0.57	0.00	0.07	—	—	—	—	—	—
Portfolio Turnover (%)	60	58	na	45	—	—	—	—	—	—
Total Assets (Millions $)	265	223	185	95	—	—	—	—	—	—

PORTFOLIO (as of 9/30/96)

Portfolio Manager: committee - 1992

Investm't Category: International Stock
- ✔ Domestic — Index
- ✔ Foreign — Sector
- Asset Allocation — State Specific

Investment Style
Large-Cap Growth	Large-Cap Value
Mid-Cap Growth	Mid-Cap Value
Small-Cap Growth	Small-Cap Value

Portfolio
4.0% cash	0.0% corp bonds
92.0% stocks	0.0% gov't bonds
3.0% preferred	0.0% muni bonds
0.0% conv't/warrants	1.0% other

SHAREHOLDER INFORMATION

Minimum Investment
Initial: $3,000   Subsequent: $50

Minimum IRA Investment
Initial: $250   Subsequent: $50

Maximum Fees
Load: none   12b-1: none
Other: none

Distributions
Income: annual   Capital Gains: annual

Exchange Options
Number Per Year: 6   Fee: none
Telephone: yes (money market fund available)

Services
IRA, pension, auto exchange, auto invest, auto withdraw

USAA Short-Term Bond
(USSBX)
General Bond

USAA Building
San Antonio, TX 78288
800-531-8722, 210-456-7211

PERFORMANCE

fund inception date: 6/1/93

	3yr Annual	5yr Annual	10yr Annual	Bull	Bear
Return (%)	5.7	na	na	19.5	-1.9
Differ from Category (+/-)	0.6 abv av	na	na	-0.8 av	2.3 abv av

Total Risk	Standard Deviation	Category Risk	Risk Index	Avg Mat
low	2.4%	blw av	0.6	2.7 yrs

	1996	1995	1994	1993	1992	1991	1990	1989	1988	1987
Return (%)	6.3	11.2	0.0	—	—	—	—	—	—	—
Differ from Category (+/-)	2.4	-3.7	2.3	—	—	—	—	—	—	—
Return, Tax-Adjusted (%)	3.9	8.5	-2.0	—	—	—	—	—	—	—

PER SHARE DATA

	1996	1995	1994	1993	1992	1991	1990	1989	1988	1987
Dividends, Net Income ($)	0.60	0.64	0.50	—	—	—	—	—	—	—
Distrib'ns, Cap Gain ($)	0.00	0.00	0.00	—	—	—	—	—	—	—
Net Asset Value ($)	9.92	9.93	9.53	—	—	—	—	—	—	—
Expense Ratio (%)	0.50	0.50	0.50	—	—	—	—	—	—	—
Yield (%)	6.04	6.44	5.24	—	—	—	—	—	—	—
Portfolio Turnover (%)	66	103	142	—	—	—	—	—	—	—
Total Assets (Millions $)	110	91	50	—	—	—	—	—	—	—

PORTFOLIO (as of 9/30/96)

Portfolio Manager: Paul Lundmark - 1993

Investm't Category: General Bond
- ✔ Domestic
- Foreign
- Asset Allocation
- Index
- Sector
- State Specific

Investment Style
- Large-Cap Growth
- Mid-Cap Growth
- Small-Cap Growth
- Large-Cap Value
- Mid-Cap Value
- Small-Cap Value

Portfolio
- 36.0% cash
- 0.0% stocks
- 0.0% preferred
- 0.0% conv't/warrants
- 51.0% corp bonds
- 4.0% gov't bonds
- 0.0% muni bonds
- 9.0% other

SHAREHOLDER INFORMATION

Minimum Investment
Initial: $3,000   Subsequent: $50

Minimum IRA Investment
Initial: $250   Subsequent: $50

Maximum Fees
Load: none   12b-1: none
Other: none

Distributions
Income: monthly   Capital Gains: annual

Exchange Options
Number Per Year: 6   Fee: none
Telephone: yes (money market fund available)

Services
IRA, pension, auto exchange, auto invest, auto withdraw

USAA Tax-Exempt CA Bond (USCBX)

USAA Building
San Antonio, TX 78288
800-531-8722, 210-456-7211

Tax-Exempt Bond

PERFORMANCE

fund inception date: 8/1/89

	3yr Annual	5yr Annual	10yr Annual	Bull	Bear
Return (%)	5.2	7.2	na	24.6	-7.9
Differ from Category (+/-)	1.0 high	0.8 high		6.2 high	-2.5 low

Total Risk	Standard Deviation	Category Risk	Risk Index	Avg Mat
blw av	6.9%	high	1.2	21.1 yrs

	1996	1995	1994	1993	1992	1991	1990	1989	1988	1987
Return (%)	5.3	21.8	-9.4	12.7	8.2	10.9	8.1	—	—	—
Differ from Category (+/-)	1.6	6.6	-4.1	0.9	-0.1	-0.5	1.7	—	—	—
Return, Tax-Adjusted (%)	5.3	21.8	-9.4	12.1	7.9	10.9	8.1	—	—	—

PER SHARE DATA

	1996	1995	1994	1993	1992	1991	1990	1989	1988	1987
Dividends, Net Income ($)	0.60	0.59	0.58	0.59	0.63	0.66	0.66	—	—	—
Distrib'ns, Cap Gain ($)	0.00	0.00	0.00	0.19	0.11	0.00	0.00	—	—	—
Net Asset Value ($)	10.71	10.76	9.36	10.94	10.44	10.36	9.97	—	—	—
Expense Ratio (%)	0.42	0.44	0.44	0.46	0.48	0.50	0.50	—	—	—
Yield (%)	5.60	5.48	6.19	5.30	5.97	6.37	6.61	—	—	—
Portfolio Turnover (%)	23	68	102	86	51	73	136	—	—	—
Total Assets (Millions $)	442	414	395	427	352	294	170	—	—	—

PORTFOLIO (as of 9/30/96)

Portfolio Manager: Robert R. Pariseau - 1995

Investm't Category: Tax-Exempt Bond
- ✔ Domestic
- Foreign
- Asset Allocation
- Index
- Sector
- ✔ State Specific

Investment Style
- Large-Cap Growth
- Mid-Cap Growth
- Small-Cap Growth
- Large-Cap Value
- Mid-Cap Value
- Small-Cap Value

Portfolio
2.0% cash	0.0% corp bonds
0.0% stocks	0.0% gov't bonds
0.0% preferred	98.0% muni bonds
0.0% conv't/warrants	0.0% other

SHAREHOLDER INFORMATION

Minimum Investment
Initial: $3,000   Subsequent: $50

Minimum IRA Investment
Initial: na   Subsequent: na

Maximum Fees
Load: none   12b-1: none
Other: none

Distributions
Income: monthly   Capital Gains: annual

Exchange Options
Number Per Year: 6   Fee: none
Telephone: yes (money market fund available)

Services
auto exchange, auto invest, auto withdraw

USAA Tax-Exempt Interm-Term (USATX)

Tax-Exempt Bond

USAA Building
San Antonio, TX 78288
800-531-8722, 210-456-7211

PERFORMANCE

fund inception date: 3/19/82

	3yr Annual	5yr Annual	10yr Annual	Bull	Bear
Return (%)	4.8	6.8	7.0	19.6	-4.7
Differ from Category (+/-)	0.6 high	0.4 av	0.3 abv av	1.2 av	0.7 abv av

Total Risk	Standard Deviation	Category Risk	Risk Index	Avg Mat
low	4.4%	blw av	0.8	9.3 yrs

	1996	1995	1994	1993	1992	1991	1990	1989	1988	1987
Return (%)	4.4	15.0	-4.1	11.4	8.4	11.1	6.7	9.2	8.6	0.9
Differ from Category (+/-)	0.7	-0.2	1.2	-0.4	0.1	-0.3	0.3	0.2	-1.4	2.3
Return, Tax-Adjusted (%)	4.4	15.0	-4.2	11.1	8.4	11.1	6.7	9.2	8.6	0.8

PER SHARE DATA

	1996	1995	1994	1993	1992	1991	1990	1989	1988	1987
Dividends, Net Income ($)	0.72	0.71	0.68	0.70	0.75	0.80	0.82	0.83	0.83	0.83
Distrib'ns, Cap Gain ($)	0.00	0.00	0.02	0.13	0.00	0.00	0.00	0.00	0.00	0.01
Net Asset Value ($)	12.92	13.08	12.02	13.26	12.68	12.41	11.93	11.98	11.76	11.61
Expense Ratio (%)	0.38	0.40	0.40	0.42	0.44	0.43	0.46	0.49	0.56	0.60
Yield (%)	5.57	5.42	5.64	5.22	5.91	6.44	6.87	6.92	7.05	7.14
Portfolio Turnover (%)	27	72	69	74	67	66	62	113	139	91
Total Assets (Millions $)	1,723	1,673	1,416	1,660	1,205	818	536	453	393	320

PORTFOLIO (as of 9/30/96)

Portfolio Manager: Clifford A. Gladson - 1993

Investm't Category: Tax-Exempt Bond
✔ Domestic   Index
   Foreign   Sector
   Asset Allocation   State Specific

Investment Style
Large-Cap Growth   Large-Cap Value
Mid-Cap Growth   Mid-Cap Value
Small-Cap Growth   Small-Cap Value

Portfolio
3.0% cash   0.0% corp bonds
0.0% stocks   0.0% gov't bonds
0.0% preferred   97.0% muni bonds
0.0% conv't/warrants 0.0% other

SHAREHOLDER INFORMATION

Minimum Investment
Initial: $3,000   Subsequent: $50

Minimum IRA Investment
Initial: na   Subsequent: na

Maximum Fees
Load: none   12b-1: none
Other: none

Distributions
Income: monthly   Capital Gains: annual

Exchange Options
Number Per Year: 6   Fee: none
Telephone: yes (money market fund available)

Services
auto exchange, auto invest, auto withdraw

USAA Tax-Exempt Long-Term (USTEX)

Tax-Exempt Bond

USAA Building
San Antonio, TX 78288
800-531-8722, 210-456-7211

PERFORMANCE

fund inception date: 3/19/82

	3yr Annual	5yr Annual	10yr Annual	Bull	Bear
Return (%)	4.4	6.8	7.3	20.7	-6.7
Differ from Category (+/-)	0.2 av	0.4 av	0.6 abv av	2.3 abv av	-1.3 blw av

Total Risk	Standard Deviation	Category Risk	Risk Index	Avg Mat
blw av	5.9%	abv av	1.1	23.2 yrs

	1996	1995	1994	1993	1992	1991	1990	1989	1988	1987
Return (%).	4.4	18.5	-8.0	12.5	8.6	12.3	6.5	10.6	12.4	-2.0
Differ from Category (+/-). .	0.7	3.3	-2.7	0.7	0.3	0.9	0.1	1.6	2.4	-0.6
Return, Tax-Adjusted (%). . .	4.4	18.5	-8.2	11.3	8.4	12.3	6.5	10.6	12.4	-2.5

PER SHARE DATA

	1996	1995	1994	1993	1992	1991	1990	1989	1988	1987
Dividends, Net Income ($)	0.78	0.80	0.77	0.84	0.89	0.92	0.94	0.95	0.95	0.98
Distrib'ns, Cap Gain ($) . . .	0.00	0.00	0.08	0.55	0.07	0.00	0.00	0.00	0.00	0.22
Net Asset Value ($)	13.42	13.63	12.22	14.18	13.90	13.73	13.09	13.21	12.84	12.31
Expense Ratio (%).	0.37	0.38	0.38	0.39	0.40	0.40	0.43	0.45	0.51	0.49
Yield (%)	5.81	5.86	6.26	5.70	6.37	6.70	7.18	7.19	7.39	7.82
Portfolio Turnover (%).	53	163	109	88	76	91	92	124	169	83
Total Assets (Millions $). .	1,909	1,910	1,661	2,013	1,784	1,637	1,306	1,145	950	791

PORTFOLIO (as of 9/30/96)

Portfolio Manager: Kenneth E. Willmann - 1982

Investm't Category: Tax-Exempt Bond
✔ Domestic　　　　　　Index
　Foreign　　　　　　　Sector
　Asset Allocation　　　State Specific

Investment Style
　Large-Cap Growth　　Large-Cap Value
　Mid-Cap Growth　　　Mid-Cap Value
　Small-Cap Growth　　Small-Cap Value

Portfolio
　3.0% cash　　　　　0.0% corp bonds
　0.0% stocks　　　　0.0% gov't bonds
　0.0% preferred　　　97.0% muni bonds
　0.0% conv't/warrants　0.0% other

SHAREHOLDER INFORMATION

Minimum Investment
Initial: $3,000　　　　Subsequent: $50

Minimum IRA Investment
Initial: na　　　　　　Subsequent: na

Maximum Fees
Load: none　　　　　　12b-1: none
Other: none

Distributions
Income: monthly　　　Capital Gains: annual

Exchange Options
Number Per Year: 6　　　　　　Fee: none
Telephone: yes (money market fund available)

Services
auto exchange, auto invest, auto withdraw

USAA Tax-Exempt NY Bond (USNYX)

Tax-Exempt Bond

USAA Building
San Antonio, TX 78288
800-531-8722, 210-456-7211

PERFORMANCE

fund inception date: 10/15/90

	3yr Annual	5yr Annual	10yr Annual	Bull	Bear
Return (%)	3.6	6.6	na	19.6	-7.9
Differ from Category (+/-)	-0.6 low	0.2 av	na	1.2 av	-2.5 low

Total Risk	Standard Deviation	Category Risk	Risk Index	Avg Mat
blw av	6.6%	high	1.2	22.8 yrs

	1996	1995	1994	1993	1992	1991	1990	1989	1988	1987
Return (%)	3.7	18.0	-9.0	13.4	8.9	13.7	—	—	—	—
Differ from Category (+/-)	0.0	2.8	-3.7	1.6	0.6	2.3	—	—	—	—
Return, Tax-Adjusted (%)	3.7	18.0	-9.0	12.7	8.6	13.7	—	—	—	—

PER SHARE DATA

	1996	1995	1994	1993	1992	1991	1990	1989	1988	1987
Dividends, Net Income ($)	0.63	0.63	0.61	0.62	0.65	0.69	—	—	—	—
Distrib'ns, Cap Gain ($)	0.00	0.00	0.00	0.28	0.11	0.00	—	—	—	—
Net Asset Value ($)	11.09	11.33	10.17	11.83	11.27	11.09	—	—	—	—
Expense Ratio (%)	0.50	0.50	0.50	0.50	0.50	0.50	—	—	—	—
Yield (%)	5.68	5.56	5.99	5.11	5.71	6.22	—	—	—	—
Portfolio Turnover (%)	74	142	124	107	111	128	—	—	—	—
Total Assets (Millions $)	56	54	45	61	42	24	—	—	—	—

PORTFOLIO (as of 9/30/96)

Portfolio Manager: Kenneth E. Willmann - 1990

Investm't Category: Tax-Exempt Bond
- ✔ Domestic
- Foreign
- Asset Allocation
- Index
- Sector
- ✔ State Specific

Investment Style
- Large-Cap Growth
- Mid-Cap Growth
- Small-Cap Growth
- Large-Cap Value
- Mid-Cap Value
- Small-Cap Value

Portfolio
- 1.0% cash
- 0.0% stocks
- 0.0% preferred
- 0.0% conv't/warrants
- 0.0% corp bonds
- 0.0% gov't bonds
- 99.0% muni bonds
- 0.0% other

SHAREHOLDER INFORMATION

Minimum Investment
Initial: $3,000   Subsequent: $50

Minimum IRA Investment
Initial: na   Subsequent: na

Maximum Fees
Load: none   12b-1: none
Other: none

Distributions
Income: monthly   Capital Gains: annual

Exchange Options
Number Per Year: 6   Fee: none
Telephone: yes (money market fund available)

Services
auto exchange, auto invest, auto withdraw

USAA Tax-Exempt Short-Term (USSTX)

Tax-Exempt Bond

USAA Building
San Antonio, TX 78288
800-531-8722, 210-456-7211

PERFORMANCE
fund inception date: 3/19/82

	3yr Annual	5yr Annual	10yr Annual	Bull	Bear
Return (%)	4.4	4.9	5.4	14.0	-0.8
Differ from Category (+/-)	0.2 av	-1.5 low	-1.3 low	-4.4 low	4.6 high

Total Risk	Standard Deviation	Category Risk	Risk Index	Avg Mat
low	1.5%	low	0.3	2.8 yrs

	1996	1995	1994	1993	1992	1991	1990	1989	1988	1987
Return (%).	4.4	8.1	0.8	5.5	5.9	7.7	5.8	7.4	6.0	2.8
Differ from Category (+/-) . .	0.7	-7.1	6.1	-6.3	-2.4	-3.7	-0.6	-1.6	-4.0	4.2
Return, Tax-Adjusted (%). . .	4.4	8.1	0.8	5.5	5.9	7.7	5.8	7.4	6.0	2.7

PER SHARE DATA

	1996	1995	1994	1993	1992	1991	1990	1989	1988	1987
Dividends, Net Income ($).	0.49	0.50	0.45	0.46	0.52	0.61	0.67	0.67	0.62	0.60
Distrib'ns, Cap Gain ($) . . .	0.00	0.00	0.00	0.00	0.00	0.00	0.00	0.00	0.00	0.03
Net Asset Value ($)	10.62	10.65	10.33	10.70	10.59	10.50	10.34	10.42	10.35	10.36
Expense Ratio (%).	0.42	0.42	0.43	0.43	0.48	0.50	0.52	0.51	0.56	0.57
Yield (%)	4.61	4.69	4.35	4.29	4.91	5.80	6.47	6.42	5.99	5.77
Portfolio Turnover (%).	35	102	101	138	107	96	87	146	148	142
Total Assets (Millions $). . .	793	776	810	954	840	602	360	258	250	226

PORTFOLIO (as of 9/30/96)

Portfolio Manager: Clifford A. Gladson - 1994

Investm't Category: Tax-Exempt Bond
✔ Domestic   Index
  Foreign   Sector
  Asset Allocation State Specific

Investment Style
  Large-Cap Growth   Large-Cap Value
  Mid-Cap Growth   Mid-Cap Value
  Small-Cap Growth   Small-Cap Value

Portfolio
  21.0% cash   0.0% corp bonds
  0.0% stocks   0.0% gov't bonds
  0.0% preferred   79.0% muni bonds
  0.0% conv't/warrants 0.0% other

SHAREHOLDER INFORMATION

Minimum Investment
Initial: $3,000   Subsequent: $50

Minimum IRA Investment
Initial: na   Subsequent: na

Maximum Fees
Load: none   12b-1: none
Other: none

Distributions
Income: monthly   Capital Gains: annual

Exchange Options
Number Per Year: no limit   Fee: none
Telephone: yes (money market fund available)

Services
auto exchange, auto invest, auto withdraw

USAA Tax-Exempt Virginia Bond (USVAX)

Tax-Exempt Bond

USAA Building
San Antonio, TX 78288
800-531-8722, 210-456-7211

PERFORMANCE

fund inception date: 10/15/90

	3yr Annual	5yr Annual	10yr Annual	Bull	Bear
Return (%)	4.8	7.0	na	21.7	-6.5
Differ from Category (+/-)	0.6 abv av	0.6 abv av	na	3.3 high	-1.1 blw av

Total Risk	Standard Deviation	Category Risk	Risk Index	Avg Mat
blw av	5.6%	av	1.0	19.7 yrs

	1996	1995	1994	1993	1992	1991	1990	1989	1988	1987
Return (%)	5.0	17.0	-6.4	12.6	8.4	11.7	—	—	—	—
Differ from Category (+/-)	1.3	1.8	-1.1	0.8	0.1	0.3	—	—	—	—
Return, Tax-Adjusted (%)	5.0	17.0	-6.4	12.2	8.2	11.7	—	—	—	—

PER SHARE DATA

	1996	1995	1994	1993	1992	1991	1990	1989	1988	1987
Dividends, Net Income ($)	0.63	0.63	0.61	0.62	0.64	0.68	—	—	—	—
Distrib'ns, Cap Gain ($)	0.00	0.00	0.00	0.14	0.06	0.00	—	—	—	—
Net Asset Value ($)	11.11	11.20	10.14	11.47	10.90	10.73	—	—	—	—
Expense Ratio (%)	0.48	0.50	0.49	0.50	0.50	0.50	—	—	—	—
Yield (%)	5.67	5.62	6.01	5.34	5.83	6.33	—	—	—	—
Portfolio Turnover (%)	27	68	92	91	87	143	—	—	—	—
Total Assets (Millions $)	285	263	215	253	182	120	—	—	—	—

PORTFOLIO (as of 9/30/96)

Portfolio Manager: Robert R. Pariseau - 1995

Investm't Category: Tax-Exempt Bond
- ✔ Domestic
- Foreign
- Asset Allocation
- Index
- Sector
- ✔ State Specific

Investment Style
- Large-Cap Growth
- Mid-Cap Growth
- Small-Cap Growth
- Large-Cap Value
- Mid-Cap Value
- Small-Cap Value

Portfolio
1.0% cash	0.0% corp bonds
0.0% stocks	0.0% gov't bonds
0.0% preferred	99.0% muni bonds
0.0% conv't/warrants	0.0% other

SHAREHOLDER INFORMATION

Minimum Investment
Initial: $3,000   Subsequent: $50

Minimum IRA Investment
Initial: na   Subsequent: na

Maximum Fees
Load: none   12b-1: none
Other: none

Distributions
Income: monthly   Capital Gains: annual

Exchange Options
Number Per Year: 6   Fee: none
Telephone: yes (money market fund available)

Services
auto exchange, auto invest, auto withdraw

United Service Gold Shares (USERX)

Gold

P.O. Box 29467
7900 Callaghan Road
San Antonio, TX 78229
800-873-8637, 512-308-1234
www.usfunds.com

PERFORMANCE

fund inception date: 6/5/70

	3yr Annual	5yr Annual	10yr Annual	Bull	Bear
Return (%)	-19.1	-10.2	-7.7	-39.2	-3.1
Differ from Category (+/-)	-19.4 low	-19.8 low	-12.0 low	-54.1 low	7.1 high

Total Risk	Standard Deviation	Category Risk	Risk Index	Beta
high	29.4%	high	1.2	0.30

	1996	1995	1994	1993	1992	1991	1990	1989	1988	1987
Return (%).............	-25.5	-26.9	-2.7	123.9	-50.9	-15.7	-34.3	64.7	-35.8	31.5
Differ from Category (+/-)	-36.7	-31.9	9.4	36.1	-35.6	-11.1	-12.0	40.3	-16.7	-0.7
Return, Tax-Adjusted (%).	-26.6	-27.8	-3.7	122.3	-51.7	-16.7	-35.5	62.6	-37.4	26.8

PER SHARE DATA

	1996	1995	1994	1993	1992	1991	1990	1989	1988	1987
Dividends, Net Income ($).	0.05	0.06	0.07	0.05	0.05	0.08	0.15	0.17	0.22	0.54
Distrib'ns, Cap Gain ($) ...	0.00	0.00	0.00	0.00	0.00	0.00	0.00	0.00	0.00	0.00
Net Asset Value ($)	1.40	1.94	2.73	2.88	1.31	2.75	3.35	5.31	3.34	5.53
Expense Ratio (%)........	1.54	1.42	1.46	1.88	1.54	1.54	1.46	1.54	1.31	1.32
Yield (%)	3.57	3.09	2.56	1.73	3.81	2.90	4.47	3.20	6.58	9.76
Portfolio Turnover (%).....	24	32	29	19	25	49	13	7	18	24
Total Assets (Millions $)...	155	175	291	337	128	208	262	356	214	340

PORTFOLIO (as of 6/30/96)

Portfolio Manager: Victor Flores - 1992

Investm't Category: Gold
- ✔ Domestic
- ✔ Foreign
-   Asset Allocation
-   Index
- ✔ Sector
-   State Specific

Investment Style

Large-Cap Growth	Large-Cap Value
Mid-Cap Growth	Mid-Cap Value
Small-Cap Growth	Small-Cap Value

Portfolio

2.0% cash	0.0% corp bonds
98.0% stocks	0.0% gov't bonds
0.0% preferred	0.0% muni bonds
0.0% conv't/warrants	0.0% other

SHAREHOLDER INFORMATION

Minimum Investment
Initial: $1,000   Subsequent: $50

Minimum IRA Investment
Initial: $1   Subsequent: $1

Maximum Fees
Load: 0.10% redemption   12b-1: none
Other: redemption fee applies for 14 days; f

Distributions
Income: Jun, Dec   Capital Gains: Dec

Exchange Options
Number Per Year: no limit   Fee: $5
Telephone: yes (money market fund available)

Services
IRA, pension, auto exchange, auto invest, auto withdraw

United Service World Gold (UNWPX)

Gold

P.O. Box 29467
7900 Callaghan Road
San Antonio, TX 78229
800-873-8637, 512-308-1234
www.usfunds.com

PERFORMANCE

fund inception date: 12/2/85

	3yr Annual	5yr Annual	10yr Annual	Bull	Bear
Return (%)	4.7	15.7	6.0	29.9	-14.5
Differ from Category (+/-)	4.4 high	6.1 high	1.7 abv av	15.0 abv av	-4.3 low

Total Risk	Standard Deviation	Category Risk	Risk Index	Beta
high	23.3%	blw av	0.9	0.86

	1996	1995	1994	1993	1992	1991	1990	1989	1988	1987
Return (%)	19.5	15.9	-17.0	89.7	-4.8	-3.4	-27.9	16.5	-18.8	31.0
Differ from Category (+/-)	8.3	10.9	-4.9	1.9	10.5	1.2	-5.6	-7.9	0.3	-1.2
Return, Tax-Adjusted (%)	16.9	15.9	-17.1	89.7	-4.8	-3.4	-27.9	16.1	-18.8	25.9

PER SHARE DATA

	1996	1995	1994	1993	1992	1991	1990	1989	1988	1987
Dividends, Net Income ($)	1.11	0.00	0.03	0.00	0.00	0.00	0.10	0.00	0.20	
Distrib'ns, Cap Gain ($)	0.00	0.00	0.00	0.00	0.00	0.00	0.00	0.00	2.10	
Net Asset Value ($)	19.16	16.96	14.63	17.65	9.30	9.76	10.10	14.00	12.10	14.90
Expense Ratio (%)	1.51	1.55	1.53	2.00	2.20	2.22	1.95	2.00	1.47	1.47
Yield (%)	5.79	0.00	0.20	0.00	0.00	0.00	0.00	0.71	0.00	1.17
Portfolio Turnover (%)	25	28	19	26	47	44	26	20	39	44
Total Assets (Millions $)	251	184	182	168	61	56	68	97	96	121

PORTFOLIO (as of 9/30/96)

Portfolio Manager: Victor Flores - 1988

Investm't Category: Gold
- ✔ Domestic
- ✔ Foreign
- Asset Allocation
- Index
- ✔ Sector
- State Specific

Investment Style
- Large-Cap Growth
- Mid-Cap Growth
- Small-Cap Growth
- Large-Cap Value
- Mid-Cap Value
- Small-Cap Value

Portfolio
2.1% cash	0.0% corp bonds
97.9% stocks	0.0% gov't bonds
0.0% preferred	0.0% muni bonds
0.0% conv't/warrants	0.0% other

SHAREHOLDER INFORMATION

Minimum Investment
Initial: $1,000   Subsequent: $50

Minimum IRA Investment
Initial: $1   Subsequent: $1

Maximum Fees
Load: 0.10% redemption   12b-1: none
Other: redemption fee applies for 14 days; *f*

Distributions
Income: Dec   Capital Gains: Dec

Exchange Options
Number Per Year: no limit   Fee: $5
Telephone: yes (money market fund available)

Services
IRA, pension, auto exchange, auto invest, auto withdraw

Value Line (VLIFX)

Growth

220 E. 42nd St.
6th Floor
New York, NY 10017
800-223-0818, 212-907-1500

PERFORMANCE
fund inception date: 1/1/50

	3yr Annual	5yr Annual	10yr Annual	Bull	Bear
Return (%)	15.6	11.5	14.5	71.1	-13.0
Differ from Category (+/-)	-0.1 av	-2.8 blw av	0.6 abv av	8.7 abv av	-6.3 low

Total Risk	Standard Deviation	Category Risk	Risk Index	Beta
abv av	11.0%	abv av	1.1	0.95

	1996	1995	1994	1993	1992	1991	1990	1989	1988	1987
Return (%).............	22.5	32.1	-4.5	6.8	4.6	48.8	-0.8	31.4	9.6	5.2
Differ from Category (+/-)..	2.4	1.8	-4.2	-7.2	-7.2	12.8	5.3	5.3	-8.5	3.2
Return, Tax-Adjusted (%)..	18.7	29.4	-8.8	4.5	0.4	46.3	-2.0	26.5	8.0	-0.6

PER SHARE DATA

	1996	1995	1994	1993	1992	1991	1990	1989	1988	1987
Dividends, Net Income ($).	0.11	0.12	0.09	0.07	0.16	0.23	0.27	0.34	0.32	0.26
Distrib'ns, Cap Gain ($) ...	2.21	1.19	2.61	1.39	2.73	0.92	0.23	1.80	0.24	2.64
Net Asset Value ($)	19.29	17.63	14.36	17.90	18.16	20.17	14.42	15.06	13.15	12.51
Expense Ratio (%).........	na	0.83	0.82	0.80	0.84	0.71	0.71	0.70	0.71	0.69
Yield (%)	0.51	0.63	0.53	0.36	0.76	1.09	1.84	2.01	2.38	1.71
Portfolio Turnover (%).....	na	78	150	120	129	109	84	125	108	118
Total Assets (Millions $)...	362	317	272	331	327	320	202	194	180	204

PORTFOLIO (as of 9/30/96)

Portfolio Manager: committee - 1990

Investm't Category: Growth

✔ Domestic	Index
Foreign	Sector
Asset Allocation	State Specific

Investment Style

Large-Cap Growth	Large-Cap Value
✔ Mid-Cap Growth	Mid-Cap Value
Small-Cap Growth	Small-Cap Value

Portfolio

17.4% cash	0.0% corp bonds
82.6% stocks	0.0% gov't bonds
0.0% preferred	0.0% muni bonds
0.0% conv't/warrants	0.0% other

SHAREHOLDER INFORMATION

Minimum Investment
Initial: $1,000   Subsequent: $100

Minimum IRA Investment
Initial: $1,000   Subsequent: $100

Maximum Fees
Load: none   12b-1: none
Other: none

Distributions
Income: quarterly   Capital Gains: Dec

Exchange Options
Number Per Year: 8   Fee: none
Telephone: yes (money market fund available)

Services
IRA, pension, auto invest, auto withdraw

Value Line Aggressive Income Trust (VAGIX)

Corporate High-Yield Bond

220 E. 42nd St.
6th Floor
New York, NY 10017
800-223-0818, 212-907-1500

PERFORMANCE

fund inception date: 2/19/86

	3yr Annual	5yr Annual	10yr Annual	Bull	Bear
Return (%)	11.2	12.9	9.1	42.6	-5.8
Differ from Category (+/-)	2.5 high	0.8 abv av	-0.2 av	9.5 high	-0.4 av

Total Risk	Standard Deviation	Category Risk	Risk Index	Avg Mat
low	4.6%	av	1.0	6.4 yrs

	1996	1995	1994	1993	1992	1991	1990	1989	1988	1987
Return (%).	19.7	20.0	-4.1	19.0	12.1	26.6	-3.7	2.3	6.2	-2.1
Differ from Category (+/-). .	4.4	2.5	-1.2	0.1	-4.0	-1.0	1.2	1.1	-6.3	-3.9
Return, Tax-Adjusted (%). .	15.7	16.0	-7.5	15.3	8.2	21.8	-8.0	-2.1	1.8	-6.9

PER SHARE DATA

	1996	1995	1994	1993	1992	1991	1990	1989	1988	1987
Dividends, Net Income ($).	0.74	0.69	0.67	0.66	0.68	0.75	0.78	0.88	0.93	1.16
Distrib'ns, Cap Gain ($) . . .	0.00	0.00	0.00	0.00	0.00	0.00	0.00	0.00	0.00	0.00
Net Asset Value ($)	8.16	7.49	6.88	7.87	7.21	7.06	6.22	7.26	7.95	8.39
Expense Ratio (%).	1.22	1.27	1.20	1.15	1.18	1.43	1.30	1.14	1.22	1.33
Yield (%)	9.06	9.21	9.73	8.38	9.43	10.62	12.54	12.12	11.69	13.82
Portfolio Turnover (%). . . .	284	221	320	148	59	36	129	95	134	110
Total Assets (Millions $). . . .	66	38	30	43	34	30	23	31	45	49

PORTFOLIO (as of 9/30/96)

Portfolio Manager: committee - 1990

Investm't Category: Corp. High-Yield Bond

✔ Domestic	Index
Foreign	Sector
Asset Allocation	State Specific

Investment Style

Large-Cap Growth	Large-Cap Value
Mid-Cap Growth	Mid-Cap Value
Small-Cap Growth	Small-Cap Value

Portfolio

4.1% cash	93.0% corp bonds
0.3% stocks	0.0% gov't bonds
1.6% preferred	0.0% muni bonds
0.9% conv't/warrants	0.0% other

SHAREHOLDER INFORMATION

Minimum Investment
Initial: $1,000   Subsequent: $250

Minimum IRA Investment
Initial: $1,000   Subsequent: $250

Maximum Fees
Load: none   12b-1: none
Other: none

Distributions
Income: monthly   Capital Gains: Dec

Exchange Options
Number Per Year: 8   Fee: none
Telephone: yes (money market fund available)

Services
IRA, pension, auto invest, auto withdraw

Value Line Asset Allocation (VLAAX)

220 E. 42nd St.
6th Floor
New York, NY 10017
800-223-0818, 212-907-1500

Balanced

PERFORMANCE

fund inception date: 8/24/93

	3yr Annual	5yr Annual	10yr Annual	Bull	Bear
Return (%)	21.2	na	na	84.0	-7.1
Differ from Category (+/-)	9.5 high	na	na	38.9 high	-1.4 blw av

Total Risk	Standard Deviation	Category Risk	Risk Index	Beta
av	8.9%	high	1.3	0.71

	1996	1995	1994	1993	1992	1991	1990	1989	1988	1987
Return (%)	26.6	36.1	3.4	—	—	—	—	—	—	—
Differ from Category (+/-)	12.4	11.5	5.0	—	—	—	—	—	—	—
Return, Tax-Adjusted (%)	20.1	32.2	2.9	—	—	—	—	—	—	—

PER SHARE DATA

	1996	1995	1994	1993	1992	1991	1990	1989	1988	1987
Dividends, Net Income ($)	0.25	0.12	0.06	—	—	—	—	—	—	—
Distrib'ns, Cap Gain ($)	2.69	1.29	0.10	—	—	—	—	—	—	—
Net Asset Value ($)	13.73	13.20	10.74	—	—	—	—	—	—	—
Expense Ratio (%)	1.38	1.76	0.47	—	—	—	—	—	—	—
Yield (%)	1.52	0.82	0.55	—	—	—	—	—	—	—
Portfolio Turnover (%)	244	211	na	—	—	—	—	—	—	—
Total Assets (Millions $)	67	49	22	—	—	—	—	—	—	—

PORTFOLIO (as of 9/30/96)

Portfolio Manager: committee - 1993

Investm't Category: Balanced

✔ Domestic	Index
Foreign	Sector
✔ Asset Allocation	State Specific

Investment Style

Large-Cap Growth	Large-Cap Value
Mid-Cap Growth	Mid-Cap Value
Small-Cap Growth	Small-Cap Value

Portfolio

26.0% cash	0.0% corp bonds
44.5% stocks	29.5% gov't bonds
0.0% preferred	0.0% muni bonds
0.0% conv't/warrants	0.0% other

SHAREHOLDER INFORMATION

Minimum Investment
Initial: $1,000   Subsequent: $100

Minimum IRA Investment
Initial: $1,000   Subsequent: $100

Maximum Fees
Load: none   12b-1: 0.25%
Other: none

Distributions
Income: annual   Capital Gains: Dec

Exchange Options
Number Per Year: 8   Fee: none
Telephone: yes (money market fund available)

Services
IRA, pension, auto invest, auto withdraw

Value Line Convertible

(VALCX)

Growth & Income

220 E. 42nd St.
6th Floor
New York, NY 10017
800-223-0818, 212-907-1500

PERFORMANCE

fund inception date: 6/3/85

	3yr Annual	5yr Annual	10yr Annual	Bull	Bear
Return (%)	11.8	12.8	10.5	46.1	-6.2
Differ from Category (+/-)	-3.5 blw av	-1.1 blw av	-2.2 low	-13.7 blw av	0.2 av

Total Risk	Standard Deviation	Category Risk	Risk Index	Beta
blw av	6.4%	low	0.7	0.47

	1996	1995	1994	1993	1992	1991	1990	1989	1988	1987
Return (%).	20.2	22.7	-5.3	14.8	13.8	28.7	-3.8	10.7	15.9	-6.2
Differ from Category (+/-). .	0.5	-7.4	-4.0	1.0	3.1	-0.4	2.1	-12.8	-0.9	-6.4
Return, Tax-Adjusted (%). .	14.7	20.2	-8.6	9.3	11.7	26.3	-6.2	8.0	13.9	-10.2

PER SHARE DATA

	1996	1995	1994	1993	1992	1991	1990	1989	1988	1987
Dividends, Net Income ($).	0.65	0.67	0.75	0.66	0.64	0.60	0.66	0.72	0.48	0.82
Distrib'ns, Cap Gain ($) . . .	1.58	0.00	0.42	1.66	0.00	0.00	0.00	0.00	0.00	0.48
Net Asset Value ($)	13.10	12.79	11.01	12.85	13.25	12.25	10.04	11.12	10.70	9.66
Expense Ratio (%).	1.07	1.08	1.07	1.10	1.14	1.19	1.05	1.03	1.06	1.04
Yield (%)	4.42	5.23	6.56	4.54	4.83	4.89	6.57	6.47	4.48	8.08
Portfolio Turnover (%). . . .	129	87	142	146	140	216	105	112	257	234
Total Assets (Millions $). . . .	68	55	45	51	41	38	34	54	61	62

PORTFOLIO (as of 9/30/96)

Portfolio Manager: committee - 1990

Investm't Category: Growth & Income
- ✔ Domestic
-   Foreign
-   Asset Allocation
-   Index
-   Sector
-   State Specific

Investment Style
-   Large-Cap Growth
- ✔ Mid-Cap Growth
-   Small-Cap Growth
-   Large-Cap Value
- ✔ Mid-Cap Value
-   Small-Cap Value

Portfolio
33.9% cash	0.0% corp bonds
4.7% stocks	0.0% gov't bonds
11.6% preferred	0.0% muni bonds
49.8% conv't/warrants	0.0% other

SHAREHOLDER INFORMATION

Minimum Investment
Initial: $1,000   Subsequent: $250

Minimum IRA Investment
Initial: $1,000   Subsequent: $250

Maximum Fees
Load: none   12b-1: none
Other: none

Distributions
Income: quarterly   Capital Gains: Dec

Exchange Options
Number Per Year: 8   Fee: none
Telephone: yes (money market fund available)

Services
IRA, pension, auto invest, auto withdraw

Value Line Income
(VALIX)
Balanced

220 E. 42nd St.
6th Floor
New York, NY 10017
800-223-0818, 212-907-1500

PERFORMANCE   fund inception date: 1/1/52

	3yr Annual	5yr Annual	10yr Annual	Bull	Bear
Return (%)	12.3	9.3	10.6	50.8	-8.1
Differ from Category (+/-)	0.6 av	-2.1 blw av	-0.2 blw av	5.7 abv av	-2.4 low

Total Risk	Standard Deviation	Category Risk	Risk Index	Beta
av	7.3%	abv av	1.1	0.70

	1996	1995	1994	1993	1992	1991	1990	1989	1988	1987
Return (%).	17.3	26.2	-4.4	8.2	1.7	28.5	1.9	22.5	12.1	-2.4
Differ from Category (+/-). .	3.1	1.6	-2.8	-6.2	-7.2	4.4	2.8	4.4	-0.1	-5.1
Return, Tax-Adjusted (%). .	12.0	23.7	-5.9	3.5	-1.2	26.5	-0.4	19.3	9.3	-7.7

PER SHARE DATA

	1996	1995	1994	1993	1992	1991	1990	1989	1988	1987
Dividends, Net Income ($).	0.24	0.25	0.21	0.22	0.27	0.31	0.38	0.46	0.39	0.42
Distrib'ns, Cap Gain ($) . . .	1.03	0.20	0.05	0.89	0.41	0.00	0.00	0.00	0.00	0.69
Net Asset Value ($)	7.37	7.37	6.21	6.77	7.29	7.86	6.39	6.66	5.84	5.57
Expense Ratio (%).	na	0.93	0.90	0.88	0.89	0.74	0.77	0.75	0.80	0.76
Yield (%)	2.85	3.30	3.35	2.87	3.50	3.94	5.94	6.90	6.67	6.70
Portfolio Turnover (%).	na	76	56	165	85	67	57	108	83	96
Total Assets (Millions $). . .	153	144	131	162	163	172	140	148	133	140

PORTFOLIO (as of 9/30/96)

Portfolio Manager: committee - 1990

Investm't Category: Balanced

✔ Domestic	Index
Foreign	Sector
✔ Asset Allocation	State Specific

Investment Style

Large-Cap Growth	Large-Cap Value
Mid-Cap Growth	Mid-Cap Value
Small-Cap Growth	Small-Cap Value

Portfolio

3.7% cash	12.0% corp bonds
59.0% stocks	15.5% gov't bonds
7.1% preferred	0.0% muni bonds
2.7% conv't/warrants	0.0% other

SHAREHOLDER INFORMATION

Minimum Investment
Initial: $1,000   Subsequent: $100

Minimum IRA Investment
Initial: $1,000   Subsequent: $100

Maximum Fees
Load: none   12b-1: none
Other: none

Distributions
Income: quarterly   Capital Gains: Dec

Exchange Options
Number Per Year: 8   Fee: none
Telephone: yes (money market fund available)

Services
IRA, pension, auto invest, auto withdraw

Value Line Leveraged Growth Investors (VALLX)

Aggressive Growth

220 E. 42nd St.
6th Floor
New York, NY 10017
800-223-0818, 212-907-1500

PERFORMANCE

fund inception date: 3/20/72

	3yr Annual	5yr Annual	10yr Annual	Bull	Bear
Return (%)	17.3	12.8	14.3	80.4	-12.9
Differ from Category (+/-)	1.5 abv av	-2.5 blw av	-0.7 av	9.3 abv av	-2.3 blw av

Total Risk	Standard Deviation	Category Risk	Risk Index	Beta
high	12.8%	blw av	0.9	1.09

	1996	1995	1994	1993	1992	1991	1990	1989	1988	1987
Return (%).............	22.3	37.0	-3.8	16.1	-2.5	46.3	-1.7	32.3	6.4	2.8
Differ from Category (+/-)..	3.2	2.7	-3.8	-3.2	-14.2	-5.8	3.7	3.9	-10.0	5.2
Return, Tax-Adjusted (%)..	18.9	33.0	-4.5	14.7	-5.7	39.7	-3.8	29.3	5.4	-4.1

PER SHARE DATA

	1996	1995	1994	1993	1992	1991	1990	1989	1988	1987
Dividends, Net Income ($).	0.00	0.09	0.11	0.05	0.15	0.22	0.36	0.38	0.43	0.45
Distrib'ns, Cap Gain ($)...	3.38	3.15	0.45	0.98	2.68	4.61	1.18	1.45	0.00	4.92
Net Asset Value ($).....	31.51	28.50	23.18	24.67	22.15	25.64	21.16	23.10	18.87	18.15
Expense Ratio (%).........	na	0.88	0.89	0.92	0.93	0.92	0.96	0.96	0.97	0.95
Yield (%)	0.00	0.28	0.46	0.19	0.60	0.72	1.61	1.54	2.27	1.95
Portfolio Turnover (%).....	na	54	49	80	208	250	94	122	143	148
Total Assets (Millions $)...	387	337	264	302	290	347	236	254	235	287

PORTFOLIO (as of 9/30/96)

Portfolio Manager: committee - 1990

Investm't Category: Aggressive Growth

✔ Domestic	Index
Foreign	Sector
Asset Allocation	State Specific

Investment Style

Large-Cap Growth	Large-Cap Value
✔ Mid-Cap Growth	Mid-Cap Value
Small-Cap Growth	Small-Cap Value

Portfolio

3.5% cash	0.0% corp bonds
96.5% stocks	0.0% gov't bonds
0.0% preferred	0.0% muni bonds
0.0% conv't/warrants	0.0% other

SHAREHOLDER INFORMATION

Minimum Investment

Initial: $1,000   Subsequent: $100

Minimum IRA Investment

Initial: $1,000   Subsequent: $100

Maximum Fees

Load: none   12b-1: none
Other: none

Distributions

Income: Dec   Capital Gains: Dec

Exchange Options

Number Per Year: 8   Fee: none
Telephone: yes (money market fund available)

Services

IRA, pension, auto invest, auto withdraw

Value Line NY Tax-Exempt Trust

(VLNYX) *Tax-Exempt Bond*

220 E. 42nd St.
6th Floor
New York, NY 10017
800-223-0818, 212-907-1500

PERFORMANCE

fund inception date: 7/1/87

	3yr Annual	5yr Annual	10yr Annual	Bull	Bear
Return (%)	3.4	6.6	na	17.6	-7.0
Differ from Category (+/-)	-0.8 low	0.2 av	na	-0.8 blw av	-1.6 low

Total Risk	Standard Deviation	Category Risk	Risk Index	Avg Mat
blw av	6.3%	high	1.1	14.4 yrs

	1996	1995	1994	1993	1992	1991	1990	1989	1988	1987
Return (%).	2.3	17.2	-7.8	13.9	9.5	14.3	4.1	7.9	10.8	—
Differ from Category (+/-) .	-1.4	2.0	-2.5	2.1	1.2	2.9	-2.3	-1.1	0.8	—
Return, Tax-Adjusted (%). . .	1.9	17.2	-8.0	12.7	9.1	14.3	4.1	7.7	10.6	—

PER SHARE DATA

	1996	1995	1994	1993	1992	1991	1990	1989	1988	1987
Dividends, Net Income ($)	0.47	0.49	0.52	0.57	0.59	0.65	0.70	0.71	0.74	—
Distrib'ns, Cap Gain ($) . . .	0.12	0.00	0.06	0.41	0.14	0.00	0.00	0.04	0.05	—
Net Asset Value ($)	10.03	10.40	9.32	10.73	10.32	10.12	9.47	9.79	9.78	—
Expense Ratio (%).	0.92	0.86	0.87	0.85	0.92	0.91	1.01	0.76	0.00	—
Yield (%)	4.63	4.71	5.54	5.11	5.64	6.42	7.39	7.22	7.52	—
Portfolio Turnover (%). . . .	119	105	54	137	124	61	39	73	17	—
Total Assets (Millions $). . . .	35	40	36	44	37	37	31	29	24	—

PORTFOLIO (as of 9/30/96)

Portfolio Manager: committee - 1990

Investm't Category: Tax-Exempt Bond

✔ Domestic	Index
Foreign	Sector
Asset Allocation	✔ State Specific

Investment Style

Large-Cap Growth	Large-Cap Value
Mid-Cap Growth	Mid-Cap Value
Small-Cap Growth	Small-Cap Value

Portfolio

6.3% cash	0.0% corp bonds
0.0% stocks	0.0% gov't bonds
0.0% preferred	93.6% muni bonds
0.0% conv't/warrants	0.1% other

SHAREHOLDER INFORMATION

Minimum Investment
Initial: $1,000   Subsequent: $250

Minimum IRA Investment
Initial: na   Subsequent: na

Maximum Fees
Load: none   12b-1: none
Other: none

Distributions
Income: monthly   Capital Gains: Dec

Exchange Options
Number Per Year: 8   Fee: none
Telephone: yes (money market fund available)

Services
auto invest, auto withdraw

Value Line Special Situations (VALSX)

Aggressive Growth

220 E. 42nd St.
6th Floor
New York, NY 10017
800-223-0818, 212-907-1500

PERFORMANCE

fund inception date: 1/1/56

	3yr Annual	5yr Annual	10yr Annual	Bull	Bear
Return (%)	11.7	8.7	8.5	63.7	-18.1
Differ from Category (+/-)	-4.1 blw av	-6.6 low	-6.5 low	-7.4 av	-7.5 low

Total Risk	Standard Deviation	Category Risk	Risk Index	Beta
high	13.9%	av	1.0	0.86

	1996	1995	1994	1993	1992	1991	1990	1989	1988	1987
Return (%)	7.2	28.9	1.0	12.9	-3.5	36.6	-4.5	21.7	3.3	-9.1
Differ from Category (+/-)	-11.9	-5.4	1.0	-6.4	-15.2	-15.5	0.9	-6.7	-13.1	-6.7
Return, Tax-Adjusted (%)	-0.1	20.9	-0.6	11.5	-3.8	34.5	-5.0	20.9	3.0	-14.2

PER SHARE DATA

	1996	1995	1994	1993	1992	1991	1990	1989	1988	1987
Dividends, Net Income ($)	0.26	0.06	0.00	0.00	0.00	0.05	0.16	0.22	0.08	0.12
Distrib'ns, Cap Gain ($)	3.75	4.49	0.96	0.74	0.14	0.85	0.00	0.00	0.00	2.55
Net Asset Value ($)	13.34	16.24	16.15	16.95	15.69	16.41	12.72	13.49	11.27	10.99
Expense Ratio (%)	na	1.06	1.10	1.06	1.09	1.04	1.11	1.08	1.16	1.01
Yield (%)	1.52	0.28	0.00	0.00	0.00	0.28	1.25	1.63	0.70	0.88
Portfolio Turnover (%)	na	10	37	39	43	37	33	66	59	41
Total Assets (Millions $)	91	98	90	91	101	129	103	116	112	123

PORTFOLIO (as of 9/30/96)

Portfolio Manager: committee - 1990

Investm't Category: Aggressive Growth
✔ Domestic	Index
Foreign	Sector
Asset Allocation	State Specific

Investment Style
Large-Cap Growth	Large-Cap Value
✔ Mid-Cap Growth	Mid-Cap Value
✔ Small-Cap Growth	Small-Cap Value

Portfolio
53.7% cash	0.0% corp bonds
46.2% stocks	0.0% gov't bonds
0.0% preferred	0.0% muni bonds
0.1% conv't/warrants	0.0% other

SHAREHOLDER INFORMATION

Minimum Investment
Initial: $1,000   Subsequent: $100

Minimum IRA Investment
Initial: $1,000   Subsequent: $100

Maximum Fees
Load: none   12b-1: none
Other: none

Distributions
Income: Dec   Capital Gains: Dec

Exchange Options
Number Per Year: 8   Fee: none
Telephone: yes (money market fund available)

Services
IRA, pension, auto invest, auto withdraw

Value Line Tax-Exempt High Yield Port (VLHYX)

Tax-Exempt Bond

220 E. 42nd St.
6th Floor
New York, NY 10017
800-223-0818, 212-907-1500

PERFORMANCE

fund inception date: 3/27/84

	3yr Annual	5yr Annual	10yr Annual	Bull	Bear
Return (%)	3.9	6.2	6.9	19.6	-7.2
Differ from Category (+/-)	-0.3 blw av	-0.2 blw av	0.2 av	1.2 av	-1.8 low

Total Risk	Standard Deviation	Category Risk	Risk Index	Avg Mat
blw av	5.9%	abv av	1.1	18.1 yrs

	1996	1995	1994	1993	1992	1991	1990	1989	1988	1987
Return (%)	3.5	16.6	-7.0	11.4	7.8	12.2	6.5	8.3	10.9	0.5
Differ from Category (+/-)	-0.2	1.4	-1.7	-0.4	-0.5	0.8	0.1	-0.7	0.9	1.9
Return, Tax-Adjusted (%)	3.5	16.6	-7.1	10.8	7.8	12.2	6.5	8.3	10.9	0.3

PER SHARE DATA

	1996	1995	1994	1993	1992	1991	1990	1989	1988	1987
Dividends, Net Income ($)	0.55	0.55	0.56	0.60	0.63	0.69	0.77	0.78	0.79	0.82
Distrib'ns, Cap Gain ($)	0.00	0.00	0.04	0.20	0.00	0.00	0.00	0.00	0.00	0.05
Net Asset Value ($)	10.77	10.95	9.89	11.27	10.86	10.68	10.17	10.30	10.26	9.99
Expense Ratio (%)	0.62	0.61	0.58	0.60	0.58	0.60	0.62	0.63	0.64	0.68
Yield (%)	5.10	5.02	5.63	5.23	5.80	6.46	7.57	7.57	7.69	8.20
Portfolio Turnover (%)	95	60	55	101	122	122	63	73	76	79
Total Assets (Millions $)	216	232	225	290	288	300	278	274	254	228

PORTFOLIO (as of 9/30/96)

Portfolio Manager: committee - 1990

Investm't Category: Tax-Exempt Bond

✔ Domestic
   Foreign
   Asset Allocation

   Index
   Sector
   State Specific

Investment Style

Large-Cap Growth   Large-Cap Value
Mid-Cap Growth   Mid-Cap Value
Small-Cap Growth   Small-Cap Value

Portfolio

5.5% cash	0.0% corp bonds
0.0% stocks	0.0% gov't bonds
0.0% preferred	93.5% muni bonds
0.0% conv't/warrants	1.0% other

SHAREHOLDER INFORMATION

Minimum Investment
Initial: $1,000   Subsequent: $250

Minimum IRA Investment
Initial: na   Subsequent: na

Maximum Fees
Load: none   12b-1: none
Other: none

Distributions
Income: monthly   Capital Gains: Dec

Exchange Options
Number Per Year: 8   Fee: none
Telephone: yes (money market fund available)

Services
auto invest, auto withdraw

Value Line US Gov't Securities (VALBX)

Mortgage-Backed Bond

220 E. 42nd St.
6th Floor
New York, NY 10017
800-223-0818, 212-907-1500

PERFORMANCE

fund inception date: 9/2/81

	3yr Annual	5yr Annual	10yr Annual	Bull	Bear
Return (%)	2.0	4.4	7.1	16.4	-9.9
Differ from Category (+/-)	-3.6 low	-1.6 low	-0.6 low	-4.7 low	-6.3 low

Total Risk	Standard Deviation	Category Risk	Risk Index	Avg Mat
blw av	4.9%	high	1.3	16.1 yrs

	1996	1995	1994	1993	1992	1991	1990	1989	1988	1987
Return (%)	3.9	14.4	-10.7	9.7	6.3	16.4	10.3	11.9	7.9	3.4
Differ from Category (+/-)	-0.5	-0.3	-9.0	2.8	0.1	2.0	0.5	-0.7	0.5	1.4
Return, Tax-Adjusted (%)	1.1	11.6	-13.2	6.0	3.3	13.2	6.9	8.1	4.4	-1.3

PER SHARE DATA

	1996	1995	1994	1993	1992	1991	1990	1989	1988	1987
Dividends, Net Income ($)	0.77	0.73	0.78	0.94	0.90	0.95	1.00	1.10	1.01	1.50
Distrib'ns, Cap Gain ($)	0.00	0.00	0.00	0.33	0.08	0.00	0.00	0.00	0.00	0.00
Net Asset Value ($)	10.93	11.28	10.52	12.62	12.68	12.89	11.96	11.80	11.57	11.67
Expense Ratio (%)	na	0.66	0.63	0.61	0.64	0.64	0.67	0.66	0.67	0.72
Yield (%)	7.04	6.47	7.41	7.25	7.05	7.37	8.36	9.32	8.72	12.85
Portfolio Turnover (%)	na	193	100	169	130	79	59	34	54	48
Total Assets (Millions $)	210	248	289	450	419	381	279	257	249	236

PORTFOLIO (as of 9/30/96)

Portfolio Manager: committee - 1990

Investm't Category: Mortgage-Backed Bond
- ✔ Domestic
- Foreign
- Asset Allocation
- Index
- Sector
- State Specific

Investment Style
- Large-Cap Growth
- Mid-Cap Growth
- Small-Cap Growth
- Large-Cap Value
- Mid-Cap Value
- Small-Cap Value

Portfolio

3.6%	cash	0.0%	corp bonds
0.0%	stocks	96.4%	gov't bonds
0.0%	preferred	0.0%	muni bonds
0.0%	conv't/warrants	0.0%	other

SHAREHOLDER INFORMATION

Minimum Investment
Initial: $1,000   Subsequent: $250

Minimum IRA Investment
Initial: $1,000   Subsequent: $250

Maximum Fees
Load: none   12b-1: none
Other: none

Distributions
Income: quarterly   Capital Gains: Dec

Exchange Options
Number Per Year: 8   Fee: none
Telephone: yes (money market fund available)

Services
IRA, pension, auto invest, auto withdraw

Van Wagoner Emerging Growth (VWEGX)

Aggressive Growth

207 E. Buffalo St.
Suite 400
Milwaukee, WI 53202
800-228-2121, 800-894-6694
networth.galt.com/vanwagoner

PERFORMANCE

fund inception date: 12/29/95

	3yr Annual	5yr Annual	10yr Annual	Bull	Bear
Return (%)	na	na	na	na	na
Differ from Category (+/-)	na	na	na	na	na

Total Risk	Standard Deviation	Category Risk	Risk Index	Beta
na	na	na	na	na

	1996	1995	1994	1993	1992	1991	1990	1989	1988	1987
Return (%)	26.8	—	—	—	—	—	—	—	—	—
Differ from Category (+/-)	7.7	—	—	—	—	—	—	—	—	—
Return, Tax-Adjusted (%)	26.8	—	—	—	—	—	—	—	—	—

PER SHARE DATA

	1996	1995	1994	1993	1992	1991	1990	1989	1988	1987
Dividends, Net Income ($)	0.00	—	—	—	—	—	—	—	—	—
Distrib'ns, Cap Gain ($)	0.00	—	—	—	—	—	—	—	—	—
Net Asset Value ($)	12.69	—	—	—	—	—	—	—	—	—
Expense Ratio (%)	na	—	—	—	—	—	—	—	—	—
Yield (%)	0.00	—	—	—	—	—	—	—	—	—
Portfolio Turnover (%)	na	—	—	—	—	—	—	—	—	—
Total Assets (Millions $)	679	—	—	—	—	—	—	—	—	—

PORTFOLIO (as of 6/30/96)

Portfolio Manager: Garrett R. Van Wagoner - 1995

Investm't Category: Aggressive Growth
- ✔ Domestic
- Foreign
- Asset Allocation
- Index
- Sector
- State Specific

Investment Style
- Large-Cap Growth
- Mid-Cap Growth
- Small-Cap Growth
- Large-Cap Value
- Mid-Cap Value
- Small-Cap Value

Portfolio
- 4.4% cash
- 95.6% stocks
- 0.0% preferred
- 0.0% conv't/warrants
- 0.0% corp bonds
- 0.0% gov't bonds
- 0.0% muni bonds
- 0.0% other

SHAREHOLDER INFORMATION

Minimum Investment
Initial: $1,000   Subsequent: $50

Minimum IRA Investment
Initial: $500   Subsequent: $50

Maximum Fees
Load: none   12b-1: 0.25%
Other: none

Distributions
Income: annual   Capital Gains: annual

Exchange Options
Number Per Year: 5   Fee: $5 (telephone)
Telephone: yes (money market fund available)

Services
IRA, pension, auto exchange, auto invest, auto withdraw

Vanguard Admiral Interm US Treas (VAITX)

Government Bond

Vanguard Financial Center
P.O. Box 2600
Valley Forge, PA 19482
800-635-1511, 610-669-1000
www.vanguard.com

PERFORMANCE

fund inception date: 12/14/92

	3yr Annual	5yr Annual	10yr Annual	Bull	Bear
Return (%)	5.6	na	na	23.4	-5.9
Differ from Category (+/-)	0.7 high	na	na	1.4 abv av	0.5 av

Total Risk	Standard Deviation	Category Risk	Risk Index	Avg Mat
blw av	5.5%	abv av	1.3	7.4 yrs

	1996	1995	1994	1993	1992	1991	1990	1989	1988	1987
Return (%)	2.0	20.5	-4.3	11.3	—	—	—	—	—	—
Differ from Category (+/-)	0.5	0.9	0.1	-0.3	—	—	—	—	—	—
Return, Tax-Adjusted (%)	-0.4	17.7	-6.5	8.6	—	—	—	—	—	—

PER SHARE DATA

	1996	1995	1994	1993	1992	1991	1990	1989	1988	1987
Dividends, Net Income ($)	0.64	0.66	0.58	0.58	—	—	—	—	—	—
Distrib'ns, Cap Gain ($)	0.00	0.00	0.00	0.12	—	—	—	—	—	—
Net Asset Value ($)	10.22	10.67	9.45	10.48	—	—	—	—	—	—
Expense Ratio (%)	0.15	0.15	0.15	0.15	—	—	—	—	—	—
Yield (%)	6.26	6.18	6.13	5.47	—	—	—	—	—	—
Portfolio Turnover (%)	64	134	102	0	—	—	—	—	—	—
Total Assets (Millions $)	668	572	319	319	—	—	—	—	—	—

PORTFOLIO (as of 9/30/96)

Portfolio Manager: Ian MacKinnon - 1992

Investm't Category: Government Bond

✔ Domestic   Index
  Foreign   Sector
  Asset Allocation   State Specific

Investment Style

Large-Cap Growth	Large-Cap Value
Mid-Cap Growth	Mid-Cap Value
Small-Cap Growth	Small-Cap Value

Portfolio

4.0% cash	0.0% corp bonds
0.0% stocks	96.0% gov't bonds
0.0% preferred	0.0% muni bonds
0.0% conv't/warrants	0.0% other

SHAREHOLDER INFORMATION

Minimum Investment
Initial: $50,000   Subsequent: $100

Minimum IRA Investment
Initial: $50,000   Subsequent: $100

Maximum Fees
Load: none   12b-1: none
Other: none

Distributions
Income: monthly   Capital Gains: annual

Exchange Options
Number Per Year: 2   Fee: none
Telephone: yes (money market fund available)

Services
IRA, pension, auto exchange, auto invest, auto withdraw

Vanguard Admiral Long-Term US Treas

(VALGX) *Government Bond*

Vanguard Financial Center
P.O. Box 2600
Valley Forge, PA 19482
800-635-1511, 610-669-1000
www.vanguard.com

PERFORMANCE

fund inception date: 12/14/92

	3yr Annual	5yr Annual	10yr Annual	Bull	Bear
Return (%)	6.2	na	na	30.1	-10.1
Differ from Category (+/-)	1.3 high	na	na	8.1 high	-3.7 low

Total Risk	Standard Deviation	Category Risk	Risk Index	Avg Mat
av	8.9%	high	2.2	21.2 yrs

	1996	1995	1994	1993	1992	1991	1990	1989	1988	1987
Return (%)	-1.1	30.0	-6.9	16.6	—	—	—	—	—	—
Differ from Category (+/-)	-2.6	10.4	-2.5	5.0	—	—	—	—	—	—
Return, Tax-Adjusted (%)	-3.6	26.7	-9.6	13.0	—	—	—	—	—	—

PER SHARE DATA

	1996	1995	1994	1993	1992	1991	1990	1989	1988	1987
Dividends, Net Income ($)	0.68	0.69	0.66	0.71	—	—	—	—	—	—
Distrib'ns, Cap Gain ($)	0.03	0.08	0.09	0.28	—	—	—	—	—	—
Net Asset Value ($)	10.26	11.12	9.22	10.71	—	—	—	—	—	—
Expense Ratio (%)	0.15	0.15	0.15	0.15	—	—	—	—	—	—
Yield (%)	6.60	6.16	7.08	6.46	—	—	—	—	—	—
Portfolio Turnover (%)	125	44	51	17	—	—	—	—	—	—
Total Assets (Millions $)	196	188	118	92	—	—	—	—	—	—

PORTFOLIO (as of 9/30/96)

Portfolio Manager: Ian MacKinnon - 1992

Investm't Category: Government Bond

✔ Domestic   Index
   Foreign   Sector
   Asset Allocation   State Specific

Investment Style

   Large-Cap Growth   Large-Cap Value
   Mid-Cap Growth   Mid-Cap Value
   Small-Cap Growth   Small-Cap Value

Portfolio

5.0% cash	0.0% corp bonds
0.0% stocks	95.0% gov't bonds
0.0% preferred	0.0% muni bonds
0.0% conv't/warrants	0.0% other

SHAREHOLDER INFORMATION

Minimum Investment
Initial: $50,000   Subsequent: $100

Minimum IRA Investment
Initial: $50,000   Subsequent: $100

Maximum Fees
Load: none   12b-1: none
Other: none

Distributions
Income: monthly   Capital Gains: annual

Exchange Options
Number Per Year: 2   Fee: none
Telephone: yes (money market fund available)

Services
IRA, pension, auto exchange, auto invest, auto withdraw

Vanguard Admiral Short-Term US Treas (VASTX)

Government Bond

Vanguard Financial Center
P.O. Box 2600
Valley Forge, PA 19482
800-635-1511, 610-669-1000
www.vanguard.com

PERFORMANCE

fund inception date: 12/14/92

	3yr Annual	5yr Annual	10yr Annual	Bull	Bear
Return (%)	5.2	na	na	18.0	-1.8
Differ from Category (+/-)	0.3 abv av	na	na	-4.0 blw av	4.6 high

Total Risk	Standard Deviation	Category Risk	Risk Index	Avg Mat
low	2.3%	low	0.6	2.3 yrs

	1996	1995	1994	1993	1992	1991	1990	1989	1988	1987
Return (%)	4.4	12.0	-0.4	6.4	—	—	—	—	—	—
Differ from Category (+/-)	2.9	-7.6	4.0	-5.2	—	—	—	—	—	—
Return, Tax-Adjusted (%)	2.1	9.5	-2.4	4.5	—	—	—	—	—	—

PER SHARE DATA

	1996	1995	1994	1993	1992	1991	1990	1989	1988	1987
Dividends, Net Income ($)	0.58	0.60	0.50	0.45	—	—	—	—	—	—
Distrib'ns, Cap Gain ($)	0.00	0.00	0.02	0.01	—	—	—	—	—	—
Net Asset Value ($)	10.05	10.20	9.67	10.23	—	—	—	—	—	—
Expense Ratio (%)	0.15	0.15	0.15	0.15	—	—	—	—	—	—
Yield (%)	5.77	5.88	5.15	4.39	—	—	—	—	—	—
Portfolio Turnover (%)	95	129	90	7	—	—	—	—	—	—
Total Assets (Millions $)	526	429	311	252	—	—	—	—	—	—

PORTFOLIO (as of 9/30/96)

Portfolio Manager: Ian MacKinnon - 1993

Investm't Category: Government Bond
- ✔ Domestic
- Foreign
- Asset Allocation
- Index
- Sector
- State Specific

Investment Style
- Large-Cap Growth
- Mid-Cap Growth
- Small-Cap Growth
- Large-Cap Value
- Mid-Cap Value
- Small-Cap Value

Portfolio
2.0% cash	0.0% corp bonds
0.0% stocks	98.0% gov't bonds
0.0% preferred	0.0% muni bonds
0.0% conv't/warrants	0.0% other

SHAREHOLDER INFORMATION

Minimum Investment
Initial: $50,000   Subsequent: $100

Minimum IRA Investment
Initial: $50,000   Subsequent: $100

Maximum Fees
Load: none   12b-1: none
Other: none

Distributions
Income: monthly   Capital Gains: annual

Exchange Options
Number Per Year: 2   Fee: none
Telephone: yes (money market fund available)

Services
IRA, pension, auto exchange, auto invest, auto withdraw

Vanguard Asset Allocation
(VAAPX)
Balanced

Vanguard Financial Center
P.O. Box 2600
Valley Forge, PA 19482
800-635-1511, 610-669-1000
www.vanguard.com

PERFORMANCE   fund inception date: 11/3/88

	3yr Annual	5yr Annual	10yr Annual	Bull	Bear
Return (%)	15.2	13.3	na	62.1	-8.4
Differ from Category (+/-)	3.5 high	1.9 abv av	na	17.0 high	-2.7 low

Total Risk	Standard Deviation	Category Risk	Risk Index	Beta
av	8.4%	high	1.2	0.81

	1996	1995	1994	1993	1992	1991	1990	1989	1988	1987
Return (%).	15.7	35.4	-2.4	13.4	7.5	25.5	-1.0	23.6	—	—
Differ from Category (+/-) . .	1.5	10.8	-0.8	-1.0	-1.4	1.4	-0.1	5.5	—	—
Return, Tax-Adjusted (%). .	12.3	32.2	-4.0	10.9	5.4	22.9	-2.7	21.2	—	—

PER SHARE DATA

	1996	1995	1994	1993	1992	1991	1990	1989	1988	1987
Dividends, Net Income ($).	0.72	0.66	0.56	0.48	0.59	0.59	0.42	0.51	—	—
Distrib'ns, Cap Gain ($) . . .	1.05	0.61	0.00	0.53	0.17	0.19	0.13	0.15	—	—
Net Asset Value ($)	17.94	17.05	13.54	14.45	13.64	13.41	11.35	12.01	—	—
Expense Ratio (%).	0.47	0.49	0.50	0.49	0.52	0.44	0.50	0.49	—	—
Yield (%)	3.79	3.73	4.13	3.20	4.27	4.33	3.65	4.19	—	—
Portfolio Turnover (%). . . .	47	34	51	31	18	44	12	52	—	—
Total Assets (Millions $). .	2,609	1,791	1,125	1,125	587	341	179	128	—	—

PORTFOLIO (as of 9/30/96)

Portfolio Manager: Thomas Hazuka - 1988

Investm't Category: Balanced
- ✔ Domestic
-   Foreign
- ✔ Asset Allocation
-   Index
-   Sector
-   State Specific

Investment Style
Large-Cap Growth	Large-Cap Value
Mid-Cap Growth	Mid-Cap Value
Small-Cap Growth	Small-Cap Value

Portfolio
25.0% cash	1.0% corp bonds
35.0% stocks	39.0% gov't bonds
0.0% preferred	0.0% muni bonds
0.0% conv't/warrants	0.0% other

SHAREHOLDER INFORMATION

Minimum Investment
Initial: $3,000   Subsequent: $100

Minimum IRA Investment
Initial: $1,000   Subsequent: $100

Maximum Fees
Load: none   12b-1: none
Other: f

Distributions
Income: semiannual   Capital Gains: annual

Exchange Options
Number Per Year: 2   Fee: none
Telephone: yes (money market fund available)

Services
IRA, pension, auto exchange, auto invest, auto withdraw

Vanguard Balanced Index
(VBINX)
Balanced

Vanguard Financial Center
P.O. Box 2600
Valley Forge, PA 19482
800-635-1511, 610-669-1000
www.vanguard.com

PERFORMANCE
fund inception date: 9/28/92

	3yr Annual	5yr Annual	10yr Annual	Bull	Bear
Return (%)	13.0	na	na	51.0	-6.6
Differ from Category (+/-)	1.3 abv av	na	na	5.9 abv av	-0.9 blw av

Total Risk	Standard Deviation	Category Risk	Risk Index	Beta
blw av	6.8%	av	1.0	0.69

	1996	1995	1994	1993	1992	1991	1990	1989	1988	1987
Return (%)	13.9	28.6	-1.6	9.9	—	—	—	—	—	—
Differ from Category (+/-)	-0.3	4.0	0.0	-4.5	—	—	—	—	—	—
Return, Tax-Adjusted (%)	12.1	26.7	-3.1	8.3	—	—	—	—	—	—

PER SHARE DATA

	1996	1995	1994	1993	1992	1991	1990	1989	1988	1987
Dividends, Net Income ($)	0.49	0.45	0.40	0.39	—	—	—	—	—	—
Distrib'ns, Cap Gain ($)	0.12	0.05	0.00	0.03	—	—	—	—	—	—
Net Asset Value ($)	13.92	12.77	10.34	10.91	—	—	—	—	—	—
Expense Ratio (%)	na	0.20	0.20	0.20	—	—	—	—	—	—
Yield (%)	3.49	3.51	3.86	3.56	—	—	—	—	—	—
Portfolio Turnover (%)	na	16	16	25	—	—	—	—	—	—
Total Assets (Millions $)	808	590	402	367	—	—	—	—	—	—

PORTFOLIO (as of 9/30/96)

Portfolio Manager: George U. Sauter, Ian MacKinnon - 1992

Investm't Category: Balanced
- ✔ Domestic
- ✔ Index
- Foreign
- Sector
- Asset Allocation
- State Specific

Investment Style
- Large-Cap Growth
- Large-Cap Value
- Mid-Cap Growth
- Mid-Cap Value
- Small-Cap Growth
- Small-Cap Value

Portfolio
1.0% cash	13.0% corp bonds
59.0% stocks	27.0% gov't bonds
0.0% preferred	0.0% muni bonds
0.0% conv't/warrants	0.0% other

SHAREHOLDER INFORMATION

Minimum Investment
Initial: $3,000   Subsequent: $100

Minimum IRA Investment
Initial: $1,000   Subsequent: $100

Maximum Fees
Load: none   12b-1: none
Other: f

Distributions
Income: quarterly   Capital Gains: annual

Exchange Options
Number Per Year: 2   Fee: none
Telephone: none

Services
IRA, pension, auto exchange, auto invest, auto withdraw

Vanguard Bond Index Interm-Term Bond (VBIIX)

General Bond

Vanguard Financial Center
P.O. Box 2600
Valley Forge, PA 19482
800-635-1511, 610-669-1000
www.vanguard.com

PERFORMANCE   fund inception date: 3/1/94

	3yr Annual	5yr Annual	10yr Annual	Bull	Bear
Return (%)	na	na	na	24.7	-3.4
Differ from Category (+/-)	na	na	na	4.4 high	0.8 abv av

Total Risk	Standard Deviation	Category Risk	Risk Index	Avg Mat
na	na	na	na	7.5 yrs

	1996	1995	1994	1993	1992	1991	1990	1989	1988	1987
Return (%).	2.5	21.0	—	—	—	—	—	—	—	—
Differ from Category (+/-).	-1.4	6.1	—	—	—	—	—	—	—	—
Return, Tax-Adjusted (%). . .	0.0	18.0	—	—	—	—	—	—	—	—

PER SHARE DATA

	1996	1995	1994	1993	1992	1991	1990	1989	1988	1987
Dividends, Net Income ($).	0.64	0.66	—	—	—	—	—	—	—	—
Distrib'ns, Cap Gain ($) . . .	0.00	0.02	—	—	—	—	—	—	—	—
Net Asset Value ($)	9.96	10.37	—	—	—	—	—	—	—	—
Expense Ratio (%).	na	0.20	—	—	—	—	—	—	—	—
Yield (%)	6.42	6.35	—	—	—	—	—	—	—	—
Portfolio Turnover (%).	na	71	—	—	—	—	—	—	—	—
Total Assets (Millions $). . .	458	345	—	—	—	—	—	—	—	—

PORTFOLIO (as of 9/30/96)

Portfolio Manager: Ian MacKinnon - 1994

Investm't Category: General Bond

✔ Domestic	✔ Index
Foreign	Sector
Asset Allocation	State Specific

Investment Style

Large-Cap Growth	Large-Cap Value
Mid-Cap Growth	Mid-Cap Value
Small-Cap Growth	Small-Cap Value

Portfolio

3.0% cash	40.0% corp bonds
0.0% stocks	57.0% gov't bonds
0.0% preferred	0.0% muni bonds
0.0% conv't/warrants	0.0% other

SHAREHOLDER INFORMATION

Minimum Investment
Initial: $3,000   Subsequent: $100

Minimum IRA Investment
Initial: $1,000   Subsequent: $100

Maximum Fees
Load: none   12b-1: none
Other: f

Distributions
Income: monthly   Capital Gains: annual

Exchange Options
Number Per Year: 2   Fee: none
Telephone: yes (money market fund available)

Services
IRA, pension, auto exchange, auto invest, auto withdraw

Vanguard Bond Index Long-Term Bond (VBLTX)

General Bond

Vanguard Financial Center
P.O. Box 2600
Valley Forge, PA 19482
800-635-1511, 610-669-1000
www.vanguard.com

PERFORMANCE

fund inception date: 3/1/94

	3yr Annual	5yr Annual	10yr Annual	Bull	Bear
Return (%)	na	na	na	30.8	-5.7
Differ from Category (+/-)	na	na	na	10.5 high	-1.5 blw av

Total Risk	Standard Deviation	Category Risk	Risk Index	Avg Mat
na	na	na	na	21.6 yrs

	1996	1995	1994	1993	1992	1991	1990	1989	1988	1987
Return (%).	-0.3	29.7	—	—	—	—	—	—	—	—
Differ from Category (+/-) .	-4.2	14.8	—	—	—	—	—	—	—	—
Return, Tax-Adjusted (%). .	-2.8	26.5	—	—	—	—	—	—	—	—

PER SHARE DATA

	1996	1995	1994	1993	1992	1991	1990	1989	1988	1987
Dividends, Net Income ($)	0.67	0.69	—	—	—	—	—	—	—	—
Distrib'ns, Cap Gain ($) . . .	0.00	0.02	—	—	—	—	—	—	—	—
Net Asset Value ($)	10.08	10.82	—	—	—	—	—	—	—	—
Expense Ratio (%)	na	0.20	—	—	—	—	—	—	—	—
Yield (%)	6.64	6.36	—	—	—	—	—	—	—	—
Portfolio Turnover (%)	na	45	—	—	—	—	—	—	—	—
Total Assets (Millions $) . . .	45	24	—	—	—	—	—	—	—	—

PORTFOLIO (as of 9/30/96)

Portfolio Manager: Ian MacKinnon - 1994

Investm't Category: General Bond

✔ Domestic   ✔ Index
✔ Foreign   Sector
   Asset Allocation   State Specific

Investment Style

Large-Cap Growth   Large-Cap Value
Mid-Cap Growth   Mid-Cap Value
Small-Cap Growth   Small-Cap Value

Portfolio

2.0%	cash	28.0%	corp bonds
0.0%	stocks	70.0%	gov't bonds
0.0%	preferred	0.0%	muni bonds
0.0%	conv't/warrants	0.0%	other

SHAREHOLDER INFORMATION

Minimum Investment
Initial: $3,000   Subsequent: $100

Minimum IRA Investment
Initial: $1,000   Subsequent: $100

Maximum Fees
Load: none   12b-1: none
Other: *f*

Distributions
Income: monthly   Capital Gains: annual

Exchange Options
Number Per Year: 2   Fee: none
Telephone: yes (money market fund available)

Services
IRA, pension, auto exchange, auto invest, auto withdraw

Vanguard Bond Index Short-Term Bond (VBISX)

General Bond

Vanguard Financial Center
P.O. Box 2600
Valley Forge, PA 19482
800-635-1511, 610-669-1000
www.vanguard.com

PERFORMANCE

fund inception date: 3/1/94

	3yr Annual	5yr Annual	10yr Annual	Bull	Bear
Return (%)	na	na	na	18.7	-1.0
Differ from Category (+/-)	na	na	na	-1.6 blw av	3.2 high

Total Risk	Standard Deviation	Category Risk	Risk Index	Avg Mat
na	na	na	na	2.4 yrs

	1996	1995	1994	1993	1992	1991	1990	1989	1988	1987
Return (%)	4.5	12.8	—	—	—	—	—	—	—	—
Differ from Category (+/-)	0.6	-2.1	—	—	—	—	—	—	—	—
Return, Tax-Adjusted (%)	2.2	10.2	—	—	—	—	—	—	—	—

PER SHARE DATA

	1996	1995	1994	1993	1992	1991	1990	1989	1988	1987
Dividends, Net Income ($)	0.58	0.62	—	—	—	—	—	—	—	—
Distrib'ns, Cap Gain ($)	0.00	0.00	—	—	—	—	—	—	—	—
Net Asset Value ($)	9.92	10.07	—	—	—	—	—	—	—	—
Expense Ratio (%)	na	0.20	—	—	—	—	—	—	—	—
Yield (%)	5.84	6.15	—	—	—	—	—	—	—	—
Portfolio Turnover (%)	na	65	—	—	—	—	—	—	—	—
Total Assets (Millions $)	324	207	—	—	—	—	—	—	—	—

PORTFOLIO (as of 9/30/96)

Portfolio Manager: Ian MacKinnon - 1994

Investm't Category: General Bond

✔ Domestic   ✔ Index
Foreign   Sector
Asset Allocation   State Specific

Investment Style
Large-Cap Growth   Large-Cap Value
Mid-Cap Growth   Mid-Cap Value
Small-Cap Growth   Small-Cap Value

Portfolio
1.0%	cash	29.0%	corp bonds
0.0%	stocks	70.0%	gov't bonds
0.0%	preferred	0.0%	muni bonds
0.0%	conv't/warrants	0.0%	other

SHAREHOLDER INFORMATION

Minimum Investment
Initial: $3,000   Subsequent: $100

Minimum IRA Investment
Initial: $1,000   Subsequent: $100

Maximum Fees
Load: none   12b-1: none
Other: *f*

Distributions
Income: monthly   Capital Gains: annual

Exchange Options
Number Per Year: 2   Fee: none
Telephone: yes (money market fund available)

Services
IRA, pension, auto exchange, auto invest, auto withdraw

Vanguard Bond Index Total Bond Mkt (VBMFX)

General Bond

Vanguard Financial Center
P.O. Box 2600
Valley Forge, PA 19482
800-635-1511, 610-669-1000
www.vanguard.com

PERFORMANCE

fund inception date: 12/9/86

	3yr Annual	5yr Annual	10yr Annual	Bull	Bear
Return (%)	6.0	6.9	8.0	23.7	-5.1
Differ from Category (+/-)	0.9 high	0.8 abv av	0.7 abv av	3.4 abv av	-0.9 av

Total Risk	Standard Deviation	Category Risk	Risk Index	Avg Mat
low	4.5%	abv av	1.2	8.8 yrs

	1996	1995	1994	1993	1992	1991	1990	1989	1988	1987
Return (%)	3.5	18.1	-2.7	9.6	7.1	15.2	8.6	13.6	7.3	1.5
Differ from Category (+/-)	-0.4	3.2	-0.4	0.5	0.6	0.5	1.3	1.9	-0.3	-0.8
Return, Tax-Adjusted (%)	1.0	15.3	-5.2	6.7	4.1	11.9	5.2	10.1	3.8	-2.0

PER SHARE DATA

	1996	1995	1994	1993	1992	1991	1990	1989	1988	1987
Dividends, Net Income ($)	0.64	0.64	0.62	0.63	0.69	0.76	0.79	0.79	0.80	0.87
Distrib'ns, Cap Gain ($)	0.00	0.00	0.00	0.11	0.09	0.02	0.00	0.00	0.00	0.00
Net Asset Value ($)	9.84	10.14	9.17	10.06	9.88	9.99	9.41	9.44	9.05	9.20
Expense Ratio (%)	na	0.20	0.18	0.18	0.20	0.16	0.21	0.24	0.30	0.14
Yield (%)	6.50	6.31	6.76	6.19	6.92	7.59	8.39	8.36	8.83	9.45
Portfolio Turnover (%)	na	36	33	50	49	31	29	33	21	77
Total Assets (Millions $)	2,941	2,405	1,730	1,540	1,066	848	276	138	58	43

PORTFOLIO (as of 9/30/96)

Portfolio Manager: Ian MacKinnon, Ken Volpert - 1986

Investm't Category: General Bond

✔ Domestic ✔ Index
  Foreign   Sector
  Asset Allocation State Specific

Investment Style

Large-Cap Growth   Large-Cap Value
Mid-Cap Growth   Mid-Cap Value
Small-Cap Growth   Small-Cap Value

Portfolio

5.7% cash	21.3% corp bonds
0.0% stocks	69.8% gov't bonds
0.0% preferred	0.0% muni bonds
0.0% conv't/warrants	3.2% other

SHAREHOLDER INFORMATION

Minimum Investment
Initial: $3,000   Subsequent: $100

Minimum IRA Investment
Initial: $1,000   Subsequent: $100

Maximum Fees
Load: none   12b-1: none
Other: f

Distributions
Income: monthly   Capital Gains: annual

Exchange Options
Number Per Year: 2   Fee: none
Telephone: yes (money market fund available)

Services
IRA, pension, auto exchange, auto invest, auto withdraw

Vanguard CA Tax-Free Ins Interm Term (VCAIX)

Tax-Exempt Bond

Vanguard Financial Center
P.O. Box 2600
Valley Forge, PA 19482
800-635-1511, 610-669-1000
www.vanguard.com

PERFORMANCE

fund inception date: 3/4/94

	3yr Annual	5yr Annual	10yr Annual	Bull	Bear
Return (%)	na	na	na	19.1	na
Differ from Category (+/-)	na	na	na	0.7 av	na

Total Risk	Standard Deviation	Category Risk	Risk Index	Avg Mat
na	na	na	na	7.2 yrs

	1996	1995	1994	1993	1992	1991	1990	1989	1988	1987
Return (%)	5.4	13.1	—	—	—	—	—	—	—	—
Differ from Category (+/-)	1.7	-2.1	—	—	—	—	—	—	—	—
Return, Tax-Adjusted (%)	5.3	13.1	—	—	—	—	—	—	—	—

PER SHARE DATA

	1996	1995	1994	1993	1992	1991	1990	1989	1988	1987
Dividends, Net Income ($)	0.50	0.51	—	—	—	—	—	—	—	—
Distrib'ns, Cap Gain ($)	0.02	0.00	—	—	—	—	—	—	—	—
Net Asset Value ($)	10.49	10.47	—	—	—	—	—	—	—	—
Expense Ratio (%)	na	0.21	—	—	—	—	—	—	—	—
Yield (%)	4.75	4.87	—	—	—	—	—	—	—	—
Portfolio Turnover (%)	na	11	—	—	—	—	—	—	—	—
Total Assets (Millions $)	343	213	—	—	—	—	—	—	—	—

PORTFOLIO (as of 9/30/96)

Portfolio Manager: Ian MacKinnon - 1994

Investm't Category: Tax-Exempt Bond
✔ Domestic   Index
  Foreign   Sector
  Asset Allocation ✔ State Specific

Investment Style
  Large-Cap Growth   Large-Cap Value
  Mid-Cap Growth   Mid-Cap Value
  Small-Cap Growth   Small-Cap Value

Portfolio
  12.0% cash   0.0% corp bonds
  0.0% stocks   0.0% gov't bonds
  0.0% preferred   88.0% muni bonds
  0.0% conv't/warrants 0.0% other

SHAREHOLDER INFORMATION

Minimum Investment
Initial: $3,000   Subsequent: $100

Minimum IRA Investment
Initial: na   Subsequent: na

Maximum Fees
Load: none   12b-1: none
Other: f

Distributions
Income: monthly   Capital Gains: annual

Exchange Options
Number Per Year: 2   Fee: none
Telephone: yes (money market fund available)

Services
auto exchange, auto invest, auto withdraw

Vanguard CA Tax-Free Ins Long-Term (VCITX)

Tax-Exempt Bond

Vanguard Financial Center
P.O. Box 2600
Valley Forge, PA 19482
800-635-1511, 610-669-1000
www.vanguard.com

PERFORMANCE

fund inception date: 4/7/86

	3yr Annual	5yr Annual	10yr Annual	Bull	Bear
Return (%)	5.4	7.6	7.4	23.2	-5.8
Differ from Category (+/-)	1.2 high	1.2 high	0.7 abv av	4.8 high	-0.4 av

Total Risk	Standard Deviation	Category Risk	Risk Index	Avg Mat
blw av	6.5%	high	1.2	12.9 yrs

	1996	1995	1994	1993	1992	1991	1990	1989	1988	1987
Return (%)	4.9	18.5	-5.7	12.8	9.3	11.0	6.9	10.4	12.1	-3.9
Differ from Category (+/-)	1.2	3.3	-0.4	1.0	1.0	-0.4	0.5	1.4	2.1	-2.5
Return, Tax-Adjusted (%)	4.6	18.5	-5.7	12.4	8.8	11.0	6.9	10.4	12.1	-3.9

PER SHARE DATA

	1996	1995	1994	1993	1992	1991	1990	1989	1988	1987
Dividends, Net Income ($)	0.59	0.60	0.60	0.60	0.63	0.64	0.65	0.67	0.68	0.66
Distrib'ns, Cap Gain ($)	0.09	0.00	0.00	0.15	0.19	0.00	0.00	0.00	0.00	0.00
Net Asset Value ($)	11.22	11.37	10.13	11.37	10.77	10.64	10.20	10.18	9.85	9.43
Expense Ratio (%)	na	0.21	0.19	0.19	0.24	0.25	0.26	0.24	0.30	0.31
Yield (%)	5.21	5.27	5.92	5.20	5.74	6.01	6.37	6.58	6.90	6.99
Portfolio Turnover (%)	na	11	28	27	54	19	6	3	4	37
Total Assets (Millions $)	1,065	985	830	1,089	852	645	391	270	132	89

PORTFOLIO (as of 9/30/96)

Portfolio Manager: Ian MacKinnon - 1986

Investm't Category: Tax-Exempt Bond
- ✔ Domestic
- Foreign
- Asset Allocation
- Index
- Sector
- ✔ State Specific

Investment Style
- Large-Cap Growth
- Mid-Cap Growth
- Small-Cap Growth
- Large-Cap Value
- Mid-Cap Value
- Small-Cap Value

Portfolio
13.0% cash	0.0% corp bonds
0.0% stocks	0.0% gov't bonds
0.0% preferred	87.0% muni bonds
0.0% conv't/warrants	0.0% other

SHAREHOLDER INFORMATION

Minimum Investment
Initial: $3,000   Subsequent: $100

Minimum IRA Investment
Initial: na   Subsequent: na

Maximum Fees
Load: none   12b-1: none
Other: *f*

Distributions
Income: monthly   Capital Gains: annual

Exchange Options
Number Per Year: 2   Fee: none
Telephone: yes (money market fund available)

Services
auto exchange, auto invest, auto withdraw

Vanguard Convertible Securites (VCVSX)

Growth & Income

Vanguard Financial Center
P.O. Box 2600
Valley Forge, PA 19482
800-635-1511, 610-669-1000
www.vanguard.com

PERFORMANCE

fund inception date: 6/17/86

	3yr Annual	5yr Annual	10yr Annual	Bull	Bear
Return (%)	8.3	11.4	9.7	36.3	-8.3
Differ from Category (+/-)	-7.0 low	-2.5 low	-3.0 low	-23.5 low	-1.9 blw av

Total Risk	Standard Deviation	Category Risk	Risk Index	Beta
av	8.9%	blw av	1.0	0.65

	1996	1995	1994	1993	1992	1991	1990	1989	1988	1987
Return (%).	15.4	16.7	-5.7	13.5	18.9	34.3	-8.2	15.8	15.7	-10.7
Differ from Category (+/-).	-4.3	-13.4	-4.4	-0.3	8.2	5.2	-2.3	-7.7	-1.1	-10.9
Return, Tax-Adjusted (%). .	10.6	14.3	-7.9	9.5	16.8	31.6	-10.6	13.2	12.9	-13.4

PER SHARE DATA

	1996	1995	1994	1993	1992	1991	1990	1989	1988	1987
Dividends, Net Income ($).	0.47	0.54	0.51	0.53	0.53	0.54	0.56	0.56	0.56	0.56
Distrib'ns, Cap Gain ($) . . .	1.29	0.14	0.18	0.91	0.00	0.00	0.00	0.00	0.00	0.12
Net Asset Value ($)	11.63	11.62	10.55	11.91	11.80	10.40	8.19	9.52	8.72	8.04
Expense Ratio (%).	na	0.75	0.73	0.71	0.85	0.81	0.88	0.84	0.88	0.85
Yield (%)	3.63	4.59	4.75	4.13	4.49	5.19	6.83	5.88	6.42	6.86
Portfolio Turnover (%).	na	46	52	81	55	57	55	55	24	13
Total Assets (Millions $). . .	169	167	170	204	135	60	45	57	68	72

PORTFOLIO (as of 9/30/96)

Portfolio Manager: Rohit M. Desai - 1986

Investm't Category: Growth & Income
- ✔ Domestic
- Foreign
- Asset Allocation
- Index
- Sector
- State Specific

Investment Style
- Large-Cap Growth
- ✔ Mid-Cap Growth
- ✔ Small-Cap Growth
- Large-Cap Value
- Mid-Cap Value
- Small-Cap Value

Portfolio
2.0% cash	0.0% corp bonds
17.0% stocks	0.0% gov't bonds
0.0% preferred	0.0% muni bonds
81.0% conv't/warrants	0.0% other

SHAREHOLDER INFORMATION

Minimum Investment
Initial: $3,000   Subsequent: $100

Minimum IRA Investment
Initial: $1,000   Subsequent: $100

Maximum Fees
Load: none   12b-1: none
Other: ƒ

Distributions
Income: quarterly   Capital Gains: annual

Exchange Options
Number Per Year: 2   Fee: none
Telephone: yes (money market fund available)

Services
IRA, pension, auto exchange, auto invest, auto withdraw

Vanguard Equity Income
(VEIPX)
Growth & Income

Vanguard Financial Center
P.O. Box 2600
Valley Forge, PA 19482
800-635-1511, 610-669-1000
www.vanguard.com

PERFORMANCE

fund inception date: 3/21/88

	3yr Annual	5yr Annual	10yr Annual	Bull	Bear
Return (%)	16.6	14.7	na	66.5	-7.0
Differ from Category (+/-)	1.3 av	0.8 av	na	6.7 abv av	-0.6 blw av

Total Risk	Standard Deviation	Category Risk	Risk Index	Beta
av	8.7%	blw av	0.9	0.82

	1996	1995	1994	1993	1992	1991	1990	1989	1988	1987
Return (%)	17.3	37.3	-1.6	14.6	9.1	25.3	-12.0	26.5	—	—
Differ from Category (+/-)	-2.4	7.2	-0.3	0.8	-1.6	-3.8	-6.1	3.0	—	—
Return, Tax-Adjusted (%)	14.8	35.0	-3.5	11.6	7.2	22.5	-14.5	23.8	—	—

PER SHARE DATA

	1996	1995	1994	1993	1992	1991	1990	1989	1988	1987
Dividends, Net Income ($)	0.64	0.60	0.57	0.61	0.59	0.65	0.73	0.70	—	—
Distrib'ns, Cap Gain ($)	0.57	0.17	0.09	0.52	0.00	0.10	0.07	0.03	—	—
Net Asset Value ($)	18.32	16.69	12.77	13.66	12.92	12.40	10.54	12.86	—	—
Expense Ratio (%)	0.42	0.45	0.43	0.40	0.44	0.46	0.48	0.44	—	—
Yield (%)	3.38	3.55	4.43	4.30	4.56	5.20	6.88	5.43	—	—
Portfolio Turnover (%)	21	31	18	15	13	9	5	8	—	—
Total Assets (Millions $)	1,440	1,102	869	1,067	835	569	398	334	—	—

PORTFOLIO (as of 9/30/96)

Portfolio Manager: Newell, Spare, Kigner, Sarnell - 1988

Investm't Category: Growth & Income

✔ Domestic   Index
  Foreign   Sector
  Asset Allocation   State Specific

Investment Style

  Large-Cap Growth   ✔ Large-Cap Value
  Mid-Cap Growth   Mid-Cap Value
  Small-Cap Growth   Small-Cap Value

Portfolio

6.0% cash	0.0% corp bonds
91.0% stocks	0.0% gov't bonds
1.0% preferred	0.0% muni bonds
2.0% conv't/warrants	0.0% other

SHAREHOLDER INFORMATION

Minimum Investment
Initial: $3,000   Subsequent: $100

Minimum IRA Investment
Initial: $1,000   Subsequent: $100

Maximum Fees
Load: none   12b-1: none
Other: f

Distributions
Income: quarterly   Capital Gains: annual

Exchange Options
Number Per Year: 2   Fee: none
Telephone: yes (money market fund available)

Services
IRA, pension, auto exchange, auto invest, auto withdraw

Vanguard Explorer

(VEXPX)

Aggressive Growth

Vanguard Financial Center
P.O. Box 2600
Valley Forge, PA 19482
800-635-1511, 610-669-1000
www.vanguard.com

PERFORMANCE

fund inception date: 12/11/67

	3yr Annual	5yr Annual	10yr Annual	Bull	Bear
Return (%)	13.2	13.6	12.9	56.0	-9.2
Differ from Category (+/-)	-2.6 blw av	-1.7 blw av	-2.1 blw av	-15.1 blw av	1.4 abv av

Total Risk	Standard Deviation	Category Risk	Risk Index	Beta
abv av	11.9%	blw av	0.8	0.77

	1996	1995	1994	1993	1992	1991	1990	1989	1988	1987
Return (%)	14.0	26.5	0.5	15.4	12.9	55.9	-10.8	9.3	25.8	-7.0
Differ from Category (+/-)	-5.1	-7.8	0.5	-3.9	1.2	3.8	-5.4	-19.1	9.4	-4.6
Return, Tax-Adjusted (%)	12.1	23.6	-1.1	11.9	12.2	55.4	-11.3	7.7	23.3	-9.2

PER SHARE DATA

	1996	1995	1994	1993	1992	1991	1990	1989	1988	1987
Dividends, Net Income ($)	0.27	0.24	0.17	0.14	0.13	0.26	0.34	0.37	0.32	0.11
Distrib'ns, Cap Gain ($)	2.83	4.00	2.25	5.17	0.78	0.00	0.00	1.01	1.59	1.96
Net Asset Value ($)	53.83	49.95	42.86	45.11	43.84	39.62	25.58	29.06	27.85	23.66
Expense Ratio (%)	na	0.68	0.70	0.73	0.69	0.56	0.67	0.58	0.65	0.62
Yield (%)	0.47	0.44	0.37	0.27	0.29	0.65	1.32	1.23	1.08	0.42
Portfolio Turnover (%)	na	66	82	51	43	49	46	16	28	9
Total Assets (Millions $)	2,223	1,647	1,121	847	620	429	237	258	264	211

PORTFOLIO (as of 9/30/96)

Portfolio Manager: John Granahan, Kenneth Abrams - 1990

Investm't Category: Aggressive Growth
- ✔ Domestic
- ✔ Foreign
-   Asset Allocation
-   Index
-   Sector
-   State Specific

Investment Style
-   Large-Cap Growth
-   Mid-Cap Growth
- ✔ Small-Cap Growth
-   Large-Cap Value
-   Mid-Cap Value
-   Small-Cap Value

Portfolio
14.0% cash	0.0% corp bonds
85.0% stocks	0.0% gov't bonds
0.0% preferred	0.0% muni bonds
1.0% conv't/warrants	0.0% other

SHAREHOLDER INFORMATION

Minimum Investment
Initial: $3,000   Subsequent: $100

Minimum IRA Investment
Initial: $1,000   Subsequent: $100

Maximum Fees
Load: none   12b-1: none
Other: *f*

Distributions
Income: annual   Capital Gains: annual

Exchange Options
Number Per Year: 2   Fee: none
Telephone: yes (money market fund available)

Services
IRA, pension, auto exchange, auto invest, auto withdraw

Vanguard Florida Insured Tax-Free (VFLTX)

Tax-Exempt Bond

Vanguard Financial Center
P.O. Box 2600
Valley Forge, PA 19482
800-635-1511, 610-669-1000
www.vanguard.com

PERFORMANCE

fund inception date: 8/31/92

	3yr Annual	5yr Annual	10yr Annual	Bull	Bear
Return (%)	5.3	na	na	21.8	-5.2
Differ from Category (+/-)	1.1 high	na	na	3.4 high	0.2 abv av

Total Risk	Standard Deviation	Category Risk	Risk Index	Avg Mat
blw av	6.3%	high	1.1	12.9 yrs

	1996	1995	1994	1993	1992	1991	1990	1989	1988	1987
Return (%)	4.1	17.7	-4.8	13.4	—	—	—	—	—	—
Differ from Category (+/-)	0.4	2.5	0.5	1.6	—	—	—	—	—	—
Return, Tax-Adjusted (%)	4.1	17.7	-4.8	13.2	—	—	—	—	—	—

PER SHARE DATA

	1996	1995	1994	1993	1992	1991	1990	1989	1988	1987
Dividends, Net Income ($)	0.55	0.55	0.55	0.53	—	—	—	—	—	—
Distrib'ns, Cap Gain ($)	0.00	0.00	0.00	0.06	—	—	—	—	—	—
Net Asset Value ($)	10.96	11.07	9.91	10.98	—	—	—	—	—	—
Expense Ratio (%)	na	0.21	0.22	0.21	—	—	—	—	—	—
Yield (%)	5.01	4.96	5.54	4.80	—	—	—	—	—	—
Portfolio Turnover (%)	na	20	43	34	—	—	—	—	—	—
Total Assets (Millions $)	515	483	328	311	—	—	—	—	—	—

PORTFOLIO (as of 9/30/96)

Portfolio Manager: Reid Smith - 1992

Investm't Category: Tax-Exempt Bond

✔ Domestic
Foreign
Asset Allocation

Index
Sector
✔ State Specific

Investment Style

Large-Cap Growth
Mid-Cap Growth
Small-Cap Growth

Large-Cap Value
Mid-Cap Value
Small-Cap Value

Portfolio

17.0% cash
0.0% stocks
0.0% preferred
0.0% conv't/warrants

0.0% corp bonds
0.0% gov't bonds
83.0% muni bonds
0.0% other

SHAREHOLDER INFORMATION

Minimum Investment
Initial: $3,000   Subsequent: $100

Minimum IRA Investment
Initial: na   Subsequent: na

Maximum Fees
Load: none   12b-1: none
Other: f

Distributions
Income: monthly   Capital Gains: annual

Exchange Options
Number Per Year: 2   Fee: none
Telephone: yes (money market fund available)

Services
auto exchange, auto invest, auto withdraw

Vanguard GNMA (VFIIX)

Mortgage-Backed Bond

Vanguard Financial Center
P.O. Box 2600
Valley Forge, PA 19482
800-635-1511, 610-669-1000
www.vanguard.com

PERFORMANCE   fund inception date: 6/27/80

	3yr Annual	5yr Annual	10yr Annual	Bull	Bear
Return (%)	6.8	6.6	8.5	25.2	-3.3
Differ from Category (+/-)	1.2 high	0.6 high	0.8 high	4.1 high	0.3 abv av

Total Risk	Standard Deviation	Category Risk	Risk Index	Avg Mat
low	3.9%	abv av	1.1	7.9 yrs

	1996	1995	1994	1993	1992	1991	1990	1989	1988	1987
Return (%)	5.2	17.0	-1.0	5.8	6.8	16.7	10.3	14.7	8.8	2.1
Differ from Category (+/-)	0.8	2.3	0.7	-1.1	0.6	2.3	0.5	2.1	1.4	0.1
Return, Tax-Adjusted (%)	2.4	13.9	-3.6	3.3	3.8	13.3	6.8	10.9	5.0	-1.4

PER SHARE DATA

	1996	1995	1994	1993	1992	1991	1990	1989	1988	1987
Dividends, Net Income ($)	0.72	0.73	0.68	0.65	0.78	0.83	0.85	0.88	0.88	0.88
Distrib'ns, Cap Gain ($)	0.00	0.00	0.00	0.00	0.00	0.00	0.00	0.00	0.00	0.00
Net Asset Value ($)	10.22	10.43	9.58	10.37	10.42	10.52	9.79	9.70	9.27	9.35
Expense Ratio (%)	0.29	0.30	0.28	0.29	0.29	0.34	0.31	0.35	0.35	0.38
Yield (%)	7.04	6.99	7.09	6.26	7.48	7.88	8.68	9.07	9.49	9.41
Portfolio Turnover (%)	7	35	2	7	1	1	9	8	22	28
Total Assets (Millions $)	7,497	6,907	5,777	7,073	6,958	5,297	2,598	2,149	1,882	1,864

PORTFOLIO (as of 9/30/96)

Portfolio Manager: Paul Kaplan - 1994

Investm't Category: Mortgage-Backed Bond
- ✔ Domestic
- Foreign
- Asset Allocation
- Index
- Sector
- State Specific

Investment Style
Large-Cap Growth	Large-Cap Value
Mid-Cap Growth	Mid-Cap Value
Small-Cap Growth	Small-Cap Value

Portfolio
2.0% cash	0.0% corp bonds
0.0% stocks	98.0% gov't bonds
0.0% preferred	0.0% muni bonds
0.0% conv't/warrants	0.0% other

SHAREHOLDER INFORMATION

Minimum Investment
Initial: $3,000   Subsequent: $100

Minimum IRA Investment
Initial: $1,000   Subsequent: $100

Maximum Fees
Load: none   12b-1: none
Other: f

Distributions
Income: monthly   Capital Gains: annual

Exchange Options
Number Per Year: 2   Fee: none
Telephone: yes (money market fund available)

Services
IRA, pension, auto exchange, auto invest, auto withdraw

836   Guide to Low-Load Mutual Funds

Vanguard High Yield Corporate (VWEHX)

Corporate High-Yield Bond

Vanguard Financial Center
P.O. Box 2600
Valley Forge, PA 19482
800-635-1511, 610-669-1000
www.vanguard.com

PERFORMANCE

fund inception date: 12/27/78

	3yr Annual	5yr Annual	10yr Annual	Bull	Bear
Return (%)	8.6	11.6	9.5	33.5	-6.1
Differ from Category (+/-)	-0.1 abv av	-0.5 abv av	0.2 high	0.4 av	-0.7 blw av

Total Risk	Standard Deviation	Category Risk	Risk Index	Avg Mat
low	4.6%	abv av	1.0	8.0 yrs

	1996	1995	1994	1993	1992	1991	1990	1989	1988	1987
Return (%)	9.5	19.1	-1.8	18.2	14.2	29.0	-5.9	1.8	13.5	2.6
Differ from Category (+/-)	-5.8	1.6	1.1	-0.7	-1.9	1.4	-1.0	0.6	1.0	0.8
Return, Tax-Adjusted (%)	6.0	15.4	-5.2	14.5	10.1	24.0	-10.7	-3.0	8.6	-2.1

PER SHARE DATA

	1996	1995	1994	1993	1992	1991	1990	1989	1988	1987
Dividends, Net Income ($)	0.68	0.67	0.67	0.69	0.73	0.77	0.91	1.00	1.01	1.00
Distrib'ns, Cap Gain ($)	0.00	0.00	0.00	0.00	0.00	0.00	0.00	0.00	0.00	0.11
Net Asset Value ($)	7.87	7.85	7.20	8.02	7.41	7.16	6.22	7.55	8.39	8.32
Expense Ratio (%)	0.34	0.34	0.32	0.34	0.34	0.40	0.38	0.41	0.41	0.45
Yield (%)	8.64	8.53	9.30	8.60	9.85	10.75	14.63	13.24	12.03	11.86
Portfolio Turnover (%)	38	33	51	83	44	61	41	48	82	67
Total Assets (Millions $)	3,524	2,899	2,120	2,529	2,033	1,452	693	895	1,164	904

PORTFOLIO (as of 9/30/96)

Portfolio Manager: Earl E. McEvoy - 1984

Investm't Category: Corp. High-Yield Bond

✔ Domestic	Index
Foreign	Sector
Asset Allocation	State Specific

Investment Style

Large-Cap Growth	Large-Cap Value
Mid-Cap Growth	Mid-Cap Value
Small-Cap Growth	Small-Cap Value

Portfolio

4.0% cash	90.0% corp bonds
0.0% stocks	6.0% gov't bonds
0.0% preferred	0.0% muni bonds
0.0% conv't/warrants	0.0% other

SHAREHOLDER INFORMATION

Minimum Investment
Initial: $3,000   Subsequent: $100

Minimum IRA Investment
Initial: $1,000   Subsequent: $100

Maximum Fees
Load: 1.00% redemption   12b-1: none
Other: redemption fee applies for 1 year; *f*

Distributions
Income: monthly   Capital Gains: annual

Exchange Options
Number Per Year: 2   Fee: none
Telephone: yes (money market fund available)

Services
IRA, pension, auto exchange, auto invest, auto withdraw

Vanguard Horizon Fd: Aggressive Growth

(VHAGX) *Aggressive Growth*

Vanguard Financial Center
P.O. Box 2600
Valley Forge, PA 19482
800-635-1511, 610-669-1000
www.vanguard.com

PERFORMANCE   fund inception date: 8/14/95

	3yr Annual	5yr Annual	10yr Annual	Bull	Bear
Return (%)	na	na	na	na	na
Differ from Category (+/-)	na	na	na	na	na

Total Risk	Standard Deviation	Category Risk	Risk Index	Beta
na	na	na	na	na

	1996	1995	1994	1993	1992	1991	1990	1989	1988	1987
Return (%)	25.1	—	—	—	—	—	—	—	—	—
Differ from Category (+/-)	6.0	—	—	—	—	—	—	—	—	—
Return, Tax-Adjusted (%)	22.5	—	—	—	—	—	—	—	—	—

PER SHARE DATA

	1996	1995	1994	1993	1992	1991	1990	1989	1988	1987
Dividends, Net Income ($)	0.18	—	—	—	—	—	—	—	—	—
Distrib'ns, Cap Gain ($)	0.71	—	—	—	—	—	—	—	—	—
Net Asset Value ($)	12.57	—	—	—	—	—	—	—	—	—
Expense Ratio (%)	na	—	—	—	—	—	—	—	—	—
Yield (%)	1.35	—	—	—	—	—	—	—	—	—
Portfolio Turnover (%)	na	—	—	—	—	—	—	—	—	—
Total Assets (Millions $)	146	—	—	—	—	—	—	—	—	—

PORTFOLIO (as of 9/30/96)

Portfolio Manager: George Sauter - 1995

Investm't Category: Aggressive Growth

✔ Domestic	Index
Foreign	Sector
Asset Allocation	State Specific

Investment Style

Large-Cap Growth	Large-Cap Value
Mid-Cap Growth	Mid-Cap Value
Small-Cap Growth	Small-Cap Value

Portfolio

1.0% cash	0.0% corp bonds
99.0% stocks	0.0% gov't bonds
0.0% preferred	0.0% muni bonds
0.0% conv't/warrants	0.0% other

SHAREHOLDER INFORMATION

Minimum Investment
Initial: $3,000   Subsequent: $100

Minimum IRA Investment
Initial: $1,000   Subsequent: $100

Maximum Fees
Load: 1.00% redemption   12b-1: none
Other: redemption fee applies for 5 years; *f*

Distributions
Income: annual   Capital Gains: annual

Exchange Options
Number Per Year: 2   Fee: none
Telephone: yes (money market fund available)

Services
IRA, pension, auto exchange, auto invest, auto withdraw

Vanguard Horizon Fd: Capital Opportunity

(VHCOX) *Aggressive Growth*

Vanguard Financial Center
P.O. Box 2600
Valley Forge, PA 19482
800-635-1511, 610-669-1000
www.vanguard.com

PERFORMANCE

fund inception date: 8/14/95

	3yr Annual	5yr Annual	10yr Annual	Bull	Bear
Return (%)	na	na	na	na	na
Differ from Category (+/-)	na	na	na	na	na

Total Risk	Standard Deviation	Category Risk	Risk Index	Beta
na	na	na	na	na

	1996	1995	1994	1993	1992	1991	1990	1989	1988	1987
Return (%)	13.4	—	—	—	—	—	—	—	—	—
Differ from Category (+/-)	-5.7	—	—	—	—	—	—	—	—	—
Return, Tax-Adjusted (%)	13.4	—	—	—	—	—	—	—	—	—

PER SHARE DATA

	1996	1995	1994	1993	1992	1991	1990	1989	1988	1987
Dividends, Net Income ($)	0.00	—	—	—	—	—	—	—	—	—
Distrib'ns, Cap Gain ($)	0.00	—	—	—	—	—	—	—	—	—
Net Asset Value ($)	11.13	—	—	—	—	—	—	—	—	—
Expense Ratio (%)	na	—	—	—	—	—	—	—	—	—
Yield (%)	0.00	—	—	—	—	—	—	—	—	—
Portfolio Turnover (%)	na	—	—	—	—	—	—	—	—	—
Total Assets (Millions $)	117	—	—	—	—	—	—	—	—	—

PORTFOLIO (as of 9/30/96)

Portfolio Manager: Frank J. Husic - 1995

Investm't Category: Aggressive Growth

✔ Domestic	Index
✔ Foreign	Sector
Asset Allocation	State Specific

Investment Style

Large-Cap Growth	Large-Cap Value
Mid-Cap Growth	Mid-Cap Value
Small-Cap Growth	Small-Cap Value

Portfolio

7.0% cash	0.0% corp bonds
93.0% stocks	0.0% gov't bonds
0.0% preferred	0.0% muni bonds
0.0% conv't/warrants	0.0% other

SHAREHOLDER INFORMATION

Minimum Investment
Initial: $3,000   Subsequent: $100

Minimum IRA Investment
Initial: $1,000   Subsequent: $100

Maximum Fees
Load: 1.00% redemption   12b-1: none
Other: redemption fee applies for 5 years; *f*

Distributions
Income: annual   Capital Gains: annual

Exchange Options
Number Per Year: 2   Fee: none
Telephone: yes (money market fund available)

Services
IRA, pension, auto exchange, auto invest, auto withdraw

Vanguard Horizon Fd: Global Asset Alloc (VHAAX)

International Stock

Vanguard Financial Center
P.O. Box 2600
Valley Forge, PA 19482
800-635-1511, 610-669-1000
www.vanguard.com

PERFORMANCE

fund inception date: 8/14/95

	3yr Annual	5yr Annual	10yr Annual	Bull	Bear
Return (%)	na	na	na	na	na
Differ from Category (+/-)	na	na	na	na	na

Total Risk	Standard Deviation	Category Risk	Risk Index	Beta
na	na	na	na	na

	1996	1995	1994	1993	1992	1991	1990	1989	1988	1987
Return (%)	9.9	—	—	—	—	—	—	—	—	—
Differ from Category (+/-)	-4.9	—	—	—	—	—	—	—	—	—
Return, Tax-Adjusted (%)	6.8	—	—	—	—	—	—	—	—	—

PER SHARE DATA

	1996	1995	1994	1993	1992	1991	1990	1989	1988	1987
Dividends, Net Income ($)	0.57	—	—	—	—	—	—	—	—	—
Distrib'ns, Cap Gain ($)	0.34	—	—	—	—	—	—	—	—	—
Net Asset Value ($)	10.59	—	—	—	—	—	—	—	—	—
Expense Ratio (%)	na	—	—	—	—	—	—	—	—	—
Yield (%)	5.21	—	—	—	—	—	—	—	—	—
Portfolio Turnover (%)	na	—	—	—	—	—	—	—	—	—
Total Assets (Millions $)	78	—	—	—	—	—	—	—	—	—

PORTFOLIO (as of 9/30/96)

Portfolio Manager: Michael J. Duffy - 1995

Investm't Category: International Stock

✔ Domestic   Index
✔ Foreign   Sector
✔ Asset Allocation   State Specific

Investment Style
Large-Cap Growth   Large-Cap Value
Mid-Cap Growth   Mid-Cap Value
Small-Cap Growth   Small-Cap Value

Portfolio
39.0%	cash	13.0%	corp bonds
6.0%	stocks	42.0%	gov't bonds
0.0%	preferred	0.0%	muni bonds
0.0%	conv't/warrants	0.0%	other

SHAREHOLDER INFORMATION

Minimum Investment
Initial: $3,000   Subsequent: $100

Minimum IRA Investment
Initial: $1,000   Subsequent: $100

Maximum Fees
Load: 1.00% redemption   12b-1: none
Other: redemption fee applies for 5 years; *f*

Distributions
Income: annual   Capital Gains: annual

Exchange Options
Number Per Year: 2   Fee: none
Telephone: yes (money market fund available)

Services
IRA, pension, auto exchange, auto invest, auto withdraw

Vanguard Horizon Fd: Global Equity (VHGEX)

International Stock

Vanguard Financial Center
P.O. Box 2600
Valley Forge, PA 19482
800-635-1511, 610-669-1000
www.vanguard.com

PERFORMANCE

fund inception date: 8/14/95

	3yr Annual	5yr Annual	10yr Annual	Bull	Bear
Return (%)	na	na	na	na	na
Differ from Category (+/-)	na	na	na	na	na

Total Risk	Standard Deviation	Category Risk	Risk Index	Beta
na	na	na	na	na

	1996	1995	1994	1993	1992	1991	1990	1989	1988	1987
Return (%)	15.5	—	—	—	—	—	—	—	—	—
Differ from Category (+/-)	0.7	—	—	—	—	—	—	—	—	—
Return, Tax-Adjusted (%)	14.4	—	—	—	—	—	—	—	—	—

PER SHARE DATA

	1996	1995	1994	1993	1992	1991	1990	1989	1988	1987
Dividends, Net Income ($)	0.14	—	—	—	—	—	—	—	—	—
Distrib'ns, Cap Gain ($)	0.19	—	—	—	—	—	—	—	—	—
Net Asset Value ($)	11.84	—	—	—	—	—	—	—	—	—
Expense Ratio (%)	na	—	—	—	—	—	—	—	—	—
Yield (%)	1.16	—	—	—	—	—	—	—	—	—
Portfolio Turnover (%)	na	—	—	—	—	—	—	—	—	—
Total Assets (Millions $)	105	—	—	—	—	—	—	—	—	—

PORTFOLIO (as of 9/30/96)

Portfolio Manager: Jeremy J. Hosking - 1995

Investm't Category: International Stock

✔ Domestic	Index
✔ Foreign	Sector
Asset Allocation	State Specific

Investment Style

Large-Cap Growth	Large-Cap Value
Mid-Cap Growth	Mid-Cap Value
Small-Cap Growth	Small-Cap Value

Portfolio

8.0% cash	0.0% corp bonds
92.0% stocks	0.0% gov't bonds
0.0% preferred	0.0% muni bonds
0.0% conv't/warrants	0.0% other

SHAREHOLDER INFORMATION

Minimum Investment
Initial: $3,000   Subsequent: $100

Minimum IRA Investment
Initial: $1,000   Subsequent: $100

Maximum Fees
Load: 1.00% redemption   12b-1: none
Other: redemption fee applies for 5 years; f

Distributions
Income: annual   Capital Gains: annual

Exchange Options
Number Per Year: 2   Fee: none
Telephone: yes (money market fund available)

Services
IRA, pension, auto exchange, auto invest, auto withdraw

Vanguard Index Trust: 500 Port (VFINX)

Growth & Income

Vanguard Financial Center
P.O. Box 2600
Valley Forge, PA 19482
800-635-1511, 610-669-1000
www.vanguard.com

PERFORMANCE

fund inception date: 8/31/76

	3yr Annual	5yr Annual	10yr Annual	Bull	Bear
Return (%)	19.5	15.0	15.0	76.9	-6.7
Differ from Category (+/-)	4.2 high	1.1 abv av	2.3 high	17.1 high	-0.3 av

Total Risk	Standard Deviation	Category Risk	Risk Index	Beta
abv av	9.7%	abv av	1.0	0.99

	1996	1995	1994	1993	1992	1991	1990	1989	1988	1987
Return (%).	22.8	37.4	1.1	9.8	7.4	30.2	-3.4	31.3	16.2	4.7
Differ from Category (+/-)	.3.1	7.3	2.4	-4.0	-3.3	1.1	2.5	7.8	-0.6	4.5
Return, Tax-Adjusted (%).	.21.7	36.1	-0.1	8.6	6.2	28.6	-4.9	28.7	14.0	3.3

PER SHARE DATA

	1996	1995	1994	1993	1992	1991	1990	1989	1988	1987
Dividends, Net Income ($).	1.28	1.22	1.17	1.12	1.12	1.14	1.17	1.20	1.10	0.69
Distrib'ns, Cap Gain ($) . .	0.25	0.13	0.20	0.03	0.10	0.12	0.10	0.75	0.32	0.17
Net Asset Value ($)	69.16	57.60	42.97	43.83	40.97	39.32	31.24	33.64	27.18	24.65
Expense Ratio (%).	na	0.20	0.19	0.19	0.19	0.20	0.22	0.21	0.22	0.26
Yield (%)	1.84	2.11	2.71	2.55	2.72	2.89	3.73	3.48	4.00	2.78
Portfolio Turnover (%). . . .	na	4	6	6	4	5	23	8	10	15
Total Assets (Millions $) .	30,312	17,371	9,356	8,272	6,547	4,345	2,173	1,803	1,055	826

PORTFOLIO (as of 9/30/96)

Portfolio Manager: George Sauter - 1987

Investm't Category: Growth & Income
- ✔ Domestic
- ✔ Index
- Foreign
- Sector
- Asset Allocation
- State Specific

Investment Style
- ✔ Large-Cap Growth
- ✔ Large-Cap Value
- Mid-Cap Growth
- Mid-Cap Value
- Small-Cap Growth
- Small-Cap Value

Portfolio

0.0% cash	0.0% corp bonds
100.0% stocks	0.0% gov't bonds
0.0% preferred	0.0% muni bonds
0.0% conv't/warrants	0.0% other

SHAREHOLDER INFORMATION

Minimum Investment
Initial: $3,000   Subsequent: $100

Minimum IRA Investment
Initial: $1,000   Subsequent: $100

Maximum Fees
Load: none   12b-1: none
Other: f

Distributions
Income: quarterly   Capital Gains: annual

Exchange Options
Number Per Year: 2   Fee: none
Telephone: none

Services
IRA, pension, auto exchange, auto invest, auto withdraw

Vanguard Index Trust: Extended Market (VEXMX)

Growth

Vanguard Financial Center
P.O. Box 2600
Valley Forge, PA 19482
800-635-1511, 610-669-1000
www.vanguard.com

PERFORMANCE

fund inception date: 12/21/87

	3yr Annual	5yr Annual	10yr Annual	Bull	Bear
Return (%)	15.6	14.7	na	63.9	-8.5
Differ from Category (+/-)	-0.1 av	0.4 av	na	1.5 av	-1.8 blw av

Total Risk	Standard Deviation	Category Risk	Risk Index	Beta
abv av	10.8%	abv av	1.0	0.89

	1996	1995	1994	1993	1992	1991	1990	1989	1988	1987
Return (%)	17.6	33.7	-1.8	14.4	12.4	41.8	-14.1	24.0	19.7	—
Differ from Category (+/-)	-2.5	3.4	-1.5	0.4	0.6	5.8	-8.0	-2.1	1.6	—
Return, Tax-Adjusted (%)	15.0	32.4	-2.8	13.5	11.4	40.4	-15.4	22.6	18.4	—

PER SHARE DATA

	1996	1995	1994	1993	1992	1991	1990	1989	1988	1987
Dividends, Net Income ($)	0.34	0.30	0.28	0.23	0.25	0.25	0.33	0.23	0.20	—
Distrib'ns, Cap Gain ($)	1.72	0.40	0.28	0.20	0.18	0.20	0.16	0.23	0.16	—
Net Asset Value ($)	26.19	24.07	18.52	19.43	17.35	15.82	11.48	13.92	11.60	—
Expense Ratio (%)	na	0.25	0.20	0.20	0.20	0.19	0.23	0.23	0.24	—
Yield (%)	1.21	1.22	1.48	1.17	1.42	1.56	2.83	1.62	1.70	—
Portfolio Turnover (%)	na	15	19	13	9	11	9	14	26	—
Total Assets (Millions $)	2,082	1,523	967	927	584	372	178	146	34	—

PORTFOLIO (as of 9/30/96)

Portfolio Manager: George Sauter - 1987

Investm't Category: Growth

✔ Domestic	✔ Index
Foreign	Sector
Asset Allocation	State Specific

Investment Style

Large-Cap Growth	Large-Cap Value
✔ Mid-Cap Growth	✔ Mid-Cap Value
✔ Small-Cap Growth	✔ Small-Cap Value

Portfolio

2.0% cash	0.0% corp bonds
98.0% stocks	0.0% gov't bonds
0.0% preferred	0.0% muni bonds
0.0% conv't/warrants	0.0% other

SHAREHOLDER INFORMATION

Minimum Investment
Initial: $3,000   Subsequent: $100

Minimum IRA Investment
Initial: $1,000   Subsequent: $100

Maximum Fees
Load: 0.50% charge   12b-1: none
Other: *f*

Distributions
Income: annual   Capital Gains: annual

Exchange Options
Number Per Year: 2   Fee: none
Telephone: none

Services
IRA, pension, auto exchange, auto invest, auto withdraw

Vanguard Index Trust: Growth Port (VIGRX)

Growth

Vanguard Financial Center
P.O. Box 2600
Valley Forge, PA 19482
800-635-1511, 610-669-1000
www.vanguard.com

PERFORMANCE

fund inception date: 11/2/92

	3yr Annual	5yr Annual	10yr Annual	Bull	Bear
Return (%)	20.7	na	na	84.2	-6.5
Differ from Category (+/-)	5.0 high	na	na	21.8 high	0.2 av

Total Risk	Standard Deviation	Category Risk	Risk Index	Beta
abv av	9.8%	av	1.0	0.98

	1996	1995	1994	1993	1992	1991	1990	1989	1988	1987
Return (%).	23.8	38.0	2.8	0.6	—	—	—	—	—	—
Differ from Category (+/-) . .	3.7	7.7	3.1	-13.4	—	—	—	—	—	—
Return, Tax-Adjusted (%). .	22.8	37.2	1.9	-0.3	—	—	—	—	—	—

PER SHARE DATA

	1996	1995	1994	1993	1992	1991	1990	1989	1988	1987
Dividends, Net Income ($)	0.22	0.20	0.21	0.21	—	—	—	—	—	—
Distrib'ns, Cap Gain ($) . . .	0.14	0.00	0.00	0.00	—	—	—	—	—	—
Net Asset Value ($)	16.91	13.97	10.28	10.20	—	—	—	—	—	—
Expense Ratio (%).	na	0.20	0.20	0.20	—	—	—	—	—	—
Yield (%)	1.29	1.43	2.04	2.05	—	—	—	—	—	—
Portfolio Turnover (%).	na	24	28	36	—	—	—	—	—	—
Total Assets (Millions $). . .	783	271	86	50	—	—	—	—	—	—

PORTFOLIO (as of 9/30/96)

Portfolio Manager: George Sauter - 1992

Investm't Category: Growth

✔ Domestic	✔ Index
Foreign	Sector
Asset Allocation	State Specific

Investment Style

✔ Large-Cap Growth	Large-Cap Value
Mid-Cap Growth	Mid-Cap Value
Small-Cap Growth	Small-Cap Value

Portfolio

1.0% cash	0.0% corp bonds
99.0% stocks	0.0% gov't bonds
0.0% preferred	0.0% muni bonds
0.0% conv't/warrants	0.0% other

SHAREHOLDER INFORMATION

Minimum Investment
Initial: $3,000   Subsequent: $100

Minimum IRA Investment
Initial: $1,000   Subsequent: $100

Maximum Fees
Load: none   12b-1: none
Other: *f*

Distributions
Income: quarterly   Capital Gains: annual

Exchange Options
Number Per Year: 2   Fee: none
Telephone: none

Services
IRA, pension, auto exchange, auto invest, auto withdraw

Vanguard Index Trust: Small Cap Stock (NAESX)

Aggressive Growth

Vanguard Financial Center
P.O. Box 2600
Valley Forge, PA 19482
800-635-1511, 610-669-1000
www.vanguard.com

PERFORMANCE

fund inception date: 1/31/74

	3yr Annual	5yr Annual	10yr Annual	Bull	Bear
Return (%)	14.7	16.2	12.4	59.7	-8.7
Differ from Category (+/-)	-1.1 av	0.9 abv av	-2.6 blw av	-11.4 av	1.9 abv av

Total Risk	Standard Deviation	Category Risk	Risk Index	Beta
abv av	11.8%	blw av	0.8	0.84

	1996	1995	1994	1993	1992	1991	1990	1989	1988	1987
Return (%)	18.1	28.7	-0.6	18.7	18.2	45.2	-18.2	10.5	24.6	-7.0
Differ from Category (+/-)	-1.0	-5.6	-0.6	-0.6	6.5	-6.9	-12.8	-17.9	8.2	-4.6
Return, Tax-Adjusted (%)	15.3	27.2	-1.9	16.5	17.2	43.4	-19.2	5.0	24.3	-8.0

PER SHARE DATA

	1996	1995	1994	1993	1992	1991	1990	1989	1988	1987
Dividends, Net Income ($)	0.27	0.23	0.22	0.18	0.18	0.18	0.18	0.13	0.05	0.00
Distrib'ns, Cap Gain ($)	1.44	0.45	0.37	0.82	0.15	0.28	0.14	2.16	0.00	1.21
Net Asset Value ($)	20.23	18.61	14.99	15.67	14.07	12.19	8.74	11.07	11.97	9.65
Expense Ratio (%)	na	0.25	0.17	0.18	0.18	0.21	0.31	1.00	0.95	0.92
Yield (%)	1.24	1.20	1.43	1.09	1.26	1.44	2.02	0.98	0.41	0.00
Portfolio Turnover (%)	na	28	na	26	26	33	40	160	68	92
Total Assets (Millions $)	1,646	971	606	488	264	131	46	33	25	24

PORTFOLIO (as of 9/30/96)

Portfolio Manager: George Sauter - 1989

Investm't Category: Aggressive Growth
- ✔ Domestic
- ✔ Index
- Foreign
- Sector
- Asset Allocation
- State Specific

Investment Style
- Large-Cap Growth
- Large-Cap Value
- Mid-Cap Growth
- Mid-Cap Value
- ✔ Small-Cap Growth
- ✔ Small-Cap Value

Portfolio
- 3.0% cash
- 0.0% corp bonds
- 97.0% stocks
- 0.0% gov't bonds
- 0.0% preferred
- 0.0% muni bonds
- 0.0% conv't/warrants
- 0.0% other

SHAREHOLDER INFORMATION

Minimum Investment
Initial: $3,000   Subsequent: $100

Minimum IRA Investment
Initial: $1,000   Subsequent: $100

Maximum Fees
Load: 0.50% charge   12b-1: none
Other: ƒ

Distributions
Income: annual   Capital Gains: annual

Exchange Options
Number Per Year: 2   Fee: none
Telephone: none

Services
IRA, pension, auto exchange, auto invest, auto withdraw

Vanguard Index Trust: Total Stock Market

Vanguard Financial Center
P.O. Box 2600
Valley Forge, PA 19482
800-635-1511, 610-669-1000
www.vanguard.com

(VTSMX) *Growth & Income*

PERFORMANCE

fund inception date: 3/16/92

	3yr Annual	5yr Annual	10yr Annual	Bull	Bear
Return (%)	17.9	na	na	71.8	-7.5
Differ from Category (+/-)	2.6 abv av	na	na	12.0 abv av	-1.1 blw av

Total Risk	Standard Deviation	Category Risk	Risk Index	Beta
abv av	9.6%	abv av	1.0	0.96

	1996	1995	1994	1993	1992	1991	1990	1989	1988	1987
Return (%)	20.9	35.7	-0.2	10.6	—	—	—	—	—	—
Differ from Category (+/-)	1.2	5.6	1.1	-3.2	—	—	—	—	—	—
Return, Tax-Adjusted (%)	19.9	34.5	-1.2	9.5	—	—	—	—	—	—

PER SHARE DATA

	1996	1995	1994	1993	1992	1991	1990	1989	1988	1987
Dividends, Net Income ($)	0.28	0.28	0.27	0.26	—	—	—	—	—	—
Distrib'ns, Cap Gain ($)	0.11	0.09	0.03	0.03	—	—	—	—	—	—
Net Asset Value ($)	17.77	15.04	11.37	11.69	—	—	—	—	—	—
Expense Ratio (%)	na	0.25	0.20	0.20	—	—	—	—	—	—
Yield (%)	1.56	1.85	2.36	2.21	—	—	—	—	—	—
Portfolio Turnover (%)	na	3	2	1	—	—	—	—	—	—
Total Assets (Millions $)	3,495	1,570	785	512	—	—	—	—	—	—

PORTFOLIO (as of 9/30/96)

Portfolio Manager: George Sauter - 1992

Investm't Category: Growth & Income
- ✔ Domestic
- ✔ Index
- Foreign
- Sector
- Asset Allocation
- State Specific

Investment Style
- ✔ Large-Cap Growth
- ✔ Large-Cap Value
- ✔ Mid-Cap Growth
- ✔ Mid-Cap Value
- Small-Cap Growth
- Small-Cap Value

Portfolio
2.0% cash	0.0% corp bonds
98.0% stocks	0.0% gov't bonds
0.0% preferred	0.0% muni bonds
0.0% conv't/warrants	0.0% other

SHAREHOLDER INFORMATION

Minimum Investment
Initial: $3,000   Subsequent: $100

Minimum IRA Investment
Initial: $1,000   Subsequent: $100

Maximum Fees
Load: none   12b-1: none
Other: f

Distributions
Income: quarterly   Capital Gains: annual

Exchange Options
Number Per Year: 2   Fee: none
Telephone: none

Services
IRA, pension, auto exchange, auto invest, auto withdraw

Vanguard Index Trust: Value Port (VIVAX)

Growth & Income

Vanguard Financial Center
P.O. Box 2600
Valley Forge, PA 19482
800-635-1511, 610-669-1000
www.vanguard.com

PERFORMANCE

fund inception date: 11/2/92

	3yr Annual	5yr Annual	10yr Annual	Bull	Bear
Return (%)	18.3	na	na	69.6	-6.7
Differ from Category (+/-)	3.0 abv av	na	na	9.8 abv av	-0.3 av

Total Risk	Standard Deviation	Category Risk	Risk Index	Beta
abv av	10.1%	abv av	1.1	1.01

	1996	1995	1994	1993	1992	1991	1990	1989	1988	1987
Return (%)	21.7	37.0	-0.7	18.1	—	—	—	—	—	—
Differ from Category (+/-)	2.0	6.9	0.6	4.3	—	—	—	—	—	—
Return, Tax-Adjusted (%)	19.6	35.5	-2.4	16.4	—	—	—	—	—	—

PER SHARE DATA

	1996	1995	1994	1993	1992	1991	1990	1989	1988	1987
Dividends, Net Income ($)	0.38	0.40	0.38	0.38	—	—	—	—	—	—
Distrib'ns, Cap Gain ($)	0.56	0.00	0.16	0.06	—	—	—	—	—	—
Net Asset Value ($)	17.02	14.80	11.12	11.73	—	—	—	—	—	—
Expense Ratio (%)	na	0.20	0.20	0.20	—	—	—	—	—	—
Yield (%)	2.16	2.70	3.36	3.22	—	—	—	—	—	—
Portfolio Turnover (%)	na	27	32	30	—	—	—	—	—	—
Total Assets (Millions $)	1,003	496	296	190	—	—	—	—	—	—

PORTFOLIO (as of 9/30/96)

Portfolio Manager: George Sauter - 1992

Investm't Category: Growth & Income
- ✔ Domestic
- ✔ Index
- Foreign
- Sector
- Asset Allocation
- State Specific

Investment Style
- Large-Cap Growth
- ✔ Large-Cap Value
- Mid-Cap Growth
- Mid-Cap Value
- Small-Cap Growth
- Small-Cap Value

Portfolio
1.0%	cash	0.0%	corp bonds
99.0%	stocks	0.0%	gov't bonds
0.0%	preferred	0.0%	muni bonds
0.0%	conv't/warrants	0.0%	other

SHAREHOLDER INFORMATION

Minimum Investment
Initial: $3,000   Subsequent: $100

Minimum IRA Investment
Initial: $1,000   Subsequent: $100

Maximum Fees
Load: none   12b-1: none
Other: f

Distributions
Income: quarterly   Capital Gains: annual

Exchange Options
Number Per Year: 2   Fee: none
Telephone: none

Services
IRA, pension, auto exchange, auto invest, auto withdraw

Vanguard Interm-Term Corporate Bond (VFICX)

Corporate Bond

Vanguard Financial Center
P.O. Box 2600
Valley Forge, PA 19482
800-635-1511, 610-669-1000
www.vanguard.com

PERFORMANCE

fund inception date: 11/1/93

	3yr Annual	5yr Annual	10yr Annual	Bull	Bear
Return (%)	6.1	na	na	25.2	-6.0
Differ from Category (+/-)	-0.2 abv av	na	na	0.4 abv av	-0.9 blw av

Total Risk	Standard Deviation	Category Risk	Risk Index	Avg Mat
blw av	5.4%	abv av	1.2	7.1 yrs

	1996	1995	1994	1993	1992	1991	1990	1989	1988	1987
Return (%)	2.7	21.3	-4.3	—	—	—	—	—	—	—
Differ from Category (+/-)	-2.5	3.3	-1.2	—	—	—	—	—	—	—
Return, Tax-Adjusted (%)	0.2	18.4	-6.6	—	—	—	—	—	—	—

PER SHARE DATA

	1996	1995	1994	1993	1992	1991	1990	1989	1988	1987
Dividends, Net Income ($)	0.63	0.65	0.57	—	—	—	—	—	—	—
Distrib'ns, Cap Gain ($)	0.01	0.00	0.00	—	—	—	—	—	—	—
Net Asset Value ($)	9.75	10.15	8.95	—	—	—	—	—	—	—
Expense Ratio (%)	0.28	0.28	0.25	—	—	—	—	—	—	—
Yield (%)	6.45	6.40	6.36	—	—	—	—	—	—	—
Portfolio Turnover (%)	78	97	74	—	—	—	—	—	—	—
Total Assets (Millions $)	604	361	151	—	—	—	—	—	—	—

PORTFOLIO (as of 9/30/96)

Portfolio Manager: Ian MacKinnon - 1993

Investm't Category: Corporate Bond

✔ Domestic	Index
Foreign	Sector
Asset Allocation	State Specific

Investment Style

Large-Cap Growth	Large-Cap Value
Mid-Cap Growth	Mid-Cap Value
Small-Cap Growth	Small-Cap Value

Portfolio

2.0%	cash	93.0%	corp bonds
0.0%	stocks	5.0%	gov't bonds
0.0%	preferred	0.0%	muni bonds
0.0%	conv't/warrants	0.0%	other

SHAREHOLDER INFORMATION

Minimum Investment
Initial: $3,000   Subsequent: $100

Minimum IRA Investment
Initial: $1,000   Subsequent: $100

Maximum Fees
Load: none   12b-1: none
Other: f

Distributions
Income: monthly   Capital Gains: annual

Exchange Options
Number Per Year: 2   Fee: none
Telephone: yes (money market fund available)

Services
IRA, pension, auto exchange, auto invest, auto withdraw

Vanguard Interm-Term US Treas (VFITX)

Government Bond

Vanguard Financial Center
P.O. Box 2600
Valley Forge, PA 19482
800-635-1511, 610-669-1000
www.vanguard.com

PERFORMANCE

fund inception date: 10/28/91

	3yr Annual	5yr Annual	10yr Annual	Bull	Bear
Return (%)	5.5	7.1	na	23.1	-6.1
Differ from Category (+/-)	0.6 abv av	0.5 abv av	na	1.1 abv av	0.3 av

Total Risk	Standard Deviation	Category Risk	Risk Index	Avg Mat
blw av	5.5%	abv av	1.4	7.4 yrs

	1996	1995	1994	1993	1992	1991	1990	1989	1988	1987
Return (%)................	1.9	20.4	-4.4	11.4	7.7	—	—	—	—	—
Differ from Category (+/-)..	0.4	0.8	0.0	-0.2	1.0	—	—	—	—	—
Return, Tax-Adjusted (%)..	-0.5	17.6	-6.7	7.9	5.1	—	—	—	—	—

PER SHARE DATA

	1996	1995	1994	1993	1992	1991	1990	1989	1988	1987
Dividends, Net Income ($).	0.64	0.66	0.59	0.62	0.67	—	—	—	—	—
Distrib'ns, Cap Gain ($) ...	0.00	0.00	0.02	0.41	0.01	—	—	—	—	—
Net Asset Value ($)	10.42	10.88	9.63	10.71	10.56	—	—	—	—	—
Expense Ratio (%)........	0.28	0.28	0.26	0.26	0.26	—	—	—	—	—
Yield (%)	6.14	6.06	6.11	5.57	6.33	—	—	—	—	—
Portfolio Turnover (%).....	56	128	118	123	32	—	—	—	—	—
Total Assets (Millions $).	1,294	1,195	844	984	604	—	—	—	—	—

PORTFOLIO (as of 9/30/96)

Portfolio Manager: Ian MacKinnon - 1991

Investm't Category: Government Bond

✔ Domestic	Index
Foreign	Sector
Asset Allocation	State Specific

Investment Style

Large-Cap Growth	Large-Cap Value
Mid-Cap Growth	Mid-Cap Value
Small-Cap Growth	Small-Cap Value

Portfolio

4.0% cash	0.0% corp bonds
0.0% stocks	96.0% gov't bonds
0.0% preferred	0.0% muni bonds
0.0% conv't/warrants	0.0% other

SHAREHOLDER INFORMATION

Minimum Investment
Initial: $3,000   Subsequent: $100

Minimum IRA Investment
Initial: $1,000   Subsequent: $100

Maximum Fees
Load: none   12b-1: none
Other: f

Distributions
Income: monthly   Capital Gains: annual

Exchange Options
Number Per Year: 2   Fee: none
Telephone: yes (money market fund available)

Services
IRA, pension, auto exchange, auto invest, auto withdraw

Vanguard Int'l Equity Index: Emerging Mkts

(VEIEX) *International Stock*

Vanguard Financial Center
P.O. Box 2600
Valley Forge, PA 19482
800-635-1511, 610-669-1000
www.vanguard.com

PERFORMANCE

fund inception date: 5/4/94

	3yr Annual	5yr Annual	10yr Annual	Bull	Bear
Return (%)	na	na	na	21.0	na
Differ from Category (+/-)	na	na	na	-3.3 blw av	na

Total Risk	Standard Deviation	Category Risk	Risk Index	Beta
na	na	na	na	na

	1996	1995	1994	1993	1992	1991	1990	1989	1988	1987
Return (%)	15.9	0.4	—	—	—	—	—	—	—	—
Differ from Category (+/-)	1.1	-8.7	—	—	—	—	—	—	—	—
Return, Tax-Adjusted (%)	15.2	-0.3	—	—	—	—	—	—	—	—

PER SHARE DATA

	1996	1995	1994	1993	1992	1991	1990	1989	1988	1987
Dividends, Net Income ($)	0.17	0.18	—	—	—	—	—	—	—	—
Distrib'ns, Cap Gain ($)	0.00	0.00	—	—	—	—	—	—	—	—
Net Asset Value ($)	12.28	10.74	—	—	—	—	—	—	—	—
Expense Ratio (%)	na	0.60	—	—	—	—	—	—	—	—
Yield (%)	1.38	1.67	—	—	—	—	—	—	—	—
Portfolio Turnover (%)	na	3	—	—	—	—	—	—	—	—
Total Assets (Millions $)	622	234	—	—	—	—	—	—	—	—

PORTFOLIO (as of 9/30/96)

Portfolio Manager: George Sauter - 1994

Investm't Category: International Stock

Domestic	✔ Index
✔ Foreign	Sector
Asset Allocation	State Specific

Investment Style

Large-Cap Growth	Large-Cap Value
Mid-Cap Growth	Mid-Cap Value
Small-Cap Growth	Small-Cap Value

Portfolio

5.0% cash	0.0% corp bonds
95.0% stocks	0.0% gov't bonds
0.0% preferred	0.0% muni bonds
0.0% conv't/warrants	0.0% other

SHAREHOLDER INFORMATION

Minimum Investment
Initial: $1,000   Subsequent: $100

Minimum IRA Investment
Initial: $1,000   Subsequent: $100

Maximum Fees
Load: 1.00% redemption   12b-1: none
Other: 1.50% transaction fee; *f*

Distributions
Income: annual   Capital Gains: annual

Exchange Options
Number Per Year: 2   Fee: none
Telephone: none

Services
IRA, pension, auto exchange, auto invest, auto
withdraw

Vanguard Int'l Equity Index: European

(VEURX) *International Stock*

Vanguard Financial Center
P.O. Box 2600
Valley Forge, PA 19482
800-635-1511, 610-669-1000
www.vanguard.com

PERFORMANCE

fund inception date: 5/1/90

	3yr Annual	5yr Annual	10yr Annual	Bull	Bear
Return (%)	14.7	13.5	na	55.1	-7.0
Differ from Category (+/-)	8.4 high	3.5 high	na	30.8 high	0.2 av

Total Risk	Standard Deviation	Category Risk	Risk Index	Beta
abv av	9.8%	blw av	1.0	0.69

	1996	1995	1994	1993	1992	1991	1990	1989	1988	1987
Return (%)	21.2	22.2	1.8	29.1	-3.4	12.4	—	—	—	—
Differ from Category (+/-)	6.4	13.1	4.9	-10.5	0.4	-0.8	—	—	—	—
Return, Tax-Adjusted (%)	20.0	21.0	0.7	28.3	-4.5	11.2	—	—	—	—

PER SHARE DATA

	1996	1995	1994	1993	1992	1991	1990	1989	1988	1987
Dividends, Net Income ($)	0.36	0.32	0.28	0.17	0.26	0.26	—	—	—	—
Distrib'ns, Cap Gain ($)	0.06	0.04	0.06	0.00	0.00	0.00	—	—	—	—
Net Asset Value ($)	16.57	14.02	11.76	11.88	9.33	9.92	—	—	—	—
Expense Ratio (%)	na	0.35	0.32	0.32	0.32	0.33	—	—	—	—
Yield (%)	2.16	2.27	2.36	1.43	2.78	2.62	—	—	—	—
Portfolio Turnover (%)	na	2	6	4	1	15	—	—	—	—
Total Assets (Millions $)	1,541	1,017	715	600	256	160	—	—	—	—

PORTFOLIO (as of 9/30/96)

Portfolio Manager: George Sauter - 1990

Investm't Category: International Stock

Domestic	✔ Index
✔ Foreign	Sector
Asset Allocation	State Specific

Investment Style

Large-Cap Growth	Large-Cap Value
Mid-Cap Growth	Mid-Cap Value
Small-Cap Growth	Small-Cap Value

Portfolio

3.0% cash	0.0% corp bonds
97.0% stocks	0.0% gov't bonds
0.0% preferred	0.0% muni bonds
0.0% conv't/warrants	0.0% other

SHAREHOLDER INFORMATION

Minimum Investment
Initial: $1,000   Subsequent: $100

Minimum IRA Investment
Initial: $1,000   Subsequent: $100

Maximum Fees
Load: 1.00% charge   12b-1: none
Other: f

Distributions
Income: annual   Capital Gains: annual

Exchange Options
Number Per Year: 2   Fee: none
Telephone: none

Services
IRA, pension, auto exchange, auto invest, auto withdraw

Vanguard Int'l Equity Index: Pacific

(VPACX) *International Stock*

Vanguard Financial Center
P.O. Box 2600
Valley Forge, PA 19482
800-635-1511, 610-669-1000
www.vanguard.com

PERFORMANCE   fund inception date: 5/1/90

	3yr Annual	5yr Annual	10yr Annual	Bull	Bear
Return (%)	2.3	3.4	na	-10.2	7.0
Differ from Category (+/-)	-4.0 blw av	-6.6 low	na	-34.5 low	14.2 high

Total Risk	Standard Deviation	Category Risk	Risk Index	Beta
high	15.4%	high	1.5	0.63

	1996	1995	1994	1993	1992	1991	1990	1989	1988	1987
Return (%).	-7.9	2.8	12.9	35.4	-18.2	10.6	—	—	—	—
Differ from Category (+/-)	-22.7	-6.3	16.0	-4.2	-14.4	-2.6	—	—	—	—
Return, Tax-Adjusted (%). .	-8.3	2.3	12.4	34.9	-18.8	10.3	—	—	—	—

PER SHARE DATA

	1996	1995	1994	1993	1992	1991	1990	1989	1988	1987
Dividends, Net Income ($).	0.09	0.12	0.08	0.06	0.05	0.05	—	—	—	—
Distrib'ns, Cap Gain ($) . .	0.00	0.00	0.06	0.05	0.10	0.00	—	—	—	—
Net Asset Value ($)	10.51	11.50	11.30	10.13	7.56	9.42	—	—	—	—
Expense Ratio (%).	na	0.35	0.32	0.32	0.32	0.32	—	—	—	—
Yield (%)	0.85	1.04	0.70	0.58	0.65	0.53	—	—	—	—
Portfolio Turnover (%). . . .	na	1	4	7	3	21	—	—	—	—
Total Assets (Millions $). .	1,023	830	697	492	206	84	—	—	—	—

PORTFOLIO (as of 9/30/96)

Portfolio Manager: George Sauter - 1990

Investm't Category: International Stock

Domestic	✔ Index
✔ Foreign	Sector
Asset Allocation	State Specific

Investment Style

Large-Cap Growth	Large-Cap Value
Mid-Cap Growth	Mid-Cap Value
Small-Cap Growth	Small-Cap Value

Portfolio

2.0% cash	0.0% corp bonds
97.0% stocks	0.0% gov't bonds
0.0% preferred	0.0% muni bonds
1.0% conv't/warrants	0.0% other

SHAREHOLDER INFORMATION

Minimum Investment
Initial: $1,000   Subsequent: $100

Minimum IRA Investment
Initial: $1,000   Subsequent: $100

Maximum Fees
Load: 0.50% charge   12b-1: none
Other: *f*

Distributions
Income: annual   Capital Gains: annual

Exchange Options
Number Per Year: 2   Fee: none
Telephone: none

Services
IRA, pension, auto exchange, auto invest, auto withdraw

Vanguard LifeStrategy: Conservative Grth (VSCGX)

Balanced

Vanguard Financial Center
P.O. Box 2600
Valley Forge, PA 19482
800-635-1511, 610-669-1000
www.vanguard.com

PERFORMANCE

fund inception date: 7/18/94

	3yr Annual	5yr Annual	10yr Annual	Bull	Bear
Return (%)	na	na	na	na	na
Differ from Category (+/-)	na	na	na	na	na

Total Risk	Standard Deviation	Category Risk	Risk Index	Beta
na	na	na	na	na

	1996	1995	1994	1993	1992	1991	1990	1989	1988	1987
Return (%)	10.3	24.3	—	—	—	—	—	—	—	—
Differ from Category (+/-)	-3.9	-0.3	—	—	—	—	—	—	—	—
Return, Tax-Adjusted (%)	8.0	22.0	—	—	—	—	—	—	—	—

PER SHARE DATA

	1996	1995	1994	1993	1992	1991	1990	1989	1988	1987
Dividends, Net Income ($)	0.53	0.47	—	—	—	—	—	—	—	—
Distrib'ns, Cap Gain ($)	0.20	0.12	—	—	—	—	—	—	—	—
Net Asset Value ($)	12.14	11.68	—	—	—	—	—	—	—	—
Expense Ratio (%)	na	0.00	—	—	—	—	—	—	—	—
Yield (%)	4.29	3.98	—	—	—	—	—	—	—	—
Portfolio Turnover (%)	na	1	—	—	—	—	—	—	—	—
Total Assets (Millions $)	455	219	—	—	—	—	—	—	—	—

PORTFOLIO (as of 6/30/96)

Portfolio Manager: committee - 1994

Investm't Category: Balanced
✔ Domestic   Index
✔ Foreign   Sector
✔ Asset Allocation   State Specific

Investment Style

Large-Cap Growth	Large-Cap Value
Mid-Cap Growth	Mid-Cap Value
Small-Cap Growth	Small-Cap Value

Portfolio

5.0% cash	40.0% corp bonds
48.0% stocks	7.0% gov't bonds
0.0% preferred	0.0% muni bonds
0.0% conv't/warrants	0.0% other

SHAREHOLDER INFORMATION

Minimum Investment
Initial: $3,000   Subsequent: $100

Minimum IRA Investment
Initial: $1,000   Subsequent: $100

Maximum Fees
Load: none   12b-1: none
Other: f

Distributions
Income: quarterly   Capital Gains: annual

Exchange Options
Number Per Year: 2   Fee: none
Telephone: yes (money market fund available)

Services
IRA, pension, auto exchange, auto invest, auto withdraw

Vanguard LifeStrategy: Growth Port (VASGX)

Balanced

Vanguard Financial Center
P.O. Box 2600
Valley Forge, PA 19482
800-635-1511, 610-669-1000
www.vanguard.com

PERFORMANCE
fund inception date: 7/18/94

	3yr Annual	5yr Annual	10yr Annual	Bull	Bear
Return (%)	na	na	na	na	na
Differ from Category (+/-)	na	na	na	na	na

Total Risk	Standard Deviation	Category Risk	Risk Index	Beta
na	na	na	na	na

	1996	1995	1994	1993	1992	1991	1990	1989	1988	1987
Return (%)	15.4	29.2	—	—	—	—	—	—	—	—
Differ from Category (+/-)	1.2	4.6	—	—	—	—	—	—	—	—
Return, Tax-Adjusted (%)	13.7	27.5	—	—	—	—	—	—	—	—

PER SHARE DATA

	1996	1995	1994	1993	1992	1991	1990	1989	1988	1987
Dividends, Net Income ($)	0.35	0.31	—	—	—	—	—	—	—	—
Distrib'ns, Cap Gain ($)	0.23	0.15	—	—	—	—	—	—	—	—
Net Asset Value ($)	13.68	12.36	—	—	—	—	—	—	—	—
Expense Ratio (%)	na	0.00	—	—	—	—	—	—	—	—
Yield (%)	2.51	2.47	—	—	—	—	—	—	—	—
Portfolio Turnover (%)	na	1	—	—	—	—	—	—	—	—
Total Assets (Millions $)	621	217	—	—	—	—	—	—	—	—

PORTFOLIO (as of 6/30/96)

Portfolio Manager: committee - 1994

Investm't Category: Balanced
✔ Domestic   Index
✔ Foreign   Sector
✔ Asset Allocation   State Specific

Investment Style
Large-Cap Growth   Large-Cap Value
Mid-Cap Growth   Mid-Cap Value
Small-Cap Growth   Small-Cap Value

Portfolio
3.0% cash   7.0% corp bonds
88.0% stocks   2.0% gov't bonds
0.0% preferred   0.0% muni bonds
0.0% conv't/warrants 0.0% other

SHAREHOLDER INFORMATION

Minimum Investment
Initial: $3,000   Subsequent: $100

Minimum IRA Investment
Initial: $1,000   Subsequent: $100

Maximum Fees
Load: none   12b-1: none
Other: f

Distributions
Income: semiannual   Capital Gains: annual

Exchange Options
Number Per Year: 2   Fee: none
Telephone: yes (money market fund available)

Services
IRA, pension, auto exchange, auto invest, auto withdraw

Vanguard LifeStrategy: Income Port (VASIX)

Balanced

Vanguard Financial Center
P.O. Box 2600
Valley Forge, PA 19482
800-635-1511, 610-669-1000
www.vanguard.com

PERFORMANCE

fund inception date: 7/18/94

	3yr Annual	5yr Annual	10yr Annual	Bull	Bear
Return (%)	na	na	na	na	na
Differ from Category (+/-)	na	na	na	na	na

Total Risk	Standard Deviation	Category Risk	Risk Index	Beta
na	na	na	na	na

	1996	1995	1994	1993	1992	1991	1990	1989	1988	1987
Return (%)	7.6	22.9	—	—	—	—	—	—	—	—
Differ from Category (+/-)	-6.6	-1.7	—	—	—	—	—	—	—	—
Return, Tax-Adjusted (%)	4.8	20.6	—	—	—	—	—	—	—	—

PER SHARE DATA

	1996	1995	1994	1993	1992	1991	1990	1989	1988	1987
Dividends, Net Income ($)	0.64	0.49	—	—	—	—	—	—	—	—
Distrib'ns, Cap Gain ($)	0.21	0.09	—	—	—	—	—	—	—	—
Net Asset Value ($)	11.55	11.54	—	—	—	—	—	—	—	—
Expense Ratio (%)	na	0.00	—	—	—	—	—	—	—	—
Yield (%)	5.44	4.21	—	—	—	—	—	—	—	—
Portfolio Turnover (%)	na	4	—	—	—	—	—	—	—	—
Total Assets (Millions $)	150	120	—	—	—	—	—	—	—	—

PORTFOLIO (as of 6/30/96)

Portfolio Manager: committee - 1994

Investm't Category: Balanced
- ✔ Domestic
- Foreign
- ✔ Asset Allocation
- Index
- Sector
- State Specific

Investment Style

Large-Cap Growth	Large-Cap Value
Mid-Cap Growth	Mid-Cap Value
Small-Cap Growth	Small-Cap Value

Portfolio

0.0% cash	58.0% corp bonds
30.0% stocks	12.0% gov't bonds
0.0% preferred	0.0% muni bonds
0.0% conv't/warrants	0.0% other

SHAREHOLDER INFORMATION

Minimum Investment
Initial: $3,000   Subsequent: $100

Minimum IRA Investment
Initial: $1,000   Subsequent: $100

Maximum Fees
Load: none   12b-1: none
Other: f

Distributions
Income: quarterly   Capital Gains: annual

Exchange Options
Number Per Year: 2   Fee: none
Telephone: yes (money market fund available)

Services
IRA, pension, auto exchange, auto invest, auto withdraw

Vanguard LifeStrategy: Moderate Grth (VSMGX)

Balanced

Vanguard Financial Center
P.O. Box 2600
Valley Forge, PA 19482
800-635-1511, 610-669-1000
www.vanguard.com

PERFORMANCE

fund inception date: 7/18/94

	3yr Annual	5yr Annual	10yr Annual	Bull	Bear
Return (%)	na	na	na	na	na
Differ from Category (+/-)	na	na	na	na	na

Total Risk	Standard Deviation	Category Risk	Risk Index	Beta
na	na	na	na	na

	1996	1995	1994	1993	1992	1991	1990	1989	1988	1987
Return (%)	12.7	27.9	—	—	—	—	—	—	—	—
Differ from Category (+/-)	-1.5	3.3	—	—	—	—	—	—	—	—
Return, Tax-Adjusted (%)	10.7	26.0	—	—	—	—	—	—	—	—

PER SHARE DATA

	1996	1995	1994	1993	1992	1991	1990	1989	1988	1987
Dividends, Net Income ($)	0.44	0.36	—	—	—	—	—	—	—	—
Distrib'ns, Cap Gain ($)	0.23	0.13	—	—	—	—	—	—	—	—
Net Asset Value ($)	12.97	12.11	—	—	—	—	—	—	—	—
Expense Ratio (%)	na	0.00	—	—	—	—	—	—	—	—
Yield (%)	3.33	2.94	—	—	—	—	—	—	—	—
Portfolio Turnover (%)	na	1	—	—	—	—	—	—	—	—
Total Assets (Millions $)	676	234	—	—	—	—	—	—	—	—

PORTFOLIO (as of 6/30/96)

Portfolio Manager: committee - 1994

Investm't Category: Balanced

✔ Domestic	Index
✔ Foreign	Sector
✔ Asset Allocation	State Specific

Investment Style

Large-Cap Growth	Large-Cap Value
Mid-Cap Growth	Mid-Cap Value
Small-Cap Growth	Small-Cap Value

Portfolio

4.0% cash	21.0% corp bonds
68.0% stocks	7.0% gov't bonds
0.0% preferred	0.0% muni bonds
0.0% conv't/warrants	0.0% other

SHAREHOLDER INFORMATION

Minimum Investment
Initial: $3,000   Subsequent: $100

Minimum IRA Investment
Initial: $1,000   Subsequent: $100

Maximum Fees
Load: none   12b-1: none
Other: *f*

Distributions
Income: semiannual   Capital Gains: annual

Exchange Options
Number Per Year: 2   Fee: none
Telephone: yes (money market fund available)

Services
IRA, pension, auto exchange, auto invest, auto withdraw

Vanguard Long-Term Corporate (VWESX)

Corporate Bond

Vanguard Financial Center
P.O. Box 2600
Valley Forge, PA 19482
800-635-1511, 610-669-1000
www.vanguard.com

PERFORMANCE

fund inception date: 6/29/73

	3yr Annual	5yr Annual	10yr Annual	Bull	Bear
Return (%)	6.6	8.7	9.4	29.1	-8.2
Differ from Category (+/-)	0.3 abv av	0.4 abv av	1.3 high	4.3 high	-3.1 low

Total Risk	Standard Deviation	Category Risk	Risk Index	Avg Mat
av	7.3%	high	1.6	20.0 yrs

	1996	1995	1994	1993	1992	1991	1990	1989	1988	1987
Return (%)	1.1	26.4	-5.3	14.4	9.7	20.9	6.2	15.1	9.6	0.1
Differ from Category (+/-)	-4.1	8.4	-2.2	2.6	0.8	3.7	2.2	5.7	0.3	-2.3
Return, Tax-Adjusted (%)	-1.9	23.3	-8.2	10.7	6.1	17.4	2.7	11.4	5.8	-3.8

PER SHARE DATA

	1996	1995	1994	1993	1992	1991	1990	1989	1988	1987
Dividends, Net Income ($)	0.61	0.62	0.61	0.63	0.68	0.70	0.71	0.73	0.74	0.77
Distrib'ns, Cap Gain ($)	0.15	0.00	0.07	0.25	0.15	0.00	0.00	0.00	0.00	0.12
Net Asset Value ($)	8.79	9.48	8.05	9.22	8.86	8.87	7.99	8.24	7.83	7.84
Expense Ratio (%)	0.31	0.32	0.30	0.31	0.31	0.37	0.34	0.38	0.37	0.41
Yield (%)	6.82	6.54	7.51	6.65	7.54	7.89	8.88	8.85	9.45	9.67
Portfolio Turnover (%)	49	43	77	50	72	62	70	60	63	47
Total Assets (Millions $)	3,535	3,356	2,552	3,168	2,629	2,006	1,192	987	711	587

PORTFOLIO (as of 9/30/96)

Portfolio Manager: Earl E. McEvoy - 1994

Investm't Category: Corp. Bond

✔ Domestic	Index
Foreign	Sector
Asset Allocation	State Specific

Investment Style

Large-Cap Growth	Large-Cap Value
Mid-Cap Growth	Mid-Cap Value
Small-Cap Growth	Small-Cap Value

Portfolio

2.0%	cash	85.0% corp bonds
0.0%	stocks	13.0% gov't bonds
0.0%	preferred	0.0% muni bonds
0.0%	conv't/warrants	0.0% other

SHAREHOLDER INFORMATION

Minimum Investment
Initial: $3,000   Subsequent: $100

Minimum IRA Investment
Initial: $1,000   Subsequent: $100

Maximum Fees
Load: none   12b-1: none
Other: *f*

Distributions
Income: monthly   Capital Gains: annual

Exchange Options
Number Per Year: 2   Fee: none
Telephone: yes (money market fund available)

Services
IRA, pension, auto exchange, auto invest, auto withdraw

Vanguard Long-Term US Treas (VUSTX)

Government Bond

Vanguard Financial Center
P.O. Box 2600
Valley Forge, PA 19482
800-635-1511, 610-669-1000
www.vanguard.com

PERFORMANCE

fund inception date: 5/19/86

	3yr Annual	5yr Annual	10yr Annual	Bull	Bear
Return (%)	5.9	8.3	8.7	29.8	-10.4
Differ from Category (+/-)	1.0 high	1.7 high	0.7 abv av	7.8 high	-4.0 low

Total Risk	Standard Deviation	Category Risk	Risk Index	Avg Mat
av	8.9%	high	2.2	21.2 yrs

	1996	1995	1994	1993	1992	1991	1990	1989	1988	1987
Return (%)	-1.3	30.0	-7.5	16.7	7.3	17.4	5.7	17.9	9.1	-3.0
Differ from Category (+/-)	-2.8	10.4	-3.1	5.1	0.6	1.7	-0.6	2.6	0.8	1.4
Return, Tax-Adjusted (%)	-3.8	26.3	-10.2	13.4	2.7	14.2	2.6	14.5	5.7	-6.1

PER SHARE DATA

	1996	1995	1994	1993	1992	1991	1990	1989	1988	1987
Dividends, Net Income ($)	0.65	0.67	0.66	0.68	0.73	0.76	0.77	0.78	0.77	0.78
Distrib'ns, Cap Gain ($)	0.01	0.22	0.07	0.17	0.69	0.00	0.00	0.00	0.00	0.03
Net Asset Value ($)	9.96	10.79	9.05	10.57	9.82	10.54	9.70	9.96	9.16	9.13
Expense Ratio (%)	0.27	0.28	0.26	0.27	0.26	0.30	0.28	0.36	0.32	0.00
Yield (%)	6.51	6.08	7.23	6.33	6.94	7.21	7.93	7.83	8.40	8.51
Portfolio Turnover (%)	105	85	7	170	89	147	83	387	182	182
Total Assets (Millions $)	952	917	644	823	856	892	698	502	150	73

PORTFOLIO (as of 9/30/96)

Portfolio Manager: Ian MacKinnon - 1986

Investm't Category: Government Bond

✔ Domestic | Index
Foreign | Sector
Asset Allocation | State Specific

Investment Style
Large-Cap Growth | Large-Cap Value
Mid-Cap Growth | Mid-Cap Value
Small-Cap Growth | Small-Cap Value

Portfolio

4.0% cash	0.0% corp bonds
0.0% stocks	96.0% gov't bonds
0.0% preferred	0.0% muni bonds
0.0% conv't/warrants	0.0% other

SHAREHOLDER INFORMATION

Minimum Investment
Initial: $3,000   Subsequent: $100

Minimum IRA Investment
Initial: $1,000   Subsequent: $100

Maximum Fees
Load: none   12b-1: none
Other: *f*

Distributions
Income: monthly   Capital Gains: annual

Exchange Options
Number Per Year: 2   Fee: none
Telephone: yes (money market fund available)

Services
IRA, pension, auto exchange, auto invest, auto withdraw

Vanguard Muni Bond Fd: High Yield (VWAHX)

Tax-Exempt Bond

Vanguard Financial Center
P.O. Box 2600
Valley Forge, PA 19482
800-635-1511, 610-669-1000
www.vanguard.com

PERFORMANCE

fund inception date: 12/27/78

	3yr Annual	5yr Annual	10yr Annual	Bull	Bear
Return (%)	5.4	7.7	8.1	21.9	-5.1
Differ from Category (+/-)	1.2 high	1.3 high	1.4 high	3.5 high	0.3 abv av

Total Risk	Standard Deviation	Category Risk	Risk Index	Avg Mat
blw av	6.0%	abv av	1.1	13.1 yrs

	1996	1995	1994	1993	1992	1991	1990	1989	1988	1987
Return (%)	4.4	18.1	-5.1	12.6	9.8	14.7	5.9	11.0	13.8	-1.6
Differ from Category (+/-)	0.7	2.9	0.2	0.8	1.5	3.3	-0.5	2.0	3.8	-0.2
Return, Tax-Adjusted (%)	4.4	18.1	-5.6	12.0	9.1	14.4	5.5	10.6	13.8	-2.2

PER SHARE DATA

	1996	1995	1994	1993	1992	1991	1990	1989	1988	1987
Dividends, Net Income ($)	0.58	0.61	0.62	0.65	0.70	0.73	0.73	0.75	0.74	0.77
Distrib'ns, Cap Gain ($)	0.00	0.00	0.17	0.21	0.25	0.10	0.14	0.11	0.00	0.20
Net Asset Value ($)	10.63	10.76	9.66	11.01	10.57	10.53	9.96	10.26	10.05	9.52
Expense Ratio (%)	0.20	0.21	0.20	0.20	0.23	0.25	0.25	0.27	0.29	0.26
Yield (%)	5.45	5.66	6.30	5.79	6.46	6.86	7.22	7.23	7.36	7.92
Portfolio Turnover (%)	19	33	50	34	64	58	82	80	40	83
Total Assets (Millions $)	2,063	1,988	1,572	1,903	1,616	1,341	1,016	941	739	654

PORTFOLIO (as of 9/30/96)

Portfolio Manager: Ian MacKinnon - 1984

Investm't Category: Tax-Exempt Bond
- ✔ Domestic
- Foreign
- Asset Allocation
- Index
- Sector
- State Specific

Investment Style
- Large-Cap Growth
- Mid-Cap Growth
- Small-Cap Growth
- Large-Cap Value
- Mid-Cap Value
- Small-Cap Value

Portfolio
17.0% cash	0.0% corp bonds
0.0% stocks	0.0% gov't bonds
0.0% preferred	83.0% muni bonds
0.0% conv't/warrants	0.0% other

SHAREHOLDER INFORMATION

Minimum Investment
Initial: $3,000   Subsequent: $100

Minimum IRA Investment
Initial: na   Subsequent: na

Maximum Fees
Load: none   12b-1: none
Other: none

Distributions
Income: monthly   Capital Gains: annual

Exchange Options
Number Per Year: 2   Fee: none
Telephone: yes (money market fund available)

Services
auto exchange, auto invest, auto withdraw

Vanguard Muni Bond Fd: Ins Long-Term (VILPX)

Tax-Exempt Bond

Vanguard Financial Center
P.O. Box 2600
Valley Forge, PA 19482
800-635-1511, 610-669-1000
www.vanguard.com

PERFORMANCE

fund inception date: 10/1/84

	3yr Annual	5yr Annual	10yr Annual	Bull	Bear
Return (%)	5.2	7.5	8.0	22.3	-6.0
Differ from Category (+/-)	1.0 high	1.1 high	1.3 high	3.9 high	-0.6 av

Total Risk	Standard Deviation	Category Risk	Risk Index	Avg Mat
blw av	6.4%	high	1.1	13.4 yrs

	1996	1995	1994	1993	1992	1991	1990	1989	1988	1987
Return (%)	4.0	18.5	-5.6	13.0	9.1	12.4	7.0	10.5	12.7	0.1
Differ from Category (+/-)	0.3	3.3	-0.3	1.2	0.8	1.0	0.6	1.5	2.7	1.5
Return, Tax-Adjusted (%)	3.8	18.5	-6.0	12.6	8.6	12.2	6.7	10.1	12.7	-0.2

PER SHARE DATA

	1996	1995	1994	1993	1992	1991	1990	1989	1988	1987
Dividends, Net Income ($)	0.67	0.67	0.70	0.70	0.74	0.77	0.79	0.83	0.82	0.84
Distrib'ns, Cap Gain ($)	0.07	0.00	0.17	0.17	0.20	0.07	0.12	0.15	0.00	0.10
Net Asset Value ($)	12.34	12.60	11.23	12.81	12.14	12.03	11.50	11.64	11.45	10.92
Expense Ratio (%)	0.20	0.21	0.20	0.20	0.23	0.25	0.25	0.29	0.29	0.26
Yield (%)	5.39	5.31	6.14	5.39	5.99	6.36	6.79	7.03	7.16	7.62
Portfolio Turnover (%)	18	7	16	30	42	33	47	36	28	50
Total Assets (Millions $)	1,992	2,017	1,737	2,161	2,004	1,701	1,250	1,018	806	685

PORTFOLIO (as of 9/30/96)

Portfolio Manager: Ian MacKinnon - 1984

Investm't Category: Tax-Exempt Bond
- ✔ Domestic
- Foreign
- Asset Allocation
- Index
- Sector
- State Specific

Investment Style
- Large-Cap Growth
- Mid-Cap Growth
- Small-Cap Growth
- Large-Cap Value
- Mid-Cap Value
- Small-Cap Value

Portfolio
9.0% cash	0.0% corp bonds
0.0% stocks	0.0% gov't bonds
0.0% preferred	91.0% muni bonds
0.0% conv't/warrants	0.0% other

SHAREHOLDER INFORMATION

Minimum Investment
Initial: $3,000   Subsequent: $100

Minimum IRA Investment
Initial: na   Subsequent: na

Maximum Fees
Load: none   12b-1: none
Other: none

Distributions
Income: monthly   Capital Gains: annual

Exchange Options
Number Per Year: 2   Fee: none
Telephone: yes (money market fund available)

Services
auto exchange, auto invest, auto withdraw

Vanguard Muni Bond Fd: Interm-Term (VWITX)

Tax-Exempt Bond

Vanguard Financial Center
P.O. Box 2600
Valley Forge, PA 19482
800-635-1511, 610-669-1000
www.vanguard.com

PERFORMANCE

fund inception date: 9/1/77

	3yr Annual	5yr Annual	10yr Annual	Bull	Bear
Return (%)	5.0	7.0	7.6	18.1	-2.9
Differ from Category (+/-)	0.8 high	0.6 abv av	0.9 high	-0.3 av	2.5 high

Total Risk	Standard Deviation	Category Risk	Risk Index	Avg Mat
low	3.9%	low	0.7	7.7 yrs

	1996	1995	1994	1993	1992	1991	1990	1989	1988	1987
Return (%)	4.1	13.6	-2.2	11.5	8.8	12.1	7.1	10.0	10.0	1.6
Differ from Category (+/-)	0.4	-1.6	3.1	-0.3	0.5	0.7	0.7	1.0	0.0	3.0
Return, Tax-Adjusted (%)	4.1	13.6	-2.6	11.3	8.5	11.9	6.8	9.8	10.0	1.3

PER SHARE DATA

	1996	1995	1994	1993	1992	1991	1990	1989	1988	1987
Dividends, Net Income ($)	0.66	0.67	0.68	0.69	0.73	0.78	0.81	0.84	0.80	0.82
Distrib'ns, Cap Gain ($)	0.00	0.00	0.15	0.07	0.12	0.07	0.09	0.06	0.00	0.09
Net Asset Value ($)	13.23	13.36	12.39	13.52	12.84	12.61	12.05	12.12	11.88	11.56
Expense Ratio (%)	0.20	0.21	0.20	0.20	0.23	0.25	0.25	0.27	0.29	0.26
Yield (%)	4.98	5.01	5.42	5.07	5.63	6.15	6.67	6.89	6.73	7.03
Portfolio Turnover (%)	15	12	18	15	32	27	54	56	89	57
Total Assets (Millions $)	6,145	5,770	4,696	5,238	3,516	2,459	1,411	1,113	851	762

PORTFOLIO (as of 9/30/96)

Portfolio Manager: Ian MacKinnon - 1981

Investm't Category: Tax-Exempt Bond
- ✔ Domestic
- Foreign
- Asset Allocation
- Index
- Sector
- State Specific

Investment Style
- Large-Cap Growth
- Mid-Cap Growth
- Small-Cap Growth
- Large-Cap Value
- Mid-Cap Value
- Small-Cap Value

Portfolio
16.0% cash	0.0% corp bonds
0.0% stocks	0.0% gov't bonds
0.0% preferred	84.0% muni bonds
0.0% conv't/warrants	0.0% other

SHAREHOLDER INFORMATION

Minimum Investment
Initial: $3,000   Subsequent: $100

Minimum IRA Investment
Initial: na   Subsequent: na

Maximum Fees
Load: none   12b-1: none
Other: none

Distributions
Income: monthly   Capital Gains: annual

Exchange Options
Number Per Year: 2   Fee: none
Telephone: yes (money market fund available)

Services
auto exchange, auto invest, auto withdraw

Vanguard Muni Bond Fd: Ltd Term (VMLTX)

Tax-Exempt Bond

Vanguard Financial Center
P.O. Box 2600
Valley Forge, PA 19482
800-635-1511, 610-669-1000
www.vanguard.com

PERFORMANCE

fund inception date: 8/31/87

	3yr Annual	5yr Annual	10yr Annual	Bull	Bear
Return (%)	4.1	5.0	na	13.5	-1.1
Differ from Category (+/-)	-0.1 av	-1.4 low	na	-4.9 low	4.3 high

Total Risk	Standard Deviation	Category Risk	Risk Index	Avg Mat
low	1.7%	low	0.3	3.3 yrs

	1996	1995	1994	1993	1992	1991	1990	1989	1988	1987
Return (%)	4.0	8.5	0.0	6.3	6.3	9.4	7.0	8.0	6.3	—
Differ from Category (+/-)	0.3	-6.7	5.3	-5.5	-2.0	-2.0	0.6	-1.0	-3.7	—
Return, Tax-Adjusted (%)	4.0	8.5	0.0	6.2	6.1	9.2	7.0	7.9	6.3	—

PER SHARE DATA

	1996	1995	1994	1993	1992	1991	1990	1989	1988	1987
Dividends, Net Income ($)	0.47	0.48	0.45	0.46	0.51	0.59	0.64	0.64	0.60	—
Distrib'ns, Cap Gain ($)	0.00	0.00	0.00	0.02	0.04	0.06	0.00	0.01	0.00	—
Net Asset Value ($)	10.71	10.76	10.37	10.82	10.65	10.56	10.27	10.22	10.09	—
Expense Ratio (%)	0.21	0.21	0.20	0.20	0.23	0.25	0.25	0.27	0.29	—
Yield (%)	4.38	4.46	4.33	4.24	4.77	5.55	6.23	6.25	5.94	—
Portfolio Turnover (%)	27	35	21	20	37	57	55	89	122	—
Total Assets (Millions $)	1,811	1,683	1,629	1,817	1,089	547	270	193	175	—

PORTFOLIO (as of 9/30/96)

Portfolio Manager: Ian MacKinnon - 1987

Investm't Category: Tax-Exempt Bond
- ✔ Domestic
- Foreign
- Asset Allocation
- Index
- Sector
- State Specific

Investment Style
- Large-Cap Growth
- Mid-Cap Growth
- Small-Cap Growth
- Large-Cap Value
- Mid-Cap Value
- Small-Cap Value

Portfolio
- 34.0% cash
- 0.0% stocks
- 0.0% preferred
- 0.0% conv't/warrants
- 0.0% corp bonds
- 0.0% gov't bonds
- 66.0% muni bonds
- 0.0% other

SHAREHOLDER INFORMATION

Minimum Investment
Initial: $3,000   Subsequent: $100

Minimum IRA Investment
Initial: na   Subsequent: na

Maximum Fees
Load: none   12b-1: none
Other: none

Distributions
Income: monthly   Capital Gains: annual

Exchange Options
Number Per Year: 2   Fee: none
Telephone: yes (money market fund available)

Services
auto exchange, auto invest, auto withdraw

Vanguard Muni Bond Fd: Long-Term (VWLTX)

Tax-Exempt Bond

Vanguard Financial Center
P.O. Box 2600
Valley Forge, PA 19482
800-635-1511, 610-669-1000
www.vanguard.com

PERFORMANCE

fund inception date: 9/1/77

	3yr Annual	5yr Annual	10yr Annual	Bull	Bear
Return (%)	5.3	7.6	8.0	22.8	-5.7
Differ from Category (+/-)	1.1 high	1.2 high	1.3 high	4.4 high	-0.3 av

Total Risk	Standard Deviation	Category Risk	Risk Index	Avg Mat
blw av	6.2%	abv av	1.1	13.3 yrs

	1996	1995	1994	1993	1992	1991	1990	1989	1988	1987
Return (%)	4.4	18.7	-5.8	13.4	9.3	13.5	6.8	11.5	12.2	-1.2
Differ from Category (+/-)	0.7	3.5	-0.5	1.6	1.0	2.1	0.4	2.5	2.2	0.2
Return, Tax-Adjusted (%)	4.3	18.7	-6.2	12.8	8.5	12.9	6.3	11.0	12.2	-2.0

PER SHARE DATA

	1996	1995	1994	1993	1992	1991	1990	1989	1988	1987
Dividends, Net Income ($)	0.58	0.59	0.61	0.62	0.68	0.73	0.72	0.75	0.74	0.78
Distrib'ns, Cap Gain ($)	0.02	0.00	0.15	0.20	0.28	0.19	0.17	0.16	0.00	0.31
Net Asset Value ($)	10.95	11.09	9.88	11.29	10.71	10.72	10.31	10.53	10.31	9.88
Expense Ratio (%)	0.20	0.21	0.20	0.20	0.23	0.25	0.25	0.27	0.29	0.26
Yield (%)	5.28	5.32	6.08	5.39	6.18	6.69	6.87	7.01	7.17	7.65
Portfolio Turnover (%)	26	35	45	36	63	62	110	99	34	67
Total Assets (Millions $)	1,155	1,114	920	1,103	1,012	887	711	680	557	523

PORTFOLIO (as of 9/30/96)

Portfolio Manager: Jerome J. Jacobs - 1988

Investm't Category: Tax-Exempt Bond
- ✔ Domestic
- Foreign
- Asset Allocation
- Index
- Sector
- State Specific

Investment Style
- Large-Cap Growth
- Mid-Cap Growth
- Small-Cap Growth
- Large-Cap Value
- Mid-Cap Value
- Small-Cap Value

Portfolio
15.0% cash	0.0% corp bonds
0.0% stocks	0.0% gov't bonds
0.0% preferred	85.0% muni bonds
0.0% conv't/warrants	0.0% other

SHAREHOLDER INFORMATION

Minimum Investment
Initial: $3,000   Subsequent: $100

Minimum IRA Investment
Initial: na   Subsequent: na

Maximum Fees
Load: none   12b-1: none
Other: none

Distributions
Income: monthly   Capital Gains: annual

Exchange Options
Number Per Year: 2   Fee: none
Telephone: yes (money market fund available)

Services
auto exchange, auto invest, auto withdraw

Vanguard Muni Bond Fd: Short-Term (VWSTX)

Tax-Exempt Bond

Vanguard Financial Center
P.O. Box 2600
Valley Forge, PA 19482
800-635-1511, 610-669-1000
www.vanguard.com

PERFORMANCE

fund inception date: 9/1/77

	3yr Annual	5yr Annual	10yr Annual	Bull	Bear
Return (%)	3.7	3.9	5.0	11.0	0.2
Differ from Category (+/-)	-0.5 low	-2.5 low	-1.7 low	-7.4 low	5.6 high

Total Risk	Standard Deviation	Category Risk	Risk Index	Avg Mat
low	0.7%	low	0.1	1.0 yrs

	1996	1995	1994	1993	1992	1991	1990	1989	1988	1987
Return (%).	3.6	5.9	1.6	3.8	4.7	7.1	6.5	7.0	5.6	4.1
Differ from Category (+/-) .	-0.1	-9.3	6.9	-8.0	-3.6	-4.3	0.1	-2.0	-4.4	5.5
Return, Tax-Adjusted (%). . .	3.6	5.9	1.6	3.7	4.6	6.9	6.5	7.0	5.6	3.9

PER SHARE DATA

	1996	1995	1994	1993	1992	1991	1990	1989	1988	1987
Dividends, Net Income ($).	0.60	0.61	0.54	0.57	0.66	0.82	0.90	0.89	0.81	0.76
Distrib'ns, Cap Gain ($) . . .	0.00	0.00	0.00	0.01	0.04	0.06	0.00	0.00	0.00	0.10
Net Asset Value ($)	15.58	15.62	15.33	15.63	15.64	15.63	15.43	15.36	15.21	15.19
Expense Ratio (%).	0.20	0.21	0.20	0.20	0.23	0.25	0.25	0.27	0.29	0.26
Yield (%)	3.85	3.90	3.52	3.64	4.20	5.22	5.83	5.79	5.32	4.97
Portfolio Turnover (%).	32	32	27	46	60	104	78	54	113	12
Total Assets (Millions $). .	1,467	1,410	1,463	1,464	1,111	874	751	704	806	834

PORTFOLIO (as of 9/30/96)

Portfolio Manager: Ian MacKinnon - 1981

Investm't Category: Tax-Exempt Bond
- ✔ Domestic
- Foreign
- Asset Allocation
- Index
- Sector
- State Specific

Investment Style
- Large-Cap Growth
- Mid-Cap Growth
- Small-Cap Growth
- Large-Cap Value
- Mid-Cap Value
- Small-Cap Value

Portfolio
- 56.0% cash
- 0.0% stocks
- 0.0% preferred
- 0.0% conv't/warrants
- 0.0% corp bonds
- 0.0% gov't bonds
- 44.0% muni bonds
- 0.0% other

SHAREHOLDER INFORMATION

Minimum Investment
Initial: $3,000   Subsequent: $100

Minimum IRA Investment
Initial: na   Subsequent: na

Maximum Fees
Load: none   12b-1: none
Other: none

Distributions
Income: monthly   Capital Gains: annual

Exchange Options
Number Per Year: 2   Fee: none
Telephone: yes (money market fund available)

Services
auto exchange, auto invest, auto withdraw

Vanguard NJ Tax Free Insured Long (VNJTX)

Tax-Exempt Bond

Vanguard Financial Center
P.O. Box 2600
Valley Forge, PA 19482
800-635-1511, 610-669-1000
www.vanguard.com

PERFORMANCE

fund inception date: 2/3/88

	3yr Annual	5yr Annual	10yr Annual	Bull	Bear
Return (%)	4.6	7.3	na	20.1	-5.7
Differ from Category (+/-)	0.4 abv av	0.9 high	na	1.7 abv av	-0.3 av

Total Risk	Standard Deviation	Category Risk	Risk Index	Avg Mat
blw av	5.9%	abv av	1.1	11.4 yrs

	1996	1995	1994	1993	1992	1991	1990	1989	1988	1987
Return (%)	3.1	17.3	-5.3	13.3	9.3	11.2	7.6	10.4	—	—
Differ from Category (+/-)	-0.6	2.1	0.0	1.5	1.0	-0.2	1.2	1.4	—	—
Return, Tax-Adjusted (%)	3.0	17.1	-5.3	13.1	8.9	11.2	7.6	10.3	—	—

PER SHARE DATA

	1996	1995	1994	1993	1992	1991	1990	1989	1988	1987
Dividends, Net Income ($)	0.61	0.62	0.62	0.63	0.65	0.67	0.69	0.70	—	—
Distrib'ns, Cap Gain ($)	0.03	0.05	0.00	0.06	0.13	0.00	0.00	0.01	—	—
Net Asset Value ($)	11.51	11.80	10.67	11.91	11.15	10.95	10.49	10.42	—	—
Expense Ratio (%)	na	0.21	0.21	0.20	0.25	0.24	0.25	0.24	—	—
Yield (%)	5.28	5.23	5.81	5.26	5.76	6.11	6.57	6.71	—	—
Portfolio Turnover (%)	na	7	13	12	34	18	7	17	—	—
Total Assets (Millions $)	848	803	653	766	588	452	252	133	—	—

PORTFOLIO (as of 9/30/96)

Portfolio Manager: Ian MacKinnon - 1988

Investm't Category: Tax-Exempt Bond
- ✔ Domestic
- Foreign
- Asset Allocation
- Index
- Sector
- ✔ State Specific

Investment Style
- Large-Cap Growth
- Mid-Cap Growth
- Small-Cap Growth
- Large-Cap Value
- Mid-Cap Value
- Small-Cap Value

Portfolio
12.0% cash	0.0% corp bonds
0.0% stocks	0.0% gov't bonds
0.0% preferred	88.0% muni bonds
0.0% conv't/warrants	0.0% other

SHAREHOLDER INFORMATION

Minimum Investment
Initial: $3,000   Subsequent: $100

Minimum IRA Investment
Initial: na   Subsequent: na

Maximum Fees
Load: none   12b-1: none
Other: f

Distributions
Income: monthly   Capital Gains: annual

Exchange Options
Number Per Year: 2   Fee: none
Telephone: yes (money market fund available)

Services
auto exchange, auto invest, auto withdraw

Vanguard NY Insured Tax-Free Fd (VNYTX)

Tax-Exempt Bond

Vanguard Financial Center
P.O. Box 2600
Valley Forge, PA 19482
800-635-1511, 610-669-1000
www.vanguard.com

PERFORMANCE

fund inception date: 4/7/86

	3yr Annual	5yr Annual	10yr Annual	Bull	Bear
Return (%)	4.9	7.4	7.4	21.0	-5.5
Differ from Category (+/-)	0.7 high	1.0 high	0.7 high	2.6 abv av	-0.1 av

Total Risk	Standard Deviation	Category Risk	Risk Index	Avg Mat
blw av	6.1%	abv av	1.1	11.7 yrs

	1996	1995	1994	1993	1992	1991	1990	1989	1988	1987
Return (%)	4.0	17.7	-5.7	13.0	9.7	12.8	6.2	10.3	11.9	-3.5
Differ from Category (+/-)	0.3	2.5	-0.4	1.2	1.4	1.4	-0.2	1.3	1.9	-2.1
Return, Tax-Adjusted (%)	3.8	17.5	-5.7	12.9	9.3	12.8	6.2	10.3	11.9	-3.5

PER SHARE DATA

	1996	1995	1994	1993	1992	1991	1990	1989	1988	1987
Dividends, Net Income ($)	0.56	0.57	0.59	0.59	0.62	0.63	0.62	0.63	0.64	0.63
Distrib'ns, Cap Gain ($)	0.04	0.06	0.00	0.01	0.14	0.00	0.00	0.00	0.00	0.00
Net Asset Value ($)	10.84	11.02	9.94	11.15	10.42	10.23	9.67	9.72	9.41	9.01
Expense Ratio (%)	na	0.22	0.22	0.19	0.23	0.27	0.31	0.34	0.40	0.35
Yield (%)	5.14	5.14	5.93	5.28	5.87	6.15	6.41	6.48	6.80	6.99
Portfolio Turnover (%)	na	10	20	10	28	19	17	10	4	31
Total Assets (Millions $)	959	870	698	826	594	431	245	175	107	77

PORTFOLIO (as of 9/30/96)

Portfolio Manager: Ian MacKinnon - 1986

Investm't Category: Tax-Exempt Bond
- ✔ Domestic
- Foreign
- Asset Allocation
- Index
- Sector
- ✔ State Specific

Investment Style
- Large-Cap Growth
- Mid-Cap Growth
- Small-Cap Growth
- Large-Cap Value
- Mid-Cap Value
- Small-Cap Value

Portfolio
13.0% cash	0.0% corp bonds
0.0% stocks	0.0% gov't bonds
0.0% preferred	87.0% muni bonds
0.0% conv't/warrants	0.0% other

SHAREHOLDER INFORMATION

Minimum Investment
Initial: $3,000   Subsequent: $100

Minimum IRA Investment
Initial: na   Subsequent: na

Maximum Fees
Load: none   12b-1: none
Other: none

Distributions
Income: monthly   Capital Gains: annual

Exchange Options
Number Per Year: 2   Fee: none
Telephone: yes (money market fund available)

Services
auto exchange, auto invest, auto withdraw

Vanguard Ohio Tax-Free Ins Long-Term (VOHIX)

Tax-Exempt Bond

Vanguard Financial Center
P.O. Box 2600
Valley Forge, PA 19482
800-635-1511, 610-669-1000
www.vanguard.com

PERFORMANCE

fund inception date: 6/18/90

	3yr Annual	5yr Annual	10yr Annual	Bull	Bear
Return (%)	4.9	7.3	na	20.6	-5.4
Differ from Category (+/-)	0.7 high	0.9 high	na	2.2 abv av	0.0 abv av

Total Risk	Standard Deviation	Category Risk	Risk Index	Avg Mat
blw av	5.8%	abv av	1.1	10.0 yrs

	1996	1995	1994	1993	1992	1991	1990	1989	1988	1987
Return (%)	4.2	16.8	-5.2	12.7	9.4	11.9	—	—	—	—
Differ from Category (+/-)	0.5	1.6	0.1	0.9	1.1	0.5	—	—	—	—
Return, Tax-Adjusted (%)	4.0	16.8	-5.2	12.6	9.0	11.9	—	—	—	—

PER SHARE DATA

	1996	1995	1994	1993	1992	1991	1990	1989	1988	1987
Dividends, Net Income ($)	0.60	0.60	0.60	0.60	0.62	0.64	—	—	—	—
Distrib'ns, Cap Gain ($)	0.05	0.00	0.00	0.03	0.14	0.00	—	—	—	—
Net Asset Value ($)	11.52	11.71	10.57	11.77	11.03	10.81	—	—	—	—
Expense Ratio (%)	na	0.21	0.23	0.21	0.31	0.27	—	—	—	—
Yield (%)	5.18	5.12	5.67	5.08	5.55	5.92	—	—	—	—
Portfolio Turnover (%)	na	7	16	10	27	20	—	—	—	—
Total Assets (Millions $)	216	198	147	172	104	62	—	—	—	—

PORTFOLIO (as of 9/30/96)

Portfolio Manager: Ian MacKinnon - 1990

Investm't Category: Tax-Exempt Bond

✔ Domestic	Index
Foreign	Sector
Asset Allocation	✔ State Specific

Investment Style

Large-Cap Growth	Large-Cap Value
Mid-Cap Growth	Mid-Cap Value
Small-Cap Growth	Small-Cap Value

Portfolio

8.0% cash	0.0% corp bonds
0.0% stocks	0.0% gov't bonds
0.0% preferred	92.0% muni bonds
0.0% conv't/warrants	0.0% other

SHAREHOLDER INFORMATION

Minimum Investment
Initial: $3,000   Subsequent: $100

Minimum IRA Investment
Initial: na   Subsequent: na

Maximum Fees
Load: none   12b-1: none
Other: *f*

Distributions
Income: monthly   Capital Gains: annual

Exchange Options
Number Per Year: 2   Fee: none
Telephone: yes (money market fund available)

Services
auto exchange, auto invest, auto withdraw

Vanguard PRIMECAP
(VPMCX)
Growth

Vanguard Financial Center
P.O. Box 2600
Valley Forge, PA 19482
800-635-1511, 610-669-1000
www.vanguard.com

PERFORMANCE

fund inception date: 11/1/84

	3yr Annual	5yr Annual	10yr Annual	Bull	Bear
Return (%)	21.3	18.0	15.0	77.7	-4.4
Differ from Category (+/-)	5.6 high	3.7 high	1.1 abv av	15.3 high	2.3 abv av

Total Risk	Standard Deviation	Category Risk	Risk Index	Beta
high	12.3%	high	1.2	1.02

	1996	1995	1994	1993	1992	1991	1990	1989	1988	1987
Return (%).	18.3	35.4	11.4	18.0	8.9	33.1	-2.8	21.6	14.6	-2.3
Differ from Category (+/-). .	-1.8	5.1	11.7	4.0	-2.9	-2.9	3.3	-4.5	-3.5	-4.3
Return, Tax-Adjusted (%). .	17.2	34.1	10.4	16.8	7.8	31.0	-3.5	19.5	13.5	-2.6

PER SHARE DATA

	1996	1995	1994	1993	1992	1991	1990	1989	1988	1987
Dividends, Net Income ($)	0.20	0.22	0.19	0.07	0.12	0.15	0.13	0.15	0.09	0.10
Distrib'ns, Cap Gain ($) . . .	0.73	0.59	0.34	0.59	0.41	0.68	0.12	0.61	0.25	0.23
Net Asset Value ($)	30.08	26.23	19.98	18.42	16.19	15.36	12.21	12.82	11.19	10.06
Expense Ratio (%).	na	0.58	0.64	0.67	0.68	0.68	0.75	0.74	0.83	0.83
Yield (%)	0.64	0.82	0.93	0.36	0.72	0.93	1.05	1.11	0.78	0.97
Portfolio Turnover (%). . . .	na	7	8	16	7	24	11	15	26	21
Total Assets (Millions $). .	4,268	3,236	1,533	790	646	486	304	279	185	164

PORTFOLIO (as of 9/30/96)

Portfolio Manager: Howard B. Schow - 1984

Investm't Category: Growth

✔ Domestic	Index
Foreign	Sector
Asset Allocation	State Specific

Investment Style

Large-Cap Growth	Large-Cap Value
✔ Mid-Cap Growth	Mid-Cap Value
Small-Cap Growth	Small-Cap Value

Portfolio

7.0% cash	0.0% corp bonds
93.0% stocks	0.0% gov't bonds
0.0% preferred	0.0% muni bonds
0.0% conv't/warrants	0.0% other

SHAREHOLDER INFORMATION

Minimum Investment
Initial: $3,000   Subsequent: $100

Minimum IRA Investment
Initial: $1,000   Subsequent: $100

Maximum Fees
Load: none   12b-1: none
Other: *f*

Distributions
Income: annual   Capital Gains: annual

Exchange Options
Number Per Year: 2   Fee: none
Telephone: yes (money market fund available)

Services
IRA, pension, auto exchange, auto invest, auto withdraw

Vanguard Penn Tax-Free Ins Long-Term (VPAIX)

Tax-Exempt Bond

Vanguard Financial Center
P.O. Box 2600
Valley Forge, PA 19482
800-635-1511, 610-669-1000
www.vanguard.com

PERFORMANCE

fund inception date: 4/7/86

	3yr Annual	5yr Annual	10yr Annual	Bull	Bear
Return (%)	5.0	7.5	7.8	20.5	-4.9
Differ from Category (+/-)	0.8 high	1.1 high	1.1 high	2.1 abv av	0.5 abv av

Total Risk	Standard Deviation	Category Risk	Risk Index	Avg Mat
blw av	5.5%	av	1.0	10.6 yrs

	1996	1995	1994	1993	1992	1991	1990	1989	1988	1987
Return (%)	4.3	16.4	-4.6	12.7	10.1	12.3	6.9	10.5	12.2	-1.3
Differ from Category (+/-)	.0.6	1.2	0.7	0.9	1.8	0.9	0.5	1.5	2.2	0.1
Return, Tax-Adjusted (%)	4.1	16.3	-4.6	12.5	9.5	12.2	6.9	10.5	12.2	-1.3

PER SHARE DATA

	1996	1995	1994	1993	1992	1991	1990	1989	1988	1987
Dividends, Net Income ($)	0.60	0.61	0.62	0.62	0.66	0.67	0.67	0.68	0.69	0.67
Distrib'ns, Cap Gain ($)	0.06	0.03	0.00	0.07	0.22	0.03	0.00	0.00	0.00	0.00
Net Asset Value ($)	11.11	11.31	10.30	11.44	10.80	10.64	10.14	10.15	9.83	9.41
Expense Ratio (%)	na	0.20	0.20	0.20	0.24	0.25	0.25	0.26	0.33	0.31
Yield (%)	5.37	5.37	6.01	5.38	5.98	6.27	6.60	6.69	7.01	7.12
Portfolio Turnover (%)	na	12	16	14	17	2	9	8	3	15
Total Assets (Millions $)	1,651	1,582	1,299	1,525	1,158	872	567	429	285	200

PORTFOLIO (as of 9/30/96)

Portfolio Manager: Ian MacKinnon - 1986

Investm't Category: Tax-Exempt Bond

✔ Domestic	Index
Foreign	Sector
Asset Allocation	✔ State Specific

Investment Style

Large-Cap Growth	Large-Cap Value
Mid-Cap Growth	Mid-Cap Value
Small-Cap Growth	Small-Cap Value

Portfolio

11.0% cash	0.0% corp bonds
0.0% stocks	0.0% gov't bonds
0.0% preferred	89.0% muni bonds
0.0% conv't/warrants	0.0% other

SHAREHOLDER INFORMATION

Minimum Investment
Initial: $3,000   Subsequent: $100

Minimum IRA Investment
Initial: na   Subsequent: na

Maximum Fees
Load: none   12b-1: none
Other: f

Distributions
Income: monthly   Capital Gains: annual

Exchange Options
Number Per Year: 2   Fee: none
Telephone: yes (money market fund available)

Services
auto exchange, auto invest, auto withdraw

Vanguard Preferred Stock

(VQIIX)

Growth & Income

Vanguard Financial Center
P.O. Box 2600
Valley Forge, PA 19482
800-635-1511, 610-669-1000
www.vanguard.com

PERFORMANCE

fund inception date: 12/3/75

	3yr Annual	5yr Annual	10yr Annual	Bull	Bear
Return (%)	7.9	9.0	8.9	33.7	-7.3
Differ from Category (+/-)	-7.4 low	-4.9 low	-3.8 low	-26.1 low	-0.9 blw av

Total Risk	Standard Deviation	Category Risk	Risk Index	Beta
blw av	6.2%	low	0.7	0.38

	1996	1995	1994	1993	1992	1991	1990	1989	1988	1987
Return (%).	8.4	25.9	-8.0	13.0	8.4	20.9	6.3	18.7	8.0	-7.8
Differ from Category (+/-)	-11.3	-4.2	-6.7	-0.8	-2.3	-8.2	12.2	-4.8	-8.8	-8.0
Return, Tax-Adjusted (%). . .	5.6	22.6	-10.7	9.5	5.2	17.4	2.6	14.9	4.2	-10.9

PER SHARE DATA

	1996	1995	1994	1993	1992	1991	1990	1989	1988	1987
Dividends, Net Income ($).	0.66	0.67	0.65	0.71	0.73	0.72	0.78	0.74	0.77	0.64
Distrib'ns, Cap Gain ($) . . .	0.00	0.00	0.00	0.14	0.00	0.00	0.00	0.00	0.00	0.12
Net Asset Value ($)	9.66	9.55	8.15	9.54	9.23	9.22	8.29	8.56	7.89	8.05
Expense Ratio (%).	na	0.52	0.51	0.53	0.58	0.63	0.65	0.67	0.66	0.64
Yield (%)	6.83	7.01	7.97	7.33	7.90	7.80	9.40	8.64	9.75	7.83
Portfolio Turnover (%).	na	20	27	45	33	18	15	42	52	67
Total Assets (Millions $). . .	290	311	278	386	186	100	56	63	73	94

PORTFOLIO (as of 9/30/96)

Portfolio Manager: Earl E. McEvoy - 1982

Investm't Category: Growth & Income
- ✔ Domestic
- Foreign
- Asset Allocation
- Index
- Sector
- State Specific

Investment Style
- ✔ Large-Cap Growth
- Mid-Cap Growth
- Small-Cap Growth
- ✔ Large-Cap Value
- Mid-Cap Value
- Small-Cap Value

Portfolio
1.0% cash	0.0% corp bonds
0.0% stocks	0.0% gov't bonds
99.0% preferred	0.0% muni bonds
0.0% conv't/warrants	0.0% other

SHAREHOLDER INFORMATION

Minimum Investment
Initial: $3,000   Subsequent: $100

Minimum IRA Investment
Initial: $1,000   Subsequent: $100

Maximum Fees
Load: none   12b-1: none
Other: *f*

Distributions
Income: quarterly   Capital Gains: annual

Exchange Options
Number Per Year: 2   Fee: none
Telephone: yes (money market fund available)

Services
IRA, pension, auto exchange, auto invest, auto withdraw

Vanguard Quantitative Port (VQNPX)

Growth & Income

Vanguard Financial Center
P.O. Box 2600
Valley Forge, PA 19482
800-635-1511, 610-669-1000
www.vanguard.com

PERFORMANCE

fund inception date: 12/10/86

	3yr Annual	5yr Annual	10yr Annual	Bull	Bear
Return (%)	18.4	15.1	15.2	74.5	-7.4
Differ from Category (+/-)	3.1 abv av	1.2 abv av	2.5 high	14.7 high	-1.0 blw av

Total Risk	Standard Deviation	Category Risk	Risk Index	Beta
abv av	10.2%	abv av	1.1	1.03

	1996	1995	1994	1993	1992	1991	1990	1989	1988	1987
Return (%)	23.0	35.9	-0.7	13.8	7.0	30.2	-2.5	31.9	16.7	4.0
Differ from Category (+/-)	3.3	5.8	0.6	0.0	-3.7	1.1	3.4	8.4	-0.1	3.8
Return, Tax-Adjusted (%)	19.6	33.4	-2.4	9.9	4.7	27.8	-3.9	30.2	15.2	2.8

PER SHARE DATA

	1996	1995	1994	1993	1992	1991	1990	1989	1988	1987
Dividends, Net Income ($)	0.40	0.42	0.39	0.39	0.44	0.47	0.47	0.47	0.35	0.25
Distrib'ns, Cap Gain ($)	1.82	0.74	0.40	1.69	0.71	0.44	0.04	0.00	0.00	0.06
Net Asset Value ($)	22.23	19.95	15.56	16.45	16.30	16.32	13.29	14.14	11.08	9.80
Expense Ratio (%)	na	0.47	0.48	0.50	0.40	0.43	0.48	0.53	0.64	0.64
Yield (%)	1.66	2.02	2.44	2.14	2.58	2.80	3.52	3.32	3.15	2.53
Portfolio Turnover (%)	na	59	71	85	51	61	81	78	50	73
Total Assets (Millions $)	1,320	909	596	530	415	334	211	175	143	149

PORTFOLIO (as of 9/30/96)

Portfolio Manager: John Nagorniak - 1986

Investm't Category: Growth & Income

✔ Domestic	Index
Foreign	Sector
Asset Allocation	State Specific

Investment Style

✔ Large-Cap Growth	✔ Large-Cap Value
Mid-Cap Growth	Mid-Cap Value
Small-Cap Growth	Small-Cap Value

Portfolio

5.0% cash	0.0% corp bonds
95.0% stocks	0.0% gov't bonds
0.0% preferred	0.0% muni bonds
0.0% conv't/warrants	0.0% other

SHAREHOLDER INFORMATION

Minimum Investment
Initial: $3,000   Subsequent: $100

Minimum IRA Investment
Initial: $1,000   Subsequent: $100

Maximum Fees
Load: none   12b-1: none
Other: *f*

Distributions
Income: semiannual   Capital Gains: annual

Exchange Options
Number Per Year: 2   Fee: none
Telephone: yes (money market fund available)

Services
IRA, pension, auto exchange, auto invest, auto withdraw

Vanguard STAR (VGSTX)
Balanced

Vanguard Financial Center
P.O. Box 2600
Valley Forge, PA 19482
800-635-1511, 610-669-1000
www.vanguard.com

PERFORMANCE
fund inception date: 3/29/85

	3yr Annual	5yr Annual	10yr Annual	Bull	Bear
Return (%)	14.2	12.8	12.1	52.1	-4.6
Differ from Category (+/-)	2.5 high	1.4 abv av	1.3 abv av	7.0 high	1.1 abv av

Total Risk	Standard Deviation	Category Risk	Risk Index	Beta
blw av	6.7%	av	1.0	0.68

	1996	1995	1994	1993	1992	1991	1990	1989	1988	1987
Return (%)...............	16.1	28.6	-0.3	10.9	10.5	24.0	-3.7	18.7	19.0	1.6
Differ from Category (+/-)..	1.9	4.0	1.3	-3.5	1.6	-0.1	-2.8	0.6	6.8	-1.1
Return, Tax-Adjusted (%)..	12.7	25.5	-2.4	8.5	8.4	20.7	-6.5	15.0	16.1	-3.3

PER SHARE DATA

	1996	1995	1994	1993	1992	1991	1990	1989	1988	1987
Dividends, Net Income ($).	0.59	0.59	0.52	0.47	0.51	0.62	0.73	0.77	0.69	0.85
Distrib'ns, Cap Gain ($) ...	0.98	0.56	0.25	0.40	0.18	0.37	0.16	0.38	0.03	0.75
Net Asset Value ($)	15.86	15.02	12.60	13.41	12.88	12.29	10.73	12.05	11.12	9.98
Expense Ratio (%).........	na	0.00	0.00	0.00	0.00	0.00	0.00	0.00	0.00	0.00
Yield (%)	3.50	3.78	4.04	3.40	3.90	4.89	6.70	6.19	6.18	7.92
Portfolio Turnover (%).....	na	13	9	3	3	11	12	7	21	0
Total Assets (Millions $)..	5,928	4,841	3,766	3,628	2,489	1,574	1,038	949	681	567

PORTFOLIO (as of 9/30/96)

Portfolio Manager: committee - 1985

Investm't Category: Balanced
- ✔ Domestic
- Foreign
- Asset Allocation
- Index
- Sector
- State Specific

Investment Style
- Large-Cap Growth
- Mid-Cap Growth
- Small-Cap Growth
- Large-Cap Value
- Mid-Cap Value
- Small-Cap Value

Portfolio
12.0%	cash	13.0%	corp bonds
63.0%	stocks	12.0%	gov't bonds
0.0%	preferred	0.0%	muni bonds
0.0%	conv't/warrants	0.0%	other

SHAREHOLDER INFORMATION

Minimum Investment
Initial: $1,000   Subsequent: $100

Minimum IRA Investment
Initial: $1,000   Subsequent: $100

Maximum Fees
Load: none   12b-1: none
Other: f

Distributions
Income: semiannual   Capital Gains: annual

Exchange Options
Number Per Year: 2   Fee: none
Telephone: yes (money market fund available)

Services
IRA, pension, auto exchange, auto invest, auto withdraw

Vanguard Short-Term Corporate (VFSTX)

Corporate Bond

Vanguard Financial Center
P.O. Box 2600
Valley Forge, PA 19482
800-635-1511, 610-669-1000
www.vanguard.com

PERFORMANCE

fund inception date: 10/29/82

	3yr Annual	5yr Annual	10yr Annual	Bull	Bear
Return (%)	5.6	6.2	7.6	19.1	-1.8
Differ from Category (+/-)	-0.7 av	-2.1 blw av	-0.5 blw av	-5.7 blw av	3.3 high

Total Risk	Standard Deviation	Category Risk	Risk Index	Avg Mat
low	2.4%	blw av	0.5	2.4 yrs

	1996	1995	1994	1993	1992	1991	1990	1989	1988	1987
Return (%)	4.7	12.7	-0.1	6.9	7.2	13.0	9.2	11.4	6.9	4.4
Differ from Category (+/-)	-0.5	-5.3	3.0	-4.9	-1.7	-4.2	5.2	2.0	-2.4	2.0
Return, Tax-Adjusted (%)	2.3	10.1	-2.3	4.4	4.2	9.9	5.8	7.9	3.7	1.1

PER SHARE DATA

	1996	1995	1994	1993	1992	1991	1990	1989	1988	1987
Dividends, Net Income ($)	0.66	0.66	0.58	0.61	0.70	0.81	0.87	0.89	0.82	0.75
Distrib'ns, Cap Gain ($)	0.00	0.00	0.00	0.09	0.16	0.00	0.00	0.00	0.00	0.18
Net Asset Value ($)	10.75	10.91	10.30	10.90	10.87	10.97	10.47	10.43	10.20	10.33
Expense Ratio (%)	0.27	0.28	0.26	0.27	0.26	0.31	0.28	0.34	0.33	0.38
Yield (%)	6.13	6.04	5.63	5.55	6.34	7.38	8.30	8.53	8.03	7.13
Portfolio Turnover (%)	62	69	61	71	99	107	121	165	258	278
Total Assets (Millions $)	4,619	3,743	2,905	3,482	2,708	1,866	796	597	498	410

PORTFOLIO (as of 9/30/96)

Portfolio Manager: Ian MacKinnon - 1982

Investm't Category: Corporate Bond
- ✔ Domestic
- Foreign
- Asset Allocation
- Index
- Sector
- State Specific

Investment Style
- Large-Cap Growth
- Mid-Cap Growth
- Small-Cap Growth
- Large-Cap Value
- Mid-Cap Value
- Small-Cap Value

Portfolio
7.0% cash	82.0% corp bonds
0.0% stocks	11.0% gov't bonds
0.0% preferred	0.0% muni bonds
0.0% conv't/warrants	0.0% other

SHAREHOLDER INFORMATION

Minimum Investment
Initial: $3,000   Subsequent: $100

Minimum IRA Investment
Initial: $1,000   Subsequent: $100

Maximum Fees
Load: none   12b-1: none
Other: f

Distributions
Income: monthly   Capital Gains: annual

Exchange Options
Number Per Year: 2   Fee: none
Telephone: yes (money market fund available)

Services
IRA, pension, auto exchange, auto invest, auto withdraw

Vanguard Short-Term Federal (VSGBX)

Mortgage-Backed Bond

Vanguard Financial Center
P.O. Box 2600
Valley Forge, PA 19482
800-635-1511, 610-669-1000
www.vanguard.com

PERFORMANCE

fund inception date: 12/28/87

	3yr Annual	5yr Annual	10yr Annual	Bull	Bear
Return (%)	5.2	5.7	na	18.3	-2.3
Differ from Category (+/-)	-0.4 blw av	-0.3 blw av	na	-2.8 low	1.3 abv av

Total Risk	Standard Deviation	Category Risk	Risk Index	Avg Mat
low	2.4%	blw av	0.6	2.4 yrs

	1996	1995	1994	1993	1992	1991	1990	1989	1988	1987
Return (%)	4.7	12.3	-1.0	7.0	6.1	12.2	9.3	11.3	5.7	—
Differ from Category (+/-)	0.3	-2.4	0.7	0.1	-0.1	-2.2	-0.5	-1.3	-1.7	—
Return, Tax-Adjusted (%)	2.3	9.8	-3.1	4.6	3.3	9.1	6.1	7.8	2.5	—

PER SHARE DATA

	1996	1995	1994	1993	1992	1991	1990	1989	1988	1987
Dividends, Net Income ($)	0.61	0.61	0.54	0.52	0.61	0.72	0.80	0.84	0.79	—
Distrib'ns, Cap Gain ($)	0.00	0.00	0.01	0.11	0.16	0.07	0.00	0.00	0.00	—
Net Asset Value ($)	10.11	10.25	9.69	10.34	10.27	10.43	10.06	9.98	9.76	—
Expense Ratio (%)	0.27	0.28	0.26	0.27	0.26	0.30	0.28	0.32	0.00	—
Yield (%)	6.03	5.95	5.56	4.97	5.84	6.85	7.95	8.41	8.09	—
Portfolio Turnover (%)	74	57	49	70	111	141	133	228	na	—
Total Assets (Millions $)	1,360	1,403	1,504	1,921	1,640	1,179	456	205	142	—

PORTFOLIO (as of 9/30/96)

Portfolio Manager: Ian MacKinnon - 1987

Investm't Category: Mortgage-Backed Bond

✔ Domestic	Index
Foreign	Sector
Asset Allocation	State Specific

Investment Style

Large-Cap Growth	Large-Cap Value
Mid-Cap Growth	Mid-Cap Value
Small-Cap Growth	Small-Cap Value

Portfolio

3.0% cash	0.0% corp bonds
0.0% stocks	97.0% gov't bonds
0.0% preferred	0.0% muni bonds
0.0% conv't/warrants	0.0% other

SHAREHOLDER INFORMATION

Minimum Investment
Initial: $3,000   Subsequent: $100

Minimum IRA Investment
Initial: $1,000   Subsequent: $100

Maximum Fees
Load: none   12b-1: none
Other: ƒ

Distributions
Income: monthly   Capital Gains: annual

Exchange Options
Number Per Year: 2   Fee: none
Telephone: yes (money market fund available)

Services
IRA, pension, auto exchange, auto invest, auto withdraw

Vanguard Short-Term US Treas (VFISX)

Government Bond

Vanguard Financial Center
P.O. Box 2600
Valley Forge, PA 19482
800-635-1511, 610-669-1000
www.vanguard.com

PERFORMANCE

fund inception date: 10/28/91

	3yr Annual	5yr Annual	10yr Annual	Bull	Bear
Return (%)	5.2	5.7	na	17.9	-1.9
Differ from Category (+/-)	0.3 abv av	-0.9 blw av	na	-4.1 blw av	4.5 high

Total Risk	Standard Deviation	Category Risk	Risk Index	Avg Mat
low	2.4%	blw av	0.6	2.4 yrs

	1996	1995	1994	1993	1992	1991	1990	1989	1988	1987
Return (%)	4.3	12.1	-0.5	6.3	6.7	—	—	—	—	—
Differ from Category (+/-)	2.8	-7.5	3.9	-5.3	0.0	—	—	—	—	—
Return, Tax-Adjusted (%)	2.0	9.5	-2.5	4.2	4.5	—	—	—	—	—

PER SHARE DATA

	1996	1995	1994	1993	1992	1991	1990	1989	1988	1987
Dividends, Net Income ($)	0.58	0.62	0.51	0.49	0.52	—	—	—	—	—
Distrib'ns, Cap Gain ($)	0.00	0.00	0.02	0.07	0.04	—	—	—	—	—
Net Asset Value ($)	10.17	10.32	9.79	10.38	10.31	—	—	—	—	—
Expense Ratio (%)	0.27	0.28	0.26	0.26	0.26	—	—	—	—	—
Yield (%)	5.70	6.00	5.19	4.68	5.02	—	—	—	—	—
Portfolio Turnover (%)	93	126	86	71	40	—	—	—	—	—
Total Assets (Millions $)	967	869	703	705	488	—	—	—	—	—

PORTFOLIO (as of 9/30/96)

Portfolio Manager: Ian MacKinnon - 1991

Investm't Category: Government Bond

- ✔ Domestic
- Foreign
- Asset Allocation
- Index
- Sector
- State Specific

Investment Style

- Large-Cap Growth
- Mid-Cap Growth
- Small-Cap Growth
- Large-Cap Value
- Mid-Cap Value
- Small-Cap Value

Portfolio

3.0% cash	0.0% corp bonds
0.0% stocks	97.0% gov't bonds
0.0% preferred	0.0% muni bonds
0.0% conv't/warrants	0.0% other

SHAREHOLDER INFORMATION

Minimum Investment
Initial: $3,000   Subsequent: $100

Minimum IRA Investment
Initial: $1,000   Subsequent: $100

Maximum Fees
Load: none   12b-1: none
Other: *f*

Distributions
Income: monthly   Capital Gains: annual

Exchange Options
Number Per Year: 2   Fee: none
Telephone: yes (money market fund available)

Services
IRA, pension, auto exchange, auto invest, auto withdraw

Vanguard Spec Port: Energy (VGENX)

Growth

Vanguard Financial Center
P.O. Box 2600
Valley Forge, PA 19482
800-635-1511, 610-669-1000
www.vanguard.com

PERFORMANCE

fund inception date: 5/23/84

	3yr Annual	5yr Annual	10yr Annual	Bull	Bear
Return (%)	18.2	17.2	15.0	57.5	0.1
Differ from Category (+/-)	2.5 abv av	2.9 high	1.1 abv av	-4.9 av	6.8 high

Total Risk	Standard Deviation	Category Risk	Risk Index	Beta
high	14.4%	high	1.4	0.86

	1996	1995	1994	1993	1992	1991	1990	1989	1988	1987
Return (%)	33.9	25.3	-1.7	26.4	6.1	0.2	-1.4	43.4	21.3	6.1
Differ from Category (+/-)	13.8	-5.0	-1.4	12.4	-5.7	-35.8	4.7	17.3	3.2	4.1
Return, Tax-Adjusted (%)	32.7	23.9	-2.9	22.6	4.6	-1.9	-4.2	40.7	19.7	-0.2

PER SHARE DATA

	1996	1995	1994	1993	1992	1991	1990	1989	1988	1987
Dividends, Net Income ($)	0.24	0.28	0.24	0.28	0.36	0.42	0.46	0.36	0.37	0.76
Distrib'ns, Cap Gain ($)	0.40	0.30	0.28	1.38	0.18	0.42	0.88	0.56	0.00	1.41
Net Asset Value ($)	22.54	17.31	14.29	15.06	13.29	13.03	13.84	15.40	11.39	9.69
Expense Ratio (%)	0.51	0.30	0.17	0.21	0.30	0.35	0.38	0.40	0.38	0.65
Yield (%)	1.04	1.59	1.64	1.70	2.67	3.12	3.12	2.25	3.24	6.84
Portfolio Turnover (%)	21	13	41	37	42	40	44	46	84	34
Total Assets (Millions $)	829	506	445	269	155	116	119	72	38	32

PORTFOLIO (as of 9/30/96)

Portfolio Manager: Ernst H. von Metzsh - 1984

Investm't Category: Growth
- ✔ Domestic
- ✔ Foreign
-   Asset Allocation
-   Index
- ✔ Sector
-   State Specific

Investment Style
-   Large-Cap Growth
-   Mid-Cap Growth
-   Small-Cap Growth
- ✔ Large-Cap Value
- ✔ Mid-Cap Value
- ✔ Small-Cap Value

Portfolio
8.0%	cash	0.0%	corp bonds
91.0%	stocks	0.0%	gov't bonds
0.0%	preferred	0.0%	muni bonds
1.0%	conv't/warrants	0.0%	other

SHAREHOLDER INFORMATION

Minimum Investment
Initial: $3,000   Subsequent: $100

Minimum IRA Investment
Initial: $1,000   Subsequent: $100

Maximum Fees
Load: 1.00% redemption   12b-1: none
Other: redemption fee applies for 1 year; *f*

Distributions
Income: annual   Capital Gains: annual

Exchange Options
Number Per Year: 3   Fee: none
Telephone: yes (money market fund available)

Services
IRA, pension, auto exchange, auto invest, auto withdraw

Vanguard Spec Port: Gold & Prec Metals

(VGPMX) *Gold*

Vanguard Financial Center
P.O. Box 2600
Valley Forge, PA 19482
800-635-1511, 610-669-1000
www.vanguard.com

PERFORMANCE

fund inception date: 5/23/84

	3yr Annual	5yr Annual	10yr Annual	Bull	Bear
Return (%)	-3.6	6.9	6.1	-2.7	-6.6
Differ from Category (+/-)	-3.9 blw av	-2.7 blw av	1.8 abv av	-17.6 low	3.6 high

Total Risk	Standard Deviation	Category Risk	Risk Index	Beta
high	20.8%	low	0.8	0.54

	1996	1995	1994	1993	1992	1991	1990	1989	1988	1987
Return (%).	-0.8	-4.5	-5.5	93.3	-19.5	4.3	-19.9	30.3	-14.2	38.7
Differ from Category (+/-)	-12.0	-9.5	6.6	5.5	-4.2	8.9	2.4	5.9	4.9	6.5
Return, Tax-Adjusted (%). .	-1.7	-5.1	-6.4	92.1	-20.3	3.2	-21.0	28.8	-15.2	33.2

PER SHARE DATA

	1996	1995	1994	1993	1992	1991	1990	1989	1988	1987
Dividends, Net Income ($)	0.21	0.17	0.31	0.21	0.18	0.25	0.32	0.34	0.26	0.48
Distrib'ns, Cap Gain ($) . . .	0.07	0.00	0.00	0.00	0.00	0.00	0.00	0.00	0.00	1.13
Net Asset Value ($)	11.63	11.98	12.72	13.78	7.24	9.21	9.07	11.73	9.27	11.11
Expense Ratio (%)	0.60	0.25	0.26	0.36	0.35	0.42	0.45	0.48	0.47	0.59
Yield (%)	1.79	1.41	2.43	1.52	2.48	2.71	3.52	2.89	2.80	3.92
Portfolio Turnover (%)	5	4	14	2	3	10	17	18	44	32
Total Assets (Millions $) . . .	521	549	639	609	173	170	156	191	124	158

PORTFOLIO (as of 9/30/96)

Portfolio Manager: David Hutchins - 1987

Investm't Category: Gold

✔ Domestic	Index
✔ Foreign	✔ Sector
Asset Allocation	State Specific

Investment Style

Large-Cap Growth	Large-Cap Value
Mid-Cap Growth	Mid-Cap Value
Small-Cap Growth	Small-Cap Value

Portfolio

7.0% cash	0.0% corp bonds
91.0% stocks	0.0% gov't bonds
1.0% preferred	0.0% muni bonds
1.0% conv't/warrants	0.0% other

SHAREHOLDER INFORMATION

Minimum Investment
Initial: $3,000   Subsequent: $100

Minimum IRA Investment
Initial: $1,000   Subsequent: $100

Maximum Fees
Load: 1.00% redemption   12b-1: none
Other: redemption fee applies for 1 year; *f*

Distributions
Income: annual   Capital Gains: annual

Exchange Options
Number Per Year: 3   Fee: none
Telephone: yes (money market fund available)

Services
IRA, pension, auto exchange, auto invest, auto withdraw

Individual Fund Listings

Vanguard Spec Port: Health Care (VGHCX)

Growth

Vanguard Financial Center
P.O. Box 2600
Valley Forge, PA 19482
800-635-1511, 610-669-1000
www.vanguard.com

PERFORMANCE

fund inception date: 5/23/84

	3yr Annual	5yr Annual	10yr Annual	Bull	Bear
Return (%)	24.5	16.2	19.9	102.9	-8.7
Differ from Category (+/-)	8.8 high	1.9 abv av	6.0 high	40.5 high	-2.0 blw av

Total Risk	Standard Deviation	Category Risk	Risk Index	Beta
abv av	10.6%	av	1.0	0.85

	1996	1995	1994	1993	1992	1991	1990	1989	1988	1987
Return (%)	21.3	45.1	9.5	11.8	-1.6	46.3	16.7	32.9	28.4	-0.6
Differ from Category (+/-)	1.2	14.8	9.8	-2.2	-13.4	10.3	22.8	6.8	10.3	-2.6
Return, Tax-Adjusted (%)	19.9	43.6	7.0	9.2	-3.3	44.9	14.7	30.7	25.2	-4.1

PER SHARE DATA

	1996	1995	1994	1993	1992	1991	1990	1989	1988	1987
Dividends, Net Income ($)	0.74	0.56	0.56	0.76	0.70	0.53	0.55	0.49	0.34	0.56
Distrib'ns, Cap Gain ($)	1.29	1.02	2.31	1.97	1.20	0.53	0.84	0.72	1.29	1.39
Net Asset Value ($)	58.35	49.82	35.47	35.07	34.01	36.50	25.69	23.21	18.43	15.70
Expense Ratio (%)	0.46	0.40	0.19	0.22	0.30	0.36	0.39	0.62	0.51	0.61
Yield (%)	1.24	1.10	1.48	2.05	1.98	1.43	2.07	2.04	1.72	3.27
Portfolio Turnover (%)	13	25	19	15	7	17	28	19	41	27
Total Assets (Millions $)	2,579	1,473	708	609	607	547	163	78	54	47

PORTFOLIO (as of 9/30/96)

Portfolio Manager: Edward Owens - 1984

Investm't Category: Growth

✔ Domestic   Index
✔ Foreign   ✔ Sector
  Asset Allocation   State Specific

Investment Style

✔ Large-Cap Growth   Large-Cap Value
  Mid-Cap Growth   Mid-Cap Value
  Small-Cap Growth   Small-Cap Value

Portfolio

11.0% cash	0.0% corp bonds
89.0% stocks	0.0% gov't bonds
0.0% preferred	0.0% muni bonds
0.0% conv't/warrants	0.0% other

SHAREHOLDER INFORMATION

Minimum Investment
Initial: $3,000   Subsequent: $100

Minimum IRA Investment
Initial: $1,000   Subsequent: $100

Maximum Fees
Load: 1.00% redemption   12b-1: none
Other: redemption fee applies for 1 year; *f*

Distributions
Income: annual   Capital Gains: annual

Exchange Options
Number Per Year: 3   Fee: none
Telephone: yes (money market fund available)

Services
IRA, pension, auto exchange, auto invest, auto withdraw

Vanguard Spec Port: Utilities Income (VGSUX)

Growth & Income

Vanguard Financial Center
P.O. Box 2600
Valley Forge, PA 19482
800-635-1511, 610-669-1000
www.vanguard.com

PERFORMANCE

fund inception date: 5/15/92

	3yr Annual	5yr Annual	10yr Annual	Bull	Bear
Return (%)	8.8	na	na	41.9	-9.5
Differ from Category (+/-)	-6.5 low	na	na	-17.9 low	-3.1 low

Total Risk	Standard Deviation	Category Risk	Risk Index	Beta
av	8.4%	blw av	0.9	0.59

	1996	1995	1994	1993	1992	1991	1990	1989	1988	1987
Return (%)	5.2	34.0	-8.6	15.0	—	—	—	—	—	—
Differ from Category (+/-)	-14.5	3.9	-7.3	1.2	—	—	—	—	—	—
Return, Tax-Adjusted (%)	3.4	31.7	-10.9	11.9	—	—	—	—	—	—

PER SHARE DATA

	1996	1995	1994	1993	1992	1991	1990	1989	1988	1987
Dividends, Net Income ($)	0.56	0.56	0.59	0.56	—	—	—	—	—	—
Distrib'ns, Cap Gain ($)	0.02	0.00	0.12	0.40	—	—	—	—	—	—
Net Asset Value ($)	12.74	12.68	9.94	11.63	—	—	—	—	—	—
Expense Ratio (%)	0.44	0.50	0.42	0.45	—	—	—	—	—	—
Yield (%)	4.38	4.41	5.86	4.65	—	—	—	—	—	—
Portfolio Turnover (%)	35	35	46	20	—	—	—	—	—	—
Total Assets (Millions $)	674	757	560	774	—	—	—	—	—	—

PORTFOLIO (as of 9/30/96)

Portfolio Manager: Mark J. Beckwith - 1996

Investm't Category: Growth & Income
- ✔ Domestic
- ✔ Foreign
-   Asset Allocation
-   Index
- ✔ Sector
-   State Specific

Investment Style
- Large-Cap Growth
- Mid-Cap Growth
- Small-Cap Growth
- ✔ Large-Cap Value
- Mid-Cap Value
- Small-Cap Value

Portfolio

1.0% cash	19.0% corp bonds
79.0% stocks	1.0% gov't bonds
0.0% preferred	0.0% muni bonds
0.0% conv't/warrants	0.0% other

SHAREHOLDER INFORMATION

Minimum Investment
Initial: $3,000   Subsequent: $100

Minimum IRA Investment
Initial: $1,000   Subsequent: $100

Maximum Fees
Load: none   12b-1: none
Other: f

Distributions
Income: quarterly   Capital Gains: annual

Exchange Options
Number Per Year: 3   Fee: none
Telephone: yes (money market fund available)

Services
IRA, pension, auto exchange, auto invest, auto withdraw

Vanguard Tax Managed Balanced Port (VTMFX)

Balanced

Vanguard Financial Center
P.O. Box 2600
Valley Forge, PA 19482
800-635-1511, 610-669-1000
www.vanguard.com

PERFORMANCE

fund inception date: 9/6/94

	3yr Annual	5yr Annual	10yr Annual	Bull	Bear
Return (%)	na	na	na	na	na
Differ from Category (+/-)	na	na	na	na	na

Total Risk	Standard Deviation	Category Risk	Risk Index	Beta
na	na	na	na	na

	1996	1995	1994	1993	1992	1991	1990	1989	1988	1987
Return (%)	12.2	24.5	—	—	—	—	—	—	—	—
Differ from Category (+/-)	-2.0	-0.1	—	—	—	—	—	—	—	—
Return, Tax-Adjusted (%)	10.9	23.2	—	—	—	—	—	—	—	—

PER SHARE DATA

	1996	1995	1994	1993	1992	1991	1990	1989	1988	1987
Dividends, Net Income ($)	0.36	0.32	—	—	—	—	—	—	—	—
Distrib'ns, Cap Gain ($)	0.00	0.00	—	—	—	—	—	—	—	—
Net Asset Value ($)	12.92	11.85	—	—	—	—	—	—	—	—
Expense Ratio (%)	na	0.20	—	—	—	—	—	—	—	—
Yield (%)	2.78	2.70	—	—	—	—	—	—	—	—
Portfolio Turnover (%)	na	5	—	—	—	—	—	—	—	—
Total Assets (Millions $)	63	38	—	—	—	—	—	—	—	—

PORTFOLIO (as of 9/30/96)

Portfolio Manager: George Sauter, Ian MacKinnon - 1994

Investm't Category: Balanced

✔ Domestic	Index
Foreign	Sector
✔ Asset Allocation	State Specific

Investment Style

Large-Cap Growth	Large-Cap Value
Mid-Cap Growth	Mid-Cap Value
Small-Cap Growth	Small-Cap Value

Portfolio

0.0% cash	0.0% corp bonds
49.0% stocks	0.0% gov't bonds
0.0% preferred	53.0% muni bonds
0.0% conv't/warrants	0.0% other

SHAREHOLDER INFORMATION

Minimum Investment
Initial: $10,000   Subsequent: $100

Minimum IRA Investment
Initial: na   Subsequent: na

Maximum Fees
Load: 1.00% redemption   12b-1: none
Other: applies to shrs held less than 5 yrs (2% for shrs held less than one yr)

Distributions
Income: quarterly   Capital Gains: annual

Exchange Options
Number Per Year: 2   Fee: none
Telephone: yes (money market fund available)

Services
auto exchange, auto invest, auto withdraw

Vanguard Tax Managed Capital Apprec Port

(VMCAX) *Growth*

Vanguard Financial Center
P.O. Box 2600
Valley Forge, PA 19482
800-635-1511, 610-669-1000
www.vanguard.com

PERFORMANCE

fund inception date: 9/6/94

	3yr Annual	5yr Annual	10yr Annual	Bull	Bear
Return (%)	na	na	na	na	na
Differ from Category (+/-)	na	na	na	na	na

Total Risk	Standard Deviation	Category Risk	Risk Index	Beta
na	na	na	na	na

	1996	1995	1994	1993	1992	1991	1990	1989	1988	1987
Return (%)	20.9	34.3	—	—	—	—	—	—	—	—
Differ from Category (+/-)	0.8	4.0	—	—	—	—	—	—	—	—
Return, Tax-Adjusted (%)	20.5	33.9	—	—	—	—	—	—	—	—

PER SHARE DATA

	1996	1995	1994	1993	1992	1991	1990	1989	1988	1987
Dividends, Net Income ($)	0.11	0.09	—	—	—	—	—	—	—	—
Distrib'ns, Cap Gain ($)	0.00	0.00	—	—	—	—	—	—	—	—
Net Asset Value ($)	15.95	13.28	—	—	—	—	—	—	—	—
Expense Ratio (%)	na	0.20	—	—	—	—	—	—	—	—
Yield (%)	0.68	0.67	—	—	—	—	—	—	—	—
Portfolio Turnover (%)	na	7	—	—	—	—	—	—	—	—
Total Assets (Millions $)	516	254	—	—	—	—	—	—	—	—

PORTFOLIO (as of 9/30/96)

Portfolio Manager: George Sauter - 1994

Investm't Category: Growth

✔ Domestic	Index
Foreign	Sector
Asset Allocation	State Specific

Investment Style

Large-Cap Growth	Large-Cap Value
Mid-Cap Growth	Mid-Cap Value
Small-Cap Growth	Small-Cap Value

Portfolio

0.0% cash	0.0% corp bonds
100.0% stocks	0.0% gov't bonds
0.0% preferred	0.0% muni bonds
0.0% conv't/warrants	0.0% other

SHAREHOLDER INFORMATION

Minimum Investment
Initial: $10,000   Subsequent: $100

Minimum IRA Investment
Initial: na   Subsequent: na

Maximum Fees
Load: 1.00% redemption   12b-1: none
Other: applies to shrs held less than 5 yrs (2% for shrs held less than one yr)

Distributions
Income: annual   Capital Gains: annual

Exchange Options
Number Per Year: 2   Fee: none
Telephone: yes (money market fund available)

Services
auto exchange, auto invest, auto withdraw

Vanguard Tax Managed Grth & Inc Port (VTGIX)

Growth & Income

Vanguard Financial Center
P.O. Box 2600
Valley Forge, PA 19482
800-635-1511, 610-669-1000
www.vanguard.com

PERFORMANCE

fund inception date: 9/6/94

	3yr Annual	5yr Annual	10yr Annual	Bull	Bear
Return (%)	na	na	na	na	na
Differ from Category (+/-)	na	na	na	na	na

Total Risk	Standard Deviation	Category Risk	Risk Index	Beta
na	na	na	na	na

	1996	1995	1994	1993	1992	1991	1990	1989	1988	1987
Return (%)	23.0	37.5	—	—	—	—	—	—	—	—
Differ from Category (+/-)	3.3	7.4	—	—	—	—	—	—	—	—
Return, Tax-Adjusted (%)	22.1	36.4	—	—	—	—	—	—	—	—

PER SHARE DATA

	1996	1995	1994	1993	1992	1991	1990	1989	1988	1987
Dividends, Net Income ($)	0.28	0.25	—	—	—	—	—	—	—	—
Distrib'ns, Cap Gain ($)	0.00	0.00	—	—	—	—	—	—	—	—
Net Asset Value ($)	15.89	13.16	—	—	—	—	—	—	—	—
Expense Ratio (%)	na	0.20	—	—	—	—	—	—	—	—
Yield (%)	1.76	1.89	—	—	—	—	—	—	—	—
Portfolio Turnover (%)	na	6	—	—	—	—	—	—	—	—
Total Assets (Millions $)	229	98	—	—	—	—	—	—	—	—

PORTFOLIO (as of 9/30/96)

Portfolio Manager: George Sauter - 1994

Investm't Category: Growth & Income

✔ Domestic   ✔ Index
  Foreign   Sector
  Asset Allocation State Specific

Investment Style

Large-Cap Growth   Large-Cap Value
Mid-Cap Growth   Mid-Cap Value
Small-Cap Growth   Small-Cap Value

Portfolio

0.0% cash	0.0% corp bonds
100.0% stocks	0.0% gov't bonds
0.0% preferred	0.0% muni bonds
0.0% conv't/warrants	0.0% other

SHAREHOLDER INFORMATION

Minimum Investment
Initial: $10,000   Subsequent: $100

Minimum IRA Investment
Initial: na   Subsequent: na

Maximum Fees
Load: 1.00% redemption   12b-1: none
Other: applies to shrs held less than 5 yrs (2% for shrs held less than one yr)

Distributions
Income: quarterly   Capital Gains: annual

Exchange Options
Number Per Year: 2   Fee: none
Telephone: yes (money market fund available)

Services
auto exchange, auto invest, auto withdraw

Vanguard US Growth Port
(VWUSX)
Growth

Vanguard Financial Center
P.O. Box 2600
Valley Forge, PA 19482
800-635-1511, 610-669-1000
www.vanguard.com

PERFORMANCE

fund inception date: 1/6/59

	3yr Annual	5yr Annual	10yr Annual	Bull	Bear
Return (%)	21.9	12.9	14.7	85.6	-5.3
Differ from Category (+/-)	6.2 high	-1.4 blw av	0.8 abv av	23.2 high	1.4 abv av

Total Risk	Standard Deviation	Category Risk	Risk Index	Beta
abv av	9.7%	blw av	0.9	0.93

	1996	1995	1994	1993	1992	1991	1990	1989	1988	1987
Return (%)	26.0	38.4	3.8	-1.5	2.7	46.7	4.1	38.2	8.7	-6.1
Differ from Category (+/-)	5.9	8.1	4.1	-15.5	-9.1	10.7	10.2	12.1	-9.4	-8.1
Return, Tax-Adjusted (%)	23.2	36.6	3.3	-2.1	2.0	45.9	3.3	37.5	8.3	-16.2

PER SHARE DATA

	1996	1995	1994	1993	1992	1991	1990	1989	1988	1987
Dividends, Net Income ($)	0.26	0.28	0.18	0.21	0.18	0.19	0.19	0.13	0.06	0.31
Distrib'ns, Cap Gain ($)	1.62	0.56	0.00	0.00	0.08	0.00	0.00	0.00	0.00	3.26
Net Asset Value ($)	23.74	20.35	15.33	14.93	15.36	15.20	10.49	10.25	7.51	6.96
Expense Ratio (%)	0.43	0.44	0.52	0.49	0.49	0.56	0.74	0.95	0.88	0.65
Yield (%)	1.02	1.33	1.17	1.40	1.16	1.25	1.81	1.26	0.79	3.03
Portfolio Turnover (%)	44	32	47	37	24	30	49	48	38	142
Total Assets (Millions $)	5,590	3,624	2,109	1,847	1,820	978	355	198	132	134

PORTFOLIO (as of 9/30/96)

Portfolio Manager: J. Parker Hall III, David Fowler - 1987

Investm't Category: Growth
✔ Domestic   Index
   Foreign   Sector
   Asset Allocation   State Specific

Investment Style
✔ Large-Cap Growth   Large-Cap Value
   Mid-Cap Growth   Mid-Cap Value
   Small-Cap Growth   Small-Cap Value

Portfolio
6.0% cash	0.0% corp bonds
94.0% stocks	0.0% gov't bonds
0.0% preferred	0.0% muni bonds
0.0% conv't/warrants	0.0% other

SHAREHOLDER INFORMATION

Minimum Investment
Initial: $3,000   Subsequent: $100

Minimum IRA Investment
Initial: $1,000   Subsequent: $100

Maximum Fees
Load: none   12b-1: none
Other: *f*

Distributions
Income: annual   Capital Gains: annual

Exchange Options
Number Per Year: 2   Fee: none
Telephone: yes (money market fund available)

Services
IRA, pension, auto exchange, auto invest, auto withdraw

Vanguard Wellesley Income (VWINX)

Balanced

Vanguard Financial Center
P.O. Box 2600
Valley Forge, PA 19482
800-635-1511, 610-669-1000
www.vanguard.com

PERFORMANCE

fund inception date: 7/1/70

	3yr Annual	5yr Annual	10yr Annual	Bull	Bear
Return (%)	10.4	10.9	11.0	41.5	-6.6
Differ from Category (+/-)	-1.3 blw av	-0.5 blw av	0.2 av	-3.6 blw av	-0.9 blw av

Total Risk	Standard Deviation	Category Risk	Risk Index	Beta
av	7.0%	av	1.0	0.56

	1996	1995	1994	1993	1992	1991	1990	1989	1988	1987
Return (%).............	9.4	28.9	-4.5	14.6	8.7	21.4	3.7	20.9	13.6	-2.0
Differ from Category (+/-) .	-4.8	4.3	-2.9	0.2	-0.2	-2.7	4.6	2.8	1.4	-4.7
Return, Tax-Adjusted (%)...	6.3	25.8	-7.2	11.5	5.7	18.2	0.5	17.0	10.2	-5.2

PER SHARE DATA

	1996	1995	1994	1993	1992	1991	1990	1989	1988	1987
Dividends, Net Income ($).	1.15	1.13	1.11	1.13	1.21	1.27	1.30	1.31	1.23	1.04
Distrib'ns, Cap Gain ($) ...	0.60	0.28	0.24	0.40	0.21	0.00	0.08	0.24	0.00	0.38
Net Asset Value ($)	20.51	20.44	17.05	19.24	18.16	18.07	16.02	16.82	15.26	14.57
Expense Ratio (%)........	na	0.35	0.34	0.33	0.35	0.40	0.45	0.45	0.51	0.49
Yield (%)	5.44	5.45	6.41	5.75	6.58	7.02	8.07	7.67	8.06	6.95
Portfolio Turnover (%).....	na	na	na	21	21	28	23	23	20	40
Total Assets (Millions $)..	7,271	7,180	5,680	6,011	3,177	1,934	1,021	787	567	494

PORTFOLIO (as of 9/30/96)

Portfolio Manager: Earl E. McEvoy, John R. Ryan - 1982

Investm't Category: Balanced
- ✔ Domestic
- Foreign
- Asset Allocation
- Index
- Sector
- State Specific

Investment Style
- Large-Cap Growth
- Mid-Cap Growth
- Small-Cap Growth
- Large-Cap Value
- Mid-Cap Value
- Small-Cap Value

Portfolio
3.0% cash	41.0% corp bonds
38.0% stocks	17.0% gov't bonds
0.0% preferred	0.0% muni bonds
1.0% conv't/warrants	0.0% other

SHAREHOLDER INFORMATION

Minimum Investment
Initial: $3,000   Subsequent: $100

Minimum IRA Investment
Initial: $1,000   Subsequent: $100

Maximum Fees
Load: none   12b-1: none
Other: ƒ

Distributions
Income: quarterly   Capital Gains: annual

Exchange Options
Number Per Year: 2   Fee: none
Telephone: yes (money market fund available)

Services
IRA, pension, auto exchange, auto invest, auto withdraw

Vanguard Wellington
(VWELX)
Balanced

Vanguard Financial Center
P.O. Box 2600
Valley Forge, PA 19482
800-635-1511, 610-669-1000
www.vanguard.com

PERFORMANCE
fund inception date: 7/1/29

	3yr Annual	5yr Annual	10yr Annual	Bull	Bear
Return (%)	15.4	13.4	12.5	57.5	-5.6
Differ from Category (+/-)	3.7 high	2.0 abv av	1.7 high	12.4 high	0.1 av

Total Risk	Standard Deviation	Category Risk	Risk Index	Beta
av	8.3%	high	1.2	0.79

	1996	1995	1994	1993	1992	1991	1990	1989	1988	1987
Return (%)...............	16.1	32.9	-0.5	13.5	7.9	23.6	-2.9	21.6	16.1	2.2
Differ from Category (+/-) . .	1.9	8.3	1.1	-0.9	-1.0	-0.5	-2.0	3.5	3.9	-0.5
Return, Tax-Adjusted (%). .	13.1	30.5	-2.3	11.0	5.6	20.8	-5.2	18.0	12.5	-0.5

PER SHARE DATA

	1996	1995	1994	1993	1992	1991	1990	1989	1988	1987
Dividends, Net Income ($).	1.06	0.97	0.88	0.92	0.94	0.96	1.01	1.02	0.96	0.98
Distrib'ns, Cap Gain ($) . .	1.11	0.28	0.03	0.38	0.16	0.23	0.00	0.60	0.57	0.14
Net Asset Value ($)	26.15	24.43	19.39	20.40	19.16	18.81	16.26	17.78	16.01	15.15
Expense Ratio (%).........	na	0.33	0.35	0.34	0.33	0.35	0.43	0.42	0.47	0.43
Yield (%)	3.88	3.92	4.53	4.42	4.86	5.04	6.21	5.54	5.79	6.40
Portfolio Turnover (%).....	na	24	32	34	24	35	33	30	28	27
Total Assets (Millions $).	16,505	12,656	8,809	8,075	5,570	3,818	2,449	2,099	1,526	1,331

PORTFOLIO (as of 9/30/96)

Portfolio Manager: P. Kaplan, E. von Metzsch - 1994

Investm't Category: Balanced
- ✔ Domestic
- ✔ Foreign
-   Asset Allocation

-   Index
-   Sector
-   State Specific

Investment Style

Large-Cap Growth	Large-Cap Value
Mid-Cap Growth	Mid-Cap Value
Small-Cap Growth	Small-Cap Value

Portfolio

3.0% cash	22.0% corp bonds
63.0% stocks	11.0% gov't bonds
0.0% preferred	0.0% muni bonds
1.0% conv't/warrants	0.0% other

SHAREHOLDER INFORMATION

Minimum Investment
Initial: $3,000   Subsequent: $100

Minimum IRA Investment
Initial: $1,000   Subsequent: $100

Maximum Fees
Load: none   12b-1: none
Other: f

Distributions
Income: quarterly   Capital Gains: annual

Exchange Options
Number Per Year: 2   Fee: none
Telephone: yes (money market fund available)

Services
IRA, pension, auto exchange, auto invest, auto withdraw

Vanguard Windsor

(VWNDX)

Growth & Income

Vanguard Financial Center
P.O. Box 2600
Valley Forge, PA 19482
800-635-1511, 610-669-1000
www.vanguard.com

this fund is closed to new investors

PERFORMANCE

fund inception date: 10/23/58

	3yr Annual	5yr Annual	10yr Annual	Bull	Bear
Return (%)	17.9	17.9	14.0	61.1	-4.0
Differ from Category (+/-)	2.6 abv av	4.0 high	1.3 abv av	1.3 av	2.4 high

Total Risk	Standard Deviation	Category Risk	Risk Index	Beta
abv av	10.9%	high	1.2	0.92

	1996	1995	1994	1993	1992	1991	1990	1989	1988	1987
Return (%)	26.3	30.1	-0.2	19.3	16.4	28.5	-15.6	15.0	28.6	1.2
Differ from Category (+/-)	6.6	0.0	1.1	5.5	5.7	-0.6	-9.7	-8.5	11.8	1.0
Return, Tax-Adjusted (%)	22.6	25.5	-3.2	16.1	13.8	24.0	-18.5	10.9	24.9	-5.8

PER SHARE DATA

	1996	1995	1994	1993	1992	1991	1990	1989	1988	1987
Dividends, Net Income ($)	0.41	0.46	0.44	0.37	0.49	0.56	0.74	0.75	0.63	0.87
Distrib'ns, Cap Gain ($)	1.33	1.38	0.86	0.89	0.38	0.84	0.32	0.85	0.55	2.21
Net Asset Value ($)	16.59	14.53	12.59	13.91	12.74	11.72	10.30	13.41	13.07	11.11
Expense Ratio (%)	na	0.45	0.45	0.40	0.26	0.30	0.37	0.41	0.46	0.43
Yield (%)	2.28	2.89	3.27	2.50	3.73	4.45	6.96	5.25	4.62	6.53
Portfolio Turnover (%)	na	32	34	25	32	36	21	34	24	46
Total Assets (Millions $)	16,981	13,646	10,672	10,610	8,832	7,822	6,523	8,062	5,826	4,565

PORTFOLIO (as of 9/30/96)

Portfolio Manager: Charles T. Freeman - 1996

Investm't Category: Growth & Income
- ✔ Domestic
- Foreign
- Asset Allocation
- Index
- Sector
- State Specific

Investment Style
- Large-Cap Growth
- Mid-Cap Growth
- Small-Cap Growth
- ✔ Large-Cap Value
- Mid-Cap Value
- Small-Cap Value

Portfolio
10.0% cash	0.0% corp bonds
89.0% stocks	1.0% gov't bonds
0.0% preferred	0.0% muni bonds
0.0% conv't/warrants	0.0% other

SHAREHOLDER INFORMATION

Minimum Investment
Initial: $3,000   Subsequent: $100

Minimum IRA Investment
Initial: $1,000   Subsequent: $100

Maximum Fees
Load: none   12b-1: none
Other: f

Distributions
Income: semiannual   Capital Gains: annual

Exchange Options
Number Per Year: 2   Fee: none
Telephone: yes (money market fund available)

Services
IRA, pension, auto exchange, auto invest, auto withdraw

Vanguard Windsor II
(VWNFX)
Growth & Income

Vanguard Financial Center
P.O. Box 2600
Valley Forge, PA 19482
800-635-1511, 610-669-1000
www.vanguard.com

PERFORMANCE

fund inception date: 6/24/85

	3yr Annual	5yr Annual	10yr Annual	Bull	Bear
Return (%)	19.4	16.7	14.6	73.7	-5.2
Differ from Category (+/-)	4.1 high	2.8 high	1.9 high	13.9 high	1.2 abv av

Total Risk	Standard Deviation	Category Risk	Risk Index	Beta
abv av	9.7%	abv av	1.1	0.96

	1996	1995	1994	1993	1992	1991	1990	1989	1988	1987
Return (%).............	24.1	38.8	-1.2	13.6	11.9	28.6	-10.0	27.8	24.7	-2.2
Differ from Category (+/-)..	4.4	8.7	0.1	-0.2	1.2	-0.5	-4.1	4.3	7.9	-2.4
Return, Tax-Adjusted (%)..	21.3	36.1	-3.3	11.4	10.1	25.6	-12.5	24.1	22.6	-6.0

PER SHARE DATA

	1996	1995	1994	1993	1992	1991	1990	1989	1988	1987
Dividends, Net Income ($)	0.63	0.57	0.55	0.51	0.52	0.61	0.73	0.74	0.56	0.61
Distrib'ns, Cap Gain ($) ...	1.15	0.69	0.47	0.50	0.22	0.44	0.28	0.61	0.00	0.80
Net Asset Value ($)	23.83	20.66	15.82	17.04	15.91	14.89	12.46	14.96	12.81	10.75
Expense Ratio (%).........	na	0.40	0.39	0.39	0.41	0.48	0.52	0.53	0.58	0.49
Yield (%)	2.52	2.66	3.37	2.90	3.22	3.97	5.72	4.75	4.37	5.28
Portfolio Turnover (%).....	na	30	24	26	23	41	20	22	25	46
Total Assets (Millions $).	15,870	11,012	7,958	7,616	5,416	3,626	2,334	2,298	1,502	1,235

PORTFOLIO (as of 9/30/96)

Portfolio Manager: Barrow, Ulrich, Tukman, Sauter - 1985

Investm't Category: Growth & Income
✔ Domestic   Index
  Foreign   Sector
  Asset Allocation   State Specific

Investment Style
  Large-Cap Growth   ✔ Large-Cap Value
  Mid-Cap Growth   Mid-Cap Value
  Small-Cap Growth   Small-Cap Value

Portfolio
  7.0% cash   0.0% corp bonds
  93.0% stocks   0.0% gov't bonds
  0.0% preferred   0.0% muni bonds
  0.0% conv't/warrants 0.0% other

SHAREHOLDER INFORMATION

Minimum Investment
Initial: $3,000   Subsequent: $100

Minimum IRA Investment
Initial: $1,000   Subsequent: $100

Maximum Fees
Load: none   12b-1: none
Other: f

Distributions
Income: semiannual   Capital Gains: annual

Exchange Options
Number Per Year: 2   Fee: none
Telephone: yes (money market fund available)

Services
IRA, pension, auto exchange, auto invest, auto withdraw

Vanguard World: Int'l Growth Port (VWIGX)

International Stock

Vanguard Financial Center
P.O. Box 2600
Valley Forge, PA 19482
800-635-1511, 610-669-1000
www.vanguard.com

PERFORMANCE

fund inception date: 9/30/85

	3yr Annual	5yr Annual	10yr Annual	Bull	Bear
Return (%)	9.8	12.5	10.0	32.4	-5.0
Differ from Category (+/-)	3.5 abv av	2.5 abv av	1.4 abv av	8.1 abv av	2.2 abv av

Total Risk	Standard Deviation	Category Risk	Risk Index	Beta
abv av	10.0%	av	1.0	0.72

	1996	1995	1994	1993	1992	1991	1990	1989	1988	1987
Return (%)	14.6	14.8	0.7	44.7	-5.8	4.7	-12.1	24.7	11.6	12.4
Differ from Category (+/-)	-0.2	5.7	3.8	5.1	-2.0	-8.5	-2.0	2.1	-3.3	0.2
Return, Tax-Adjusted (%)	13.0	13.7	0.1	44.2	-6.7	3.6	-14.3	23.3	8.0	5.9

PER SHARE DATA

	1996	1995	1994	1993	1992	1991	1990	1989	1988	1987
Dividends, Net Income ($)	0.19	0.20	0.18	0.11	0.21	0.19	0.20	0.15	0.16	0.13
Distrib'ns, Cap Gain ($)	0.55	0.21	0.00	0.00	0.00	0.12	0.68	0.28	1.07	2.43
Net Asset Value ($)	16.46	15.02	13.43	13.51	9.41	10.21	10.05	12.42	10.30	10.34
Expense Ratio (%)	0.56	0.58	0.46	0.59	0.58	0.67	0.68	0.64	0.67	0.66
Yield (%)	1.11	1.31	1.34	0.81	2.23	1.83	1.86	1.18	1.40	1.01
Portfolio Turnover (%)	22	31	28	51	58	49	45	50	71	77
Total Assets (Millions $)	5,521	3,676	2,927	2,127	878	869	733	685	462	472

PORTFOLIO (as of 9/30/96)

Portfolio Manager: Richard R. Foulkes - 1981

Investm't Category: International Stock

Domestic	Index
✔ Foreign	Sector
Asset Allocation	State Specific

Investment Style

Large-Cap Growth	Large-Cap Value
Mid-Cap Growth	Mid-Cap Value
Small-Cap Growth	Small-Cap Value

Portfolio

1.0% cash	0.0% corp bonds
99.0% stocks	0.0% gov't bonds
0.0% preferred	0.0% muni bonds
0.0% conv't/warrants	0.0% other

SHAREHOLDER INFORMATION

Minimum Investment
Initial: $3,000   Subsequent: $100

Minimum IRA Investment
Initial: $1,000   Subsequent: $100

Maximum Fees
Load: none   12b-1: none
Other: f

Distributions
Income: annual   Capital Gains: annual

Exchange Options
Number Per Year: 2   Fee: none
Telephone: yes (money market fund available)

Services
IRA, pension, auto exchange, auto invest, auto withdraw

Vanguard/Morgan Growth
(VMRGX)
Growth

Vanguard Financial Center
P.O. Box 2600
Valley Forge, PA 19482
800-635-1511, 610-669-1000
www.vanguard.com

PERFORMANCE   fund inception date: 12/31/68

	3yr Annual	5yr Annual	10yr Annual	Bull	Bear
Return (%)	18.1	14.1	14.5	77.4	-9.2
Differ from Category (+/-)	2.4 abv av	-0.2 av	0.6 abv av	15.0 high	-2.5 blw av

Total Risk	Standard Deviation	Category Risk	Risk Index	Beta
abv av	11.5%	abv av	1.1	1.05

	1996	1995	1994	1993	1992	1991	1990	1989	1988	1987
Return (%).	23.3	35.9	-1.7	7.3	9.5	29.3	-1.6	22.6	22.3	5.0
Differ from Category (+/-). .	3.2	5.6	-1.4	-6.7	-2.3	-6.7	4.5	-3.5	4.2	3.0
Return, Tax-Adjusted (%). .	19.8	32.5	-2.9	3.7	7.7	25.9	-4.7	19.9	18.3	-1.7

PER SHARE DATA

	1996	1995	1994	1993	1992	1991	1990	1989	1988	1987
Dividends, Net Income ($).	0.14	0.15	0.14	0.18	0.18	0.28	0.34	0.28	0.24	0.20
Distrib'ns, Cap Gain ($) . . .	1.53	1.15	0.31	1.35	0.52	0.86	0.80	0.59	0.98	2.45
Net Asset Value ($)	15.63	14.09	11.36	12.01	12.65	12.20	10.40	11.72	10.27	9.39
Expense Ratio (%).	na	0.49	0.50	0.49	0.48	0.46	0.55	0.51	0.55	0.46
Yield (%)	0.81	0.98	1.19	1.34	1.36	2.14	3.03	2.27	2.13	1.68
Portfolio Turnover (%). . . .	na	76	84	72	64	52	73	27	32	43
Total Assets (Millions $) .	2,091	1,471	1,074	1,135	1,116	956	696	732	621	537

PORTFOLIO (as of 9/30/96)

Portfolio Manager: Nagorniak, Sauter, Husic, Rands - 1990

Investm't Category: Growth
✔ Domestic	Index
Foreign	Sector
Asset Allocation	State Specific

Investment Style
Large-Cap Growth	Large-Cap Value
✔ Mid-Cap Growth	Mid-Cap Value
Small-Cap Growth	Small-Cap Value

Portfolio
9.0% cash	0.0% corp bonds
91.0% stocks	0.0% gov't bonds
0.0% preferred	0.0% muni bonds
0.0% conv't/warrants	0.0% other

SHAREHOLDER INFORMATION

Minimum Investment
Initial: $3,000   Subsequent: $100

Minimum IRA Investment
Initial: $1,000   Subsequent: $100

Maximum Fees
Load: none   12b-1: none
Other: *f*

Distributions
Income: Dec   Capital Gains: Dec

Exchange Options
Number Per Year: 2   Fee: none
Telephone: yes (money market fund available)

Services
IRA, pension, auto exchange, auto invest, auto withdraw

Vanguard/Trustees' Equity—Int'l Port (VTRIX)

International Stock

Vanguard Financial Center
P.O. Box 2600
Valley Forge, PA 19482
800-635-1511, 610-669-1000
www.vanguard.com

PERFORMANCE

fund inception date: 5/16/83

	3yr Annual	5yr Annual	10yr Annual	Bull	Bear
Return (%)	8.3	8.6	10.4	20.0	-1.4
Differ from Category (+/-)	2.0 abv av	-1.4 blw av	1.8 high	-4.3 blw av	5.8 high

Total Risk	Standard Deviation	Category Risk	Risk Index	Beta
av	9.3%	blw av	0.9	0.60

	1996	1995	1994	1993	1992	1991	1990	1989	1988	1987
Return (%)	10.2	9.6	5.2	30.4	-8.8	9.8	-12.2	25.9	18.7	23.8
Differ from Category (+/-)	-4.6	0.5	8.3	-9.2	-5.0	-3.4	-2.1	3.3	3.8	11.6
Return, Tax-Adjusted (%)	3.9	6.3	3.9	29.0	-10.1	8.0	-14.3	22.7	12.8	9.7

PER SHARE DATA

	1996	1995	1994	1993	1992	1991	1990	1989	1988	1987
Dividends, Net Income ($)	0.82	0.79	0.56	0.81	0.67	0.77	0.95	0.79	0.99	0.75
Distrib'ns, Cap Gain ($)	5.77	2.51	0.63	0.00	0.28	0.61	1.01	2.08	4.58	18.32
Net Asset Value ($)	27.54	31.11	31.48	31.04	24.44	27.78	26.60	32.44	28.27	28.66
Expense Ratio (%)	na	0.47	0.34	0.40	0.42	0.38	0.44	0.46	0.51	0.50
Yield (%)	2.46	2.34	1.74	2.60	2.71	2.71	3.44	2.28	3.01	1.59
Portfolio Turnover (%)	na	47	40	39	51	46	18	25	14	48
Total Assets (Millions $)	952	988	1,053	982	678	878	796	645	467	657

PORTFOLIO (as of 9/30/96)

Portfolio Manager: Wilson Phillips, Robin Apps - 1996

Investm't Category: International Stock
- Domestic
- ✔ Foreign
- Asset Allocation
- Index
- Sector
- State Specific

Investment Style
- Large-Cap Growth
- Mid-Cap Growth
- Small-Cap Growth
- Large-Cap Value
- Mid-Cap Value
- Small-Cap Value

Portfolio
4.0%	cash	0.0%	corp bonds
96.0%	stocks	0.0%	gov't bonds
0.0%	preferred	0.0%	muni bonds
0.0%	conv't/warrants	0.0%	other

SHAREHOLDER INFORMATION

Minimum Investment
Initial: $3,000   Subsequent: $100

Minimum IRA Investment
Initial: $1,000   Subsequent: $100

Maximum Fees
Load: none   12b-1: none
Other: *f*

Distributions
Income: quarterly   Capital Gains: annual

Exchange Options
Number Per Year: 2   Fee: none
Telephone: yes (money market fund available)

Services
IRA, pension, auto exchange, auto invest, auto withdraw

Vanguard/Trustees' Equity—US Port (VTRSX)

Growth & Income

Vanguard Financial Center
P.O. Box 2600
Valley Forge, PA 19482
800-635-1511, 610-669-1000
www.vanguard.com

PERFORMANCE

fund inception date: 1/31/80

	3yr Annual	5yr Annual	10yr Annual	Bull	Bear
Return (%)	15.7	14.1	12.8	65.6	-10.7
Differ from Category (+/-)	0.4 av	0.2 av	0.1 av	5.8 abv av	-4.3 low

Total Risk	Standard Deviation	Category Risk	Risk Index	Beta
abv av	10.7%	high	1.2	1.02

	1996	1995	1994	1993	1992	1991	1990	1989	1988	1987
Return (%).	21.2	33.2	-4.0	17.2	6.4	26.5	-8.4	17.2	24.6	1.6
Differ from Category (+/-). .	1.5	3.1	-2.7	3.4	-4.3	-2.6	-2.5	-6.3	7.8	1.4
Return, Tax-Adjusted (%). .	15.3	31.3	-4.5	14.4	4.6	25.2	-10.1	11.8	21.6	-5.2

PER SHARE DATA

	1996	1995	1994	1993	1992	1991	1990	1989	1988	1987
Dividends, Net Income ($).	0.67	0.61	0.34	0.43	0.67	0.71	1.08	0.88	0.97	0.72
Distrib'ns, Cap Gain ($) . . .	6.78	1.05	0.03	2.16	0.86	0.00	0.00	3.81	1.00	5.88
Net Asset Value ($)	37.08	37.01	29.09	30.65	28.43	28.20	22.90	26.15	26.35	22.77
Expense Ratio (%).	na	0.56	0.73	0.90	0.65	0.44	0.52	0.51	0.58	0.52
Yield (%)	1.52	1.60	1.16	1.31	2.28	2.51	4.71	2.93	3.54	2.51
Portfolio Turnover (%).	na	77	151	139	209	84	81	72	90	44
Total Assets (Millions $). . .	161	137	112	118	68	114	99	120	115	122

PORTFOLIO (as of 9/30/96)

Portfolio Manager: John Geewax - 1992

Investm't Category: Growth & Income
- ✔ Domestic
- Foreign
- Asset Allocation
- Index
- Sector
- State Specific

Investment Style
- ✔ Large-Cap Growth
- ✔ Mid-Cap Growth
- Small-Cap Growth
- ✔ Large-Cap Value
- ✔ Mid-Cap Value
- Small-Cap Value

Portfolio
1.0%	cash	0.0%	corp bonds
99.0%	stocks	0.0%	gov't bonds
0.0%	preferred	0.0%	muni bonds
0.0%	conv't/warrants	0.0%	other

SHAREHOLDER INFORMATION

Minimum Investment
Initial: $3,000   Subsequent: $100

Minimum IRA Investment
Initial: $1,000   Subsequent: $100

Maximum Fees
Load: none   12b-1: none
Other: f

Distributions
Income: quarterly   Capital Gains: annual

Exchange Options
Number Per Year: 2   Fee: none
Telephone: yes (money market fund available)

Services
IRA, pension, auto exchange, auto invest, auto withdraw

WPG Gov't Securities
(WPGVX)
General Bond

One New York Plaza
31st Floor
New York, NY 10004
800-223-3332, 212-908-9500
www.mediasource.com/weis-
speckgreer/index.html

PERFORMANCE

fund inception date: 2/20/86

	3yr Annual	5yr Annual	10yr Annual	Bull	Bear
Return (%)	2.3	4.2	6.7	16.5	-9.4
Differ from Category (+/-)	-2.8 low	-1.9 low	-0.6 blw av	-3.8 blw av	-5.2 low

Total Risk	Standard Deviation	Category Risk	Risk Index	Avg Mat
low	4.5%	abv av	1.2	5.6 yrs

	1996	1995	1994	1993	1992	1991	1990	1989	1988	1987
Return (%)	3.8	13.3	-8.9	8.9	5.4	13.9	8.9	14.0	7.6	2.3
Differ from Category (+/-)	-0.1	-1.6	-6.6	-0.2	-1.1	-0.8	1.6	2.3	0.0	0.0
Return, Tax-Adjusted (%)	1.5	10.6	-11.4	5.4	2.1	10.8	5.7	10.4	4.5	-0.7

PER SHARE DATA

	1996	1995	1994	1993	1992	1991	1990	1989	1988	1987
Dividends, Net Income ($)	0.53	0.58	0.64	0.79	0.77	0.79	0.82	0.87	0.76	0.71
Distrib'ns, Cap Gain ($)	0.00	0.00	0.01	0.15	0.16	0.00	0.00	0.00	0.00	0.07
Net Asset Value ($)	9.19	9.38	8.82	10.37	10.40	10.79	10.22	10.18	9.74	9.77
Expense Ratio (%)	na	0.82	0.80	0.81	0.78	0.81	0.75	0.76	0.82	0.87
Yield (%)	5.76	6.18	7.24	7.50	7.29	7.32	8.02	8.54	7.80	7.21
Portfolio Turnover (%)	na	375	115	97	137	190	184	159	130	108
Total Assets (Millions $)	129	171	216	335	263	193	130	90	78	74

PORTFOLIO (as of 9/30/96)

Portfolio Manager: Daniel S. Vanivort - 1995

Investm't Category: General Bond
- ✔ Domestic
-   Foreign
-   Asset Allocation
-   Index
-   Sector
-   State Specific

Investment Style
- Large-Cap Growth
- Mid-Cap Growth
- Small-Cap Growth
- Large-Cap Value
- Mid-Cap Value
- Small-Cap Value

Portfolio
31.7% cash	0.0% corp bonds
0.0% stocks	68.3% gov't bonds
0.0% preferred	0.0% muni bonds
0.0% conv't/warrants	0.0% other

SHAREHOLDER INFORMATION

Minimum Investment
Initial: $2,500   Subsequent: $100

Minimum IRA Investment
Initial: $250   Subsequent: $1

Maximum Fees
Load: none   12b-1: 0.50%
Other: none

Distributions
Income: monthly   Capital Gains: annual

Exchange Options
Number Per Year: 6   Fee: none
Telephone: yes (money market fund available)

Services
IRA, pension, auto invest, auto withdraw

WPG Growth & Income
(WPGFX)
Growth & Income

One New York Plaza
31st Floor
New York, NY 10004
800-223-3332, 212-908-9500
www.mediasource.com/weis-
speckgreer/index.html

PERFORMANCE

fund inception date: 7/31/79

	3yr Annual	5yr Annual	10yr Annual	Bull	Bear
Return (%)	16.0	14.2	13.8	65.0	-8.7
Differ from Category (+/-)	0.7 av	0.3 av	1.1 abv av	5.2 av	-2.3 low

Total Risk	Standard Deviation	Category Risk	Risk Index	Beta
abv av	9.6%	abv av	1.0	0.91

	1996	1995	1994	1993	1992	1991	1990	1989	1988	1987
Return (%)	24.4	32.7	-5.5	9.5	13.8	40.7	-10.4	27.6	9.4	6.7
Differ from Category (+/-)	4.7	2.6	-4.2	-4.3	3.1	11.6	-4.5	4.1	-7.4	6.5
Return, Tax-Adjusted (%)	19.2	31.9	-6.7	5.7	7.9	40.2	-15.6	26.5	5.2	6.1

PER SHARE DATA

	1996	1995	1994	1993	1992	1991	1990	1989	1988	1987
Dividends, Net Income ($)	0.55	0.36	0.62	0.89	0.51	0.22	0.39	0.23	0.26	0.00
Distrib'ns, Cap Gain ($)	4.37	0.03	0.09	1.93	4.68	0.00	4.10	0.46	2.84	0.38
Net Asset Value ($)	29.32	27.90	21.36	23.34	23.89	25.82	18.53	25.27	20.47	21.72
Expense Ratio (%)	na	1.22	1.23	1.26	1.34	1.48	1.56	1.41	1.53	1.19
Yield (%)	1.63	1.28	2.89	3.52	1.78	0.85	1.72	0.89	1.11	0.00
Portfolio Turnover (%)	na	79	71	86	76	89	91	67	42	84
Total Assets (Millions $)	84	67	61	62	49	42	29	38	35	40

PORTFOLIO (as of 9/30/96)

Portfolio Manager: Roy Knutsen - 1992

Investm't Category: Growth & Income
- ✔ Domestic   Index
- ✔ Foreign   Sector
-   Asset Allocation State Specific

Investment Style
- ✔ Large-Cap Growth ✔ Large-Cap Value
-   Mid-Cap Growth   Mid-Cap Value
-   Small-Cap Growth   Small-Cap Value

Portfolio
3.9% cash	0.0% corp bonds
94.8% stocks	0.0% gov't bonds
0.0% preferred	0.0% muni bonds
1.3% conv't/warrants	0.0% other

SHAREHOLDER INFORMATION

Minimum Investment
Initial: $2,500   Subsequent: $100

Minimum IRA Investment
Initial: $250   Subsequent: $1

Maximum Fees
Load: none   12b-1: 0.50%
Other: none

Distributions
Income: annual   Capital Gains: annual

Exchange Options
Number Per Year: 6   Fee: none
Telephone: yes (money market fund available)

Services
IRA, pension, auto invest, auto withdraw

WPG Quantitative Equity

(WPGQX)

Growth & Income

One New York Plaza
31st Floor
New York, NY 10004
800-223-3332, 212-908-9500
www.mediasource.com/weis-
speckgreer/index.html

PERFORMANCE

fund inception date: 1/4/93

	3yr Annual	5yr Annual	10yr Annual	Bull	Bear
Return (%)	16.6	na	na	66.0	-7.4
Differ from Category (+/-)	1.3 av	na	na	6.2 abv av	-1.0 blw av

Total Risk	Standard Deviation	Category Risk	Risk Index	Beta
av	9.3%	av	1.0	0.93

	1996	1995	1994	1993	1992	1991	1990	1989	1988	1987
Return (%)	18.5	33.3	0.3	—	—	—	—	—	—	—
Differ from Category (+/-)	-1.2	3.2	1.6	—	—	—	—	—	—	—
Return, Tax-Adjusted (%)	7.8	33.3	-0.7	—	—	—	—	—	—	—

PER SHARE DATA

	1996	1995	1994	1993	1992	1991	1990	1989	1988	1987
Dividends, Net Income ($)	0.26	0.00	0.10	—	—	—	—	—	—	—
Distrib'ns, Cap Gain ($)	2.39	0.00	0.05	—	—	—	—	—	—	—
Net Asset Value ($)	5.89	7.24	5.44	—	—	—	—	—	—	—
Expense Ratio (%)	na	1.00	1.14	—	—	—	—	—	—	—
Yield (%)	3.14	0.00	1.82	—	—	—	—	—	—	—
Portfolio Turnover (%)	na	26	46	—	—	—	—	—	—	—
Total Assets (Millions $)	108	133	73	—	—	—	—	—	—	—

PORTFOLIO (as of 9/30/96)

Portfolio Manager: Daniel J. Cardell - 1996

Investm't Category: Growth & Income
- ✔ Domestic
- Foreign
- Asset Allocation
- Index
- Sector
- State Specific

Investment Style
- Large-Cap Growth
- Mid-Cap Growth
- Small-Cap Growth
- ✔ Large-Cap Value
- Mid-Cap Value
- Small-Cap Value

Portfolio
0.0%	cash	0.0% corp bonds
100.0%	stocks	0.0% gov't bonds
0.0%	preferred	0.0% muni bonds
0.0%	conv't/warrants	0.0% other

SHAREHOLDER INFORMATION

Minimum Investment
Initial: $5,000   Subsequent: $500

Minimum IRA Investment
Initial: $250   Subsequent: $1

Maximum Fees
Load: none   12b-1: 0.50%
Other: none

Distributions
Income: annual   Capital Gains: annual

Exchange Options
Number Per Year: 6   Fee: none
Telephone: yes (money market fund available)

Services
IRA, pension, auto invest, auto withdraw

WPG Tudor (TUDRX)

Aggressive Growth

One New York Plaza
31st Floor
New York, NY 10004
800-223-3332, 212-908-9500
www.mediasource.com/weis-
speckgreer/index.html

PERFORMANCE

fund inception date: 3/14/69

	3yr Annual	5yr Annual	10yr Annual	Bull	Bear
Return (%)	14.8	12.5	13.7	79.0	-17.8
Differ from Category (+/-)	-1.0 av	-2.8 blw av	-1.3 blw av	7.9 abv av	-7.2 low

Total Risk	Standard Deviation	Category Risk	Risk Index	Beta
high	17.1%	abv av	1.2	1.21

	1996	1995	1994	1993	1992	1991	1990	1989	1988	1987
Return (%)	18.8	41.1	-9.9	13.3	5.1	45.8	-5.2	25.0	15.1	1.1
Differ from Category (+/-)	-0.3	6.8	-9.9	-6.0	-6.6	-6.3	0.2	-3.4	-1.3	3.5
Return, Tax-Adjusted (%)	11.0	39.6	-12.1	7.9	2.8	45.1	-12.9	23.7	13.8	-0.1

PER SHARE DATA

	1996	1995	1994	1993	1992	1991	1990	1989	1988	1987
Dividends, Net Income ($)	0.14	0.00	0.00	0.00	0.14	0.28	0.23	0.16	0.03	0.00
Distrib'ns, Cap Gain ($)	7.10	1.01	1.78	4.73	1.91	0.00	6.78	0.74	0.82	0.86
Net Asset Value ($)	23.28	26.24	19.34	23.40	24.85	25.68	17.85	25.97	21.65	19.64
Expense Ratio (%)	na	1.30	1.28	1.25	1.21	1.17	1.11	1.10	1.14	1.03
Yield (%)	0.46	0.00	0.00	0.00	0.52	1.09	0.93	0.59	0.13	0.00
Portfolio Turnover (%)	na	123	109	118	89	90	73	94	89	113
Total Assets (Millions $)	195	167	143	242	273	264	162	185	163	149

PORTFOLIO (as of 9/30/96)

Portfolio Manager: Melville Straus - 1973

Investm't Category: Aggressive Growth
- ✔ Domestic
- ✔ Foreign
- Asset Allocation

- Index
- Sector
- State Specific

Investment Style
- Large-Cap Growth
- ✔ Mid-Cap Growth
- ✔ Small-Cap Growth

- Large-Cap Value
- Mid-Cap Value
- Small-Cap Value

Portfolio
0.0% cash	0.0% corp bonds
99.0% stocks	0.0% gov't bonds
0.0% preferred	0.0% muni bonds
1.0% conv't/warrants	0.0% other

SHAREHOLDER INFORMATION

Minimum Investment
Initial: $2,500   Subsequent: $100

Minimum IRA Investment
Initial: $250   Subsequent: $1

Maximum Fees
Load: none   12b-1: 0.50%
Other: none

Distributions
Income: annual   Capital Gains: annual

Exchange Options
Number Per Year: 6   Fee: none
Telephone: yes (money market fund available)

Services
IRA, pension, auto invest, auto withdraw

Warburg Pincus
Balanced—Common

335 Madison Ave.
15th Floor
New York, NY 10017
800-257-5614, 212-878-0600

(WAPBX) *Balanced*

PERFORMANCE
fund inception date: 10/6/88

	3yr Annual	5yr Annual	10yr Annual	Bull	Bear
Return (%)	14.5	12.3	na	51.7	-3.4
Differ from Category (+/-)	2.8 high	0.9 av	na	6.6 high	2.3 high

Total Risk	Standard Deviation	Category Risk	Risk Index	Beta
av	8.0%	high	1.2	0.61

	1996	1995	1994	1993	1992	1991	1990	1989	1988	1987
Return (%).	12.8	31.5	1.2	10.7	7.5	25.1	3.0	19.4	—	—
Differ from Category (+/-).	-1.4	6.9	2.8	-3.7	-1.4	1.0	3.9	1.3	—	—
Return, Tax-Adjusted (%). .	11.8	30.3	-4.1	6.6	2.3	22.0	0.7	16.4	—	—

PER SHARE DATA

	1996	1995	1994	1993	1992	1991	1990	1989	1988	1987
Dividends, Net Income ($).	0.18	0.16	0.35	0.45	0.54	0.38	0.43	0.45	—	—
Distrib'ns, Cap Gain ($) . . .	0.15	0.14	1.50	0.97	1.46	0.59	0.27	0.41	—	—
Net Asset Value ($)	12.63	11.50	9.00	10.73	11.00	12.12	10.49	10.88	—	—
Expense Ratio (%).	1.53	1.53	0.00	0.00	0.67	1.40	1.40	1.40	—	—
Yield (%)	1.40	1.37	3.33	3.84	4.33	2.98	3.99	3.98	—	—
Portfolio Turnover (%). . . .	108	107	32	30	93	76	76	na	—	—
Total Assets (Millions $). . . .	33	12	0	0	0	1	1	1	—	—

PORTFOLIO (as of 9/30/96)

Portfolio Manager: D. Christensen, A.
Orphanos - 1994

Investm't Category: Balanced
- ✔ Domestic
- Foreign
- Asset Allocation
- Index
- Sector
- State Specific

Investment Style
- Large-Cap Growth
- Mid-Cap Growth
- Small-Cap Growth
- Large-Cap Value
- Mid-Cap Value
- Small-Cap Value

Portfolio
7.7% cash	3.2% corp bonds
56.6% stocks	22.9% gov't bonds
1.0% preferred	0.0% muni bonds
7.9% conv't/warrants	0.7% other

SHAREHOLDER INFORMATION

Minimum Investment
Initial: $1,000   Subsequent: $100

Minimum IRA Investment
Initial: $500   Subsequent: $100

Maximum Fees
Load: none   12b-1: 0.25%
Other: none

Distributions
Income: quarterly   Capital Gains: annual

Exchange Options
Number Per Year: 36   Fee: none
Telephone: yes (money market fund available)

Services
IRA, pension, auto exchange, auto invest, auto
withdraw

Warburg Pincus Cap Apprec—Common

335 Madison Ave.
15th Floor
New York, NY 10017
800-257-5614, 212-878-0600

(CUCAX) *Growth*

PERFORMANCE

fund inception date: 7/17/87

	3yr Annual	5yr Annual	10yr Annual	Bull	Bear
Return (%)	18.2	15.5	na	75.8	-8.8
Differ from Category (+/-)	2.5 abv av	1.2 abv av	na	13.4 abv av	-2.1 blw av

Total Risk	Standard Deviation	Category Risk	Risk Index	Beta
abv av	10.5%	av	1.0	0.97

	1996	1995	1994	1993	1992	1991	1990	1989	1988	1987
Return (%)	23.2	38.1	-2.9	15.8	7.6	26.2	-5.5	26.7	21.3	—
Differ from Category (+/-)	3.1	7.8	-2.6	1.8	-4.2	-9.8	0.6	0.6	3.2	—
Return, Tax-Adjusted (%)	19.6	33.4	-4.9	13.0	5.8	25.6	-6.3	24.5	19.9	—

PER SHARE DATA

	1996	1995	1994	1993	1992	1991	1990	1989	1988	1987
Dividends, Net Income ($)	0.09	0.05	0.00	0.07	0.05	0.11	0.21	0.35	0.19	—
Distrib'ns, Cap Gain ($)	1.80	2.03	0.98	1.18	0.75	0.05	0.00	0.23	0.13	—
Net Asset Value ($)	16.94	15.32	12.66	14.06	13.24	13.06	10.48	11.31	9.39	—
Expense Ratio (%)	na	1.12	1.05	1.01	1.06	1.08	1.04	1.10	1.07	—
Yield (%)	0.48	0.28	0.00	0.45	0.35	0.83	2.00	3.03	1.99	—
Portfolio Turnover (%)	na	146	51	48	56	40	37	37	33	—
Total Assets (Millions $)	465	256	145	158	120	122	83	57	31	—

PORTFOLIO (as of 9/30/96)

Portfolio Manager: George Wiper, Susan Black - 1994

Investm't Category: Growth
- ✔ Domestic
- ✔ Foreign
- Asset Allocation
- Index
- Sector
- State Specific

Investment Style
- ✔ Large-Cap Growth
- ✔ Mid-Cap Growth
- Small-Cap Growth
- ✔ Large-Cap Value
- ✔ Mid-Cap Value
- Small-Cap Value

Portfolio
9.3%	cash	0.0% corp bonds
90.7%	stocks	0.0% gov't bonds
0.0%	preferred	0.0% muni bonds
0.0%	conv't/warrants	0.0% other

SHAREHOLDER INFORMATION

Minimum Investment
Initial: $2,500   Subsequent: $100

Minimum IRA Investment
Initial: $500   Subsequent: $100

Maximum Fees
Load: none   12b-1: none
Other: none

Distributions
Income: annual   Capital Gains: annual

Exchange Options
Number Per Year: 36   Fee: none
Telephone: yes (money market fund available)

Services
IRA, pension, auto exchange, auto invest, auto withdraw

Warburg Pincus Emerging Grth—Common (CUEGX)

335 Madison Ave.
15th Floor
New York, NY 10017
800-257-5614, 212-878-0600

Aggressive Growth

PERFORMANCE

fund inception date: 1/22/88

	3yr Annual	5yr Annual	10yr Annual	Bull	Bear
Return (%)	16.5	15.9	na	76.5	-12.9
Differ from Category (+/-)	0.7 abv av	0.6 abv av	na	5.4 abv av	-2.3 blw av

Total Risk	Standard Deviation	Category Risk	Risk Index	Beta
high	14.5%	av	1.0	0.89

	1996	1995	1994	1993	1992	1991	1990	1989	1988	1987
Return (%).	9.8	46.2	-1.5	18.1	12.1	56.1	-10.0	21.8	—	—
Differ from Category (+/-) .	-9.3	11.9	-1.5	-1.2	0.4	4.0	-4.6	-6.6	—	—
Return, Tax-Adjusted (%). . .	9.7	43.9	-1.5	16.2	11.5	55.0	-10.4	20.1	—	—

PER SHARE DATA

	1996	1995	1994	1993	1992	1991	1990	1989	1988	1987
Dividends, Net Income ($).	0.00	0.00	0.00	0.00	0.00	0.17	0.13	0.38	—	—
Distrib'ns, Cap Gain ($) . . .	0.06	1.75	0.00	1.35	0.37	0.19	0.00	0.15	—	—
Net Asset Value ($)	33.22	30.30	21.99	22.31	20.07	18.23	11.92	13.37	—	—
Expense Ratio (%).	na	1.26	1.22	1.23	1.24	1.25	1.25	1.25	—	—
Yield (%)	0.00	0.00	0.00	0.00	0.00	0.92	1.09	2.81	—	—
Portfolio Turnover (%).	na	84	60	68	63	98	107	100	—	—
Total Assets (Millions $).	1,129	557	222	183	110	75	23	26	—	—

PORTFOLIO (as of 9/30/96)

Portfolio Manager: Beth Dater, Steven Lurito - 1988

Investm't Category: Aggressive Growth
- ✔ Domestic
- ✔ Foreign
-    Asset Allocation
-    Index
-    Sector
-    State Specific

Investment Style
- Large-Cap Growth
- Mid-Cap Growth
- ✔ Small-Cap Growth
- Large-Cap Value
- Mid-Cap Value
- Small-Cap Value

Portfolio
6.7% cash	0.0% corp bonds
92.9% stocks	0.0% gov't bonds
0.4% preferred	0.0% muni bonds
0.0% conv't/warrants	0.0% other

SHAREHOLDER INFORMATION

Minimum Investment
Initial: $2,500   Subsequent: $100

Minimum IRA Investment
Initial: $500   Subsequent: $100

Maximum Fees
Load: none   12b-1: none
Other: none

Distributions
Income: annual   Capital Gains: annual

Exchange Options
Number Per Year: 36   Fee: none
Telephone: yes (money market fund available)

Services
IRA, pension, auto exchange, auto invest, auto withdraw

Warburg Pincus Emerging Mkts—Common (WPEMX)

335 Madison Ave.
15th Floor
New York, NY 10017
800-257-5614, 212-878-0600

International Stock

PERFORMANCE

fund inception date: 1/3/95

	3yr Annual	5yr Annual	10yr Annual	Bull	Bear
Return (%)	na	na	na	na	na
Differ from Category (+/-)	na	na	na	na	na

Total Risk	Standard Deviation	Category Risk	Risk Index	Beta
na	na	na	na	na

	1996	1995	1994	1993	1992	1991	1990	1989	1988	1987
Return (%)	9.9	—	—	—	—	—	—	—	—	—
Differ from Category (+/-)	-4.9	—	—	—	—	—	—	—	—	—
Return, Tax-Adjusted (%)	9.7	—	—	—	—	—	—	—	—	—

PER SHARE DATA

	1996	1995	1994	1993	1992	1991	1990	1989	1988	1987
Dividends, Net Income ($)	0.02	—	—	—	—	—	—	—	—	—
Distrib'ns, Cap Gain ($)	0.05	—	—	—	—	—	—	—	—	—
Net Asset Value ($)	12.59	—	—	—	—	—	—	—	—	—
Expense Ratio (%)	na	—	—	—	—	—	—	—	—	—
Yield (%)	0.15	—	—	—	—	—	—	—	—	—
Portfolio Turnover (%)	na	—	—	—	—	—	—	—	—	—
Total Assets (Millions $)	222	—	—	—	—	—	—	—	—	—

PORTFOLIO (as of 9/30/96)

Portfolio Manager: Richard King, Nicholas Horsley - 1994

Investm't Category: International Stock
- Domestic
- ✔ Foreign
- Asset Allocation
- Index
- Sector
- State Specific

Investment Style
- Large-Cap Growth
- Mid-Cap Growth
- Small-Cap Growth
- Large-Cap Value
- Mid-Cap Value
- Small-Cap Value

Portfolio

2.3% cash	0.0% corp bonds
96.0% stocks	0.0% gov't bonds
0.2% preferred	0.0% muni bonds
1.4% conv't/warrants	0.1% other

SHAREHOLDER INFORMATION

Minimum Investment
Initial: $2,500   Subsequent: $100

Minimum IRA Investment
Initial: $500   Subsequent: $100

Maximum Fees
Load: none   12b-1: 0.25%
Other: none

Distributions
Income: annual   Capital Gains: annual

Exchange Options
Number Per Year: 36   Fee: none
Telephone: yes (money market fund available)

Services
IRA, pension, auto exchange, auto invest, auto withdraw

Warburg Pincus Fixed Income—Common

(CUFIX) *General Bond*

335 Madison Ave.
15th Floor
New York, NY 10017
800-257-5614, 212-878-0600

PERFORMANCE

fund inception date: 8/17/87

	3yr Annual	5yr Annual	10yr Annual	Bull	Bear
Return (%)	6.4	7.4	na	23.5	-3.8
Differ from Category (+/-)	1.3 high	1.3 high	na	3.2 abv av	0.4 abv av

Total Risk	Standard Deviation	Category Risk	Risk Index	Avg Mat
low	3.5%	av	0.9	5.0 yrs

	1996	1995	1994	1993	1992	1991	1990	1989	1988	1987
Return (%).	5.5	15.1	-0.7	11.1	6.7	16.8	2.8	9.2	8.5	—
Differ from Category (+/-) . .	1.6	0.2	1.6	2.0	0.2	2.1	-4.5	-2.5	0.9	—
Return, Tax-Adjusted (%) . . .	3.2	12.2	-3.3	8.5	4.0	13.7	-0.8	5.4	4.9	—

PER SHARE DATA

	1996	1995	1994	1993	1992	1991	1990	1989	1988	1987
Dividends, Net Income ($) .	0.57	0.68	0.67	0.56	0.67	0.70	0.86	0.93	0.87	—
Distrib'ns, Cap Gain ($) . . .	0.00	0.00	0.00	0.09	0.00	0.00	0.00	0.00	0.01	—
Net Asset Value ($)	10.15	10.19	9.49	10.24	9.82	9.86	9.09	9.69	9.75	—
Expense Ratio (%)	na	0.75	0.75	0.75	0.75	0.75	0.75	0.75	0.74	—
Yield (%)	5.61	6.67	7.06	5.42	6.82	7.09	9.46	9.59	8.91	—
Portfolio Turnover (%)	na	182	179	227	122	151	132	78	56	—
Total Assets (Millions $) . . .	156	121	105	84	66	59	57	71	80	—

PORTFOLIO (as of 9/30/96)

Portfolio Manager: D. Christensen, A. Van Daalen - 1991

Investm't Category: General Bond
✔ Domestic   Index
✔ Foreign   Sector
  Asset Allocation State Specific

Investment Style
  Large-Cap Growth   Large-Cap Value
  Mid-Cap Growth   Mid-Cap Value
  Small-Cap Growth   Small-Cap Value

Portfolio
  2.8% cash   12.6% corp bonds
  2.3% stocks   56.2% gov't bonds
  5.4% preferred   0.0% muni bonds
  0.9% conv't/warrants 19.8% other

SHAREHOLDER INFORMATION

Minimum Investment
Initial: $2,500   Subsequent: $100

Minimum IRA Investment
Initial: $500   Subsequent: $100

Maximum Fees
Load: none   12b-1: none
Other: none

Distributions
Income: monthly   Capital Gains: annual

Exchange Options
Number Per Year: 36   Fee: none
Telephone: yes (money market fund available)

Services
IRA, pension, auto exchange, auto invest, auto withdraw

Warburg Pincus Global Fixed Income (CGFIX)

International Bond

335 Madison Ave.
15th Floor
New York, NY 10017
800-257-5614, 212-878-0600

PERFORMANCE

fund inception date: 11/1/90

	3yr Annual	5yr Annual	10yr Annual	Bull	Bear
Return (%)	6.4	8.0	na	27.6	-6.3
Differ from Category (+/-)	0.4 av	1.4 abv av	na	-3.6 av	3.2 abv av

Total Risk	Standard Deviation	Category Risk	Risk Index	Avg Mat
low	4.4%	blw av	0.6	6.7 yrs

	1996	1995	1994	1993	1992	1991	1990	1989	1988	1987
Return (%)	9.9	16.0	-5.5	19.6	2.1	14.7	—	—	—	—
Differ from Category (+/-)	-1.4	0.0	2.1	4.3	-3.1	-0.3	—	—	—	—
Return, Tax-Adjusted (%)	6.5	12.6	-6.8	16.3	-1.5	12.3	—	—	—	—

PER SHARE DATA

	1996	1995	1994	1993	1992	1991	1990	1989	1988	1987
Dividends, Net Income ($)	0.93	0.85	0.36	0.74	0.88	0.59	—	—	—	—
Distrib'ns, Cap Gain ($)	0.00	0.00	0.00	0.13	0.12	0.00	—	—	—	—
Net Asset Value ($)	11.01	10.90	10.16	11.13	10.06	10.84	—	—	—	—
Expense Ratio (%)	na	0.95	0.95	0.49	0.45	1.09	—	—	—	—
Yield (%)	8.44	7.79	3.54	6.57	8.64	5.44	—	—	—	—
Portfolio Turnover (%)	na	128	178	109	93	186	—	—	—	—
Total Assets (Millions $)	141	80	84	69	16	12	—	—	—	—

PORTFOLIO (as of 9/30/96)

Portfolio Manager: D. Christensen, L. Bhandari - 1990

Investm't Category: International Bond
- ✔ Domestic
- ✔ Foreign
- Asset Allocation
- Index
- Sector
- State Specific

Investment Style
- Large-Cap Growth
- Mid-Cap Growth
- Small-Cap Growth
- Large-Cap Value
- Mid-Cap Value
- Small-Cap Value

Portfolio
- 14.1% cash
- 0.0% stocks
- 1.1% preferred
- 6.6% conv't/warrants
- 42.0% corp bonds
- 36.2% gov't bonds
- 0.0% muni bonds
- 0.0% other

SHAREHOLDER INFORMATION

Minimum Investment
Initial: $2,500   Subsequent: $100

Minimum IRA Investment
Initial: $500   Subsequent: $100

Maximum Fees
Load: none   12b-1: none
Other: none

Distributions
Income: quarterly   Capital Gains: annual

Exchange Options
Number Per Year: 36   Fee: none
Telephone: yes (money market fund available)

Services
IRA, pension, auto exchange, auto invest, auto withdraw

Warburg Pincus Grth & Inc—Common (RBEGX)

335 Madison Ave.
15th Floor
New York, NY 10017
800-257-5614, 212-878-0600

Growth & Income

PERFORMANCE

fund inception date: 10/6/88

	3yr Annual	5yr Annual	10yr Annual	Bull	Bear
Return (%)	8.5	13.5	na	22.8	0.6
Differ from Category (+/-)	-6.8 low	-0.4 blw av	na	-37.0 low	7.0 high

Total Risk	Standard Deviation	Category Risk	Risk Index	Beta
high	12.1%	high	1.3	0.72

	1996	1995	1994	1993	1992	1991	1990	1989	1988	1987
Return (%).............	-1.2	20.4	7.5	35.7	8.5	13.0	4.0	20.9	—	—
Differ from Category (+/-)	-20.9	-9.7	8.8	21.9	-2.2	-16.1	9.9	-2.6	—	—
Return, Tax-Adjusted (%)..	-1.4	18.1	6.8	26.4	7.9	11.6	1.2	18.4	—	—

PER SHARE DATA

	1996	1995	1994	1993	1992	1991	1990	1989	1988	1987
Dividends, Net Income ($).	0.05	0.20	0.10	0.12	0.16	0.26	0.41	0.40	—	—
Distrib'ns, Cap Gain ($) ...	0.00	0.81	0.18	3.97	0.00	0.16	0.54	0.30	—	—
Net Asset Value ($)	15.15	15.39	13.64	12.95	12.56	11.73	10.77	11.29	—	—
Expense Ratio (%)........	1.21	1.22	1.28	1.14	1.25	1.30	1.40	1.40	—	—
Yield (%)	0.33	1.23	0.72	0.70	1.27	2.18	3.62	3.45	—	—
Portfolio Turnover (%).....	94	109	150	344	175	41	98	111	—	—
Total Assets (Millions $)...	540	985	628	34	30	23	1	1	—	—

PORTFOLIO (as of 9/30/96)

Portfolio Manager: Brian S. Posner - 1997

Investm't Category: Growth & Income
✔ Domestic	Index
✔ Foreign	Sector
Asset Allocation	State Specific

Investment Style
Large-Cap Growth	Large-Cap Value
✔ Mid-Cap Growth	✔ Mid-Cap Value
Small-Cap Growth	Small-Cap Value

Portfolio
2.9% cash	0.0% corp bonds
97.1% stocks	0.0% gov't bonds
0.0% preferred	0.0% muni bonds
0.0% conv't/warrants	0.0% other

SHAREHOLDER INFORMATION

Minimum Investment
Initial: $1,000   Subsequent: $100

Minimum IRA Investment
Initial: $500   Subsequent: $100

Maximum Fees
Load: none   12b-1: none
Other: none

Distributions
Income: quarterly   Capital Gains: annual

Exchange Options
Number Per Year: 36   Fee: none
Telephone: yes (money market fund available)

Services
IRA, pension, auto exchange, auto invest, auto withdraw

Warburg Pincus Interm Maturity Gov't (CUIGX)

Government Bond

335 Madison Ave.
15th Floor
New York, NY 10017
800-257-5614, 212-878-0600

PERFORMANCE

fund inception date: 8/22/88

	3yr Annual	5yr Annual	10yr Annual	Bull	Bear
Return (%)	5.3	5.9	na	19.5	-3.5
Differ from Category (+/-)	0.4 abv av	-0.7 av	na	-2.5 av	2.9 abv av

Total Risk	Standard Deviation	Category Risk	Risk Index	Avg Mat
low	3.6%	av	0.9	6.5 yrs

	1996	1995	1994	1993	1992	1991	1990	1989	1988	1987
Return (%)	2.2	16.2	-1.8	7.3	6.6	14.9	8.9	11.5	—	—
Differ from Category (+/-)	0.7	-3.4	2.6	-4.3	-0.1	-0.8	2.6	-3.8	—	—
Return, Tax-Adjusted (%)	-0.3	13.5	-4.0	3.7	2.7	12.0	5.9	8.2	—	—

PER SHARE DATA

	1996	1995	1994	1993	1992	1991	1990	1989	1988	1987
Dividends, Net Income ($)	0.57	0.59	0.55	0.52	0.85	0.75	0.78	0.82	—	—
Distrib'ns, Cap Gain ($)	0.11	0.08	0.00	0.63	0.34	0.00	0.00	0.00	—	—
Net Asset Value ($)	9.91	10.38	9.55	10.29	10.67	11.15	10.42	10.33	—	—
Expense Ratio (%)	na	0.60	0.60	0.60	0.60	0.57	0.50	0.50	—	—
Yield (%)	5.68	5.64	5.75	4.76	7.72	6.72	7.48	7.93	—	—
Portfolio Turnover (%)	na	105	115	108	166	39	113	23	—	—
Total Assets (Millions $)	47	55	44	64	99	104	75	52	—	—

PORTFOLIO (as of 9/30/96)

Portfolio Manager: D. Christensen, A. Van Daalen - 1989

Investm't Category: Government Bond
- ✔ Domestic
- Foreign
- Asset Allocation
- Index
- Sector
- State Specific

Investment Style
- Large-Cap Growth
- Mid-Cap Growth
- Small-Cap Growth
- Large-Cap Value
- Mid-Cap Value
- Small-Cap Value

Portfolio
2.5% cash	0.0% corp bonds
0.0% stocks	67.2% gov't bonds
0.0% preferred	0.0% muni bonds
0.0% conv't/warrants	30.3% other

SHAREHOLDER INFORMATION

Minimum Investment
Initial: $2,500   Subsequent: $100

Minimum IRA Investment
Initial: $500   Subsequent: $100

Maximum Fees
Load: none   12b-1: none
Other: none

Distributions
Income: monthly   Capital Gains: annual

Exchange Options
Number Per Year: 36   Fee: none
Telephone: yes (money market fund available)

Services
IRA, pension, auto exchange, auto invest, auto withdraw

Warburg Pincus Int'l Equity—Common (CUIEX)

335 Madison Ave.
15th Floor
New York, NY 10017
800-257-5614, 212-878-0600

International Stock

PERFORMANCE

fund inception date: 5/2/89

	3yr Annual	5yr Annual	10yr Annual	Bull	Bear
Return (%)	6.9	12.0	na	19.5	-6.7
Differ from Category (+/-)	0.6 av	2.0 abv av	na	-4.8 blw av	0.5 av

Total Risk	Standard Deviation	Category Risk	Risk Index	Beta
high	13.3%	abv av	1.3	0.77

	1996	1995	1994	1993	1992	1991	1990	1989	1988	1987
Return (%)	10.5	10.3	0.1	51.2	-4.4	20.6	-4.6	—	—	—
Differ from Category (+/-)	-4.3	1.2	3.2	11.6	-0.6	7.4	5.5	—	—	—
Return, Tax-Adjusted (%)	9.0	8.9	-0.9	51.0	-4.8	19.4	-5.9	—	—	—

PER SHARE DATA

	1996	1995	1994	1993	1992	1991	1990	1989	1988	1987
Dividends, Net Income ($)	0.47	0.62	0.10	0.03	0.05	0.32	0.39	—	—	—
Distrib'ns, Cap Gain ($)	0.37	0.00	0.52	0.03	0.12	0.00	0.01	—	—	—
Net Asset Value ($)	20.84	19.64	18.38	18.98	12.60	13.36	11.35	—	—	—
Expense Ratio (%)	na	1.39	1.44	1.48	1.49	1.50	1.46	—	—	—
Yield (%)	2.21	3.15	0.52	0.15	0.39	2.39	3.43	—	—	—
Portfolio Turnover (%)	na	39	17	22	53	54	66	—	—	—
Total Assets (Millions $)	2,978	2,220	1,551	506	99	76	40	—	—	—

PORTFOLIO (as of 9/30/96)

Portfolio Manager: Richard H. King, committee - 1989

Investm't Category: International Stock
- Domestic
- ✔ Foreign
- Asset Allocation
- Index
- Sector
- State Specific

Investment Style
- Large-Cap Growth
- Mid-Cap Growth
- Small-Cap Growth
- Large-Cap Value
- Mid-Cap Value
- Small-Cap Value

Portfolio
3.5% cash	0.0% corp bonds
94.8% stocks	0.0% gov't bonds
0.2% preferred	0.0% muni bonds
1.3% conv't/warrants	0.2% other

SHAREHOLDER INFORMATION

Minimum Investment
Initial: $2,500   Subsequent: $100

Minimum IRA Investment
Initial: $500   Subsequent: $100

Maximum Fees
Load: none   12b-1: none
Other: none

Distributions
Income: annual   Capital Gains: annual

Exchange Options
Number Per Year: 36   Fee: none
Telephone: yes (money market fund available)

Services
IRA, pension, auto exchange, auto invest, auto withdraw

Warburg Pincus Japan OTC—Common (WPJPX)

International Stock

335 Madison Ave.
15th Floor
New York, NY 10017
800-257-5614, 212-878-0600

PERFORMANCE

fund inception date: 9/30/94

	3yr Annual	5yr Annual	10yr Annual	Bull	Bear
Return (%)	na	na	na	na	na
Differ from Category (+/-)	na	na	na	na	na

Total Risk	Standard Deviation	Category Risk	Risk Index	Beta
na	na	na	na	na

	1996	1995	1994	1993	1992	1991	1990	1989	1988	1987
Return (%)	-13.1	-1.1	—	—	—	—	—	—	—	—
Differ from Category (+/-)	-27.9	-10.2	—	—	—	—	—	—	—	—
Return, Tax-Adjusted (%)	-13.4	-2.7	—	—	—	—	—	—	—	—

PER SHARE DATA

	1996	1995	1994	1993	1992	1991	1990	1989	1988	1987
Dividends, Net Income ($)	0.00	0.37	—	—	—	—	—	—	—	—
Distrib'ns, Cap Gain ($)	0.08	0.00	—	—	—	—	—	—	—	—
Net Asset Value ($)	7.85	9.13	—	—	—	—	—	—	—	—
Expense Ratio (%)	na	1.41	—	—	—	—	—	—	—	—
Yield (%)	0.00	4.05	—	—	—	—	—	—	—	—
Portfolio Turnover (%)	na	82	—	—	—	—	—	—	—	—
Total Assets (Millions $)	116	212	—	—	—	—	—	—	—	—

PORTFOLIO (as of 9/30/96)

Portfolio Manager: R. King, N. Horsley, S. Abe - 1994

Investm't Category: International Stock
Domestic	Index
✔ Foreign	Sector
Asset Allocation	State Specific

Investment Style
Large-Cap Growth	Large-Cap Value
Mid-Cap Growth	Mid-Cap Value
Small-Cap Growth	Small-Cap Value

Portfolio
6.7%	cash	0.0%	corp bonds
92.3%	stocks	0.0%	gov't bonds
0.0%	preferred	0.0%	muni bonds
1.0%	conv't/warrants	0.0%	other

SHAREHOLDER INFORMATION

Minimum Investment
Initial: $2,500   Subsequent: $100

Minimum IRA Investment
Initial: $500   Subsequent: $100

Maximum Fees
Load: 1.00% redemption   12b-1: 0.25%
Other: redemption fee applies for 6 months

Distributions
Income: annual   Capital Gains: annual

Exchange Options
Number Per Year: 36   Fee: none
Telephone: yes (money market fund available)

Services
IRA, pension, auto exchange, auto invest, auto withdraw

Warburg Pincus NY Interm Muni (CNMBX)

335 Madison Ave.
15th Floor
New York, NY 10017
800-257-5614, 212-878-0600

Tax-Exempt Bond

PERFORMANCE

fund inception date: 4/1/87

	3yr Annual	5yr Annual	10yr Annual	Bull	Bear
Return (%)	4.3	6.0	na	15.1	-2.3
Differ from Category (+/-)	0.1 av	-0.4 blw av	na	-3.3 low	3.1 high

Total Risk	Standard Deviation	Category Risk	Risk Index	Avg Mat
low	2.8%	low	0.5	5.7 yrs

	1996	1995	1994	1993	1992	1991	1990	1989	1988	1987
Return (%)	4.3	9.5	-0.6	9.8	7.5	9.4	5.9	6.8	6.3	—
Differ from Category (+/-)	0.6	-5.7	4.7	-2.0	-0.8	-2.0	-0.5	-2.2	-3.7	—
Return, Tax-Adjusted (%)	3.9	9.1	-0.6	9.4	7.3	9.4	5.9	6.8	6.3	—

PER SHARE DATA

	1996	1995	1994	1993	1992	1991	1990	1989	1988	1987
Dividends, Net Income ($)	0.45	0.45	0.45	0.46	0.49	0.56	0.59	0.59	0.54	—
Distrib'ns, Cap Gain ($)	0.12	0.11	0.00	0.13	0.04	0.00	0.00	0.00	0.00	—
Net Asset Value ($)	10.26	10.40	10.03	10.55	10.16	9.97	9.64	9.68	9.63	—
Expense Ratio (%)	na	0.60	0.60	0.58	0.55	0.55	0.55	0.56	0.54	—
Yield (%)	4.33	4.28	4.48	4.30	4.80	5.61	6.12	6.09	5.60	—
Portfolio Turnover (%)	na	105	167	116	48	67	70	74	145	—
Total Assets (Millions $)	79	72	76	73	50	35	23	21	27	—

PORTFOLIO (as of 9/30/96)

Portfolio Manager: S. Parente, D. Christensen - 1992

Investm't Category: Tax-Exempt Bond
✔ Domestic   Index
  Foreign   Sector
  Asset Allocation   ✔ State Specific

Investment Style
  Large-Cap Growth   Large-Cap Value
  Mid-Cap Growth   Mid-Cap Value
  Small-Cap Growth   Small-Cap Value

Portfolio
  1.8% cash   0.0% corp bonds
  0.0% stocks   0.0% gov't bonds
  0.0% preferred   98.2% muni bonds
  0.0% conv't/warrants   0.0% other

SHAREHOLDER INFORMATION

Minimum Investment
Initial: $2,500   Subsequent: $100

Minimum IRA Investment
Initial: na   Subsequent: na

Maximum Fees
Load: none   12b-1: none
Other: none

Distributions
Income: monthly   Capital Gains: annual

Exchange Options
Number Per Year: 36   Fee: none
Telephone: yes (money market fund available)

Services
auto exchange, auto invest, auto withdraw

Warburg Pincus Post-Vent Cap—Common (WPVCX)

Aggressive Growth

335 Madison Ave.
15th Floor
New York, NY 10017
800-257-5614, 212-878-0600

PERFORMANCE
fund inception date: 9/29/95

	3yr Annual	5yr Annual	10yr Annual	Bull	Bear
Return (%)	na	na	na	na	na
Differ from Category (+/-)	na	na	na	na	na

Total Risk	Standard Deviation	Category Risk	Risk Index	Beta
na	na	na	na	na

	1996	1995	1994	1993	1992	1991	1990	1989	1988	1987
Return (%)	17.2	—	—	—	—	—	—	—	—	—
Differ from Category (+/-)	-1.9	—	—	—	—	—	—	—	—	—
Return, Tax-Adjusted (%)	17.2	—	—	—	—	—	—	—	—	—

PER SHARE DATA

	1996	1995	1994	1993	1992	1991	1990	1989	1988	1987
Dividends, Net Income ($)	0.00	—	—	—	—	—	—	—	—	—
Distrib'ns, Cap Gain ($)	0.00	—	—	—	—	—	—	—	—	—
Net Asset Value ($)	16.24	—	—	—	—	—	—	—	—	—
Expense Ratio (%)	na	—	—	—	—	—	—	—	—	—
Yield (%)	0.00	—	—	—	—	—	—	—	—	—
Portfolio Turnover (%)	na	—	—	—	—	—	—	—	—	—
Total Assets (Millions $)	166	—	—	—	—	—	—	—	—	—

PORTFOLIO (as of 9/30/96)

Portfolio Manager: Elizabeth Dater, Steve Lurito - 1995

Investm't Category: Aggressive Growth
- ✔ Domestic
- ✔ Foreign
- Asset Allocation
- Index
- Sector
- State Specific

Investment Style
Large-Cap Growth / Large-Cap Value
Mid-Cap Growth / Mid-Cap Value
Small-Cap Growth / Small-Cap Value

Portfolio
7.6% cash	0.0% corp bonds
92.4% stocks	0.0% gov't bonds
0.0% preferred	0.0% muni bonds
0.0% conv't/warrants	0.0% other

SHAREHOLDER INFORMATION

Minimum Investment
Initial: $2,500   Subsequent: $100

Minimum IRA Investment
Initial: $500   Subsequent: $100

Maximum Fees
Load: none   12b-1: 0.25%
Other: none

Distributions
Income: annual   Capital Gains: annual

Exchange Options
Number Per Year: 36   Fee: none
Telephone: yes (money market fund available)

Services
IRA, pension, auto exchange, auto invest, auto withdraw

Warburg Pincus Small Co Value (WPSVX)

335 Madison Ave.
15th Floor
New York, NY 10017
800-257-5614, 212-878-0600

Aggressive Growth

PERFORMANCE

	3yr Annual	5yr Annual	10yr Annual	Bull	Bear
Return (%)	na	na	na	na	na
Differ from Category (+/-)	na	na	na	na	na

Total Risk	Standard Deviation	Category Risk	Risk Index	Beta
na	na	na	na	na

	1996	1995	1994	1993	1992	1991	1990	1989	1988	1987
Return (%)	56.1	—	—	—	—	—	—	—	—	—
Differ from Category (+/-)	37.0	—	—	—	—	—	—	—	—	—
Return, Tax-Adjusted (%)	55.6	—	—	—	—	—	—	—	—	—

PER SHARE DATA

	1996	1995	1994	1993	1992	1991	1990	1989	1988	1987
Dividends, Net Income ($)	0.00	—	—	—	—	—	—	—	—	—
Distrib'ns, Cap Gain ($)	0.17	—	—	—	—	—	—	—	—	—
Net Asset Value ($)	15.44	—	—	—	—	—	—	—	—	—
Expense Ratio (%)	na	—	—	—	—	—	—	—	—	—
Yield (%)	0.00	—	—	—	—	—	—	—	—	—
Portfolio Turnover (%)	na	—	—	—	—	—	—	—	—	—
Total Assets (Millions $)	97	—	—	—	—	—	—	—	—	—

PORTFOLIO (as of 9/30/96)

Portfolio Manager: Elizabeth Dates - 1995

Investm't Category: Aggressive Growth

✔ Domestic	Index
✔ Foreign	Sector
Asset Allocation	State Specific

Investment Style

Large-Cap Growth	Large-Cap Value
Mid-Cap Growth	Mid-Cap Value
Small-Cap Growth	Small-Cap Value

Portfolio

10.4% cash	0.0% corp bonds
89.6% stocks	0.0% gov't bonds
0.0% preferred	0.0% muni bonds
0.0% conv't/warrants	0.0% other

SHAREHOLDER INFORMATION

Minimum Investment
Initial: $2,500   Subsequent: $100

Minimum IRA Investment
Initial: $500   Subsequent: $50

Maximum Fees
Load: none   12b-1: 0.25%
Other: none

Distributions
Income: annual   Capital Gains: annual

Exchange Options
Number Per Year: 36   Fee: none
Telephone: yes (money market fund available)

Services
IRA, pension, auto exchange, auto invest, auto withdraw

Wasatch Aggressive Equity (WAAEX)

Aggressive Growth

68 S. Main St.
Salt Lake City, UT 84101
800-551-1700, 801-533-0778

PERFORMANCE

fund inception date: 11/18/86

	3yr Annual	5yr Annual	10yr Annual	Bull	Bear
Return (%)	12.4	12.7	13.8	52.9	-9.6
Differ from Category (+/-)	-3.4 blw av	-2.6 blw av	-1.2 blw av	-18.2 blw av	1.0 av

Total Risk	Standard Deviation	Category Risk	Risk Index	Beta
high	13.0%	blw av	0.9	0.66

	1996	1995	1994	1993	1992	1991	1990	1989	1988	1987
Return (%)	5.1	28.1	5.4	22.4	4.7	50.4	7.8	32.0	-1.5	-4.9
Differ from Category (+/-)	-14.0	-6.2	5.4	3.1	-7.0	-1.7	13.2	3.6	-17.9	-2.5
Return, Tax-Adjusted (%)	3.6	27.3	3.2	20.3	3.6	47.5	7.8	32.0	-1.7	-7.9

PER SHARE DATA

	1996	1995	1994	1993	1992	1991	1990	1989	1988	1987
Dividends, Net Income ($)	0.00	0.00	0.00	0.00	0.00	0.72	0.00	0.00	0.04	0.01
Distrib'ns, Cap Gain ($)	1.22	0.54	1.51	1.22	0.66	0.18	0.00	0.00	0.00	1.04
Net Asset Value ($)	23.86	23.87	19.06	19.50	16.95	16.82	11.78	10.92	8.27	8.44
Expense Ratio (%)	1.50	1.47	1.50	1.50	1.51	1.51	1.56	1.50	1.50	1.26
Yield (%)	0.00	0.00	0.00	0.00	0.00	4.23	0.00	0.00	0.48	0.10
Portfolio Turnover (%)	73	29	64	70	32	41	74	82	71	58
Total Assets (Millions $)	218	294	55	29	15	9	3	1	0	0

PORTFOLIO (as of 9/30/96)

Portfolio Manager: Samuel S. Stewart Jr. - 1986

Investm't Category: Aggressive Growth
✔ Domestic	Index
✔ Foreign	Sector
Asset Allocation	State Specific

Investment Style
Large-Cap Growth	Large-Cap Value
Mid-Cap Growth	Mid-Cap Value
✔ Small-Cap Growth	Small-Cap Value

Portfolio
4.2% cash	0.0% corp bonds
94.4% stocks	0.0% gov't bonds
0.0% preferred	0.0% muni bonds
1.4% conv't/warrants	0.0% other

SHAREHOLDER INFORMATION

Minimum Investment
Initial: $2,000   Subsequent: $100

Minimum IRA Investment
Initial: $1,000   Subsequent: $100

Maximum Fees
Load: none   12b-1: none
Other: none

Distributions
Income: annual   Capital Gains: annual

Exchange Options
Number Per Year: 4   Fee: none
Telephone: yes (money market fund available)

Services
IRA, pension, auto invest, auto withdraw

Wasatch Growth
(WGROX)
Growth

68 S. Main St.
Salt Lake City, UT 84101
800-551-1700, 801-533-0778

PERFORMANCE   fund inception date: 11/18/86

	3yr Annual	5yr Annual	10yr Annual	Bull	Bear
Return (%)	18.8	14.3	14.1	86.1	-10.4
Differ from Category (+/-)	3.1 abv av	0.0 av	0.2 av	23.7 high	-3.7 low

Total Risk	Standard Deviation	Category Risk	Risk Index	Beta
abv av	11.3%	abv av	1.1	0.64

	1996	1995	1994	1993	1992	1991	1990	1989	1988	1987
Return (%)	16.5	40.4	2.6	11.1	4.7	40.8	10.3	24.8	3.1	-4.2
Differ from Category (+/-)	-3.6	10.1	2.9	-2.9	-7.1	4.8	16.4	-1.3	-15.0	-6.2
Return, Tax-Adjusted (%)	14.0	39.5	-4.7	8.5	3.4	37.9	7.0	24.3	2.6	-5.5

PER SHARE DATA

	1996	1995	1994	1993	1992	1991	1990	1989	1988	1987
Dividends, Net Income ($)	0.07	0.05	0.00	0.00	0.00	0.61	0.80	0.11	0.10	0.02
Distrib'ns, Cap Gain ($)	1.31	0.29	3.93	1.37	0.66	0.28	0.16	0.00	0.00	0.39
Net Asset Value ($)	17.19	15.96	11.61	15.14	14.90	14.87	11.20	11.02	8.92	8.75
Expense Ratio (%)	1.50	1.50	1.50	1.50	1.49	1.51	1.87	1.50	1.50	na
Yield (%)	0.37	0.30	0.00	0.00	0.00	4.02	7.04	0.99	1.12	0.21
Portfolio Turnover (%)	62	88	163	104	40	37	69	63	88	na
Total Assets (Millions $)	97	61	8	16	16	13	5	4	2	2

PORTFOLIO (as of 9/30/96)

Portfolio Manager: Sam S. Stewart, Jeff Cardon - 1986

Investm't Category: Growth
✔ Domestic   Index
✔ Foreign   Sector
  Asset Allocation   State Specific

Investment Style
  Large-Cap Growth   Large-Cap Value
  Mid-Cap Growth   Mid-Cap Value
✔ Small-Cap Growth   Small-Cap Value

Portfolio
  4.6% cash   0.0% corp bonds
  90.6% stocks   0.0% gov't bonds
  0.0% preferred   0.0% muni bonds
  2.7% conv't/warrants 2.1% other

SHAREHOLDER INFORMATION

Minimum Investment
Initial: $2,000   Subsequent: $100

Minimum IRA Investment
Initial: $1,000   Subsequent: $100

Maximum Fees
Load: none   12b-1: none
Other: none

Distributions
Income: annual   Capital Gains: annual

Exchange Options
Number Per Year: 4   Fee: none
Telephone: yes (money market fund available)

Services
IRA, pension, auto invest, auto withdraw

Wasatch Micro-Cap
(WMICX)
Aggressive Growth

68 S. Main St.
Salt Lake City, UT 84101
800-551-1700, 801-533-0778

PERFORMANCE

fund inception date: 6/19/95

	3yr Annual	5yr Annual	10yr Annual	Bull	Bear
Return (%)	na	na	na	na	na
Differ from Category (+/-)	na	na	na	na	na

Total Risk	Standard Deviation	Category Risk	Risk Index	Beta
na	na	na	na	na

	1996	1995	1994	1993	1992	1991	1990	1989	1988	1987
Return (%)	13.6	—	—	—	—	—	—	—	—	—
Differ from Category (+/-)	-5.5	—	—	—	—	—	—	—	—	—
Return, Tax-Adjusted (%)	11.8	—	—	—	—	—	—	—	—	—

PER SHARE DATA

	1996	1995	1994	1993	1992	1991	1990	1989	1988	1987
Dividends, Net Income ($)	0.00	—	—	—	—	—	—	—	—	—
Distrib'ns, Cap Gain ($)	0.18	—	—	—	—	—	—	—	—	—
Net Asset Value ($)	3.03	—	—	—	—	—	—	—	—	—
Expense Ratio (%)	2.50	—	—	—	—	—	—	—	—	—
Yield (%)	0.00	—	—	—	—	—	—	—	—	—
Portfolio Turnover (%)	84	—	—	—	—	—	—	—	—	—
Total Assets (Millions $)	79	—	—	—	—	—	—	—	—	—

PORTFOLIO (as of 9/30/96)

Portfolio Manager: Sam Stewart Jr., Robert Gardiner - 1995

Investm't Category: Aggressive Growth
- ✔ Domestic
- ✔ Foreign
-   Asset Allocation
-   Index
-   Sector
-   State Specific

Investment Style
- Large-Cap Growth
- Mid-Cap Growth
- Small-Cap Growth
- Large-Cap Value
- Mid-Cap Value
- Small-Cap Value

Portfolio
8.7% cash	0.0% corp bonds
90.3% stocks	0.0% gov't bonds
0.0% preferred	0.0% muni bonds
0.0% conv't/warrants	1.0% other

SHAREHOLDER INFORMATION

Minimum Investment
Initial: $2,000   Subsequent: $100

Minimum IRA Investment
Initial: $1,000   Subsequent: $100

Maximum Fees
Load: none   12b-1: none
Other: none

Distributions
Income: annual   Capital Gains: annual

Exchange Options
Number Per Year: 4   Fee: none
Telephone: yes (money market fund available)

Services
IRA, pension, auto invest, auto withdraw

Wasatch Mid-Cap

(WAMCX)

Aggressive Growth

68 S. Main St.
Salt Lake City, UT 84101
800-551-1700, 801-533-0778

PERFORMANCE

fund inception date: 8/24/92

	3yr Annual	5yr Annual	10yr Annual	Bull	Bear
Return (%)	21.1	na	na	94.5	-12.6
Differ from Category (+/-)	5.3 high	na	na	23.4 high	-2.0 blw av

Total Risk	Standard Deviation	Category Risk	Risk Index	Beta
high	19.2%	high	1.3	1.12

	1996	1995	1994	1993	1992	1991	1990	1989	1988	1987
Return (%).	3.5	58.7	8.1	-3.0	—	—	—	—	—	—
Differ from Category (+/-)	-15.6	24.4	8.1	-22.3	—	—	—	—	—	—
Return, Tax-Adjusted (%). . .	3.5	58.2	8.0	-3.0	—	—	—	—	—	—

PER SHARE DATA

	1996	1995	1994	1993	1992	1991	1990	1989	1988	1987
Dividends, Net Income ($).	0.00	0.00	0.00	0.00	—	—	—	—	—	—
Distrib'ns, Cap Gain ($) . . .	0.00	0.18	0.02	0.00	—	—	—	—	—	—
Net Asset Value ($)	18.94	18.29	11.64	10.79	—	—	—	—	—	—
Expense Ratio (%).	1.75	1.75	1.75	1.74	—	—	—	—	—	—
Yield (%)	0.00	0.00	0.00	0.00	—	—	—	—	—	—
Portfolio Turnover (%). . . .	121	46	213	113	—	—	—	—	—	—
Total Assets (Millions $). . .	105	130	1	1	—	—	—	—	—	—

PORTFOLIO (as of 9/30/96)

Portfolio Manager: Sam S. Stewart, Karey Barker - 1992

Investm't Category: Aggressive Growth
- ✔ Domestic
- ✔ Foreign
- Asset Allocation
- Index
- Sector
- State Specific

Investment Style
- Large-Cap Growth
- ✔ Mid-Cap Growth
- ✔ Small-Cap Growth
- Large-Cap Value
- Mid-Cap Value
- Small-Cap Value

Portfolio
3.1% cash	0.0% corp bonds
97.4% stocks	0.0% gov't bonds
0.0% preferred	0.0% muni bonds
0.0% conv't/warrants	0.0% other

SHAREHOLDER INFORMATION

Minimum Investment
Initial: $2,000   Subsequent: $100

Minimum IRA Investment
Initial: $1,000   Subsequent: $100

Maximum Fees
Load: none   12b-1: none
Other: none

Distributions
Income: annual   Capital Gains: annual

Exchange Options
Number Per Year: 4   Fee: none
Telephone: yes (money market fund available)

Services
IRA, pension, auto invest, auto withdraw

Wayne Hummer Growth
(WHGRX)
Growth

300 S. Wacker Drive
Chicago, IL 60606
800-621-4477, 312-431-1700

fund inception date: 12/30/83

	3yr Annual	5yr Annual	10yr Annual	Bull	Bear
Return (%)	11.4	9.6	11.9	45.5	-6.9
Differ from Category (+/-)	-4.3 low	-4.7 low	-2.0 low	-16.9 low	-0.2 av

Total Risk	Standard Deviation	Category Risk	Risk Index	Beta
av	9.5%	blw av	0.9	0.82

	1996	1995	1994	1993	1992	1991	1990	1989	1988	1987
Return (%)	11.8	24.8	-1.0	3.5	10.3	28.8	5.0	24.0	7.0	9.2
Differ from Category (+/-)	-8.3	-5.5	-0.7	-10.5	-1.5	-7.2	11.1	-2.1	-11.1	7.2
Return, Tax-Adjusted (%)	10.2	23.5	-1.9	2.8	9.5	27.5	2.6	22.6	5.9	6.0

PER SHARE DATA

	1996	1995	1994	1993	1992	1991	1990	1989	1988	1987
Dividends, Net Income ($)	0.28	0.31	0.30	0.31	0.28	0.38	0.44	0.23	0.24	0.23
Distrib'ns, Cap Gain ($)	1.00	0.48	0.21	0.03	0.14	0.16	0.75	0.36	0.16	1.19
Net Asset Value ($)	27.50	25.81	21.34	22.06	21.64	20.02	16.00	16.41	13.74	13.22
Expense Ratio (%)	1.06	1.07	1.07	1.12	1.23	1.36	1.50	1.50	1.50	1.50
Yield (%)	0.98	1.17	1.39	1.40	1.28	1.88	2.62	1.37	1.72	1.59
Portfolio Turnover (%)	6	3	2	1	3	13	3	12	10	28
Total Assets (Millions $)	101	100	87	98	79	50	26	24	20	18

PORTFOLIO (as of 9/30/96)

Portfolio Manager: Tom Rouland - 1987

Investm't Category: Growth
- ✔ Domestic
- Foreign
- Asset Allocation
- Index
- Sector
- State Specific

Investment Style
- Large-Cap Growth
- Mid-Cap Growth
- Small-Cap Growth
- Large-Cap Value
- ✔ Mid-Cap Value
- Small-Cap Value

Portfolio
0.0% cash	0.0% corp bonds
98.9% stocks	1.1% gov't bonds
0.0% preferred	0.0% muni bonds
0.0% conv't/warrants	0.0% other

SHAREHOLDER INFORMATION

Minimum Investment
Initial: $1,000   Subsequent: $500

Minimum IRA Investment
Initial: $500   Subsequent: $200

Maximum Fees
Load: none   12b-1: none
Other: none

Distributions
Income: quarterly   Capital Gains: Apr, Dec

Exchange Options
Number Per Year: no limit   Fee: none
Telephone: yes (money market fund available)

Services
IRA, pension, auto invest

Wayne Hummer Income

(WHICX)

Corporate Bond

300 S. Wacker Drive
Chicago, IL 60606
800-621-4477, 312-431-1700

PERFORMANCE

fund inception date: 12/1/92

	3yr Annual	5yr Annual	10yr Annual	Bull	Bear
Return (%)	5.2	na	na	20.7	-5.0
Differ from Category (+/-)	-1.1 blw av	na	na	-4.1 av	0.1 av

Total Risk	Standard Deviation	Category Risk	Risk Index	Avg Mat
low	4.1%	av	0.9	11.9 yrs

	1996	1995	1994	1993	1992	1991	1990	1989	1988	1987
Return (%)	3.5	15.5	-2.6	10.7	—	—	—	—	—	—
Differ from Category (+/-)	-1.7	-2.5	0.5	-1.1	—	—	—	—	—	—
Return, Tax-Adjusted (%)	1.1	12.6	-5.1	8.1	—	—	—	—	—	—

PER SHARE DATA

	1996	1995	1994	1993	1992	1991	1990	1989	1988	1987
Dividends, Net Income ($)	0.93	1.01	0.95	0.93	—	—	—	—	—	—
Distrib'ns, Cap Gain ($)	0.00	0.00	0.00	0.04	—	—	—	—	—	—
Net Asset Value ($)	14.98	15.41	14.27	15.62	—	—	—	—	—	—
Expense Ratio (%)	0.91	0.94	1.13	1.39	—	—	—	—	—	—
Yield (%)	6.20	6.55	6.65	5.93	—	—	—	—	—	—
Portfolio Turnover (%)	46	32	86	141	—	—	—	—	—	—
Total Assets (Millions $)	24	26	25	36	—	—	—	—	—	—

PORTFOLIO (as of 9/30/96)

Portfolio Manager: David Poitras - 1992

Investm't Category: Corporate Bond

✔ Domestic	Index
Foreign	Sector
Asset Allocation	State Specific

Investment Style

Large-Cap Growth	Large-Cap Value
Mid-Cap Growth	Mid-Cap Value
Small-Cap Growth	Small-Cap Value

Portfolio

1.8% cash	62.6% corp bonds
0.0% stocks	35.6% gov't bonds
0.0% preferred	0.0% muni bonds
0.0% conv't/warrants	0.0% other

SHAREHOLDER INFORMATION

Minimum Investment
Initial: $2,500   Subsequent: $1,000

Minimum IRA Investment
Initial: $2,000   Subsequent: $500

Maximum Fees
Load: none   12b-1: none
Other: none

Distributions
Income: monthly   Capital Gains: Apr, Dec

Exchange Options
Number Per Year: no limit   Fee: none
Telephone: yes (money market fund available)

Services
IRA, pension, auto invest

Weitz Series Value Port

(WVALX)

Growth

One Pacific Place Suite 600
1125 S. 103 St.
Omaha, NE 68124
800-232-4161, 402-391-1980

PERFORMANCE   fund inception date: 5/9/86

	3yr Annual	5yr Annual	10yr Annual	Bull	Bear
Return (%)	13.9	15.0	13.1	57.2	-6.8
Differ from Category (+/-)	-1.8 blw av	0.7 abv av	-0.8 blw av	-5.2 av	-0.1 av

Total Risk	Standard Deviation	Category Risk	Risk Index	Beta
abv av	9.8%	av	0.9	0.83

	1996	1995	1994	1993	1992	1991	1990	1989	1988	1987
Return (%)	18.7	38.3	-9.9	19.9	13.5	27.6	-5.3	22.1	16.4	-0.7
Differ from Category (+/-)	-1.4	8.0	-9.6	5.9	1.7	-8.4	0.8	-4.0	-1.7	-2.7
Return, Tax-Adjusted (%)	16.7	35.0	-11.1	18.7	11.5	25.4	-6.7	19.0	15.1	-2.9

PER SHARE DATA

	1996	1995	1994	1993	1992	1991	1990	1989	1988	1987
Dividends, Net Income ($)	0.12	0.41	0.02	0.02	0.27	0.32	0.37	0.42	0.31	0.48
Distrib'ns, Cap Gain ($)	1.10	1.08	0.69	0.58	0.54	0.39	0.06	0.62	0.00	0.11
Net Asset Value ($)	20.59	18.38	14.43	16.80	14.54	13.58	11.22	12.31	10.97	9.70
Expense Ratio (%)	1.35	1.42	1.41	1.35	1.40	1.49	1.46	1.50	1.50	1.50
Yield (%)	0.55	2.10	0.13	0.11	1.79	2.29	3.28	3.24	2.82	4.89
Portfolio Turnover (%)	40	28	23	23	35	28	49	25	67	54
Total Assets (Millions $)	259	149	107	106	49	32	23	24	11	8

PORTFOLIO (as of 9/30/96)

Portfolio Manager: Wallace R. Weitz - 1986

Investm't Category: Growth

✔ Domestic	Index
Foreign	Sector
Asset Allocation	State Specific

Investment Style

Large-Cap Growth	Large-Cap Value
Mid-Cap Growth	✔ Mid-Cap Value
Small-Cap Growth	Small-Cap Value

Portfolio

5.5% cash	0.6% corp bonds
86.8% stocks	5.6% gov't bonds
1.5% preferred	0.0% muni bonds
0.0% conv't/warrants	0.0% other

SHAREHOLDER INFORMATION

Minimum Investment
Initial: $25,000   Subsequent: $1

Minimum IRA Investment
Initial: $2,000   Subsequent: $1

Maximum Fees
Load: none   12b-1: none
Other: none

Distributions
Income: na   Capital Gains: annual

Exchange Options
Number Per Year: no limit   Fee: none
Telephone: yes (money market fund not available)

Services
IRA, pension, auto invest

Weston Century Capital Port (NCCPX)

Growth

Wellesley Office Park
20 William
Wellesley, MA 02181
617-239-0445

PERFORMANCE

fund inception date: 1/31/89

	3yr Annual	5yr Annual	10yr Annual	Bull	Bear
Return (%)	13.6	10.9	na	51.1	-6.6
Differ from Category (+/-)	-2.1 blw av	-3.4 low	na	-11.3 blw av	0.1 av

Total Risk	Standard Deviation	Category Risk	Risk Index	Beta
abv av	9.8%	av	0.9	0.89

	1996	1995	1994	1993	1992	1991	1990	1989	1988	1987
Return (%)	14.5	28.0	0.0	13.8	0.5	36.4	-4.8	—	—	—
Differ from Category (+/-)	-5.6	-2.3	0.3	-0.2	-11.3	0.4	1.3	—	—	—
Return, Tax-Adjusted (%)	11.5	24.7	-2.4	13.8	-3.4	35.2	-5.5	—	—	—

PER SHARE DATA

	1996	1995	1994	1993	1992	1991	1990	1989	1988	1987
Dividends, Net Income ($)	0.08	0.28	0.22	0.00	0.16	0.11	0.17	—	—	—
Distrib'ns, Cap Gain ($)	1.33	1.01	0.76	0.00	1.56	0.26	0.00	—	—	—
Net Asset Value ($)	13.99	13.63	11.94	12.93	11.36	13.02	9.82	—	—	—
Expense Ratio (%)	na	1.61	1.60	1.54	1.58	1.76	1.90	—	—	—
Yield (%)	0.52	1.91	1.73	0.00	1.23	0.82	1.73	—	—	—
Portfolio Turnover (%)	na	206	107	133	224	156	286	—	—	—
Total Assets (Millions $)	65	51	36	38	32	39	40	—	—	—

PORTFOLIO (as of 9/30/96)

Portfolio Manager: Wayne Grzecki - 1995

Investm't Category: Growth

✔ Domestic	Index
✔ Foreign	Sector
Asset Allocation	State Specific

Investment Style

Large-Cap Growth	Large-Cap Value
✔ Mid-Cap Growth	Mid-Cap Value
✔ Small-Cap Growth	Small-Cap Value

Portfolio

0.0% cash	0.0% corp bonds
0.0% stocks	0.0% gov't bonds
0.0% preferred	0.0% muni bonds
0.0% conv't/warrants	100.0% other

SHAREHOLDER INFORMATION

Minimum Investment
Initial: $5,000   Subsequent: $100

Minimum IRA Investment
Initial: $1,000   Subsequent: $100

Maximum Fees
Load: none   12b-1: 0.25%
Other: none

Distributions
Income: annual   Capital Gains: annual

Exchange Options
Number Per Year: no limit   Fee: none
Telephone: yes (money market fund not available)

Services
IRA, pension, auto invest, auto withdraw

Weston Century I Port

(NCIPX)

Balanced

Wellesley Office Park
20 William
Wellesley, MA 02181
617-239-0445

	3yr Annual	5yr Annual	10yr Annual	Bull	Bear
Return (%)	10.3	9.7	na	39.2	-6.3
Differ from Category (+/-)	-1.4 blw av	-1.7 blw av	na	-5.9 blw av	-0.6 blw av

Total Risk	Standard Deviation	Category Risk	Risk Index	Beta
blw av	6.7%	blw av	1.0	0.65

	1996	1995	1994	1993	1992	1991	1990	1989	1988	1987
Return (%)	12.0	22.8	-2.5	15.5	2.8	22.8	-0.8	—	—	—
Differ from Category (+/-)	-2.2	-1.8	-0.9	1.1	-6.1	-1.3	0.1	—	—	—
Return, Tax-Adjusted (%)	9.3	20.1	-4.9	14.6	-0.9	21.1	-2.6	—	—	—

PER SHARE DATA

	1996	1995	1994	1993	1992	1991	1990	1989	1988	1987
Dividends, Net Income ($)	0.27	0.34	0.39	0.23	0.37	0.37	0.45	—	—	—
Distrib'ns, Cap Gain ($)	0.80	0.57	0.47	0.00	1.00	0.05	0.00	—	—	—
Net Asset Value ($)	12.61	12.32	10.94	12.08	10.67	11.72	9.92	—	—	—
Expense Ratio (%)	na	1.72	1.60	1.54	1.58	1.76	1.90	—	—	—
Yield (%)	2.01	2.63	3.41	1.90	3.17	3.14	4.53	—	—	—
Portfolio Turnover (%)	na	191	107	133	224	156	286	—	—	—
Total Assets (Millions $)	41	31	22	23	17	19	18	—	—	—

PORTFOLIO (as of 9/30/96)

Portfolio Manager: Wayne Grzecki - 1995

Investm't Category: Balanced
- ✔ Domestic
- ✔ Foreign
- ✔ Asset Allocation
- Index
- Sector
- State Specific

Investment Style
- Large-Cap Growth
- Mid-Cap Growth
- Small-Cap Growth
- Large-Cap Value
- Mid-Cap Value
- Small-Cap Value

Portfolio
0.0% cash	0.0% corp bonds
0.0% stocks	0.0% gov't bonds
0.0% preferred	0.0% muni bonds
0.0% conv't/warrants	100.0% other

SHAREHOLDER INFORMATION

Minimum Investment
Initial: $5,000   Subsequent: $100

Minimum IRA Investment
Initial: $1,000   Subsequent: $100

Maximum Fees
Load: none   12b-1: 0.25%
Other: none

Distributions
Income: quarterly   Capital Gains: annual

Exchange Options
Number Per Year: no limit   Fee: none
Telephone: yes (money market fund not available)

Services
IRA, pension, auto invest, auto withdraw

William Blair Mutual Fds: Growth (WBGSX)

Growth

222 W. Adams
Chicago, IL 60606
800-742-7272, 312-364-8000
www.wmblair.com

PERFORMANCE

fund inception date: 3/20/46

	3yr Annual	5yr Annual	10yr Annual	Bull	Bear
Return (%)	17.4	15.0	15.7	66.8	-5.3
Differ from Category (+/-)	1.7 abv av	0.7 abv av	1.8 high	4.4 abv av	1.4 abv av

Total Risk	Standard Deviation	Category Risk	Risk Index	Beta
abv av	11.3%	abv av	1.1	0.92

	1996	1995	1994	1993	1992	1991	1990	1989	1988	1987
Return (%)	17.9	29.1	6.4	15.5	7.6	44.3	-2.1	30.4	7.1	7.9
Differ from Category (+/-)	-2.2	-1.2	6.7	1.5	-4.2	8.3	4.0	4.3	-11.0	5.9
Return, Tax-Adjusted (%)	16.5	27.6	4.2	12.2	5.1	42.0	-4.9	22.0	3.6	3.1

PER SHARE DATA

	1996	1995	1994	1993	1992	1991	1990	1989	1988	1987
Dividends, Net Income ($)	0.01	0.03	0.02	0.03	0.04	0.07	0.13	0.13	0.16	0.13
Distrib'ns, Cap Gain ($)	0.54	0.45	0.71	1.04	0.76	0.45	0.58	2.14	0.79	1.37
Net Asset Value ($)	13.48	11.90	9.60	9.73	9.39	9.49	6.97	7.84	7.81	8.21
Expense Ratio (%)	na	0.65	0.71	0.78	0.83	0.90	0.87	0.91	0.92	0.87
Yield (%)	0.07	0.24	0.19	0.27	0.39	0.70	1.72	1.30	1.86	1.35
Portfolio Turnover (%)	na	32	46	55	27	33	34	45	18	22
Total Assets (Millions $)	509	362	182	149	111	91	62	67	59	66

PORTFOLIO (as of 9/30/96)

Portfolio Manager: James Barber, Mark Fuller III - 1993

Investm't Category: Growth
- ✔ Domestic
- Foreign
- Asset Allocation
- Index
- Sector
- State Specific

Investment Style
- Large-Cap Growth
- ✔ Mid-Cap Growth
- Small-Cap Growth
- Large-Cap Value
- Mid-Cap Value
- Small-Cap Value

Portfolio
3.3% cash	0.0% corp bonds
96.7% stocks	0.0% gov't bonds
0.0% preferred	0.0% muni bonds
0.0% conv't/warrants	0.0% other

SHAREHOLDER INFORMATION

Minimum Investment
Initial: $5,000   Subsequent: $1,000

Minimum IRA Investment
Initial: $2,000   Subsequent: $1,000

Maximum Fees
Load: none   12b-1: none
Other: none

Distributions
Income: Jul, Dec   Capital Gains: Dec

Exchange Options
Number Per Year: 4   Fee: none
Telephone: yes (money market fund available)

Services
IRA, pension, auto invest, auto withdraw

William Blair Mutual Fds: Income (WBRRX)

General Bond

222 W. Adams
Chicago, IL 60606
800-742-7272, 312-364-8000
www.wmblair.com

PERFORMANCE

fund inception date: 9/25/90

	3yr Annual	5yr Annual	10yr Annual	Bull	Bear
Return (%)	5.3	6.2	na	19.5	-3.0
Differ from Category (+/-)	0.2 av	0.1 av	na	-0.8 av	1.2 abv av

Total Risk	Standard Deviation	Category Risk	Risk Index	Avg Mat
low	3.0%	blw av	0.8	4.0 yrs

	1996	1995	1994	1993	1992	1991	1990	1989	1988	1987
Return (%)	3.0	14.3	-0.8	7.8	7.1	18.0	—	—	—	—
Differ from Category (+/-)	-0.9	-0.6	1.5	-1.3	0.6	3.3	—	—	—	—
Return, Tax-Adjusted (%)	0.7	11.6	-3.2	4.9	3.8	13.6	—	—	—	—

PER SHARE DATA

	1996	1995	1994	1993	1992	1991	1990	1989	1988	1987
Dividends, Net Income ($)	0.61	0.65	0.64	0.66	0.82	1.01	—	—	—	—
Distrib'ns, Cap Gain ($)	0.00	0.00	0.00	0.16	0.08	0.14	—	—	—	—
Net Asset Value ($)	10.27	10.57	9.85	10.58	10.60	10.77	—	—	—	—
Expense Ratio (%)	na	0.68	0.68	0.70	0.88	0.92	—	—	—	—
Yield (%)	5.93	6.14	6.49	6.14	7.67	9.25	—	—	—	—
Portfolio Turnover (%)	na	54	63	114	47	64	—	—	—	—
Total Assets (Millions $)	151	147	143	205	136	83	—	—	—	—

PORTFOLIO (as of 9/30/96)

Portfolio Manager: Bentley Myer - 1993

Investm't Category: General Bond
- ✔ Domestic
- Foreign
- Asset Allocation
- Index
- Sector
- State Specific

Investment Style
- Large-Cap Growth
- Mid-Cap Growth
- Small-Cap Growth
- Large-Cap Value
- Mid-Cap Value
- Small-Cap Value

Portfolio
21.0% cash	0.0% corp bonds	
0.0% stocks	56.2% gov't bonds	
0.0% preferred	0.0% muni bonds	
0.0% conv't/warrants	22.8% other	

SHAREHOLDER INFORMATION

Minimum Investment
Initial: $5,000   Subsequent: $1,000

Minimum IRA Investment
Initial: $2,000   Subsequent: $1,000

Maximum Fees
Load: none   12b-1: none
Other: none

Distributions
Income: monthly   Capital Gains: Dec

Exchange Options
Number Per Year: 4   Fee: none
Telephone: yes (money market fund available)

Services
IRA, pension, auto invest, auto withdraw

William Blair Mutual Fds: Int'l Growth (WBIGX)

222 W. Adams
Chicago, IL 60606
800-742-7272, 312-364-8000
www.wmblair.com

International Stock

PERFORMANCE

fund inception date: 10/1/92

	3yr Annual	5yr Annual	10yr Annual	Bull	Bear
Return (%)	5.7	na	na	14.5	-3.1
Differ from Category (+/-)	-0.6 blw av	na	na	-9.8 blw av	4.1 high

Total Risk	Standard Deviation	Category Risk	Risk Index	Beta
av	9.2%	low	0.9	0.55

	1996	1995	1994	1993	1992	1991	1990	1989	1988	1987
Return (%)	10.2	7.2	-0.1	33.8	—	—	—	—	—	—
Differ from Category (+/-)	-4.6	-1.9	3.0	-5.8	—	—	—	—	—	—
Return, Tax-Adjusted (%)	9.1	6.7	-1.9	32.7	—	—	—	—	—	—

PER SHARE DATA

	1996	1995	1994	1993	1992	1991	1990	1989	1988	1987
Dividends, Net Income ($)	0.06	0.13	0.02	0.03	—	—	—	—	—	—
Distrib'ns, Cap Gain ($)	0.42	0.00	0.78	0.32	—	—	—	—	—	—
Net Asset Value ($)	13.95	13.12	12.36	13.18	—	—	—	—	—	—
Expense Ratio (%)	na	1.48	1.51	1.71	—	—	—	—	—	—
Yield (%)	0.41	0.99	0.15	0.22	—	—	—	—	—	—
Portfolio Turnover (%)	na	77	40	83	—	—	—	—	—	—
Total Assets (Millions $)	104	89	71	40	—	—	—	—	—	—

PORTFOLIO (as of 9/30/96)

Portfolio Manager: George Greig - 1996

Investm't Category: International Stock
Domestic	Index
✔ Foreign	Sector
Asset Allocation	State Specific

Investment Style
Large-Cap Growth	Large-Cap Value
Mid-Cap Growth	Mid-Cap Value
Small-Cap Growth	Small-Cap Value

Portfolio
4.6% cash	0.0% corp bonds
88.1% stocks	0.0% gov't bonds
4.0% preferred	0.0% muni bonds
0.0% conv't/warrants	3.3% other

SHAREHOLDER INFORMATION

Minimum Investment
Initial: $5,000   Subsequent: $1,000

Minimum IRA Investment
Initial: $2,000   Subsequent: $1,000

Maximum Fees
Load: none   12b-1: none
Other: none

Distributions
Income: Dec   Capital Gains: Dec

Exchange Options
Number Per Year: 4   Fee: none
Telephone: yes (money market fund available)

Services
IRA, pension, auto invest, auto withdraw

World Fds: Vontobel Europacific (VNEPX)

International Stock

1500 Forest Ave.
Suite 223
Richmond, VA 23229
800-527-9500, 804-285-8211

PERFORMANCE

fund inception date: 1/1/85

	3yr Annual	5yr Annual	10yr Annual	Bull	Bear
Return (%)	7.0	11.0	na	29.3	-9.8
Differ from Category (+/-)	0.7 av	1.0 av	na	5.0 abv av	-2.6 blw av

Total Risk	Standard Deviation	Category Risk	Risk Index	Beta
abv av	10.9%	abv av	1.1	0.78

	1996	1995	1994	1993	1992	1991	1990	1989	1988	1987
Return (%)	16.9	10.8	-5.4	40.8	-2.4	18.7	-12.5	10.6	7.6	—
Differ from Category (+/-)	2.1	1.7	-2.3	1.2	1.4	5.5	-2.4	-12.0	-7.3	—
Return, Tax-Adjusted (%)	13.5	9.1	-5.6	40.8	-2.9	18.7	-12.7	10.4	7.3	—

PER SHARE DATA

	1996	1995	1994	1993	1992	1991	1990	1989	1988	1987
Dividends, Net Income ($)	0.60	0.17	0.08	0.00	0.14	0.00	0.05	0.05	0.06	—
Distrib'ns, Cap Gain ($)	1.19	0.70	0.00	0.00	0.00	0.00	0.00	0.00	0.00	—
Net Asset Value ($)	18.22	17.13	16.23	17.22	12.23	12.67	10.67	12.24	11.11	—
Expense Ratio (%)	na	1.53	1.54	1.77	1.98	2.71	2.76	3.00	2.99	—
Yield (%)	3.09	0.95	0.49	0.00	1.14	0.00	0.46	0.40	0.54	—
Portfolio Turnover (%)	na	68	34	10	27	3	61	85	19	—
Total Assets (Millions $)	149	129	138	136	47	25	10	2	2	—

PORTFOLIO (as of 9/30/96)

Portfolio Manager: Fabrizio Pierallini - 1994

Investm't Category: International Stock

Domestic	Index
✔ Foreign	Sector
Asset Allocation	State Specific

Investment Style

Large-Cap Growth	Large-Cap Value
Mid-Cap Growth	Mid-Cap Value
Small-Cap Growth	Small-Cap Value

Portfolio

3.7% cash	0.0% corp bonds
96.3% stocks	0.0% gov't bonds
0.0% preferred	0.0% muni bonds
0.0% conv't/warrants	0.0% other

SHAREHOLDER INFORMATION

Minimum Investment
Initial: $1,000   Subsequent: $50

Minimum IRA Investment
Initial: $1,000   Subsequent: $50

Maximum Fees
Load: none   12b-1: none
Other: none

Distributions
Income: annual   Capital Gains: annual

Exchange Options
Number Per Year: no limit   Fee: none
Telephone: yes (money market fund not available)

Services
IRA, auto invest, auto withdraw

World Fds: Vontobel US Value (VUSVX)

Growth

1500 Forest Ave.
Suite 223
Richmond, VA 23229
800-527-9500, 804-285-8211

PERFORMANCE

fund inception date: 3/30/90

	3yr Annual	5yr Annual	10yr Annual	Bull	Bear
Return (%)	19.4	15.9	na	69.5	-2.8
Differ from Category (+/-)	3.7 high	1.6 abv av	na	7.1 abv av	3.9 high

Total Risk	Standard Deviation	Category Risk	Risk Index	Beta
av	9.3%	blw av	0.9	0.83

	1996	1995	1994	1993	1992	1991	1990	1989	1988	1987
Return (%)	21.2	40.3	0.0	6.0	15.9	37.2	—	—	—	—
Differ from Category (+/-)	1.1	10.0	0.3	-8.0	4.1	1.2	—	—	—	—
Return, Tax-Adjusted (%)	16.1	37.1	-5.6	5.7	12.8	34.5	—	—	—	—

PER SHARE DATA

	1996	1995	1994	1993	1992	1991	1990	1989	1988	1987
Dividends, Net Income ($)	0.21	0.04	0.25	0.08	0.17	0.06	—	—	—	—
Distrib'ns, Cap Gain ($)	2.08	1.11	2.14	0.00	0.99	0.74	—	—	—	—
Net Asset Value ($)	13.78	13.25	10.26	12.64	12.00	11.36	—	—	—	—
Expense Ratio (%)	na	1.50	1.62	1.82	1.96	2.54	—	—	—	—
Yield (%)	1.32	0.27	2.01	0.63	1.30	0.49	—	—	—	—
Portfolio Turnover (%)	na	95	98	137	100	166	—	—	—	—
Total Assets (Millions $)	69	54	30	34	31	21	—	—	—	—

PORTFOLIO (as of 9/30/96)

Portfolio Manager: Edwin Walczak - 1990

Investm't Category: Growth
- ✔ Domestic
- Foreign
- Asset Allocation
- Index
- Sector
- State Specific

Investment Style
- Large-Cap Growth
- Mid-Cap Growth
- Small-Cap Growth
- ✔ Large-Cap Value
- Mid-Cap Value
- Small-Cap Value

Portfolio

6.8% cash	0.0% corp bonds
70.9% stocks	0.0% gov't bonds
0.0% preferred	0.0% muni bonds
0.0% conv't/warrants	22.3% other

SHAREHOLDER INFORMATION

Minimum Investment
Initial: $1,000   Subsequent: $50

Minimum IRA Investment
Initial: $1,000   Subsequent: $50

Maximum Fees
Load: none   12b-1: none
Other: none

Distributions
Income: annual   Capital Gains: annual

Exchange Options
Number Per Year: no limit   Fee: none
Telephone: yes (money market fund not available)

Services
IRA, auto invest, auto withdraw

Yacktman (YACKX)

Growth

303 W. Madison St.
Chicago, IL 60606
800-525-8258, 312-201-9480

Appendix A
Special Types of Funds

ASSET ALLOCATION FUNDS
BB&K Diversa
Berwyn Income
Blanchard Global Growth
CGM Mutual
Columbia Balanced
Crabbe Huson Asset Allocation—Prim
Dreyfus Asset Allocation Total Return
Fidelity Asset Manager
Fidelity Asset Manager: Growth
Fidelity Asset Manager: Income
Fidelity Balanced
Fidelity Global Balanced
Flex Muirfield Fd
Fremont Global
Hotchkis & Wiley Balanced Income
IAI Balanced
INVESCO Industrial Income
INVESCO Value Trust: Total Return
Jurika & Voyles Balanced /J
Maxus Equity
Maxus Income
Montgomery Asset Allocation—R
Northeast Investors Trust
Permanent Portfolio
Preferred Asset Allocation
Schwab Asset Director: Balanced Growth
Schwab Asset Director: High Growth
SteinRoe Balanced
Strong Asset Allocation
T. Rowe Price Personal Strat Fds: Bal
T. Rowe Price Personal Strat Fds: Inc
T. Rowe Price Spectrum: Income
USAA Invest Trust: Cornerstone Strategy
USAA Invest Trust: Growth & Tax Strategy
USAA Invest Trust: Growth Strategy
Value Line Asset Allocation
Value Line Income

Vanguard Asset Allocation
Vanguard Horizon Fd: Global Asset Alloc
Vanguard LifeStrategy: Conservative Grth
Vanguard LifeStrategy: Growth Port
Vanguard LifeStrategy: Income Port
Vanguard LifeStrategy: Moderate Grth
Vanguard Tax Managed Balanced Port
Weston Century I Port

FUNDS INVESTING IN FUNDS

API Trust: Growth
Flex Muirfield Fd
Markman Moderate Growth
Rightime Fund
T. Rowe Price Spectrum: Growth
T. Rowe Price Spectrum: Income
Vanguard LifeStrategy: Conservative Grth
Vanguard LifeStrategy: Growth Port
Vanguard LifeStrategy: Income Port
Vanguard LifeStrategy: Moderate Grth
Vanguard STAR
Weston Century Capital Port
Weston Century I Port

GLOBAL FUNDS

American Century Glbl Natural Resources
Blanchard Global Growth
Bull & Bear Global Income
Columbia Int'l Stock
Dreyfus Global Growth
Fidelity Global Balanced
Fidelity Global Bond
Fidelity Int'l Growth & Income
Fidelity Worldwide
Founders Worldwide Growth
Fremont Global
Gabelli Global Telecommunications
INVESCO Worldwide Communications
Janus Worldwide
Legg Mason Global Gov't Trust/Prim
Lexington Global
Lexington Ramirez Global Income
Lexington Worldwide Emerging Mkts
Loomis Sayles Global Bond
Montgomery Global Communications
Montgomery Global Opportunities

Montgomery Select 50—R
Payden & Rygel Global Fixed Income—A
Robertson Stephens Contrarian
Robertson Stephens Glbl Low Priced Stk
Robertson Stephens Glbl Natrl Res
Scout Worldwide
Scudder Global
Scudder Global Bond
Scudder Global Discovery
Strong Short-Term Global Bond
T. Rowe Price Int'l: Global Gov't Bd
Tweedy Browne Global Value
USAA Invest Trust: World Growth
Vanguard Horizon Fd: Global Asset Alloc
Vanguard Horizon Fd: Global Equity
Warburg Pincus Global Fixed Income

INDEX MUTUAL FUNDS

American Gas Index
Dreyfus Midcap Index
Dreyfus S&P 500 Index
Fidelity Market Index
Galaxy II: Large Co Index
Galaxy II: Small Co Index
Galaxy II: US Treasury Index—Retail
Galaxy II: Utility Index
Schwab 1000
Schwab Capital Trust: Int'l Index
Schwab Capital Trust: Small Cap Index
SSgA: S&P 500 Index
T. Rowe Price Equity Index
Vanguard Balanced Index
Vanguard Bond Index Interm-Term Bond
Vanguard Bond Index Long-Term Bond
Vanguard Bond Index Short-Term Bond
Vanguard Bond Index Total Bond Mkt
Vanguard Index Trust: Small Cap Stock
Vanguard Index Trust: 500 Port
Vanguard Index Trust: Extended Market
Vanguard Index Trust: Growth Port
Vanguard Index Trust: Total Stock Market
Vanguard Index Trust: Value Port
Vanguard Int'l Equity Index: Emerging Mkts
Vanguard Int'l Equity Index: European
Vanguard Int'l Equity Index: Pacific
Vanguard Tax Managed Grth & Inc Port

SECTOR FUNDS

American Century Global Gold
American Gas Index
Americas Utility
Blanchard Precious Metals
Bull & Bear Gold Investors Ltd
Century Shares Trust
CGM Realty
Cohen & Steers Realty Shares
Fidelity Real Estate Investment Port
Fidelity Sel Air Transportation
Fidelity Sel American Gold
Fidelity Sel Automotive
Fidelity Sel Biotechnology
Fidelity Sel Brokerage & Investment
Fidelity Sel Chemicals
Fidelity Sel Computers
Fidelity Sel Construction & Housing
Fidelity Sel Consumer Industries
Fidelity Sel Defense & Aerospace
Fidelity Sel Developing Communications
Fidelity Sel Electronics
Fidelity Sel Energy
Fidelity Sel Energy Service
Fidelity Sel Environmental Services
Fidelity Sel Financial Services
Fidelity Sel Food & Agriculture
Fidelity Sel Health Care
Fidelity Sel Home Finance
Fidelity Sel Industrial Equipment
Fidelity Sel Industrial Materials
Fidelity Sel Insurance
Fidelity Sel Leisure
Fidelity Sel Medical Delivery
Fidelity Sel Multimedia
Fidelity Sel Natural Gas
Fidelity Sel Paper & Forest Products
Fidelity Sel Precious Metals & Minerals
Fidelity Sel Regional Banks
Fidelity Sel Retailing
Fidelity Sel Software & Computer
Fidelity Sel Technology
Fidelity Sel Telecommunications
Fidelity Sel Transportation
Fidelity Sel Utilities Growth
Fidelity Utilities Income

Gabelli Global Telecommunications
Galaxy II: Utility Index
INVESCO Strat Port—Environmental
INVESCO Strat Port—Energy
INVESCO Strat Port—Financial Svcs
INVESCO Strat Port—Gold
INVESCO Strat Port—Health Science
INVESCO Strat Port—Leisure
INVESCO Strat Port—Technology
INVESCO Strat Port—Utilities
INVESCO Worldwide Communications
Lexington Goldfund
Lindner Utility
Markman Moderate Growth
Montgomery Global Communications
PBHG Technology & Communications
Robertson Stephens Glbl Natrl Res
Robertson Stephens Information Age
Scudder Gold
Strong American Utilities
T. Rowe Price Health Sciences
T. Rowe Price New Era
T. Rowe Price Science & Technology
United Service Gold Shares
United Service World Gold
USAA Invest Trust: Gold
Vanguard Spec Port: Energy
Vanguard Spec Port: Gold & Prec Metals
Vanguard Spec Port: Utilities Income
VanguardSpecPort: Health Care

SMALL CAPITALIZATION STOCK FUNDS
American Century Global Gold
American Gas Index
Americas Utility
Blanchard Precious Metals
Bull & Bear Gold Investors Ltd
Century Shares Trust
CGM Realty
Cohen & Steers Realty Shares
Fidelity Real Estate Investment Port
Fidelity Sel Air Transportation
Fidelity Sel American Gold
Fidelity Sel Automotive
Fidelity Sel Biotechnology
Fidelity Sel Brokerage & Investment

Fidelity Sel Chemicals
Fidelity Sel Computers
Fidelity Sel Construction & Housing
Fidelity Sel Consumer Industries
Fidelity Sel Defense & Aerospace
Fidelity Sel Developing Communications
Fidelity Sel Electronics
Fidelity Sel Energy
Fidelity Sel Energy Service
Fidelity Sel Environmental Services
Fidelity Sel Financial Services
Fidelity Sel Food & Agriculture
Fidelity Sel Health Care
Fidelity Sel Home Finance
Fidelity Sel Industrial Equipment
Fidelity Sel Industrial Materials
Fidelity Sel Insurance
Fidelity Sel Leisure
Fidelity Sel Medical Delivery
Fidelity Sel Multimedia
Fidelity Sel Natural Gas
Fidelity Sel Paper & Forest Products
Fidelity Sel Precious Metals & Minerals
Fidelity Sel Regional Banks
Fidelity Sel Retailing
Fidelity Sel Software & Computer
Fidelity Sel Technology
Fidelity Sel Telecommunications
Fidelity Sel Transportation
Fidelity Sel Utilities Growth
Fidelity Utilities Income
Gabelli Global Telecommunications
Galaxy II: Utility Index
INVESCO Strat Port—Environmental
INVESCO Strat Port—Energy
INVESCO Strat Port—Financial Svcs
INVESCO Strat Port—Gold
INVESCO Strat Port—Health Science
INVESCO Strat Port—Leisure
INVESCO Strat Port—Technology
INVESCO Strat Port—Utilities
INVESCO Worldwide Communications
Lexington Goldfund
Lindner Utility
Markman Moderate Growth
Montgomery Global Communications

PBHG Technology & Communications
Robertson Stephens Glbl Natrl Res
Robertson Stephens Information Age
Scudder Gold
Strong American Utilities
T. Rowe Price Health Sciences
T. Rowe Price New Era
T. Rowe Price Science & Technology
United Service Gold Shares
United Service World Gold
USAA Invest Trust: Gold
Vanguard Spec Port: Energy
Vanguard Spec Port: Gold & Prec Metals
Vanguard Spec Port: Utilities Income
Vanguard Spec Port: Health Care

SOCIALLY CONSCIOUS FUNDS

Aquinas Balanced
Aquinas Equity Income
Aquinas Fixed Income
Domini Social Equity
Dreyfus Third Century
Pax World

STATE-SPECIFIC TAX-EXEMPT BOND FUNDS

Arizona
Benham Arizona Interm-Term Muni

California
Benham CA High Yield Muni
Benham CA Insured Tax-Free
Benham CA Interm-Term Tax-Free
Benham CA Long-Term Tax-Free
Benham CA Ltd-Term Tax-Free
California Tax-Free Income
Dreyfus CA Interm Muni Bond
Dreyfus CA Tax-Exempt Bond
Dreyfus General CA Muni Bond
Fidelity CA Insured Muni Income
Fidelity CA Muni Income
Fidelity Spartan CA Interm Muni Income
Fidelity Spartan CA Muni Income
Fremont CA Interm Tax-Free
SAFECO CA Tax-Free Income

Schwab CA Long-Term Tx Fr Bond
Schwab CA Short Interm Tx Fr Bond
Scudder CA Tax-Free
T. Rowe Price CA Tax-Free Bond
USAA Tax-Exempt CA Bond
Vanguard CA Tax-Free Ins Interm Term
Vanguard CA Tax-Free Ins Long-Term

Connecticut
1784 Conn Tax-Exempt Income
Dreyfus Conn Interm Muni Bond
Fidelity Spartan Conn Muni Income

Florida
Dreyfus Florida Interm Muni Bond
Fidelity Spartan Florida Muni Income
T. Rowe Price FL Ins Interm Tax-Free
USAA Florida Tax Free Income
Vanguard Florida Insured Tax-Free

Georgia
T. Rowe Price GA Tax-Free Bond

Hawaii
First Hawaii Muni Bond

Kentucky
Dupree KY Tax-Free Income
Dupree KY Tx Fr Short-To-Medium

Massachusetts
1784 MA Tax-Exempt Income
Dreyfus MA Interm Muni Bond
Dreyfus MA Tax-Exempt Bond
Fidelity MA Muni Income
Scudder MA Ltd Tax-Free
Scudder MA Tax-Free

Maryland
Fidelity Spartan MD Muni Income
Rushmore Fund for Tax-Free Invest: MD
T. Rowe Price MD Short Term Tax Free
T. Rowe Price MD Tax-Free Bond

Michigan
Fidelity Michigan Muni Income

Minnesota
Fidelity Minnesota Muni Income
Sit Minnesota Tax-Free Income

New Jersey
Dreyfus NJ Interm Muni Bond
Dreyfus NJ Muni Bond
Fidelity Spartan NJ Muni Income
T. Rowe Price NJ Tax-Free Bond
Vanguard NJ Tax Free Insured Long

New York
Dreyfus General NY Muni Bond
Dreyfus NY Insured Tax-Exempt
Dreyfus NY Interm Tax-Exempt
Dreyfus NY Tax-Exempt Bond
Fidelity NY Insured Muni Income
Fidelity NY Muni Income
Fidelity Spartan NY Interm Muni Income
Fidelity Spartan NY Muni Income
Fundamental New York Muni
Scudder NY Tax-Free
T. Rowe Price NY Tax-Free Bond
USAA Tax-Exempt NY Bond
Value Line NY Tax-Exempt Trust
Vanguard NY Insured Tax-Free Fd
Warburg Pincus NY Interm Muni

Ohio
Fidelity Ohio Muni Income
Scudder Ohio Tax-Free
Vanguard Ohio Tax-Free Ins Long-Term

Oregon
Crabbe Huson Oregon Tax-Free—Prim

Pennsylvania
Dreyfus Penn Interm Muni Bond
Fidelity Spartan Penn Muni Income
Scudder Penn Tax-Free
Vanguard Penn Tax-Free Ins Long-Term

Rhode Island
1784 Rhode Island Tax-Exempt Income

Virginia
GIT Tax-Free Trust: Virginia Port
Rushmore Fund for Tax-Free Invest: VA
T. Rowe Price VA Tax-Free Bond
USAA Tax-Exempt Virginia Bond

Wisconsin
Heartland Wisconsin Tax-Free

Appendix B
Changes to the Funds

FUND NAME CHANGES

Former	*Current*
Benham Equity Growth	American Century Equity Growth
Benham Glbl Natural Resources Index	American Century Glbl Natural Resources
Benham Gold Equities	American Century Global Gold
Benham GNMA Income	Benham GNMA
Benham Income & Growth	American Century Income & Growth
Benham Long-Term Treasury & Agency	Benham Long-Term Treasury
Benham Nat'l Tax-Free Interm Term	Benham Interm-Term Tax-Free
Benham Nat'l Tax-Free Long-Term	Benham Long-Term Tax-Free
Benham Short-Term Treasury & Agency	Benham Short-Term Treasury
Benham Treasury Note	Benham Interm-Term Treasury
Benham Utilities Income	American Century Utilities
Caldwell & Orkin Aggressive Growth	Caldwell & Orkin Market Opportunity
Dreyfus Int'l Equity	Dreyfus Int'l Growth
Fidelity High Yield Tax-Free Port	Fidelity Muni Income
Fidelity Sel Consumer Products	Fidelity Sel Consumer Industries
International Equity	Schroder Capital Int'l—Inv
Leeb Personal Finance	Megatrend
National Industries	Stonebridge Growth
SBSF	KEY Fund
SBSF Convertible Securities	KEY Convertible Securities
Seven Seas Series Growth & Income	SSgA: Growth & Income
Seven Seas Series—Matrix Equity	SSgA: Matrix Equity
Seven Seas Series—S&P 500	SSgA: S&P 500 Index
Seven Seas Series Yield Plus	SSgA: Yield Plus
Sit Growth	Sit Mid Cap Growth
Sit Growth & Income	Sit Large Cap Growth
Twentieth Century Balanced	American Century Balanced Investors
Twentieth Century Int'l Equity	Twentieth Century Int'l Growth
Twentieth Century Long-Term Bond	Benham Bond
Twentieth Century Tax-Exempt Interm	Benham Interm-Term Tax-Exempt
Twentieth Century Tax-Exempt Long	Benham Long-Term Tax-Exempt
Twentieth Century Tax-Exempt Short	Benham Ltd-Term Tax-Exempt
Twentieth Century US Gov't Short Term	Benham Short-Term Gov't
Twentieth Century Value	American Century Value

INVESTMENT CATEGORY CHANGES

Fund Name	Old	New
AmSouth Mutual Fds: Ltd Maturity	General Bond	Corporate Bond
Brundage Story & Rose Sh Interm Fxd	General Bond	Mortgage-Backed Bond
Century Shares Trust	Growth	Growth and Income
Fidelity Spartan Gov't Income	Mortgage-Backed Bond	Government Bond
Fidelity Spartan Investment Grade	Corporate Bond	General Bond
Fidelity Spartan Ltd Maturity Gov't	Mortgage-Backed Bond	Government Bond
Fidelity Spartan Short Interm Gov't	General Bond	Government Bond
Janus Twenty	Growth	Aggressive Growth
Maxus Equity	Growth	Growth & Income
SteinRoe Growth & Income	Growth	Growth & Income
Strong Schafer Value	Growth & Income	Growth
Vanguard Short-Term Federal	General Bond	Mortgage-Backed Bond

FUNDS DROPPED FROM THE GUIDE

Fund	Reason Eliminated
American Heritage	Total assets below 25 million for two consecutive years
Bartlett Fixed Income	Merged into Legg Mason Income Trust: US Gov't Intermediate/Primary Shares
Blanchard American Equity	Merged into Virtus Style Manager Large Cap Fund
Bull & Bear Muni Income	Converted to a closed-end fund
Bull & Bear US & Overseas	Total assets below 25 million for two consecutive years
Bull & Bear US Gov't Securities	Converted to a closed-end fund
Cal Muni	Total assets below 25 million for two consecutive years
Cappiello-Rushmore Utility Income	Total assets below 25 million for two consecutive years
Corefund Equity Index	Multiple class structure: Class A-5.0% front-end load
Dreyfus Edison Electric Index	Liquidated
Eaton Vance Short-Term Treasury	Brokerage firm fund
Evergreen—Class Y	Imposed multiple load structure
Evergreen American Retirement—Class Y	Imposed multiple load structure
Evergreen Foundation—Class Y	Imposed multiple load structure
Evergreen Global Real Estate—Class Y	Imposed multiple load structure
Evergreen Growth & Income—Class Y	Imposed multiple load structure
Evergreen High Grade Tax-Free—Class Y	Imposed multiple load structure
Evergreen Limited Market—Class Y	Imposed multiple load structure
Evergreen Short-Interm Muni—Class Y	Imposed multiple load structure
Evergreen Total Return—Class Y	Imposed multiple load structure

Fidelity Muni Bond..Now distributed through financial interme-
diaries as Fidelity Advisor
Fidelity Short-Term World Income.................Merged into Fidelity Short Term Bond
Fidelity Spartan Long-Term Gov't..................Merged into Fidelity Spartan Gov't Income
Flex Growth...Total assets below 25 million for two con-
secutive years
Flex Bond ....Total assets below 25 million for two con-
secutive years
Fundamental US Gov't Strat Income..............Total assets below 25 million for two con-
secutive years
Gintel ERISA ....Merged into Gintel Fund
Mutual Beacon...Imposed multiple load structure
Mutual Discovery..Imposed multiple load structure
Mutual Qualified...Imposed multiple load structure
Mutual Shares..Imposed multiple load structure
Pacifica Asset Preservation.............................Merged into Stagecoach Money Mrkt Insti-
tutional Class
Pacifica Short Term CA Tax-Free ....Merged into Stagecoach CA Tax-Free
Pegasus (formerly Woodward) Equity Index.Imposed multiple load structure
Permanent Port—Versatile Bond ....Total assets below 25 million for two con-
secutive years
Portico Bond IMMDEX—Retail........................Imposed 12b-1 fee and 2% front-end load
Portico Interm Bond Market—Retail..............Total assets below 25 million for two con-
secutive years
Portico Tax-Exempt Interm Bond—Retail .....Total assets below 25 million for two con-
secutive years
Portico Short Term Bond Market—Retail......Imposed 12b-1 fee and 2% front-end load
Prudential Gov't Sec Trust Short Interm........Brokerage firm fund
Salomon Brothers Capital..................................Imposed multiple load structure
Salomon Brothers Opportunity........................Imposed multiple load structure
Schroder US Equity...Total assets below 25 million for two con-
secutive years
Selected US Gov't Income.................................Total assets below 25 million for two con-
secutive years
SteinRoe Limited Maturity Income.................Liquidated
Strong Insured Muni Bond...............................Strong Insured Municipal merged into
Strong Municipal
T. Rowe Price Short-Term US Gov't ....Information not supplied
UAM C & B Balanced...Established for institutional investors
UAM C & B Equity ....Established for institutional investors
UAM DSI Disciplined Value.............................Established for institutional investors
UAM DSI Limited Maturity Bond ....Established for institutional investors
UAM ICM Small Company Port......................Established for institutional investors
UAM Sterling Partners Balanced ....Established for institutional investors
UAM TS & W International Equity..................Established for institutional investors
Value Line Intermediate Bond.........................Total assets below 25 million for two con-
secutive years

Vista Bond ....Multiple class structure: Cl A-4.5% front-
                                            end fee; Cl B-5%; Cl I-Institutional

Vista Equity...Multiple class structure: Cl A-4.5% front-
                                            end load; Cl B-5% back-end load; Cl C-
                                            Institutional

Vista Short-Term Bond....................................Multiple class structure: Cl A-1.5% front-
                                            end load & 12b-1; Cl B-back-end load; Cl
                                            C-Institutional

Woodward (now Pegasus) Equity Index.......Imposed multiple load structure

Index

Dreyfus NY Insured Tax-Exempt 52, **225**, 932

Dreyfus NY Interm Tax-Exempt 50, **226**, 932

Dreyfus NY Tax-Exempt Bond 52, **227**, 932

Dreyfus Penn Interm Muni Bond 50, **229**, 932

Dreyfus S&P 500 Index 42, **230**, 926

Dreyfus Short—Interm Gov't 46, **231**

Dreyfus Short—Interm Muni Bond 50, **232**

Dreyfus Short-Term Income 45, **233**

Dreyfus Special Growth—Investor 32, 38, **234**

Dreyfus Strategic Income 48, **235**

Dreyfus Third Century 42, **236**, 930

Dupree KY Tax-Free Income 51, **237**, 931

Dupree KY Tx Fr Short-To-Medium 50, **238**, 931

E

Eaton Vance Short-Term Treasury 935

Eclipse Financial Asset Tr: Balanced 44, **239**

Eclipse Financial Asset Tr: Equity 39, 55, **240**

Evergreen American Retirement—Class Y 935

Evergreen Foundation—Class Y 935

Evergreen Global Real Estate—Class Y 935

Evergreen Growth & Income—Class Y 935

Evergreen High Grade Tax-Free—Class Y 935

Evergreen Limited Market—Class Y 935

Evergreen Short-Interm Muni—Class Y 935

Evergreen Total Return—Class Y 935

Evergreen—Class Y 935

F

Fairmont 38, **242**

FAM Value 41, 56, **241**

Fidelity Aggressive Muni 51, **243**

Fidelity Asset Manager 44, **244**, 924

Fidelity Asset Manager: Growth 44, **245**, 924

Fidelity Asset Manager: Income 45, **246**, 924

Fidelity Balanced 45, **247**, 924

Fidelity Blue Chip Growth 41, **248**

Fidelity CA Insured Muni Income 50, **249**, 930

Fidelity CA Muni Income 49, **250**, 930

Fidelity Canada 53, **251**

Fidelity Capital & Income 46, **252**

Fidelity Capital Appreciation 41, **253**

Fidelity Contrafund 33, 34, 39, **254**

Fidelity Convertible Securities 43, **255**

Fidelity Disciplined Equity 41, **256**

Fidelity Diversified Int'l 52, **257**

Fidelity Dividend Growth 35, 39, **258**

Fidelity Emerging Growth 37, 56, **259**

Fidelity Emerging Markets 53, **260**

Fidelity Equity Income 42, **261**

Fidelity Equity Income II 43, **262**

Fidelity Europe 52, **263**

Fidelity Europe Capital Appreciation 52, **264**

Fidelity Export 32, 38, **265**

Fidelity Fifty 37, **266**

Fidelity Fund 42, **267**

Fidelity Ginnie Mae 47, **268**

Fidelity Global Balanced 54, **269**, 924, 925

Fidelity Global Bond 54, **270**, 925

Fidelity Gov't Securities 46, **271**

Fidelity Growth & Income Port 33, 42, **272**

Fidelity Growth Co 33, 37, **273**

Fidelity High Yield Tax-Free Port 934

Fidelity Hong Kong & China 32, 52, **274**

Fidelity Insured Muni Income 51, **275**

Fidelity Interm Bond 48, **276**

Fidelity Int'l Growth & Income 53, **277**, 925

Fidelity Int'l Value 53, **278**

Fidelity Investment Grade Bond 48, **279**

Fidelity Japan 32, 54, **280**

Fidelity Japan Small Companies 32, 54,

Fidelity Sel Utilities Growth 43, **339**, 927, 929

Fidelity Short—Interm Gov't 46, **340**

Fidelity Short-Term Bond 45, **341**

Fidelity Short-Term World Income 936

Fidelity Small Cap Stock 37, 56, **342**

Fidelity Southeast Asia 53, **343**

Fidelity Spartan Aggressive Muni 50, **344**

Fidelity Spartan CA Interm Muni Income 49, **345**, 930

Fidelity Spartan CA Muni Income 49, **346**, 930

Fidelity Spartan Conn Muni Income 50, **347**, 931

Fidelity Spartan Florida Muni Income 50, **348**, 931

Fidelity Spartan Ginnie Mae 47, **349**

Fidelity Spartan Gov't Income 46, **350**, 935

Fidelity Spartan High Income 46, **351**

Fidelity Spartan Interm Muni Income 49, **352**

Fidelity Spartan Investment Grade Bond 48, **353**, 935

Fidelity Spartan Long-Term Gov't 936

Fidelity Spartan Ltd Maturity Gov't 46, **354**, 935

Fidelity Spartan MD Muni Income 50, **355**, 931

Fidelity Spartan Muni Income 49, **356**

Fidelity Spartan NJ Muni Income 50, **357**, 932

Fidelity Spartan NY Interm Muni Income 50, **358**, 932

Fidelity Spartan NY Muni Income 49, **359**, 932

Fidelity Spartan Penn Muni Income 50, **360**, 932

Fidelity Spartan Short Interm Gov't 46, **361**, 935

Fidelity Spartan Short Interm Muni Inc 50, **362**

Fidelity Spartan Short-Term Bond 45, **363**

Fidelity Stock Selector 40, **364**

Fidelity Trend 40, **365**

Fidelity Utilities Income 43, **366**, 927, 929

Fidelity Value 34, 40, **367**

Fidelity Worldwide 53, **368**, 925

Fiduciary Capital Growth 40, **369**

First Eagle Fund of America 34, 35, 39, **370**

First Eagle Int'l 53, **371**

First Hawaii Muni Bond 50, **372**, 931

Flex Bond 936

Flex Growth 936

Flex Muirfield Fd 41, **373**, 924, 925

Founders Balanced 44, **374**

Founders Blue Chip 42, **375**

Founders Discovery 36, 56, **376**

Founders Frontier 37, 56, **377**

Founders Gov't Securities 46, **378**

Founders Growth 33, 40, **379**

Founders Passport 52, **380**

Founders Special 33, 37, **381**

Founders Worldwide Growth 53, **382**, 925

Fremont Bond 48, **383**

Fremont CA Interm Tax-Free 51, **384**, 930

Fremont Global 53, **385**, 924, 925

Fremont Growth 39, **386**

Fremont Int'l Growth 53, **387**

Fremont US Micro Cap 32, 36, 55, **388**

Fundamental New York Muni 32, 52, **389**, 932

Fundamental US Gov't Strat Income 936

G

Gabelli Asset 33, 41, **393**

Gabelli Global Telecommunications 53, **394**, 925, 928, 929

Gabelli Growth 40, **395**

Galaxy II: Large Co Index 42, **396**, 926

Galaxy II: Small Co Index 37, 56, **397**, 926

Galaxy II: US Treasury Index—Retail 46, **398**, 926

Galaxy II: Utility Index 43, 926, 928, 929

Gateway Index Plus 43, **400**

Gintel 38, **401**

Gintel ERISA 936

GIT Equity Trust: Special Growth 38, 56, **390**

GIT Tax-Free Trust

R

Rainier Investment: Small/Mid Cap Equity 36, 55, **586**

Reich & Tang Equity 40, **587**

Reynolds Blue Chip Growth 41, **588**

Rightime Fund 41, **589**, 925

Robertson Stephens Contrarian 52, **590**, 926

Robertson Stephens Developing Century 52, **591**

Robertson Stephens Emerging Growth 36, 55, **592**

Robertson Stephens Glbl Low Priced Stk 52, **593**, 926

Robertson Stephens Glbl Natrl Res 32, 52, **594**, 926, 928, 930

Robertson Stephens Information Age 36, **595**, 928, 930

Robertson Stephens Value + Growth 35, 37, 56, **596**

Royce: Equity Income 43, **597**

Royce: Micro-Cap 34, 37, 56, **598**

Royce: Penn Mutual 41, 56, **599**

Royce: Premier 40, 56, **600**

Rushmore Fund for Tax-Free Invest: MD 51, **601**, 931

Rushmore Fund for Tax-Free Invest: VA 51, **602**, 933

S

SAFECO CA Tax-Free Income 51, **603**, 930

SAFECO Equity 33, 34, 35, 42, **604**

SAFECO GNMA 47, **605**

SAFECO Growth 36, 55, **606**

SAFECO High Yield Bond 46, **607**

SAFECO Income 44, **608**

SAFECO Muni Bond 51, **609**

SAFECO Northwest 41, **610**

Salomon Brothers Capital 936

Salomon Brothers Opportunity 936

SBSF 934

SBSF Convertible Securities 934

Schroder Capital Int'l—Inv 53, **618**, 934

Schroder US Equity 936

Schwab 1000 42, **619**, 926

Schwab Asset Director: Balanced Growth 45, **620**, 924

Schwab Asset Director: High Growth 44, **621**, 924

Schwab CA Long-Term Tx Fr Bond 49, **622**, 931

Schwab CA Short Interm Tx Fr Bond 50, **623**, 931

Schwab Capital Trust: Int'l Index 53, **624**, 926

Schwab Capital Trust: Small Cap Index 37, 56, **625**, 926

Schwab Long-Term Tax-Free Bond 50, **626**

Schwab Short/Interm Gov't Bond 46, **627**

Schwab Short/Interm Tax-Free Bond 51, **628**

Schwartz Value 40, 56, **629**

Scout Bond 48, **630**

Scout Regional 41, 56, **631**

Scout Stock 43, **632**

Scout Worldwide 53, **633**, 926

Scudder CA Tax-Free 51, **634**, 931

Scudder Development 38, 56, **635**

Scudder Emerging Markets Income 54, **636**

Scudder Equity Trust: Capital Growth 40, **637**

Scudder Equity Trust: Value 39, **638**

Scudder Global 53, **640**, 926

Scudder Global Bond 54, **641**, 926

Scudder Global Discovery 52, **642**, 926

Scudder GNMA 47, **639**

Scudder Gold 55, **643**, 928, 930

Scudder Greater Europe Growth 52, **644**

Scudder Growth & Income 42, **645**

Scudder Int'l 53, **646**

Scudder Int'l Bond 54, **647**

Scudder Int'l: Latin America 52, **648**

Scudder Int'l: Pacific Opport Fd 54, **649**

Scudder Ltd Term Tax-Free 50, **650**

Scudder MA Ltd Tax Free 51, **651**, 931

Scudder MA Tax-Free 50, **652**, 931

Scudder Muni Tr: High Yield Tax-Free 49

Scudder Muni Trust: High Yield Tax-

Strong Short-Term Global Bond 54, **716**, 926

Strong Short-Term Muni Bond 49, **717**

Strong Small Cap 36, 55, **718**

Strong Total Return 43, **719**

Strong Value 40, **720**

T

T. Rowe Price Balanced 44, **721**

T. Rowe Price Blue Chip Growth 35, 41, **722**

T. Rowe Price CA Tax-Free Bond 49, **723**, 931

T. Rowe Price Capital Appreciation 40, **724**

T. Rowe Price Capital Opportunity 37, **725**

T. Rowe Price Dividend Growth 42, **726**

T. Rowe Price Equity Income 42, **727**

T. Rowe Price Equity Index 42, **728**, 926

T. Rowe Price FL Ins Interm Tax-Free 51, **729**, 931

T. Rowe Price GA Tax-Free Bond 50, **730**, 931

T. Rowe Price GNMA 47, **731**

T. Rowe Price Growth & Income 41, **732**

T. Rowe Price Growth Stock 39, **733**

T. Rowe Price Health Sciences 36, **734**, 928, 930

T. Rowe Price High Yield 46, **735**

T. Rowe Price Int'l: Bond 54, **736**

T. Rowe Price Int'l: Discovery 53, **737**

T. Rowe Price Int'l: Emerging Mkts Stock 53, **738**

T. Rowe Price Int'l: European Stock 52, **739**

T. Rowe Price Int'l: Global Gov't Bd 54, **740**, 926

T. Rowe Price Int'l: Japan 32, 54, **741**

T. Rowe Price Int'l: Latin America 52, **742**

T. Rowe Price Int'l: New Asia 53, **743**

T. Rowe Price Int'l: Stock 53, **744**

T. Rowe Price MD Sh Term Tax Free 51, **745**, 931

T. Rowe Price MD Tax-Free Bond 50, **746**, 931

T. Rowe Price Mid-Cap Growth 35, 39, **747**

T. Rowe Price New America Growth 33, 40, **750**

T. Rowe Price New Era 39, **751**, 928, 930

T. Rowe Price New Horizons 33, 34, 35, 37, 56, **752**

T. Rowe Price New Income 49, **753**

T. Rowe Price NJ Tax-Free Bond 51, **748**, 932

T. Rowe Price NY Tax-Free Bond 51, **749**, 932

T. Rowe Price OTC 36, 56, **754**

T. Rowe Price Personal Strat Fds: Bal 44, **755**, 924

T. Rowe Price Personal Strat Fds: Inc 44, **756**, 924

T. Rowe Price Science & Technology 34, 35, 37, **757**, 928, 930

T. Rowe Price Short-Term Bond 48, **758**

T. Rowe Price Short-Term US Gov't 48, **759**, 936

T. Rowe Price Small Cap Value 34, 39, 55, **760**

T. Rowe Price Spectrum: Growth 42, **761**, 925

T. Rowe Price Spectrum: Income 45, **762**, 924, 925

T. Rowe Price Summit Fds: Ltd Term Bond 48, **763**

T. Rowe Price Summit Fds: Muni Interm 49, **764**

T. Rowe Price Tax-Free High Yield 49, **765**

T. Rowe Price Tax-Free Income 51, **766**

T. Rowe Price Tax-Free Ins Interm Bond 50, **767**

T. Rowe Price Tax-Free Short Interm 50, **768**

T. Rowe Price US Treasury Interm 46, **769**

T. Rowe Price US Treasury Long-Term 32, 47, **770**

T. Rowe Price VA Tax-Free Bond 50, **771**, 933

T. Rowe Price Value 39, **772**

Third Avenue Value 34, 44, **773**

W

Y

ABOUT AAII

WHAT IS AAII?

The American Association of Individual Investors is an independent, not-for-profit organization that was formed in 1978 to assist individuals in becoming effective managers of their own investments.

AAII achieves this aim through publications, nationwide seminars, home study texts, educational videos, and local chapters that focus on investing and investment techniques. Current membership is 175,000.

The *AAII Journal* is the primary benefit of membership. It is published 10 times a year. The focus is on providing information and how-to articles that help the individual learn investment fundamentals. The *Journal* does not promote a specific viewpoint or recommend specific investments, and it does not accept advertising. In March every member receives a new edition of *The Individual Investor's Guide to Low-Load Mutual Funds*.

NATIONWIDE SEMINARS

AAII holds seminars across the country taught by university finance professors on the topics of stock analysis, financial planning, retirement and estate planning, mutual funds, portfolio management, and the fundamentals of investing.

LOCAL CHAPTERS

AAII sponsors over 60 local chapters throughout the U.S. AAII members organize presentations given by investment professionals. Members who are interested in attending these meetings also benefit from talking to like-minded investors.

OTHER EDUCATIONAL PRODUCTS

Members can buy AAII educational materials at reduced prices.

FOR ONLY $49 A YEAR

Membership in AAII is $49, which includes a subscription to the *AAII Journal*, *The Individual Investor's Guide to Low-Load Mutual Funds* (published in March), a yearly tax planning guide (published in mid-November), and reduced fees for seminars and educational publications.

To join AAII or order products, call AAII at (800) 428-2244 or (312) 280-0170
or send E-mail to AAIIMembr@aol.com (please specify Dept. 222).